# CHRYSLER NEON
## 1995-99 REPAIR MANUAL

**Covers all U.S. and Canadian models of Dodge and Plymouth Neon**

by Christine Sheeky, S.A.E.

CHILTON *Automotive Books*

PUBLISHED BY HAYNES NORTH AMERICA, Inc.

Manufactured in USA
© 1998 Haynes North America, Inc.
ISBN 0-8019-8971-X
Library of Congress Catalog Card No. 98-71354
4567890123  9876543210

**Haynes Publishing Group**
Sparkford Nr Yeovil
Somerset BA22 7JJ England

**Haynes North America, Inc**
861 Lawrence Drive
Newbury Park
California 91320 USA

ABCDE
F

# Contents

# Contents

**DRIVE TRAIN  7**

**SUSPENSION AND STEERING  8**

**BRAKES  9**

**BODY AND TRIM  10**

**GLOSSARY**

**MASTER INDEX**

## SAFETY NOTICE

Proper service and repair procedures are vital to the safe, reliable operation of all motor vehicles, as well as the personal safety of those performing repairs. This manual outlines procedures for servicing and repairing vehicles using safe, effective methods. The procedures contain many NOTES, CAUTIONS and WARNINGS which should be followed, along with standard procedures to eliminate the possibility of personal injury or improper service which could damage the vehicle or compromise its safety.

It is important to note that repair procedures and techniques, tools and parts for servicing motor vehicles, as well as the skill and experience of the individual performing the work vary widely. It is not possible to anticipate all of the conceivable ways or conditions under which vehicles may be serviced, or to provide cautions as to all possible hazards that may result. Standard and accepted safety precautions and equipment should be used when handling toxic or flammable fluids, and safety goggles or other protection should be used during cutting, grinding, chiseling, prying, or any other process that can cause material removal or projectiles.

Some procedures require the use of tools specially designed for a specific purpose. Before substituting another tool or procedure, you must be completely satisfied that neither your personal safety, nor the performance of the vehicle will be endangered.

Although information in this manual is based on industry sources and is complete as possible at the time of publication, the possibility exists that some car manufacturers made later changes which could not be included here. While striving for total accuracy, the authors or publishers cannot assume responsibility for any errors, changes or omissions that may occur in the compilation of this data.

## PART NUMBERS

Part numbers listed in this reference are not recommendations by Haynes North America, Inc. for any product brand name. They are references that can be used with interchange manuals and aftermarket supplier catalogs to locate each brand supplier's discrete part number.

## SPECIAL TOOLS

Special tools are recommended by the vehicle manufacturer to perform their specific job. Use has been kept to a minimum, but where absolutely necessary, they are referred to in the text by the part number of the tool manufacturer. These tools can be purchased, under the appropriate part number, from your local dealer or regional distributor, or an equivalent tool can be purchased locally from a tool supplier or parts outlet. Before substituting any tool for the one recommended, read the SAFETY NOTICE at the top of this page.

## ACKNOWLEDGMENTS

The publisher expresses appreciation to Chrysler Corporation for their generous assistance.

# 1

# GENERAL INFORMATION AND MAINTENANCE

## HOW TO USE THIS BOOK

Chilton's Total Car Care manual for the Dodge and Plymouth Neon is intended to help you learn more about the inner workings of your vehicle and save you money on its maintenance and repairs.

The beginning of the book will likely be referred to the most, since that is where you will find information for maintenance and tune-up. The other sections deal with the more complex systems of your vehicle. Operating systems from engine through brakes are covered to the extent that the average do-it-yourselfer becomes mechanically involved. This book will not explain such things as rebuilding a differential for the simple reason that the expertise required and the investment in special tools make this task uneconomical. It will, however, give you detailed instructions to help you change your own brake pads and shoes, replace spark plugs, and perform many more jobs that can save you money, give you personal satisfaction and help you avoid expensive problems.

A secondary purpose of this book is a reference for owners who want to understand their vehicle and/or their mechanics better. In this case, no tools at all are required.

### Where to Begin

Before removing any bolts, read through the entire procedure. This will give you the overall view of what tools and supplies will be required. There is nothing more frustrating than having to walk to the bus stop on Monday morning because you were short one bolt on Sunday afternoon. So read ahead and plan ahead. Each operation should be approached logically and all procedures thoroughly understood before attempting any work.

All sections contain adjustments, maintenance, removal and installation procedures, and in some cases, repair or overhaul procedures. When repair is not considered practical, we tell you how to remove the part and then how to install the new or rebuilt replacement. In this way, you at least save the labor costs. Backyard repair of some components is just not practical.

### Avoiding Trouble

Many procedures in this book require you to "label and disconnect . . ." a group of lines, hoses or wires. Don't be lulled into thinking you can remember where everything goes—you won't. If you hook up vacuum or fuel lines incorrectly, the vehicle will run poorly, if at all. If you hook up electrical wiring incorrectly, you may instantly learn a very expensive lesson.

You don't need to know the official or engineering name for each hose or line. A piece of masking tape on the hose and a piece on its fitting will allow you to assign your own label such as the letter A or a short name. As long as you remember your own code, the lines can be reconnected by matching similar letters or names. Do remember that tape will dissolve in gasoline or other fluids; if a component is to be washed or cleaned, use another method of identification. A permanent felt-tipped marker can be very handy for marking metal parts. Remove any tape or paper labels after assembly.

### Maintenance or Repair?

It's necessary to mention the difference between maintenance and repair. Maintenance includes routine inspections, adjustments, and replacement of parts which show signs of normal wear. Maintenance compensates for wear or deterioration. Repair implies that something has broken or is not working. A need for repair is often caused by lack of maintenance. Example: draining and refilling the automatic transmission fluid is maintenance recommended by the manufacturer at specific mileage intervals. Failure to do this can ruin the transmission/transaxle, requiring very expensive repairs. While no maintenance program can prevent items from breaking or wearing out, a general rule can be stated: MAINTENANCE IS CHEAPER THAN REPAIR.

Two basic mechanic's rules should be mentioned here. First, whenever the left side of the vehicle or engine is referred to, it is meant to specify the driver's side. Conversely, the right side of the vehicle means the passenger's side. Second, most screws and bolts are removed by turning counterclockwise, and tightened by turning clockwise.

Safety is always the most important rule. Constantly be aware of the dangers involved in working on an automobile and take the proper precautions. See the information in this section regarding SERVICING YOUR VEHICLE SAFELY and the SAFETY NOTICE on the acknowledgment page.

### Avoiding the Most Common Mistakes

Pay attention to the instructions provided. There are 3 common mistakes in mechanical work:

1. Incorrect order of assembly, disassembly or adjustment. When taking something apart or putting it together, performing steps in the wrong order usually just costs you extra time; however, it CAN break something. Read the entire procedure before beginning disassembly. Perform everything in the order in which the instructions say you should, even if you can't immediately see a reason for it. When you're taking apart something that is very intricate, you might want to draw a picture of how it looks when assembled at one point in order to make sure you get everything back in its proper position. We will supply exploded views whenever possible. When making adjustments, perform them in the proper order; often, one adjustment affects another, and you cannot expect even satisfactory results unless each adjustment is made only when it cannot be changed by any other.

2. Overtorquing (or undertorquing). While it is more common for overtorquing to cause damage, undertorquing may allow a fastener to vibrate loose causing serious damage. Especially when dealing with aluminum parts, pay attention to torque specifications and utilize a torque wrench in assembly. If a torque figure is not available, remember that if you are using the right tool to perform the job, you will probably not have to strain yourself to get a fastener tight enough. The pitch of most threads is so slight that the tension you put on the wrench will be multiplied many times in actual force on what you are tightening. A good example of how critical torque is can be seen in the case of spark plug installation, especially where you are putting the plug into an aluminum cylinder head. Too little torque can fail to crush the gasket, causing leakage of combustion gases and consequent overheating of the plug and engine parts. Too much torque can damage the threads or distort the plug, changing the spark gap.

There are many commercial products available for ensuring that fasteners won't come loose, even if they are not torqued just right (a very common brand is Loctite®). If you're worried about getting something together tight enough to hold, but loose enough to avoid mechanical damage during assembly, one of these products might offer substantial insurance. Before choosing a thread-locking compound, read the label on the package and make sure the product is compatible with the materials, fluids, etc. involved.

3. Crossthreading. This occurs when a part such as a bolt is screwed into a nut or casting at the wrong angle and forced. Crossthreading is more likely to occur if access is difficult. It helps to clean and lubricate fasteners, then to start threading with the part to be installed positioned straight in. Then, start the bolt, spark plug, etc. with your fingers. If you encounter resistance, unscrew the part and start over again at a different angle until it can be inserted and turned several times without much effort. Keep in mind that many parts, especially spark plugs, have tapered threads, so that gentle turning will automatically bring the part you're threading to the proper angle, but only if you don't force it or resist a change in angle. Don't put a wrench on the part until it's been tightened a couple of turns by hand. If you suddenly encounter resistance, and the part has not seated fully, don't force it. Pull it back out to make sure it's clean and threading properly.

Always take your time and be patient; once you have some experience, working on your vehicle may well become an enjoyable hobby.

## TOOLS AND EQUIPMENT

♦ **See Figures 1 thru 15**

Naturally, without the proper tools and equipment it is impossible to properly service your vehicle. It would also be virtually impossible to catalog every tool that you would need to perform all of the operations in this book. Of course, It would be unwise for the amateur to rush out and buy an expensive set of tools on the theory that he/she may need one or more of them at some time.

The best approach is to proceed slowly, gathering a good quality set of those tools that are used most frequently. Don't be misled by the low cost of bargain tools It is far better to spend a little more for better quality. Forged wrenches, 6 or 12-point sockets and fine tooth ratchets are by far preferable to their less expensive counterparts. As any good mechanic can tell you, there are few worse experiences than trying to work on a vehicle with bad tools. Your monetary savings will be far outweighed by frustration and mangled knuckles.

Begin accumulating those tools that are used most frequently: those associated with routine maintenance and tune-up. In addition to the normal assortment of screwdrivers and pliers, you should have the following tools:

• Wrenches/sockets and combination open end/box end wrenches in sizes from ⅛–¾ in. or 3mm–19mm (depending on whether your vehicle uses standard or metric fasteners) and a ¹³⁄₁₆ in. or ⅝ in. spark plug socket (depending on plug type).

➡ **If possible, buy various length socket drive extensions. Universal-joint and wobble extensions can be extremely useful, but be careful when using them, as they can change the amount of torque applied to the socket.**

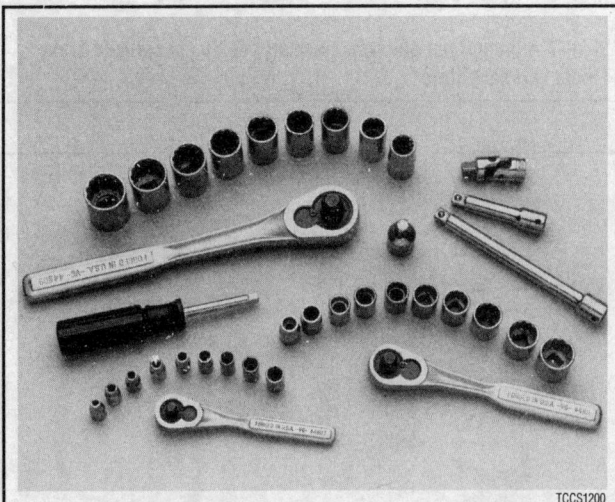

Fig. 1 All but the most basic procedures will require an assortment of ratchets and sockets

TCCS1200

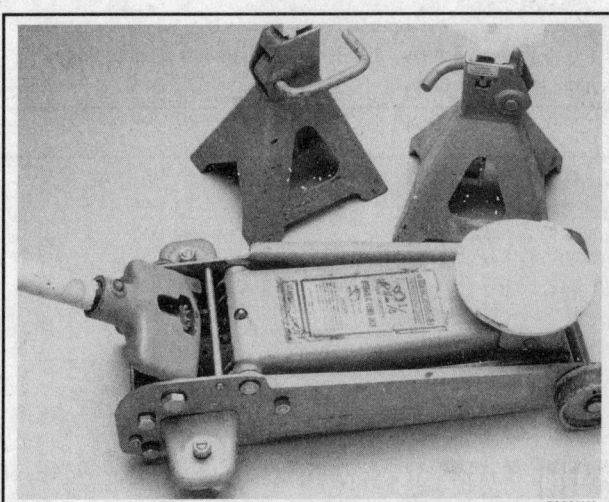

Fig. 3 A hydraulic floor jack and a set of jackstands are essential for lifting and supporting the vehicle

TCCS1202

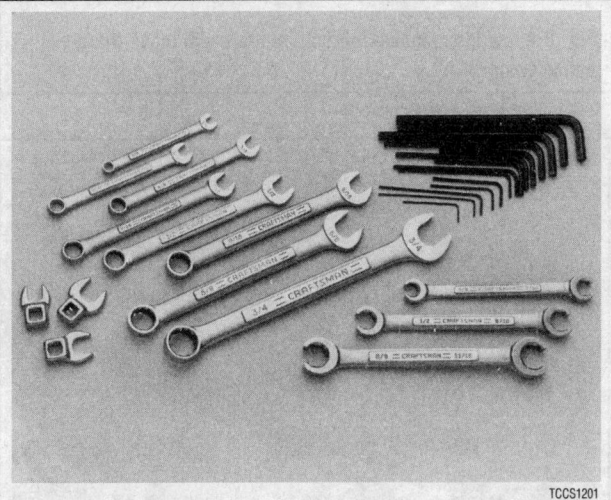

Fig. 2 In addition to ratchets, a good set of wrenches and hex keys will be necessary

TCCS1201

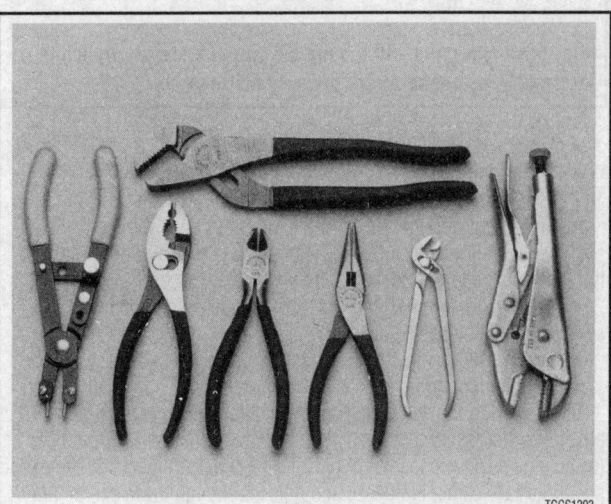

Fig. 4 An assortment of pliers, grippers and cutters will be handy for old rusted parts and stripped bolt heads

TCCS1203

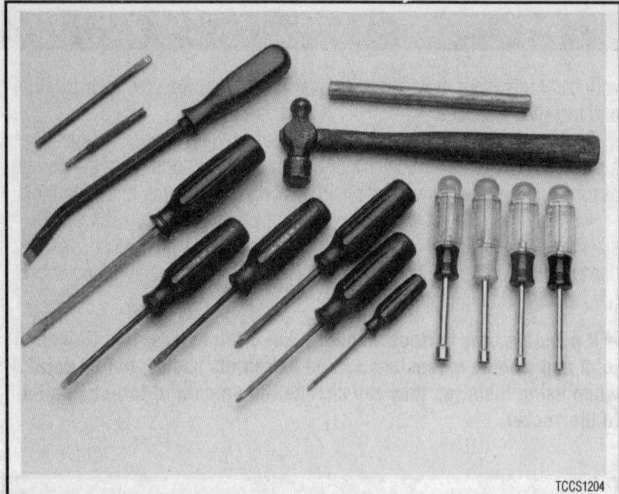

Fig. 5 Various drivers, chisels and prybars are great tools to have in your toolbox

TCCS1204

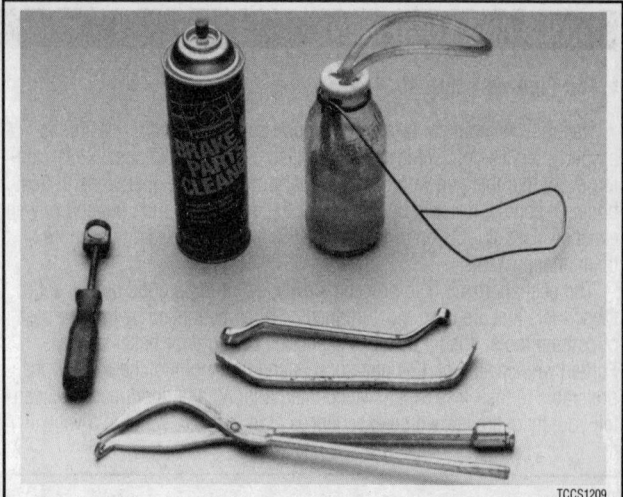

Fig. 7 Although not always necessary, using specialized brake tools will save time

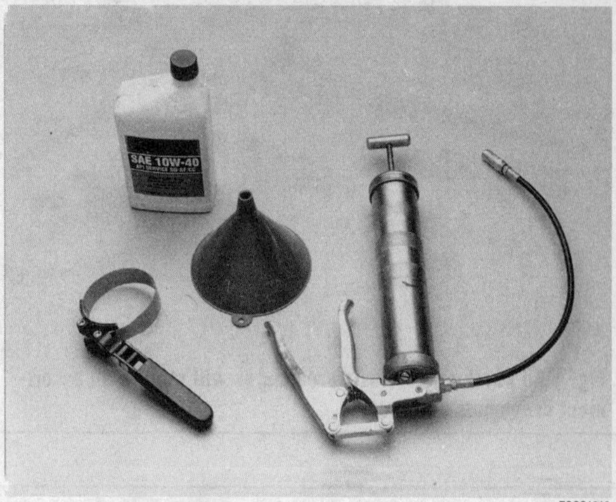

TCCS1209

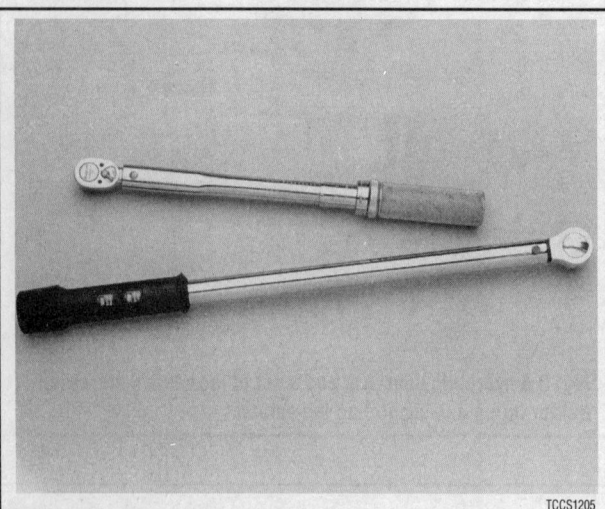

Fig. 6 Many repairs will require the use of a torque wrench to assure the components are properly fastened

TCCS1205

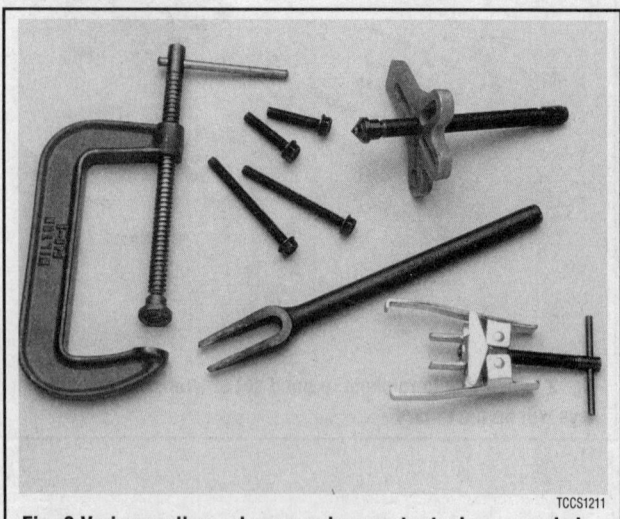

Fig. 8 A few inexpensive lubrication tools will make maintenance easier

TCCS1210

- Jackstands for support.
- Oil filter wrench.
- Spout or funnel for pouring fluids.
- Grease gun for chassis lubrication (unless your vehicle is not equipped with any grease fittings—for details, please refer to information on Fluids and Lubricants found later in this section).
- Hydrometer for checking the battery (unless equipped with a sealed, maintenance-free battery).
- A container for draining oil and other fluids.
- Rags for wiping up the inevitable mess.

In addition to the above items there are several others that are not absolutely necessary, but handy to have around. These include Oil Dry® (or an equivalent oil absorbent gravel—such as cat litter) and the usual supply of lubricants, antifreeze and fluids, although these can be purchased as needed. This is a basic list for routine maintenance, but only your personal needs and desire can accurately determine your list of tools.

After performing a few projects on the vehicle, you'll be amazed at the other tools and non-tools on your workbench. Some useful household items are: a large turkey baster or siphon, empty coffee cans and ice trays (to store parts), ball of twine, electrical tape for wiring, small rolls of colored tape for tagging lines or hoses, markers and pens, a note pad,

Fig. 9 Various pullers, clamps and separator tools are needed for many larger, more complicated repairs

TCCS1211

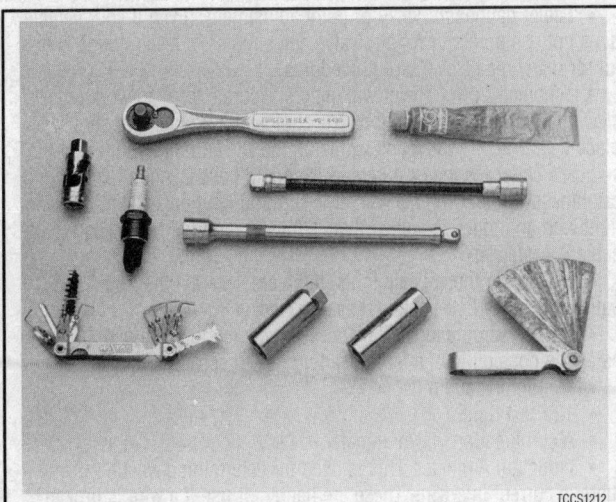

TCCS1212

**Fig. 10 A variety of tools and gauges should be used for spark plug gapping and installation**

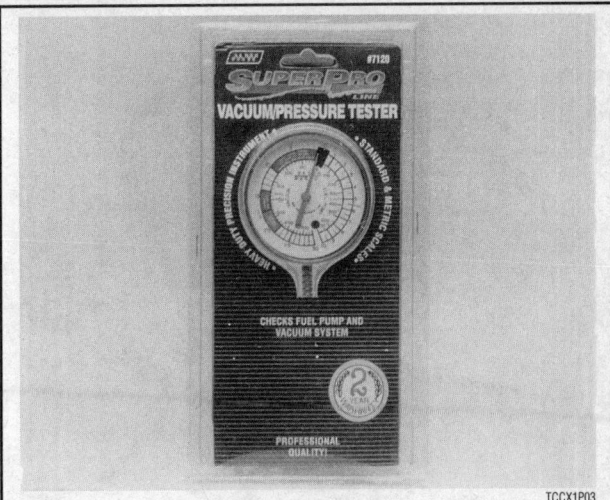

TCCX1P03

**Fig. 13 A vacuum/pressure tester is necessary for many testing procedures**

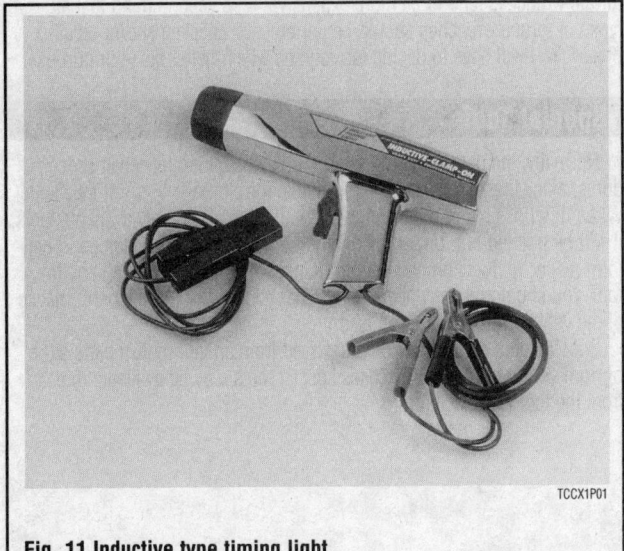

TCCX1P01

**Fig. 11 Inductive type timing light**

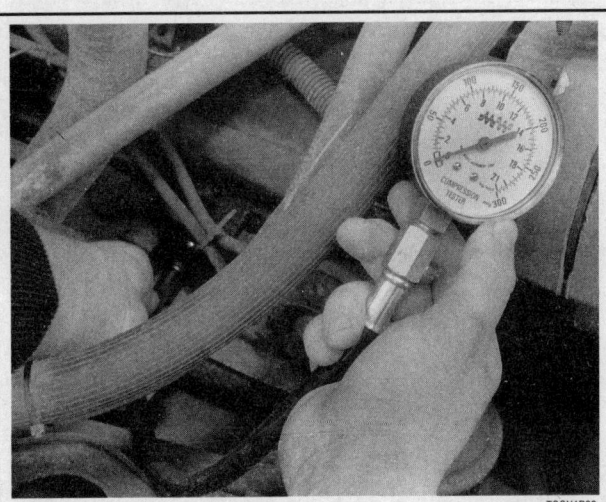

TCCX1P02

**Fig. 12 A screw-in type compression gauge is recommended for compression testing**

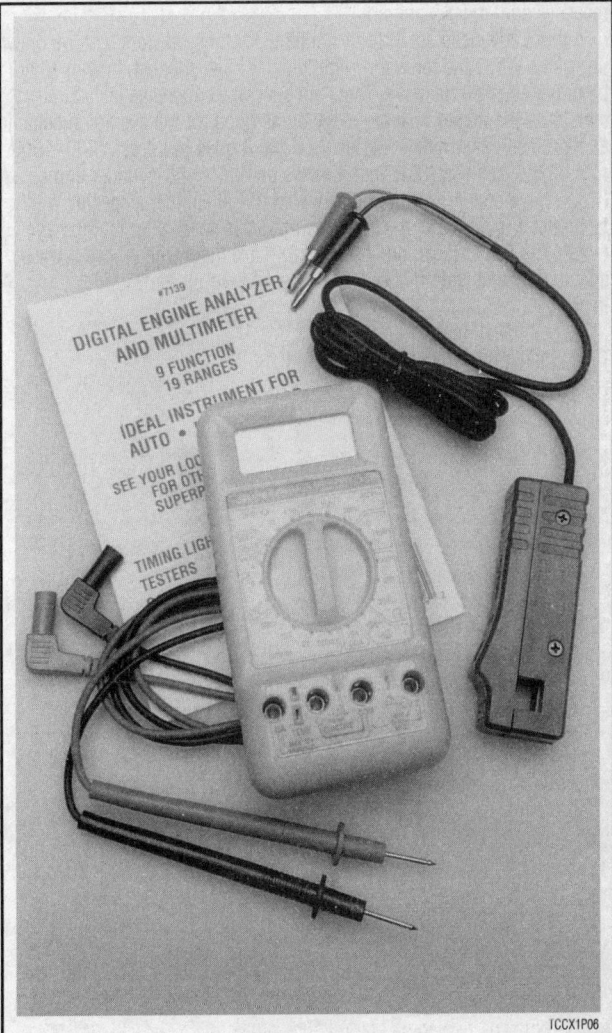

TCCX1P06

**Fig. 14 Most modern automotive multimeters incorporate many helpful features**

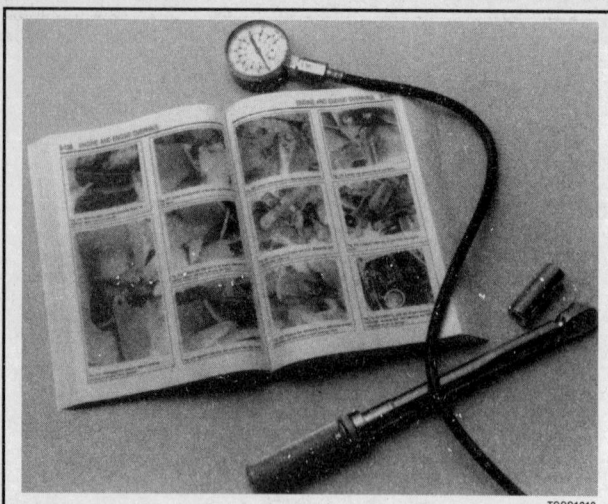

**Fig. 15 Proper information is vital, so always have a Chilton Total Car Care manual handy**

golf tees (for plugging vacuum lines), metal coat hangers or a roll of mechanics's wire (to hold things out of the way), dental pick or similar long, pointed probe, a strong magnet, and a small mirror (to see into recesses and under manifolds).

A more advanced set of tools, suitable for tune-up work, can be drawn up easily. While the tools are slightly more sophisticated, they need not be outrageously expensive. There are several inexpensive tach/dwell meters on the market that are every bit as good for the average mechanic as a professional model. Just be sure that it goes to a least 1200–1500 rpm on the tach scale and that it works on 4, 6 and 8-cylinder engines. (If you have one or more vehicles with a diesel engine, a special tachometer is required since diesels don't use spark plug ignition systems). The key to these purchases is to make them with an eye towards adaptability and wide range. A basic list of tune-up tools could include:

- Tach/dwell meter.
- Spark plug wrench and gapping tool.

- Feeler gauges for valve or point adjustment. (Even if your vehicle does not use points or require valve adjustments, a feeler gauge is helpful for many repair/overhaul procedures).

A tachometer/dwell meter will ensure accurate tune-up work on vehicles without electronic ignition. The choice of a timing light should be made carefully. A light which works on the DC current supplied by the vehicle's battery is the best choice; it should have a xenon tube for brightness. On any vehicle with an electronic ignition system, a timing light with an inductive pickup that clamps around the No. 1 spark plug cable is preferred.

In addition to these basic tools, there are several other tools and gauges you may find useful. These include:

- Compression gauge. The screw-in type is slower to use, but eliminates the possibility of a faulty reading due to escaping pressure.
- Manifold vacuum gauge.
- 12V test light.
- A combination volt/ohmmeter
- Induction Ammeter. This is used for determining whether or not there is current in a wire. These are handy for use if a wire is broken somewhere in a wiring harness.

As a final note, you will probably find a torque wrench necessary for all but the most basic work. The beam type models are perfectly adequate, although the newer click types (breakaway) are easier to use. The click type torque wrenches tend to be more expensive. Also keep in mind that all types of torque wrenches should be periodically checked and/or recalibrated. You will have to decide for yourself which better fits your purpose.

## Special Tools

Normally, the use of special factory tools is avoided for repair procedures, since these are not readily available for the do-it-yourself mechanic. When it is possible to perform the job with more commonly available tools, it will be pointed out, but occasionally, a special tool was designed to perform a specific function and should be used. Before substituting another tool, you should be convinced that neither your safety nor the performance of the vehicle will be compromised.

Special tools can usually be purchased from an automotive parts store or from your dealer. In some cases special tools may be available directly from the tool manufacturer.

# DIAGNOSTIC TEST EQUIPMENT

Modern vehicles equipped with computer-controlled fuel, emission and ignition systems require modern electronic tools to diagnose problems. Many of these tools are designed solely for the professional mechanic and are too costly and difficult to use for the average do-it-yourselfer. However, various automotive aftermarket companies have introduced products that address the needs of the average home mechanic, providing sophisticated information at affordable cost. Consult your local auto parts store to determine what is available for your vehicle.

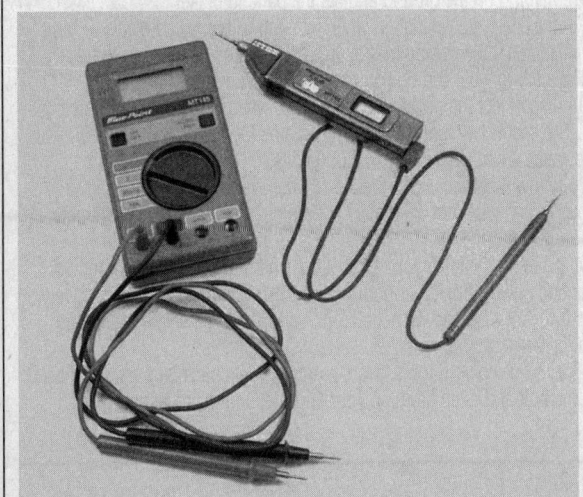

**Digital multimeters** come in a variety of styles and are a "must-have" for any serious home mechanic. Digital multimeters measure voltage (volts), resistance (ohms) and sometimes current (amperes). These versatile tools are used for checking all types of electrical or electronic components

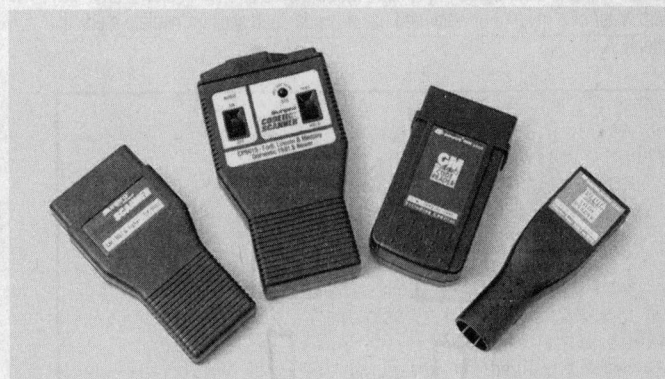

**Trouble code tools** allow the home mechanic to extract the "fault code" number from an on-board computer that has sensed a problem (usually indicated by a Check Engine light). Armed with this code, the home mechanic can focus attention on a suspect system or component

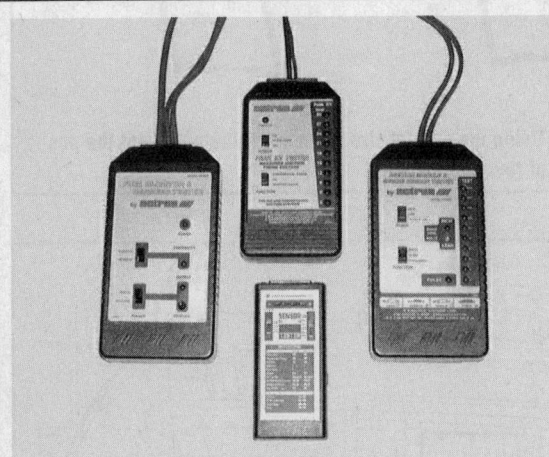

**Sensor testers** perform specific checks on many of the sensors and actuators used on today's computer-controlled vehicles. These testers can check sensors both on or off the vehicle, as well as test the accompanying electrical circuits

**Hand-held scanners** represent the most sophisticated of all do-it-yourself diagnostic tools. These tools do more than just access computer codes like the code readers above; they provide the user with an actual interface into the vehicle's computer. Comprehensive data on specific makes and models will come with the tool, either built-in or as a separate cartridge

## SERVICING YOUR VEHICLE SAFELY

▶ **See Figures 16, 17, 18 and 19**

It is virtually impossible to anticipate all of the hazards involved with automotive maintenance and service, but care and common sense will prevent most accidents.

The rules of safety for mechanics range from "don't smoke around gasoline," to "use the proper tool(s) for the job." The trick to avoiding injuries is to develop safe work habits and to take every possible precaution.

### Do's

• Do keep a fire extinguisher and first aid kit handy.
• Do wear safety glasses or goggles when cutting, drilling, grinding or prying, even if you have 20–20 vision. If you wear glasses for the sake of vision, wear safety goggles over your regular glasses.
• Do shield your eyes whenever you work around the battery. Batteries contain sulfuric acid. In case of contact with the eyes or skin, flush the area with water or a mixture of water and baking soda, then seek immediate medical attention.

• Do use safety stands (jackstands) for any undervehicle service. Jacks are for raising vehicles; jackstands are for making sure the vehicle stays raised until you want it to come down. Whenever the vehicle is raised, block the wheels remaining on the ground and set the parking brake.
• Do use adequate ventilation when working with any chemicals or hazardous materials. Like carbon monoxide, the asbestos dust resulting from some brake lining wear can be hazardous in sufficient quantities.
• Do disconnect the negative battery cable when working on the electrical system. The secondary ignition system contains EXTREMELY HIGH VOLTAGE. In some cases it can even exceed 50,000 volts.
• Do follow manufacturer's directions whenever working with potentially hazardous materials. Most chemicals and fluids are poisonous if taken internally.
• Do properly maintain your tools. Loose hammerheads, mushroomed punches and chisels, frayed or poorly grounded electrical cords, excessively worn screwdrivers, spread wrenches (open end), cracked sockets, slipping ratchets, or faulty droplight sockets can cause accidents.
• Likewise, keep your tools clean; a greasy wrench can slip off a bolt head, ruining the bolt and often harming your knuckles in the process.

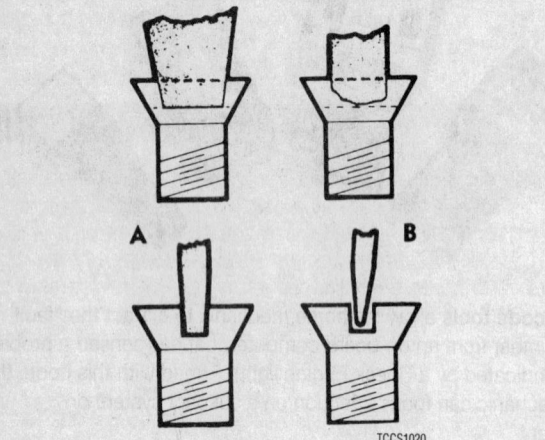

**Fig. 16 Screwdrivers should be kept in good condition to prevent injury or damage which could result if the blade slips from the screw**

**Fig. 18 Using the correct size wrench will help prevent the possibility of rounding off a nut**

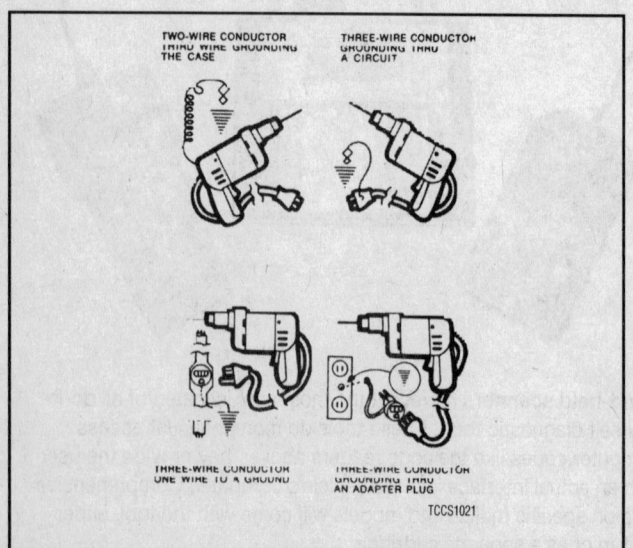

**Fig. 17 Power tools should always be properly grounded**

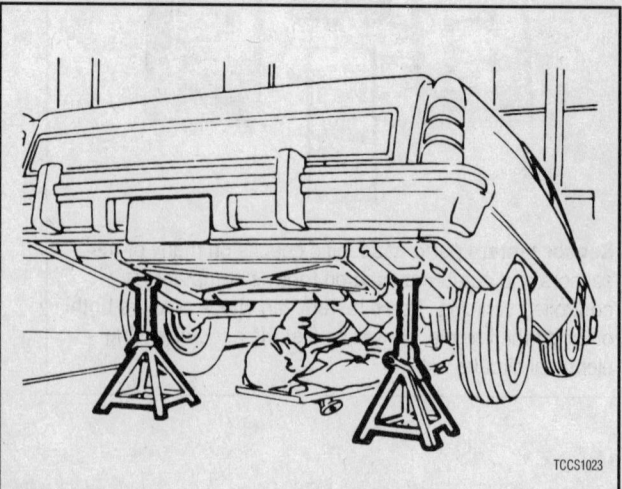

**Fig. 19 NEVER work under a vehicle unless it is supported using safety stands (jackstands)**

• Do use the proper size and type of tool for the job at hand. Do select a wrench or socket that fits the nut or bolt. The wrench or socket should sit straight, not cocked.

• Do, when possible, pull on a wrench handle rather than push on it, and adjust your stance to prevent a fall.

• Do be sure that adjustable wrenches are tightly closed on the nut or bolt and pulled so that the force is on the side of the fixed jaw.

• Do strike squarely with a hammer; avoid glancing blows.

• Do set the parking brake and block the drive wheels if the work requires a running engine.

## Don'ts

• Don't run the engine in a garage or anywhere else without proper ventilation—EVER! Carbon monoxide is poisonous; it takes a long time to leave the human body and you can build up a deadly supply of it in your system by simply breathing in a little every day. You may not realize you are slowly poisoning yourself. Always use power vents, windows, fans and/or open the garage door.

• Don't work around moving parts while wearing loose clothing. Short sleeves are much safer than long, loose sleeves. Hard-toed shoes with neoprene soles protect your toes and give a better grip on slippery surfaces. Jewelry such as watches, fancy belt buckles, beads or body adornment of any kind is not safe working around a vehicle. Long hair should be tied back under a hat or cap.

• Don't use pockets for toolboxes. A fall or bump can drive a screwdriver

deep into your body. Even a rag hanging from your back pocket can wrap around a spinning shaft or fan.

• Don't smoke when working around gasoline, cleaning solvent or other flammable material.

• Don't smoke when working around the battery. When the battery is being charged, it gives off explosive hydrogen gas.

• Don't use gasoline to wash your hands; there are excellent soaps available. Gasoline contains dangerous additives which can enter the body through a cut or through your pores. Gasoline also removes all the natural oils from the skin so that bone dry hands will suck up oil and grease.

• Don't service the air conditioning system unless you are equipped with the necessary tools and training. When liquid or compressed gas refrigerant is released to atmospheric pressure it will absorb heat from whatever it contacts. This will chill or freeze anything it touches. Although refrigerant is normally non-toxic, R-12 becomes a deadly poisonous gas in the presence of an open flame. One good whiff of the vapors from burning refrigerant can be fatal.

• Don't use screwdrivers for anything other than driving screws! A screwdriver used as an prying tool can snap when you least expect it, causing injuries. At the very least, you'll ruin a good screwdriver.

• Don't use a bumper or emergency jack (that little ratchet, scissors, or pantograph jack supplied with the vehicle) for anything other than changing a flat! These jacks are only intended for emergency use out on the road; they are NOT designed as a maintenance tool. If you are serious about maintaining your vehicle yourself, invest in a hydraulic floor jack of at least a 1½ ton capacity, and at least two sturdy jackstands.

## FASTENERS, MEASUREMENTS AND CONVERSIONS

### Bolts, Nuts and Other Threaded Retainers

▶ See Figures 20, 21, 22 and 23

Although there are a great variety of fasteners found in the modern car or truck, the most commonly used retainer is the threaded fastener (nuts, bolts, screws, studs, etc). Most threaded retainers may be reused, provided that they are not damaged in use or during the repair. Some retainers (such as stretch bolts or torque prevailing nuts) are designed to deform when tightened or in use and should not be reinstalled.

Whenever possible, we will note any special retainers which should be replaced during a procedure. But you should always inspect the condition of a retainer when it is removed and replace any that show signs of damage. Check all threads for rust or corrosion which can increase the torque necessary to achieve the desired clamp load for which that fastener was originally selected. Additionally, be sure that the driver surface of the fastener has not been compromised by rounding or other damage. In some cases a driver surface may become only partially rounded, allowing the driver to catch in only one direction. In many of these occurrences, a fastener may be installed and tightened, but the driver would not be able to

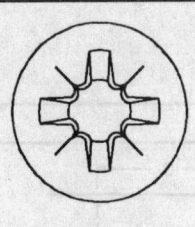

POZIDRIVE

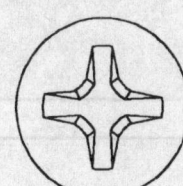

PHILLIPS RECESS

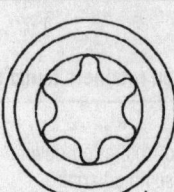

TORX®

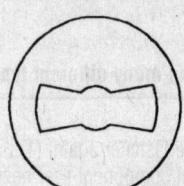

CLUTCH RECESS

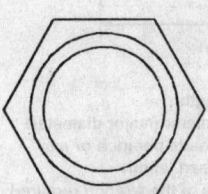

INDENTED HEXAGON

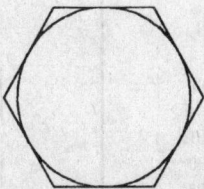

HEXAGON TRIMMED

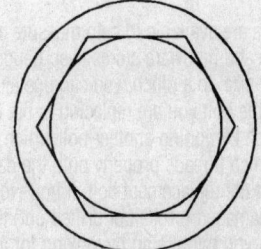

HEXAGON WASHER HEAD

TCCS1037

Fig. 20 Here are a few of the most common screw/bolt driver styles

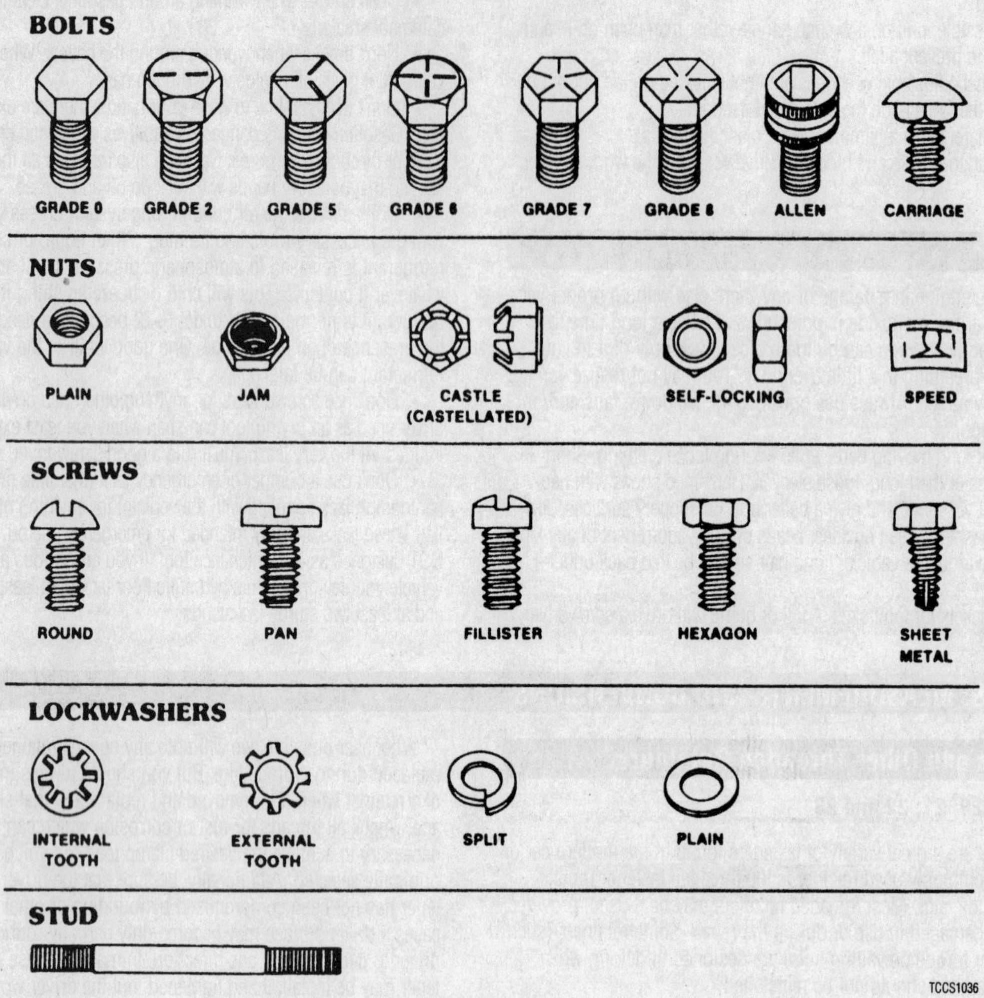

## BOLTS

GRADE 0    GRADE 2    GRADE 5    GRADE 6    GRADE 7    GRADE 8    ALLEN    CARRIAGE

## NUTS

PLAIN    JAM    CASTLE (CASTELLATED)    SELF-LOCKING    SPEED

## SCREWS

ROUND    PAN    FILLISTER    HEXAGON    SHEET METAL

## LOCKWASHERS

INTERNAL TOOTH    EXTERNAL TOOTH    SPLIT    PLAIN

## STUD

TCCS1036

**Fig. 21 There are many different types of threaded retainers found on vehicles**

grip and loosen the fastener again. (This could lead to frustration down the line should that component ever need to be disassembled again).

If you must replace a fastener, whether due to design or damage, you must ALWAYS be sure to use the proper replacement. In all cases, a retainer of the same design, material and strength should be used. Markings on the heads of most bolts will help determine the proper strength of the fastener. The same material, thread and pitch must be selected to assure proper installation and safe operation of the vehicle afterwards.

Thread gauges are available to help measure a bolt or stud's thread. Most automotive and hardware stores keep gauges available to help you select the proper size. In a pinch, you can use another nut or bolt for a thread gauge. If the bolt you are replacing is not too badly damaged, you can select a match by finding another bolt which will thread in its place. If you find a nut which threads properly onto the damaged bolt, then use that nut to help select the replacement bolt. If however, the bolt you are replacing is so badly damaged (broken or drilled out) that its threads cannot be used as a gauge, you might start by looking for another bolt (from the same assembly or a similar location on your vehicle) which will thread into the damaged bolt's mounting. If so, the other bolt can be used to select a nut; the nut can then be used to select the replacement bolt.

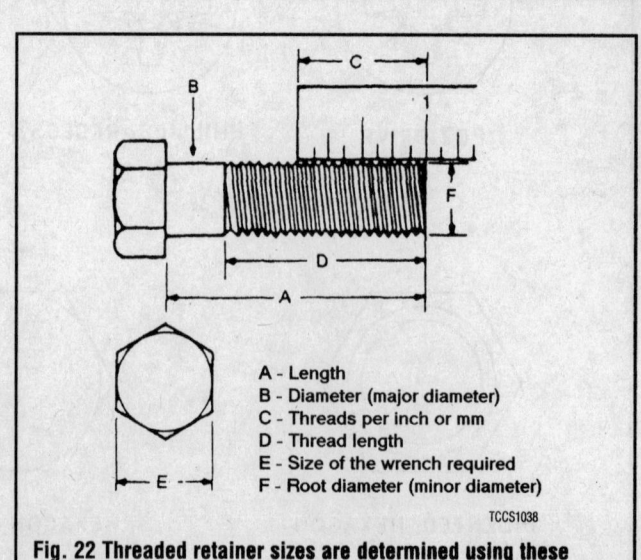

A - Length
B - Diameter (major diameter)
C - Threads per inch or mm
D - Thread length
E - Size of the wrench required
F - Root diameter (minor diameter)

TCCS1038

**Fig. 22 Threaded retainer sizes are determined using these measurements**

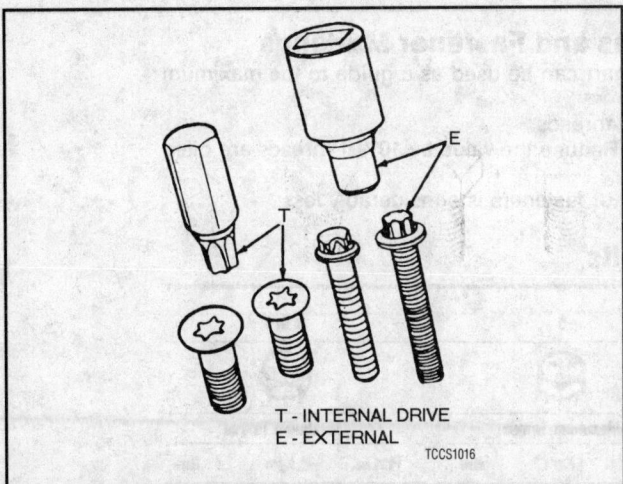

T - INTERNAL DRIVE
E - EXTERNAL

TCCS1016

**Fig. 23 Special fasteners such as these Torx® head bolts are used by manufacturers to discourage people from working on vehicles without the proper tools**

In all cases, be absolutely sure you have selected the proper replacement. Don't be shy, you can always ask the store clerk for help.

### ✳✳ WARNING

**Be aware that when you find a bolt with damaged threads, you may also find the nut or drilled hole it was threaded into has also been damaged. If this is the case, you may have to drill and tap the hole, replace the nut or otherwise repair the threads. NEVER try to force a replacement bolt to fit into the damaged threads.**

### Torque

Torque is defined as the measurement of resistance to turning or rotating. It tends to twist a body about an axis of rotation. A common example of this would be tightening a threaded retainer such as a nut, bolt or screw. Measuring torque is one of the most common ways to help assure that a threaded retainer has been properly fastened.

When tightening a threaded fastener, torque is applied in three distinct areas, the head, the bearing surface and the clamp load. About 50 percent of the measured torque is used in overcoming bearing friction. This is the friction between the bearing surface of the bolt head, screw head or nut face and the base material or washer (the surface on which the fastener is rotating). Approximately 40 percent of the applied torque is used in overcoming thread friction. This leaves only about 10 percent of the applied torque to develop a useful clamp load (the force which holds a joint together). This means that friction can account for as much as 90 percent of the applied torque on a fastener.

### TORQUE WRENCHES

#### ▶ See Figures 24 and 25

In most applications, a torque wrench can be used to assure proper installation of a fastener. Torque wrenches come in various designs and most automotive supply stores will carry a variety to suit your needs. A torque wrench should be used any time we supply a specific torque value for a fastener. A torque wrench can also be used if you are following the general guidelines in the accompanying charts. Keep in mind that because there is no worldwide standardization of fasteners, the charts are a general guideline and should be used with caution. Again, the general rule of "if you are using the right tool for the job, you should not have to strain to tighten a fastener" applies here.

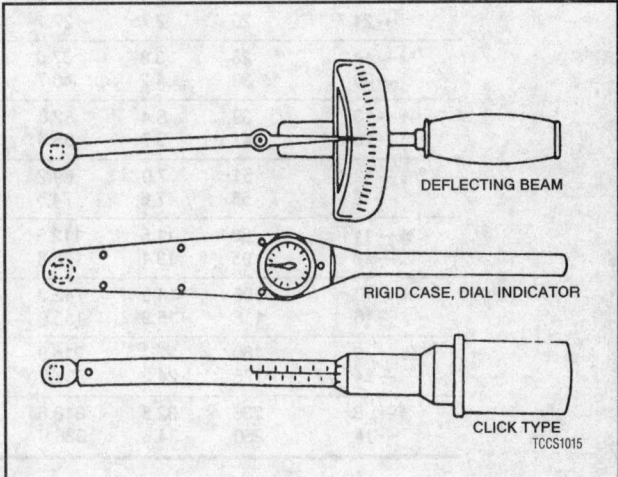

DEFLECTING BEAM

RIGID CASE, DIAL INDICATOR

CLICK TYPE

TCCS1015

**Fig. 24 Various styles of torque wrenches are usually available at your local automotive supply store**

## Standard Torque Specifications and Fastener Markings

In the absence of specific torques, the following chart can be used as a guide to the maximum safe torque of a particular size/grade of fastener.

- There is no torque difference for fine or coarse threads.
- Torque values are based on clean, dry threads. Reduce the value by 10% if threads are oiled prior to assembly.
- The torque required for aluminum components or fasteners is considerably less.

### U.S. Bolts

| SAE Grade Number | 1 or 2 | | | 5 | | | 6 or 7 | | |
|---|---|---|---|---|---|---|---|---|---|
| Number of lines always 2 less than the grade number. |  | | |  | | |  | | |
| Bolt Size (Inches)—(Thread) | **Maximum Torque** | | | **Maximum Torque** | | | **Maximum Torque** | | |
| | Ft./Lbs. | Kgm | Nm | Ft./Lbs. | Kgm | Nm | Ft./Lbs. | Kgm | Nm |
| ¼ — 20 | 5 | 0.7 | 6.8 | 8 | 1.1 | 10.8 | 10 | 1.4 | 13.5 |
| — 28 | 6 | 0.8 | 8.1 | 10 | 1.4 | 13.6 | | | |
| ⁵⁄₁₆ — 18 | 11 | 1.5 | 14.9 | 17 | 2.3 | 23.0 | 19 | 2.6 | 25.8 |
| — 24 | 13 | 1.8 | 17.6 | 19 | 2.6 | 25.7 | | | |
| ⅜ — 16 | 18 | 2.5 | 24.4 | 31 | 4.3 | 42.0 | 34 | 4.7 | 46.0 |
| — 24 | 20 | 2.75 | 27.1 | 35 | 4.8 | 47.5 | | | |
| ⁷⁄₁₆ — 14 | 28 | 3.8 | 37.0 | 49 | 6.8 | 66.4 | 55 | 7.6 | 74.5 |
| — 20 | 30 | 4.2 | 40.7 | 55 | 7.6 | 74.5 | | | |
| ½ — 13 | 39 | 5.4 | 52.8 | 75 | 10.4 | 101.7 | 85 | 11.75 | 115.2 |
| — 20 | 41 | 5.7 | 55.6 | 85 | 11.7 | 115.2 | | | |
| ⁹⁄₁₆ — 12 | 51 | 7.0 | 69.2 | 110 | 15.2 | 149.1 | 120 | 16.6 | 162.7 |
| — 18 | 55 | 7.6 | 74.5 | 120 | 16.6 | 162.7 | | | |
| ⅝ — 11 | 83 | 11.5 | 112.5 | 150 | 20.7 | 203.3 | 167 | 23.0 | 226.5 |
| — 18 | 95 | 13.1 | 128.8 | 170 | 23.5 | 230.5 | | | |
| ¾ — 10 | 105 | 14.5 | 142.3 | 270 | 37.3 | 366.0 | 280 | 38.7 | 379.6 |
| — 16 | 115 | 15.9 | 155.9 | 295 | 40.8 | 400.0 | | | |
| ⅞ — 9 | 160 | 22.1 | 216.9 | 395 | 54.6 | 535.5 | 440 | 60.9 | 596.5 |
| — 14 | 175 | 24.2 | 237.2 | 435 | 60.1 | 589.7 | | | |
| 1 — 8 | 236 | 32.5 | 318.6 | 590 | 81.6 | 799.9 | 660 | 91.3 | 894.8 |
| — 14 | 250 | 34.6 | 338.9 | 660 | 91.3 | 849.8 | | | |

### Metric Bolts

| Relative Strength Marking | 4.6, 4.8 | | | 8.8 | | |
|---|---|---|---|---|---|---|
| Bolt Markings |  | | |  | | |
| Bolt Size Thread Size x Pitch (mm) | **Maximum Torque** | | | **Maximum Torque** | | |
| | Ft./Lbs. | Kgm | Nm | Ft./Lbs. | Kgm | Nm |
| 6 x 1.0 | 2–3 | .2–.4 | 3–4 | 3–6 | 4–.8 | 5–8 |
| 8 x 1.25 | 6–8 | .8–1 | 8–12 | 9–14 | 1.2–1.9 | 13–19 |
| 10 x 1.25 | 12–17 | 1.5–2.3 | 16–23 | 20–29 | 2.7–4.0 | 27–39 |
| 12 x 1.25 | 21–32 | 2.9–4.4 | 29–43 | 35–53 | 4.8–7.3 | 47–72 |
| 14 x 1.5 | 35–52 | 4.8–7.1 | 48–70 | 57–85 | 7.8–11.7 | 77–110 |
| 16 x 1.5 | 51–77 | 7.0–10.6 | 67–100 | 90–120 | 12.4–16.5 | 130–160 |
| 18 x 1.5 | 74–110 | 10.2–15.1 | 100–150 | 130–170 | 17.9–23.4 | 180–230 |
| 20 x 1.5 | 110–140 | 15.1–19.3 | 150–190 | 190–240 | 26.2–46.9 | 160–320 |
| 22 x 1.5 | 150–190 | 22.0–26.2 | 200–260 | 250–320 | 34.5–44.1 | 340–430 |
| 24 x 1.5 | 190–240 | 26.2–46.9 | 260–320 | 310–410 | 42.7–56.5 | 420–550 |

TCCS1098

Fig. 25 Standard and metric bolt torque specifications based on bolt strengths—WARNING: use only as a guide

## Beam Type

▶ **See Figure 26**

The beam type torque wrench is one of the most popular types. It consists of a pointer attached to the head that runs the length of the flexible beam (shaft) to a scale located near the handle. As the wrench is pulled, the beam bends and the pointer indicates the torque using the scale.

## Click (Breakaway) Type

▶ **See Figure 27**

Another popular design of torque wrench is the click type. To use the click type wrench you pre-adjust it to a torque setting. Once the torque is reached, the wrench has a reflex signaling feature that causes a momentary breakaway of the torque wrench body, sending an impulse to the operator's hand.

## Pivot Head Type

▶ **See Figures 27 and 28**

Some torque wrenches (usually of the click type) may be equipped with a pivot head which can allow it to be used in areas of limited access. BUT, it must be used properly. To hold a pivot head wrench, grasp the handle lightly, and as you pull on the handle, it should be floated on the pivot point. If the handle comes in contact with the yoke extension during the process of pulling, there is a very good chance the torque readings will be inaccurate because this could alter the wrench loading point. The design of the handle is usually such as to make it inconvenient to deliberately misuse the wrench.

➡️ It should be mentioned that the use of any U-joint, wobble or extension will have an effect on the torque readings, no matter what type of wrench you are using. For the most accurate readings, install the socket directly on the wrench driver. If necessary, straight extensions (which hold a socket directly under the wrench driver) will have the least effect on the torque reading. Avoid any extension that alters the length of the wrench from the handle to the head/driving point (such as a crow's foot). U-joint or Wobble extensions can greatly affect the readings; avoid their use at all times.

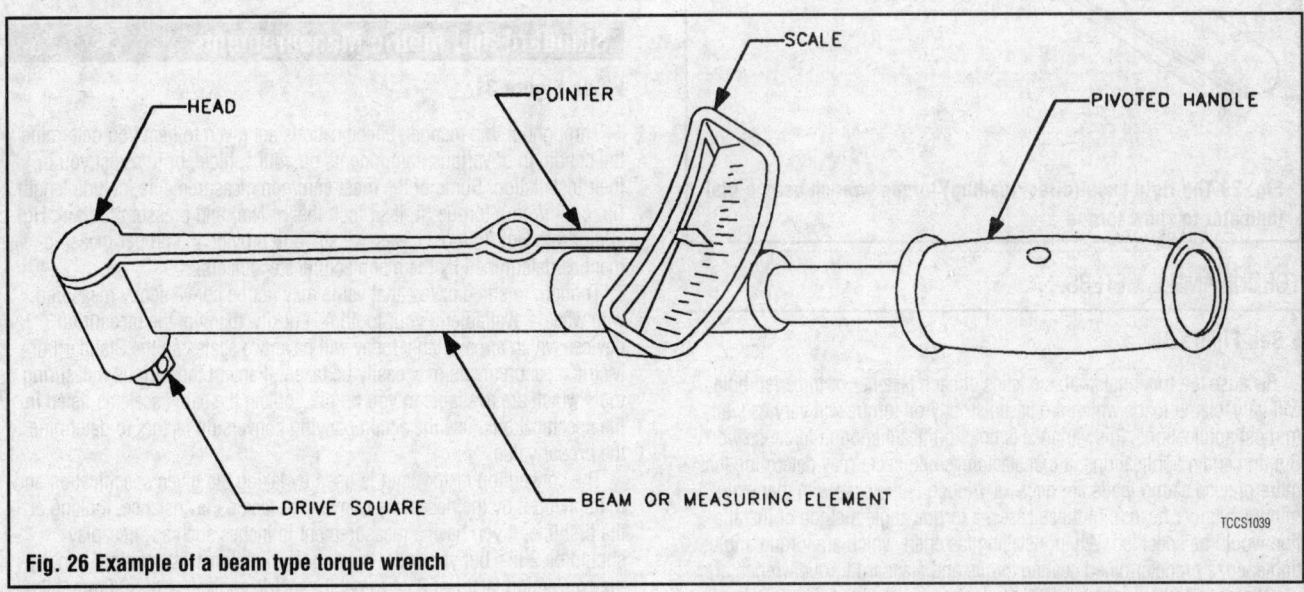

Fig. 26 Example of a beam type torque wrench

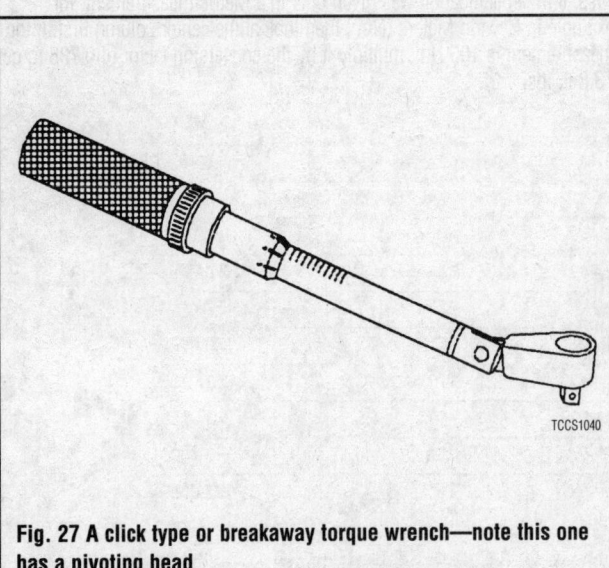

Fig. 27 A click type or breakaway torque wrench—note this one has a pivoting head

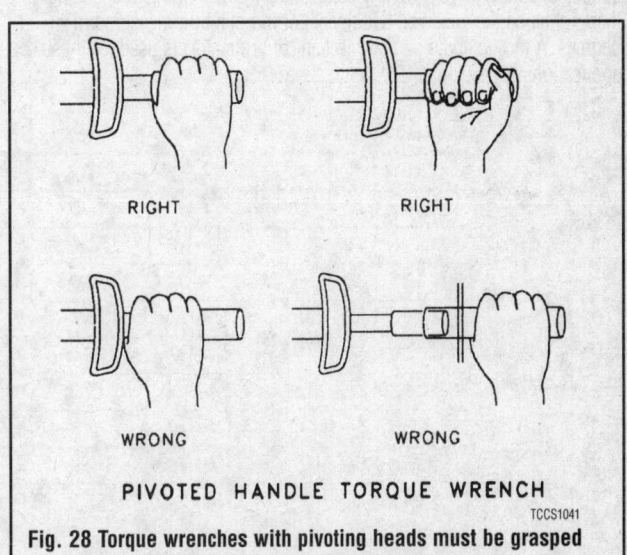

Fig. 28 Torque wrenches with pivoting heads must be grasped and used properly to prevent an incorrect reading

## Rigid Case (Direct Reading)

▶ **See Figure 29**

A rigid case or direct reading torque wrench is equipped with a dial indicator to show torque values. One advantage of these wrenches is that they can be held at any position on the wrench without affecting accuracy. These wrenches are often preferred because they tend to be compact, easy to read and have a great degree of accuracy.

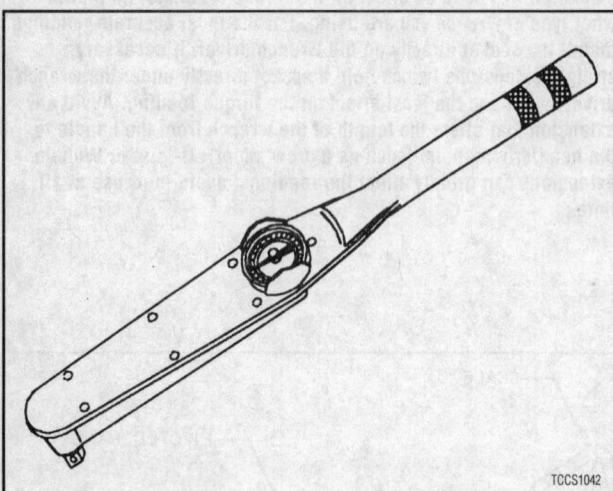

TCCS1042

**Fig. 29 The rigid case (direct reading) torque wrench uses a dial indicator to show torque**

## TORQUE ANGLE METERS

▶ **See Figure 30**

Because the frictional characteristics of each fastener or threaded hole will vary, clamp loads which are based strictly on torque will vary as well. In most applications, this variance is not significant enough to cause worry. But, in certain applications, a manufacturer's engineers may determine that more precise clamp loads are necessary (such is the case with many aluminum cylinder heads). In these cases, a torque angle method of installation would be specified. When installing fasteners which are torque angle tightened, a predetermined seating torque and standard torque wrench are usually used first to remove any compliance from the joint. The fastener is then tightened the specified additional portion of a turn measured in degrees. A torque angle gauge (mechanical protractor) is used for these applications.

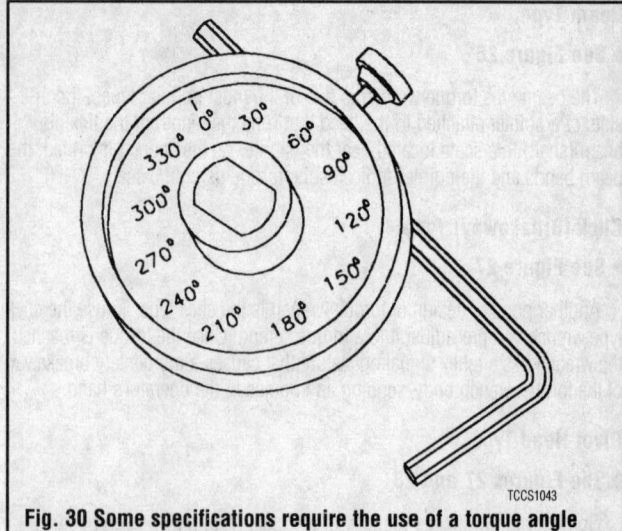

TCCS1043

**Fig. 30 Some specifications require the use of a torque angle meter (mechanical protractor)**

## Standard and Metric Measurements

▶ **See Figure 31**

Throughout this manual, specifications are given to help you determine the condition of various components on your vehicle, or to assist you in their installation. Some of the most common measurements include length (in. or cm/mm), torque (ft. lbs., inch lbs. or Nm) and pressure (psi, in. Hg, kPa or mm Hg). In most cases, we strive to provide the proper measurement as determined by the manufacturer's engineers.

Though, in some cases, that value may not be conveniently measured with what is available in your toolbox. Luckily, many of the measuring devices which are available today will have two scales so the Standard or Metric measurements may easily be taken. If any of the various measuring tools which are available to you do not contain the same scale as listed in the specifications, use the accompanying conversion factors to determine the proper value.

The conversion factor chart is used by taking the given specification and multiplying it by the necessary conversion factor. For instance, looking at the first line, if you have a measurement in inches such as "free-play should be 2 in." but your ruler reads only in millimeters, multiply 2 in. by the conversion factor of 25.4 to get the metric equivalent of 50.8mm. Likewise, if the specification was given only in a Metric measurement, for example in Newton Meters (Nm), then look at the center column first. If the measurement is 100 Nm, multiply it by the conversion factor of 0.738 to get 73.8 ft. lbs.

# CONVERSION FACTORS

## LENGTH–DISTANCE

| | | | | |
|---|---|---|---|---|
| Inches (in.) | x 25.4 | = Millimeters (mm) | x .0394 | = Inches |
| Feet (ft.) | x .305 | = Meters (m) | x 3.281 | = Feet |
| Miles | x 1.609 | = Kilometers (km) | x .0621 | = Miles |

## VOLUME

| | | | | |
|---|---|---|---|---|
| Cubic Inches (in3) | x 16.387 | = Cubic Centimeters | x .061 | = in3 |
| IMP Pints (IMP pt.) | x .568 | = Liters (L) | x 1.76 | = IMP pt. |
| IMP Quarts (IMP qt.) | x 1.137 | = Liters (L) | x .88 | = IMP qt. |
| IMP Gallons (IMP gal.) | x 4.546 | = Liters (L) | x .22 | = IMP gal. |
| IMP Quarts (IMP qt.) | x 1.201 | = US Quarts (US qt.) | x .833 | = IMP qt. |
| IMP Gallons (IMP gal.) | x 1.201 | = US Gallons (US gal.) | x .833 | = IMP gal. |
| Fl. Ounces | x 29.573 | = Milliliters | x .034 | = Ounces |
| US Pints (US pt.) | x .473 | = Liters (L) | x 2.113 | = Pints |
| US Quarts (US qt.) | x .946 | = Liters (L) | x 1.057 | = Quarts |
| US Gallons (US gal.) | x 3.785 | = Liters (L) | x .264 | = Gallons |

## MASS–WEIGHT

| | | | | |
|---|---|---|---|---|
| Ounces (oz.) | x 28.35 | = Grams (g) | x .035 | = Ounces |
| Pounds (lb.) | x .454 | = Kilograms (kg) | x 2.205 | = Pounds |

## PRESSURE

| | | | | |
|---|---|---|---|---|
| Pounds Per Sq. In. (psi) | x 6.895 | = Kilopascals (kPa) | x .145 | = psi |
| Inches of Mercury (Hg) | x .4912 | = psi | x 2.036 | = Hg |
| Inches of Mercury (Hg) | x 3.377 | = Kilopascals (kPa) | x .2961 | = Hg |
| Inches of Water ($H_2O$) | x .07355 | = Inches of Mercury | x 13.783 | = $H_2O$ |
| Inches of Water ($H_2O$) | x .03613 | = psi | x 27.684 | = $H_2O$ |
| Inches of Water ($H_2O$) | x .248 | = Kilopascals (kPa) | x 4.026 | = $H_2O$ |

## TORQUE

| | | | | |
|---|---|---|---|---|
| Pounds–Force Inches (in–lb) | x .113 | = Newton Meters (N·m) | x 8.85 | = in–lb |
| Pounds–Force Feet (ft–lb) | x 1.356 | = Newton Meters (N·m) | x .738 | = ft–lb |

## VELOCITY

| | | | | |
|---|---|---|---|---|
| Miles Per Hour (MPH) | x 1.609 | = Kilometers Per Hour (KPH) | x .621 | = MPH |

## POWER

| | | | | |
|---|---|---|---|---|
| Horsepower (Hp) | x .745 | = Kilowatts | x 1.34 | = Horsepower |

## FUEL CONSUMPTION*

| | | |
|---|---|---|
| Miles Per Gallon IMP (MPG) | x .354 | = Kilometers Per Liter (Km/L) |
| Kilometers Per Liter (Km/L) | x 2.352 | = IMP MPG |
| Miles Per Gallon US (MPG) | x .425 | = Kilometers Per Liter (Km/L) |
| Kilometers Per Liter (Km/L) | x 2.352 | = US MPG |

*It is common to covert from miles per gallon (mpg) to liters/100 kilometers (1/100 km), where mpg (IMP) x 1/100 km = 282 and mpg (US) x 1/100 km = 235.

## TEMPERATURE

Degree Fahrenheit (°F)  = (°C x 1.8) + 32
Degree Celsius (°C)  = (°F – 32) x .56

TCCS1044

**Fig. 31 Standard and metric conversion factors chart**

## SERIAL NUMBER IDENTIFICATION

### Vehicle

▶ See Figures 32 and 33

The Vehicle Identification Number (VIN) is stamped on a plate located on the top left hand side (driver's side) of the instrument panel. It can be seen by looking through the windshield. The VIN is made up of 17 digits in a combination of numbers and letters that contain specific information regarding the vehicle.

### Engine

▶ See Figures 34 and 35

The engine code is represented by the eighth character in the VIN and identifies the engine type, displacement, fuel system and manufacturing division.

The engine identification code is either stamped onto the engine block or found on a label affixed to the engine. This code supplies information about the manufacturing plant location and time of manufacture.

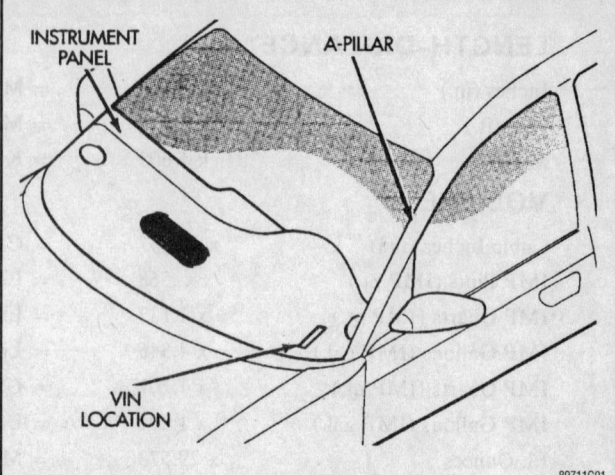

Fig. 32 The VIN plate is mounted to the dash panel and is visible through the windshield

| POSITION | INTERPRETATION | CODE = DESCRIPTION |
|---|---|---|
| 1 | Country of Origin | 1 = United states<br>3 = Mexico |
| 2 | Make | B = Dodge<br>P = Plymouth |
| 3 | Vehicle Type | 3 = Passenger Car |
| 4 | Pass. Safety | E = Active Restraints, Driver & Passenger Airbags |
| 5 | Car Line | S = Neon/Neon Expresso |
| 6 | Series | 2 = Low Line<br>4 = High Line<br>6 = Sport |
| 7 | Body Style | 2 = 2 Door Pillared Hardtop<br>7 = 4 Door Pillared Hardtop |
| 8 | Engine | C = 2.0L 4 Cyl. 16V<br>Y = 2.0L 4 Cyl. DOHC |
| 9 | Check Digit | |
| 10 | Model Year | W = 1998 |
| 11 | Assembly Plant | D = Belvidere<br>T = Toluca |
| 12 Thru 17 | Vehicle Build Sequence | 6 digit number assigned by assembly plant. |

89711G02

Fig. 33 Vehicle Identification Number (VIN) decoding

## VEHICLE IDENTIFICATION CHART

| Engine Code | | | | | | Model Year | |
|---|---|---|---|---|---|---|---|
| Code | Liters | Cu. In. (cc) | Cyl. | Fuel Sys. | Eng. Mfg. | Code | Year |
| C | 2.0 | 121.8 (1996) | 4 | MPI | Chrysler | S | 1995 |
| Y | 2.0 | 121.8 (1996) | 4 | MPI | Chrysler | T | 1996 |
| | | | | | | V | 1997 |
| | | | | | | W | 1998 |
| | | | | | | X | 1999 |

MPI - Multi-Port electronic fuel Injection

88271C01

Fig. 34 Location of the engine identification number—2.0L SOHC engine

89711G20

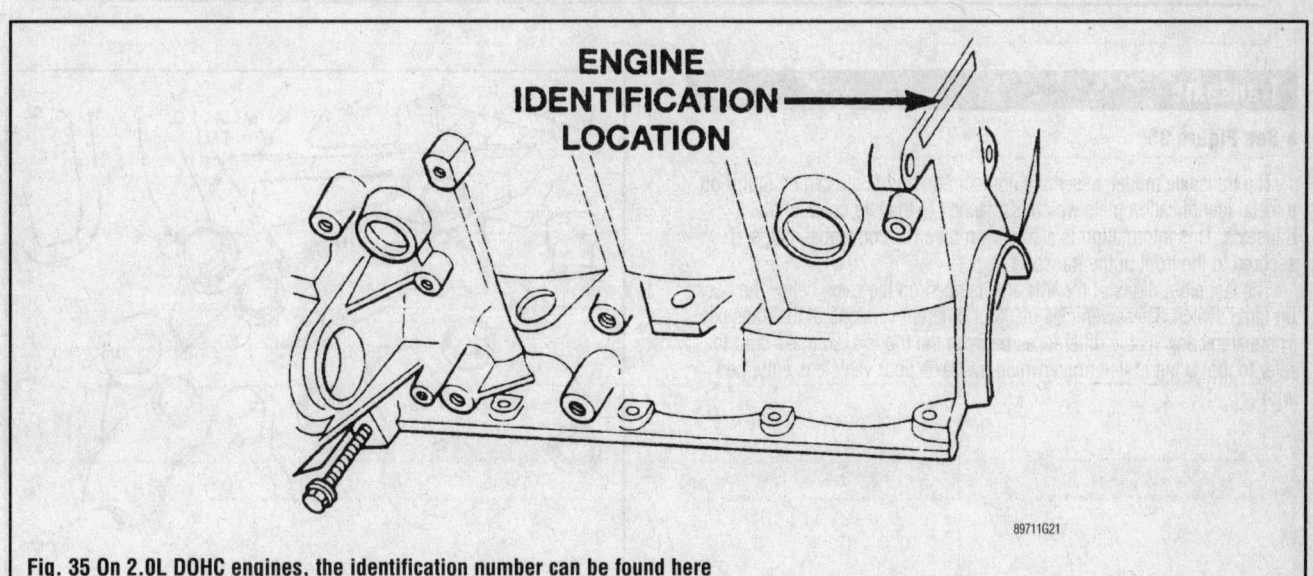

Fig. 35 On 2.0L DOHC engines, the identification number can be found here

89711G21

## ENGINE IDENTIFICATION

| Year | Model | Engine Displacement Liters (cc) | Engine Series (ID/VIN) | Fuel System | No. of Cylinders | Engine Type |
|------|-------|-------------------------------|----------------------|-------------|-----------------|-------------|
| 1995 | Neon | 2.0 (1996) | C | MPI | 4 | SOHC |
|      | Neon | 2.0 (1996) | Y | MPI | 4 | DOHC |
| 1996 | Neon | 2.0 (1996) | C | MPI | 4 | SOHC |
|      | Neon | 2.0 (1996) | Y | MPI | 4 | DOHC |
| 1997 | Neon | 2.0 (1996) | C | MPI | 4 | SOHC |
|      | Neon | 2.0 (1996) | Y | MPI | 4 | DOHC |
| 1998 | Neon | 2.0 (1996) | C | MPI | 4 | SOHC |
|      | Neon | 2.0 (1996) | Y | MPI | 4 | DOHC |
| 1999 | Neon | 2.0 (1996) | C | MPI | 4 | SOHC |
|      | Neon | 2.0 (1996) | Y | MPI | 4 | DOHC |

MPI - Multi-Port electronic fuel Injection

SOHC - Single OverHead Cam

DOHC - Dual OverHead Cam

89711C02

## GENERAL ENGINE SPECIFICATIONS

| Year | Engine ID/VIN | Engine Displacement Liters (cc) | Fuel System Type | Net Horsepower @ rpm | Net Torque @ rpm (ft. lbs.) | Bore x Stroke (in.) | Compression Ratio | Oil Pressure @ rpm |
|------|--------------|-------------------------------|-----------------|---------------------|----------------------------|---------------------|-------------------|-------------------|
| 1995 | C | 2.0 (1996) | MPI | 132 @ 6000 | 129 @ 5000 | 3.44 x 3.27 | 9.8:1 | 25-80@3000 |
|      | Y | 2.0 (1996) | MPI | 150 @ 6500 | 133 @ 5500 | 3.44 x 3.27 | 9.6:1 | 25-80@3000 |
| 1996 | C | 2.0 (1996) | MPI | 132 @ 6000 | 129 @ 5000 | 3.44 x 3.27 | 9.8:1 | 25-80@3000 |
|      | Y | 2.0 (1996) | MPI | 150 @ 6500 | 133 @ 5500 | 3.44 x 3.27 | 9.6:1 | 25-80@3000 |
| 1997 | C | 2.0 (1996) | MPI | 132 @ 6000 | 129 @ 5000 | 3.44 x 3.27 | 9.8:1 | 25-80@3000 |
|      | Y | 2.0 (1996) | MPI | 150 @ 6500 | 133 @ 5500 | 3.44 x 3.27 | 9.6:1 | 25-80@3000 |
| 1998 | C | 2.0 (1996) | MPI | 132 @ 6000 | 129 @ 5000 | 3.44 x 3.27 | 9.8:1 | 25-80@3000 |
|      | Y | 2.0 (1996) | MPI | 150 @ 6500 | 133 @ 5500 | 3.44 x 3.27 | 9.6:1 | 25-80@3000 |
| 1999 | C | 2.0 (1996) | MPI | 132 @ 6000 | 129 @ 5000 | 3.44 x 3.27 | 9.8:1 | 25-80@3000 |
|      | Y | 2.0 (1996) | MPI | 150 @ 6500 | 133 @ 5500 | 3.44 x 3.27 | 9.6:1 | 25-80@3000 |

89713C01

## Transaxle

▶ See Figure 36

The transaxle model, assembly number and build date can be found on a metal identification plate which is attached to the end cover of the transaxle. This information is also shown on a bar code label that is secured to the front of the transaxle.

The last eight digits of the VIN are stamped on the case, below the back-up lamp switch. These vehicles use four different versions of the transaxle. There aren't any visible differences between the models, so make sure to refer to the ID tag to determine which transaxle your vehicle is equipped with.

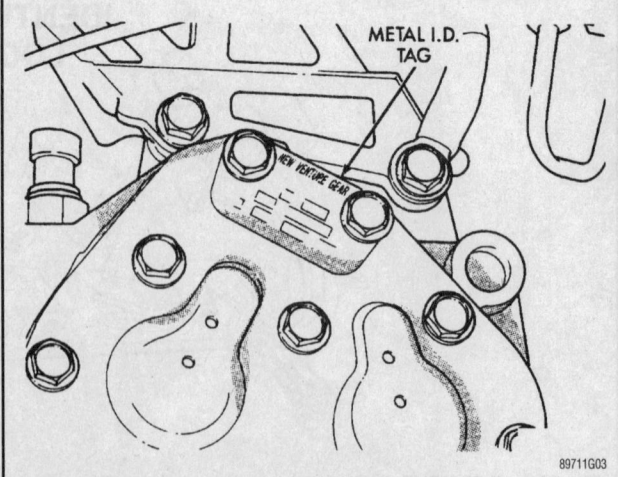

89711G03

Fig. 36 There is a metal identification plate located on the transaxle case

## MAINTENANCE COMPONENT LOCATIONS—SOHC ENGINES

1. Radiator
2. Upper radiator hose
3. Engine oil dipstick
4. Radiator fill cap
5. Coolant overflow hose
6. Coolant recovery reservoir
7. Air cleaner
8. Spark plug wires
9. Engine oil fill cap
10. Brake master cylinder reservoir
11. Battery
12. PCV valve
13. Power steering fluid reservoir

89711P01

**MAINTENANCE COMPONENT LOCATIONS—DOHC ENGINES**

1. Radiator
2. Upper radiator hose
3. Engine oil dipstick
4. Spark plugs & wires
5. PCV valve
6. Engine oil fill cap
7. Coolant overflow hose
8. Coolant recovery reservoir
9. Power steering fluid reservoir
10. Air cleaner
11. Brake master cylinder
12. Battery

Proper maintenance and tune-up is the key to long and trouble-free vehicle life, and the work can yield its own rewards. Studies have shown that a properly tuned and maintained vehicle can achieve better gas mileage than an out-of-tune vehicle. As a conscientious owner and driver, set aside a Saturday morning, say once a month, to check or replace items which could cause major problems later. Keep your own personal log to jot down which services you performed, how much the parts cost you, the date, and the exact odometer reading at the time. Keep all receipts for such items as engine oil and filters, so that they may be referred to in case of related problems or to determine operating expenses. As a do-it-yourselfer, these receipts are the only proof you have that the required maintenance was performed. In the event of a warranty problem, these receipts will be invaluable.

The literature provided with your vehicle when it was originally delivered includes the factory recommended maintenance schedule. If you no longer have this literature, replacement copies are usually available from the dealer. A maintenance schedule is provided later in this section, in case you do not have the factory literature.

## Air Cleaner (Element)

### REMOVAL & INSTALLATION

▶ **See Figures 37 thru 45**

1. Remove the retainers then detach the air intake tube from the air cleaner housing.
2. Unfasten the retaining clamps on top of the air cleaner housing, then remove the lid. On 1996–99 models, rotate the front of the housing forward, then lift the front away from the air cleaner housing.
3. Remove the air cleaner element and replace it with a new one.
4. Wipe the air cleaner housing out using a damp cloth. Check the lid gasket, if equipped, to ensure that it has a tight seal.

**To install:**

5. Place the air cleaner element into the housing.

➡**When installing the air cover, make sure the retaining tabs are properly positioned in the slots.**

6. On 1996–99 models, rotate the front of the housing forward, then lower into place and position the tabs in the slots. Fasten the retaining clamps on top of the air cleaner housing.
7. Attach the air intake tube to the air cleaner. Secure using the retainers. Note that the air intake tube has a piece protruding from it for alignment purposes during installation.

Fig. 38 On 1995 models, start by loosening the screw to relieve tension from the air inlet duct retaining clamp

Fig. 39 . . . then separate the duct from the air cleaner assembly

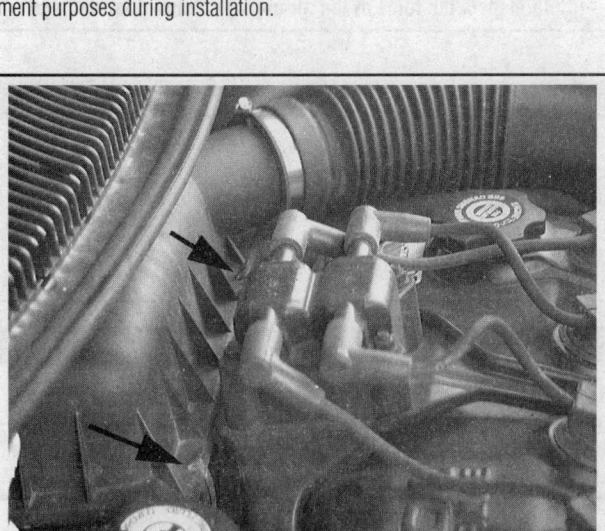

Fig. 37 Note the two retaining clamps on the front of the air cleaner assembly—1995 models shown

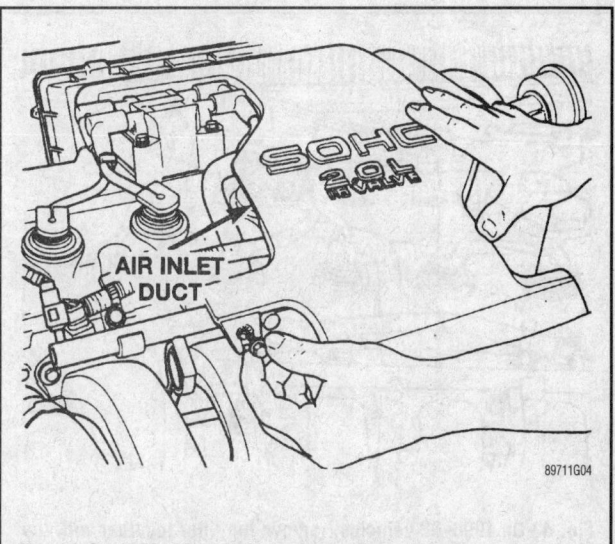

Fig. 40 On 1996–99 models, unfasten the retainers . . .

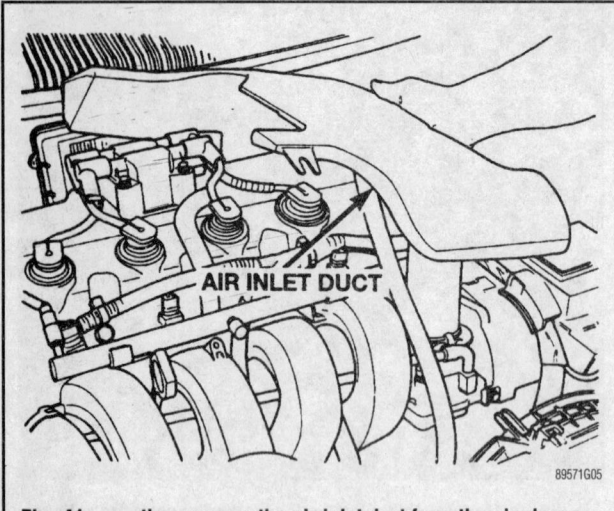

Fig. 41 . . . then remove the air inlet duct from the air cleaner and manifold

Fig. 44 On 1995 models, the air cleaner element can now be removed from the housing

Fig. 42 Unlatch the clamps, then remove the air cleaner assembly lid

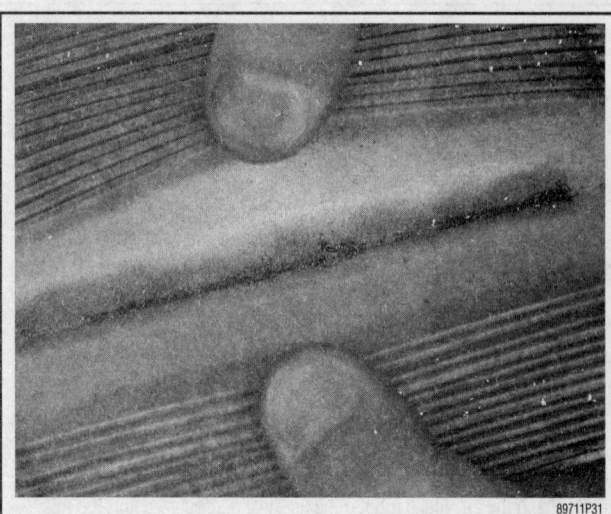

Fig. 45 Inspect the folds of the air cleaner element for damage

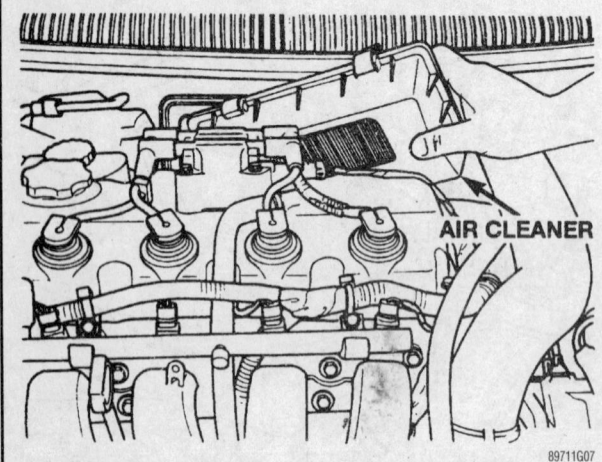

Fig. 43 On 1996–99 vehicles, remove the filter together with the housing lid

## Fuel Filter

A fuel filter, which is located on the frame rail in front of the fuel tank is used on 1995 vehicles. On 1996–99 vehicles, a combination fuel filter/pressure regulator assembly is used, which is located on the top of the fuel pump module.

### REMOVAL & INSTALLATION

### ✳✳ CAUTION

**Do not allow fuel spray or fuel vapors to come in contact with a spark or open flame. Keep a dry chemical fire extinguisher nearby. Never store fuel in an open container due to risk of fire or explosion.**

#### 1995 Vehicles

▶ **See Figures 46 and 47**

1. Properly relieve the fuel system pressure, as outlined in Section 5 of this manual.

2. If not done already, disconnect the negative battery cable.

3. Raise and safely support the vehicle.

4. If necessary, unfasten the retainers then remove the shield covering the fuel filter and pump assembly.

5. Unfasten the quick-connect fittings from the fuel pump module and chassis fuel supply tube. Refer to Section 5 for information regarding quick-connect fittings.

➡The fuel lines are permanently attached to the fuel filter. The ends of the fuel supply and return lines have different size quick-connect fittings. The larger quick-connect fittings attach to the large nipple on the fuel pump module. The smaller fitting connects to the small nipple on the fuel pump module.

6. Remove the fuel filter mounting screw, then remove the fuel filter from the vehicle.

**To install:**

7. Position the fuel filter on the frame rail and secure with the retaining screw. Tighten the screw to 85 inch lbs. (9.5 Nm).

8. Apply a thin coating of clean engine oil to the fuel filter nipples, then attach the quick-connect fuel lines. Refer to Section 5 for details.

9. Carefully lower the vehicle, then connect the negative battery cable.

## 1996–99 Vehicles

▶ **See Figures 48 and 49**

1. Properly relieve the fuel system pressure, as outlined in Section 5 of this manual.

2. If not done already, disconnect the negative battery cable.

3. Raise and safely support the vehicle.

4. Unfasten the quick-connect fuel supply line from the filter/regulator nipple.

5. Depress the locking spring tab, located on the side of the fuel filter/regulator, then rotate 90° and pull out. Make sure the upper and lower O-rings are still on the filter assembly.

**To install:**

6. Lightly coat the filter O-rings with clean engine oil. Insert the filter into the opening in the fuel pump module, then align the 2 hold-down tabs with the flange.

7. While applying downward pressure, rotate the filter clockwise until the spring tab catches in the locating slot.

8. Attach the fuel line to the filter/regulator assembly.

9. Carefully lower the vehicle, then connect the negative battery cable.

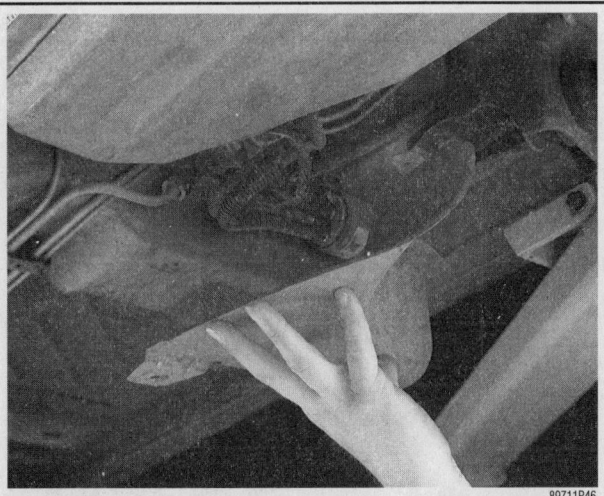

Fig. 46 On some vehicles, you will have to remove a cover for access to the fuel filter

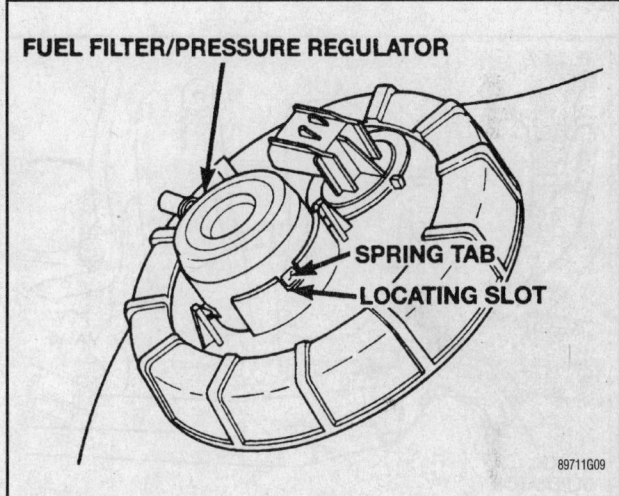

Fig. 48 Depress the spring tab, then rotate and pull the filter assembly out

Fig. 47 View of the fuel filter (1) and lines (2) attaching to the fuel pump (3)

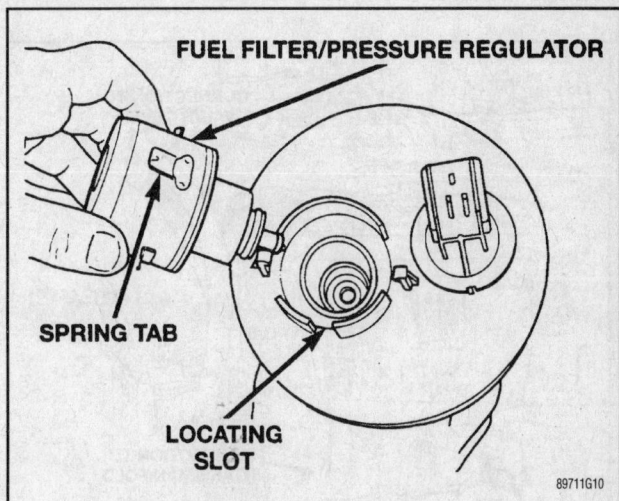

Fig. 49 To install the filter, align the spring tab with the locating slot

## PCV Valve

The Positive Crankcase Ventilation (PCV) valve is part of a system which is designed to protect the atmosphere from harmful vapors. Blow-by gas from the crankcase, as well as fumes from crankcase oil are diverted into the combustion chamber where they are burned during engine operation. Proper operation of this system will improve engine performance as well as decrease the amount of harmful vapors released into the atmosphere.

### REMOVAL & INSTALLATION

▶ See Figures 50, 51, 52, 53 and 54

1. Disconnect the negative battery cable.
2. If necessary for access, unfasten the starter wiring, then position the wiring harness aside.
3. If necessary, use a pair of pliers to unfasten the crankcase hose retaining clamps, then disconnect the ventilation hoses from the PCV valve.
4. Remove the PCV valve from the camshaft (rocker) cover or the hose, as applicable.

**To install:**

5. Install the PCV valve into the rocker cover or attach to the hose, as necessary.

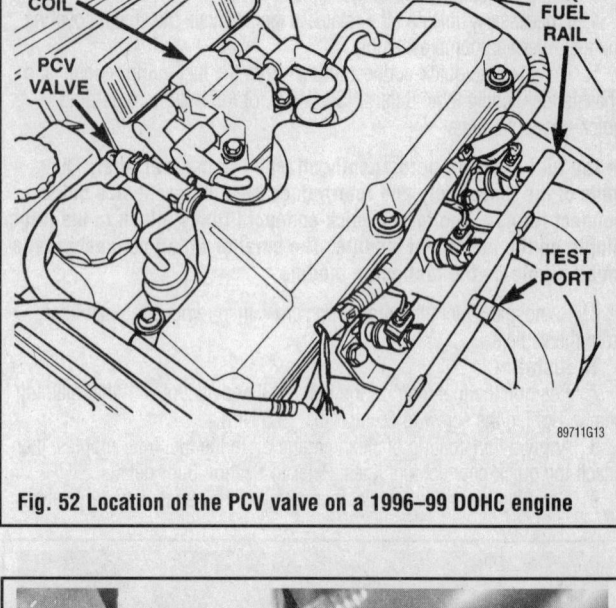

Fig. 52 Location of the PCV valve on a 1996–99 DOHC engine

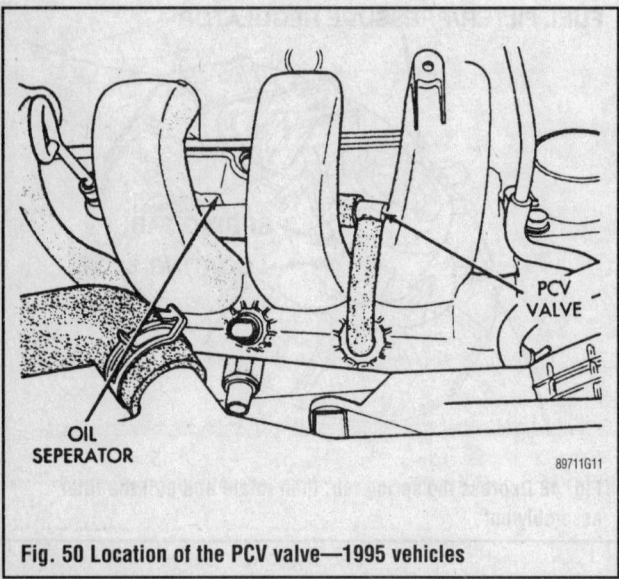

Fig. 50 Location of the PCV valve—1995 vehicles

Fig. 53 You may have to unfasten the starter wiring and reposition the wiring harness to get to the PCV valve

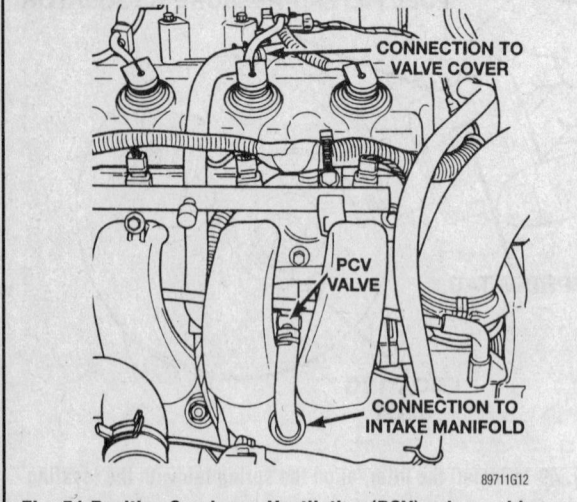

Fig. 51 Positive Crankcase Ventilation (PCV) valve and hose locations—1996–99 SOHC engines

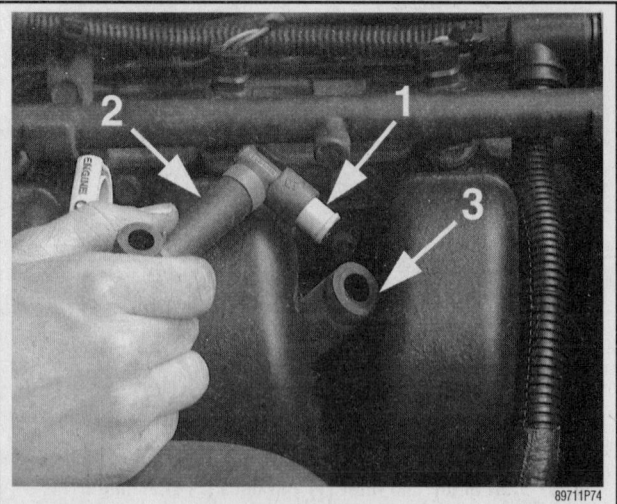

Fig. 54 Remove the PCV valve (1) and oil separator hose (2) from the PCV hose (3)

6. Reconnect the ventilation hoses to the valve. If necessary, use a pair of pliers to secure the hose clamps.

7. If removed, reposition the wiring harness, then attach the starter wiring.

8. Connect the negative battery cable.

## Evaporative Canister

This system is designed to limit gasoline vapor, which normally escapes from the fuel tank, from discharging into the atmosphere. Vapor absorption is accomplished through the use of the charcoal canister which stores the vapors until they can be removed and burned in the combustion process.

### SERVICING

▶ **See Figure 55**

The evaporative canister is mounted to a bracket located behind the front fascia on the passenger's side of the vehicle.

Check the evaporative emission control system every 15,000 miles. The evaporative canister does not require periodic service. Inspect the fuel vapor lines and the vacuum hoses for proper connections and correct routing, as well as condition. Replace clogged, damaged or deteriorated parts as necessary. Refer to the Vehicle Emission Control Information Label, located under the hood, for routing of the canister hoses.

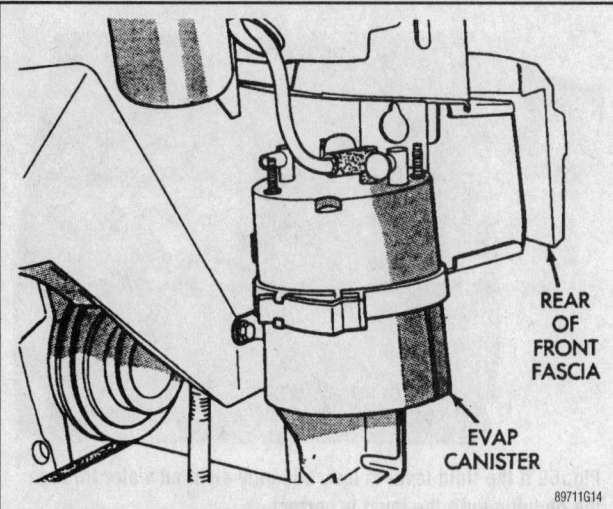

REAR
OF
FRONT
FASCIA

EVAP
CANISTER

89711G14

**Fig. 55 The evaporative canister is attached to a bracket behind the passenger's side front fascia**

➡**The evaporative system uses a special type of hoses. If it becomes necessary to replace any of the hoses, use only fuel resistant hoses.**

## Battery

### PRECAUTIONS

Always use caution when working on or near the battery. Never allow a tool to bridge the gap between the negative and positive battery terminals. Also, be careful not to allow a tool to provide a ground between the positive cable/terminal and any metal component on the vehicle. Either of these conditions will cause a short circuit, leading to sparks and possible personal injury.

Do not smoke, have an open flame or create sparks near a battery; the gases contained in the battery are very explosive and, if ignited, could cause severe injury or death.

All batteries, regardless of type, should be carefully secured by a battery hold-down device. If this is not done, the battery terminals or casing may crack from stress applied to the battery during vehicle operation. A battery which is not secured may allow acid to leak out, making it discharge faster; such leaking corrosive acid can also eat away at components under the hood.

Always visually inspect the battery case for cracks, leakage and corrosion. A white corrosive substance on the battery case or on nearby components would indicate a leaking or cracked battery. If the battery is cracked, it should be replaced immediately.

### GENERAL MAINTENANCE

▶ **See Figures 56 and 57**

A battery that is not sealed must be checked periodically for electrolyte level. You cannot add water to a sealed maintenance-free battery (though not all maintenance-free batteries are sealed); however, a sealed battery must also be checked for proper electrolyte level, as indicated by the color of the built-in hydrometer "eye."

TCCA1G02

**Fig. 56 A typical location for the built-in hydrometer on maintenance-free batteries**

89711P37

**Fig. 57 This battery has corrosion around the negative battery cable and terminal which must be cleaned off**

Always keep the battery cables and terminals free of corrosion. Check these components about once a year. Refer to the removal, installation and cleaning procedures outlined in this section.

Keep the top of the battery clean, as a film of dirt can help completely discharge a battery that is not used for long periods. A solution of baking soda and water may be used for cleaning, but be careful to flush this off with clear water. DO NOT let any of the solution into the filler holes. Baking soda neutralizes battery acid and will de-activate a battery cell.

Batteries in vehicles which are not operated on a regular basis can fall victim to parasitic loads (small current drains which are constantly drawing current from the battery). Normal parasitic loads may drain a battery on a vehicle that is in storage and not used for 6–8 weeks. Vehicles that have additional accessories such as a cellular phone, an alarm system or other devices that increase parasitic load may discharge a battery sooner. If the vehicle is to be stored for 6–8 weeks in a secure area and the alarm system, if present, is not necessary, the negative battery cable should be disconnected at the onset of storage to protect the battery charge.

Remember that constantly discharging and recharging will shorten battery life. Take care not to allow a battery to be needlessly discharged.

## BATTERY FLUID

Check the battery electrolyte level at least once a month, or more often in hot weather or during periods of extended vehicle operation. On non-sealed batteries, the level can be checked either through the case on translucent batteries or by removing the cell caps on opaque-cased types. The electrolyte level in each cell should be kept filled to the split ring inside each cell, or the line marked on the outside of the case.

If the level is low, add only distilled water through the opening until the level is correct. Each cell is separate from the others, so each must be checked and filled individually. Distilled water should be used, because the chemicals and minerals found in most drinking water are harmful to the battery and could significantly shorten its life.

If water is added in freezing weather, the vehicle should be driven several miles to allow the water to mix with the electrolyte. Otherwise, the battery could freeze.

Although some maintenance-free batteries have removable cell caps for access to the electrolyte, the electrolyte condition and level on all sealed maintenance-free batteries must be checked using the built-in hydrometer "eye." The exact type of eye varies between battery manufacturers, but most apply a sticker to the battery itself explaining the possible readings. When in doubt, refer to the battery manufacturer's instructions to interpret battery condition using the built-in hydrometer.

➡**Although the readings from built-in hydrometers found in sealed batteries may vary, a green eye usually indicates a properly charged battery with sufficient fluid level. A dark eye is normally an indicator of a battery with sufficient fluid, but one which may be low in charge. And a light or yellow eye is usually an indication that electrolyte supply has dropped below the necessary level for battery (and hydrometer) operation. In this last case, sealed batteries with an insufficient electrolyte level must usually be discarded.**

### Checking the Specific Gravity

▶ See Figures 58, 59 and 60

A hydrometer is required to check the specific gravity on all batteries that are not maintenance-free. On batteries that are maintenance-free, the specific gravity is checked by observing the built-in hydrometer "eye" on the top of the battery case. Check with your battery's manufacturer for proper interpretation of its built-in hydrometer readings.

### ⁘ CAUTION

**Battery electrolyte contains sulfuric acid. If you should splash any on your skin or in your eyes, flush the affected area with plenty of clear water. If it lands in your eyes, get medical help immediately.**

TCCA1P07

**Fig. 58 On non-maintenance-free batteries, the fluid level can be checked through the case on translucent models; the cell caps must be removed on other models**

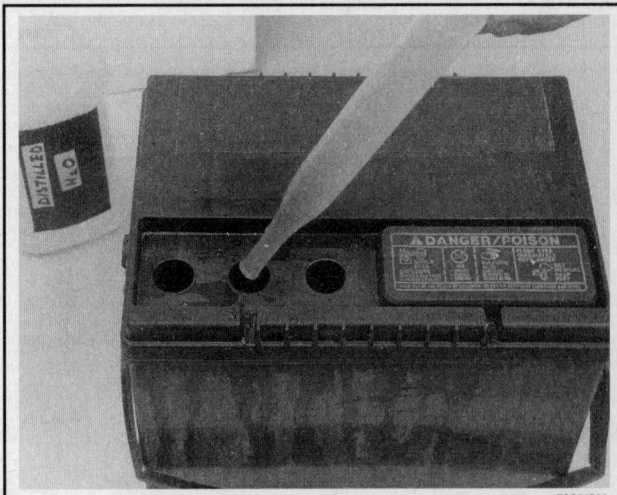

TCCA1P08

**Fig. 59 If the fluid level is low, add only distilled water through the opening until the level is correct**

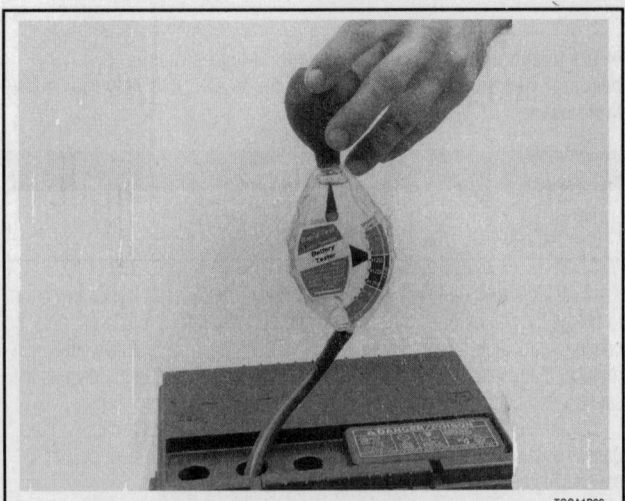

TCCA1P09

**Fig. 60 Check the specific gravity of the battery's electrolyte with a hydrometer**

The fluid (sulfuric acid solution) contained in the battery cells will tell you many things about the condition of the battery. Because the cell plates must be kept submerged below the fluid level in order to operate, maintaining the fluid level is extremely important. And, because the specific gravity of the acid is an indication of electrical charge, testing the fluid can be an aid in determining if the battery must be replaced. A battery in a vehicle with a properly operating charging system should require little maintenance, but careful, periodic inspection should reveal problems before they leave you stranded.

As stated earlier, the specific gravity of a battery's electrolyte level can be used as an indication of battery charge. At least once a year, check the specific gravity of the battery. It should be between 1.20 and 1.26 on the gravity scale. Most auto supply stores carry a variety of inexpensive battery testing hydrometers. These can be used on any non-sealed battery to test the specific gravity in each cell.

The battery testing hydrometer has a squeeze bulb at one end and a nozzle at the other. Battery electrolyte is sucked into the hydrometer until the float is lifted from its seat. The specific gravity is then read by noting the position of the float. If gravity is low in one or more cells, the battery should be slowly charged and checked again to see if the gravity has come up. Generally, if after charging, the specific gravity between any two cells varies more than 50 points (0.50), the battery should be replaced, as it can no longer produce sufficient voltage to guarantee proper operation.

## CABLES

▶ See Figures 61, 62, 63, 64 and 65

Once a year (or as necessary), the battery terminals and the cable clamps should be cleaned. Loosen the clamps and remove the cables, negative cable first. On batteries with posts on top, the use of a puller specially made for this purpose is recommended. These are inexpensive and available in most auto parts stores. Side terminal battery cables are secured with a small bolt.

Clean the cable clamps and the battery terminal with a wire brush, until all corrosion, grease, etc., is removed and the metal is shiny. It is especially important to clean the inside of the clamp thoroughly (an old knife is useful here), since a small deposit of foreign material or oxidation there will prevent a sound electrical connection and inhibit either starting or charging. Special tools are available for cleaning these parts, one type for conventional top post batteries and another type for side terminal batteries. It is also a good idea to apply some dielectric grease to the terminal, as this will aid in the prevention of corrosion.

After the clamps and terminals are clean, reinstall the cables, negative cable last; DO NOT hammer the clamps onto battery posts. Tighten the

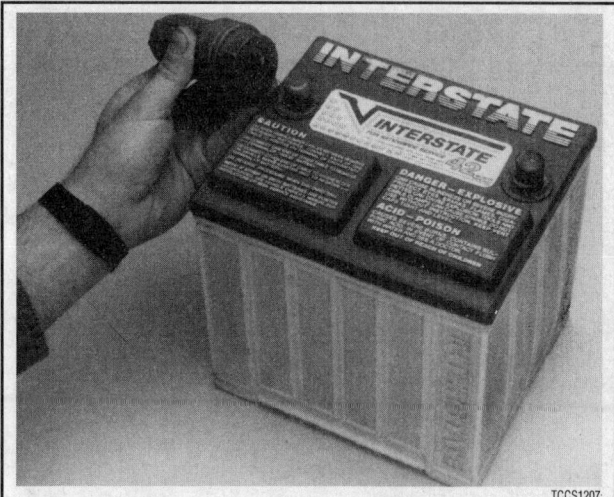
Fig. 62 The underside of this special battery tool has a wire brush to clean post terminals

Fig. 63 Place the tool over the battery posts and twist to clean until the metal is shiny

Fig. 61 Maintenance is performed with household items and with special tools like this post cleaner

Fig. 64 A special tool is available to pull the clamp from the post

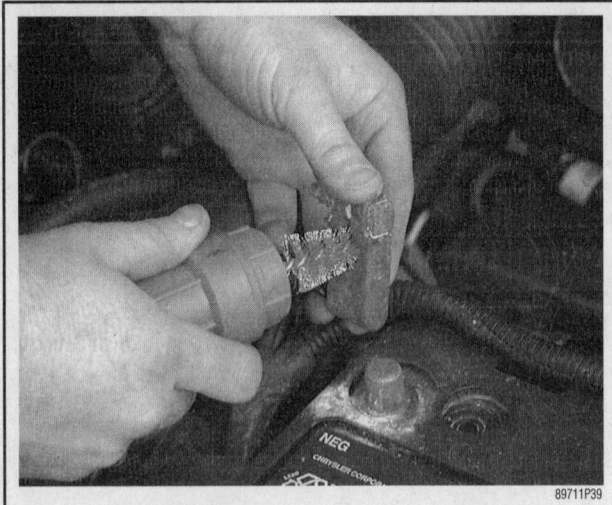

Fig. 65 The cable ends should be cleaned as well

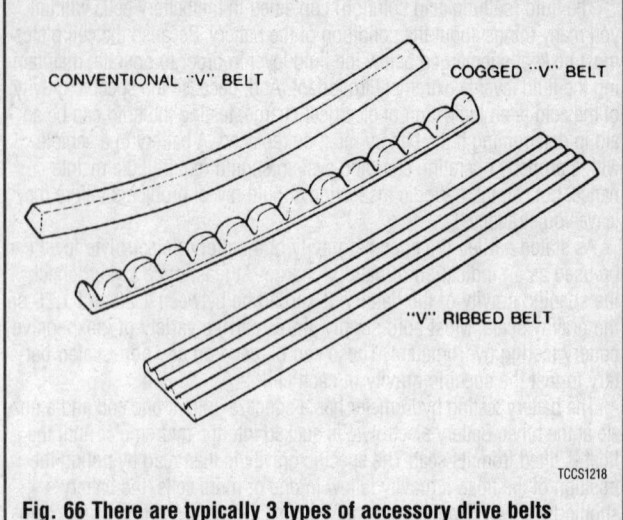

Fig. 66 There are typically 3 types of accessory drive belts found on vehicles today

clamps securely, but do not distort them. Give the clamps and terminals a thin external coating of grease after installation, to retard corrosion.

Check the cables at the same time that the terminals are cleaned. If the cable insulation is cracked or broken, or if the ends are frayed, the cable should be replaced with a new cable of the same length and gauge.

## CHARGING

### ❊❊ CAUTION

**The chemical reaction which takes place in all batteries generates explosive hydrogen gas. A spark can cause the battery to explode and splash acid. To avoid serious personal injury, be sure there is proper ventilation and take appropriate fire safety precautions when connecting, disconnecting, or charging a battery and when using jumper cables.**

A battery should be charged at a slow rate to keep the plates inside from getting too hot. However, if some maintenance-free batteries are allowed to discharge until they are almost "dead," they may have to be charged at a high rate to bring them back to "life." Always follow the charger manufacturer's instructions on charging the battery.

## REPLACEMENT

When it becomes necessary to replace the battery, select one with an amperage rating equal to or greater than the battery originally installed. Deterioration and just plain aging of the battery cables, starter motor, and associated wires makes the battery's job harder in successive years. The slow increase in electrical resistance over time makes it prudent to install a new battery with a greater capacity than the old.

## Belts

### INSPECTION

▶ **See Figures 66 thru 71**

Inspect the belts for signs of glazing or cracking. A glazed belt will be perfectly smooth from slippage, while a good belt will have a slight texture of fabric visible. Cracks will usually start at the inner edge of the belt and run outward. All worn or damaged drive belts should be replaced immediately. It is best to replace all drive belts at one time, as a preventive maintenance measure, during this service operation.

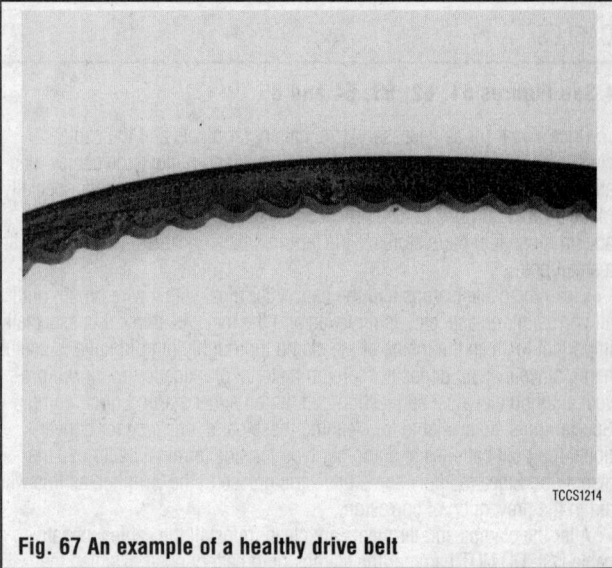

Fig. 67 An example of a healthy drive belt

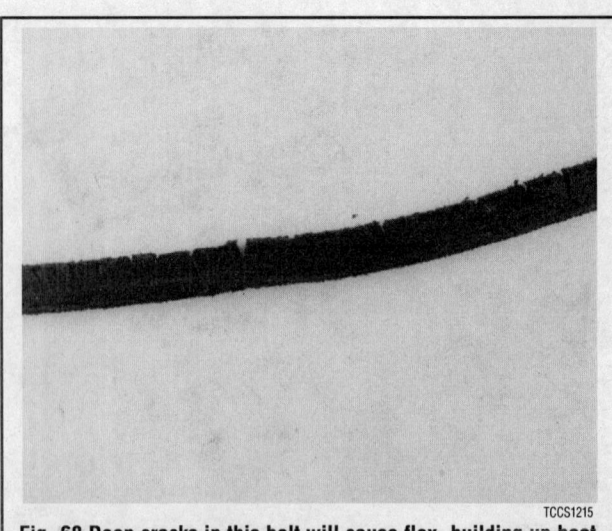

Fig. 68 Deep cracks in this belt will cause flex, building up heat that will eventually lead to belt failure

Fig. 69 The cover of this belt is worn, exposing the critical reinforcing cords to excessive wear

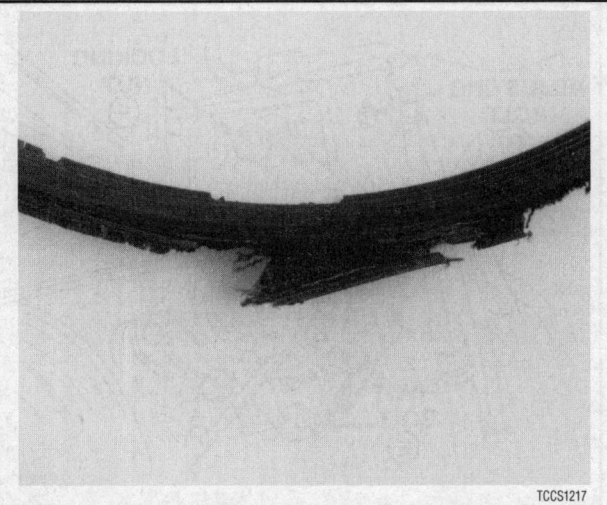

Fig. 70 Installing too wide a belt can result in serious belt wear and/or breakage

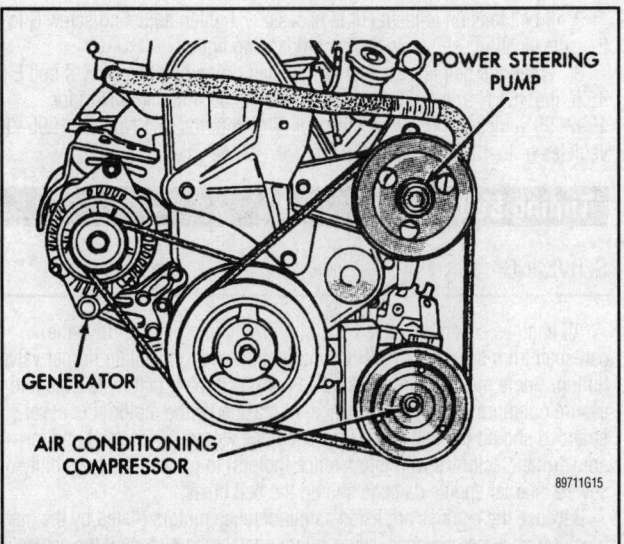

Fig. 71 It is essential to route the accessory drive belts properly

REMOVAL, INSTALLATION & ADJUSTMENT

### A/C Compressor and Power Steering Pump

▶ See Figures 72, 73, 74, 75 and 76

1. Loosen the power steering pump locking bolts A and B and pivot bolt C to remove and install or adjust the belt.

2. If necessary, adjust the belt tension by using a ½ in. breaker bar to apply torque to the square hole D on the idler/power steering pivot bracket. Adjust the tension to the specifications given in the accompanying figure. On 1998–99 models, adjust the belt using a tension gauge only.

3. When the belt is installed, or properly adjusted, tighten the locking bolt A to 20 ft. lbs. (27 Nm), bolt B to 20 ft. lbs. (27 Nm), then tighten pivot bolt C to 45 ft. lbs. (61 Nm) for 1995–96 vehicles or to 40 ft. lbs. (54 Nm) for 1997–99 vehicles.

### Alternator Drive Belt

▶ See Figures 76 and 77

1. Loosen pivot bolt E then T-bolt locking nut F and adjusting bolt G to remove and install or adjust the belt.

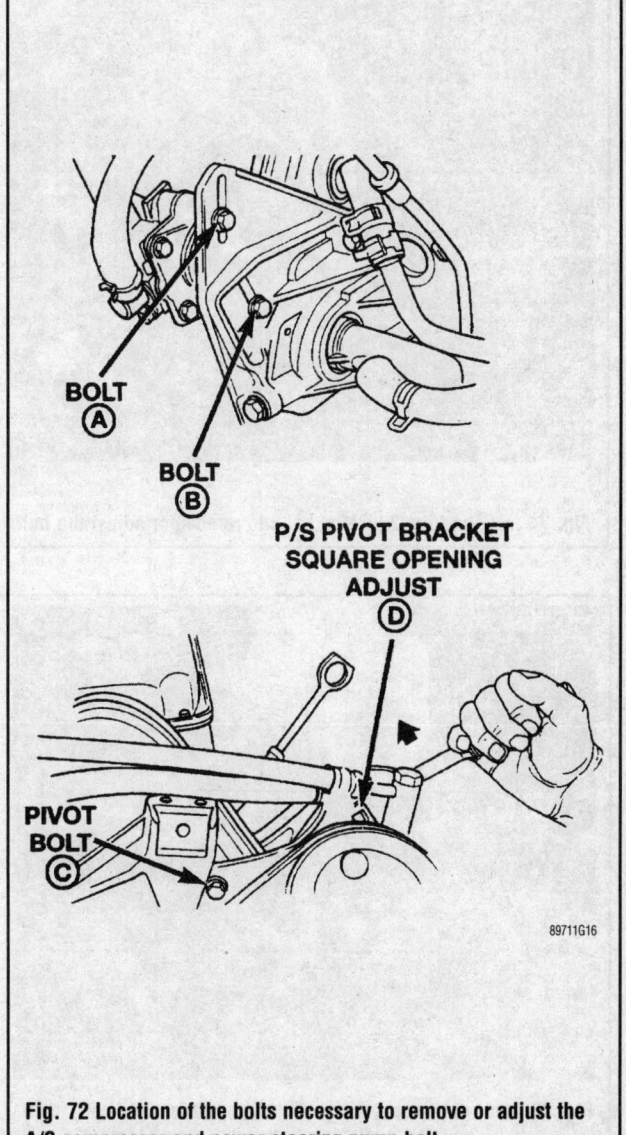

Fig. 72 Location of the bolts necessary to remove or adjust the A/C compressor and power steering pump belt

Fig. 73 You must loosen the pivot bolt . . .

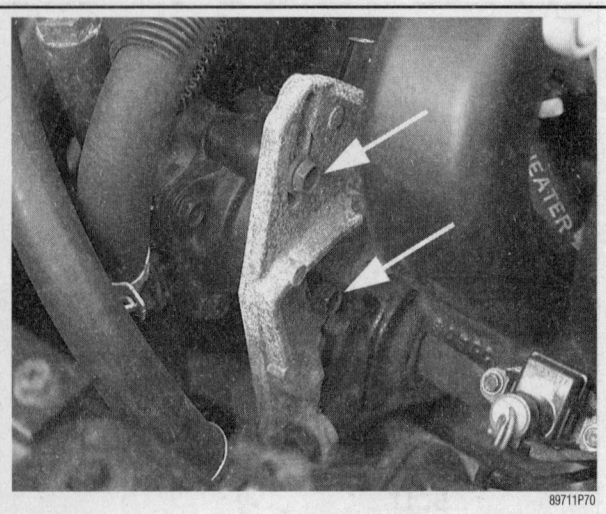

Fig. 74 . . . and the 2 locking bolts to remove or adjust the belt

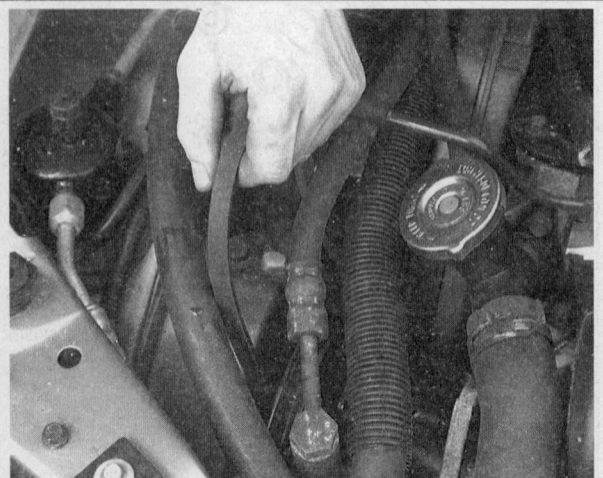

Fig. 75 After all the necessary retainers are loosened or removed, as necessary, you can remove the belt

| Accessory Drive Belt | Gauge | Torque |
|---|---|---|
| Power Steering Pump and Air Conditioning Compressor | New 135 lb. | 121 N·m (90 ft. lbs.) |
| | Used 100 lb. | 81 N·m (60 ft. lbs.) |
| Generator | New 135 lb. | 121 N·m (90 ft. lbs.) |
| | Used 100 lb. | 81 N·m (60 ft. lbs.) |

Fig. 76 Accessory drive belt tensioner gauge chart. Do not use the torque figures for 1997–99 models

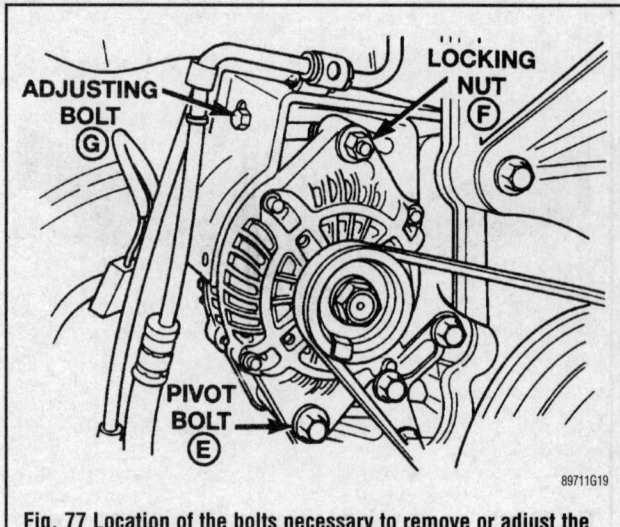

Fig. 77 Location of the bolts necessary to remove or adjust the alternator drive belt

2. If belt tension adjustment is necessary, tighten adjusting screw G to the specifications shown in the accompanying figure.

3. When the belt is installed, or adjusted properly, tighten pivot bolt E to 45 ft. lbs. (61 Nm) for 1995–96 vehicles or to 40 ft. lbs. (54 Nm) for 1997–99 vehicles, Tighten locking nut F to 45 ft. lbs. (61 Nm) for 1995–96 vehicles or to 40 ft. lbs. (54 Nm) for 1997–99 vehicles.

## Timing Belt

### SERVICING

All engines covered by this manual utilize timing belts to drive the camshaft from the crankshaft's turning motion and to maintain proper valve timing. Some manufacturer's schedule periodic timing belt replacement to assure optimum engine performance, to make sure the motorist is never stranded should the belt break (as the engine will stop instantly) and for some (manufacturer's with interference motors) to prevent the possibility of severe internal engine damage should the belt break.

Because the engines are listed as interference motors (listed by the manufacturer as a motor whose valves might contact the pistons if the camshaft was rotated separately from the crankshaft), Chrysler corporation recommends changing the timing belt at 105,000 miles (168,000km) for vehicles operated under normal service conditions or 102,000 miles (163,000km) for vehicles operated under severe conditions.

You would be wise to check the belt periodically to make sure it has not become damaged or worn. Generally speaking, a severely worn belt may cause engine performance to drop dramatically, but a damaged belt (which could give out suddenly) may not give as much warning. In general, any time the engine timing cover(s) is(are) removed you should inspect the belt for premature parting, severe cracks or missing teeth.

## Hoses

### INSPECTION

▶ See Figures 78, 79, 80 and 81

Upper and lower radiator hoses along with the heater hoses should be checked for deterioration, leaks and loose hose clamps at least every 15,000 miles (24,000 km). It is also wise to check the hoses periodically in early spring and at the beginning of the fall or winter when you are performing other maintenance. A quick visual inspection could discover a

weakened hose which might have left you stranded if it had remained unrepaired.

Whenever you are checking the hoses, make sure the engine and cooling system are cold. Visually inspect for cracking, rotting or collapsed hoses, and replace as necessary. Run your hand along the length of the hose. If a weak or swollen spot is noted when squeezing the hose wall, the hose should be replaced.

### REMOVAL & INSTALLATION

1. Remove the radiator pressure cap.

### ✳✳ CAUTION

**Never remove the pressure cap while the engine is running, or personal injury from scalding hot coolant or steam may result. If possible, wait until the engine has cooled to remove the pressure cap. If this is not possible, wrap a thick cloth around the pressure cap and turn it slowly to the stop. Step back while the pressure is released from the cooling system. When you are sure all the pressure has been released, use the cloth to turn and remove the cap.**

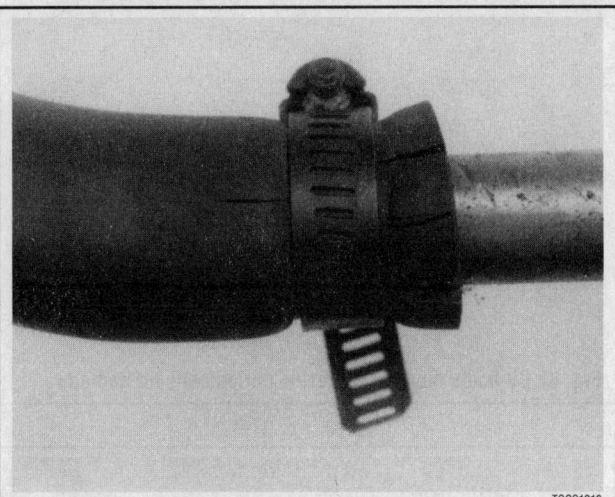

TCCS1219

Fig. 78 The cracks developing along this hose are a result of age-related hardening

TCCS1221

Fig. 80 A soft spongy hose (identifiable by the swollen section) will eventually burst and should be replaced

TCCS1220

Fig. 79 A hose clamp that is too tight can cause older hoses to separate and tear on either side of the clamp

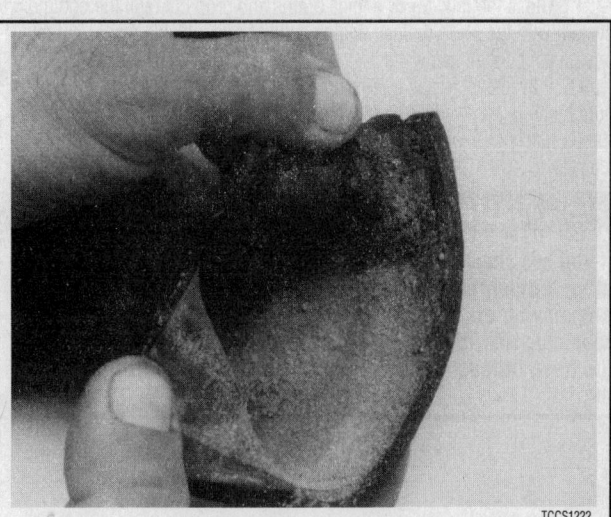

TCCS1222

Fig. 81 Hoses are likely to deteriorate from the inside if the cooling system is not periodically flushed

2. Position a clean container under the radiator and/or engine draincock or plug, then open the drain and allow the cooling system to drain to an appropriate level. For some upper hoses, only a little coolant must be drained. To remove hoses positioned lower on the engine, such as a lower radiator hose, the entire cooling system must be emptied.

### ※※ CAUTION

**When draining coolant, keep in mind that cats and dogs are attracted by ethylene glycol antifreeze, and are quite likely to drink any that is left in an uncovered container or in puddles on the ground. This will prove fatal in sufficient quantity. Always drain coolant into a sealable container. Coolant may be reused unless it is contaminated or several years old.**

3. Loosen the hose clamps at each end of the hose requiring replacement. Clamps are usually either of the spring tension type (which require pliers to squeeze the tabs and loosen) or of the screw tension type (which require screw or hex drivers to loosen). Pull the clamps back on the hose away from the connection.

4. Twist, pull and slide the hose off the fitting, taking care not to damage the neck of the component from which the hose is being removed.

➡**If the hose is stuck at the connection, do not try to insert a screwdriver or other sharp tool under the hose end in an effort to free it, as the connection and/or hose may become damaged. Heater connections especially may be easily damaged by such a procedure. If the hose is to be replaced, use a single-edged razor blade to make a slice along the portion of the hose which is stuck on the connection, perpendicular to the end of the hose. Do not cut deep so as to prevent damaging the connection. The hose can then be peeled from the connection and discarded.**

5. Clean both hose mounting connections. Inspect the condition of the hose clamps and replace them, if necessary.

**To install:**

6. Dip the ends of the new hose into clean engine coolant to ease installation.

7. Slide the clamps over the replacement hose, then slide the hose ends over the connections into position.

8. Position and secure the clamps at least ¼ in. (6.35mm) from the ends of the hose. Make sure they are located beyond the raised bead of the connector.

9. Close the radiator or engine drains and properly refill the cooling system with the clean drained engine coolant or a suitable mixture of ethylene glycol coolant and water.

10. If available, install a pressure tester and check for leaks. If a pressure tester is not available, run the engine until normal operating temperature is reached (allowing the system to naturally pressurize), then check for leaks.

### ※※ CAUTION

**If you are checking for leaks with the system at normal operating temperature, BE EXTREMELY CAREFUL not to touch any moving or hot engine parts. Once temperature has been reached, shut the engine OFF, and check for leaks around the hose fittings and connections which were removed earlier.**

### CV-Boots

INSPECTION

▶ **See Figures 82 and 83**

The CV (Constant Velocity) boots should be checked for damage each time the oil is changed and any other time the vehicle is raised for service. These boots keep water, grime, dirt and other damaging matter from entering the CV-joints. Any of these could cause early CV-joint failure which can be expensive to repair. Heavy grease thrown around the inside of the front wheel(s) and on the brake caliper/drum can be an indication of a torn boot. Thoroughly check the boots for missing clamps and tears. If the boot is damaged, it should be replaced immediately. Please refer to Section 7 for procedures.

TCCS1011

Fig. 82 CV-boots must be inspected periodically for damage

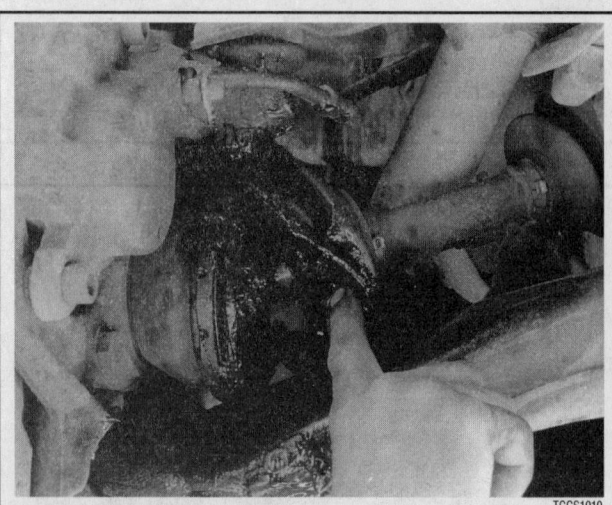
TCCS1010

Fig. 83 A torn boot should be replaced immediately

## Spark Plugs

▶ See Figure 84

A typical spark plug consists of a metal shell surrounding a ceramic insulator. A metal electrode extends downward through the center of the insulator and protrudes a small distance. Located at the end of the plug and attached to the side of the outer metal shell is the side electrode. The side electrode bends in at a 90⁻ angle so that its tip is just past and parallel to the tip of the center electrode. The distance between these two electrodes (measured in thousandths of an inch or hundredths of a millimeter) is called the spark plug gap.

The spark plug does not produce a spark but instead provides a gap across which the current can arc. The coil produces anywhere from 20,000 to 50,000 volts (depending on the type and application) which travels through the wires to the spark plugs. The current passes along the center electrode and jumps the gap to the side electrode, and in doing so, ignites the air/fuel mixture in the combustion chamber.

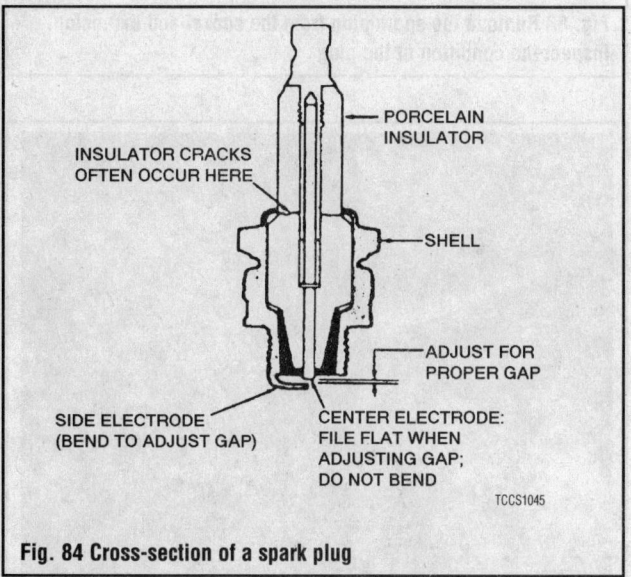

**Fig. 84 Cross-section of a spark plug**

## SPARK PLUG HEAT RANGE

▶ See Figure 85

Spark plug heat range is the ability of the plug to dissipate heat. The longer the insulator (or the farther it extends into the engine), the hotter the plug will operate; the shorter the insulator (the closer the electrode is to the block's cooling passages) the cooler it will operate. A plug that absorbs little heat and remains too cool will quickly accumulate deposits of oil and carbon since it is not hot enough to burn them off. This leads to plug fouling and consequently to misfiring. A plug that absorbs too much heat will have no deposits but, due to the excessive heat, the electrodes will burn away quickly and might possibly lead to preignition or other ignition problems. Preignition takes place when plug tips get so hot that they glow sufficiently to ignite the air/fuel mixture before the actual spark occurs. This early ignition will usually cause a pinging during low speeds and heavy loads.

The general rule of thumb for choosing the correct heat range when picking a spark plug is: if most of your driving is long distance, high speed travel, use a colder plug; if most of your driving is stop and go, use a hotter plug. Original equipment plugs are generally a good compromise between

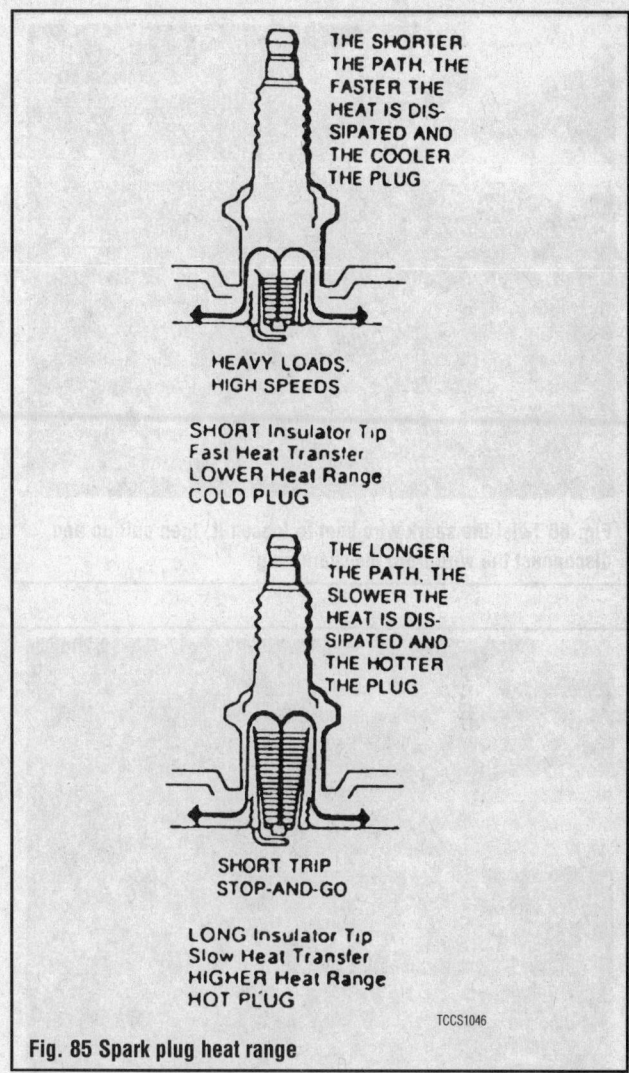

**Fig. 85 Spark plug heat range**

the 2 styles and most people never have the need to change their plugs from the factory-recommended heat range.

## REMOVAL & INSTALLATION

▶ See Figures 86, 87, 88 and 89

A set of spark plugs usually requires replacement after about 30,000 miles (48,000 km), depending on your style of driving. In normal operation plug gap increases about 0.001 in. (0.025mm) for every 2500 miles (4000 km). As the gap increases, the plug's voltage requirement also increases. It requires a greater voltage to jump the wider gap and about two to three times as much voltage to fire the plug at high speeds than at idle. The improved air/fuel ratio control of modern fuel injection combined with the higher voltage output of modern ignition systems will often allow an engine to run significantly longer on a set of standard spark plugs, but keep in mind that efficiency will drop as the gap widens (along with fuel economy and power).

When you're removing spark plugs, work on one at a time. Don't start by removing the plug wires all at once, because, unless you number them, they may become mixed up. Take a minute before you begin and number the wires with tape.

Fig. 86 Twist the spark wire boot to loosen it, then pull up and disconnect the wire from the spark plug

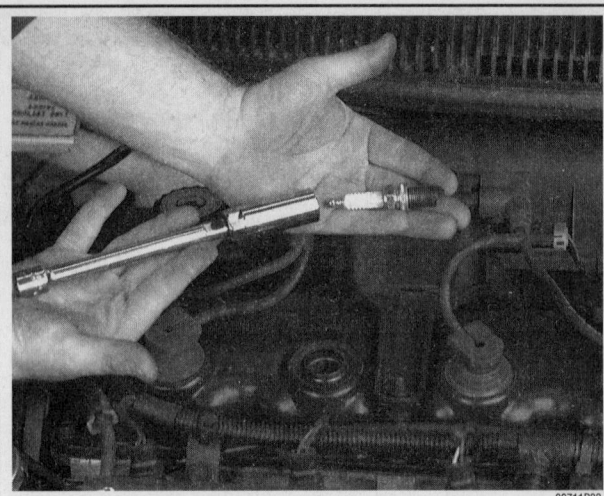

Fig. 88 Remove the spark plug from the socket and extension. Inspect the condition of the plug

Fig. 87 Use a ratchet and an extension with a spark plug socket to loosen and remove the plug from the bore

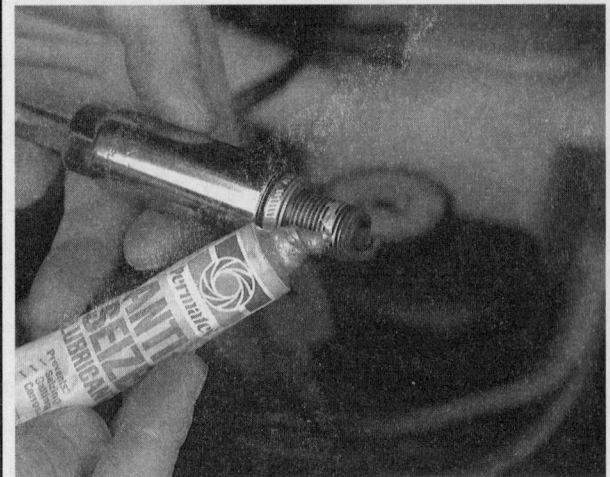

Fig. 89 Apply a thin coat of anti-seize lubricant to the spark plug threads

1. Disconnect the negative battery cable, and if the vehicle has been run recently, allow the engine to thoroughly cool.

➡ **It may be easier to remove the plug wire from the ignition coil before trying to disconnect it from the spark plug.**

2. Carefully twist the spark plug wire boot to loosen it, then pull upward and remove the boot from the plug. Be sure to pull on the boot and not on the wire, otherwise the connector located inside the boot may become separated.

3. Using compressed air, blow any water or debris from the spark plug well to assure that no harmful contaminants are allowed to enter the combustion chamber when the spark plug is removed. If compressed air is not available, use a rag or a brush to clean the area.

➡ **Remove the spark plugs when the engine is cold, if possible, to prevent damage to the threads. If removal of the plugs is difficult, apply a few drops of penetrating oil or silicone spray to the area around the base of the plug, and allow it a few minutes to work.**

4. Using a spark plug socket that is equipped with a rubber insert to properly hold the plug, turn the spark plug counterclockwise to loosen and remove the spark plug from the bore.

### ✷✷ WARNING

**Be sure not to use a flexible extension on the socket. Use of a flexible extension may allow a shear force to be applied to the plug. A shear force could break the plug off in the cylinder head, leading to costly and frustrating repairs.**

**To install:**

5. Inspect the spark plug boot for tears or damage. If a damaged boot is found, the spark plug wire must be replaced.

6. Using a wire feeler gauge, check and adjust the spark plug gap. When using a gauge, the proper size should pass between the electrodes with a slight drag. The next larger size should not be able to pass while the next smaller size should pass freely.

7. Apply a thin coat of anti-seize lubricant to the spark plug threads

8. Carefully thread the plug into the bore by hand. If resistance is felt before the plug is almost completely threaded, back the plug out and begin threading again. In small, hard to reach areas, an old spark plug wire and boot could be used as a threading tool. The boot will hold the plug while you twist the end of the wire and the wire is supple enough to twist before it would allow the plug to crossthread.

### ✳✳ WARNING

**Do not use the spark plug socket to thread the plugs. Always carefully thread the plug by hand or using an old plug wire to prevent the possibility of crossthreading and damaging the cylinder head bore.**

9. Carefully tighten the spark plug to 20 ft. lbs. (28 Nm).

10. Apply a small amount of silicone dielectric compound to the end of the spark plug lead or inside the spark plug boot to prevent sticking, then install the boot to the spark plug and push until it clicks into place. The click may be felt or heard, then gently pull back on the boot to assure proper contact.

11. If removed, connect the spark plug wire to its corresponding ignition coil terminal.

12. Connect the negative battery cable.

## INSPECTION & GAPPING

▶ **See Figures 90 thru 100**

Check the plugs for deposits and wear. If they are not going to be replaced, clean the plugs thoroughly. Remember that any kind of deposit will decrease the efficiency of the plug. Plugs can be cleaned on a spark plug cleaning machine, which can sometimes be found in service stations, or you can do an acceptable job of cleaning with a stiff brush. If the plugs are cleaned, the electrodes must be filed flat. Use an ignition points file, not an emery board or the like, which will leave deposits. The electrodes must be filed perfectly flat with sharp edges; rounded edges reduce the spark plug voltage by as much as 50%.

Check spark plug gap before installation. The ground electrode (the L-shaped one connected to the body of the plug) must be parallel to the center electrode and the specified size wire gauge (please refer to the Tune-Up Specifications chart for details) must pass between the electrodes with a slight drag.

➡**NEVER adjust the gap on a used platinum type spark plug.**

Always check the gap on new plugs as they are not always set correctly at the factory. Do not use a flat feeler gauge when measuring the gap on a used plug, because the reading may be inaccurate. A round-wire type gapping tool is the best way to check the gap. The correct gauge should pass through the electrode gap with a slight drag. If you're in doubt, try one size smaller and one larger. The smaller gauge should go through easily, while the larger one shouldn't go through at all. Wire gapping tools usually have a bending tool attached. Use that to adjust the side electrode until the proper distance is obtained. Absolutely never attempt to bend the center electrode. Also, be careful not to bend the side electrode too far or too often as it may weaken and break off within the engine, requiring removal of the cylinder head to retrieve it.

### Spark Plug Wires

## TESTING

▶ **See Figure 101**

At every tune-up/inspection, visually check the spark plug cables for burns cuts, or breaks in the insulation. Check the boots and the nipples on the coil. Replace any damaged wiring.

TCCS2135

**Fig. 90 A normally worn spark plug should have light tan or gray deposits on the firing tip**

TCCS2136

**Fig. 91 A carbon fouled plug, identified by soft, sooty, black deposits, may indicate an improperly tuned vehicle. Check the air cleaner, ignition components and engine control system**

Fig. 92 A variety of tools and gauges are needed for spark plug service

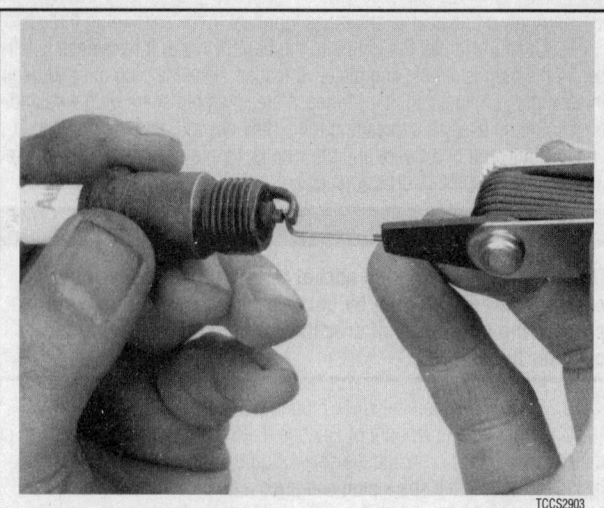

Fig. 94 Checking the spark plug gap with a feeler gauge

Fig. 93 A physically damaged spark plug may be evidence of severe detonation in that cylinder. Watch that cylinder carefully between services, as a continued detonation will not only damage the plug, but could also damage the engine

Fig. 95 An oil fouled spark plug indicates an engine with worn piston rings and/or bad valve seals allowing excessive oil to enter the chamber

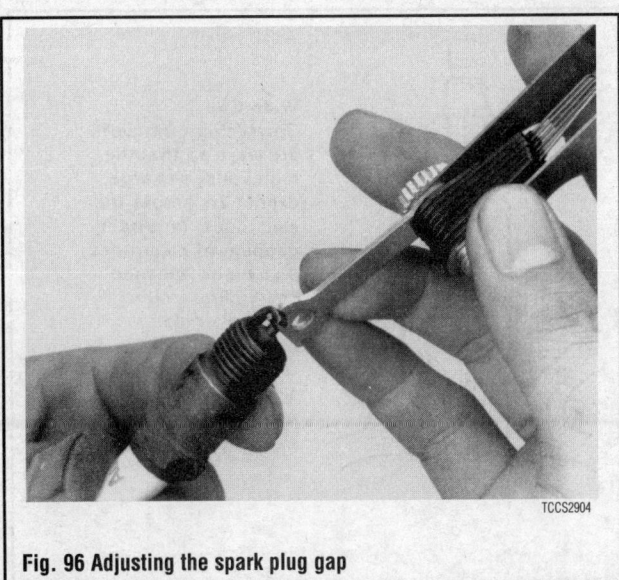

TCCS2904

Fig. 96 Adjusting the spark plug gap

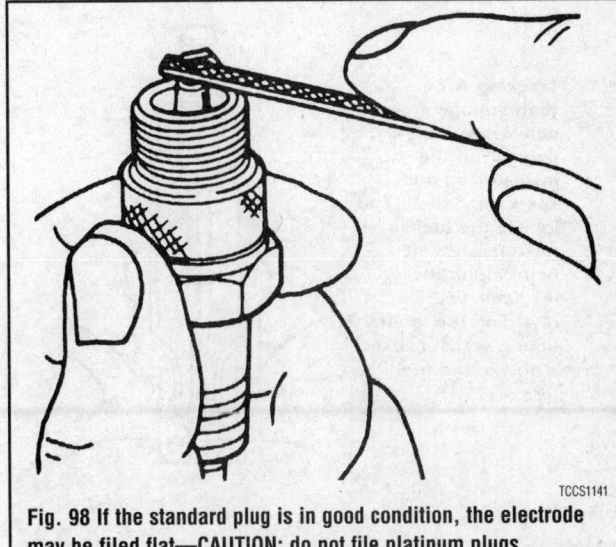

TCCS1141

Fig. 98 If the standard plug is in good condition, the electrode may be filed flat—CAUTION: do not file platinum plugs

TCCS2139

Fig. 97 This spark plug has been left in the engine too long, as evidenced by the extreme gap—Plugs with such an extreme gap can cause misfiring and stumbling accompanied by a noticeable lack of power

TCCS2140

Fig. 99 A bridged or almost bridged spark plug, identified by a build-up between the electrodes caused by excessive carbon or oil build-up on the plug

**Tracking Arc**
High voltage arcs between a fouling deposit on the insulator tip and spark plug shell. This ignites the fuel/air mixture at some point along the insulator tip, retarding the ignition timing which causes a power and fuel loss.

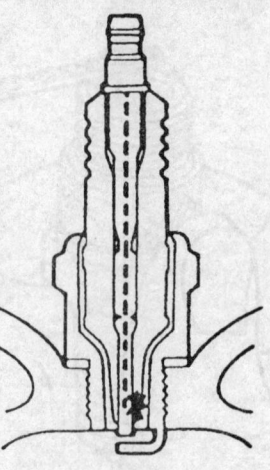

**Wide Gap**
Spark plug electrodes are worn so that the high voltage charge cannot arc across the electrodes. Improper gapping of electrodes on new or "cleaned" spark plugs could cause a similar condition. Fuel remains unburned and a power loss results.

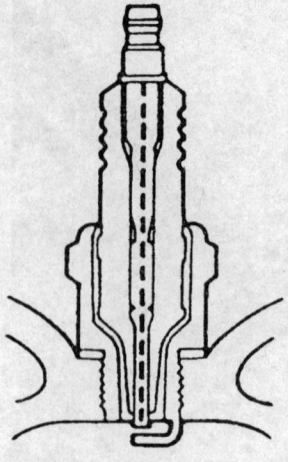

**Flashover**
A damaged spark plug boot, along with dirt and moisture, could permit the high voltage charge to short over the insulator to the spark plug shell or the engine. A buttress insulator design helps prevent high voltage flashover.

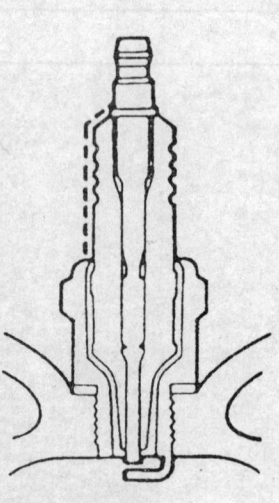

**Fouled Spark Plug**
Deposits that have formed on the insulator tip may become conductive and provide a "shunt" path to the shell. This prevents the high voltage from arcing between the electrodes. A power and fuel loss is the result.

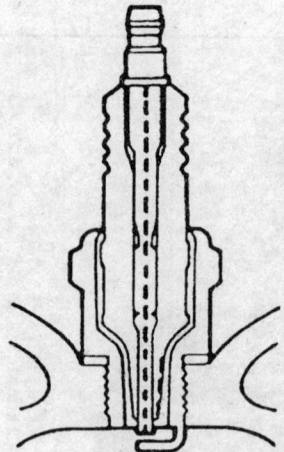

**Bridged Electrodes**
Fouling deposits between the electrodes "ground out" the high voltage needed to fire the spark plug. The arc between the electrodes does not occur and the fuel air mixture is not ignited. This causes a power loss and exhausting of raw fuel.

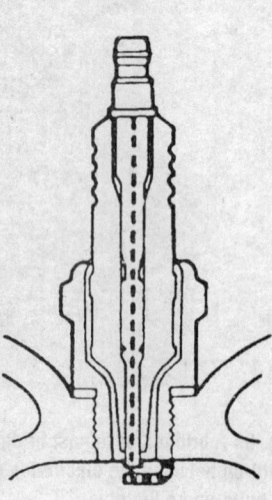

**Cracked Insulator**
A crack in the spark plug insulator could cause the high voltage charge to "ground out." Here, the spark does not jump the electrode gap and the fuel air mixture is not ignited. This causes a power loss and raw fuel is exhausted.

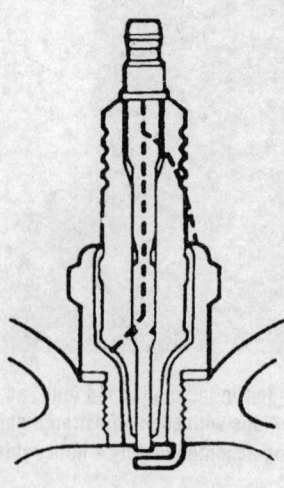

TCCS201A

**Fig. 100 Inspect the spark plug to determine engine running conditions**

**Fig. 101 Disconnect the spark plug wire, then check the resistance with an ohmmeter**

Every 50,000 miles (80,000 Km) or 60 months, the resistance of the wires should be checked with an ohmmeter. Wires with excessive resistance will cause misfiring, and may make the engine difficult to start in damp weather.

To check resistance, disconnect the spark plug wire from the plug and ignition coil, then use an ohmmeter to measure the resistance.

For 1995 vehicle the resistance should be 250–1,000 ohms per inch or 3,000–12,000 ohms per foot.

For 1996–99 SOHC engines, the resistance should be follows:

1. Cables #1 and #4: 3,500–4,900 ohms.
2. Cables #2 and #3: 2,950–4,100 ohms.

For 1996–99 DOHC engine, the resistance should be as follows:

3. Cables #1 and #4: 3,050–4,250 ohms.
4. Cables #2 and #3: 2300–3,300 ohms.

If resistance falls outside of specifications, the cable(s) should be replaced with new ones.

## REMOVAL & INSTALLATION

▸ **See Figure 102**

➡ **As the spark plug wires must be routed and connected properly, if all of the wires must be disconnected from the spark plugs or from the ignition coil pack at the same time, be sure to tag the wires to assure proper reconnection.**

When installing a new set of spark plug wires, replace the wires one at a time so there will be no mix-up. Start by replacing the longest cable first. Twist the boot of the spark plug wire ½ turn in each direction before pulling if off. Install the boot firmly over the spark plug. Route the wire exactly the same as the original. Insert the nipple firmly onto the tower on the ignition coil. Be sure to apply silicone dielectric compound to the spark plug wire boots and tower connectors prior to installation.

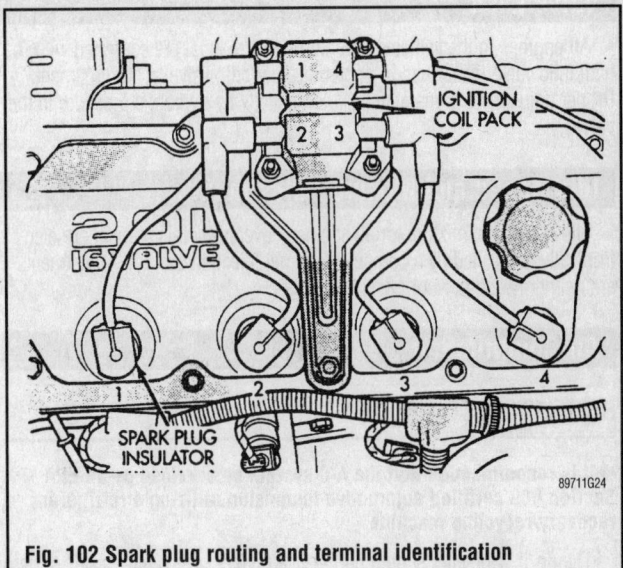

**Fig. 102 Spark plug routing and terminal identification**

## GASOLINE ENGINE TUNE-UP SPECIFICATIONS

| Year | Engine ID/VIN | Engine Displacement Liters (cc) | Spark Plugs Gap (in.) | Ignition Timing (deg.) MT | Ignition Timing (deg.) AT | Fuel Pump (psi) | Idle Speed (rpm) MT | Idle Speed (rpm) AT | Valve Clearance In. | Valve Clearance Ex. |
|------|---------------|---------------------------------|-----------------------|-----|-----|-----|-----|-----|-----|-----|
| 1995 | C | 2.0 (1996) | 0.033-0.038 | ① | ① | 48 | ② | ② | HYD | HYD |
|      | Y | 2.0 (1996) | 0.033-0.038 | ① | ① | 48 | ② | ② | HYD | HYD |
| 1996 | C | 2.0 (1996) | 0.033-0.038 | ① | ① | 48 | ② | ② | HYD | HYD |
|      | Y | 2.0 (1996) | 0.033-0.038 | ① | ① | 48 | ② | ② | HYD | HYD |
| 1997 | C | 2.0 (1996) | 0.033-0.038 | ① | ① | 49 | ② | ② | HYD | HYD |
|      | Y | 2.0 (1996) | 0.033-0.038 | ① | ① | 49 | ② | ② | HYD | HYD |
| 1998 | C | 2.0 (1996) | 0.033-0.038 | ① | ① | 49 | ② | ② | HYD | HYD |
|      | Y | 2.0 (1996) | 0.033-0.038 | ① | ① | 49 | ② | ② | HYD | HYD |
| 1999 | C | 2.0 (1996) | 0.033-0.038 | ① | ① | 49 | ② | ② | HYD | HYD |
|      | Y | 2.0 (1996) | 0.033-0.038 | ① | ① | 49 | ② | ② | HYD | HYD |

NOTE: The Vehicle Emission Control Information Label often reflects specification changes made during production. The label figures must be used if they differ from those in this chart.

HYD - Hydraulic

① The ignition timing is controlled by the PCM and is not adjustable.

② Refer to the Vehicle Emission Control Information Label for proper specification

When installing the wires, on SOHC engines, make sure the dual plastic clip holds the #1 and #2 cables off of the valve cover and that the PCV hose plastic clip holds the #3 cable away from the metal PCV clamp and edge of air duct. On DOHC engines, make sure the plastic clip on the PCV hose is positioned so the cable clip is beneath the hose, and that the #1 cable is snapped into this clip to protect it from the metal PCV clamp.

## Ignition Timing

### GENERAL INFORMATION

All engines in the vehicles covered by this manual are equipped with distributorless ignition systems. Accordingly, ignition timing is controlled by the Powertrain Control Module (PCM) and is not adjustable.

## Valve Lash

All engines in the vehicles covered by this manual are equipped with hydraulic valve lifters that do not require periodic valve lash adjustment. Proper adjustment is maintained automatically by hydraulic pressure in the valves.

## Idle Speed and Mixture Adjustment

Idle speed and mixture for all engines covered by this manual are electronically controlled by a computerized fuel injection system. Adjustments are neither necessary nor possible.

## Air Conditioning

### SYSTEM SERVICE & REPAIR

➡It is recommended that the A/C system be serviced by an EPA Section 609 certified automotive technician utilizing a refrigerant recovery/recycling machine.

The do-it-yourselfer should not service his/her own vehicle's A/C system for many reasons, including legal concerns, personal injury, environmental damage and cost. The following are some of the reasons why you may decide not to service your own vehicle's A/C system.

According to the U.S. Clean Air Act, it is a federal crime to service or repair (involving the refrigerant) a Motor Vehicle Air Conditioning (MVAC) system for money without being EPA certified. It is also illegal to vent R-134a refrigerant into the atmosphere.

State and/or local laws may be more strict than the federal regulations, so be sure to check with your state and/or local authorities for further information. For further federal information on the legality of servicing your A/C system, call the EPA Stratospheric Ozone Hotline.

➡Federal law dictates that a fine of up to $25,000 may be levied on people convicted of venting refrigerant into the atmosphere. Additionally, the EPA may pay up to $10,000 for information or services leading to a criminal conviction of the violation of these laws.

When servicing an A/C system you run the risk of handling or coming in contact with refrigerant, which may result in skin or eye irritation or frostbite. Although low in toxicity (due to chemical stability), inhalation of concentrated refrigerant fumes is dangerous and can result in death; cases of fatal cardiac arrhythmia have been reported in people accidentally subjected to high levels of refrigerant. Some early symptoms include loss of concentration and drowsiness.

Also, refrigerants can decompose at high temperatures (near gas heaters or open flame), which may result in hydrofluoric acid, hydrochloric acid and phosgene (a fatal nerve gas).

R-134a refrigerant is a greenhouse gas which, if allowed to vent into the atmosphere, will contribute to global warming (the Greenhouse Effect).

It is usually more economically feasible to have a certified MVAC automotive technician perform A/C system service to your vehicle. While it is illegal to service an A/C system without the proper equipment, the home mechanic would have to purchase an expensive refrigerant recovery/recycling machine to service his/her own vehicle.

### PREVENTIVE MAINTENANCE

Although the A/C system should not be serviced by the do-it-yourselfer, preventive maintenance can be practiced and A/C system inspections can be performed to help maintain the efficiency of the vehicle's A/C system. For preventive maintenance, perform the following:

• The easiest and most important preventive maintenance for your A/C system is to be sure that it is used on a regular basis. Running the system for five minutes each month (no matter what the season) will help ensure that the seals and all internal components remain lubricated.

➡Some newer vehicles automatically operate the A/C system compressor whenever the windshield defroster is activated. When running, the compressor lubricates the A/C system components; therefore, the A/C system would not need to be operated each month.

• In order to prevent heater core freeze-up during A/C operation, it is necessary to maintain a proper antifreeze protection. Use a hand-held coolant tester (hydrometer) to periodically check the condition of the antifreeze in your engine's cooling system.

➡Antifreeze should not be used longer than the manufacturer specifies.

• For efficient operation of an air conditioned vehicle's cooling system, the radiator cap should have a holding pressure which meets manufacturer's specifications. A cap which fails to hold these pressures should be replaced.

• Any obstruction of or damage to the condenser configuration will restrict air flow which is essential to its efficient operation. It is, therefore, a good rule to keep this unit clean and in proper physical shape.

➡Bug screens which are mounted in front of the condenser (unless they are original equipment) are regarded as obstructions.

• The condensation drain tube expels any water, which accumulates on the bottom of the evaporator housing, into the engine compartment. If this tube is obstructed, the air conditioning performance can be restricted and condensation buildup can spill over onto the vehicle's floor.

### SYSTEM INSPECTION

Although the A/C system should not be serviced by the do-it-yourselfer, preventive maintenance can be practiced and A/C system inspections can be performed to help maintain the efficiency of the vehicle's A/C system. For A/C system inspection, perform the following:

The easiest and often most important check for the air conditioning system consists of a visual inspection of the system components. Visually inspect the air conditioning system for refrigerant leaks, damaged compressor clutch, abnormal compressor drive belt tension and/or condition, plugged evaporator drain tube, blocked condenser fins, disconnected or broken wires, blown fuses, corroded connections and poor insulation.

A refrigerant leak will usually appear as an oily residue at the leakage point in the system. The oily residue soon picks up dust or dirt particles from the surrounding air and appears greasy. Through time, this will build up and appear to be a heavy dirt impregnated grease.

For a thorough visual and operational inspection, check the following:

• Check the surface of the radiator and condenser for dirt, leaves or other material which might block air flow.

• Check for kinks in hoses and lines. Check the system for leaks.

• Make sure the drive belt is properly tensioned. When the air conditioning is operating, make sure the drive belt is free of noise or slippage.

• Make sure the blower motor operates at all appropriate positions, then check for distribution of the air from all outlets with the blower on **HIGH** or **MAX**.

➡️**Keep in mind that under conditions of high humidity, air discharged from the A/C vents may not feel as cold as expected, even if the system is working properly. This is because vaporized moisture in humid air retains heat more effectively than dry air, thereby making humid air more difficult to cool.**

• Make sure the air passage selection lever is operating correctly. Start the engine and warm it to normal operating temperature, then make sure the temperature selection lever is operating correctly.

## Windshield Wiper (Elements)

### ELEMENT (REFILL) CARE & REPLACEMENT

▶ **See Figures 103 thru 112**

For maximum effectiveness and longest element life, the windshield and wiper blades should be kept clean. Dirt, tree sap, road tar and so on will cause streaking, smearing and blade deterioration if left on the glass. It is advisable to wash the windshield carefully with a commercial glass cleaner at least once a month. Wipe off the rubber blades with the wet rag afterwards. Do not attempt to move wipers across the windshield by hand; damage to the motor and drive mechanism will result.

To inspect and/or replace the wiper blade elements, place the wiper switch in the **LOW** speed position and the ignition switch in the **ACC** position. When the wiper blades are approximately vertical on the windshield, turn the ignition switch to **OFF**.

Examine the wiper blade elements. If they are found to be cracked, bro-

ken or torn, they should be replaced immediately. Replacement intervals will vary with usage, although ozone deterioration usually limits element life to about one year. If the wiper pattern is smeared or streaked, or if the blade chatters across the glass, the elements should be replaced. It is easiest and most sensible to replace the elements in pairs.

If your vehicle is equipped with aftermarket blades, there are several different types of refills and your vehicle might have any kind. Aftermarket blades and arms rarely use the exact same type blade or refill as the original equipment. Here are some typical aftermarket blades; not all may be available for your vehicle:

The Anco® type uses a release button that is pushed down to allow the refill to slide out of the yoke jaws. The new refill slides back into the frame and locks in place.

Some Trico® refills are removed by locating where the metal backing strip or the refill is wider. Insert a small screwdriver blade between the frame and metal backing strip. Press down to release the refill from the retaining tab.

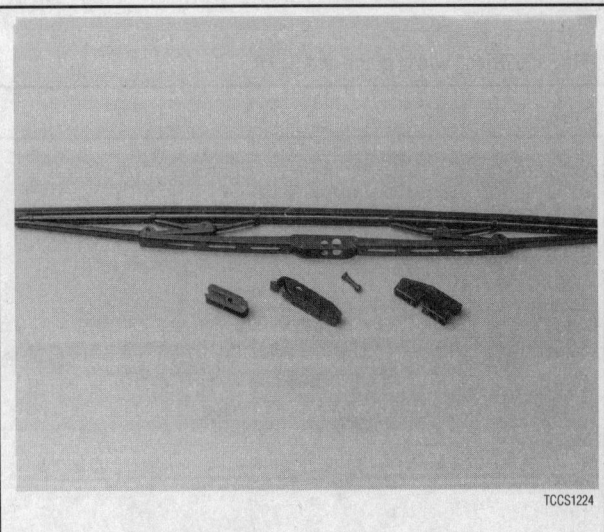

**Fig. 104 Lexor® wiper blade and fit kit**

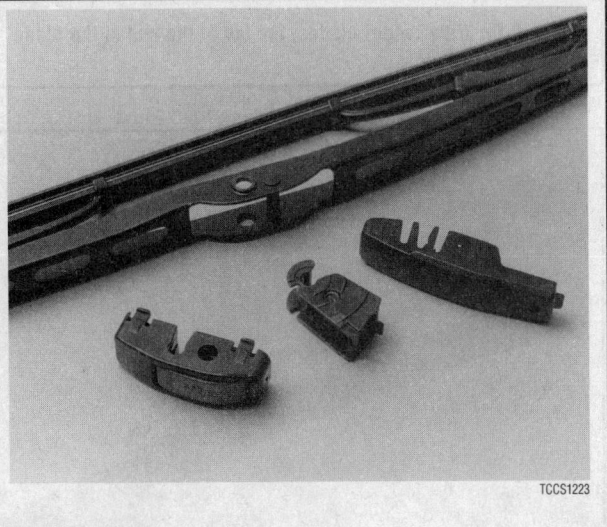

**Fig. 103 Bosch® wiper blade and fit kit**

**Fig. 105 Pylon® wiper blade and adapter**

Fig. 106 Trico® wiper blade and fit kit

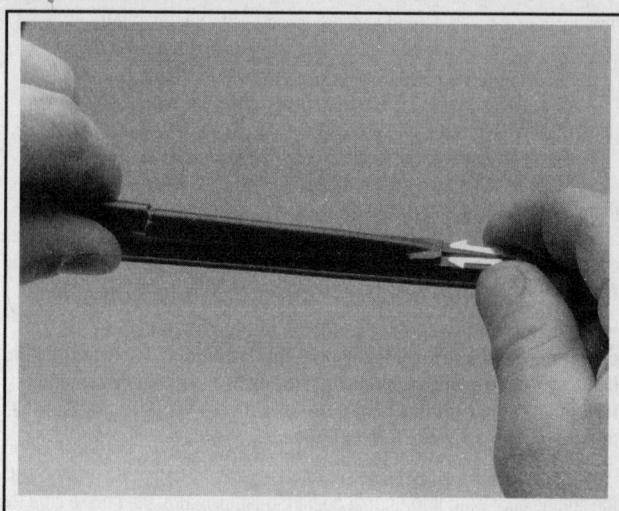

Fig. 109 On Pylon® inserts, the clip at the end has to be removed prior to sliding the insert off

Fig. 107 Tripledge® wiper blade and fit kit

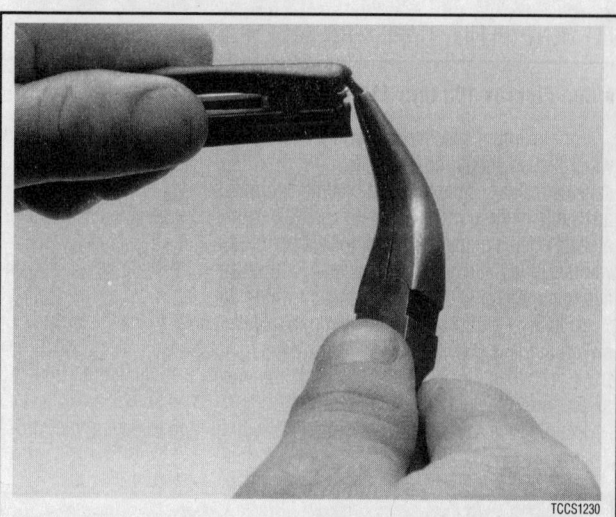

Fig. 110 On Trico® wiper blades, the tab at the end of the blade must be turned up . . .

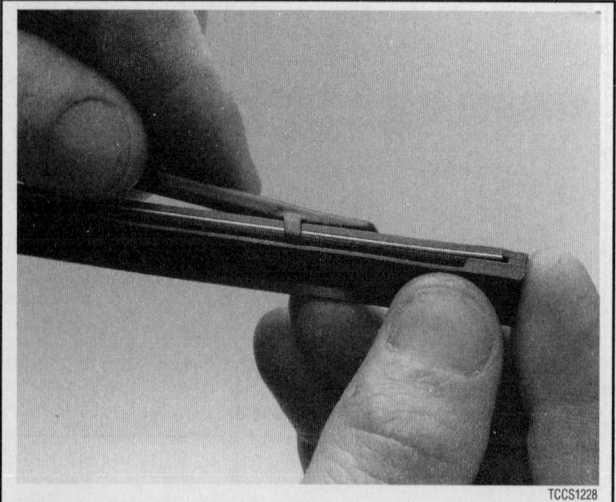

Fig. 108 To remove and install a Lexor® wiper blade refill, slip out the old insert and slide in a new one

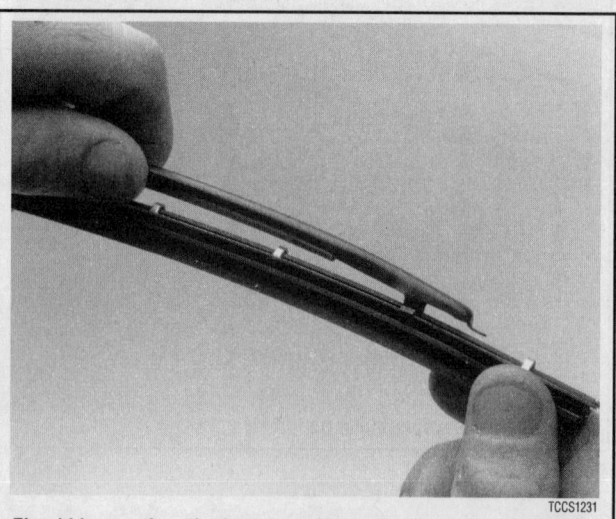

Fig. 111 . . . then the insert can be removed. After installing the replacement insert, bend the tab back

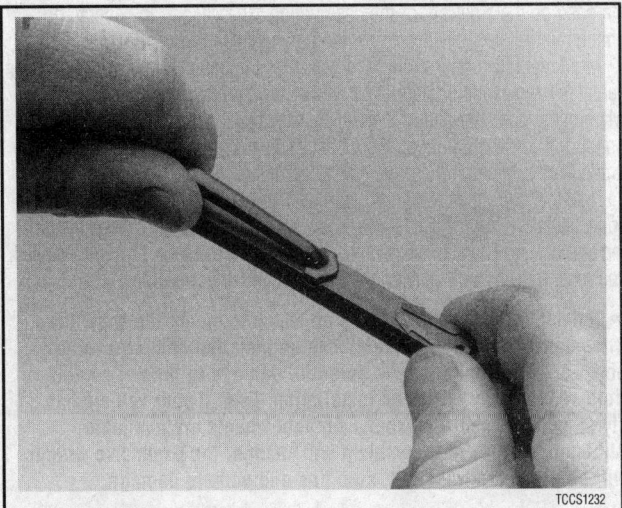

**Fig. 112 The Tripledge® wiper blade insert is removed and installed using a securing clip**

Other types of Trico® refills have two metal tabs which are unlocked by squeezing them together. The rubber filler can then be withdrawn from the frame jaws. A new refill is installed by inserting the refill into the front frame jaws and sliding it rearward to engage the remaining frame jaws. There are usually four jaws; be certain when installing that the refill is engaged in all of them. At the end of its travel, the tabs will lock into place on the front jaws of the wiper blade frame.

Another type of refill is made from polycarbonate. The refill has a simple locking device at one end which flexes downward out of the groove into which the jaws of the holder fit, allowing easy release. By sliding the new refill through all the jaws and pushing through the slight resistance when it reaches the end of its travel, the refill will lock into position.

To replace the Tridon® refill, it is necessary to remove the wiper blade. This refill has a plastic backing strip with a notch about 1 in. (25mm) from the end. Hold the blade (frame) on a hard surface so that the frame is tightly bowed. Grip the tip of the backing strip and pull up while twisting counter-clockwise. The backing strip will snap out of the retaining tab. Do this for the remaining tabs until the refill is free of the blade. The length of these refills is molded into the end and they should be replaced with identical types.

Regardless of the type of refill used, be sure to follow the part manufacturer's instructions closely. Make sure that all of the frame jaws are engaged as the refill is pushed into place and locked. If the metal blade holder and frame are allowed to touch the glass during wiper operation, the glass will be scratched.

## Tires and Wheels

Common sense and good driving habits will afford maximum tire life. Fast starts, sudden stops and hard cornering are hard on tires and will shorten their useful life span. Make sure that you don't overload the vehicle or run with incorrect pressure in the tires. Both of these practices will increase tread wear.

➡**For optimum tire life, keep the tires properly inflated, rotate them often and have the wheel alignment checked periodically.**

Inspect your tires frequently. Be especially careful to watch for bubbles in the tread or sidewall, deep cuts or underinflation. Replace any tires with bubbles in the sidewall. If cuts are so deep that they penetrate to the cords, discard the tire. Any cut in the sidewall of a radial tire renders it unsafe. Also look for uneven tread wear patterns that may indicate the front end is out of alignment or that the tires are out of balance.

## TIRE ROTATION

▶ **See Figures 113 and 114**

Tires must be rotated periodically to equalize wear patterns that vary with a tire's position on the vehicle. Tires will also wear in an uneven way as the front steering/suspension system wears to the point where the alignment should be reset.

Rotating the tires will ensure maximum life for the tires as a set, so you will not have to discard a tire early due to wear on only part of the tread. Regular rotation is required to equalize wear.

When rotating "unidirectional tires," make sure that they always roll in the same direction. This means that a tire used on the left side of the vehicle must not be switched to the right side and vice-versa. Such tires should only be rotated front-to-rear or rear-to-front, while always remaining on the same side of the vehicle. These tires are marked on the

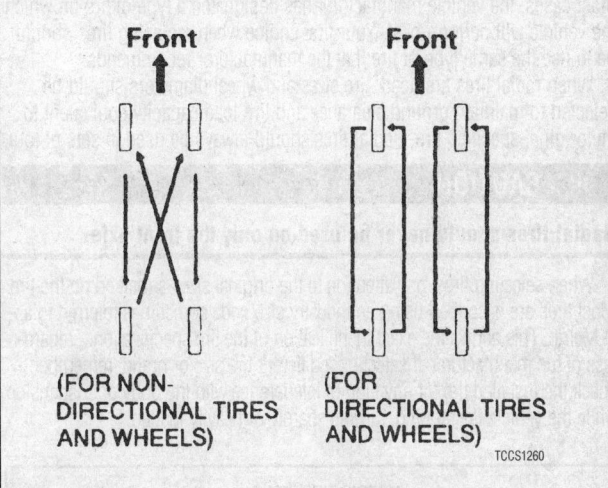

**Fig. 113 Compact spare tires must NEVER be used in the rotation pattern**

**Fig. 114 Unidirectional tires are identifiable by sidewall arrows and/or the word "rotation"**

sidewall as to the direction of rotation; observe the marks when reinstalling the tire(s).

Some styled or "mag" wheels may have different offsets front to rear. In these cases, the rear wheels must not be used up front and vice-versa. Furthermore, if these wheels are equipped with unidirectional tires, they cannot be rotated unless the tire is remounted for the proper direction of rotation.

➡**The compact or space-saver spare is strictly for emergency use. It must never be included in the tire rotation or placed on the vehicle for everyday use.**

## TIRE DESIGN

▶ **See Figure 115**

For maximum satisfaction, tires should be used in sets of four. Mixing of different types (radial, bias-belted, fiberglass belted) must be avoided. In most cases, the vehicle manufacturer has designated a type of tire on which the vehicle will perform best. Your first choice when replacing tires should be to use the same type of tire that the manufacturer recommends.

When radial tires are used, tire sizes and wheel diameters should be selected to maintain ground clearance and tire load capacity equivalent to the original specified tire. Radial tires should always be used in sets of four.

### ✳✳ CAUTION

**Radial tires should never be used on only the front axle.**

When selecting tires, pay attention to the original size as marked on the tire. Most tires are described using an industry size code sometimes referred to as P-Metric. This allows the exact identification of the tire specifications, regardless of the manufacturer. If selecting a different tire size or brand, remember to check the installed tire for any sign of interference with the body or suspension while the vehicle is stopping, turning sharply or heavily loaded.

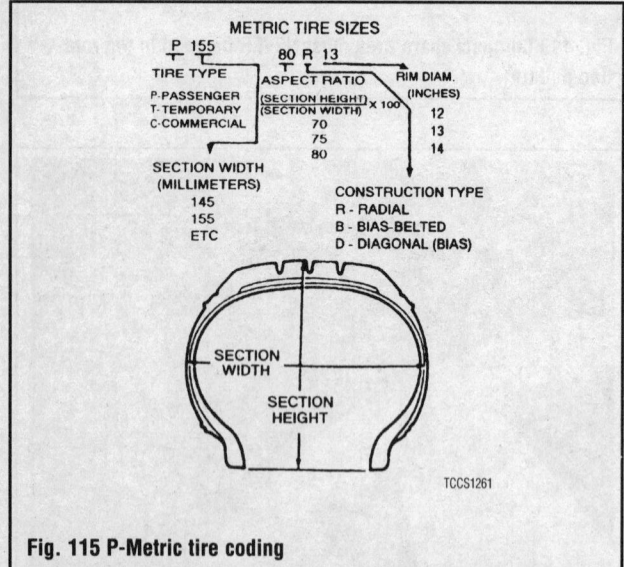

Fig. 115 P-Metric tire coding

### Snow Tires

Good radial tires can produce a big advantage in slippery weather, but in snow, a street radial tire does not have sufficient tread to provide traction and control. The small grooves of a street tire quickly pack with snow and the tire behaves like a billiard ball on a marble floor. The more open, chunky tread of a snow tire will self-clean as the tire turns, providing much better grip on snowy surfaces.

To satisfy municipalities requiring snow tires during weather emergencies, most snow tires carry either an M + S designation after the tire size

stamped on the sidewall, or the designation "all-season." In general, no change in tire size is necessary when buying snow tires.

Most manufacturers strongly recommend the use of 4 snow tires on their vehicles for reasons of stability. If snow tires are fitted only to the drive wheels, the opposite end of the vehicle may become very unstable when braking or turning on slippery surfaces. This instability can lead to unpleasant endings if the driver can't counteract the slide in time.

Note that snow tires, whether 2 or 4, will affect vehicle handling in all non-snow situations. The stiffer, heavier snow tires will noticeably change the turning and braking characteristics of the vehicle. Once the snow tires are installed, you must re-learn the behavior of the vehicle and drive accordingly.

➡**Consider buying extra wheels on which to mount the snow tires. Once done, the "snow wheels" can be installed and removed as needed. This eliminates the potential damage to tires or wheels from seasonal removal and installation. Even if your vehicle has styled wheels, see if inexpensive steel wheels are available. Although the look of the vehicle will change, the expensive wheels will be protected from salt, curb hits and pothole damage.**

## TIRE STORAGE

If they are mounted on wheels, store the tires at proper inflation pressure. All tires should be kept in a cool, dry place. If they are stored in the garage or basement, do not let them stand on a concrete floor; set them on strips of wood, a mat or a large stack of newspaper. Keeping them away from direct moisture is of paramount importance. Tires should not be stored upright, but in a flat position.

## INFLATION & INSPECTION

▶ **See Figures 116 thru 125**

The importance of proper tire inflation cannot be overemphasized. A tire employs air as part of its structure. It is designed around the supporting strength of the air at a specified pressure. For this reason, improper inflation drastically reduces the tire's ability to perform as intended. A tire will lose some air in day-to-day use; having to add a few pounds of air periodically is not necessarily a sign of a leaking tire.

Two items should be a permanent fixture in every glove compartment: an accurate tire pressure gauge and a tread depth gauge. Check the tire pressure (including the spare) regularly with a pocket type gauge. Too often, the gauge on the end of the air hose at your corner garage is not accurate because it suffers too much abuse. Always check tire pressure when the tires are cold, as pressure increases with temperature. If you must move the vehicle to check the

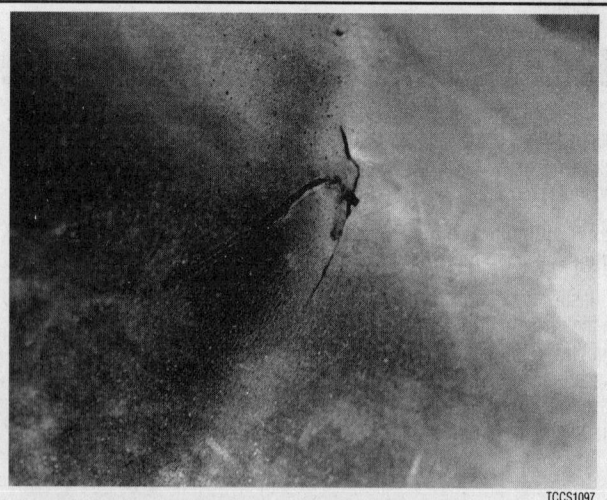

Fig. 116 Tires should be checked frequently for any sign of puncture or damage

tire inflation, do not drive more than a mile before checking. A cold tire is generally one that has not been driven for more than three hours.

A plate or sticker is normally provided somewhere in the vehicle (door post, hood, tailgate or trunk lid) which shows the proper pressure for the tires. Never counteract excessive pressure build-up by bleeding off air pressure (letting some air out). This will cause the tire to run hotter and wear quicker.

### ✳✳ CAUTION

**Never exceed the maximum tire pressure embossed on the tire! This is the pressure to be used when the tire is at maximum loading, but it is rarely the correct pressure for everyday driving. Consult the owner's manual or the tire pressure sticker for the correct tire pressure.**

Once you've maintained the correct tire pressures for several weeks, you'll be familiar with the vehicle's braking and handling personality. Slight adjustments in tire pressures can fine-tune these characteristics, but never change the cold pressure specification by more than 2 psi. A slightly softer tire pressure will give a softer ride but also yield lower fuel mileage. A slightly harder tire will give crisper dry road handling but can cause skid-

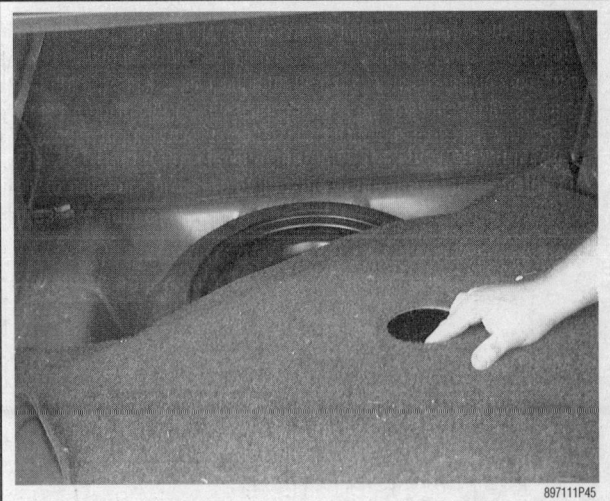

Fig. 119 . . . then remove the panel for access to the spare tire

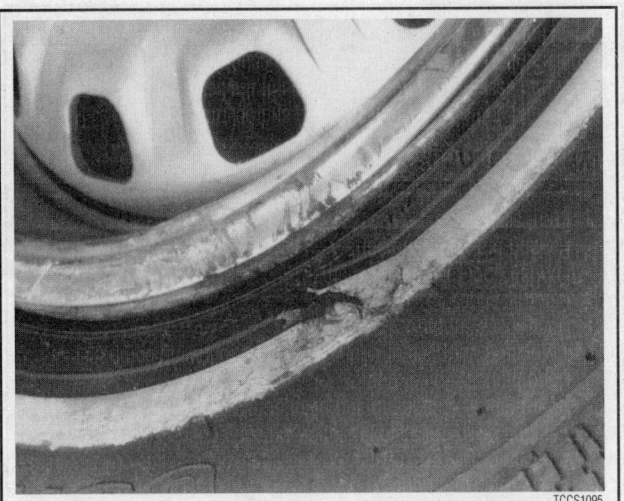

Fig. 117 Tires with deep cuts, or cuts which show bulging should be replaced immediately

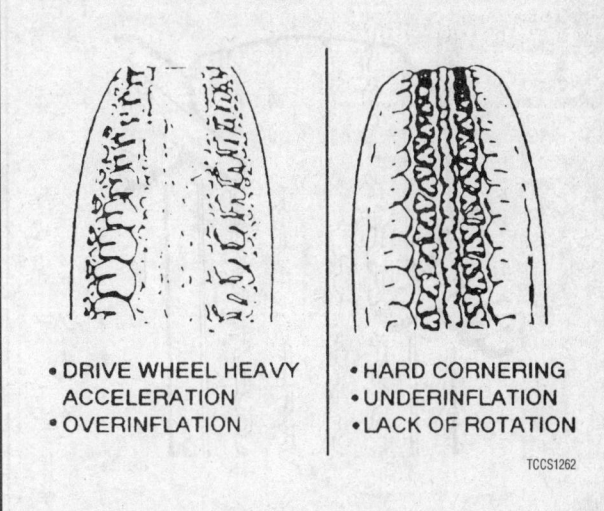

• DRIVE WHEEL HEAVY ACCELERATION
• OVERINFLATION

• HARD CORNERING
• UNDERINFLATION
• LACK OF ROTATION

Fig. 120 Examples of inflation-related tire wear patterns

Fig. 118 Check the inflation pressure of the spare as well. Unfasten the panel retainer . . .

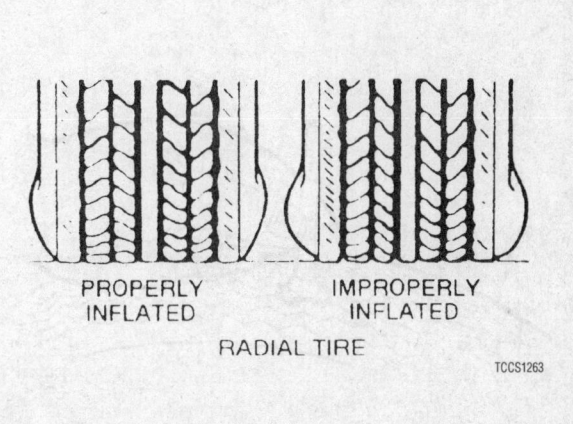

PROPERLY INFLATED

IMPROPERLY INFLATED

RADIAL TIRE

Fig. 121 Radial tires have a characteristic sidewall bulge; don't try to measure pressure by looking at the tire. Use a quality air pressure gauge

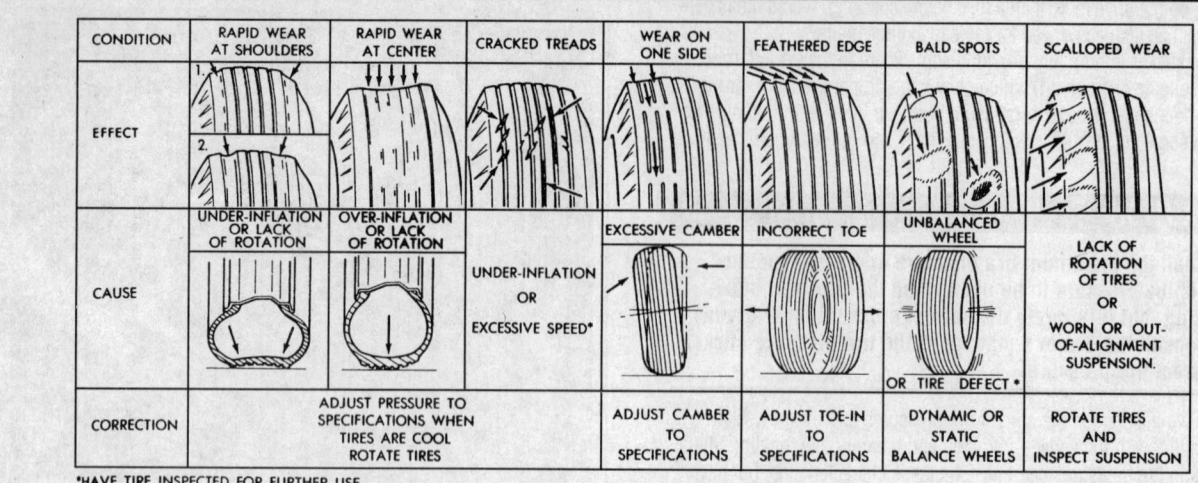

| CONDITION | RAPID WEAR AT SHOULDERS | RAPID WEAR AT CENTER | CRACKED TREADS | WEAR ON ONE SIDE | FEATHERED EDGE | BALD SPOTS | SCALLOPED WEAR |
|---|---|---|---|---|---|---|---|
| EFFECT | | | | | | | |
| CAUSE | UNDER-INFLATION OR LACK OF ROTATION | OVER-INFLATION OR LACK OF ROTATION | UNDER-INFLATION OR EXCESSIVE SPEED* | EXCESSIVE CAMBER | INCORRECT TOE | UNBALANCED WHEEL OR TIRE DEFECT * | LACK OF ROTATION OF TIRES OR WORN OR OUT-OF-ALIGNMENT SUSPENSION. |
| CORRECTION | ADJUST PRESSURE TO SPECIFICATIONS WHEN TIRES ARE COOL ROTATE TIRES | | | ADJUST CAMBER TO SPECIFICATIONS | ADJUST TOE-IN TO SPECIFICATIONS | DYNAMIC OR STATIC BALANCE WHEELS | ROTATE TIRES AND INSPECT SUSPENSION |

*HAVE TIRE INSPECTED FOR FURTHER USE.

TCCS1267

**Fig. 122 Common tire wear patterns and causes**

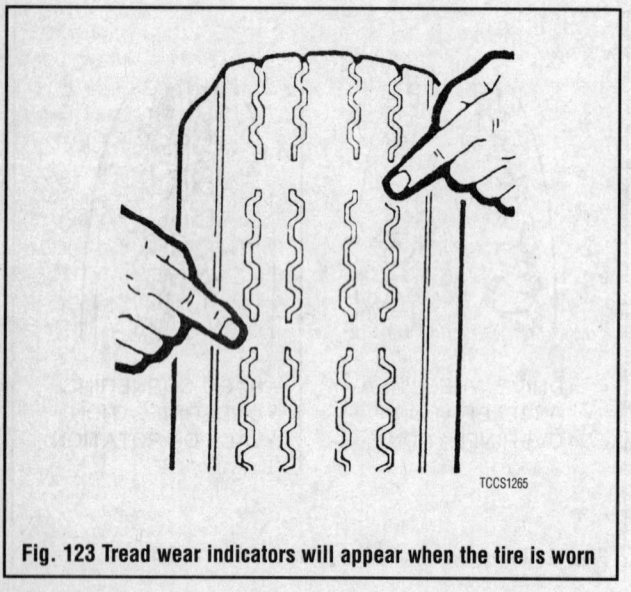

**Fig. 123 Tread wear indicators will appear when the tire is worn**

TCCS1265

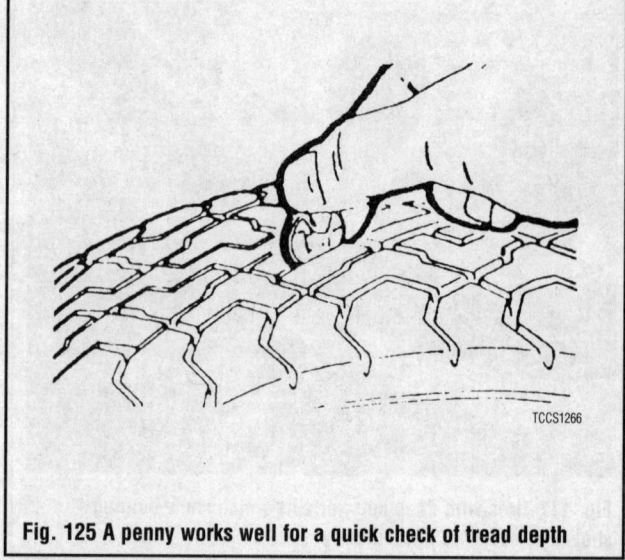

TCCS1266

**Fig. 125 A penny works well for a quick check of tread depth**

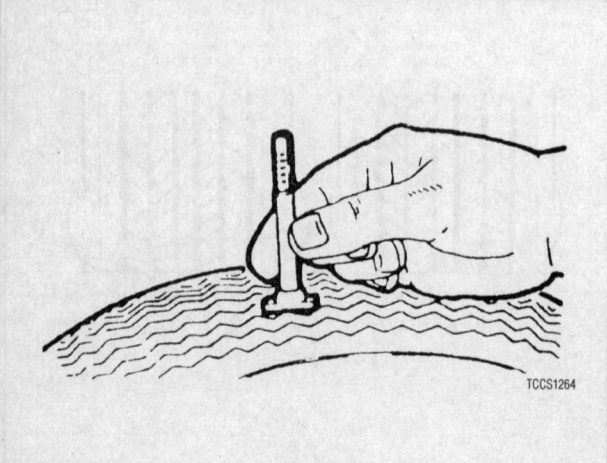

TCCS1264

**Fig. 124 Accurate tread depth indicators are inexpensive and handy**

ding on wet surfaces. Unless you're fully attuned to the vehicle, stick to the recommended inflation pressures.

All tires made since 1968 have built-in tread wear indicator bars that show up as $\frac{1}{2}$ in. (13mm) wide smooth bands across the tire when $\frac{1}{16}$ in. (1.5mm) of tread remains. The appearance of tread wear indicators means that the tires should be replaced. In fact, many states have laws prohibiting the use of tires with less than this amount of tread.

You can check your own tread depth with an inexpensive gauge or by using a Lincoln head penny. Slip the Lincoln penny (with Lincoln's head upside-down) into several tread grooves. If you can see the top of Lincoln's head in 2 adjacent grooves, the tire has less than $\frac{1}{16}$ in. (1.5mm) tread left and should be replaced. You can measure snow tires in the same manner by using the "tails" side of the Lincoln penny. If you can see the top of the Lincoln memorial, it's time to replace the snow tire(s).

## CARE OF SPECIAL WHEELS

If you have invested money in magnesium, aluminum alloy or sport wheels, special precautions should be taken to make sure your investment is not wasted and that your special wheels look good for the life of the vehicle.

Special wheels are easily damaged and/or scratched. Occasionally check the rims for cracking, impact damage or air leaks. If any of these are found, replace the wheel. But in order to prevent this type of damage and the costly replacement of a special wheel, observe the following precautions:

• Use extra care not to damage the wheels during removal, installation, balancing, etc. After removal of the wheels from the vehicle, place them on a mat or other protective surface. If they are to be stored for any length of time, support them on strips of wood. Never store tires and wheels upright; the tread may develop flat spots.

• When driving, watch for hazards; it doesn't take much to crack a wheel.

• When washing, use a mild soap or non-abrasive dish detergent (keeping in mind that detergent tends to remove wax). Avoid cleansers with abrasives or the use of hard brushes. There are many cleaners and polishes for special wheels.

• If possible, remove the wheels during the winter. Salt and sand used for snow removal can severely damage the finish of a wheel.

• Make certain the recommended lug nut torque is never exceeded or the wheel may crack. Never use snow chains on special wheels; severe scratching will occur.

## FLUIDS AND LUBRICANTS

### Fluid Disposal

Used fluids such as engine oil, transmission fluid, antifreeze and brake fluid are hazardous wastes and must be disposed of properly. Before draining any fluids, consult with your local authorities; in many areas waste oil, etc. is being accepted as a part of recycling programs. A number of service stations and auto parts stores are also accepting waste fluids for recycling.

Be sure of the recycling center's policies before draining any fluids, as many will not accept different fluids that have been mixed together.

### Fuel and Engine Oil Recommendations

#### FUEL

➡ **Some fuel additives contain chemicals that can damage the catalytic converter and/or oxygen sensor. Read all of the labels carefully before using any additive in the engine or fuel system.**

All Neons are designed to run on unleaded fuel. The use of a leaded fuel in a car requiring unleaded fuel will plug the catalytic converter and render it inoperative. It will also increase exhaust backpressure to the point where engine output will be severely reduced. The minimum octane rating of the unleaded fuel being used must be at least 87, which usually means regular unleaded, but some high performance engines may require higher ratings. Fuel should be selected for the brand and octane which performs best with your engine. Judge a gasoline by its ability to prevent pinging, its engine starting capabilities (cold and hot) and general all weather performance.

As far as the octane rating is concerned, refer to the general engine specifications chart in Section 3 of this manual to find your engine and its compression ratio. If the compression ratio is 9.0:1 or lower, in most cases a regular unleaded grade of gasoline can be used. If the compression ratio is higher than 9.0:1 use a premium grade of unleaded fuel.

The use of a fuel too low in octane (a measure of anti-knock quality) will result in spark knock. Since many factors such as altitude, terrain, air temperature and humidity affect operating efficiency, knocking may result even though the recommended fuel is being used. If persistent knocking occurs, it may be necessary to switch to a higher grade of fuel. Continuous or heavy knocking may result in engine damage.

➡ **Your engine's fuel requirement can change with time, mainly due to carbon build-up, which will in turn change the compression ratio. If you engine pings, knocks or diesels (runs with the ignition OFF) switch to a higher grade of fuel. Sometimes, just changing brands will cure the problem. If it becomes necessary to retard the timing from the specifications, don't change it more than a few degrees. Retarded timing will reduce power output and fuel mileage, in addition to making the engine run hotter.**

#### OIL

▶ **See Figures 126 and 127**

The Society Of Automotive Engineer (SAE) grade number indicates the viscosity of the engine oil and thus its ability to lubricate at a given temperature. The lower the SAE grade number, the lighter the oil; the lower the viscosity, the easier it is to crank the engine in cold weather. Oil viscosities should be chosen from those oils recommended for the lowest anticipated temperatures during the oil change interval. With the proper viscosity, you will be assured of easy cold starting and sufficient engine protection.

Multi-viscosity oils (5W-30, 10W-30 etc.) offer the important advantage of being adaptable to temperature extremes. They allow easy starting at low temperatures, yet they give good protection at high speeds and engine temperatures. This is a decided advantage in changeable climates or in long distance driving.

The American Petroleum Institute (API) designation indicates the classification of engine oil used under certain given operating conditions. Only oil designated for Service SH, or latest superseding oil grade, should be used. Oils of the SH type perform a variety of functions inside the engine in addition to their basic function as a lubricant. Through a balanced system of metallic detergents and polymeric dispersants, the oil prevents the formation of high and low temperature deposits and also keeps sludge and particles of dirt in suspension. Acids, particularly sulfuric acid, as well as other byproducts of combustion, are neutralized. Both the SAE grade number and the API designation can be found on the side of the oil bottle.

Fig. 126 Look for the API oil identification label when choosing your engine oil

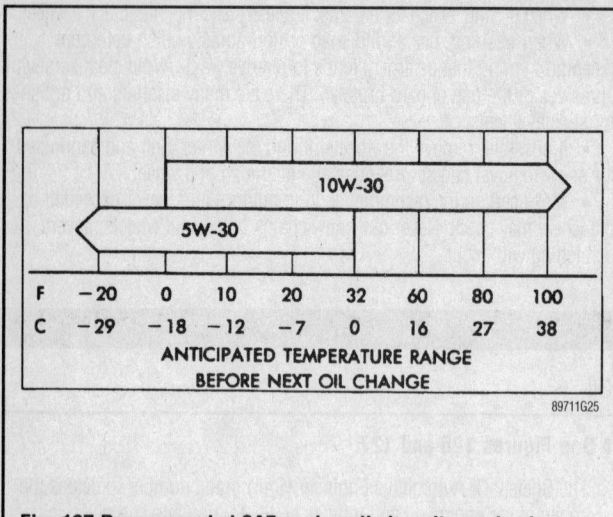

Fig. 127 Recommended SAE engine oil viscosity grades for gasoline engines

Fig. 128 Pull the engine oil dipstick out of the tube

## Synthetic Oils

There are excellent synthetic and fuel-efficient oils available that, under the right circumstances, can help provide better fuel mileage and better engine protection. However, these advantages come at a price, which can be significantly more than the price per quart of conventional motor oils.

Before pouring any synthetic oils into your car's engine, you should consider the condition of the engine and the type of driving you do. It is also wise to check the vehicle manufacturer's position on synthetic oils.

Generally, it is best to avoid the use of synthetic oil in both brand new and older, high mileage engines. New engines require a proper break-in, and the synthetics are so slippery that they can impede this; most manufacturers recommend that you wait at least 5,000 miles (8,000 km) before switching to a synthetic oil. Conversely, older engines are looser and tend to lose more oil; synthetics will slip past worn parts more readily than regular oil. If your car already leaks oil, (due to worn parts or bad seals/gaskets), it may leak more with a synthetic inside.

Consider your type of driving. If most of your accumulated mileage is on the highway at higher, steadier speed, a synthetic oil will reduce friction and probably help deliver better fuel mileage. Under such ideal highway conditions, the oil change interval can be extended, as long as the oil filter can operated effectively for the extended life of the oil. If the filter can't do its job for this extended period, dirt and sludge will build up in your engine's crankcase, sump, oil pump and lines, no matter what type of oil is used. If using synthetic oil in this manner, your should continue to change the oil filter at the recommended intervals.

Cars used under harder, stop-and-go, short hop circumstances should always be serviced more frequently, and for these cars synthetic oil may not be a wise investment. Because of the necessary shorter change interval needed for this type of driving, you cannot take advantage of the long recommended change interval of most synthetic oils.

## Engine

### OIL LEVEL CHECK

▶ See Figures 128 and 129

Every time you stop for fuel, check the engine oil making sure the engine has fully warmed and the vehicle is parked on a level surface. Because it takes some time for the oil to drain back to the oil pan, you should wait a few minutes before checking your oil. If you are doing this at a fuel stop, first fill the fuel tank, then open the hood and check the oil, but don't get so

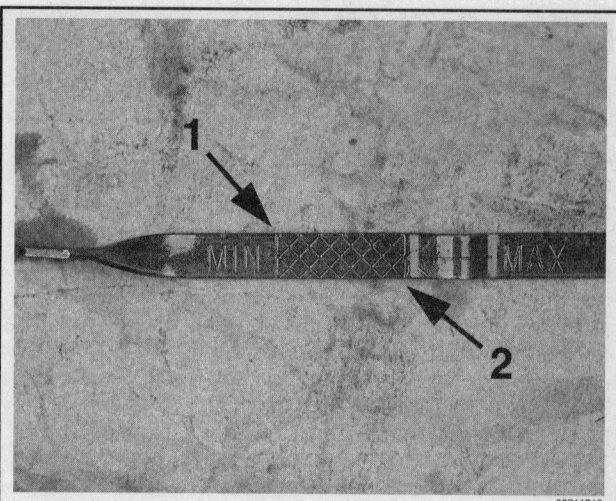

Fig. 129 The oil level should be within the crosshatched area between the MIN (1) and MAX (2) marks

carried away as to forget to pay for the fuel. Most station attendants won't believe that you forgot.

1. Make sure the car is parked on level ground.

2. When checking the oil level, it is best for the engine to be at normal operating temperature, although checking the oil immediately after stopping will lead to a false reading. Wait a few minutes after turning off the engine to allow the oil to drain back into the crankcase.

3. Open the hood and locate the dipstick which will be in a guide tube mounted in the upper engine block. Pull the dipstick from its tube, wipe it clean (using a clean, lint free rag) and then reinsert it.

4. Pull the dipstick out again and, holding it horizontally, read the oil level. The oil should be in the crosshatched area between the MIN and MAX marks on the dipstick. If the oil is below the MIN mark, add oil of the proper viscosity through the capped opening in the top of the valve cover. See the oil and fuel recommendations listed earlier in this section for the proper viscosity and rating of oil to use.

5. Insert the dipstick and check the oil level again after adding any oil. Approximately one quart of oil will raise the level from the MIN mark to the MAX mark. Be sure not to overfill the crankcase and waste the oil. Excess oil will generally be consumed at an accelerated rate.

## ⁂ WARNING

**DO NOT** overfill the crankcase. It may result in oil-fouled spark plugs, oil leaks cause by oil seal failure or engine damage due to oil foaming.

6. Close the hood.

## OIL & FILTER CHANGE

▶ **See Figures 130 thru 140**

## ⁂ CAUTION

The EPA warns that prolonged contact with used engine oil may cause a number of skin disorders, including cancer! You should make every effort to minimize your exposure to used engine oil. Protective gloves should be worn when changing the oil. Wash your hands and any other exposed skin areas as soon as possible after exposure to used engine oil. Soap and water, or waterless hand cleaner should be used.

The manufacturer's recommended oil change interval is 7500 miles (12,000 km) under normal operating conditions. We recommend an oil change interval of 3000–3500 miles (4800–5600 km) under normal conditions; more frequently under severe conditions such as when the average trip is less than 4 miles (6 km), the engine is operated for extended periods at idle or low-speed, when towing a trailer or operating is dusty areas.

In addition, we recommend that the filter be replaced EVERY time the oil is changed.

➡**Please be considerate of the environment. Dispose of waste oil properly by taking it to a service station, municipal facility or recycling center.**

1. Run the engine until it reaches normal operating temperature. The turn the engine **OFF**.
2. Raise and safely support the front of the vehicle using jackstands.
3. Slide a drain pan of at least 5 quarts capacity under the oil pan. Wipe the drain plug and surrounding area clean using an old rag.
4. Loosen the drain plug using a ratchet, short extension and socket, or a box-wrench. Turn the plug out by hand, using a rag to shield your fingers from the hot oil. By keeping an inward pressure on the plug as you unscrew it, oil won't escape past the threads and you can remove it without being burned by hot oil.

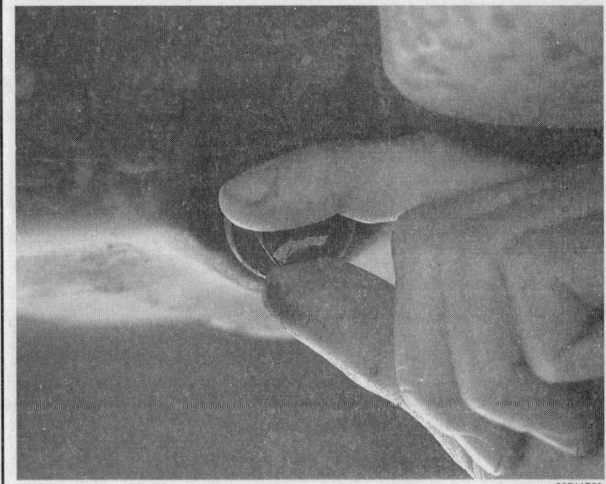
Fig. 131 Finish unthreading the oil pan drain plug by hand . . .

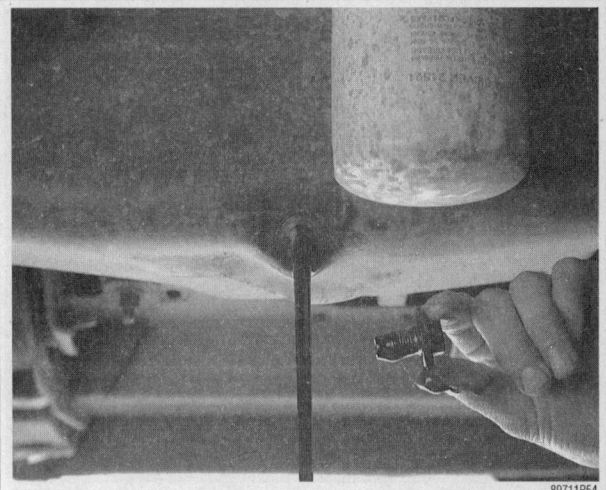
Fig. 132 . . . then quickly withdraw the plug and allow the fluid to drain into a suitable container

Fig. 130 Use a wrench or socket to loosen the drain plug

Fig. 133 Loosen the oil filter. This can be done with a strap type wrench (shown)

**Fig. 134 A cup type adapter can also be used . . .**

**Fig. 135 . . . as well as filter pliers**

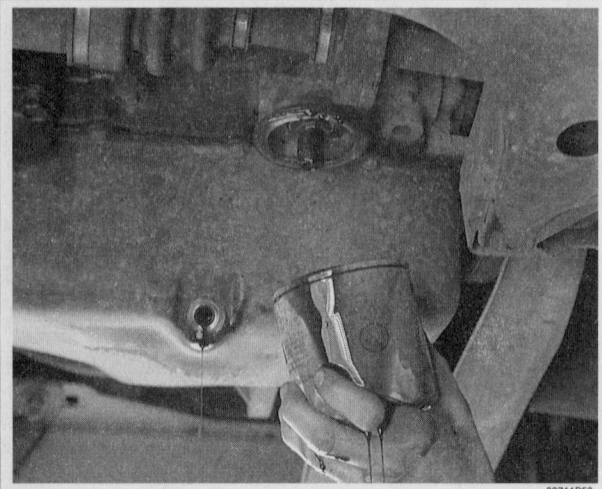

**Fig. 136 Carefully lower the filter, then empty it into the drain pan**

5.  Quickly withdraw the plug and move your hands out of the way, but be careful not to drop the plug into the drain pan, as fishing it out can be an unpleasant mess..

6.  Move the drain pan under the oil filter. Use a strap-type or cap-type wrench or oil filter pliers to loosen the oil filter. Cover your hand with a rag, and spin the filter off by hand; turn it slowly. Keep in mind that it's holding about one quart of dirty, hot oil.

➡ **Be careful when removing the oil filter, because the filter contains about 1 quart of hot, dirty oil.**

7.  Empty the old oil filter into the drain pan, then properly dispose of the filter.

8.  Using a clean shop towel, wipe off the filter adapter on the engine block. Be sure the towel does not leave any lint which could clog an oil passage. Allow the oil to drain completely, then reinstall the drain plug. Do not overtighten the plug.

9.  Coat the rubber gasket on the new filter with fresh oil. Spin the filter onto the adapter by hand until it contacts the mounting surface. Tighten the filter to 15 ft. lbs. (20 Nm). Do NOT overtighten the filter.

10.  Carefully lower the vehicle.

11.  Refill the crankcase with the correct amount of fresh engine oil. Please refer to the Capacities chart in this section.

**Fig. 137 Use a clean, lint free rag to clean the filter mounting boss**

**Fig. 138 Before installing a new oil filter, lightly coat the rubber gasket with clean oil**

Fig. 139 Remove the engine oil fill cap . . .

Fig. 140 . . . then fill the crankcase with the proper type and amount of oil, using a funnel to avoid a mess

12. Check the oil level on the dipstick. It is normal or the level to be a bit above the full mark until the engine is run and the new filter is filled with oil. Start the engine and allow it to idle for a few minutes.

### ✳✳✳ CAUTION

**Do not run the engine above idle speed until it has built up oil pressure, as indicated when the oil light goes out.**

13. Shut off the engine and allow the oil to flow back to the crankcase for a minute, then recheck the oil level. Check around the filter and drain plug for any leaks, and correct as necessary.

When you have finished this job, you will notice that you now possess four or five quarts of dirty oil. The best thing to do is to pour it into plastic jugs, such as milk or old antifreeze containers. Then, locate a service station or automotive parts store where you can pour it into their used oil tank for recycling.

➡**Improperly disposing of used motor oil not only pollutes the environment, it violates Federal law. Dispose of waste oil properly.**

## Manual Transaxle

### FLUID RECOMMENDATIONS

The proper fluid for all manual transaxles is Mopar® type M.S. 9417 manual transaxle fluid. Do NOT use Hypoid gear lube, engine oil and/or automatic transmission fluid should, as this may cause damage. The manufacturer does not give an interval for manual transaxle fluid change, however the fluid should be drained and refilled if water contamination is suspected. If the oil is foamy or looks milky, it should be replaced.

### LEVEL CHECK

▶ **See Figure 141**

You should check the manual transaxle for leaks and proper fluid level each time the vehicle is raised. To check the oil level, perform the following:
1. Raise and safely support the vehicle. Make sure the vehicle is raised level and evenly for an accurate reading.

➡**The transaxle fill plug is accessible through the left fender well.**

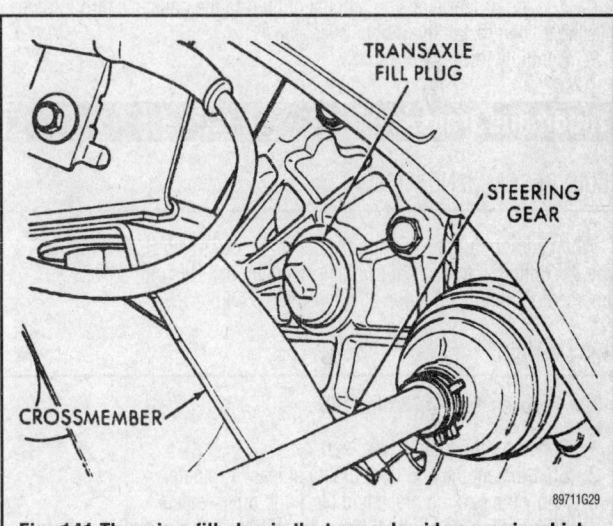

Fig. 141 There is a fill plug in the transaxle side cover in which you can check and add fluid

2. Remove the fill plug from the transaxle side cover. If the fluid level is within 3/16 in. (4mm) of the fill plug opening, the fluid level is fine.
3. If the fluid level is 3/16 in. (4mm) below the bottom of the fill plug opening or lower, you should add the proper type of fluid through the filler hole, until the proper level is reached.

### DRAIN & REFILL

▶ **See Figure 142**

1. Raise and safely support the vehicle in a level position.
2. Place a suitable drain pan under the transaxle drain plug.
3. Remove the rubber fill plug, located on the left side of the transaxle differential area.
4. Use a wrench to loosen the drain plug, then remove the drain plug from the transaxle and allow the fluid to drain completely into the pan.
5. After the fluid has drained completely, install the drain plug and tighten to 20 ft. lbs. (28 Nm).

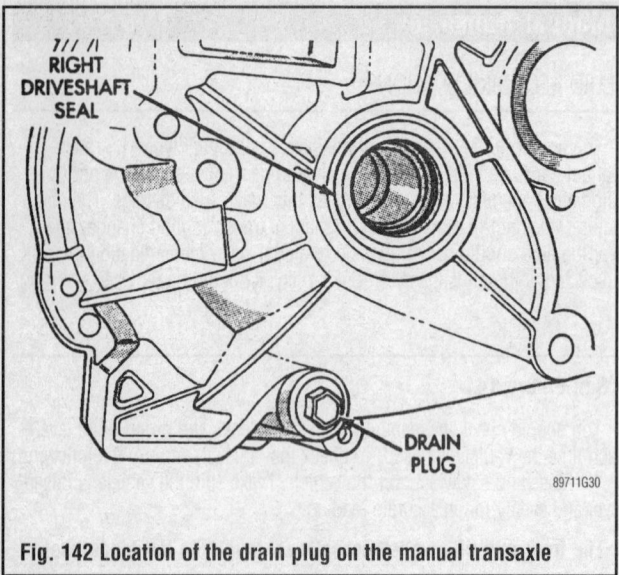

Fig. 142 Location of the drain plug on the manual transaxle

6. Add the proper type and amount of fluid to the transaxle through the filler hole, then install the rubber filler plug.

7. Carefully lower the vehicle.

## Automatic Transaxle

### FLUID RECOMMENDATIONS

When adding fluid or refilling the transaxle, use MOPAR® ATF Plus 3 type 7176 fluid. If this is not available, you can use Dexron II®(or its superceding fluid type) automatic transmission fluid.

### LEVEL CHECK

▶ **See Figures 143, 144 and 145**

1. Park the vehicle on a level surface.
2. Start the engine and let it run for at least 1 minute.
3. Apply the parking brake and block the drive wheels.
4. With the brakes applied, move the shift lever through all the gear ranges, ending in **P**.

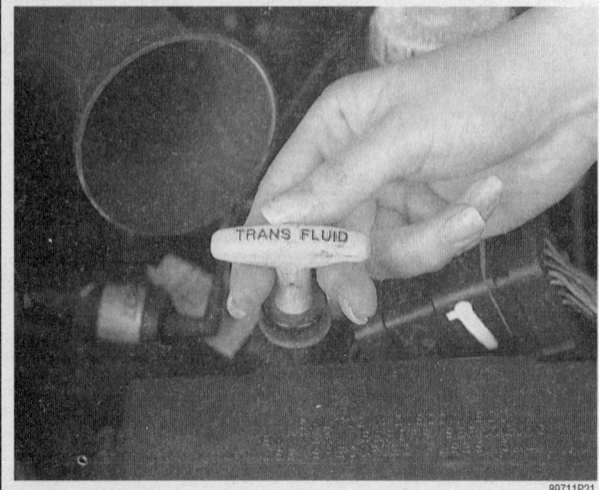

Fig. 143 Pull the dipstick out, wipe it clean then reinsert it fully until it is completely seated

Fig. 144 Depending upon engine temperature, the fluid level should either be between the WARM or HOT holes in the dipstick

Fig. 145 Use a long necked funnel when adding automatic transaxle fluid, to avoid making a mess

➡The fluid level must be checked with the engine running at slow idle, with the car level, and the fluid at least at room temperature. The correct fluid level cannot be read if you have just driven the car for a long time at high speed, city traffic in hot weather or if the car has been pulling a trailer. In these cases, wait at least 30 minutes for the fluid to cool down.

5. Remove the dipstick, then determine of the fluid is hot or warm. Hot fluid is about 180°F (82°C) that is the normal operating temperature after the vehicle has been driven al least 15 miles. The fluid is too hot to touch. Warm is when the fluid is about 85–125°F (29–52°C).

6. Wipe the dipstick clean, with a lint free rag, then reinsert it fully it is seated.

7. Remove the dipstick again and note the reading. If the fluid is hot, the reading should be within the cross hatched area marked "HOT" between the upper two holes in the dipstick. If the fluid level is warm, the fluid level should be within the lower two holes in the area marked "WARM".

8. If the fluid level is low, use a funnel to add the proper type and amount of transaxle fluid to bring to the correct level, through the dipstick tube. It generally takes less than a pint. DO NOT overfill the transaxle! If the fluid level is within specifications, simply push the dipstick back into the filler tube completely.

**⁂ WARNING**

To avoid getting any dirt or water in the transaxle, always make sure the dipstick is fully seated in the tube.

## DRAIN, REFILL & FILTER REPLACEMENT

▶ **See Figures 146 thru 156**

The car should be driven approximately 15 miles (24 km) to warm the transaxle fluid before the pan is removed.

➡**The fluid should be drained while the transaxle is warm.**

1. Raise and safely support the vehicle with jackstands.
2. Place a suitable drain pan under the transaxle fluid pan.
3. Loosen the automatic transaxle fluid pan bolts.

**⁂ WARNING**

Be careful not to damage the mating surfaces of the oil pan and case. Any damage could result in fluid leaks.

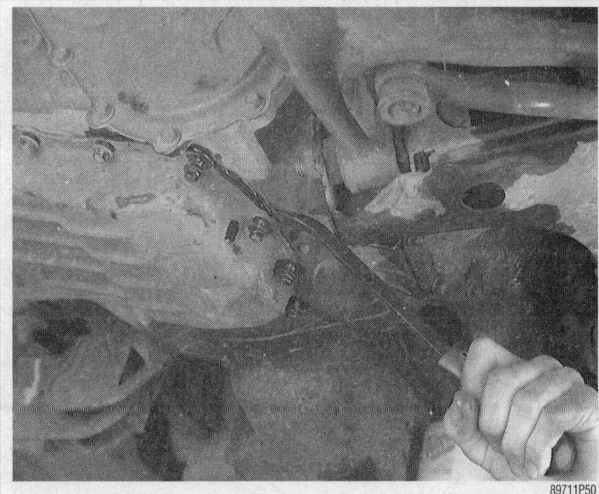

Fig. 148 Carefully pry the pan, being sure not to damage the mating surfaces . . .

Fig. 146 Loosen the transaxle oil pan mounting bolts

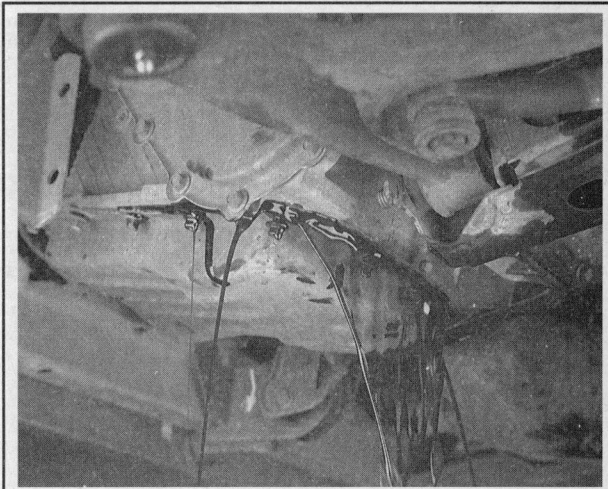

Fig. 149 . . . then allow the fluid to drain completely into a suitable container

Fig. 147 Your vehicle may have a plastic wiring harness nipple that must be removed from the pan

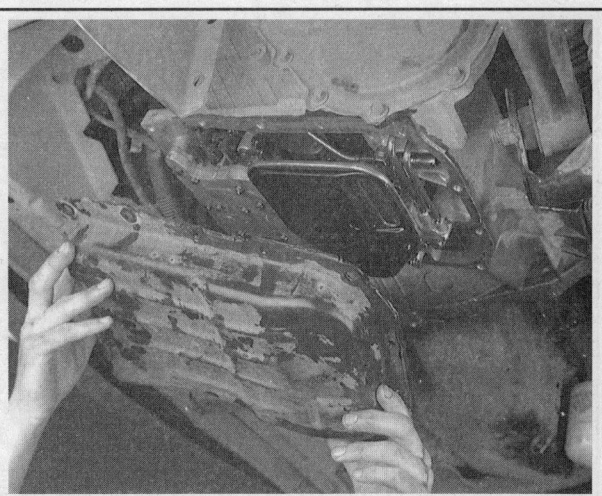

Fig. 150 Once the fluid has drained, remove the bolts and lower the pan

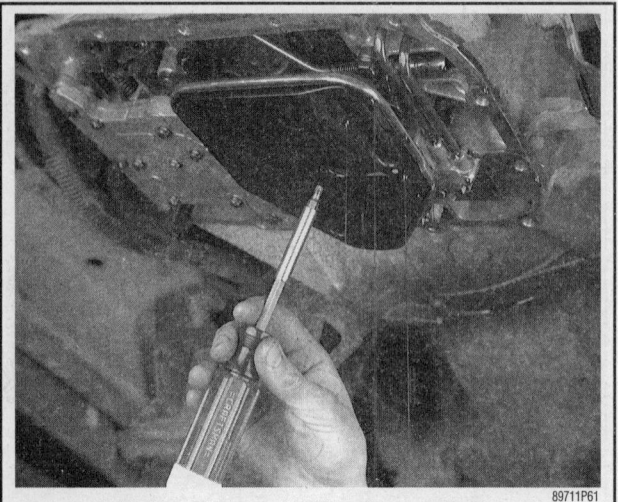

Fig. 151 Unfasten the filter-to-transaxle body screws . . .

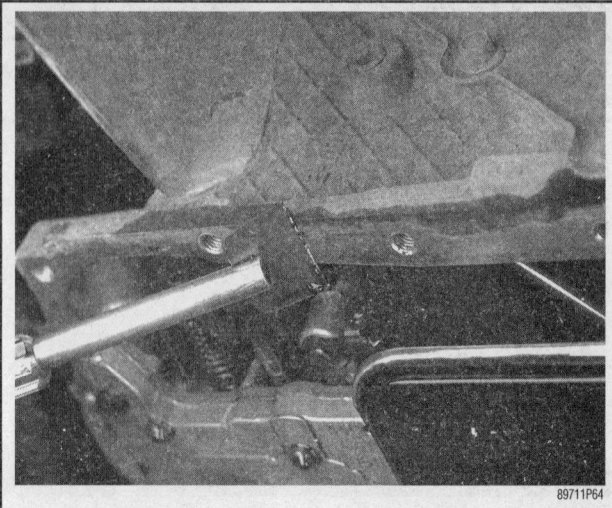

Fig. 154 . . . and the transaxle gasket surface

Fig. 152 . . . then remove the filter from the transaxle

Fig. 155 After cleaning the magnet, place it back into the pan in its original position

Fig. 153 Use a gasket scraper to clean the old sealant from the transaxle fluid pan . . .

Fig. 156 Run a THIN bead of sealant around the edge of the transaxle pan and bolt holes

4. Lightly tap the pan at one corner with a rubber mallet or carefully pry the fluid pan loose and allow the fluid to drain.

5. Remove the remaining bolts, then remove the pan. Thoroughly clean the gasket mating surfaces.

6. If necessary, unfasten the retaining screws, then remove the filter.

**To install:**

7. If removed, install a new filter and gasket on the throttle valve body. Tighten the retaining screws to 40 inch lbs. (5 Nm). Make the filter gasket is aligned properly before removal.

### ✳✳ WARNING

**Be careful not to use too much sealant when installing the fluid pan as this could flow over into the pan and mix with the fluid when the pan is tightened!**

8. Clean the oil pan and magnet. Use a thin bead of suitable adhesive sealant on the edge of the transaxle pan and around the bolt holes, then install the pan and secure with the retaining bolts. Tighten the bolts to 14 ft. lbs. (19 Nm).

9. Carefully lower the vehicle.

10. Pour 4 quarts of the proper automatic transaxle fluid through the dipstick tube. Make sure to use a funnel to avoid making a mess!

11. Start the engine and allow to idle for at least a minute. With the parking brake on and the brakes depressed, move the gear selector through each position, ending in the Park or Neutral position.

12. Check the fluid level and add just enough fluid to bring the level to ⅛ in. below the ADD mark.

13. Allow the engine to fully warm up to normal operating temperature, then check the fluid level. The fluid level should be in the HOT range. If not, add the proper amount of fluid to bring it up to that level. If the fluid level is within specifications, simply push the dipstick back into the filler tube completely.

### ✳✳ WARNING

**To avoid getting any dirt or water in the transaxle, always make sure the dipstick is fully seated in the tube.**

## Cooling System

### ✳✳ CAUTION

**Never remove the radiator cap under any conditions while the engine is hot! Failure to follow these instructions could result in damage to the cooling system, engine and/or personal injury. To avoid having scalding hot coolant or steam blow out of the radiator, use extreme care whenever you are removing the radiator cap. Wait until the engine has cooled, then wrap a thick cloth around radiator cap and turn it slowly to the first stop. Step back while the pressure is released from the cooling system. When you are sure the pressure has been released, press down on the radiator cap (still have the cloth in position), turn and remove the cap.**

### FLUID RECOMMENDATIONS

The cooling system should be inspected, flushed and refilled with fresh coolant at least every 30,000 miles (48,000 km) or 24 months. If the coolant is left in the system too long, it loses its ability to prevent rust and corrosion.

When the coolant is being replaced, use a good quality antifreeze that is safe to be used with aluminum cooling system components. The ratio of antifreeze to water should always be a 50/50 mixture. This ratio will ensure the proper balance of cooling ability, corrosion protection and antifreeze protection. At this ratio, the antifreeze protection should be good to −34°F (−37°C). If greater antifreeze protection is needed, the ratio should not exceed 70% antifreeze to 30% water.

### LEVEL CHECK

▶ **See Figures 157, 158 and 159**

➡ **When checking the coolant level, the radiator cap need not be removed. Simply check the coolant level in the recovery bottle or surge tank.**

Check the coolant level in the recovery tank, usually mounted near the firewall, to the right of the passenger side strut tower. The coolant recovery tank level should be between the ADD and FULL marks on the side of the recovery tank, when the engine is at normal operating temperature. Only add coolant to the recovery tank as necessary to bring the system up to a proper level.

### ✳✳ CAUTION

**Should it be necessary to remove the radiator cap, make sure the system has had time to cool, reducing the internal pressure.**

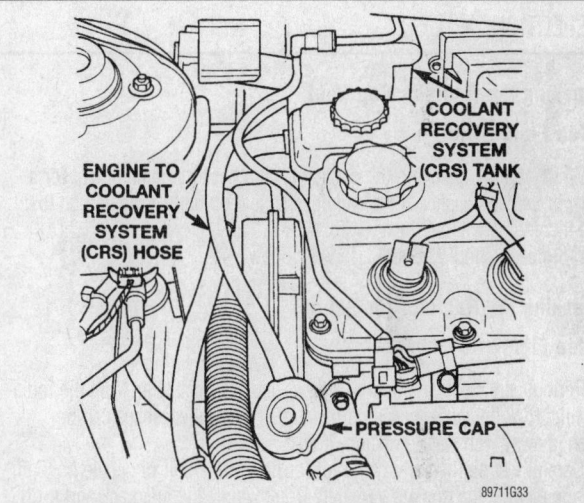

Fig. 157 The coolant recovery tank is located near the power steering fluid reservoir and the passenger side strut tower

Fig. 158 The coolant level should be between the ADD (1) and FULL (2) marks on the coolant recovery reservoir

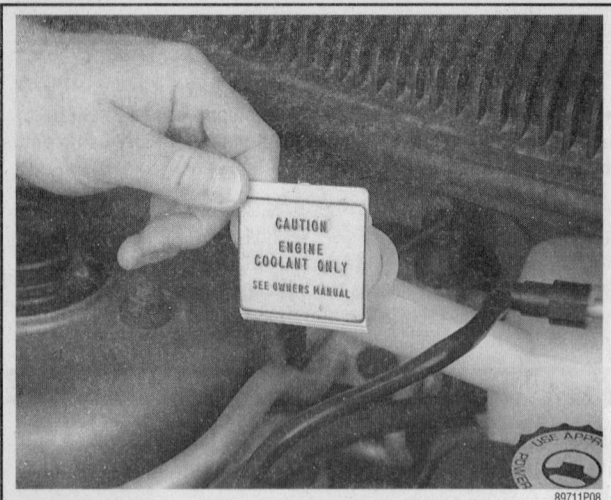

Fig. 159 If the level is low, add coolant through the recovery reservoir cap

## INSPECTION

### Checking the Radiator Cap Seal

▶ See Figure 160

While you are checking the coolant level, check the radiator cap for a worn or cracked gasket. If the cap doesn't seal properly, fluid will be lost and the engine will overheat.

Worn caps should be replaced with a new one.

### Checking the Radiator for Debris

▶ See Figure 161

Periodically clean any debris; leaves, paper, insects, etc. from the radiator fins. Pick the large pieces off by hand. The smaller pieces can be washed away with water pressure from a hose.

Carefully straighten any bent radiator fins with a pair of needle nose pliers. Be careful, the fins are very soft. Don't wiggle the fins back and forth too much. Straighten them once and try not move them again.

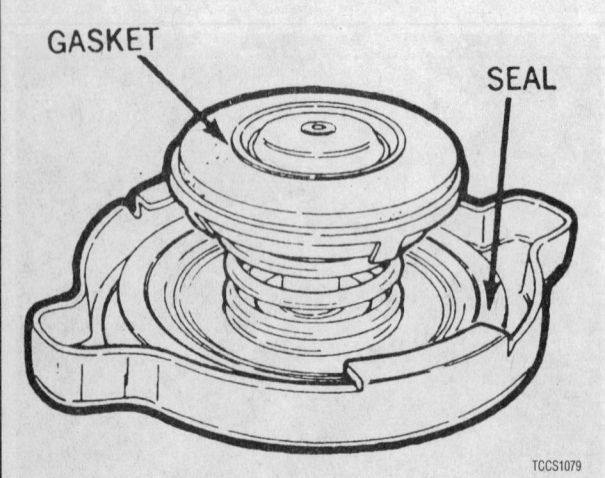

Fig. 160 Be sure the rubber gasket on the radiator cap has a tight seal

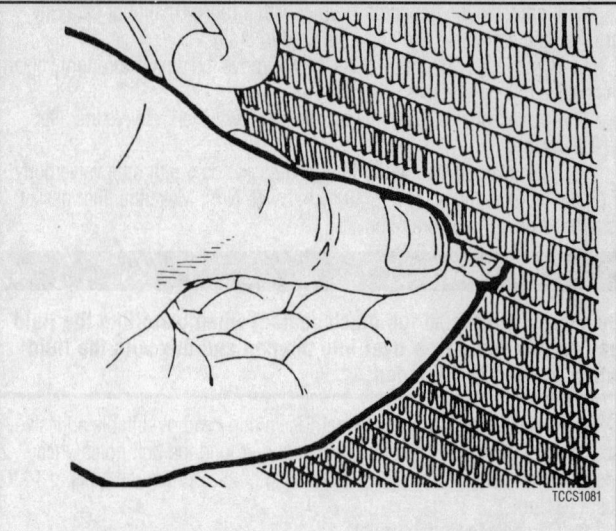

Fig. 161 Periodically removal all debris from the radiator fins

## DRAIN & REFILL

▶ See Figures 162 thru 167

### ✳✳ CAUTION

When draining the coolant, keep in mind that cats and dogs are attracted by ethylene glycol antifreeze and are quite likely to drink any that is left in an uncovered container or in puddles on the ground. This will prove fatal in sufficient quantity. Always drain the coolant into a sealable container. Coolant should be reused until it is contaminated or several years old. To avoid injuries from scalding fluid and steam, DO NOT remove the radiator cap while the engine and radiator are still hot.

1. Make sure the engine is cool and the vehicle is parked on a level surface.
2. Remove the recovery tank cap.
3. Place a fluid catch pan under the radiator. Turn the radiator drain-

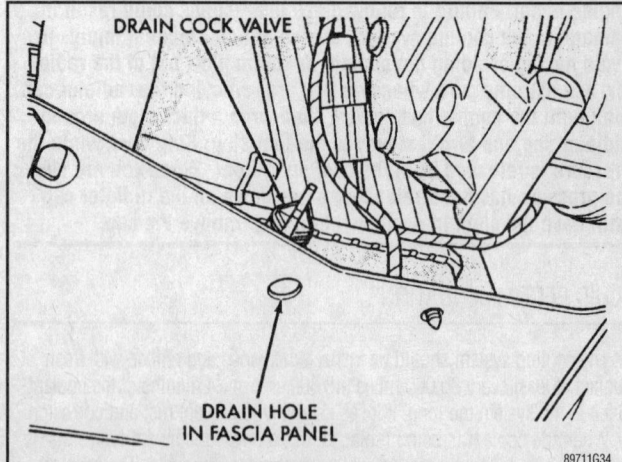

Fig. 162 The draincock valve is found at the bottom corner of the radiator. There is also a hole in the fasica panel which the coolant drains through

Fig. 163 The radiator draincock opens by turning it counterclockwise

Fig. 165 NEVER remove the radiator cap when the engine is hot!

Fig. 164 Attaching a piece of tubing to the valve helps prevent mess during coolant draining

Fig. 166 If the system was drained, fill the radiator to the bottom of the filler neck

cock counterclockwise to open, then allow the coolant to drain. The coolant should drain out of the recovery tank first.

### ✳ CAUTION

**Never open, service or drain the radiator or cooling system when hot; serious burns can occur from the steam and hot coolant. Also, when draining engine coolant, keep in mind that cats and dogs are attracted to ethylene glycol antifreeze and could drink any that is left in an uncovered container or in puddles on the ground. This will prove fatal in sufficient quantities. Always drain coolant into a sealable container. Coolant should be reused unless it is contaminated or is several years old.**

4. Remove the radiator cap by performing the following:
   a. Slowly rotate the cap counterclockwise to the detent.
   b. If any residual pressure is present, WAIT until the hissing stops.
   c. After the hissing noise has ceased, press down on the cap and continue rotating it counterclockwise to remove it.
5. If equipped, remove the engine block drain plug.

Fig. 167 Fill the coolant recovery reservoir up to the FULL mark

6. Allow the coolant to drain completely from the vehicle.

7. Close the radiator drain valve, then reinstall any block drains which were removed.

➡ **When filling the cooling system, be careful not to spill any coolant on the drive belts or alternator.**

8. Using a 50/50 mixture of antifreeze and clean water, fill the radiator to the bottom of the filler neck and the coolant tank to the FULL mark.

9. Install the radiator cap, then place the cap back on the recovery bottle or surge tank.

10. Start the engine. Select heat on the climate control panel and turn the temperature valve to full warm. Run the engine until it reaches normal operating temperature. Check to make sure there is hot air flowing from the floor ducts.

11. Check the fluid level in the recovery tank and add as necessary.

## FLUSHING & CLEANING

1. Refer to the drain and refill procedure in this section, then drain the cooling system.

2. Close the drain valve.

➡ **A flushing solution may be used. Ensure it is safe for use with aluminum cooling system components. Follow the directions on the container.**

3. If using a flushing solution, remove the thermostat. Reinstall the thermostat housing.

4. Add sufficient water to fill the system.

5. Start the engine and run for a few minutes. Drain the system.

6. If using a flushing solution, disconnect the heater hose that connects the cylinder head to the heater core (that end of the hose will clamp to a fitting on the firewall. Connect a water hose to the end of the heater hose that runs to the cylinder head and run water into the system until it begins to flow out of the top of the radiator.

7. Allow the water to flow out of the radiator until it is clear.

8. Reconnect the heater hose.

9. Drain the cooling system.

10. Reinstall the thermostat.

11. Empty the coolant reservoir or surge tank and flush it.

12. Fill the cooling system, using the correct ratio of antifreeze and water, to the bottom of the filler neck. Fill the reservoir or surge tank to the FULL mark.

13. Install the radiator cap, making sure that the arrows align with the overflow tube.

## Brake Master Cylinder

### FLUID RECOMMENDATIONS

Use only MOPAR®, or equivalent brake fluid meeting DOT 3 specifications from a clean, sealed container. Using any other type of fluid may result in severe brake system damage.

### ❈❈ WARNING

**Brake fluid damages paint. It also absorbs moisture from the air; never leave a container or the master cylinder uncovered longer than necessary. All parts in contact with the brake fluid (master cylinder, hoses, plunger assemblies and etc.) must be kept clean, since any contamination of the brake fluid will adversely affect braking performance.**

## LEVEL CHECK

▶ **See Figures 168, 169, 170 and 171**

It should be obvious how important the brake system is to safe operation of your vehicle. The brake fluid is key to the proper operation of your vehicle. Low levels of fluid indicate a need for service (there may be a leak in the system or the brake pads may just be worn and in need of replacement). In any case, the brake fluid level should be inspected at least during every oil change, but more often is desirable. Every time you open the hood is a good time to glance at the master cylinder reservoir.

To check the fluid level, look on the side of the reservoir to see how high the fluid level is against the markings on the side of the reservoir. The level should be at the full mark. If not, remove the reservoir cap, then add the proper amount of DOT-3 brake fluid to bring the level up to FULL.

When making additions of brake fluid, use only fresh, uncontaminated brake fluid which meets or exceeds DOT-3 standards. Be careful not to spill any brake fluid on painted surfaces, as it will quickly eat the paint. Do not

Fig. 168 Before removing the brake master cylinder reservoir cap, clean it off to avoid getting any dirt in the reservoir

Fig. 169 The brake fluid level should be between the MIN (1) and FULL (2) marks

Fig. 170 Remove the brake master cylinder reservoir lid . . .

Fig. 172 After wiping off the power steering cap/dipstick, remove it from the reservoir

Fig. 171 . . . then add fluid from a sealed container, until the level reaches the FULL mark

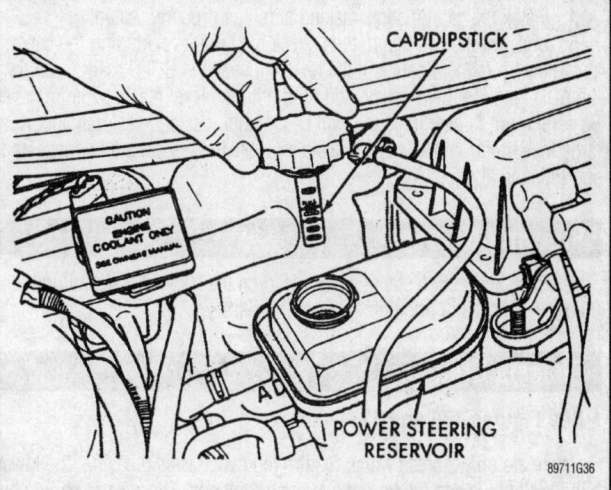

Fig. 173 When checking the power steering fluid level, hold the cap vertically with the tip of the dipstick pointing downward

allow the brake fluid container or the master cylinder to remain open any longer than necessary; brake fluid absorbs moisture from the air, reducing the fluid's effectiveness and causing corrosion in the lines.

## Power Steering Pump

### FLUID RECOMMENDATIONS

When adding fluid or making a complete fluid change, always use Mopar® Power Steering Fluid or equivalent. NEVER use automatic transmission fluid. Failure to use the proper fluid may cause hose and seal damage and fluid leaks.

### LEVEL CHECK

▶ See Figures 172, 173, 174 and 175

1. Park the vehicle on a level surface with the engine at normal operating temperatures, then turn the engine **OFF** and remove the ignition key.
2. Use a rag to clean all the dirt and oil residue from the power steering pump reservoir cap/dipstick.

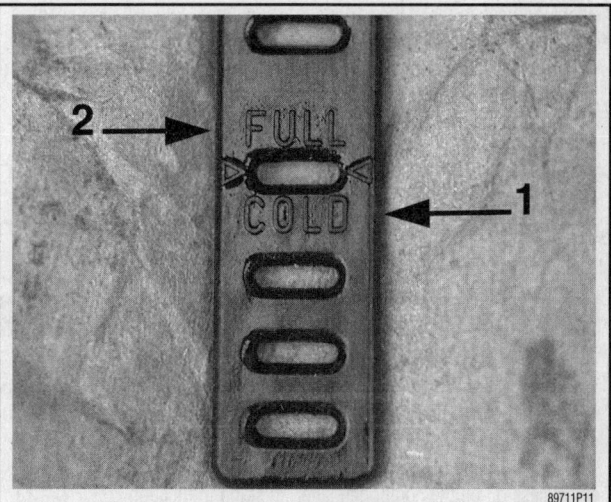

Fig. 174 If at room temperature and the level is below the COLD (1) mark, you must add fluid until it reaches the FULL (2) mark

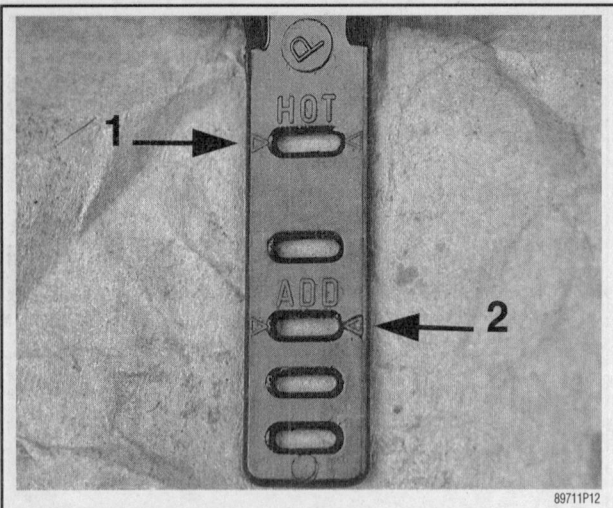

**Fig. 175 When the engine is at operating temperature, the level should be between the HOT (1) and ADD (2) marks**

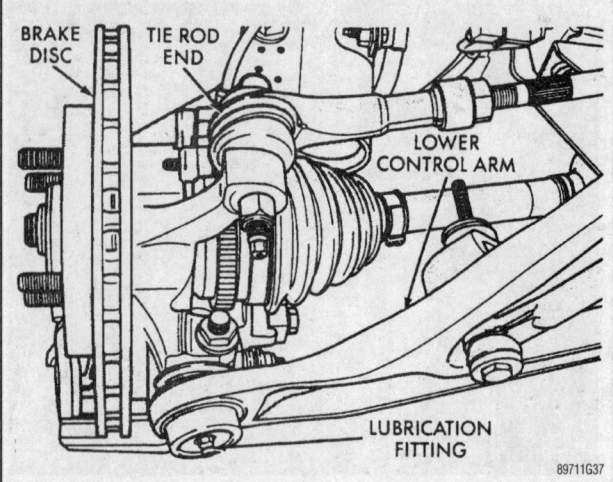

**Fig. 176 Location of the tie-rod end and ball joint grease fitting locations**

3. Remove the reservoir cap/dipstick and wipe off the fluid.
4. Install the cap/dipstick, making sure it is properly seated.
5. Unscrew the cap again, then check the fluid level holding the cap above the tip of the dipstick. If the level is below the COLD mark or below the ADD mark on the dipstick, add fluid until the level reaches the full level. Be careful not to overfill as this will cause fluid loss and seal damage. A large loss in the system may indicate a problem. This should be inspected and repaired at once.

## Steering Gear

The rack and pinion steering gear used on the Neon is a sealed unit; no fluid level checks or additions are ever necessary.

## Chassis Greasing

▶ See Figures 176 and 177

There are only 2 areas which require regular chassis greasing: the lower ball joint fittings and the tie rod end to strut fittings. These parts should be greased every 12 months or 7,500 miles (12,000km.) with Mopar, multi-mileage lube or equivalent.

If you choose to do this job yourself, you will need to purchase a hand operated grease gun, if you do not own one already, and a long flexible extension hose to reach the various grease fittings. You will also need a cartridge of the appropriate grease.

First, use a clean cloth to wipe the dirt from around the grease fitting and joint seal. Press the fitting on the grease gun hose onto the grease fitting on the suspension or steering linkage component. Pump a few shots of grease into the fitting, until the rubber boot on the joint begins to expand, indicating that the joint is full. Remove the gun from the fitting. Be careful not to overfill the joints, which will rupture the rubber boots, allowing the entry of dirt. You can keep the grease fittings clean by covering them with a small square of tin foil.

## Body Lubrication and Maintenance

The body mechanisms and linkages should be inspected, cleaned and lubricated as necessary to preserve correct operation and to avoid wear and corrosion. Before you lubricate a component, make sure to wipe any dirt or grease from the surface with a suitable rag. If necessary, you can also use a suitable cleaning solvent to clean the surface off. And don't forget to wipe any excess oil off the component after finishing lubrication.

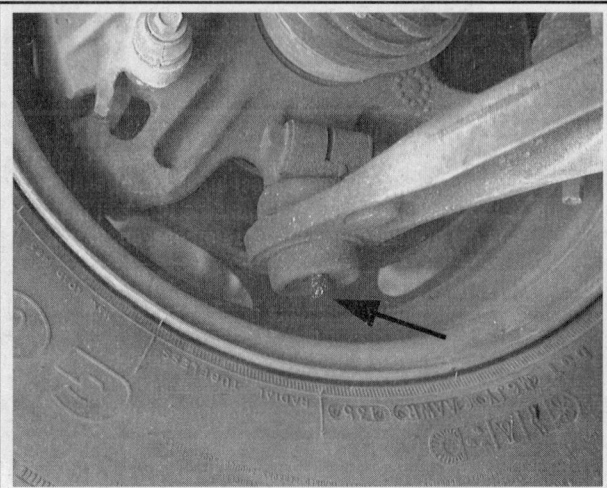

**Fig. 177 The ball joint grease fitting should be cleaned and filled with a grease gun**

To be sure the hood latch works properly, use engine oil to lubricate the latch, safety catch and hood hinges, as necessary. Apply Mopar®, or equivalent, multi-purpose grease, sparingly to all pivot and slide contact areas.
Use engine oil to lubricate the following components:
• Door hinges—hinge pin and pivot points
• Hood hinges—pivot points
Use Mopar® Lubriplate or equivalent on the following components:
• Door check straps
• Ash tray slides
• Fuel fill door latch mechanism
• Parking brake moving parts
• Front seat tracks

## Wheel Bearings

Neons are equipped with sealed hub and bearing assemblies. The hub and bearing assembly is non-serviceable. If the assembly is damaged, the complete unit must be replaced. Refer to Section 8 for the hub/bearing removal and installation procedure.

## TRAILER TOWING

### General Recommendations

Your vehicle was primarily designed to carry passengers and cargo. It is important to remember that towing a trailer will place additional loads on your vehicles engine, drivetrain, steering, braking and other systems. However, if you decide to tow a trailer, using the prior equipment is a must.

Local laws may require specific equipment such as trailer brakes or fender mounted mirrors. Check your local laws.

### Trailer Weight

The weight of the trailer is the most important factor. A good weight-to-horsepower ratio is about 35:1, 35 lbs. of Gross Combined Weight (GCW) for every horsepower your engine develops. Multiply the engine's rated horsepower by 35 and subtract the weight of the vehicle passengers and luggage. The number remaining is the approximate ideal maximum weight you should tow, although a numerically higher axle ratio can help compensate for heavier weight.

### Hitch (Tongue) Weight

**♦ See Figure 178**

Calculate the hitch weight in order to select a proper hitch. The weight of the hitch is usually 9-11% of the trailer gross weight and should be measured with the trailer loaded. Hitches fall into various categories: those that mount on the frame and rear bumper, the bolt-on type, or the weld-on distribution type used for larger trailers. Axle mounted or clamp-on bumper hitches should never be used.

Check the gross weight rating of your trailer. Tongue weight is usually figured as 10% of gross trailer weight. Therefore, a trailer with a maximum gross weight of 2000 lbs. will have a maximum tongue weight of 200 lbs. Class I trailers fall into this category. Class II trailers are those with a gross weight rating of 2000–3000 lbs., while Class III trailers fall into the 3500–6000 lbs. category. Class IV trailers are those over 6000 lbs. and are for use with fifth wheel trucks, only.

When you've determined the hitch that you'll need, follow the manufacturer's installation instructions, exactly, especially when it comes to fastener torques. The hitch will subjected to a lot of stress and good hitches come with hardened bolts. Never substitute an inferior bolt for a hardened bolt.

### Cooling

ENGINE
***

#### Oil Cooler

Aftermarket engine oil coolers are helpful for prolonging engine oil life and reducing overall engine temperatures. Both of these factors increase engine life. While not absolutely necessary in towing Class I and some Class II trailers, they are recommended for heavier Class II and all Class III towing. Engine oil cooler systems usually consist of an adapter, screwed on in place of the oil filter, a remote filter mounting and a multi-tube, finned heat exchanger, which is mounted in front of the radiator or air conditioning condenser.

## JUMP STARTING A DEAD BATTERY

**♦ See Figure 179**

Whenever a vehicle is jump started, precautions must be followed in order to prevent the possibility of personal injury. Remember that batteries contain a small amount of explosive hydrogen gas which is a by-product of battery charging. Sparks should always be avoided when working around batteries, especially when attaching jumper cables. To

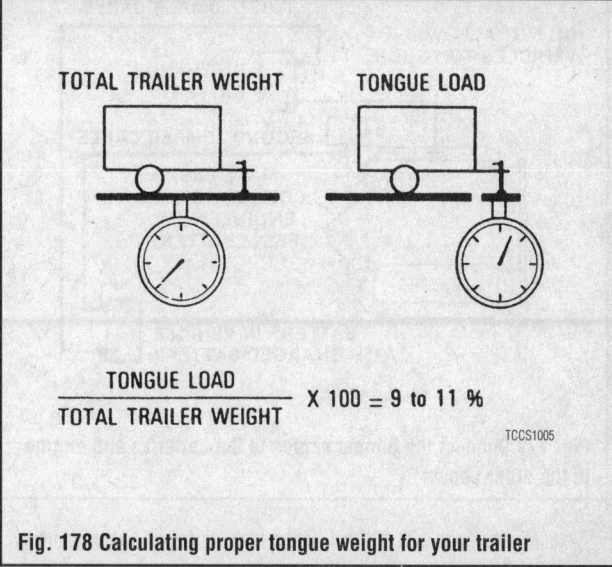

**Fig. 178 Calculating proper tongue weight for your trailer**

TRANSAXLE
***

An automatic transaxle is usually recommended for trailer towing. Modern automatics have proven reliable and, of course, easy to operate, in trailer towing. The increased load of a trailer, however, causes an increase in the temperature of the automatic transaxle fluid. Heat is the worst enemy of an automatic transaxle. As the temperature of the fluid increases, the life of the fluid decreases.

It is essential, therefore, that you install an automatic transaxle cooler. The cooler, which consists of a multi-tube, finned heat exchanger, is usually installed in front of the radiator or air conditioning compressor, and hooked in-line with the transaxle cooler tank inlet line. Follow the cooler manufacturer's installation instructions.

Select a cooler of at least adequate capacity, based upon the combined gross weights of the vehicle and trailer.

Cooler manufacturers recommend that you use an aftermarket cooler in addition to, and not instead of, the present cooling tank in your radiator. If you do want to use it in place of the radiator cooling tank, get a cooler at least two sizes larger than normally necessary.

**➡A transaxle cooler can, sometimes, cause slow or harsh shifting in the transaxle during cold weather, until the fluid has a chance to come up to normal operating temperature. Some coolers can be purchased with or retrofitted with a temperature bypass valve which will allow fluid flow through the cooler only when the fluid has reached above a certain operating temperature.**

### Handling A Trailer

Towing a trailer with ease and safety requires a certain amount of experience. It's a good idea to learn the feel of a trailer by practicing turning, stopping and backing in an open area such as an empty parking lot.

minimize the possibility of accidental sparks, follow the procedure carefully.

### ✳✳ CAUTION

**NEVER hook the batteries up in a series circuit or the entire electrical system will go up in smoke, including the starter!**

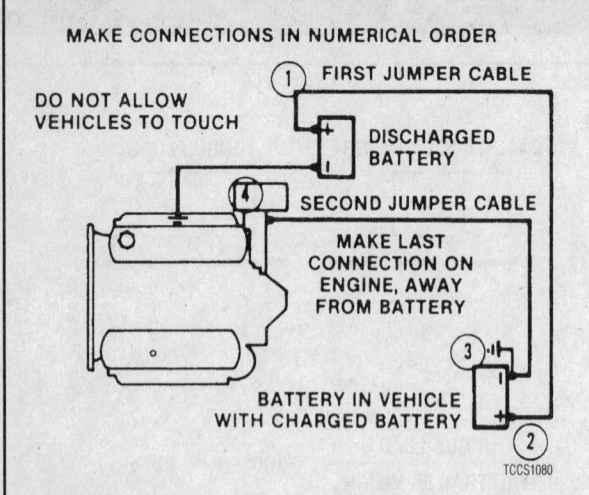

MAKE CONNECTIONS IN NUMERICAL ORDER

**Fig. 179 Connect the jumper cables to the batteries and engine in the order shown**

Vehicles equipped with a diesel engine may utilize two 12 volt batteries. If so, the batteries are connected in a parallel circuit (positive terminal to positive terminal, negative terminal to negative terminal). Hooking the batteries up in parallel circuit increases battery cranking power without increasing total battery voltage output. Output remains at 12 volts. On the other hand, hooking two 12 volt batteries up in a series circuit (positive terminal to negative terminal, positive terminal to negative terminal) increases total battery output to 24 volts (12 volts plus 12 volts).

## Jump Starting Precautions

• Be sure that both batteries are of the same voltage. Vehicles covered by this manual and most vehicles on the road today utilize a 12 volt charging system.
• Be sure that both batteries are of the same polarity (have the same terminal, in most cases NEGATIVE grounded).
• Be sure that the vehicles are not touching or a short could occur.
• On serviceable batteries, be sure the vent cap holes are not obstructed.
• Do not smoke or allow sparks anywhere near the batteries.
• In cold weather, make sure the battery electrolyte is not frozen. This can occur more readily in a battery that has been in a state of dis-charge.
• Do not allow electrolyte to contact your skin or clothing.

## Jump Starting Procedure

1. Make sure that the voltages of the 2 batteries are the same. Most batteries and charging systems are of the 12 volt variety.
2. Pull the jumping vehicle (with the good battery) into a position so the jumper cables can reach the dead battery and that vehicle's engine. Make sure that the vehicles do NOT touch.

3. Place the transmissions/transaxles of both vehicles in **Neutral** (MT) or **P** (AT), as applicable, then firmly set their parking brakes.

➡️**If necessary for safety reasons, the hazard lights on both vehicles may be operated throughout the entire procedure without significantly increasing the difficulty of jumping the dead battery.**

4. Turn all lights and accessories OFF on both vehicles. Make sure the ignition switches on both vehicles are turned to the **OFF** position.
5. Cover the battery cell caps with a rag, but do not cover the terminals.
6. Make sure the terminals on both batteries are clean and free of corrosion or proper electrical connection will be impeded. If necessary, clean the battery terminals before proceeding.
7. Identify the positive (+) and negative (&minus;) terminals on both batteries.
8. Connect the first jumper cable to the positive (+) terminal of the dead battery, then connect the other end of that cable to the positive (+) terminal of the booster (good) battery.
9. Connect one end of the other jumper cable to the negative (&minus;) terminal on the booster battery and the final cable clamp to an engine bolt head, alternator bracket or other solid, metallic point on the engine with the dead battery. Try to pick a ground on the engine that is positioned away from the battery in order to minimize the possibility of the 2 clamps touching should one loosen during the procedure. DO NOT connect this clamp to the negative (–) terminal of the bad battery.

### ✳✳ CAUTION

**Be very careful to keep the jumper cables away from moving parts (cooling fan, belts, etc.) on both engines.**

10. Check to make sure that the cables are routed away from any moving parts, then start the donor vehicle's engine. Run the engine at moderate speed for several minutes to allow the dead battery a chance to receive some initial charge.
11. With the donor vehicle's engine still running slightly above idle, try to start the vehicle with the dead battery. Crank the engine for no more than 10 seconds at a time and let the starter cool for at least 20 seconds between tries. If the vehicle does not start in 3 tries, it is likely that something else is also wrong or that the battery needs additional time to charge.
12. Once the vehicle is started, allow it to run at idle for a few seconds to make sure that it is operating properly.
13. Turn ON the headlights, heater blower and, if equipped, the rear defroster of both vehicles in order to reduce the severity of voltage spikes and subsequent risk of damage to the vehicles' electrical systems when the cables are disconnected. This step is especially important to any vehicle equipped with computer control modules.
14. Carefully disconnect the cables in the reverse order of connection. Start with the negative cable that is attached to the engine ground, then the negative cable on the donor battery. Disconnect the positive cable from the donor battery and finally, disconnect the positive cable from the formerly dead battery. Be careful when disconnecting the cables from the positive terminals not to allow the alligator clips to touch any metal on either vehicle or a short and sparks will occur.

## JACKING

♦ **See Figures 180, 181, 182, 183 and 184**

Your vehicle was supplied with a jack for emergency road repairs. This jack is fine for changing a flat tire or other short term procedures not requiring you to go beneath the vehicle. If it is used in an emergency situation, carefully follow the instructions provided either with the jack or in your owner's manual. Do not attempt to use the jack on any portions of the vehicle other than specified by the vehicle manufacturer. Always block the diagonally opposite wheel when using a jack.

A more convenient way of jacking is the use of a garage or floor jack. You may use the floor jack to raise the front of the vehicle by placing the jack under the jacking pad located in the front of the vehicle, then placing

jackstands under the frame rails to safely support the vehicle. To raise the rear of the vehicle, place the floor jack under the center of the rear crossmember, then place jackstands under the frame rails.

Never place the jack under the radiator, engine or transmission components. Severe and expensive damage will result when the jack is raised. Additionally, never jack under the floorpan or bodywork; the metal will deform.

Whenever you plan to work under the vehicle, you must support it on jackstands or ramps. Never use cinder blocks or stacks of wood to support the vehicle, even if you're only going to be under it for a few minutes. Never crawl under the vehicle when it is supported only by the tire-changing jack or other floor jack.

➡Always position a block of wood or small rubber pad on top of the jack or jackstand to protect the lifting point's finish when lifting or supporting the vehicle.

Small hydraulic, screw, or scissors jacks are satisfactory for raising the vehicle. Drive-on trestles or ramps are also a handy and safe way to both raise and support the vehicle. Be careful though, some ramps may be too steep to drive your vehicle onto without scraping the front bottom panels. Never support the vehicle on any suspension member (unless specifically instructed to do so by a repair manual) or by an underbody panel.

## Jacking Precautions

The following safety points cannot be overemphasized:
- Always block the opposite wheel or wheels to keep the vehicle from rolling off the jack.
- When raising the front of the vehicle, firmly apply the parking brake.
- When the drive wheels are to remain on the ground, leave the vehicle in gear to help prevent it from rolling.
- Always use jackstands to support the vehicle when you are working underneath. Place the stands beneath the vehicle's jacking brackets. Before climbing underneath, rock the vehicle a bit to make sure it is firmly supported.

Fig. 182 Place the jack under the center of the rear crossmember to raise the vehicle

Fig. 180 To raise the front of the vehicle, place a suitable floor jack squarely under the jacking pad

Fig. 183 Once the vehicle is raised to the proper height, place jackstands to properly support the vehicle

Fig. 181 Front jackstand placement points

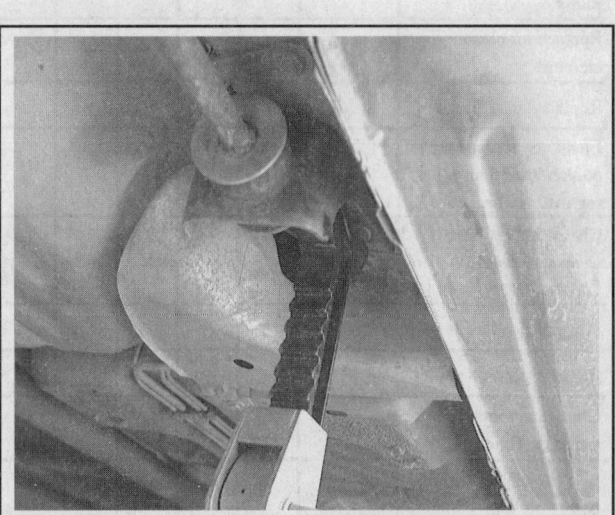
Fig. 184 The jackstands supporting the rear of the vehicle should be placed in the niche in the frame as shown

## CAPACITIES

| Year | Model | Engine ID/VIN | Engine Displacement Liters (cc) | Engine Oil with Filter | Transmission (pts.) | | Transfer Case (pts.) | Drive Axle | | Fuel Tank (gal.) | Cooling System (qts.) |
|------|-------|---------------|----------------------------------|------------------------|-------|------|----------------------|-------------------|----------------|------------------|------------------------|
| | | | | | 5-Spd | Auto. | | Front (pts.) | Rear (pts.) | | |
| 1995 | Neon | C | 2.0 (1996) | 4.5 | ① | ② | — | — | — | 11 | 7.4 |
| | Neon | Y | 2.0 (1996) | 4.5 | ① | ② | — | — | — | 11 | 7.4 |
| 1996 | Neon | C | 2.0 (1996) | 4.5 | 4.0-4.6 | ③ | — | — | — | 12.5 | 6.5 |
| | Neon | Y | 2.0 (1996) | 4.5 | 4.0-4.6 | ③ | — | — | — | 12.5 | 6.5 |
| 1997 | Neon | C | 2.0 (1996) | 4.5 | 4.0-4.6 | ③ | — | — | — | 12.5 | 6.5 |
| | Neon | Y | 2.0 (1996) | 4.5 | 4.0-4.6 | ③ | — | — | — | 12.5 | 6.5 |
| 1998 | Neon | C | 2.0 (1996) | 4.5 | 4.0-4.6 | ③ | — | — | — | 12.5 | 6.5 |
| | Neon | Y | 2.0 (1996) | 4.5 | 4.0-4.6 | ③ | — | — | — | 12.5 | 6.5 |
| 1999 | Neon | C | 2.0 (1996) | 4.5 | 4.0-4.6 | ③ | — | — | — | 12.5 | 6.5 |
| | Neon | Y | 2.0 (1996) | 4.5 | 4.0-4.6 | ③ | — | — | — | 12.5 | 6.5 |

**NOTE:** All capacities are approximate. Add fluid gradually and check to be sure a proper fluid level is obtained

① Fill to bottom of fill hole

② Pan removal: 8.0 pts.
Overhaul (with torque converter): 17.6 pts.

③ Overhaul fill capacity with torque converter empty
31TH: 17.8 pts
31TH (fleet vehicles): 19.4 pts.

89711C04

## NORMAL MAINTENANCE INTERVALS

| TO BE SERVICED | TYPE OF SERVICE | VEHICLE MILEAGE INTERVAL (x1000) | | | | | | | | | | | | | | | |
|----------------|-----------------|------|----|------|----|------|----|------|----|------|----|------|----|------|-----|-------|-----|
| | | 7.5 | 15 | 22.5 | 30 | 37.5 | 45 | 52.5 | 60 | 67.5 | 75 | 82.5 | 90 | 97.5 | 105 | 112.5 | 120 |
| Change engine oil | R | ✔ | ✔ | ✔ | ✔ | ✔ | ✔ | ✔ | ✔ | ✔ | ✔ | ✔ | ✔ | ✔ | ✔ | ✔ | ✔ |
| Replace engine oil filter | R | | ✔ | | ✔ | | ✔ | | ✔ | | ✔ | | ✔ | | ✔ | | ✔ |
| Adjust drive belt tension | A | | ✔ | | ✔ | | ✔ | | ✔ | | ✔ | | ✔ | | ✔ | | ✔ |
| Inspect the front brake pads and rear brake pads/linings | S/I | | | ✔ | | | ✔ | | | ✔ | | | ✔ | | | ✔ | |
| Lubricate front ball joints | L | | | | ✔ | | | | ✔ | | | | ✔ | | | | ✔ |
| Replace air cleaner element | R | | | | ✔ | | | | ✔ | | | | ✔ | | | | ✔ |
| Replace spark plugs | R | | | | ✔ | | | | ✔ | | | | ✔ | | | | ✔ |
| Flush and replace the coolant (at 36 mos. regardless of mileage) | R | | | | | | ✔ | | | | | | ✔ | | | | |
| Check and replace, if necessary, the PCV valve | S/I | | | | | | | | ✔ | | | | | | | | ✔ |
| Replace drive belts | R | | | | | | | | ✔ | | | | | | | | ✔ |
| Replace ignition cables | R | | | | | | | | ✔ | | | | | | | | ✔ |
| Change automatic transaxle fluid | R | | | | | | | | | | | | | ✔ | | | |
| Replace engine timing belt | R | | | | | | | | | | | | | | ✔ | | |

R - Replace     S/I - Inspect and service, if needed     L - Lubricate     A - Adjust     C - Clean

89711C05

## SEVERE MAINTENANCE INTERVALS

| TO BE SERVICED | TYPE OF SERVICE | VEHICLE MILEAGE INTERVAL (x1000) | | | | | | | | | | | | | | | | | | | |
|---|---|---|---|---|---|---|---|---|---|---|---|---|---|---|---|---|---|---|---|---|---|
| | | 3 | 6 | 9 | 12 | 15 | 18 | 21 | 24 | 27 | 30 | 33 | 36 | 39 | 42 | 45 | 48 | 51 | 54 | 57 | 60 |
| Change engine oil | R | ✓ | ✓ | ✓ | ✓ | ✓ | ✓ | ✓ | ✓ | ✓ | ✓ | ✓ | ✓ | ✓ | ✓ | ✓ | ✓ | ✓ | ✓ | ✓ | ✓ |
| Replace engine oil filter | R | | ✓ | | ✓ | | ✓ | | ✓ | | ✓ | | ✓ | | ✓ | | ✓ | | ✓ | | ✓ |
| Inspect the front brake pads and rear brake pads/linings | S/I | | | ✓ | | | ✓ | | | ✓ | | | ✓ | | | ✓ | | | ✓ | | |
| Adjust drive belt tension | A | | | | | ✓ | | | | | ✓ | | | | | ✓ | | | | | ✓ |
| Inspect the air cleaner element and replace if necessary | R | | | | | ✓ | | | | | ✓ | | | | | ✓ | | | | | ✓ |
| Change the automatic transaxle fluid and filter | R | | | | | ✓ | | | | | ✓ | | | | | ✓ | | | | | ✓ |
| Check and replace, if necessary, the PCV valve | S/I | | | | | | | | | | ✓ | | | | | | | | | | ✓ |
| Lubricate front ball joints | L | | | | | | | | | | ✓ | | | | | | | | | | ✓ |
| Replace the air cleaner element | R | | | | | | | | | | ✓ | | | | | | | | | | ✓ |
| Replace spark plugs | R | | | | | | | | | | ✓ | | | | | | | | | | ✓ |
| Flush and replace the coolant | R | | | | | | | | | | | | ✓ | | | | | | | | |
| Replace drive belts | R | | | | | | | | | | | | | | | | | | | | ✓ |
| Replace ignition cables | R | | | | | | | | | | | | | | | | | | | | ✓ |
| Change automatic transaxle fluid | R | | | | | | | | | | | | | | | | | | | | ✓ |
| Replace engine timing belt ① | R | | | | | | | | | | | | | | | | | | | | |

① Replace the engine timing belt at 105,000 miles (168,000km)

R - Replace    S/I - Inspect and service, if needed    L - Lubricate    A - Adjust    C - Clean

## FREQUENT OPERATION MAINTENANCE (SEVERE SERVICE)

If a vehicle is operated under any of the following conditions it is considered severe service, and you should use this chart:
- Towing a trailer or using a camper or car-top carrier.
- Repeated short trips of less than 5 miles in temperatures below freezing, or trips of less than 10 miles in any temperature.
- Extensive idling or low-speed driving for long distances as in heavy commercial use, such as delivery, taxi or police cars.
- Operating on rough, muddy or salt-covered roads.
- Operating on unpaved or dusty roads.
- Driving in extremely hot (over 90°) conditions.

89711C06

## ENGLISH TO METRIC CONVERSION: MASS (WEIGHT)

Current **mass** measurement is expressed in pounds and ounces (lbs. & ozs.). The metric unit of mass (or weight) is the kilogram (kg). Even although this table does not show conversion of masses (weights) larger than 15 lbs, it is easy to calculate larger units by following the data immediately below.

To convert ounces (oz.) to grams (g): multiply th number of ozs. by 28
To convert grams (g) to ounces (oz.): multiply the number of grams by .035

To convert pounds (lbs.) to kilograms (kg): multiply the number of lbs. by .45
To convert kilograms (kg) to pounds (lbs.): multiply the number of kilograms by 2.2

| lbs | kg | lbs | kg | oz | kg | oz | kg |
|------|------|-----|-----|-----|-------|-----|-------|
| 0.1 | 0.04 | 0.9 | 0.41 | 0.1 | 0.003 | 0.9 | 0.024 |
| 0.2 | 0.09 | 1 | 0.4 | 0.2 | 0.005 | 1 | 0.03 |
| 0.3 | 0.14 | 2 | 0.9 | 0.3 | 0.008 | 2 | 0.06 |
| 0.4 | 0.18 | 3 | 1.4 | 0.4 | 0.011 | 3 | 0.08 |
| 0.5 | 0.23 | 4 | 1.8 | 0.5 | 0.014 | 4 | 0.11 |
| 0.6 | 0.27 | 5 | 2.3 | 0.6 | 0.017 | 5 | 0.14 |
| 0.7 | 0.32 | 10 | 4.5 | 0.7 | 0.020 | 10 | 0.28 |
| 0.8 | 0.36 | 15 | 6.8 | 0.8 | 0.023 | 15 | 0.42 |

## ENGLISH TO METRIC CONVERSION: TEMPERATURE

To convert Fahrenheit (°F) to Celsius (°C): take number of °F and subtract 32; multiply result by 5; divide result by 9

To convert Celsius (°C) to Fahrenheit (°F): take number of °C and multiply by 9; divide result by 5; add 32 to total

| Fahrenheit (F) | Celsius (C) | Celsius (C) | Fahrenheit (F) | Fahrenheit (F) | Celsius (C) | Celsius (C) | Fahrenheit (F) | Fahrenheit (F) | Celsius (C) | Celsius (C) | Fahrenheit (F) |
|------|------|------|------|------|------|------|------|------|------|------|------|
| °F | °C | °C | °F | °F | °C | °C | °F | °F | °C | °C | °F |
| −40 | −40 | −38 | −36.4 | 80 | 26.7 | 18 | 64.4 | 215 | 101.7 | 80 | 176 |
| −35 | −37.2 | −36 | −32.8 | 85 | 29.4 | 20 | 68 | 220 | 104.4 | 85 | 185 |
| −30 | −34.4 | −34 | −29.2 | 90 | 32.2 | 22 | 71.6 | 225 | 107.2 | 90 | 194 |
| −25 | −31.7 | −32 | −25.6 | 95 | 35.0 | 24 | 75.2 | 230 | 110.0 | 95 | 202 |
| −20 | −28.9 | −30 | −22 | 100 | 37.8 | 26 | 78.8 | 235 | 112.8 | 100 | 212 |
| −15 | −26.1 | −28 | −18.4 | 105 | 40.6 | 28 | 82.4 | 240 | 115.6 | 105 | 221 |
| −10 | −23.3 | −26 | −14.8 | 110 | 43.3 | 30 | 86 | 245 | 118.3 | 110 | 230 |
| −5 | −20.6 | −24 | −11.2 | 115 | 46.1 | 32 | 89.6 | 250 | 121.1 | 115 | 239 |
| 0 | −17.8 | −22 | −7.6 | 120 | 48.9 | 34 | 93.2 | 255 | 123.9 | 120 | 248 |
| 1 | −17.2 | −20 | −4 | 125 | 51.7 | 36 | 96.8 | 260 | 126.6 | 125 | 257 |
| 2 | −16.7 | −18 | −0.4 | 130 | 54.4 | 38 | 100.4 | 265 | 129.4 | 130 | 266 |
| 3 | −16.1 | −16 | 3.2 | 135 | 57.2 | 40 | 104 | 270 | 132.2 | 135 | 275 |
| 4 | −15.6 | −14 | 6.8 | 140 | 60.0 | 42 | 107.6 | 275 | 135.0 | 140 | 284 |
| 5 | −15.0 | −12 | 10.4 | 145 | 62.8 | 44 | 112.2 | 280 | 137.8 | 145 | 293 |
| 10 | −12.2 | −10 | 14 | 150 | 65.6 | 46 | 114.8 | 285 | 140.6 | 150 | 302 |
| 15 | −9.4 | −8 | 17.6 | 155 | 68.3 | 48 | 118.4 | 290 | 143.3 | 155 | 311 |
| 20 | −6.7 | −6 | 21.2 | 160 | 71.1 | 50 | 122 | 295 | 146.1 | 160 | 320 |
| 25 | −3.9 | −4 | 24.8 | 165 | 73.9 | 52 | 125.6 | 300 | 148.9 | 165 | 329 |
| 30 | −1.1 | −2 | 28.4 | 170 | 76.7 | 54 | 129.2 | 305 | 151.7 | 170 | 338 |
| 35 | 1.7 | 0 | 32 | 175 | 79.4 | 56 | 132.8 | 310 | 154.4 | 175 | 347 |
| 40 | 4.4 | 2 | 35.6 | 180 | 82.2 | 58 | 136.4 | 315 | 157.2 | 180 | 356 |
| 45 | 7.2 | 4 | 39.2 | 185 | 85.0 | 60 | 140 | 320 | 160.0 | 185 | 365 |
| 50 | 10.0 | 6 | 42.8 | 190 | 87.8 | 62 | 143.6 | 325 | 162.8 | 190 | 374 |
| 55 | 12.8 | 8 | 46.4 | 195 | 90.6 | 64 | 147.2 | 330 | 165.6 | 195 | 383 |
| 60 | 15.6 | 10 | 50 | 200 | 93.3 | 66 | 150.8 | 335 | 168.3 | 200 | 392 |
| 65 | 18.3 | 12 | 53.6 | 205 | 96.1 | 68 | 154.4 | 340 | 171.1 | 205 | 401 |
| 70 | 21.1 | 14 | 57.2 | 210 | 98.9 | 70 | 158 | 345 | 173.9 | 210 | 410 |
| 75 | 23.9 | 16 | 60.8 | 212 | 100.0 | 75 | 167 | 350 | 176.7 | 215 | 414 |

TCCS1C01

## ENGLISH TO METRIC CONVERSION: LENGTH

To convert inches (ins.) to millimeters (mm): multiply number of inches by 25.4

To convert millimeters (mm) to inches (ins.): multiply number of millimeters by .04

| Inches | | Decimals | Milli-meters | Inches to millimeters inches | mm | Inches | | Decimals | Milli-meters | Inches to millimeters inches | mm |
|---|---|---|---|---|---|---|---|---|---|---|---|
| | 1/64 | 0.051625 | 0.3969 | 0.0001 | 0.00254 | | 33/64 | 0.515625 | 13.0969 | 0.6 | 15.24 |
| 1/32 | | 0.03125 | 0.7937 | 0.0002 | 0.00508 | 17/32 | | 0.53125 | 13.4937 | 0.7 | 17.78 |
| | 3/64 | 0.046875 | 1.1906 | 0.0003 | 0.00762 | | 35/64 | 0.546875 | 13.8906 | 0.8 | 20.32 |
| 1/16 | | 0.0625 | 1.5875 | 0.0004 | 0.01016 | 9/16 | | 0.5625 | 14.2875 | 0.9 | 22.86 |
| | 5/64 | 0.078125 | 1.9844 | 0.0005 | 0.01270 | | 37/64 | 0.578125 | 14.6844 | 1 | 25.4 |
| 3/32 | | 0.09375 | 2.3812 | 0.0006 | 0.01524 | 19/32 | | 0.59375 | 15.0812 | 2 | 50.8 |
| | 7/64 | 0.109375 | 2.//81 | 0.0007 | 0.01778 | | 39/64 | 0.609375 | 15.4781 | 3 | 76.2 |
| 1/8 | | 0.125 | 3.1750 | 0.0008 | 0.02032 | 5/8 | | 0.625 | 15.8750 | 4 | 101.6 |
| | 9/64 | 0.140625 | 3.5719 | 0.0009 | 0.02286 | | 41/64 | 0.640625 | 16.2719 | 5 | 127.0 |
| 5/32 | | 0.15625 | 3.9687 | 0.001 | 0.0254 | 21/32 | | 0.65625 | 16.6687 | 6 | 152.4 |
| | 11/64 | 0.171875 | 4.3656 | 0.002 | 0.0508 | | 43/64 | 0.671875 | 17.0656 | 7 | 177.8 |
| 3/16 | | 0.1875 | 4.7625 | 0.003 | 0.0762 | 11/16 | | 0.6875 | 17.4625 | 8 | 203.2 |
| | 13/64 | 0.203125 | 5.1594 | 0.004 | 0.1016 | | 45/64 | 0.703125 | 17.8594 | 9 | 228.6 |
| 7/32 | | 0.21875 | 5.5562 | 0.005 | 0.1270 | 23/32 | | 0.71875 | 18.2562 | 10 | 254.0 |
| | 15/64 | 0.234375 | 5.9531 | 0.006 | 0.1524 | | 47/64 | 0.734375 | 18.6531 | 11 | 279.4 |
| 1/4 | | 0.25 | 6.3500 | 0.007 | 0.1778 | 3/4 | | 0.75 | 19.0500 | 12 | 304.8 |
| | 17/64 | 0.265625 | 6.7469 | 0.008 | 0.2032 | | 49/64 | 0.765625 | 19.4469 | 13 | 330.2 |
| 9/32 | | 0.28125 | 7.1437 | 0.009 | 0.2286 | 25/32 | | 0.78125 | 19.8437 | 14 | 355.6 |
| | 19/64 | 0.296875 | 7.5406 | 0.01 | 0.254 | | 51/64 | 0.796875 | 20.2406 | 15 | 381.0 |
| 5/16 | | 0.3125 | 7.9375 | 0.02 | 0.508 | 13/16 | | 0.8125 | 20.6375 | 16 | 406.4 |
| | 21/64 | 0.328125 | 8.3344 | 0.03 | 0.762 | | 53/64 | 0.828125 | 21.0344 | 17 | 431.8 |
| 11/32 | | 0.34375 | 8.7312 | 0.04 | 1.016 | 27/32 | | 0.84375 | 21.4312 | 18 | 457.2 |
| | 23/64 | 0.359375 | 9.1281 | 0.05 | 1.270 | | 55/64 | 0.859375 | 21.8281 | 19 | 482.6 |
| 3/8 | | 0.375 | 9.5250 | 0.06 | 1.524 | 7/8 | | 0.875 | 22.2250 | 20 | 508.0 |
| | 25/64 | 0.390625 | 9.9219 | 0.07 | 1.778 | | 57/64 | 0.890625 | 22.6219 | 21 | 533.4 |
| 13/32 | | 0.40625 | 10.3187 | 0.08 | 2.032 | 29/32 | | 0.90625 | 23.0187 | 22 | 558.8 |
| | 27/64 | 0.421875 | 10.7156 | 0.09 | 2.286 | | 59/64 | 0.921875 | 23.4156 | 23 | 584.2 |
| 7/16 | | 0.4375 | 11.1125 | 0.1 | 2.54 | 15/16 | | 0.9375 | 23.8125 | 24 | 609.6 |
| | 29/64 | 0.453125 | 11.5094 | 0.2 | 5.08 | | 61/64 | 0.953125 | 24.2094 | 25 | 635.0 |
| 15/32 | | 0.46875 | 11.9062 | 0.3 | 7.62 | 31/32 | | 0.96875 | 24.6062 | 26 | 660.4 |
| | 31/64 | 0.484375 | 12.3031 | 0.4 | 10.16 | | 63/64 | 0.984375 | 25.0031 | 27 | 690.6 |
| 1/2 | | 0.5 | 12.7000 | 0.5 | 12.70 | | | | | | |

## ENGLISH TO METRIC CONVERSION: TORQUE

To convert foot-pounds (ft. lbs.) to Newton-meters: multiply the number of ft. lbs. by 1.3

To convert inch-pounds (in. lbs.) to Newton-meters: multiply the number of in. lbs. by .11

| in lbs | N-m | in lbs | N-m | in lbs | N-m | in lbs | N-m | in lbs | N-m |
|---|---|---|---|---|---|---|---|---|---|
| 0.1 | 0.01 | 1 | 0.11 | 10 | 1.13 | 19 | 2.15 | 28 | 3.16 |
| 0.2 | 0.02 | 2 | 0.23 | 11 | 1.24 | 20 | 2.26 | 29 | 3.28 |
| 0.3 | 0.03 | 3 | 0.34 | 12 | 1.36 | 21 | 2.37 | 30 | 3.39 |
| 0.4 | 0.04 | 4 | 0.45 | 13 | 1.47 | 22 | 2.49 | 31 | 3.50 |
| 0.5 | 0.06 | 5 | 0.56 | 14 | 1.58 | 23 | 2.60 | 32 | 3.62 |
| 0.6 | 0.07 | 6 | 0.68 | 15 | 1.70 | 24 | 2.71 | 33 | 3.73 |
| 0.7 | 0.08 | 7 | 0.78 | 16 | 1.81 | 25 | 2.82 | 34 | 3.84 |
| 0.8 | 0.09 | 8 | 0.90 | 17 | 1.92 | 26 | 2.94 | 35 | 3.95 |
| 0.9 | 0.10 | 9 | 1.02 | 18 | 2.03 | 27 | 3.05 | 36 | 4.0 |

## ENGLISH TO METRIC CONVERSION: TORQUE

Torque is now expressed as either foot-pounds (ft./lbs.) or inch-pounds (in./lbs.). The metric measurement unit for torque is the Newton-meter (Nm). This unit—the Nm—will be used for all SI metric torque references, both the present ft./lbs. and in./lbs.

| ft lbs | N-m | ft lbs | N-m | ft lbs | N-m | ft lbs | N-m |
|--------|-----|--------|-----|--------|-----|--------|-----|
| 0.1 | 0.1 | 33 | 44.7 | 74 | 100.3 | 115 | 155.9 |
| 0.2 | 0.3 | 34 | 46.1 | 75 | 101.7 | 116 | 157.3 |
| 0.3 | 0.4 | 35 | 47.4 | 76 | 103.0 | 117 | 158.6 |
| 0.4 | 0.5 | 36 | 48.8 | 77 | 104.4 | 118 | 160.0 |
| 0.5 | 0.7 | 37 | 50.7 | 78 | 105.8 | 119 | 161.3 |
| 0.6 | 0.8 | 38 | 51.5 | 79 | 107.1 | 120 | 162.7 |
| 0.7 | 1.0 | 39 | 52.9 | 80 | 108.5 | 121 | 164.0 |
| 0.8 | 1.1 | 40 | 54.2 | 81 | 109.8 | 122 | 165.4 |
| 0.9 | 1.2 | 41 | 55.6 | 82 | 111.2 | 123 | 166.8 |
| 1 | 1.3 | 42 | 56.9 | 83 | 112.5 | 124 | 168.1 |
| 2 | 2.7 | 43 | 58.3 | 84 | 113.9 | 125 | 169.5 |
| 3 | 4.1 | 44 | 59.7 | 85 | 115.2 | 126 | 170.8 |
| 4 | 5.4 | 45 | 61.0 | 86 | 116.6 | 127 | 172.2 |
| 5 | 6.8 | 46 | 62.4 | 87 | 118.0 | 128 | 173.5 |
| 6 | 8.1 | 47 | 63.7 | 88 | 119.3 | 129 | 174.9 |
| 7 | 9.5 | 48 | 65.1 | 89 | 120.7 | 130 | 176.2 |
| 8 | 10.8 | 49 | 66.4 | 90 | 122.0 | 131 | 177.6 |
| 9 | 12.2 | 50 | 67.8 | 91 | 123.4 | 132 | 179.0 |
| 10 | 13.6 | 51 | 69.2 | 92 | 124.7 | 133 | 180.3 |
| 11 | 14.9 | 52 | 70.5 | 93 | 126.1 | 134 | 181.7 |
| 12 | 16.3 | 53 | 71.9 | 94 | 127.4 | 135 | 183.0 |
| 13 | 17.6 | 54 | 73.2 | 95 | 128.8 | 136 | 184.4 |
| 14 | 18.9 | 55 | 74.6 | 96 | 130.2 | 137 | 185.7 |
| 15 | 20.3 | 56 | 75.9 | 97 | 131.5 | 138 | 187.1 |
| 16 | 21.7 | 57 | 77.3 | 98 | 132.9 | 139 | 188.5 |
| 17 | 23.0 | 58 | 78.6 | 99 | 134.2 | 140 | 189.8 |
| 18 | 24.4 | 59 | 80.0 | 100 | 135.6 | 141 | 191.2 |
| 19 | 25.8 | 60 | 81.4 | 101 | 136.9 | 142 | 192.5 |
| 20 | 27.1 | 61 | 82.7 | 102 | 138.3 | 143 | 193.9 |
| 21 | 28.5 | 62 | 84.1 | 103 | 139.6 | 144 | 195.2 |
| 22 | 29.8 | 63 | 85.4 | 104 | 141.0 | 145 | 196.6 |
| 23 | 31.2 | 64 | 86.8 | 105 | 142.4 | 146 | 198.0 |
| 24 | 32.5 | 65 | 88.1 | 106 | 143.7 | 147 | 199.3 |
| 25 | 33.9 | 66 | 89.5 | 107 | 145.1 | 148 | 200.7 |
| 26 | 35.2 | 67 | 90.8 | 108 | 146.4 | 149 | 202.0 |
| 27 | 36.6 | 68 | 92.2 | 109 | 147.8 | 150 | 203.4 |
| 28 | 38.0 | 69 | 93.6 | 110 | 149.1 | 151 | 204.7 |
| 29 | 39.3 | 70 | 94.9 | 111 | 150.5 | 152 | 206.1 |
| 30 | 40.7 | 71 | 96.3 | 112 | 151.8 | 153 | 207.4 |
| 31 | 42.0 | 72 | 97.6 | 113 | 153.2 | 154 | 208.8 |
| 32 | 43.4 | 73 | 99.0 | 114 | 154.6 | 155 | 210.2 |

TCCS1C03

**ENGLISH TO METRIC CONVERSION: FORCE**

Force is presently measured in pounds (lbs.). This type of measurement is used to measure spring pressure, specifically how many pounds it takes to compress a spring. Our present force unit (the pound) will be replaced in SI metric measurements by the Newton (N). This term will eventually see use in specifications for electric motor brush spring pressures, valve spring pressures, etc.

To convert pounds (lbs.) to Newton (N): multiply the number of lbs. by 4.45

| lbs | N | lbs | N | lbs | N | oz | N |
|------|-------|-----|-------|-----|-------|----|------|
| 0.01 | 0.04 | 21 | 93.4 | 59 | 262.4 | 1 | 0.3 |
| 0.02 | 0.09 | 22 | 97.9 | 60 | 266.9 | 2 | 0.6 |
| 0.03 | 0.13 | 23 | 102.3 | 61 | 271.3 | 3 | 0.8 |
| 0.04 | 0.18 | 24 | 106.8 | 62 | 275.8 | 4 | 1.1 |
| 0.05 | 0.22 | 25 | 111.2 | 63 | 280.2 | 5 | 1.4 |
| 0.06 | 0.27 | 26 | 115.6 | 64 | 284.6 | 6 | 1.7 |
| 0.07 | 0.31 | 27 | 120.1 | 65 | 289.1 | 7 | 2.0 |
| 0.08 | 0.36 | 28 | 124.6 | 66 | 293.6 | 8 | 2.2 |
| 0.09 | 0.40 | 29 | 129.0 | 67 | 298.0 | 9 | 2.5 |
| 0.1 | 0.4 | 30 | 133.4 | 68 | 302.5 | 10 | 2.8 |
| 0.2 | 0.9 | 31 | 137.9 | 69 | 306.9 | 11 | 3.1 |
| 0.3 | 1.3 | 32 | 142.3 | 70 | 311.4 | 12 | 3.3 |
| 0.4 | 1.8 | 33 | 146.8 | 71 | 315.8 | 13 | 3.6 |
| 0.5 | 2.2 | 34 | 151.2 | 72 | 320.3 | 14 | 3.9 |
| 0.6 | 2.7 | 35 | 155.7 | 73 | 324.7 | 15 | 4.2 |
| 0.7 | 3.1 | 36 | 160.1 | 74 | 329.2 | 16 | 4.4 |
| 0.8 | 3.6 | 37 | 164.6 | 75 | 333.6 | 17 | 4.7 |
| 0.9 | 4.0 | 38 | 169.0 | 76 | 338.1 | 18 | 5.0 |
| 1 | 4.4 | 39 | 173.5 | 77 | 342.5 | 19 | 5.3 |
| 2 | 8.9 | 40 | 177.9 | 78 | 347.0 | 20 | 5.6 |
| 3 | 13.4 | 41 | 182.4 | 79 | 351.4 | 21 | 5.8 |
| 4 | 17.8 | 42 | 186.8 | 80 | 355.9 | 22 | 6.1 |
| 5 | 22.2 | 43 | 191.3 | 81 | 360.3 | 23 | 6.4 |
| 6 | 26.7 | 44 | 195.7 | 82 | 364.8 | 24 | 6.7 |
| 7 | 31.1 | 45 | 200.2 | 83 | 369.2 | 25 | 7.0 |
| 8 | 35.6 | 46 | 204.6 | 84 | 373.6 | 26 | 7.2 |
| 9 | 40.0 | 47 | 209.1 | 85 | 378.1 | 27 | 7.5 |
| 10 | 44.5 | 48 | 213.5 | 86 | 382.6 | 28 | 7.8 |
| 11 | 48.9 | 49 | 218.0 | 87 | 387.0 | 29 | 8.1 |
| 12 | 53.4 | 50 | 224.4 | 88 | 391.4 | 30 | 8.3 |
| 13 | 57.8 | 51 | 226.9 | 89 | 395.9 | 31 | 8.6 |
| 14 | 62.3 | 52 | 231.3 | 90 | 400.3 | 32 | 8.9 |
| 15 | 66.7 | 53 | 235.8 | 91 | 404.8 | 33 | 9.2 |
| 16 | 71.2 | 54 | 240.2 | 92 | 409.2 | 34 | 9.4 |
| 17 | 75.6 | 55 | 244.6 | 93 | 413.7 | 35 | 9.7 |
| 18 | 80.1 | 56 | 249.1 | 94 | 418.1 | 36 | 10.0 |
| 19 | 84.5 | 57 | 253.6 | 95 | 422.6 | 37 | 10.3 |
| 20 | 89.0 | 58 | 258.0 | 96 | 427.0 | 38 | 10.6 |

TCCS1C04

## ENGLISH TO METRIC CONVERSION: LIQUID CAPACITY

Liquid or fluid capacity is presently expressed as pints, quarts or gallons, or a combination of all of these. In the metric system the liter (l) will become the basic unit. Fractions of a liter would be expressed as deciliters, centiliters, or most frequently (and commonly) as milliliters.

To convert pints (pts.) to liters (l): multiply the number of pints by .47
To convert liters (l) to pints (pts.): multiply the number of liters by 2.1
To convert quarts (qts.) to liters (l): multiply the number of quarts by .95

To convert liters (l) to quarts (qts.): multiply the number of liters by 1.06
To convert gallons (gals.) to liters (l): multiply the number of gallons by 3.8
To convert liters (l) to gallons (gals.): multiply the number of liters by .26

| gals | liters | qts | liters | pts | liters |
|------|--------|-----|--------|-----|--------|
| 0.1 | 0.38 | 0.1 | 0.10 | 0.1 | 0.05 |
| 0.2 | 0.76 | 0.2 | 0.19 | 0.2 | 0.10 |
| 0.3 | 1.1 | 0.3 | 0.28 | 0.3 | 0.14 |
| 0.4 | 1.5 | 0.4 | 0.38 | 0.4 | 0.19 |
| 0.5 | 1.9 | 0.5 | 0.47 | 0.5 | 0.24 |
| 0.6 | 2.3 | 0.6 | 0.57 | 0.6 | 0.28 |
| 0.7 | 2.6 | 0.7 | 0.66 | 0.7 | 0.33 |
| 0.8 | 3.0 | 0.8 | 0.76 | 0.8 | 0.38 |
| 0.9 | 3.4 | 0.9 | 0.85 | 0.9 | 0.43 |
| 1 | 3.8 | 1 | 1.0 | 1 | 0.5 |
| 2 | 7.6 | 2 | 1.9 | 2 | 1.0 |
| 3 | 11.4 | 3 | 2.8 | 3 | 1.4 |
| 4 | 15.1 | 4 | 3.8 | 4 | 1.9 |
| 5 | 18.9 | 5 | 4.7 | 5 | 2.4 |
| 6 | 22.7 | 6 | 5.7 | 6 | 2.8 |
| 7 | 26.5 | 7 | 6.6 | 7 | 3.3 |
| 8 | 30.3 | 8 | 7.6 | 8 | 3.8 |
| 9 | 34.1 | 9 | 8.5 | 9 | 4.3 |
| 10 | 37.8 | 10 | 9.5 | 10 | 4.7 |
| 11 | 41.6 | 11 | 10.4 | 11 | 5.2 |
| 12 | 45.4 | 12 | 11.4 | 12 | 5.7 |
| 13 | 49.2 | 13 | 12.3 | 13 | 6.2 |
| 14 | 53.0 | 14 | 13.2 | 14 | 6.6 |
| 15 | 56.8 | 15 | 14.2 | 15 | 7.1 |
| 16 | 60.6 | 16 | 15.1 | 16 | 7.6 |
| 17 | 64.3 | 17 | 16.1 | 17 | 8.0 |
| 18 | 68.1 | 18 | 17.0 | 18 | 8.5 |
| 19 | 71.9 | 19 | 18.0 | 19 | 9.0 |
| 20 | 75.7 | 20 | 18.9 | 20 | 9.5 |
| 21 | 79.5 | 21 | 19.9 | 21 | 9.9 |
| 22 | 83.2 | 22 | 20.8 | 22 | 10.4 |
| 23 | 87.0 | 23 | 21.8 | 23 | 10.9 |
| 24 | 90.8 | 24 | 22.7 | 24 | 11.4 |
| 25 | 94.6 | 25 | 23.6 | 25 | 11.8 |
| 26 | 98.4 | 26 | 24.6 | 26 | 12.3 |
| 27 | 102.2 | 27 | 25.5 | 27 | 12.8 |
| 28 | 106.0 | 28 | 26.5 | 28 | 13.2 |
| 29 | 110.0 | 29 | 27.4 | 29 | 13.7 |
| 30 | 113.5 | 30 | 28.4 | 30 | 14.2 |

TCCS1C05

## ENGLISH TO METRIC CONVERSION: PRESSURE

The basic unit of pressure measurement used today is expressed as pounds per square inch (psi). The metric unit for psi will be the kilopascal (kPa). This will apply to either fluid pressure or air pressure, and will be frequently seen in tire pressure readings, oil pressure specifications, fuel pump pressure, etc.

To convert pounds per square inch (psi) to kilopascals (kPa): multiply the number of psi by 6.89

| Psi | kPa | Psi | kPa | Psi | kPa | Psi | kPa |
|---|---|---|---|---|---|---|---|
| 0.1 | 0.7 | 37 | 255.1 | 82 | 565.4 | 127 | 875.6 |
| 0.2 | 1.4 | 38 | 262.0 | 83 | 572.3 | 128 | 882.5 |
| 0.3 | 2.1 | 39 | 268.9 | 84 | 579.2 | 129 | 889.4 |
| 0.4 | 2.8 | 40 | 275.8 | 85 | 586.0 | 130 | 896.3 |
| 0.5 | 3.4 | 41 | 282.7 | 86 | 592.9 | 131 | 903.2 |
| 0.6 | 4.1 | 42 | 289.6 | 87 | 599.8 | 132 | 910.1 |
| 0.7 | 4.8 | 43 | 296.5 | 88 | 606.7 | 133 | 917.0 |
| 0.8 | 5.5 | 44 | 303.4 | 89 | 613.6 | 134 | 923.9 |
| 0.9 | 6.2 | 45 | 310.3 | 90 | 620.5 | 135 | 930.8 |
| 1 | 6.9 | 46 | 317.2 | 91 | 627.4 | 136 | 937.7 |
| 2 | 13.8 | 47 | 324.0 | 92 | 634.3 | 137 | 944.6 |
| 3 | 20.7 | 48 | 331.0 | 93 | 641.2 | 138 | 951.5 |
| 4 | 27.6 | 49 | 337.8 | 94 | 648.1 | 139 | 958.4 |
| 5 | 34.5 | 50 | 344.7 | 95 | 655.0 | 140 | 965.2 |
| 6 | 41.4 | 51 | 351.6 | 96 | 661.9 | 141 | 972.2 |
| 7 | 48.3 | 52 | 358.5 | 97 | 668.8 | 142 | 979.0 |
| 8 | 55.2 | 53 | 365.4 | 98 | 675.7 | 143 | 985.9 |
| 9 | 62.1 | 54 | 372.3 | 99 | 682.6 | 144 | 992.8 |
| 10 | 69.0 | 55 | 379.2 | 100 | 689.5 | 145 | 999.7 |
| 11 | 75.8 | 56 | 386.1 | 101 | 696.4 | 146 | 1006.6 |
| 12 | 82.7 | 57 | 393.0 | 102 | 703.3 | 147 | 1013.5 |
| 13 | 89.6 | 58 | 399.9 | 103 | 710.2 | 148 | 1020.4 |
| 14 | 96.5 | 59 | 406.8 | 104 | 717.0 | 149 | 1027.3 |
| 15 | 103.4 | 60 | 413.7 | 105 | 723.9 | 150 | 1034.2 |
| 16 | 110.3 | 61 | 420.6 | 106 | 730.8 | 151 | 1041.1 |
| 17 | 117.2 | 62 | 427.5 | 107 | 737.7 | 152 | 1048.0 |
| 18 | 124.1 | 63 | 434.4 | 108 | 744.6 | 153 | 1054.9 |
| 19 | 131.0 | 64 | 441.3 | 109 | 751.5 | 154 | 1061.8 |
| 20 | 137.9 | 65 | 448.2 | 110 | 758.4 | 155 | 1068.7 |
| 21 | 144.8 | 66 | 455.0 | 111 | 765.3 | 156 | 1075.6 |
| 22 | 151.7 | 67 | 461.9 | 112 | 772.2 | 157 | 1082.5 |
| 23 | 158.6 | 68 | 468.8 | 113 | 779.1 | 158 | 1089.4 |
| 24 | 165.5 | 69 | 475.7 | 114 | 786.0 | 159 | 1096.3 |
| 25 | 172.4 | 70 | 482.6 | 115 | 792.9 | 160 | 1103.2 |
| 26 | 179.3 | 71 | 489.5 | 116 | 799.8 | 161 | 1110.0 |
| 27 | 186.2 | 72 | 496.4 | 117 | 806.7 | 162 | 1116.9 |
| 28 | 193.0 | 73 | 503.3 | 118 | 813.6 | 163 | 1123.8 |
| 29 | 200.0 | 74 | 510.2 | 119 | 820.5 | 164 | 1130.7 |
| 30 | 206.8 | 75 | 517.1 | 120 | 827.4 | 165 | 1137.6 |
| 31 | 213.7 | 76 | 524.0 | 121 | 834.3 | 166 | 1144.5 |
| 32 | 220.6 | 77 | 530.9 | 122 | 841.2 | 167 | 1151.4 |
| 33 | 227.5 | 78 | 537.8 | 123 | 848.0 | 168 | 1158.3 |
| 34 | 234.4 | 79 | 544.7 | 124 | 854.9 | 169 | 1165.2 |
| 35 | 241.3 | 80 | 551.6 | 125 | 861.8 | 170 | 1172.1 |
| 36 | 248.2 | 81 | 558.5 | 126 | 868.7 | 171 | 1179.0 |

TCCS1C06

## ENGLISH TO METRIC CONVERSION: PRESSURE

The basic unit of pressure measurement used today is expressed as pounds per square inch (psi). The metric unit for psi will be the kilopascal (kPa). This will apply to either fluid pressure or air pressure, and will be frequently seen in tire pressure readings, oil pressure specifications, fuel pump pressure, etc.

To convert pounds per square inch (psi) to kilopascals (kPa): multiply the number of psi by 6.89

| Psi | kPa | Psi | kPa | Psi | kPa | Psi | kPa |
|---|---|---|---|---|---|---|---|
| 172 | 1185.9 | 216 | 1489.3 | 260 | 1792.6 | 304 | 2096.0 |
| 173 | 1192.8 | 217 | 1496.2 | 261 | 1799.5 | 305 | 2102.9 |
| 174 | 1199.7 | 218 | 1503.1 | 262 | 1806.4 | 306 | 2109.8 |
| 175 | 1206.6 | 219 | 1510.0 | 263 | 1813.3 | 307 | 2116.7 |
| 176 | 1213.5 | 220 | 1516.8 | 264 | 1820.2 | 308 | 2123.6 |
| 177 | 1220.4 | 221 | 1523.7 | 265 | 1827.1 | 309 | 2130.5 |
| 178 | 1227.3 | 222 | 1530.6 | 266 | 1834.0 | 310 | 2137.4 |
| 179 | 1234.2 | 223 | 1537.5 | 267 | 1840.9 | 311 | 2144.3 |
| 180 | 1241.0 | 224 | 1544.4 | 268 | 1847.8 | 312 | 2151.2 |
| 181 | 1247.9 | 225 | 1551.3 | 269 | 1854.7 | 313 | 2158.1 |
| 182 | 1254.8 | 226 | 1558.2 | 270 | 1861.6 | 314 | 2164.9 |
| 183 | 1261.7 | 227 | 1565.1 | 271 | 1868.5 | 315 | 2171.8 |
| 184 | 1268.6 | 228 | 1572.0 | 272 | 1875.4 | 316 | 2178.7 |
| 185 | 1275.5 | 229 | 1578.9 | 273 | 1882.3 | 317 | 2185.6 |
| 186 | 1282.4 | 230 | 1585.8 | 274 | 1889.2 | 318 | 2192.5 |
| 187 | 1289.3 | 231 | 1592.7 | 275 | 1896.1 | 319 | 2199.4 |
| 188 | 1296.2 | 232 | 1599.6 | 276 | 1903.0 | 320 | 2206.3 |
| 189 | 1303.1 | 233 | 1606.5 | 277 | 1909.8 | 321 | 2213.2 |
| 190 | 1310.0 | 234 | 1613.4 | 278 | 1916.7 | 322 | 2220.1 |
| 191 | 1316.9 | 235 | 1620.3 | 279 | 1923.6 | 323 | 2227.0 |
| 192 | 1323.8 | 236 | 1627.2 | 280 | 1930.5 | 324 | 2233.9 |
| 193 | 1330.7 | 237 | 1634.1 | 281 | 1937.4 | 325 | 2240.8 |
| 194 | 1337.6 | 238 | 1641.0 | 282 | 1944.3 | 326 | 2247.7 |
| 195 | 1344.5 | 239 | 1647.8 | 283 | 1951.2 | 327 | 2254.6 |
| 196 | 1351.4 | 240 | 1654.7 | 284 | 1958.1 | 328 | 2261.5 |
| 197 | 1358.3 | 241 | 1661.6 | 285 | 1965.0 | 329 | 2268.4 |
| 198 | 1365.2 | 242 | 1668.5 | 286 | 1971.9 | 330 | 2275.3 |
| 199 | 1372.0 | 243 | 1675.4 | 287 | 1978.8 | 331 | 2282.2 |
| 200 | 1378.9 | 244 | 1682.3 | 288 | 1985.7 | 332 | 2289.1 |
| 201 | 1385.8 | 245 | 1689.2 | 289 | 1992.6 | 333 | 2295.9 |
| 202 | 1392.7 | 246 | 1696.1 | 290 | 1999.5 | 334 | 2302.8 |
| 203 | 1399.6 | 247 | 1703.0 | 291 | 2006.4 | 335 | 2309.7 |
| 204 | 1406.5 | 248 | 1709.9 | 292 | 2013.3 | 336 | 2316.6 |
| 205 | 1413.4 | 249 | 1716.8 | 293 | 2020.2 | 337 | 2323.5 |
| 206 | 1420.3 | 250 | 1723.7 | 294 | 2027.1 | 338 | 2330.4 |
| 207 | 1427.2 | 251 | 1730.6 | 295 | 2034.0 | 339 | 2337.3 |
| 208 | 1434.1 | 252 | 1737.5 | 296 | 2040.8 | 240 | 2344.2 |
| 209 | 1441.0 | 253 | 1744.4 | 297 | 2047.7 | 341 | 2351.1 |
| 210 | 1447.9 | 254 | 1751.3 | 298 | 2054.6 | 342 | 2358.0 |
| 211 | 1454.8 | 255 | 1758.2 | 299 | 2061.5 | 343 | 2364.9 |
| 212 | 1461.7 | 256 | 1765.1 | 300 | 2068.4 | 344 | 2371.8 |
| 213 | 1468.7 | 257 | 1772.0 | 301 | 2075.3 | 345 | 2378.7 |
| 214 | 1475.5 | 258 | 1778.8 | 302 | 2082.2 | 346 | 2385.6 |
| 215 | 1482.4 | 259 | 1785.7 | 303 | 2089.1 | 347 | 2392.5 |

TCCS1C07

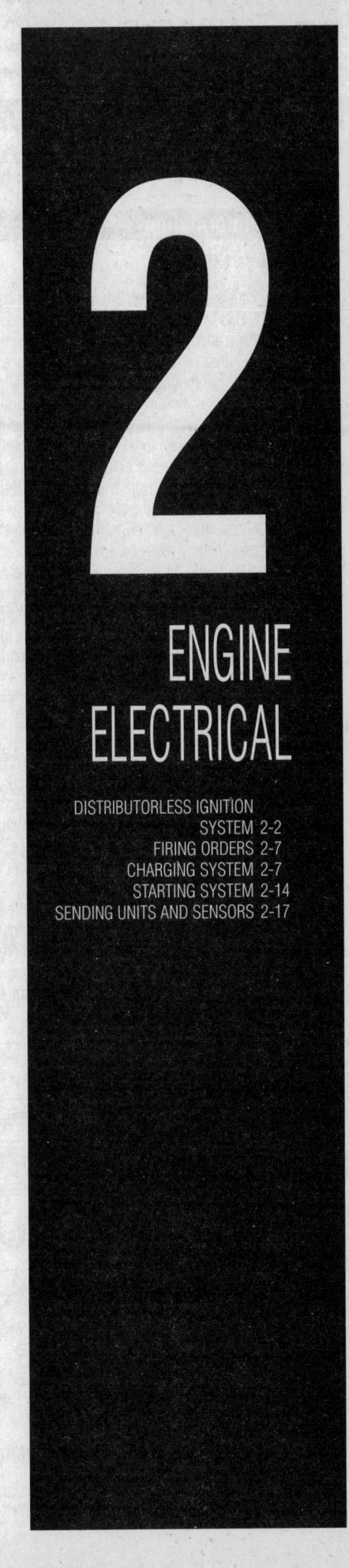

# 2

# ENGINE ELECTRICAL

## DISTRIBUTORLESS IGNITION SYSTEM

➡**For information on understanding electricity and troubleshooting electrical circuits, please refer to Section 6 of this manual.**

### General Information

◆ **See Figures 1 thru 7**

The distributorless ignition system is referred to as the Direct Ignition System (DIS). This system's three main components are the coil pack, the crankshaft sensor, and the camshaft sensor. The crankshaft and camshaft sensors are hall effect devices. These devices use the change in a magnetic field (from an internal magnet) to sense whether a slot is present on the camshaft sprocket or a window is present on the torque converter driveplate. When a slot or window is sensed, the sensors switch (sensor) input voltage from high (5.0 volts) to low (less than 0.3 volts). As the slot or window passes, the input voltage is switched back to high (5.0 volts). These changes in input voltage allow the engine controller to compute engine speed, crankshaft position, and camshaft position.

The ignition system is regulated by the Powertrain Control Module (PCM). The PCM supplies battery voltage to the ignition coil through the Auto Shutdown (ASD) relay. The PCM also controls the ground circuit for the ignition coil. By switching the ground path for the coil on and off, the PCM adjusts the ignition timing to meet changing engine operating conditions.

During the crank-start period the PCM advances ignition timing a set amount. During engine operation, the amount of spark advance provided by the PCM is determined by these input factors:

- Coolant temperature
- Engine RPM
- Available manifold vacuum

The PCM also regulates the fuel injection system.

The camshaft position sensor provides fuel injection synchronization and cylinder identification information. The sensor generates pulses that are the input sent to the PCM. The PCM interprets the camshaft position sensor input (along with the crankshaft position sensor input) to determine crankshaft position. The PCM uses the crankshaft position sensor input to determine injector sequence and ignition timing.

The camshaft position sensor is mounted to the rear of the cylinder head. A target magnet attaches to the rear of the camshaft and indexes to the correct position. The target magnet has four different poles arranged in an asymmetrical pattern. As the target magnet rotates, the camshaft position sensor recognizes the change in polarity. The sensor switches from high (5 volts) to low (0.3 volts) as the target magnet rotates. When the north pole of the target magnet passes under the sensor, the output switches high. The sensor output switches low when the south pole of the target magnet passes underneath.

The PCM uses the camshaft position sensor to determine injector sequence. The PCM determines ignition timing from the crankshaft position sensor. Once the crankshaft position has been determined, the PCM begins energizing the injectors in sequence.

The crankshaft position sensor is mounted to the engine block behind the alternator, just above the oil filter. The second crankshaft counterweight has machined into it two sets of four timing reference notches including a 60 degree signature notch. From the crankshaft position sensor input, the PCM determines engine speed and crankshaft angle (position). The notches generate pulses front high to low in the crankshaft position sensor output voltage. When a metal portion of the counterweight aligns with the crankshaft position sensor, the sensor output voltage goes low (less than 0.5 volts). When a notch aligns with the sensor, voltage goes high (5.0 volts). As a group of notches pass under the sensor the output voltage switches from low (metal) to high (notch) then back to low.

From the frequency of the output voltage pulses, the PCM calculates

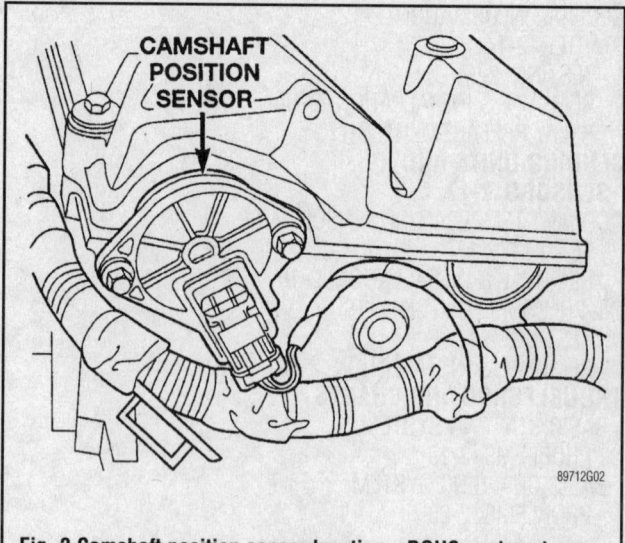

Fig. 2 Camshaft position sensor location—DOHC engine shown

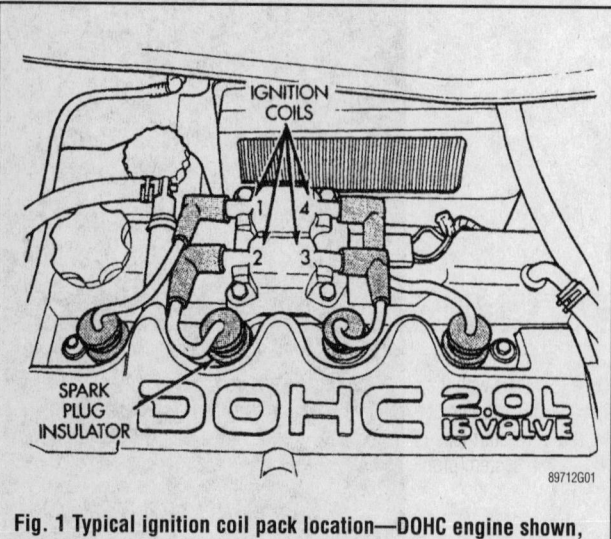

Fig. 1 Typical ignition coil pack location—DOHC engine shown, SOHC similar

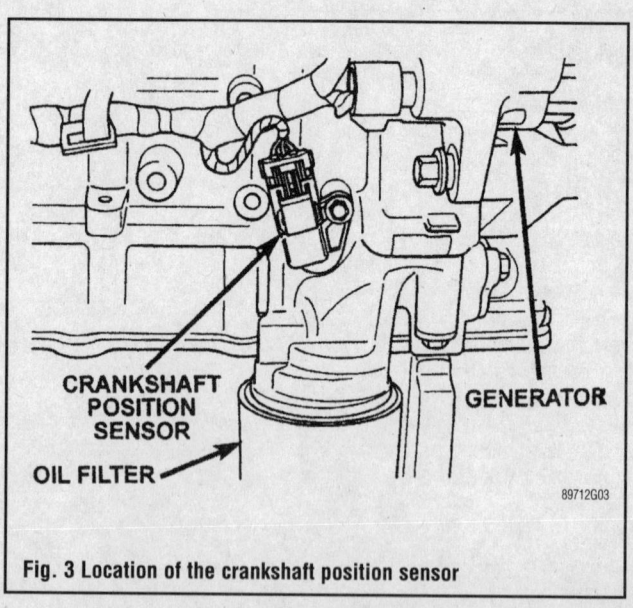

Fig. 3 Location of the crankshaft position sensor

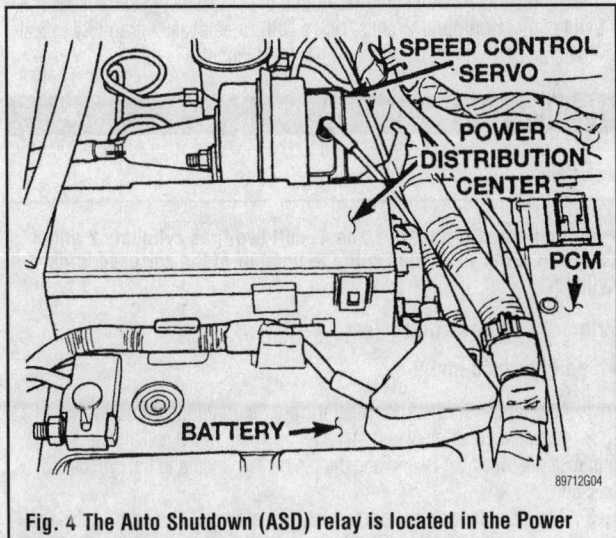

Fig. 4 The Auto Shutdown (ASD) relay is located in the Power Distribution Center (PDC)

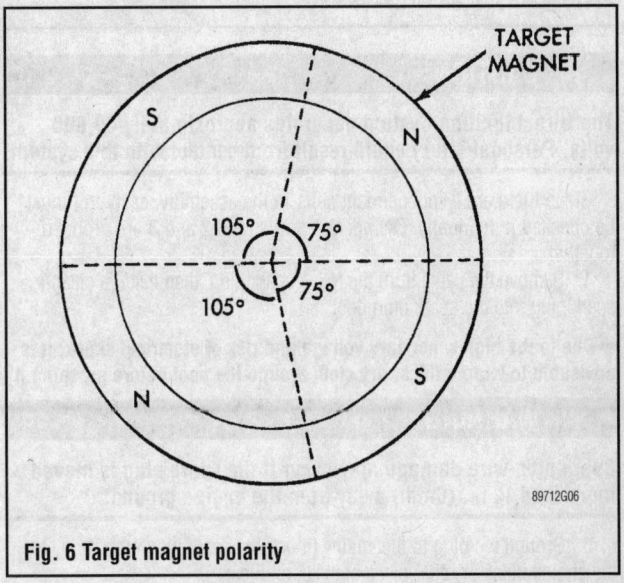

Fig. 6 Target magnet polarity

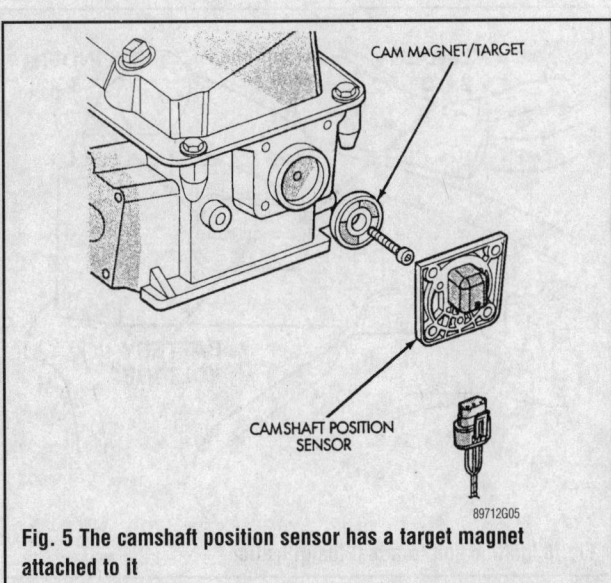

Fig. 5 The camshaft position sensor has a target magnet attached to it

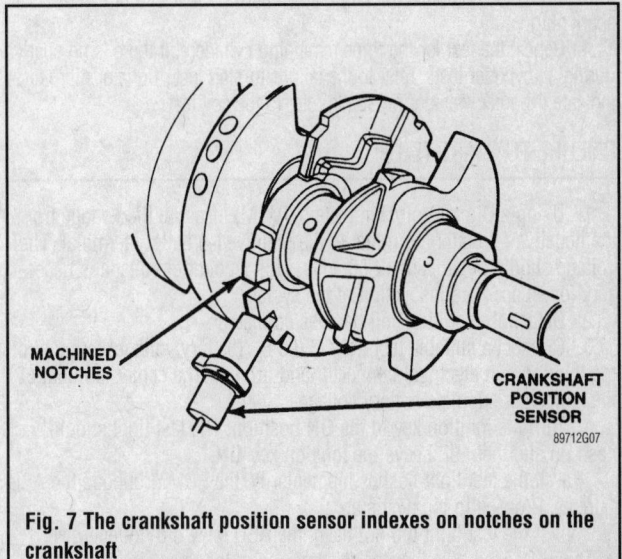

Fig. 7 The crankshaft position sensor indexes on notches on the crankshaft

engine speed. The width of the pulses represent the amount of time the output voltage stays high before switching back to low. The period of time the voltage stays high before returning to low is called a pulse width. the faster the engine is operating, the smaller the pulse width.

By counting the pulses and referencing the pulse from the 60 degree signature notch, the PCM calculates crankshaft angle (position). In each group of timing reference notches, the first notch represents 69 degrees Before Top Dead Center (BTDC). The second notch represents 49 degrees BTDC. The third notch represents 29 degrees. The last notch in each set represents 9 degrees BTDC.

The timing reference notches are machined at 20 degree increments. Front the voltage pulse-width, the PCM tells the difference between the timing reference notches and the 60 degree reference notches. The 60 degree signature notch produces a longer pulse-width than the smaller timing reference notches. If the camshaft position sensor input switches front high to low when the 60 degree signature notch passes under the crankshaft position sensor, the PCM knows cylinder No. 1 is the next cylinder at TDC.

The ignition coil assembly consists of 2 coils molded together. The assembly is mounted on the top of the engine. The number of each coil appears on the front of the coil pack.

High tension leads route to each cylinder from the coil. The coil fires two spark plugs every power stroke. One plug is the cylinder under compression, the other cylinder fires on the exhaust stroke. The PCM determines which of the coils to charge and fire at the correct time. The coil's low primary resistance allows the PCM to fully charge the coil for each firing.

## Diagnosis and Testing

To test the ignition system perform the test procedures in a particular sequence. Start with the secondary spark test, commence to the coil test (located under the coil procedures later in this section) and finally perform the failure-to-start test. Performing the tests in this order will narrow down the ignition system problem in the easiest manner.

## SECONDARY SPARK TEST

**✳✳ CAUTION**

**The Direct Ignition System generates approximately 40,000 volts. Personal injury could result from contact with this system.**

Since there are 2 independent coils in the assembly, each coil must be checked individually. Cylinders 1 and 4, and 2 and 3 are grouped together.

1. Remove the cable from the No. 1 spark plug, then insert a clean spark plug into the spark plug boot.

➡Due to the high secondary voltage and risk of electrical shock, it is advisable to wrap a thick, dry cloth around the boot before grasping it.

**✳✳ WARNING**

**Spark plug wire damage may occur if the spark plug is moved more than ¼ in. (6mm) away from the engine ground.**

2. Ground the plug to the engine (touch the spark plug metal body to the engine block or other piece of metal on the car).
3. Crank the engine and look for spark across the electrodes of the spark plug.
4. Repeat the test for the three remaining cylinders. If there is no spark during all cylinder tests, refer to the failure-to-start test. If one or more tests indicate irregular, weak or no spark, refer to the coil test.

## FAILURE TO START TEST

1. Using a Digital Volt/Ohmmeter (DVOM) measure the voltage from the negative (-) battery terminal to the positive (+) battery terminal. The voltage should be at least 12.66 volts. This amount of voltage is necessary for an accurate inspection of the system.
2. Detach the ignition coil harness connector.
3. Connect a suitable test light to the B+ (battery voltage) terminal of the ignition coil electrical connector and ground. The center terminal of the connector supplies battery voltage.
4. Turn the ignition key to the **ON** position. The test light should flash on and then off. Leave the ignition key **ON**.
    a. If the test light flashes momentarily, the PCM grounded the ASD relay. Proceed to the next step.
    b. If the test light did not flash, the ASD relay did not energize. This is caused by either the relay or one of the relay circuits.
5. Crank the engine. (If the key was placed in the **OFF** position in Step 4, turn the key to the **ON** position before cranking. Wait for the test light to flash once, then crank the engine).
    a. If the test light momentarily flashes during cranking, the PCM is not receiving a camshaft/crankshaft position sensor signal.. A DRB or equivalent scan tool must be used to test the sensor and related circuitry.
    b. For 1995 vehicles, if the test light did not flash during cranking, unplug the camshaft position sensor connector. Turn the ignition key to the **OFF** position. Turn the key to the **ON** position, wait for the test light to momentarily flash once, then crank the engine. If the test light momentarily flashes, the camshaft position sensor is shorted and must be replaced. If the light did not flash when the engine was cranked, the cause of the no-start condition is in either the crankshaft or camshaft position sensor 8-volt supply circuit to the crankshaft position sensor 5-volt output or ground circuits. Use a DRB or equivalent scan tool to test the crankshaft position sensor and related circuitry.
    c. For 1996–99 vehicles, if the test light did not flash during cranking, unplug the crankshaft position sensor connector. Turn the ignition key to the **OFF** position. Turn the key to the **ON** position, wait for the test light to momentarily flash once, then crank the engine. If the test light momentarily flashes, the crankshaft position sensor is shorted and must be replaced. If the light did not flash when the engine was cranked, the cause of the no-start condition is in either the crankshaft or camshaft

position sensor 8-volt supply circuit to the crankshaft position sensor 5-volt output or ground circuits. Use a DRB or equivalent scan tool to test the crankshaft position sensor and related circuitry.

**Ignition Coil Pack**

### TESTING

➡Coil one fires cylinders 1 and 4, coil two fires cylinders 2 and 3. Each coil tower is labeled with the number of the corresponding cylinder.

**Primary Coil Resistance Test**

◆ See Figures 8 and 9

1. Unplug the electrical connector from the ignition coil pack.
2. Measure the primary resistance of each coil. At the coil, connect an ohmmeter between the B+ pin and the pin corresponding to the cylinders in question.
3. The resistance on the primary side of each coil should be 0.45–0.65 ohms. Replace the coil if not within specifications.

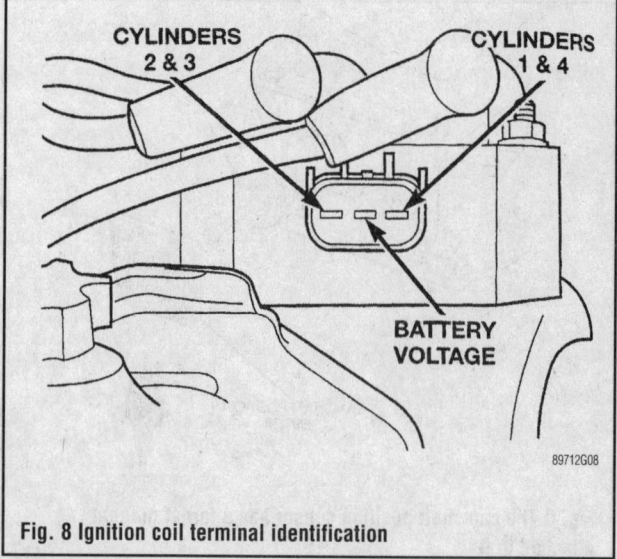

Fig. 8 Ignition coil terminal identification

Fig. 9 Detach the coil connector, then measure primary resistance with an ohmmeter

## Secondary Coil Resistance Test

▶ **See Figures 10 and 11**

1. Disconnect the spark plug wires from the secondary towers of the ignition coil.

2. Use an ohmmeter to measure the secondary resistance of the coil between towers 1 and 4, then between towers 2 and 3.

3. The secondary resistance should be 11,000–14,000 ohms. If resistance is not within specifications, the coil must be replaced.

## REMOVAL & INSTALLATION

▶ **See Figures 12 thru 17**

1. Disconnect the negative battery cable.
2. Tag and unplug the spark plug wires from the ignition coil.

3. Detach the electrical connector from the ignition coil.

4. Remove the ignition coil mounting nuts, then remove the ignition coil pack from the vehicle.

**To install:**

5. Install the ignition coil pack and secure with the mounting nuts.

6. Attach the electrical connector to the ignition coil.

7. Connect the spark plug wires to the coil, as tagged during removal. Make sure the wires are installed correctly and that the cables snap onto the towers.

8. Connect the negative battery cable.

## Crankshaft and Camshaft Position Sensors

For position sensor information, please refer to Section 4 of this manual.

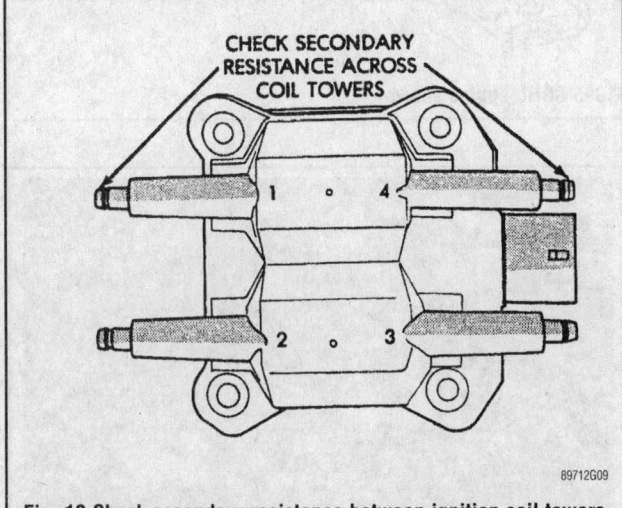

Fig. 10 Check secondary resistance between ignition coil towers 1 and 4, and coil towers 2 and 3

Fig. 11 To measure secondary resistance, place the ohmmeter leads on the 2 and 3 cylinder coil towers

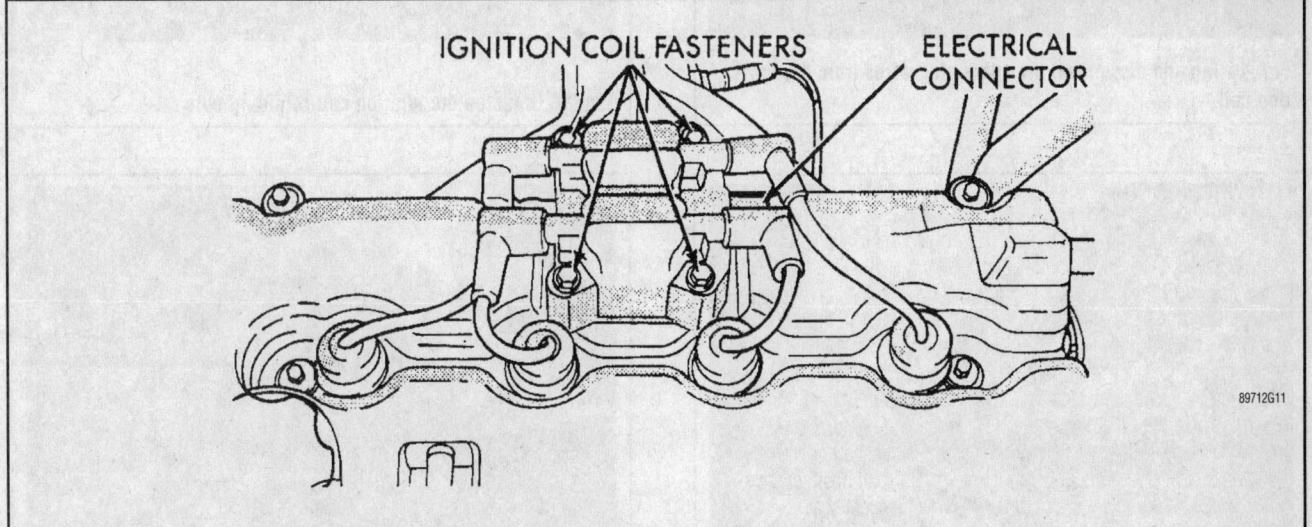

Fig. 12 View of the ignition coil, fasteners and electrical connector—DOHC engine shown

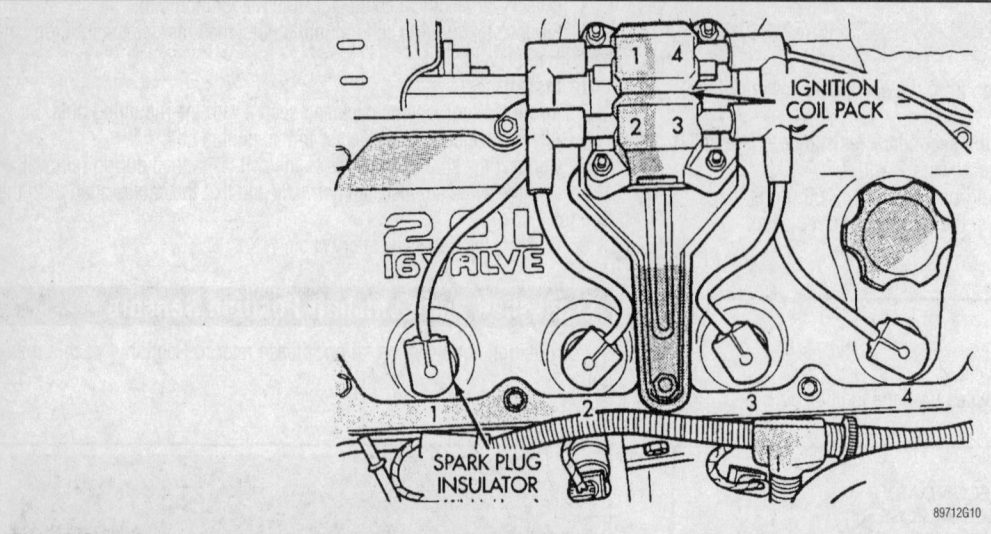

Fig. 13 On some vehicles, the ignition coil pack is mounted to a bracket—1995 SOHC engine shown

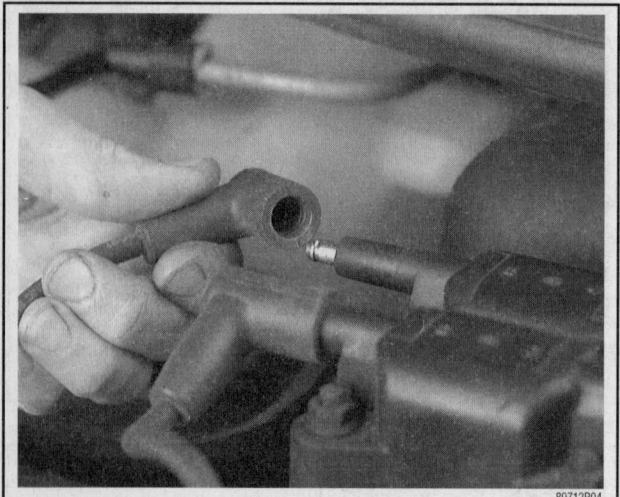

Fig. 14 Tag and disconnect the spark plug wires from the ignition coil

Fig. 16 Unfasten the ignition coil retaining nuts . . .

Fig. 15 Unplug the ignition coil electrical connector

Fig. 17 . . . then lift the ignition coil up off the mounting studs

## FIRING ORDERS

▶ See Figure 18

➡ To avoid confusion, remove and tag the spark plug wires one at a time, for replacement.

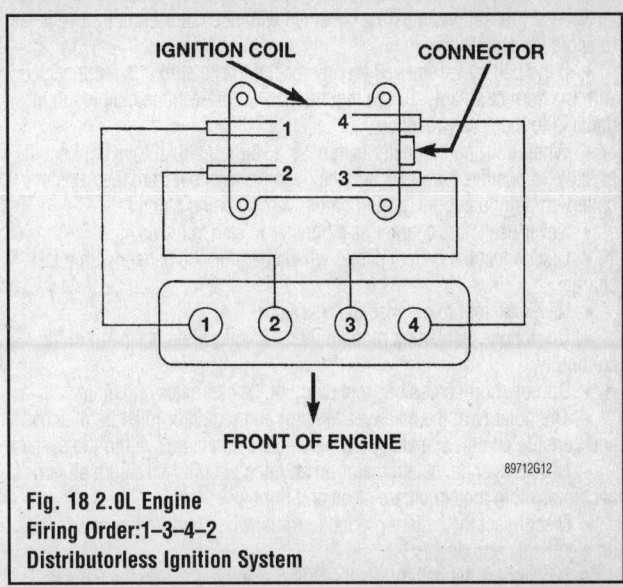

Fig. 18 2.0L Engine
Firing Order:1–3–4–2
Distributorless Ignition System

## CHARGING SYSTEM

### General Information

The automobile charging system provides electrical power for operation of the vehicle's ignition system, starting system and all electrical accessories. The battery serves as an electrical surge or storage tank, storing (in chemical form) the energy originally produced by the engine driven generator. The system also provides a means of regulating output to protect the battery from being overcharged and to avoid excessive voltage to the accessories.

The storage battery is a chemical device incorporating parallel lead plates in a tank containing a sulfuric acid/water solution. Adjacent plates are slightly dissimilar, and the chemical reaction of the two dissimilar plates produces electrical energy when the battery is connected to a load such as the starter motor. The chemical reaction is reversible, so that when the alternator is producing a voltage (electrical pressure) greater than that produced by the battery, electricity is forced into the battery, and the battery is returned to its fully charged state.

Newer automobiles use alternating current alternators, because they are more efficient, can be rotated at higher speeds, and have fewer brush problems. In an alternator, the field usually rotates while all the current produced passes only through the stator winding. The brushes bear against continuous slip rings. This causes the current produced to periodically reverse the direction of its flow. Diodes (electrical one way valves) block the flow of current from traveling in the wrong direction. A series of diodes is wired together to permit the alternating flow of the stator to be rectified back to 12 volts DC for use by the vehicle's electrical system.

The voltage regulating function is performed by a regulator. The regulator is often built in to the alternator; this system is termed an integrated or internal regulator.

An alternator differs from a DC shunt generator in that the armature is stationary, and is called the stator, while the field rotates and is called the rotor. The higher current values in the alternator's stator are conducted to the external circuit through fixed leads and connections, rather than through a rotating commutator and brushes as in a DC generator. This eliminates a major point of maintenance.

The rotor assembly is supported in the drive end frame by a ball bearing and at the other end by a roller bearing. These bearings are lubricated during assembly and require no maintenance. There are six diodes in the end frame assembly. These diodes are electrical check valves that also change the alternating current developed within the stator windings to a Direct Current (DC) at the output (BAT) terminal. Three of these diodes are negative

and are mounted flush with the end frame while the other three are positive and are mounted into a strip called a heat sink. The positive diodes are easily identified as the ones within small cavities or depressions.

The alternator charging system is a negative (–) ground system which consists of an alternator, a regulator, a charge indicator, a storage battery and wiring connecting the components, and fuse link wire.

The alternator is belt-driven from the engine. Energy is supplied from the alternator/regulator system to the rotating field through two brushes to two slip-rings. The slip-rings are mounted on the rotor shaft and are connected to the field coil. This energy supplied to the rotating field from the battery is called excitation current and is used to initially energize the field to begin the generation of electricity. Once the alternator starts to generate electricity, the excitation current comes from its own output rather than the battery.

The alternator produces power in the form of alternating current. The alternating current is rectified by 6 diodes into direct current. The direct current is used to charge the battery and power the rest of the electrical system.

When the ignition key is turned **ON**, current flows from the battery, through the charging system indicator light on the instrument panel, to the voltage regulator, and to the alternator. Since the alternator is not producing any current, the alternator warning light comes on. When the engine is started, the alternator begins to produce current and turns the alternator light off. As the alternator turns and produces current, the current is divided in two ways: part to the battery(to charge the battery and power the electrical components of the vehicle), and part is returned to the alternator (to enable it to increase its output). In this situation, the alternator is receiving current from the battery and from itself. A voltage regulator is wired into the current supply to the alternator to prevent it from receiving too much current which would cause it to put out too much current. Conversely, if the voltage regulator does not allow the alternator to receive enough current, the battery will not be fully charged and will eventually go dead.

The battery is connected to the alternator at all times, whether the ignition key is turned **ON** or not. If the battery were shorted to ground, the alternator would also be shorted. This would damage the alternator. To prevent this, a fuse link is installed in the wiring between the battery and the alternator. If the battery is shorted, the fuse link melts, protecting the alternator.

An alternator is better that a conventional, DC shunt generator because it is lighter and more compact, because it is designed to supply the battery and accessory circuits through a wide range of engine speeds, and because it eliminates the necessary maintenance of replacing brushes and servicing commutators.

## Alternator Precautions

Several precautions must be observed with alternator-equipped vehicles to avoid damage to the unit.

• If the battery is removed for any reason, make sure it is reconnected with the correct polarity. Reversing the battery connections may result in damage to the 1-way rectifiers.

• When utilizing a booster battery as a starting aid, always connect the positive to positive terminals and the negative terminal from the booster battery to a good engine ground on the vehicle being started.

• Never use a fast charger as a booster to start vehicles.

• Disconnect the battery cables when charging the battery with a fast charger.

• Never attempt to polarize the alternator.

• Do not use test lamps of more than 12 volts when checking diode continuity.

• Do not short across or ground any of the alternator terminals.

• The polarity of the battery, alternator and regulator must be matched and considered before making any electrical connections within the system.

• Never separate the alternator on an open circuit. Make sure all connections within the circuit are clean and tight.

• Disconnect the battery ground terminal when performing any service on electrical components.

• Disconnect the battery if arc welding is to be done on the vehicle.

## Alternator

### TESTING

#### Voltage Drop Test

*1995 VEHICLES*

▶ See Figure 19

➡The alternator output wire voltage drop test shows the amount of voltage drop across the alternator output wire between the alternator B+ terminal and the battery positive post.

1. Before beginning the test, make sure the vehicle has a fully charged battery.

2. Using an ohmmeter, check the alternator ground path. Resistance between the alternator housing to the engine should not exceed 0.3 milliohms. If the resistance is higher, clean the surfaces between the alternator and the mounting bracket thoroughly and make sure all fasteners are tightened to the proper specifications.

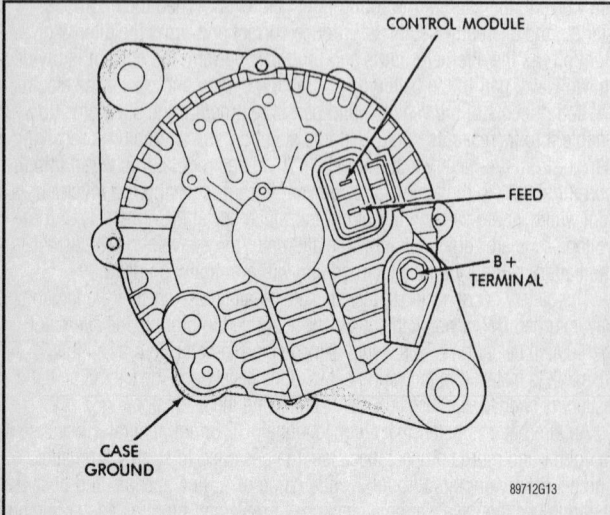

**Fig. 19 Alternator wiring connection locations—1995 vehicles**

3. Using a 0–18 volt scale voltmeter, connect the positive lead to the alternator (B+) output terminal. Connect the negative lead to the battery positive post.

4. Connect an engine tachometer, according to the manufacturers directions.

5. Make sure the parking brake is fully engaged.

6. Place the transaxle in Neutral, then start the engine. Let the engine warm up for about 2 minutes.

7. Operate the blower motor on high speed.

8. Turn the headlight high beams on.

9. Increase the engine speed to about 2,400 rpm.

10. Check the voltmeter, the reading should not be over 0.8 volts. If a higher voltage is shown, inspect, clean and tighten all connections between the alternator B+ terminal and the battery positive post.

➡A voltage drop test can be performed at each connection to find a connection with excessive voltage drop.

11. If the voltage drop tests are OK, reduce the engine speed, turn off the headlights and blower motor, then turn the ignition **OFF**.

*1996–99 VEHICLES*

▶ See Figure 19

➡These tests will show the amount of voltage drop across the alternator output wire from the alternator output (B+) terminal to the battery positive post. They will also show the amount of voltage drop from the ground (-) terminal on the alternator.

A voltmeter with a 0–18 volt DC scale should be used for these tests. By repositioning the voltmeter test leads, the point of high resistance (voltage drop) can easily be found. Test points on the alternator can be reached by either removing the air cleaner housing or below by raising the vehicle.

1. Before starting the test, make sure the battery is in good condition and is fully charged. Check the conditions of the battery cables.

2. Start the engine, let it warm up to normal operating temperatures, then turn the engine **OFF**.

3. Connect an engine tachometer, following the manufacturers directions.

4. Make sure the parking brake is fully engaged.

5. Start the engine, then place the blower on High, and turn the high beams interior lamps On.

6. Bring the engine speed up to 2,400 rpm and hold there.

7. To test the ground (-) circuitry, perform the following:

a. Touch the negative lead of the voltmeter directly to the positive battery post.

b. Touch the positive lead of the voltmeter to the B+ output terminal stud on the alternator (NOT the terminal mounting nut). The voltage should be no higher than 0.6 volts. If the voltage is higher than 0.6 volts, touch the test lead to the terminal mounting stud nut, and then to the wiring connector. If the voltage is now below 0.6 volts, look for dirty, loose or poor connections at this point. A voltage drop test may be performed at each ground (-) connection in the circuit to locate the excessive resistance.

8. To test the positive (+) circuitry, perform the following:

a. Touch the positive lead of the voltmeter directly to the negative battery post.

b. Touch the negative lead of the voltmeter to the ground terminal stud on the alternator case (NOT the terminal mounting nut). The voltage should be no higher than 0.3 volts. If the voltage is higher than 0.3 volts, touch the test lead to the terminal mounting stud nut, and then to the wiring connector. If the voltage is now below 0.3 volts, look for dirty, loose or poor connections at this point. A voltage drop test may be performed at each positive (+) connection in the circuit to locate the excessive resistance.

9. This test can also be performed between the alternator case and the engine. If the test voltage is higher than 0.3 volts, check for corrosion at the alternator mounting points or loose alternator mounting.

## Output Voltage Test

### 1995 VEHICLES

▶ See Figures 20 thru 25

➡The output voltage test determines whether or not the alternator is capable of delivering output current to satisfy the vehicle electrical load requirements.

1. Before starting the test, make sure the vehicle has a fully charged battery.

2. Connect voltmeter leads across battery terminals, as shown in the accompanying figure.

3. Record base battery voltage which is with all electrical loads and the ignition switch OFF.

4. Fully engage the parking brake, then make sure the transaxle in Park (A/T) or Neutral (M/T).

5. Using a jumper wire, attach a jumper wire from K20 terminal to ground, as shown in the accompanying figures.

6. Start the engine and allow to warm up to normal operating temperatures.

7. With the engine at operating temperatures, record the battery voltage at engine speed of 1,8 rpm with no other electrical loads. The battery voltage should not be more than 2.7 volts above the base battery voltage. If battery voltage is higher than 2.7 volts, refer to the Overcharge test.

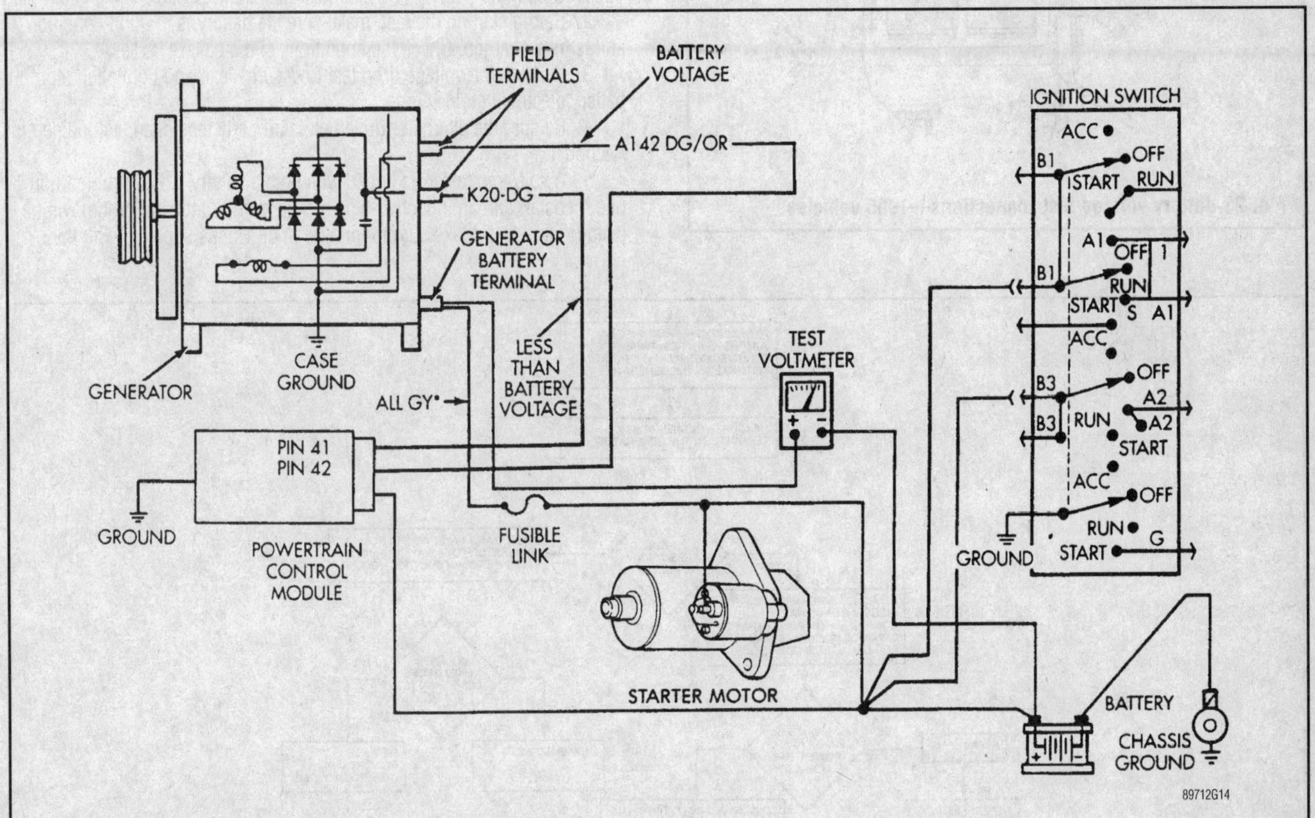

Fig. 20 Output voltage test wiring schematic—1995 vehicles

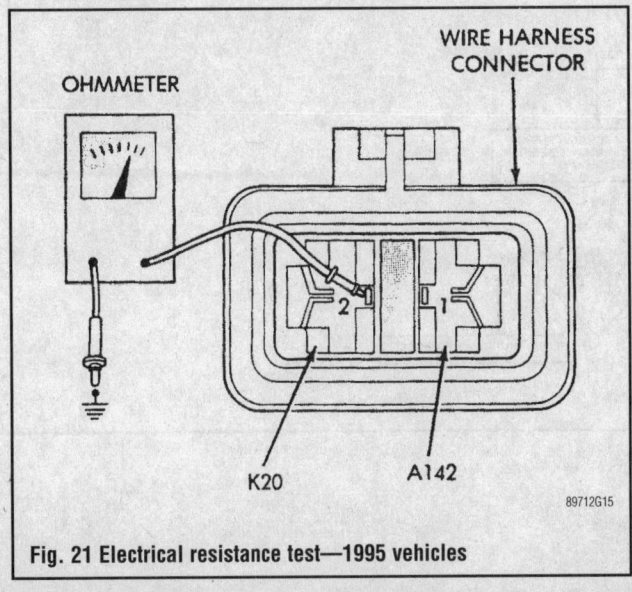

Fig. 21 Electrical resistance test—1995 vehicles

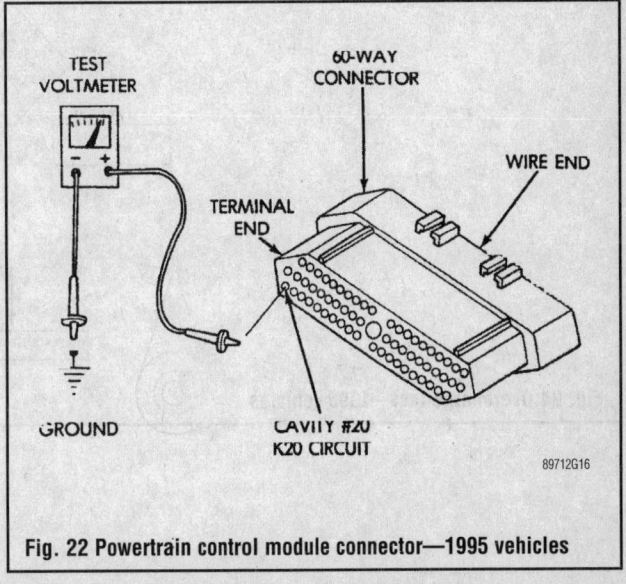

Fig. 22 Powertrain control module connector—1995 vehicles

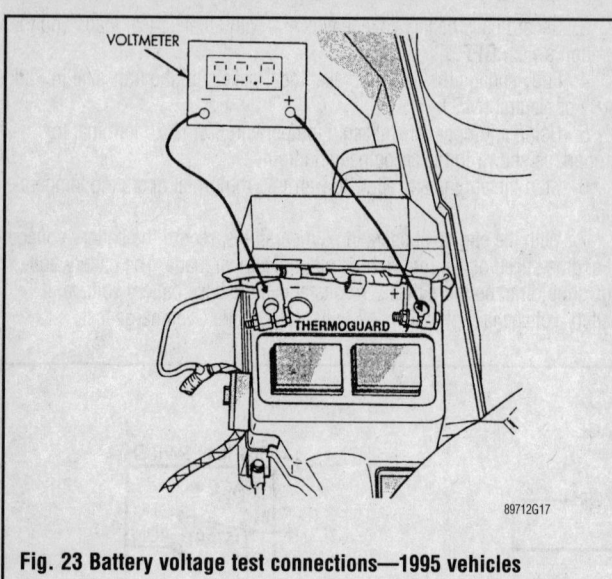

VOLTMETER

THERMOGUARD

89712G17

Fig. 23 Battery voltage test connections—1995 vehicles

8. Record the battery voltage with the engine at 2,400 rpm and the following conditions:
   • A/C blower motor on High, if equipped.
   • Heater blower motor on High.
   • Headlights on high beam.

9. The battery voltage should be a minimum of 0.4 volts above base battery voltage. If the battery voltage is below 0.4 volts, refer to the Low or No Voltage Test.

10. After the output voltage tests are finished, turn off the blower motor and headlights, then turn the ignition switch **OFF**.

### 1996–99 VEHICLES

1. Determine if any DTC's exist, as outlined in Section 4.

2. Before starting the test, make sure the battery is in good condition and is fully charged. Check the conditions of the battery cables.

3. Perform the voltage drop test to ensure clean and tight alternator/battery electrical connections.

4. Be sure the alternator drive belt is properly tensioned, as outlined in Section 1.

5. A volt/amp tester equipped with both a battery lad control (carbon pile rheostat) and an inductive-type pickup clamp (ammeter probe) will be used for this test. Make sure to follows all directions supplied with the

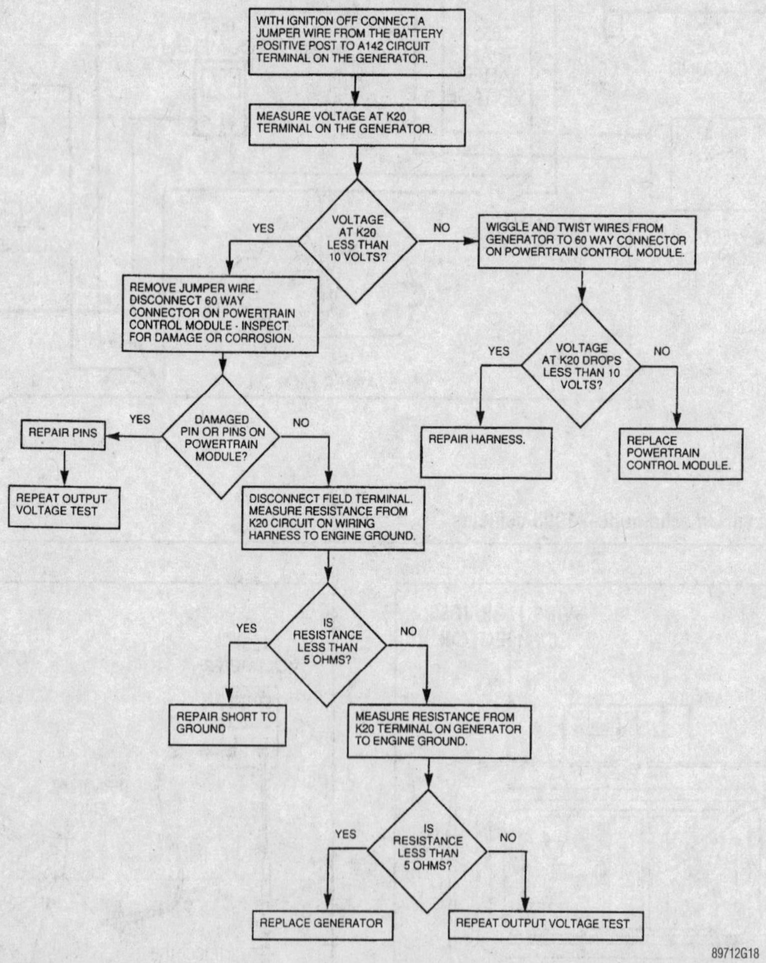

---

WITH IGNITION OFF CONNECT A JUMPER WIRE FROM THE BATTERY POSITIVE POST TO A142 CIRCUIT TERMINAL ON THE GENERATOR.

↓

MEASURE VOLTAGE AT K20 TERMINAL ON THE GENERATOR.

↓

VOLTAGE AT K20 LESS THAN 10 VOLTS?

— YES → REMOVE JUMPER WIRE. DISCONNECT 60 WAY CONNECTOR ON POWERTRAIN CONTROL MODULE - INSPECT FOR DAMAGE OR CORROSION.

— NO → WIGGLE AND TWIST WIRES FROM GENERATOR TO 60 WAY CONNECTOR ON POWERTRAIN CONTROL MODULE.

↓

VOLTAGE AT K20 DROPS LESS THAN 10 VOLTS?

— YES → REPAIR HARNESS.

— NO → REPLACE POWERTRAIN CONTROL MODULE.

DAMAGED PIN OR PINS ON POWERTRAIN MODULE?

— YES → REPAIR PINS → REPEAT OUTPUT VOLTAGE TEST

— NO → DISCONNECT FIELD TERMINAL. MEASURE RESISTANCE FROM K20 CIRCUIT ON WIRING HARNESS TO ENGINE GROUND.

↓

IS RESISTANCE LESS THAN 5 OHMS?

— YES → REPAIR SHORT TO GROUND

— NO → MEASURE RESISTANCE FROM K20 TERMINAL ON GENERATOR TO ENGINE GROUND.

↓

IS RESISTANCE LESS THAN 5 OHMS?

— YES → REPLACE GENERATOR

— NO → REPEAT OUTPUT VOLTAGE TEST

89712G18

Fig. 24 Overcharge test—1995 vehicles

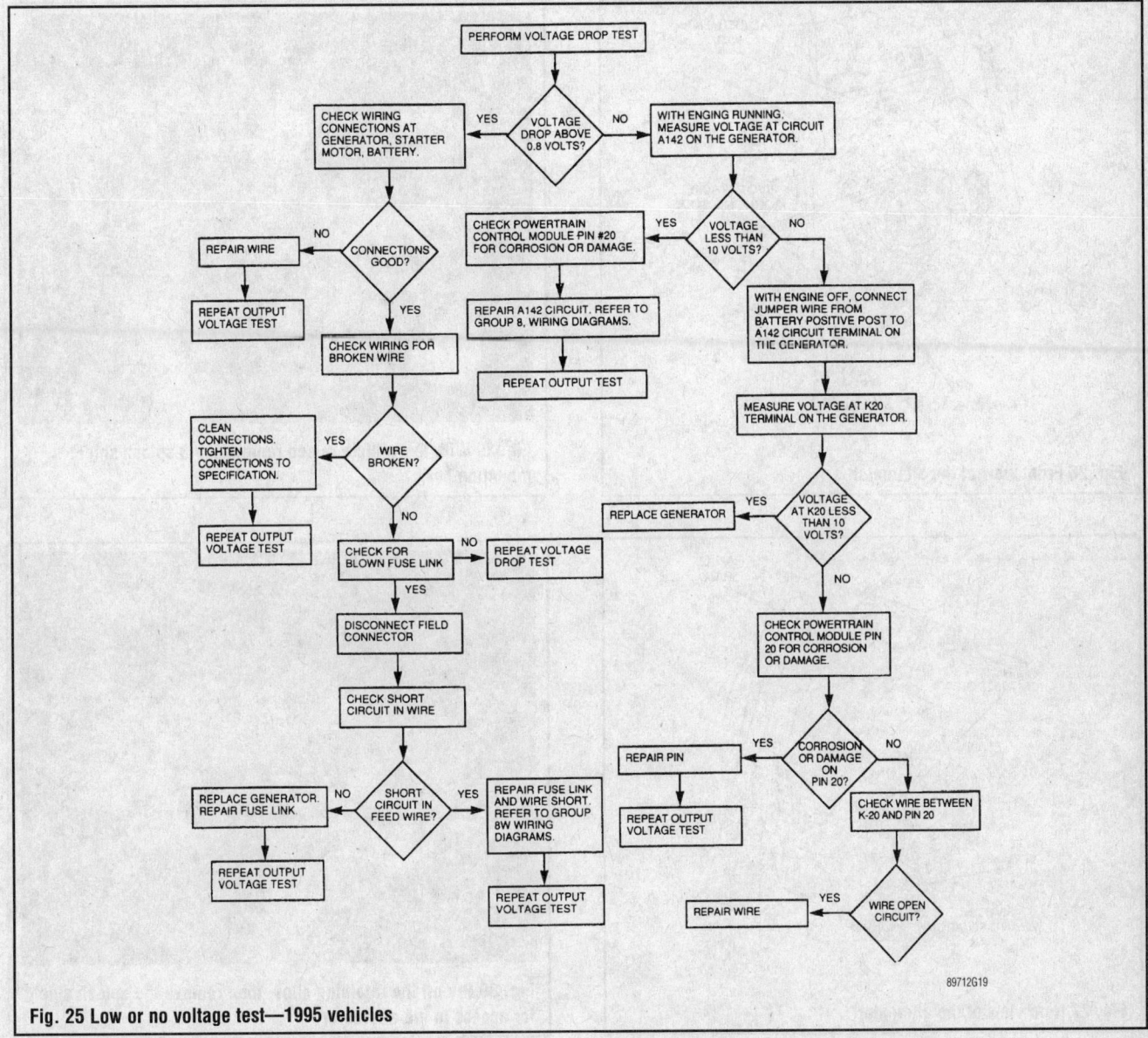

**Fig. 25 Low or no voltage test—1995 vehicles**

tester. If you are using a tester equipped with an inductive-type clamp, you don't have to remove the wiring from the alternator.

6. Start the engine and let run until it reaches normal operating temperature, then shut the engine **OFF**.

7. Make sure all electrical accessories and lights are turned off.

8. Connect the volt/amp tester leads to the battery. Be sure the carbon pile rheostat control is in the OPEN or OFF position before connection the leads.

9. Connect the inductive camp (ammeter probe), following the instructions supplied with the test equipment.

10. If a volt/amp tester is not equipped with an engine tachometer, connect a separate tachometer to the engine.

11. Fully engage the parking brake.

12. Start the engine, then bring the engine speed up to 2,500 rpm.

### ✳✳ WARNING

**This load test must be performed within 15 seconds to prevent damage to the test equipment!**

13. With the engine speed held at 2,500 rpm, slowly adjust the rheostat control (load) on the tester to get the highest amperage reading. Do not let the voltage drop below 12 volts. Record the reading. On certain brands of

test equipment, this load will be applied automatically. Make sure to read the operating manual supplied with test equipment.

14. The ammeter reading must meet the minimum test amps specification which is 75 amps.

15. Rotate the load control to the OFF position.

16. Continue holding the engine speed at 2,500 rpm. If the EVR circuitry is OK, the amperage should drop below 15–20 amps. With all of the electrical accessories and vehicle lighting off, this could take several minutes of engine operation.

17. After procedure is complete, remove the volt/amp tester.

### REMOVAL & INSTALLATION

▶ **See Figures 26 thru 38**

1. Disconnect the negative battery cable.

2. Loosen, but do not remove the alternator adjusting nut.

3. Turn the front wheels completely to the right, then raise and safely support the vehicle.

4. Unfasten the retainers, then remove the plastic lower splash shield.

5. Unfasten the alternator field circuit wiring connector. You must squeeze the locking tab to release it.

6. Remove the B+ terminal nut and wire.

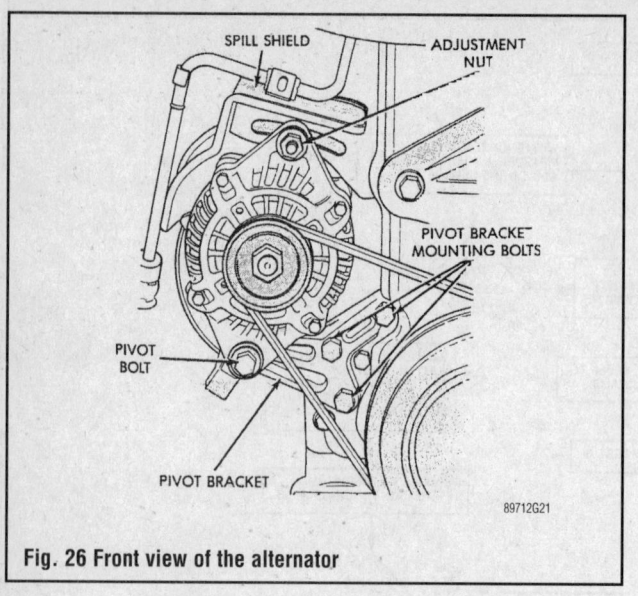

Fig. 26 Front view of the alternator

Fig. 29 With the vehicle raised remove the 3 splash shield mounting bolts

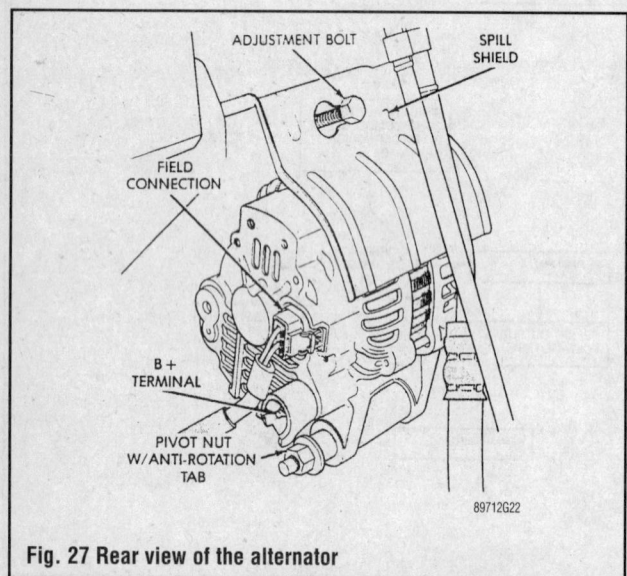

Fig. 27 Rear view of the alternator

Fig. 30 Pry off the retaining clips, then remove the splash shield for access to the alternator

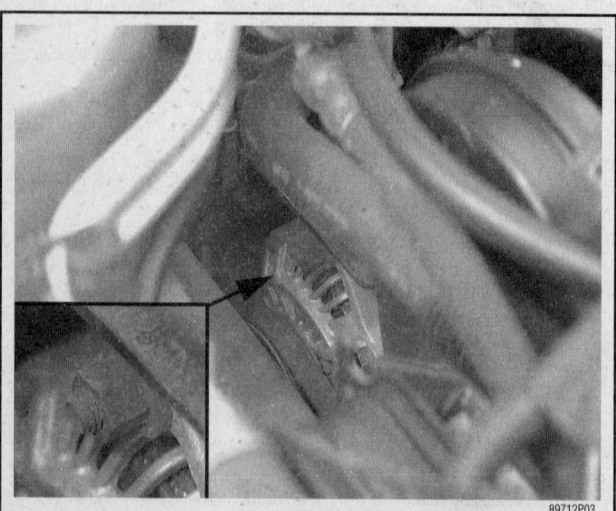

Fig. 28 Loosen the adjusting bolt, located at the top of the alternator

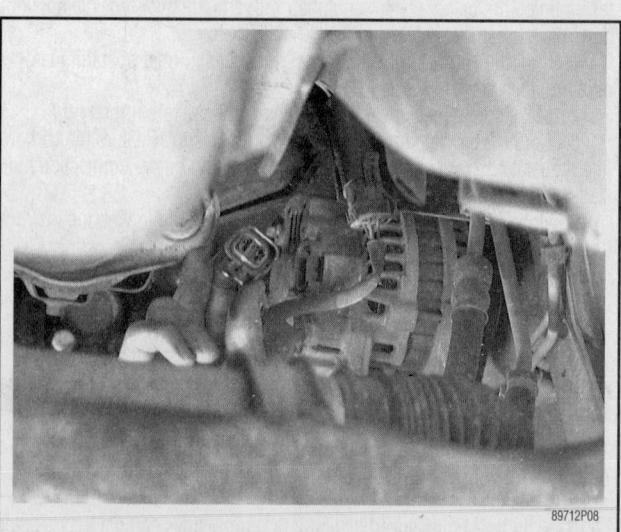

Fig. 31 Unplug the alternator electrical connector

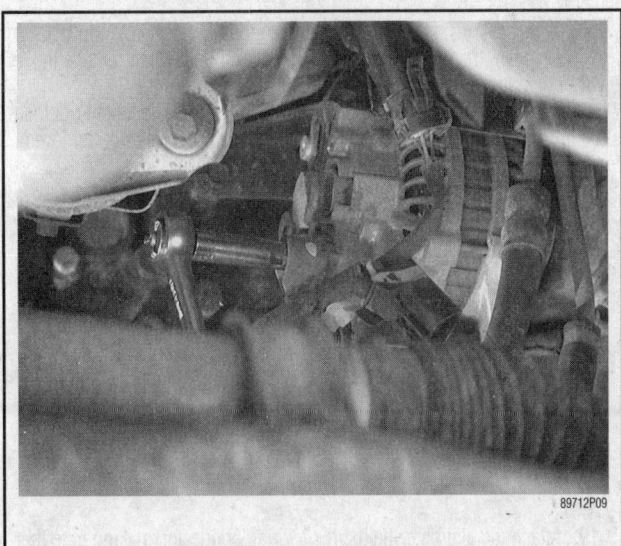

**Fig. 32 Unfasten the B+ terminal nut and wire**

**Fig. 35 Remove the bottom pivot bolt and anti-rotation tab**

**Fig. 33 Loosen, but do not remove the bottom pivot bolt . . .**

**Fig. 36 Remove the 3 pivot bracket mounting bolts . . .**

**Fig. 34 . . . then pull the belt off the pulleys and remove from the vehicle**

**Fig. 37 . . . then remove the alternator from the vehicle**

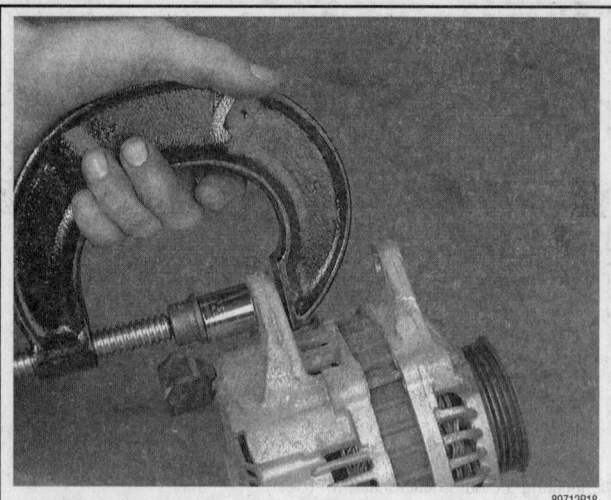

**Fig. 38 If the alternator is difficult to install, you can use a C-clamp to drive the sleeve back into the mounting ear**

7. Loosen the alternator pivot bolt, but do not remove it.

8. Remove the alternator drive belt. The alternator spill shield does not have to be removed.

9. If necessary, remove the bottom pivot bolt and anti-rotation tab.

10. Unfasten the three mounting pivot bracket bolts, then remove the pivot bolt and bracket.

11. Holding the alternator in one hand, remove the adjustment nut then slide the alternator off the T-bolt. The T-bolt does not have to be removed. Lower the alternator and remove through the wheel well.

**To install:**

12. You may need to use a C-clamp to drive the sleeve into the mounting ear for installation clearance.

13. Position the alternator in the vehicle, sliding it onto the T-bolt. Install the adjusting nut.

14. Install the bracket and pivot bolt, then install the three mounting pivot bracket bolts. Tighten the bolts to 40 ft. lbs. (54 Nm).

15. If removed, install the anti-rotation tab and bottom pivot bolt hand-tight.

16. Install the alternator drive belt.

17. Tighten the alternator pivot bolt to 40 ft. lbs. (54 Nm).

18. Install the B+ terminal wire and nut. Tighten the nut to 75 inch lbs. (9 Nm).

19. Attach the alternator field circuit wiring connector, making sure the locking tabs are engaged.

20. Install the splash shield, then carefully lower the vehicle.

21. Tighten the adjusting nut.

22. Connect the negative battery cable. Adjust the alternator belt, as outlined in Section 1 of this manual.

## STARTING SYSTEM

### General Information

The battery and starting motor are linked by very heavy electrical cables designed to minimize resistance to the flow of current. Generally, the major power supply cable that leaves the battery goes directly to the starter, while other electrical system needs are supplied by a smaller cable. During starter operation, power flows from the battery to the starter and is grounded through the vehicle's frame/body or engine and the battery's negative ground strap.

The starter is a specially designed, direct current electric motor capable of producing a great amount of power for its size. One thing that allows the motor to produce a great deal of power is its tremendous rotating speed. It drives the engine through a tiny pinion gear (attached to the starter's armature), which drives the very large flywheel ring gear at a greatly reduced speed. Another factor allowing it to produce so much power is that only intermittent operation is required of it. Thus, little allowance for air circulation is necessary, and the windings can be built into a very small space.

The starter solenoid is a magnetic device which employs the small current supplied by the start circuit of the ignition switch. This magnetic action moves a plunger which mechanically engages the starter and closes the heavy switch connecting it to the battery. The starting switch circuit usually consists of the starting switch contained within the ignition switch, a neutral safety switch or clutch pedal switch, and the wiring necessary to connect these in series with the starter solenoid or relay.

The pinion, a small gear, is mounted to a one way drive clutch. This clutch is splined to the starter armature shaft. When the ignition switch is moved to the **START** position, the solenoid plunger slides the pinion toward the flywheel ring gear via a collar and spring. If the teeth on the pinion and flywheel match properly, the pinion will engage the flywheel immediately. If the gear teeth butt one another, the spring will be compressed and will force the gears to mesh as soon as the starter turns far enough to allow them to do so. As the solenoid plunger reaches the end of its travel, it closes the contacts that connect the battery and starter, then the engine is cranked.

As soon as the engine starts, the flywheel ring gear begins turning fast enough to drive the pinion at an extremely high rate of speed. At this point, the one-way clutch begins allowing the pinion to spin faster than the starter shaft so that the starter will not operate at excessive speed. When the ignition switch is released from the starter position, the solenoid is de-energized, and a spring pulls the gear out of mesh interrupting the current flow to the starter.

Some starters employ a separate relay, mounted away from the starter, to switch the motor and solenoid current on and off. The relay replaces the solenoid electrical switch, but does not eliminate the need for a solenoid mounted on the starter used to mechanically engage the starter drive gears. The relay is used to reduce the amount of current the starting switch must carry.

### Starter

#### TESTING

**Testing Preparation**

Before commencing with the starting system diagnostics, verify:
- The battery top posts, and terminals are clean.
- The alternator drive belt tension and condition is correct.
- The battery state-of-charge is correct.
- The battery cable connections at the starter and engine block are clean and free from corrosion.
- The wiring harness connectors and terminals are clean and free from corrosion.
- Proper circuit grounding.

**Starter Feed Circuit**

▶ **See Figures 39 and 40**

### ✳✳ CAUTION

**For 1995 vehicles, the ignition system must be disabled to prevent engine start while performing the following tests. For 1996–99 vehicles, the ignition and fuel systems must be disabled to prevent engine start while performing the tests.**

1. Connect a volt-ampere tester to the battery terminals. You can use a multimeter if it has an inductive clamp for reading high amperage.

2. For 1995 vehicles, disable the ignition system by unplugging the ignition coil electrical connector.

3. For 1996–99 vehicles, disable the ignition and fuel systems by dis-

connecting the Automatic Shutdown (ASD) relay, located in the Power Distribution Center (PDC) in the engine compartment.

4. Verify that all lights and accessories are Off, and the transaxle shift selector is in Park (automatic) or Neutral (manual). Set the parking brake.

5. Rotate and hold the ignition switch in the **START** position. Observe the volt-ampere tester:
- If the voltage reads above 9.6 volts, and the amperage draw reads above 250 amps, go to the starter feed circuit resistance test (following this test).
- If the voltage reads 12.4 volts or greater and the amperage reads 0–10 amps, refer to the starter control circuit test.
- If the voltage reads below 9.6 volts and the amperage draw reads above 300 amps, the trouble is within the starter.

### ✷✷ WARNING

**Do not overheat the starter motor or draw the battery voltage below 9.6 volts during cranking operations.**

6. After the starting system problems have been corrected, verify the battery state of charge and charge the battery if necessary. Disconnect all of the testing equipment and connect the ignition coil cable or ignition coil connector. Start the vehicle several times to assure the problem was corrected.

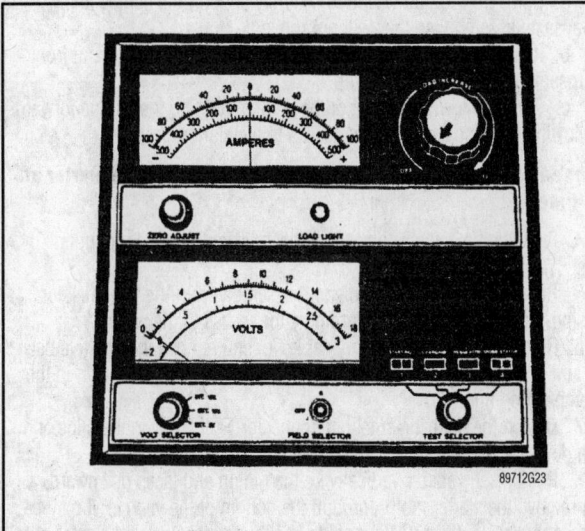

Fig. 39 This test requires the use of a volt ampere tester

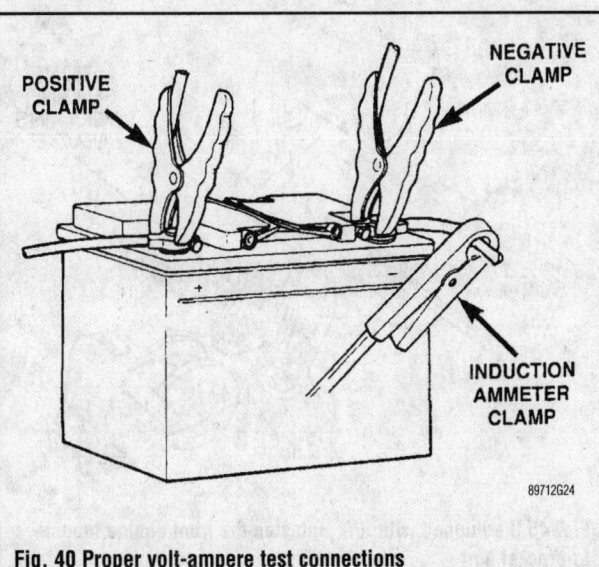

Fig. 40 Proper volt-ampere test connections

### Starter Feed Circuit Resistance

▶ See Figures 41, 42, 43 and 44

Before proceeding with this test, refer to the battery tests and starter feed circuit test. The following test will require a voltmeter, which is capable of accuracy to 0.1 volt.

### ✷✷ CAUTION

**For 1995 vehicles, the ignition system must be disabled to prevent engine start while performing the following tests. For 1996–99 vehicles, the ignition and fuel systems must be disabled to prevent engine start while performing the tests.**

1. For 1995 vehicles, disable the ignition system by unplugging the ignition coil electrical connector.

2. For 1996–99 vehicles, disable the ignition and fuel systems by disconnecting the Automatic Shutdown (ASD) relay, located in the Power Distribution Center (PDC) in the engine compartment.

3. With all wiring harnesses and components (except for the coils) properly connected, perform the following:

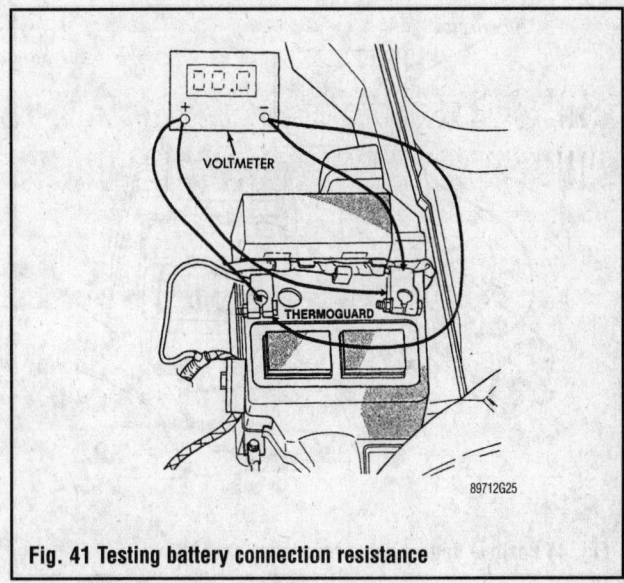

Fig. 41 Testing battery connection resistance

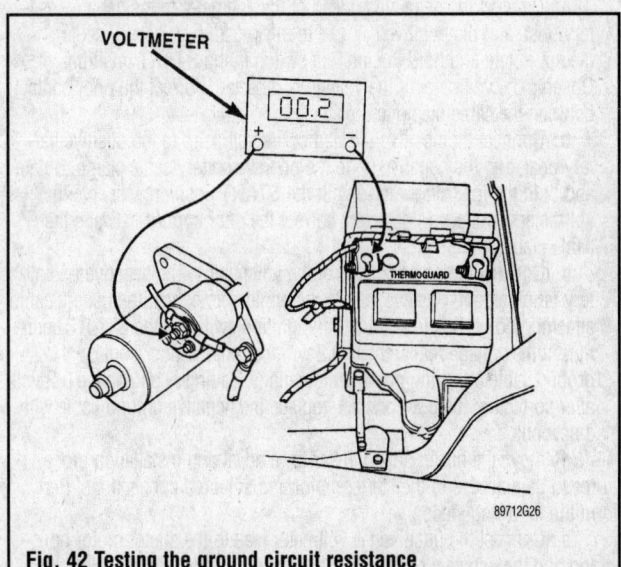

Fig. 42 Testing the ground circuit resistance

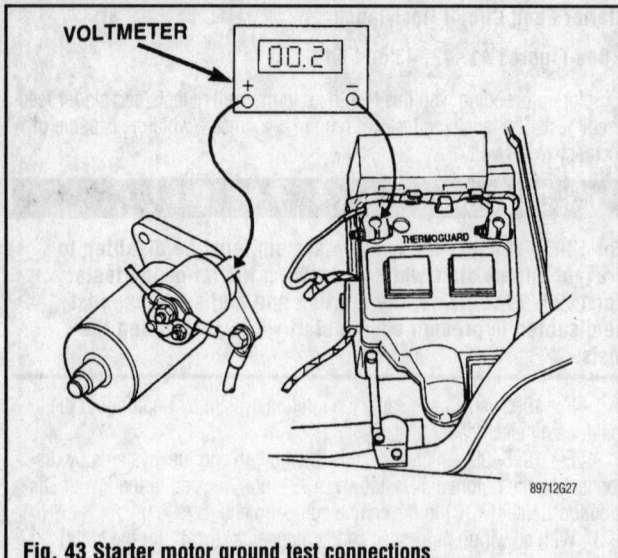

**Fig. 43 Starter motor ground test connections**

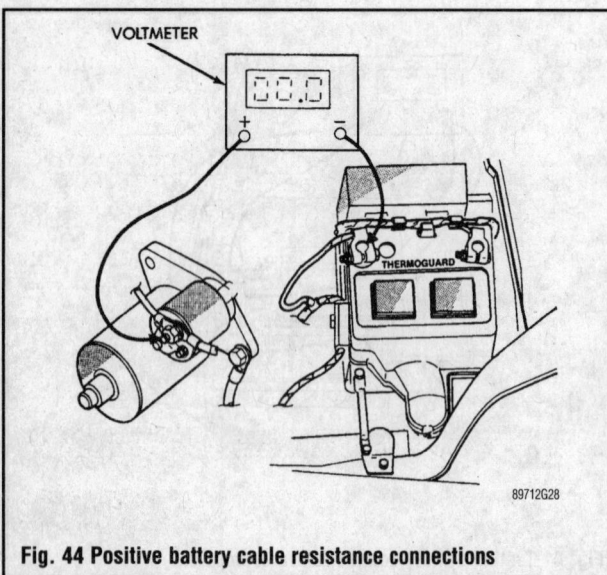

**Fig. 44 Positive battery cable resistance connections**

a. Connect the negative (-) lead of the voltmeter to the negative battery post, and the positive (+) lead to the negative (-) battery cable clamp. Rotate and hold the ignition switch in the **START** position. Observe the voltmeter. If the voltage is detected, correct the poor contact between the cable clamp and post.

b. Connect the positive (+) lead of the voltmeter to the positive battery post, and the negative (-) to the positive battery cable clamp. Rotate and hold the ignition switch key in the **START** position. Observe the voltmeter. If voltage is detected, correct the poor contact between the cable clamp and post.

c. Connect the negative lead of the voltmeter to the negative (-) battery terminal, and positive lead to the engine block near the battery cable attaching point. Rotate and hold the ignition switch in the **START** position. If the voltage reads above 0.2 volt, correct the poor contact at ground cable attaching point. If the voltage reading is still above 0.2 volt after correcting the poor contact, replace the negative ground cable with a new one.

4. Remove the heater shield. Refer to removal and installation procedures to gain access to the starter motor and solenoid connections. Perform the following steps:

a. Connect the positive (+) voltmeter lead to the starter motor housing and the negative (-) lead to the negative battery terminal. Hold the ignition switch key in the **START** position. If the voltage reads above 0.2 volt, correct the poor starter to engine ground.

b. Connect the positive (+) voltmeter lead to the positive battery terminal, and the negative lead to the battery cable terminal on the starter solenoid. Rotate and hold the ignition key in the **START** position. If the voltage reads above 0.2 volt, correct poor contact at the battery cable to the solenoid connection. If the reading is still above 0.2 volt after correcting the poor contacts, replace the positive battery cable with a new one.

c. If the resistance tests did not detect feed circuit failures, refer to the starter solenoid test.

## REMOVAL & INSTALLATION

▶ See Figures 45, 46 and 47

➡ **This starter motor removal procedure is time consuming. An alternate method of removing the starter would be to remove the engine fan(s) and radiator, then remove the starter motor from the top of the engine. If you chose to go this route, radiator and fan removal can be found in Section 3 of this manual.**

1. Disconnect the negative battery cable.
2. Raise and safely support the vehicle.
3. If equipped with A/C, perform the following:

a. Use a floor or jack stand to securely support the engine and transaxle assembly so they will not rotate.

b. Remove the front engine mount bolt from the insulator and front crossmember mounting bracket.

c. Carefully lower the front of the engine, rotating the engine forward allowing more space for easier access to the starter.

➡ **For easier removal, do not remove the wiring from the starter at this time.**

4. Remove the 2 starter motor-to-transmission housing mounting bolts.

5. Remove the starter and solenoid assembly from the transmission housing. Position the starter accordingly for access to the wiring.

6. Remove the positive battery cable nut and remove the positive battery and alternator output wire from the starter. The wiring is shown in the accompanying figure.

7. Detach the push-on solenoid connector. Pull back on the slide and push down on the rear tab to release the lock.

8. Position the starter vertically so the pinion end faces downward, then remove the starter motor through the bottom of the vehicle. It may be necessary to move the A/C lines aside slightly to maneuver the starter out of the vehicle.

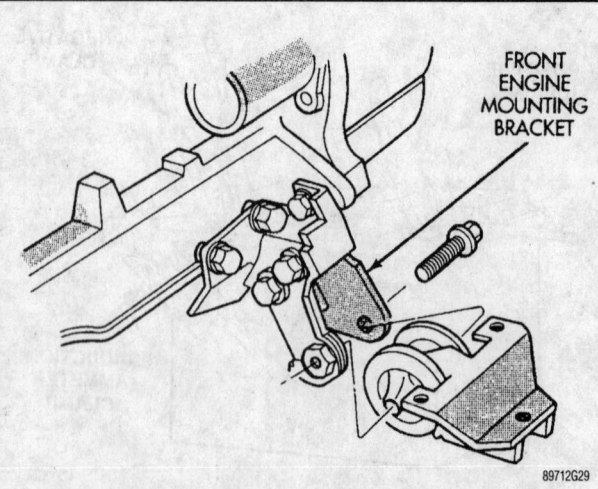

**Fig. 45 If equipped with A/C, unfasten the front engine mount-to-bracket bolt**

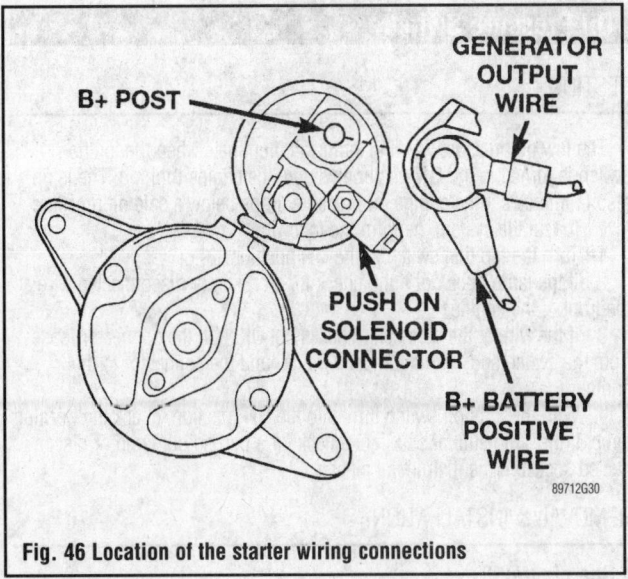

**Fig. 46 Location of the starter wiring connections**

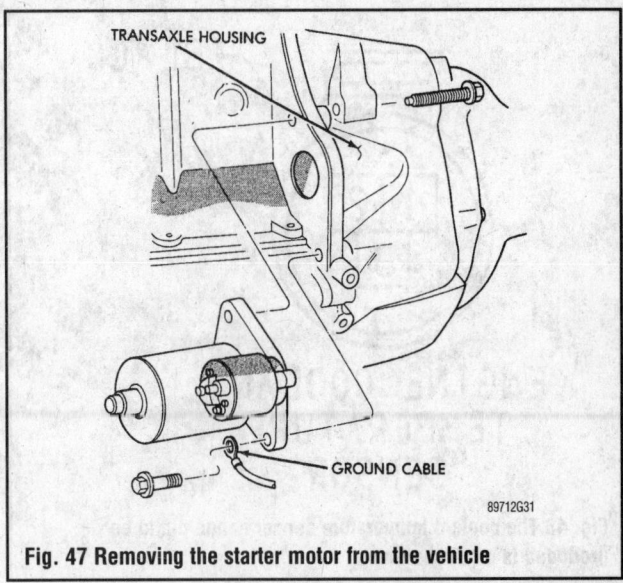

**Fig. 47 Removing the starter motor from the vehicle**

**To install:**

➡ **Clean the corrosion and dirt from the cable and wire terminals before fastening the wiring to the solenoid.**

9. Connect the positive battery and alternator output wire to the starter solenoid post.

### ⁂ WARNING

**It is imperative that the alternator output terminal be connected to the positive battery terminal of the starter solenoid for proper starting and charging system operation.**

10. Connect the push-on wiring until it is fully engaged.
11. Position the starter face into the transmission housing. Support the starter in the pilot and start the top bolt.

## SENDING UNITS AND SENSORS

➡ **This section describes the operating principles of sending units, warning lights and gauges. Sensors which provide information to the Electronic Control Module (ECM) are covered in Section 4 of this manual.**

Instrument panels contain a number of indicating devices (gauges and warning lights). These devices are composed of two separate components. One is the sending unit, mounted on the engine or other remote part of the vehicle, and the other is the actual gauge or light in the instrument panel.

Several types of sending units exist, however most can be characterized as being either a pressure type or a resistance type. Pressure type sending units convert liquid pressure into an electrical signal which is sent to the gauge. Resistance type sending units are most often used to measure temperature and use variable resistance to control the current flow back to the indicating device. Both types of sending units are connected in series by a wire to the battery (through the ignition switch). When the ignition is turned **ON**, current flows from the battery through the indicating device and on to the sending unit.

12. Attach the ground cable to the lower mounting bolt and start the bolt.
13. Make sure the starter is aligned properly before tightening the mounting bolts to 40 ft. lbs. (54 Nm).
14. If equipped with A/C, perform the following:
   a. Using a floor jack to carefully raise the engine and transaxle assembly to its original position.
   b. Install the front engine mount bolt through the insulator and front crossmember mounting bracket. Tighten the bolt to 40 ft. lbs. (54 Nm).
15. Carefully lower the vehicle, then connect the negative battery cable.

### RELAY REPLACEMENT

The relay is located in the Power Distribution Center (PDC) in the engine compartment. Refer to the underside of the PDC cover for starter relay location. Simply unplug the relay to replace it.

## Coolant Temperature Sensor

### TESTING

▶ **See Figure 48**

1. Detach the coolant temperature sensor electrical connector.
2. Turn the ignition switch to the **ON** position. The temperature gauge should be at its lowest position.
3. Ground the temperature gauge sending unit connector pin 3, as shown in the accompanying figure. Turn the ignition switch **ON**. The temperature gauge should be at its highest position. After the seat belt lamp goes out, the cluster should chime for about 8 seconds.
   a. If OK, check the temperature sending unit connector for proper connection. If connections are OK, replace the sending unit.
   b. If not OK, and the high temperature chime should but the gauge shows cold, replace the gauge assembly. If the gauge still does not work, replace the printed circuit board.

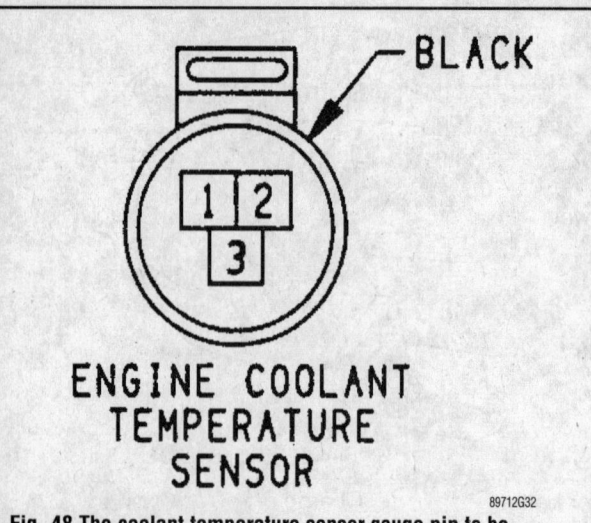

Fig. 48 The coolant temperature sensor gauge pin to be grounded is on the bottom

## REMOVAL & INSTALLATION

▶ **See Figure 49**

1. Disconnect the negative battery cable.
2. Unplug the sensor electrical connector.
3. Remove the sensor from the vehicle.
**To install:**
4. Install the sensor in the vehicle and tighten securely.
5. Attach the electrical connector to the sensor.
6. Connect the negative battery cable.

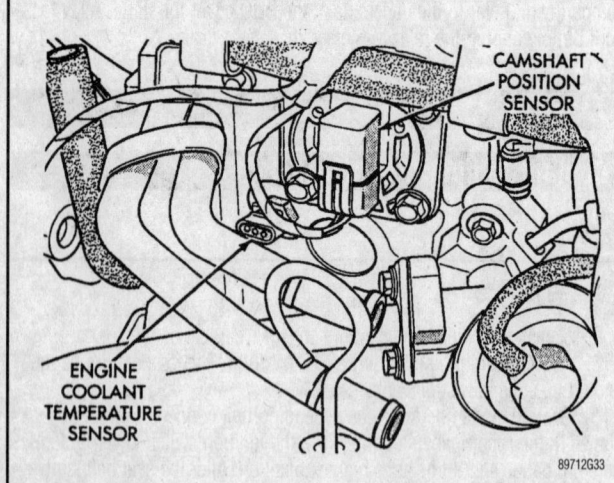

Fig. 49 The coolant temperature sensor (which controls the gauge) is located near the camshaft position sensor

## Oil Pressure Switch

### TESTING

The low oil pressure warning lamp will illuminate when the ignition switch is turned to the **ON** position without the engine running. The lamp also illuminates if the engine oil pressure drops below a safe oil pressure level. To test the system, perform the following:

1. Turn the ignition switch to the **ON** position.
2. If the lamp does not light, check for a broken or disconnected wire at the front of the engine.
3. If the wire at the connector checks out OK, pull the connector loose from the switch and, with a jumper wire, ground the connector to the engine.
4. With the ignition switch turned to the **ON** position, check the warning lamp. If the lamp still fails to light, check for a burned out lamp or disconnected socket in the instrument cluster.

### REMOVAL & INSTALLATION

▶ **See Figure 50**

1. Disconnect the negative battery cable.
2. Unplug the switch electrical connector.
3. Remove the switch from the vehicle.
**To install:**
4. Install the switch in the vehicle and tighten securely.
5. Attach the electrical connector to the switch.
6. Connect the negative battery cable.

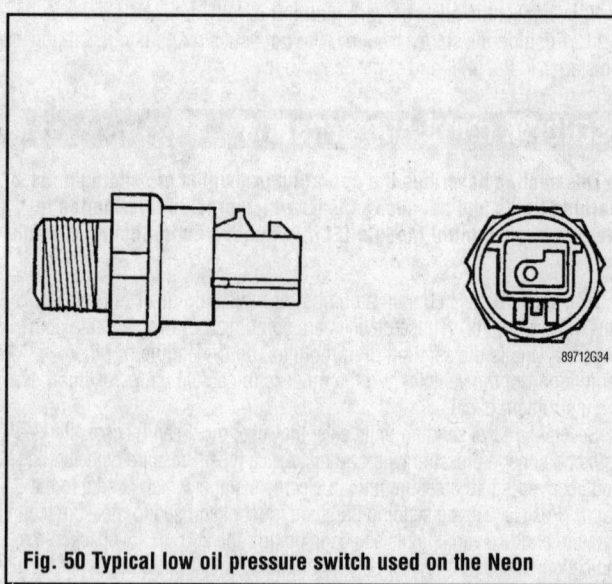

Fig. 50 Typical low oil pressure switch used on the Neon

## Troubleshooting Basic Starting System Problems

| Problem | Cause | Solution |
|---|---|---|
| Starter motor rotates engine slowly | • Battery charge low or battery defective | • Charge or replace battery |
| | • Defective circuit between battery and starter motor | • Clean and tighten, or replace cables |
| | • Low load current | • Bench-test starter motor. Inspect for worn brushes and weak brush springs. |
| | • High load current | • Bench-test starter motor. Check engine for friction, drag or coolant in cylinders. Check ring gear-to-pinion gear clearance. |
| Starter motor will not rotate engine | • Battery charge low or battery defective | • Charge or replace battery |
| | • Faulty solenoid | • Check solenoid ground. Repair or replace as necessary. |
| | • Damaged drive pinion gear or ring gear | • Replace damaged gear(s) |
| | • Starter motor engagement weak | • Bench-test starter motor |
| | • Starter motor rotates slowly with high load current | • Inspect drive yoke pull-down and point gap, check for worn end bushings, check ring gear clearance |
| | • Engine seized | • Repair engine |
| Starter motor drive will not engage (solenoid known to be good) | • Defective contact point assembly | • Repair or replace contact point assembly |
| | • Inadequate contact point assembly ground | • Repair connection at ground screw |
| | • Defective hold-in coil | • Replace field winding assembly |
| Starter motor drive will not disengage | • Starter motor loose on flywheel housing | • Tighten mounting bolts |
| | • Worn drive end busing | • Replace bushing |
| | • Damaged ring gear teeth | • Replace ring gear or driveplate |
| | • Drive yoke return spring broken or missing | • Replace spring |
| Starter motor drive disengages prematurely | • Weak drive assembly thrust spring | • Replace drive mechanism |
| | • Hold-in coil defective | • Replace field winding assembly |
| Low load current | • Worn brushes | • Replace brushes |
| | • Weak brush springs | • Replace springs |

TCCS2C01

## Troubleshooting Basic Charging System Problems

| Problem | Cause | Solution |
|---|---|---|
| Noisy alternator | • Loose mountings<br>• Loose drive pulley<br>• Worn bearings<br>• Brush noise<br>• Internal circuits shorted (High pitched whine) | • Tighten mounting bolts<br>• Tighten pulley<br>• Replace alternator<br>• Replace alternator<br>• Replace alternator |
| Squeal when starting engine or accelerating | • Glazed or loose belt | • Replace or adjust belt |
| Indicator light remains on or ammeter indicates discharge (engine running) | • Broken belt<br>• Broken or disconnected wires<br>• Internal alternator problems<br>• Defective voltage regulator | • Install belt<br>• Repair or connect wiring<br>• Replace alternator<br>• Replace voltage regulator/alternator |
| Car light bulbs continually burn out— battery needs water continually | • Alternator/regulator overcharging | • Replace voltage regulator/alternator |
| Car lights flare on acceleration | • Battery low<br>• Internal alternator/regulator problems | • Charge or replace battery<br>• Replace alternator/regulator |
| Low voltage output (alternator light flickers continually or ammeter needle wanders) | • Loose or worn belt<br>• Dirty or corroded connections<br>• Internal alternator/regulator problems | • Replace or adjust belt<br>• Clean or replace connections<br>• Replace alternator/regulator |

TCCS2C02

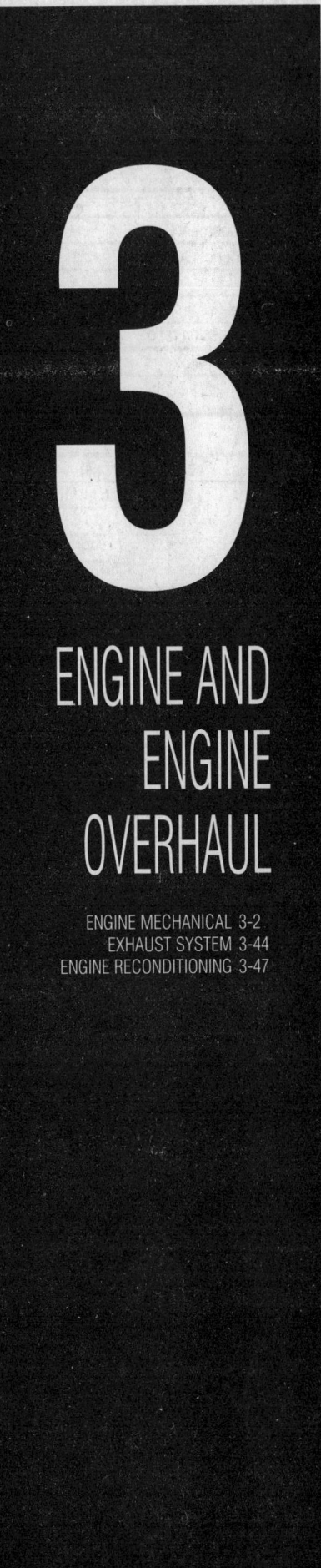

# 3

# ENGINE AND ENGINE OVERHAUL

**ENGINE MECHANICAL**

### 2.0 L (VIN C) ENGINE SPECIFICATIONS

| Description | English | Metric |
|---|---|---|
| Type | Inline Single Overhead Cam (SOHC) | |
| Displacement | 121.8 in. | 2.0 (1,996cc) |
| Number of Cylinders | 4 | |
| Bore | 3.445 in. | 87.5mm |
| Stroke | 3.267 in. | 83.0mm |
| Compression ratio | 9.8:1 | |
| Cylinder Block | | |
|     Diameter | 3.4446-3.4452 in. | 87.4924-87.5076mm |
|     Out-of-round (max.) | 0.002 in. | 0.051mm |
|     Taper (max.) | 0.002 in. | 0.051mm |
| Pistons (Federal Emissions) | | |
|     Clearance at 11/16 in. (17.5mm) from bottom of skirt | 0.0002-0.0015 in. | 0.006-0.038mm |
|     Weight | | |
|         1995-96 vehicles | 11.75-12.10 oz. | 333-343 grams |
|         1997-99 vehicles | 11.47-11.82 oz. | 325-335 grams |
|     Land clearance (diametrical) | | |
|         1995-96 vehicles | 0.029-0.031 in. | 0.734-0.797 |
|         1997-99 vehicles | 0.029-0.031 in. | 0.734-0.797mm |
|     Piston length | 2.520 in. | 64mm |
|     Piston ring groove depth | | |
|         No. 1 | 0.1057-0.165 in. | 3.989-4.188mm |
|         No. 2 | 0.176-0.184 in. | 4.462-4.661mm |
|         No. 3 | 0.151-0.163 in. | 3.847-4.131mm |
| Pistons (Low Emission Vehicle - LEV) | | |
|     Clearance at 0.42 in. (10.42mm) from bottom of skirt | 0.0008-0.0020 in. | 0.018-0.50mm |
|     Weight | 11.29-11.60 oz. | 320-329 grams |
|     Land clearance (diametrical) | 0.0299-0.0312 in. | 0.758-0.790mm |
|     Piston length | 2.197 in. | 55.8mm |
|     Piston ring groove depth | | |
|         No. 1 | 0.157-0.165 in. | 3.989-4.188mm |
|         No. 2 | 0.176-0.184 in. | 4.462-4.661mm |
|         No. 3 | 0.151-0.163 in. | 3.847-4.131mm |
| Piston pins | | |
|     Clearance in piston | | |
|         1995-96 vehicles | 0.0002-0.0007 in. | 0.005-0.018mm |
|         1997-99 vehicles | | |
|     In rod (interference) | 0.0007-0.0017 in. | 0.018-0.043mm |
|     Diameter | 0.8267-0.8269 in. | 20.998-21.003mm |
|     End play | None | |
|     Length | 2.943-2.963 in. | 74.75-75.25mm |
| Piston rings | | |
|     Ring gap | | |
|         Top compression ring | 0.009-0.020 in. | 0.23-0.52mm |
|         2nd compression ring | 0.019-0.031 in. | 0.49-0.78mm |
|         Oil control (steel rails) | 0.009-0.026 in. | 0.23-0.66mm |
|     Ring side clearance | | |
|         Top and 2nd compression rings | 0.0010-0.0026 in. | 0.025-0.065mm |
|         Oil ring (pack) | 0.002-0.0070 in. | 0.004-0.178mm |
|     Ring width | | |
|         Compression rings | 0.046-0.047 in. | 1.17-1.19mm |
|         Oil ring (pack) | 0.1124-0.1184 in. | 2.854-3.008mm |

## 2.0 L (VIN C) ENGINE SPECIFICATIONS

| Description | English | Metric |
|---|---|---|
| **Connecting Rods** | | |
| Bearing clearance | 0.001-0.023 in. | 0.026-0.059mm |
| Piston pin bore clearance | 0.8252-0.8260 in. | 20.96-20.98mm |
| Large end bore diameter | 2.0075-2.0081 in. | 50.991-51.005mm |
| Side clearance | 0.005-0.015 in. | 0.13-0.38mm |
| Total weight (less bearing) | 1.20 lbs. | 543 grams |
| **Crankshaft** | | |
| Connecting rod journal diameter | 1.8894-1.8900 in. | 47.9924-48.0076mm |
| Out-of-round (max.) | 0.0001 in. | 0.0035mm |
| Taper (max.) | 0.0001 in. | 0.0035mm |
| Main bearing diametrical clearance | | |
| No. 1-5 | 0.0008-0.0024 in. | 0.022-0.062mm |
| End play | 0.0035-0.0094 in. | 0.09-0.24mm |
| **Main Bearing Journals** | | |
| Diameter | 2.0469-2.0475 in. | 51.9924-52.0076mm |
| Out-of-round (max.) | 0.0001 in. | 0.0035mm |
| Taper (max.) | 0.0001 in. | 0.0038mm |
| **Rocker Arms** | | |
| Rocker arm shaft diameter | 0.7860-0.7867 in. | 19.996-19.984mm |
| Rocker arm shaft retainers (width) | | |
| Intake (all) | 1.12 in. | 28.46mm |
| Exhaust | | |
| 1 & 5 | 1.14 in. | 29.20mm |
| 2, 3 & 4 | 1.59 in. | 40.45mm |
| Rocker arm/hydraulic lash adjuster | | |
| Rocker arm inside diameter | 0.787-0.788 in. | 20.00-20.02mm |
| Rocker arm shaft clearance | 0.0006-0.0021 in. | 0.016-0.054mm |
| Body diameter | 0.9035-0.9040 in. | 22.949-22.962mm |
| Plunger travel minimum (dry) | 0.087 in. | 2.2mm |
| Rocker arm ratio | 1.4:1 | |
| **Camshaft** | | |
| No. 1 | 1.622-1.6228 in. | 41.20-41.221mm |
| No. 2 | 1.637-1.638 in. | 41.6-41.621mm |
| No. 3 | 1.653-1.654 in. | 42.0-42.021mm |
| No. 4 | 1.669-1.670 in. | 42.4-42.421mm |
| No. 5 | 1.685-1.6858 in. | 42.8-42.821mm |
| **Bearing Journal Diameter** | | |
| No. 1 | 1.619-1.6199 in. | 41.128-41.147mm |
| No. 2 | 1.634-1.635 in. | 41.528-41.547mm |
| No. 3 | 1.650-1.651 in. | 41.928-41.947mm |
| No. 4 | 1.666-1.688 in. | 42.328-42.374mm |
| No. 5 | 1.682-1.6829 in. | 42.728-42.747mm |
| Diametrical bearing clearance | 0.0027-0.0030 in. | 0.053-0.093mm |
| Max. allowable | 0.0047 in. | 0.12mm |
| End play | 0.0059 in. | 0.05-0.39mm |
| **Valves and valve springs** | | |
| Lift (zero lash) | | |
| Intake | | |
| 1995-96 vehicles | 0.307 in. | 7.8mm |
| 1997-99 vehicles | 0.283 in. | 7.2mm |
| Exhaust | 0.277 in. | 7.03mm |

89713C03

## 2.0 L (VIN C) ENGINE SPECIFICATIONS

| Description | English | Metric |
|---|:---:|:---:|
| Valve timing exhaust valve | | |
|    Closes (ATDC) | 5.4° | |
|    Opens (BBDC) | 43.7° | |
|    Duration | 229.1° | |
| Valve timing intake valve | | |
|    Closes (ATDC) | | |
|       1995 vehicles | 41.7° | |
|       1996-99 vehicles | 41.1° | |
|    Opens (BBDC) | | |
|       1995 vehicles | 4.9° | |
|       1996-99 vehicles | 13.9° | |
|    Duration | | |
|       1995 vehicles | 216.8° | |
|       1996-99 vehicles | 207.2° | |
|    Valve overlap | | |
|       1995 vehicles | 0.5° | |
|       1996-99 vehicles | 0° | |
| Valve seat | | |
|    Angle | 45° | |
|    Runout (max.) | 0.002 in. | 0.050mm |
|    Width (finish) | | |
|       Intake and exhaust | | |
|          1995-97 vehicles | 0.035-0.051 in. | 0.9-1.3mm |
|          1998-99 vehicles | 0.030-0.049 in. | 0.75-1.25mm |
| Valve guide finished | | |
|    Diameter I.D. | 0.235-0.236 in. | 5.975-6.000mm |
|    Guide bore diameter (std.) | 0.4330-0.4338 in. | 11.0-11.02mm |
| Valves | 1.89 in. | 48mm |
|    Face angle (intake and exhaust) | 45-45.5° | |
|    Head diameter | | |
|       Intake | 1.303-1.313 in. | 32.12-33.37mm |
|       Exhaust | 1.124-1.135 in. | 28.57-28.83mm |
| Valve margin | | |
|    Intake | 0.0452-0.0582 in. | 1.15-1.48mm |
|    Exhaust | 0.058-0.071 in. | 1.475-1.805mm |
| Valve length (overall) | | |
|    Intake | 4.515-4.535 in. | 114.69-115.19mm |
|    Exhaust | 4.603-4.623 in. | 109.59-110.09mm |
| Valve stem tip height | | |
|    Intake | | |
|       1995-96 vehicles | 1.891 in. | 48.04mm |
|       1997-99 vehicles | 1.77-1.81 in. | 45.01-46.07mm |
|    Exhaust | | |
|       1995-96 vehicles | 1.889 in. | 47.99mm |
|       1997-99 vehicles | 1.71-1.75 in. | 43.51-44.57mm |
| Stem diameter | | |
|    Intake | 0.234-0.234 in. | 5.934-5.952mm |
|    Exhaust | 0.233-0.233 in. | 5.906-5.924mm |
| Stem-to-guide clearance | | |
|    Intake | 0.0018-0.0025 in. | 0.048-0.066mm |
|    Exhaust | 0.0029-0.0037 in. | 0.0736-0.094mm |
|    Max. allowable intake | 0.003 in. | 0.076mm |
|    Max. allowable exhaust | 0.004 in. | 0.101mm |

## 2.0 L (VIN C) ENGINE SPECIFICATIONS

| Description | English | Metric |
|---|---|---|
| Valve springs | | |
| Free length (approx.) | 1.747 in. | 44.4mm |
| Installed height | 1.580 in. | 40.18mm |
| Spring tension (valve closed) | | |
| 1995-96 vehicles | 75 lbs. @ 1.54 in. | 333 N @ 39.2mm |
| Spring tension (valve open) | | |
| 1995-96 vehicles | 176 lbs. @ 1.24 in. | 482 N @ 31.4mm |
| Nominal force (valve closed) | | |
| 1997-99 vehicles | 67 lbs. @ 1.57 in. | 91 lbs. @ 39.8mm |
| Nominal force (valve open) | | |
| 1997 vehicles | 160 lbs. @ 1.26 in. | 160 lbs. @ 32.6mm |
| 1998-99 vehicles | 176 lbs. @ 1.28 in. | 239 Nm @ 32.6mm |

89713C05

## 2.0 L (VIN Y) ENGINE SPECIFICATIONS

| Description | English | Metric |
|---|---|---|
| Type | Inline Dual Overhead Cam (DOHC) | |
| Displacement | 121.8 in. | 2.0 (1,996cc) |
| Number of Cylinders | 4 | |
| Bore | 3.445 in. | 87.5mm |
| Stroke | 3.267 in. | 83.0mm |
| Compression ratio | 9.6:1 | |
| **Cylinder Block** | | |
| Bore diameter | 3.4446-3.4452 in. | 87.4924-87.5076mm |
| Out-of-round (max.) | 0.002 in. | 0.051mm |
| Taper (max.) | 0.002 in. | 0.051mm |
| **Pistons** | | |
| Clearance at 11/16 in. (17.5mm) from bottom of skirt | | |
| 1995-96 vehicles | 0.0005-0.0017 in. | 0.012-0.044mm |
| 1997-99 vehicles | 0.0007-0.0020 in. | 0.018-0.050mm |
| Weight | | |
| 1995-96 vehicles | 11.85-12.20 oz. | 336-346 grams |
| 1997-99 vehicles | 11.99-12.34 oz. | 340-350 grams |
| Land clearance (diametrical) | 0.029-0.031 in. | 0.740-0.803mm |
| Piston length | 2.551 in. | 64.8mm |
| Piston ring groove depth | | |
| No. 1 | 0.157-0.163 in. | 3.983-4.132mm |
| No. 2 | 0.175-0.181 in. | 4.456-4.605mm |
| No. 3 | 0.151-0.160 in. | 3.841-4.075mm |
| **Piston pins** | | |
| Clearance in piston | 0.0003-0.0008 in. | 0.008-0.020mm |
| In rod (interference) | 0.0007-0.0017 in. | 0.018-0.043mm |
| Diameter | 0.8267-0.8269 in. | 20.998-21.003mm |
| End play | None | |
| Length | 2.943-2.963 in. | 74.75-75.25mm |
| **Piston rings** | | |
| Ring gap | | |
| Top compression ring | 0.009-0.020 in. | 0.23-0.52mm |
| 2nd compression ring | 0.019-0.031 in. | 0.49-0.78mm |
| Oil control (steel rails) | 0.009-0.026 in. | 0.23-0.66mm |
| Ring side clearance | | |
| Top and 2nd compression rings | 0.0010-0.0026 in. | 0.025-0.065mm |
| Oil ring (pack) | 0.002-0.0070 in. | 0.004-0.178mm |
| Ring width | | |
| Compression rings | 0.046-0.047 in. | 1.17-1.19mm |
| Oil ring (pack) | 0.1124-0.1184 in. | 2.854-3.008mm |
| **Connecting Rods** | | |
| Bearing clearance | 0.001-0.023 in. | 0.026-0.059mm |
| Piston pin bore clearance | 0.8252-0.8260 in. | 20.96-20.98mm |
| Large end bore diameter | 2.0075-2.0081 in. | 50.991-51.005mm |
| Side clearance | 0.005-0.015 in. | 0.13-0.38mm |
| Total weight (less bearing) | 1.20 lbs. | 543 grams |
| **Crankshaft** | | |
| Connecting rod journal diameter | 1.8894-1.8900 in. | 47.9924-48.0076mm |
| Out-of-round (max.) | 0.0001 in. | 0.0035mm |
| Taper (max.) | 0.0001 in. | 0.0035mm |
| Main bearing diametrical clearance | | |
| No. 1-5 | 0.0008-0.0024 in. | 0.022-0.062mm |
| End play | 0.0035-0.0094 in. | 0.09-0.24mm |

89713C06

## 2.0 L (VIN Y) ENGINE SPECIFICATIONS

| Description | English | Metric |
|---|---|---|
| **Main Bearing Journals** | | |
| Diameter | 2.0469-2.0475 in. | 51.9924-52.0076mm |
| Out-of-round (max.) | 0.0001 in. | 0.0035mm |
| Taper (max.) | 0.0001 in. | 0.0038mm |
| **Camshaft** | | |
| Bearing bore diameter | | |
|     No. 1-6 | 1.021-1.022 in. | 25.951-25.970mm |
| Diametrical bearing clearance | 0.0027-0.0030 in. | 0.069-0.071mm |
| End Play | 1.669-1.670 in. | 42.4-42.421mm |
|     1995-96 vehicles | 0.0019-0.0066 in. | 0.050-0.070mm |
|     1997-99 vehicles | 0.002-0.006 in. | 0.05-0.15mm |
| Bearing journal diameter | | |
|     No. 1-6 | 1.021-1.022 in. | 25.951-25.970mm |
| Lift (zero lash) | | |
|     Intake | 0.344 in. | 8.75mm |
|     Exhaust | 0.314 in. | 8.00mm |
| **Valve Timing (at 5 degrees of lift)** | | |
| 1995-96 vehicles | | |
|     Exhaust valve closes (ATDC) | 5.4° | |
|     Exhaust valve opens (BBDC) | 43.7° | |
|     Duration | 229.1° | |
|     Intake valve closes (ABDC) | 41.7° | |
|     Intake valve opens (ATDC) | 4.9° | |
|     Duration | 216.8° | |
|     Valve overlap | 5° | |
| 1997-99 vehicles | | |
|     Intake valve closes (ABDC) | 38° | |
|     Intake valve opens (BTDC) | 1.2° | |
|     Intake valve duration | 219.2° | |
|     Exhaust valve closes (BTDC) | 3° | |
|     Exhaust valve opens (BBDC) | 42° | |
|     Exhaust valve duration | 219° | |
|     Valve overlap | 0° | |
| **Cylinder Head** | | |
| Material | Cast aluminum | |
| Gasket thickness (compressed) | 0.045 in. | 1.15mm |
| Valve seat angle | 44.5-45° | |
| Runout (max.) | 0.002 in. | 0.050mm |
| Width (finished) | | |
|     Intake and exhaust | 0.035-0.051 in. | 0.9-1.3mm |
| Valve guide finished diameter | 0.235-0.236 in. | 5.975-6.000mm |
| Guide bore diameter (standard) | 0.4330-0.4338 in. | 11.0-11.02mm |
| **Valves** | | |
| Head diameter | | |
|     Intake | 1.365-1.375 in. | 34.67-34.93mm |
|     Exhaust | 1.195-1.195 in. | 30.37-30.36mm |
| Valve margin | | |
|     Intake | 0.0452-0.0582 in. | 1.15-1.48mm |
|     Exhaust | 0.058-0.071 in. | 1.475-1.805mm |
| Length | | |
|     Intake | 4.389-4.409 in. | 111.49-111.99mm |
|     Exhaust | 4.314-4.334 in. | 109.59-110.09mm |

89713C07

## 2.0 L (VIN Y) ENGINE SPECIFICATIONS

| Description | | English | Metric |
|---|---|---|---|
| Valve stem tip height | | | |
| | Intake | 1.891 in. | 48.04mm |
| | Exhaust | 1.889 in. | 47.99mm |
| Stem diameter | | | |
| | Intake | 0.234-0.234 in. | 5.934-5.952mm |
| | Exhaust | 0.233-0.233 in. | 5.906-5.924mm |
| Stem-to-guide clearance | | | |
| | Intake | 0.0009-0.0025 in. | 0.023-0.066mm |
| | Exhaust | 0.002-0.0037 in. | 0.051-0.094mm |
| Maximum allowable | | | |
| | Intake | 0.003 in. | 0.076mm |
| | Exhaust | 0.004 in. | 0.101mm |
| Valve spring | | | |
| | Free length (approx.) | 1.811 in. | 46mm |
| Spring tension | | | |
| | Valve closed | 55-60 lbs. @ 1.496 in. | 246-270 N @ 38.0mm |
| | Valve open | 123-137 lbs. @ 1.53 in. | 549-611 N @ 29.3mm |

89713C08

## Engine

### REMOVAL & INSTALLATION

▶ **See Figures 1, 2, 3, 4 and 5**

In the process of removing the engine, you will come across a number of steps which call for the removal of a separate component or system, such as "disconnect the exhaust system" or "remove the radiator." In most instances, a detailed removal procedure can be found elsewhere in this manual.

It is virtually impossible to list each individual wire and hose which must be disconnected, simply because so many different model and engine combinations have been manufactured. Careful observation and common sense are the best possible approaches to any repair procedure.

Removal and installation of the engine can be made easier if you follow these basic points:

- If you have to drain any of the fluids, use a suitable container.
- Always tag any wires or hoses and, if possible, the components they came from before disconnecting them.

- Because there are so many bolts and fasteners involved, store and label the retainers from components separately in muffin pans, jars or coffee cans. This will prevent confusion during installation.
- After unbolting the transmission or transaxle, always make sure it is properly supported.
- If it is necessary to disconnect the air conditioning system, have this service performed by a qualified technician using a recovery/recycling station. If the system does not have to be disconnected, unbolt the compressor and set it aside.
- When unbolting the engine mounts, always make sure the engine is properly supported. When removing the engine, make sure that any lifting devices are properly attached to the engine. It is recommended that if your engine is supplied with lifting hooks, your lifting apparatus be attached to them.
- Lift the engine from its compartment slowly, checking that no hoses, wires or other components are still connected.
- After the engine is clear of the compartment, place it on an engine stand or workbench.
- After the engine has been removed, you can perform a partial or full teardown of the engine using the procedures outlined in this manual.

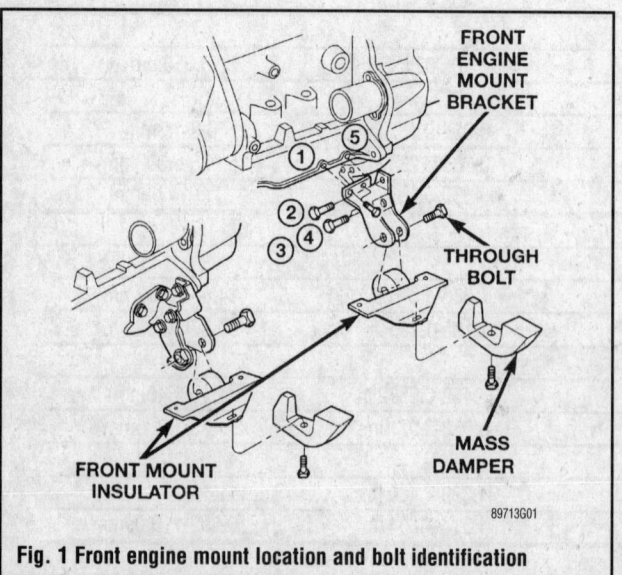

Fig. 1 Front engine mount location and bolt identification

89713G01

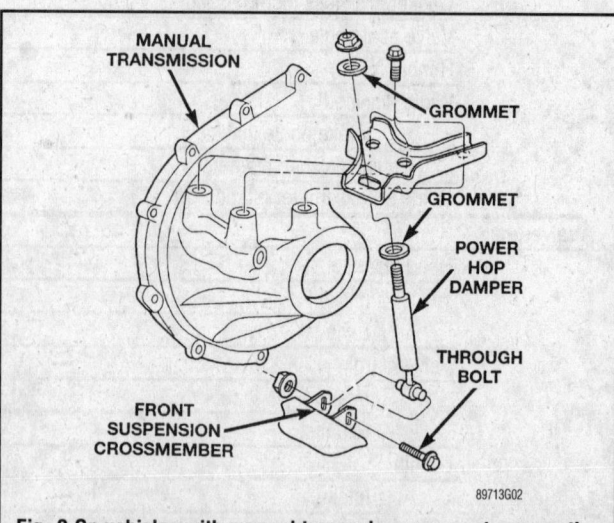

Fig. 2 On vehicles with manual transaxles, you must remove the power hop damper

89713G02

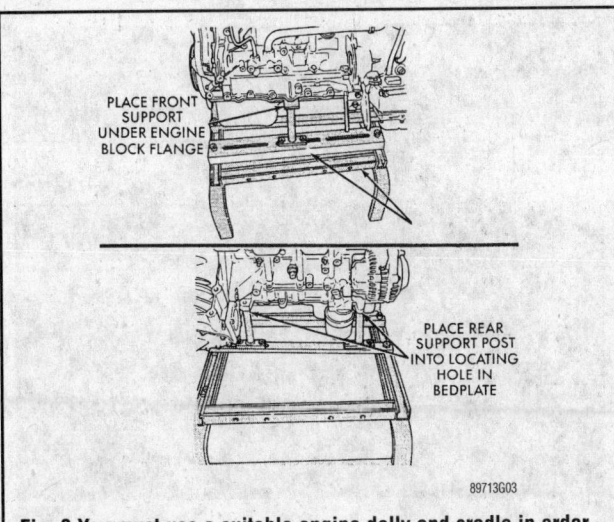

**Fig. 3 You must use a suitable engine dolly and cradle in order to remove the engine**

1. If equipped with A/C, take the vehicle to a reputable repair shop to the have the system discharged and evacuated.

➡**If your vehicle is equipped with air conditioning, refer to Section 1 for information regarding the implications of servicing your A/C system yourself. Only a MVAC-trained, EPA-certified, automotive technician should service the A/C system or its components.**

2. Properly relieve the fuel system pressure, as outlined in Section 5 of this manual.

3. Disconnect the negative, then the positive battery cables. Remove the battery and the battery tray. Set the PCM aside.

4. Drain the cooling system into a suitable container.

5. Remove the upper radiator hose, radiator and fan module assembly. Remove the lower radiator hose.

6. If equipped with an automatic transaxle, disconnect and plug the transaxle cooler lines.

7. Disconnect the clutch cable (manual transaxles) and transmission shift linkage.

8. Disconnect the throttle body linkage.

9. Detach the engine wiring harness.

10. Disconnect the heater hoses.

11. Raise and safely support the vehicle, then remove the right inner splash shield.

12. Remove the accessory drive belts.

13. Remove the halfshafts, as outlined in Section 7 of this manual.

14. Disconnect the exhaust pipe from the manifold.

15. Support the engine and transaxle assembly with a suitable jack, then remove the front engine mount.

16. On 1996–99 vehicles equipped with manual transaxle, remove the power hop damper.

17. Carefully lower the vehicle.

18. Remove the air cleaner assembly.

19. Unbolt the power steering pump and reservoir and position them aside.

20. If equipped, remove the A/C compressor.

21. Remove the ground straps to body.

22. Raise the vehicle enough to allow a suitable engine dolly and cradle to be placed under the engine.

23. Loosen the engine support posts in order to allow movement for positioning onto the engine locating holes and flange on the engine bedplate. Carefully lower the vehicle and position the cradle until the engine is resting on the support posts. Tighten the mounts to the cradle frame. This will keep the support posts from moving when removing or installing the engine and transmission.

24. Install safety straps around the engine to the cradle; tighten straps and lock them into position.

25. Raise the vehicle enough to see if the straps are tight enough to hold the cradle assembly to the engine.

26. Lower the vehicle so the weight of the engine and transaxle ONLY is on the cradle.

27. Remove the engine and transaxle mount through-bolts.

28. Raise the vehicle slowly, it might be necessary to move the engine/transaxle assembly with the cradle to allow to remove around the body flanges.

**To install:**

29. Installation is the reverse of the removal procedure. Please note the following important steps.

30. Tighten the front engine mount retainers as follows (bolt specifications are on accompanying figure):

a. If the engine mount bracket was removed, tighten bolt 1 to 20 inch lbs. (3 Nm) and bolts 2,3 and 4 to 80 ft. lbs. (108 Nm).

b. If the engine mount bracket was removed, tighten bolts 5 and 1 to 40 ft. lbs. (54 Nm).

c. Tighten the engine mount bracket-to-insulator assembly through-bolt to 40 ft. lbs. (54 Nm).

d. Tighten the insulator assembly nuts to the lower radiator cross-member torque to 40 ft. lbs. (54 Nm).

e. Tighten the mass damper bolt to 40 ft .lbs. (54 Nm).

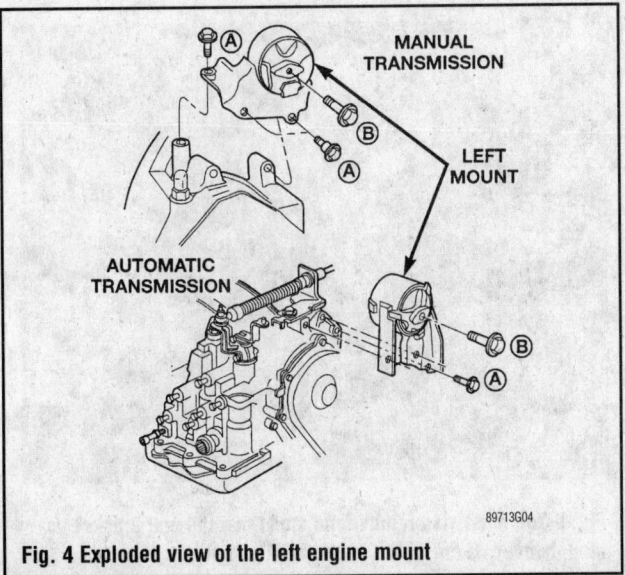

**Fig. 4 Exploded view of the left engine mount**

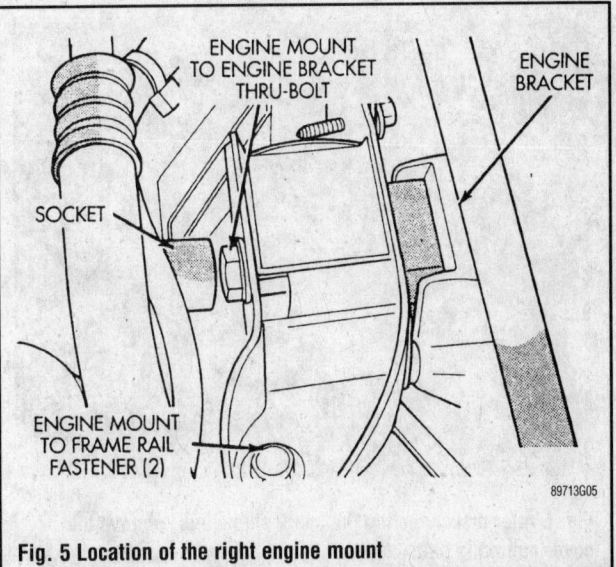

**Fig. 5 Location of the right engine mount**

31. Tighten the left engine mount as follows:
   a. To 40 ft. lbs. (54 Nm) for (A) fasteners
   b. To 80 ft. lbs. (108 Nm) for (B) fasteners.
32. Tighten the right engine mount as follows:
   a. Engine mount-to-rail fasteners to 40 ft. lbs. (54 Nm).
   b. Engine mount-to-engine bracket to 80 ft. lbs. (108 Nm).
33. Tighten the power hop damper retainers to 40 ft. lbs. (54 Nm).
34. After all components are installed, perform the camshaft and crankshaft timing relearn procedure as follows:
   a. Connect a DRB or equivalent scan tool to the Data Link Connector (located under the instrument panel, near the steering column).
   b. Turn the ignition switch **ON**, and access the "miscellaneous" screen.
   c. Select "re-learn cam/crank" option and follow the directions on the scan tool screen.
35. If equipped with A/C, take your vehicle to a reputable repair shop to have the A/C system recharged.

## Rocker Arm (Valve) Cover

### REMOVAL & INSTALLATION

▶ **See Figures 6 thru 14**

1. Disconnect the negative battery cable.
2. If equipped, remove the air cleaner inlet duct.
3. Remove the ignition coil pack.
4. Unfasten the valve cover retaining bolts, then remove the valve cover.
5. Remove and discard the cover gasket. Inspect the spark plug well gaskets and replace if necessary. Thoroughly clean the cover and cylinder head mating surfaces. Make sure the cylinder head cover mating surfaces is flat.

**To install:**

### ❊❊ WARNING

**Do not let any oil or solvents come in contact with the timing belt, as they can deteriorate the rubber and cause tooth skipping.**

6. Install new gasket(s). For DOHC engines, apply a suitable RTV sealant at the camshaft cap corners and at the top edges of the ½ round seal. Position the cover on the head and install the retainers.

Fig. 7 Remove the ignition coil mounting bracket retainers . . .

Fig. 8 . . . then lift the coil assembly up and off of the valve cover

Fig. 6 After disconnecting the spark plug wires, remove the cover mounting bolts

Fig. 9 You must also remove the studs that the coil bracket mounts over. There is one in the front and one in the rear

**Fig. 10 After all of the retainers are removed, you can lift the valve cover off**

**Fig. 11 While the valve cover is off, inspect the spark plug tube seals and replace if necessary**

**Fig. 12 Remove and discard the gasket and replace with a new one during installation**

**Fig. 13 Use rag and suitable solvent to clean the mating surfaces**

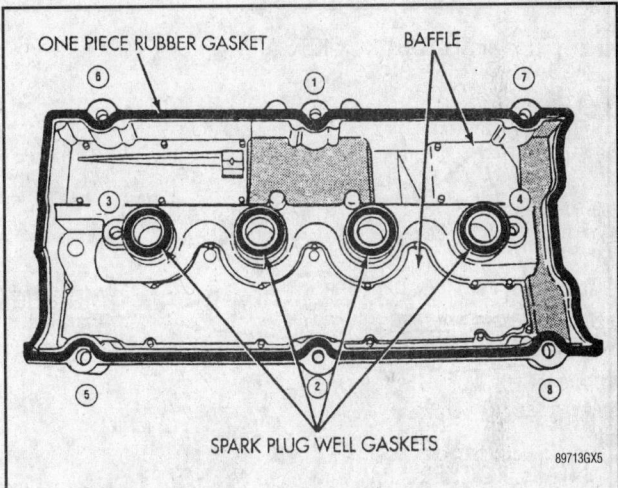

**Fig. 14 Rocker arm (valve) cover gasket locations and tightening sequence**

7. For SOHC engines, tighten the retainers to 9 ft. lbs. (12 Nm).
8. For DOHC engines, tighten the retainers in order, as follows:
   a. Step 1: Tighten all fasteners to 40 inch lbs. (4.5 Nm).
   b. Step 2: Tighten all fasteners to 6.5 inch lbs. (9 Nm).
   c. Step 3: Tighten all fasteners to 9 ft. lbs. (12 Nm).
9. Install the ignition coil pack. Tighten the retainers to 17 ft. lbs. (23 Nm) for SOHC engines or to 9 ft. lbs. (12 Nm) for DOHC engines.
10. If equipped, install the air cleaner inlet duct.
11. Connect the negative battery cable.

## Rocker Arm/Shafts

### REMOVAL & INSTALLATION

▶ See Figures 15, 16, 17, 18 and 19

This procedure applies to SOHC engines only. On DOHC engines, the valves are actuated directly by the camshafts.
1. Disconnect the negative battery cable.
2. Remove the cylinder head cover, as outlined earlier in this section.

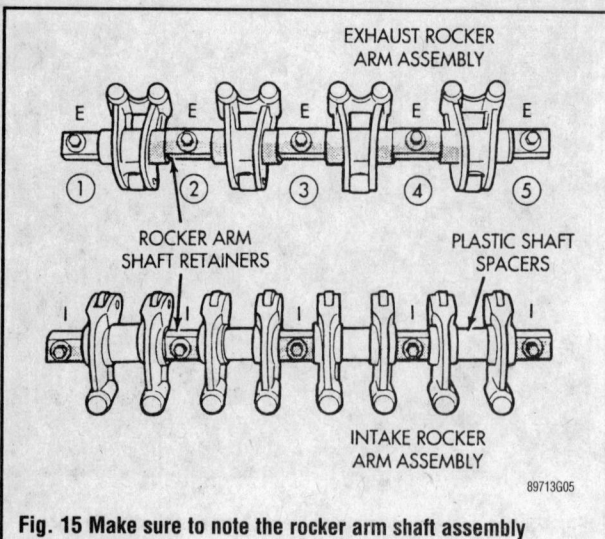

Fig. 15 Make sure to note the rocker arm shaft assembly installed positions

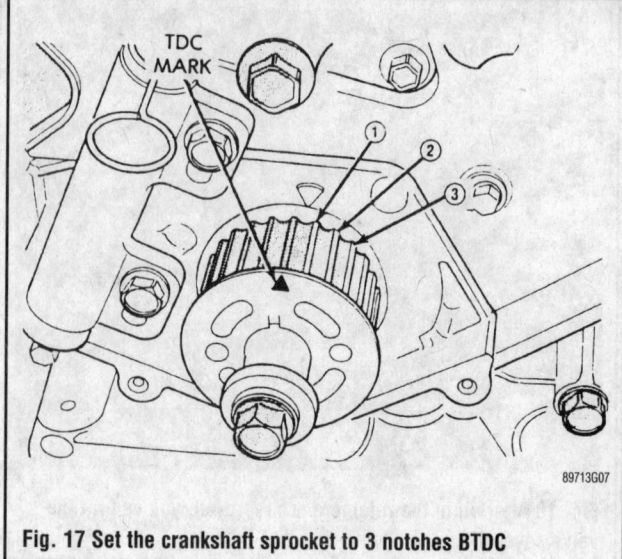

Fig. 17 Set the crankshaft sprocket to 3 notches BTDC

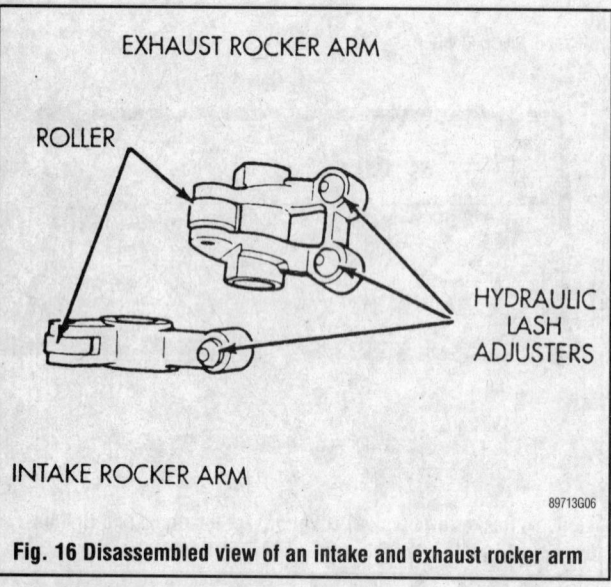

Fig. 16 Disassembled view of an intake and exhaust rocker arm

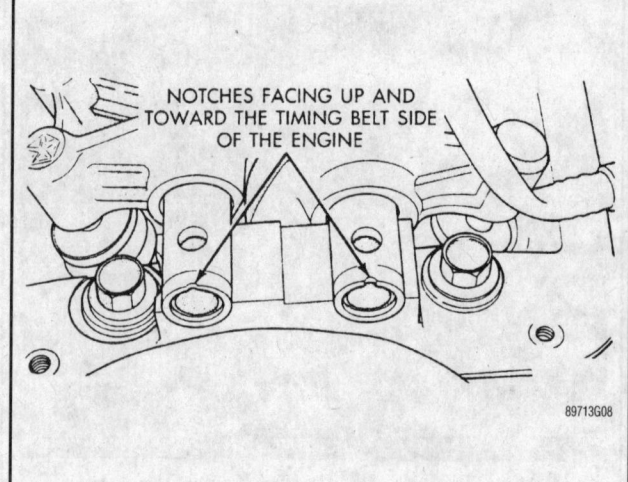

Fig. 18 Make sure the notch in the rocker arm shafts points up and toward the timing belt side of the engine

➡**Make sure to note the installed positions of the rocker arm shaft assemblies before removal.**

3. Loosen the rocker arm shaft attaching fasteners.

4. Remove the rocker arm shaft assembly from the cylinder head.

5. If necessary, disassemble the rocker arm assemblies by removing the attaching bolts from the shaft.

6. Slide the rocker arms and spacers off the shaft. Make sure to keep the spacers and rocker arms in their original locations for installation.

7. Inspect the rocker arm for scoring, wear on the roller or damage to the rocker arm and replace if necessary. Check the location where the rocker arms mount to the shafts for war or damage. Replace if damaged or worn. The rocker arm shaft is hollow and is used a lubrication oil duct. Check the oil holes for clogs with a small piece of wire, and clean as required. Lubricate the rocker arms and spacers. Make sure to install in their original locations.

**To install:**

**※※ WARNING**

**You MUST set the crankshaft to 3 notches before TDC before installing the rocker arm shafts.**

8. Set the crankshaft sprocket to TDC by aligning the mark on the sprocket with the arrow on the oil pump housing, then back off to 3 notches before TDC, as shown in the accompanying figure.

9. Install the rocker arm/hydraulic lash adjuster assembly making sure that the adjusters are at least partially full of oil. This is indicated by little or no plunger travel when the lash adjuster is depressed. If there is excessive plunger travel, place the rocker arm assembly into clean engine oil and pump the plunger until the lash adjuster travel is taken up. If travel is not reduced, replace the assembly. The hydraulic lash adjuster and rocker arm are serviced as an assembly.

10. Install the rocker arm and shaft assemblies with the NOTCH in the rocker arm shafts pointing up and toward the timing belt side of the engine. Install the retainers in their original positions on the exhaust and intake shafts.

**※※ WARNING**

**When installing the intake rocker arm shaft assembly, be sure the plastic spacers do not interfere with the spark plug tubes. If the spacers do interfere, rotate until they are at the proper angle. To avoid damaging the spark plug tubes, do not try to rotate the spacers by forcing the shaft down.**

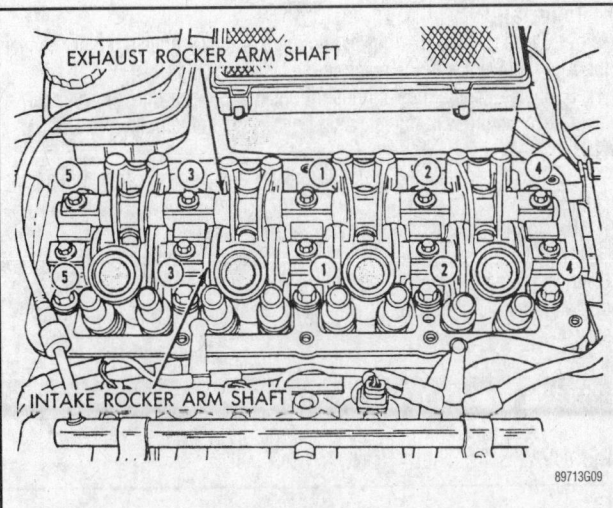

**Fig. 19 You must tighten the rocker arm shaft assembly bolts in the proper sequence**

11. Tighten the bolts to 17 ft. lbs. (23 Nm) for 1995 vehicles or to 21 ft. lbs. (28 Nm) in the sequence shown in the accompanying figure.

12. Install the rocker arm (valve) cover, as outlined earlier in this section.

13. Connect the negative battery cable.

## Thermostat

### REMOVAL & INSTALLATION

▶ **See Figures 20 thru 26**

1. Disconnect the negative battery cable.
2. Drain the cooling system to a level below the thermostat.
3. Disconnect the coolant recovery system hose from the thermostat housing.
4. If necessary, you can unfasten the upper radiator hose clamp, then slide the hose off the fitting.
5. Unfasten the thermostat/engine outlet housing connector bolts, then remove the housing. Remove the thermostat from the engine.
6. Remove the O-ring, then thoroughly clean the sealing surfaces.

**Fig. 20 Disconnect the coolant recovery reservoir hose from the nipple on the thermostat housing**

**Fig. 21 Use pliers to unfasten the upper radiator hose clamp, then disconnect the hose from the fitting**

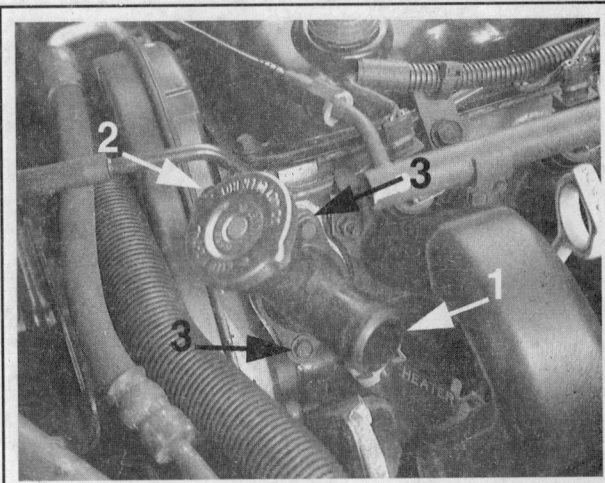

**Fig. 22 View of the radiator outlet fitting (1), recovery reservoir nipple (2) and mounting bolts (3)**

**Fig. 23 After unfastening the bolts, pull the housing away to reveal the thermostat**

Fig. 24 Pull the thermostat and O-ring assembly from the engine

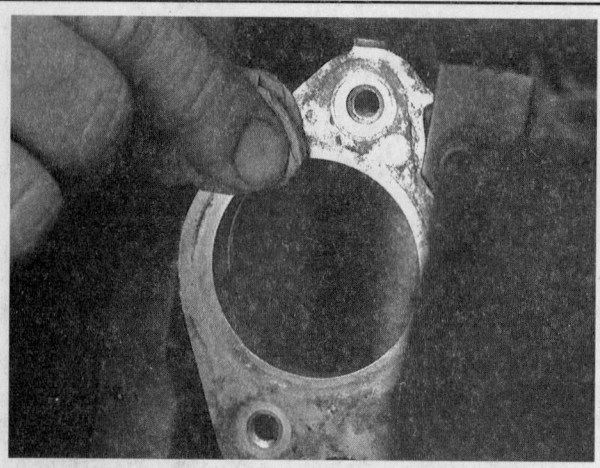

Fig. 25 You should thoroughly clean the housing mating surfaces before installing the thermostat

Fig. 26 Note that the vent should face up (see arrow) when installing the thermostat

**To install:**

7. Place the new thermostat into the thermostat housing/outlet connector. Align the vent with the notch in the cylinder head.

8. Install the thermostat housing/outlet connector onto the cylinder head, then secure with the retaining bolts. Tighten the bolts to 9.2 ft. lbs. (12.5 Nm).

9. If removed, attach the upper radiator hose and secure with the hose clamp.

10. Connect the coolant recovery system hose.

11. Fill the cooling system with the proper type and quantity of fluid. Connect the negative battery cable. Start the engine and let it warm up to operating temperatures, then recheck the coolant level and add if necessary.

## Intake Manifold

### REMOVAL & INSTALLATION

#### SOHC Engine

▶ See Figures 27 thru 40

1. Disconnect the negative battery cable.
2. Remove the fresh air inlet duct from the air cleaner.

### ✳✳ CAUTION

**Observe all applicable safety precautions when working around fuel. Whenever servicing the fuel system, always work in a well ventilated area. Do not allow fuel spray or vapors to come in contact with a spark or open flame. Keep a dry chemical fire extinguisher near the work area. Always keep fuel in a container specifically designed for fuel storage; also, always properly seal fuel containers to avoid the possibility of fire or explosion.**

3. Properly relieve the fuel system pressure, as outlined in Section 5.

4. Remove the throttle body, as outlined in Section 5 of this manual.

5. Remove the clean air duct and upper air filter housing.

6. Wrap towels around the fitting to catch any spilled fuel, then disconnect the fuel supply line quick-connect from the fuel tube assembly.

7. Unfasten the fuel rail attaching screws, then remove the fuel rail from the engine. Make sure to cover the injector openings.

Fig. 27 Remove the fuel rail, and place clean rags in the injector openings to prevent debris from entering them

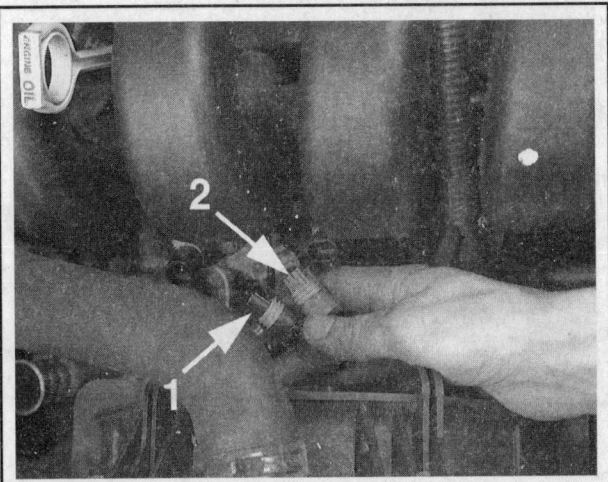

Fig. 28 Unplug the MAP sensor (1) and IAT sensor (2) electrical connectors

Fig. 31 Unfasten the EGR tube-to-intake manifold bolts . . .

Fig. 29 Detach the knock sensor electrical connector

Fig. 32 . . . then separate the tube and remove the gasket

Fig. 30 After unfastening the starter relay connector, unclip the wiring harness and position it aside

Fig. 33 Use a pair of needle nose pliers to unfasten the hose clamp . . .

Fig. 34 . . . then disconnect the brake booster vacuum hose

Fig. 37 Remove and discard the intake manifold retaining bolts and studs . . .

Fig. 35 Disconnect the PCV vapor hose

Fig. 38 . . . then remove the intake manifold from the vehicle

Fig. 36 Remove the intake manifold-to-inlet water tube support fastener

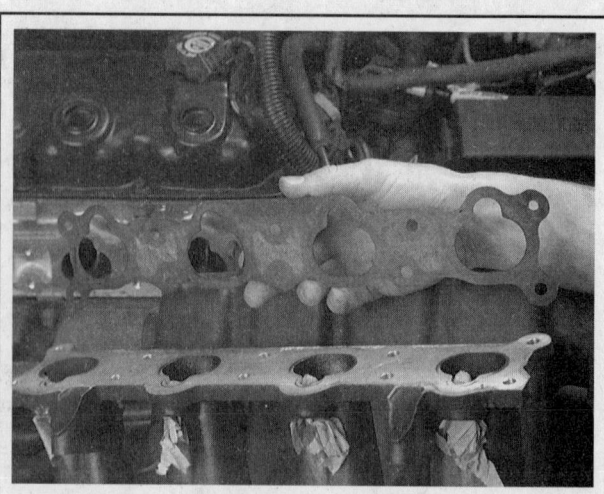

Fig. 39 Remove the gaskets and seals and replace with new ones during installation

**Do NOT set the fuel injectors on their tips, as this may damage them.**

8. Detach the electrical connector(s) from the MAP and IAT sensors. On early models there are 2 sensors, on later models they are combined into 1 sensor.

9. Unplug the knock sensor electrical connector.

10. Disconnect the wiring from the starter, then unclip the wiring harness and position it out of the way.

11. Remove the EGR tube bolts at the intake manifold, then remove the tube from the manifold. Remove the gasket.

12. Disconnect the brake booster vacuum hose.

13. Disconnect the PCV vapor hose.

14. Unfasten the intake manifold-to-inlet water tube support fastener.

15. Remove and discard the intake manifold retainers. Remove the intake manifold from the vehicle.

16. Remove and discard the gaskets and seals. Thoroughly clean the gasket mating surfaces.

**To install:**

17. Position new gaskets and seals, then install the intake manifold. Install new retainers and tighten them in the sequence shown in the accompanying figure to 9 ft. lbs. (12 Nm).

18. Install the intake manifold-to-water inlet support fastener and tighten to 9 ft. lbs. (12 Nm).

19. Remove the covering from the fuel injector holes and make sure the holes are clean. Install the fuel rail assembly to the intake manifold and tighten the screws to 17 ft. lbs. (23 Nm).

20. Connect the PCV and brake booster vacuum hoses.

21. Inspect the fuel line quick-connect fittings for damage and replace if necessary. Apply a small amount of clean engine oil to the fuel inlet tube. Connect the fuel supply hose to the fuel rail assembly. Check to be sure the connection is fastened securely by pulling on the connector.

22. Install the throttle body. Tighten the fastener to 16 ft. lbs. (22 Nm). Install the transmission-to-throttle body support bracket and tighten to 9 ft. lbs. (12 Nm) at the throttle body first. Next, tighten the bracket at the transmission.

23. Attach the MAP and IAT electrical connector(s).

24. Connect the knock sensor wiring and the wiring at the starter. Fasten the wiring harness to the intake manifold tab.

25. Attach the Idle Air Control (IAC) motor and Throttle Position Sensor (TPS) wiring connectors.

26. Connect the vacuum hoses to the throttle body.

27. Install accelerator, kickdown and speed control cables to their bracket and connect them to the throttle lever.

28. Loosely assemble the EGR tube to the intake manifold finger-tight, then tighten the retainers to 95 inch lbs. (11 Nm).

29. Install the clean air duct to the air filter housing, then tighten the clamp to 30 inch lbs. (3 Nm).

30. Connect the negative battery cable.

31. Attach the fresh air duct to the air cleaner and tighten the wing nut securely.

### DOHC Engine

◆ **See Figures 41, 42 and 43**

1. Disconnect the negative battery cable.

2. Loosen the wing nut on the intake, then remove the fresh air inlet duct.

3. Properly relieve the fuel system pressure, as outlined in Section 5 of this manual.

**Observe all applicable safety precautions when working around fuel. Whenever servicing the fuel system, always work in a well ventilated area. Do not allow fuel spray or vapors to come in contact with a spark or open flame. Keep a dry chemical fire extinguisher near the work area. Always keep fuel in a container specifically designed for fuel storage; also, always properly seal fuel containers to avoid the possibility of fire or explosion.**

4. Wrap towels around the fitting to catch any spilled fuel, then disconnect the fuel supply line quick-connect from the fuel tube assembly.

5. Remove the clean air inlet duct.

6. Detach the coolant temperature sensor electrical connector.

7. Disconnect the heater hose from the intake manifold and the heater tube from the bottom of the intake manifold.

8. Disconnect the upper radiator and coolant recovery hoses.

**Do not allow the injectors to rest on their tips, as this may cause damage.**

9. Unfasten the attaching screws, then remove the fuel rail from the engine. Cover the injector openings with a suitable covering to prevent debris from entering the ports.

10. Remove the accelerator, kickdown and speed control (if equipped) cables from the throttle lever and bracket.

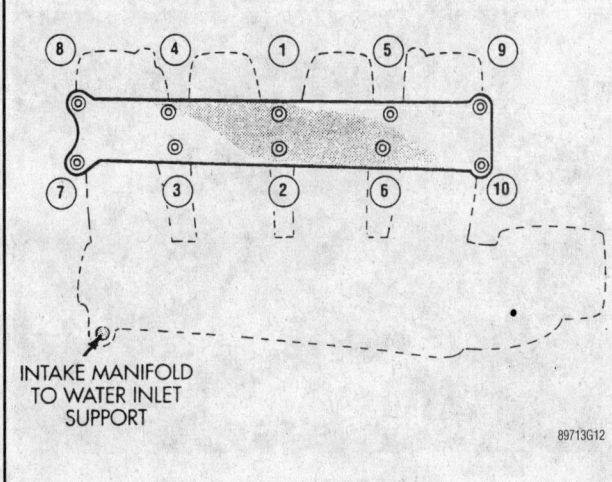

**Fig. 40 Intake manifold retainer tightening sequence—SOHC engines**

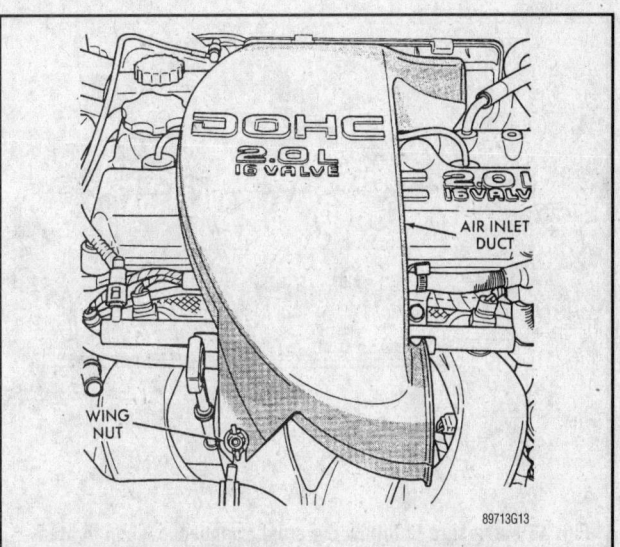

**Fig. 41 The fresh air inlet duct is secured with a wing nut**

11. Detach the Idle Air Control (IAC) motor and Throttle Position Sensor (TPS) wiring connectors.

12. Tag and disconnect the vacuum hoses from the throttle body, then remove the throttle body from the vehicle.

13. Detach the Manifold Absolute Pressure (MAP) and Intake Air Temperature (IAT) sensor electrical connector. Disconnect the vapor and brake booster hoses.

14. Detach the knock sensor electrical connector and disconnect the wiring harness from the tab located on the heater tube.

15. Disconnect the wiring from the starter.

16. Unfasten the EGR tube bolts at the valve and at the intake manifold. Remove the tube from the engine.

17. Remove the intake manifold fasteners, then remove the upper and lower intake manifold assemblies. If necessary, you can separate the upper and lower manifolds.

18. Remove and discard the gaskets, then thoroughly clean all of the gasket mating surfaces.

**To install:**

19. If separated, position a new gasket, then assemble the lower manifold to the upper, then tighten the retaining bolts to 21 ft. lbs. (28 Nm) in the sequence shown in the accompanying figure.

20. Position a new gasket on the cylinder head, then install the intake manifold on the head. Tighten the fasteners to 21 ft. lbs. (28 Nm).

21. Remove the covering from the fuel injector holes and make sure the holes are clean. Install the fuel rail assembly to the intake manifold and tighten the screws to 17 ft. lbs. (23 Nm).

22. Connect the PCV and brake booster vacuum hoses.

23. Inspect the fuel line quick-connect fittings for damage and replace if necessary. Apply a small amount of clean engine oil to the fuel inlet tube. Connect the fuel supply hose to the fuel rail assembly. Check to be sure the connection is fastened securely by pulling on the connector.

24. Connect the heater tube and hose to the intake manifold.

25. Attach the upper radiator hose and coolant recovery reservoir hose.

26. Attach the coolant temperature sensor wiring.

27. Install the throttle body. Tighten the fastener to 16 ft. lbs. (22 Nm).

28. Attach the MAP and IAT electrical connector.

29. Connect the knock sensor wiring and the wiring at the starter. Fasten the wiring harness to the heater tube tab.

30. Attach the Idle Air Control (IAC) motor and Throttle Position Sensor (TPS) wiring connectors.

31. Connect the vacuum hoses to the throttle body.

32. Install accelerator, kickdown and speed control cables to their bracket and connect them to the throttle lever.

33. Loosely assemble the EGR tube to valve and the intake manifold finger-tight. Tighten the tube fasteners to the at the EGR valve first to 95 inch lbs., then tighten the intake manifold side retainers to 95 inch lbs. (11 Nm).

34. Install the clean air duct to the air filter housing, then tighten the clamp to 25 inch lbs. (3 Nm).

35. Connect the negative battery cable.

36. Attach the fresh air duct to the air cleaner and tighten the wing nut securely.

## Exhaust Manifold

### REMOVAL & INSTALLATION

▶ See Figures 44 thru 57

1. Disconnect the negative battery cable.

2. Remove the air cleaner assembly and bracket.

3. Unfasten the retainers, then separate the exhaust pipe from the manifold. If Low Emission Vehicle (LEV) equipped, discard the manifold-to-flex joint gasket.

4. Unbolt the power steering pump reservoir and position it aside. Do NOT disconnect the fluid lines.

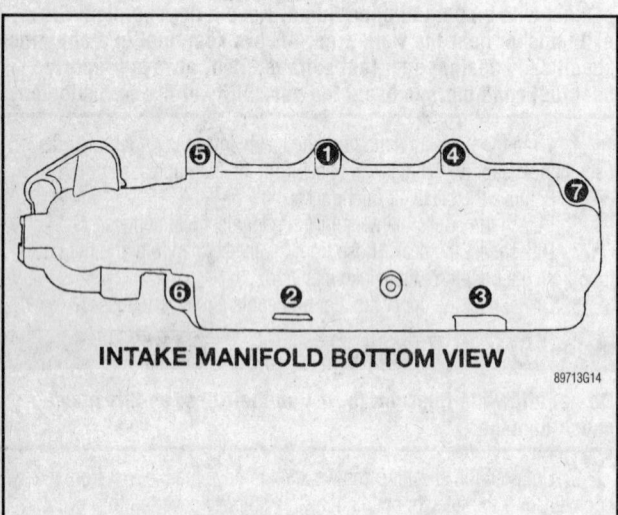

INTAKE MANIFOLD BOTTOM VIEW

89713G14

**Fig. 42 Lower-to-upper intake manifold bolt tightening sequence—DOHC engines**

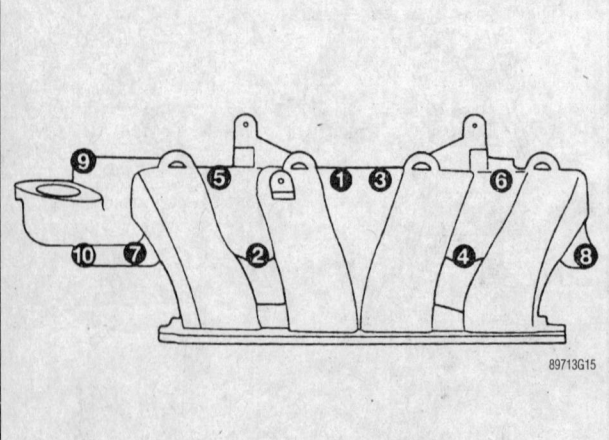

89713G15

**Fig. 43 Make sure to follow the proper sequence when tightening the intake manifold-to-cylinder head retainers**

89713P84

**Fig. 44 Remove the air cleaner lid and element, then remove the air cleaner assembly mounting bolts**

Fig. 45 Make sure to remove all of the air cleaner assembly retainers . . .

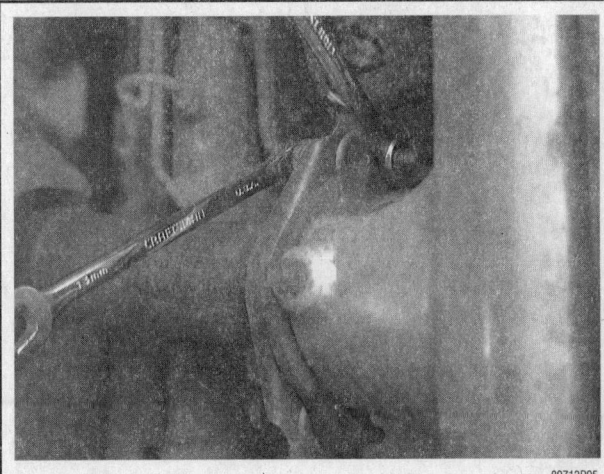

Fig. 48 Remove the retainers, then separate the exhaust pipe from the manifold

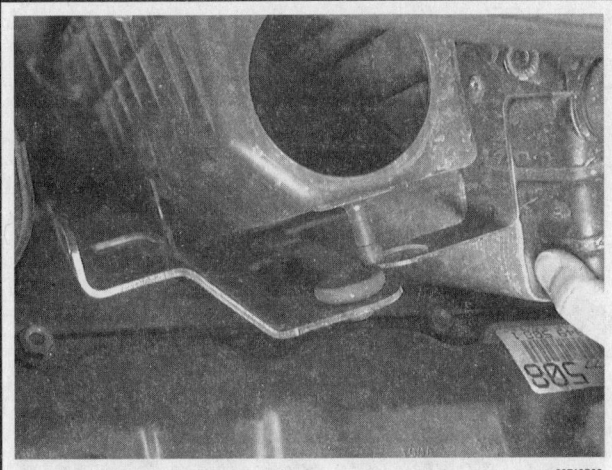

Fig. 46 . . . then remove the air cleaner assembly from the vehicle

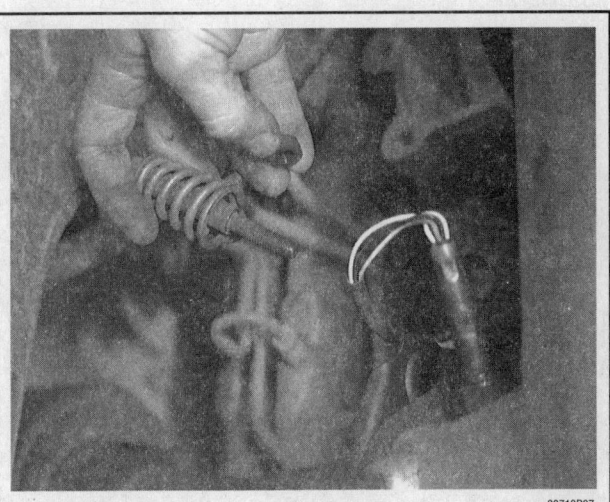

Fig. 49 View of the exhaust pipe-to-manifold retainers

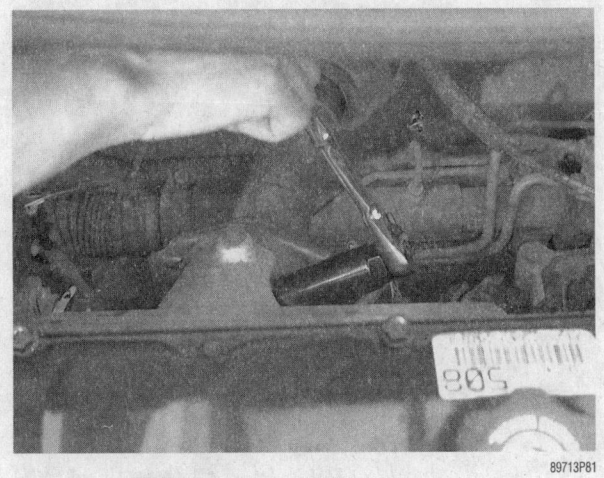

Fig. 47 Once the air cleaner assembly is removed, you can loosen and remove the oxygen sensor if necessary

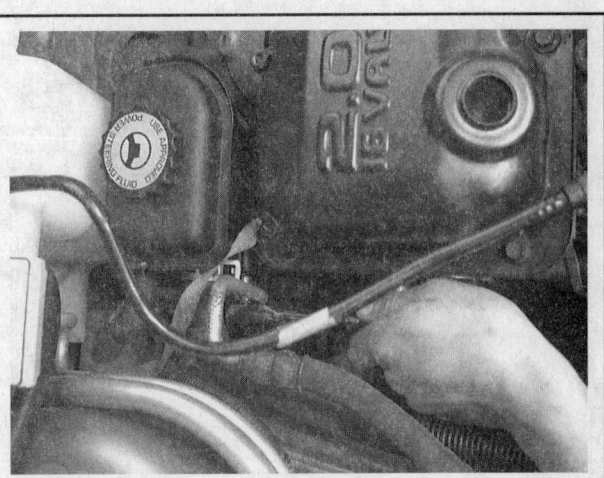

Fig. 50 To access the heat shield, unfasten the power steering reservoir mounting bolts . . .

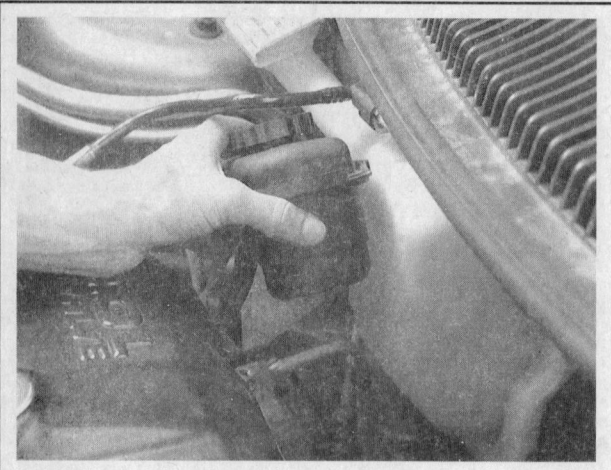

Fig. 51 . . . then position the power steering reservoir aside, but do not disconnect the fluid lines

Fig. 54 Loosen the alternator bracket bolt shown . . .

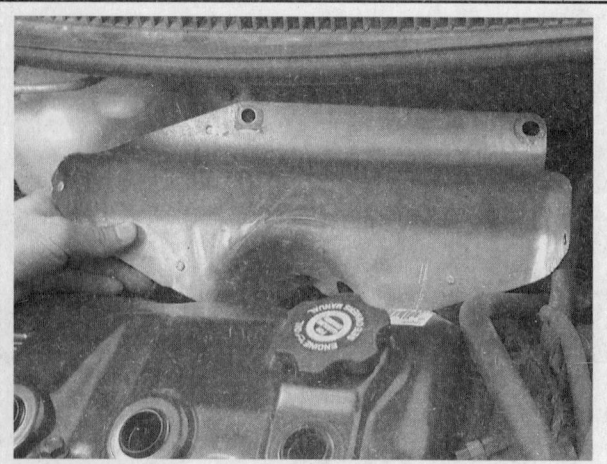

Fig. 52 Remove the retainers, then remove the exhaust manifold heat shield

Fig. 55 . . . in order to remove the outer exhaust manifold bolt

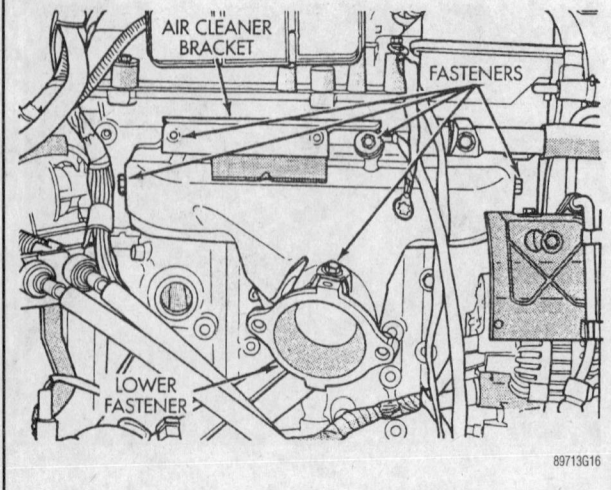

Fig. 53 Location of the exhaust manifold heat shield fasteners

Fig. 56 Unfasten the remaining exhaust manifold mounting bolts

Fig. 57 . . . then remove the exhaust manifold from the vehicle

Fig. 58 Use pliers to unfasten the clamps, then disconnect the upper radiator hose

5. Unfasten the retainers, then remove the exhaust manifold heat shield.

6. For 1996–99 vehicles, detach the upstream heated oxygen sensor connector.

➡It may be necessary to loosen the alternator bracket bolt to remove the outer exhaust manifold bolt.

7. Remove the 8 exhaust manifold retaining fasteners, then remove the exhaust manifold and gasket.

8. Discard the gasket, then thoroughly clean the mating surfaces.

**To install:**

9. Position a new gasket and the exhaust manifold it their proper positions. Apply Mopar stud and bearing mount, or equivalent, to the fasteners. Install the fasteners and tighten to 17 ft. lbs. (23 Nm), starting at the center and working outward in both directions. Repeat this procedure until all fasteners are tightened to specifications.

10. If loosened, tighten the alternator bracket bolt.

11. Install the exhaust manifold heat shield.

12. Place the power steering pump reservoir in position and secure with the mounting bolts.

13. If necessary, attach the upstream heated oxygen sensor.

14. Install the air cleaner bracket and assembly.

15. If Low Emission Vehicle (LEV) equipped, replace the manifold-to-flex fold gasket.

16. Attach the exhaust pipe to the manifold and tighten to 21 ft. lbs. (28 Nm).

17. Connect the negative battery cable.

## Radiator

### REMOVAL & INSTALLATION

◗ See Figures 58 thru 72

1. Disconnect the negative battery cable.

### ✳✳ CAUTION

**Never remove the cylinder block plug or the radiator draincock with the system hot and under pressure, as serious burns could occur.**

2. Drain the cooling system into a suitable container.
3. Remove the engine air inlet duct.
4. Disconnect the upper radiator hose from the radiator.

Fig. 59 If you disconnect the cooler lines from the transaxle, you will spill less coolant

Fig. 60 Remove the radiator-to-battery strut (1) and ground strap (2)

Fig. 61 Remove the battery, unfasten the retainers, then remove the battery tray

Fig. 64 Unfasten the fan mounting bolts . . .

Fig. 62 Unplug the first fan motor electrical connector . . .

Fig. 65 . . . then remove the left side fan . . .

Fig. 63 . . . then unplug the other fan connector

Fig. 66 . . . and the right side fan from the vehicle

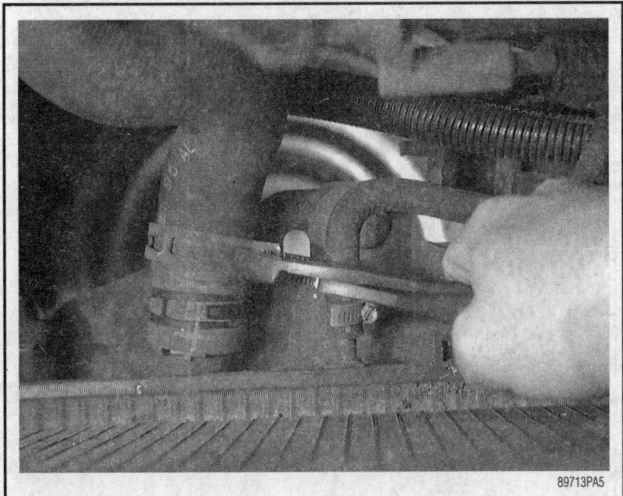

Fig. 67 Unfasten the hose clamp, then disconnect the lower radiator hose

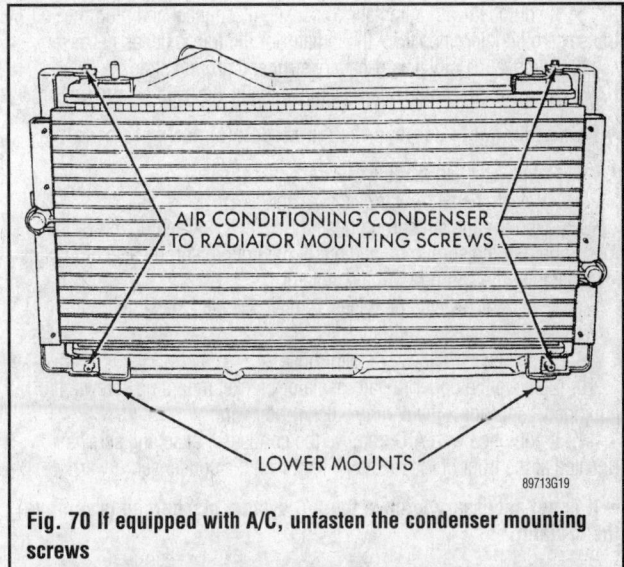

Fig. 70 If equipped with A/C, unfasten the condenser mounting screws

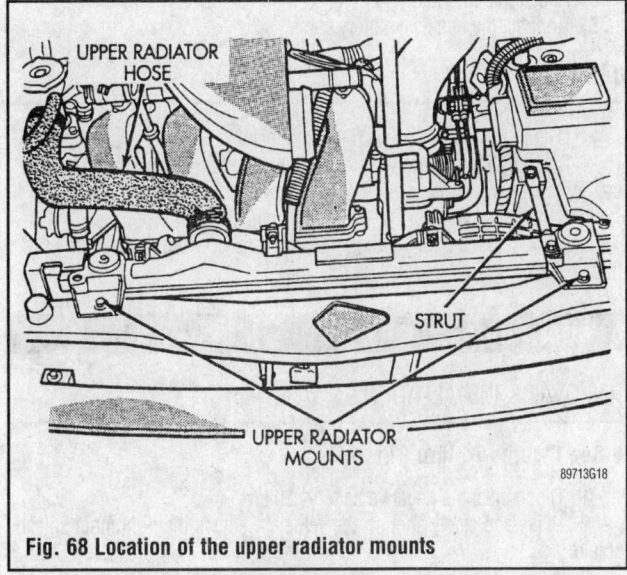

Fig. 68 Location of the upper radiator mounts

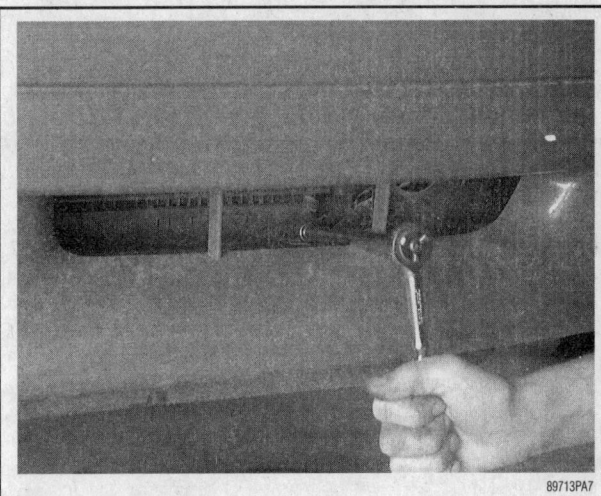

Fig. 71 You can access the condenser mounting bolts at the front of the radiator

Fig. 69 Remove the upper radiator mounting bolts

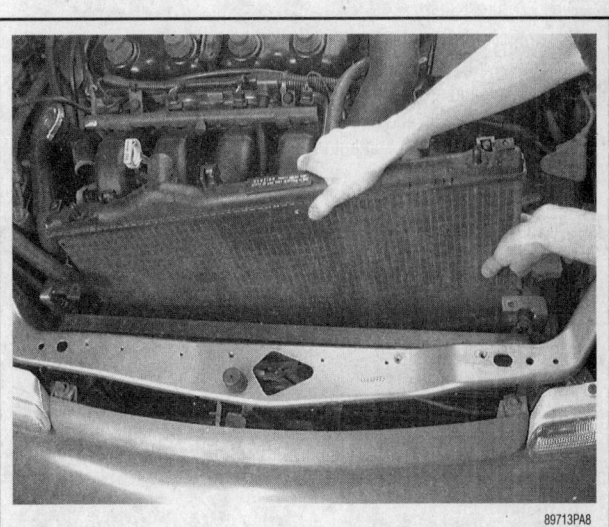

Fig. 72 Carefully lift the radiator from the engine compartment

5. If equipped with automatic transaxle, disconnect and plug the transaxle oil cooler lines from the radiator or the transaxle, as necessary.

6. Remove the radiator-to-battery strut and ground strap.

7. If equipped with dual fans, remove the battery and battery tray.

➥ **Be careful not to damage the fan module(s) during removal.**

8. Remove the fan module assembly, as follows:
   a. Detach the fan motor electrical connector.
   b. Remove the fan shroud retaining screws, located on top of the shroud. Lift the shroud up and out of the bottom shroud attaching clips separating the shroud from the radiator.
   c. For vehicles with dual fans, remove the left side fan first, then remove the right side module last.

9. Disconnect the lower radiator hose.

10. Remove the upper radiator isolator bracket mounting screws. If equipped, disconnect the engine block heater wire.

11. If equipped with A/C, remove the condenser attaching screws (located at the front of the radiator), then lean the condenser forward.

➥ **It is not necessary to have the A/C system discharged to remove the radiator.**

12. You can not lift the radiator free from the engine compartment. Be very careful not the damage the radiator cooling fins or water tubes during removal.

**To install:**

13. Slide the radiator down into position behind the radiator support (yoke).

14. If equipped, attach the A/C condenser to the radiator with the 4 mounting screws and tighten to 50 inch lbs. (5.4 Nm). Then, seat the assembly lower rubber isolators into the mounting holes provided in the lower crossmember.

15. Tighten the radiator isolator mounting bracket screws to 90 inch lbs. (10 Nm). The radiator should have clearance to move upward about 0.25 in. (58mm) after installed.

16. Connect the lower radiator hose, making sure to align the hose and position the clamp so it will not interfere with any other engine components.

17. If equipped, unplug and connect the automatic transmission hoses. Tighten the hose clamps to 35 inch lbs. (4 Nm).

18. Slide the fan module down into the clip(s) on the lower radiator flange. For vehicles with dual fans, install the right fan module first, then install the left fan module. Install the retaining screws and tighten to 65 inch lbs. (7.5 Nm).

19. Attach the cooling fan electrical connector.

20. Connect the upper radiator hose. Make sure the hose is aligned and position the clamp so it will not interfere with other engine components.

21. If equipped with dual fans, install the battery tray and battery. Connect the positive battery cable.

22. Connect the negative battery cable. Make sure the draincock is closed and all block plugs are installed, then fill the cooling system with the proper type and amount of coolant.

23. Start the engine and allow it to reach normal operating temperatures. Check the coolant system and automatic transaxle for proper fluid levels. Add as necessary.

## Engine Fan

### REMOVAL & INSTALLATION

▶ **See Figure 73**

1. Disconnect the negative battery cable.
2. Detach the fan motor leads from the module.
3. Unfasten the fan module fasteners from the radiator, then remove the module from the vehicle.

**To install:**

4. Position the fan module to the radiator. Install the shroud-to-radiator fasteners and tighten to 65 inch lbs. (7.5 Nm).

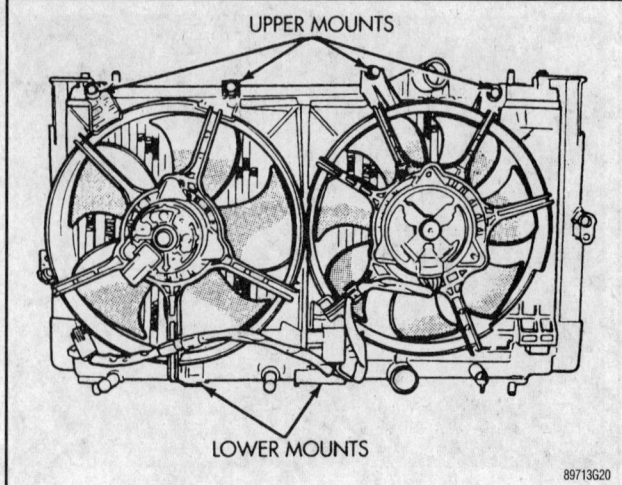

**Fig. 73 Location of the fan module assembly upper and lower mounts**

5. Attach the fan motor lead.
6. Connect the negative battery cable.

### TESTING

1. Detach the fan motor electrical connector.
2. Connect the fan wire with #14 gauge wire to a known-good 12-volt battery, observing good polarity.
3. If the fan runs normally, the motor is functioning properly.
4. If not, replace the fan module using the procedure located earlier in this section.

## Water Pump

### REMOVAL & INSTALLATION

▶ **See Figures 74 thru 81**

1. Disconnect the negative battery cable.
2. Raise and safely support the vehicle. Remove the right inner splash shield.

**Fig. 74 Unfasten the timing belt tensioner bracket retaining bolts . . .**

Fig. 75 . . . then remove the bracket fo access the rear cover retainers

Fig. 78 Unfasten the water pump retaining bolts . . .

Fig. 76 Remove three 3 inner timing belt cover retaining bolts . . .

Fig. 79 . . . then pull the water pump away from the cylinder block

Fig. 77 . . . then remove the inner timing belt cover to access the water pump

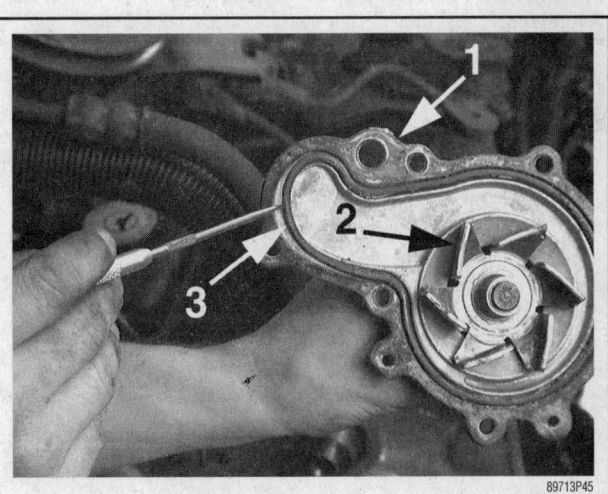

Fig. 80 View of the water pump body (1), impeller (2) and O-ring (3)

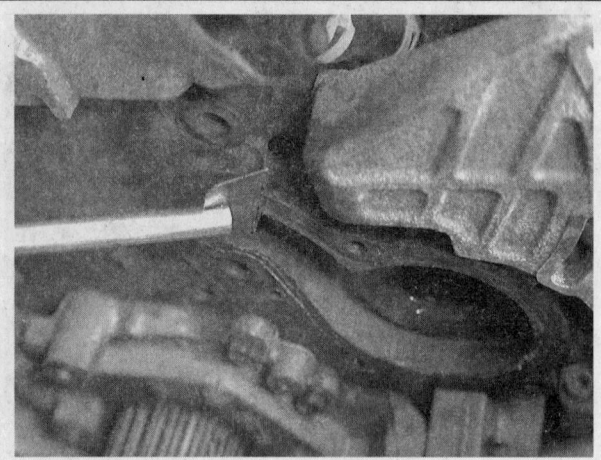

Fig. 81 Thoroughly clean the water pump and cylinder head mating surfaces

3. Remove the accessory drive belts and power steering pump.

4. Drain the cooling system into a suitable container.

5. Securely support the engine from the bottom, then remove the right engine mount.

6. Remove the power steering pump bracket bolts, then set the pump and bracket assembly aside, but the power steering lines do not need to be disconnected.

7. Remove the right engine mount bracket.

8. Remove the timing belt tensioner and timing belt, as outlined later in this section.

9. Remove the camshaft sprocket(s) and inner timing belt cover, as outlined in this section.

10. Unfasten the water pump-to-engine attaching screws, then remove the water pump from the engine.

11. Remove and discard the water pump O-ring, and thoroughly clean the mating surfaces.

**To install:**

12. Install a new O-ring gasket in the water pump O-ring groove. Hold the O-ring in place with a few small dabs of suitable silicone sealant.

### ✳✳ WARNING

**Before proceeding, make sure the O-ring gasket is properly seated in the water pump groove before tightening the screws. A improperly installed O-ring could cause a coolant leak.**

13. Position the water pump to the block and install the retainers. Tighten the retainers to 9 ft. lbs. (12 Nm). Use a pressure tester to pressurize the cooling system to 15 psi and check the water pump shaft seal and O-ring for leaks.

14. Rotate the pump by hand to check for freedom of movement.

15. Install the inner timing belt cover, timing belt and tensioner.

16. Install the right engine mount bracket and engine mount.

17. Refill the cooling system with the proper type and amount of coolant.

18. Install the power steering pump and accessory drive belts.

19. Connect the negative battery cable.

20. Use a DRB or equivalent scan tool to perform the camshaft and crankshaft timing relearn procedure, as follows:

    a. Connect the scan tool to the Data Link Connector (located under the instrument panel, near the steering column).

    b. Turn the ignition switch **ON**, and access the "miscellaneous" screen.

    c. Select the "re-learn cam/crank" option, then follow the instructions on the scan tool screen.

## Cylinder Head

REMOVAL & INSTALLATION

♦ **See Figures 82 thru 99**

1. Disconnect the negative battery cable.

2. Properly relieve the fuel system pressure, as outlined in Section 5 of this manual.

3. Drain the cooling system into a suitable container.

4. Remove the air cleaner inlet duct and air cleaner. Tag and disconnect all vacuum lines, electrical wiring and fuel lines from the throttle body.

5. Remove the throttle linkage.

6. Remove the accessory drive belts, as outlined in Section 1.

7. Disconnect the power brake vacuum hose from the intake manifold.

8. Raise and safely support the vehicle, then separate the exhaust pipe from the manifold. Carefully lower the vehicle.

9. Unbolt the power steering pump and set aside. Do NOT disconnect the fluid lines!

10. Detach the ignition coil pack wiring connector, then remove the coil pack and bracket from the engine.

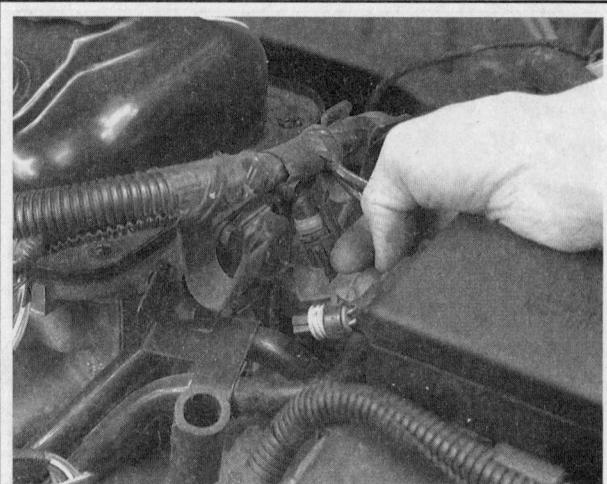

Fig. 82 Detach the cam position and other necessary connectors

Fig. 83 Unfasten the bolts securing any brackets attached to the head . . .

Fig. 84 . . . then remove the bracket from the head

Fig. 87 . . . then remove the exhaust rocker arm shaft assembly from the cylinder head

Fig. 85 Remove the retainers, then remove the rocker arm (valve) cover

Fig. 88 Remove the oil separator assembly retaining bolts, then remove the assembly

Fig. 86 Remove the intake rocker arm shaft assembly . . .

Fig. 89 Unfasten the clamps, then disconnect the heater hoses

Fig. 90 Remove any remaining lines or hoses

Fig. 93 If they are reusable, fabricate a holder to keep the bolts in their original positions for installation

Fig. 91 Loosen the cylinder head bolts, starting from the center and working outward

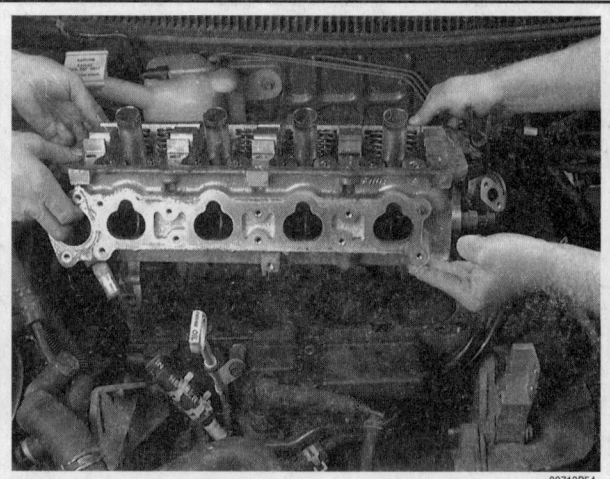

Fig. 94 It can be advantageous to have an assistant help you lift the cylinder head off the engine

Fig. 92 Remove the cylinder head bolts and inspect their condition in order to determine if they can be reused

Fig. 95 Remove and discard the cylinder head gasket. NEVER reuse this gasket!

**Fig. 96 With rags stuffed into the combustion chambers, use a gasket scraper to carefully clean the engine block surface**

**Fig. 97 While you have the head on a workbench, thoroughly clean the gasket mating surfaces, then inspect for damage**

**Fig. 98 Always use a torque wrench to tighten the head bolts, making sure to follow the proper sequence**

**Fig. 99 Cylinder head bolt tightening sequence**

11. Detach the cam sensor and fuel injector electrical connectors.

12. For 1996–99 vehicles, remove the intake manifold.

13. For SOHC engines, remove the timing belt and camshaft sprocket.

14. For DOHC engines, remove the timing belt, timing belt tensioner and camshaft sprocket. Remove the inner timing belt cover.

15. Remove the rocker arm (valve) cover.

16. For SOHC engine, remove the rocker arm shaft assemblies.

17. For DOHC engines, remove the camshaft and cam follower assemblies.

18. For SOHC engines, if necessary, remove the oil separator assembly bolts, then remove the oil separator.

19. For SOHC engines, unfasten the hose clamps, then disconnect the heater hoses. Remove any remaining hoses or lines.

20. Use a ratchet to unfasten the cylinder head bolts, working from the center outward, then remove the cylinder head from the engine block.

21. The cylinder head bolts must be inspected before they can be reused. If the threads of bolts are stretched, they must be replaced. Check for thread stretching by holding a scale or other straight edge against the threads. If all the threads do not contact the scale, the bolts must be replaced.

### ✸✸ WARNING

**Use only a plastic scraper to clean the mating surfaces. NEVER use metal, as this may gouge the metal surfaces and cause leaks!**

22. Cover the combustion chambers, then use a plastic scraper to thoroughly and carefully clean the engine block and cylinder head mating surfaces.

23. The cylinder head must be cleaned and inspected prior to installation. Please refer to the engine reconditioning portion of the section for further details and information.

**To install:**

24. Position a new gasket on the engine block, then place the cylinder head over the gasket.

25. Apply a thin coat of engine oil to the cylinder head bolt threads. The 4 short bolts 4.33 in. (110mm) are installed in positions 7, 8, 9 and 10, as shown in the accompanying figure.

26. For SOHC engines, tighten the cylinder head bolts, in the sequence shown, to the following specifications:

    a. Step 1: Tighten the bolts to 25 ft. lbs. (34 Nm).

    b. Step 2: Tighten the bolts to 50 ft. lbs. (68 Nm).

    c. Step 3: Loosen, then re-tighten the bolts to 50 ft. lbs. (68 Nm).

    d. Step 4: Tighten all bolts an additional ¼ turn. Do NOT use a torque wrench for this step.

27. For DOHC engines, tighten the cylinder head bolts, in the sequence shown, to the following specifications:

    a. Step 1: Tighten bolts 16 to 25 ft. lbs. (34 Nm) and bolts 710 to 20 ft. lbs. (28 Nm).

    b. Step 2: Tighten bolts 16 to 50 ft. lbs. (68 Nm) and bolts 710 to 20 ft. lbs. (28 Nm).

    c. Step 3: Loosen, then re-tighten bolts 16 to 50 ft. lbs. (68 Nm) and bolts 710 to 20 ft. lbs. (28 Nm).

    d. Step 4: Tighten all bolts an additional ¼ turn. Do NOT use a torque wrench for this step.

28. The remainder of installation is the reverse of the removal procedure.

29. Connect the negative battery cable.

30. Fill the cooling system with the proper amount and type of coolant.

31. Use a DRB or equivalent scan tool to perform the camshaft and crankshaft timing relearn procedure, as follows:

    a. Connect the scan tool to the Data Link Connector (located under the instrument panel, near the steering column).

    b. Turn the ignition switch **ON**, and access the "miscellaneous" screen.

    c. Select the "re-learn cam/crank" option, then follow the instructions on the scan tool screen.

## Oil Pan

### REMOVAL & INSTALLATION

#### 1995 Vehicles

▶ **See Figure 100**

1. Raise and safely support the vehicle.
2. Drain the engine oil into a suitable container.
3. Unfasten the pan retaining bolts, then lower the oil pan from the engine.
4. Thoroughly clean all of the gasket mating surfaces.

**To install:**

5. Apply suitable silicone sealer to the oil pump-to-engine block parting line, as shown in the accompanying figure.
6. Position the oil pan gasket to the block, using silicone sealer to hold the gasket in place.
7. Install the oil pan and secure with the retaining bolts. Tighten the bolts to 85 inch lbs. (9.5 Nm).
8. Carefully lower the vehicle. Fill the crankcase with the proper type and amount of engine oil.

9. Start the engine and check for leaks, then recheck the fluid level and add as necessary.

#### 1996–97 Vehicles

▶ **See Figure 100**

1. Raise and safely support the vehicle.
2. Drain the engine oil into a suitable container.
3. Remove the transmission bending bracket.
4. Support the engine and transaxle assembly, then remove the front engine mount and bracket.
5. Remove the transmission inspection cover.
6. If equipped with A/C, remove the oil filter and adapter.
7. Unfasten the retainers, then remove the oil pan.
8. Thoroughly clean the gasket mating surfaces.

**To install:**

9. Apply suitable silicone sealer to the oil pump-to-engine block parting line, as shown in the accompanying figure.
10. Position a new oil pan gasket on the pan.
11. Install the pan, then tighten the retainers to 105 inch lbs. (12 Nm).
12. If removed, install the oil filter and adapter.
13. Install the transmission inspection cover.
14. Install the front engine mount and bracket.
15. Install the transmission bending bracket.
16. Carefully lower the vehicle. Fill the crankcase with the proper type and amount of engine oil.
17. Start the engine and check for leaks, then recheck the fluid level and add as necessary.

#### 1998–99 Vehicles

▶ **See Figures 100 and 101**

1. Raise and safely support the vehicle.
2. Drain the engine oil into a suitable container.
3. Properly support the engine and transaxle assembly, then remove the front engine mount bracket.
4. Remove the powertrain bending strut.
5. Remove the structural collar from the oil pan-to-transaxle.
6. Remove the transaxle lower dust cover.
7. If equipped with A/C, remove the oil filter and adapter.
8. Unfasten the retaining bolts, then remove the oil pan.
9. Thoroughly clean the gasket mating surfaces.

**To install:**

10. Apply suitable silicone sealer to the oil pump-to-engine block parting line, as shown in the accompanying figure.

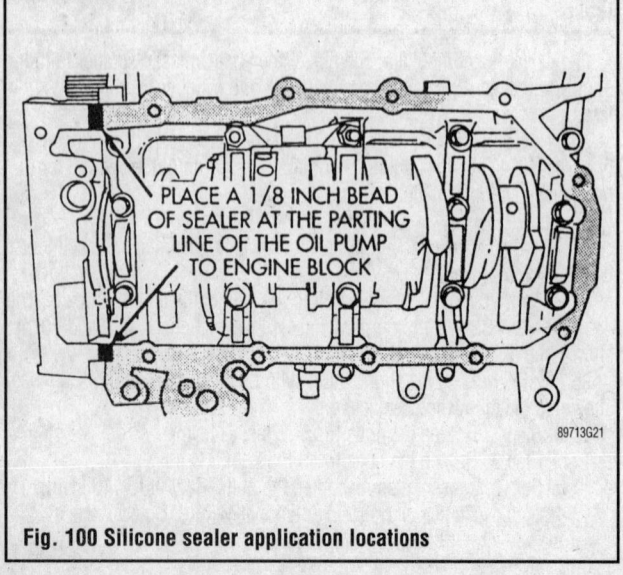

PLACE A 1/8 INCH BEAD OF SEALER AT THE PARTING LINE OF THE OIL PUMP TO ENGINE BLOCK

89713G21

**Fig. 100 Silicone sealer application locations**

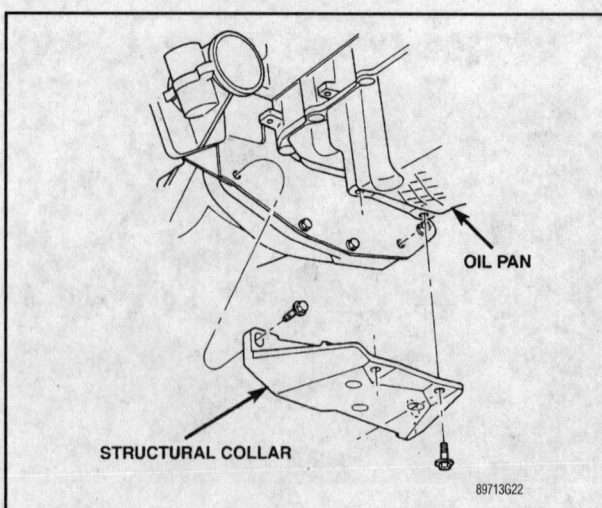

OIL PAN

STRUCTURAL COLLAR

89713G22

**Fig. 101 Exploded view of the structural collar mounting—1998–99 vehicles**

11. Position a new oil pan gasket on the pan.
12. Install the pan, then tighten the retainers to 105 inch lbs. (12 Nm).
13. If removed, install the oil filter and adapter.
14. Install the transaxle lower dust cover.
15. Install the powertrain bending strut.
16. Install the front engine mount and bracket.

### ✳✳ WARNING

**You MUST follow the proper tightening sequence for the structural collar or damage to the collar or oil pan may occur!**

17. Install the structural collar, then tighten the retainers as follows:
  a. Step 1: Install the collar-to-oil pan bolts and tighten to 30 inch lbs. (3 Nm).
  b. Step 2: Install the collar-to-transaxle bolts and tighten to 80 ft. lbs. (108 Nm).
  c. Step 3: Final-tighten the collar-to-oil pan bolts to 40 ft. lbs. (54 Nm).
18. Carefully lower the vehicle. Fill the crankcase with the proper type and amount of engine oil.
19. Start the engine and check for leaks, then recheck the fluid level and add as necessary.

## Oil Pump

### REMOVAL & INSTALLATION

▶ **See Figures 102 thru 111**

1. Disconnect the negative battery cable.
2. Remove the timing belt, as outlined later in this section.
3. Raise and safely support the vehicle.
4. Drain the engine oil into a suitable container.
5. Remove the oil pan, as outlined earlier.

6. Remove the crankshaft sprocket using a suitable puller.
7. Remove the oil pickup tube.
8. Remove the oil pump and the front crankshaft seal.
9. Remove the oil pump cover screws, then lift the cover off.
10. Remove the oil pump rotors.
11. Wash all parts in a suitable solvent, then inspect carefully for damage or wear, as follows:
  a. Clean all parts thoroughly. The mating surface of the oil pump should be smooth. Replace the pump cover if it is scratched or grooved.
  b. Lay a straightedge across the pump cover surface. If a 0.003 in. (0.076mm) feeler gauge can be inserted between the cover and the straight edge, the cover should be replaced.
  c. Measure the thickness and diameter of the outer rotor. If the outer rotor thickness measures 0.301 in. (7.64mm) or less, or if the diameter is 3.148 in. (79.95mm) or less, replace the outer rotor.
  d. If the inner rotor measures 0.301 in. (7.64mm) or less, replace the inner rotor.
  e. Slide the outer rotor into the pump housing, press to one side with your fingers and measure the clearance between the rotor and the housing. If the measurement is 0.015 in. (0.39mm) or more, replace the housing only f the outer rotor is within specification.
  f. Install the inner rotor into the pump housing, If the clearance between the inner and outer rotors is 0.008 ion. (0.203mm) or more, replace both rotors.
  g. Place a straightedge across the face of the pump housing, between the bolt holes. If a feeler gauge of 0.004 in. (0.102mm) or more can be inserted between the rotors and the straightedge. replace the pump assembly ONLY if the rotors are within specifications.
  h. Inspect the oil pressure relief valve plunger for scoring and free operation in its bore. Small marks may be removed with 400-grit wet or dry sandpaper.
  i. The relief valve spring has a free length of about 2.39 in. (60.7mm) and should test between 18–19 lbs. when compressed to 1.60 in. (4.05mm). Replace the spring if it falls outside of specifications.

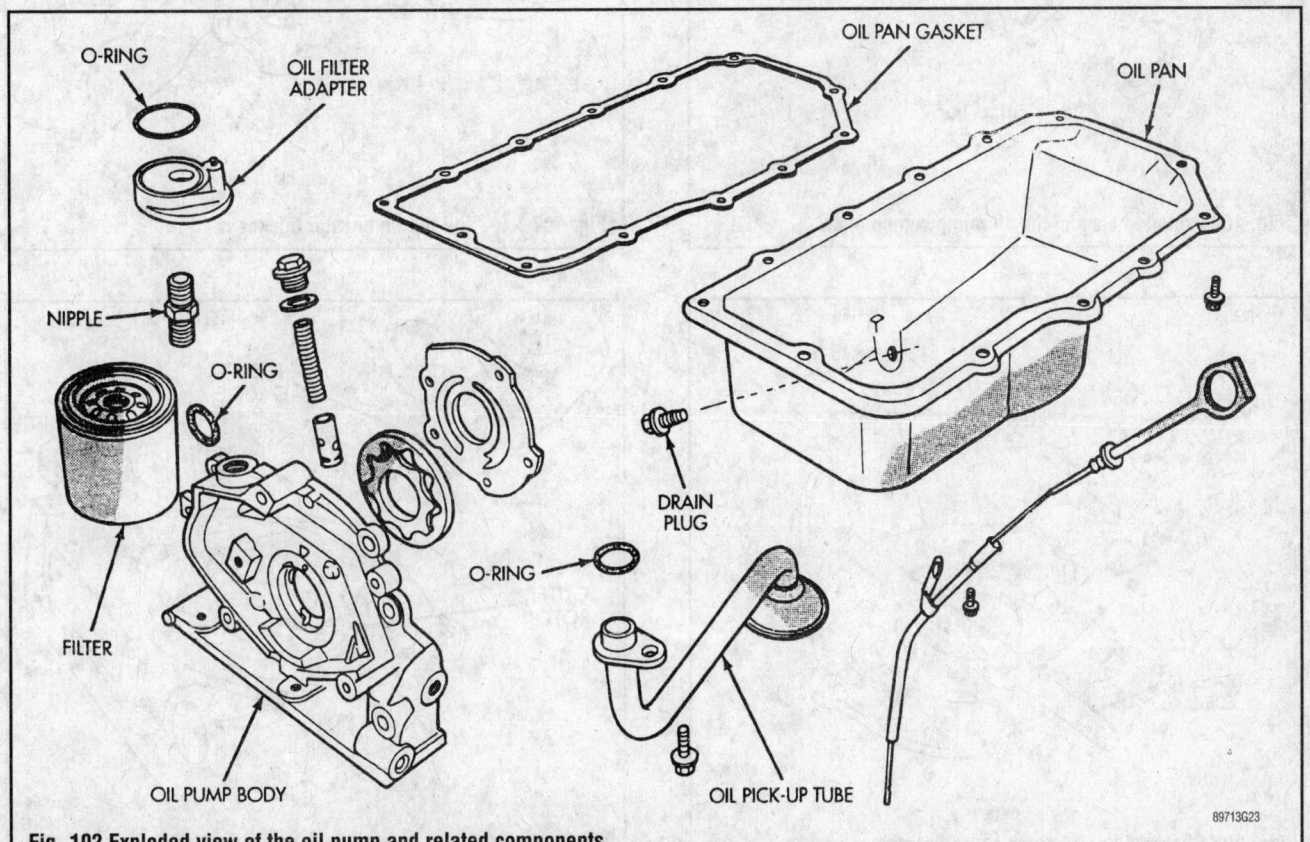

Fig. 102 Exploded view of the oil pump and related components

89713G23

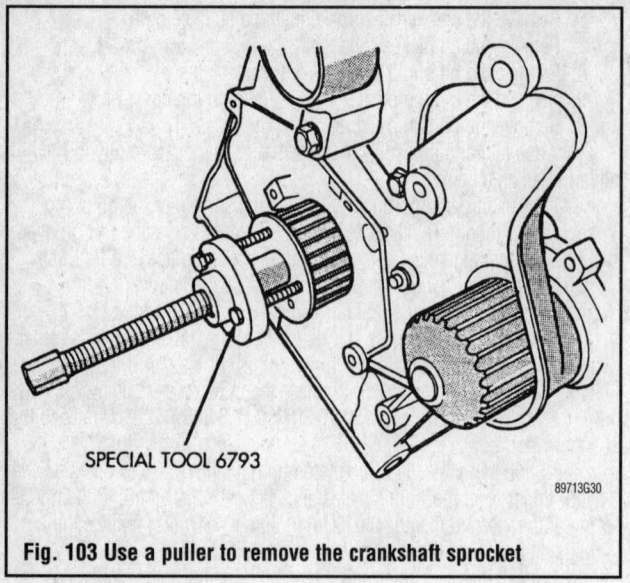

Fig. 103 Use a puller to remove the crankshaft sprocket

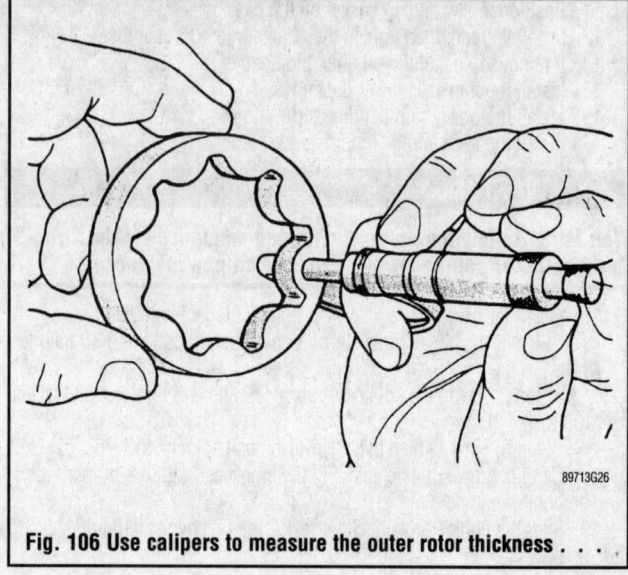

Fig. 106 Use calipers to measure the outer rotor thickness . . .

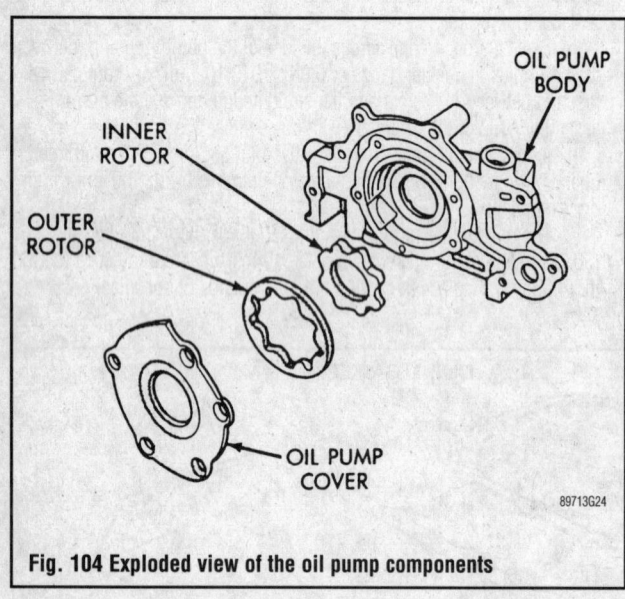

Fig. 104 Exploded view of the oil pump components

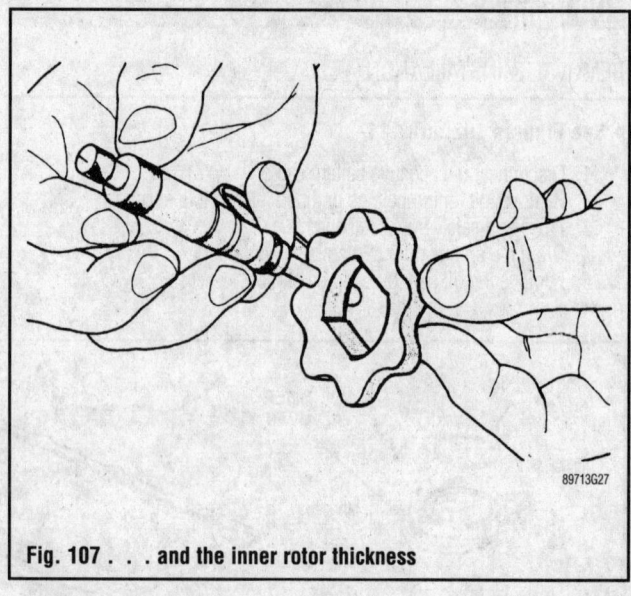

Fig. 107 . . . and the inner rotor thickness

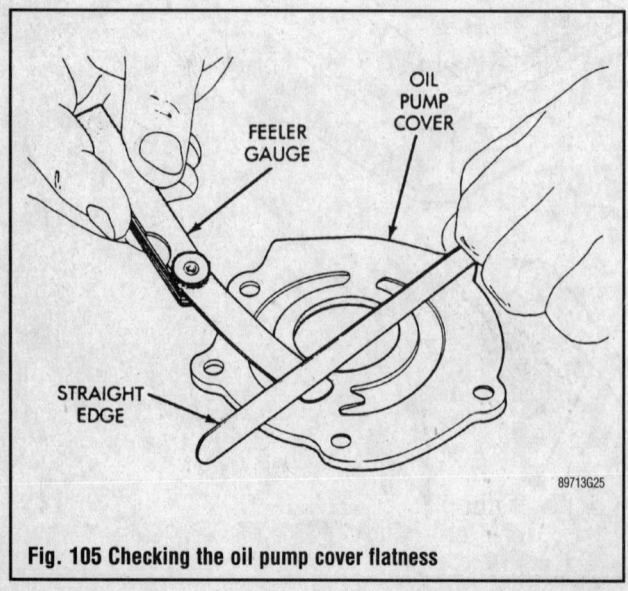

Fig. 105 Checking the oil pump cover flatness

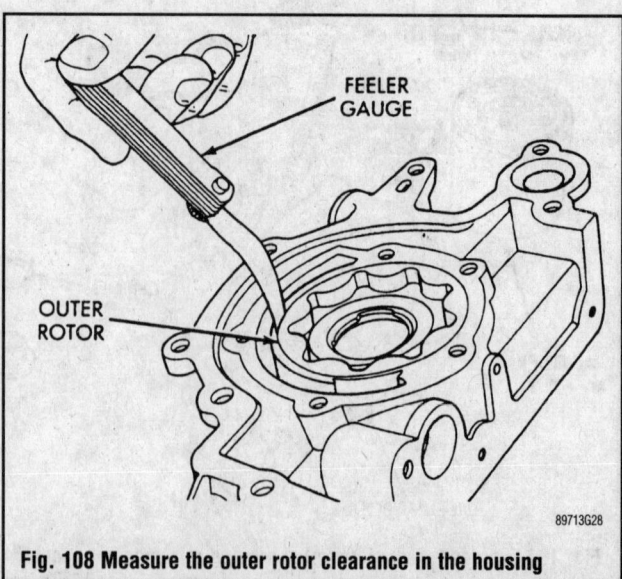

Fig. 108 Measure the outer rotor clearance in the housing

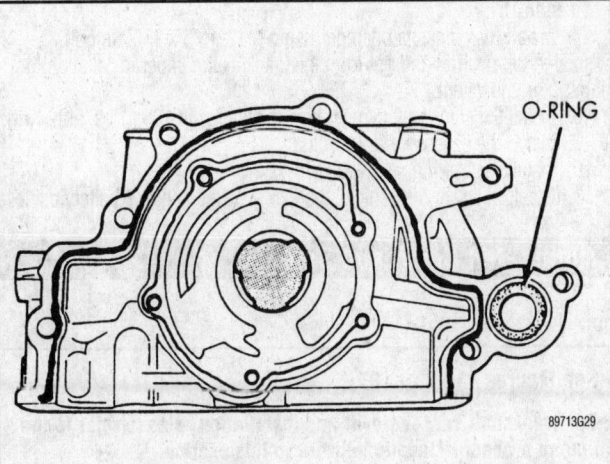

**Fig. 109 Apply a small amount of gasket maker to the pump body cover mounting surface**

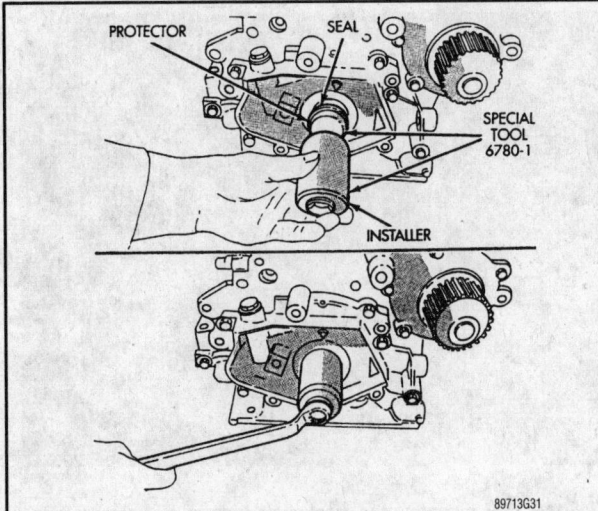

**Fig. 110 Use a suitable driver tool to install the crankshaft seal**

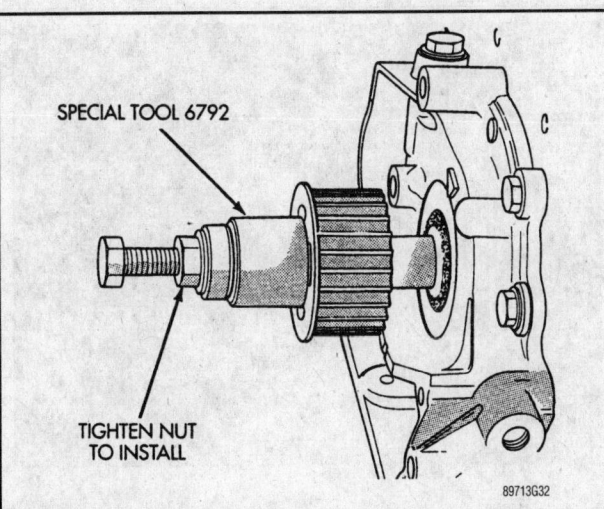

**Fig. 111 A special tool is available to install the crankshaft sprocket**

j. If the oil pressure is low and the pump is within specifications, inspect for worn engine bearings or other reasons for oil pressure loss.

**To install:**

12. Assemble the pump, using new parts as required. Install the inner rotor with the chamfer facing the cast iron oil pump cover.

13. Apply Mopar or equivalent gasket maker to the oil pump as shown in the accompanying figure. Install the oil ring into the oil pump body discharge passage.

14. Prime the oil pump before installation by filling the rotor cavity with engine oil.

15. Align the oil pump rotor flats with the flats on the crankshaft as your install the oil pump to the block.

### ✳✳ WARNING

**The front crankshaft seal MUST be out of the pump to align, or damage may result.**

16. Tighten all of the pump attaching bolts to 21 ft. lbs. (28 Nm).

17. Install a new front crankshaft seal using seal driver tool 6780 or equivalent.

18. Install the crankshaft sprocket using a suitable crankshaft damper installation tool.

19. Install the oil pump pick-up tube and oil pan.

20. Install the timing belt.

21. Carefully lower the vehicle. Fill the crankcase with the proper type and amount of engine oil.

22. Start the engine and check for leaks, then recheck the fluid level and add as necessary.

## Crankshaft Damper

### REMOVAL & INSTALLATION

▶ See Figures 112, 113, 114 and 115

1. Disconnect the negative battery cable.

2. Raise and safely support the vehicle. Remove the right side wheel and tire assembly.

3. Remove the right inner splash shield.

4. Remove the accessory drive belts.

5. Break the crankshaft damper bolt loose, but do not remove it.

6. Attach a suitable 3-jawed puller to the crankshaft damper, then tighten the center bolt and remove the damper bolt and damper.

**Fig. 112 After the splash shield is removed, break the crankshaft damper loose**

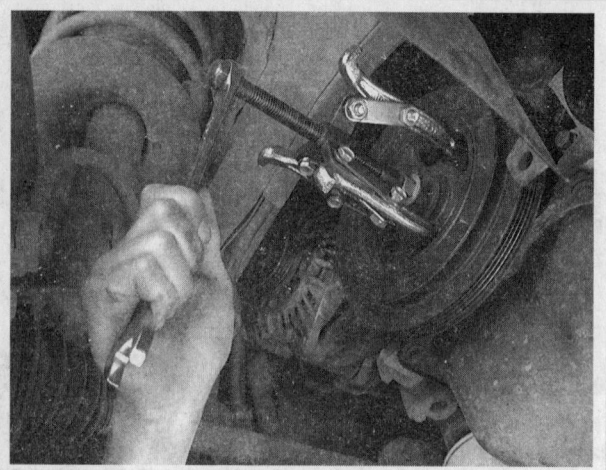

**Fig. 113 Attach a suitable 3-jawed puller to the crankshaft damper and tighten the center bolt . . .**

**Fig. 114 . . . to remove the crankshaft damper bolt and damper**

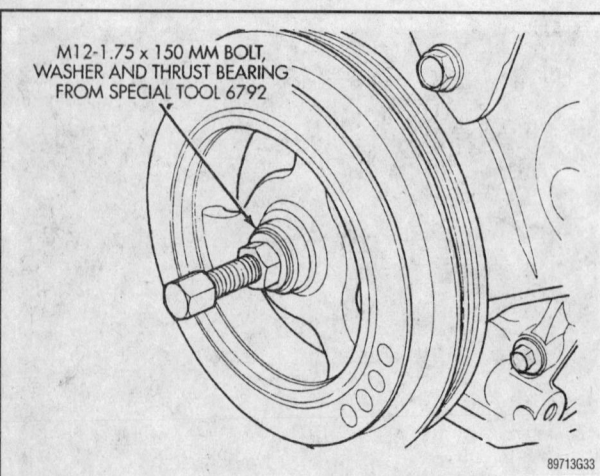

**Fig. 115 Install the crankshaft damper using the bolt, washer, thrust bearing and nut from the crankshaft damper installation tool kit**

**To install:**

7. Install the crankshaft damper using M12-1.75 x 150mm bolt, washer, thrust bearing and nut from the crankshaft damper installation tool kit 6792 or equivalent.

8. Install the crankshaft damper bolt and tighten to 105 ft. lbs. (142 Nm).

9. Install the accessory drive belts.

10. Install the right inner splash shield.

11. Carefully lower the vehicle, then connect the negative battery cable.

## Timing Belt Cover and Seal

### REMOVAL & INSTALLATION

▶ **See Figures 116 thru 127**

➡ For crankshaft seal removal and installation, please refer to the oil pump procedure location earlier in this section.

1. Disconnect the negative battery cable.
2. Remove the accessory drive belts.
3. Raise and safely support the vehicle, then remove the right inner splash shield.

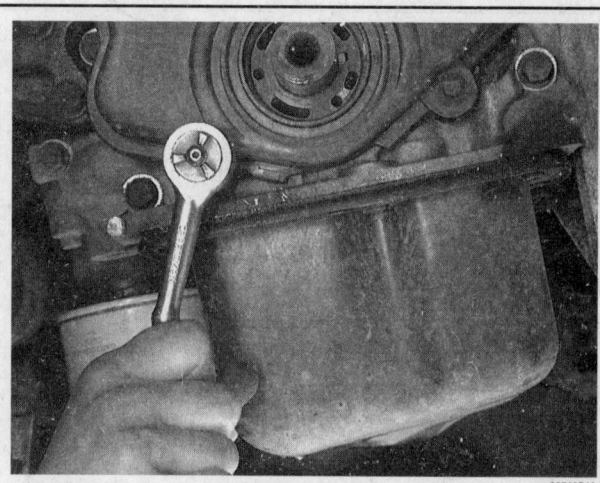

**Fig. 116 After removing the crankshaft damper, you can remove the timing belt cover lower fasteners**

**Fig. 117 Safely and carefully support the engine with a suitable floor jack and block of wood under the oil pan**

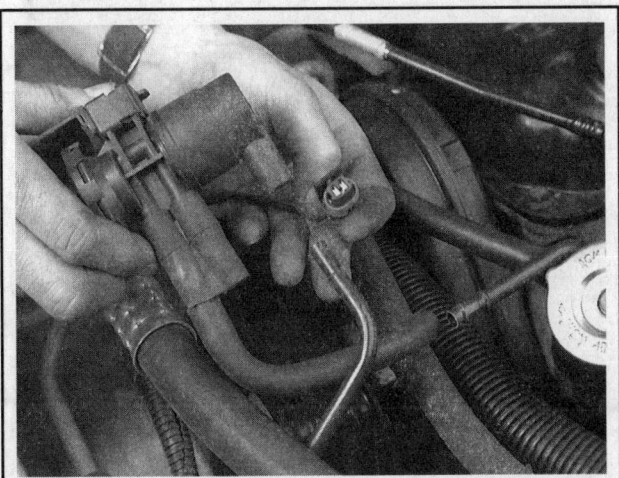

Fig. 118 Disconnect the hoses, detach the connector, then remove the purge solenoid

Fig. 121 Once the bolt is loosened, you can withdraw it through the access hole . . .

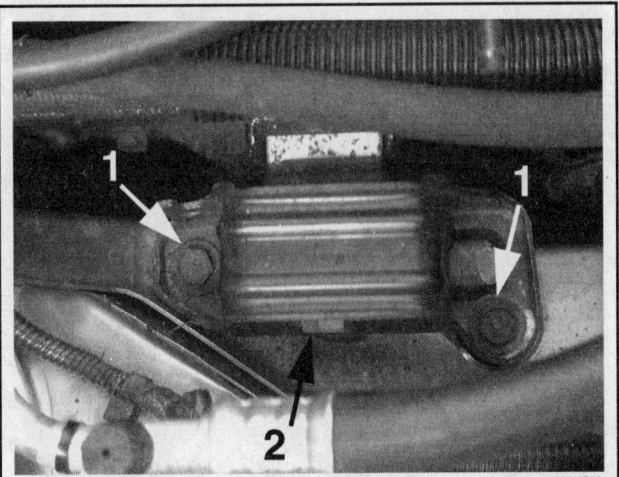

Fig. 119 The right engine mount is secured with two vertical bolts (1) and a horizontal insulator bolt (2)

Fig. 122 . . . then you can remove the right side engine mount

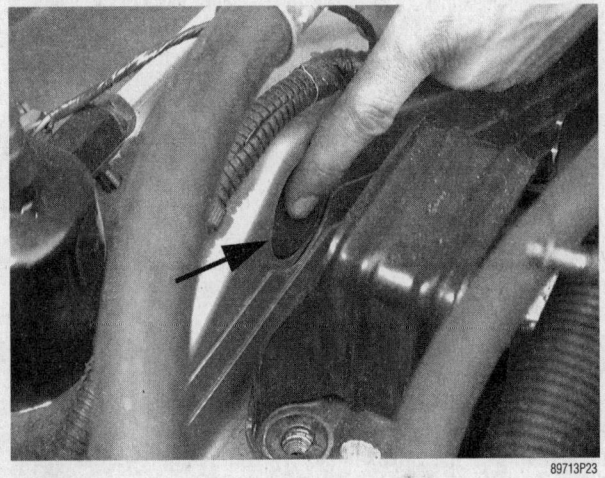

Fig. 120 Remove the plug (see arrow) in order to access the insulator bolt

Fig. 123 For added space, unbolt the power steering pump and position it aside. Do NOT disconnect the fluid lines!

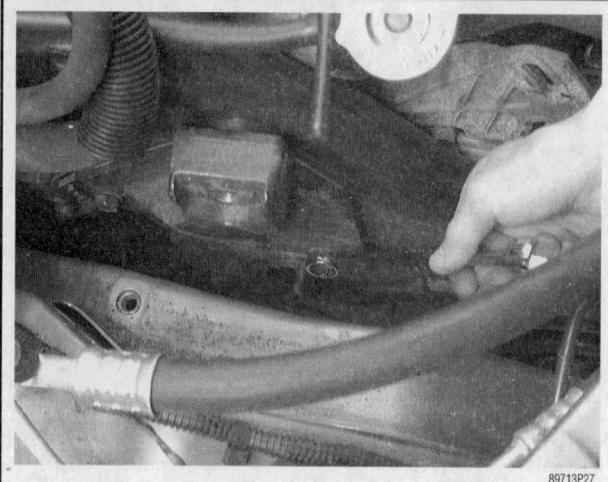

Fig. 124 Unfasten the engine mount bracket retaining bolts (you may have the raise the engine with the jack for access)

Fig. 125 Then, remove the engine mount bracket. Keep in mind it may take some maneuvering to remove it from the vehicle

Fig. 126 Remove any remaining retainers, then remove the timing belt cover from the engine

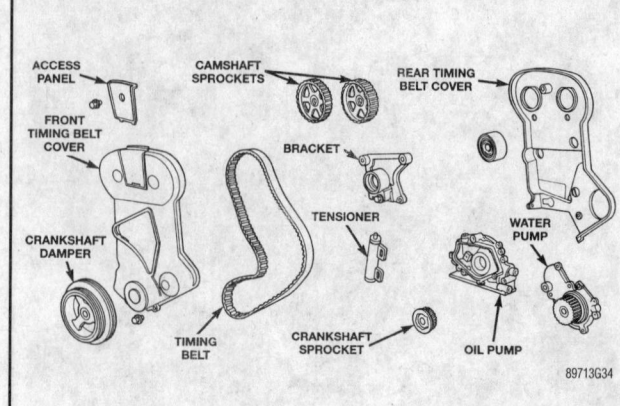

Fig. 127 Timing belt cover and fastener location—DOHC engine shown, SOHC similar

4. Remove the crankshaft damper, as outlined earlier in this section.
5. Remove the lower timing belt cover fasteners.
6. Carefully lower the vehicle, then support the engine with a floor jack and block of wood under the oil pan. NEVER place the jack directly on the oil pan, use a block of wood to disperse the weight of the engine.
7. Disconnect the hoses, unplug the connector and remove the purge solenoid.
8. Unfasten the retainers, then remove the right engine mount. You will have to remove the access plug to get to the insulator bolt.
9. Unbolt the power steering pump and position it aside for more working space. Do NOT disconnect the power steering fluid lines!
10. Remove the right engine mount bracket.
11. Unfasten the remaining retainers, then remove the timing belt cover from the engine.

**To install:**
12. Install the front timing belt cover and secure with the upper and/or side fasteners.
13. Install the right engine mount bracket.
14. Reposition the power steering pump and bolt it securely in place.
15. Install the right engine mount, then remove the jack from under the oil pan.
16. Install the purge solenoid and attach the connector and hoses.
17. Install the lower timing belt fasteners.
18. Install the crankshaft damper, as outlined earlier in this section.
19. Install the inner splash shield, then carefully lower the vehicle.
20. Install the accessory drive belts.
21. Raise and safely support the vehicle, then install the right inner splash shield.
22. Carefully lower the vehicle, then connect the negative battery cable.

## Timing Belt and Sprockets

### INSPECTION

▶ See Figures 128 thru 135

### ✳✳ WARNING

**Timing belt maintenance is extremely important! All Neon models utilize an interference-type, non-free-wheeling engine. If the timing belt breaks, the valves in the cylinder head may strike the pistons, causing potentially serious (also time-consuming and expensive) engine damage. The recommended replacement interval for the timing belt is 102,000 miles (163,000km), or sooner.**

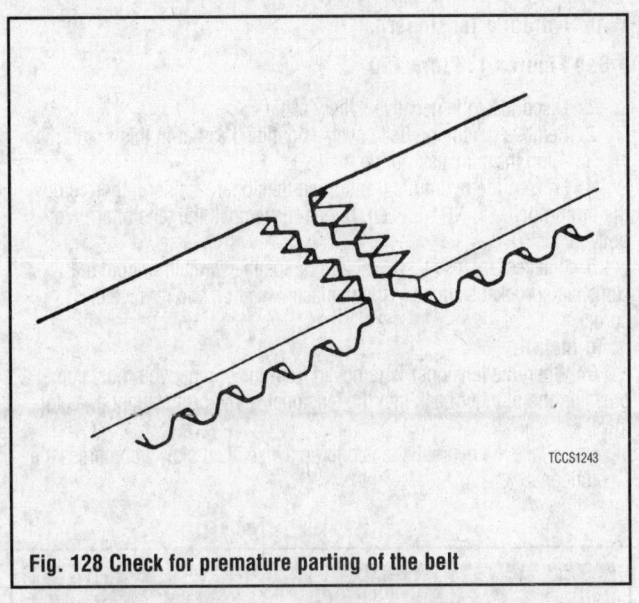

Fig. 128 Check for premature parting of the belt

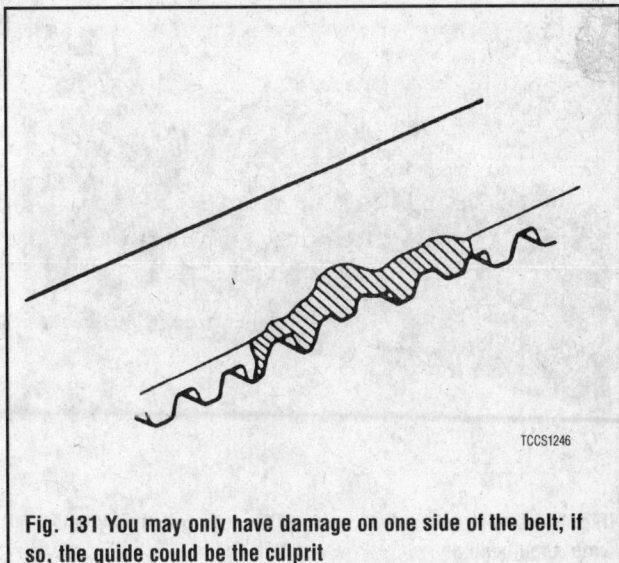

Fig. 131 You may only have damage on one side of the belt; if so, the guide could be the culprit

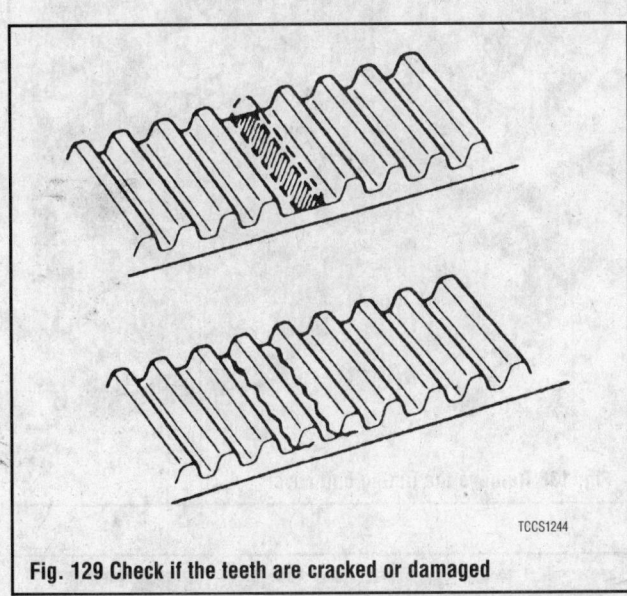

Fig. 129 Check if the teeth are cracked or damaged

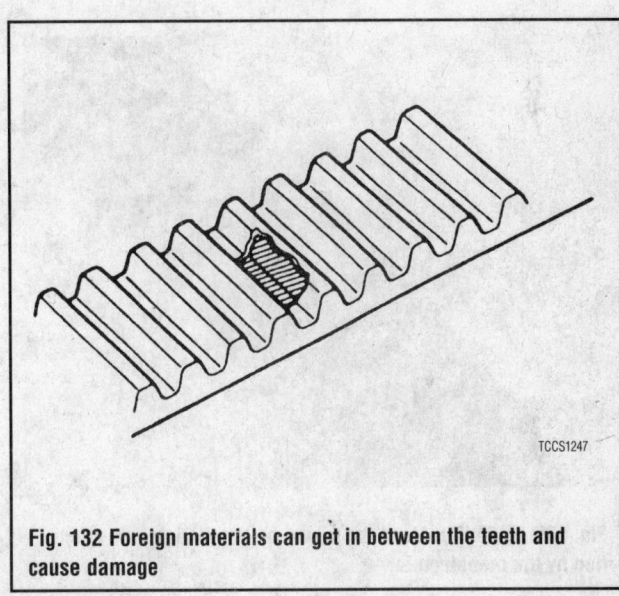

Fig. 132 Foreign materials can get in between the teeth and cause damage

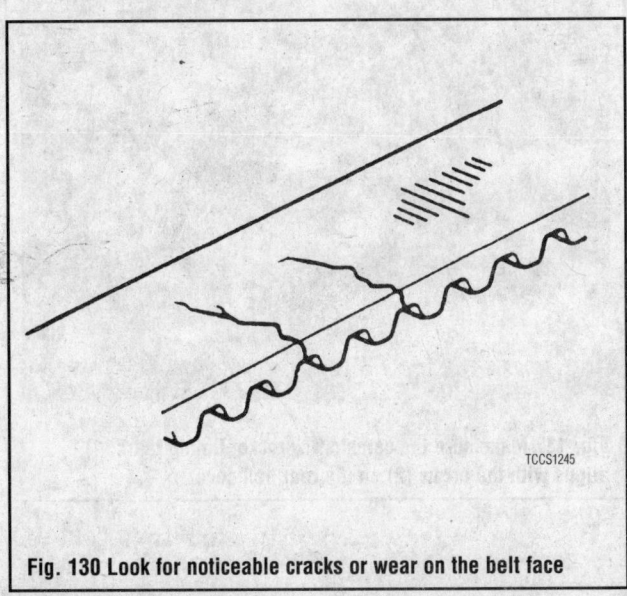

Fig. 130 Look for noticeable cracks or wear on the belt face

Fig. 133 Inspect the timing belt for cracks, fraying, glazing or damage of any kind

Fig. 134 Damage on only one side of the timing belt may indicate a faulty guide

Fig. 135 ALWAYS replace the timing belt at the interval specified by the manufacturer

You would be wise to check the belt periodically to make sure it has not become damaged or worn. Generally speaking, a severely worn belt may cause engine performance to drop dramatically, but a damaged belt (which could give out suddenly) may not give as much warning. In general, any time the engine timing cover(s) is(are) removed you should inspect the belt for premature parting, severe cracks or missing teeth. Also, an access plug or cover is provided in the upper portion of the timing cover so that camshaft timing can be checked without cover removal. If timing is found to be off, cover removal and further belt inspection or replacement is necessary.

## REMOVAL & INSTALLATION

### ❊❊ WARNING

**NEVER rotate the camshaft(s) or crankshaft after the timing belt is removed! This could damage the valve train components. Always align the timing marks before removing the timing belt.**

### With Hydraulic Tensioner

▶ See Figures 136 thru 150

1. Disconnect the negative battery cable.
2. Remove the timing belt cover, as outlined earlier in this section.
3. Align the camshaft timing marks.
4. Loosen the hydraulic timing belt tensioner retainers, then remove the timing belt. Do NOT loosen, tighten or remove the tensioner pivot bolt.
5. If necessary, use a special tool or spanner wrench to hold the camshaft sprocket stationary, then unfasten the bolt and remove the sprocket.

**To install:**

6. When the tensioner is removed from the engine, you must compression the plunger back into the tensioner body for installation, as follows:

   a. Place the hydraulic tensioner in a vise, then slowly compress the plunger.

Fig. 136 Remove the timing belt cover

Fig. 137 Make sure the camshaft sprocket timing mark (1) aligns with the arrow (2) on the rear belt cover . . .

Fig. 138 . . . and the crankshaft sprocket timing mark (1) is aligned with the arrow (2)

Fig. 141 . . . then remove the timing belt from the sprockets

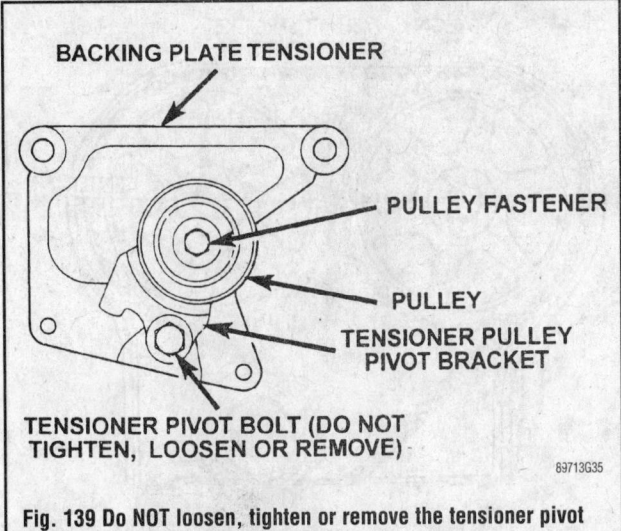

BACKING PLATE TENSIONER

PULLEY FASTENER

PULLEY

TENSIONER PULLEY PIVOT BRACKET

TENSIONER PIVOT BOLT (DO NOT TIGHTEN, LOOSEN OR REMOVE)

Fig. 139 Do NOT loosen, tighten or remove the tensioner pivot bolt

Fig. 142 If necessary, use the special tool or a spanner wrench to hold the cam sprocket, then unfasten the bolt and remove the sprocket

Fig. 140 Remove the 2 timing belt tensioner retaining bolts . . .

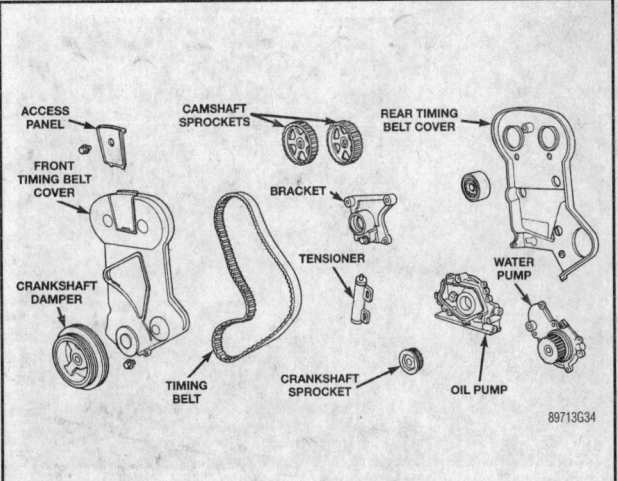

ACCESS PANEL

CAMSHAFT SPROCKETS

REAR TIMING BELT COVER

FRONT TIMING BELT COVER

BRACKET

CRANKSHAFT DAMPER

TENSIONER

WATER PUMP

TIMING BELT

CRANKSHAFT SPROCKET

OIL PUMP

Fig. 143 Exploded view of the timing belt and related components—DOHC with hydraulic tensioner shown, SOHC similar

Fig. 144 Install the timing belt tensioner in a vise

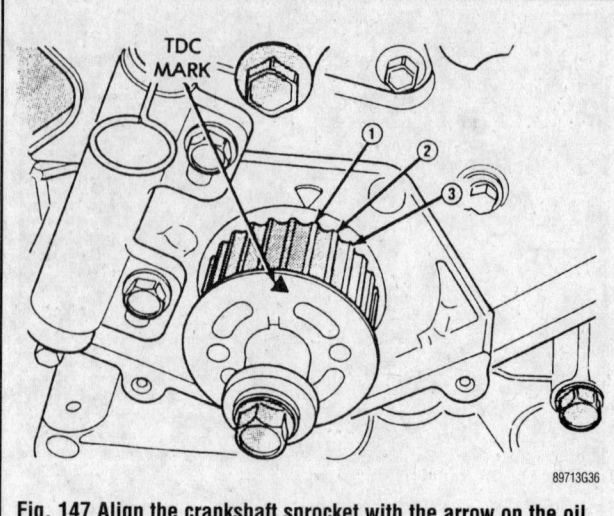

Fig. 147 Align the crankshaft sprocket with the arrow on the oil pump housing, then back off 3 notches for TDC

Fig. 145 Use the vise to slowly compress the tensioner plunger so the holes in the plunger and the body align . . .

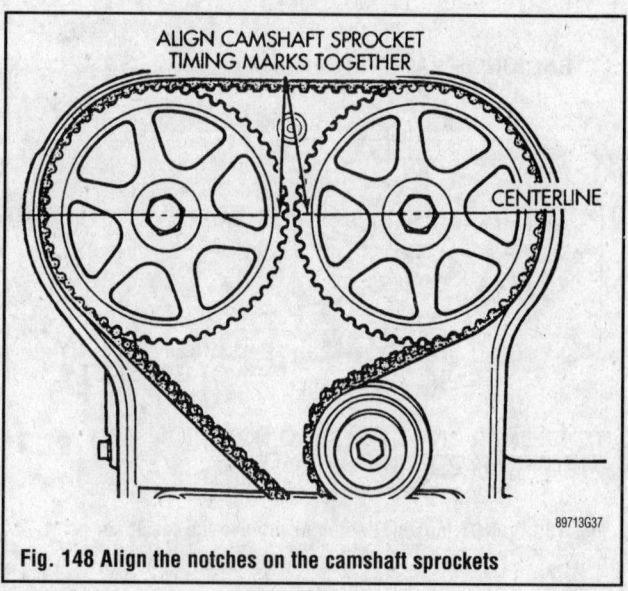

Fig. 148 Align the notches on the camshaft sprockets

Fig. 146 . . . then insert a ⁵⁄₆₄ in. (1.9mm) Allen wrench through the holes to hold the plunger in place

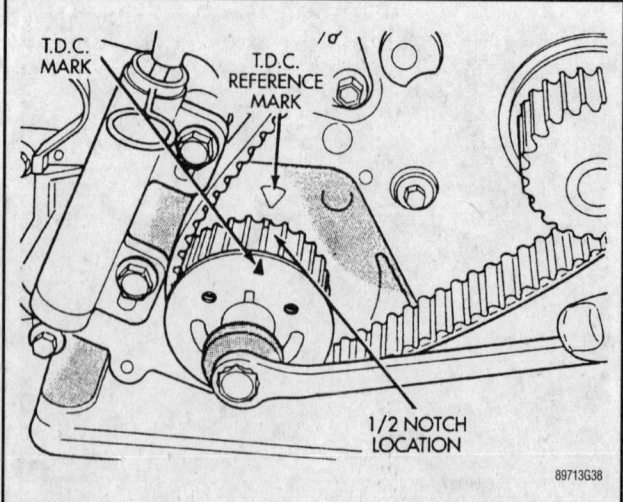

Fig. 149 Rotate the crankshaft ½ tooth counterclockwise from Top Dead Center (TDC)

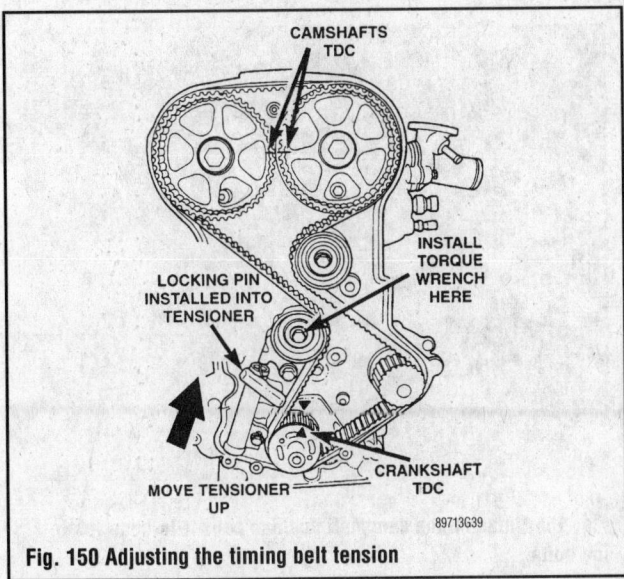

Fig. 150 Adjusting the timing belt tension

➥Index the tensioner in the vise the same way it is installed on the engine. This will ensure proper pin orientation when the tensioner is installed on the engine.

7. When the plunger is compressed into the tensioner body, install a 5/64 in. (9mm) hex pin through the body and plunger. This will keep the plunger in place until the tensioner is installed.

8. If removed, install the camshaft sprocket(s) and secure with the retaining bolts.

9. Set the crankshaft sprocket to TDC by aligning the sprocket with the arrow on the oil pump housing, then back off 3 notches before TDC.

10. Set the camshaft timing marks together by aligning the notches on the sprockets.

11. Rotate the crankshaft ½ tooth counterclockwise from TDC.

12. Install the timing belt in this direction. Starting at the crankshaft, go around the water pump sprocket, idler pulley, camshaft sprockets and then around the tensioner pulley.

13. Move the crankshaft sprocket to TDC to take up the belt slack. Install the tensioner to the block but do not tighten the fasteners yet.

14. Using a torque wrench on the tensioner pulley, apply 21 ft. lbs. (28 Nm). or torque to the tensioner.

15. With torque being applied to the tensioner pulley, move the tensioner up against the tensioner pulley bracket and tighten the fasteners to 23 ft. lbs. (31 Nm).

16. Pull the tensioner plunger pin. The pretension is correct when the pin can be removed and installed freely.

17. Rotate the crankshaft 2 revolutions and check the alignment of the timing marks.

18. Install the front timing belt cover, as outlined earlier in this section.

### With Mechanical Tensioner

▶ See Figures 151, 152, 153 and 154

1. Disconnect the negative battery cable.
2. Remove the timing belt cover, as outlined earlier in this section.

### ❈❈ WARNING

**Align the camshaft and crankshaft timing marks before removing the timing belt by rotating the engine with the crankshaft. NEVER rotate the camshaft once the timing belt has been removed because damage to the valve components may occur.**

3. Align the camshaft timing mark(s) and crankshaft timing mark with the arrow on the oil pump housing.

4. Insert an 8mm Allen wrench into the timing belt tensioner. Insert the

long end of the 1/8 in. (3mm) Allen wrench into the pin hole on the front of the tensioner.

5. Rotate the tensioner counterclockwise with the Allen wrench, while pushing in lightly with the 1/8 in. (3mm) Allen wrench, until it slides into the locking hole.

6. Remove the timing belt from the engine.

7. If necessary, remove the tensioner by unfastening the attaching bolts. The timing belt tensioner is serviced as an assembly. To prevent premature timing belt failure and engine damage, DO NOT separate the tensioner pulley from the mounting bracket.

8. If necessary, use a special tool or spanner wrench to hold the camshaft sprocket stationary, then unfasten the bolt and remove the sprocket.

**To install:**

9. If removed, install the camshaft sprocket(s) and secure with the retaining bolts.

10. If removed, install the timing belt tensioner. Install the retaining bolts and tighten to 21 ft. lbs. (28 Nm).

11. Set the crankshaft sprocket to TDC by aligning the sprocket with the arrow on the oil pump housing, then back off 3 notches before TDC.

12. Set the camshaft timing marks together by aligning the notches on the sprockets.

13. Rotate the crankshaft ½ tooth counterclockwise from TDC.

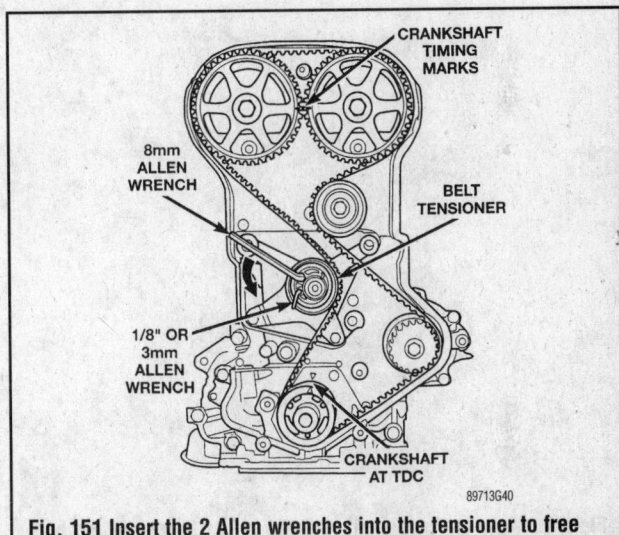

Fig. 151 Insert the 2 Allen wrenches into the tensioner to free the timing belt

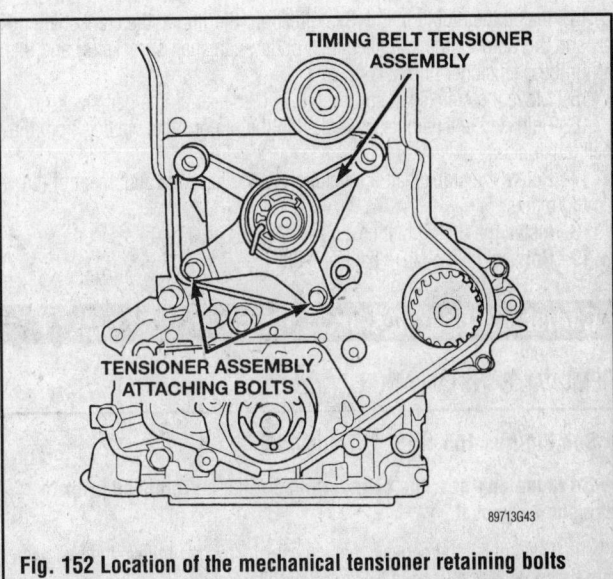

Fig. 152 Location of the mechanical tensioner retaining bolts

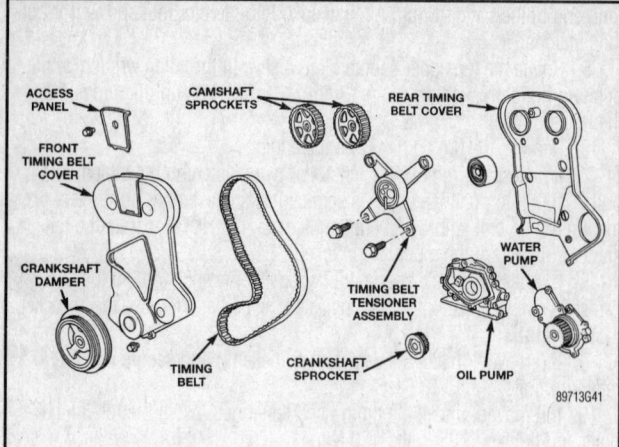

Fig. 153 Exploded view of the timing belt and related components—DOHC with mechanical tensioner shown, SOHC similar

Fig. 155 Unfasten the camshaft position sensor-to-head retaining bolts

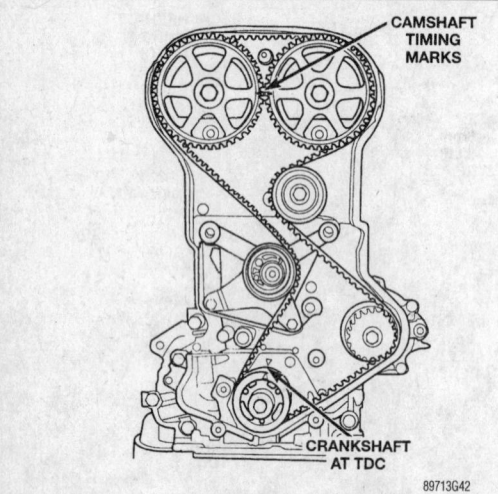

Fig. 154 Move the crankshaft sprocket to TDC to take up the belt slack

Fig. 156 Pull the camshaft position sensor (1) away from the target magnet (2) on the cylinder head

14. Install the timing belt in this direction. Starting at the crankshaft, go around the water pump sprocket, idler pulley, camshaft sprocket(s) and then around the tensioner pulley.

15. Move the crankshaft sprocket to TDC to take up the belt slack.

16. Release the tensioner by removing the pin or Allen wrench from the belt tensioner.

17. Rotate the crankshaft 2 revolutions and check the alignment of the timing marks.

18. Install the timing belt cover, as outlined earlier in this section.

19. Connect the negative battery cable.

## Camshaft, Bearings and Lifters

### REMOVAL & INSTALLATION

▶ See Figures 155, 156, 157 and 158

➡On these engines, the cylinder head must be removed prior to camshaft removal.

1. Disconnect the negative battery cable. Properly relieve the fuel system pressure, as outlined in Section 5 of this manual.

Fig. 157 Carefully slide the camshaft from the rear of the cylinder head, being careful not to damage the lobes

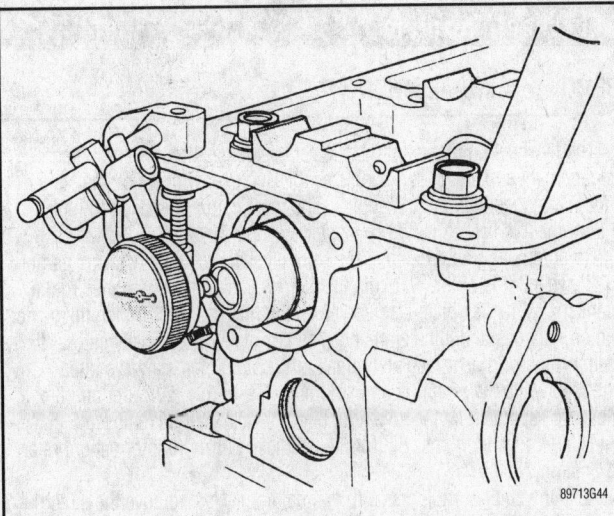

**Fig. 158 Use a dial indicator to measure camshaft end-play**

2. Remove the cylinder head, as outlined earlier in this section.

3. Remove the camshaft sensor and camshaft target magnet.

4. Carefully slide the camshaft from the rear of the cylinder head. Be very careful not to damage the camshaft during removal.

5. Inspect the camshaft and related components for wear as outlined later in this section.

**To install:**

6. Lubricate the camshaft journals with oil, then install the camshaft without the rocker arm assemblies installed.

7. Install the camshaft target magnet into the end of the camshaft. Tighten the mounting screw to 30 inch lbs. (3.4 Nm).

8. Install the camshaft position sensor and tighten the retaining screws to 80 inch lbs. (9 Nm).

9. Measure the camshaft end-play using the following procedure:

   a. Mount a suitable dial indicator to a stationary point on the cylinder head.

   b. Using a suitable tool, move the camshaft to the rearward limits of travel.

   c. Zero the dial indicator.

   d. Move the camshaft forward to the limits of travel and read the dial indicator. The end-play travel should be 0.005–0.013 in. (0.13–0.33mm).

10. Install the front camshaft seal. The camshaft must be installed before the seal is installed.

11. Install the cylinder head.

12. Install the rear timing belt cover.

13. Install the camshaft sprocket and tighten the bolt to 85 ft. lbs. (115 Nm).

14. Install the timing belt tensioner and timing belt.

15. Install the rocker arm shaft assemblies in the same position as they were removed. Tighten the rocker arm assemblies in the sequence shown in the accompanying illustration to 21 ft. lbs. (28 Nm).

16. Install the rocker arm (valve) cover.

17. Connect the negative battery cable.

## INSPECTION

Check the camshaft journals for scratches and worn areas. If light scratches are found, you can remove them carefully with 400-grit sandpaper. If deep scratches are found, replace the camshaft check the cylinder head for damage. Replace the cylinder head if worn of damaged. Check the lobes for pitting and wear. If the lobes show signs of wear, check the corresponding rocker arm roller for wear or damage. Replace the rocker arm/hydraulic lash adjuster if worn or damaged. If the lobes show signs of pitting on the nose, flank or base circle, the camshaft must be replaced.

## Rear Main Seal

### REMOVAL & INSTALLATION

▶ **See Figures 159, 160 and 161**

1. Insert a ³⁄₁₆ in. flat-bladed screwdriver between the dust lip and the metal case of the crankshaft seal. Angle the screwdriver through the dust lip against the metal case of the seal. Pry out the seal.

### ❊❊ WARNING

**Do NOT let the screwdriver blade contact the crankshaft seal surface. Contact of the screwdriver blade against the crankshaft edge (chamfer) is permitted.**

To install:

### ❊❊ WARNING

**If the crankshaft edge (chamfer) has any burrs or scratches on the, you can clean it up with 400 grit sand paper to prevent seal damage during installation of the new seal.**

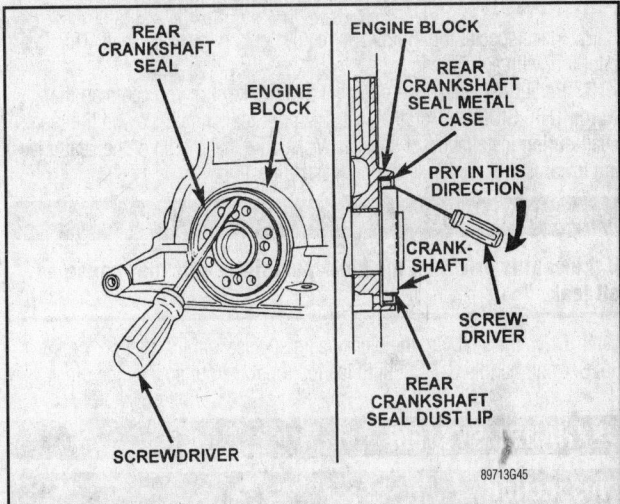

**Fig. 159 When prying the seal out, be sure to use the screwdriver at the proper angle**

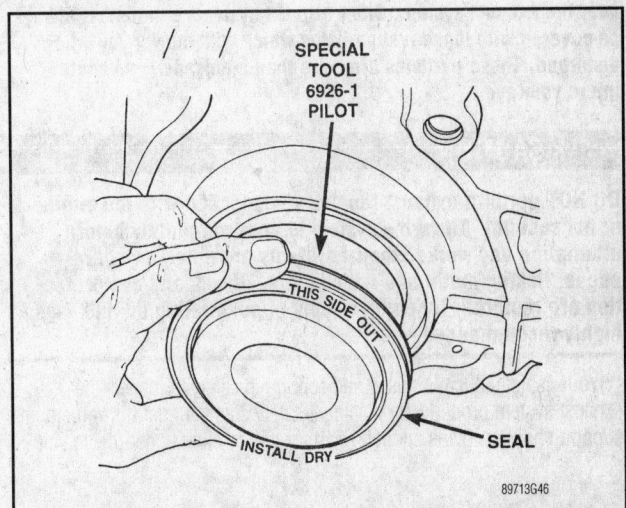

**Fig. 160 Place a proper size pilot tool with a magnetic base on the crankshaft**

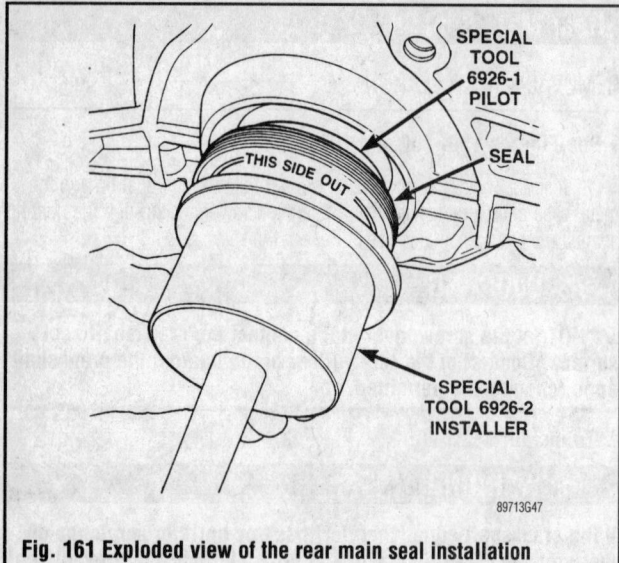

**Fig. 161 Exploded view of the rear main seal installation**

➡**No lubrication is necessary when installing the seal.**

2. Place special tool 6926-1, or equivalent on the crankshaft. This is a pilot tool with a magnetic base.

3. Position the seal over the pilot tool. Make sure you can read the words THIS SIDE OUT on the seal. The pilot tool should stay on the crankshaft during installation of the seal. Make sure that the lip of the seal if facing towards the crankcase during installation.

### ⚙ WARNING

**If the seal is driven in the block past flush, this may cause an oil leak.**

4. Drive the seal into the block using special seal installation tools 6926-2 and handle C-4171 until the tool bottoms out against the block.

## EXHAUST SYSTEM

### Inspection

▸ See Figures 162 thru 168

➡**Safety glasses should be worn at all times when working on or near the exhaust system. Older exhaust systems will almost always be covered with loose rust particles which will shower you when disturbed. These particles are more than a nuisance and could injure your eye.**

### ⚙ CAUTION

**DO NOT perform exhaust repairs or inspection with the engine or exhaust hot. Allow the system to cool completely before attempting any work. Exhaust systems are noted for sharp edges, flaking metal and rusted bolts. Gloves and eye protection are required. A healthy supply of penetrating oil and rags is highly recommended.**

Your vehicle must be raised and supported safely to inspect the exhaust system properly. By placing 4 safety stands under the vehicle for support should provide enough room for you to slide under the vehicle

## Flywheel/Flexplate

### REMOVAL & INSTALLATION

The flywheel on manual transaxle cars serves as the forward clutch engagement surface. It also serves as the ring gear with which the starter pinion engages to crank the engine. The most common reason to replace the flywheel is broken teeth on the starter ring gear.

On automatic transaxle cars, the torque converter actually forms part of the flywheel. It is bolted to a thin flexplate which, in turn, is bolted to the crankshaft. The flex plate also serves as the ring gear with which the starter pinion engages in engine cranking. The flex plate occasionally cracks; the teeth on the ring gear may also break, especially if the starter is often engaged while the pinion is still spinning. The torque converter and flex plate are separated so the converter and transaxle can be removed together.

1. Remove the transaxle from the vehicle. For more information, refer to Section 7.

2. On vehicles equipped with manual transaxles, remove the clutch assembly from the flywheel, as described in Section 7.

3. Support the flywheel in a secure manner (the flywheel on manual transaxle-equipped vehicles can be heavy).

4. Matchmark the flywheel/flexplate to the rear flange of the crankshaft.

5. Remove the attaching bolts and pull the flywheel/flexplate from the crankshaft.

**To install:**

6. Clean the flywheel/flexplate attaching bolts, the flywheel/flexplate and the rear crankshaft mounting flange.

7. Position the flywheel/flexplate onto the crankshaft flange so that the matchmarks align.

8. Coat the threads of the attaching bolts with Loctite® Thread Locker 271, or equivalent, to help ensure that the attaching bolts will not work loose. Install the bolts finger-tight.

9. Tighten the attaching bolts in a crisscross fashion in 3 even steps to 70 ft. lbs. (95 Nm).

10. For manual transaxle-equipped vehicles, install the clutch assembly. For more information, refer to Section 7.

11. Install the transaxle, as described in Section 7.

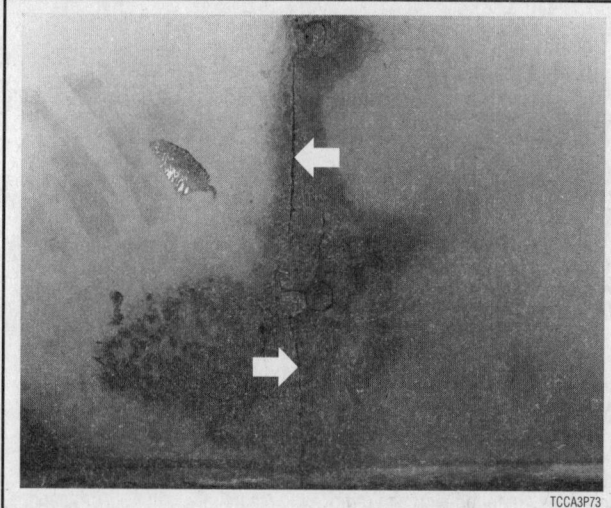

**Fig. 162 Cracks in the muffler are a guaranteed leak**

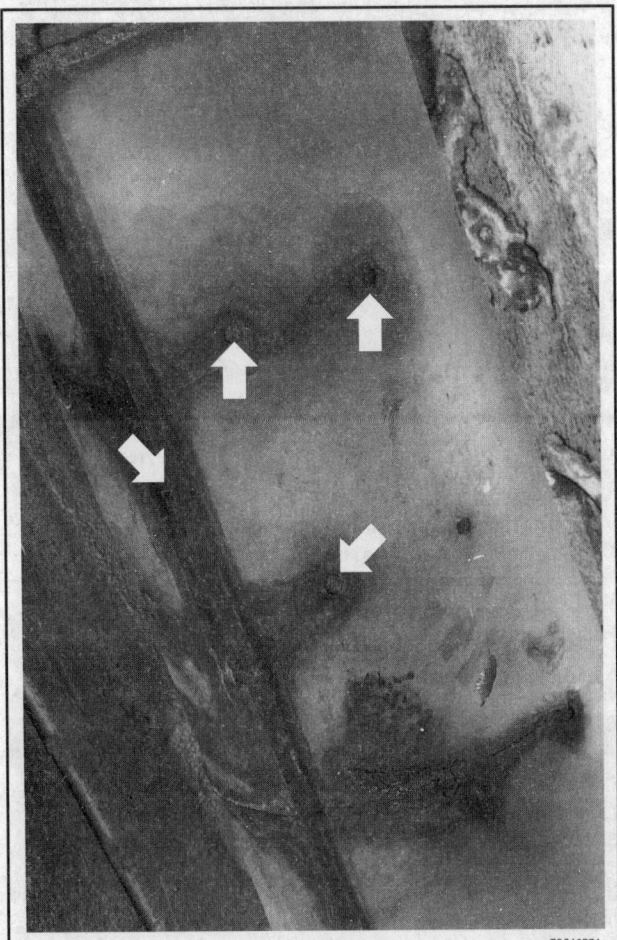

Fig. 163 Check the muffler for rotted spot welds and seams

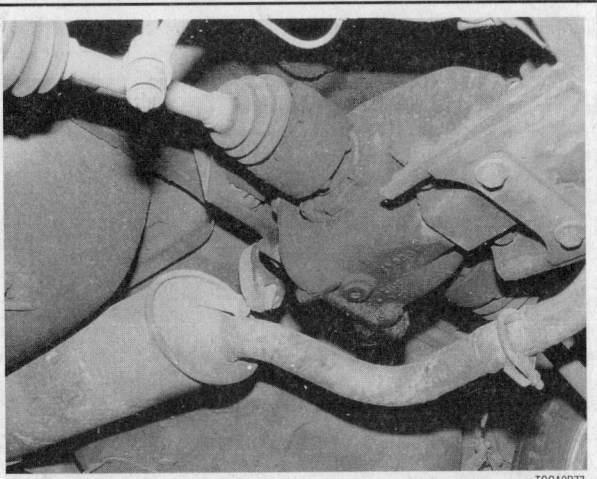

Fig. 164 Make sure the exhaust components are not contacting the body or suspension

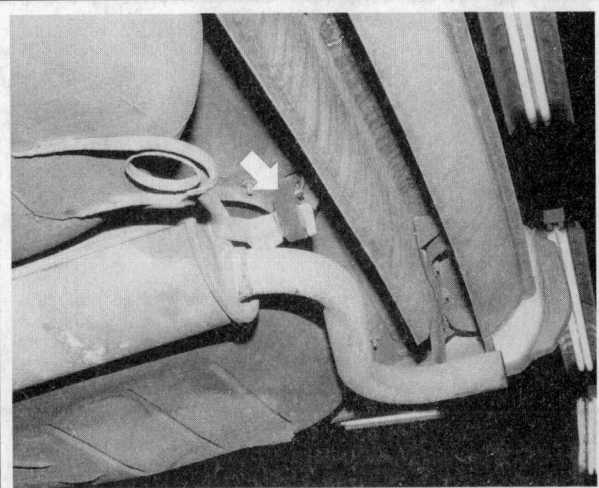

Fig. 165 Check for overstretched or torn exhaust hangers

Fig. 166 Example of a badly deteriorated exhaust pipe

and inspect the system completely. Start the inspection at the exhaust manifold or turbocharger pipe where the header pipe is attached and work your way to the back of the vehicle. On dual exhaust systems, remember to inspect both sides of the vehicle. Check the complete exhaust system for open seams, holes loose connections, or other deterioration which could permit exhaust fumes to seep into the passenger compartment. Inspect all mounting brackets and hangers for deterioration, some models may have rubber O-rings that can be overstretched and non-supportive. These components will need to be replaced if found. It has always been a practice to use a pointed tool to poke up into the exhaust system where the deterioration spots are to see whether or not they crumble. Some models may have heat shield covering certain parts of the exhaust system, it will be necessary to remove these shields to have the exhaust visible for inspection also.

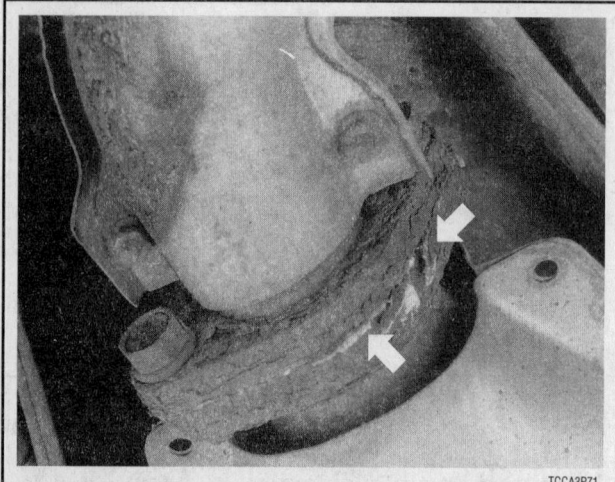

Fig. 167 Inspect flanges for gaskets that have deteriorated and need replacement

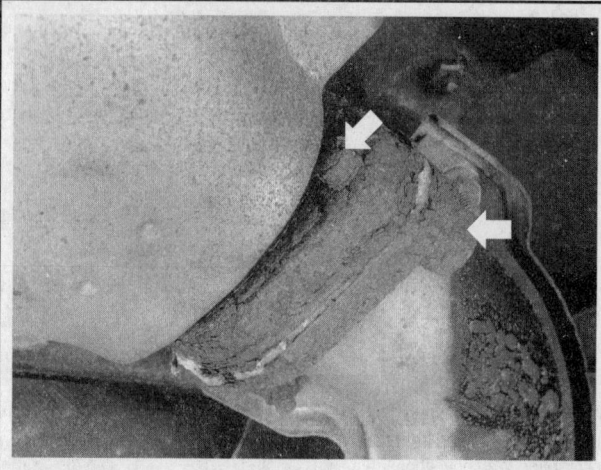

Fig. 169 Nuts and bolts will be extremely difficult to remove when deteriorated with rust

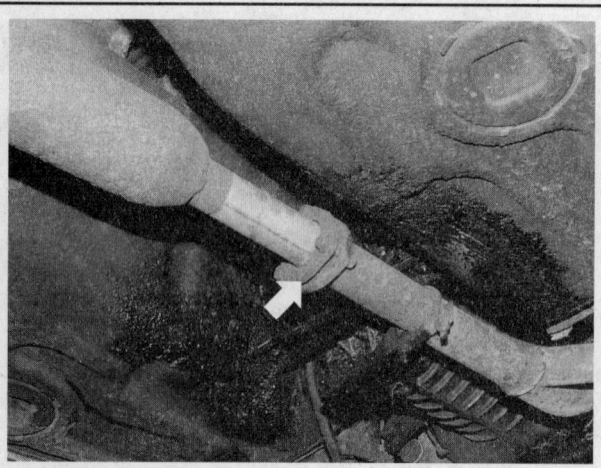

Fig. 168 Some systems, like this one, use large O-rings (donuts) in between the flanges

## REPLACEMENT

▶ See Figure 169

There are basically two types of exhaust systems. One is the flange type where the component ends are attached with bolts and a gasket in-between. The other exhaust system is the slip joint type. These components slip into one another using clamps to retain them together.

### ✳✳ CAUTION

**Allow the exhaust system to cool sufficiently before spraying a solvent exhaust fasteners. Some solvents are highly flammable and could ignite when sprayed on hot exhaust components.**

Before removing any component of the exhaust system, ALWAYS squirt a liquid rust dissolving agent onto the fasteners for ease of removal. A lot of knuckle skin will be saved by following this rule. It may even be wise to spray the fasteners and allow them to sit overnight.

### Flange Type

▶ See Figure 170

### ✳✳ CAUTION

**Do NOT perform exhaust repairs or inspection with the engine or exhaust hot. Allow the system to cool completely before attempting any work. Exhaust systems are noted for sharp edges, flaking metal and rusted bolts. Gloves and eye protection are required. A healthy supply of penetrating oil and rags is highly recommended. Never spray liquid rust dissolving agent onto a hot exhaust component.**

Before removing any component on a flange type system, ALWAYS squirt a liquid rust dissolving agent onto the fasteners for ease of removal. Start by unbolting the exhaust piece at both ends (if required). When unbolting the headpipe from the manifold, make sure that the bolts are free

Fig. 170 Example of a flange type exhaust system joint

before trying to remove them. if you snap a stud in the exhaust manifold, the stud will have to be removed with a bolt extractor, which often means removal of the manifold itself. Next, disconnect the component from the mounting; slight twisting and turning may be required to remove the component completely from the vehicle. You may need to tap on the component with a rubber mallet to loosen the component. If all else fails, use a hacksaw to separate the parts. An oxy-acetylene cutting torch may be faster but the sparks are DANGEROUS near the fuel tank, and at the very least, accidents could happen, resulting in damage.

### Slip Joint Type

▶ **See Figure 171**

Before removing any component on the slip joint type exhaust system, ALWAYS squirt a liquid rust dissolving agent onto the fasteners for ease of removal. Start by unbolting the exhaust piece at both ends (if required). When unbolting the headpipe from the manifold, make sure that the bolts are free before trying to remove them. if you snap a stud in the exhaust manifold, the stud will have to be removed with a bolt extractor, which often means removal of the manifold itself. Next, remove the mounting U-bolts from around the exhaust pipe you are extracting from the vehicle. Don't be surprised if the U-bolts break while removing the nuts. Loosen the exhaust pipe from any mounting brackets retaining it to the floor pan and separate the components.

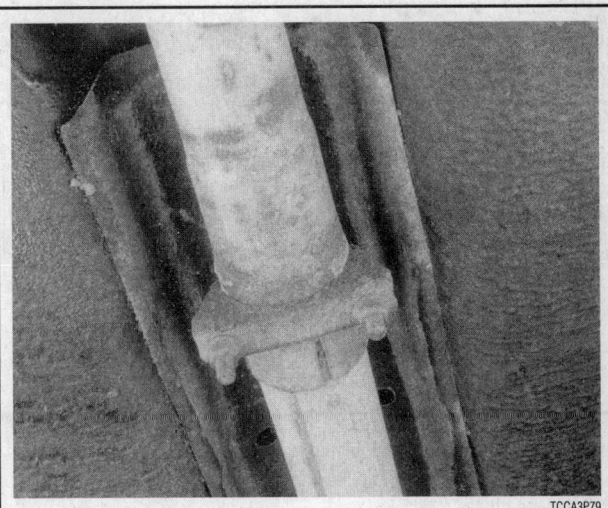

TCCA3P79

Fig. 171 Example of a common slip joint type system

## ENGINE RECONDITIONING

### Determining Engine Condition

Anything that generates heat and/or friction will eventually burn or wear out (ie. a light bulb generates heat, therefore its life span is limited). With this in mind, a running engine generates tremendous amounts of both; friction is encountered by the moving and rotating parts inside the engine and heat is created by friction and combustion of the fuel. However, the engine has systems designed to help reduce the effects of heat and friction and provide added longevity. The oiling system reduces the amount of friction encountered by the moving parts inside the engine, while the cooling system reduces heat created by friction and combustion. If either system is not maintained, a break-down will be inevitable. Therefore, you can see how regular maintenance can affect the service life of your vehicle. If you do not drain, flush and refill your cooling system at the proper intervals, deposits will begin to accumulate in the radiator, thereby reducing the amount of heat it can extract from the coolant. The same applies to your oil and filter; if it is not changed often enough it becomes laden with contaminates and is unable to properly lubricate the engine. This increases friction and wear.

There are a number of methods for evaluating the condition of your engine. A compression test can reveal the condition of your pistons, piston rings, cylinder bores, head gasket(s), valves and valve seats. An oil pressure test can warn you of possible engine bearing, or oil pump failures. Excessive oil consumption, evidence of oil in the engine air intake area and/or bluish smoke from the tail pipe may indicate worn piston rings, worn valve guides and/or valve seals. As a general rule, an engine that uses no more than one quart of oil every 1000 miles is in good condition. Engines that use one quart of oil or more in less than 1000 miles should first be checked for oil leaks. If any oil leaks are present, have them fixed before determining how much oil is consumed by the engine, especially if blue smoke is not visible at the tail pipe.

### COMPRESSION TEST

▶ **See Figure 172**

A noticeable lack of engine power, excessive oil consumption and/or poor fuel mileage measured over an extended period are all indicators of internal engine wear. Worn piston rings, scored or worn cylinder bores, blown head gaskets, sticking or burnt valves, and worn valve seats are all possible culprits. A check of each cylinder's compression will help locate the problem.

➡A screw-in type compression gauge is more accurate than the type you simply hold against the spark plug hole. Although it takes slightly longer to use, it's worth the effort to obtain a more accurate reading.

1. Make sure that the proper amount and viscosity of engine oil is in the crankcase, then ensure the battery is fully charged.
2. Warm-up the engine to normal operating temperature, then shut the engine **OFF**.
3. Disable the ignition system.
4. Label and disconnect all of the spark plug wires from the plugs.
5. Thoroughly clean the cylinder head area around the spark plug ports, then remove the spark plugs.
6. Set the throttle plate to the fully open (wide-open throttle) position. You can block the accelerator linkage open for this, or you can have an assistant fully depress the accelerator pedal.
7. Install a screw-in type compression gauge into the No. 1 spark plug hole until the fitting is snug.

TCCS3801

Fig. 172 A screw-in type compression gauge is more accurate and easier to use without an assistant

## ✳ WARNING

**Be careful not to crossthread the spark plug hole.**

8. According to the tool manufacturer's instructions, connect a remote starting switch to the starting circuit.

9. With the ignition switch in the **OFF** position, use the remote starting switch to crank the engine through at least five compression strokes (approximately 5 seconds of cranking) and record the highest reading on the gauge.

10. Repeat the test on each cylinder, cranking the engine approximately the same number of compression strokes and/or time as the first.

11. Compare the highest readings from each cylinder to that of the others. The indicated compression pressures are considered within specifications if the lowest reading cylinder is within 75 percent of the pressure recorded for the highest reading cylinder. For example, if your highest reading cylinder pressure was 150 psi (1034 kPa), then 75 percent of that would be 113 psi (779 kPa). So the lowest reading cylinder should be no less than 113 psi (779 kPa).

12. If a cylinder exhibits an unusually low compression reading, pour a tablespoon of clean engine oil into the cylinder through the spark plug hole and repeat the compression test. If the compression rises after adding oil, it means that the cylinder's piston rings and/or cylinder bore are damaged or worn. If the pressure remains low, the valves may not be seating properly (a valve job is needed), or the head gasket may be blown near that cylinder. If compression in any two adjacent cylinders is low, and if the addition of oil doesn't help raise compression, there is leakage past the head gasket. Oil and coolant in the combustion chamber, combined with blue or constant white smoke from the tail pipe, are symptoms of this problem. However, don't be alarmed by the normal white smoke emitted from the tail pipe during engine warm-up or from cold weather driving. There may be evidence of water droplets on the engine dipstick and/or oil droplets in the cooling system if a head gasket is blown.

### OIL PRESSURE TEST

Check for proper oil pressure at the sending unit passage with an externally mounted mechanical oil pressure gauge (as opposed to relying on a factory installed dash-mounted gauge). A tachometer may also be needed, as some specifications may require running the engine at a specific rpm.

1. With the engine cold, locate and remove the oil pressure sending unit.

2. Following the manufacturer's instructions, connect a mechanical oil pressure gauge and, if necessary, a tachometer to the engine.

3. Start the engine and allow it to idle.

4. Check the oil pressure reading when cold and record the number. You may need to run the engine at a specified rpm, so check the specifications chart located earlier in this section.

5. Run the engine until normal operating temperature is reached (upper radiator hose will feel warm).

6. Check the oil pressure reading again with the engine hot and record the number. Turn the engine **OFF**.

7. Compare your hot oil pressure reading to that given in the chart. If the reading is low, check the cold pressure reading against the chart. If the cold pressure is well above the specification, and the hot reading was lower than the specification, you may have the wrong viscosity oil in the engine. Change the oil, making sure to use the proper grade and quantity, then repeat the test.

Low oil pressure readings could be attributed to internal component wear, pump related problems, a low oil level, or oil viscosity that is too low. High oil pressure readings could be caused by an overfilled crankcase, too high of an oil viscosity or a faulty pressure relief valve.

## Buy or Rebuild?

Now that you have determined that your engine is worn out, you must make some decisions. The question of whether or not an engine is worth rebuilding is largely a subjective matter and one of personal worth. Is the engine a popular one, or is it an obsolete model? Are parts available? Will it get acceptable gas mileage once it is rebuilt? Is the car it's being put into worth keeping? Would it be less expensive to buy a new engine, have your engine rebuilt by a pro, rebuild it yourself or buy a used engine from a salvage yard? Or would it be simpler and less expensive to buy another car? If you have considered all these matters and more, and have still decided to rebuild the engine, then it is time to decide how you will rebuild it.

➡ **The editors at Chilton feel that most engine machining should be performed by a professional machine shop. Don't think of it as wasting money, rather, as an assurance that the job has been done right the first time. There are many expensive and specialized tools required to perform such tasks as boring and honing an engine block or having a valve job done on a cylinder head. Even inspecting the parts requires expensive micrometers and gauges to properly measure wear and clearances. Also, a machine shop can deliver to you clean, and ready to assemble parts, saving you time and aggravation. Your maximum savings will come from performing the removal, disassembly, assembly and installation of the engine and purchasing or renting only the tools required to perform the above tasks. Depending on the particular circumstances, you may save 40 to 60 percent of the cost doing these yourself.**

A complete rebuild or overhaul of an engine involves replacing all of the moving parts (pistons, rods, crankshaft, camshaft, etc.) with new ones and machining the non-moving wearing surfaces of the block and heads. Unfortunately, this may not be cost effective. For instance, your crankshaft may have been damaged or worn, but it can be machined undersize for a minimal fee.

So, as you can see, you can replace everything inside the engine, but, it is wiser to replace only those parts which are really needed, and, if possible, repair the more expensive ones. Later in this section, we will break the engine down into its two main components: the cylinder head and the engine block. We will discuss each component, and the recommended parts to replace during a rebuild on each.

## Engine Overhaul Tips

Most engine overhaul procedures are fairly standard. In addition to specific parts replacement procedures and specifications for your individual engine, this section is also a guide to acceptable rebuilding procedures. Examples of standard rebuilding practice are given and should be used along with specific details concerning your particular engine.

Competent and accurate machine shop services will ensure maximum performance, reliability and engine life. In most instances it is more profitable for the do-it-yourself mechanic to remove, clean and inspect the component, buy the necessary parts and deliver these to a shop for actual machine work.

Much of the assembly work (crankshaft, bearings, piston rods, and other components) is well within the scope of the do-it-yourself mechanic's tools and abilities. You will have to decide for yourself the depth of involvement you desire in an engine repair or rebuild.

### TOOLS

The tools required for an engine overhaul or parts replacement will depend on the depth of your involvement. With a few exceptions, they will be the tools found in a mechanic's tool kit (see Section 1 of this manual). More in-depth work will require some or all of the following:

- A dial indicator (reading in thousandths) mounted on a universal base
- Micrometers and telescope gauges
- Jaw and screw-type pullers
- Scraper
- Valve spring compressor
- Ring groove cleaner
- Piston ring expander and compressor
- Ridge reamer

- Cylinder hone or glaze breaker
- Plastigage®
- Engine stand

The use of most of these tools is illustrated in this section. Many can be rented for a one-time use from a local parts jobber or tool supply house specializing in automotive work.

Occasionally, the use of special tools is called for. See the information on Special Tools and the Safety Notice in the front of this book before substituting another tool.

## OVERHAUL TIPS

Aluminum has become extremely popular for use in engines, due to its low weight. Observe the following precautions when handling aluminum parts:
- Never hot tank aluminum parts (the caustic hot tank solution will eat the aluminum.
- Remove all aluminum parts (identification tag, etc.) from engine parts prior to the tanking.
- Always coat threads lightly with engine oil or anti-seize compounds before installation, to prevent seizure.
- Never overtighten bolts or spark plugs especially in aluminum threads.

When assembling the engine, any parts that will be exposed to frictional contact must be prelubed to provide lubrication at initial start-up. Any product specifically formulated for this purpose can be used, but engine oil is not recommended as a prelube in most cases.

When semi-permanent (locked, but removable) installation of bolts or nuts is desired, threads should be cleaned and coated with Loctite® or another similar, commercial non-hardening sealant.

## CLEANING

▶ **See Figures 173, 174, 175 and 176**

Before the engine and its components are inspected, they must be thoroughly cleaned. You will need to remove any engine varnish, oil sludge and/or carbon deposits from all of the components to insure an accurate inspection. A crack in the engine block or cylinder head can easily become overlooked if hidden by a layer of sludge or carbon.

Most of the cleaning process can be carried out with common hand tools and readily available solvents or solutions. Carbon deposits can be chipped away using a hammer and a hard wooden chisel. Old gasket material and varnish or sludge can usually be removed using a scraper and/or cleaning solvent. Extremely stubborn deposits may require the use of a

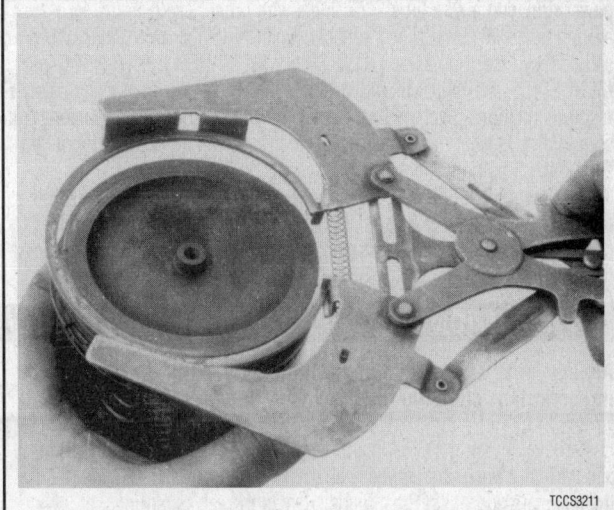
TCCS3211
**Fig. 174 Use a ring expander tool to remove the piston rings**

TCCS3208
**Fig. 175 Clean the piston ring grooves using a ring groove cleaner tool, or . . .**

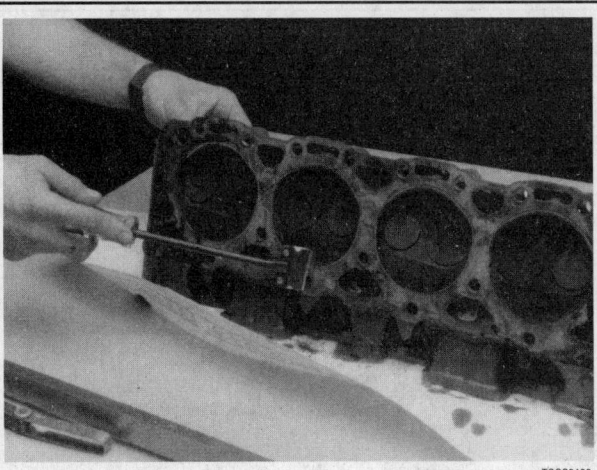
TCCS3132
**Fig. 173 Use a gasket scraper to remove the old gasket material from the mating surfaces**

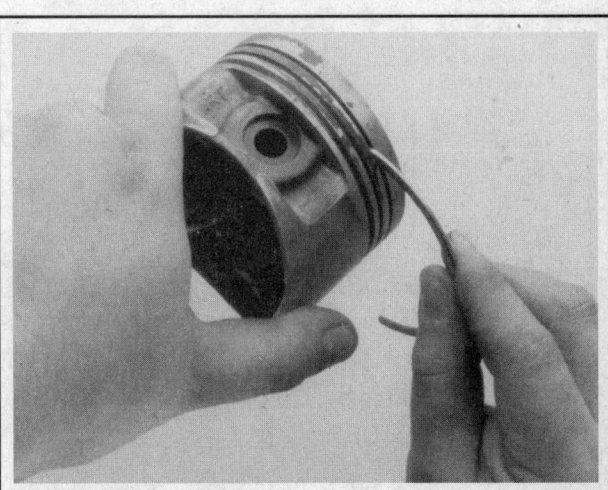
TCCS3911
**Fig. 176 . . . use a piece of an old ring to clean the grooves. Be careful, the ring can be quite sharp**

power drill with a wire brush. If using a wire brush, use extreme care around any critical machined surfaces (such as the gasket surfaces, bearing saddles, cylinder bores, etc.). USE OF A WIRE BRUSH IS NOT RECOMMENDED ON ANY ALUMINUM COMPONENTS. Always follow any safety recommendations given by the manufacturer of the tool and/or solvent. You should always wear eye protection during any cleaning process involving scraping, chipping or spraying of solvents.

An alternative to the mess and hassle of cleaning the parts yourself is to drop them off at a local garage or machine shop. They will, more than likely, have the necessary equipment to properly clean all of the parts for a nominal fee.

### ❊❊ CAUTION

**Always wear eye protection during any cleaning process involving scraping, chipping or spraying of solvents.**

Remove any oil galley plugs, freeze plugs and/or pressed-in bearings and carefully wash and degrease all of the engine components including the fasteners and bolts. Small parts such as the valves, springs, etc., should be placed in a metal basket and allowed to soak. Use pipe cleaner type brushes, and clean all passageways in the components. Use a ring expander and remove the rings from the pistons. Clean the piston ring grooves with a special tool or a piece of broken ring. Scrape the carbon off of the top of the piston. You should never use a wire brush on the pistons. After preparing all of the piston assemblies in this manner, wash and degrease them again.

### ❊❊ WARNING

**Use extreme care when cleaning around the cylinder head valve seats. A mistake or slip may cost you a new seat.**

When cleaning the cylinder head, remove carbon from the combustion chamber with the valves installed. This will avoid damaging the valve seats.

REPAIRING DAMAGED THREADS

▶ **See Figures 177, 178, 179, 180 and 181**

Several methods of repairing damaged threads are available. Heli-Coil® (shown here), Keenserts® and Microdot® are among the most widely used. All involve basically the same principle—drilling out stripped threads, tapping the hole and installing a prewound insert—making welding, plugging and oversize fasteners unnecessary.

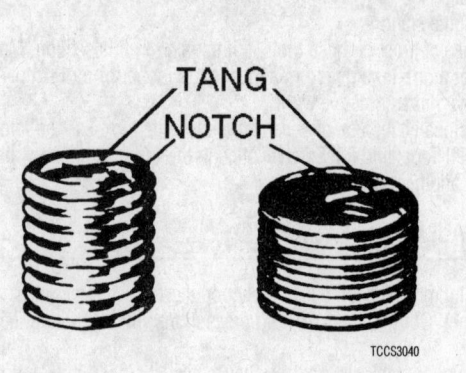

Fig. 178 Standard thread repair insert (left), and spark plug thread insert

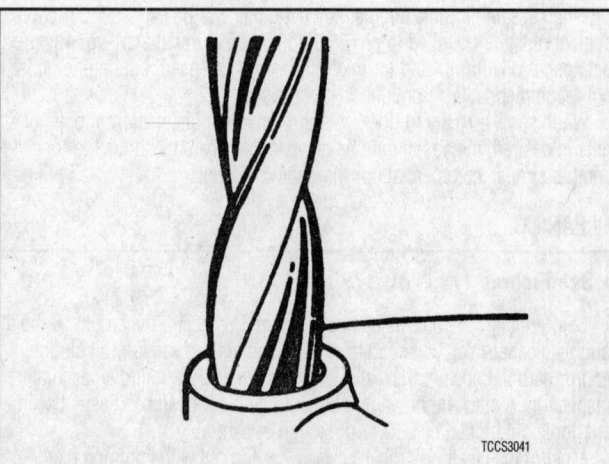

Fig. 179 Drill out the damaged threads with the specified size bit. Be sure to drill completely through the hole or to the bottom of a blind hole

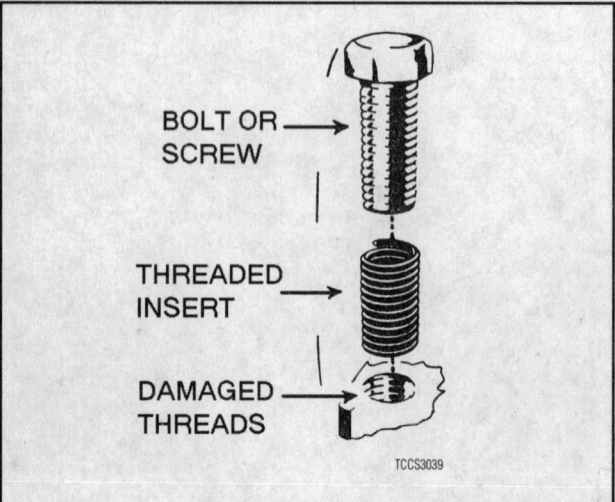

Fig. 177 Damaged bolt hole threads can be replaced with thread repair inserts

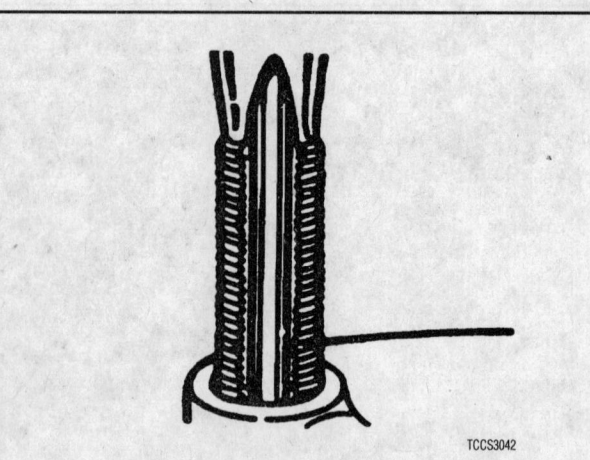

Fig. 180 Using the kit, tap the hole in order to receive the thread insert. Keep the tap well oiled and back it out frequently to avoid clogging the threads

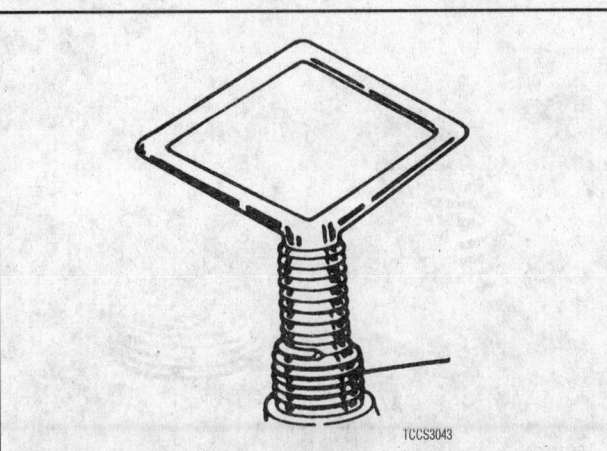

**Fig. 181 Screw the insert onto the installer tool until the tang engages the slot. Thread the insert into the hole until it is ¼–½ turn below the top surface, then remove the tool and break off the tang using a punch**

Two types of thread repair inserts are usually supplied: a standard type for most inch coarse, inch fine, metric course and metric fine thread sizes and a spark lug type to fit most spark plug port sizes. Consult the individual tool manufacturer's catalog to determine exact applications. Typical thread repair kits will contain a selection of prewound threaded inserts, a tap (corresponding to the outside diameter threads of the insert) and an installation tool. Spark plug inserts usually differ because they require a tap equipped with pilot threads and a combined reamer/tap section. Most manufacturers also supply blister-packed thread repair inserts separately in addition to a master kit containing a variety of taps and inserts plus installation tools.

Before attempting to repair a threaded hole, remove any snapped, broken or damaged bolts or studs. Penetrating oil can be used to free frozen threads. The offending item can usually be removed with locking pliers or using a screw/stud extractor. After the hole is clear, the thread can be repaired, as shown in the series of accompanying illustrations and in the kit manufacturer's instructions.

## Engine Preparation

To properly rebuild an engine, you must first remove it from the vehicle, then disassemble and diagnose it. Ideally you should place your engine on an engine stand. This affords you the best access to the engine components. Follow the manufacturer's directions for using the stand with your particular engine. Remove the flywheel or flexplate before installing the engine to the stand.

Now that you have the engine on a stand, and assuming that you have drained the oil and coolant from the engine, it's time to strip it of all but the necessary components. Before you start disassembling the engine, you may want to take a moment to draw some pictures, or fabricate some labels or containers to mark the locations of various components and the bolts and/or studs which fasten them. Modern day engines use a lot of little brackets and clips which hold wiring harnesses and such, and these holders are often mounted on studs and/or bolts that can be easily mixed up. The manufacturer spent a lot of time and money designing your vehicle, and they wouldn't have wasted any of it by haphazardly placing brackets, clips or fasteners on the vehicle. If it's present when you disassemble it, put it back when you assemble, you will regret not remembering that little bracket which holds a wire harness out of the path of a rotating part.

You should begin by unbolting any accessories still attached to the engine, such as the water pump, power steering pump, alternator, etc. Then, unfasten any manifolds (intake or exhaust) which were not removed during the engine removal procedure. Finally, remove any covers remaining on the engine such as the rocker arm, front or timing cover and oil pan. Some front covers may require the vibration damper and/or crank pulley to be removed beforehand. The idea is to reduce the engine to the bare necessities (cylinder head(s), valve train, engine block, crankshaft, pistons and connecting rods), plus any other `in block' components such as oil pumps, balance shafts and auxiliary shafts.

Finally, remove the cylinder head(s) from the engine block and carefully place on a bench. Disassembly instructions for each component follow later in this section.

## Cylinder Head

There are two basic types of cylinder heads used on today's automobiles: the Overhead Valve (OHV) and the Overhead Camshaft (OHC). The latter can also be broken down into two subgroups: the Single Overhead Camshaft (SOHC) and the Dual Overhead Camshaft (DOHC). Generally, if there is only a single camshaft on a head, it is just referred to as an OHC head. Also, an engine with an OHV cylinder head is also known as a pushrod engine.

Most cylinder heads these days are made of an aluminum alloy due to its light weight, durability and heat transfer qualities. However, cast iron was the material of choice in the past, and is still used on many vehicles today. Whether made from aluminum or iron, all cylinder heads have valves and seats. Some use two valves per cylinder, while the more hi-tech engines will utilize a multi-valve configuration using 3, 4 and even 5 valves per cylinder. When the valve contacts the seat, it does so on precision machined surfaces, which seals the combustion chamber. All cylinder heads have a valve guide for each valve. The guide centers the valve to the seat and allows it to move up and down within it. The clearance between the valve and guide can be critical. Too much clearance and the engine may consume oil, lose vacuum and/or damage the seat. Too little, and the valve can stick in the guide causing the engine to run poorly if at all, and possibly causing severe damage. The last component all cylinder heads have are valve springs. The spring holds the valve against its seat. It also returns the valve to this position when the valve has been opened by the valve train or camshaft. The spring is fastened to the valve by a retainer and valve locks (sometimes called keepers). Aluminum heads will also have a valve spring shim to keep the spring from wearing away the aluminum.

An ideal method of rebuilding the cylinder head would involve replacing all of the valves, guides, seats, springs, etc. with new ones. However, depending on how the engine was maintained, often this is not necessary. A major cause of valve, guide and seat wear is an improperly tuned engine. An engine that is running too rich, will often wash the lubricating oil out of the guide with gasoline, causing it to wear rapidly. Conversely, an engine which is running too lean will place higher combustion temperatures on the valves and seats allowing them to wear or even burn. Springs fall victim to the driving habits of the individual. A driver who often runs the engine rpm to the redline will wear out or break the springs faster then one that stays well below it. Unfortunately, mileage takes it toll on all of the parts. Generally, the valves, guides, springs and seats in a cylinder head can be machined and re-used, saving you money. However, if a valve is burnt, it may be wise to replace all of the valves, since they were all operating in the same environment. The same goes for any other component on the cylinder head. Think of it as an insurance policy against future problems related to that component.

Unfortunately, the only way to find out which components need replacing, is to disassemble and carefully check each piece. After the cylinder head(s) are disassembled, thoroughly clean all of the components.

## DISASSEMBLY

◆ **See Figures 182 and 183**

Whether it is a single or dual overhead camshaft cylinder head, the disassembly procedure is relatively unchanged. One aspect to pay attention to is careful labeling of the parts on the dual camshaft cylinder head. There will be an intake camshaft and followers as well as an exhaust camshaft and followers and they must be labeled as such. In some cases, the components are identical and could easily be installed incorrectly. DO NOT MIX THEM UP! Determining which is which is very simple; the intake camshaft and components are on the same side of the head as was the intake manifold. Conversely, the exhaust camshaft and components are on the same side of the head as was the exhaust manifold.

### *CUP TYPE CAMSHAFT FOLLOWERS*

◆ **See Figures 184, 185 and 186**

Most cylinder heads with cup type camshaft followers will have the valve spring, retainer and locks recessed within the follower's bore. You will need a C-clamp style valve spring compressor tool, an OHC spring removal tool (or equivalent) and a small magnet to disassemble the head.

1. If not already removed, remove the camshaft(s) and/or followers. Mark their positions for assembly.
2. Position the cylinder head to allow use of a C-clamp style valve spring compressor tool.

TCCA3P62

**Fig. 183 Example of a multi-valve cylinder head. Note how it has 2 intake and 2 exhaust valve ports**

TCCA3P54

**Fig. 182 Exploded view of a valve, seal, spring, retainer and locks from an OHC cylinder head**

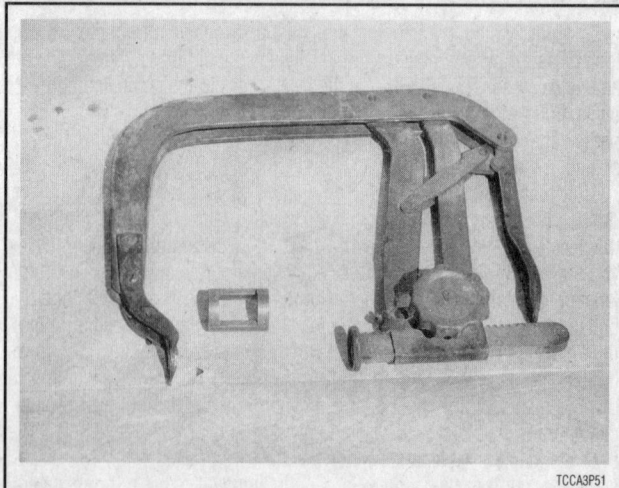

TCCA3P51

**Fig. 184 C-clamp type spring compressor and an OHC spring removal tool (center) for cup type followers**

Fig. 185 Most cup type follower cylinder heads retain the camshaft using bolt-on bearing caps

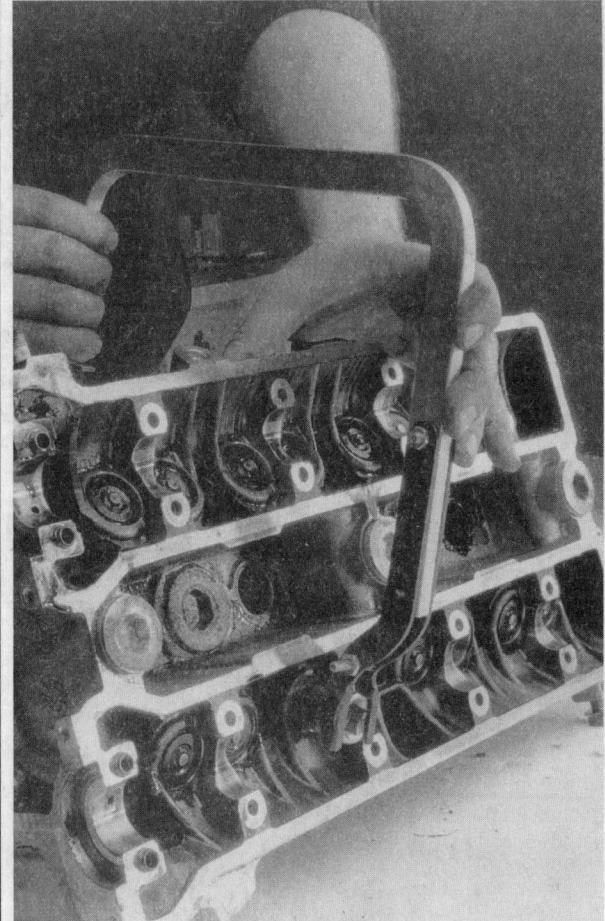

Fig. 186 Position the OHC spring tool in the follower bore, then compress the spring with a C-clamp type tool

➡It is preferred to position the cylinder head gasket surface facing you with the valve springs facing the opposite direction and the head laying horizontal.

3. With the OHC spring removal adapter tool positioned inside of the follower bore, compress the valve spring using the C-clamp style valve spring compressor.

4. Remove the valve locks. A small magnetic tool or screwdriver will aid in removal.

5. Release the compressor tool and remove the spring assembly.

6. Withdraw the valve from the cylinder head.

7. If equipped, remove the valve seal.

➡Special valve seal removal tools are available. Regular or needlenose type pliers, if used with care, will work just as well. If using ordinary pliers, be sure not to damage the follower bore. The follower and its bore are machined to close tolerances and any damage to the bore will effect this relationship.

8. If equipped, remove the valve spring shim. A small magnetic tool or screwdriver will aid in removal.

9. Repeat Steps 3 through 8 until all of the valves have been removed.

### ROCKER ARM TYPE CAMSHAFT FOLLOWERS

#### ▶ See Figures 187 thru 195

Most cylinder heads with rocker arm-type camshaft followers are easily disassembled using a standard valve spring compressor. However, certain models may not have enough open space around the spring for the standard tool and may require you to use a C-clamp style compressor tool instead.

1. If not already removed, remove the rocker arms and/or shafts and the camshaft. If applicable, also remove the hydraulic lash adjusters. Mark their positions for assembly.

2. Position the cylinder head to allow access to the valve spring.

3. Use a valve spring compressor tool to relieve the spring tension from the retainer.

➡Due to engine varnish, the retainer may stick to the valve locks. A gentle tap with a hammer may help to break it loose.

4. Remove the valve locks from the valve tip and/or retainer. A small magnet may help in removing the small locks.

5. Lift the valve spring, tool and all, off of the valve stem.

6. If equipped, remove the valve seal. If the seal is difficult to remove

Fig. 187 Example of the shaft mounted rocker arms on some OHC heads

Fig. 188 Another example of the rocker arm type OHC head. This model uses a follower under the camshaft

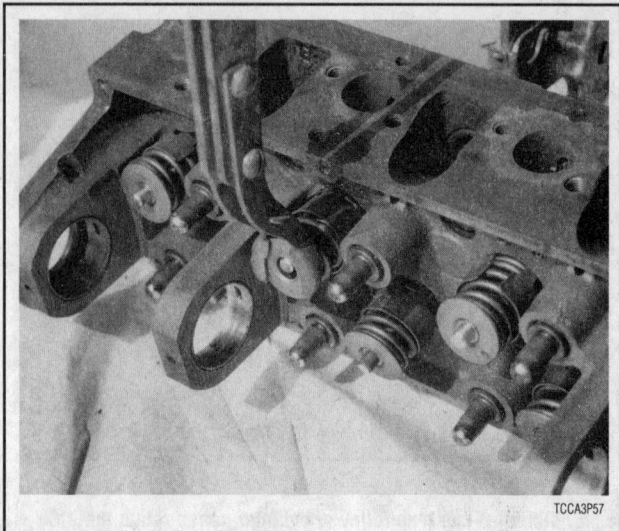

Fig. 191 Compress the valve spring . . .

Fig. 189 Before the camshaft can be removed, all of the followers must first be removed . . .

Fig. 192 . . . then remove the valve locks from the valve stem and spring retainer

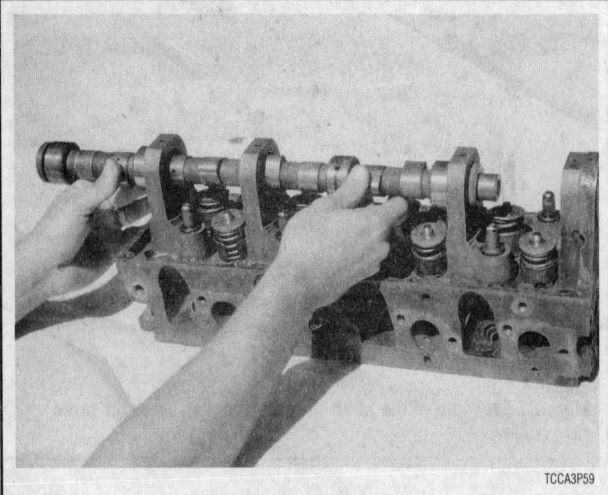

Fig. 190 . . . then the camshaft can be removed by sliding it out (shown), or unbolting a bearing cap (not shown)

Fig. 193 Remove the valve spring and retainer from the cylinder head

**Fig. 194 Remove the valve seal from the guide. Some gentle prying or pliers may help to remove stubborn ones**

**Fig. 195 All aluminum and some cast iron heads will have these valve spring shims. Remove all of them as well**

with the valve in place, try removing the valve first, then the seal. Follow the steps below for valve removal.

7. Position the head to allow access for withdrawing the valve.

➡ **Cylinder heads that have seen a lot of miles and/or abuse may have mushroomed the valve lock grove and/or tip, causing difficulty in removal of the valve. If this has happened, use a metal file to carefully remove the high spots around the lock grooves and/or tip. Only file it enough to allow removal.**

8. Remove the valve from the cylinder head.

9. If equipped, remove the valve spring shim. A small magnetic tool or screwdriver will aid in removal.

10. Repeat Steps 3 though 9 until all of the valves have been removed.

## INSPECTION

Now that all of the cylinder head components are clean, it's time to inspect them for wear and/or damage. To accurately inspect them, you will need some specialized tools:

- A 01 in. micrometer for the valves
- A dial indicator or inside diameter gauge for the valve guides
- A spring pressure test gauge

If you do not have access to the proper tools, you may want to bring the components to a shop that does.

### Valves

▶ **See Figures 196 and 197**

The first thing to inspect are the valve heads. Look closely at the head, margin and face for any cracks, excessive wear or burning. The margin is the best place to look for burning. It should have a squared edge with an even width all around the diameter. When a valve burns, the margin will look melted and the edges rounded. Also inspect the valve head for any signs of tulipping. This will show as a lifting of the edges or dishing in the center of the head and will usually not occur to all of the valves. All of the heads should look the same, any that seem dished more than others are probably bad. Next, inspect the valve lock grooves and valve tips. Check for any burrs around the lock grooves, especially if you had to file them to remove the valve. Valve tips should appear flat, although slight rounding with high mileage engines is normal. Slightly worn valve tips will need to be machined flat. Last, measure the valve stem diameter with the micrometer. Measure the area that rides within the guide, especially towards the tip where most of the wear occurs. Take several measurements along its length and compare them to each other. Wear should be even along the length

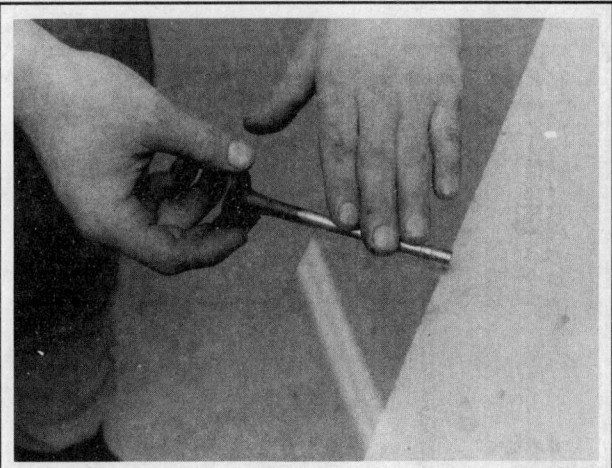

**Fig. 196 Valve stems may be rolled on a flat surface to check for bends**

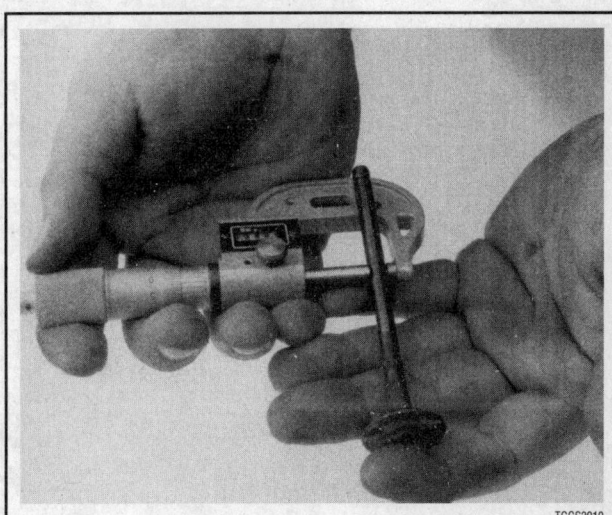

**Fig. 197 Use a micrometer to check the valve stem diameter**

with little to no taper. If no minimum diameter is given in the specifications, then the stem should not read more than 0.001 in. (0.025mm) below the specification. Any valves that fail these inspections should be replaced.

## Springs, Retainers and Valve Locks

▶ **See Figures 198 and 199**

The first thing to check is the most obvious, broken springs. Next check the free length and squareness of each spring. If applicable, insure to distinguish between intake and exhaust springs. Use a ruler and/or carpenters square to measure the length. A carpenters square should be used to check the springs for squareness. If a spring pressure test gauge is available, check each springs rating and compare to the specifications chart. Check the readings against the specifications given. Any springs that fail these inspections should be replaced.

The spring retainers rarely need replacing, however they should still be checked as a precaution. Inspect the spring mating surface and the valve lock retention area for any signs of excessive wear. Also check for any signs of cracking. Replace any retainers that are questionable.

Valve locks should be inspected for excessive wear on the outside contact area as well as on the inner notched surface. Any locks which appear worn or broken and its respective valve should be replaced.

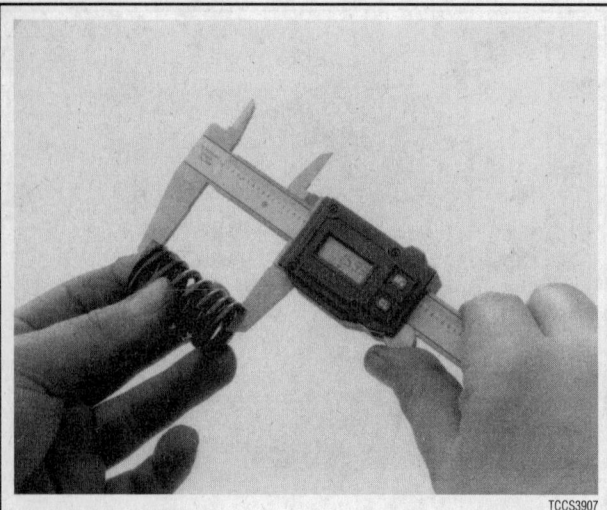

Fig. 198 Use a caliper to check the valve spring free-length

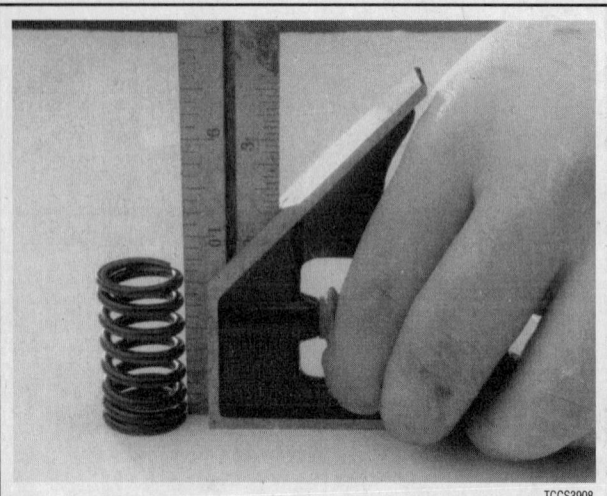

Fig. 199 Check the valve spring for squareness on a flat surface; a carpenter's square can be used

## Cylinder Head

There are several things to check on the cylinder head: valve guides, seats, cylinder head surface flatness, cracks and physical damage.

### VALVE GUIDES

▶ **See Figure 200**

Now that you know the valves are good, you can use them to check the guides, although a new valve, if available, is preferred. Before you measure anything, look at the guides carefully and inspect them for any cracks, chips or breakage. Also if the guide is a removable style (as in most aluminum heads), check them for any looseness or evidence of movement. All of the guides should appear to be at the same height from the spring seat. If any seem lower (or higher) from another, the guide has moved. Mount a dial indicator onto the spring side of the cylinder head. Lightly oil the valve stem and insert it into the cylinder head. Position the dial indicator against the valve stem near the tip and zero the gauge. Grasp the valve stem and wiggle towards and away from the dial indicator and observe the readings. Mount the dial indicator 90 degrees from the initial point and zero the gauge and again take a reading. Compare the two readings for a out of round condition. Check the readings against the specifications given. An Inside Diameter (I.D.) gauge designed for valve guides will give you an accurate valve guide bore measurement. If the I.D. gauge is used, compare the readings with the specifications given. Any guides that fail these inspections should be replaced or machined.

Fig. 200 A dial gauge may be used to check valve stem-to-guide clearance; read the gauge while moving the valve stem

### VALVE SEATS

A visual inspection of the valve seats should show a slightly worn and pitted surface where the valve face contacts the seat. Inspect the seat carefully for severe pitting or cracks. Also, a seat that is badly worn will be recessed into the cylinder head. A severely worn or recessed seat may need to be replaced. All cracked seats must be replaced. A seat concentricity gauge, if available, should be used to check the seat run-out. If run-out exceeds specifications the seat must be machined (if no specification is given use 0.002 in. or 0.051mm).

### CYLINDER HEAD SURFACE FLATNESS

▶ **See Figures 201 and 202**

After you have cleaned the gasket surface of the cylinder head of any old gasket material, check the head for flatness.

Place a straightedge across the gasket surface. Using feeler gauges, determine the clearance at the center of the straightedge and across the cylinder head at several points. Check along the centerline and diagonally

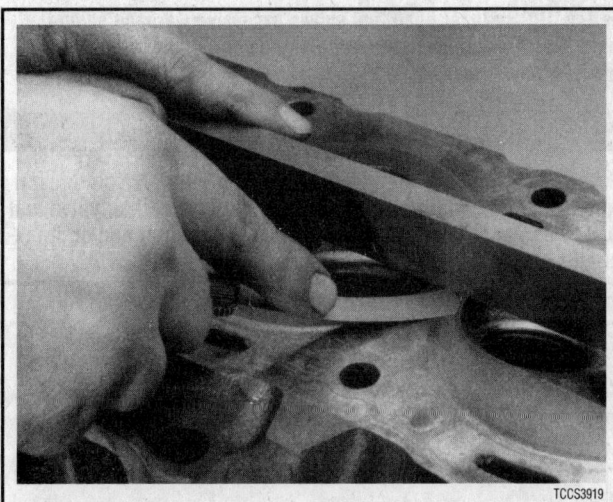

**Fig. 201 Check the head for flatness across the center of the head surface using a straightedge and feeler gauge**

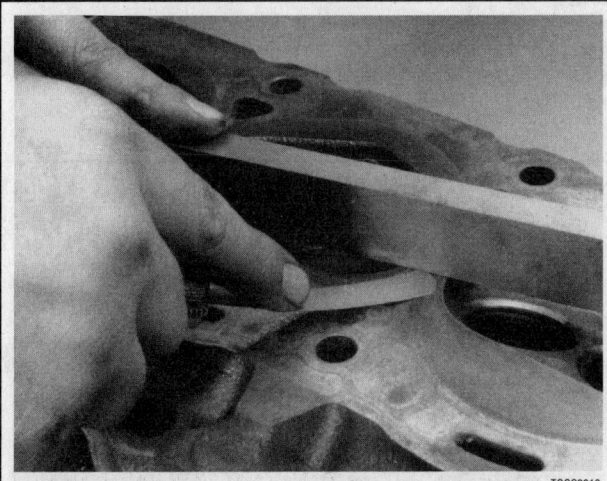

**Fig. 202 Checks should also be made along both diagonals of the head surface**

on the head surface. If the warpage exceeds 0.003 in. (0.076mm) within a 6.0 in. (15.2cm) span, or 0.006 in. (0.152mm) over the total length of the head, the cylinder head must be resurfaced. After resurfacing the heads of a V-type engine, the intake manifold flange surface should be checked, and if necessary, milled proportionally to allow for the change in its mounting position.

### CRACKS AND PHYSICAL DAMAGE

Generally, cracks are limited to the combustion chamber, however, it is not uncommon for the head to crack in a spark plug hole, port, outside of the head or in the valve spring/rocker arm area. The first area to inspect is always the hottest: the exhaust seat/port area.

A visual inspection should be performed, but just because you don't see a crack does not mean it is not there. Some more reliable methods for inspecting for cracks include Magnaflux®, a magnetic process or Zyglo®, a dye penetrant. Magnaflux® is used only on ferrous metal (cast iron) heads. Zyglo® uses a spray on fluorescent mixture along with a black light to reveal the cracks. It is strongly recommended to have your cylinder head checked professionally for cracks, especially if the engine was known to have overheated and/or leaked or consumed coolant. Contact a local shop for availability and pricing of these services.

Physical damage is usually very evident. For example, a broken mounting ear from dropping the head or a bent or broken stud and/or bolt. All of these defects should be fixed or, if unrepairable, the head should be replaced.

### Camshaft and Followers

Inspect the camshaft(s) and followers as described earlier in this section.

### REFINISHING & REPAIRING

Many of the procedures given for refinishing and repairing the cylinder head components must be performed by a machine shop. Certain steps, if the inspected part is not worn, can be performed yourself inexpensively. However, you spent a lot of time and effort so far, why risk trying to save a couple bucks if you might have to do it all over again?

### Valves

Any valves that were not replaced should be refaced and the tips ground flat. Unless you have access to a valve grinding machine, this should be done by a machine shop. If the valves are in extremely good condition, as well as the valve seats and guides, they may be lapped in without performing machine work.

It is a recommended practice to lap the valves even after machine work has been performed and/or new valves have been purchased. This insures a positive seal between the valve and seat.

#### LAPPING THE VALVES

➡Before lapping the valves to the seats, read the rest of the cylinder head section to insure that any related parts are in acceptable enough condition to continue.

➡Before any valve seat machining and/or lapping can be performed, the guides must be within factory recommended specifications.

1. Invert the cylinder head.
2. Lightly lubricate the valve stems and insert them into the cylinder head in their numbered order.
3. Raise the valve from the seat and apply a small amount of fine lapping compound to the seat.
4. Moisten the suction head of a hand-lapping tool and attach it to the head of the valve.
5. Rotate the tool between the palms of both hands, changing the position of the valve on the valve seat and lifting the tool often to prevent grooving.
6. Lap the valve until a smooth, polished circle is evident on the valve and seat.
7. Remove the tool and the valve. Wipe away all traces of the grinding compound and store the valve to maintain its lapped location.

### ✳✳ WARNING

**Do not get the valves out of order after they have been lapped. They must be put back with the same valve seat with which they were lapped.**

### Springs, Retainers and Valve Locks

There is no repair or refinishing possible with the springs, retainers and valve locks. If they are found to be worn or defective, they must be replaced with new (or known good) parts.

### Cylinder Head

Most refinishing procedures dealing with the cylinder head must be performed by a machine shop. Read the sections below and review your inspection data to determine whether or not machining is necessary.

## VALVE GUIDE

➠**If any machining or replacements are made to the valve guides, the seats must be machined.**

Unless the valve guides need machining or replacing, the only service to perform is to thoroughly clean them of any dirt or oil residue.

There are only two types of valve guides used on automobile engines: the replaceable-type (all aluminum heads) and the cast-in integral-type (most cast iron heads). There are four recommended methods for repairing worn guides.

- Knurling
- Inserts
- Reaming oversize
- Replacing

Knurling is a process in which metal is displaced and raised, thereby reducing clearance, giving a true center, and providing oil control. It is the least expensive way of repairing the valve guides. However, it is not necessarily the best, and in some cases, a knurled valve guide will not stand up for more than a short time. It requires a special knurlizer and precision reaming tools to obtain proper clearances. It would not be cost effective to purchase these tools, unless you plan on rebuilding several of the same cylinder head.

Installing a guide insert involves machining the guide to accept a bronze insert. One style is the coil-type which is installed into a threaded guide. Another is the thin-walled insert where the guide is reamed oversize to accept a split-sleeve insert. After the insert is installed, a special tool is then run through the guide to expand the insert, locking it to the guide. The insert is then reamed to the standard size for proper valve clearance.

Reaming for oversize valves restores normal clearances and provides a true valve seat. Most cast-in type guides can be reamed to accept an valve with an oversize stem. The cost factor for this can become quite high as you will need to purchase the reamer and new, oversize stem valves for all guides which were reamed. Oversizes are generally 0.003 to 0.030 in. (0.076 to 0.762mm), with 0.015 in. (0.381mm) being the most common.

To replace cast-in type valve guides, they must be drilled out, then reamed to accept replacement guides. This must be done on a fixture which will allow centering and leveling off of the original valve seat or guide, otherwise a serious guide-to-seat misalignment may occur making it impossible to properly machine the seat.

Replaceable-type guides are pressed into the cylinder head. A hammer and a stepped drift or punch may be used to install and remove the guides. Before removing the guides, measure the protrusion on the spring side of the head and record it for installation. Use the stepped drift to hammer out the old guide from the combustion chamber side of the head. When installing, determine whether or not the guide also seals a water jacket in the head, and if it does, use the recommended sealing agent. If there is no water jacket, grease the valve guide and its bore. Use the stepped drift, and hammer the new guide into the cylinder head from the spring side of the cylinder head. A stack of washers the same thickness as the measured protrusion may help the installation process.

## VALVE SEATS

➠**Before any valve seat machining can be performed, the guides must be within factory recommended specifications.**

➠**If any machining or replacements were made to the valve guides, the seats must be machined.**

If the seats are in good condition, the valves can be lapped to the seats, and the cylinder head assembled. See the valves section for instructions on lapping.

If the valve seats are worn, cracked or damaged, they must be serviced by a machine shop. The valve seat must be perfectly centered to the valve guide, which requires very accurate machining.

## CYLINDER HEAD SURFACE

If the cylinder head is warped, it must be machined flat. If the warpage is extremely severe, the head may need to be replaced. In some instances, it may be possible to straighten a warped head enough to allow machining. In either case, contact a professional machine shop for service.

➠Any OHC cylinder head that shows excessive warpage should have the camshaft bearing journals align bored after the cylinder head has been resurfaced.

### ✳✳ WARNING

**Failure to align bore the camshaft bearing journals could result in severe engine damage including but not limited to: valve and piston damage, connecting rod damage, camshaft and/or crankshaft breakage.**

## CRACKS AND PHYSICAL DAMAGE

Certain cracks can be repaired in both cast iron and aluminum heads. For cast iron, a tapered threaded insert is installed along the length of the crack. Aluminum can also use the tapered inserts, however welding is the preferred method. Some physical damage can be repaired through brazing or welding. Contact a machine shop to get expert advice for your particular dilemma.

## ASSEMBLY

◆ **See Figure 203**

The first step for any assembly job is to have a clean area in which to work. Next, thoroughly clean all of the parts and components that are to be assembled. Finally, place all of the components onto a suitable work space and, if necessary, arrange the parts to their respective positions.

TCCA3P64

**Fig. 203 Once assembled, check the valve clearance and correct as needed**

## CUP TYPE CAMSHAFT FOLLOWERS

To install the springs, retainers and valve locks on heads which have these components recessed into the camshaft follower's bore, you will need a small screwdriver-type tool, some clean white grease and a lot of patience. You will also need the C-clamp style spring compressor and the OHC tool used to disassemble the head.

1. Lightly lubricate the valve stems and insert all of the valves into the cylinder head. If possible, maintain their original locations.
2. If equipped, install any valve spring shims which were removed.
3. If equipped, install the new valve seals, keeping the following in mind:

- If the valve seal presses over the guide, lightly lubricate the outer guide surfaces.
- If the seal is an O-ring type, it is installed just after compressing the spring but before the valve locks.

4. Place the valve spring and retainer over the stem.

5. Position the spring compressor and the OHC tool, then compress the spring.

6. Using a small screwdriver as a spatula, fill the valve stem side of the lock with white grease. Use the excess grease on the screwdriver to fasten the lock to the driver.

7. Carefully install the valve lock, which is stuck to the end of the screwdriver, to the valve stem then press on it with the screwdriver until the grease squeezes out. The valve lock should now be stuck to the stem.

8. Repeat Steps 6 and 7 for the remaining valve lock.

9. Relieve the spring pressure slowly and insure that neither valve lock becomes dislodged by the retainer.

10. Remove the spring compressor tool.

11. Repeat Steps 2 through 10 until all of the springs have been installed.

12. Install the followers, camshaft(s) and any other components that were removed for disassembly.

### ROCKER ARM TYPE CAMSHAFT FOLLOWERS

1. Lightly lubricate the valve stems and insert all of the valves into the cylinder head. If possible, maintain their original locations.

2. If equipped, install any valve spring shims which were removed.

3. If equipped, install the new valve seals, keeping the following in mind:

• If the valve seal presses over the guide, lightly lubricate the outer guide surfaces.

• If the seal is an O-ring type, it is installed just after compressing the spring but before the valve locks.

4. Place the valve spring and retainer over the stem.

5. Position the spring compressor tool and compress the spring.

6. Assemble the valve locks to the stem.

7. Relieve the spring pressure slowly and insure that neither valve lock becomes dislodged by the retainer.

8. Remove the spring compressor tool.

9. Repeat Steps 2 through 8 until all of the springs have been installed.

10. Install the camshaft(s), rockers, shafts and any other components that were removed for disassembly.

## Engine Block

### GENERAL INFORMATION

A thorough overhaul or rebuild of an engine block would include replacing the pistons, rings, bearings, timing belt/chain assembly and oil pump. For OHV engines also include a new camshaft and lifters. The block would then have the cylinders bored and honed oversize (or if using removable cylinder sleeves, new sleeves installed) and the crankshaft would be cut undersize to provide new wearing surfaces and perfect clearances. However, your particular engine may not have everything worn out. What if only the piston rings have worn out and the clearances on everything else are still within factory specifications? Well, you could just replace the rings and put it back together, but this would be a very rare example. Chances are, if one component in your engine is worn, other components are sure to follow, and soon. At the very least, you should always replace the rings, bearings and oil pump. This is what is commonly called a "freshen up".

### Cylinder Ridge Removal

Because the top piston ring does not travel to the very top of the cylinder, a ridge is built up between the end of the travel and the top of the cylinder bore.

Pushing the piston and connecting rod assembly past the ridge can be difficult, and damage to the piston ring lands could occur. If the ridge is not removed before installing a new piston or not removed at all, piston ring breakage and piston damage may occur.

➡ It is always recommended that you remove any cylinder ridges before removing the piston and connecting rod assemblies. If you know that new pistons are going to be installed and the engine block will be bored oversize, you may be able to forego this step. However, some ridges may actually prevent the assemblies from being removed, necessitating its removal.

There are several different types of ridge reamers on the market, none of which are inexpensive. Unless a great deal of engine rebuilding is anticipated, borrow or rent a reamer.

1. Turn the crankshaft until the piston is at the bottom of its travel.

2. Cover the head of the piston with a rag.

3. Follow the tool manufacturers instructions and cut away the ridge, exercising extreme care to avoid cutting too deeply.

4. Remove the ridge reamer, the rag and as many of the cuttings as possible. Continue until all of the cylinder ridges have been removed.

### DISASSEMBLY

#### ▶ See Figures 204 and 205

The engine disassembly instructions following assume that you have the engine mounted on an engine stand. If not, it is easiest to disassemble the engine on a bench or the floor with it resting on the bellhousing or transmission mounting surface. You must be able to access the connecting rod fasteners and turn the crankshaft during disassembly. Also, all engine covers (timing, front, side, oil pan, whatever) should have already been removed. Engines which are seized or locked up may not be able to be completely disassembled, and a core (salvage yard) engine should be purchased.

If not done during the cylinder head removal, remove the timing chain/belt and/or gear/sprocket assembly. Remove the oil pick-up and pump assembly and, if necessary, the pump drive. If equipped, remove any balance or auxiliary shafts. If necessary, remove the cylinder ridge from the top of the bore. See the cylinder ridge removal procedure earlier in this section.

Rotate the engine over so that the crankshaft is exposed. Use a number punch or scribe and mark each connecting rod with its respective cylinder number. The cylinder closest to the front of the engine is always number 1. However, depending on the engine placement, the front of the engine could either be the flywheel or damper/pulley end. Generally the front of the engine faces the front of the vehicle. Use a number punch or scribe and also mark the main bearing caps from front to rear with the front most cap being number 1 (if there are five caps, mark them 1 through 5, front to rear).

TCCS3803

**Fig. 204 Place rubber hose over the connecting rod studs to protect the crankshaft and cylinder bores from damage**

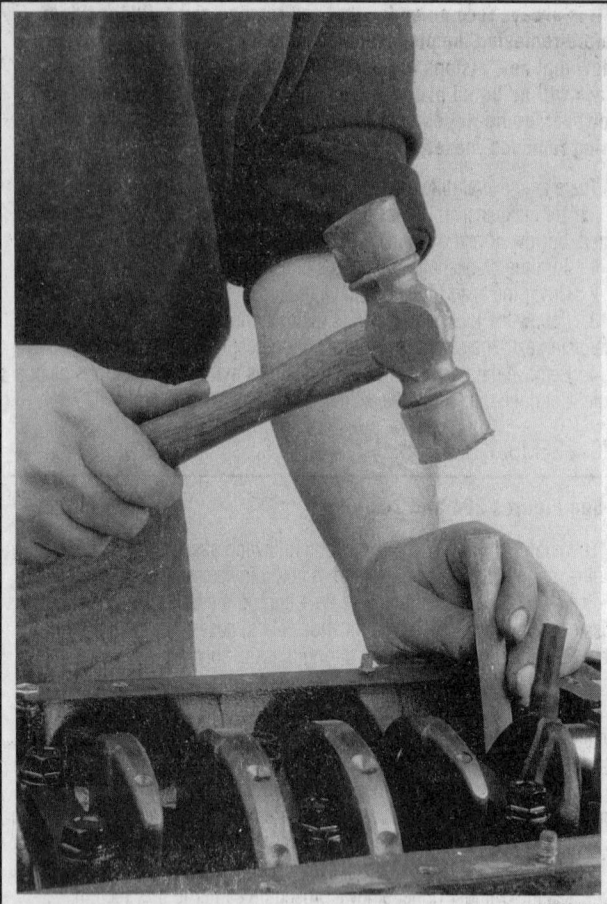

TCCS3804

**Fig. 205 Carefully tap the piston out of the bore using a wooden dowel**

### ✳✳ WARNING

**Take special care when pushing the connecting rod up from the crankshaft because the sharp threads of the rod bolts/studs will score the crankshaft journal. Insure that special plastic caps are installed over them, or cut two pieces of rubber hose to do the same.**

Again, rotate the engine, this time to position the number one cylinder bore (head surface) up. Turn the crankshaft until the number one piston is at the bottom of its travel, this should allow the maximum access to its connecting rod. Remove the number one connecting rods fasteners and cap and place two lengths of rubber hose over the rod bolts/studs to protect the crankshaft from damage. Using a sturdy wooden dowel and a hammer, push the connecting rod up about 1 in. (25mm) from the crankshaft and remove the upper bearing insert. Continue pushing or tapping the connecting rod up until the piston rings are out of the cylinder bore. Remove the piston and rod by hand, put the upper half of the bearing insert back into the rod, install the cap with its bearing insert installed, and hand-tighten the cap fasteners. If the parts are kept in order in this manner, they will not get lost and you will be able to tell which bearings came form what cylinder if any problems are discovered and diagnosis is necessary. Remove all the other piston assemblies in the same manner. On V-style engines, remove all of the pistons from one bank, then reposition the engine with the other cylinder bank head surface up, and remove that banks piston assemblies.

The only remaining component in the engine block should now be the crankshaft. Loosen the main bearing caps evenly until the fasteners can be turned by hand, then remove them and the caps. Remove the crankshaft from the engine block. Thoroughly clean all of the components.

## INSPECTION

Now that the engine block and all of its components are clean, it's time to inspect them for wear and/or damage. To accurately inspect them, you will need some specialized tools:

- Two or three separate micrometers to measure the pistons and crankshaft journals
- A dial indicator
- Telescoping gauges for the cylinder bores
- A rod alignment fixture to check for bent connecting rods

If you do not have access to the proper tools, you may want to bring the components to a shop that does.

Generally, you shouldn't expect cracks in the engine block or its components unless it was known to leak, consume or mix engine fluids, it was severely overheated, or there was evidence of bad bearings and/or crankshaft damage. A visual inspection should be performed on all of the components, but just because you don't see a crack does not mean it is not there. Some more reliable methods for inspecting for cracks include Magnaflux®, a magnetic process or Zyglo®, a dye penetrant. Magnaflux® is used only on ferrous metal (cast iron). Zyglo® uses a spray on fluorescent mixture along with a black light to reveal the cracks. It is strongly recommended to have your engine block checked professionally for cracks, especially if the engine was known to have overheated and/or leaked or consumed coolant. Contact a local shop for availability and pricing of these services.

### Engine Block

#### ENGINE BLOCK BEARING ALIGNMENT

Remove the main bearing caps and, if still installed, the main bearing inserts. Inspect all of the main bearing saddles and caps for damage, burrs or high spots. If damage is found, and it is caused from a spun main bearing, the block will need to be align-bored or, if severe enough, replacement. Any burrs or high spots should be carefully removed with a metal file.

Place a straightedge on the bearing saddles, in the engine block, along the centerline of the crankshaft. If any clearance exists between the straightedge and the saddles, the block must be align-bored.

Align-boring consists of machining the main bearing saddles and caps by means of a flycutter that runs through the bearing saddles.

#### DECK FLATNESS

The top of the engine block where the cylinder head mounts is called the deck. Insure that the deck surface is clean of dirt, carbon deposits and old gasket material. Place a straightedge across the surface of the deck along its centerline and, using feeler gauges, check the clearance along several points. Repeat the checking procedure with the straightedge placed along both diagonals of the deck surface. If the reading exceeds 0.003 in. (0.076mm) within a 6.0 in. (15.2cm) span, or 0.006 in. (0.152mm) over the total length of the deck, it must be machined.

#### CYLINDER BORES

▶ See Figure 206

The cylinder bores house the pistons and are slightly larger than the pistons themselves. A common piston-to-bore clearance is 0.0015–0.0025 in. (0.0381mm–0.0635mm). Inspect and measure the cylinder bores. The bore should be checked for out-of-roundness, taper and size. The results of this inspection will determine whether the cylinder can be used in its existing size and condition, or a rebore to the next oversize is required (or in the case of removable sleeves, have replacements installed).

The amount of cylinder wall wear is always greater at the top of the cylinder than at the bottom. This wear is known as taper. Any cylinder that has a taper of 0.0012 in. (0.305mm) or more, must be rebored. Measurements are taken at a number of positions in each cylinder: at the top, middle and bottom and at two points at each position; that is, at a point 90 degrees from the crankshaft centerline, as well as a point parallel to the crankshaft centerline. The measurements are made with either a special dial indicator or a telescopic gauge and micrometer. If the necessary precision

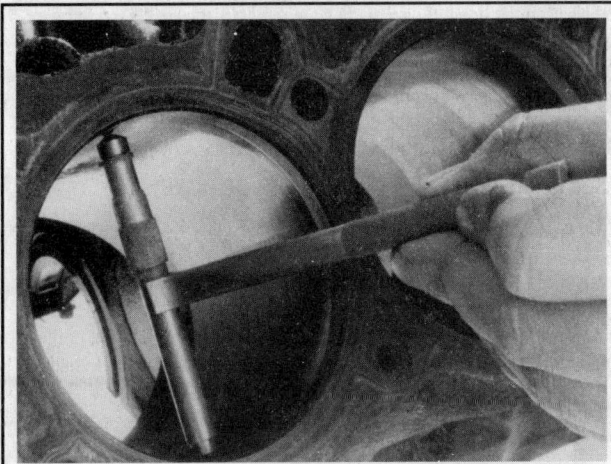

**Fig. 206 Use a telescoping gauge to measure the cylinder bore diameter—take several readings within the same bore**

tools to check the bore are not available, take the block to a machine shop and have them mike it. Also if you don't have the tools to check the cylinder bores, chances are you will not have the necessary devices to check the pistons, connecting rods and crankshaft. Take these components with you and save yourself an extra trip.

For our procedures, we will use a telescopic gauge and a micrometer. You will need one of each, with a measuring range which covers your cylinder bore size.

1. Position the telescopic gauge in the cylinder bore, loosen the gauges lock and allow it to expand.

➡ **Your first two readings will be at the top of the cylinder bore, then proceed to the middle and finally the bottom, making a total of six measurements.**

2. Hold the gauge square in the bore, 90 degrees from the crankshaft centerline, and gently tighten the lock. Tilt the gauge back to remove it from the bore.

3. Measure the gauge with the micrometer and record the reading.

4. Again, hold the gauge square in the bore, this time parallel to the crankshaft centerline, and gently tighten the lock. Again, you will tilt the gauge back to remove it from the bore.

5. Measure the gauge with the micrometer and record this reading. The difference between these two readings is the out-of-round measurement of the cylinder.

6. Repeat steps 1 through 5, each time going to the next lower position, until you reach the bottom of the cylinder. Then go to the next cylinder, and continue until all of the cylinders have been measured.

The difference between these measurements will tell you all about the wear in your cylinders. The measurements which were taken 90 degrees from the crankshaft centerline will always reflect the most wear. That is because at this position is where the engine power presses the piston against the cylinder bore the hardest. This is known as thrust wear. Take your top, 90 degree measurement and compare it to your bottom, 90 degree measurement. The difference between them is the taper. When you measure your pistons, you will compare these readings to your piston sizes and determine piston-to-wall clearance.

## Crankshaft

Inspect the crankshaft for visible signs of wear or damage. All of the journals should be perfectly round and smooth. Slight scores are normal for a used crankshaft, but you should hardly feel them with your fingernail. When measuring the crankshaft with a micrometer, you will take readings at the front and rear of each journal, then turn the micrometer 90 degrees and take two more readings, front and rear. The difference between the front-to-rear readings is the journal taper and the first-to-90 degree reading is the

out-of-round measurement. Generally, there should be no taper or out-of-roundness found, however, up to 0.0005 in. (0.0127mm) for either can be overlooked. Also, the readings should fall within the factory specifications for journal diameters.

If the crankshaft journals fall within specifications, it is recommended that it be polished before being returned to service. Polishing the crankshaft insures that any minor burrs or high spots are smoothed, thereby reducing the chance of scoring the new bearings.

### Pistons and Connecting Rods

#### PISTONS

▶ **See Figure 207**

The piston should be visually inspected for any signs of cracking or burning (caused by hot spots or detonation), and scuffing or excessive wear on the skirts. The wristpin attaches the piston to the connecting rod. The piston should move freely on the wrist pin, both sliding and pivoting. Grasp the connecting rod securely, or mount it in a vise, and try to rock the piston back and forth along the centerline of the wristpin. There should not be any excessive play evident between the piston and the pin. If there are C-clips retaining the pin in the piston then you have wrist pin bushings in the rods. There should not be any excessive play between the wrist pin and the rod bushing. Normal clearance for the wrist pin is approx. 0.001–0.002 in. (0.025mm–0.051mm).

Use a micrometer and measure the diameter of the piston, perpendicular to the wrist pin, on the skirt. Compare the reading to its original cylinder measurement obtained earlier. The difference between the two readings is the piston-to-wall clearance. If the clearance is within specifications, the piston may be used as is. If the piston is out of specification, but the bore is not, you will need a new piston. If both are out of specification, you will need the cylinder rebored and oversize pistons installed. Generally if two or more pistons/bores are out of specification, it is best to rebore the entire block and purchase a complete set of oversize pistons.

**Fig. 207 Measure the piston's outer diameter, perpendicular to the wrist pin, with a micrometer**

#### CONNECTING ROD

You should have the connecting rod checked for straightness at a machine shop. If the connecting rod is bent, it will unevenly wear the bearing and piston, as well as place greater stress on these components. Any bent or twisted connecting rods must be replaced. If the rods are straight and the wrist pin clearance is within specifications, then only the bearing end of the rod need be checked. Place the connecting rod into a vice, with the bearing inserts in place, install the cap to the rod and torque the fasteners to specifications. Use a telescoping gauge and carefully measure the inside diameter of the bearings. Compare this reading to the rods original crankshaft journal diameter measurement. The difference is the oil clearance. If the oil clearance is not within specifications, install new bearings in the rod and take another measurement. If the clearance is still out of specifications, and the crankshaft is not, the rod will need to be reconditioned by a machine shop.

➡**You can also use Plastigage® to check the bearing clearances. The assembling section has complete instructions on its use.**

### Camshaft

Inspect the camshaft and lifters/followers as described earlier in this section.

### Bearings

All of the engine bearings should be visually inspected for wear and/or damage. The bearing should look evenly worn all around with no deep scores or pits. If the bearing is severely worn, scored, pitted or heat blued, then the bearing, and the components that use it, should be brought to a machine shop for inspection. Full-circle bearings (used on most camshafts, auxiliary shafts, balance shafts, etc.) require specialized tools for removal and installation, and should be brought to a machine shop for service.

### Oil Pump

➡**The oil pump is responsible for providing constant lubrication to the whole engine and so it is recommended that a new oil pump be installed when rebuilding the engine.**

Completely disassemble the oil pump and thoroughly clean all of the components. Inspect the oil pump gears and housing for wear and/or damage. Insure that the pressure relief valve operates properly and there is no binding or sticking due to varnish or debris. If all of the parts are in proper working condition, lubricate the gears and relief valve, and assemble the pump.

## REFINISHING

▶ **See Figure 208**

Almost all engine block refinishing must be performed by a machine shop. If the cylinders are not to be rebored, then the cylinder glaze can be removed with a ball hone. When removing cylinder glaze with a ball hone, use a light or penetrating type oil to lubricate the hone. Do not allow the hone to run dry as this may cause excessive scoring of the cylinder bores

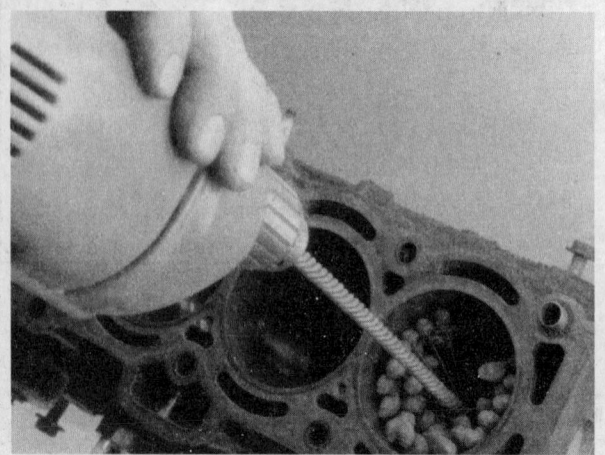

Fig. 208 Use a ball type cylinder hone to remove any glaze and provide a new surface for seating the piston rings

and wear on the hone. If new pistons are required, they will need to be installed to the connecting rods. This should be performed by a machine shop as the pistons must be installed in the correct relationship to the rod or engine damage can occur.

### Pistons and Connecting Rods

▶ **See Figure 209**

Only pistons with the wrist pin retained by C-clips are serviceable by the home-mechanic. Press fit pistons require special presses and/or heaters to remove/install the connecting rod and should only be performed by a machine shop.

All pistons will have a mark indicating the direction to the front of the engine and the must be installed into the engine in that manner. Usually it is a notch or arrow on the top of the piston, or it may be the letter F cast or stamped into the piston.

Fig. 209 Most pistons are marked to indicate positioning in the engine (usually a mark means the side facing the front)

#### *C-CLIP TYPE PISTONS*

1. Note the location of the forward mark on the piston and mark the connecting rod in relation.
2. Remove the C-clips from the piston and withdraw the wrist pin.

➡**Varnish build-up or C-clip groove burrs may increase the difficulty of removing the wrist pin. If necessary, use a punch or drift to carefully tap the wrist pin out.**

3. Insure that the wrist pin bushing in the connecting rod is usable, and lubricate it with assembly lube.
4. Remove the wrist pin from the new piston and lubricate the pin bores on the piston.
5. Align the forward marks on the piston and the connecting rod and install the wrist pin.
6. The new C-clips will have a flat and a rounded side to them. Install both C-clips with the flat side facing out.
7. Repeat all of the steps for each piston being replaced.

## ASSEMBLY

Before you begin assembling the engine, first give yourself a clean, dirt free work area. Next, clean every engine component again. The key to a good assembly is cleanliness.

Mount the engine block into the engine stand and wash it one last time using water and detergent (dishwashing detergent works well). While washing it, scrub the cylinder bores with a soft bristle brush and thoroughly clean all of the oil passages. Completely dry the engine and spray the entire assembly down with an anti-rust solution such as WD-40® or similar product. Take a clean lint-free rag and wipe up any excess anti-rust solution from the bores, bearing saddles, etc. Repeat the final cleaning process on the crankshaft. Replace any freeze or oil galley plugs which were removed during disassembly.

## Crankshaft

▶ **See Figures 210, 211, 212 and 213**

1. Remove the main bearing inserts from the block and bearing caps.
2. If the crankshaft main bearing journals have been refinished to a definite undersize, install the correct undersize bearing. Be sure that the bearing inserts and bearing bores are clean. Foreign material under inserts will distort bearing and cause failure.
3. Place the upper main bearing inserts in bores with tang in slot.

➡**The oil holes in the bearing inserts must be aligned with the oil holes in the cylinder block.**

4. Install the lower main bearing inserts in bearing caps.
5. Clean the mating surfaces of block and rear main bearing cap.
6. Carefully lower the crankshaft into place. Be careful not to damage bearing surfaces.
7. Check the clearance of each main bearing by using the following procedure:

a. Place a piece of Plastigage® or its equivalent, on bearing surface across full width of bearing cap and about ¼ in. off center.

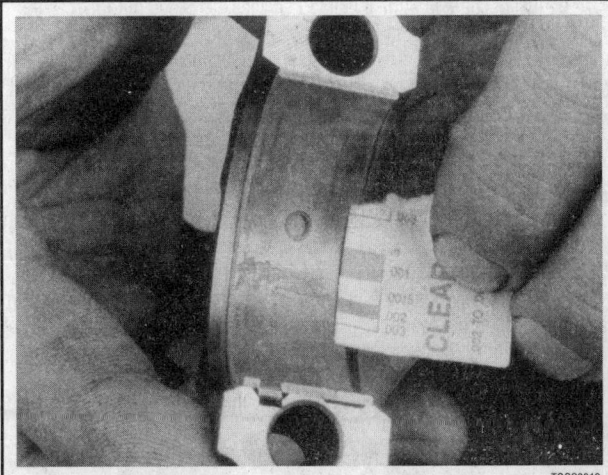

Fig. 211 After the cap is removed again, use the scale supplied with the gauging material to check the clearance

Fig. 212 A dial gauge may be used to check crankshaft end-play

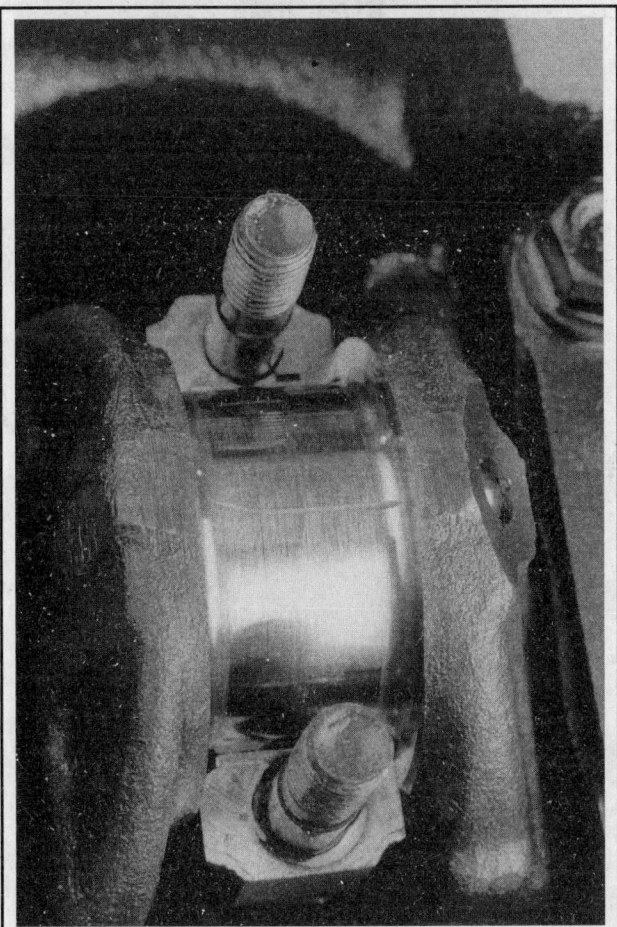

Fig. 210 Apply a strip of gauging material to the bearing journal, then install and torque the cap

Fig. 213 Carefully pry the crankshaft back and forth while reading the dial gauge for end-play

b. Install cap and tighten bolts to specifications. Do not turn crankshaft while Plastigage® is in place.

c. Remove the cap. Using the supplied Plastigage® scale, check width of Plastigage® at widest point to get maximum clearance. Difference between readings is taper of journal.

d. If clearance exceeds specified limits, try a 0.001 in. or 0.002 in. undersize bearing in combination with the standard bearing. Bearing clearance must be within specified limits. If standard and 0.002 in. undersize bearing does not bring clearance within desired limits, refinish crankshaft journal, then install undersize bearings.

8. After the bearings have been fitted, apply a light coat of engine oil to the journals and bearings. Install the rear main bearing cap. Install all bearing caps except the thrust bearing cap. Be sure that main bearing caps are installed in original locations. Tighten the bearing cap bolts to specifications.

9. Install the thrust bearing cap with bolts finger-tight.

10. Pry the crankshaft forward against the thrust surface of upper half of bearing.

11. Hold the crankshaft forward and pry the thrust bearing cap to the rear. This aligns the thrust surfaces of both halves of the bearing.

12. Retain the forward pressure on the crankshaft. Tighten the cap bolts to specifications.

13. Measure the crankshaft end-play as follows:

a. Mount a dial gauge to the engine block and position the tip of the gauge to read from the crankshaft end.

b. Carefully pry the crankshaft toward the rear of the engine and hold it there while you zero the gauge.

c. Carefully pry the crankshaft toward the front of the engine and read the gauge.

d. Confirm that the reading is within specifications. If not, install a new thrust bearing and repeat the procedure. If the reading is still out of specifications with a new bearing, have a machine shop inspect the thrust surfaces of the crankshaft, and if possible, repair it.

14. Rotate the crankshaft so as to position the first rod journal to the bottom of its stroke.

15. Install the rear main seal.

### Pistons and Connecting Rods

▶ **See Figures 214, 215, 216 and 217**

1. Before installing the piston/connecting rod assembly, oil the pistons, piston rings and the cylinder walls with light engine oil. Install connecting rod bolt protectors or rubber hose onto the connecting rod bolts/studs. Also perform the following:

a. Select the proper ring set for the size cylinder bore.

b. Position the ring in the bore in which it is going to be used.

c. Push the ring down into the bore area where normal ring wear is not encountered.

d. Use the head of the piston to position the ring in the bore so that the ring is square with the cylinder wall. Use caution to avoid damage to the ring or cylinder bore.

e. Measure the gap between the ends of the ring with a feeler gauge. Ring gap in a worn cylinder is normally greater than specification. If the ring gap is greater than the specified limits, try an oversize ring set.

f. Check the ring side clearance of the compression rings with a feeler gauge inserted between the ring and its lower land according to specification. The gauge should slide freely around the entire ring circumference without binding. Any wear that occurs will form a step at the inner portion of the lower land. If the lower lands have high steps, the piston should be replaced.

2. Unless new pistons are installed, be sure to install the pistons in the cylinders from which they were removed. The numbers on the connecting rod and bearing cap must be on the same side when installed in the cylinder bore. If a connecting rod is ever transposed from one engine or cylinder to another, new bearings should be fitted and the connecting rod should be numbered to correspond with the new cylinder number. The notch on the piston head goes toward the front of the engine.

3. Install all of the rod bearing inserts into the rods and caps.

4. Install the rings to the pistons. Install the oil control ring first, then the second compression ring and finally the top compression ring. Use a piston ring expander tool to aid in installation and to help reduce the chance of breakage.

5. Make sure the ring gaps are properly spaced around the circumference of the piston. Fit a piston ring compressor around the piston and slide the piston and connecting rod assembly down into the cylinder bore, pushing it in with the wooden hammer handle. Push the piston down until it is only

TCCS3923

**Fig. 214 Checking the piston ring-to-ring groove side clearance using the ring and a feeler gauge**

TCCS3917

**Fig. 215 The notch on the side of the bearing cap matches the tang on the bearing insert**

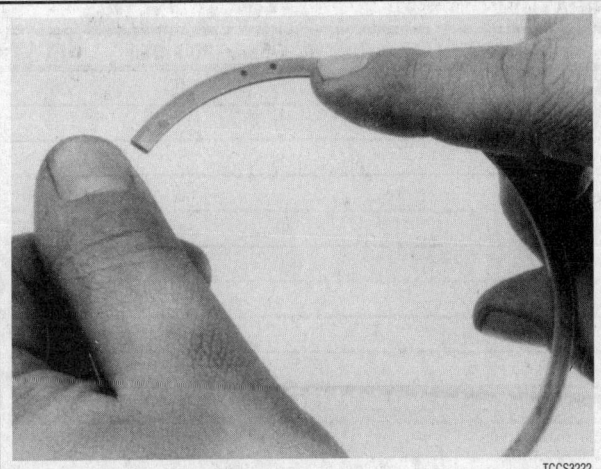

Fig. 216 Most rings are marked to show which side of the ring should face up when installed to the piston

Fig. 217 Install the piston and rod assembly into the block using a ring compressor and the handle of a hammer

slightly below the top of the cylinder bore. Guide the connecting rod onto the crankshaft bearing journal carefully, to avoid damaging the crankshaft.

6. Check the bearing clearance of all the rod bearings, fitting them to the crankshaft bearing journals. Follow the procedure in the crankshaft installation above.

7. After the bearings have been fitted, apply a light coating of assembly oil to the journals and bearings.

8. Turn the crankshaft until the appropriate bearing journal is at the bottom of its stroke, then push the piston assembly all the way down until the connecting rod bearing seats on the crankshaft journal. Be careful not to allow the bearing cap screws to strike the crankshaft bearing journals and damage them.

9. After the piston and connecting rod assemblies have been installed, check the connecting rod side clearance on each crankshaft journal.

10. Prime and install the oil pump and the oil pump intake tube.

### OHV Engines

#### CAMSHAFT, LIFTERS AND TIMING ASSEMBLY

1. Install the camshaft.
2. Install the lifters/followers into their bores.
3. Install the timing gears/chain assembly.

#### CYLINDER HEAD(S)

1. Install the cylinder head(s) using new gaskets.
2. Assemble the rest of the valve train (pushrods and rocker arms and/or shafts).

### OHC Engines

#### CYLINDER HEAD(S)

1. Install the cylinder head(s) using new gaskets.
2. Install the timing sprockets/gears and the belt/chain assemblies.

### Engine Covers and Components

Install the timing cover(s) and oil pan. Refer to your notes and drawings made prior to disassembly and install all of the components that were removed. Install the engine into the vehicle.

## Engine Start-up and Break-in

### STARTING THE ENGINE

Now that the engine is installed and every wire and hose is properly connected, go back and double check that all coolant and vacuum hoses are connected. Check that you oil drain plug is installed and properly tightened. If not already done, install a new oil filter onto the engine. Fill the crankcase with the proper amount and grade of engine oil. Fill the cooling system with a 50/50 mixture of coolant/water.

1. Connect the vehicle battery.
2. Start the engine. Keep your eye on your oil pressure indicator; if it does not indicate oil pressure within 10 seconds of starting, turn the vehicle off.

### ❋❋ WARNING

**Damage to the engine can result if it is allowed to run with no oil pressure. Check the engine oil level to make sure that it is full. Check for any leaks and if found, repair the leaks before continuing. If there is still no indication of oil pressure, you may need to prime the system.**

3. Confirm that there are no fluid leaks (oil or other).
4. Allow the engine to reach normal operating temperature (the upper radiator hose will be hot to the touch).
5. If necessary, set the ignition timing.
6. Install any remaining components such as the air cleaner (if removed for ignition timing) or body panels which were removed.

### BREAKING IT IN

Make the first miles on the new engine, easy ones. Vary the speed but do not accelerate hard. Most importantly, do not lug the engine, and avoid sustained high speeds until at least 100 miles. Check the engine oil and coolant levels frequently. Expect the engine to use a little oil until the rings seat. Change the oil and filter at 500 miles, 1500 miles, then every 3000 miles past that.

### KEEP IT MAINTAINED

Now that you have just gone through all of that hard work, keep yourself from doing it all over again by thoroughly maintaining it. Not that you may not have maintained it before, heck you could have had one to two hundred thousand miles on it before doing this. However, you may have bought the vehicle used, and the previous owner did not keep up on maintenance. Which is why you just went through all of that hard work. See?

## TORQUE SPECIFICATIONS

| Component | ft. lbs. | inch lbs. | Nm |
|---|---|---|---|
| Camshaft sensor pick up bolts | | 85 | 9.6 |
| Camshaft sprocket bolt | 85 | | 115 |
| Collar—Oil pan-to-transaxle | | | |
|     Step 1: Collar-to-oil pan bolts | | 30 | 3 |
|     Step 2: Collar-to-transaxle bolts | 80 | | 108 |
|     Step 3: Collar-to-oil pan bolts | 40 | | 54 |
| Crankshaft main bearing cap/bedplate | | | |
|   SOHC engines | | | |
|     M8 bedplate bolts | | | |
|       1995 vehicles | 25 | | 34 |
|       1996-99 vehicles | 22 | | 30 |
|     M11 bedplate bolts | 60 | | 81 |
|   DOHC engines | | | |
|     M8 bedplate bolts | 22 | | 30 |
|     M11 bedplate bolts | 60 | | 81 |
| Crankshaft damper bolt | 105 | | 142 |
| Cylinder head bolts | | Refer to procedure | |
| Cylinder head cover bolts | 9 | | 12 |
| Drive plate-to-crankshaft bolts | 70 | | 95 |
| Engine mount bracket bolts | | | |
|   SOHC engines | | | |
|     1995-97 vehicles | 30 | | 41 |
|     1998-99 vehicles | 45 | | 61 |
|   DOHC engines | 30 | | 41 |
| Exhaust manifold-to-cylinder head bolts | 17 | | 23 |
| Exhaust manifold head shield bolts | | | |
|   SOHC engines | 9 | | 12 |
|   DOHC engines | 11 | | 15 |
| Front mount torque bracket bolts | | | |
|   SOHC engines | 24 | | 33 |
| Front powertrain bending strut | | | |
|   SOHC engines | | | |
|     Long bolts | 75 | | 101 |
|     Short bolts | 45 | | 61 |
| Intake manifold bolts | | | |
|   SOHC engines | 9 | | 12 |
|   DOHC engines | 21 | | 28 |
| Oil filter adapter | | | |
|   Fastener | | | |
|     1995 vehicles | 40 | | 54 |
|     1996-99 vehicles | 60 | | 80 |
|   Oil filter | 15 | | 20 |
| Oil pan | | | |
|   SOHC engines | | | |
|     Bolts | 9 | | 12 |
|     Drain Plug | | | |
|       1995-96 vehicles | 25 | | 34 |
|       1997-99 vehicles | 20 | | 27 |

## TORQUE SPECIFICATIONS

| Component | ft. lbs. | inch lbs. | Nm |
|---|---|---|---|
| Oil Pan | | | |
|   DOHC engines | | | |
|     Bolts | 9 | | 12 |
|     Drain plug | 25 | | 34 |
| Oil pump retainers | | | |
|   Oil pump attaching bolts | 21 | | 28 |
|   Oil pump cover fastener | 9 | | 12 |
|   Oil pump pick-up tube bolt | 21 | | 28 |
|   Oil pump relief valve cap | | | |
|     SOHC engines | 30 | | 41 |
|     DOHC engines | 40 | | 55 |
| Rear torque bracket | | | |
|   SOHC engines | | | |
|     Bolts w/ automatic transaxle | 80 | | 110 |
|     Bolts w/ manual transaxle | 45 | | 61 |
| Rocker arm shaft bolts | | | |
|   SOHC engines | 21 | | 28 |
| Spark Plugs | 21 | | 28 |
| Thermostat housing bolts | 17 | | 23 |
| Timing belt cover | 9 | | 12 |
| Timing belt tensioner retainers | | | |
|   SOHC engines | | | |
|     1995-97 vehicles | | | |
|       Timing belt tensioner bolts | 23 | | 31 |
|       Timing belt tensioner pivot bracket bolt | 23 | | 31 |
|     1998-99 vehicles | | | |
|       Mechanical timing belt tensioner assembly | 21 | | 28 |
|       Hydraulic timing belt tensioner assembly | | | |
|         Pulley bolt | 50 | | 68 |
|         Pivot bracket bolt | 23 | | 31 |
|         Tensioner bolts | 23 | | 31 |
|   DOHC engines | | | |
|     1995-97 vehicles | | | |
|       Timing belt tensioner bolts | 21 | | 28 |
|       Timing belt tensioner pulley bolts | 30 | | 41 |
|       Timing belt tensioner pulley bolt (1997 only) | 50 | | 68 |
|     1998-99 vehicles | | | |
|       Mechanical timing belt tensioner assembly | 21 | | 28 |
|       Hydraulic timing belt tensioner assembly bolts | 23 | | 31 |
|       Timing belt idler pulley | 45 | | 61 |
| Water pump mounting bolts | 9 | | 12 |

89713C10

## USING A VACUUM GAUGE

*White needle = steady needle*     *Dark needle = drifting needle*

The vacuum gauge is one of the most useful and easy-to-use diagnostic tools. It is inexpensive, easy to hook up, and provides valuable information about the condition of your engine.

**Indication: Normal engine in good condition**

Gauge reading: Steady, from 17–22 in./Hg.

**Indication: Sticking valve or ignition miss**

Gauge reading: Needle fluctuates from 15–20 in./Hg. at idle

**Indication: Late ignition or valve timing, low compression, stuck throttle valve, leaking carburetor or manifold gasket.**

Gauge reading: Low (15–20 in./Hg.) but steady

**Indication: Improper carburetor adjustment, or minor intake leak at carburetor or manifold**

**NOTE: Bad fuel injector O-rings may also cause this reading.**

Gauge reading: Drifting needle

**Indication: Weak valve springs, worn valve stem guides, or leaky cylinder head gasket (vibrating excessively at all speeds).**

**NOTE: A plugged catalytic converter may also cause this reading.**

Gauge reading: Needle fluctuates as engine speed increases

**Indication: Burnt valve or improper valve clearance. The needle will drop when the defective valve operates.**

Gauge reading: Steady needle, but drops regularly

**Indication: Choked muffler or obstruction in system. Speed up the engine. Choked muffler will exhibit a slow drop of vacuum to zero.**

Gauge reading: Gradual drop in reading at idle

**Indication: Worn valve guides**

Gauge reading: Needle vibrates excessively at idle, but steadies as engine speed increases

TCCS3C01

## Troubleshooting Engine Mechanical Problems

| Problem | Cause | Solution |
|---|---|---|
| External oil leaks | • Cylinder head cover RTV sealant broken or improperly seated | • Replace sealant; inspect cylinder head cover sealant flange and cylinder head sealant surface for distortion and cracks |
| | • Oil filler cap leaking or missing | • Replace cap |
| | • Oil filter gasket broken or improperly seated | • Replace oil filter |
| | • Oil pan side gasket broken, improperly seated or opening in RTV sealant | • Replace gasket or repair opening in sealant; inspect oil pan gasket flange for distortion |
| | • Oil pan front oil seal broken or improperly seated | • Replace seal; inspect timing case cover and oil pan seal flange for distortion |
| | • Oil pan rear oil seal broken or improperly seated | • Replace seal; inspect oil pan rear oil seal flange; inspect rear main bearing cap for cracks, plugged oil return channels, or distortion in seal groove |
| | • Timing case cover oil seal broken or improperly seated | • Replace seal |
| | • Excess oil pressure because of restricted PCV valve | • Replace PCV valve |
| | • Oil pan drain plug loose or has stripped threads | • Repair as necessary and tighten |
| | • Rear oil gallery plug loose | • Use appropriate sealant on gallery plug and tighten |
| | • Rear camshaft plug loose or improperly seated | • Seat camshaft plug or replace and seal, as necessary |
| Excessive oil consumption | • Oil level too high | • Drain oil to specified level |
| | • Oil with wrong viscosity being used | • Replace with specified oil |
| | • PCV valve stuck closed | • Replace PCV valve |
| | • Valve stem oil deflectors (or seals) are damaged, missing, or incorrect type | • Replace valve stem oil deflectors |
| | • Valve stems or valve guides worn | • Measure stem-to-guide clearance and repair as necessary |
| | • Poorly fitted or missing valve cover baffles | • Replace valve cover |
| | • Piston rings broken or missing | • Replace broken or missing rings |
| | • Scuffed piston | • Replace piston |
| | • Incorrect piston ring gap | • Measure ring gap, repair as necessary |
| | • Piston rings sticking or excessively loose in grooves | • Measure ring side clearance, repair as necessary |
| | • Compression rings installed upside down | • Repair as necessary |
| | • Cylinder walls worn, scored, or glazed | • Repair as necessary |

TCCS3C02

## Troubleshooting Engine Mechanical Problems

| Problem | Cause | Solution |
| --- | --- | --- |
| Excessive oil consumption (cont.) | • Piston ring gaps not properly staggered<br>• Excessive main or connecting rod bearing clearance | • Repair as necessary<br>• Measure bearing clearance, repair as necessary |
| No oil pressure | • Low oil level<br>• Oil pressure gauge, warning lamp or sending unit inaccurate<br>• Oil pump malfunction<br>• Oil pressure relief valve sticking<br><br>• Oil passages on pressure side of pump obstructed<br><br>• Oil pickup screen or tube obstructed<br>• Loose oil inlet tube | • Add oil to correct level<br>• Replace oil pressure gauge or warning lamp<br>• Replace oil pump<br>• Remove and inspect oil pressure relief valve assembly<br>• Inspect oil passages for obstruction<br>• Inspect oil pickup for obstruction<br>• Tighten or seal inlet tube |
| Low oil pressure | • Low oil level<br>• Inaccurate gauge, warning lamp or sending unit<br>• Oil excessively thin because of dilution, poor quality, or improper grade<br>• Excessive oil temperature<br><br>• Oil pressure relief spring weak or sticking<br>• Oil inlet tube and screen assembly has restriction or air leak<br><br><br><br>• Excessive oil pump clearance<br>• Excessive main, rod, or camshaft bearing clearance | • Add oil to correct level<br>• Replace oil pressure gauge or warning lamp<br>• Drain and refill crankcase with recommended oil<br>• Correct cause of overheating engine<br>• Remove and inspect oil pressure relief valve assembly<br>• Remove and inspect oil inlet tube and screen assembly. (Fill inlet tube with lacquer thinner to locate leaks.)<br>• Measure clearances<br>• Measure bearing clearances, repair as necessary |
| High oil pressure | • Improper oil viscosity<br><br>• Oil pressure gauge or sending unit inaccurate<br>• Oil pressure relief valve sticking closed | • Drain and refill crankcase with correct viscosity oil<br>• Replace oil pressure gauge<br>• Remove and inspect oil pressure relief valve assembly |
| Main bearing noise | • Insufficient oil supply<br><br>• Main bearing clearance excessive<br><br>• Bearing insert missing<br>• Crankshaft end-play excessive<br><br>• Improperly tightened main bearing cap bolts<br>• Loose flywheel or drive plate<br><br>• Loose or damaged vibration damper | • Inspect for low oil level and low oil pressure<br>• Measure main bearing clearance, repair as necessary<br>• Replace missing insert<br>• Measure end-play, repair as necessary<br>• Tighten bolts with specified torque<br>• Tighten flywheel or drive plate attaching bolts<br>• Repair as necessary |

TCCS3C03

## Troubleshooting Engine Mechanical Problems

| Problem | Cause | Solution |
|---|---|---|
| Connecting rod bearing noise | • Insufficient oil supply | • Inspect for low oil level and low oil pressure |
| | • Carbon build-up on piston | • Remove carbon from piston crown |
| | • Bearing clearance excessive or bearing missing | • Measure clearance, repair as necessary |
| | • Crankshaft connecting rod journal out-of-round | • Measure journal dimensions, repair or replace as necessary |
| | • Misaligned connecting rod or cap | • Repair as necessary |
| | • Connecting rod bolts tightened improperly | • Tighten bolts with specified torque |
| Piston noise | • Piston-to-cylinder wall clearance excessive (scuffed piston) | • Measure clearance and examine piston |
| | • Cylinder walls excessively tapered or out-of-round | • Measure cylinder wall dimensions, rebore cylinder |
| | • Piston ring broken | • Replace all rings on piston |
| | • Loose or seized piston pin | • Measure piston-to-pin clearance, repair as necessary |
| | • Connecting rods misaligned | • Measure rod alignment, straighten or replace |
| | • Piston ring side clearance excessively loose or tight | • Measure ring side clearance, repair as necessary |
| | • Carbon build-up on piston is excessive | • Remove carbon from piston |
| Valve actuating component noise | • Insufficient oil supply | • Check for:<br>(a) Low oil level<br>(b) Low oil pressure<br>(c) Wrong hydraulic tappets<br>(d) Restricted oil gallery<br>(e) Excessive tappet to bore clearance |
| | • Rocker arms or pivots worn | • Replace worn rocker arms or pivots |
| | • Foreign objects or chips in hydraulic tappets | • Clean tappets |
| | • Excessive tappet leak-down | • Replace valve tappet |
| | • Tappet face worn | • Replace tappet; inspect corresponding cam lobe for wear |
| | • Broken or cocked valve springs | • Properly seat cocked springs; replace broken springs |
| | • Stem-to-guide clearance excessive | • Measure stem-to-guide clearance, repair as required |
| | • Valve bent | • Replace valve |
| | • Loose rocker arms | • Check and repair as necessary |
| | • Valve seat runout excessive | • Regrind valve seat/valves |
| | • Missing valve lock | • Install valve lock |
| | • Excessive engine oil | • Correct oil level |

TCCS3C04

## Troubleshooting Engine Performance

| Problem | Cause | Solution |
|---|---|---|
| Hard starting (engine cranks normally) | • Faulty engine control system component | • Repair or replace as necessary |
| | • Faulty fuel pump | • Replace fuel pump |
| | • Faulty fuel system component | • Repair or replace as necessary |
| | • Faulty ignition coil | • Test and replace as necessary |
| | • Improper spark plug gap | • Adjust gap |
| | • Incorrect ignition timing | • Adjust timing |
| | • Incorrect valve timing | • Check valve timing; repair as necessary |
| Rough idle or stalling | • Incorrect curb or fast idle speed | • Adjust curb or fast idle speed (If possible) |
| | • Incorrect ignition timing | • Adjust timing to specification |
| | • Improper feedback system operation | • Refer to Chapter 4 |
| | • Faulty EGR valve operation | • Test EGR system and replace as necessary |
| | • Faulty PCV valve air flow | • Test PCV valve and replace as necessary |
| | • Faulty TAC vacuum motor or valve | • Repair as necessary |
| | • Air leak into manifold vacuum | • Inspect manifold vacuum connections and repair as necessary |
| | • Faulty distributor rotor or cap | • Replace rotor or cap (Distributor systems only) |
| | • Improperly seated valves | • Test cylinder compression, repair as necessary |
| | • Incorrect ignition wiring | • Inspect wiring and correct as necessary |
| | • Faulty ignition coil | • Test coil and replace as necessary |
| | • Restricted air vent or idle passages | • Clean passages |
| | • Restricted air cleaner | • Clean or replace air cleaner filter element |
| Faulty low-speed operation | • Restricted idle air vents and passages | • Clean air vents and passages |
| | • Restricted air cleaner | • Clean or replace air cleaner filter element |
| | • Faulty spark plugs | • Clean or replace spark plugs |
| | • Dirty, corroded, or loose ignition secondary circuit wire connections | • Clean or tighten secondary circuit wire connections |
| | • Improper feedback system operation | • Refer to Chapter 4 |
| | • Faulty ignition coil high voltage wire | • Replace ignition coil high voltage wire (Distributor systems only) |
| | • Faulty distributor cap | • Replace cap (Distributor systems only) |
| Faulty acceleration | • Incorrect ignition timing | • Adjust timing |
| | • Faulty fuel system component | • Repair or replace as necessary |
| | • Faulty spark plug(s) | • Clean or replace spark plug(s) |
| | • Improperly seated valves | • Test cylinder compression, repair as necessary |
| | • Faulty ignition coil | • Test coil and replace as necessary |

TCCS3C05

## Troubleshooting Engine Performance

| Problem | Cause | Solution |
|---|---|---|
| Faulty acceleration (cont.) | • Improper feedback system operation | • Refer to Chapter 4 |
| Faulty high speed operation | • Incorrect ignition timing<br>• Faulty advance mechanism | • Adjust timing (if possible)<br>• Check advance mechanism and repair as necessary (Distributor systems only) |
| | • Low fuel pump volume<br>• Wrong spark plug air gap or wrong plug<br>• Partially restricted exhaust manifold, exhaust pipe, catalytic converter, muffler, or tailpipe<br>• Restricted vacuum passages<br>• Restricted air cleaner | • Replace fuel pump<br>• Adjust air gap or install correct plug<br><br>• Eliminate restriction<br><br><br>• Clean passages<br>• Cleaner or replace filter element as necessary |
| | • Faulty distributor rotor or cap | • Replace rotor or cap (Distributor systems only) |
| | • Faulty ignition coil<br>• Improperly seated valve(s) | • Test coil and replace as necessary<br>• Test cylinder compression, repair as necessary |
| | • Faulty valve spring(s) | • Inspect and test valve spring tension, replace as necessary |
| | • Incorrect valve timing | • Check valve timing and repair as necessary |
| | • Intake manifold restricted | • Remove restriction or replace manifold |
| | • Worn distributor shaft | • Replace shaft (Distributor systems only) |
| | • Improper feedback system operation | • Refer to Chapter 4 |
| Misfire at all speeds | • Faulty spark plug(s)<br>• Faulty spark plug wire(s)<br>• Faulty distributor cap or rotor | • Clean or relace spark plug(s)<br>• Replace as necessary<br>• Replace cap or rotor (Distributor systems only) |
| | • Faulty ignition coil<br>• Primary ignition circuit shorted or open intermittently<br>• Improperly seated valve(s) | • Test coil and replace as necessary<br>• Troubleshoot primary circuit and repair as necessary<br>• Test cylinder compression, repair as necessary |
| | • Faulty hydraulic tappet(s)<br>• Improper feedback system operation<br>• Faulty valve spring(s) | • Clean or replace tappet(s)<br>• Refer to Chapter 4<br><br>• Inspect and test valve spring tension, repair as necessary |
| | • Worn camshaft lobes<br>• Air leak into manifold | • Replace camshaft<br>• Check manifold vacuum and repair as necessary |
| | • Fuel pump volume or pressure low<br>• Blown cylinder head gasket<br>• Intake or exhaust manifold passage(s) restricted | • Replace fuel pump<br>• Replace gasket<br>• Pass chain through passage(s) and repair as necessary |
| Power not up to normal | • Incorrect ignition timing<br>• Faulty distributor rotor | • Adjust timing<br>• Replace rotor (Distributor systems only) |

TCCS3C06

## Troubleshooting Engine Performance

| Problem | Cause | Solution |
|---|---|---|
| Power not up to normal (cont.) | • Incorrect spark plug gap | • Adjust gap |
| | • Faulty fuel pump | • Replace fuel pump |
| | • Faulty fuel pump | • Replace fuel pump |
| | • Incorrect valve timing | • Check valve timing and repair as necessary |
| | • Faulty ignition coil | • Test coil and replace as necessary |
| | • Faulty ignition wires | • Test wires and replace as necessary |
| | • Improperly seated valves | • Test cylinder compression and repair as necessary |
| | • Blown cylinder head gasket | • Replace gasket |
| | • Leaking piston rings | • Test compression and repair as necessary |
| | • Improper feedback system operation | • Refer to Chapter 4 |
| Intake backfire | • Improper ignition timing | • Adjust timing |
| | • Defective EGR component | • Repair as necessary |
| | • Defective TAC vacuum motor or valve | • Repair as necessary |
| Exhaust backfire | • Air leak into manifold vacuum | • Check manifold vacuum and repair as necessary |
| | • Faulty air injection diverter valve | • Test diverter valve and replace as necessary |
| | • Exhaust leak | • Locate and eliminate leak |
| Ping or spark knock | • Incorrect ignition timing | • Adjust timing |
| | • Distributor advance malfunction | • Inspect advance mechanism and repair as necessary (Distributor systems only) |
| | • Excessive combustion chamber deposits | • Remove with combustion chamber cleaner |
| | • Air leak into manifold vacuum | • Check manifold vacuum and repair as necessary |
| | • Excessively high compression | • Test compression and repair as necessary |
| | • Fuel octane rating excessively low | • Try alternate fuel source |
| | • Sharp edges in combustion chamber | • Grind smooth |
| | • EGR valve not functioning properly | • Test EGR system and replace as necessary |
| Surging (at cruising to top speeds) | • Low fuel pump pressure or volume | • Replace fuel pump |
| | • Improper PCV valve air flow | • Test PCV valve and replace as necessary |
| | • Air leak into manifold vacuum | • Check manifold vacuum and repair as necessary |
| | • Incorrect spark advance | • Test and replace as necessary |
| | • Restricted fuel filter | • Replace fuel filter |
| | • Restricted air cleaner | • Clean or replace air cleaner filter element |
| | • EGR valve not functioning properly | • Test EGR system and replace as necessary |
| | • Improper feedback system operation | • Refer to Chapter 4 |

TCCS3C07

## Troubleshooting the Serpentine Drive Belt

| Problem | Cause | Solution |
|---|---|---|
| Tension sheeting fabric failure (woven fabric on outside circumference of belt has cracked or separated from body of belt) | • Grooved or backside idler pulley diameters are less than minimum recommended<br>• Tension sheeting contacting (rubbing) stationary object<br>• Excessive heat causing woven fabric to age<br>• Tension sheeting splice has fractured | • Replace pulley(s) not conforming to specification<br>• Correct rubbing condition<br>• Replace belt<br>• Replace belt |
| Noise (objectional squeal, squeak, or rumble is heard or felt while drive belt is in operation) | • Belt slippage<br>• Bearing noise<br>• Belt misalignment<br>• Belt-to-pulley mismatch<br>• Driven component inducing vibration<br>• System resonant frequency inducing vibration | • Adjust belt<br>• Locate and repair<br>• Align belt/pulley(s)<br>• Install correct belt<br>• Locate defective driven component and repair<br>• Vary belt tension within specifications. Replace belt. |
| Rib chunking (one or more ribs has separated from belt body) | • Foreign objects imbedded in pulley grooves<br>• Installation damage<br>• Drive loads in excess of design specifications<br>• Insufficient internal belt adhesion | • Remove foreign objects from pulley grooves<br>• Replace belt<br>• Adjust belt tension<br>• Replace belt |
| Rib or belt wear (belt ribs contact bottom of pulley grooves) | • Pulley(s) misaligned<br>• Mismatch of belt and pulley groove widths<br>• Abrasive environment<br>• Rusted pulley(s)<br>• Sharp or jagged pulley groove tips<br>• Rubber deteriorated | • Align pulley(s)<br>• Replace belt<br>• Replace belt<br>• Clean rust from pulley(s)<br>• Replace pulley<br>• Replace belt |
| Longitudinal belt cracking (cracks between two ribs) | • Belt has mistracked from pulley groove<br>• Pulley groove tip has worn away rubber-to-tensile member | • Replace belt<br>• Replace belt |
| Belt slips | • Belt slipping because of insufficient tension<br>• Belt or pulley subjected to substance (belt dressing, oil, ethylene glycol) that has reduced friction<br>• Driven component bearing failure<br>• Belt glazed and hardened from heat and excessive slippage | • Adjust tension<br>• Replace belt and clean pulleys<br>• Replace faulty component bearing<br>• Replace belt |
| "Groove jumping" (belt does not maintain correct position on pulley, or turns over and/or runs off pulleys) | • Insufficient belt tension<br>• Pulley(s) not within design tolerance<br>• Foreign object(s) in grooves | • Adjust belt tension<br>• Replace pulley(s)<br>• Remove foreign objects from grooves |

TCCS3C09

## Troubleshooting the Serpentine Drive Belt

| Problem | Cause | Solution |
|---|---|---|
| "Groove jumping" (belt does not maintain correct position on pulley, or turns over and/or runs off pulleys) | • Excessive belt speed<br><br>• Pulley misalignment<br>• Belt-to-pulley profile mismatched<br>• Belt cordline is distorted | • Avoid excessive engine acceleration<br>• Align pulley(s)<br>• Install correct belt<br>• Replace belt |
| Belt broken (Note: identify and correct problem before replacement belt is installed) | • Excessive tension<br><br>• Tensile members damaged during belt installation<br>• Belt turnover<br>• Severe pulley misalignment<br>• Bracket, pulley, or bearing failure | • Replace belt and adjust tension to specification<br>• Replace belt<br><br>• Replace belt<br>• Align pulley(s)<br>• Replace defective component and belt |
| Cord edge failure (tensile member exposed at edges of belt or separated from belt body) | • Excessive tension<br>• Drive pulley misalignment<br>• Belt contacting stationary object<br>• Pulley irregularities<br>• Improper pulley construction<br>• Insufficient adhesion between tensile member and rubber matrix | • Adjust belt tension<br>• Align pulley<br>• Correct as necessary<br>• Replace pulley<br>• Replace pulley<br>• Replace belt and adjust tension to specifications |
| Sporadic rib cracking (multiple cracks in belt ribs at random intervals) | • Ribbed pulley(s) diameter less than minimum specification<br>• Backside bend flat pulley(s) diameter less than minimum<br>• Excessive heat condition causing rubber to harden<br>• Excessive belt thickness<br>• Belt overcured<br>• Excessive tension | • Replace pulley(s)<br><br>• Replace pulley(s)<br><br>• Correct heat condition as necessary<br>• Replace belt<br>• Replace belt<br>• Adjust belt tension |

TCCS3C10

## Troubleshooting the Cooling System

| Problem | Cause | Solution |
|---|---|---|
| High temperature gauge indication—overheating | · Coolant level low<br>· Improper fan operation<br>· Radiator hose(s) collapsed<br>· Radiator airflow blocked | · Replenish coolant<br>· Repair or replace as necessary<br>· Replace hose(s)<br>· Remove restriction (bug screen, fog lamps, etc.) |
| | · Faulty pressure cap<br>· Ignition timing incorrect<br>· Air trapped in cooling system<br>· Heavy traffic driving | · Replace pressure cap<br>· Adjust ignition timing<br>· Purge air<br>· Operate at fast idle in neutral intermittently to cool engine<br>· Install proper component(s) |
| | · Incorrect cooling system component(s) installed<br>· Faulty thermostat<br>· Water pump shaft broken or impeller loose<br>· Radiator tubes clogged<br>· Cooling system clogged<br>· Casting flash in cooling passages | · Replace thermostat<br>· Replace water pump<br><br>· Flush radiator<br>· Flush system<br>· Repair or replace as necessary. Flash may be visible by removing cooling system components or removing core plugs. |
| | · Brakes dragging<br>· Excessive engine friction<br>· Antifreeze concentration over 68% | · Repair brakes<br>· Repair engine<br>· Lower antifreeze concentration percentage |
| | · Missing air seals<br>· Faulty gauge or sending unit | · Replace air seals<br>· Repair or replace faulty component |
| | · Loss of coolant flow caused by leakage or foaming<br>· Viscous fan drive failed | · Repair or replace leaking component, replace coolant<br>· Replace unit |
| Low temperature indication—undercooling | · Thermostat stuck open<br>· Faulty gauge or sending unit | · Replace thermostat<br>· Repair or replace faulty component |
| Coolant loss—boilover | · Overfilled cooling system<br><br>· Quick shutdown after hard (hot) run<br>· Air in system resulting in occasional "burping" of coolant<br>· Insufficient antifreeze allowing coolant boiling point to be too low<br>· Antifreeze deteriorated because of age or contamination<br>· Leaks due to loose hose clamps, loose nuts, bolts, drain plugs, faulty hoses, or defective radiator | · Reduce coolant level to proper specification<br>· Allow engine to run at fast idle prior to shutdown<br>· Purge system<br><br>· Add antifreeze to raise boiling point<br><br>· Replace coolant.<br><br>· Pressure test system to locate source of leak(s) then repair as necessary |

TCCS3C11

## Troubleshooting the Cooling System

| Problem | Cause | Solution |
|---|---|---|
| Coolant loss—boilover | • Faulty head gasket<br>• Cracked head, manifold, or block<br>• Faulty radiator cap | • Replace head gasket<br>• Replace as necessary<br>• Replace cap |
| Coolant entry into crankcase or cylinder(s) | • Faulty head gasket<br>• Crack in head, manifold or block | • Replace head gasket<br>• Replace as necessary |
| Coolant recovery system inoperative | • Coolant level low<br>• Leak in system<br><br>• Pressure cap not tight or seal missing, or leaking<br>• Pressure cap defective<br>• Overflow tube clogged or leaking<br>• Recovery bottle vent restricted | • Replenish coolant to FULL mark<br>• Pressure test to isolate leak and repair as necessary<br>• Repair as necessary<br><br>• Replace cap<br>• Repair as necessary<br>• Remove restriction |
| Noise | • Fan contacting shroud<br><br><br>• Loose water pump impeller<br>• Glazed fan belt<br>• Loose fan belt<br>• Rough surface on drive pulley<br>• Water pump bearing worn<br><br>• Belt alignment | • Reposition shroud and inspect engine mounts (on electric fans inspect assembly)<br>• Replace pump<br>• Apply silicone or replace belt<br>• Adjust fan belt tension<br>• Replace pulley<br>• Remove belt to isolate. Replace pump.<br>• Check pulley alignment. Repair as necessary. |
| No coolant flow through heater core | • Restricted return inlet in water pump<br>• Heater hose collapsed or restricted<br>• Restricted heater core<br>• Restricted outlet in thermostat housing<br>• Intake manifold bypass hole in cylinder head restricted<br>• Faulty heater control valve<br>• Intake manifold coolant passage restricted | • Remove restriction<br><br>• Remove restriction or replace hose<br>• Remove restriction or replace core<br>• Remove flash or restriction<br><br>• Remove restriction<br><br>• Replace valve<br>• Remove restriction or replace intake manifold |

NOTE: *Immediately after shutdown, the engine enters a condition known as heat soak. This is caused by the cooling system being inoperative while engine temperature is still high. If coolant temperature rises above boiling point, expansion and pressure may push some coolant out of the radiator overflow tube. If this does not occur frequently it is considered normal.*

TCCS3C12

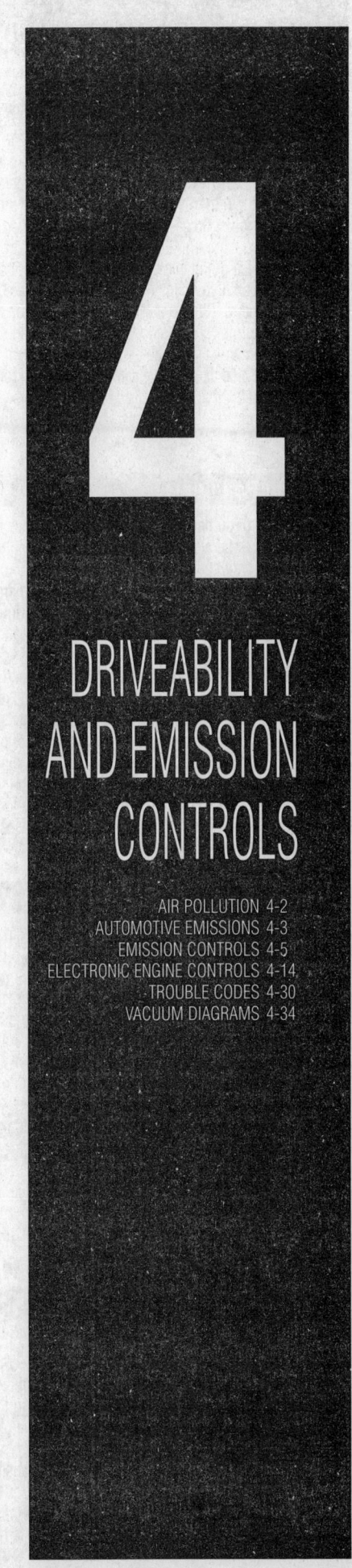

# 4

# DRIVEABILITY AND EMISSION CONTROLS

## AIR POLLUTION

The earth's atmosphere, at or near sea level, consists approximately of 78 percent nitrogen, 21 percent oxygen and 1 percent other gases. If it were possible to remain in this state, 100 percent clean air would result. However, many varied sources allow other gases and particulates to mix with the clean air, causing our atmosphere to become unclean or polluted.

Some of these pollutants are visible while others are invisible, with each having the capability of causing distress to the eyes, ears, throat, skin and respiratory system. Should these pollutants become concentrated in a specific area and under certain conditions, death could result due to the displacement or chemical change of the oxygen content in the air. These pollutants can also cause great damage to the environment and to the many man made objects that are exposed to the elements.

To better understand the causes of air pollution, the pollutants can be categorized into 3 separate types, natural, industrial and automotive.

### Natural Pollutants

Natural pollution has been present on earth since before man appeared and continues to be a factor when discussing air pollution, although it causes only a small percentage of the overall pollution problem. It is the direct result of decaying organic matter, wind born smoke and particulates from such natural events as plain and forest fires (ignited by heat or lightning), volcanic ash, sand and dust which can spread over a large area of the countryside.

Such a phenomenon of natural pollution has been seen in the form of volcanic eruptions, with the resulting plume of smoke, steam and volcanic ash blotting out the sun's rays as it spreads and rises higher into the atmosphere. As it travels into the atmosphere the upper air currents catch and carry the smoke and ash, while condensing the steam back into water vapor. As the water vapor, smoke and ash travel on their journey, the smoke dissipates into the atmosphere while the ash and moisture settle back to earth in a trail hundreds of miles long. In some cases, lives are lost and millions of dollars of property damage result.

### Industrial Pollutants

Industrial pollution is caused primarily by industrial processes, the burning of coal, oil and natural gas, which in turn produce smoke and fumes. Because the burning fuels contain large amounts of sulfur, the principal ingredients of smoke and fumes are sulfur dioxide and particulate matter. This type of pollutant occurs most severely during still, damp and cool weather, such as at night. Even in its less severe form, this pollutant is not confined to just cities. Because of air movements, the pollutants move for miles over the surrounding countryside, leaving in its path a barren and unhealthy environment for all living things.

Working with Federal, State and Local mandated regulations and by carefully monitoring emissions, big business has greatly reduced the amount of pollutant introduced from its industrial sources, striving to obtain an acceptable level. Because of the mandated industrial emission clean up, many land areas and streams in and around the cities that were formerly barren of vegetation and life, have now begun to move back in the direction of nature's intended balance.

### Automotive Pollutants

The third major source of air pollution is automotive emissions. The emissions from the internal combustion engines were not an appreciable problem years ago because of the small number of registered vehicles and the nation's small highway system. However, during the early 1950's, the trend of the American people was to move from the cities to the surrounding suburbs. This caused an immediate problem in transportation because the majority of suburbs were not afforded mass transit conveniences. This lack of transportation created an attractive market for the automobile manufacturers, which resulted in a dramatic increase in the number of vehicles produced and sold, along with a marked increase in highway construction

between cities and the suburbs. Multi-vehicle families emerged with a growing emphasis placed on an individual vehicle per family member. As the increase in vehicle ownership and usage occurred, so did pollutant levels in and around the cities, as suburbanites drove daily to their businesses and employment, returning at the end of the day to their homes in the suburbs.

It was noted that a smoke and fog type haze was being formed and at times, remained in suspension over the cities, taking time to dissipate. At first this "smog," derived from the words "smoke" and "fog," was thought to result from industrial pollution but it was determined that automobile emissions shared the blame. It was discovered that when normal automobile emissions were exposed to sunlight for a period of time, complex chemical reactions would take place.

It is now known that smog is a photo chemical layer which develops when certain oxides of nitrogen (NOx) and unburned hydrocarbons (HC) from automobile emissions are exposed to sunlight. Pollution was more severe when smog would become stagnant over an area in which a warm layer of air settled over the top of the cooler air mass, trapping and holding the cooler mass at ground level. The trapped cooler air would keep the emissions from being dispersed and diluted through normal air flows. This type of air stagnation was given the name "Temperature Inversion."

## TEMPERATURE INVERSION

In normal weather situations, surface air is warmed by heat radiating from the earth's surface and the sun's rays. This causes it to rise upward, into the atmosphere. Upon rising it will cool through a convection type heat exchange with the cooler upper air. As warm air rises, the surface pollutants are carried upward and dissipated into the atmosphere.

When a temperature inversion occurs, we find the higher air is no longer cooler, but is warmer than the surface air, causing the cooler surface air to become trapped. This warm air blanket can extend from above ground level to a few hundred or even a few thousand feet into the air. As the surface air is trapped, so are the pollutants, causing a severe smog condition. Should this stagnant air mass extend to a few thousand feet high, enough air movement with the inversion takes place to allow the smog layer to rise above ground level but the pollutants still cannot dissipate. This inversion can remain for days over an area, with the smog level only rising or lowering from ground level to a few hundred feet high. Meanwhile, the pollutant levels increase, causing eye irritation, respiratory problems, reduced visibility, plant damage and in some cases, even disease.

This inversion phenomenon was first noted in the Los Angeles, California area. The city lies in terrain resembling a basin and with certain weather conditions, a cold air mass is held in the basin while a warmer air mass covers it like a lid.

Because this type of condition was first documented as prevalent in the Los Angeles area, this type of trapped pollution was named Los Angeles Smog, although it occurs in other areas where a large concentration of automobiles are used and the air remains stagnant for any length of time.

## HEAT TRANSFER

Consider the internal combustion engine as a machine in which raw materials must be placed so a finished product comes out. As in any machine operation, a certain amount of wasted material is formed. When we relate this to the internal combustion engine, we find that through the input of air and fuel, we obtain power during the combustion process to drive the vehicle. The by-product or waste of this power is, in part, heat and exhaust gases with which we must dispose.

The heat from the combustion process can rise to over 4000°F (2204°C). The dissipation of this heat is controlled by a ram air effect, the use of cooling fans to cause air flow and a liquid coolant solution surrounding the combustion area to transfer the heat of combustion through the cylinder walls and into the coolant. The coolant is then directed to a thin-finned, multi-tubed radiator, from which the excess heat is transferred to the atmosphere by 1 of the 3 heat transfer methods, conduction, convection or radiation.

The cooling of the combustion area is an important part in the control of exhaust emissions. To understand the behavior of the combustion and transfer of its heat, consider the air/fuel charge. It is ignited and the flame front burns progressively across the combustion chamber until the burning charge reaches the cylinder walls. Some of the fuel in contact with the walls is not hot enough to burn, thereby snuffing out or quenching the combustion process. This leaves unburned fuel in the combustion chamber. This

unburned fuel is then forced out of the cylinder and into the exhaust system, along with the exhaust gases.

Many attempts have been made to minimize the amount of unburned fuel in the combustion chambers due to quenching, by increasing the coolant temperature and lessening the contact area of the coolant around the combustion area. However, design limitations within the combustion chambers prevent the complete burning of the air/fuel charge, so a certain amount of the unburned fuel is still expelled into the exhaust system, regardless of modifications to the engine.

## AUTOMOTIVE EMISSIONS

Before emission controls were mandated on internal combustion engines, other sources of engine pollutants were discovered along with the exhaust emissions. It was determined that engine combustion exhaust produced approximately 60 percent of the total emission pollutants, fuel evaporation from the fuel tank and carburetor vents produced 20 percent, with the final 20 percent being produced through the crankcase as a by-product of the combustion process.

## Exhaust Gases

The exhaust gases emitted into the atmosphere are a combination of burned and unburned fuel. To understand the exhaust emission and its composition, we must review some basic chemistry.

When the air/fuel mixture is introduced into the engine, we are mixing air, composed of nitrogen (78 percent), oxygen (21 percent) and other gases (1 percent) with the fuel, which is 100 percent hydrocarbons (HC), in a semi-controlled ratio. As the combustion process is accomplished, power is produced to move the vehicle while the heat of combustion is transferred to the cooling system. The exhaust gases are then composed of nitrogen, a diatomic gas ($N_2$), the same as was introduced in the engine, carbon dioxide ($CO_2$), the same gas that is used in beverage carbonation, and water vapor ($H_2O$). The nitrogen ($N_2$), for the most part, passes through the engine unchanged, while the oxygen ($O_2$) reacts (burns) with the hydrocarbons (HC) and produces the carbon dioxide ($CO_2$) and the water vapors ($H_2O$). If this chemical process would be the only process to take place, the exhaust emissions would be harmless. However, during the combustion process, other compounds are formed which are considered dangerous. These pollutants are hydrocarbons (HC), carbon monoxide (CO), oxides of nitrogen (NOx) oxides of sulfur (SOx) and engine particulates.

### HYDROCARBONS

Hydrocarbons (HC) are essentially fuel which was not burned during the combustion process or which has escaped into the atmosphere through fuel evaporation. The main sources of incomplete combustion are rich air/fuel mixtures, low engine temperatures and improper spark timing. The main sources of hydrocarbon emission through fuel evaporation on most vehicles used to be the vehicle's fuel tank and carburetor float bowl.

To reduce combustion hydrocarbon emission, engine modifications were made to minimize dead space and surface area in the combustion chamber. In addition, the air/fuel mixture was made more lean through the improved control which feedback carburetion and fuel injection offers and by the addition of external controls to aid in further combustion of the hydrocarbons outside the engine. Two such methods were the addition of air injection systems, to inject fresh air into the exhaust manifolds and the installation of catalytic converters, units that are able to burn traces of hydrocarbons without affecting the internal combustion process or fuel economy.

To control hydrocarbon emissions through fuel evaporation, modifications were made to the fuel tank to allow storage of the fuel vapors during periods of engine shut-down. Modifications were also made to the air intake system so that at specific times during engine operation, these vapors may be purged and burned by blending them with the air/fuel mixture.

### CARBON MONOXIDE

Carbon monoxide is formed when not enough oxygen is present during the combustion process to convert carbon (C) to carbon dioxide ($CO_2$). An increase in the carbon monoxide (CO) emission is normally accompanied by an increase in the hydrocarbon (HC) emission because of the lack of oxygen to completely burn all of the fuel mixture.

Carbon monoxide (CO) also increases the rate at which the photo chemical smog is formed by speeding up the conversion of nitric oxide (NO) to nitrogen dioxide ($NO_2$). To accomplish this, carbon monoxide (CO) combines with oxygen ($O_2$) and nitric oxide (NO) to produce carbon dioxide ($CO_2$) and nitrogen dioxide ($NO_2$). ($CO + O_2 + NO = CO_2 + NO_2$).

The dangers of carbon monoxide, which is an odorless and colorless toxic gas are many. When carbon monoxide is inhaled into the lungs and passed into the blood stream, oxygen is replaced by the carbon monoxide in the red blood cells, causing a reduction in the amount of oxygen supplied to the many parts of the body. This lack of oxygen causes headaches, lack of coordination, reduced mental alertness and, should the carbon monoxide concentration be high enough, death could result.

### NITROGEN

Normally, nitrogen is an inert gas. When heated to approximately 2500°F (1371°C) through the combustion process, this gas becomes active and causes an increase in the nitric oxide (NO) emission.

Oxides of nitrogen (NOx) are composed of approximately 97–98 percent nitric oxide (NO). Nitric oxide is a colorless gas but when it is passed into the atmosphere, it combines with oxygen and forms nitrogen dioxide ($NO_2$). The nitrogen dioxide then combines with chemically active hydrocarbons (HC) and when in the presence of sunlight, causes the formation of photochemical smog.

#### Ozone

To further complicate matters, some of the nitrogen dioxide ($NO_2$) is broken apart by the sunlight to form nitric oxide and oxygen. ($NO_2 + $ sunlight $= NO + O$). This single atom of oxygen then combines with diatomic (meaning 2 atoms) oxygen ($O_2$) to form ozone ($O_3$). Ozone is one of the smells associated with smog. It has a pungent and offensive odor, irritates the eyes and lung tissues, affects the growth of plant life and causes rapid deterioration of rubber products. Ozone can be formed by sunlight as well as electrical discharge into the air.

The most common discharge area on the automobile engine is the secondary ignition electrical system, especially when inferior quality spark plug cables are used. As the surge of high voltage is routed through the secondary cable, the circuit builds up an electrical field around the wire, which acts upon the oxygen in the surrounding air to form the ozone. The faint glow along the cable with the engine running that may be visible on a dark night, is called the "corona discharge." It is the result of the electrical field passing from a high along the cable, to a low in the surrounding air, which forms the ozone gas. The combination of corona and ozone has been a major cause of cable deterioration. Recently, different and better quality insulating materials have lengthened the life of the electrical cables.

Although ozone at ground level can be harmful, ozone is beneficial to the earth's inhabitants. By having a concentrated ozone layer called the "ozonosphere," between 10 and 20 miles (1632 km) up in the atmosphere, much of the ultra violet radiation from the sun's rays are absorbed and screened. If this ozone layer were not present, much of the earth's surface would be burned, dried and unfit for human life.

## OXIDES OF SULFUR

Oxides of sulfur (SOx) were initially ignored in the exhaust system emissions, since the sulfur content of gasoline as a fuel is less than 1/10 of 1 percent. Because of this small amount, it was felt that it contributed very little to the overall pollution problem. However, because of the difficulty in solving the sulfur emissions in industrial pollutions and the introduction of catalytic converter to the automobile exhaust systems, a change was mandated. The automobile exhaust system, when equipped with a catalytic converter, changes the sulfur dioxide ($SO_2$) into sulfur trioxide ($SO_3$).

When this combines with water vapors ($H_2O$), a sulfuric acid mist ($H_2SO_4$) is formed and is a very difficult pollutant to handle since it is extremely corrosive. This sulfuric acid mist that is formed, is the same mist that rises from the vents of an automobile battery when an active chemical reaction takes place within the battery cells.

When a large concentration of vehicles equipped with catalytic converters are operating in an area, this acid mist may rise and be distributed over a large ground area causing land, plant, crop, paint and building damage.

## PARTICULATE MATTER

A certain amount of particulate matter is present in the burning of any fuel, with carbon constituting the largest percentage of the particulates. In gasoline, the remaining particulates are the burned remains of the various other compounds used in its manufacture. When a gasoline engine is in good internal condition, the particulate emissions are low but as the engine wears internally, the particulate emissions increase. By visually inspecting the tail pipe emissions, a determination can be made as to where an engine defect may exist. An engine with light gray or blue smoke emitting from the tail pipe normally indicates an increase in the oil consumption through burning due to internal engine wear. Black smoke would indicate a defective fuel delivery system, causing the engine to operate in a rich mode. Regardless of the color of the smoke, the internal part of the engine or the fuel delivery system should be repaired to prevent excess particulate emissions.

Diesel and turbine engines emit a darkened plume of smoke from the exhaust system because of the type of fuel used. Emission control regulations are mandated for this type of emission and more stringent measures are being used to prevent excess emission of the particulate matter. Electronic components are being introduced to control the injection of the fuel at precisely the proper time of piston travel, to achieve the optimum in fuel ignition and fuel usage. Other particulate after-burning components are being tested to achieve a cleaner emission.

Good grades of engine lubricating oils should be used, which meet the manufacturers specification. Cut-rate oils can contribute to the particulate emission problem because of their low flash or ignition temperature point. Such oils burn prematurely during the combustion process causing emission of particulate matter.

The cooling system is an important factor in the reduction of particulate matter. The optimum combustion will occur, with the cooling system operating at a temperature specified by the manufacturer. The cooling system must be maintained in the same manner as the engine oiling system, as each system is required to perform properly in order for the engine to operate efficiently for a long time.

## Crankcase Emissions

Crankcase emissions are made up of water, acids, unburned fuel, oil fumes and particulates. These emissions are classified as hydrocarbons

(HC) and are formed by the small amount of unburned, compressed air/fuel mixture entering the crankcase from the combustion area (between the cylinder walls and piston rings) during the compression and power strokes. The head of the compression and combustion help to form the remaining crankcase emissions.

Since the first engines, crankcase emissions were allowed into the atmosphere through a road draft tube, mounted on the lower side of the engine block. Fresh air came in through an open oil filler cap or breather. The air passed through the crankcase mixing with blow-by gases. The motion of the vehicle and the air blowing past the open end of the road draft tube caused a low pressure area (vacuum) at the end of the tube. Crankcase emissions were simply drawn out of the road draft tube into the air.

To control the crankcase emission, the road draft tube was deleted. A hose and/or tubing was routed from the crankcase to the intake manifold so the blow-by emission could be burned with the air/fuel mixture. However, it was found that intake manifold vacuum, used to draw the crankcase emissions into the manifold, would vary in strength at the wrong time and not allow the proper emission flow. A regulating valve was needed to control the flow of air through the crankcase.

Testing, showed the removal of the blow-by gases from the crankcase as quickly as possible, was most important to the longevity of the engine. Should large accumulations of blow-by gases remain and condense, dilution of the engine oil would occur to form water, soots, resins, acids and lead salts, resulting in the formation of sludge and varnishes. This condensation of the blow-by gases occurs more frequently on vehicles used in numerous starting and stopping conditions, excessive idling and when the engine is not allowed to attain normal operating temperature through short runs.

## Evaporative Emissions

Gasoline fuel is a major source of pollution, before and after it is burned in the automobile engine. From the time the fuel is refined, stored, pumped and transported, again stored until it is pumped into the fuel tank of the vehicle, the gasoline gives off unburned hydrocarbons (HC) into the atmosphere. Through the redesign of storage areas and venting systems, the pollution factor was diminished, but not eliminated, from the refinery standpoint. However, the automobile still remained the primary source of vaporized, unburned hydrocarbon (HC) emissions.

Fuel pumped from an underground storage tank is cool but when exposed to a warmer ambient temperature, will expand. Before controls were mandated, an owner might fill the fuel tank with fuel from an underground storage tank and park the vehicle for some time in warm area, such as a parking lot. As the fuel would warm, it would expand and should no provisions or area be provided for the expansion, the fuel would spill out of the filler neck and onto the ground, causing hydrocarbon (HC) pollution and creating a severe fire hazard. To correct this condition, the vehicle manufacturers added overflow plumbing and/or gasoline tanks with built in expansion areas or domes.

However, this did not control the fuel vapor emission from the fuel tank. It was determined that most of the fuel evaporation occurred when the vehicle was stationary and the engine not operating. Most vehicles carry 5–25 gallons (19–95 liters) of gasoline. Should a large concentration of vehicles be parked in one area, such as a large parking lot, excessive fuel vapor emissions would take place, increasing as the temperature increases.

To prevent the vapor emission from escaping into the atmosphere, the fuel systems were designed to trap the vapors while the vehicle is stationary, by sealing the system from the atmosphere. A storage system is used to collect and hold the fuel vapors from the carburetor (if equipped) and the fuel tank when the engine is not operating. When the engine is started, the storage system is then purged of the fuel vapors, which are drawn into the engine and burned with the air/fuel mixture.

**EMISSION CONTROLS**

**EMISSION COMPONENT LOCATIONS—DOHC ENGINES**

1. Idle air control valve (on throttle body)
2. Throttle position sensor (on throttle body)
3. MAP/IAT sensor
4. Engine coolant temperature sensor
5. PCV valve
6. Upstream heated O₂ sensor (mounted in exhaust manifold outlet flange)
7. Camshaft position sensor
8. EGR valve (under air intake duct)
9. Electronic EGR transducer
10. Powertrain control module

8974P00

## EMISSION COMPONENT LOCATIONS—SOHC ENGINES

1. Idle air control valve (on throttle body)
2. Throttle position sensor (on throttle body)
3. PCV valve
4. Knock sensor
5. Intake air temperature sensor
6. Manifold absolute pressure sensor
7. Engine coolant temperature sensor
8. Upstream heated O₂ sensor (threaded in exhaust manifold outlet flange)
9. Camshaft position sensor (mounted to end of cylinder head)
10. EGR valve (located under air intake duct)
11. Powertrain control module

89714P01

## Crankcase Ventilation System

### OPERATION

▶ **See Figures 1, 2 and 3**

All vehicles are equipped with a Positive Crankcase Ventilation (PCV) system. In this system, the intake manifold vacuum removes crankcase vapors and piston blow-by from the engine. The emissions pass through the PCV valve into the intake manifold where they become part of the set air/fuel ratio. They are burned and released with the exhaust gases. The air cleaner provides make up are when the engine does not have enough vapor or blow-by gases. In this system, fresh air does not enter the crankcase. The PCV system is composed of a PCV valve, oil separator (1995 engines only) and connecting hoses.

The PCV valve has a spring loaded plunger. The plunger meters the amount of crankcase vapors routed into the combustion chamber, depend-

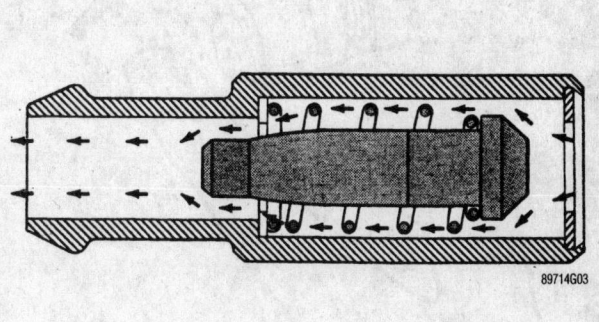

Fig. 3 Maximum vapor flow exists when there is a moderate intake manifold vacuum

ing upon intake manifold vacuum. When the engine is not operating or during engine backfire, the spring forces the plunger back against the seat, preventing vapors from flowing through the valve. When the engine is at idle or cruising, high manifold vacuum is present. At these times, manifold vacuum is able to completely compress the spring and pull the plunger to the top of the valve. There is minimal vapor flow through the valve in this position. During periods of moderate manifold vacuum, the plunger is only pulled part of the way back from the inlet, resulting in maximum vapor flow.

On 1995 engines, the PCV system also includes an oil separator. The crankcase vapors enter the bottom of the separator, then oil accumulated in the separator drains back into the crankcase from an outlet in the bottom of the separator. The PCV valve on these engines, connects to the separator and to intake manifold vacuum. Make-up air is provided to the separator by a hose attached to the air cleaner air tube.

### COMPONENT TESTING

▶ **See Figure 4**

### ❊❊ CAUTION

**ALWAYS block the drive wheels and apply the parking brake anytime you are performing a test or adjustment in which the engine must be running!**

1. With the engine idling, detach the vapor hose from the PCV valve. If the valve is not obstructed, a hissing noise will be heard as air passes through the valve. Also, a strong vacuum should be felt when you place your finger over the valve inlet.
2. Attach the hose to the PCV valve. Disconnect the make-up air hose from the air plenum at the rear of the engine. Hold a piece of rigid paper loosely over the end of the make-up air hose.
3. After allowing about 1 minute for the crankcase pressure to decrease, the paper should draw up against the hose with a noticeable force. If the engine does not draw the paper against the grommet after installing a new valve, replace the valve hose.
4. Turn the engine **OFF**. Remove the PCV valve from the intake manifold, then shake the valve. The valve is OK if a rattling noise is heard as the valve is shaken.
5. If any of the previous tests fail, replace the PCV valve and/or hose and retest the system. Do not try to clean and reuse the old PCV valve. It should be replaced with a new one.

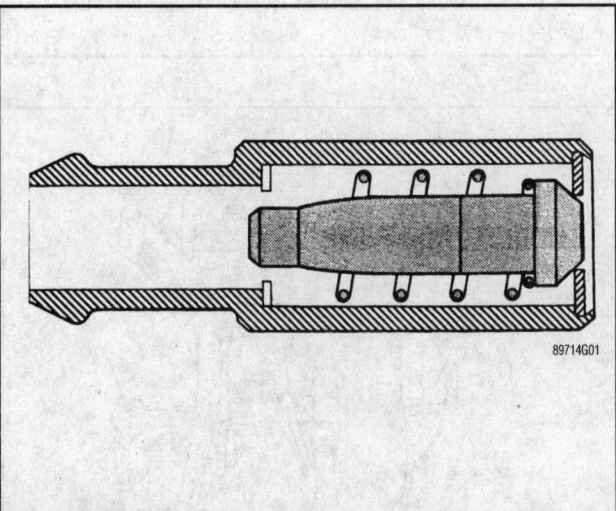

Fig. 1 When the engine is off or backfiring, there is no vapor flow

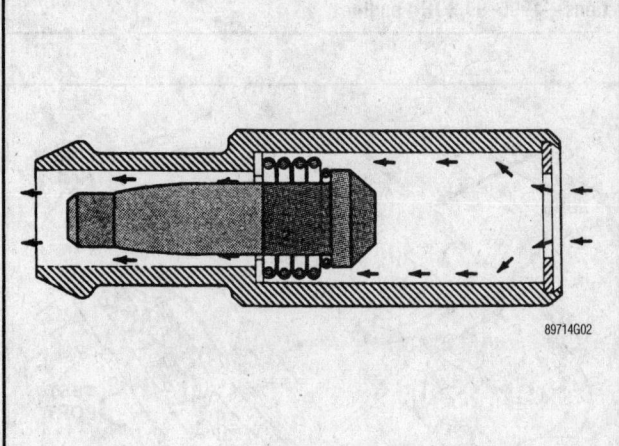

Fig. 2 During a condition of high manifold vacuum, there is a minimal amount of vapor flow

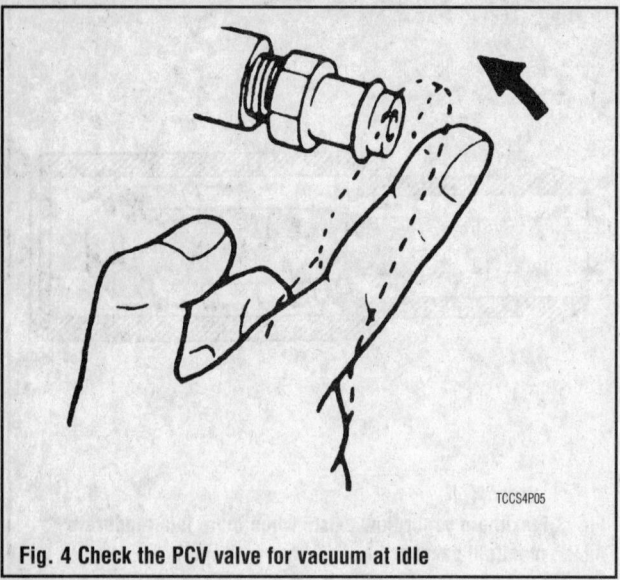

Fig. 4 Check the PCV valve for vacuum at idle

## REMOVAL & INSTALLATION

### PCV Valve

▶ See Figures 5, 6, 7 and 8

1. Disconnect the negative battery cable.
2. If necessary, use a pair of pliers to unfasten the crankcase hose retaining clamps, then disconnect the ventilation hoses from the PCV valve.
3. Remove the PCV valve from the camshaft (rocker) cover or the hose, as applicable.

**To install:**

4. Install the PCV valve into the rocker cover or attach to the hose, as necessary.
5. Reconnect the ventilation hoses to the valve. If necessary, use a pair of pliers to secure the hose clamps.
6. Connect the negative battery cable.

### Oil Separator

▶ See Figures 5 and 6

1. Disconnect the negative battery cable.
2. Remove the intake manifold from the vehicle as outlined in Section 3 of this manual.

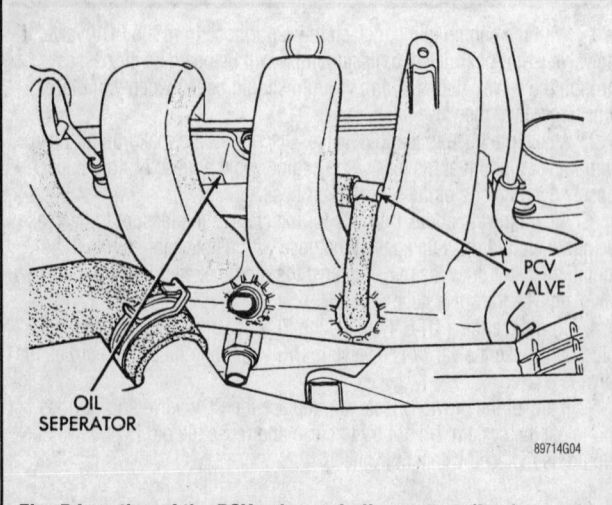

Fig. 5 Location of the PCV valve and oil separator (intake manifold installed)—1995 vehicles

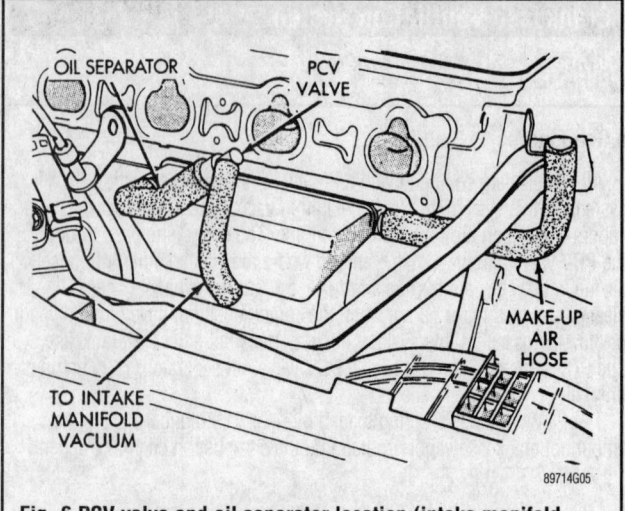

Fig. 6 PCV valve and oil separator location (intake manifold removed)—1995 vehicles

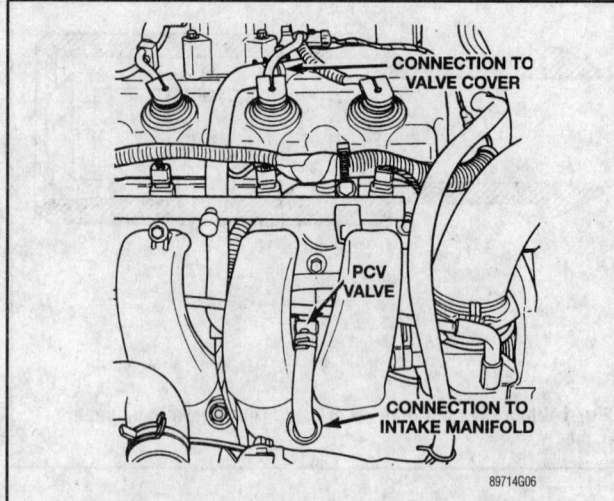

Fig. 7 Positive Crankcase Ventilation (PCV) valve and hose locations—1996–99 SOHC engines

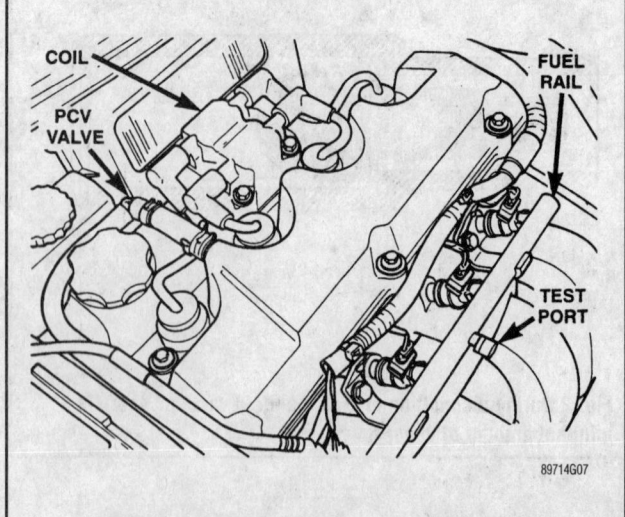

Fig. 8 Location of the PCV valve on a 1996–99 DOHC engine

➡Constant tension hose clamps are used on the separator hoses. During removal and installation, you should use the special clamp tools (No. 6094), available for this purpose.

    3. Disconnect the PCV valve hose from the oil separator.

    4. Unfasten the hose clamps, then detach the 2 hoses from the bottom of the separator.

    5. Remove the 2 separator-to-block retaining bolts, then remove the separator from the vehicle.

**To install:**

    6. Position the separator in the vehicle, and secure with the 2 retaining bolt.

➡An identification number or letter is stamped into the tongue of the constant tension clamps. If you need to replace a clamp, make sure to get an original replacement clamp with a matching number or letter.

    7. Connect the 2 hoses to the bottom of the separator, then secure the hoses with the clamps.

    8. Attach the PCV valve hose to the oil separator.

    9. Install the intake manifold, as outlined in Section 3 of this manual.

    10. Connect the negative battery cable.

## Evaporative Emission Controls

### OPERATION

The evaporation control system prevents the emission of fuel tank vapors into the atmosphere. When fuel evaporates in the fuel tank, the vapors pass through vent hoses or tubes to a charcoal filled evaporative canister. This canister holds the vapors temporarily. The Powertrain Control Module (PCM) allows intake manifold vacuum to draw vapors into the combustion chambers during certain operating conditions. The evaporation control system is made up of the following components:

### Rollover Valve

All vehicles are equipped with a rollover valve. This valve is a safely feature which prevents fuel flow through the fuel tank vent valve hoses, should the vehicle roll over in an accident. All vehicles pass a 360° rollover.

### EVAP Canister

#### ▶ See Figure 9

All vehicles used a sealed, maintenance free evaporative (EVAP) canister. Fuel tank pressure vents into the canister. The canister temporarily holds

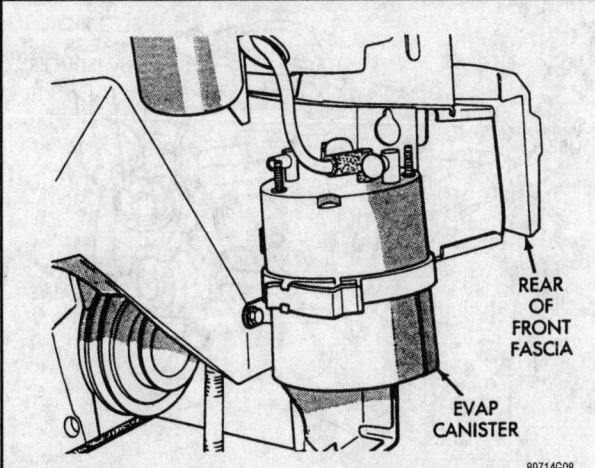

**Fig. 9 The evaporative canister is mounted to a bracket found behind the front fascia on the passenger's side of the vehicle**

the fuel vapors until intake manifold vacuum draws them into the combustion chamber. The PCM purges the canister through the duty cycle EVAP purge solenoid. The canister is purged at intervals and engine conditions predetermined by the PCM.

The canister mounts to a bracket located behind the front passenger's side fascia. The vacuum and vapor tubes connect to the top of the canister.

### Duty Cycle Evaporative Purge Solenoid Valve

#### ▶ See Figure 10

The duty cycle EVAP purge solenoid regulates the rate of vapor flow from the EVAP canister to the throttle body. The PCM operates the solenoid. During the cold start warm up period and the hot start time delay, the PCM does not energize the solenoid. When de-energized, no vapors are purged.

When purging, the PCM energizes and de-energizes the solenoid about 5–10 times per second, depending upon operation conditions. The PCM varies the vapor flow rate by changing the solenoid pulse width. Pulse width is the amount of time the solenoid energizes.

The solenoid is attached to a bracket that is secured to the front engine mount. The solenoid will not operate properly unless it is installed with the electrical connector at the top.

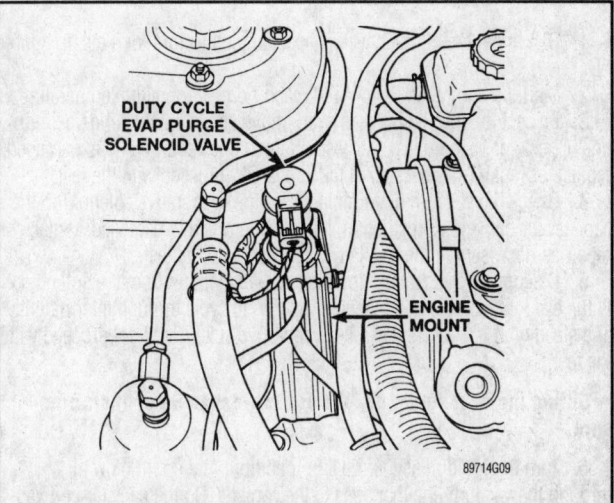

**Fig. 10 The duty cycle evaporative purge solenoid valve is located near the front engine mount**

### Pressure-Vacuum Filler Cap

#### ▶ See Figure 11

A pressure vacuum relief cap is used to seal the fuel tank. Tightening the cap on the fuel filler tube creates a seal between them. The relief valves in the cap are a safety feature which prevent possible excessive pressure or vacuum in the fuel tank. Excessive fuel tank pressure could be caused by a malfunction in the system to damage to the vent lines.

When the cap is removed, the seal is broken and fuel tank pressure is relieved. If the filler cap ever needs to be replaced, make sure to get the correct part.

### Leak Detection Pump

Some vehicles use a leak detection pump which is a device used to find leaks in the evaporative emission system. The pump has a 3-port solenoid, a pump that contains a switch, a spring loaded canister vent valve seal, 2 check valves and a spring/diaphragm.

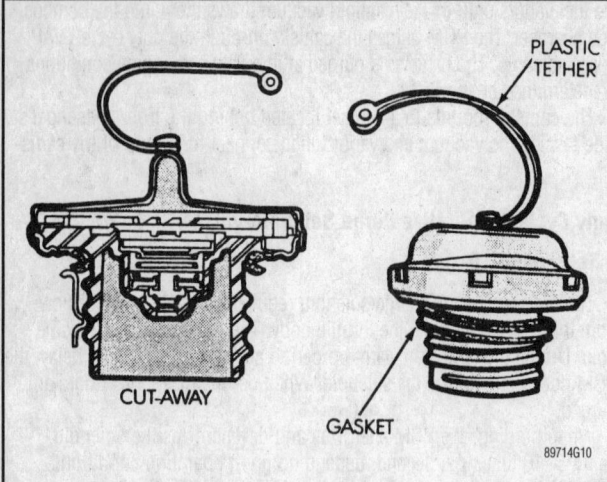

**Fig. 11 If you ever have to replace the gas tank cap, make sure you get the proper one for your vehicle**

## COMPONENT TESTING

### Evaporative System Check

1. Before beginning the check, inspect all connectors for a clean, tight fit.
2. Start the engine and allow it to reach normal operating temperatures.
3. Inspect the throttle body-to-evaporative emission solenoid vacuum line. Check for vacuum leaks or restrictions. If the vacuum line is damaged, replace or repair as necessary. If the line is OK, proceed with the test.
4. Check the vacuum line running from the evaporative solenoid to the canister for damage or restriction. If the vacuum line is damaged, replace or repair as necessary. If the line is OK, proceed with the test.
5. Disconnect the canister-to-solenoid vacuum line from the solenoid. Is the evaporative solenoid allowing vacuum to cycle through intermittently at a steady rate? If not, replace the evaporative solenoid. If so, proceed with the test.

➡**During the next steps, do NOT use more than 5 psi of air pressure.**

6. Turn the ignition key to the **OFF** position. Attempt to blow air through the vacuum line that goes to the canister. Do the canister and vacuum line allow air to pass? If so, the purge solenoid and hoses are OK. If not, proceed with the test.
7. Disconnect the solenoid-to-canister vacuum line from the canister. Try to blow air through the vacuum line that goes to the canister. Does the line let air pass? If so, replace the evaporative canister. If not, repair or replace the vacuum line, as necessary.

## REMOVAL & INSTALLATION

### Evaporative Canister

1. Disconnect the negative battery cable.
2. Raise and safely support the vehicle. Remove the front passenger's side wheel and tire assembly.
3. Remove the retainers, then remove the splash shield.
4. Tag and disconnect the vacuum lines from the evaporative canister.
5. Push the locking tab on the electrical connector to unlock and remove the connector.
6. Unafsten the 3 retaining nuts, then remove the canister from the mounting bracket.
   **To install:**
7. Install the evaporative canister to the bracket, then secure with the retaining nuts. Tighten to 50 inch lbs. (5.6 Nm).

8. Attach the electrical connector to the pump, then push the locking tab to lock the connector in place.
9. Connect the vacuum lines to the canister, as tagged during removal.
10. Install the splash shield, securing it with the retainers.
11. Install the wheel and tire assembly, then carefully lower the vehicle.
12. Connect the negative battery cable.

### Leak Detection Pump

1. Disconnect the negative battery cable.
2. Remove the evaporative canister from the vehicle.
3. Remove the pump and bracket, as an assembly.
4. Remove the pump from the bracket.
   **To install:**
5. Install the pump and bracket assembly to the body, then tighten the retaining bolts to 90 inch lbs. (10 Nm).
6. Install the evaporative canister, as outlined earlier.
7. Connect the negative battery cable.

## Exhaust Gas Recirculation System

### OPERATION

▶ **See Figures 12, 13 and 14**

The Exhaust Gas Recirculation (EGR) system reduces oxides of Nitrogen (NOx) in the engine exhaust and helps prevent detonation (engine knock). Under normal operating conditions, engine cylinder temperature can reach over 3000°F. The formation of NOx increases proportionally with the combustion temperature. To reduce the emission of these oxides, the cylinder temperature must be lowered. The system allows a predetermined amount of hot exhaust gas to recirculate and dilute the incoming air/fuel mixture. The diluted mixture lowers temperatures during combustion. The EGR system consists of the following components:

- EGR tube
- EGR valve
- Electronic EGR Transducer (EET)
- Connecting hoses

The electronic EGR transducer container an electrically operated solenoid and a backpressure transducer. The Powertrain Control Module (PCM) operated the solenoid, determining when to energize the solenoid. Exhaust system backpressure controls the transducer.

When the PCM energizes the solenoid, vacuum doesn't reach the transducer. Vacuum flows to the transducer when the PCM de-energizes the solenoid. When exhaust system backpressure becomes high enough, it

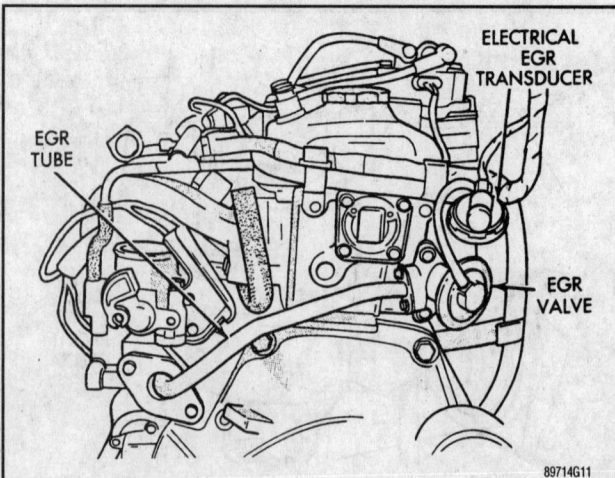

**Fig. 12 Exhaust Gas Recirculation (EGR) system components— 1995 vehicles shown**

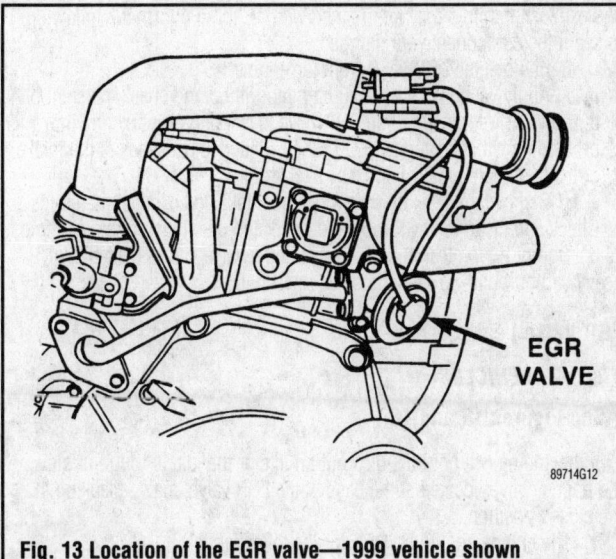

**Fig. 13 Location of the EGR valve—1999 vehicle shown**

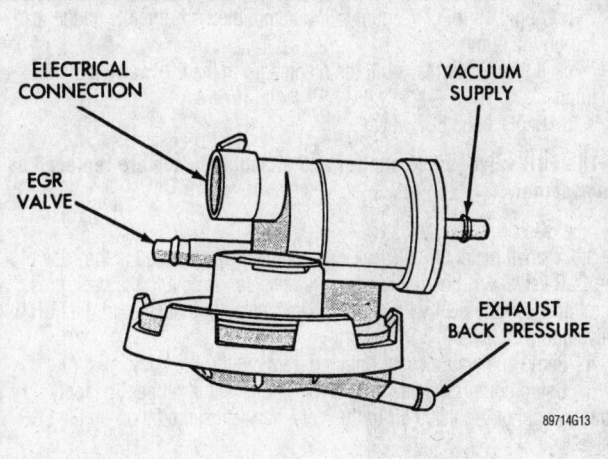

**Fig. 14 Electronic EGR Transducer (EET) vacuum hose connection identification**

fully closes a bleed valve in the transducer. When the PCM de-energizes the solenoid and back-pressure closes the transducer bleed valve, vacuum flows through the transducer to operate the EGR valve.

De-engergizing the solenoid, but not fully closing the transducer bleed hole (because of low back-pressure), varies the strength of vacuum applied to the EGR valve. Varying the strength of the vacuum changes the amount of EGR supplied to the engine. This provides the correct amount of exhaust gas recirculation for different operating conditions. This system does not allow EGR at idle.

## COMPONENT TESTING

### EGR System On-Board Diagnostics

The PCM performs an on-board diagnostic check of the EGR system. The diagnostic system uses t he electronic EGR transducer for the system tests.

The check activates only during certain conditions. When the conditions are met, the PCM energizes the transducer solenoid to disable the EGR. The PCM checks for a change the heated oxygen sensor signal. If the air/fuel ratio goes lean, the PCM will try to enrich the mixture. The PCM records a Diagnostic Trouble Code (DTC) if the EGR system is not operating properly. After

registering a DTC, then PCM turns on the Check Engine lamp (malfunction indicator) after 2 consecutive trips. There are 2 types of failures sensed by the PCM; a short or open in the circuit or a mechanical failure or loss of vacuum. The Malfunction Indicator Lamp (MIL) denotes the need for service.

If you find a problem indicated by the MIL and a DTC is set, first check for proper operation of the EGR system. If the system tests properly check the system using Chrysler's DRB® or equivalent scan tool. Make sure to follow all of the instructions included with the scan tool.

### EGR System Test

> ⁛ **CAUTION**
>
> **ALWAYS block the drive wheels and apply the parking brake anytime you are performing a test or adjustment in which the engine must be running!**

#### 1995–96 VEHICLES

A failed or malfunctioning EGR system can cause engine spark knock, hesitation, rough idle, stalling and/or increased emissions. The make sure the EGR system is operating properly, all passages and moving parts must be clean of deposits that could cause plugging or sticking. Make sure the hoses don't leak and replace any components that do leak.

Check the hose connections between the intake manifold, EGR solenoid and transducer and the EGR valve. Replace any hardened, cracked or leaking hoses. Repair or replace faulty connectors.

1. Check the EGR control system and EGR valve with the engine fully warmed up and running. With the transmission in Neutral and the throttle closed, allow the engine to idle for about 70 seconds.

2. Abruptly accelerate the engine to about 2,000 rpm, but NOT over 3,000 rpm. The EGR valve stem should move when accelerating the engine.

3. Repease the test a few times to confirm movement. If the valve stem moves, the EGR system is operating properly. If the stem doesn't move, then EGR system is not operating properly.

#### 1997–99 VEHICLES

▶ See Figures 15 and 16

1. Check the condition of all EGR system hoses and tubes for leaks, blockage, cracks, kinks or hardening. Repair or replace as necessary before beginning the test.

2. Make sure the hoses at both the EGR valve and EGR valve control are connected properly and the electrical connector is firmly attached at the valve control.

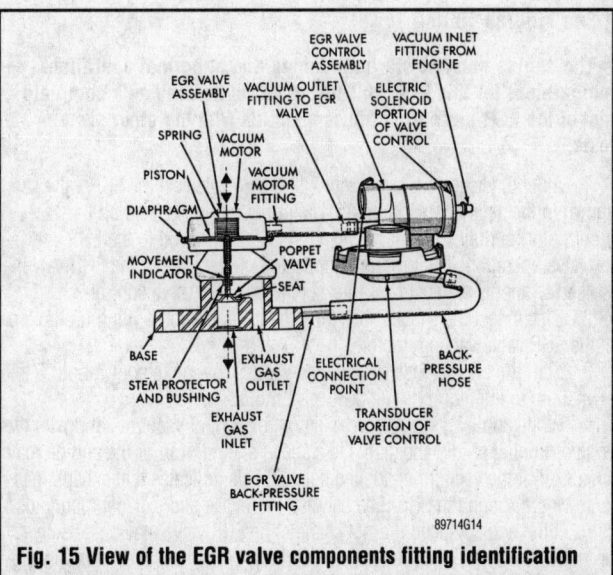

**Fig. 15 View of the EGR valve components fitting identification**

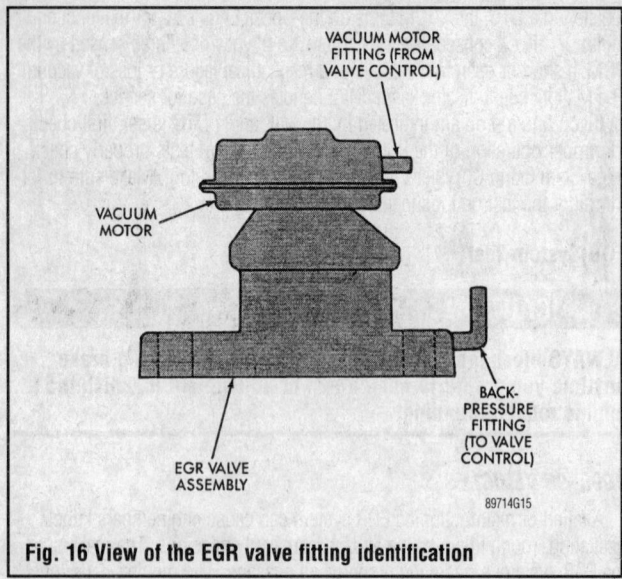

VACUUM MOTOR
FITTING (FROM
VALVE CONTROL)

VACUUM
MOTOR

BACK-
PRESSURE
FITTING
(TO VALVE
CONTROL)

EGR VALVE
ASSEMBLY

89714G15

**Fig. 16 View of the EGR valve fitting identification**

3. To check EGR system operation, connect the DRB® or equivalent scan tool to the 16-way data link connector. (The data link connector is located on the lower edge of the instrument panel near the steering column.) Make sure the follow all of the manufacturers instructions when connecting the scan tool and testing the EGR system.

4. After checking the system with the scan tool, proceed to the remaining EGR valve control tests.

### EGR Gas Flow Test

Use this test to see if exhaust gas is flowing through the EGR system

#### 1995–96 VEHICLES

1. Connect a suitable hand held vacuum pump to the EGR valve vacuum motor.

2. With the engine running at idle speed, slowly apply vacuum. Engine speed should begin to drop when the applied vacuum reaches 2.0–3.5 in. Hg. Engine speed may drop quickly or the engine may even stall. This indicates that EGR gas is flowing through the system.

3. if the engine speed doesn't drop when applying the vacuum, remove both the EGR valve and EGR tube and check for plugged passages and clean or replace, as necessary.

#### 1997–99 VEHICLES

▶ See Figures 15 and 16

➡The engine must be started, running and at normal operation temperature for this test. This test is not to be used as a complete test of the EGR system, but in conjunction with the other system tests.

1. All engines are equipped with 2 fittings located on the EGR valve, as shown in the accompanying figure. The upper fitting (located on the vacuum motor) supplies engine vacuum to a diaphragm within the EGR valve for valve operation. The lower fitting(located on the base of the EGR valve) is used to supply exhaust back-pressure to the EGR valve control.

2. Disconnect the rubber hose from the vacuum motor fitting on the top of the EGR valve vacuum motor.

3. Start the engine. Use a hand held vacuum gauge to apply about 5 in. of vacuum to the fitting on the EGR valve motor.

4. While applying vacuum, a minimum of 3 in. of vacuum , and with the engine running at idle speed, the idle speed should drop or the engine may even stall, if the vacuum is applied quickly. This indicates that exhaust gas is flowing through the EGR tube between the intake and exhaust manifolds.

5. If the engine speed did not change, the EGR valve may be defective or the EGR tube may be plugged with carbon, or the passages in the intake

and exhaust manifold may be plugged with carbon. Perform the following to see if the components are plugged:

a. Remove the EGR valve from the engine.

b. Apply vacuum to the vacuum motor fitting and check the stem on the valve. If it's moving, then EGR valve is working properly and the problem is either a plugged EGR tube or plugged passages at the intake or exhaust manifolds (refer to the next step).

c. Remove the EGR tube between the intake and exhaust manifolds. Check and clean the EGR tube and its related openings on the manifolds.

6. Do not try to clean the EGR valve. If the valve shows evidence of heavy carbon build-up near the base, replace it.

### EGR Valve Leakage Test

#### 1997–99 VEHICLES

▶ See Figures 15 and 16

If the engine will not idle, dies out on idle or the idle is rough or slow, the poppet valve, located at the base of the EGR valve, may be leaking in the closed position.

1. The engine should be **OFF** for the following test.

2. Disconnect the rubber hose from the fitting at the top (vacuum motor) side of the EGR valve, and perform the following:

a. Connect a hand-held vacuum pump to this fitting.

b. Apply 15 in. of vacuum to the pump, then observe the gauge reading on the pump.

c. If the vacuum falls off, the diaphragm in the EGR valve has ruptured.

d. Replace the EGR valve.

➡The EGR valve, valve control and attaching hoses are replaced as an assembly.

e. Go on to the next step.

3. A small metal fitting (back-pressure fitting) is located at the base of the EGR valve. A rubber back-pressure hose connects it to the back-pressure fitting on the EGR valve control. Disconnect this hose from the EGR valve fitting.

4. Remove the air cleaner housing from the throttle body.

5. Using compressed air with an air nozzle with a rubber tip, apply about 50 psi of regulated air to the metal back-pressure fitting on the EGR valve.

6. By hand, open the throttle to the wide open position. Air should NOT be heard coming from the intake manifold while apply air pressure to the fitting.

7. If air CAN be heard coming from the intake manifold, the poppet valve is leaking at the bottom of the EGR valve. Replace the EGR valve.

## REMOVAL & INSTALLATION

### EGR Valve and Electric Transducer

▶ See Figures 12 and 13, and 17 thru 22

➡If the EGR system is operating incorrectly and component replacement is necessary, keep in mind that because they are calibrated together, they must be replaced together.

On 1995 vehicles, the EGR valve and EET attach to the rear of the cylinder head. On 1996–99 vehicles,. the EGR valve is attaches to the rear of the cylinder head and the EGR transducer is attached to the air inlet duct.

1. Disconnect the negative battery cable.

2. If necessary for access, disconnect the air inlet tube and unclip the fuse box.

3. For 1996–98 vehicles, remove the EGR transducer from the air inlet duct.

4. For 1996–99 vehicles, remove the air inlet duct.

5. Unfasten the EGR tube-to-EGR valve screws/bolts.

6. Remove the EGR valve mounting screws.

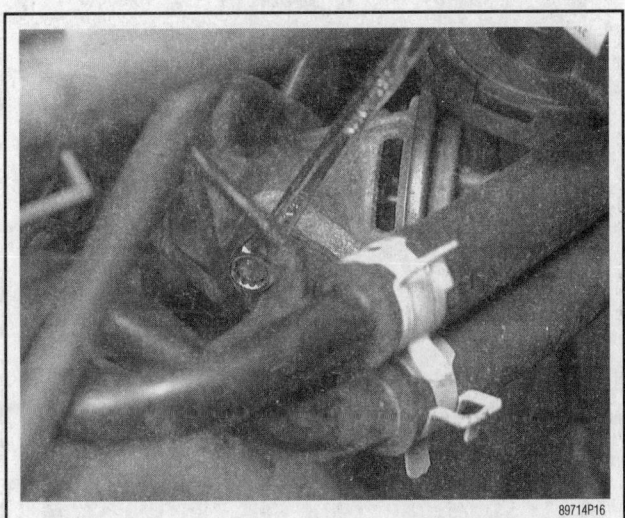

Fig. 17 Unfasten the EGR tube-to-valve mounting bolts

Fig. 20 Unplug the solenoid electrical connector

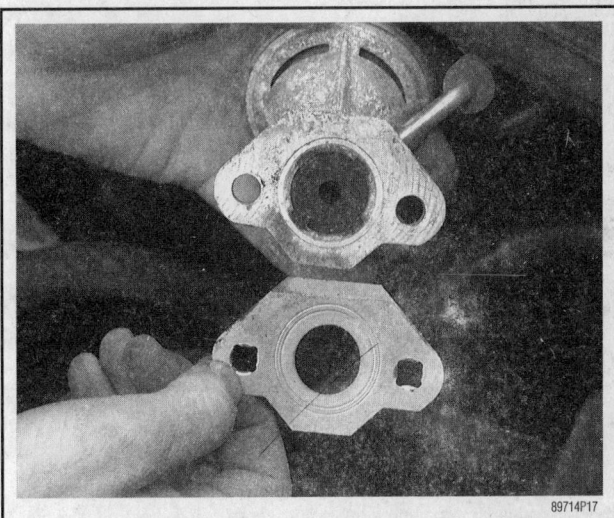

Fig. 18 Remove the EGR valve mounting bolts

Fig. 21 Remove and discard the bottom of the EGR valve

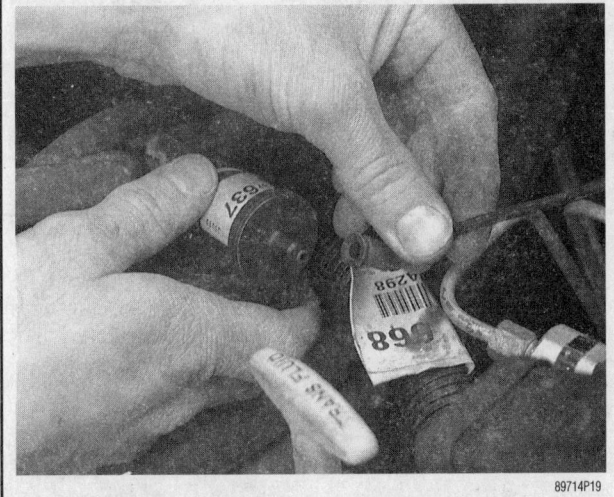

Fig. 19 Disconnect the vacuum line from the solenoid

Fig. 22 Don't forget to remove the EGR tube-to-valve gasket

7. Detach the vacuum supply tube from the EET solenoid.

8. Unplug the electrical connector from the solenoid.

9. Remove the EGR valve and transducer.

10. Remove and discard the old gaskets. Thoroughly clean the gasket mating surfaces and/or passages.

**To install:**

11. Using new gaskets, loosely install the EGR valve.

12. Finger-tighten the EGR tube fasteners.

13. Tighten the EGR tube fasteners to 95 inch lbs. (100 Nm).

14. Tighten the EGR valve mounting screws to 16 ft. lbs. (22 Nm).

15. If removed, install the air inlet duct.

16. Attach the vacuum supply tube and the electrical connector to the solenoid.

17. For 1996–99 vehicles, install the EGR transducer onto the air inlet duct.

18. If removed, fasten the fuse box in position and connect the air inlet tube.

19. Connect the negative battery cable.

### EGR Tube

▶ See Figure 23

The EGR tube attaches to the intake manifold plenum below the throttle body and EGR valve.

1. Disconnect the negative battery cable.

2. Remove the screws attaching the EGR tube to the intake manifold.

3. Unfasten the EGR tube-to-EGR valve screws.

4. Remove the EGR tube from the vehicle. Make sure to clean the gasket surface on the EGR valve and wipe the grommet on the intake manifold clean.

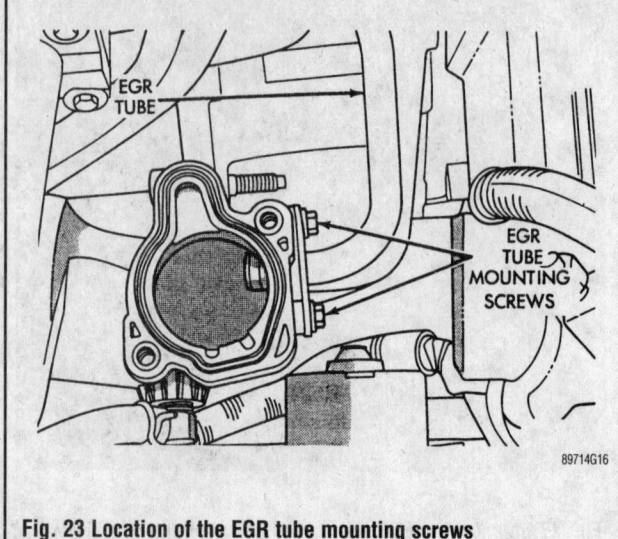

Fig. 23 Location of the EGR tube mounting screws

**To install:**

➡ **The rubber grommet that seals the EGR tube-to-intake manifold connection is reusable.**

5. Loosely install the EGR tube and fasteners.

6. Tighten the EGR tube-to-intake manifold plenum and EGR tube-to-EGR valve screws to 95 inch lbs.

7. Connect the negative battery cable.

## ELECTRONIC ENGINE CONTROLS

### Powertrain Control Module (PCM)

#### OPERATION

▶ See Figures 24, 25, 26 and 27

The heart of the electronic control system, which is found on the vehicles covered by this manual, is a Powertrain Control Module (PCM). The module gathers information from various sensors, then controls fuel supply and engine emission systems. The PCM controls the engine and related emissions systems. It may also control the manual transaxle shift lamp or the shift functions of the electronically controlled automatic transmission.

Care must be taken when handling these expensive components in order to protect them from damage. Carefully follow all instructions included with the replacement part. Avoid touching pins or connectors to prevent damage from static electricity.

### ❋❋ WARNING

**To prevent the possibility of permanent control module damage, the ignition switch MUST always be OFF when disconnecting power from or reconnecting power to the module. This includes unplugging the module connector, disconnecting the negative battery cable, removing the module fuse or even attempting to jump your dead battery using jumper cables.**

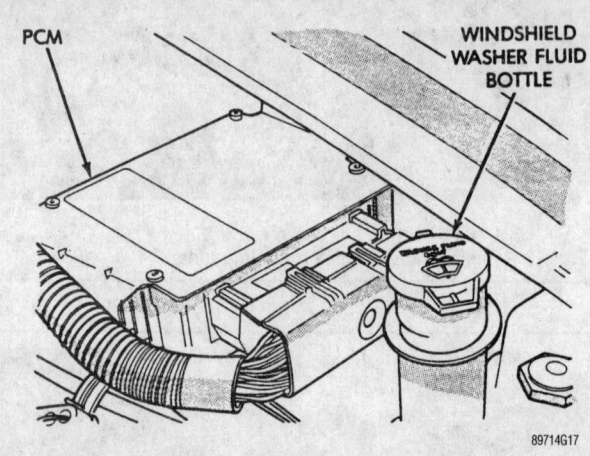

Fig. 24 The PCM is attached to the inner fender panel, next to the windshield washer bottle—1995 vehicle shown

In the event of an PCM failure, the system will default to a pre-programmed set of values. These are compromise values which allow the engine to operate, although at a reduced efficiency. This is variously known as the default, limp-in or back-up mode. Driveability is almost always affected when the PCM enters this mode.

| CAV | WIRE COLOR | DESCRIPTION | CAV | WIRE COLOR | DESCRIPTION |
|---|---|---|---|---|---|
| 1 | BK/GY* | IGNITION COIL DRIVER #2 | 37 | TN/BK* | CHARGING SYSTEM INDICATOR LAMP |
| 2 | BK/TN* | POWER GROUND | 38 | BR | FUEL PUMP RELAY |
| 3 | YL/WT* | FUEL INJECTOR #3 | 39 | GY/YL* | EGR SOLENOID |
| 4 | WT/DB* | FUEL INJECTOR #1 | 40 | TN/RD* | SPEED CONTROL VACUUM SOLENOID |
| 5 | WT/OR* | VEHICLE SPEED SENSOR | 41 | DG | GENERATOR FIELD |
| 6 | BK/RD* | INTAKE AIR TEMPERATURE SENSOR | 42 | DG/OR* | IGNITION SENSE |
| 7 | DG/BK* | DOWNSTREAM HEATED OXYGEN SENSOR | 43 | VT/WT* | 5 VOLT SUPPLY (FOR MAP AND TPS) |
| 8 | BK/DG* | UPSTREAM HEATED OXYGEN SENSOR | 44 | OR | 9 VOLT SUPPLY |
| 9 | LG | DATA LINK | 45 | | |
| 10 | OR/DB* | THROTTLE POSITION SENSOR | 46 | | |
| 11 | RD/WT* | DIRECT BATTERY VOLTAGE | 47 | YL/RD* | SPEED CONTROL SERVO |
| 12 | | | 48 | GY/LB* | TACHOMETER |
| 13 | | | 49 | VT/LG | BATTERY TEMPERATURE SENSOR SIGNAL |
| 14 | YL/BK* | IDLE AIR CONTROL MOTOR DRIVER #2 | 50 | BR/YL* | PARK/NEUTRAL SWITCH |
| 15 | GY/RD* | IDLE AIR CONTROL MOTOR DRIVER #3 | 51 | BK/LB* | SENSOR GROUND |
| 16 | PK/BK* | DUTY CYCLE EVAP PURGE SOLENOID | 52 | BK/WT* | SIGNAL GROUND |
| 17 | OR/BK* | TORQUE CONVERTOR CLUTCH SOLENOID (AUTO. TRANS.) | 53 | | |
| 18 | DB/YL* | AUTOMATIC SHUTDOWN RELAY | 54 | LG/BK* | IGNITION SWITCH |
| 19 | DB/PK* | RADIATOR FAN RELAY | 55 | | |
| 20 | | | 56 | WT | POWER STEERING PRESSURE SWITCH |
| 21 | DB/YL* | IGNITION COIL DRIVER #1 | 57 | | |
| 22 | BK/TN* | POWER GROUND | 58 | | |
| 23 | TN | FUEL INJECTOR #2 | 59 | DB/OR* | A/C COMPRESSOR CLUTCH RELAY |
| 24 | LB/BR* | FUEL INJECTOR #4 | 60 | LG/RD* | SPEED CONTROL VENT SOLENOID |
| 25 | GY/BK* | CRANKSHAFT POSITION SENSOR | | | |
| 26 | TN/YL* | CAMSHAFT POSITION SENSOR | | | |
| 27 | BK/LG* | KNOCK SENSOR | | | |
| 28 | TN/BK* | ENGINE COOLANT TEMPERATURE SENSOR | | | |
| 29 | DG/RD* | MAP SENSOR | | | |
| 30 | PK | DATA LINK | | | |
| 31 | RD/LG* | SPEED CONTROL SELECT SIGNAL | | | |
| 32 | WT/PK* | BRAKE SWITCH | | | |
| 33 | BR/OR* | A/C PRESSURE SWITCH | | | |
| 34 | VT/BK* | IDLE AIR CONTROL MOTOR DRIVER #4 | | | |
| 35 | BR/WT* | IDLE AIR CONTROL MOTOR DRIVER #1 | | | |
| 36 | BK/PK* | MALFUNCTION INDICATOR LAMP | | | |

| WIRE COLOR CODES | | | | | |
|---|---|---|---|---|---|
| BK | BLACK | LB | LIGHT BLUE | VT | VIOLET |
| BR | BROWN | LG | LIGHT GREEN | WT | WHITE |
| DB | DARK BLUE | OR | ORANGE | YL | YELLOW |
| DG | DARK GREEN | PK | PINK | * | WITH TRACER |
| GY | GRAY | RD | RED | | |
| | | TN | TAN | | |

CONNECTOR TERMINAL SIDE SHOWN

89714G52

**Fig. 25 Powertrain Control Module (PCM) 60-way connector identification—1995 vehicles**

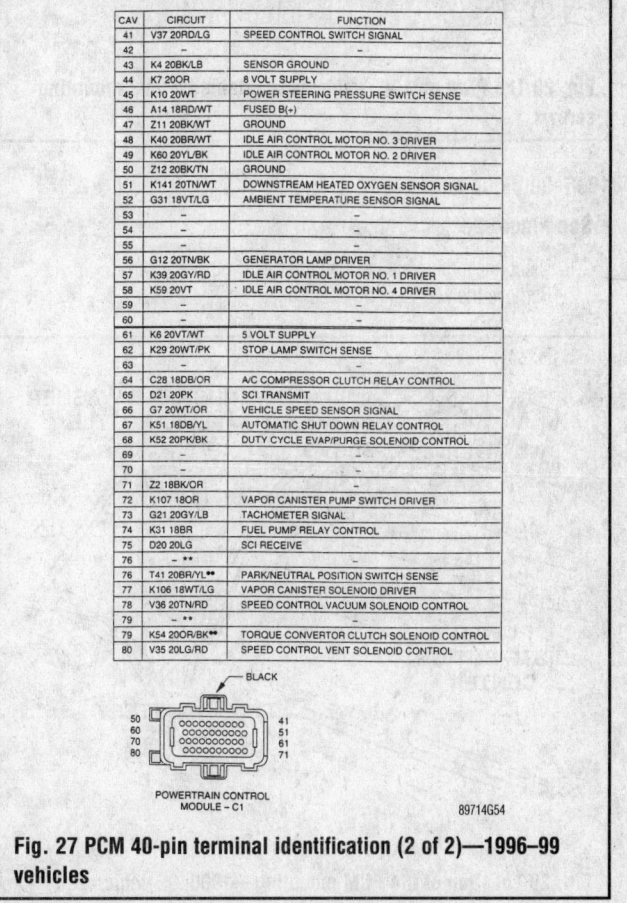

| CAV | CIRCUIT | FUNCTION |
|---|---|---|
| 1 | – | – |
| 2 | K19 18BK/GY | IGNITION COIL NO. 1, 3 DRIVER |
| 3 | K17 18DB/TN | IGNITION COIL NO. 2, 4 DRIVER |
| 4 | K20 18DG | GENERATOR FIELD DRIVER |
| 5 | V32 20YL/RD | SPEED CONTROL FEED |
| 6 | A142 18DG/OR | AUTOMATIC SHUT DOWN RELAY OUTPUT |
| 7 | K13 18YL/WT | INJECTOR NO. 3 DRIVER |
| 8 | G3 20BK/PK | CHECK ENGINE LAMP DRIVER |
| 9 | – | – |
| 10 | Z12 18BK/TN | GROUND |
| 11 | – | – |
| 12 | – | – |
| 13 | K11 18WT/DB | INJECTOR NO. 1 DRIVER |
| 14 | – | – |
| 15 | – | – |
| 16 | K14 18LB/BR | INJECTOR NO. 4 DRIVER |
| 17 | K12 18TN | INJECTOR NO. 2 DRIVER |
| 18 | K173 20LG | RAD FAN PULSE CONTROL |
| 19 | – | – |
| 20 | F12 18DB/WT | FUSED IGNITION SWITCH OUTPUT (RUN/START) |
| 21 | – | – |
| 22 | – | – |
| 23 | G4 20DB | FUEL LEVEL SENSOR SIGNAL |
| 24 | K42 20BK/LG* | KNOCK SENSOR SIGNAL |
| 24 | K42 20DB/LG* | KNOCK SENSOR SIGNAL |
| 25 | – | – |
| 26 | K2 20TN/DB* | ENGINE COOLANT TEMPERATURE SENSOR SIGNAL |
| 26 | K2 20TN/BK* | ENGINE COOLANT TEMPERATURE SENSOR SIGNAL |
| 27 | – | – |
| 28 | – | – |
| 29 | – | – |
| 30 | K41 20BK/DG | UPSTREAM HEATED OXYGEN SENSOR SIGNAL |
| 31 | – | – |
| 32 | K24 20GY/BK | CRANKSHAFT POSITION SENSOR SIGNAL |
| 33 | K44 20TN/YL | CAMSHAFT POSITION SENSOR SIGNAL |
| 34 | – | – |
| 35 | K22 20OR/DB | THROTTLE POSITION SENSOR SIGNAL |
| 36 | K1 18DG/RD | MANIFOLD ABSOLUTE PRESSURE SENSOR SIGNAL |
| 37 | K21 18BK/RD | INTAKE AIR TEMPERATURE SENSOR SIGNAL |
| 38 | C20 18BR/OR | A/C SWITCH SENSE |
| 39 | – | – |
| 40 | K35 20GY/YL | EXHAUST GAS RECIRCULATION SOLENOID CONTROL |

BLACK

40 30 20 10

* 2.0L (SOHC) ENGINE
** 2.0L (DOHC) ENGINE
** MTX
** ATX

POWERTRAIN CONTROL MODULE – C2

89714G53

**Fig. 26 PCM 40-pin terminal identification (1 of 2)—1996–99 vehicles**

| CAV | CIRCUIT | FUNCTION |
|---|---|---|
| 41 | V37 20RD/LG | SPEED CONTROL SWITCH SIGNAL |
| 42 | – | – |
| 43 | K4 20BK/LB | SENSOR GROUND |
| 44 | K7 20OR | 8 VOLT SUPPLY |
| 45 | K10 20WT | POWER STEERING PRESSURE SWITCH SENSE |
| 46 | A14 18RD/WT | FUSED B(+) |
| 47 | Z11 20BK/WT | GROUND |
| 48 | K40 20BR/WT | IDLE AIR CONTROL MOTOR NO. 3 DRIVER |
| 49 | K60 20YL/BK | IDLE AIR CONTROL MOTOR NO. 2 DRIVER |
| 50 | Z12 20BK/TN | GROUND |
| 51 | K141 20TN/WT | DOWNSTREAM HEATED OXYGEN SENSOR SIGNAL |
| 52 | G31 18VT/LG | AMBIENT TEMPERATURE SENSOR SIGNAL |
| 53 | – | – |
| 54 | – | – |
| 55 | – | – |
| 56 | G12 20TN/BK | GENERATOR LAMP DRIVER |
| 57 | K39 20GY/RD | IDLE AIR CONTROL MOTOR NO. 1 DRIVER |
| 58 | K59 20VT | IDLE AIR CONTROL MOTOR NO. 4 DRIVER |
| 59 | – | – |
| 60 | – | – |
| 61 | K6 20VT/WT | 5 VOLT SUPPLY |
| 62 | K29 20WT/PK | STOP LAMP SWITCH SENSE |
| 63 | – | – |
| 64 | C28 18DB/OR | A/C COMPRESSOR RELAY CONTROL |
| 65 | D21 20PK | SCI TRANSMIT |
| 66 | G7 20WT/OR | VEHICLE SPEED SENSOR SIGNAL |
| 67 | K51 18DB/YL | AUTOMATIC SHUT DOWN RELAY CONTROL |
| 68 | K52 20PK/BK | DUTY CYCLE EVAP/PURGE SOLENOID CONTROL |
| 69 | – | – |
| 70 | – | – |
| 71 | Z2 18BK/OR | – |
| 72 | K107 18OR | VAPOR CANISTER PUMP SWITCH DRIVER |
| 73 | G21 20GY/LB | TACHOMETER SIGNAL |
| 74 | K31 18BR | FUEL PUMP RELAY CONTROL |
| 75 | D20 20LG | SCI RECEIVE |
| 76 | – ** | – |
| 76 | T41 20BR/YL** | PARK/NEUTRAL POSITION SWITCH SENSE |
| 77 | K106 18WT/LG | VAPOR CANISTER SOLENOID DRIVER |
| 78 | V36 20TN/RD | SPEED CONTROL VACUUM SOLENOID CONTROL |
| 79 | – ** | – |
| 79 | K54 20OR/BK** | TORQUE CONVERTOR CLUTCH SOLENOID CONTROL |
| 80 | V35 20LG/RD | SPEED CONTROL VENT SOLENOID CONTROL |

BLACK

50 60 70 80   41 51 61 71

POWERTRAIN CONTROL MODULE – C1

89714G54

**Fig. 27 PCM 40-pin terminal identification (2 of 2)—1996–99 vehicles**

REMOVAL & INSTALLATION

### 1995 Vehicles

▶ **See Figure 28**

1. Disconnect the negative battery cable.
2. Remove the attaching the PCM to the body.
3. Lift the PCM partially up, then detach the 60-way connector from the PCM.
4. Remove the PCM from the vehicle.

**To install:**

5. Attach the 60-way connector to the PCM. Tighten the connector screw to 40 inch lbs. (4.7 Nm).
6. Position the PCM in the vehicle, then install the mounting screws and tighten to 80 inch lbs. (9 Nm).
7. Connect the negative battery cable.

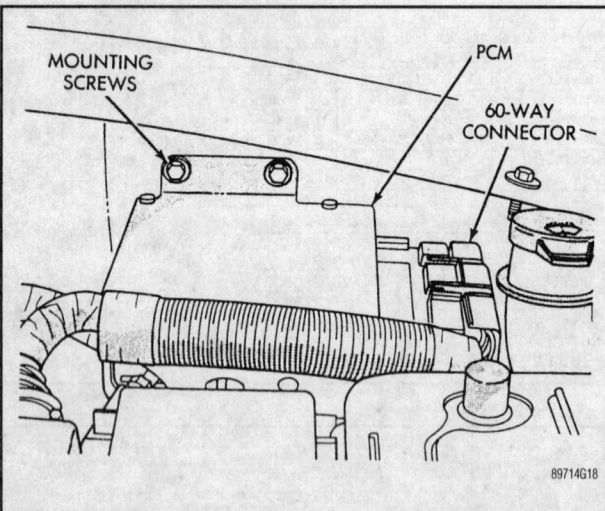

**Fig. 28 The PCM on 1995 vehicles is retained with 2 mounting screws**

### 1996–99 Vehicles

▶ **See Figure 29**

1. Disconnect the negative then the positive battery cables.
2. Remove the windshield washer bottle neck.

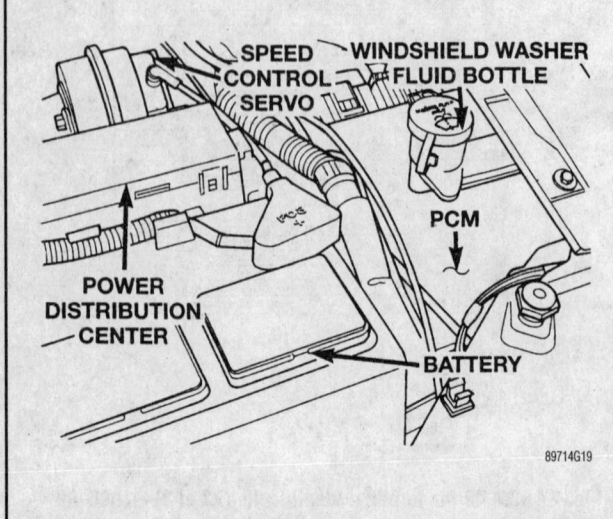

**Fig. 29 Location of the PCM mounting—1996–99 vehicles**

3. Squeeze the tabs on the power distribution center while pulling the center up to remove it from the bracket. Position the power distribution center aside for access to the PCM bracket screws.
4. Unfasten the PCM-to-body screws.
5. Lift the PCM partially up and detach the two 40-way electrical connectors.
6. Remove the PCM from the vehicle.

**To install:**

7. Attach the two 40-way electrical connectors to the PCM.
8. Install the PCM, tightening the retaining screws to 80 inch lbs. (9 Nm).
9. Install the power distributor center by pushing it down into the brackets.
10. Install the washer bottle neck.
11. Connect the positive, then the negative battery cables.

## Heated Oxygen Sensor

OPERATION

▶ **See Figures 30 and 31**

As a vehicle accrues mileage, the catalytic converter deteriorates. The deterioration results in a less effective catalyst. To monitor catalytic con-

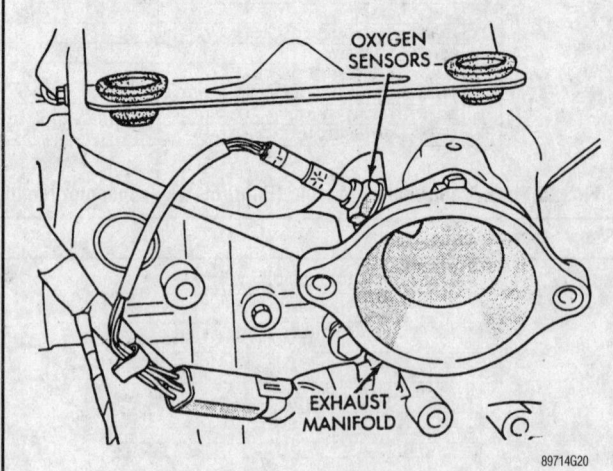

**Fig. 30 The upstream heated oxygen sensor is threaded into the outlet flange of the exhaust manifold**

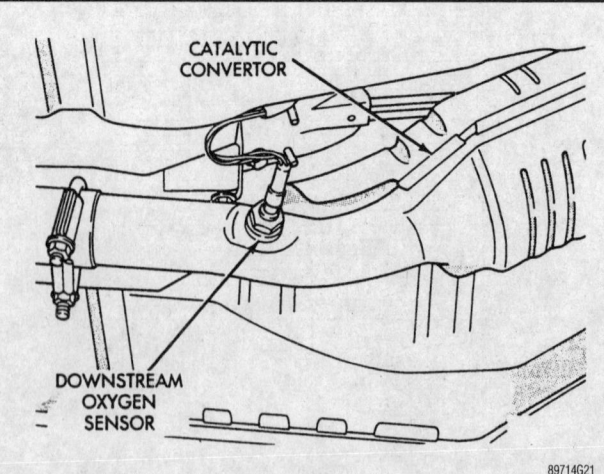

**Fig. 31 The downstream heated oxygen sensor is threaded into the exhaust pipe behind the catalytic converter**

verter deterioration, the fuel injection system uses two heated oxygen sensors. One sensor upstream of the catalytic converter and one downstream of the converter.

The PCM compares the reading from the sensors to calculate the catalytic converter oxygen storage capacity and storage efficiency. Also the PCM uses the upstream heater oxygen sensor input when adjusting the injector pulse width. When the catalytic converter efficiency drops below preset emission criterion, the PCM stores a Diagnostic Trouble Code (DTC) and illuminates the Malfunction Indicator Lamp (MIL).

The automatic shutdown relay supplies battery voltage to both of the heated oxygen sensors. The sensors have heating elements which reduce the amount of time it takes for the sensors to reach operating temperature.

## TESTING

### ▶ See Figure 32

1. Visually check the connector, making sure it is properly attached and all of the terminals are straight, tight and free of corrosion.
2. Use an ohmmeter to test the heating element of the heated oxygen sensors.
3. Detach the electrical connector from each oxygen sensor. The white wires in the sensor connector are the power and ground circuits for the heater elements.
4. Connect the ohmmeter test leads to the terminals of the white wires in the heated oxygen sensor connector.
5. Replace the heated oxygen sensor is the resistance is not 5–7 ohms for 1995 vehicles or 4–7 ohms for 1996–99 vehicles.
6. Backprobe with a high impedance averaging voltmeter (set to the DC voltage scale) between the oxygen sensor (02S) signal wire and battery ground.
7. Verify that the 02S voltage fluctuates rapidly between 0.40–0.60 volts.
8. If the 02S voltage is stabilized at the middle of the specified range (approximately 0.45–0.55 volts) or if the 02S voltage fluctuates very slowly between the specified range (02S signal crosses 0.5 volts less than 5 times in ten seconds), the 02S may be faulty.
9. If the 02S voltage stabilizes at either end of the specified range, the PCM is probably not able to compensate for a mechanical problem such as a vacuum leak or a faulty pressure regulator. These types of mechanical problems will cause the 02S to sense a constant lean or constant rich mixture. The mechanical problem will first have to be repaired and then the 02S test repeated.

10. Pull a vacuum hose located after the throttle plate. Voltage should drop to approximately 0.12 volts (while still fluctuating rapidly). This tests the ability of the 02S to detect a lean mixture condition. Reattach the vacuum hose.
11. Richen the mixture using a propane enrichment tool. Voltage should rise to approximately 0.90 volts (while still fluctuating rapidly). This tests the ability of the 02S to detect a rich mixture condition.
12. If the 02S voltage is above or below the specified range, the 02S and/or the 02S wiring may be faulty. Check the wiring for any breaks, repair as necessary and repeat the test.

➡Before installing a new oxygen sensor, perform a visual inspection. Black, sooty deposits on the sensor tip may indicate a rich air/fuel mixture. White gritty deposits could be an internal antifreeze leak. Brown deposits indicate oil consumption. All of these contaminants can damage a new sensor.

## REMOVAL & INSTALLATION

### Upstream Heated Oxygen Sensor

### ▶ See Figures 33 and 34

1. Disconnect the negative battery cable.
2. Raise and safely support the vehicle.
3. Unplug the upstream oxygen sensor connector.
4. Remove the sensor using a suitable oxygen sensor crow foot wrench. After removing the sensor, the exhaust manifold must be cleaned with an 18mm x 1.5 + 6E tap.

**To install:**

5. New oxygen sensors will be packaged with a special anti-seize compound already applied to the threads. If you a reinstalling the old sensor, the sensor threads must be coated with fresh anti-seize compound. You must use the correct type of anti-seize compound containing liquid graphite and glass beads. This is not a conventional anti-seize paste. the graphite will tend to burn away, but the glass beads will remain. The use of a regular compound may electrically insulator the sensor, rendering it inoperative. You must coat the threads with an electrically conductive anti-seize compound.
6. Carefully thread the sensor into the bore, then tighten to 20 ft. lbs. (28 Nm).
7. Attach the oxygen sensor electrical connector.
8. Carefully lower the vehicle, then connect the negative battery cable.

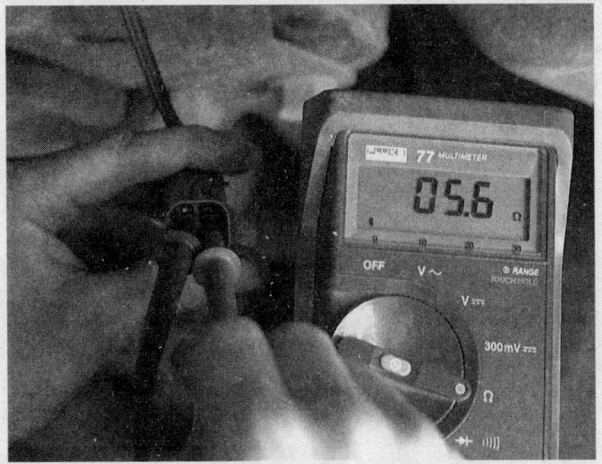

**Fig. 32 Test resistance with an ohmmeter. This 1995 vehicle is within specifications**

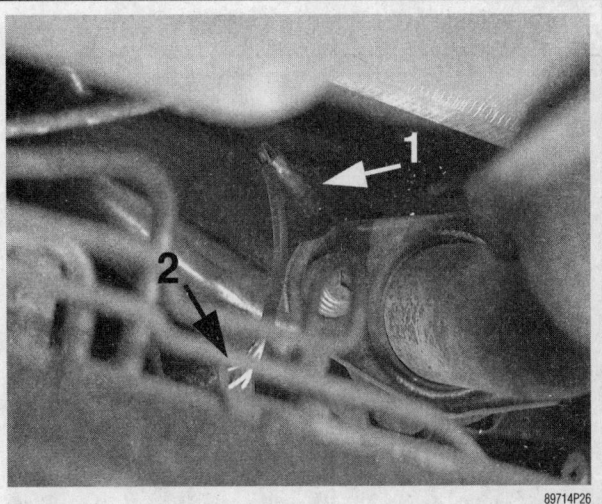

**Fig. 33 Upstream heated oxygen sensor (1) and wiring (2)**

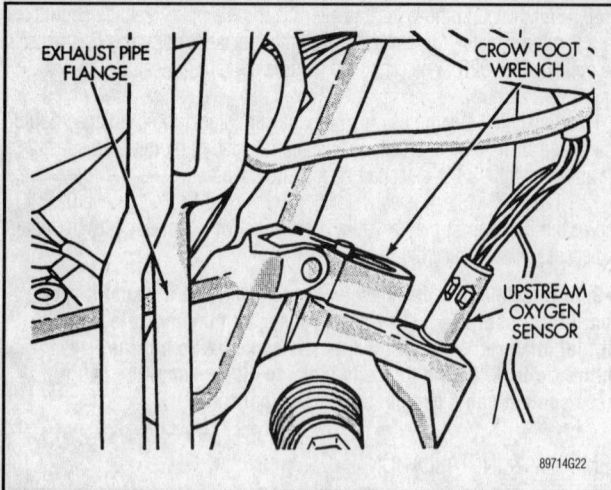

Fig. 34 Use a crow foot wrench to loosen the upstream heated oxygen sensor

Fig. 36 Location of the downstream oxygen sensor connector (see arrow)

### Downstream Heated Oxygen Sensor

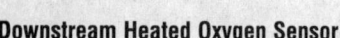

▶ See Figures 35, 36, 37, 38 and 39

1. Disconnect the negative battery cable.
2. Raise and safely support the vehicle.
3. Unplug the electrical connector from the downstream oxygen sensor.
4. Detach the sensor electrical harness from the clips along the body.
5. Remove the sensor using a suitable oxygen sensor crow foot wrench. After removing the sensor, the exhaust manifold must be cleaned with an 18mm x 1.5 + 6E tap.

**To install:**

6. New oxygen sensors will be packaged with a special anti-seize compound already applied to the threads. If you a reinstalling the old sensor, the sensor threads must be coated with fresh anti-seize compound. You must use the correct type of anti-seize compound containing liquid graphite and glass beads. This is not a conventional anti-seize paste. the graphite will tend to burn away, but the glass beads will remain. The use of a regular compound may electrically insulator the sensor, rendering it inoperative. You must coat the threads with an electrically conductive anti-seize compound.

7. Carefully thread the sensor into the bore, then tighten to 20 ft. lbs. (28 Nm).

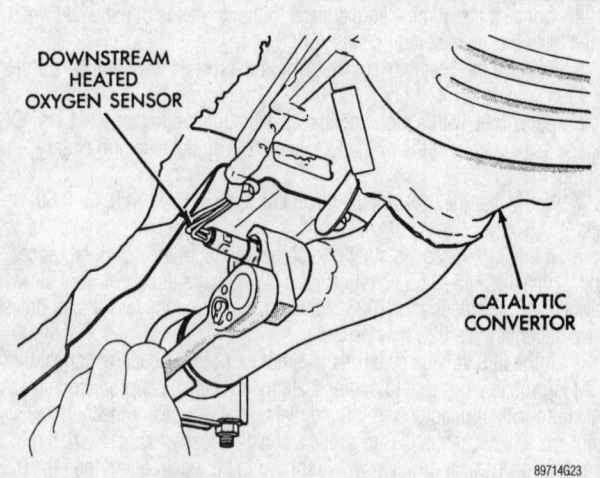

Fig. 37 Because the angle, you should use a crow foot wrench to remove the downstream oxygen sensor

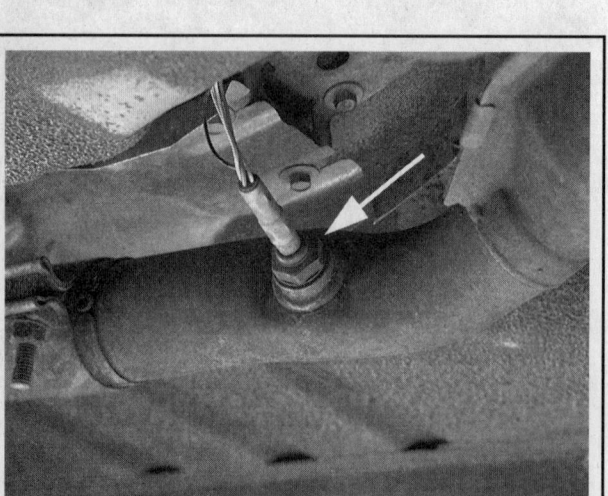

Fig. 35 The downstream O$_2$ sensor is threaded into the exhaust pipe behind the catalytic converter

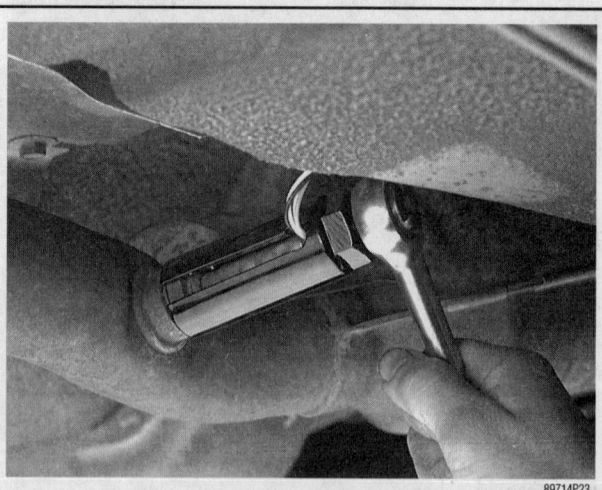

Fig. 38 There are also special sockets available specifically for the purpose of removing the sensor

**Fig. 39 Remove the oxygen sensor from the exhaust pipe**

8. Route the sensor electrical harness through the clips along the body.
9. Attach the oxygen sensor electrical connector.
10. Carefully lower the vehicle, then connect the negative battery cable.

## Idle Air Control Motor

### OPERATION

▶ See Figure 40

The Idle Air Control (IAC) motor, attached to the side of the throttle body, is operated by the PCM. The PCM adjusts engine idle speed through the idle air control motor to compensate for load on the engine, or changes in coolant temperature or barometric pressure.

The throttle body has an air passage that provides air for the engine during closed throttle idle. The idle air control motor pintle protrudes into the air bypass passage and regulates the air flow through it. The PCM adjusts the idle speed by moving the IAC motor pintle in and out of the bypass passage. The speed is based on various sensor and switch inputs received by the PCM.

### TESTING

Visually check the connector, making sure it is properly attached and all of the terminals are straight, tight and free of corrosion.

You need to have access to a DRB® or equivalent scan tool to accurately test the Idle Air Control (IAC) motor and related circuits. Make sure to carefully follow all of the scan tool manufacturers directions when testing the IAC motor.

If you do not have access to a scan tool, this simple test should give you an indication if the circuit is working properly:

1. First attach a tachometer to the engine, then start the engine.
2. Observe the idle speed. Pull a vacuum hose (like the one leading from the brake booster to the intake manifold). The idle speed should rise, then fall as the IAC motor tries to compensate for the vacuum leak. 3. Reattach the vacuum hose. The idle should drop, then stabilize.
4. If the engine reacted as indicated, the circuit Is probably OK.

### REMOVAL & INSTALLATION

▶ See Figures 41 and 42

➡You will need to have access to a DRB® or equivalent scan tool when installing the IAC motor, as the IAC motor pintle must be properly retracted if it is more than 1 in. (25mm).

1. Disconnect the negative battery cable.
2. Disconnect the EVAP purge hose from the throttle body.
3. Remove the throttle body from the vehicle, as outlined in
4. Detach the electrical connectors from the IAC motor and Throttle Position (TP) sensor.
5. Unfasten the IAC motor mounting screws from the throttle body, then remove the motor from the throttle body. Make sure the O-ring is removed with the motor. Remove and discard the O-ring.

When servicing throttle body components, always install the components with new O-rings and seals, when applicable. Do NOT use any lubricants on the O-rings or seals, as damage may result. If you're having trouble, use a little water to help ease installation.

**To install:**

6. The new IAC motor has a new O-ring installed on it. Measure the pintle on the new IAC valve. If it is longer than 1 in. (25mm), it must be retracted using the Idle Air control Motor Open/Close test on the DRB® or equivalent scan tool. Note that the battery must be connected for this test.

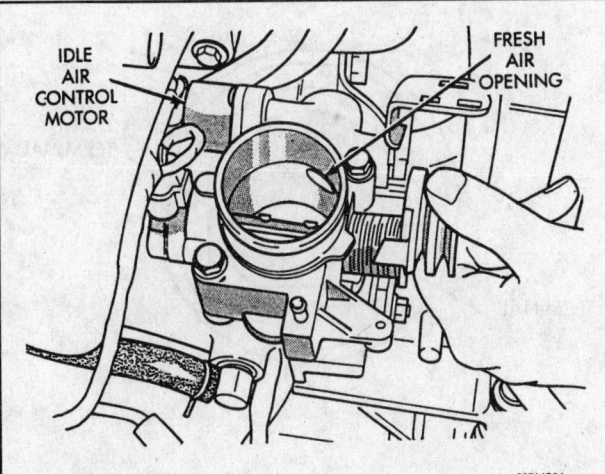

**Fig. 40 The Idle Air Control (IAC) valve is mounted to the side of the throttle body**

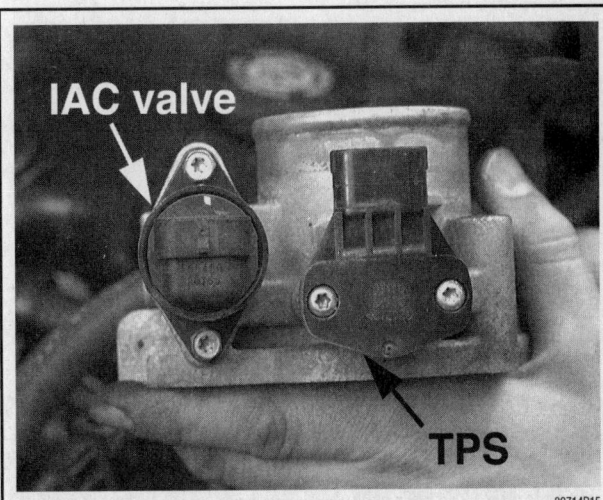

**Fig. 41 The IAC valve and TPS are mounted to the throttle body**

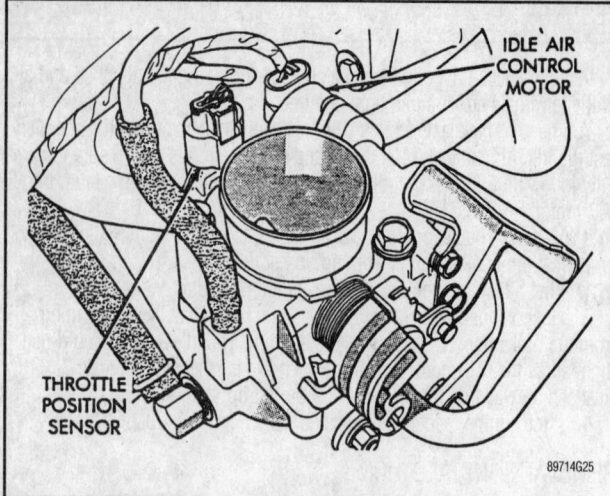

Fig. 42 The IAC motor and TP sensor are secured with screws, and share an electrical wiring harness

7. If the old IAC motor is being installed, place a new O-ring on the motor.

8. Carefully plate the IAC motor into the throttle body and install the retaining screws. Tighten the screws to 17 inch lbs. (2 Nm).

9. Attach the electrical connectors to the IAC motor and TP sensor.

10. Install the throttle body. Connect the EVAP purge hose to the throttle body nipple.

11. Connect the negative battery cable.

## Coolant Temperature Sensor

### OPERATION

▶ See Figures 43 and 44

The PCM determines engine coolant temperature from the coolant temperature sensor. The combination coolant temperature sensor has two elements. One supplies a coolant temperature signal to the PCM, and the other element provides a coolant temperature signal to the instrument panel

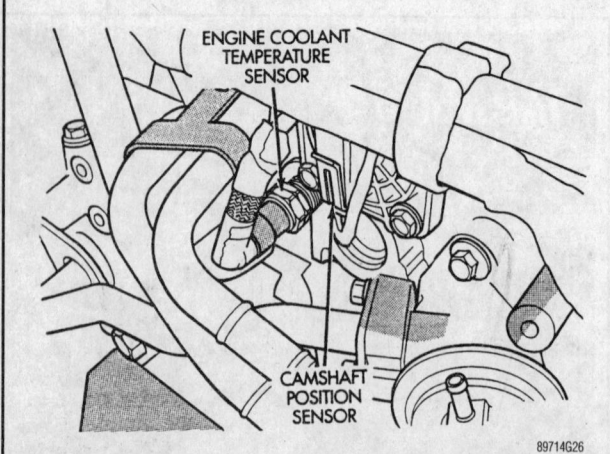

Fig. 43 On SOHC engines, the coolant temperature sensor is threaded into the rear of the cylinder head, next to the camshaft position sensor

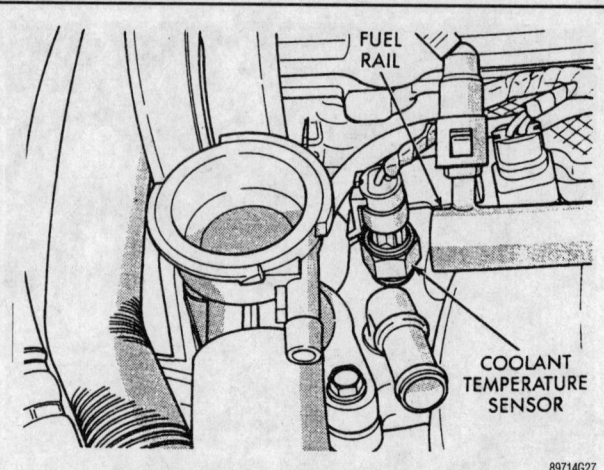

Fig. 44 On DOHC engines, the coolant temperature sensor is threaded into the intake manifold, next to the thermostat housing

gauge cluster. As coolant temperature changes, the coolant temperature sensor's resistance changes, resulting in a different input voltage to the PCM and gauge. When the air is cold, the PCM provides a slightly richer air/fuel ratio and higher idle speed until the proper normal operating temperature is reached.

### TESTING

▶ See Figures 45 and 46

1. Visually check the connector, making sure it is attached properly and all of the terminals are straight, tight and free of corrosion.

2. With the ignition **OFF**, detach the electrical connector from the coolant temperature sensor.

3. Connect a digital ohmmeter to terminals A and B (shown in the accompanying figure). The ohmmeter should read as follows:

a. With the engine and sensor at normal operating temperature, about 200°F, the DVOM should read about 700–1,000 ohms.

b. With the engine and sensor at room temperature, about 70°F, the DVOM should read about 7,000–13,000 ohms.

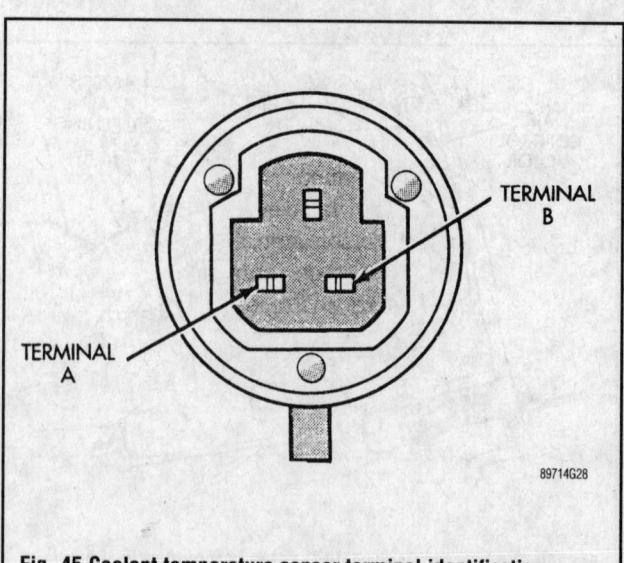

Fig. 45 Coolant temperature sensor terminal identification

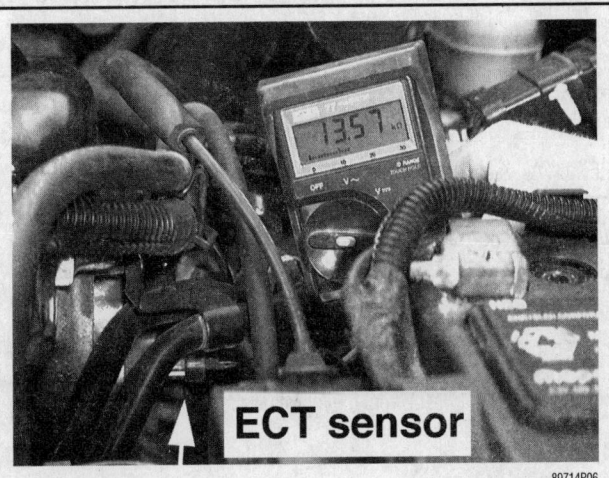

Fig. 46 Attach an ohmmeter to the ECT sensor and measure the resistance

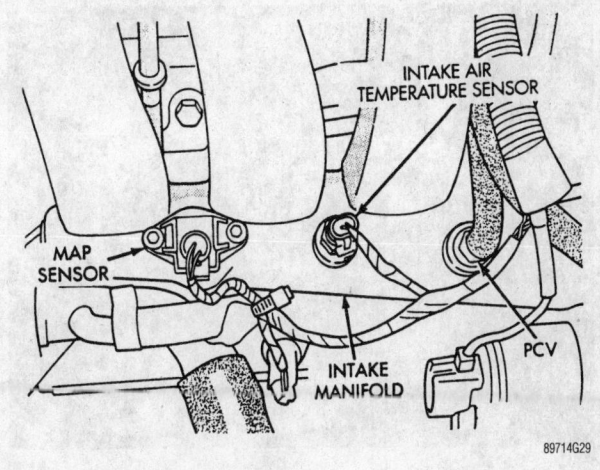

Fig. 47 The IAT sensor and MAP sensor thread into the intake manifold on 1995 vehicles

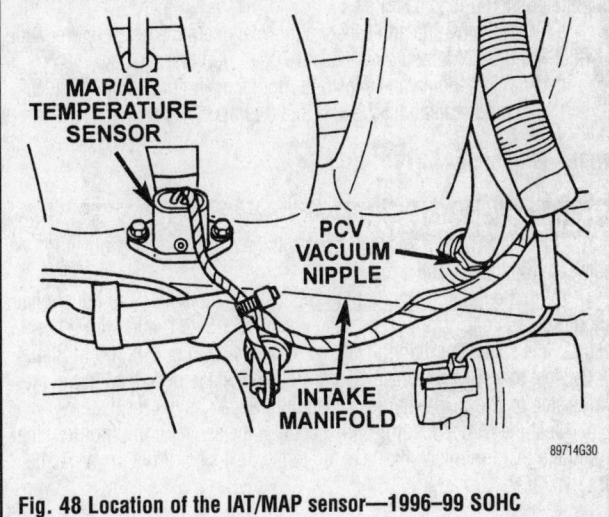

Fig. 48 Location of the IAT/MAP sensor—1996–99 SOHC engines

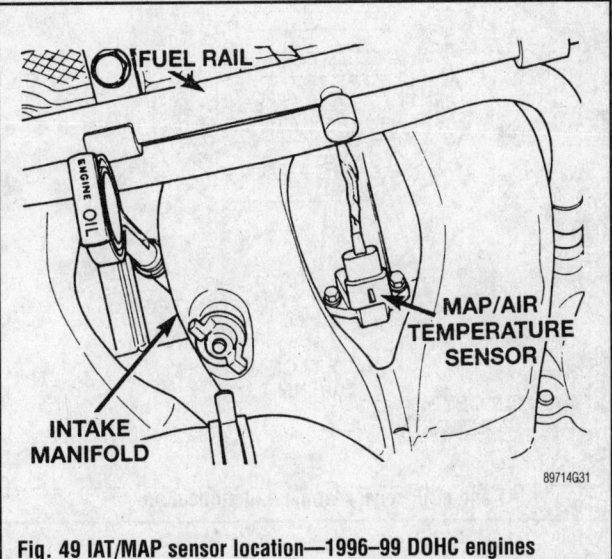

Fig. 49 IAT/MAP sensor location—1996–99 DOHC engines

## REMOVAL & INSTALLATION

▶ See Figures 45 and 46

➡New sensors have sealant already applied to the threads.

1. Disconnect the negative battery cable.
2. Drain the coolant into a suitable container, until it is at a level below the coolant temperature sensor.
3. Detach the coolant temperature sensor electrical connector.
4. Use a suitable wrench or ratchet, as applicable, to loosen and remove the coolant temperature sensor.

**To install:**

5. Install the coolant sensor and tighten to 60 inch lbs. (70 Nm) for 1995 vehicles or to 13.5 ft. lbs. (18 Nm) for 1996–99 vehicles.
6. Attach the electrical connector to the coolant temperature sensor.
7. Connect the negative battery cable. Fill the cooling system with the proper type and quantity of coolant.

## Intake Air Temperature Sensor

### OPERATION

▶ See Figures 47, 48 and 49

The Intake Air Temperature (IAT) sensor measures the temperature of the intake air as it enters the engine. The sensor supplies one of the inputs the PCM uses to determine injector pulse width and spark advance. AS the intake air temperature varies, the IAT sensor's resistance changes resulting in a different input voltage to the PCM.

On 1995 vehicles, the IAT sensor threads into the intake manifold. On 1996–99 vehicles, the IAT and Manifold Absolute Pressure (MAP) sensors are combined into a single sensor which is attached to the intake manifold.

### TESTING

▶ See Figure 50

**1995 Vehicles**

1. Visually check the connector, making sure it is attached properly and all of the terminals are straight, tight and free of corrosion.
2. With the ignition key **OFF**, detach the wire harness connector from the IAT sensor.

**Fig. 50 At room temperature, the IAT sensor resistance should be approximately 7,000–13,000 ohms**

3. Connect a digital ohmmeter (DVOM) to the sensor terminals. The ohmmeter should read as follows:

  a. With the engine and sensor at normal operating temperature, about 200°F, the DVOM should read about 700–1,000 ohms.

  b. With the engine and sensor at room temperature, about 70°F, the DVOM should read about 7,000–13,000 ohms.

### 1996–99 Vehicles

▶ **See Figure 51**

1. Test the IAT/MAP sensor output voltage at the sensor connector, between terminals 1 and 4.

2. With the ignition **ON**, but the engine NOT running, the output voltage should be 45 volts. The voltage should drop to 1.5–2.1 volts with a hot, neutral idle speed condition. If OK, go to next step. If not OK, go to Step 4.

3. Test the PCM terminal 36 for the same voltage described in the previous step to check wire harness condition. Repair as necessary.

4. Test the MAP sensor ground circuit at the sensor connector terminal 1 and the PCM terminal 43. If OK, go to the next step. If not, repair as necessary.

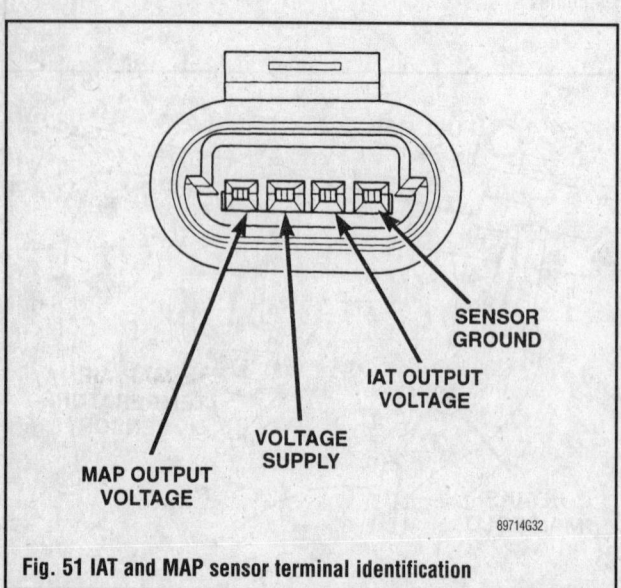

**Fig. 51 IAT and MAP sensor terminal identification**

5. Test the MAP sensor supply voltage between sensor connector terminal 3 and 1 with the ignition key **ON**. The voltage should be about 3.5–4.5 volts. There should also be 3.5–4.5 volts at terminal 61 of the PCM. If OK, replace the MAP sensor. If not, repair or replace the wire harness as required.

### REMOVAL & INSTALLATION

#### 1995 Vehicles

▶ **See Figure 47, 52, 53, and 54**

1. Disconnect the negative battery cable.
2. Remove the engine cover.
3. Detach the electrical connector from the sensor.
4. Remove the sensor from the intake manifold.
**To install:**
5. Thread the sensor into the intake manifold and tighten to 20 ft. lbs. (28 Nm).
6. Attach the electrical connector to the sensor.

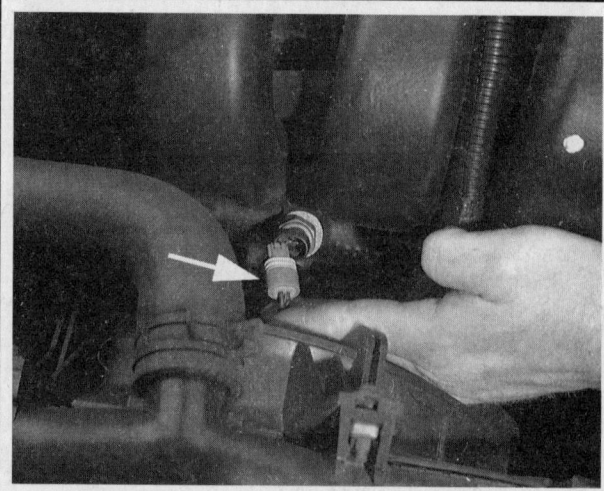

**Fig. 52 Detach the IAT sensor electrical connector**

**Fig. 53 Use a ratchet and extension with a deep socket to loosen . . .**

**Fig. 54 . . . then remove the IAT sensor from the intake manifold**

7. Install the engine cover.
8. Connect the negative battery cable.

### 1996–99 Vehicles

#### SOHC ENGINES

▶ See Figure 48

1. Disconnect the negative battery cable.
2. Detach the electrical connector from the MAP/IAT sensor.
3. Unfasten the sensor mounting screws, then remove the sensor from the vehicle.
   **To install:**
4. Insert the sensor into the intake manifold, but make sure not to damage the O-ring seal.
5. Tighten the mounting screws to 20 inch lbs. (2 Nm) for vehicles with a plastic intake manifold. For vehicles with an aluminum intake manifold, tighten the sensor to 30 inch lbs. (3 Nm).
6. Attach the electrical connector to the sensor.
7. Connect the negative battery cable.

#### DOHC ENGINES

▶ See Figure 49

1. Disconnect the negative battery cable.
2. Remove the air inlet duct wing nut and duct from the intake manifold.
3. Detach the electrical connector from the IAT/MAP sensor.
4. Unfasten the sensor mounting screws, then remove the sensor from the vehicle.
   **To install:**
5. Insert the sensor into the intake manifold, but make sure not to damage the O-ring seal.
6. Tighten the mounting screws to 20 inch lbs. (2 Nm) for vehicles with a plastic intake manifold. For vehicles with an aluminum intake manifold, tighten the sensor to 30 inch lbs. (3 Nm).
7. Attach the sensor electrical connector.
8. Install the air inlet duct to the intake manifold and secure with the wing nut. Make sure the duct doesn't interfere with the spark plug wires.
9. Connect the negative battery cable.

## Manifold Absolute Pressure Sensor

### OPERATION

#### 1995 Vehicles

▶ See Figure 47

➡On 1996–99 vehicles, the IAT and Manifold Absolute Pressure (MAP) sensors are combined into a single sensor which is attached to the intake manifold. Refer to the IAT sensor information, located earlier in this section for operation, testing and removal and installation.

The PCM supplies 5 volts of direct current to the Manifold Absolute Pressure (MAP) sensor. The MAP sensor then converts the intake manifold pressure into voltage. The PCM monitors the MAP sensor output voltage. As vacuum increases, the MAP sensor voltage decreases proportionately. Also, as vacuum decreases, the MAP sensor voltage increases proportionally.

With the ignition key **ON**, before the engine is started, the PCM determines atmospheric air pressure from the MAP sensor voltage. While the engine operates, the PCM figures out intake manifold pressure from the MAP sensor voltage. Based on the MAP sensor voltage and inputs from other sensors, the PCM adjusts spark advance and the air/fuel ratio. The MAP sensor is mounted to the intake manifold.

### TESTING

#### 1995 Vehicles

▶ See Figures 55 and 56

### ❋❋ WARNING

**When testing the MAP sensor, make sure the harness wires do not become damaged by the test meter probes.**

1. Visually check the connector, making sure it is attached properly and all of the terminals are straight, tight and free of corrosion.
2. Test the MAP sensor output voltage at the sensor connector between terminals 1 and 3, as shown in the accompanying figure.

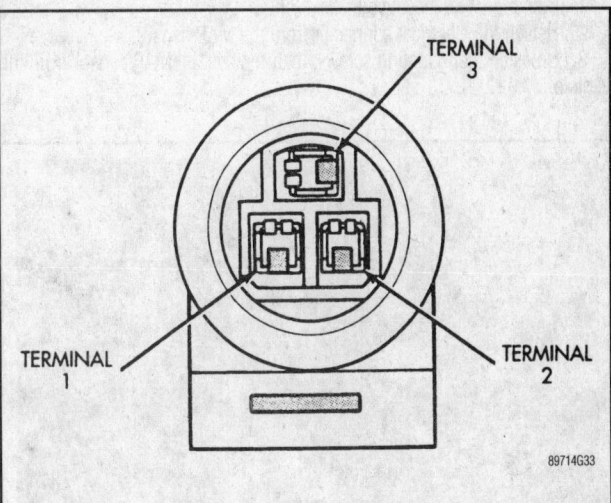

**Fig. 55 MAP sensor connector terminal identification—1995 vehicles**

Fig. 56 Check the sensor supply voltage

3. With the ignition switch **ON** and the engine not running, then output voltage should be 4.5 volts. If OK, go to next step. If not OK, go to step 4.

4. Test the PCM terminal 29 for the same voltage described in the previous step to make sure the wire harness is OK. Repair as necessary.

5. Test the MAP sensor ground circuit at the sensor connector terminal 1 and PCM terminal 51. If OK, go to the next step. If not OK, repair as necessary.

6. Test the MAP sensor supply voltage between the sensor connector terminals 2 and 1 with the ignition key in the **ON** position. The voltage should be about 3.5–5.5 volts. There should also be 3.5–5.5 volts at terminal 43 of the PCM. If OK, replace the MAP sensor. If not, repair or replace the wire harness as required.

## REMOVAL & INSTALLATION

### 1995 Vehicles

▶ See Figures 47, 57 and 58

1. Disconnect the negative battery cable.
2. Detach the electrical connector from the MAP sensor.
3. Unfasten the mounting screws, then remove the MAP sensor from the vehicle.

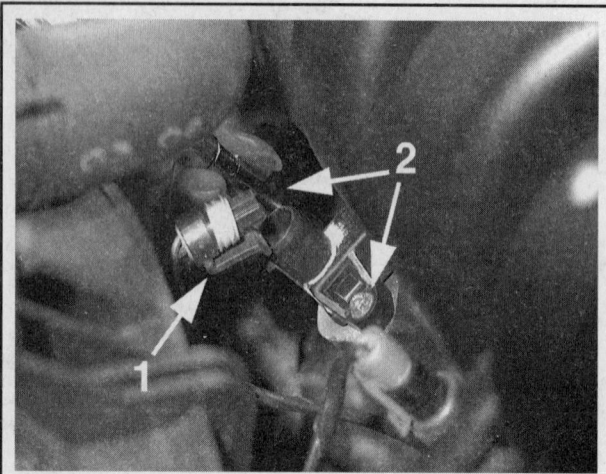

Fig. 57 Unfasten the connector (1), remove the retaining screws (2) . . .

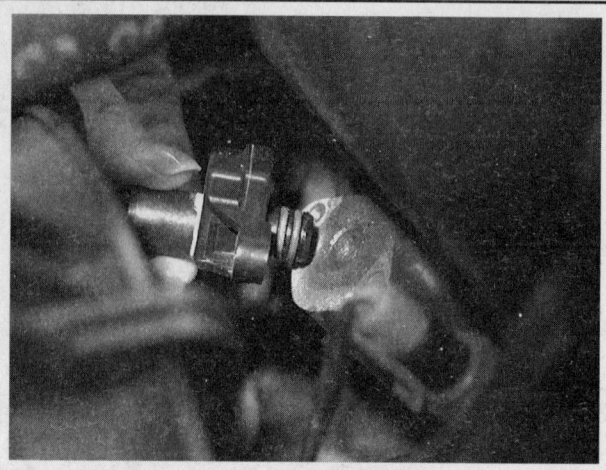

Fig. 58 . . . then remove the MAP sensor from the intake manifold

**To install:**

4. Insert the sensor into the intake manifold, but be careful not to damage the sensor O-ring seal.
5. Tighten the sensor mounting screws to 20 inch lbs. (2 Nm).
6. Attach the sensor electrical connector.
7. Connect the negative battery cable.

## Throttle Position Sensor

### OPERATION

▶ See Figure 59

The Throttle Position Sensor (TPS) is mounted to the side of the throttle body and connects to the throttle blade shaft. The TPS is a variable resistor that provides the PCM with an input signal (voltage). The signal represents throttle blade position. As the position of the throttle blade changes, the resistance of the TPS changes.

The PCM supplies about 5 volts of DC current to the TPS. The TPS output voltage (input signal to the PCM) represents throttle blade position. For 1995 vehicles, the TPS output voltage to the PCM varies from about 0.5 volt at idle to a maximum of 3.7 volts at wide open throttle. For 1996–99

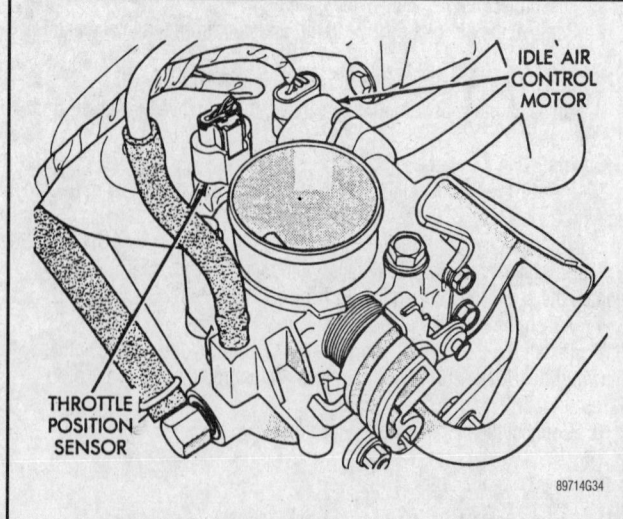

Fig. 59 Throttle Position Sensor (TPS) location—1995 vehicles

vehicles, the TPS output voltage to the PCM varies from about 0.35–1.03 volts at idle to a maximum of 3.1–4.0 volts at wide open throttle.

Along with inputs from other sensors, the PCM uses the TPS input to determine current engine operating conditions. The PCM also adjusts fuel injector pulse width and ignition timing based on these inputs.

## TESTING

### 1995 Vehicles

⏵ See Figures 60, 61, 62 and 63

➡ The TPS can be tested using a digital ohmmeter. The center terminal of the sensor is the output terminal.

1. Visually check the connector, making sure it is attached properly and all of the terminals are straight, tight and free of corrosion.
2. Turn the ignition switch to the **ON** position.

3. Attach a digital multimeter and check the output voltage at the center terminal wire of the sensor connector.
4. For a general sensor check.
   a. Turn the ignition key to the **ON** position with the engine **OFF**.
   b. Attach a digital ohmmeter to the TPS as shown in the accompanying figure.
   c. Measure the resistance with the throttle closed, with the throttle about half way open and at wide open throttle.
   d. The resistance should increase smoothly as the throttle plate is opened,
5. Check the output voltage at idle and at Wide Open Throttle (WOT). At idle, the TPS output voltage should be about 0.5 volts. At WOT, the output voltage should about 3.7 volts. The output voltage should gradually increase as the throttle plate moves slowly from idle to WOT.
6. Before replacing the TPS, check for spread terminals and also inspect the PCM connections.

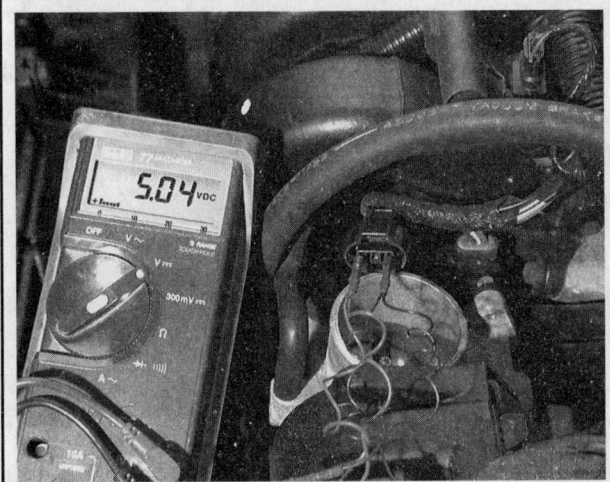

Fig. 60 Check the output voltage at the TPS connector

Fig. 62 Then, measure the resistance with the throttle plate partially open.

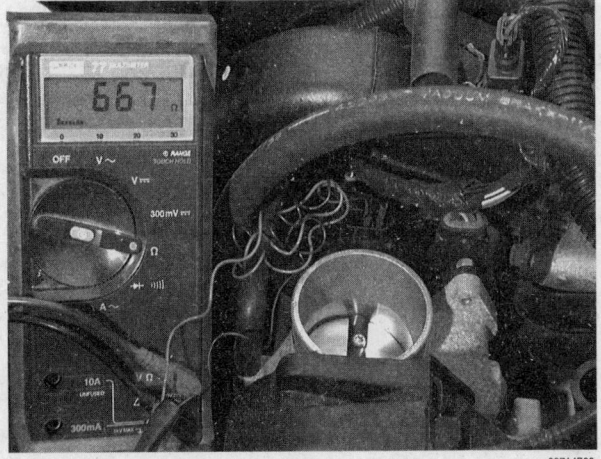

Fig. 61 Attach a DVOM to the TPS and measure the resistance with the throttle plate closed

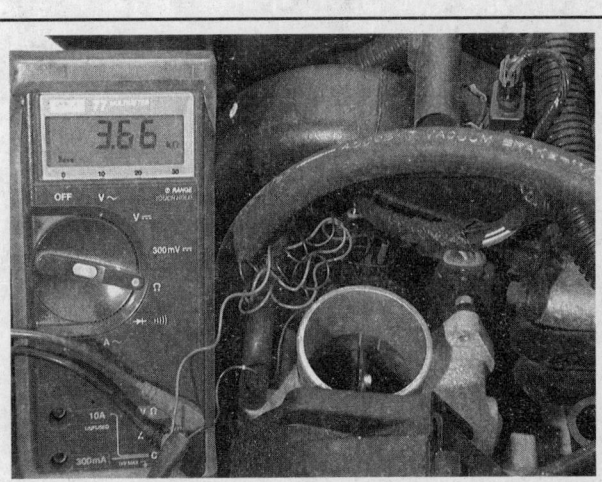

Fig. 63 Finally, measure the resistance at WOT. The resistance should increase smoothly as the throttle is opened

**1996–99 Vehicles**

▶ **See Figures 64 and 65**

➡In order to perform a complete test of the TPS and related circuits, you must use a DRB® or equivalent scan tool, and following the manufacturers directions. To check the Throttle Position Sensor (TPS) only, proceed with the following test.

1. The TPS can be tested using a digital ohmmeter. The center terminal of the sensor is the output terminal. One of the other terminals is a 5 volt supply and the remaining terminal is ground.
2. Connect the DVOM between the center and sensor ground terminals.
3. With the ignition switch in the **ON** position, check the output voltage at the center terminal wire of the connector. Check the output voltage at idle and at Wide Open Throttle (WOT).
4. For 1996 vehicles, at idle, the TPS output voltage should be about 0.38–1.03 volts. At WOT, the output voltage should be about 3.1–4.0 volts. The output voltage should gradually increase as the throttle plate moves slowly from idle to WOT.
5. For 1997–99 vehicles, at idle, the TPS output voltage should be about 0.38–1.20 volts. At WOT, the output voltage should be about 3.1–4.4

volts. The output voltage should gradually increase as the throttle plate moves slowly from idle to WOT.

## REMOVAL & INSTALLATION

▶ **See Figures 41, 59, 66, 67 and 68**

1. Disconnect the negative battery cable.
2. Disconnect the EVAP purge hose from the throttle body.
3. Detach the electrical connector from the IAC motor and the TPS.
4. Remove the throttle body from the vehicle, as outlined in
5. Unfasten the mounting screws, then remove the TPS from the throttle body.

**To install:**

6. The throttle shaft end of the throttle body slides into a socket in the TPS. The socket has 2 tabs inside it. The throttle shaft rests against the tabs. When indexed correctly the TPS can rotate clockwise a few degrees to line up the mounting screw holes with the screw holes in the throttle body. The TPS has slight tension when rotated into position. If it is difficult to rotate the TPS into position, install the sensor with the throttle shaft on the other side of the tabs in the socket.
7. Install the sensor mounting screws and tighten to 17 inch lbs. (2 Nm).

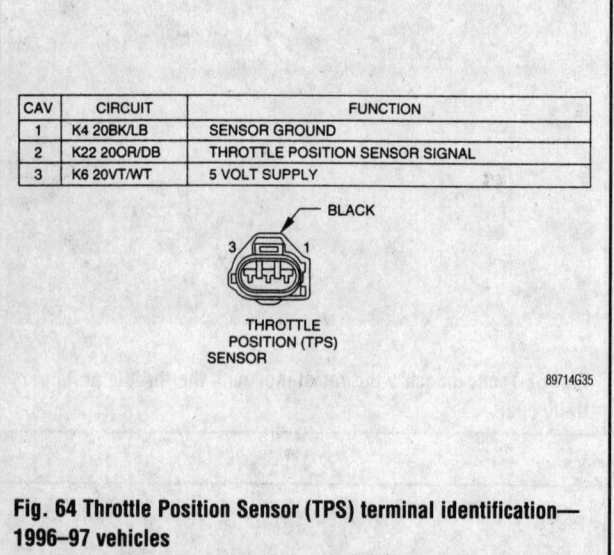

| CAV | CIRCUIT | FUNCTION |
|---|---|---|
| 1 | K4 20BK/LB | SENSOR GROUND |
| 2 | K22 20OR/DB | THROTTLE POSITION SENSOR SIGNAL |
| 3 | K6 20VT/WT | 5 VOLT SUPPLY |

BLACK

THROTTLE
POSITION (TPS)
SENSOR

89714G35

**Fig. 64 Throttle Position Sensor (TPS) terminal identification—1996–97 vehicles**

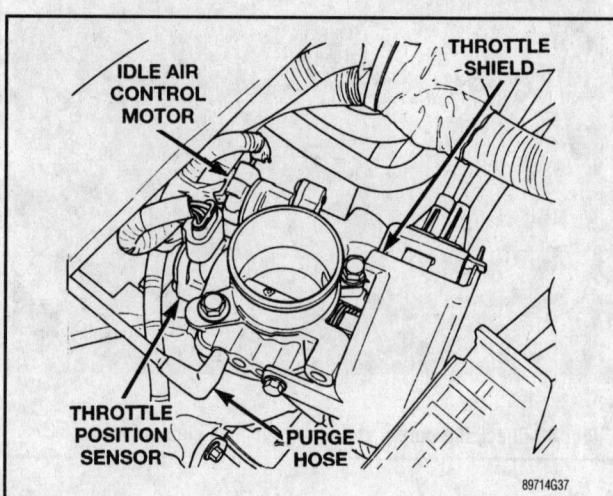

89714G37

**Fig. 66 View of the TPS and related components—1999 SOHC engine shown**

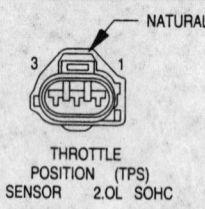

NATURAL

THROTTLE
POSITION (TPS)
SENSOR 2.0L SOHC

| CAV | CIRCUIT | FUNCTION |
|---|---|---|
| 1 | K4 20BK/LB | SENSOR GROUND |
| 2 | K22 20OR/DB | THROTTLE POSITION SENSOR SIGNAL |
| 3 | K6 20VT/WT | 5 VOLT SUPPLY |

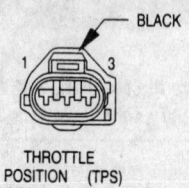

BLACK

THROTTLE
POSITION (TPS)
SENSOR 2.0L DOHC

| CAV | CIRCUIT | FUNCTION |
|---|---|---|
| 1 | K6 20VT/WT | 5 VOLT SUPPLY |
| 2 | K22 20OR/DB | THROTTLE POSITION SENSOR SIGNAL |
| 3 | K4 20BK/LB | SENSOR GROUND |

89714G36

**Fig. 65 Throttle Position Sensor (TPS) terminal identification—1999 vehicles**

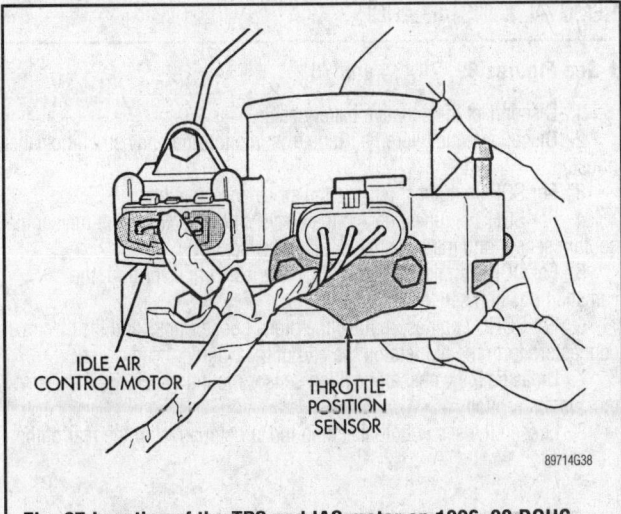

**Fig. 67 Location of the TPS and IAC motor on 1996–99 DOHC engines. Note that they share a wiring harness**

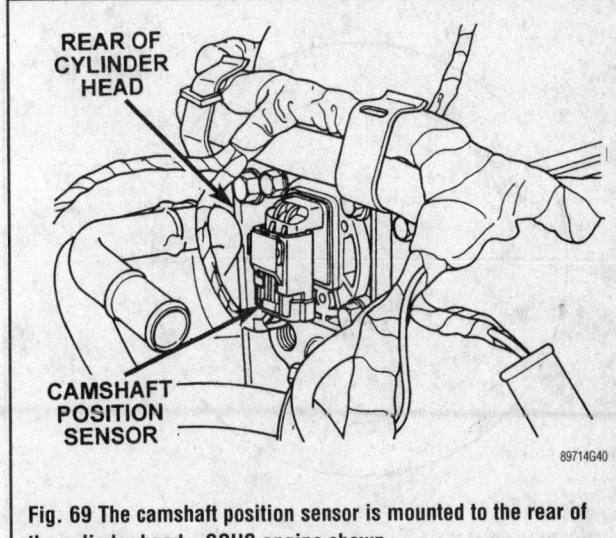

**Fig. 69 The camshaft position sensor is mounted to the rear of the cylinder head—SOHC engine shown**

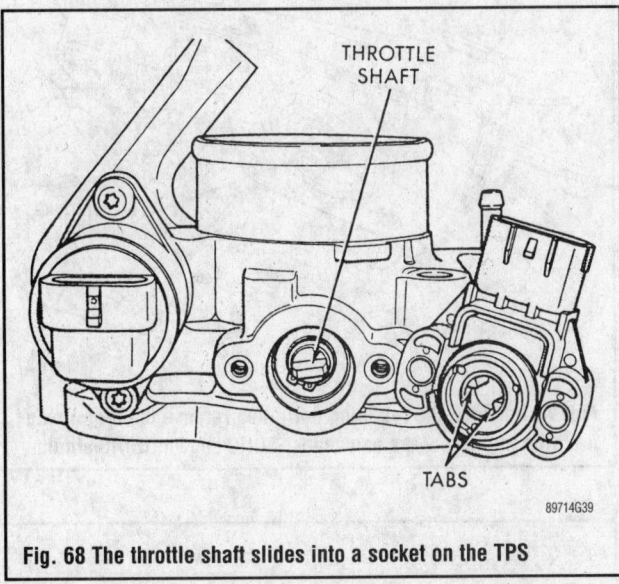

**Fig. 68 The throttle shaft slides into a socket on the TPS**

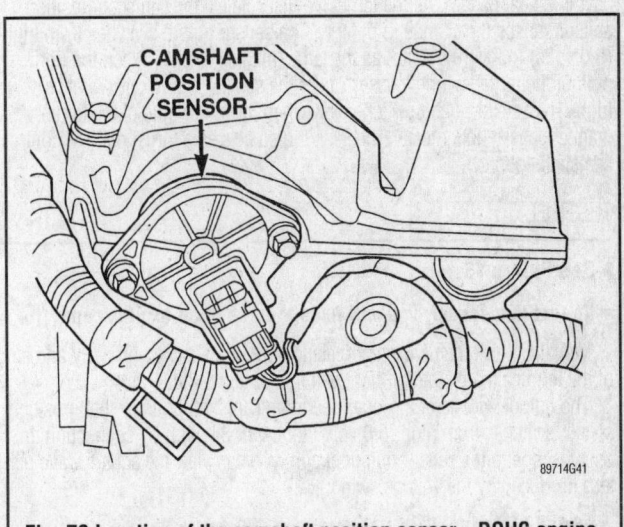

**Fig. 70 Location of the camshaft position sensor—DOHC engine shown**

8. After installing the TPS, the throttle plate should be closed. If the throttle plate is open, install the sensor on the other side of the tabs in the socket.

9. Install the throttle body, as outlined in Section 5.

10. Attach the electrical connectors to the IAC motor and TPS.

11. Connect the EVAP purge hose to the throttle body nipple.

12. Connect the negative battery cable.

## Camshaft Position Sensor

### OPERATION

▶ **See Figures 69, 70, 71 and 72**

The camshaft position sensor (along with the crankshaft position sensor) provides inputs to the PCM to determine fuel injection synchronization and cylinder identification. From these inputs, the PCM determines crankshaft position. The camshaft position sensor is attached to the rear of the cylinder head.

A target magnet attaches to the rear of the camshaft and indexes to the proper position. The target magnet has four different poles arranges in an

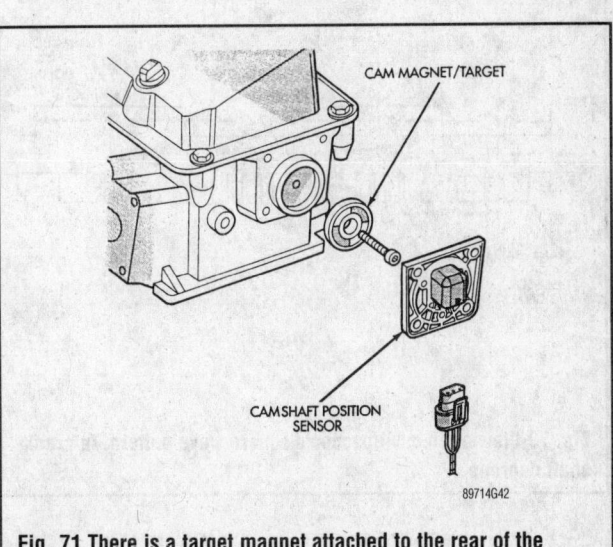

**Fig. 71 There is a target magnet attached to the rear of the camshaft**

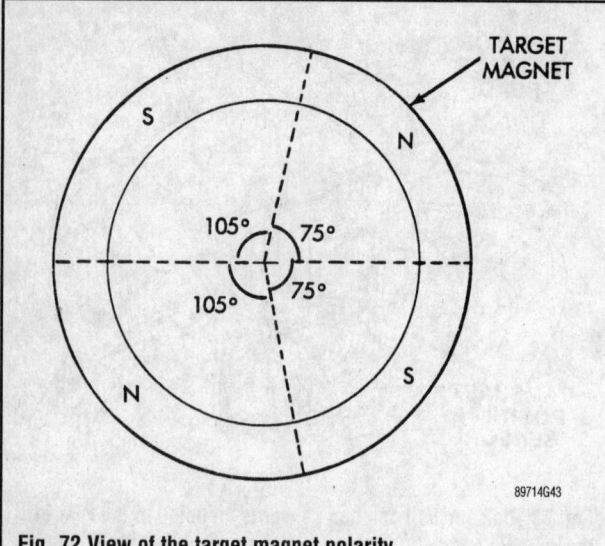

Fig. 72 View of the target magnet polarity

asymmetrical pattern. As the target magnet rotates, the camshaft position sensor senses the change in polarity. The sensor output switches from high (5.0 volts) to low (0.5 volts) as the target magnet rotates. When the north pole of the target magnet passes under the sensor, the output switches high. The sensor output switches low when the south pole of the target magnet passes underneath. The sensor also acts as a thrust plate to control camshaft endplay.

## TESTING

### ▶ See Figure 73

➡ To test this sensor, you will need the use of an oscilloscope.

Visually check the connector, making sure it is attached properly and all of the terminals are straight, tight and free of corrosion.

The output voltage of a proper operating camshaft or crankshaft position sensor switches from high (5.0 volts) to low (0.3 volts). By connecting an oscilloscope to the sensor output circuit, you can view the square wave pattern produced by the voltage swing.

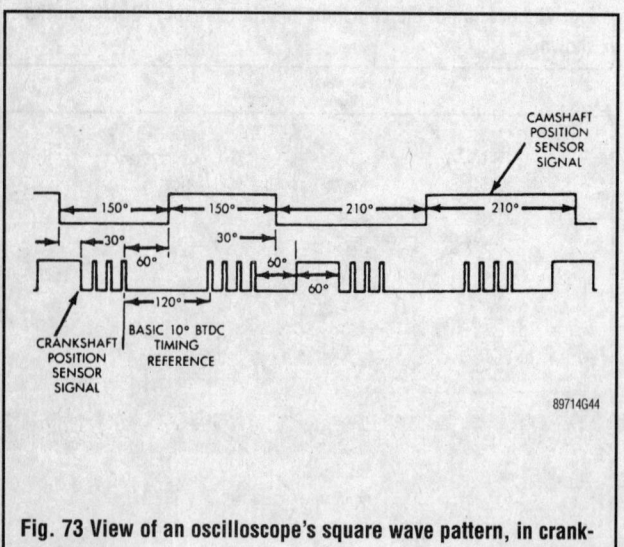

Fig. 73 View of an oscilloscope's square wave pattern, in crankshaft degrees

## REMOVAL & INSTALLATION

### ▶ See Figures 69, 70, 74 and 75

1. Disconnect the negative battery cable.
2. Disconnect the filtered air tube from the throttle body and air cleaner housing.
3. For SOHC engines, remove the air cleaner inlet tube.
4. For SOHC engines, detach the electrical connectors from the engine coolant sensor and the camshaft position sensor.
5. For DOHC engines, unplug the electrical connector from the camshaft position sensor.
6. For SOHC engines, remove the brake booster hose and the electrical connectors form the holders on the end of the cylinder head cover.
7. Unfasten the camshaft position sensor mounting screws, then remove the sensor.
8. Loosen the screw/bolt attaching the target magnet to the rear of the camshaft.

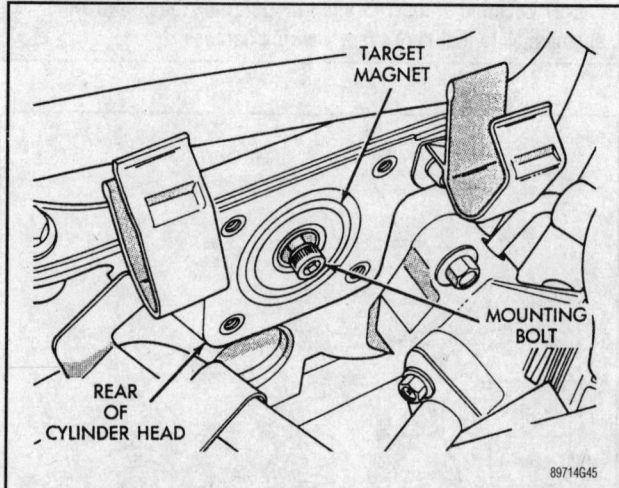

Fig. 74 Unfasten the retaining bolt, then remove the target magnet from the rear of the camshaft—SOHC shown, DOHC similar

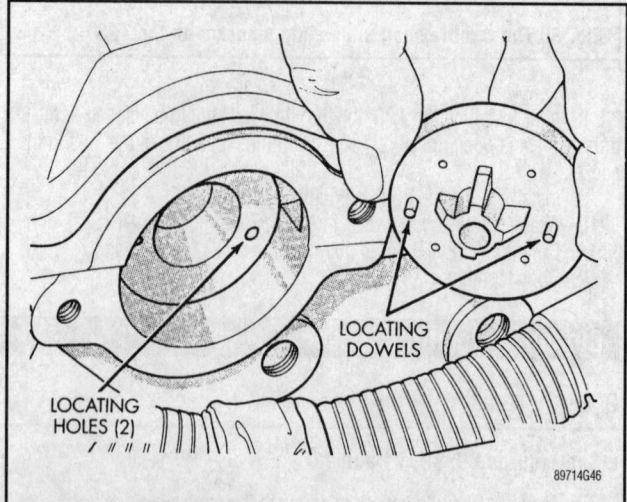

Fig. 75 The target magnet has 2 locating dowels for proper alignment during installation

**To install:**

➡️ **The target magnet has 2 locating dowels which fit into the machined locating holes in the end of the camshaft.**

9. Install the target magnet in the end of the camshaft. Tighten the retainer to 30 inch lbs. (3.4 Nm).
10. Install the camshaft position sensor. Tighten the sensor mounting screws to 80 inch lbs. (9 Nm).
11. For SOHC engines, place the brake booster hose and the electrical harness in the holders on the end of the valve cover.
12. Attach the electrical connector(s) to the camshaft position sensor and coolant temperature sensor (if necessary).
13. Install the air cleaner inlet tube and the filtered air tube.
14. Connect the negative battery cable.

## Crankshaft Position Sensor

### OPERATION

▶ **See Figure 76**

The PCM determines what cylinder to fire from the crankshaft position sensor input and the camshaft position sensor input. The second crankshaft counterweight has two sets of four timing reference notches, including a 60° signature notch. From the crankshaft position sensor input, the PCM determines engine speed and crankshaft angle (position).

The notches generate pulses from high to low in the crankshaft position sensor output voltage. When a metal portion of the counterweight aligns with the crankshaft position sensor, the sensor output voltage goes low (less than 0.5 volts). when a notch aligns with the sensor, voltage goes high (5.0 volts). As a group of notches pass under the sensor, the output voltage switches from low (metal) to high (notch) then back to low.

If available, an oscilloscope can display the square wave patterns of each voltage pulse. From the width of the output voltage pulses, the PCM calculates engine speed, The width of the pulses represent the amount of time the output voltage stays high before switching back to low. The period of time the sensor output voltage stays high before switching back to low is referred to as pulse width. The faster the engine is operating, the smaller the pulse width on the oscilloscope.

By counting the pulses and referencing the pulse from the 60° signature notch, the PCM calculates the crankshaft angle (position). In each group of timing reference notches, the first notch represents 69° Before Top Dead Center (BTDC). The second notch represents 49° BTDC. The third notch represents 29° BTDC. The last notch in each set represents 9° BTDC.

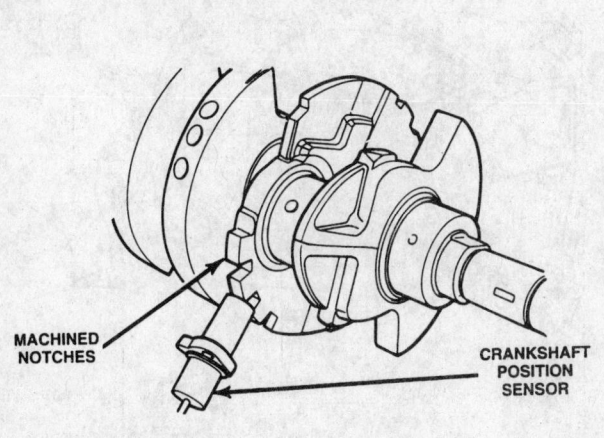

**MACHINED NOTCHES**

**CRANKSHAFT POSITION SENSOR**

89714G47

**Fig. 76 Timing reference notches**

The timing reference notches are machined at 20° increments. From the voltage pulse width, the PCM tells the difference between the timing reference notches and the 60° signature notch. The 60° signature notch produces a longer pulse width than the smaller timing reference notches. If the camshaft position sensor input switches from high to low when the 60° signature notch passes under the crankshaft position sensor, the PCM knows cylinder number on is the next cylinder at TDC.

The crankshaft position sensor is mounted to the engine block behind the alternator, just above the oil filter.

### TESTING

▶ **See Figure 73**

➡️ **To test this sensor, you will need the use of an oscilloscope.**

Visually check the connector, making sure it is attached properly and all of the terminals are straight, tight and free of corrosion.

The output voltage of a proper operating camshaft or crankshaft position sensor switches from high (5.0 volts) to low (0.3 volts). By connecting an oscilloscope to the sensor output circuit, you can view the square wave pattern produced by the voltage swing.

### REMOVAL & INSTALLATION

▶ **See Figure 77**

1. Disconnect the negative battery cable.
2. Detach the crankshaft position sensor electrical connector.
3. Unfasten the sensor mounting screw, then remove the sensor from the vehicle.

**To install:**
4. Install the sensor in the vehicle and secure with the retaining screw.
5. Attach the crankshaft position sensor electrical connector.
6. Connect the negative battery cable.

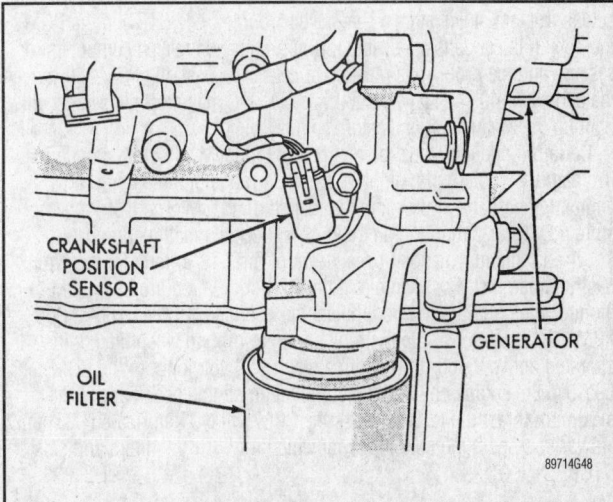

**CRANKSHAFT POSITION SENSOR**

**GENERATOR**

**OIL FILTER**

89714G48

**Fig. 77 The crankshaft position sensor is mounted to the engine block, behind the alternator just above the oil filter**

## Knock Sensor

### OPERATION

▶ **See Figure 78**

Visually check the connector, making sure it is attached properly and all of the terminals are straight, tight and free of corrosion.

These vehicles are equipped with a knock sensor, which is threaded into the side of the cylinder block in front of the starter. When the knock sensor

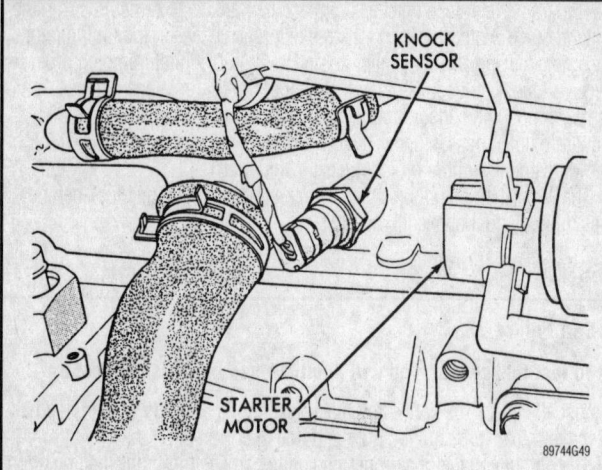

**Fig. 78 You can find the knock sensor in front of the starter, threaded into the side of the cylinder block**

detects a knock in one of the cylinders, it sends an input signal to the PCM. In response, the PCM retards ignition timing for all cylinders by a scheduled amount.

Knock sensors contain a piezoelectric material which sends an input voltage (signal) to the PCM. As the intensity of the engine knock vibration increases, the knock sensor output voltage also increases.

## TESTING

A number of factors affect the engine knock sensor. A few of these are: ignition timing, cylinder pressure, fuel octane, etc. The knock sensor produces an AC voltage whose amplitude increased with the increase of engine knock. The knock sensor can be tested with a digital voltmeter. The RMS voltage at about 20mVac (at about 700 rpm) and increased to about 600mVac (5000 rpm). If the output falls outside of this range, a Diagnostic Trouble Code (DTC) will set.

## REMOVAL & INSTALLATION

◗ **See Figure 78**

1. Disconnect the negative battery cable.
2. Unplug the electrical connector from the knock sensor.
3. Use a crow's foot wrench to remove the knock sensor from the vehicle.

**To install:**

4. Install the sensor in the vehicle and tighten to 7 ft. lbs. (10 Nm). Make sure not to over or under-tighten the sensor, as is could adversely effect knock sensor performance causing improper spark control.
5. Attach the knock sensor electrical connector.
6. Connect the negative battery cable.

## TROUBLE CODES

### General Information

The Powertrain Control Module (PCM) monitors many different circuits in the fuel injection, ignition, emissions and engine systems. If the PCM senses a problem with a monitored circuit often enough to indicate an actual problem, it will store a Diagnostic Trouble Code (DTC) in the PCM's memory. If the code is applicable to a non-emission related component or system, and the problem is repaired or ceases to exist, the PCM will cancel the code after 40 engine warm up cycles. A DTC that affect emissions will light up the Malfunction Indicator Lamp (MIL).

Certain guidelines must be met before the PCM will store a code in it's memory. The criteria might be a certain range of the engine RPM, engine temperature and/or input voltage to the PCM. The PCM may not store a DTC for a monitored circuit even though a malfunction has occurred. This may happen because on of the DTC criteria for the circuit has not been met. For example, if the DTC criteria required the PCM to monitor the circuit only when the engine operated between 750–2,000 RPM . If the sensor's output circuit shorts to ground when the engine operated above 2,400 RPM, (with a result of 0 volt input to the PCM),. Because the engine condition occurred at an engine speed above the maximum threshold (2,000 RPM), the PCM will NOT store a DTC. There are various operating conditions for which the PCM monitors and sets DTC's.

➥**Various diagnostic procedures may actually cause a diagnostic monitor to set a DTC. For example, disconnecting a spark plug wire to perform a spark test may set the misfire code. When a repair is completed and verified, use Chryslers DRB® or equivalent scan tool to erase all DTC's, therefore putting out the MIL.**

As a functional test, the Malfunction Indicator Lamp (MIL) lights up at the ignition key **ON** position before engine cranking. Whenever the PCM sets a DTC, that affects emissions, it lights up the MIL. If a problem is detected, the PCM sends a message to the instrument cluster, illuminating the lamp. The PCM will light up the MIL only for codes that affect vehicle emissions. The MIL stays on constantly when the PCM has entered Limp-In mode or found a failed emission component or system. The MIL stays on until the DTC is erased.

The MIL will either flash or light up constantly when the PCM detects active engine misfire. Also, the PCM may reset (turn off) the MIL when one of the following conditions occur:

• PCM does not detect the malfunction for 3 successive trips (except misfire and fuel system monitors).
• PCM does not detect a malfunction while performing three consecutive engine misfire or fuel system tests. The PCM perform these tests while the engine is operating within 375 RPM of and within 10% or the lead of the operating condition at which the problem was first detected.

### Diagnostic Connector

◗ **See Figures 79 and 80**

There is a Data Link Connector (diagnostic connector), located inside the vehicle, under the instrument panel to the left of the steering column. The

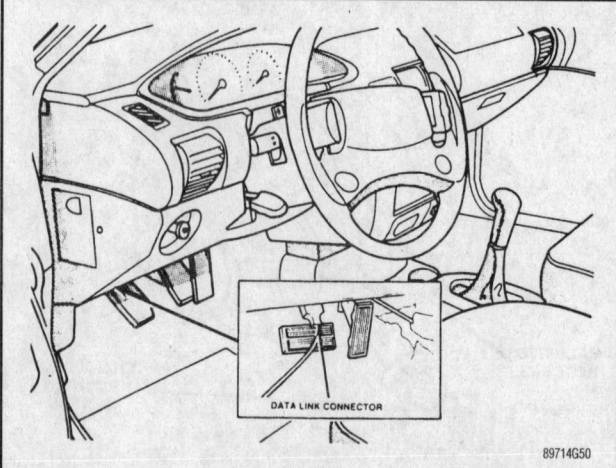

**Fig. 79 The Data Link Connector can be found under the dash panel, to the left of the steering wheel—1995 vehicle shown**

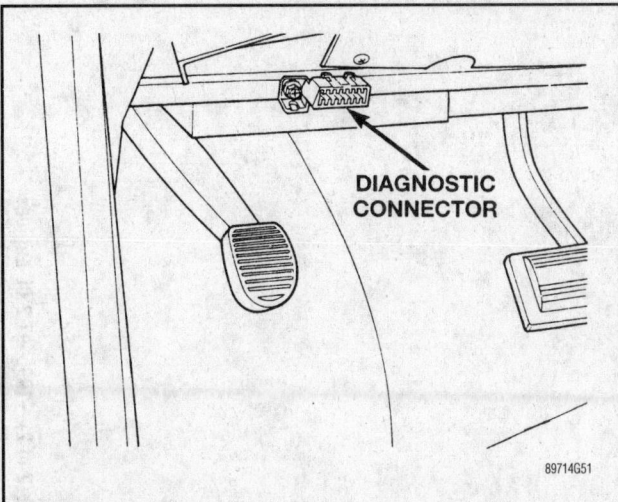

**Fig. 80 The diagnostic connector is the link between the scan tool and the PCM**

diagnostic connector is used as a link between the DRB® or equivalent scan tool and the PCM. The PCM communicates with the scan tool through the data link receive and transmit circuits. You can connect the scan tool to the data link connector to access any stored DTC's.

## Visual Inspection

➡This is a general procedure and the specific steps may differ from vehicle-to-vehicle; adjust the procedure as necessary.

When a fault code is exhibited by the engine computer it is a good idea to perform this general inspection to make sure that the cause is not a loose wire or a dirty connection.

Perform a visual inspection for loose, disconnected or mis-routed wires and hoses before diagnosing or servicing the fuel injection system. A visual check saves unnecessary test and diagnostic time. A thorough visual inspection includes the following:

1. Check for correct spark plug cable routing. Ensure the cables are completely connected to the spark plugs and distributor.
2. Check ignition coil electrical connections.
3. Verify the electrical connector is attached to the purge solenoid.
4. Verify vacuum connection at the purge solenoid is secure and not leaking.
5. Verify the electrical connector is attached to the MAP sensor.
6. Check the MAP sensor hose (if so equipped) at the MAP sensor assembly and at the vacuum connection at the intake plenum fitting.
7. Check the alternator wiring connections. Ensure the accessory drive belt has proper tension.
8. Verify the hoses are securely attached to the vapor canister.
9. Verify the engine ground strap is attached at the engine and dash panel.
10. Ensure the heated oxygen sensor connector is attached to the wiring harness.
11. Verify that the distributor connector (if so equipped) is connected to the harness connector.
12. Verify that the coolant temperature sensor connector is attached to the wiring harness.
13. Check that the vacuum hose connection at the fuel pressure regulator and intake plenum.
14. Ensure that the harness connector is securely attached to each fuel injector.
15. Check the oil pressure sending unit electrical connection.
16. Check the hose connections at the throttle body.
17. Check the throttle body electrical connections.
18. Check the PCV system hose connections.
19. If equipped, check the EGR system vacuum hose connections.
20. If equipped, check the EGR tube to intake plenum connections.

21. Inspect the electronic EGR transducer solenoid electrical connector.
22. Ensure that the vacuum connections at the electronic EGR transducer is secure and not leaking.
23. Check the power brake booster and speed connections.
24. Inspect the engine harness to main harness connections.
25. Check all automatic transaxle electrical connections, if so equipped.
26. Check the vehicle speed sensor electrical connector.
27. Inspect the PCM electrical connector(s) for damage or spread terminals. Verify that the 60-way connector is fully inserted into the socket of the PCM. Ensure wires are not stretched or pulled out of the connector.
28. Check the air conditioning, starter, automatic shutdown relay, fuel pump, and radiator fan relay connections.
29. Check the battery cable connections.
30. Check the hose and electrical connections at the fuel pump. Ensure that the connector is making contact with the terminals on the pump.

## Reading Codes

▶ See Figures 81, 82, 83, 84 and 85

On all 1995–97 vehicles, you can access the DTC's in two ways, listed as follows:
• The preferred and most accurate way of reading a DTC is by using Chrysler's DRB® or equivalent scan tool. The scan tool supplies detailed diagnostic information which can be used for more accurate and specific diagnosis of the code.
• The second way of reading DTC's is by observing the number of flashes displayed at the Malfunction Indicator Lamp (MIL). The MIL is shown on the instrument panel as the Check Engine lamp. This method should be used as a "quick test" only. You should always use a scan tool to get the most detailed information.

On 1998–99 vehicles, the only way to retrieve DTC's is by using a DRB® or equivalent scan tool.

➡Keep in mind that DTC's are the result of a system or circuit failure, but may not directly identify the failed component(s).

### READING DTC'S USING A SCAN TOOL

1. Connect Chrysler's Diagnostic Readout Box (DRB) or equivalent scan tool to the data link (diagnostic) connector. This connector is located at the lower edge of the instrument panel, near the steering column.

➡Always make sure to follow the manufacturer's instructions when using a scan tool.

**Fig. 81 The Data Link Connector (DLC) is located under the instrument panel to the left of the steering column**

## 1995-97 DIAGNOSTIC TROUBLE CODE (DTC) APPLICATIONS

| MIL Code | Scan Tool Code | DRB Scan Tool Display |
|---|---|---|
| 11 ① | P1390 | Timing belt skipped 1 tooth or more |
| 11 ① | P1391 | Intermittent loss of CMP or CKP |
| 12 ② | | Battery disconnect |
| 13 ① | P1297 | No change in MAP from from start to run |
| 14 ① | P0107 | MAP sensor voltage too low |
| 14 ① | P0108 | MAP sensor voltage too high |
| 15 ① | P0500 | No vehicle speed sensor signal |
| 17 ① | P0125 | Closed loop temperature not reached |
| 21 ① | P0131 | Upstream O2S shorted to ground |
| 21 ① | P0132 | Upstream O2S shorted to voltage |
| 21 ① | P0133 | Upstream O2S response |
| 21 ① | P0134 | Upstream O2S stays at center |
| 21 ① | P0135 | Upstream O2S heater failure |
| 21 ① | P0137 | Downstream O2S shorted to ground |
| 21 ① | P0138 | Downstream O2S shorted to voltage |
| 21 ① | P0139 | Downstream O2S response |
| 21 ① | P0141 | Downstream O2S heater failure |
| 22 ① | P0117 | ECT sensor voltage too low |
| 22 ① | P0118 | ECT sensor voltage too high |
| 23 ① | P0112 | Intake air temperature voltage low |
| 23 ① | P0113 | Intake air temperature voltage high |
| 24 ① | P0121 | TPS voltage does not agree with MAP |
| 24 ① | P0122 | Throttle position sensor voltage low |
| 24 ① | P0123 | Throttle position sensor voltage high |
| 25 ① | P0505 | Idle air control motor circuits |
| 25 ① | P1294 | Target idle not reached |
| 25 ① | P1299 | Vacuum leak found (IAC fully seated) |
| 27 ① | P0201 | Injector #1 control circuit |
| 27 ① | P0202 | Injector #2 control circuit |
| 27 ① | P0203 | Injector #3 control circuit |
| 27 ① | P0204 | Injector #4 control circuit |
| 31 ① | P0441 | Evap purge flow monitor failure |
| 31 ① | P0443 | EVAP solenoid circuit |
| 32 ① | P0401 | EGR system failure |
| 32 ① | P0403 | EGR solenoid circuit |
| 33 ② | | A/C clutch relay circuit |
| 34 ② | | Speed control solenoid circuits |
| 35 ② | | High speed fan relay circuit check |
| 35 ② | | Low speed fan relay circuit check |
| 35 ② | P1491 | Radiator fan control relay circuit |
| 37 ① | P0740 | Torque converter clutch no rpm drop at lockup |
| 37 ① | P0743 | Torque converter clutch solenoid circuit |
| 37 ① | P1899 | Park/Neutral switch failure |
| 41 ① | | Generator field not switching properly |
| 42 ② | | Fuel pump relay control circuit |
| 43 ① | P0300 | Multiple cylinder misfire |
| 43 ① | P0301 | Cylinder #1 misfire |
| 43 ① | P0302 | Cylinder #2 misfire |

89714C01

**Fig. 82 Diagnostic trouble code chart (1 of 2)—1995-97 engines**

## 1995-97 DIAGNOSTIC TROUBLE CODE (DTC) APPLICATIONS

| MIL Code | Scan Tool Code | DRB Scan Tool Display |
|---|---|---|
| 43 ① | P0303 | Cylinder #3 misfire |
| 43 ① | P0304 | Cylinder #4 misfire |
| 43 ① | P0351 | Ignition coil #1 primary circuit |
| 43 ① | P0352 | Ignition coil #2 primary circuit |
| 44 ③ | | Battery temperature sensor volts out of limit |
| 44 ③ | P1492 | Battery temperature sensor voltage too high |
| 44 ③ | P1493 | Battery temperature sensor voltage too low |
| 46 ③ | | Charging system voltage too high |
| 47 ③ | | Charging system voltage too low |
| 51 ① | P0171 | Fuel system lean |
| 52 ① | P0172 | Fuel system rich |
| 53 ① | P0601 | Internal controller failure |
| 53 ① | P0600 | PCM failure SPI communications |
| 54 ① | P0340 | No cam signal at PCM |
| 55 ② | | Completion of fault code display on Check Engine Lamp |
| 62 | P1697 | PCM failure SRI mile not stored |
| 63 ① | P1696 | PCM failure EEPROM write denied |
| 65 ① | P0551 | Power steering switch failure |
| 72 ① | P0420 | Catalytic converter efficiency failure |

89714C02

Check engine lamp will illuminate during engine operation if this DTC was recorded
Check engine lamp will not illuminate at all times if this DTC was recorded. Cycle the ignition key and observe the flashed code
Alternator lamp illuminated

**Fig. 83 Diagnostic trouble code chart (2 of 2)—1995-97 2.0L engines**

## 1998-99 DIAGNOSTIC TROUBLE CODE (DTC) APPLICATIONS

| Hex Code | Scan Tool Code | DRB Scan Tool Display |
|---|---|---|
| 1 | P0340 | No cam signal at PCM |
| 2 | P0601 | Internal controller failure |
| 5 | P1682 | Charging system voltage too low |
| 6 | P1597 | Charging system voltage too high |
| 0A | P1388 | Auto shutdown relay control circuit |
| 0B | P0622 | Alternator field not switching properly |
| 0C | P0743 | Torque converter clutch solenoid/trans. relay circuits |
| 0E | P1491 | Radiator fan control relay circuits |
| 0F | P1595 | Speed control solenoid circuits |
| 10 | P0645 | A/C clutch relay circuit |
| 11 | P0403 | EGR solenoid circuit |
| 12 | P0443 | EVAP purge solenoid circuit |
| 13 | P0203 | Injector #3 control circuit |
| 14 | P0202 | Injector #2 control circuit |
| 15 | P0201 | Injector #1 control circuit |
| 19 | P0505 | Idle air control motor circuits |
| 1A | P0122 | Throttle position sensor voltage low |
| 1B | P0123 | Throttle position sensor voltage high |
| 1E | P0117 | ECT sensor voltage too low |
| 1F | P0118 | ECT sensor voltage too high |
| 20 | P0134 | Right rear upstream O2S stays at center |
| 21 | P1281 | Engine is cold too long |
| 23 | P0500 | No vehicle speed sensor signal |
| 24 | P0107 | MAP sensor voltage too low |
| 25 | P0108 | MAP sensor voltage too high |
| 27 | P1297 | No change in MAP from start to run |
| 28 | P0320 | No crank reference signal at PCM |
| 2A | P0352 | Ignition coil #2 primary circuits |
| 2B | P0351 | Ignition coil #1 primary circuits |
| 2C | P1389 | No ASD relay output voltage at PCM |
| 2E | P0401 | EGR system failure |
| 30 | P1697 | PCM failure SRI miles not stored |
| 31 | P1696 | PCM failure; EEPROM write denied |
| 39 | P0112 | Intake air temperature sensor voltage low |
| 3A | P0113 | Intake air temperature sensor voltage high |
| 3C | P0106 | Barometric pressure out of range |
| 3D | P0204 | Injector #4 control circuit |
| 3E | P0132 | Right rear upstream O2S shorted to voltage |
| 44 | P0600 | PCM failure, SPI communications |
| 52 | P1683 | S/C power relay circuit |
| 65 | P1282 | Fuel pump relay control circuit |
| 66 | P0133 | Right bank upstream O2S slow response |
| 67 | P0135 | Right rear upstream O2S heater failure |
| 69 | P0141 | Right rear downstream O2S heater failure |
| 6A | P0300 | Multiple cylinder misfire |
| 6B | P0301 | Cylinder #1 misfire |
| 6C | P0302 | Cylinder #2 misfire |
| 6D | P0303 | Cylinder #3 misfire |

89714C03

**Fig. 84 Diagnostic trouble code chart (1 of 2)—1998–99 engines**

## 1998-99 DIAGNOSTIC TROUBLE CODE (DTC) APPLICATIONS

| Hex Code | Scan Tool Code | DRB Scan Tool Display |
|---|---|---|
| 6E | P0304 | Cylinder #4 misfire |
| 70 | P0420 | Right rear catalyst efficiency failure |
| 71 | P0441 | Incorrect purge flow |
| 72 | P1899 | P/N switch stuck in park or in gear |
| 73 | P0551 | Power steering switch failure |
| 76 | P0172 | Right rear fuel system rich |
| 77 | P0171 | Right rear fuel system lean |
| 7E | P0138 | Right rear downstream O2S shorted to voltage |
| 80 | P0125 | Closed loop temperature not reached |
| 81 | P0140 | Right rear downstream O2S stays at center |
| 84 | P0121 | TPS voltage does not agree with MAP |
| 85 | P1390 | Timing belt skipped 1 tooth or more |
| 8A | P1294 | Target idle not reached |
| 91 | P1299 | Vacuum leak found (IAC fully seated) |
| 92 | P1496 | 5 volt supply output too low |
| 94 | P0740 | Torque converter clutch no rpm drop at lockup |
| 95 | P0462 | Fuel level sending unit voltage too low |
| 96 | P0463 | Fuel level sending unit voltage too high |
| 97 | P0460 | Fuel level unit no change over miles |
| 98 | P0703 | Brake switch stuck, pressed or released |
| 99 | P1493 | Ambient battery temperature sensor voltage too low |
| 9A | P1492 | Ambient battery temperature sensor voltage too high |
| 9B | P0131 | Right rear upstream O2S shorted to ground |
| 9C | P0137 | Right rear downstream O2S shorted to ground |
| 9D | P1391 | Intermittent loss of CMP or CKP |
| A0 | P0442 | Evap leak monitor; small leak detected |
| A1 | P0455 | Evap leak monitor; large leak detected |
| B7 | P1495 | Leak detection pump solenoid circuit |
| B8 | P1494 | Leak detect pump switch or mechanical fault |
| BA | P1398 | Misfire adaptive numerator at limit |
| BB | P1486 | Evap hose pinched |
| C0 | P1195 | Catalyst monitor slow O2 upstream |

89714C04

**Fig. 85 Diagnostic trouble code chart (2 of 2)—1998–99 engines**

2. Turn the ignition switch **ON**, and access the "Read Fault" screen with the scan tool.

3. Record all of the DTC's and "freeze frame" information shown on the scan tool.

## READING CODES USING MIL (CHECK ENGINE) LAMP

➡**Be advised that the MIL or CHECK ENGINE light can only perform a limited number of functions and it is a good idea to have the system checked with a scan tool to double check the circuit function.**

1. Within a period of 5 seconds, cycle the ignition key **ON–OFF–ON–OFF–ON**.

2. Count the number of times the MIL (check engine lamp) on the instrument panel flashes on and off. The number of flashes represents the trouble code. There is a short pause between the flashes representing the

1st and 2nd digits of the code. Longer pauses are used to separate individual 2-digit trouble codes.

An example of a flashed DTC is as follows:
- Lamp flashes 4 times, pauses, then flashes 6 more times. This denotes a DTC number 46.
- Lamp flashes 5 times, pauses, then flashes 5 more times. This indicates a DTC number 55. DTC 55 will always be the last code to be displayed.

### Clearing Codes

Erase the DTC's with Chrysler's DRB® or equivalent scan tool, using the "Erase Trouble Code" data screen on the scan tool. Do NOT erase any DTC's until the malfunctions have been checked and repairs been performed.

### VACUUM DIAGRAMS

Following are vacuum diagrams for most of the engine and emissions package combinations covered by this manual. Because vacuum circuits will vary based on various engine and vehicle options, always refer first to the vehicle emission control information label, if present. Should the label be missing, or should vehicle be equipped with a different engine from the

vehicle's original equipment, refer to the diagrams below for the same or similar configuration.

If you wish to obtain a replacement emissions label, most manufacturers make the labels available for purchase. The labels can usually be ordered from a local dealer.

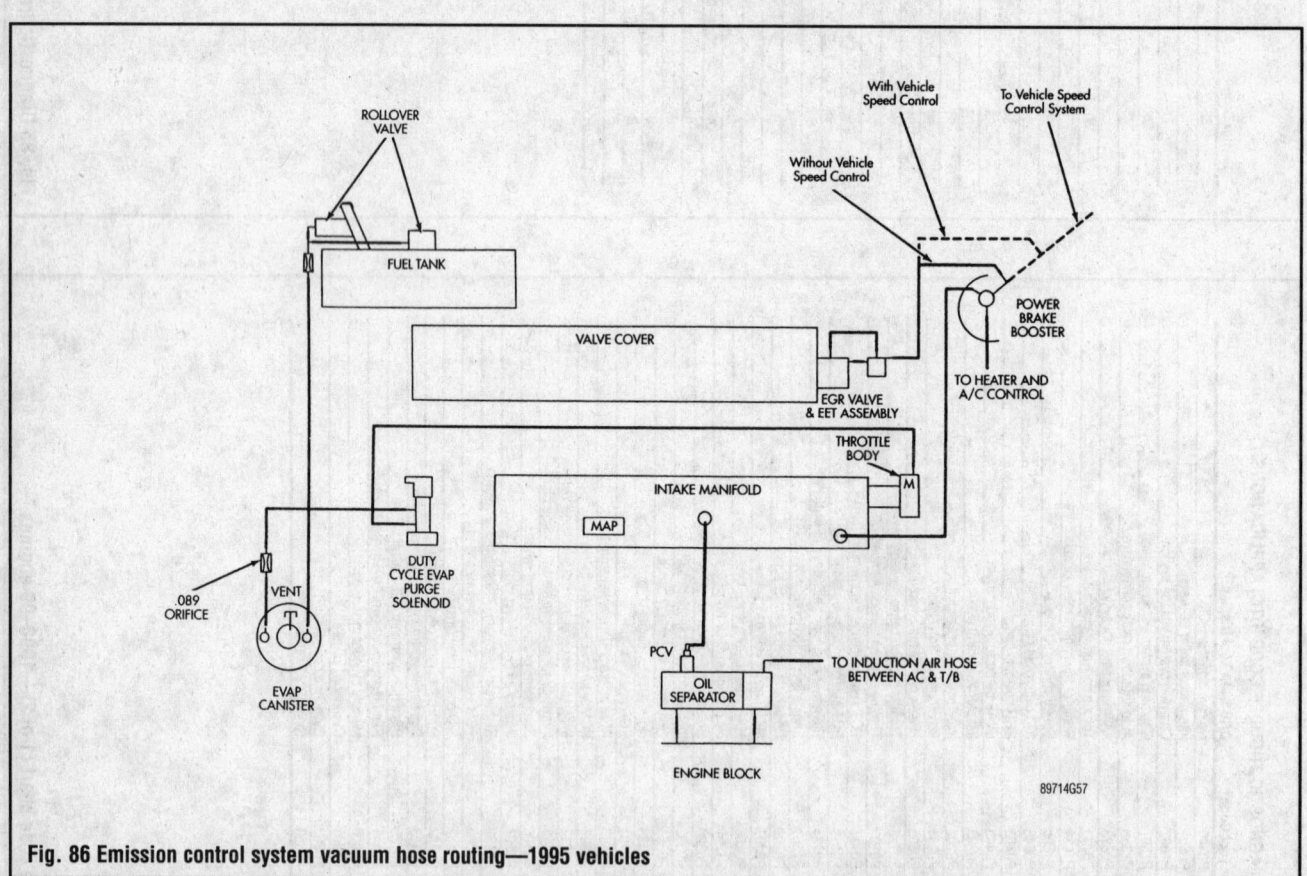

**Fig. 86 Emission control system vacuum hose routing—1995 vehicles**

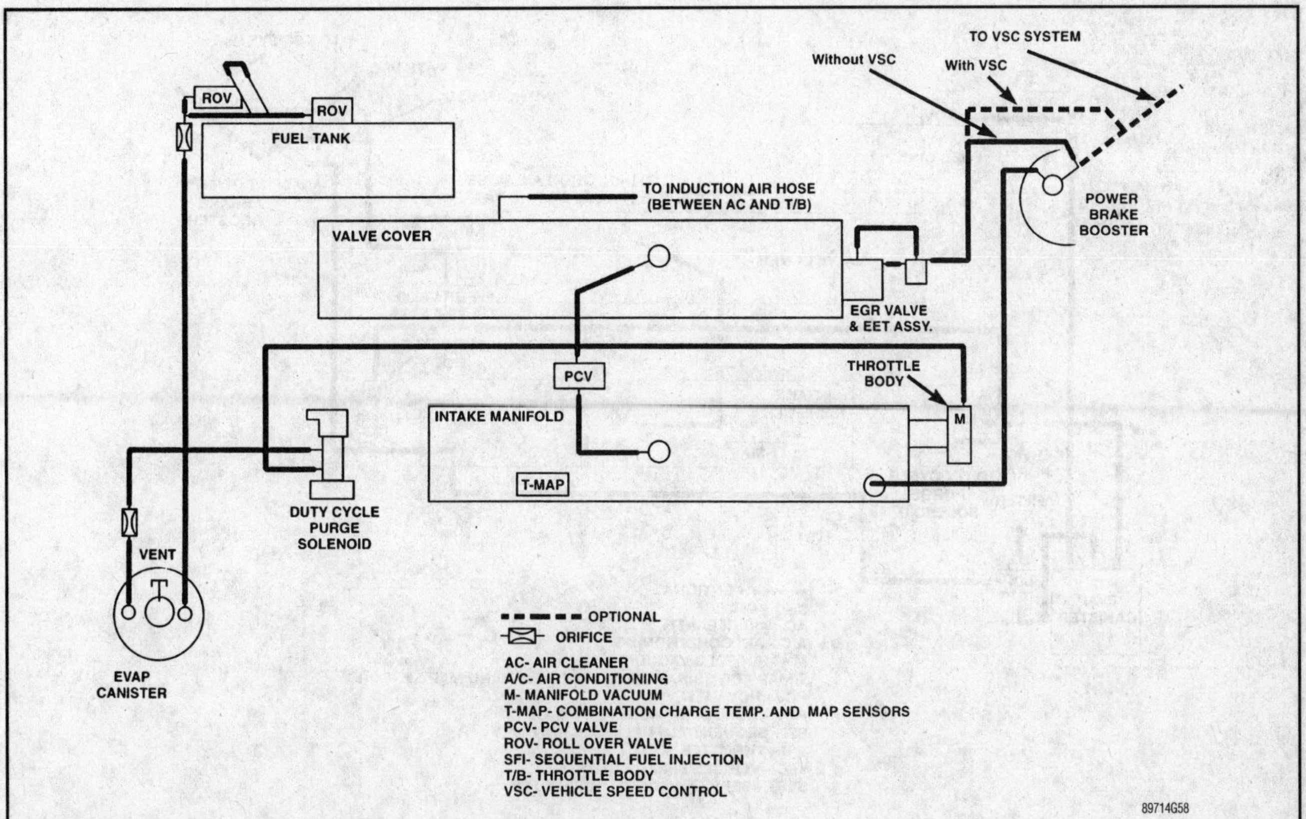

Fig. 87 Emission control system vacuum hose routing—1996 SOHC engines

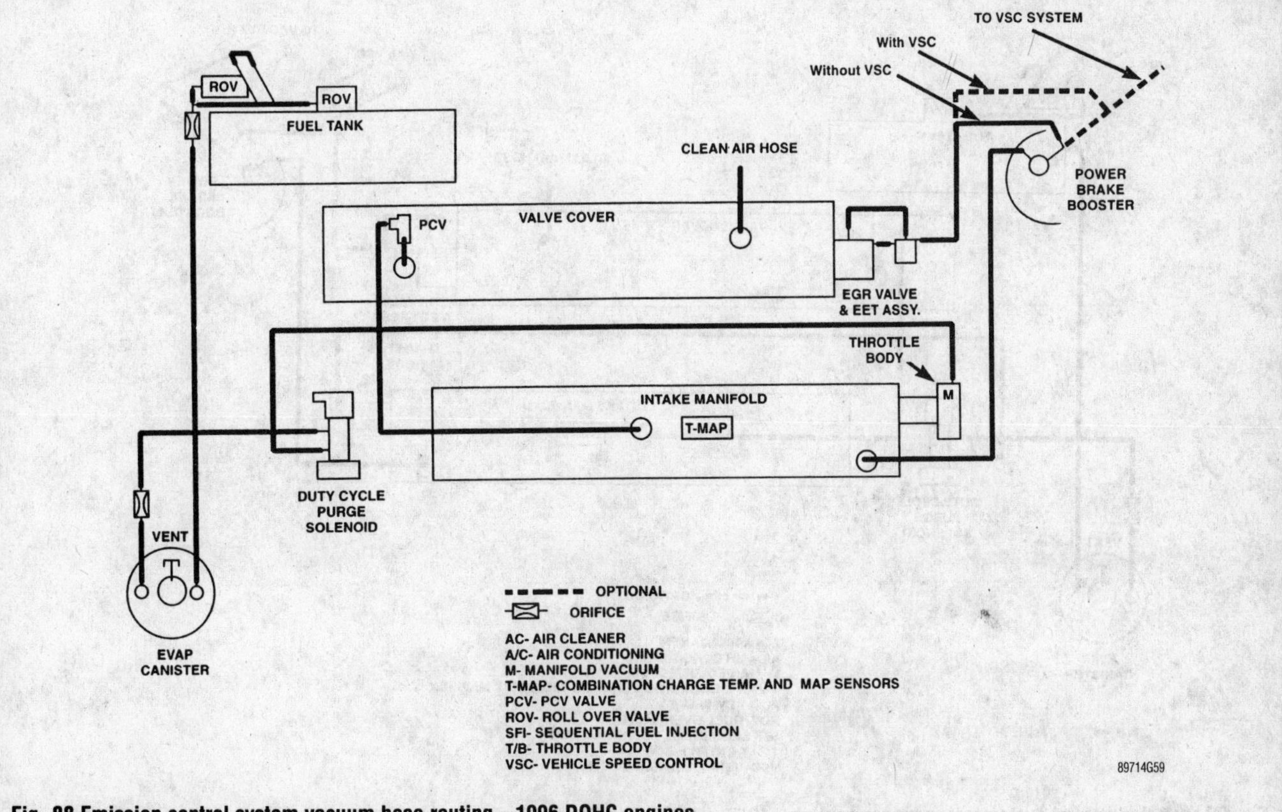

Fig. 88 Emission control system vacuum hose routing—1996 DOHC engines

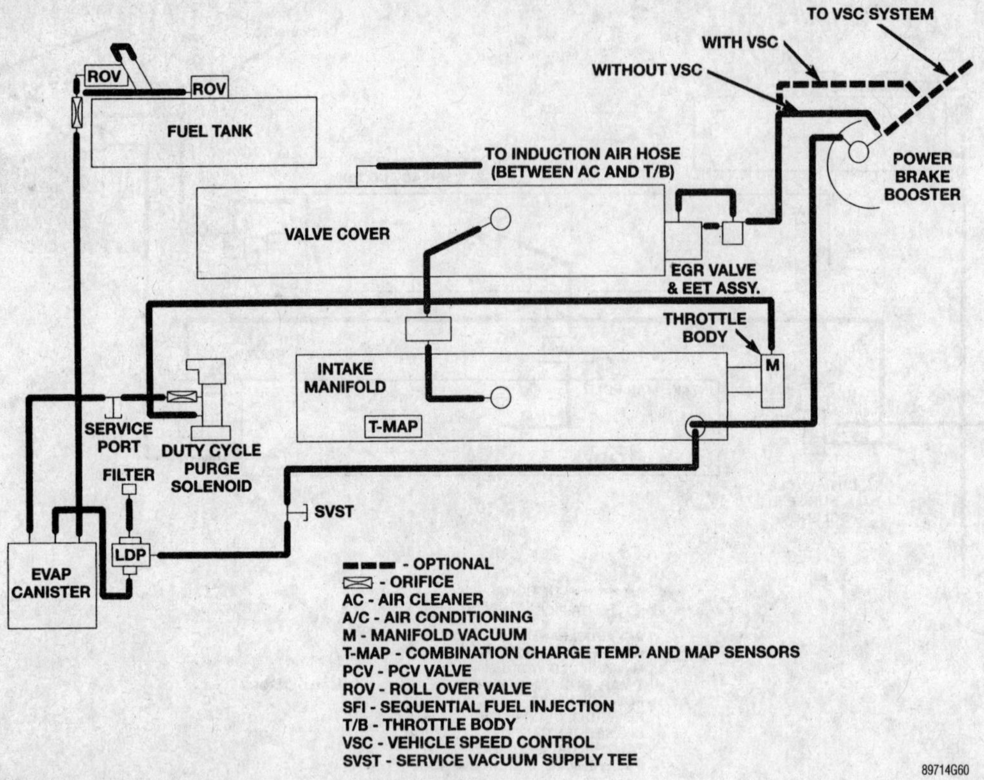

ROV
ROV
FUEL TANK

TO VSC SYSTEM
WITH VSC
WITHOUT VSC
POWER BRAKE BOOSTER

TO INDUCTION AIR HOSE (BETWEEN AC AND T/B)

VALVE COVER

EGR VALVE & EET ASSY.

THROTTLE BODY
M

INTAKE MANIFOLD
T-MAP

SERVICE PORT

DUTY CYCLE PURGE SOLENOID

FILTER

SVST

EVAP CANISTER

LDP

- - - - - OPTIONAL
- ORIFICE
AC - AIR CLEANER
A/C - AIR CONDITIONING
M - MANIFOLD VACUUM
T-MAP - COMBINATION CHARGE TEMP. AND MAP SENSORS
PCV - PCV VALVE
ROV - ROLL OVER VALVE
SFI - SEQUENTIAL FUEL INJECTION
T/B - THROTTLE BODY
VSC - VEHICLE SPEED CONTROL
SVST - SERVICE VACUUM SUPPLY TEE

89714G60

**Fig. 89 Emission control system vacuum hose routing—1997–99 SOHC engines**

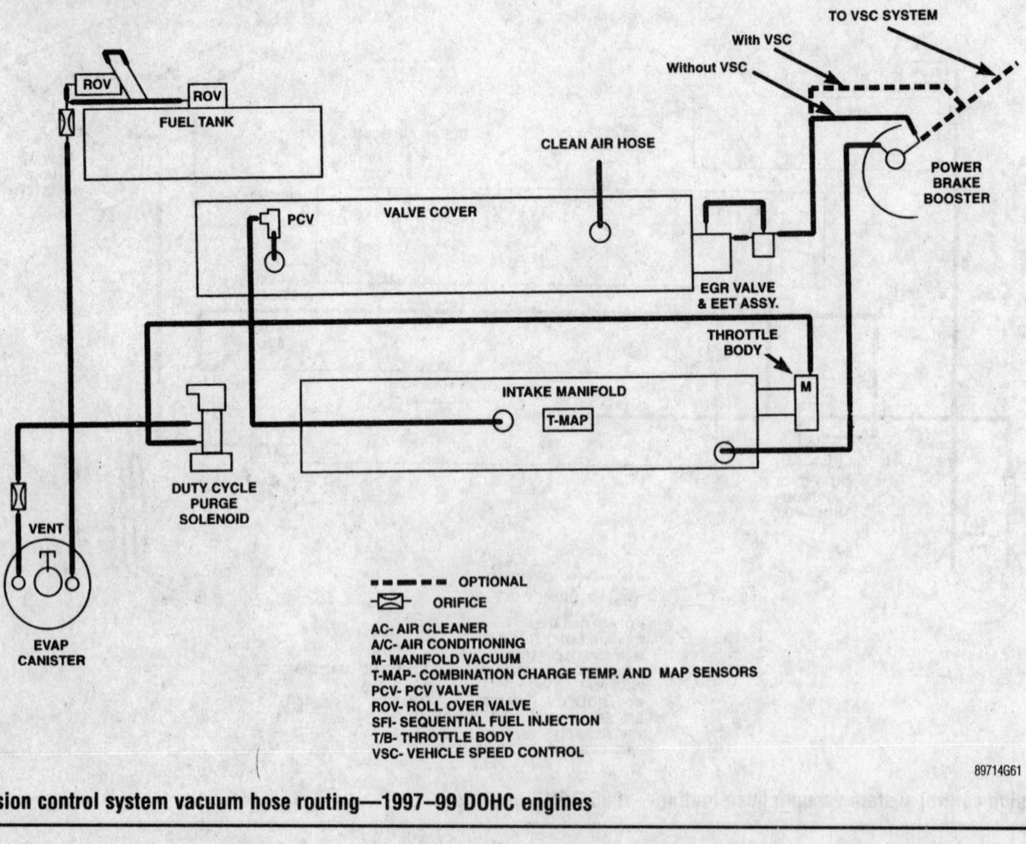

ROV
ROV
FUEL TANK

TO VSC SYSTEM
With VSC
Without VSC
POWER BRAKE BOOSTER

CLEAN AIR HOSE

PCV
VALVE COVER

EGR VALVE & EET ASSY.

THROTTLE BODY
M

INTAKE MANIFOLD
T-MAP

DUTY CYCLE PURGE SOLENOID

VENT

EVAP CANISTER

- - - - - OPTIONAL
- ORIFICE
AC- AIR CLEANER
A/C- AIR CONDITIONING
M- MANIFOLD VACUUM
T-MAP- COMBINATION CHARGE TEMP. AND MAP SENSORS
PCV- PCV VALVE
ROV- ROLL OVER VALVE
SFI- SEQUENTIAL FUEL INJECTION
T/B- THROTTLE BODY
VSC- VEHICLE SPEED CONTROL

89714G61

**Fig. 90 Emission control system vacuum hose routing—1997–99 DOHC engines**

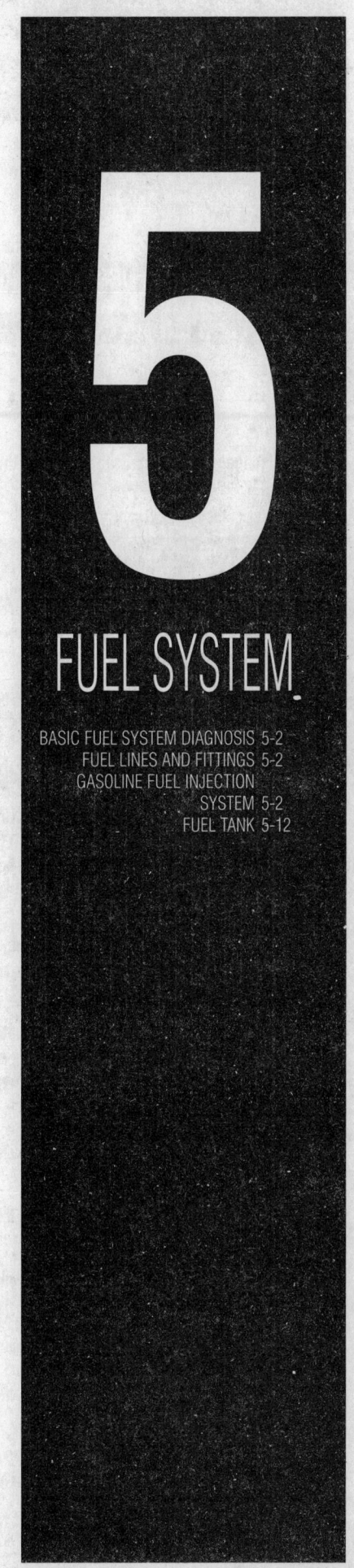

# 5

# FUEL SYSTEM

## BASIC FUEL SYSTEM DIAGNOSIS

When there is a problem starting or driving a vehicle, two of the most important checks involve the ignition and the fuel systems. The questions most mechanics attempt to answer first, "is there spark?" and "is there fuel?" will often lead to solving most basic problems. For ignition system diagnosis and testing, please refer to the information on engine electrical components and ignition systems found earlier in this manual. If the ignition system checks out (there is spark), then you must determine if the fuel system is operating properly (is there fuel?).

## FUEL LINES AND FITTINGS

### Quick-Connect Fittings

REMOVAL & INSTALLATION

♦ See Figure 1

➡ When disengaging a quick-connect fitting, the retainer will remain on the fuel tube nipple.

1. Disconnect the negative battery cable.

### ✺ CAUTION

**You MUST relieve the fuel system pressure before disconnecting any quick-connect fittings.**

2. Properly relieve the fuel system pressure, as outlined later in this section.
3. Squeeze the retainer tabs together and pull the fuel tube/quick-connect fitting assembly off of the fuel tube nipple. The retainer will remain on the tube.
**To install:**

### ✺ WARNING

**Never install a quick-connect fitting without the retainer being either on the fuel tube or already in the quick-connect fitting. In either case, make sure the retainer locks securely into the quick-connect fitting by firmly pulling on the fuel tube and fitting to ensure it is fastened.**

4. Using a clean, lint free cloth, clean the fuel tube nipple and retainer.
5. Before connecting the fitting to the fuel tube, coat the tube nipple with clean 30 weight engine oil.

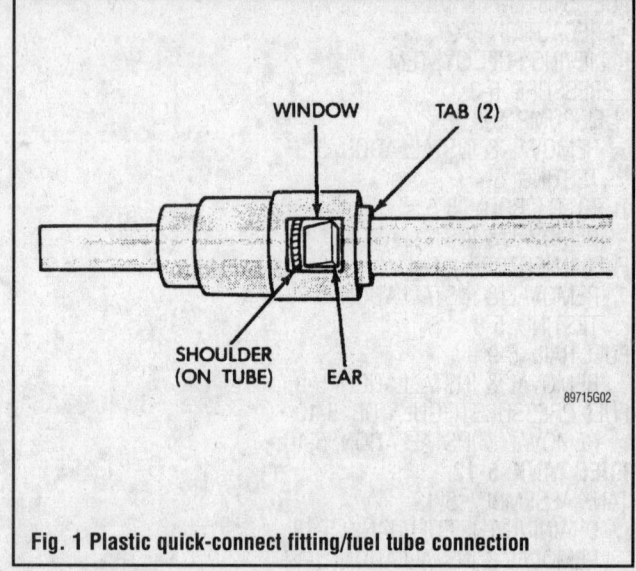

**Fig. 1 Plastic quick-connect fitting/fuel tube connection**

6. Push the quick-connect fitting over the fuel tube until the retainer seats and a click is heard.
7. The plastic quick-connect fitting has windows in the sides of the casing. When the fitting completely attaches to the fuel tube, the retainer locking ears and the fuel tube shoulder are visible in the windows. If they are not visible, the retainer was not installed properly. Do NOT count on the audible click to confirm a secure connection.
8. Use a DRB or equivalent scan tool to pressurize the fuel system and check for leaks.

## GASOLINE FUEL INJECTION SYSTEM

### General Information

The Multi-port Fuel Injection (MFI) system is electronically controlled by the Powertrain Control Module (PCM), based on data from various sensors. The PCM controls the fuel flow, idle speed and ignition timing.

Fuel is supplied to the injectors by an electric in-tank fuel pump and is distributed to the respective injectors via the main fuel pipe. The fuel pressure applied to the injector is constant and higher than the pressure in the intake manifold. The pressure is controlled by the fuel pressure regulator. The excess fuel is returned to the fuel tank through the fuel return pipe.

When an electric current flows in the injector, the injector valve is fully opened to supply fuel. Since the fuel pressure is constant, the amount of the fuel injected from the injector into the manifold is increased or decreased in proportion to the time the electric current flows. Based on PCM signals, the injectors inject fuel to the cylinder manifold ports in firing order.

Air enters the air intake plenum or manifold through the throttle body. In the intake manifold, the air is mixed with the fuel from the injectors and is drawn into the cylinder. The air flow rate is controlled according to the degree of the throttle valve and the servo motor openings.

The system is monitored through a number of sensors which feed information on engine conditions and requirements to the PCM. The PCM calculates the injection time and rate according to the signals from the sensors.

### Fuel System Service Precaution

Safety is an important factor when servicing the fuel system. Failure to conduct maintenance and repairs in a safe manner may result in serious personal injury. Maintenance and testing of the vehicle's fuel system components can be accomplished safely and effectively by adhering to the following rules and guidelines.

• To avoid the possibility of fire and personal injury, always disconnect the negative battery cable unless the repair or test procedure requires that battery voltage be applied.

• Always relieve the fuel system pressure prior to disconnecting any fuel system component (injector, fuel rail, pressure regulator, etc.), fitting or fuel line connection. Exercise extreme caution whenever relieving fuel system pressure to avoid exposing skin, face and eyes to fuel spray. Please be advised that fuel under pressure may penetrate the skin or any part of the body that it contacts.

• Always place a shop towel or cloth around the fitting or connection prior to loosening to absorb any excess fuel due to spillage. Ensure that all fuel spillage is quickly removed from engine surfaces. Ensure that all fuel soaked cloths or towels are deposited into a suitable waste container.

• Always keep a dry chemical (Class B) fire extinguisher near the work area.

• Do not allow fuel spray or fuel vapors to come into contact with a spark or open flame.

• Always use a backup wrench when loosening and tightening fuel line connection fittings. This will prevent unnecessary stress and torsion to fuel line piping. Always follow the proper torque specifications.

• Always replace worn fuel fitting O-rings. Do not substitute fuel hose where fuel pipe is installed.

## Relieving Fuel System Pressure

▶ See Figures 2 and 3

### ※※ CAUTION

**You MUST relieve the fuel system pressure before servicing any components of the fuel system. Service vehicles in well ventilated areas and avoid ignition sources. NEVER smoke while servicing the vehicle!**

1. Disconnect the negative battery cable.
2. Remove the fuel filler cap.
3. Remove the protective cap from the fuel pressure port on the fuel rail.

Fig. 2 There is a test port (1) located under a cap you must remove to relieve the fuel pressure

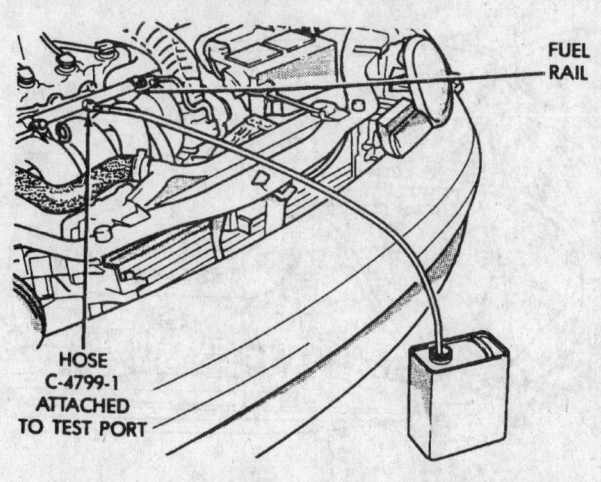

Fig. 3 Relieve the fuel system, allowing the pressure to bleed off through the hose into the container

4. Place the open end of a suitable fuel pressure release hose (tool C-4799-1 or equivalent) into an approved gasoline container. Connect the other end of the hose to the fuel pressure test port. The fuel pressure will bleed off through the hose into the gasoline container.

➡**Fuel pressure gauge kit C-4799-B contains hose C-4799-1.**

5. The vehicle is now safe for servicing.
6. After you are finished working on the fuel system, don't forget to install the fuel filler cap.

## Fuel Pump

The fuel pump is integral with the pump module, which also contains the fuel reservoir, level sensor, inlet strainer and fuel pressure regulator. The inlet strainer, fuel pressure regulator and level sensor are the only serviceable items. If the fuel pump requires service, replace the entire fuel pump module.

### REMOVAL & INSTALLATION

#### 1995 Vehicles

▶ See Figures 4 and 5

1. Disconnect the negative battery cable.
2. Properly relieve the fuel system pressure.
3. Raise and safely support the vehicle.
4. Drain the fuel tank, as outlined under the fuel tank removal and installation procedure.

### ※※ WARNING

**The fuel reservoir of the fuel pump module does not empty out when the tank is drained. The fuel in the reservoir will spill out when the module is removed.**

5. Disconnect the fuel lines from the fuel pump module by depressing the quick-connect retainers with your thumb and fore-finger.
6. Using a hammer and brass drift punch, carefully tap the lock ring counterclockwise to release the pump.
7. Remove the fuel pump and O-ring seal from the tank. Discard the old seal.

**To install:**

8. Wipe the area of the tank clean, then place a new O-ring seal in proper position on the pump.
9. Position the fuel pump in the tank with the locking ring.
10. Using a hammer and brass drift, drive the ring around in a clockwise direction to lock the pump in place.

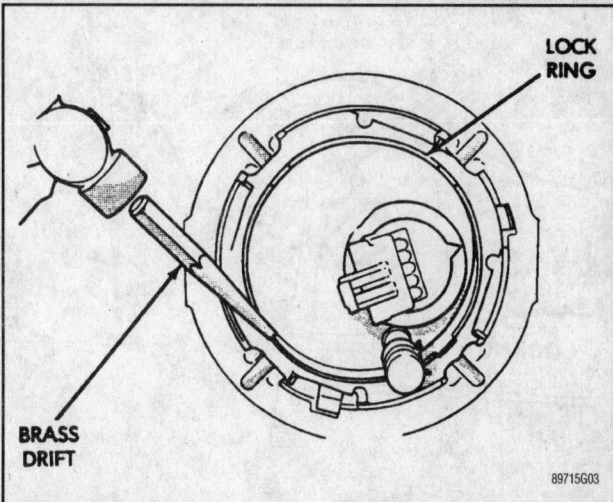

Fig. 4 Carefully tap the lock ring counterclockwise to release the fuel pump

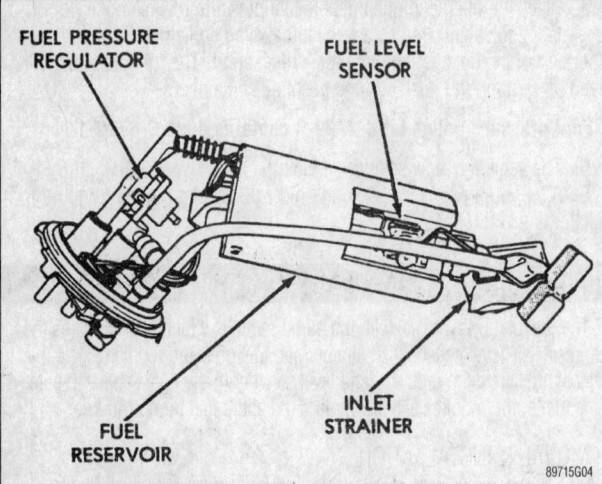

FUEL PRESSURE REGULATOR

FUEL LEVEL SENSOR

INLET STRAINER

FUEL RESERVOIR

89715G04

**Fig. 5 The fuel module assembly contains the pump, pressure regulator, reservoir, inlet strainer and level sensor**

### ✳✳ CAUTION

**Do not overtighten the pump lock ring, as this may cause a fuel leak.**

11. Carefully lower the vehicle.
12. Fill the fuel tank, the check for leaks.
13. Connect the negative battery cable.

#### 1996–99 Vehicles

▶ See Figure 6

1. Disconnect the negative battery cable.
2. Properly relieve the fuel system pressure.
3. Raise and safely support the vehicle.
4. Drain the fuel tank, as outlined under the fuel tank removal and installation procedure.

### ✳✳ WARNING

**The fuel reservoir of the fuel pump module does not empty out when the tank is drained. The fuel in the reservoir will spill out when the module is removed.**

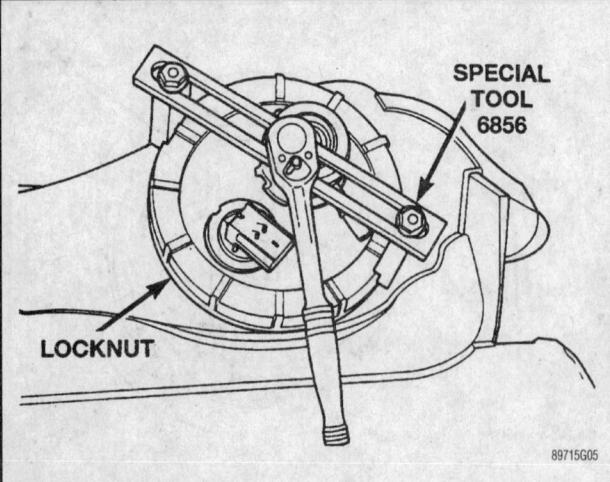

SPECIAL TOOL 6856

LOCKNUT

89715G05

**Fig. 6 To loosen the fuel pump module locknut, use a ratchet and spanner wrench**

5. Disconnect the fuel lines from the fuel pump module by depressing the quick-connect retainers with your thumb and fore-finger.
6. Slide the fuel pump module electrical lock to unlock it.
7. Detach the electrical connection from the fuel pump module, by pushing down on the connector retainer and pulling the connector off of the module.
8. Use a transmission jack to safely support the fuel tank, then remove the bolts from the fuel tank straps.
9. Carefully lower the tank slightly for access to the module.
10. Use a ratchet and spanner wrench to remove the fuel pump module locknut.
11. Remove the fuel pump and O-ring seal from the tank. Discard the old seal.

**To install:**

12. Wipe the area of the tank clean, then place a new O-ring seal in position in the tank opening.
13. Position the fuel pump in the tank. Make sure the alignment tab on the underside of the fuel pump module flange sits in the notch on the fuel tank.
14. Position the locknut over the fuel pump module.
15. Using the ratchet and spanner wrench, tighten the locknut to 41 ft. lbs. (55 Nm).
16. Carefully lower the vehicle, then check for leaks.
17. Connect the negative battery cable.

### TESTING

▶ See Figure 7

The fuel pump operates at about 49 psi (338 kPa). The fuel system pressure is checked at the test port on the fuel rail.

1. Remove the cap from the fuel pressure test port on the fuel rail.
2. Connect a suitable fuel pressure gauge to the test port.
3. Unplug the fuel pump connector. Apply 12 volts directly to the fuel pump connector.
4. Note the gauge reading and compare with the following:
• If the gauge reading equals approximately 49 psi (338 kPa), no further testing is required. If the pressure is not correct, record the reading.
• If the fuel pressure is below specifications, check for a restricted fuel pump inlet strainer. If its restricted, replace the inlet strainer. If not restricted, check for an incorrectly operating fuel filter/regulator or fuel pump and replace as necessary.
• If the fuel pressure is above specifications (54 psi or higher), check for a kinked or restricted fuel supply line. If the line is not kinked or restricted, check for a restriction in the chassis fuel supply line or for

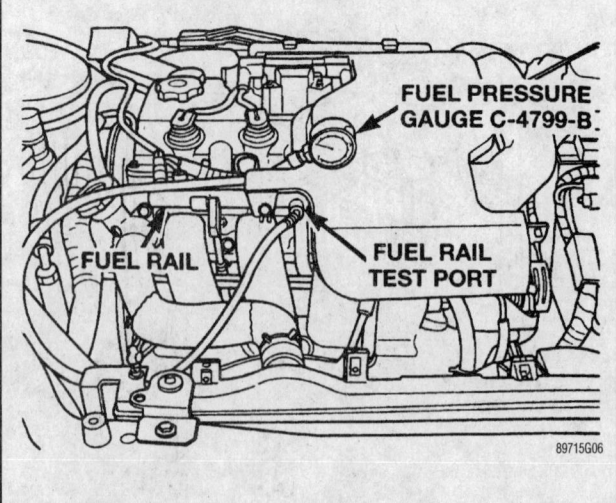

FUEL PRESSURE GAUGE C-4799-B

FUEL RAIL

FUEL RAIL TEST PORT

89715G06

**Fig. 7 Attach a suitable fuel pressure gauge to the test port**

kinked or plugged fuel supply line. If none of the lines are restricted, replace the filter/regulator.

5. After the test is complete, remove the test equipment and reconnect the fuel pump harness.

## Throttle Body

### REMOVAL & INSTALLATION

▶ See Figures 8 thru 20

1. Disconnect the negative battery cable.
2. Remove the retaining bolts, then remove the throttle body cable cover.
3. For vehicles with manual transaxles, perform the following to remove the throttle cables:
   a. Remove the throttle cable from the throttle body cam.
   b. Compress the retaining tabs on the cable, then slide the cable out of the bracket.
   c. If equipped with cruise control, remove the speed control cable from the throttle lever by sliding the clasp out of the hole used for the throttle cable.

4. For vehicles with automatic transaxles, perform the following to remove the throttle cables:
   a. Remove the throttle cable from the throttle body cam.
   b. Compress the retaining tabs on the cable and slide the cable out of the bracket.
   c. Hold the throttle lever in the wide open position. Using finger-pressure only, remove the kickdown cable by PUSHING the connector off of the lever nail head. DO NOT attempt to pull the connector off perpendicular to the lever.
   d. Compress the retaining tabs on the cable and slide the cable out of the bracket.
   e. If equipped with cruise control, hold the throttle lever in the wide open position. Using finger pressure only, remove the speed control cable by PUSHING the connector off the lever nail head. DO NOT try to pull the connector off perpendicular to the lever.
   f. Compress the retaining tabs on the cable, then slide the cable out of the bracket.

5. Remove the 2 screws holding the cable mounting bracket and support bracket.
6. Remove the throttle body mounting bolts.
7. Disconnect the EVAP purge hose.

Fig. 8 Unfasten the throttle body cable cover retaining bolts . . .

Fig. 10 Pull the throttle cable forward to create some slack in the line

Fig. 9 . . . then lift the cover up and off the throttle body for access to the cables

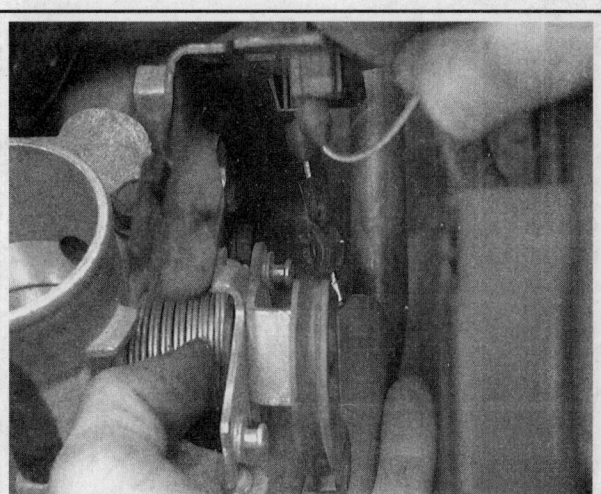
Fig. 11 Unhook the cable clasp from the throttle lever, then push the transmission kickdown cable off of the head

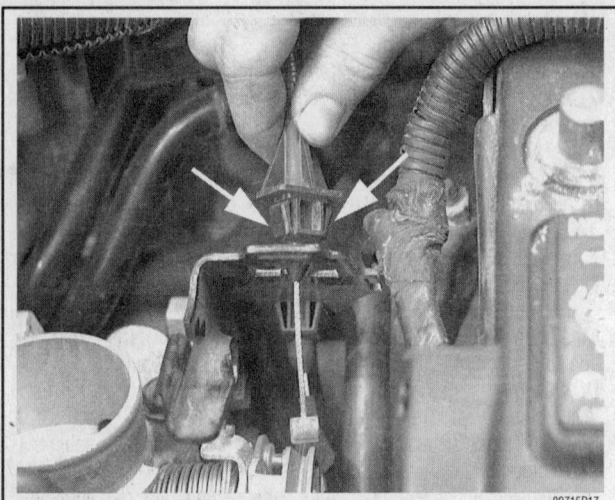

Fig. 12 Compress the cable retaining tabs (see arrows), then slide the cable out of the bracket

Fig. 15 Remove the 2 throttle body mounting bolts

Fig. 13 Remove the 2 cable and support mounting bracket retaining bolts . . .

Fig. 16 Don't forget to disconnect any hoses necessary for throttle body removal

Fig. 14 . . . then remove the bracket from the throttle body

Fig. 17 In order to unplug the TPS and IAC connectors, partially lift the throttle body up . . .

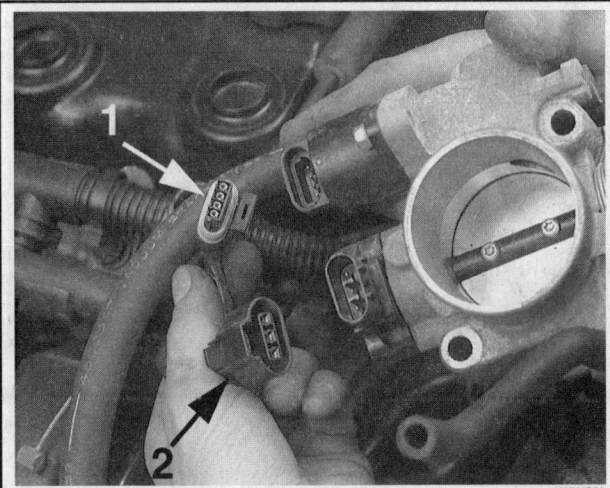

Fig. 18 . . . then detach the IAC valve (1) and TPS connectors (2) and remove the throttle body from the intake manifold

Fig. 19 Remove and inspect the throttle body gasket. If it is in good condition, you can reuse it

Fig. 20 The TPS (1) and IAC valve (2) are mounted to the side of the throttle body

8. Partially lift the throttle body, detach the IAC valve and TPS electrical connectors, then remove the throttle body from the vehicle.

9. The rubber O-ring is reusable, so wipe it clean and inspect it. If it's in good condition, you can reinstall it. If not, replace it with a new one.

**To install:**

10. Attach the electrical connection(s) to the throttle body.

11. Position the throttle body on the intake manifold. Install the mounting bolts and tighten to 9 ft. lbs. (12 Nm).

12. Attach the cable mounting bracket and support bracket and secure with the 2 mounting screws.

13. Connect the EVAP purge hose.

14. Install the cable housing(s) retainer tabs into the bracket.

15. Install the throttle cables, using the following procedures:

   a. From the engine compartment, rotate the throttle lever forward to the wide open position and install the throttle cable clasp.

   b. If equipped with cruise control, rotate the throttle lever forward to the wide open throttle position and slide the speed control cable connector onto the nail head.

   c. Rotate the throttle lever forward to the wide open position and slide the kickdown cable connector onto the nail head.

16. Install the throttle cable cover and tighten the retaining bolt(s) to 50 inch lbs. (5.6 Nm).

17. Connect the negative battery cable.

## Fuel Injector(s)

### REMOVAL & INSTALLATION

▶ See Figures 21 thru 26

1. Disconnect the negative battery cable.

2. Properly relieve the fuel system pressure.

3. Remove the fuel rail, as outlined later in this section.

4. Unfasten the fuel injector-to-rail retaining clip, then pull the fuel injector out of the rail.

5. Use a small awl to carefully remove the O-rings from each end of the injector. Discard the O-rings and replace with new ones during installation.

**To install:**

6. Install new O-rings on each end of the injector.

7. Lightly coat the upper O-ring of the injector with clean engine oil.

8. Install the injector in the cup on the fuel rail, then secure with the retaining clip.

9. Install the fuel rail, as outlined later in this section.

10. Connect the negative battery cable.

Fig. 21 Remove the injector-to-fuel rail retaining clip . . .

Fig. 22 . . . then pull the fuel injector up and out of the fuel rail

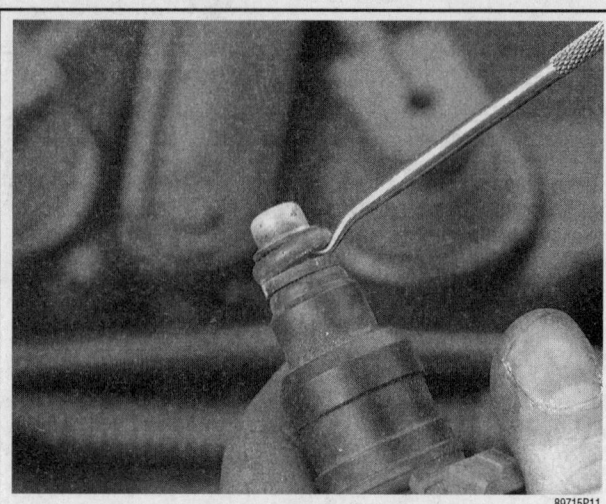

Fig. 25 Use an awl to carefully remove the O-ring from the top end of the fuel injector

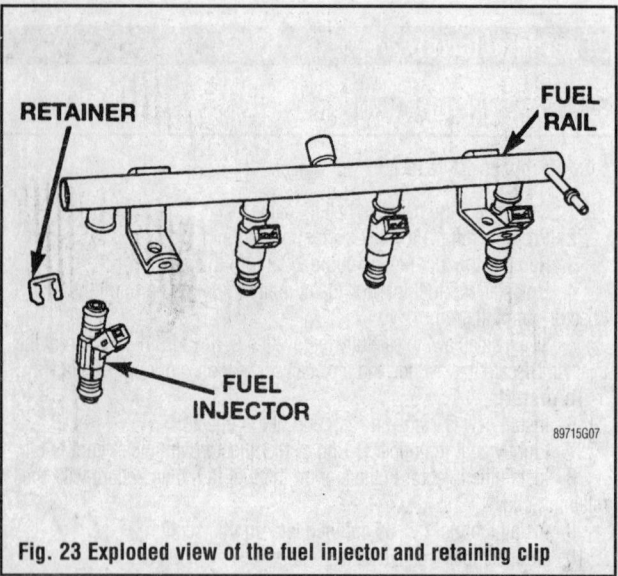

Fig. 23 Exploded view of the fuel injector and retaining clip

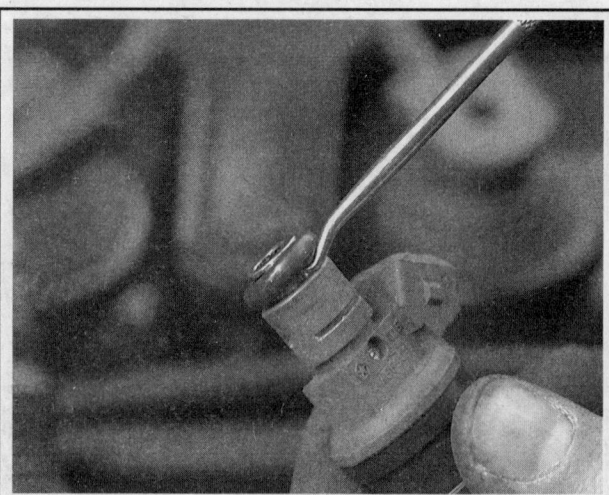

Fig. 26 Don't forget to remove the O-ring from the bottom end of the injector

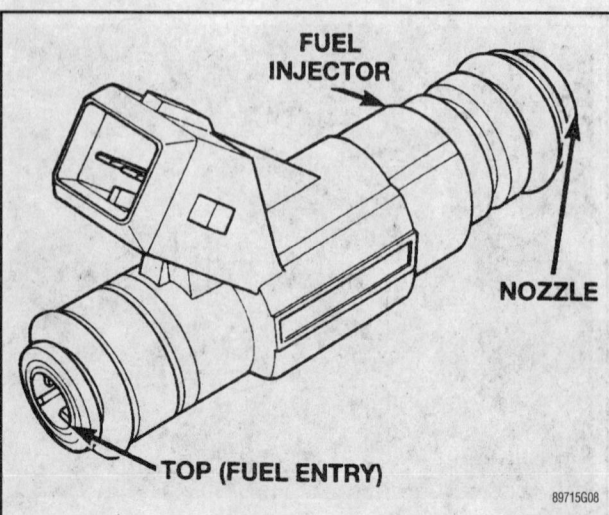

Fig. 24 The fuel injector has O-rings at each end which must be replaced before installation

## TESTING

### ▶ See Figure 27

1. Unplug the injector electrical connector.
2. Using an ohmmeter, test the injector resistance across the injector terminals. The reading should be approximately 12 ohms at 68°F (20°C).
   a. If the resistance falls outside specifications, replace the faulty injector.
   b. If the resistance is within specifications, proceed with the testing.
3. Place a 12 volt test lamp across injector electrical connector terminals. Watch the test lamp while cranking the engine and compare with the following:
   a. If the test lamp does not flash, check the power feed and ground circuits between the PCM and the injector connector. Refer to the wiring diagrams in Section 6 for wire colors. If the circuits are faulty, repair them. If the circuits are OK, test the engine control system should be tested.
   b. If the test lamp flashes, proceed with the testing.
4. Check for fuel delivery at the suspect injector by removing the injector from the fuel rail and check for fuel and/or restrictions in the rail or injector fuel inlet. Compare your results with the following:

Fig. 27 Connect an ohmmeter to the fuel injector terminals and measure the resistance

a. If there is no fuel present at the injector, replace the plugged injector, or clean the restricted passage, as necessary.

b. If there is fuel present at the injector, proceed with the testing.

5. With the injector removed from the fuel rail, connect a 12 volt source to one terminal on the injector connector and a ground wire to the other terminal. The injector should "click" each time the ground wire is connected and disconnected to and from the terminal.

6. If the injector "clicks", it is OK. If it does not "click" it must be replaced.

## Fuel Rail

### REMOVAL & INSTALLATION

▶ **See Figures 28 thru 34**

1. Disconnect the negative battery cable.
2. Properly relieve the fuel system pressure, as outlined earlier in this section.
3. Unfasten the wiring harness retainer from the fuel rail bracket. Unplug the fuel injector electrical connectors.

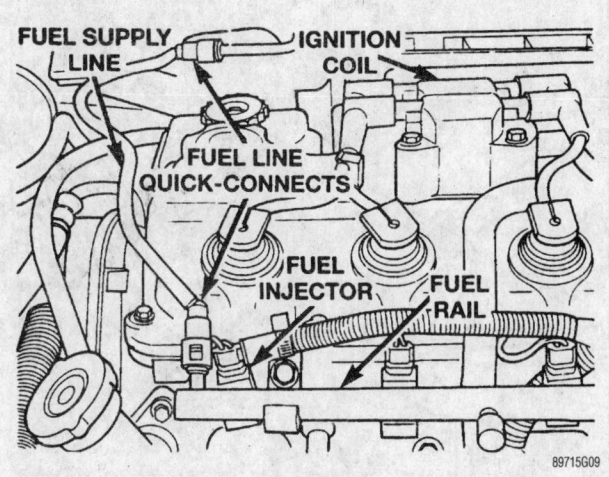

Fig. 28 Location of the fuel rail, injectors and related components

Fig. 29 Unclip the wiring harness retainer from the fuel rail bracket

Fig. 30 Detach the fuel injector electrical connectors

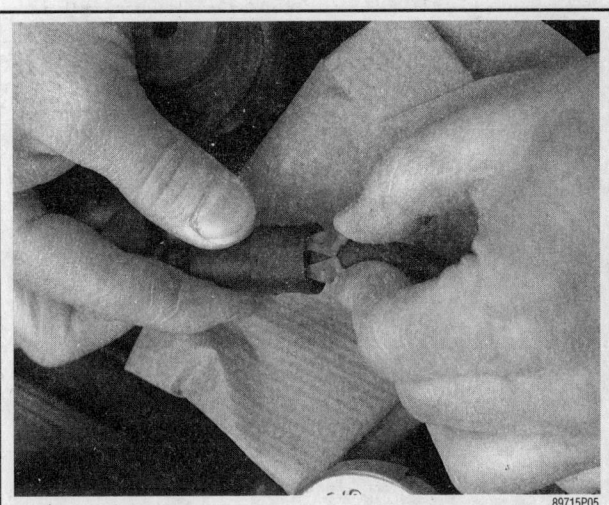

Fig. 31 Place a towel under the quick-connect fitting, then squeeze the tabs . . .

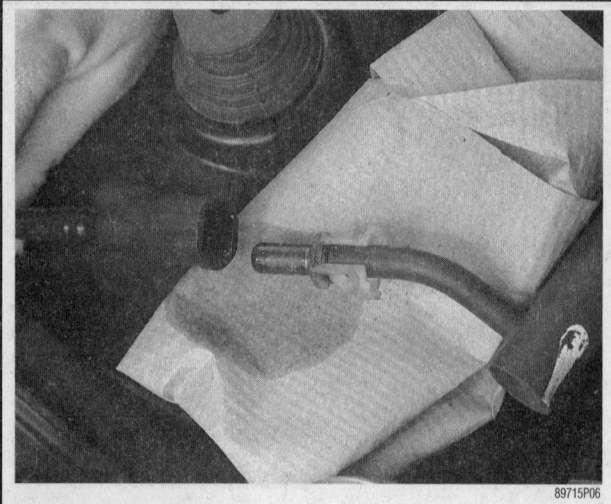

Fig. 32 . . . and separate the quick-connect fuel line fitting

Fig. 33 Remove the fuel rail assembly retaining bolts . . .

Fig. 34 . . . then pull up on the fuel rail while twisting the injectors to remove the rail from the vehicle

4. Place a shop rag under the quick-connect fitting, then disconnect the fuel supply tube from the fuel rail.

5. Unfasten the fuel rail assembly retaining bolts, then lift the fuel rail off the intake manifold. You have to pull up on the rail while twisting the injectors to the remove the rail from the vehicle.

6. Cover the fuel rail injector openings in the intake manifold to prevent debris from entering while the rail is removed.

**To install:**

7. Apply a light coating of clean engine oil to the O-ring on the nozzle end of each injector. Remove the covering from the injector openings.

8. Insert the fuel injector nozzles into the openings in the intake manifold. Seat the injectors in place. Tighten the fuel rail mounting screws to 15–17 ft. lbs. (20–23 Nm).

9. Attach the electrical connectors to the fuel injectors.

10. Attach the quick-connect fuel supply line to the fuel rail, as outlined earlier in this section.

11. Connect the negative battery cable.

## Fuel Pressure Regulator

### REMOVAL & INSTALLATION

#### 1995 Vehicles

♦ See Figures 35, 36 and 37

The fuel pressure regulator is part of the fuel pump module. Remove the module from the fuel tank for access to the regulator.

1. Disconnect the negative battery cable.

2. Properly relieve the fuel system pressure.

3. Remove the fuel pump module, as outlined earlier in this section.

4. Spread the tabs on the pressure regulator retainer.

5. Use a suitable prytool to carefully pry the regulator out of the housing.

6. Make sure both the upper and lower O-rings were removed with the regulator.

**To install:**

7. Lightly lubricate the O-rings with clean engine oil, then place then into the fuel pump module opening.

8. Push the regulator into the opening in the pump module.

9. Fold the tabs on the regulator retainer over the tabs on the housing.

10. Install the fuel pump module, as outlined earlier in this section.

11. Connect the negative battery cable.

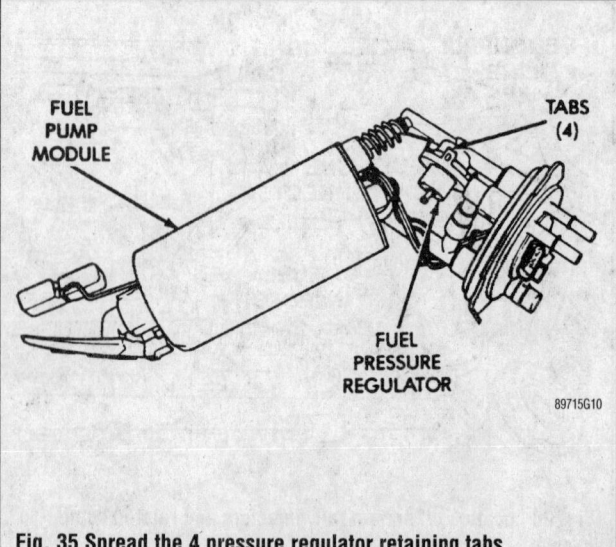

Fig. 35 Spread the 4 pressure regulator retaining tabs . . .

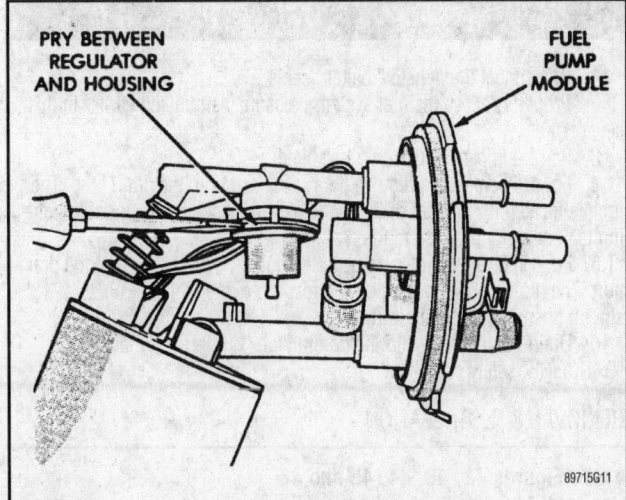

Fig. 36 . . . then carefully pry the pressure regulator from the housing

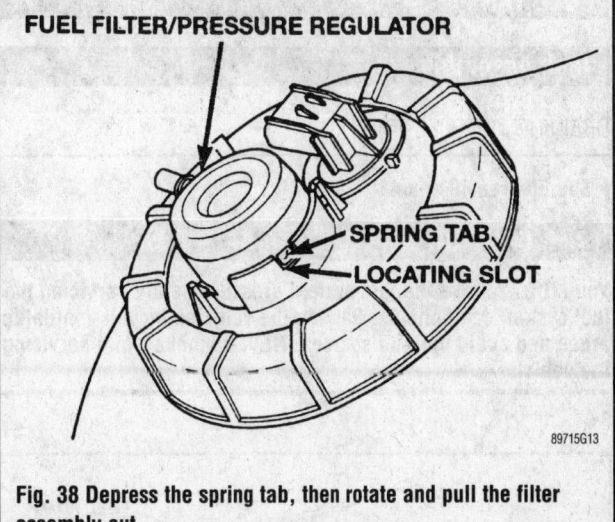

Fig. 38 Depress the spring tab, then rotate and pull the filter assembly out

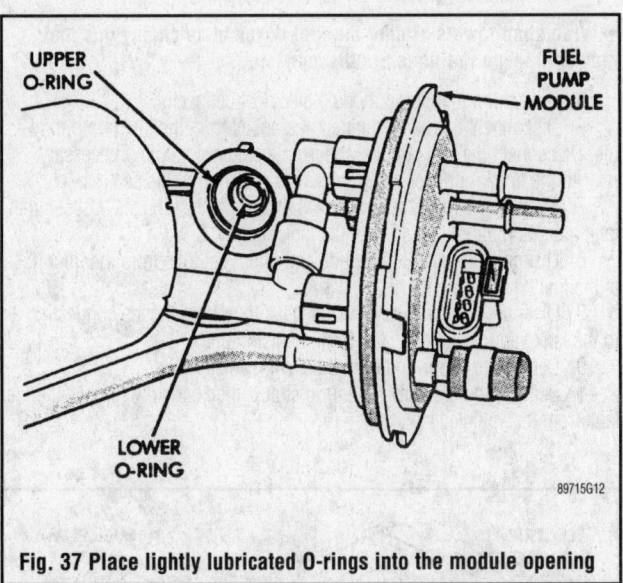

Fig. 37 Place lightly lubricated O-rings into the module opening

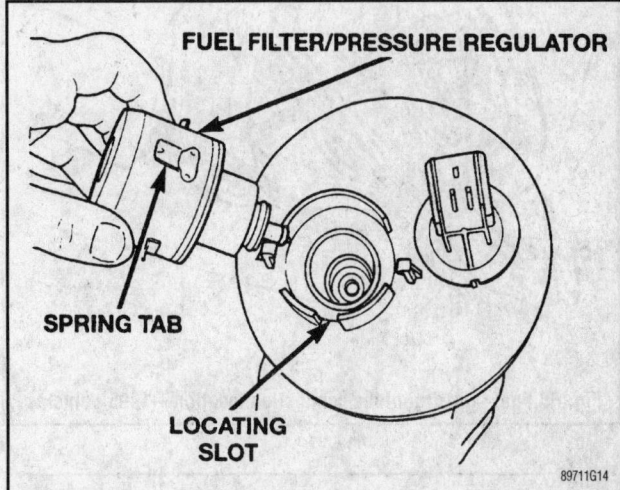

Fig. 39 To install the filter, align the spring tab with the locating slot

## 1996–99 Vehicles

▶ See Figures 38 and 39

➡These vehicles use a integral fuel filter/pressure regulator, mounted on the top of the fuel pump module. Fuel pump module removal is not necessary.

1. Properly relieve the fuel system pressure, as outlined in Section 5 of this manual.
2. If not done already, disconnect the negative battery cable.
3. Raise and safely support the vehicle.
4. Unfasten the quick-connect fuel supply line from the filter/regulator nipple.

5. Depress the locking spring tab, located on the side of the fuel filter/regulator, then rotate 90° and pull out. Make sure the upper and lower O-rings are still on the filter assembly.

**To install:**
6. Lightly coat the filter O-rings with clean engine oil. Insert the filter into the opening in the fuel pump module, then align the 2 hold-down tabs with the flange.
7. While applying downward pressure, rotate the filter clockwise until the spring tab catches in the locating slot.
8. Attach the fuel line to the filter/regulator assembly.
9. Carefully lower the vehicle, the connect the negative battery cable.

## FUEL TANK

### Tank Assembly

DRAINING THE FUEL TANK

♦ **See Figures 40 and 41**

### ✳✳ CAUTION

**You MUST relieve the fuel system pressure before servicing the fuel system components. Service the vehicles in well ventilated areas and avoid ignition sources. NEVER smoke while servicing the vehicle.**

1. Disconnect the negative battery cable.
2. Properly relieve the fuel system pressure, as outlined earlier in this section.
3. Raise and safely support the vehicle.
4. For 1995 vehicles, remove the rubber cap from the drain tube. The tube is located on the rear of the fuel tank. Connect either a portable holding tank or a siphon hose to the drain tube.
5. For 1996–99 vehicles, remove the quick-connect cap from the drain port. The drain port is located on the rear top of the fuel tank. Push a siphon hose into the drain port.
6. Drain the fuel tank into the holding tank or a properly labeled "GASOLINE" safety container.

REMOVAL & INSTALLATION

♦ **See Figures 42, 43, 44, 45 and 46**

1. Disconnect the negative battery cable.
2. Properly relieve the fuel system pressure.
3. Raise and safely support the vehicle.
4. Drain the fuel tank into an approved container.

➡**Wrap shop towels around the fuel hoses to catch any gas that may spill when the lines are disconnected.**

5. Detach the fuel pump module electrical connector.
6. Disconnect the quick-connect fuel tubes from the fuel pump module. Disconnect the fuel supply tube from the chassis tube. If necessary, refer to the quick-connect fitting information earlier in this section.
7. Support the fuel tank securely with a transmission jack. Loosen the tank mounting straps, then lower the tank slightly.
8. Disconnect the fuel filler tube and filler vent tube from the filler hose at the fuel tank.
9. Disconnect the fuel filler vapor relief tube from the tee connecting it to the tank vapor relief tube and EVAP canister tube.
10. Detach the vapor line from the EVAP canister tube.
11. Remove the fuel tank mounting straps, then carefully remove the fuel tank from the vehicle.

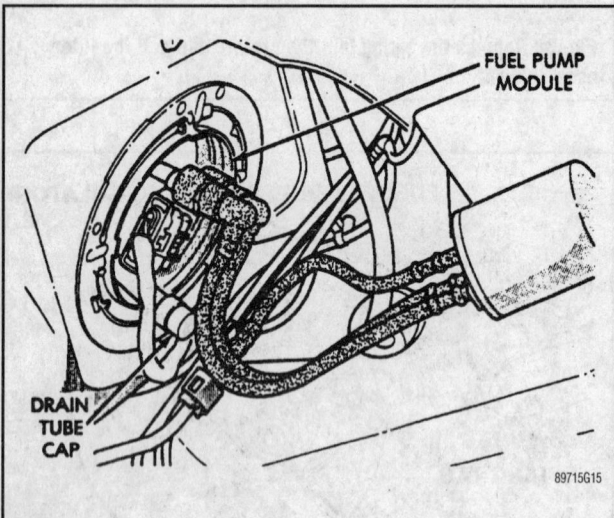

Fig. 40 Fuel tank drain tube connection location—1995 vehicles

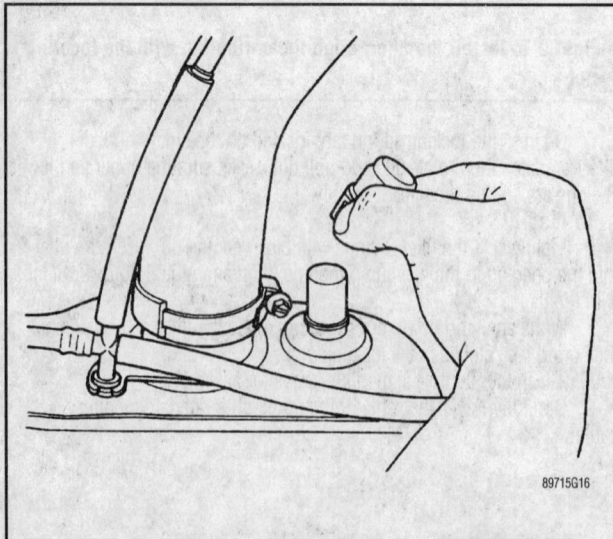

Fig. 41 Location of the fuel tank drain port—1996–99 vehicles

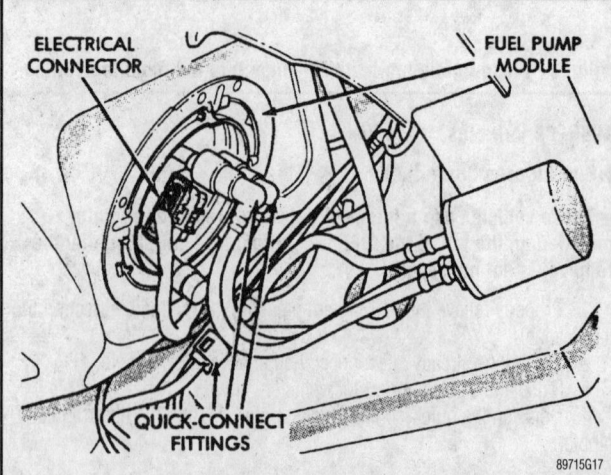

Fig. 42 Location of the fuel pump module electrical connector—1995 vehicle shown

**To install:**

12. Position the fuel tank onto the transmission jack.

13. Raise the tank into position. Connect the fuel filler tube tank inlet nipple.

14. Tighten the fuel tank strap nuts to 17 ft. lbs. (23 Nm). Remove the transmission jack. Make sure the straps are not twisted or bent.

15. Attach the quick-connect fuel tubes to the pump module and chassis fuel tube.

16. Connect the fuel vapor tube to the tee, then to the EVAP canister tube.

17. Attach the fuel pump module electrical connector.

18. Carefully lower the vehicle.

19. Fill the fuel tank, install the filler cap, then connect the negative battery cable.

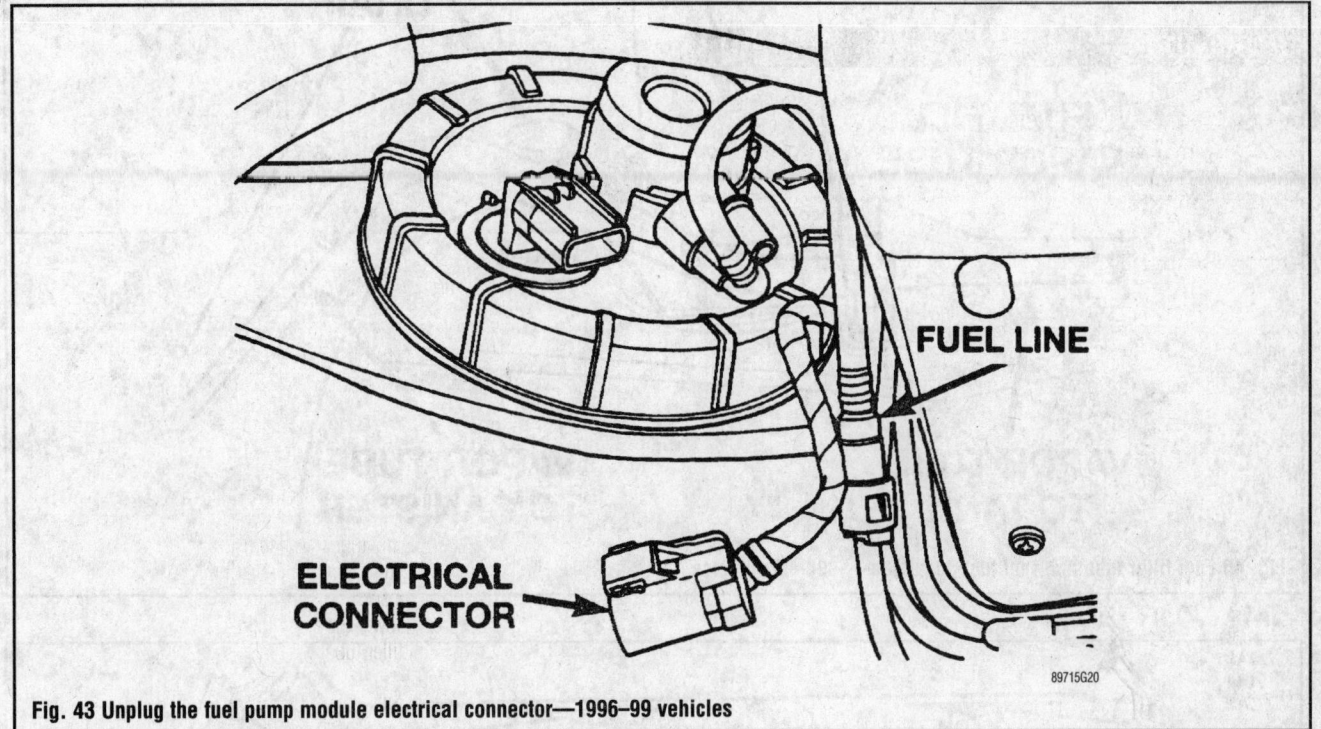

Fig. 43 Unplug the fuel pump module electrical connector—1996–99 vehicles

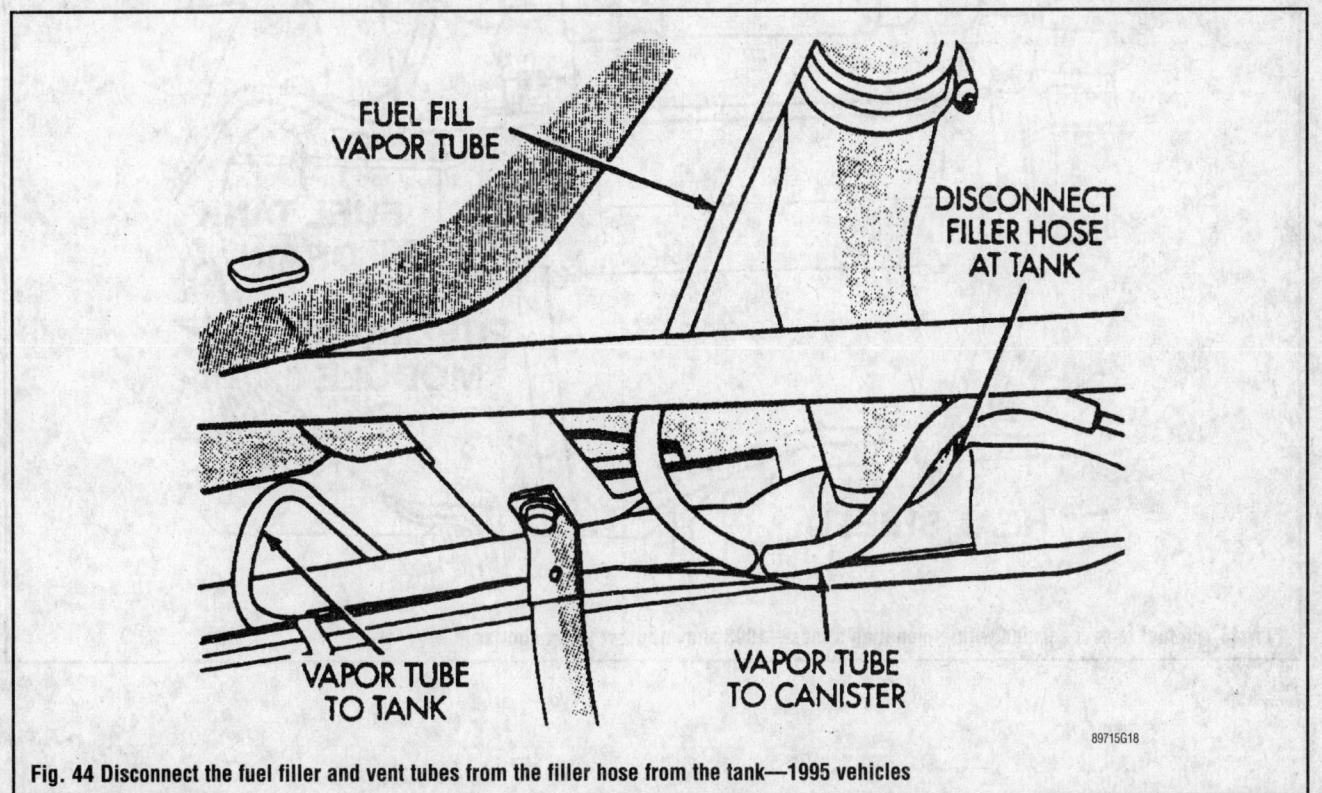

Fig. 44 Disconnect the fuel filler and vent tubes from the filler hose from the tank—1995 vehicles

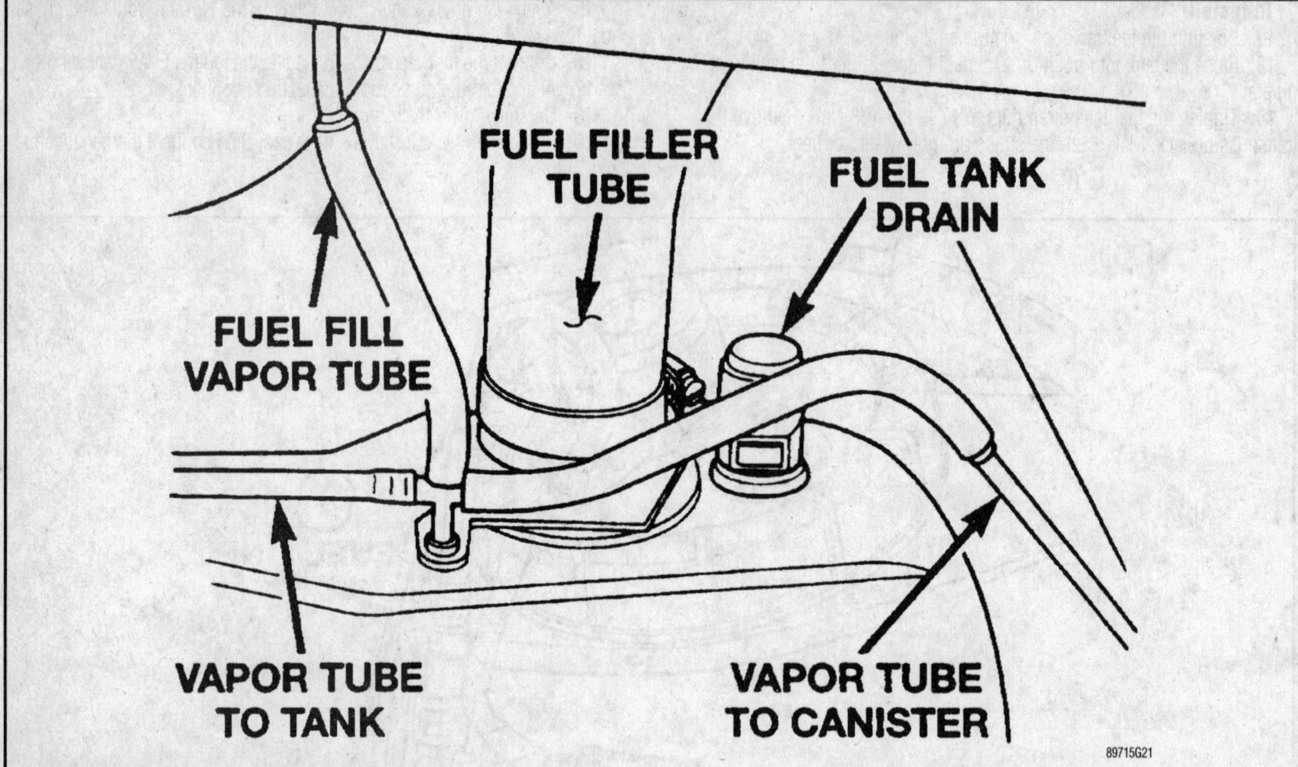

**FUEL FILL VAPOR TUBE**

**FUEL FILLER TUBE**

**FUEL TANK DRAIN**

**VAPOR TUBE TO TANK**

**VAPOR TUBE TO CANISTER**

89715G21

Fig. 45 Fuel filler tube and vent tube locations—1996–99 vehicles

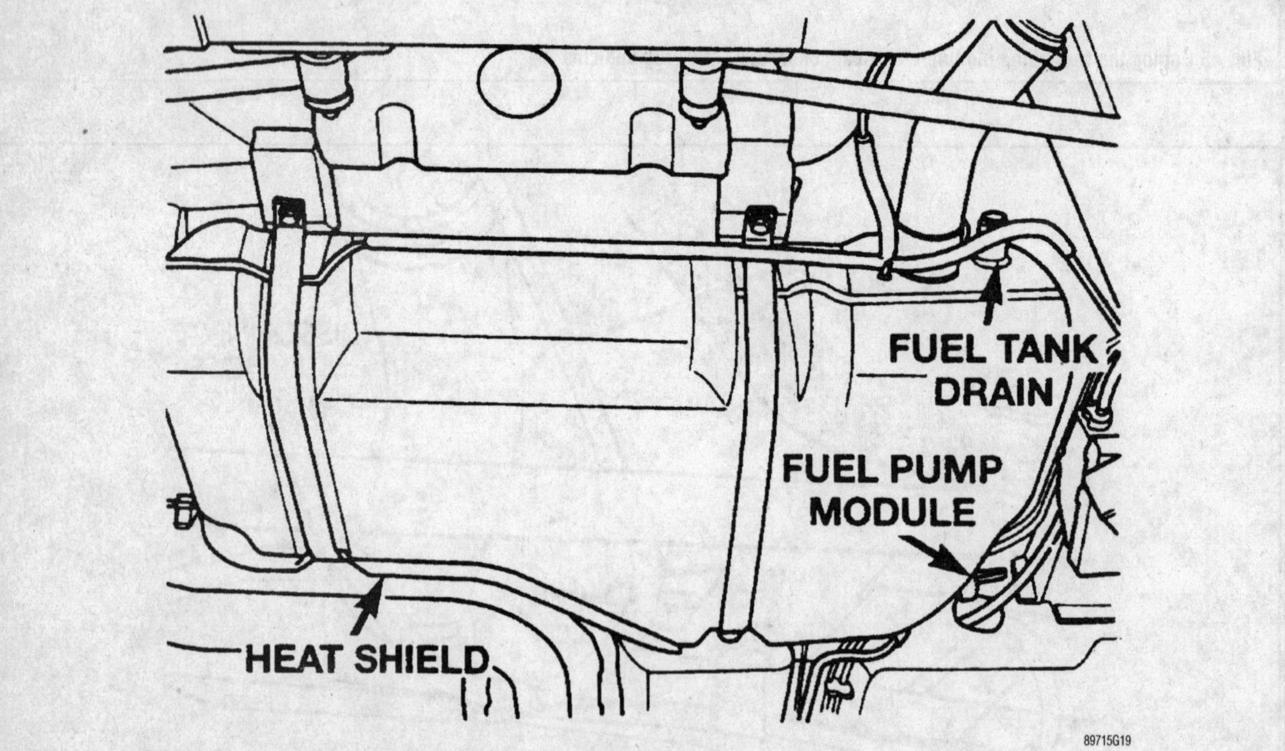

**FUEL TANK DRAIN**

**FUEL PUMP MODULE**

**HEAT SHIELD**

89715G19

Fig. 46 The fuel tank is secured with 2 mounting straps—1998 shown, other years similar

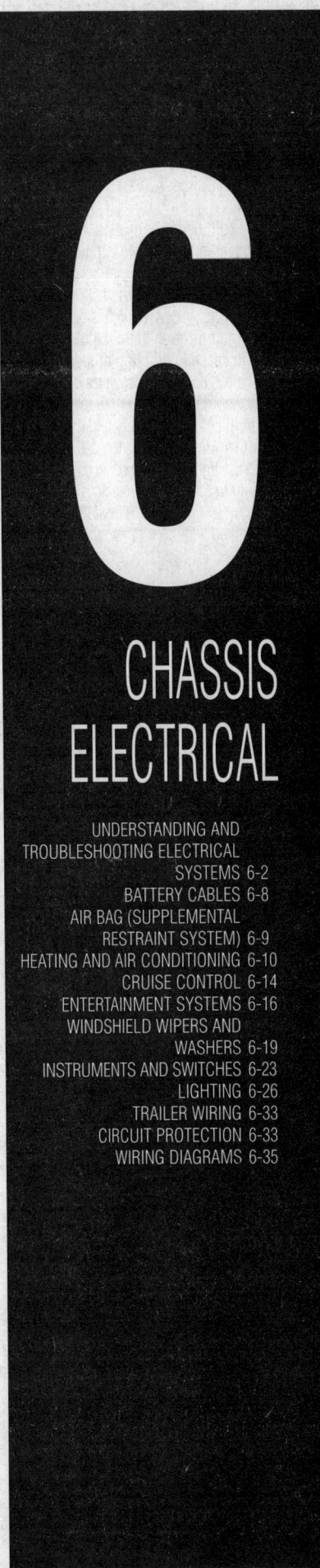

# 6

## CHASSIS ELECTRICAL

## UNDERSTANDING AND TROUBLESHOOTING ELECTRICAL SYSTEMS

### Basic Electrical Theory

♦ **See Figure 1**

For any 12 volt, negative ground, electrical system to operate, the electricity must travel in a complete circuit. This simply means that current (power) from the positive terminal (+) of the battery must eventually return to the negative terminal (-) of the battery. Along the way, this current will travel through wires, fuses, switches and components. If, for any reason, the flow of current through the circuit is interrupted, the component fed by that circuit will cease to function properly.

Perhaps the easiest way to visualize a circuit is to think of connecting a light bulb (with two wires attached to it) to the battery—one wire attached to the negative (-) terminal of the battery and the other wire to the positive (+) terminal. With the two wires touching the battery terminals, the circuit would be complete and the light bulb would illuminate. Electricity would follow a path from the battery to the bulb and back to the battery. It's easy to see that with longer wires on our light bulb, it could be mounted anywhere. Further, one wire could be fitted with a switch so that the light could be turned on and off.

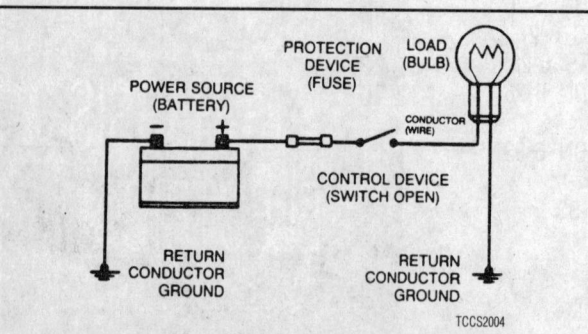

TCCS2004

**Fig. 1 This example illustrates a simple circuit. When the switch is closed, power from the positive (+) battery terminal flows through the fuse and the switch, and then to the light bulb. The light illuminates and the circuit is completed through the ground wire back to the negative (-) battery terminal. In reality, the two ground points shown in the illustration are attached to the metal chassis of the vehicle, which completes the circuit back to the battery**

The normal automotive circuit differs from this simple example in two ways. First, instead of having a return wire from the bulb to the battery, the current travels through the chassis of the vehicle. Since the negative (-) battery cable is attached to the chassis and the chassis is made of electrically conductive metal, the chassis of the vehicle can serve as a ground wire to complete the circuit. Secondly, most automotive circuits contain multiple components which receive power from a single circuit. This lessens the amount of wire needed to power components on the vehicle.

### THE WATER ANALOGY

Electricity is the flow of electrons—hypothetical particles thought to constitute the basic "stuff" of electricity. Many people have been taught electrical theory using an analogy with water. In a comparison with water flowing through a pipe, the electrons would be the water.

The flow of electricity can be measured much like the flow of water through a pipe. The unit of measurement used is amperes, frequently abbreviated as amps (a). When connected to a circuit, an ammeter will measure the actual amount of current flowing through the circuit. When relatively few electrons flow through a circuit, the amperage is low. When many electrons flow, the amperage is high.

Just as water pressure is measured in units such as pounds per square inch (psi), electrical pressure is measured in units called volts (v). When a voltmeter is connected to a circuit, it is measuring the electrical pressure. The higher the voltage, the more current will flow through the circuit. The lower the voltage, the less current will flow.

While increasing the voltage in a circuit will increase the flow of current, the actual flow depends not only on voltage, but also on the resistance of the circuit. Resistance is the amount of force necessary to push the current through the circuit. The standard unit for measuring resistance is an ohm (W or omega). Resistance in a circuit varies depending on the amount and type of components used in the circuit. The main factors which determine resistance are:

• Material—some materials have more resistance than others. Those with high resistance are said to be insulators. Rubber is one of the best insulators available, as it allows little current to pass. Low resistance materials are said to be conductors. Copper wire is among the best conductors. Most vehicle wiring is made of copper.

• Size—the larger the wire size being used, the less resistance the wire will have. This is why components which use large amounts of electricity usually have large wires supplying current to them.

• Length—for a given thickness of wire, the longer the wire, the greater the resistance. The shorter the wire, the less the resistance. When determining the proper wire for a circuit, both size and length must be considered to design a circuit that can handle the current needs of the component.

• Temperature—with many materials, the higher the temperature, the greater the resistance. This principle is used in many of the sensors on the engine.

### OHM'S LAW

The preceding definitions may lead the reader into believing that there is no relationship between current, voltage and resistance. Nothing can be further from the truth. The relationship between current, voltage and resistance can be summed up by a statement known as Ohm's law.

Voltage (E) is equal to amperage (I) times resistance (R): $E = I \times R$
Other forms of the formula are $R = E/I$ and $I = E/R$

In each of these formulas, E is the voltage in volts, I is the current in amps and R is the resistance in ohms. The basic point to remember is that as the resistance of a circuit goes up, the amount of current that flows in the circuit will go down, if voltage remains the same.

### Electrical Components

### POWER SOURCE

The power source for 12 volt automotive electrical systems is the battery. In most modern vehicles, the battery is a lead/acid electrochemical device consisting of six 2 volt subsections (cells) connected in series, so that the unit is capable of producing approximately 12 volts of electrical pressure. Each subsection consists of a series of positive and negative plates held a short distance apart in a solution of sulfuric acid and water.

The two types of plates are of dissimilar metals. This sets up a chemical reaction, and it is this reaction which produces current flow from the battery when its positive and negative terminals are connected to an electrical load. The power removed from the battery is replaced by the alternator, which forces electrons back through the battery, reversing the normal flow, and restoring the battery to its original chemical state.

### GROUND

Two types of grounds are used in automotive electric circuits: Direct ground components are grounded through their mounting points. All other components use some sort of ground wire which is attached to the body or chassis of the vehicle. The electrical current runs through the chassis of the vehicle and returns to the battery through the ground (-) cable; if you look, you'll see that the battery ground cable connects between the battery and the body or chassis of the vehicle.

➡ It should be noted that a good percentage of electrical problems can be traced to bad grounds.

## PROTECTIVE DEVICES

▶ See Figure 2

It is possible for large surges of current to pass through the electrical system of your vehicle. If this surge of current were to reach the load in the circuit, it could burn it out or severely damage it. To prevent this, fuses, circuit breakers and/or fusible links are connected into the supply wires of the electrical system. These items are nothing more than a built-in weak spot in the system. When an abnormal amount of current flows through the system, these protective devices work as follows to protect the circuit:

• Fuse—when an excessive electrical current passes through a fuse, the fuse "blows" (the conductor melts) and opens the circuit, preventing the passage of current.

• Circuit Breaker—a circuit breaker is basically a self-repairing fuse. It will open the circuit in the same fashion as a fuse, but when the surge subsides, the circuit breaker can be reset and does not need replacement.

• Fusible Link—a fusible link (fuse link or main link) is a short length of special, Hypalon high temperature insulated wire that acts as a fuse. When an excessive electrical current passes through a fusible link, the thin gauge wire inside the link melts, creating an intentional open to protect the circuit. To repair the circuit, the link must be replaced. Some newer type fusible links are housed in plug-in modules, which are simply replaced like a fuse, while older type fusible links must be cut and spliced if they melt. Since this link is very early in the electrical path, it's the first place to look if nothing on the vehicle works, but the battery seems to be charged and is properly connected.

### ✴✴ CAUTION

**Always replace fuses, circuit breakers and fusible links with identically rated components. Under no circumstances should a component of higher or lower amperage rating be substituted.**

## SWITCHES & RELAYS

▶ See Figures 3 and 4

Switches are used in electrical circuits to control the passage of current. The most common use is to open and close circuits between the battery and the various electric devices in the system. Switches are rated according to the amount of amperage they can handle. If a sufficient amperage rated switch is not used in a circuit, the switch could overload and cause damage.

Some electrical components which require a large amount of current to operate use a special switch called a relay. Since these circuits carry a large amount of current, the thickness of the wire in the circuit is also greater. If this large wire were connected from the load to the control

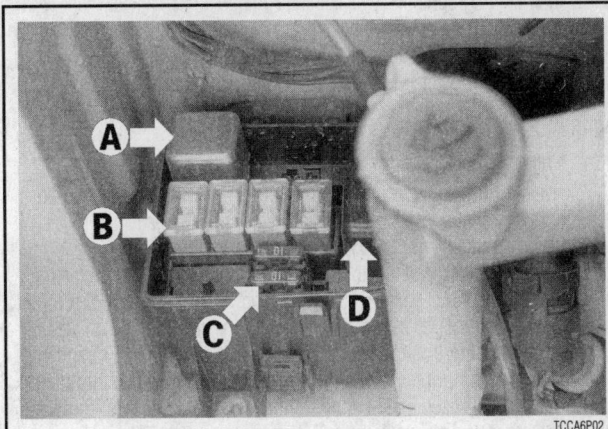

A. Relay         C. Fuse
B. Fusible link    D. Flasher

Fig. 3 The underhood fuse and relay panel usually contains fuses, relays, flashers and fusible links

switch on the dashboard, the switch would have to carry the high amperage load and the dash would be twice as large to accommodate the increased size of the wiring harness. To prevent these problems, a relay is used.

Relays are composed of a coil and a switch. These two components are linked together so that when one operates, the other operates at the same time. The large wires in the circuit are connected from the battery to one side of the relay switch and from the opposite side of the relay switch to the load. Most relays are normally open, preventing current from passing through the circuit. Additional, smaller wires are connected from the relay coil to the control switch for the circuit and from the opposite side of the relay coil to ground. When the control switch is turned on, it grounds the smaller wire to the relay coil, causing the coil to operate. The coil pulls the relay switch closed, sending power to the component without routing it through the inside of the vehicle. Some common circuits which may use relays are the horn, headlights, starter, electric fuel pump and rear window defogger systems.

Fig. 2 Most vehicles use one or more fuse panels. This one is located in the driver's side kick panel

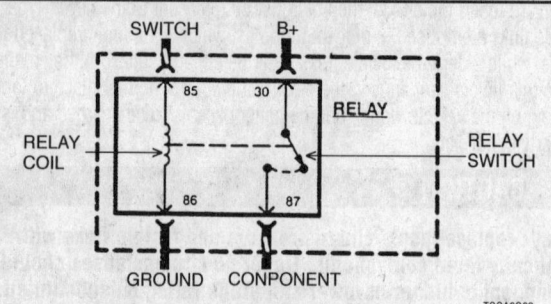

**Fig. 4 Relays are composed of a coil and a switch. These two components are linked together so that when one operates, the other operates at the same time. The large wires in the circuit are connected from the battery to one side of the relay switch (B+) and from the opposite side of the relay switch to the load (component). Smaller wires are connected from the relay coil to the control switch for the circuit and from the opposite side of the relay coil to ground**

## LOAD

Every complete circuit must include a "load" (something to use the electricity coming from the source). Without this load, the battery would attempt to deliver its entire power supply from one pole to another. The electricity would take a short cut to ground and cause a great amount of damage to other components in the circuit by developing a tremendous amount of heat. This condition could develop sufficient heat to melt the insulation on all the surrounding wires and reduce a multiple wire cable to a lump of plastic and copper.

## WIRING & HARNESSES

The average automobile contains about ½ mile of wiring, with hundreds of individual connections. To protect the many wires from damage and to keep them from becoming a confusing tangle, they are organized into bundles, enclosed in plastic or taped together and called wiring harnesses. Different harnesses serve different parts of the vehicle. Individual wires are color coded to help trace them through a harness where sections are hidden from view.

Automotive wiring or circuit conductors can be either single strand wire, multi-strand wire or printed circuitry. Single strand wire has a solid metal core and is usually used inside such components as alternators, motors, relays and other devices. Multi-strand wire has a core made of many small strands of wire twisted together into a single conductor. Most of the wiring in an automotive electrical system is made up of multi-strand wire, either as a single conductor or grouped together in a harness. All wiring is color coded on the insulator, either as a solid color or as a colored wire with an identification stripe. A printed circuit is a thin film of copper or other conductor that is printed on an insulator backing. Occasionally, a printed circuit is sandwiched between two sheets of plastic for more protection and flexibility. A complete printed circuit, consisting of conductors, insulating material and connectors for lamps or other components is called a printed circuit board. Printed circuitry is used in place of individual wires or harnesses in places where space is limited, such as behind instrument panels.

Since automotive electrical systems are very sensitive to changes in resistance, the selection of properly sized wires is critical when systems are repaired. A loose or corroded connection or a replacement wire that is too small for the circuit will add extra resistance and an additional voltage drop to the circuit.

The wire gauge number is an expression of the cross-section area of the conductor. The most common system for expressing wire size is the American Wire Gauge (AWG) system. As gauge number increases, area decreases and the wire becomes smaller. An 18 gauge wire is smaller than a 4 gauge wire. A wire with a higher gauge number will carry less current than a wire with a lower gauge number. Gauge wire size refers to the size of the strands of the conductor, not the size of the complete wire. It is possible, therefore, to have two wires of the same gauge with different diameters because one may have thicker insulation than the other.

12 volt automotive electrical systems generally use 10, 12, 14, 16 and 18 gauge wire. Main power distribution circuits and larger accessories usually use 10 and 12 gauge wire. Battery cables are usually 4 or 6 gauge, although 1 and 2 gauge wires are occasionally used.

It is essential to understand how a circuit works before trying to figure out why it doesn't. An electrical schematic shows the electrical current paths when a circuit is operating properly. Schematics break the entire electrical system down into individual circuits. In a schematic, no attempt is made to represent wiring and components as they physically appear on the vehicle; switches and other components are shown as simply as possible. Face views of harness connectors show the cavity or terminal locations in all multi-pin connectors to help locate test points.

## CONNECTORS

#### ♦ See Figures 5 and 6

Three types of connectors are commonly used in automotive applications—weatherproof, molded and hard shell.

• Weatherproof—these connectors are most commonly used in the engine compartment or where the connector is exposed to the elements.

**Fig. 5 Hard shell (left) and weatherproof (right) connectors have replaceable terminals**

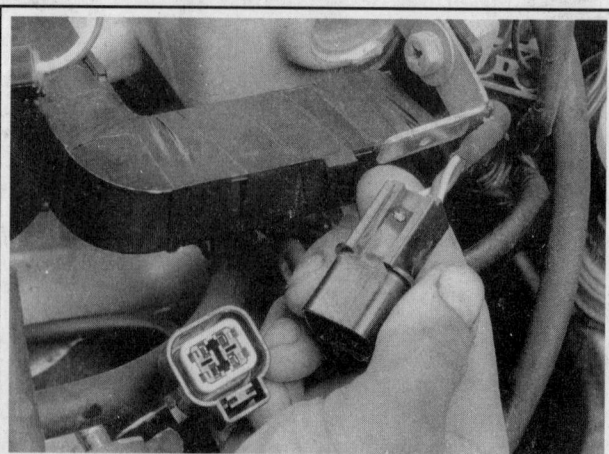

**Fig. 6 Weatherproof connectors are most commonly used in the engine compartment or where the connector is exposed to the elements**

Terminals are protected against moisture and dirt by sealing rings which provide a weathertight seal. All repairs require the use of a special terminal and the tool required to service it. Unlike standard blade type terminals, these weatherproof terminals cannot be straightened once they are bent. Make certain that the connectors are properly seated and all of the sealing rings are in place when connecting leads.

• Molded—these connectors require complete replacement of the connector if found to be defective. This means splicing a new connector assembly into the harness. All splices should be soldered to insure proper contact. Use care when probing the connections or replacing terminals in them, as it is possible to create a short circuit between opposite terminals. If this happens to the wrong terminal pair, it is possible to damage certain components. Always use jumper wires between connectors for circuit checking and NEVER probe through weatherproof seals.

• Hard Shell—unlike molded connectors, the terminal contacts in hard-shell connectors can be replaced. Replacement usually involves the use of a special terminal removal tool that depresses the locking tangs (barbs) on the connector terminal and allows the connector to be removed from the rear of the shell. The connector shell should be replaced if it shows any evidence of burning, melting, cracks, or breaks. Replace individual terminals that are burnt, corroded, distorted or loose.

### Test Equipment

Pinpointing the exact cause of trouble in an electrical circuit is most times accomplished by the use of special test equipment. The following describes different types of commonly used test equipment and briefly explains how to use them in diagnosis. In addition to the information covered below, the tool manufacturer's instructions booklet (provided with the tester) should be read and clearly understood before attempting any test procedures.

### JUMPER WIRES

### ✳✳ CAUTION

**Never use jumper wires made from a thinner gauge wire than the circuit being tested. If the jumper wire is of too small a gauge, it may overheat and possibly melt. Never use jumpers to bypass high resistance loads in a circuit. Bypassing resistances, in effect, creates a short circuit. This may, in turn, cause damage and fire. Jumper wires should only be used to bypass lengths of wire.**

Jumper wires are simple, yet extremely valuable, pieces of test equipment. They are basically test wires which are used to bypass sections of a circuit. Although jumper wires can be purchased, they are usually fabricated from lengths of standard automotive wire and whatever type of connector (alligator clip, spade connector or pin connector) that is required for the particular application being tested. In cramped, hard-to-reach areas, it is advisable to have insulated boots over the jumper wire terminals in order to prevent accidental grounding. It is also advisable to include a standard automotive fuse in any jumper wire. This is commonly referred to as a "fused jumper". By inserting an in-line fuse holder between a set of test leads, a fused jumper wire can be used for bypassing open circuits. Use a 5 amp fuse to provide protection against voltage spikes.

Jumper wires are used primarily to locate open electrical circuits, on either the ground (-) side of the circuit or on the power (+) side. If an electrical component fails to operate, connect the jumper wire between the component and a good ground. If the component operates only with the jumper installed, the ground circuit is open. If the ground circuit is good, but the component does not operate, the circuit between the power feed and component may be open. By moving the jumper wire successively back from the component toward the power source, you can isolate the area of the circuit where the open is located. When the component stops functioning, or the power is cut off, the open is in the segment of wire between the jumper and the point previously tested.

You can sometimes connect the jumper wire directly from the battery to the "hot" terminal of the component, but first make sure the component uses 12 volts in operation. Some electrical components, such as fuel injec-

tors, are designed to operate on about 4 volts, and running 12 volts directly to these components will cause damage.

### TEST LIGHTS

#### ▶ See Figure 7

The test light is used to check circuits and components while electrical current is flowing through them. It is used for voltage and ground tests. To use a 12 volt test light, connect the ground clip to a good ground and probe wherever necessary with the pick. The test light will illuminate when voltage is detected. This does not necessarily mean that 12 volts (or any particular amount of voltage) is present; it only means that some voltage is present. It is advisable before using the test light to touch its ground clip and probe across the battery posts or terminals to make sure the light is operating properly.

### ✳✳ WARNING

**Do not use a test light to probe electronic ignition spark plug or coil wires. Never use a pick-type test light to probe wiring on computer controlled systems unless specifically instructed to do so. Any wire insulation that is pierced by the test light probe should be taped and sealed with silicone after testing.**

Like the jumper wire, the 12 volt test light is used to isolate opens in circuits. But, whereas the jumper wire is used to bypass the open to operate the load, the 12 volt test light is used to locate the presence of voltage in a circuit. If the test light illuminates, there is power up to that point in the circuit; if the test light does not illuminate, there is an open circuit (no power). Move the test light in successive steps back toward the power source until the light in the handle illuminates. The open is between the probe and a point which was previously probed.

The self-powered test light is similar in design to the 12 volt test light, but contains a 1.5 volt penlight battery in the handle. It is most often used in place of a multimeter to check for open or short circuits when power is isolated from the circuit (continuity test).

The battery in a self-powered test light does not provide much current. A weak battery may not provide enough power to illuminate the test light even when a complete circuit is made (especially if there is high resistance in the circuit). Always make sure that the test battery is strong. To check the battery, briefly touch the ground clip to the probe; if the light glows brightly, the battery is strong enough for testing.

➡A self-powered test light should not be used on any computer controlled system or component. The small amount of electricity transmitted by the test light is enough to damage many electronic automotive components.

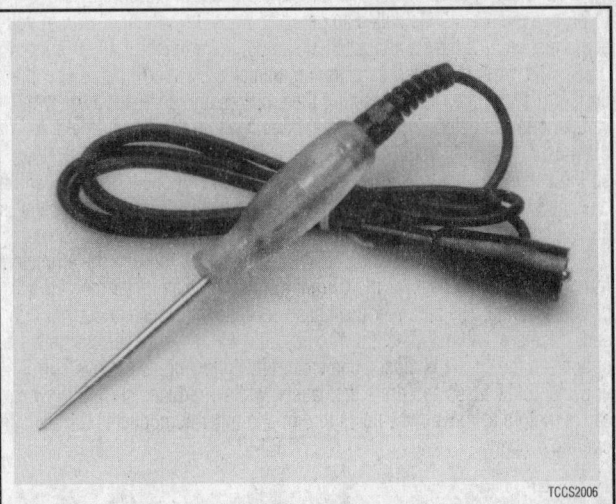

TCCS2006

**Fig. 7 A 12 volt test light is used to detect the presence of voltage in a circuit**

## MULTIMETERS

Multimeters are an extremely useful tool for troubleshooting electrical problems. They can be purchased in either analog or digital form and have a price range to suit any budget. A multimeter is a voltmeter, ammeter and ohmmeter (along with other features) combined into one instrument. It is often used when testing solid state circuits because of its high input impedance (usually 10 megaohms or more). A brief description of the multimeter main test functions follows:

• Voltmeter—the voltmeter is used to measure voltage at any point in a circuit, or to measure the voltage drop across any part of a circuit. Voltmeters usually have various scales and a selector switch to allow the reading of different voltage ranges. The voltmeter has a positive and a negative lead. To avoid damage to the meter, always connect the negative lead to the negative (-) side of the circuit (to ground or nearest the ground side of the circuit) and connect the positive lead to the positive (+) side of the circuit (to the power source or the nearest power source). Note that the negative voltmeter lead will always be black and that the positive voltmeter will always be some color other than black (usually red).

• Ohmmeter—the ohmmeter is designed to read resistance (measured in ohms) in a circuit or component. All ohmmeters will have a selector switch which permits the measurement of different ranges of resistance (usually the selector switch allows the multiplication of the meter reading by 10, 100, 1,000 and 10,000). Since the meters are powered by an internal battery, the ohmmeter can be used as a self-powered test light. When the ohmmeter is connected, current from the ohmmeter flows through the circuit or component being tested. Since the ohmmeter's internal resistance and voltage are known values, the amount of current flow through the meter depends on the resistance of the circuit or component being tested. The ohmmeter can also be used to perform a continuity test for suspected open circuits. In using the meter for making continuity checks, do not be concerned with the actual resistance readings. Zero resistance, or any ohm reading, indicates continuity in the circuit. Infinite resistance indicates an opening in the circuit. A high resistance reading where there should be none indicates a problem in the circuit. Checks for short circuits are made in the same manner as checks for open circuits, except that the circuit must be isolated from both power and normal ground. Infinite resistance indicates no continuity to ground, while zero resistance indicates a dead short to ground.

### ✳✳ WARNING

**Never use an ohmmeter to check the resistance of a component or wire while there is voltage applied to the circuit.**

• Ammeter—an ammeter measures the amount of current flowing through a circuit in units called amperes or amps. At normal operating voltage, most circuits have a characteristic amount of amperes, called "current draw" which can be measured using an ammeter. By referring to a specified current draw rating, then measuring the amperes and comparing the two values, one can determine what is happening within the circuit to aid in diagnosis. An open circuit, for example, will not allow any current to flow, so the ammeter reading will be zero. A damaged component or circuit will have an increased current draw, so the reading will be high. The ammeter is always connected in series with the circuit being tested. All of the current that normally flows through the circuit must also flow through the ammeter; if there is any other path for the current to follow, the ammeter reading will not be accurate. The ammeter itself has very little resistance to current flow and, therefore, will not affect the circuit, but it will measure current draw only when the circuit is closed and electricity is flowing. Excessive current draw can blow fuses and drain the battery, while a reduced current draw can cause motors to run slowly, lights to dim and other components to not operate properly.

## Troubleshooting Electrical Systems

When diagnosing a specific problem, organized troubleshooting is a must. The complexity of a modern automotive vehicle demands that you approach any problem in a logical, organized manner. There are certain troubleshooting techniques which are standard:

• Establish when the problem occurs. Does the problem appear only under certain conditions? Were there any noises, odors or other unusual symptoms?

Isolate the problem area. To do this, make some simple tests and observations, then eliminate the systems that are working properly. Check for obvious problems, such as broken wires and loose or dirty connections. Always check the obvious before assuming something complicated is the cause.

• Test for problems systematically to determine the cause once the problem area is isolated. Are all the components functioning properly? Is there power going to electrical switches and motors. Performing careful, systematic checks will often turn up most causes on the first inspection, without wasting time checking components that have little or no relationship to the problem.

• Test all repairs after the work is done to make sure that the problem is fixed. Some causes can be traced to more than one component, so a careful verification of repair work is important in order to pick up additional malfunctions that may cause a problem to reappear or a different problem to arise. A blown fuse, for example, is a simple problem that may require more than another fuse to repair. If you don't look for a problem that caused a fuse to blow, a shorted wire (for example) may go undetected.

Experience has shown that most problems tend to be the result of a fairly simple and obvious cause, such as loose or corroded connectors, bad grounds or damaged wire insulation which causes a short. This makes careful visual inspection of components during testing essential to quick and accurate troubleshooting.

## Testing

### OPEN CIRCUITS

▶ **See Figure 8**

1. Isolate the circuit from power and ground.
2. Connect the self-powered test light or ohmmeter ground clip to a good ground and probe sections of the circuit sequentially.
3. If the light is out or there is infinite resistance, the open is between the probe and the circuit ground.
4. If the light is on or the meter shows continuity, the open is between the probe and end of the circuit toward the power source.

### SHORT CIRCUITS

➡**Never use a self-powered test light to perform checks for opens or shorts when power is applied to the electrical system under test. The 12 volt vehicle power will quickly burn out the light bulb in the test light.**

1. Isolate the circuit from power and ground.
2. Connect the self-powered test light or ohmmeter ground clip to a good ground and probe any easy-to-reach test point in the circuit.
3. If the light comes on or there is continuity, there is a short somewhere in the circuit.
4. To isolate the short, probe a test point at either end of the isolated circuit (the light should be on or the meter should indicate continuity).
5. Leave the test light probe engaged and sequentially open connectors or switches, remove parts, etc. until the light goes out or continuity is broken.
6. When the light goes out, the short is between the last two circuit components which were opened.

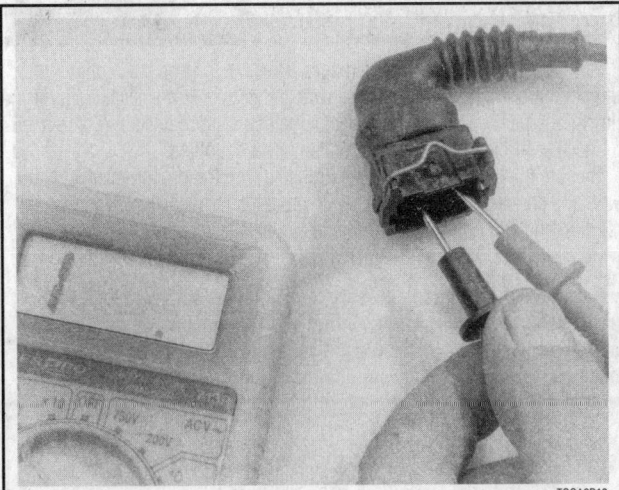

Fig. 8 The infinite reading on this multimeter (1 . ) indicates that the circuit is open

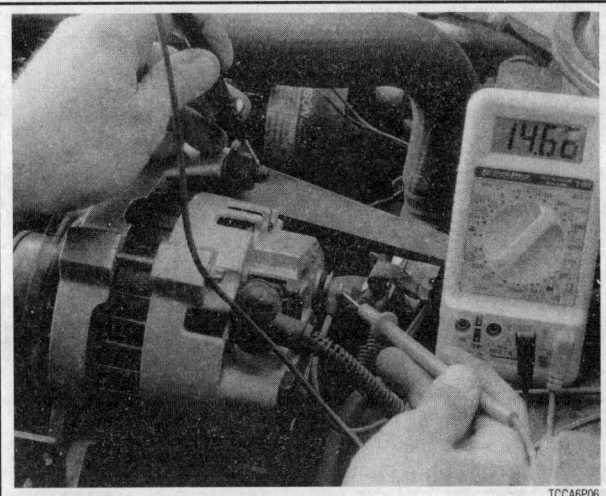

Fig. 10 Testing voltage output between the alternator's BAT terminal and ground. This voltage reading is normal

## VOLTAGE

▶ See Figures 9 and 10

This test determines voltage available from the battery and should be the first step in any electrical troubleshooting procedure. Many electrical problems, especially on computer controlled systems, can be caused by a low state of charge in the battery. Excessive corrosion at the battery cable terminals can cause poor contact that will prevent proper charging and full battery current flow.

1. Set the voltmeter selector switch to the 20V position.
2. Connect the multimeter negative lead to the battery's negative (-) post or terminal and the positive lead to the battery's positive (+) post or terminal.
3. Turn the ignition switch **ON** to provide a load.
4. A well charged battery should register over 12 volts. If the meter reads below 11.5 volts, the battery power may be insufficient to operate the electrical system properly.

## VOLTAGE DROP

▶ See Figure 11

When current flows through a load, the voltage beyond the load drops. This voltage drop is due to the resistance created by the load and also by small resistances created by corrosion at the connectors and damaged insulation on the wires. The maximum allowable voltage drop under load is critical, especially if there is more than one load in the circuit, since all voltage drops are cumulative.

1. Set the voltmeter selector switch to the 20 volt position.
2. Connect the multimeter negative lead to a good ground.
3. Operate the circuit and check the voltage prior to the first component (load).
4. There should be little or no voltage drop in the circuit prior to the first component. If a voltage drop exists, the wire or connectors in the circuit are suspect.

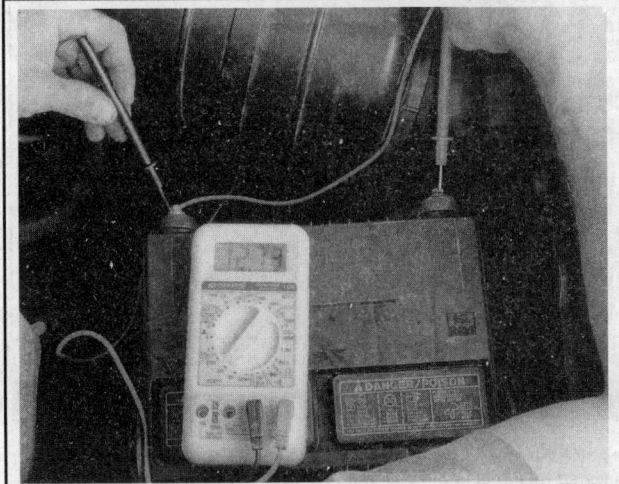

Fig. 9 Using a multimeter to check battery voltage. This battery is fully charged

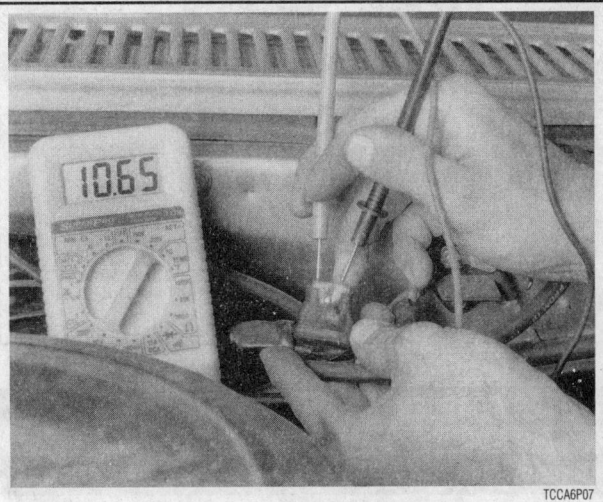

Fig. 11 This voltage drop test revealed high resistance (low voltage) in the circuit

5. While operating the first component in the circuit, probe the ground side of the component with the positive meter lead and observe the voltage readings. A small voltage drop should be noticed. This voltage drop is caused by the resistance of the component.

6. Repeat the test for each component (load) down the circuit.

7. If a large voltage drop is noticed, the preceding component, wire or connector is suspect.

## RESISTANCE

♦ See Figures 12 and 13

### ※ WARNING

**Never use an ohmmeter with power applied to the circuit. The ohmmeter is designed to operate on its own power supply. The normal 12 volt automotive electrical system current could damage the meter!**

1. Isolate the circuit from the vehicle's power source.

2. Ensure that the ignition key is **OFF** when disconnecting any components or the battery.

3. Where necessary, also isolate at least one side of the circuit to be checked, in order to avoid reading parallel resistances. Parallel circuit resistances will always give a lower reading than the actual resistance of either of the branches.

4. Connect the meter leads to both sides of the circuit (wire or component) and read the actual measured ohms on the meter scale. Make sure the selector switch is set to the proper ohm scale for the circuit being tested, to avoid misreading the ohmmeter test value.

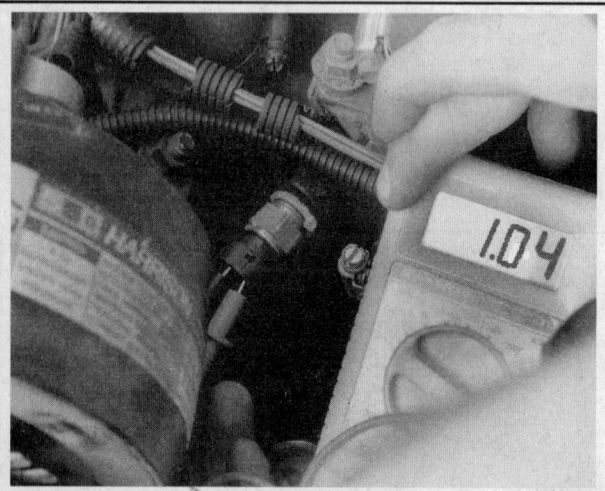

Fig. 12 Checking the resistance of a coolant temperature sensor with an ohmmeter. Reading is 1.04 kilohms

## Wire and Connector Repair

Almost anyone can replace damaged wires, as long as the proper tools and parts are available. Automotive wire and terminals are available to fit almost any need. Even the specialized weatherproof, molded and hard shell connectors are now available from aftermarket suppliers.

Be sure the ends of all the wires are fitted with the proper terminal hardware and connectors. Wrapping a wire around a stud is never a permanent solution and will only cause trouble later. Replace wires one at a time to avoid confusion. Always route wires exactly the same as the factory.

➡️ If connector repair is necessary, only attempt it if you have the proper tools. Weatherproof and hard shell connectors require special tools to release the pins inside the connector. Attempting to repair these connectors with conventional hand tools will damage them.

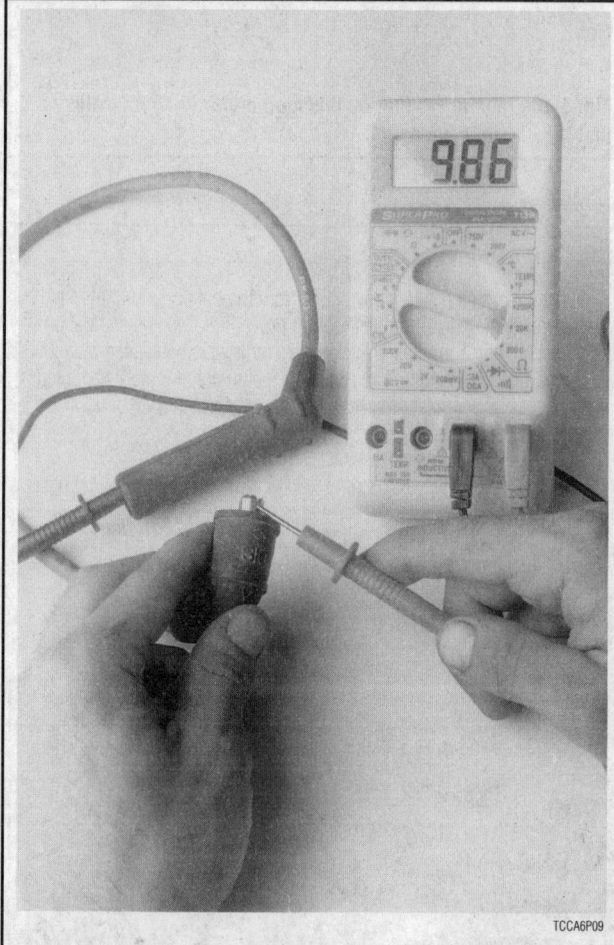

Fig. 13 Spark plug wires can be checked for excessive resistance using an ohmmeter

## BATTERY CABLES

### Disconnecting the Cables

♦ See Figures 14 and 15

When working on any electrical component on the vehicle, it is always a good idea to disconnect the negative (-) battery cable. This will prevent potential damage to many sensitive electrical components such as the Engine Control Module (ECM), radio, alternator, etc.

➡️ Any time you disengage the battery cables, it is recommended that you disconnect the negative (-) battery cable first. This will prevent your accidentally grounding the positive (+) terminal to the body of the vehicle when disconnecting it, thereby preventing damage to the above mentioned components.

Before you disconnect the cable(s), first turn the ignition to the **OFF** position. This will prevent a draw on the battery which could cause arcing

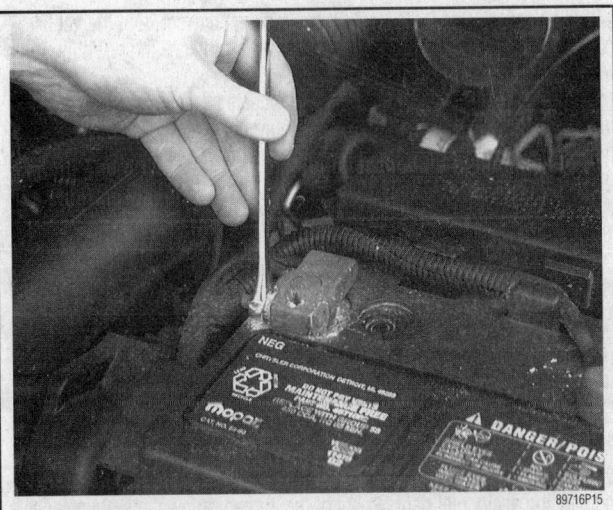

Fig. 14 ALWAYS disconnect the negative battery cable before servicing any electrical components by loosening the nut . . .

Fig. 15 . . . then pulling the cable up and off the terminal

(electricity trying to ground itself to the body of a vehicle, just like a spark plug jumping the gap) and, of course, damaging some components such as the alternator diodes.

When the battery cable(s) are reconnected (negative cable last), be sure to check that your lights, windshield wipers and other electrically operated safety components are all working correctly. If your vehicle contains an Electronically Tuned Radio (ETR), don't forget to also reset your radio stations. Ditto for the clock.

## AIR BAG (SUPPLEMENTAL RESTRAINT SYSTEM)

### General Information

▶ See Figures 16 and 17

The Supplemental Restraint System (SRS), found on all vehicles covered by this manual, is designed to be used along with the front seat belts to reduce the risk or amount of injury by deploying one or both air bags during certain frontal collisions.

The air bag system is made up of left and right front impact sensors, air bag modules for the driver (in the steering wheel) and front passenger (right side instrument panel above the glove compartment), SRS diagnosis unit (with a safing sensor) and a SRS warning lamp in the instrument cluster.

The SRS system is designed to deploy when the safing sensor, along with either or both of the impact sensors simultaneously activate while the ignition is **ON**. The sensors will activate during front or near-frontal impacts of moderate to severe force.

### SERVICE PRECAUTIONS

When working on the SRS or any components which require the removal of the air bag, adhere to all of these precautions to minimize the risks of personal injury or component damage:

• Before attempting to diagnose, remove or install the air bag system components, you must first detach and isolate the negative (-) battery

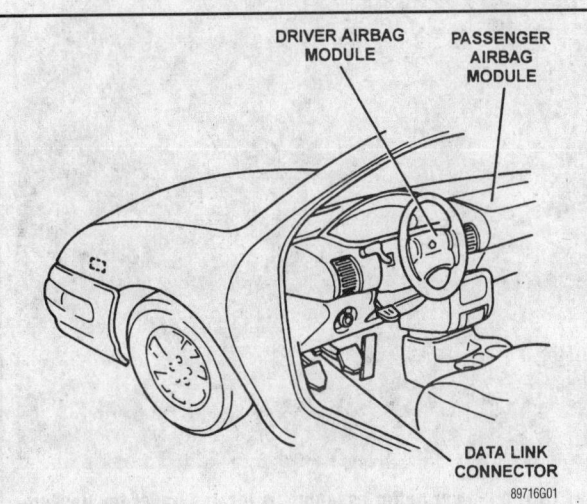

Fig. 16 The driver's side air bag inflator module is mounted to the steering wheel

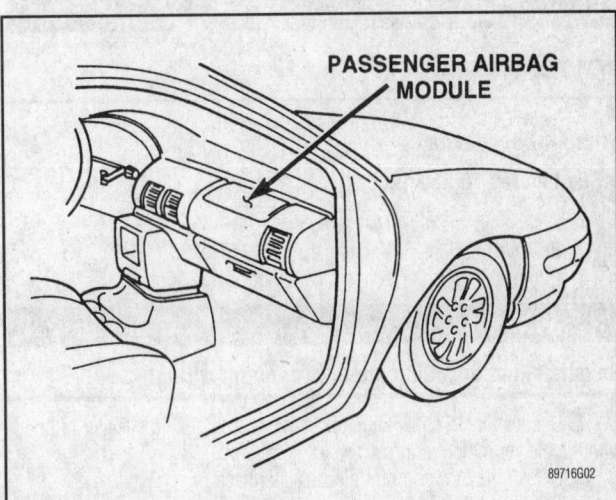

Fig. 17 There is also a passenger side air bag module located above the glove compartment

cable. Failure to do so could result in accidental deployment and possible personal injury.

• When an undeployed air bag assembly is to be removed from the steering wheel, after detaching the negative battery cable, allow the system capacitor to discharge for two minutes before commencing with the air bag system component removal.

• Replace the air bag system components only with Mopar® specified replacement parts, or equivalent. Substitute parts may visually appear interchangeable, but internal differences may result in inferior occupant protection.

• The fasteners, screws, and bolts originally used for the SRS have special coatings and are specifically designed for the SRS. They must never be replaced with any substitutes. Anytime a new fastener is needed, replace with the correct fasteners provided in the service package or fasteners listed in the parts books.

### Handling A Live Air Bag Module

At no time should any source of electricity be permitted near the inflator on the back of the module. When carrying a live module, the trim cover should be pointed away from the body to minimize injury in the event of accidental deployment. In addition, if the module is placed on a bench or other surface, the plastic trim cover should be face up to minimize movement in case of accidental deployment.

When handling a steering column with an air bag module attached, never place the column on the floor or other surface with the steering wheel or module face down.

### Handling A Deployed Air Bag Module

The vehicle interior may contain a very small amount of sodium hydroxide powder, a by-product of air bag deployment. Since this powder can irritate the skin, eyes, nose or throat, be sure to wear safety glasses, rubber gloves and long sleeves during cleanup.

If you find that the cleanup is irritating your skin, run cool water over the affected area. Also, if you experience nasal or throat irritation, exit the vehicle for fresh air until the irritation ceases. If irritation continues, see a physician.

Begin the cleanup by putting tape over the two air bag exhaust vents so that no additional powder will find its way into the vehicle interior. Then remove the air bag and air bag module from the vehicle.

Use a vacuum cleaner to remove any residual powder from the vehicle interior. Work from the outside in so that you avoid kneeling or sitting in an uncleaned area.

Be sure to vacuum the heater and A/C outlets as well. In fact it's a good idea to run the blower on low and to vacuum up any powder expelled from the plenum. You may need to vacuum the interior of the car a second time to recover all of the powder.

Check with the local authorities before disposing of the deployed bag and module in your trash.

After an air bag has been deployed, the air bag module and clockspring must be replaced because they cannot be reused. Other air bag system components should be replaced with new ones if damaged.

### DISARMING THE SYSTEM

To disarm the SRS, simply detach the negative battery cable from the battery. Isolate the battery cable by taping up any exposed metal areas of the cable. This will keep the cable from inadvertently contacting the battery and causing accidental deployment of the air bag. Allow the system capacitor to discharge for at least 2 minutes, although 10 minutes is recommended to allow the dissipation of any residual energy.

### ARMING THE SYSTEM

After finishing the service procedures, you must perform the following procedure:

1. Connect a DRB or equivalent scan tool to the Data Link Connector (DLC), located at the right side of the steering column and at the lower edge of the lower instrument panel.
2. Turn the ignition key to the **ON** position. Get out of the vehicle with the scan tool. Make sure you are using the latest version of the proper cartridge.
3. After making sure no one is in the vehicle, remove the tape, then reconnect the negative battery cable.
4. Read and record any stored Diagnostic Trouble Codes (DTCs). If any diagnostic trouble codes are recorded, take your vehicle to a reputable repair shop for diagnosis.
5. If there are no DTCs, and if the airbag warning lamp either fails to light, with the ignition switch ON, or the light goes on and stays on, there is a system malfunction. If any of these conditions exist, you should take your vehicle to a reputable repair shop for diagnosis.

## HEATING AND AIR CONDITIONING

### Blower Motor

#### REMOVAL & INSTALLATION

**With Air Conditioning**

▶ **See Figures 18 and 19**

1. Disconnect the negative battery cable.
2. Remove the right side scuff plate.
3. Pull back the carpet from the passenger's side floor.

### ❊❊ WARNING

**Be careful not to cut into the blower motor wiring!**

4. Use a suitable utility knife to cut the wheel housing silencer in line with the blower motor wiring.
5. Detach the blower motor electrical connector.
6. For right-hand drive vehicles, remove the motor cover.
7. Unfasten the three blower motor retaining screws, then lower the blower motor assembly from the unit housing.

89716P56

**Fig. 18 The blower motor assembly is located under the passenger's side dash panel**

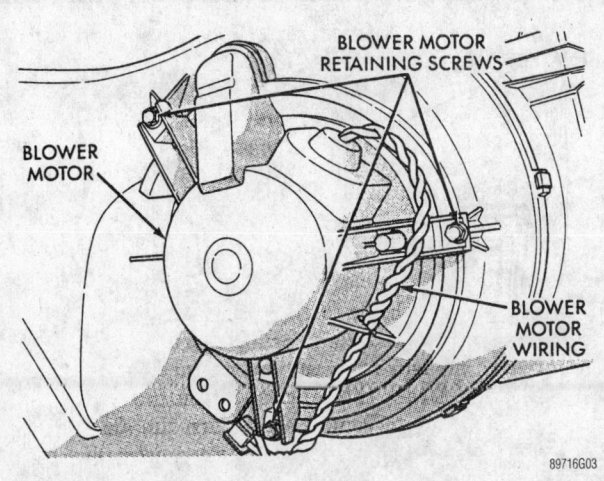

**Fig. 19 Blower motor mounting and location of the retaining screws and wiring—vehicles with A/C**

**To install:**

8. Raise the blower motor into position in the unit housing and secure with the three retaining screws.
9. If removed, install the motor cover.
10. Attach the blower motor electrical connector.
11. Use tape to secure the silencer into position.
12. Reposition the passenger's side floor carpeting.
13. Install the right side scuff plate.
14. Connect the negative battery cable.

#### Without Air Conditioning

▶ **See Figure 20**

1. Disconnect the negative battery cable.
2. Detach the blower motor electrical connector.
3. Grasp the blower motor, while pulling down on the tab. Turn the motor about ⅛ of a turn counterclockwise, then remove the blower motor from the unit housing.

**To install:**

4. Position the blower motor in the unit housing and turn the assembly ⅛ of a turn to lock in place.

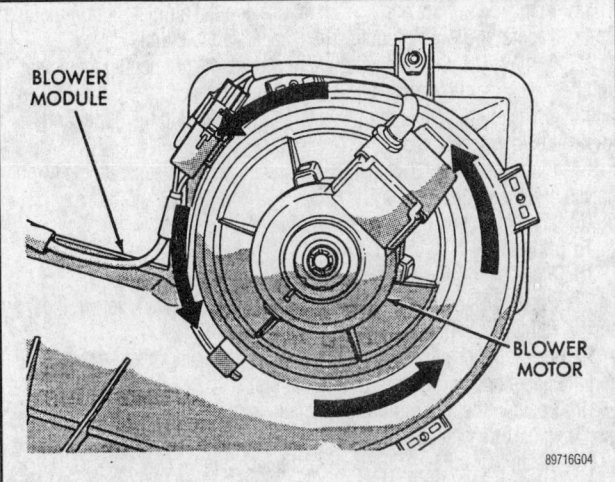

**Fig. 20 On vehicles without A/C, turn the motor assembly ⅛ of a turn to unlock it from the unit**

5. Attach the blower motor electrical connector.
6. Connect the negative battery cable.

### Heater Core

#### REMOVAL & INSTALLATION

▶ **See Figures 21 thru 26**

➡ **In order to remove the heater core, you must first remove the HVAC unit housing, then disassemble the unit to remove the core.**

1. If equipped with A/C, have the A/C system discharged by a reputable automotive technician utilizing a recovery/recycling machine before detaching the A/C system. Refer to the A/C system precautions presented in Section 1.
2. Disconnect the negative battery cable.
3. Remove the instrument panel from the vehicle, as outlined in Section 10 of this manual.
4. Drain the cooling system into a suitable container, then disconnect

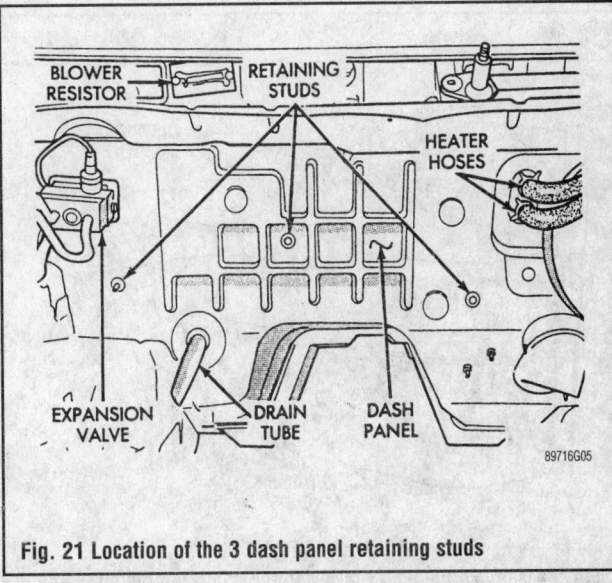

**Fig. 21 Location of the 3 dash panel retaining studs**

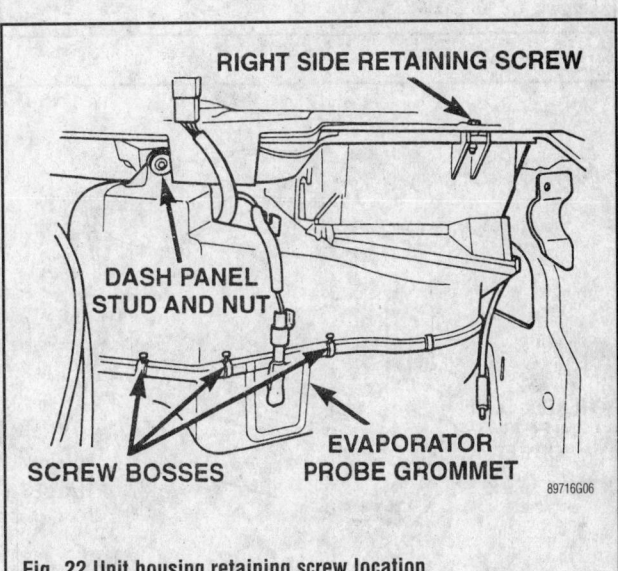

**Fig. 22 Unit housing retaining screw location**

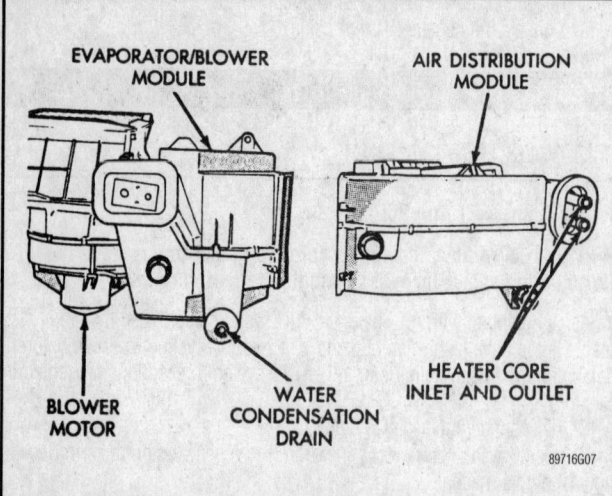

Fig. 23 You must remove the retainers, then separate the air distribution module from the evaporator/blower module

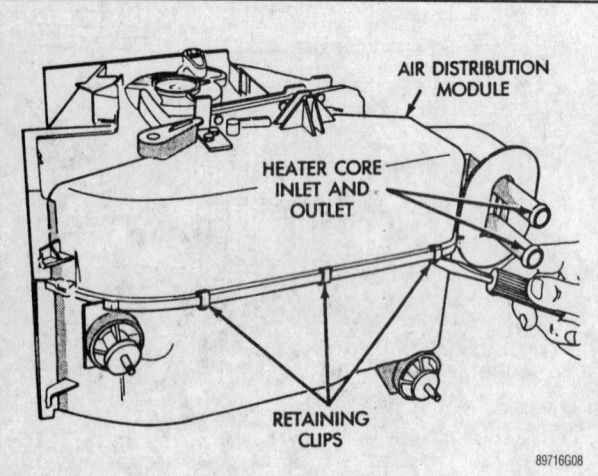

Fig. 24 Remove the upper-to-lower housing retaining clips and screws . . .

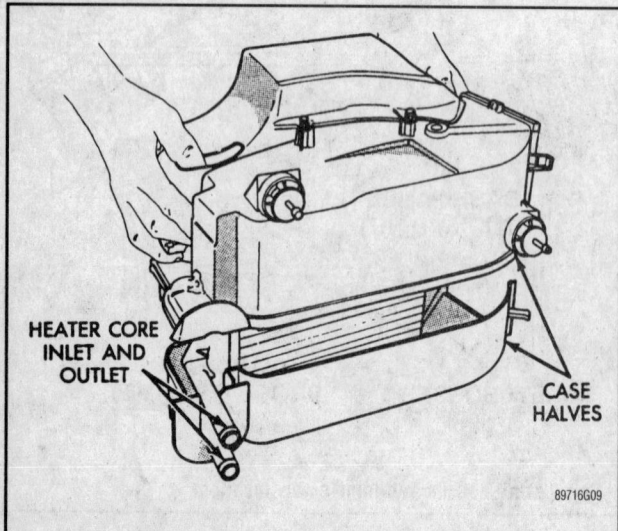

Fig. 25 . . . then separate the two halves of the module

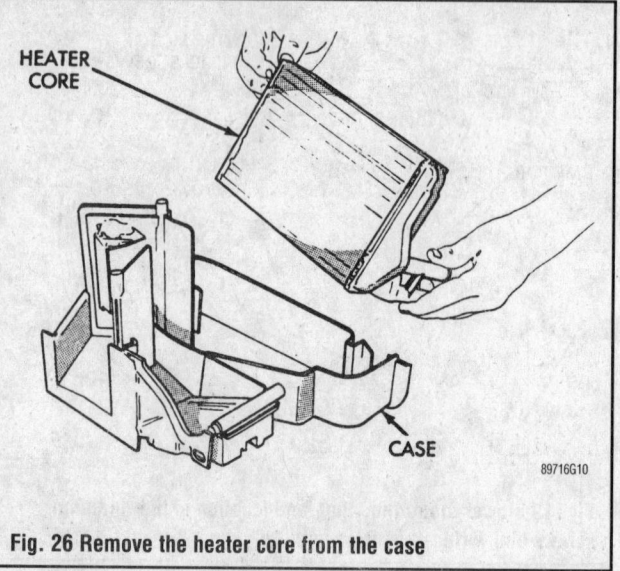

Fig. 26 Remove the heater core from the case

the heater hoses from the dash panel. Plug the heater core outlets to prevent coolant from spilling during unit housing removal.

5. If equipped with A/C, perform the following:

   a. Remove the suction line from the expansion valve. Place a piece of tap over the open refrigerant line to prevent the system from being contaminated.

   b. Remove the expansion valve from the evaporator. Place a piece of tap over the open evaporator fitting to prevent dirt and/or moisture from entering the evaporator.

   c. Disconnect the rubber drain tube extension from the condensation drain tube.

6. Remove the 3 retaining nuts located in the engine compartment on the dash panel.

7. Unfasten the right side retaining screw.

8. Remove the remaining nut located on the dash panel stud.

9. Detach the blue 5-way connector from the plenum. The module wiring harness must be removed with the module.

10. Remove the unit housing from the vehicle.

➡For right-hand drive vehicles, the unit housing does not separate. It is a one piece unit and must be replaced as an assembly.

11. Remove the clips and screws that secure the air distribution module to the evaporator/blower module. Then, separate the 2 units.

12. Remove the panel opening foam seal, demister opening foam seal, and heater core tube foam seals from the unit.

13. Unfasten the retaining clips and screws that hold the upper and lower housings together.

14. Place the unit in the upside down position, then separate the two halves of the module.

15. Lift the heater core up and out of the case.

**To install:**

16. Place the heater core in the case.

17. Position the upper and lower halves of the module together, then secure with the retaining screws and clips.

18. Install the heater core tube foam seals, demister opening foam seal and the panel opening foam seal into the unit.

19. Position the air distribution module to the evaporator/blower module. Then, secure with the retaining screws and clips.

20. Install the unit housing in the vehicle.

21. Attach the blue 5-way connector to the plenum.

22. Install the nut located on the dash panel stud and the right side retaining screw.

23. Install the 3 retaining nuts to the dash panel in the engine compartment.

24. The remainder of installation is the reverse of the removal procedure.

25. Instrument panel installation procedures can be found in Section 10 of this manual.
26. Connect the negative battery cable.
27. Have the A/C system evacuated, recharged and leak tested by a reputable automotive technician utilizing a recovery/recycling apparatus.

## Air Conditioning Components

### REMOVAL & INSTALLATION

Repair or service of air conditioning components is not covered by this manual, because of the risk of personal injury or death, and because of the legal ramifications of servicing these components without the proper EPA certification and experience. Cost, personal injury or death, environmental damage, and legal considerations (such as the fact that it is a federal crime to vent refrigerant into the atmosphere), dictate that the A/C components on your vehicle should be serviced only by a Motor Vehicle Air Conditioning (MVAC) trained, and EPA certified automotive technician.

➡If your vehicle's A/C system uses R-12 refrigerant and is in need of recharging, the A/C system can be converted over to R-134a refrigerant (less environmentally harmful and expensive). Refer to Section 1 for additional information on R-12 to R-134a conversions, and for additional considerations dealing with your vehicle's A/C system.

## Control Cables

### REMOVAL & INSTALLATION

▶ **See Figures 27, 28, 29 and 30**

The following procedure can be used to remove either the mode control or temperature control cable, as necessary.

➡**Control cable replacement does not require instrument panel removal.**

1. Disconnect the negative battery cable. You should wait a minimum of 2 minutes before proceeding to allow the SRS system capacitor ample time to discharge.
2. Remove the right side upper instrument panel bezel, as follows:
    a. Using a trim panel removal tool, carefully pry up on the top cover and cluster bezel to remove it.

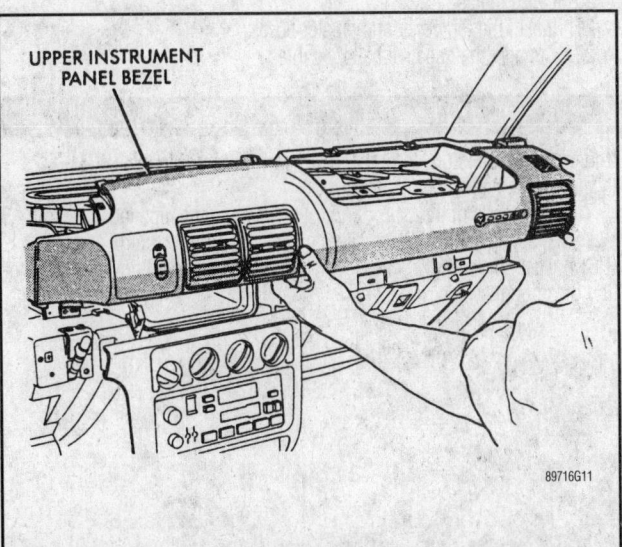
Fig. 27 Remove the right side upper instrument panel bezel

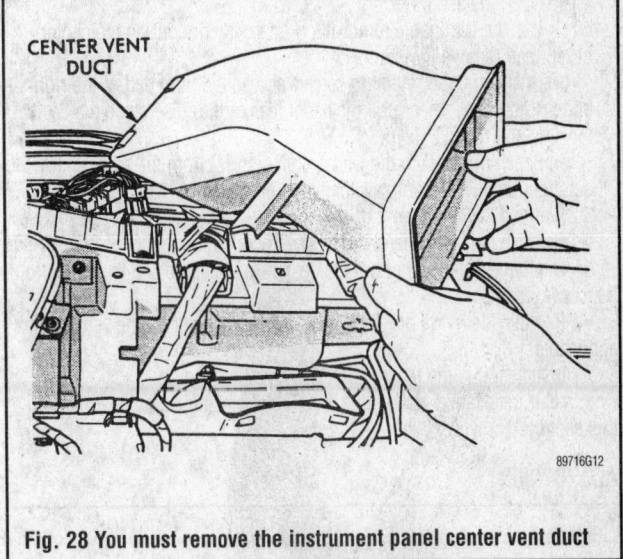
Fig. 28 You must remove the instrument panel center vent duct

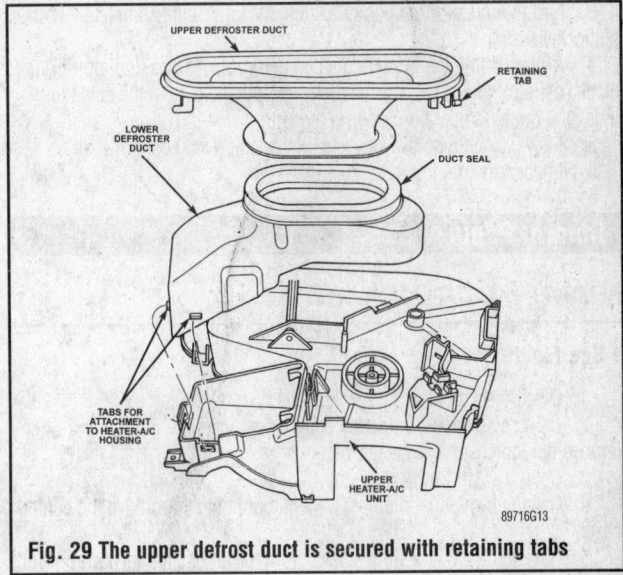
Fig. 29 The upper defrost duct is secured with retaining tabs

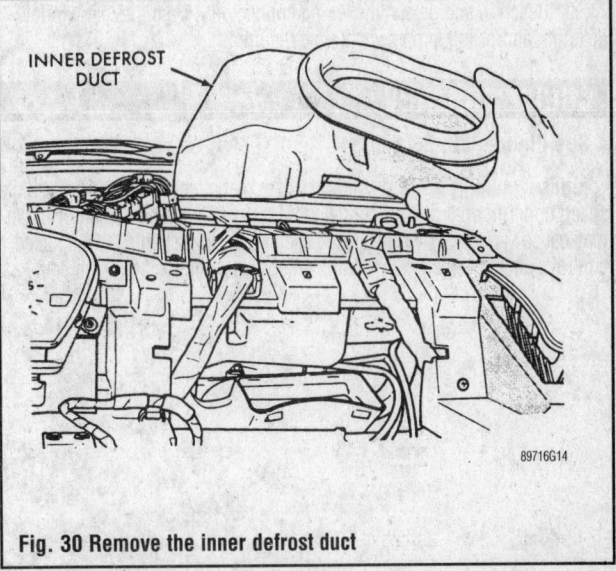
Fig. 30 Remove the inner defrost duct

b. Open the ash tray.

c. Use the trim panel removal tool to gently pry out on the center bezel, then remove the bezel.

d. Unfasten the 6 retaining screws across the front part of the right upper trim panel. Then, pull the panel rearward to disengage the 3 locator pins and remove them.

e. Reach in a detach the wiring connector(s) from the rear window defogger and/or fog lamp switch(s), as necessary.

3. Remove the center vent duct.

4. Remove the upper defrost duct and inner defrost duct.

5. Disconnect the cable from the heater unit, then detach the cable from the control panel.

6. Remove the mode or temperature control cable from the vehicle, as applicable.

7. Installation is the reverse of the removal procedure.

8. After installation, make sure to adjust the cable, as outlined later in this section.

## ADJUSTMENT

1. Attach the cable to the actuator arm on the mode/temperature door and clip the back casing against the stop.

2. Fasten the other end of the cable to the instrument panel control.

3. Turn the mode or temperature knob, as applicable, completely counterclockwise.

4. While holding the knob in the counterclockwise position, pull on the black casing of the cable. This will take up any free play in the cable and index the mode/temperature door to the knob.

5. Snap the cable hold-down clip into position to secure the cable.

6. If necessary, remount the control.

## Control Panel

### REMOVAL & INSTALLATION

▶ **See Figure 31**

1. Disconnect and isolate the negative battery cable.

2. Using a suitable trim panel removal tool, carefully pry up and remove the top cover and cluster bezel.

3. Open the ash tray.

4. Use the trim panel remover to gently pry out and remove the center bezel.

5. Unfasten the 6 attaching screws from the across the forward portion of the right upper trim panel. Pull the panel rearward to disengage the 3 locator pins and remove.

6. Reach in and detach the wiring connector(s) from the rear window defogger and/or fog lamp switch(s) as required.

## CRUISE CONTROL

▶ **See Figures 32, 33 and 34**

Cruise control is a speed control system that maintains a desired vehicle speed under normal driving conditions. However, steep grades up or down may cause variations in the selected speeds. On these vehicles, the speed control system is electrically controlled and vacuum operated. The elec-

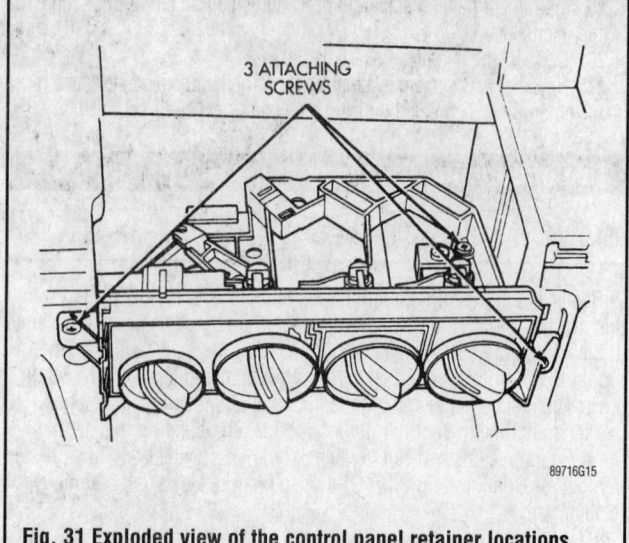

Fig. 31 Exploded view of the control panel retainer locations

7. If equipped with Remove Keyless Entry (RKE), remove the 2 screws holding the module and lay over the instrument cluster.

8. Gently pull on the center A/C outlet duct to remove it.

9. Remove the 3 attaching screws from the corners of the control. There are 2 retaining in the front and one retaining from the top rear.

10. Pull the control rearward and detach the wiring connector.

11. Use a prytool to disengage the cable attachment clips, then remove the control in the vehicle.

**To install:**

12. Connect the cable to the control panel, make sure they are securely retained by the clips.

13. Attach the electrical connector to the control, then position the control in the vehicle.

14. Install the 3 control assembly retaining screws.

15. Install the center A/C outlet duct.

16. If equipped with RKE, reposition the module and install the 2 retaining screws.

17. Attach the wiring to the rear window defogger and/or fog lamp switch as necessary.

18. Fasten the right upper trim panel, making sure the locator pins are engaged, then secure with the 6 retaining screws.

19. Install the center bezel making sure the retaining clips are secured.

20. Close the ash tray.

21. Install the top cover and cluster bezel.

22. Connect the negative battery cable.

tronic control is integrated in the Powertrain Control Module (PCM), located in the engine compartment.

The main parts of the cruise control system are the functional control switches, speed control servo, servo cable, Powertrain Control Module (PCM), vacuum reservoir and the release switches, including the dual function brake light switch.

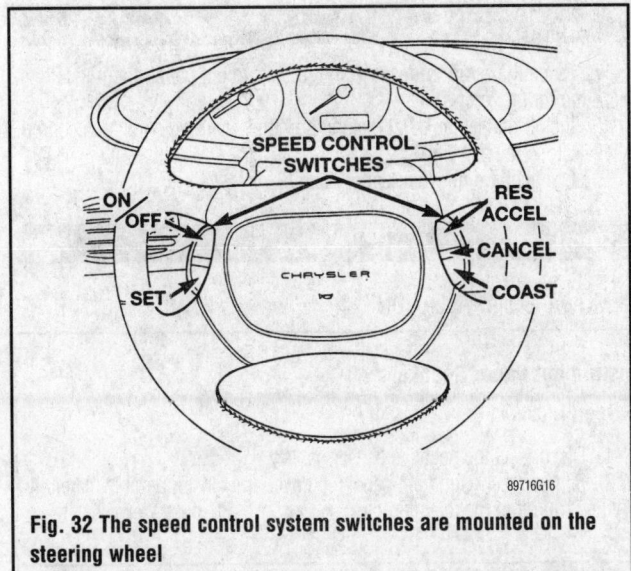

Fig. 32 The speed control system switches are mounted on the steering wheel

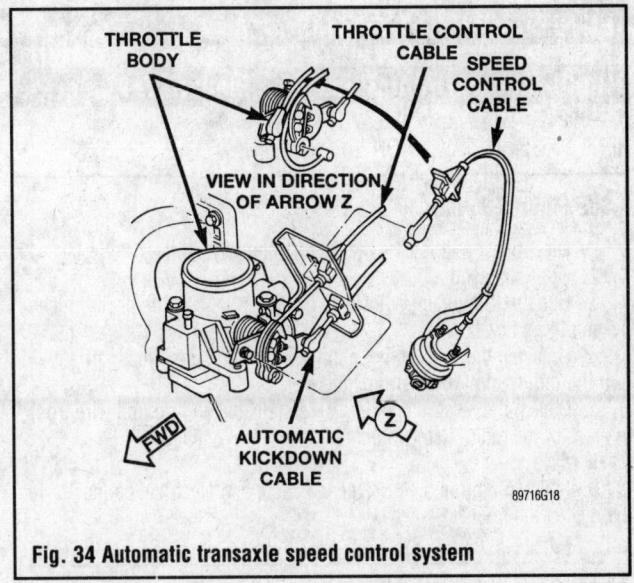

Fig. 34 Automatic transaxle speed control system

The cruise control module assembly contains a low speed limit which will prevent system engagement below 30 mph (50 km/h). The module is controlled by the functional switches located on a lever on the steering column or steering wheel and on the instrument panel.

The release switches are mounted on the brake/clutch/accelerator pedal bracket. When the brake or clutch pedal is depressed, the cruise control system is electrically disengaged and the throttle is returned to the idle position.

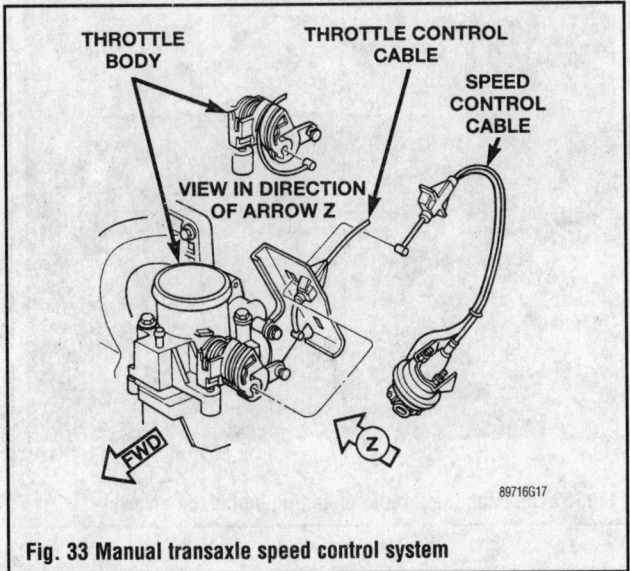

Fig. 33 Manual transaxle speed control system

## CRUISE CONTROL TROUBLESHOOTING

| Problem | Possible Cause |
|---|---|
| Will not hold proper speed | Incorrect cable adjustment |
| | Binding throttle linkage |
| | Leaking vacuum servo diaphragm |
| | Leaking vacuum tank |
| | Faulty vacuum or vent valve |
| | Faulty stepper motor |
| | Faulty transducer |
| | Faulty speed sensor |
| | Faulty cruise control module |
| Cruise intermittently cuts out | Clutch or brake switch adjustment too tight |
| | Short or open in the cruise control circuit |
| | Faulty transducer |
| | Faulty cruise control module |
| Vehicle surges | Kinked speedometer cable or casing |
| | Binding throttle linkage |
| | Faulty speed sensor |
| | Faulty cruise control module |
| Cruise control inoperative | Blown fuse |
| | Short or open in the cruise control circuit |
| | Faulty brake or clutch switch |
| | Leaking vacuum circuit |
| | Faulty cruise control switch |
| | Faulty stepper motor |
| | Faulty transducer |
| | Faulty speed sensor |
| | Faulty cruise control module |

Note: Use this chart as a guide. Not all systems will use the components listed.

TCCA6C01

## ENTERTAINMENT SYSTEMS

### Radio Receiver/Amplifier/Tape Player/CD Player

#### REMOVAL & INSTALLATION

▶ See Figures 35 thru 40

1. Disconnect and isolate the negative battery cable.
2. Open the ash tray.
3. Use the trim panel remover to gently pry out and remove the center mounting bezel.
4. Unfasten the 2 radio mounting screws and bolts, then partially pull the radio out of the instrument panel.
5. Detach the electrical wiring, antenna cable and ground wire from the rear of the radio. Remove the radio from the vehicle.

**To install:**

6. Attach the ground wire, antenna cable and electrical connector to the rear of the radio.

7. Place the radio in position in the instrument panel, then install the 2 mounting screws.
8. Install the center bezel making sure the retaining clips are secured.
9. Close the ash tray.
10. Connect the negative battery cable.

### Speakers

#### REMOVAL & INSTALLATION

**Instrument Panel Speakers**

▶ See Figure 41

1. Disconnect the negative battery cable.
2. Remove the instrument panel top cover and cluster bezel by carefully prying it up off of the retaining clips.

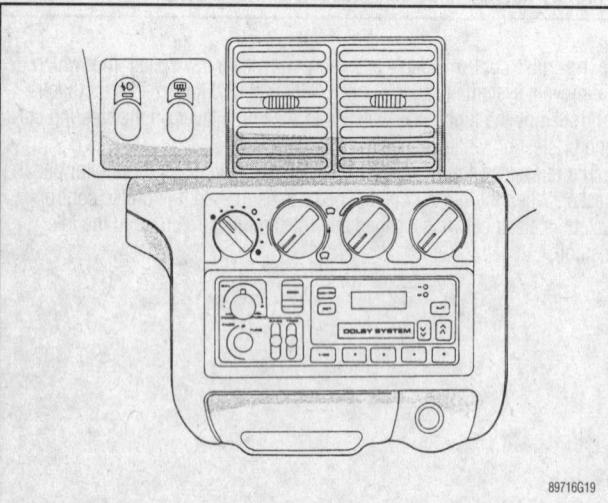

Fig. 35 The center mounting bezel surrounds the radio and heater controls

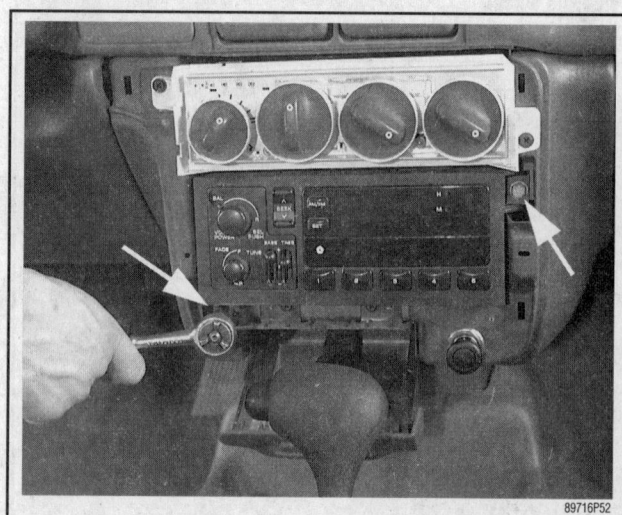

Fig. 37 Unfasten the 2 radio mounting bolts (see arrows) . . .

Fig. 36 Carefully pry the center mounting bezel out to remove it

Fig. 38 . . . partially pull the radio out of its mounting bracket to access the wiring

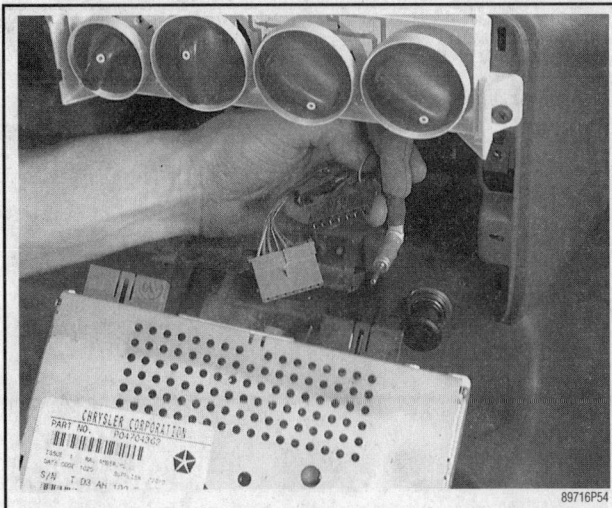

Fig. 39 Unplug the radio connectors and the antenna lead, then remove the radio from the vehicle

3. Unfasten the speaker retaining screws.
4. Partially lift the speaker up, detach the electrical connector, then remove the speaker from the vehicle.
**To install:**
5. Attach the electrical connector to the speaker, then position in the instrument panel.
6. Install the speaker retaining screws.
7. Install the instrument panel top cover and cluster bezel.
8. Connect the negative battery cable.

**Front Door Speakers**

▶ **See Figures 42, 43 and 44**

1. Disconnect the negative battery cable.
2. Remove the door trim panel, as outlined in Section 10 of this manual.
3. Remove the 3 speaker retaining screws.
4. Partially lift the speaker out, detach the electrical connector, then remove the speaker from the door.
**To install:**
5. Attach the electrical connector, then position the speaker in the door.

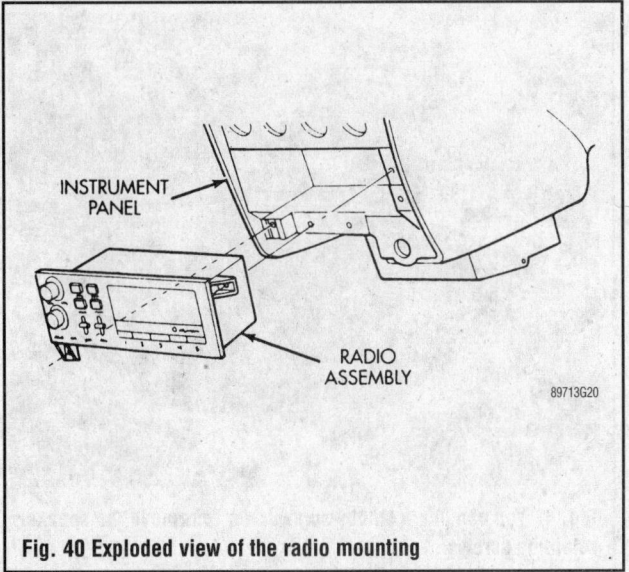

Fig. 40 Exploded view of the radio mounting

Fig. 42 After removing the door trim panel, unfasten the speaker retaining screws . . .

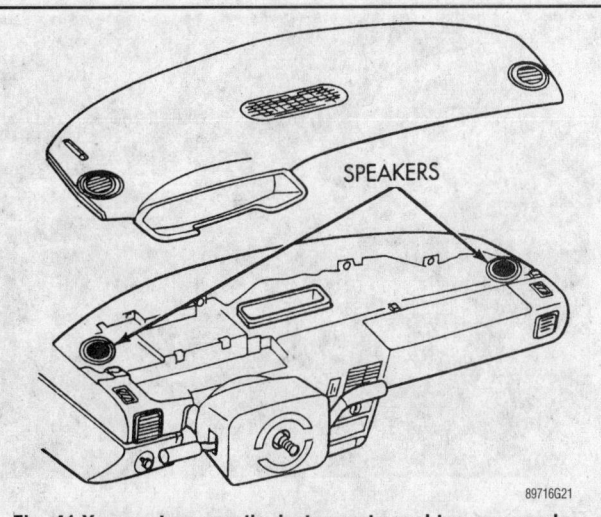

Fig. 41 You must remove the instrument panel top cover and cluster bezel to access the speakers

Fig. 43 . . . then pull the speaker away from the door, unplug the connector and remove it from the vehicle

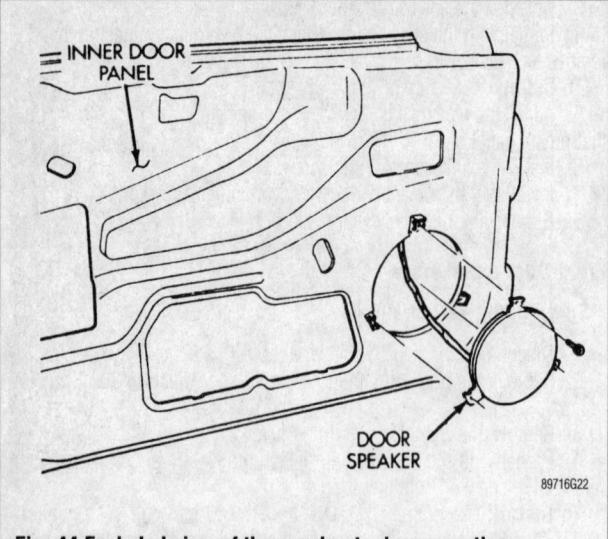

Fig. 44 Exploded view of the speaker-to-door mounting

Fig. 46 . . . then partially remove the shelf trim panel by sliding it down to the seat back position

6. Install the 3 speaker retaining screws.
7. Install the door trim panel, as outlined in Section 10 of this manual.
8. Connect the negative battery cable.

**Rear Speakers**

▶ **See Figures 45 thru 52**

1. Disconnect the negative battery cable.
2. Remove the rear seat and seat back. Remove the seat cushion, seat back and seat belt anchor bolts.
3. Pry out the seat belt trim bezel along the rearward edge.
4. Partially remove the shelf trim panel, sliding it down to the seat back position.
5. Remove the speaker retaining screws.
6. Partially pull the speaker up out of its mounting position, then unplug the connector and remove the speaker from the vehicle.
7. Installation is the reverse of the removal procedure. After attaching the speaker wiring, it is a good idea to connect the negative battery cable and turn the radio on so you can see if the speakers work before you install the seats.

Fig. 47 You can use a stubby screwdriver to remove the speaker retaining screws . . .

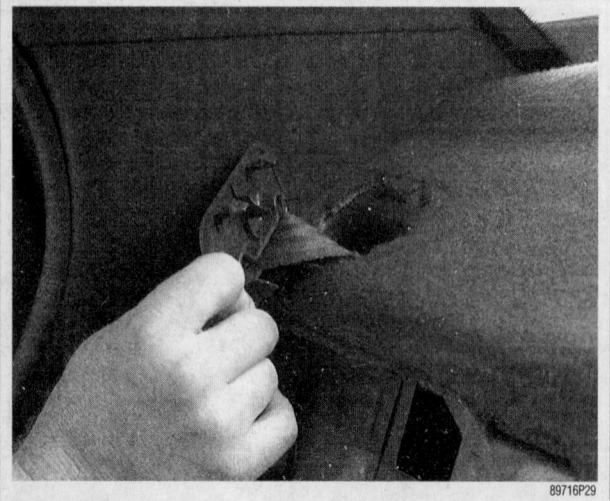

Fig. 45 After removing the rear seat and seat back, unclip the seat belt trim bezel . . .

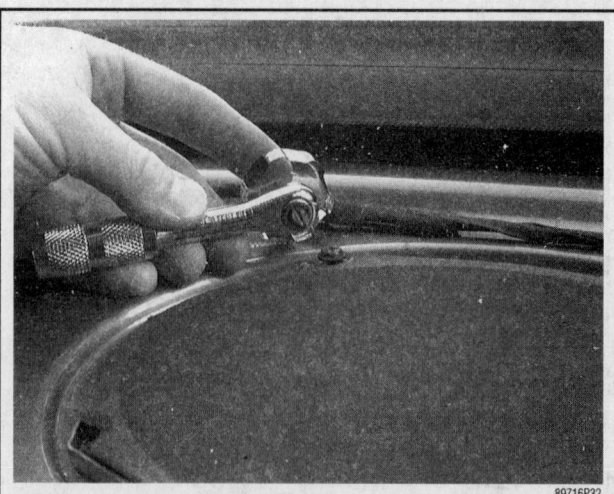

Fig. 48 . . . however there are tools, such as this 90° ratcheting screwdriver . . .

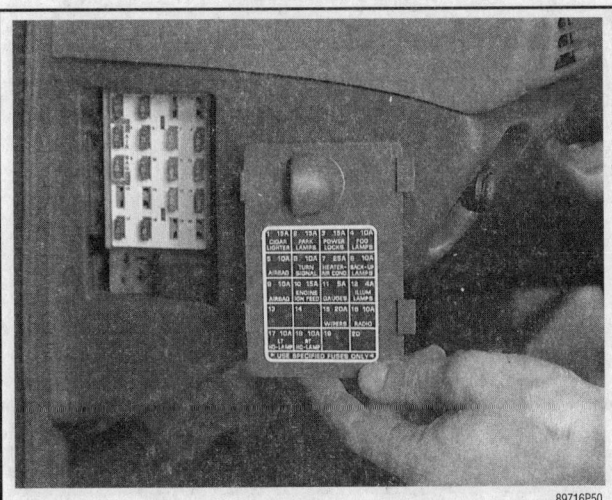

Fig. 49 . . . that can make the job a lot easier and less time consuming

Fig. 51 . . . then unplug the connector and remove the speaker from the vehicle

Fig. 50 Pull the speaker partially up and out of its mounting position . . .

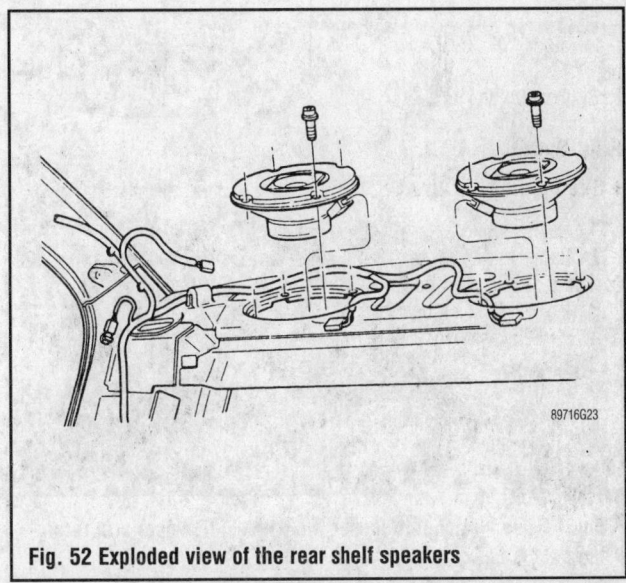

Fig. 52 Exploded view of the rear shelf speakers

## WINDSHIELD WIPERS AND WASHERS

### Windshield Wiper Blade and Arm

REMOVAL & INSTALLATION

▶ See Figures 53, 54, 55, 56 and 57

1. Place the wipers are in the **PARK** position, then turn the ignition **OFF**.
2. Disconnect the negative battery cable.
3. Remove the cap from the wiper arm.
4. Remove the wiper arm retaining nut.
5. Use a rocking motion to pull the wiper blade and arm from the pivot.

**To install:**

6. Position the wiper blade and arm on the pivot, making sure it is proper seated. Make sure wiper arms so that the heel of the blade is on the park line of the windshield.
7. Install the nut on the wiper arm, tighten securely, then install the nut cap.
8. Connect the negative battery cable.

Fig. 53 Remove the windshield wiper arm nut cover

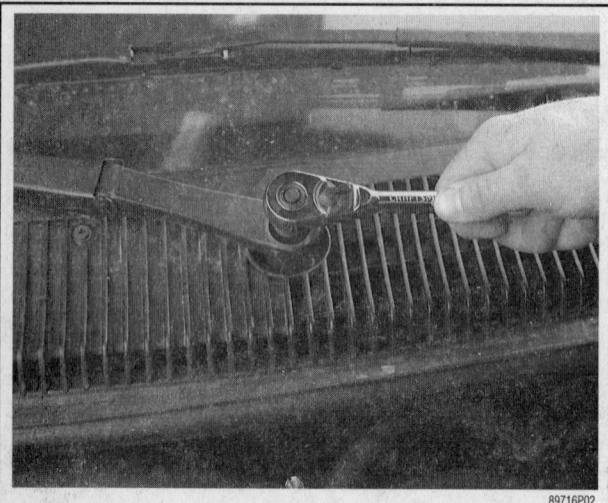

Fig. 54 Use a ratchet to loosen the windshield wiper arm retaining nut . . .

Fig. 55 . . . then remove the nut from the arm

Fig. 56 It's a good idea to matchmark the wiper arm position before removing it

Fig. 57 Remove the wiper arm from the pivot using a rocking motion then pulling it off the pivot

## Windshield Wiper Motor

### REMOVAL & INSTALLATION

▶ See Figures 58 thru 67

1. Disconnect the negative battery cable.
2. Remove the wiper arm and blade assemblies, as outlined earlier in this section.
3. Remove the rear hood seal with the cowl top plastic screen.
4. Detach the motor wire connector at the front plenum wall.
5. Remove the wiper module retainers.
6. Remove the ground strap bolt, then remove the strap and position it out of the way.
7. Remove the wiper motor and linkage from the vehicle.
8. If necessary, you can separate the motor from the linkage as follows:
   a. Remove the linkage from the motor crank.
   b. Insert a prytool between the crank and the linkage, then twist the prytool and lift straight up on the linkage.
   c. Remove the motor mounting screws, then remove the motor.
9. Installation is the reverse of the removal procedure.

Fig. 58 Unfasten the cowl retaining screws . . .

Fig. 61 If necessary you can unclip the connector and position it out of the way

Fig. 59 . . . then remove the cowl panel off for access to the wiper motor

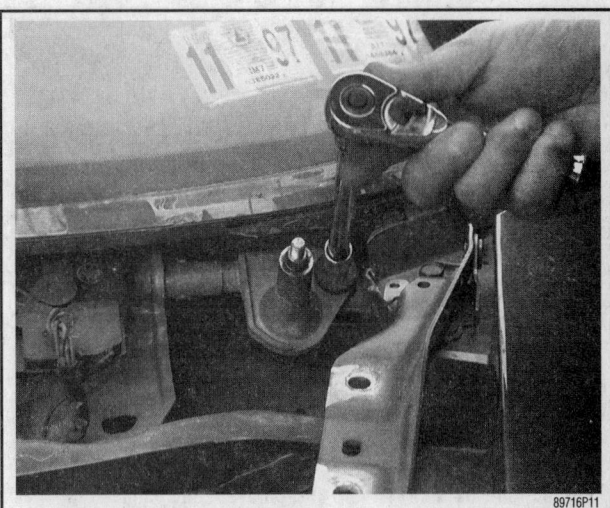

Fig. 62 Unfasten the wiper module retainers

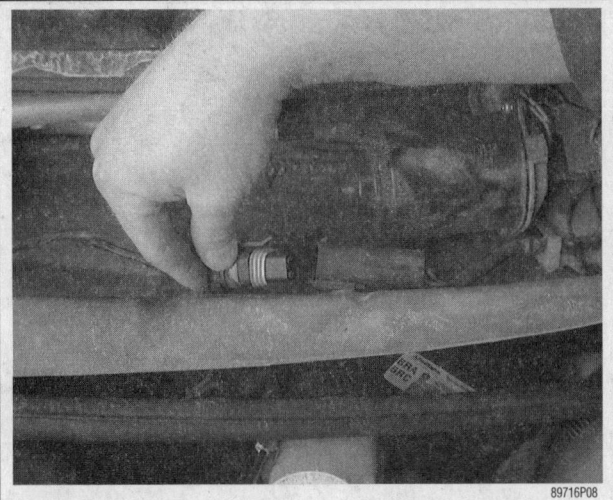

Fig. 60 Detach the electrical connector from the wiper motor

Fig. 63 Unfasten the grounding strap retaining bolt . . .

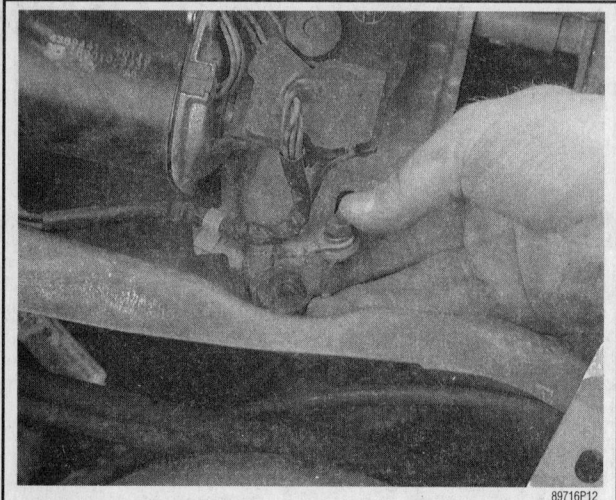

Fig. 64 . . . then remove the grounding strap and position out of the way

Fig. 65 After all the retainers are removed, and connectors detached, remove the windshield wiper motor and linkage assembly from the vehicle

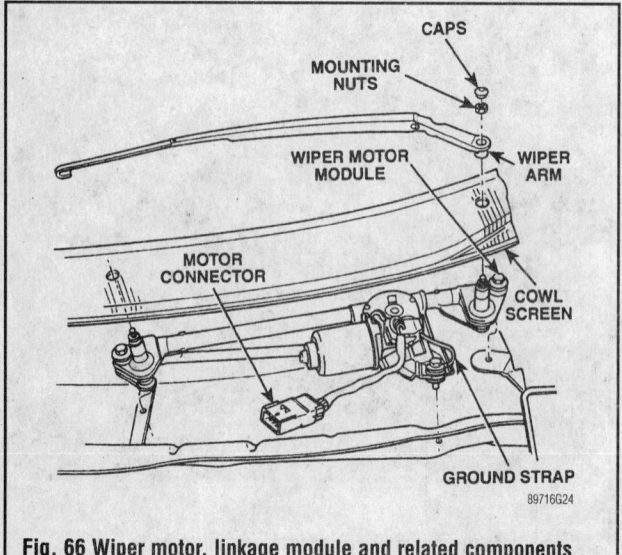

Fig. 66 Wiper motor, linkage module and related components

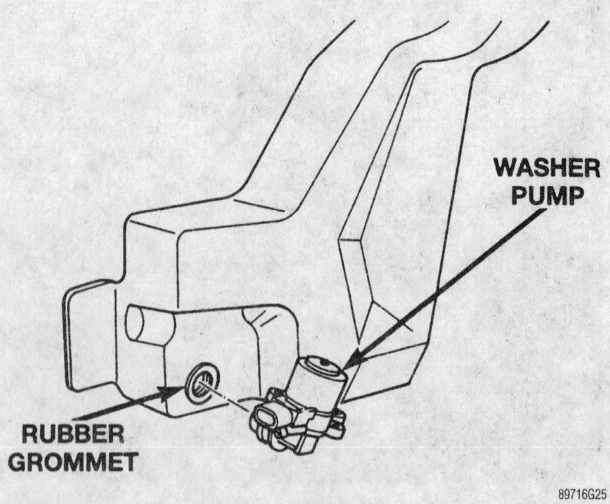

Fig. 67 View of the wiper motor (1), and linkage-to-motor crank attachment (2)

10. Make sure to lubricate the socket with multi-purpose grease.
11. Observe the following specifications during installation:
   a. Tighten the motor mounting screws to 45–55 inch lbs. (5–6 Nm).
   b. Tighten the drive link nut to 8–9 ft. lbs. (11–12 Nm).
   c. Tighten the module mounting screws to 60–80 inch lbs. (7–9 Nm).

## Windshield Washer Pump

### REMOVAL & INSTALLATION

▶ **See Figure 68**

1. Disconnect the negative battery cable.
2. Raise and safely support the vehicle.
3. Detach the electrical connector from the reservoir pump.
4. Place a suitable drain pan under the reservoir, then disconnect the washer hose from the pump and allow the reservoir to drain into the pan.
5. Carefully pry the pump away from the reservoir and out of the

Fig. 68 The washer fluid pump is mounted in the side of the reservoir

retaining grommet. Be careful not to puncture the reservoir when removing the pump.

  6. Remove and discard the rubber grommet.

**To install:**

  7. Place a new rubber grommet in the reservoir.

  8. Place the pump into position, then push it onto the grommet until it is fully seated.

  9. Attach the reservoir pump electrical connector.

  10. Carefully lower the vehicle.

  11. Fill the windshield washer reservoir with the proper type and amount of fluid.

  12. Connect the negative battery cable, then check the system for proper operation.

## INSTRUMENTS AND SWITCHES

### Instrument Cluster

REMOVAL & INSTALLATION

▶ **See Figures 69 thru 76**

➡ **When handling or storing the instrument cluster, make sure that the overlays are not damaged. If you put the cluster down, make sure it is in the face up position or the gauge operation will be damaged.**

  1. Disconnect the negative battery cable.

  2. Remove the instrument panel top cover and bezel by carefully prying it up to disengage the retaining clips.

  3. Unfasten the four screws attaching the cluster housing to the base panel.

  4. Pull the cluster rearward to disengage it from the base panel, then remove the cluster from the vehicle.

  5. If necessary, you can replace the cluster bulb(s) by accessing them from the rear of the cluster. The bulbs are identified on the rear of the cluster.

Fig. 69 Carefully pry the instrument top cover and bezel up to remove it

Fig. 71 Remove the 4 cluster-to-panel mounting screws

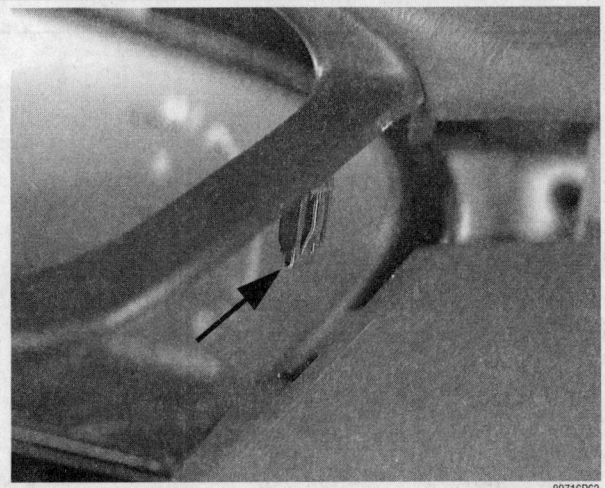
Fig. 70 The top cover and bezel are secured with retaining clips (see arrow)

Fig. 72 Pull the cluster rearward to detach it from the base panel and remove it from the vehicle

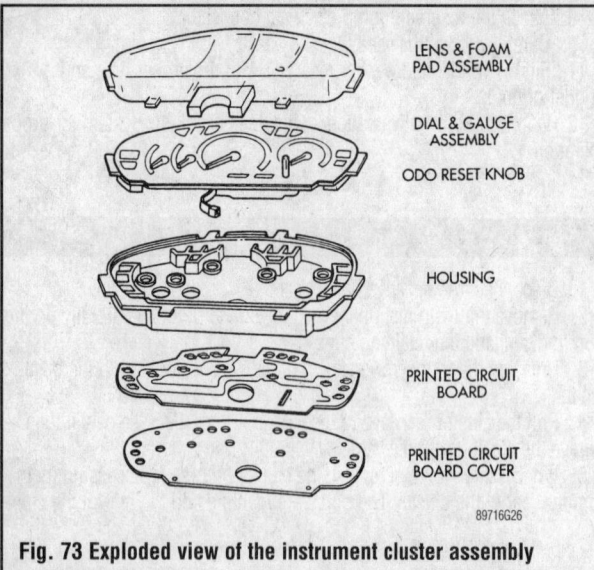

LENS & FOAM PAD ASSEMBLY

DIAL & GAUGE ASSEMBLY

ODO RESET KNOB

HOUSING

PRINTED CIRCUIT BOARD

PRINTED CIRCUIT BOARD COVER

89716G26

**Fig. 73 Exploded view of the instrument cluster assembly**

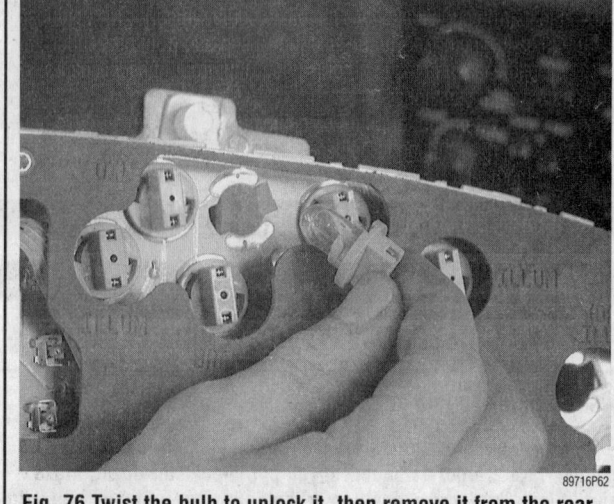

89716P62

**Fig. 76 Twist the bulb to unlock it, then remove it from the rear side of the instrument cluster**

**To install:**

6.  Position the cluster and press firmly in place.
7.  Install the four cluster housing-to-base panel screws.
8.  Install the instrument panel top cover and bezel by pushing it into place.
9.  Connect the negative battery cable.

## Gauges

REMOVAL & INSTALLATION

▶ **See Figures 73 and 77**

1.  Disconnect the negative battery cable.
2.  Remove the instrument cluster from the vehicle.

➡**When handling or storing the instrument cluster, make sure that the overlays are not damaged. If you put the cluster down, make sure it is in the face up position or the gauge operation will be damaged.**

3.  Remove the attaching screws from the printed circuit board cover. The bottom screws attaching the lens to the housing can be accessed without removing the foam pad.

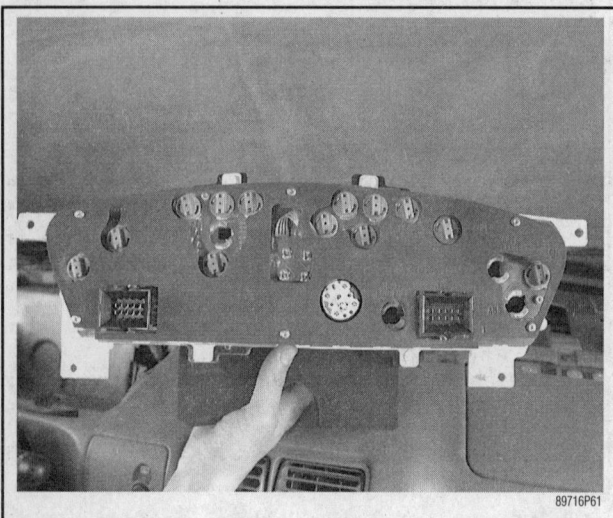

89716P61

**Fig. 74 Rear view of the instrument cluster**

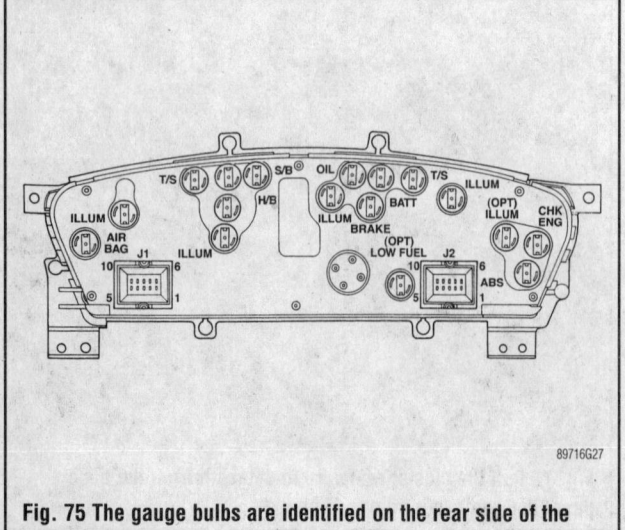

89716G27

**Fig. 75 The gauge bulbs are identified on the rear side of the instrument cluster**

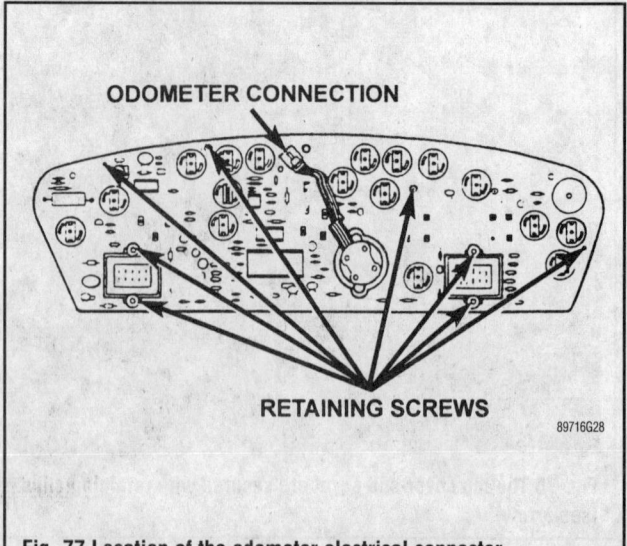

ODOMETER CONNECTION

RETAINING SCREWS

89716G28

**Fig. 77 Location of the odometer electrical connector**

4. Detach the odometer connector.
5. Remove the lens attaching screws, then remove the lens.
6. Carefully pry out the dial and gauge assembly.
7. Installation is the reverse of the removal procedure.

## Windshield Wiper Switch

### REMOVAL & INSTALLATION

The windshield wiper switch and the intermittent wiper relay is built into a multi-function combination switch that is mounted on the steering column. Refer to Section 8 for removal and installation procedures.

## Headlight Switch

### REMOVAL & INSTALLATION

▶ **See Figure 78**

1. Disconnect the negative battery cable.
2. Remove the steering column cover and liner.
3. Remove the 3 screws securing the headlight switch mounting plate to the instrument panel.
4. Pull the headlight switch and mounting plate rearward from the instrument panel opening.
5. Detach both the 9-way and ground connectors from the switch.
6. Remove the switch knob by depressing the release button on the bottom of the switch and pulling the knob out from the switch.
7. Snap the headlight switch bezel out of the mounting plate in order to access the mounting plate retaining nut.
8. Remove the headlight switch, mounting plate, and retaining nut, then separate the switch from the mounting plate.
9. Installation is the reverse of the removal procedure.

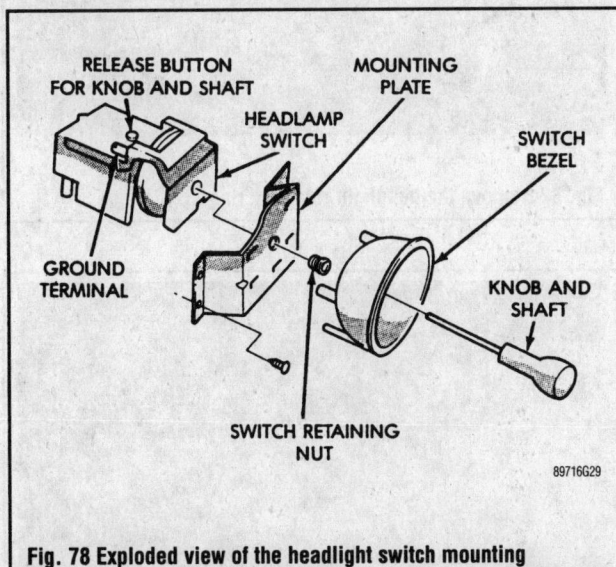

Fig. 78 Exploded view of the headlight switch mounting

## Back-up Light Switch

### REMOVAL & INSTALLATION

**Manual Transaxle**

▶ **See Figure 79**

➡The back-up lamp switch is located on the top left front side of the transaxle case.

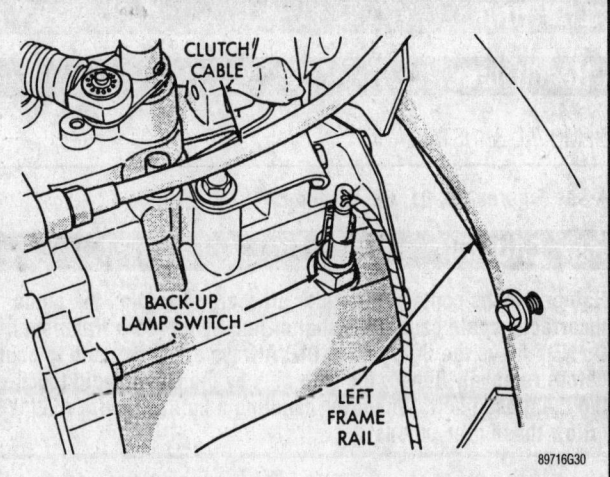

Fig. 79 Location of the back-up light switch—vehicles with manual transaxles

1. Disconnect the negative battery cable.
2. Raise and safely support the vehicle.
3. From the bottom side of the vehicle, detach the wiring connector from the switch.
4. Unscrew the switch from the transaxle case.
5. Installation is the reverse of the removal procedure. You must use Teflon® tape on the switch threads.

### ✴✴ WARNING

**Do NOT overtighten the switch.**

6. After installation, make sure the back-up lamps are working properly.

**Automatic Transaxle**

➡On vehicles equipped with automatic transaxles, the park/neutral and back-up light switch are combined into a single switch.

1. Disconnect the negative battery cable.
2. Place a suitable drain pan under the transaxle.
3. Unscrew the switch from the transaxle case, letting the fluid drain into the pan.
4. Move the gear selector lever to PARK, then to the NEUTRAL position, and check to see if the switch operating lever fingers are centered in the switch opening.
**To install:**
5. Screw the switch, with a new seal, into the transaxle case and tighten to 24 ft. lbs. (33 Nm). Test the switch with the test lamp.
6. Add fluid to the transaxle to bring it up to the proper level.
7. The back-up lamp switch circuit is through the 2 outside terminals of the three terminal switch.
8. To test the switch, remove the wiring connector from the switch and test for continuity between the 2 outside pines.
9. Continuity should exist only with the transaxle in the REVERSE position.

## Ignition Switch

### REMOVAL & INSTALLATION

The ignition switch is mounted in the steering column. For removal and installation procedures, please refer to Section 8 of this manual.

## LIGHTING

### Headlights

REMOVAL & INSTALLATION

▶ **See Figures 80, 81, 82, 83 and 84**

### ✳ CAUTION

**Halogen bulbs contain gas under pressure. Handling the bulbs incorrectly could cause it to shatter into flying glass fragments. Do NOT leave the light switch ON. Always allow the bulb to cool before removal. Handle the bulb only by the base; avoid touching the glass itself. Whenever handling a halogen bulb, ALWAYS follow these precautions:**

• Turn the headlight switch **OFF** and allow the bulb to cool before changing it. Leave the switch **OFF** until the change is complete.

• ALWAYS wear eye protection when changing a halogen bulb.
• Handle the bulb only by its base. Avoid touching the glass.
• DO NOT drop or scratch the bulb.
• Keep dirt and moisture away from the bulb.
• Place the used bulb in the new bulb's carton and dispose of it properly.

1. Open the vehicle's hood and secure it in an upright position.
2. Disconnect the negative battery cable.
3. Detach the headlight electrical connector.
4. Remove the retaining ring holding the bulb to the back of the headlight module.
5. Pull the bulb from the back of the headlight module. Hold the bulb by its base only, try not to touch the glass itself.

**To install:**

6. Holding the bulb by the base, place it in the headlight module, then secure with the retaining ring.
7. Attach the electrical connector to the bulb.
8. Connect the negative battery cable and check the headlight operation.

Fig. 80 The headlight bulb and socket are accessed through the engine compartment

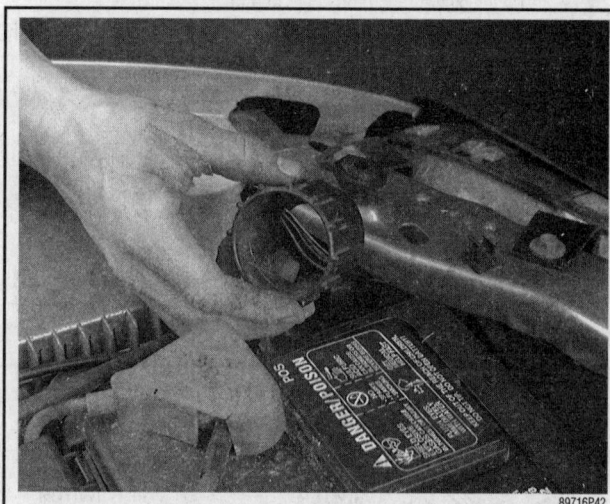

Fig. 82 Remove the headlight retaining ring . . .

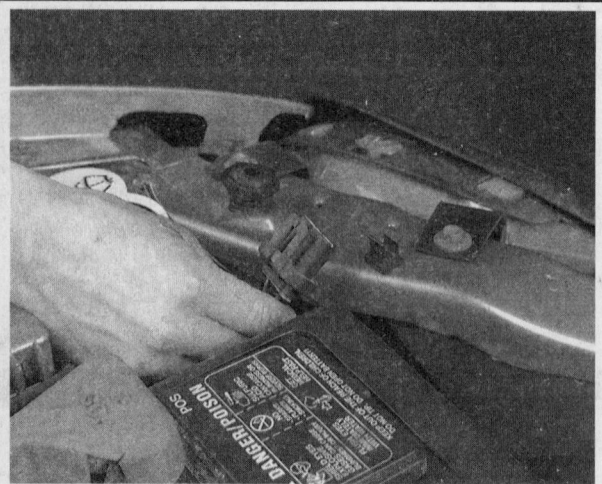

Fig. 81 Unplug the headlight electrical connector

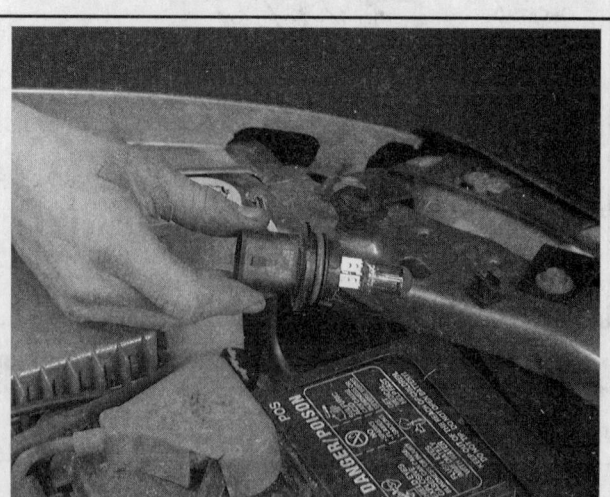

Fig. 83 . . . then, holding it by its base ONLY, pull the headlight bulb out

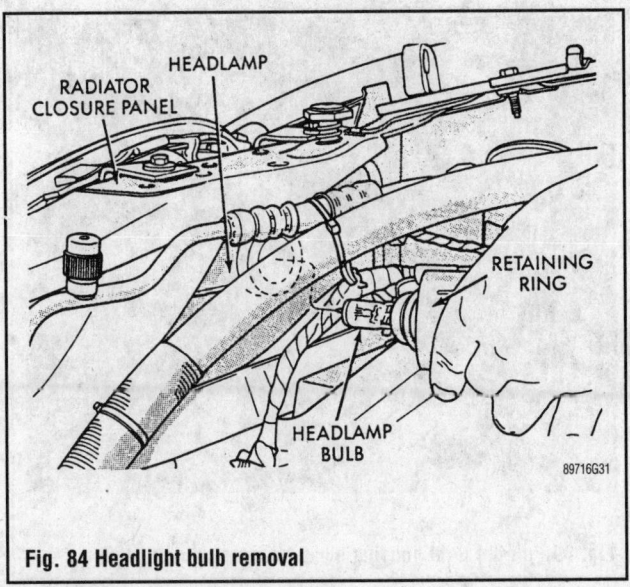

**Fig. 84 Headlight bulb removal**

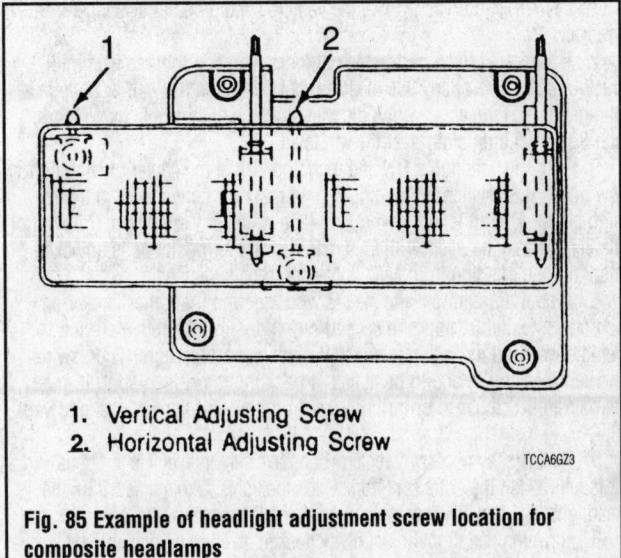

1. Vertical Adjusting Screw
2. Horizontal Adjusting Screw

**Fig. 85 Example of headlight adjustment screw location for composite headlamps**

## AIMING THE HEADLIGHTS

▶ **See Figures 85, 86 and 87**

The headlights must be properly aimed to provide the best, safest road illumination. The lights should be checked for proper aim and adjusted as necessary. Certain state and local authorities have requirements for headlight aiming; these should be checked before adjustment is made.

### ✳ CAUTION

**About once a year, when the headlights are replaced or any time front end work is performed on your vehicle, the headlight should be accurately aimed by a reputable repair shop using the proper equipment. Headlights not properly aimed can make it virtually impossible to see and may blind other drivers on the road, possibly causing an accident. Note that the following procedure is a temporary fix, until you can take your vehicle to a repair shop for a proper adjustment.**

Headlight adjustment may be temporarily made using a wall, as described below, or on the rear of another vehicle. When adjusted, the lights should not glare in oncoming car or truck windshields, nor should they illuminate the passenger compartment of vehicles driving in front of you. These adjustments are rough and should always be fine-tuned by a repair shop which is equipped with headlight aiming tools. Improper adjustments may be both dangerous and illegal.

For most of the vehicles covered by this manual, horizontal and vertical aiming of each sealed beam unit is provided by two adjusting screws which move the retaining ring and adjusting plate against the tension of a coil spring. There is no adjustment for focus; this is done during headlight manufacturing.

➡ **Because the composite headlight assembly is bolted into position, no adjustment should be necessary or possible. Some applications, however, may be bolted to an adjuster plate or may be retained by adjusting screws. If so, follow this procedure when adjusting the lights, BUT always have the adjustment checked by a reputable shop.**

Before removing the headlight bulb or disturbing the headlamp in any way, note the current settings in order to ease headlight adjustment upon reassembly. If the high or low beam setting of the old lamp still works, this can be done using the wall of a garage or a building:

1. Park the vehicle on a level surface, with the fuel tank about ½ full and with the vehicle empty of all extra cargo (unless normally carried). The vehicle should be facing a wall which is no less than 6 feet (1.8m) high and

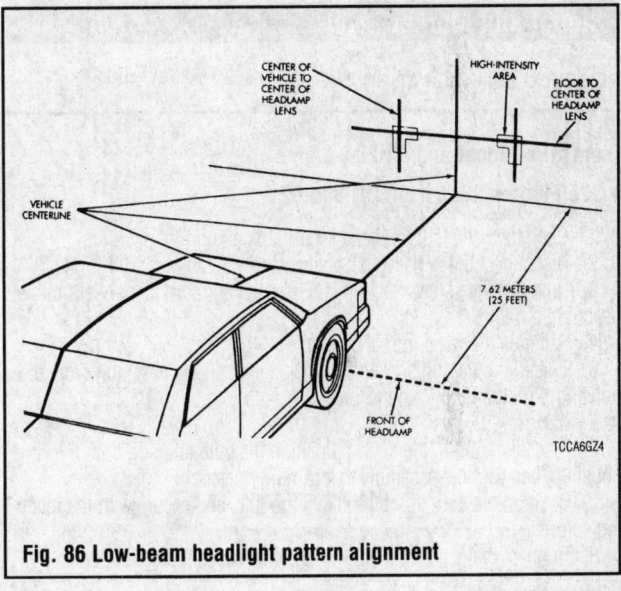

**Fig. 86 Low-beam headlight pattern alignment**

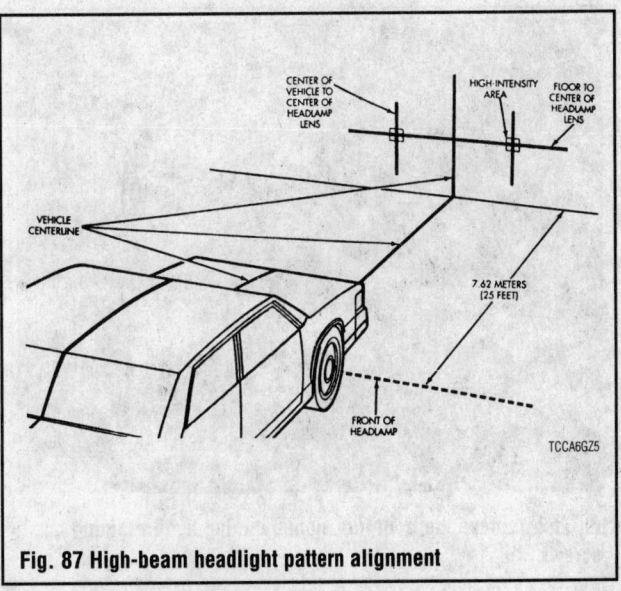

**Fig. 87 High-beam headlight pattern alignment**

12 feet (3.7m) wide. The front of the vehicle should be about 25 feet from the wall.

2. If aiming is to be performed outdoors, it is advisable to wait until dusk in order to properly see the headlight beams on the wall. If done in a garage, darken the area around the wall as much as possible by closing shades or hanging cloth over the windows.

3. Turn the headlights **ON** and mark the wall at the center of each light's low beam, then switch on the brights and mark the center of each light's high beam. A short length of masking tape which is visible from the front of the vehicle may be used. Although marking all four positions is advisable, marking one position from each light should be sufficient.

4. If neither beam on one side is working, and if another like-sized vehicle is available, park the second one in the exact spot where the vehicle was and mark the beams using the same-side light. Then switch the vehicles so the one to be aimed is back in the original spot. It must be parked no closer to or farther away from the wall than the second vehicle.

5. Perform any necessary repairs, but make sure the vehicle is not moved, or is returned to the exact spot from which the lights were marked. Turn the headlights **ON** and adjust the beams to match the marks on the wall.

6. Have the headlight adjustment checked as soon as possible by a reputable repair shop.

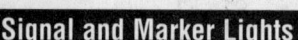

## Signal and Marker Lights

### REMOVAL & INSTALLATION

#### Front Turn Signal and Parking Lights

▶ See Figures 88, 89, 90, 91 and 92

1. Open the vehicle's hood and secure it in an upright position.
2. Disconnect the negative battery cable.
3. Unfasten the screws securing the parking and turn signal light to the headlight module.
4. Separate the lamp from the module.
5. Twist the bulb and socket to unlock, then pull the assembly from the housing. Pull the bulb from the socket.

**To install:**

6. Place the bulb in the socket. Position the bulb and socket in the housing, then turn the assembly to lock it into place.
7. Position the light to the headlight module, and secure with the retaining screws.
8. Connect the negative battery cable, then check the light operation.

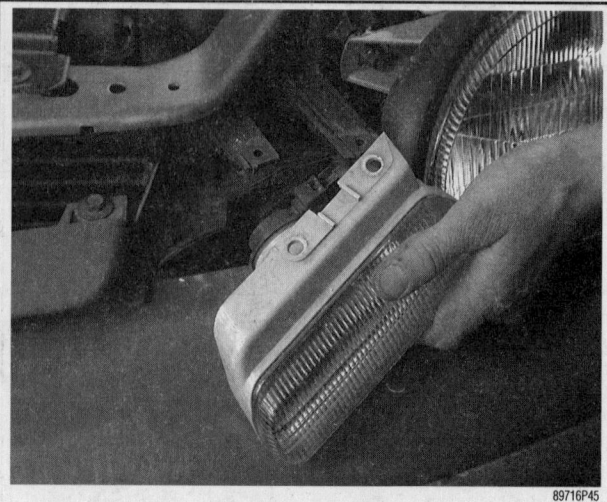

Fig. 89 Pull the light housing away from the vehicle

Fig. 90 Twist the bulb and socket to unlock it, pull it from the housing . . .

Fig. 88 Remove the front turn signal/parking light retaining screws

Fig. 91 . . . then pull the bulb from the socket and replace if necessary

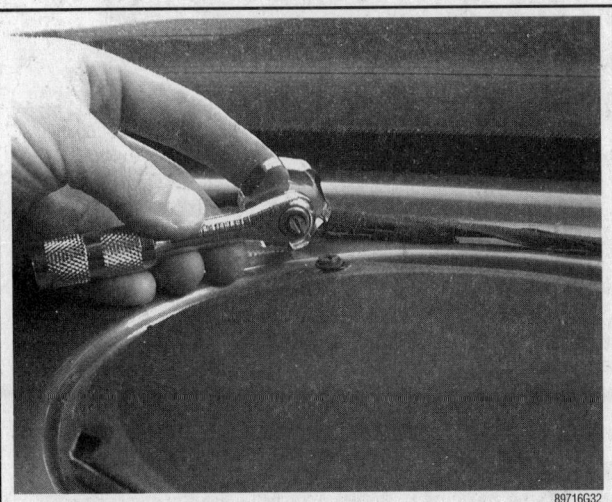

Fig. 92 You must remove the parking/turn signal light housing to remove the bulb

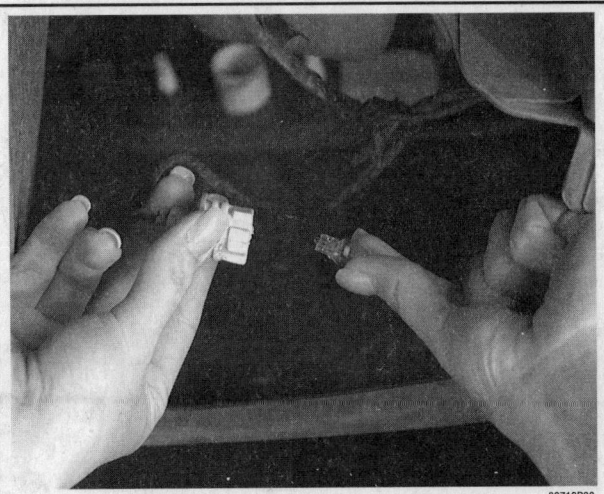

Fig. 94 Twist and unlock the socket, then carefully pull the bulb out of the socket

### Side Marker Light

▶ See Figures 93 and 94

1. Disconnect the negative battery cable.
2. Raise and safely support the vehicle. The vehicle only has to be raised enough for you to access the light inside the front bumper.
3. Reach behind the front bumper fascia in forward of the front wheel.
4. Turn the bulb and socket to unlock it, then pull the assembly from the rear of the housing.
5. Carefully pull the bulb straight out of the socket.

**To install:**

6. Place a new bulb in the socket.
7. Position the bulb and socket in the rear of the housing and turn to lock into position.
8. Carefully lower the vehicle.
9. Connect the negative battery cable, then check the light operation.

### Rear Turn Signal, Brake and Parking Lights

▶ See Figures 95, 96, 97 and 98

1. Disconnect the negative battery cable, then open the trunk.
2. Separate the trunk lining from the rear closure panel to gain access to the back of the tail light.
3. Rotate and remove the bulb socket from the tail light, through the openings in the rear closure panel.
4. Pull the bulb from the socket.

**To install:**

5. Push the bulb into the socket.
6. Install the bulb socket into the tail light through the openings in the rear closure panel, then rotate to lock into place.
7. Install the trunk lining to the rear closure panel.
8. Close the trunk lid.
9. Connect the negative battery cable.

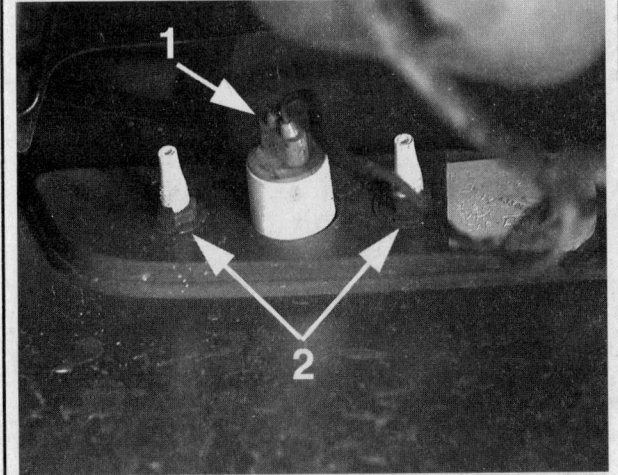

Fig. 93 The side marker light connector (1) and retainers (2) must be accessed from under the vehicle

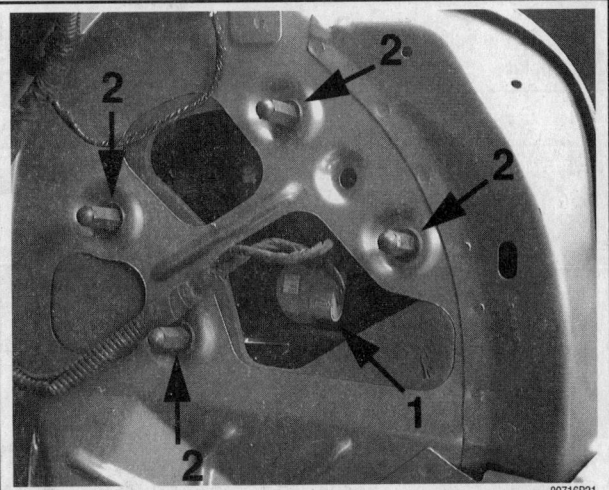

Fig. 95 Rear turn signal/brake light bulb connector (1) and lens assembly retainers (2)

**Fig. 96 Twist the bulb and socket to unlock, then pull the assembly from the rear of the lens**

89716P22

**Fig. 97 If the bulb has burnt out , pull the bulb from the socket and replace**

89716P23

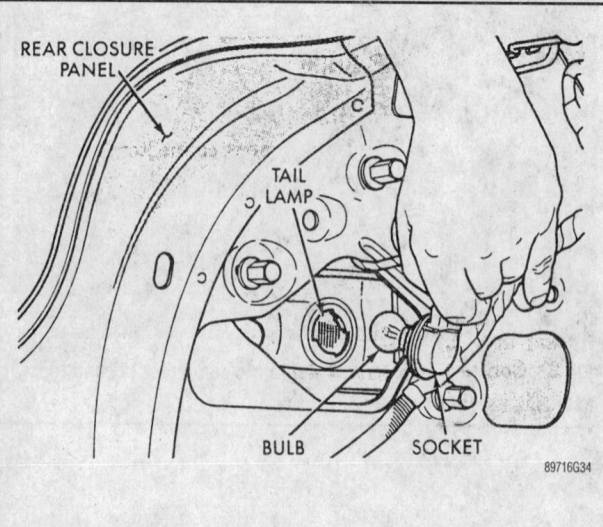

**Fig. 98 Exploded view of the tail, brake and turn signal light**

89716G34

### High-mount Brake Light

**♦ See Figures 99, 100 and 101**

1. Disconnect the negative battery cable, then open the trunk.
2. Rotate and remove the bulb socket from the high-mount brake light housing.
3. Pull the bulb from the socket.

**To install:**

4. Push the bulb into the socket.
5. Position the bulb socket in the housing, then rotate to lock into place.
6. Close the trunk, connect the negative battery cable, then check light operation.

### Dome Light

**♦ See Figures 102 and 103**

1. Disconnect the negative battery cable.
2. Insert a small prytool between the headliner and dome lamp lens.
3. Carefully pry downward on the four corners of the lamp lens.

**Fig. 99 Twist the high-mount brake light bulb and socket to unlock it, pull it from the lens . . .**

89716P24

**Fig. 100 . . . then remove the bulb from the socket and replace if necessary**

89716P25

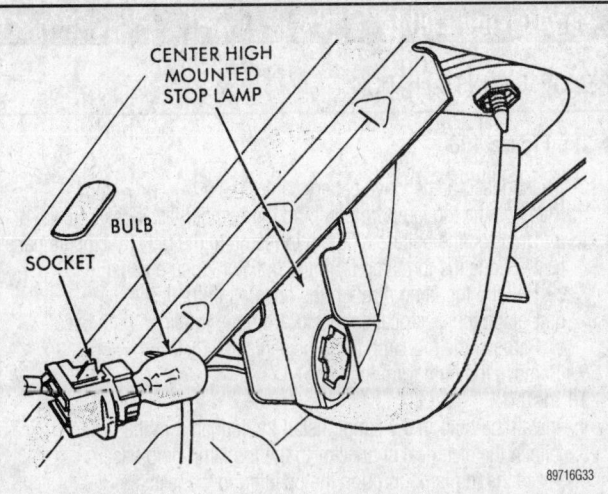

**Fig. 101 Exploded view of the center high-mount brake light and bulb**

4. Separate the lens from the lamp.
5. Pull the bulb from the lamp socket.
**To install:**
6. Position the bulb into the socket and snap into place.
7. Position the lens onto the lamp and snap securely into place.
8. Connect the negative battery cable.

**License Plate Lights**

▶ **See Figures 104, 105, 106 and 107**

1. Disconnect the negative battery cable.
2. Remove the screws holding the license plate lamp to the rear bumper fascia.
3. Separate the lamp from the bumper.
4. Remove the bulb socket from the lamp, then pull the bulb from the socket.
**To install:**
5. Push the bulb into the socket.
6. Place the bulb socket into the lamp.
7. Position the lamp into the bumper then install the screws holding the lamp to the rear bumper.
8. Connect the negative battery cable.

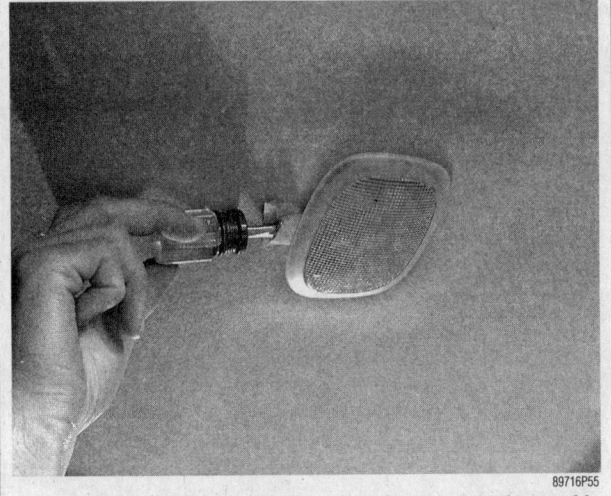

**Fig. 102 Place a piece of paper towel under the prytool to avoid damaging the headlining material**

**Fig. 104 The license plate light is accessed through the opening in the rear bumper**

**Fig. 103 Remove the lens, then pull the bulb downward to remove it**

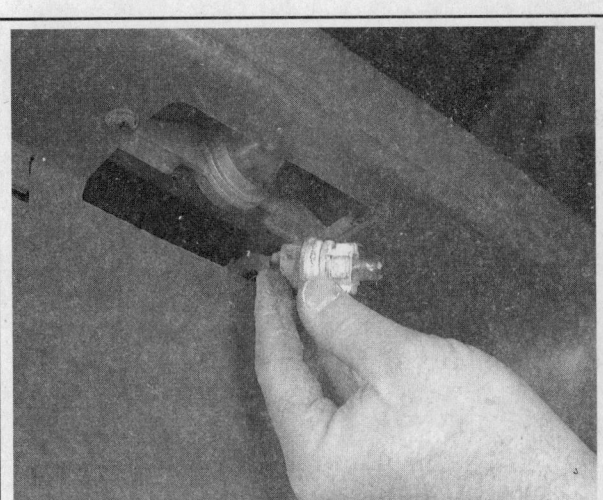

**Fig. 105 Pull the license plate bulb and socket from its lens . . .**

**Fig. 106 . . . then remove the bulb from the assembly and replace**

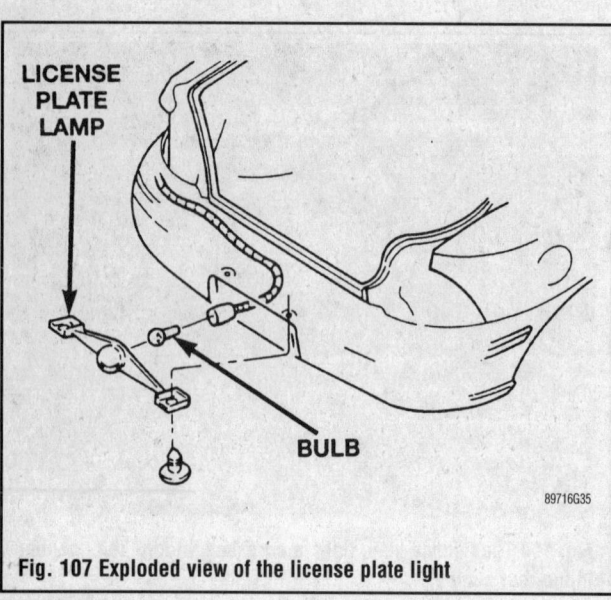

**Fig. 107 Exploded view of the license plate light**

## Fog/Driving Lights

REMOVAL & INSTALLATION

▶ **See Figure 108**

1. Disconnect the negative battery cable.
2. Remove the fog lamp from behind the bumper fascia, as follows:
   a. Unfasten the bolt holding the fog lamp to the radiator closure panel.
   b. Separate the fog lamp from the radiator closure panel.
   c. Pull the fog lamp through the opening in the fascia.
   d. Detach the electrical connector from the fog lamp bulb base.
   e. Remove the fog lamp from the vehicle.
3. Remove the bulb from the lamp.

**To install:**

4. Install the bulb in the lamp. Install the fog lamp in the vehicle.
5. Attach the electrical connector to the fog lamp bulb base.
6. Place the fog lamp through the opening in the fascia.
7. Position the fog lamp to the radiator closure panel.
8. Install the bolt holding the fog lamp to the radiator closure panel.
9. Connect the negative battery cable.

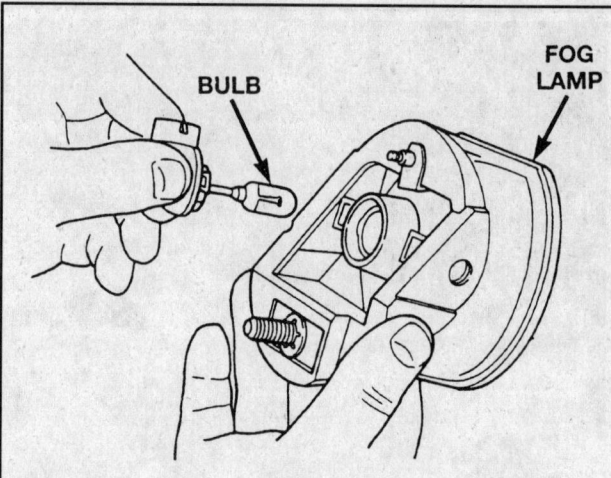

**Fig. 108 Once the fog lamp is removed from the bumper, you can remove the bulb**

## EXTERIOR LAMPS

| LAMP | BULB |
| --- | --- |
| Back-up | 3157 |
| Center High Mounted Stop | 921 |
| Fog | GE 881 |
| Headlamp | 9007 |
| License Plate | 168 |
| Park/Turn Signal | 3157NA |
| Tail/Stop/Turn Signal | 3157 |
| Front Side Marker | 168 |

## INTERIOR LAMPS

| LAMP | BULB |
| --- | --- |
| A/C and Heater Control | 203 |
| Ash Receiver | 161 |
| Cigar Lighter | 203 |
| Dome Lamp | 578 |
| Gear Selector Console W/Auto | 161 |
| Glove Compartment | 194 |
| Ignition Lock | 161 |
| Instrument Panel and Cluster | PC194 |
| Rear Cargo | 912 |
| Underhood | 105 |

## TRAILER WIRING

Wiring the vehicle for towing is fairly easy. There are a number of good wiring kits available and these should be used, rather than trying to design your own.

All trailers will need brake lights and turn signals as well as tail lights and side marker lights. Most areas require extra marker lights for overwide trailers. Also, most areas have recently required back-up lights for trailers, and most trailer manufacturers have been building trailers with back-up lights for several years.

Additionally, some Class I, most Class II and just about all Class III and IV trailers will have electric brakes. Add to this number an accessories wire, to operate trailer internal equipment or to charge the trailer's battery, and you can have as many as seven wires in the harness.

Determine the equipment on your trailer and buy the wiring kit necessary. The kit will contain all the wires needed, plus a plug adapter set which includes the female plug, mounted on the bumper or hitch, and the male plug, wired into, or plugged into the trailer harness.

When installing the kit, follow the manufacturer's instructions. The color coding of the wires is usually standard throughout the industry. One point to note: some domestic vehicles, and most imported vehicles, have separate turn signals. On most domestic vehicles, the brake lights and rear turn signals operate with the same bulb. For those vehicles with separate turn signals, you can purchase an isolation unit so that the brake lights won't blink whenever the turn signals are operated, or, you can go to your local electronics supply house and buy four diodes to wire in series with the brake and turn signal bulbs. Diodes will isolate the brake and turn signals. The choice is yours. The isolation units are simple and quick to install, but far more expensive than the diodes. The diodes, however, require more work to install properly, since they require the cutting of each bulb's wire and soldering in place of the diode.

One, final point, the best kits are those with a spring loaded cover on the vehicle mounted socket. This cover prevents dirt and moisture from corroding the terminals. Never let the vehicle socket hang loosely; always mount it securely to the bumper or hitch.

## CIRCUIT PROTECTION

### Fuses

The main fuse block on these vehicles is located on the left side of the dash, behind an access panel. These is also a Power Distribution Center (PDC) which can be found under the hood.

Each fuse block uses miniature fuses which are designed for increased circuit protection and greater reliability. The compact fuse is a blade terminal design which allows easy pull-out/push-in removal and replacement.

Although the fuses are interchangeable, the amperage values are not. The values are usually molded in bold, color coded, easy to read numbers on the fuse body. Use only fuses of equal replacement valve.

REPLACEMENT

▶ **See Figures 109, 110, 111, 112 and 113**

1. Remove the fuse block access panel or cover.
2. Locate the fuse for the circuit in question.

➡**When replacing the fuse, DO NOT use one with a higher amperage rating.**

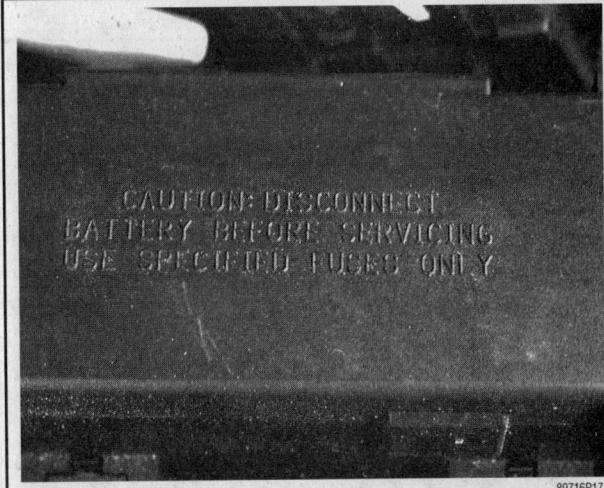

Fig. 110 There is also a fuse box located in the engine compartment, under a protective lid

Fig. 109 Most fuse block covers have a label which identifies the fuses

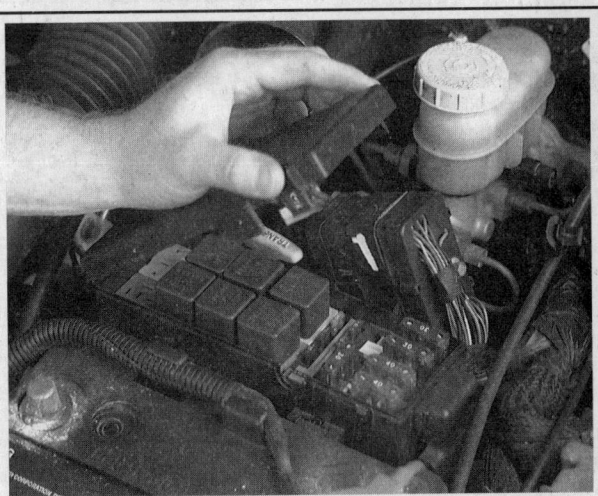

Fig. 111 Unlatch the retaining clamps, then remove the fuse block lid

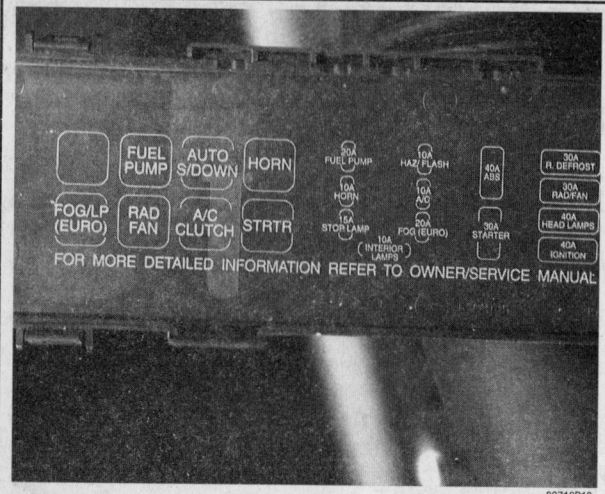

**Fig. 112 The underside of the lid has fuse identification information**

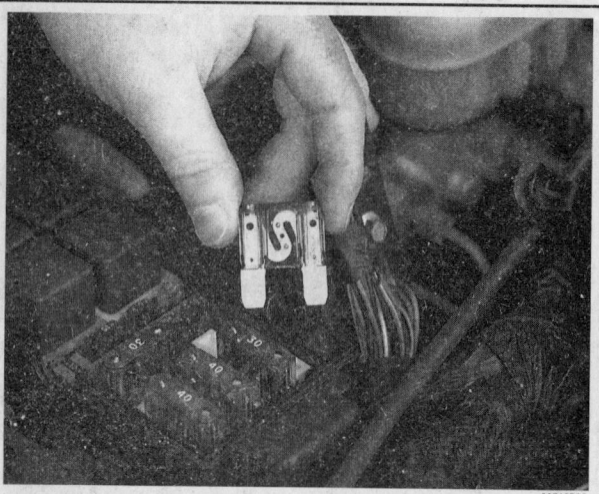

**Fig. 113 Pull the suspect fuse from the block and check the element**

3. Check the fuse by pulling it from the fuse block and observing the element. If it is broken, install a replacement fuse of the same amperage rating. If the fuse blows again, check the circuit for a short to ground or faulty device in the circuit protected by the fuse.

4. Continuity can also be checked with the fuse installed in the fuse block with the use of a test light connected across the 2 test points on the end of the fuse. If the test light lights, replace the fuse. Check the circuit for a short to ground or faulty device in the circuit protected by the fuse.

## Fusible Links

In addition to circuit breakers and fuses, the wiring harness incorporates fusible links to protect the wiring. Links are used rather than a fuse, in wiring circuits that are not normally fused, such as the ignition circuit. The fusible links are color coded red in the charging and load circuits to match the color coding of the circuits they protect. Each link is four gauges smaller than the cable it protects, and is marked on the insulation with the gauge size because the insulation makes it appear heavier than it really is. The engine compartment wiring harness has several fusible links. The same size wire with a special Hypalon insulation must be used when replacing a fusible link.

➡**For more details, see the information on fusible links at the beginning of this section.**

On these vehicles, there is a fusible link placed between the output terminal of the alternator and the engine starter motor terminal.

## Circuit Breakers

Circuit breakers differ from fuses in that they are reusable. Circuit breakers open when the flow of current exceeds specified value and will close after a few seconds when current flow returns to normal. Some of the circuits protected by circuit breakers include electric windows and power accessories. Circuit breakers are used in these applications due to the fact that they must operate at times under prolonged high current flow due to demand, even though there is not malfunction in the circuit.

There are 2 types of circuit breakers. The first type opens when high current flow is detected. A few seconds after the excessive current flow has been removed, the circuit breaker will close. If the high current flow is experienced again, the circuit will open again.

The second type is referred to as the Positive Temperature Coefficient (PTC) circuit breaker. When excessive current flow passes through the PTC circuit breaker, the circuit is not opened, but its resistance increases. As the device heats up with the increase in current flow, the resistance increases to the point where the circuit is effectively open. Unlike other circuit breakers, the PTC circuit breaker will not reset until circuit is opened, removing voltage from the terminals. Once the voltage is removed, the circuit breaker will not reset until the circuit is opened, remove voltage from the terminals. Once the voltage is removed, the circuit breaker will re-close within a few seconds.

Various circuit breakers are located under the instrument panel. In order to gain access to these components, it may be necessary to first remove the under dash padding. Most of the circuit breakers are located in the power distribution center or the fuse panel. Replace the circuit breaker by unplugging the old one and plugging in the new one. Confirm proper circuit operation.

## Flashers

### REPLACEMENT

Flashers are located either on the bottom of the fuse block or on a module under the dash. They are replaced by simply pulling them straight out. Note that the prongs are arranged in such a way that the flasher must be properly oriented before attempting to install it. Turn the flasher until the orientation of the prongs is correct and simply push it firmly in until the prongs are fully engaged.

# INDEX OF WIRING DIAGRAMS

89716W01

## SAMPLE DIAGRAM: HOW TO READ & INTERPRET WIRING DIAGRAMS

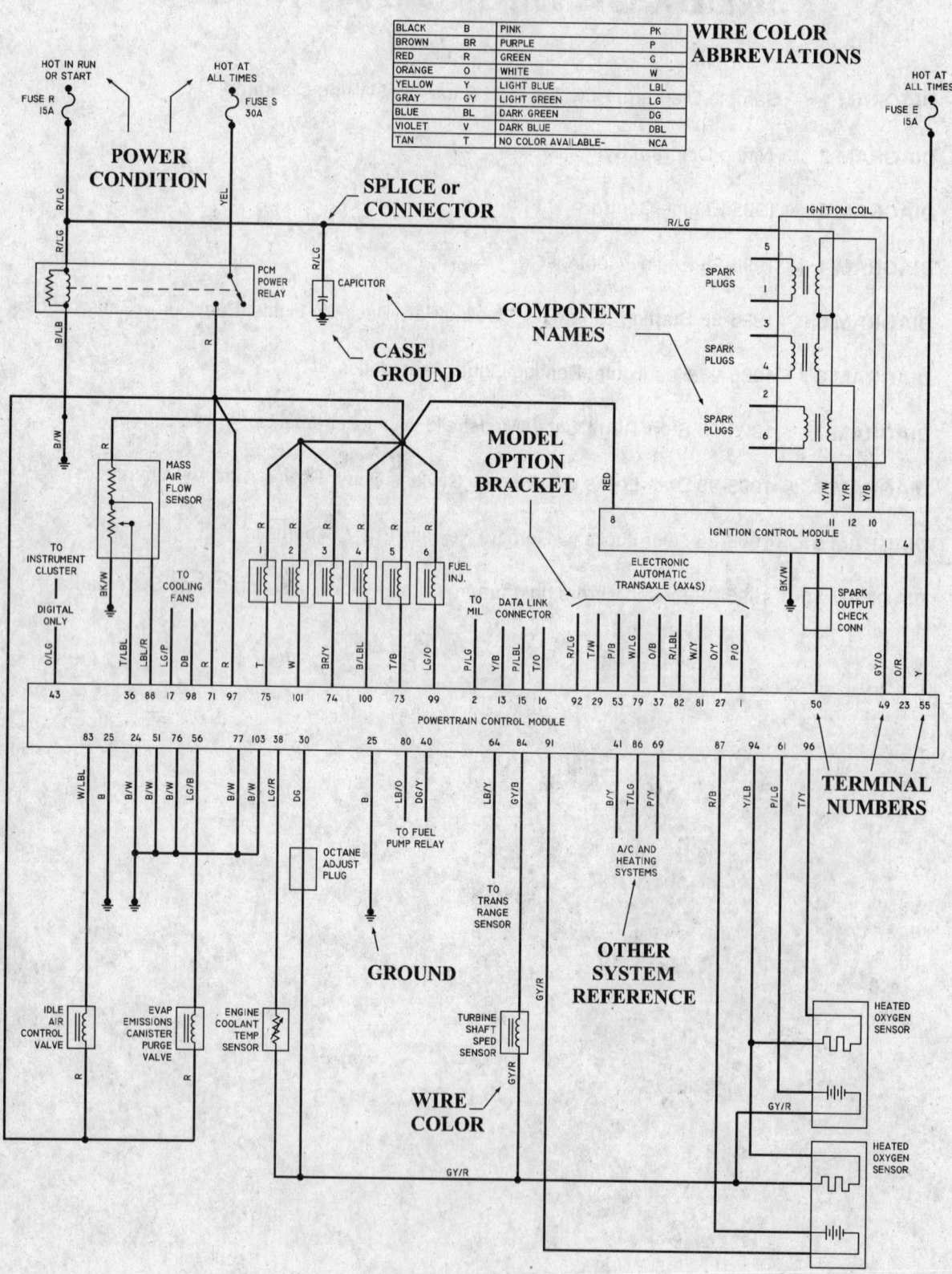

**DIAGRAM 1**

TCCA6W01

# WIRING DIAGRAM SYMBOLS

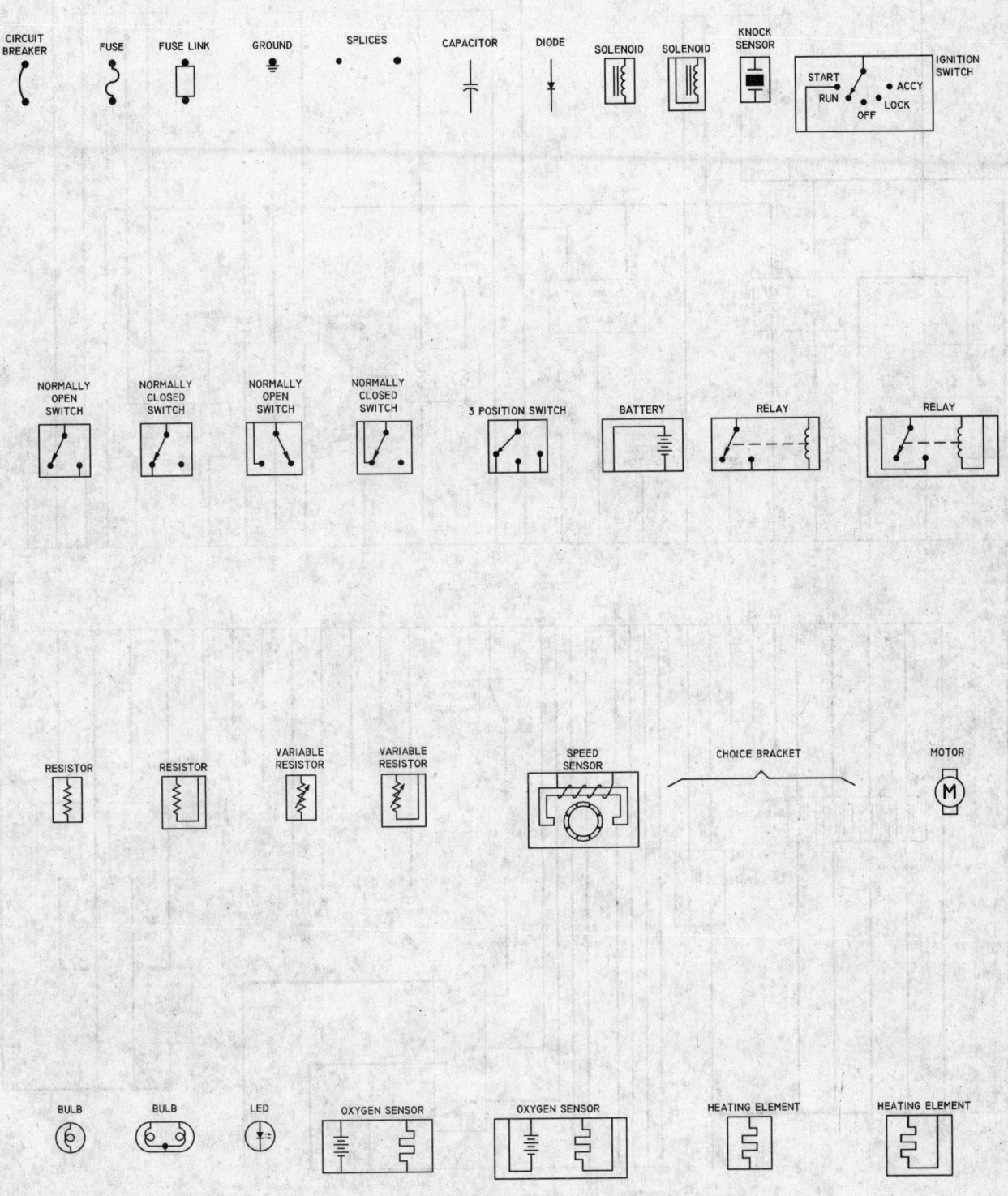

**DIAGRAM 2**

TCCA6W02

## 1995 Neon Engine Schematics

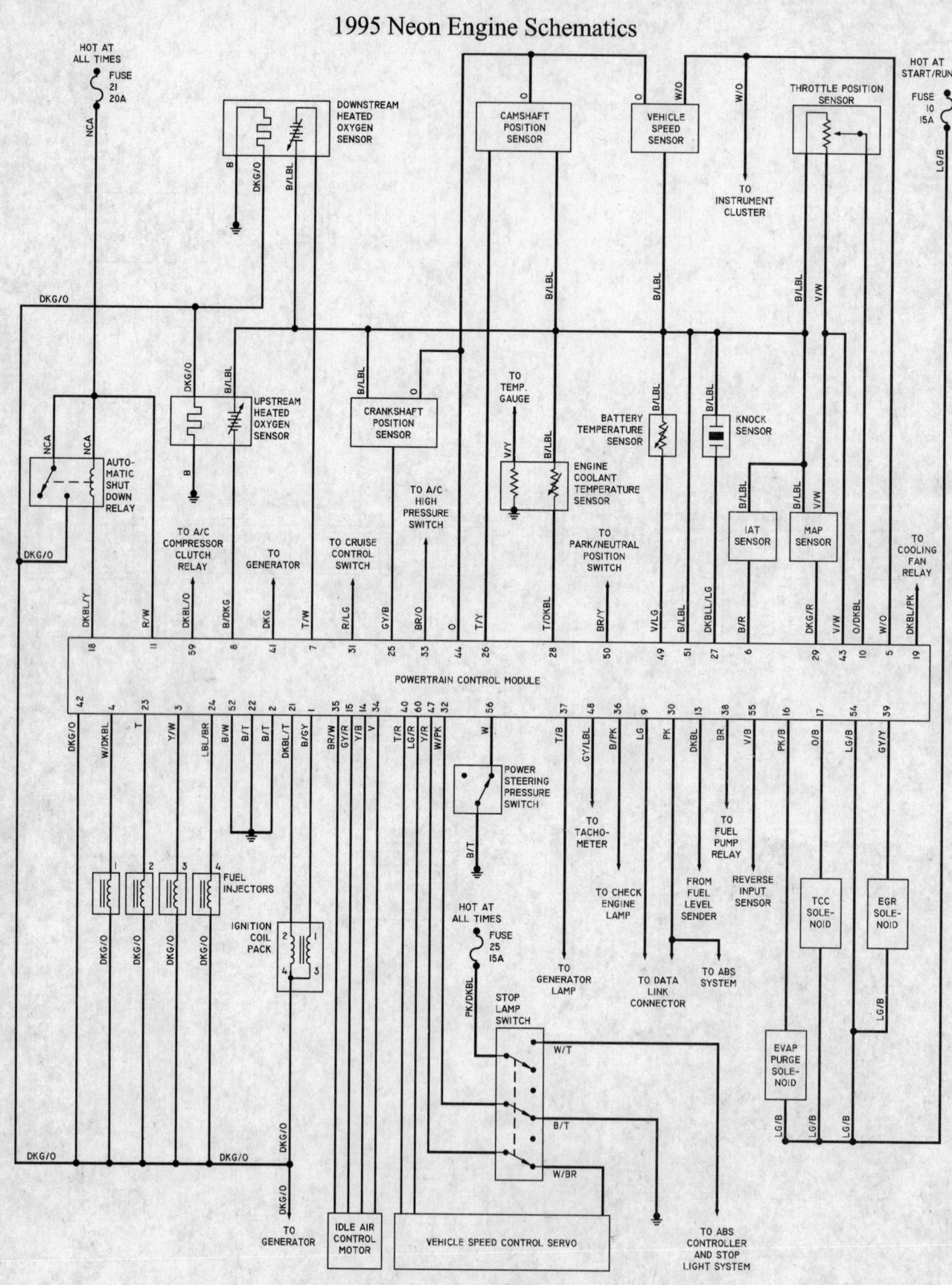

**DIAGRAM 3**

89716E01

## 1996-98 Neon Engine Schematics

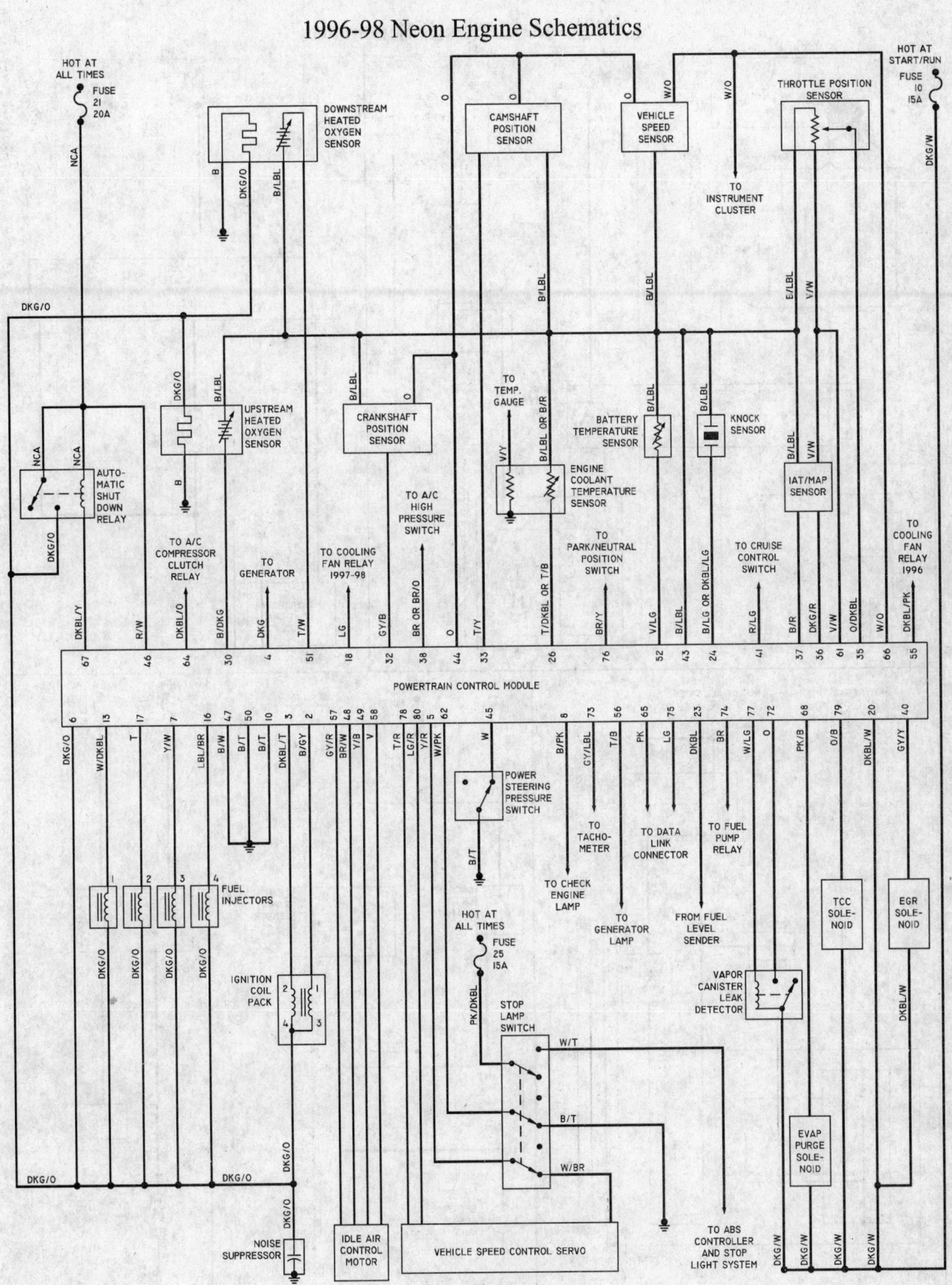

DIAGRAM 4

89716E02

## 1995-98 Neon Chassis Schematics

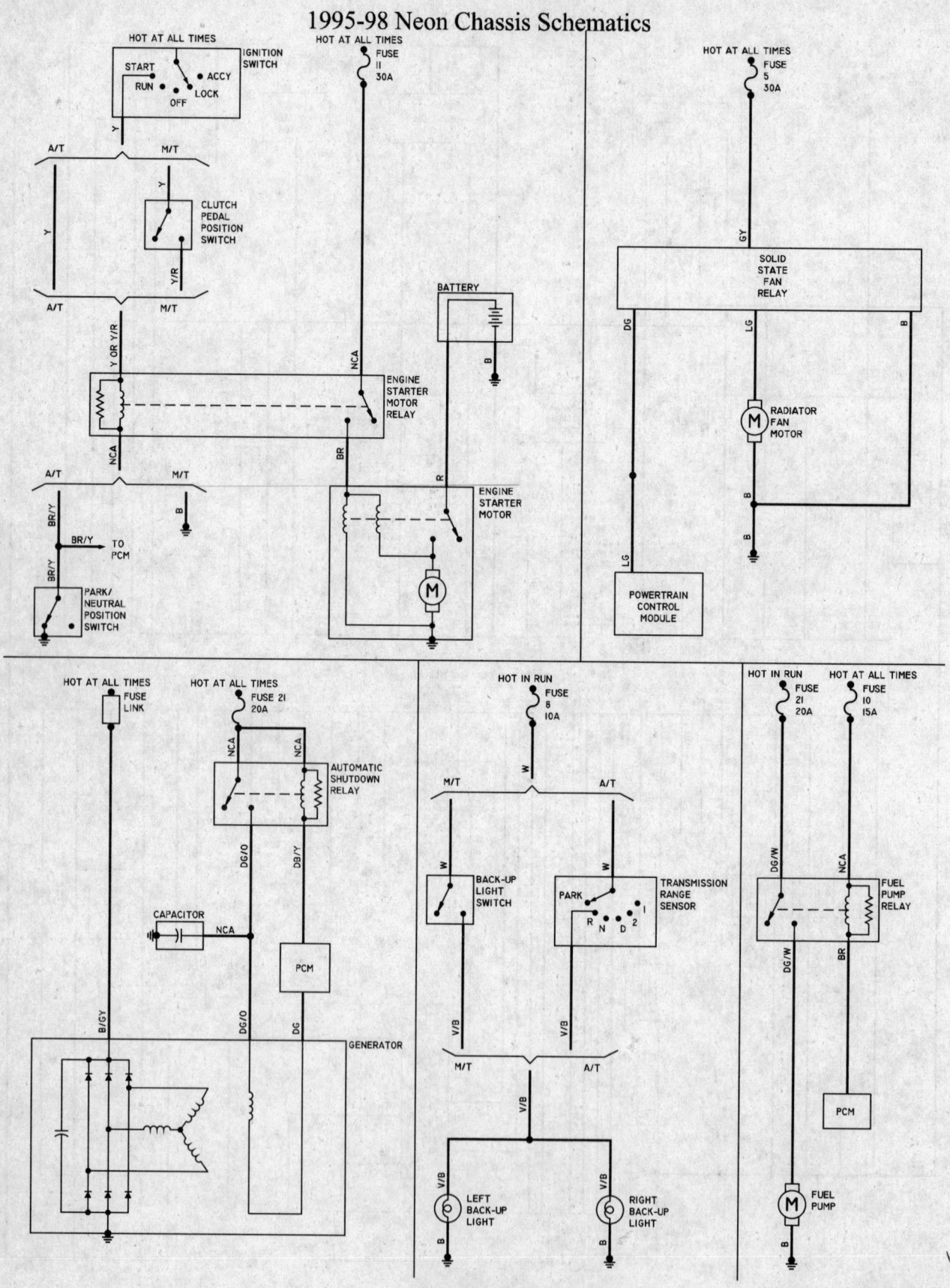

**DIAGRAM 5**

89716B01

## 1995-98 Neon Chassis Schematics

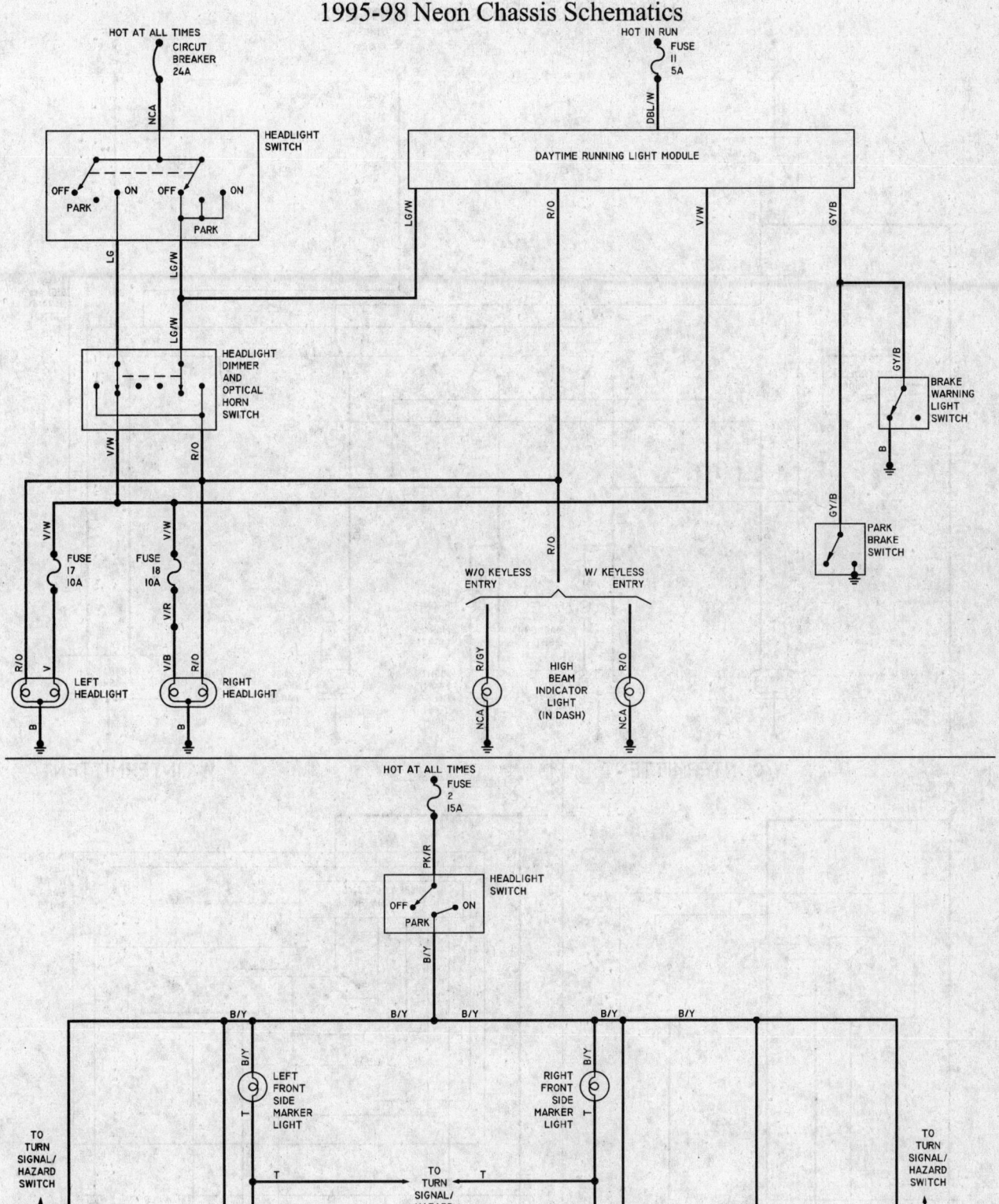

**DIAGRAM 6**

89716B02

## 1995-98 Neon Chassis Schematics

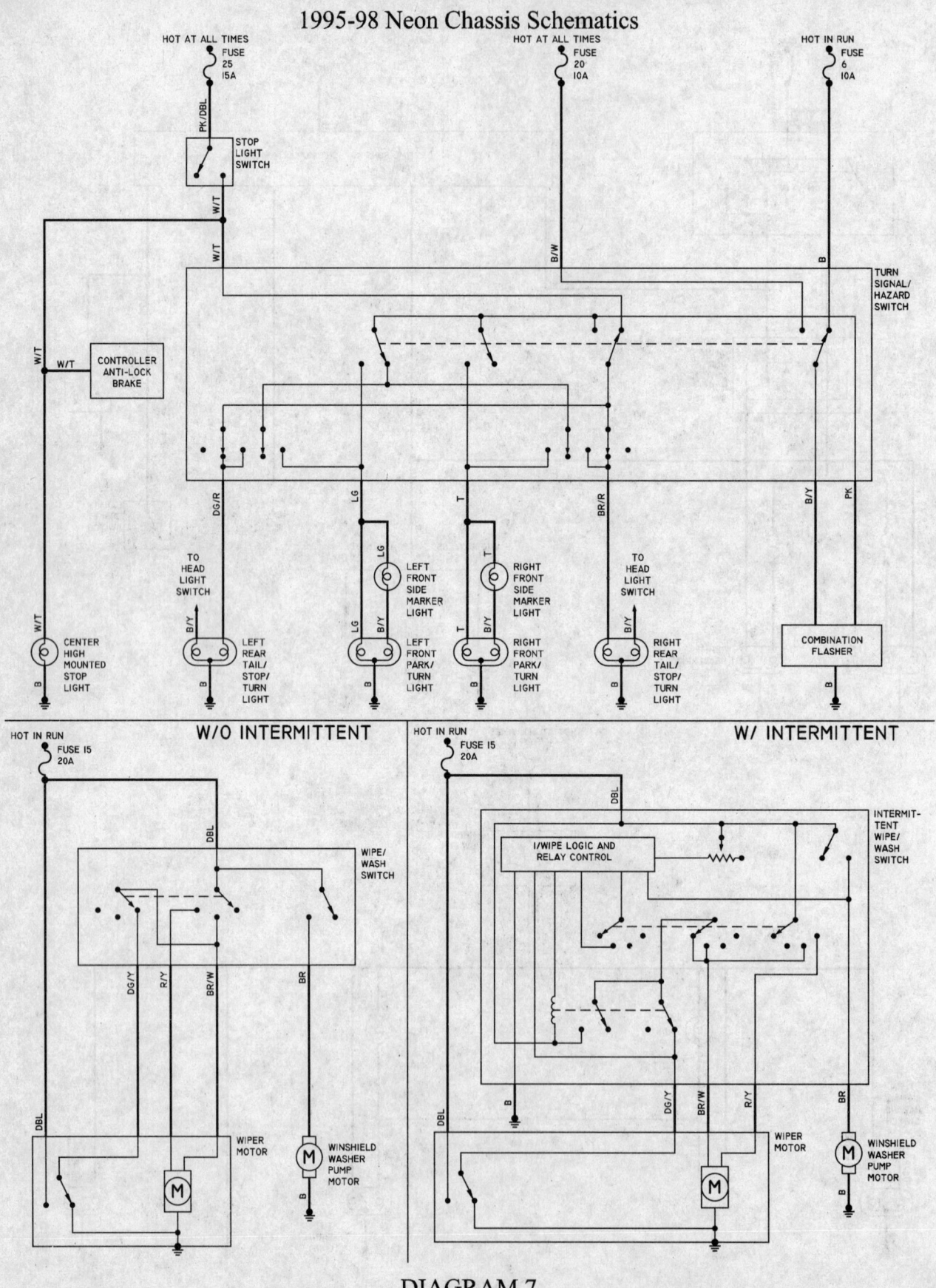

DIAGRAM 7

89716B03

## 1995-98 Neon Chassis Schematics

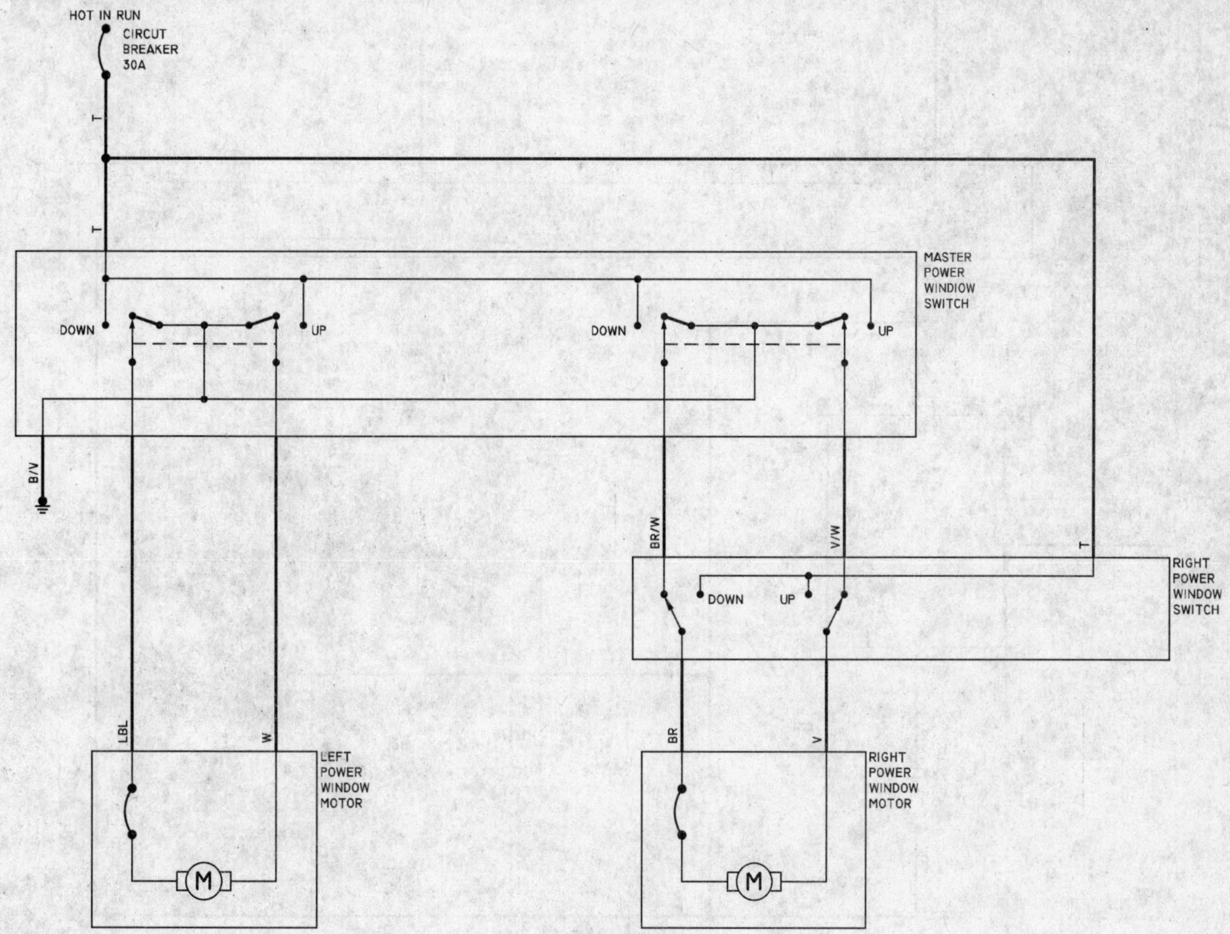

W/O REMOTE KEYLESS ENTRY

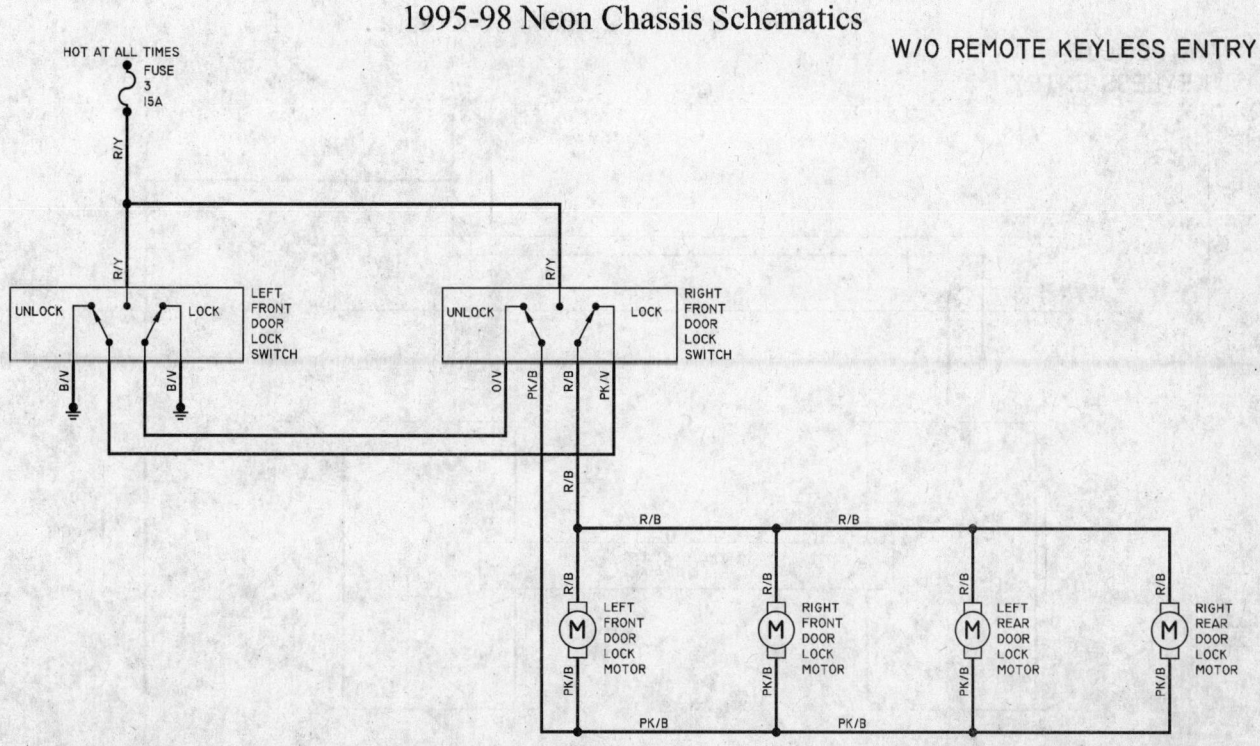

DIAGRAM 8

89716B04

## 1996-98 Neon Chassis Schematic

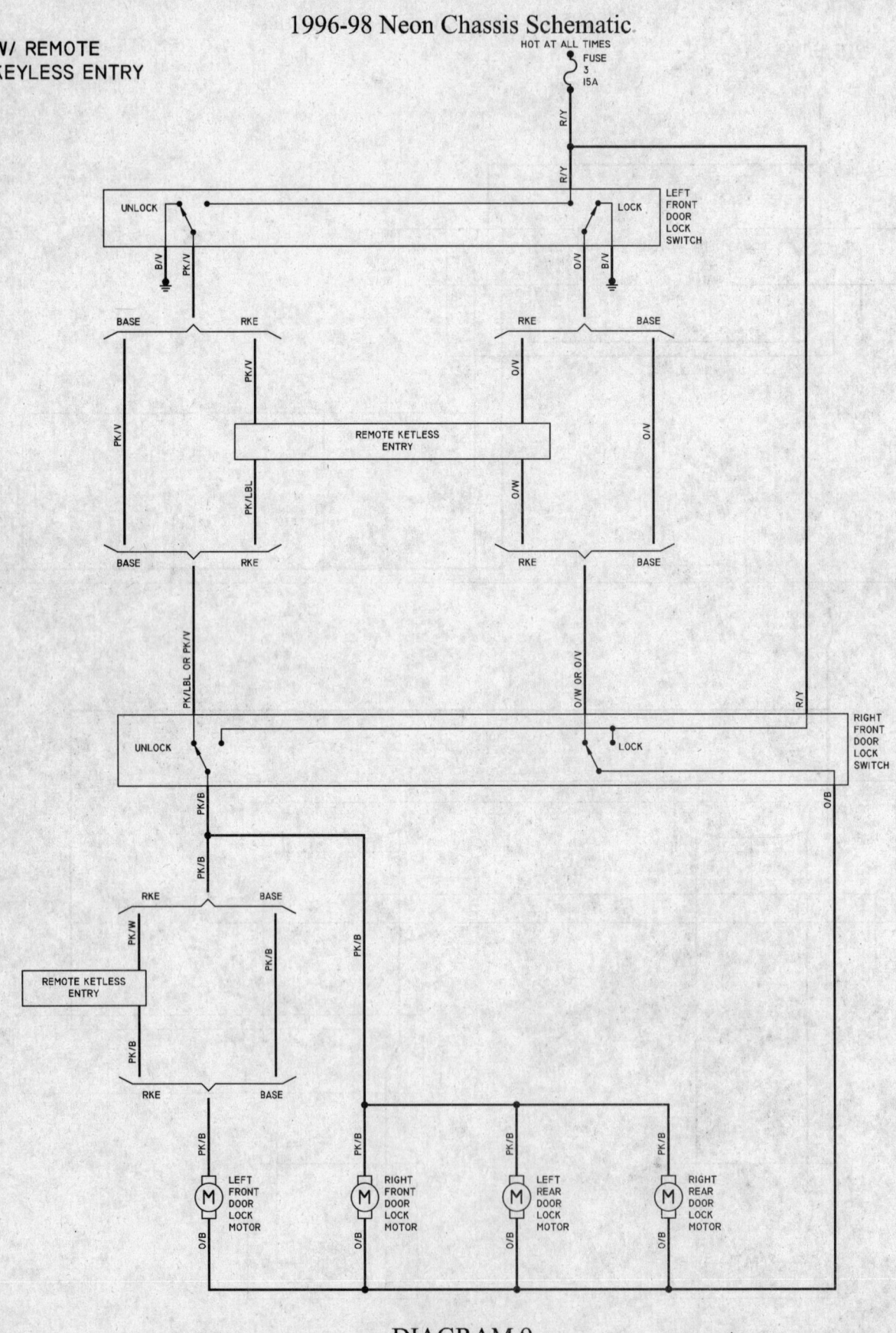

W/ REMOTE
KEYLESS ENTRY

HOT AT ALL TIMES
FUSE
3
15A

REMOTE KETLESS
ENTRY

REMOTE KETLESS
ENTRY

LEFT
FRONT
DOOR
LOCK
SWITCH

RIGHT
FRONT
DOOR
LOCK
SWITCH

LEFT
FRONT
DOOR
LOCK
MOTOR

RIGHT
FRONT
DOOR
LOCK
MOTOR

LEFT
REAR
DOOR
LOCK
MOTOR

RIGHT
REAR
DOOR
LOCK
MOTOR

**DIAGRAM 9**

89716B05

## 1995-98 Neon Chassis Schematics

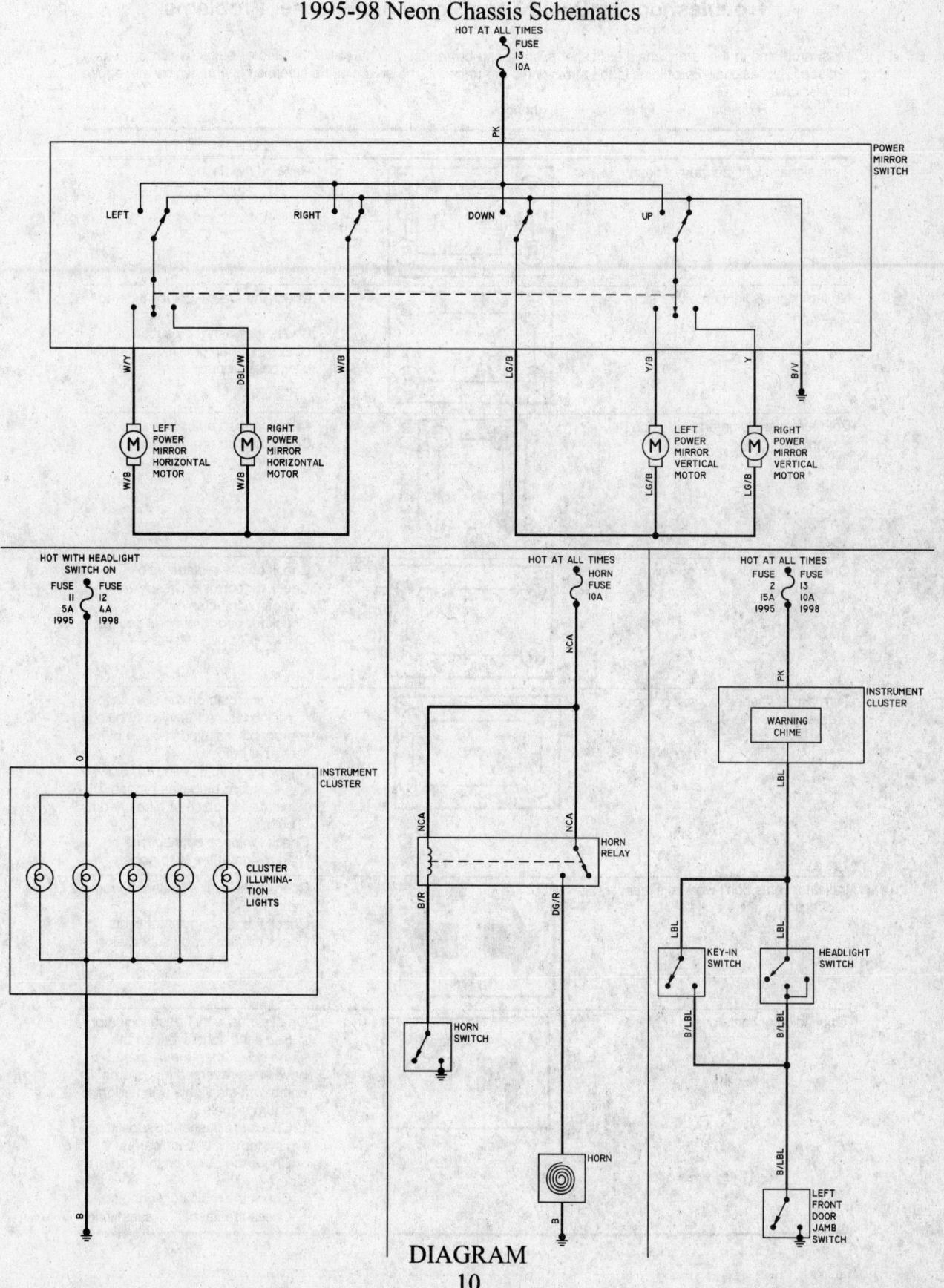

**DIAGRAM 10**

89716B06

## Troubleshooting Basic Turn Signal and Flasher Problems

Most problems in the turn signals or flasher system can be reduced to defective flashers or bulbs, which are easily replaced. Occasionally, problems in the turn signals are traced to the switch in the steering column, which will require professional service.

F = Front     R = Rear     ● = Lights off     ○ = Lights on

| Problem | | Solution |
|---|---|---|
| Turn signals light, but do not flash | | · Replace the flasher |
| No turn signals light on either side | | · Check the fuse. Replace if defective.<br>· Check the flasher by substitution<br>· Check for open circuit, short circuit or poor ground |
| Both turn signals on one side don't work | | · Check for bad bulbs<br>· Check for bad ground in both housings |
| One turn signal light on one side doesn't work | | · Check and/or replace bulb<br>· Check for corrosion in socket. Clean contacts.<br>· Check for poor ground at socket |
| Turn signal flashes too fast or too slow | | · Check any bulb on the side flashing too fast. A heavy-duty bulb is probably installed in place of a regular bulb.<br>· Check the bulb flashing too slow. A standard bulb was probably installed in place of a heavy-duty bulb.<br>· Check for loose connections or corrosion at the bulb socket |
| Indicator lights don't work in either direction | | · Check if the turn signals are working<br>· Check the dash indicator lights<br>· Check the flasher by substitution |
| One indicator light doesn't light | | · On systems with 1 dash indicator: See if the lights work on the same side. Often the filaments have been reversed in systems combining stoplights with taillights and turn signals. Check the flasher by substitution<br>· On systems with 2 indicators: Check the bulbs on the same side Check the indicator light bulb Check the flasher by substitution |

TCCA6C02

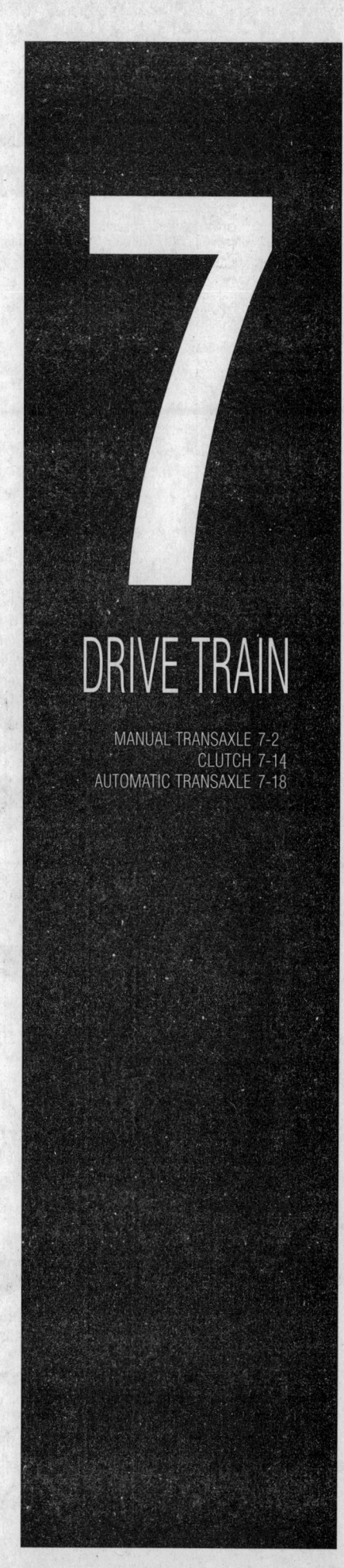

# 7
## DRIVE TRAIN

## MANUAL TRANSAXLE

### Understanding the Manual Transaxle

Because of the way an internal combustion engine breathes, it can produce torque, or twisting force, only within a narrow speed range. Most modern, overhead valve pushrod engines must turn at about 2500 rpm to produce their peak torque. By 4500 rpm they are producing so little torque that continued increases in engine speed produce no power increases. The torque peak on overhead camshaft engines is generally much higher, but much narrower.

The manual transaxle and clutch are employed to vary the relationship between engine speed and the speed of the wheels so that adequate engine power can be produced under all circumstances. The clutch allows engine torque to be applied to the transaxle input shaft gradually, due to mechanical slippage. Consequently, the vehicle may be started smoothly from a full stop. The transaxle changes the ratio between the rotating speeds of the engine and the wheels by the use of gears. The gear ratios allow full engine power to be applied to the wheels during acceleration at low speeds and at highway/passing speeds.

In a front wheel drive transaxle, power is usually transmitted from the input shaft to a mainshaft or output shaft located slightly beneath and to the side of the input shaft. The gears of the mainshaft mesh with gears on the input shaft, allowing power to be carried from one to the other. All forward gears are in constant mesh and are free from rotating with the shaft unless the synchronizer and clutch is engaged. Shifting from one gear to the next causes one of the gears to be freed from rotating with the shaft and locks another to it. Gears are locked and unlocked by internal dog clutches which slide between the center of the gear and the shaft. The forward gears employ synchronizers; friction members which smoothly bring gear and shaft to the same speed before the toothed dog clutches are engaged.

### Back-up Light Switch

#### REMOVAL & INSTALLATION

For back-up light switch removal and installation, please refer to Section 6 of this manual.

### Manual Transaxle Assembly

#### REMOVAL & INSTALLATION

▶ See Figures 1 thru 9

1. Disconnect the negative, then the positive battery cables.
2. Pull the Power Distribution Center (PDC) up and out of its holding bracket. Position the PDC aside for working clearance.
3. Remove the battery heat shield, then remove the battery from the vehicle. Remove the battery tray from the engine compartment. If equipped, disconnect the cruise control.
4. Remove the vehicle speed sensor wire.
5. Detach the back-up lamp switch wiring from the transaxle.

#### ✳✳ WARNING

**Pry with equal amounts of force on both sides of the shifter cable isolator bushing to avoid damaging the cable isolator bushing.**

6. Use 2 prytools to disconnect both gear shift cable ends from the transaxle shift levers.
7. Remove the clutch housing vent cap, exposing the clutch cable end and clutch release lever. Then, remove the clutch cable from the transaxle bellhousing.
8. Unfasten the retaining bolts, then remove the shift cable (linkage) mounting bracket.

9. If equipped, remove the accelerator cable shield.
10. Remove the intake manifold support bracket and the upper starter bolt.
11. Remove the upper bellhousing bolt.
12. Install a suitable engine bridge fixture and support the engine securely.
13. Raise and safely support the vehicle, then remove the front wheel and tire assemblies.
14. Position a suitable drain pan under the vehicle, then drain the transaxle.
15. Remove both front halfshafts, as outlined later in this section.

#### ✳✳ WARNING

**When installing the halfshafts, new driveshaft retaining clips MUST be used. NEVER reuse the old clips. If you do not use new clips, the inner CV-joint may disengage.**

16. Remove the power hop damper and bracket.
17. Remove the lower starter mounting bolt.
18. Remove the transaxle-to-rear lateral bending strut from the engine and transaxle.

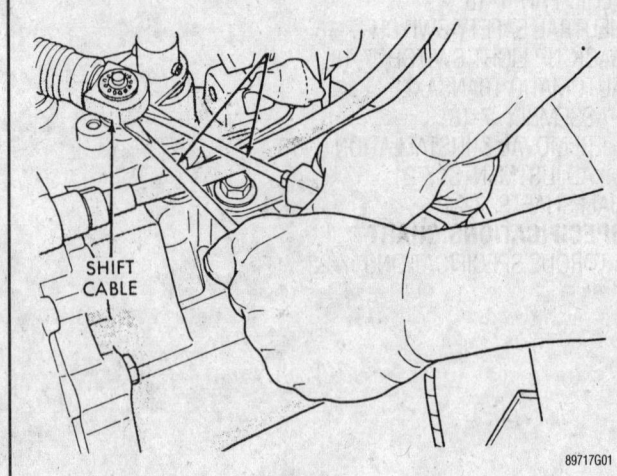

Fig. 1 Use 2 prytools to disconnect the gear shift cable ends from the shift levers

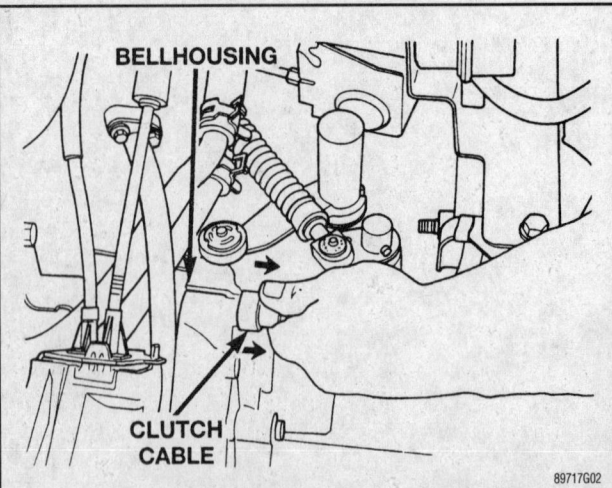

Fig. 2 Pull the clutch cable backward, to disconnect the clutch cable from the bellhousing

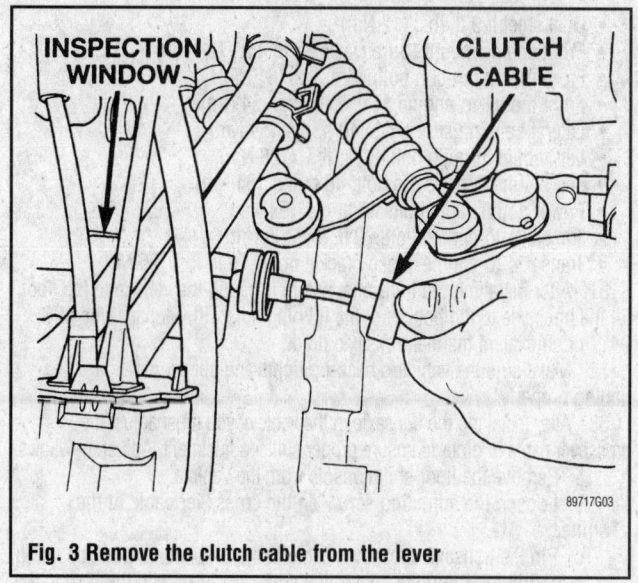

**Fig. 3 Remove the clutch cable from the lever**

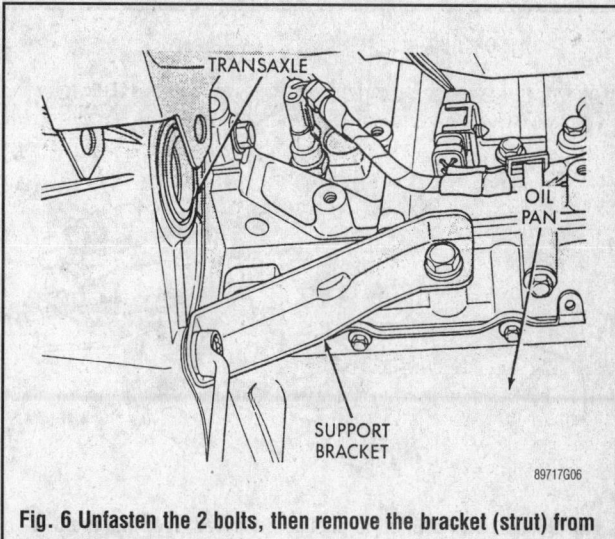

**Fig. 6 Unfasten the 2 bolts, then remove the bracket (strut) from the engine and transaxle**

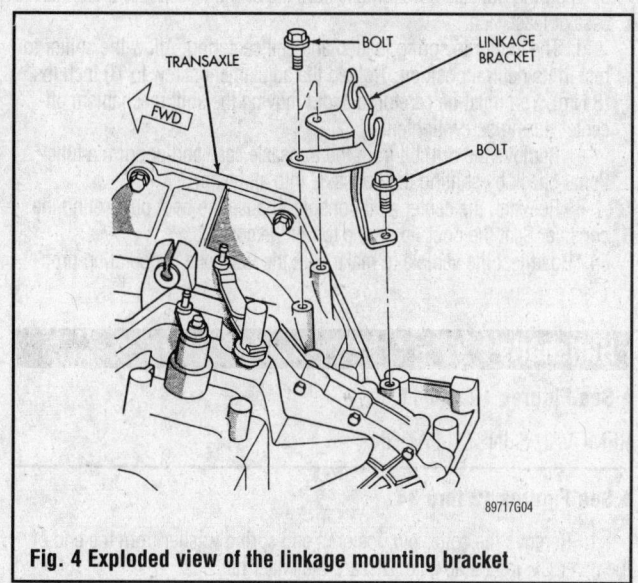

**Fig. 4 Exploded view of the linkage mounting bracket**

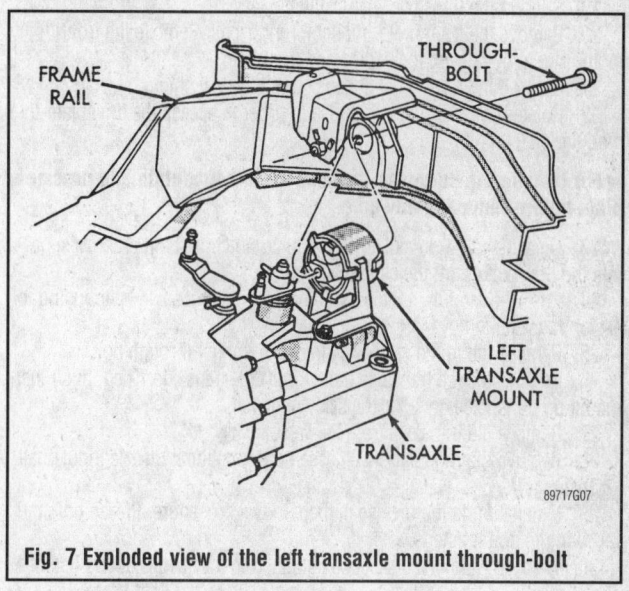

**Fig. 7 Exploded view of the left transaxle mount through-bolt**

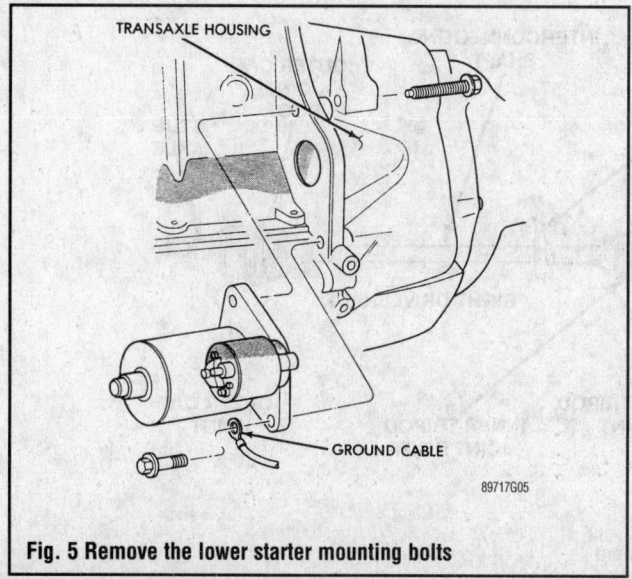

**Fig. 5 Remove the lower starter mounting bolts**

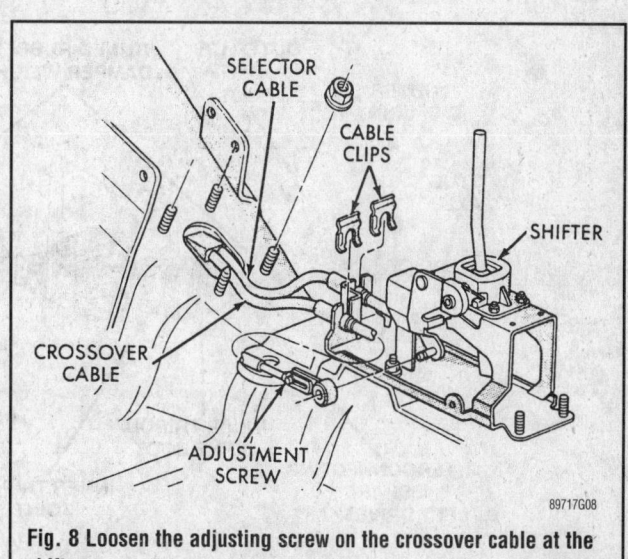

**Fig. 8 Loosen the adjusting screw on the crossover cable at the shifter**

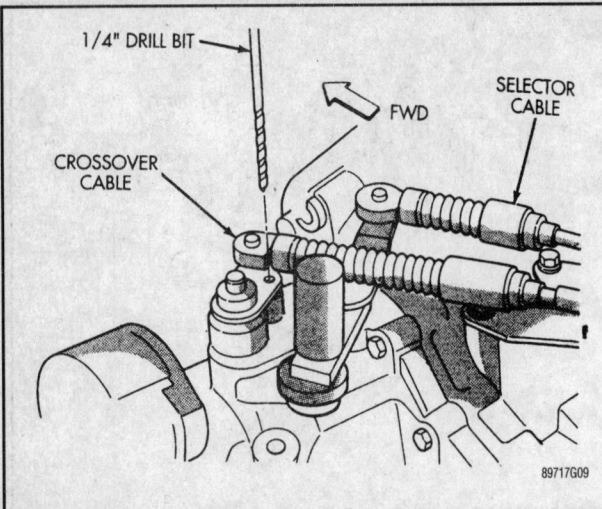

**Fig. 9 Insert a ¼ drill bit to pin the crossover lever into the 3–4 neutral position**

19. Support the transaxle with a suitable jack.
20. Remove the front motor mount through-bolt. Remove the front motor mount bolts from the engine and transaxle.
21. Remove the lower dust shield screw and dust shield.
22. Rotate the crankshaft clockwise in order to access the driveplate-to-modular clutch bolts.

➡ **For installation purposes, matchmark the driveplate and pressure plate before removing any bolts.**

23. Unfasten the 4 driveplate-to-modular clutch bolts in order to separate the driveplate from the clutch.
24. Push the modular clutch assembly into the transaxle bellhousing for easier transaxle removal.
25. Remove the frame rail-to-left transaxle mount through bolt.
26. Remove the left transaxle mount from the transaxle. Then, push the mount up to get clearance for transaxle removal.
27. Remove the transaxle from the vehicle.
28. Remove the modular clutch assembly from the transaxle input shaft.
**To install:**
29. Installation is the reverse of the removal procedure. Please note the following important steps.
30. The following items must be tightened to the specifications listed.

- Dust shield: 9 ft. lbs. (12 Nm)
- Front engine mount-to-transaxle:80 ft. lbs. (108 Nm)
- Front mount through bolt: 45 ft. lbs. (61 Nm)
- Front mount-to-engine bolt: 40 ft. lbs. (54 Nm)
- Lateral bending strut bolts: 40 ft. lbs. (54 Nm)
- Left mount through bolt: 80 ft. lbs. (108 Nm)
- Left mount-to-transaxle bolt: 40 ft. lbs. (54 Nm)
- Power hop damper bolts:40 ft. lbs. (54 Nm)
- Transaxle-to-engine bolt: 70 ft. lbs. (95 Nm)
- Transaxle-to-engine intake bracket bolts: 70 ft. lbs. (95 Nm)

31. After installing the transaxle, before lowering the vehicle to the floor, fill the transaxle to the bottom of the fill plug hole with Mopar® type M.S. 9417 or equivalent manual transaxle fluid.
32. Make sure the vehicle's back-up lights and speedometer are functioning properly.
33. After installing the transaxle in the vehicle, you must adjust the crossover cable in order to ensure proper shifter adjustment. Adjust as follows:
  a. Remove the floor shift console from the vehicle.
  b. Loosen the adjusting screw on the crossover cable at the shifter.
  c. Pin the transaxle crossover cable in the 3–4 neutral position using a ¼ in. drill bit. Align the hole in the crossover lever with the hole in the boss on the transaxle case. Make sure the drill bit goes into the transaxle case at least ½in.
  d. The shifter is spring loaded and self centering. Allow the shifter to rest in its neutral position. Tighten the adjustment screw to 70 inch lbs. (8 Nm). You must be careful to avoid moving the shift mechanism off-center during screw tightening.
  e. Remove the drill bit from the transaxle case and perform a functional check by shifting the transaxle into all gears.
  f. Reinstall the center shift console. Blouse the boot out around the console. Seat the boot lip on the top of the console.
34. Road test the vehicle to make sure the transaxle is operating properly.

## Halfshafts

▶ **See Figures 10 and 11**

REMOVAL & INSTALLATION

▶ **See Figures 12 thru 34**

1. Remove the cotter pin, lock nut and spring washer from the end of the outer CV-joint stub axle. Discard the cotter pin.

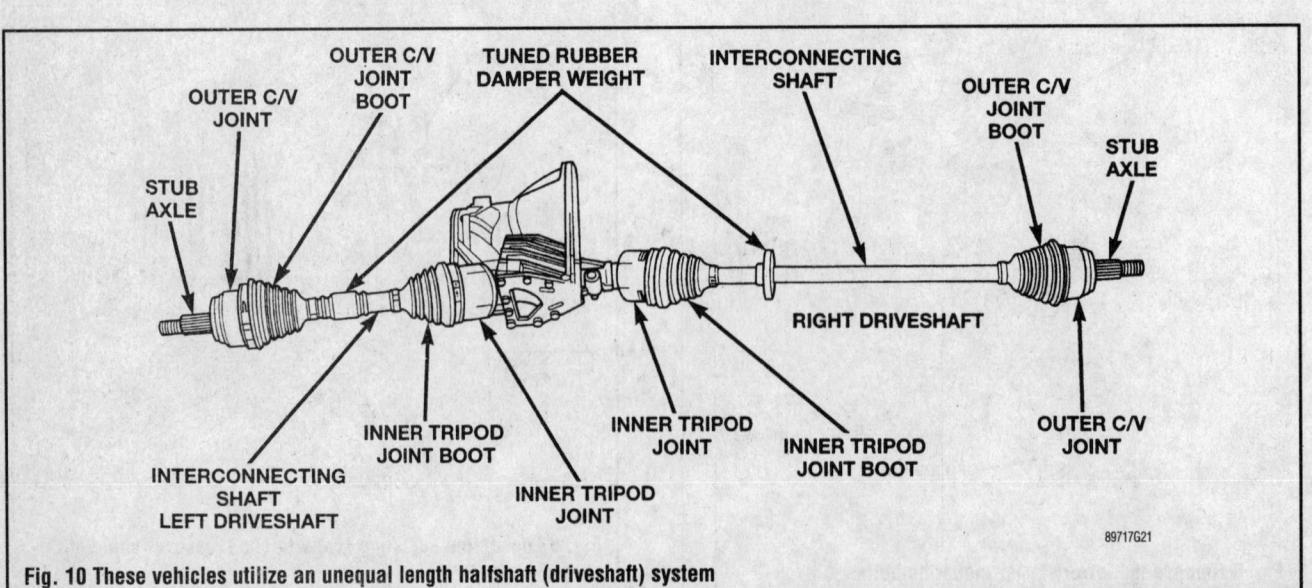

**Fig. 10 These vehicles utilize an unequal length halfshaft (driveshaft) system**

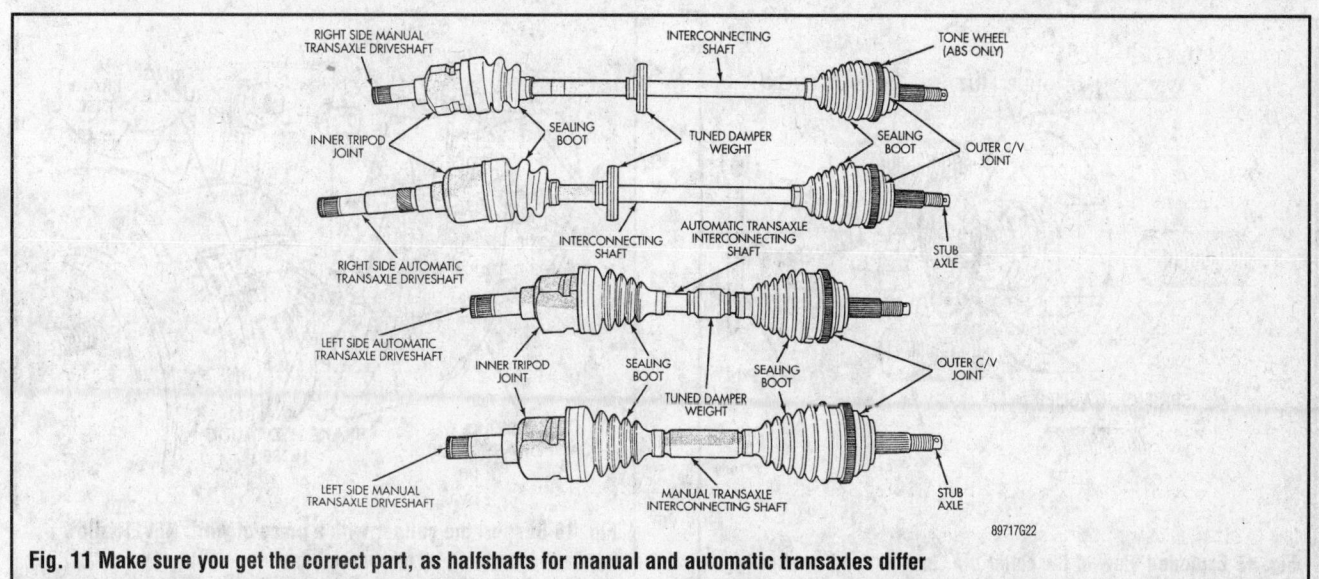

**Fig. 11 Make sure you get the correct part, as halfshafts for manual and automatic transaxles differ**

2. With the vehicle on the ground and brakes applied, loosen, but do not remove the stub axle-to-hub and bearing retaining nut. The front hub and driveshaft are splined together and retained by the hub nut.

3. Raise and safely support the vehicle with jack stands.

4. Remove the front wheel and tire assembly.

5. Unfasten the front caliper-to-steering knuckle bolts.

6. Remove the caliper from the steering knuckle by lifting the bottom of the caliper away from the steering knuckle and then remove the top of the caliper out from under the steering knuckle.

7. Support the caliper out of the way by suspending it with a piece from the strut. Do NOT allow the caliper to hang by the brake hose.

8. Remove the rotor from the hub.

9. Remove the nut attaching the outer tie rod end to the steering knuckle, as follows:

   a. Hold the tie rod end stud with a 1/32 in. socket while loosening and removing the nut.

10. Separate the tie rod end stud from the steering knuckle using a side puller.

11. Remove the nut and bolt holding the ball joint stud into the steering knuckle.

**Fig. 13 Remove the lock nut . . .**

**Fig. 12 Straighten the cotter pin, then use needle-nose pliers to remove it from the lock nut**

**Fig. 14 . . . and spring washer from the end of the stub axle**

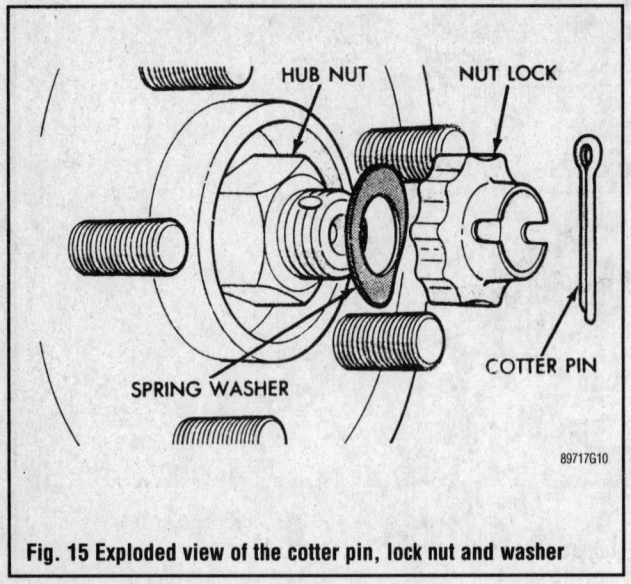

**Fig. 15 Exploded view of the cotter pin, lock nut and washer**

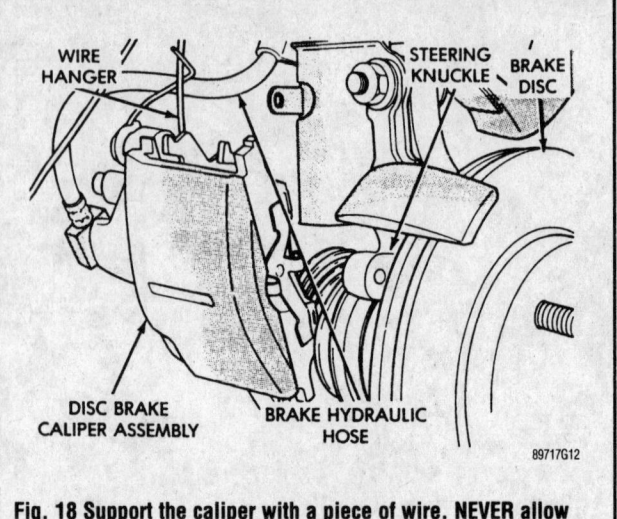

**Fig. 18 Support the caliper with a piece of wire. NEVER allow the caliper to hang by the brake hose**

**Fig. 16 Have an assistant apply the brakes, then loosen the hub nut. Do not remove it at this time**

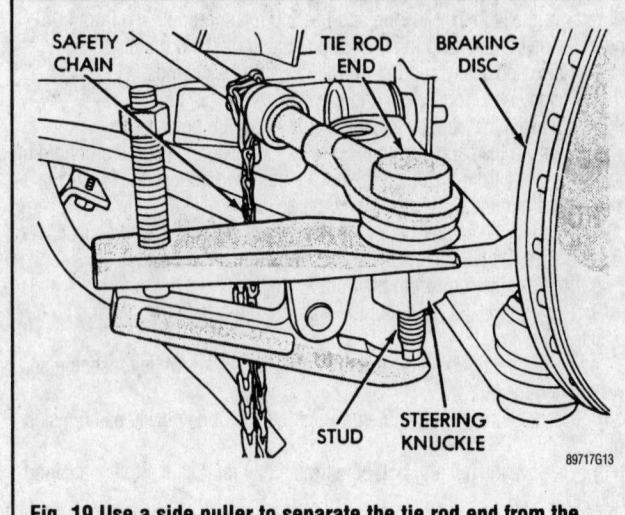

**Fig. 19 Use a side puller to separate the tie rod end from the steering knuckle**

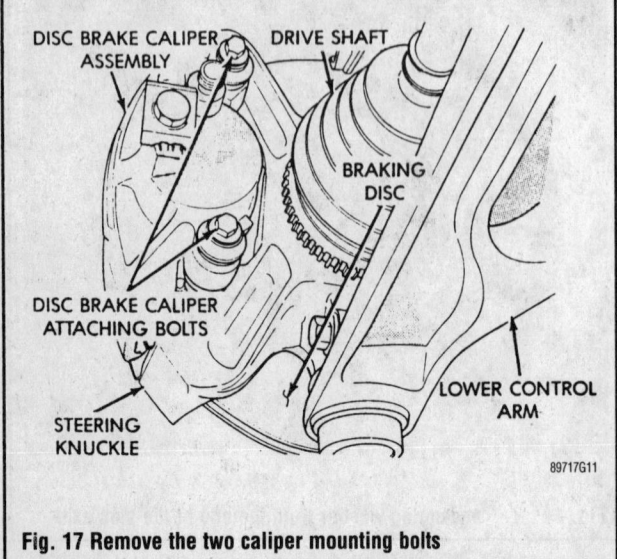

**Fig. 17 Remove the two caliper mounting bolts**

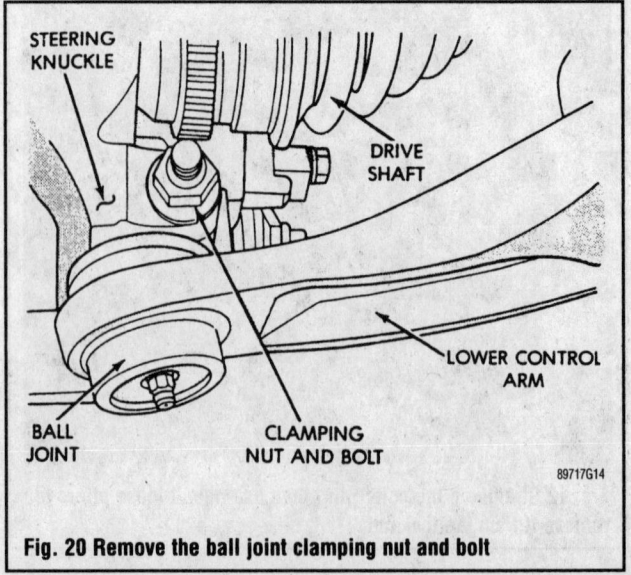

**Fig. 20 Remove the ball joint clamping nut and bolt**

Fig. 21 While holding the steering knuckle clamping bolt, loosen the nut . . .

Fig. 24 . . . then separate the lower ball joint stud from the steering knuckle

Fig. 22 . . . then remove the clamping nut and bolt

Fig. 25 Remove the hub nut and washer

Fig. 23 Pry down on the lower control arm . . .

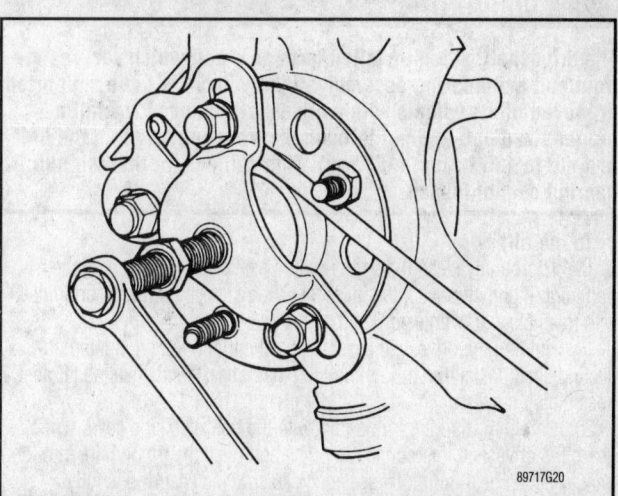

Fig. 26 With a prytool positioned to prevent the hub from turning, use the puller to separate the outer stud axle from the hub and bearing

**Be careful when separating the ball joint stud from the steering knuckle, so the ball joint seal does not get damaged.**

12. Separate the ball joint stud from the steering knuckle by prying down on the lower control arm.

13. For 1998–99 vehicles, perform the following steps:

  a. Remove the hub and bearing-to-stub axle retaining nut.

  b. Install a suitable puller on the hub and bearing assembly, using the lug nuts to hold it in place.

  c. Install a wheel lug nut on wheel stud to protect the threads on the stud. Install a flat-bladed prytool to keep the hub from turning. Using the puller, force the outer stub axle from the hub and bearing.

**Be careful when separating the inner CV-joint during this operation. Do not let the driveshaft hang by the inner CV-joint, the driveshaft must be supported.**

14. Pull the steering knuckle assembly out and away from the outer CV-joint of the driveshaft assembly. Support the outer end of the driveshaft assembly.

15. Insert a pry bar between the inner tripod joint and the transaxle case. Pry against the inner tripod joint until the joint retaining snapring is disengaged from the transaxle side gear.

➡ **Inner tripod joint removal is easier if you apply outward pressure on the joint as you hit the punch with a hammer.**

16. For 1996–99 vehicles, remove the inner tripod joints from the side gears of the transaxle using a punch to dislodge the inner tripod joint retaining ring from the transaxle side gear. If removing the right side inner tripod joint, position the punch against the inner tripod joint. Hit the punch sharply with a hammer to dislodge the right inner joint from the side gear. If removing the left side inner tripod joint, position the punch in the groove of the inner tripod joint. Hit the punch sharply with a hammer to dislodge the left inner tripod joint from the side gear.

17. Hold the inner tripod joint and interconnecting shaft of the driveshaft assembly. Remove the inner tripod joint from the transaxle by pulling it straight out of the transaxle side gear and transaxle oil seal. When removing the tripod joint, do not let the spline or snapring drag across the sealing lip of the transaxle-to-tripod joint oil seal.

**The driveshaft, when installed, acts as a bolt which secures the from hub and bearing assembly. If the vehicle is to be supported or moved on its wheels with a driveshaft removed, install a proper sized bolt and nut through the front hub. Tighten the bolt and nut to 135 ft. lbs. (183 Nm). This will ensure that the hub bearing cannot loosen.**

**To install:**

18. Thoroughly clean the spline and oil seal sealing surface on the tripod joint. Lightly lubricate the oil seal sealing surface on the tripod joint with fresh clean transmission fluid.

19. Holding the driveshaft assembly by the tripod joint and interconnecting shaft, install the tripod joint into the transaxle side gear as far as possible by hand.

20. Carefully align the tripod joint with the transaxle side gears. Then, grasp the driveshaft interconnecting shaft and push the tripod joint into the transaxle side gear until fully seated. Make sure the snapring is fully engaged with the side gear by trying to remove the tripod joint from the transaxle by hand. If the snapring is fully seated with the side gear, the tripod joint will not be removable by hand.

Fig. 27 Pull the steering knuckle assembly out, away from the outer CV-joint

Fig. 28 Pry against the inner tripod joint until the snapring disengages from the transaxle side gear

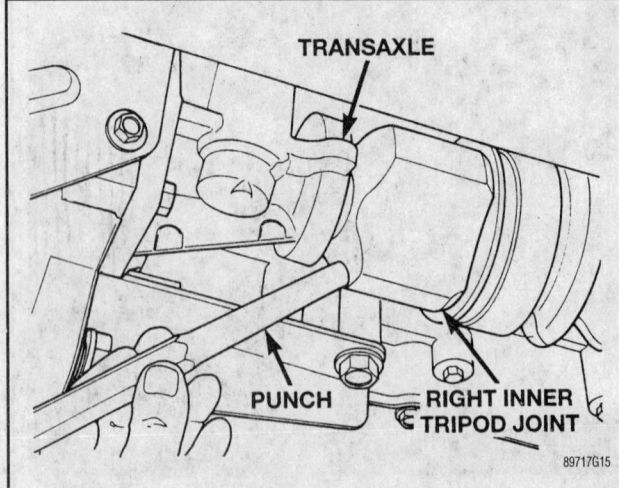
Fig. 29 Separating the right inner tripod joint from the transaxle

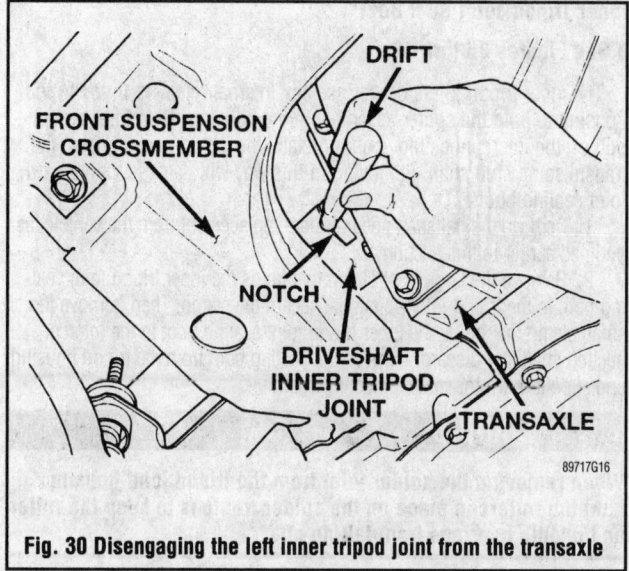

Fig. 30 Disengaging the left inner tripod joint from the transaxle

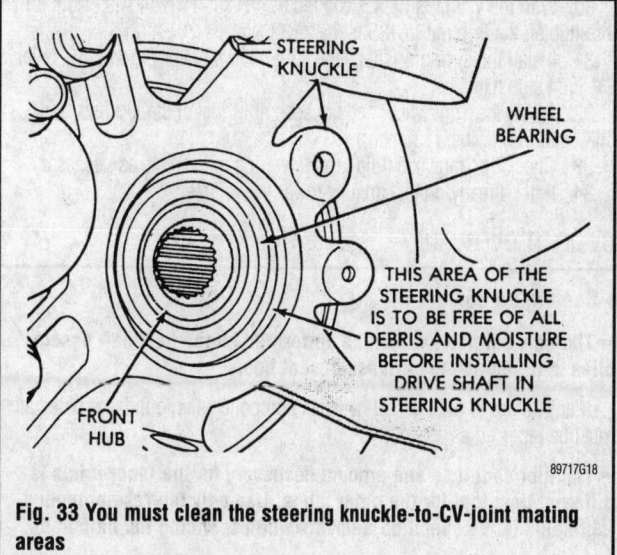

Fig. 33 You must clean the steering knuckle-to-CV-joint mating areas

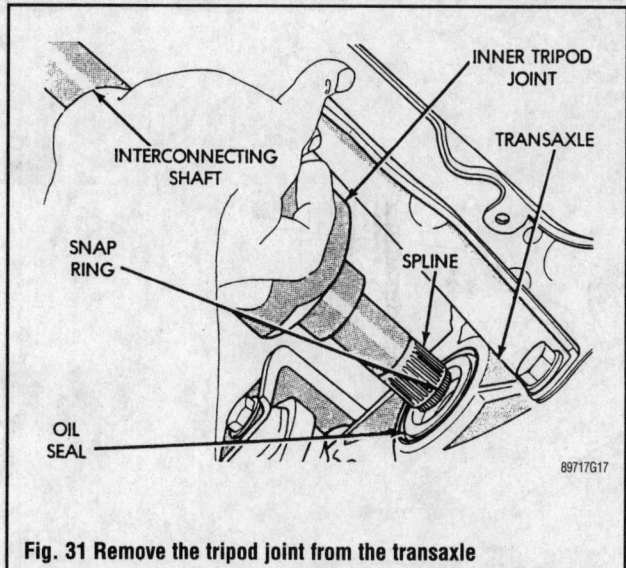

Fig. 31 Remove the tripod joint from the transaxle

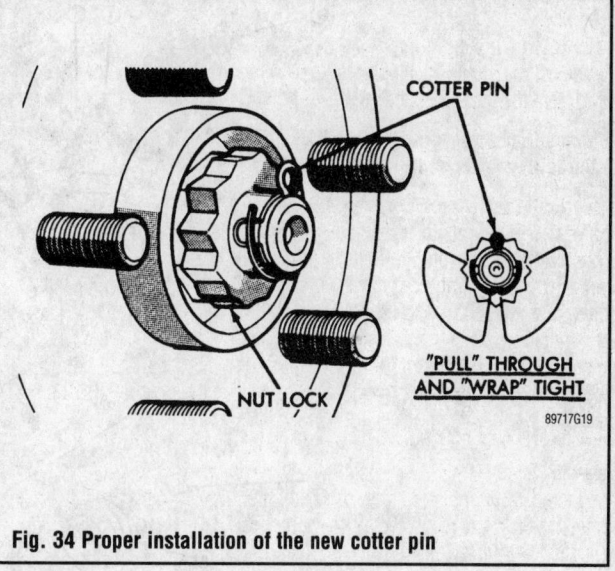

Fig. 34 Proper installation of the new cotter pin

Fig. 32 Carefully remove the halfshaft, being sure not to let the spline or snapring drag across anything

21. Clean all debris and moisture out of the steering knuckle.

22. Make sure that the outer CV-joint, which fits into the steering knuckle, has no debris or moisture on it before installing into the steering knuckle.

23. Slide the driveshaft back into the front hub. Install the steering knuckle into the ball joint stud.

24. Install a NEW steering knuckle-to-ball joint stud bolt and nut. Tighten the nut and bolt to 70 ft. lbs. (95 Nm).

25. Insert the tie rod end into the steering knuckle. Start the tie rod end-to-steering knuckle nut onto the stud of the tie rod end. While holding the stud of the tie rod end stationary, tighten the nut. Then, using a crow foot and 11/32 in socket, tighten the tie rod end nut to 45 ft. lbs. (61 Nm).

26. Install the rotor back onto the hub and bearing assembly.

27. Position the caliper on the steering knuckle. Slide the top of the caliper under the top abutment on the steering knuckle, then install the bottom of the caliper against the bottom abutment of the steering knuckle.

28. Install the caliper-to-knuckle bolts and tighten to 23 ft. lbs. (31 Nm).

29. Clean all foreign matter from the threads of the outer CV-joint stub axle. Install hub nut and washer onto the threads of the stub axle and tighten the nut.

30. With the vehicle's brakes applied to prevent the axle shaft from turning, tighten the hub nut to 135 ft. lbs. (183 Nm).

31. Install the spring washer, lock nut and new cotter pin into the outer CV-joint stub axle.

32. Install the front wheel and tire assembly. Install the lug nuts and tighten to 100 ft. lbs. (135 Nm).

33. Check the transaxle fluid level, lowering the vehicle as necessary.

34. If not already done, carefully lower the vehicle.

## CV-JOINT OVERHAUL

▶ **See Figure 35**

➡ **The only service that can be performed on the halfshaft assemblies is to replace the driveshaft seal boots.**

If any failure to the internal halfshaft components is found, the halfshaft must be replaced as assembly.

➡ **The lubricant type and amount necessary for the inner joints is different than that for the outer joints. Use only the recommended lubricants in the specified amounts when servicing the halfshafts.**

## Inner Tripod Joint Seal Boot

▶ **See Figures 36 thru 46**

The inner tripod joints do not use any internal retainers in the tripod housing to hold the spider assembly in the housing. Therefore, do not pull on the interconnecting shaft to detach the tripod housing from the transmission stub shaft. Removing in this way will damage the inboard joint sealing boots.

1. Remove the halfshaft needing boot replacement from the vehicle, as outlined earlier in this section.

2. Remove the large boot clamp that holds the inner tripod joint sealing boot to the tripod joint housing. Discard the clamp. Then, remove the small clamp that holds the inner tripod joint sealing boot to the interconnecting shaft and discard. Remove the sealing boot from the tripod housing and slide it down the interconnecting shaft.

### ✷✷ WARNING

**When removing the spider joint from the tripod joint housing, hold the rollers in place on the spider trunions to keep the roller and needle bearings from falling off.**

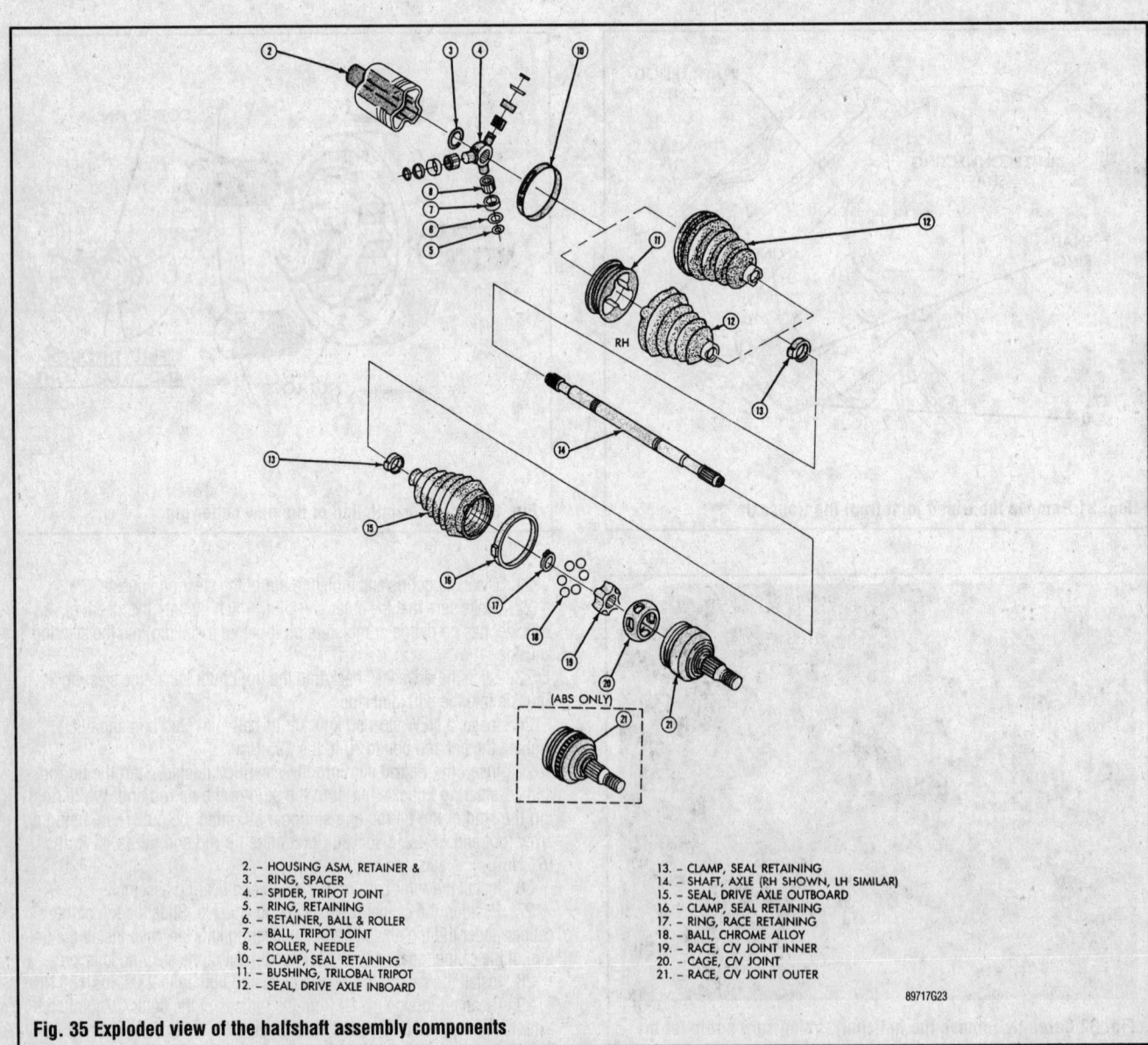

2. – HOUSING ASM, RETAINER &
3. – RING, SPACER
4. – SPIDER, TRIPOT JOINT
5. – RING, RETAINING
6. – RETAINER, BALL & ROLLER
7. – BALL, TRIPOT JOINT
8. – ROLLER, NEEDLE
10. – CLAMP, SEAL RETAINING
11. – BUSHING, TRILOBAL TRIPOT
12. – SEAL, DRIVE AXLE INBOARD

13. – CLAMP, SEAL RETAINING
14. – SHAFT, AXLE (RH SHOWN, LH SIMILAR)
15. – SEAL, DRIVE AXLE OUTBOARD
16. – CLAMP, SEAL RETAINING
17. – RING, RACE RETAINING
18. – BALL, CHROME ALLOY
19. – RACE, CV JOINT INNER
20. – CAGE, CV JOINT
21. – RACE, CV JOINT OUTER

89717G23

**Fig. 35 Exploded view of the halfshaft assembly components**

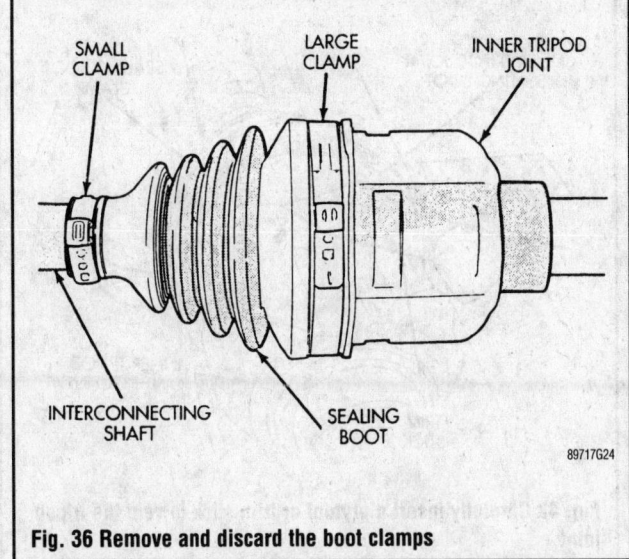

**Fig. 36 Remove and discard the boot clamps**

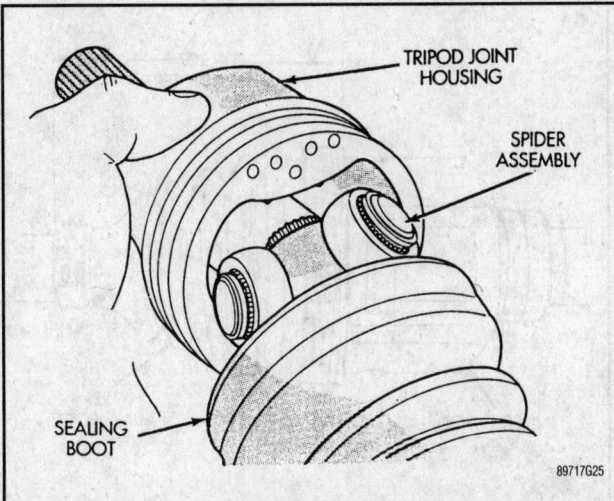

**Fig. 37 Remove the interconnecting shaft and spider assembly from the tripod joint housing**

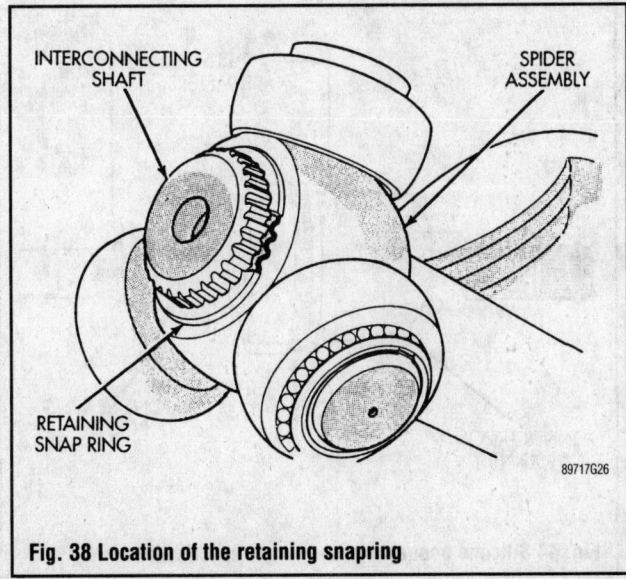

**Fig. 38 Location of the retaining snapring**

3. Slide the interconnecting shaft and spider assembly out of the tripod joint housing.

4. Remove the snapring that holds the spider assembly to the interconnecting shaft. Remove the spider assembly from the interconnecting shaft. If the spider won't come off by hand, you can remove it by tapping the spider with a brass drift. Do NOT hit the outer tripod bearings trying to remove the spider assembly from the interconnecting shaft.

5. Slide the sealing boot off the interconnecting shaft.

6. Thoroughly clean and inspect the spider assembly, tripod joint housing, and interconnecting shaft for any signs of excessive wear. If any parts show extreme wear, the halfshaft must be replaced.

**To install:**

➡ **The inner tripod joint sealing boots are make from two different types of material. High temperature applications use silicone rubber, whereas standard temperature applications use Hytrel® plastic. The silicone sealing boots are soft and pliable. The Hytrel® sealing boots are stiff and rigid. The replacement sealing boot MUST BE the same type of material as the sealing boot that was removed.**

7. Slide the inner tripod joint seal boot retaining clamp onto the interconnecting shaft. Then, slide the replacement inner tripod joint sealing boot onto the interconnecting shaft. The inner tripod joint seal boot MUST be positioned on the interconnecting shaft, so the raised bead on the inside of the seal boot is in the groove on the interconnecting shaft.

8. Install the spider assembly onto the interconnecting shaft with the chamfer on the spider assembly toward the interconnecting shaft. The spider must be installed on the inter connecting shaft far enough to fully install the retaining snapring. If the spider assembly will not fully install by hand, you can tap the spider body with a brass drift. Do NOT hit the outer tripod bearings trying to install the spider on the interconnecting shaft.

9. Install the spider assembly to the interconnecting shaft retaining snapring into the groove on the end of the interconnecting shaft. Be sure the snapring is fully seated into the groove on the interconnecting shaft.

10. Distribute ½ the amount of the grease provided in the seal boot service package (DO NOT USE ANY OTHER TYPE OF GREASE) into the tripod housing. Put the remaining amount into the sealing boot.

11. Align the tripod housing with the spider assembly and then slide the tripod housing over the spider assembly and interconnecting shaft.

12. Install the inner tripod joint seal boot to the interconnecting shaft clamp evenly on the sealing boot.

13. Clean the sealing boot onto the interconnecting shaft using a suitable crimper. Place the crimping tool over the bridge of the clamp. Tighten the nut on the tool until the jaws of the tool are closed completely together, face-to-face.

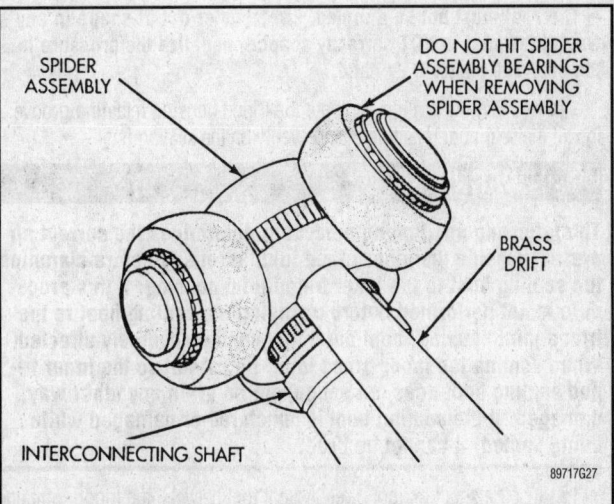

**Fig. 39 If difficulty is encountered, use a brass drift to tap the spider**

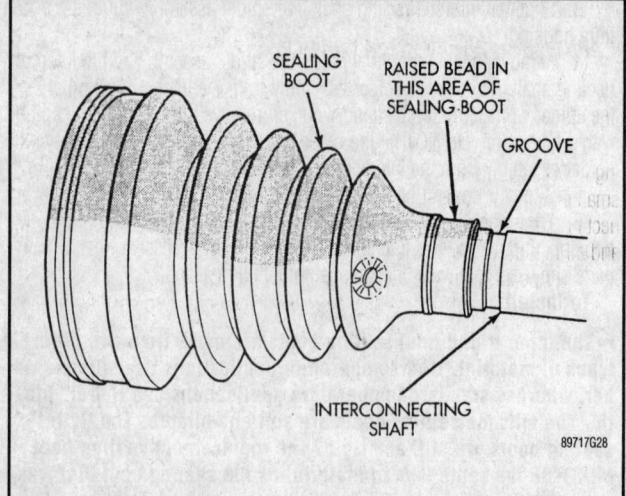

Fig. 40 Installation of the sealing boot on the interconnecting shaft

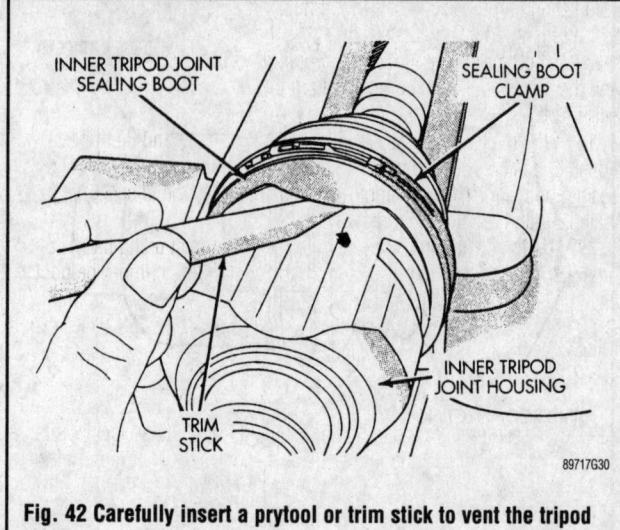

Fig. 42 Carefully insert a prytool or trim stick to vent the tripod joint

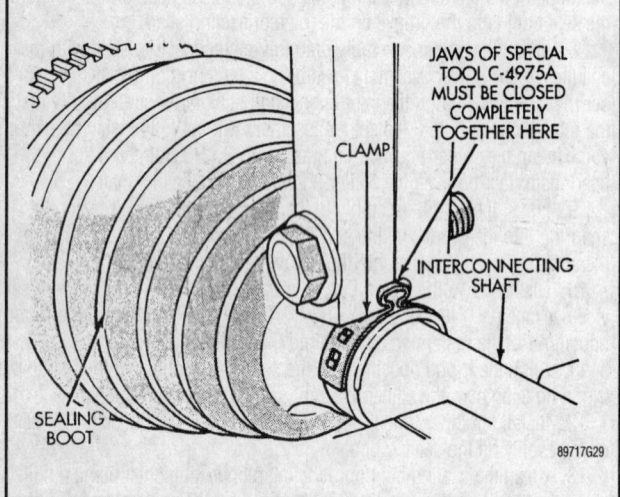

Fig. 41 Tighten the nut on the crimping tool until the jaws are completely closed, face-to-face

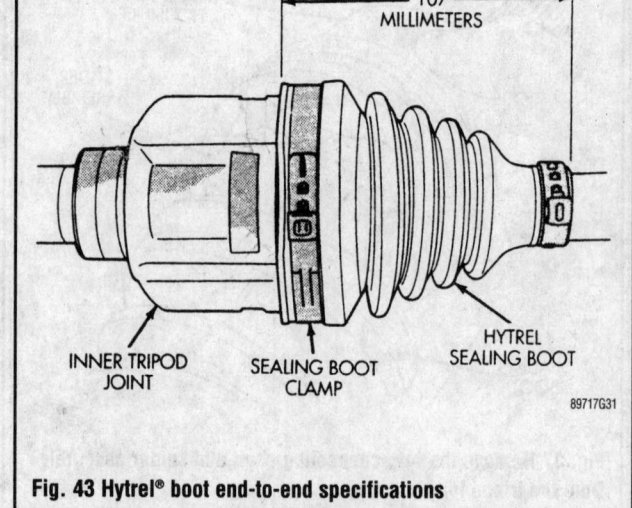

Fig. 43 Hytrel® boot end-to-end specifications

➡The seal must not be dimpled, stretched or out-of-shape in any way. If the seal is NOT correctly shaped, equalize the pressure in the seal and shape it by hand.

14. Position the sealing boot into the tripod housing retaining groove. Install the seal boot retaining clamp evenly on the sealing boot.

### ✳✳ WARNING

The following positioning procedure determines the correct air pressure inside the inner tripod joint assembly before clamping the sealing boot to the inner tripod joint housing. If this procedure is not performed before clamping the sealing boot to the tripod joint housing, boot durability can be adversely affected. When venting the inner tripod joint, be careful so the inner tripod sealing boot does not get punctured or, in any other way, damaged. If the sealing boot is punctured or damaged while being vented, it cannot be used.

15. Insert a small prytool or equivalent tool between the tripod joint and sealing boot to vent the inner tripod joint assembly. When inserting the prytool between the tripod housing and the sealing boot, make sure the tool is

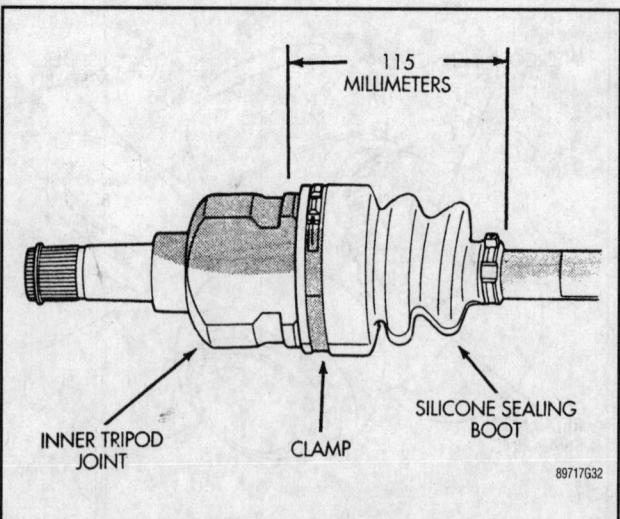

Fig. 44 Silicone boot end-to-end length specifications

held flat and firmly against the tripod housing. If this is not done, damage to the sealing boot can occur. If the inner tripod joint has a Hytrel® (hard plastic) boot, make sure the tool is places between the soft rubber insert and the tripod housing, and not the hard plastic sealing boot and soft rubber insert.

16. With the tool inserted between the sealing boot and the tripod joint housing, position the inner tripod joint on the driveshaft until the correct sealing boot edge-to-edge length is attained for the type of sealing boot material being used. Then remove the tool.

17. Clamp the tripod sealing boot to the tripod joint using the proper procedure for the type of boot clamp. If the boot uses a crimp-type boot clamp, clamp the sealing boot onto the tripod housing using crimping tool C-4975-A or equivalent. Place the tool over the bridge of the clamp, then tighten the nut on the tool until the jaws are closed completely together, face-to-face.

18. If the boot uses low profile, latching type boot clamps, clamp the sealing boot onto the tripod housing using a suitable clamp locking tool, as shown in the accompanying figure. Place the prongs of the clamp locking tool in the holes of the clamp. Squeeze the tool together until the top band of the clamp is latched behind the 2 tabs on the lower band of the clamp.

19. Install the halfshaft in the vehicle, as outlined earlier in this section.

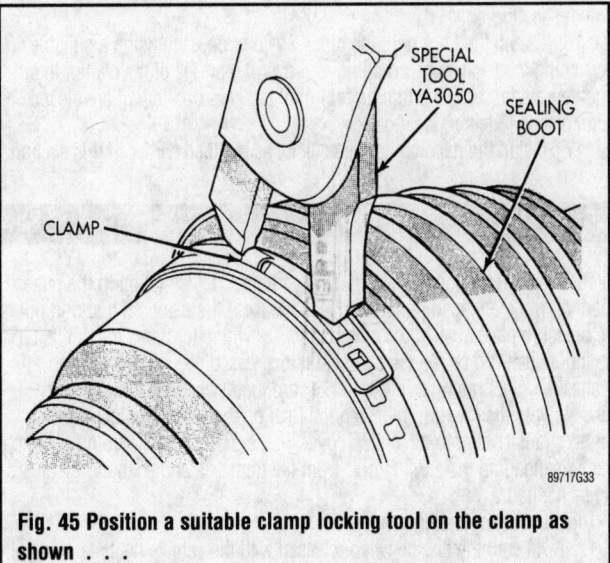

Fig. 45 Position a suitable clamp locking tool on the clamp as shown . . .

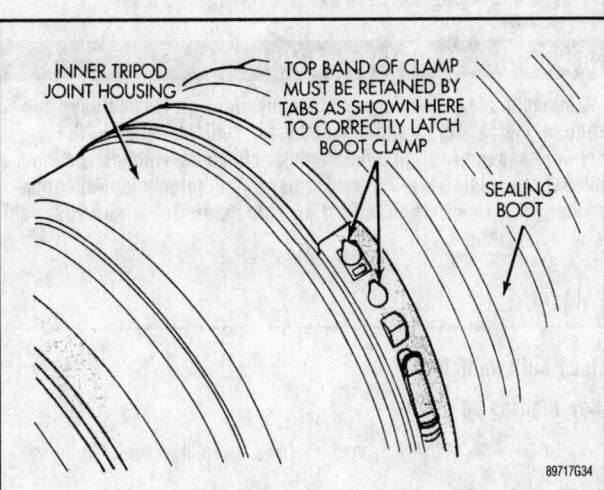

Fig. 46 . . . then squeeze the tool together in order to properly install the clamp

### Outer CV-Joint Seal Boot

▶ See Figures 36, 40, 47, 48 and 49

1. Remove the halfshaft needing boot replacement from the vehicle, as outlined earlier in this section.

2. Remove the large boot clamp that holds the inner tripod joint sealing boot to the tripod joint housing. Discard the clamp. Then, remove the small clamp that holds the inner tripod joint sealing boot to the interconnecting shaft and discard. Remove the sealing boot from the tripod housing and slide it down the interconnecting shaft.

3. Wipe away the grease to expose the outer CV-joint.

4. Remove the outer CV-joint from the interconnecting shaft by performing the following:

   a. Place the interconnecting shaft in a soft jawed vise.

   b. Using a soft-faced hammer, sharply hit the end of the CV-joint housing to dislodge the housing from the internal circlip on the Interconnecting shaft.

   c. Slide the outer CV-joint off the end of the interconnecting shaft; the joint may have to be tapped off using a soft-faced hammer.

5. Use a pair of snapring pliers to remove the large circlip from the interconnecting shaft before trying to remove the outer CV-joint sealing boot.

6. Slide the faulty boot off the interconnecting shaft.

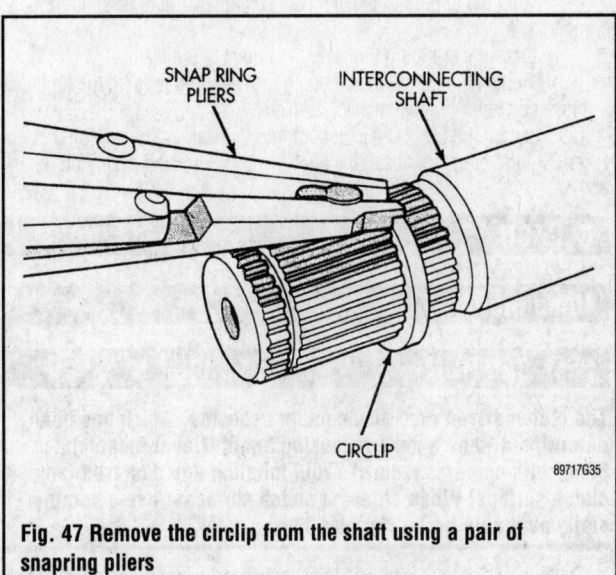

Fig. 47 Remove the circlip from the shaft using a pair of snapring pliers

7. Throughly clean and inspect the outer CV-joint and interconnecting joint for signs of excessive wear. If any parts show extreme wear, the halfshaft must be replaced.

### To install:

8. Slide the new boot-to-interconnecting shaft retaining clamp onto the interconnecting shaft. Slide the outer CV-joint assembly boot onto the interconnecting shaft. The boot must be positioned on the interconnecting shaft so the raised bead of the inside of the seal boot is in the groove on the interconnecting shaft.

9. Align the splines on the interconnecting shaft with the splines on the cross of the outer CV-joint and start the outer CV-joint onto the interconnecting shaft.

10. Install the outer CV-joint onto the interconnecting shaft by using a soft-faced hammer and tapping the end of the stub axle (with the nut installed) until the outer CV-joint is fully seated on the shaft.

11. The outer CV-joint must be installed on the interconnecting shaft until the cross of the CV-joint is seated against the circlip on the shaft.

12. Place ½ of the grease provided with the boot service package (DO NOT USE ANY OTHER TYPE OF GREASE) into the outer CV-joint housing. Place the remaining grease into the boot.

13. Install the outer CV-joint boot to the interconnecting shaft clamp evenly on the sealing boot.

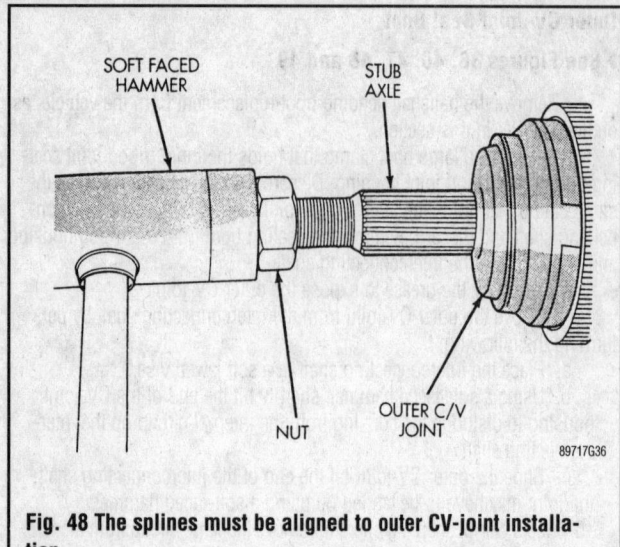

**Fig. 48 The splines must be aligned to outer CV-joint installation**

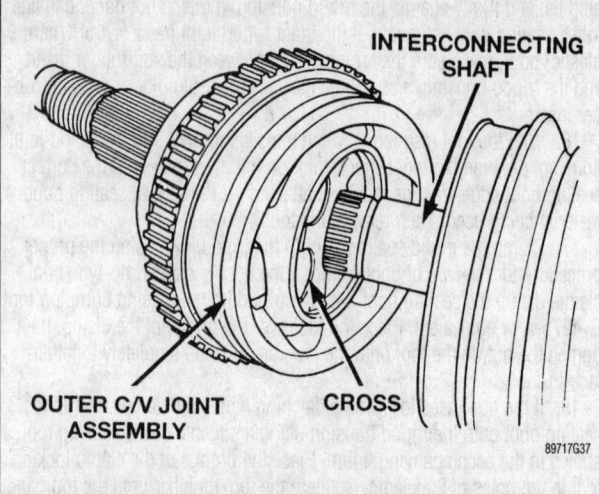

**Fig. 49 The outer CV-joint must be installed until the cross of the joint is seated against the shaft circlip**

14. Clamp the boot onto the interconnecting shaft using a suitable crimper, as follows:

   a. Place the crimping tool over the bridge of the clamp.

   b. Tighten the nut on the crimping tool until the jaws on the tool are closed completely together, face-to-face.

15. Position the outer CV-joint boot into its retaining groove on the outer CV-joint housing. Install the boot-to-housing clamp evenly on the housing. Install the sealing boot-to-outer CV-joint retaining clamp evenly on the sealing boot.

16. Clamp the boot onto the outer CV-joint housing using a suitable crimping tool. Place the crimping tool over the bridge of the clamp, then tighten the nut on the crimping tool until the jaws on the tool are closed completely together, face-to-face.

17. Install the halfshaft in the vehicle, as outlined earlier in this section.

# CLUTCH

## Understanding the Clutch

### ✳✳ CAUTION

**The clutch driven disc may contain asbestos, which has been determined to be a cancer causing agent. Never clean clutch surfaces with compressed air! Avoid inhaling any dust from any clutch surface! When cleaning clutch surfaces, use a commercially available brake cleaning fluid.**

The purpose of the clutch is to disconnect and connect engine power at the transaxle. A vehicle at rest requires a lot of engine torque to get all that weight moving. An internal combustion engine does not develop a high starting torque (unlike steam engines) so it must be allowed to operate without any load until it builds up enough torque to move the vehicle. Torque increases with engine rpm. The clutch allows the engine to build up torque by physically disconnecting the engine from the transaxle, relieving the engine of any load or resistance.

The transfer of engine power to the transaxle (the load) must be smooth and gradual; if it weren't, drive line components would wear out or break quickly. This gradual power transfer is made possible by gradually releasing the clutch pedal. The clutch disc and pressure plate are the connecting link between the engine and transaxle. When the clutch pedal is released, the disc and plate contact each other (the clutch is engaged) physically joining the engine and transaxle. When the pedal is pushed inward, the disc and plate separate (the clutch is disengaged) disconnecting the engine from the transaxle.

Most clutches utilize a single plate, dry friction disc with a diaphragm-style spring pressure plate. The clutch disc has a splined hub which attaches the disc to the input shaft. The disc has friction material where it contacts the flywheel and pressure plate. Torsion springs on the disc help absorb engine torque pulses. The pressure plate applies pressure to the clutch disc, holding it tight against the surface of the flywheel. The clutch operating mechanism consists of a release bearing, fork and cylinder assembly.

The release fork and actuating linkage transfer pedal motion to the release bearing. In the engaged position (pedal released) the diaphragm spring holds the pressure plate against the clutch disc, so engine torque is transmitted to the input shaft. When the clutch pedal is depressed, the release bearing pushes the diaphragm spring center toward the flywheel. The diaphragm spring pivots the fulcrum, relieving the load on the pressure plate. Steel spring straps riveted to the clutch cover lift the pressure plate from the clutch disc, disengaging the engine drive from the transaxle and enabling the gears to be changed.

The clutch is operating properly if:

1. It will stall the engine when released with the vehicle held stationary.

2. The shift lever can be moved freely between 1st and reverse gears when the vehicle is stationary and the clutch disengaged.

## Driven Disc and Pressure Plate

➡**Vehicles made at the Toluca assembly plant, in Mexico have conventional clutch and flywheel assembles. Vehicles made at the Belvidere assembly plant have modular clutch assemblies. As the removal procedures are different, refer to the Vehicle Identification Number (VIN) information in Section 1, to determine where your vehicle was assembled.**

### REMOVAL & INSTALLATION

**Toluca Built Vehicles**

▶ **See Figures 50 thru 60**

1. Remove the transaxle from the vehicle, as outlined earlier in this section.

2. Matchmark the position of the clutch cover and flywheel for proper alignment during installation.

3. Install a suitable clutch alignment tool through the clutch disc hub to prevent the clutch disc from falling and damaging the facings.

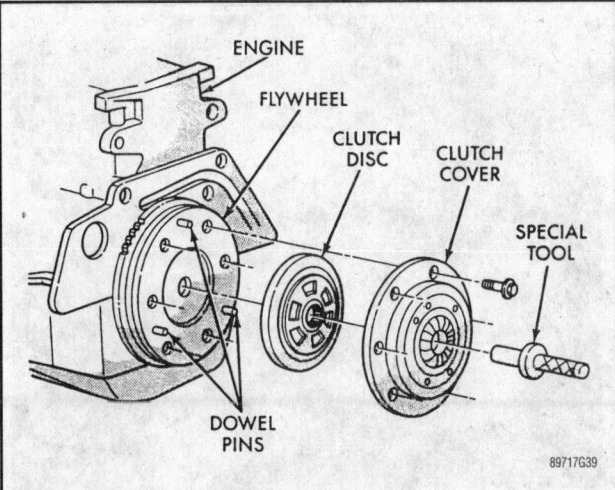

Fig. 50 Exploded view of the conventional clutch components—vehicles built in Toluca

Fig. 52 . . . then carefully remove the clutch and pressure plate assembly from the flywheel

4. Loosen the clutch cover attaching bolts, one or two turns at a time, in a criss-cross pattern. This release the spring pressure gradually, avoiding cover damage.

➡Do NOT touch the clutch disc facing with oily or dirty hands. Oil or dirt transferred from your hands onto the clutch disc may cause clutch chatter.

5. Remove the clutch pressure plate, cover assembly and disc from the flywheel. Handle the components carefully to avoid contaminating the friction surfaces.

6. Inspect for oil leakage through the engine rear main bearing oil seal and transaxle input shaft seal. If there is leakage, it should be fixed at this time.

7. The friction faces of the flywheel and pressure place should not have excessive discoloration, burned areas, cracks, deep grooves or ridges. Replace parts as required.

8. Clean the flywheel face with medium sandpaper, then wipe the surface with mineral spirits. If the surface is severely scored, heat checked, cracked or warped, replace the flywheel.

9. The heavy side of the flywheel is indicated by a white paint mark, near the outside diameter. To minimize the effects of flywheel unbalance, perform the following installation procedure:

Fig. 53 Check across the flywheel surface, it should be flat

Fig. 51 Loosen and remove the clutch and pressure plate bolts evenly, a little at a time . . .

Fig. 54 If necessary, lock the flywheel in place and remove the retaining bolts . . .

Fig. 55 . . . then remove the flywheel from the crankshaft in order replace it or have it machined

Fig. 58 Install a clutch alignment arbor, to align the clutch assembly during installation

Fig. 56 Upon installation, it is usually a good idea to apply a thread-locking compound to the flywheel bolts

Fig. 59 You may want to use a thread locking compound on the clutch assembly bolts

Fig. 57 Be sure that the flywheel surface is clean, before installing the clutch

Fig. 60 Be sure to use a torque wrench to tighten all bolts

a. Loosely assembly the flywheel to the crankshaft. If available, use new flywheel attaching bolts which have sealant on the threads. If new bolts are not available, apply Loctite® sealant to the threads of the original bolts. This sealant is required to prevent engine oil leakage.

b. Rotate the flywheel and crankshaft until the white paint (heavy side) is at the 12 o'clock position.

c. Tighten the flywheel attaching bolts, in a criss-cross pattern, to 70 ft. lbs. (95 Nm).

10. The clutch disc should be handled without touching the facings. Replace the disc if the facings show grease or oil soakage, or wear to within less than 0.008 in. (0.20mm) of the rivet heads. The splines on the disc hub and transaxle input shaft should be a snug fit without signs of excessive wear. Metallic portions of the disc assembly should be dry, clean and not discolored from excessive heat. Each of the arched springs between the facings should be tight.

11. Wipe the friction surface of the pressure plate with mineral spirits.

12. Using a straight edge, check the pressure plate for flatness. The pressure plate friction area should be flat to slightly concave, with the inner diameter 0.000–0.0039 in. (0.0–0.1mm) below the outer diameter. It should also be free from discoloration, burned areas, cracks, grooves or ridges.

13. Using a surface plate, test the cover for flatness. All sections around the attaching bolt holes should be in contact with the surface plate within 0.015 in. (0.381mm).

14. The cover should be a snug fit on the flywheel dowels. If the clutch assembly does not meet these requirements, it should be replaced.

**To install:**

15. Mount the clutch assembly on the flywheel with the disc centered on the alignment tool, being careful to properly align the dowels and the alignment marks made before removal. The flywheel side of the clutch disc is marked for proper installation. If the new clutch or flywheel is installed, align the orange cover balance spot as close as possible to the orange flywheel balance spot. Apply pressure to the alignment tool. Center the tip of the tool into the crankshaft and the sliding cone into the clutch fingers. Tighten the clutch attaching bolts sufficiently to hold the disc in position.

16. To avoid distorting the clutch cover, tighten the bolts gradually, a few turns at a time. Use a criss-cross pattern until all bolts are seated. Tighten the bolts to a final torque of 21 ft. lbs. (28 Nm).

17. Remove the clutch alignment tool.

18. Install the transaxle, as outlined earlier in this section.

**Belvidere Built Vehicles**

▶ **See Figure 61**

1. Disconnect the negative battery cable.
2. Remove the starter wiring, then remove the starter motor assembly.
3. Remove the rear and front transaxle brackets.
4. Unfasten the modular clutch assembly works.
5. Remove the transaxle from the vehicle, as outlined earlier in this section. The transaxle and modular clutch come out as an assembly.
6. Remove the modular clutch assembly from the transaxle input shaft. Handle the components carefully to avoid contaminating the friction surface.
7. Inspect for oil leakage through the engine rear main bearing oil seal and transaxle input shaft seal. If any leakage is noted, it should be fixed at this time.

**To install:**

➡**Always use new bolts when mounting the modular clutch assembly to the drive plate.**

8. Mount the modular clutch assembly onto the input shaft. Install the transaxle.

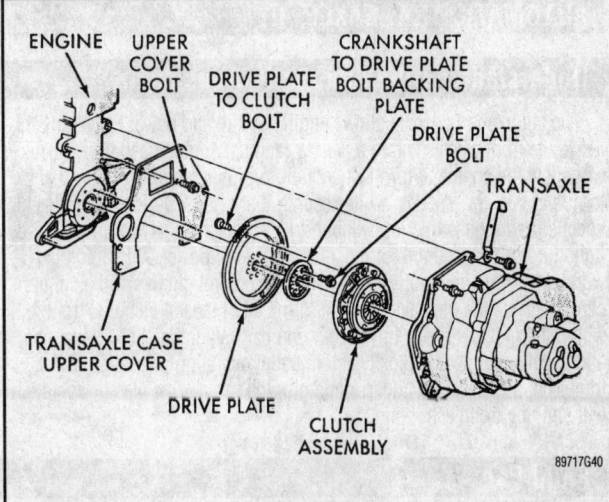

**Fig. 61 The transaxle and modular clutch are removed as an assembly**

9. To avoid distorting the drive plate, tighten the bolts gradually a few turns at a time. Use a criss-cross pattern, until all bolts are seated. Tighten the bolts to a final torque of 55 ft. lbs. (75 Nm).

10. Install the clutch inspection cover.
11. Install the transaxle lower support brackets.
12. Install the starter assembly, then attach the wiring.
13. Connect the negative battery cable.

## Release Bearing and Fork

### REMOVAL & INSTALLATION

1. Remove the transaxle from the vehicle.
2. Move the lever and bearing assembly to a vertical in-line position. Grasp the release lever with 2 hands in the pivot stud socket area. Pull with even pressure and the lever will pop off with the pivot-stud. Do NOT use a prytool or screwdriver to pop the lever off. This may damage the spring clip on the lever.
3. As a unit, remove the fork from the bearing thrust plate. Be careful not to damage the bearing retention tabs.
4. Check the bearing condition. The bearing is a pre-lubricated, sealed unit and should not be immersed in oil or solvent.
5. The bearing should turn smoothly when held in the hand under a light thrust load. A light drag, caused by the lubricant fill, is considered normal. If the bearing is noisy, rough or dry, you must replace the bearing.
6. Check the condition of the pivot stud spring clips on the back side of the clutch fork. If the clips are broken or distorted, the fork must be replaced.

**To install:**

7. The pivot ball pocket in the fork is Teflon® coated and should be installed without any lubrication, such as grease. Using grease will break down the Teflon® coating. Be sure the ball stud and fork pocket are clean of contamination and dirt.
8. Assemble the fork to the bearing. The small pegs on the bearing must go over the fork arms.
9. Slide the bearing and fork assembly onto the input shaft bearing retainer, as a unit.
10. Snap the clutch fork onto the pivot ball.
11. Install the transaxle assembly, as outlined earlier in this section.

## AUTOMATIC TRANSAXLE

### Understanding the Automatic Transaxle

The automatic transaxle allows engine torque and power to be transmitted to the front wheels within a narrow range of engine operating speeds. It will allow the engine to turn fast enough to produce plenty of power and torque at very low speeds, while keeping it at a sensible rpm at high vehicle speeds (and it does this job without driver assistance). The transaxle uses a light fluid as the medium for the transmission of power. This fluid also works in the operation of various hydraulic control circuits and as a lubricant. Because the transaxle fluid performs all of these functions, trouble within the unit can easily travel from one part to another. For this reason, and because of the complexity and unusual operating principles of the transaxle, a very sound understanding of the basic principles of operation will simplify troubleshooting.

### Fluid Pan

For automatic transaxle fluid pan removal and filter replacement, please refer to Section 1 of this manual.

### Neutral Safety/Back-up Light Switch

For neutral safety/back-up light switch removal and installation, please refer to Section 6 of this manual.

### Automatic Transaxle Assembly

#### REMOVAL & INSTALLATION

▶ **See Figures 62 thru 74**

The transaxle and torque converter must be removed as an assembly; otherwise the torque converter drive plate, pump bushing or oil seal may be damaged. The drive plate will not support a load; therefore, none of the weight of the transaxle should be allowed to rest on the plate during removal.

1. Disconnect the negative, then the positive battery cables.
2. Pull the Power Distribution Center (PDC) up and out of its holding bracket. Set the PDC aside to gain clearance.
3. Remove the battery heat shield, then remove the battery from the engine compartment. Remove the battery tray from the engine compartment. If equipped, disconnect the cruise control.
4. Remove the vehicle speed sensor wiring.
5. Disconnect the neutral safety switch and torque converter control wiring from the transaxle.

> ⚙ **WARNING**
>
> Pry up on both sides of the shift cable isolator bushing, evenly, to avoid damaging the cable isolator bushing.

6. Disconnect the gear shift cable end from the transaxle shift lever. Remove the bracket bolt from the transaxle.
7. Remove the throttle pressure control cable from the lever. Then, remove the bracket bolts from the transaxle.
8. Remove the transaxle dipstick tube.
9. Disconnect the transaxle oil cooler lines, and plug them to prevent contamination from entering.
10. Remove the throttle pressure control cable support bracket bolts. Remove the upper bellhousing bolts and upper starter bolt.
11. Install a suitable engine bridge fixture, then support the engine.

12. Raise and safely support the vehicle, then remove the front wheel and tire assemblies.

> ⚙ **WARNING**
>
> When installing the halfshafts, new retaining clips must be used. Do NOT reuse the old clips. Failure to use new clips could cause the inner CV-joint to disengage.

13. Remove both front halfshafts, as outlined earlier in this section.

> ⚙ **WARNING**
>
> On 1998–99 vehicles, then exhaust flex joint must be disconnected from the exhaust manifold anytime the engine is lowered. If the engine is lowered while the flex pipe is attached, damage will occur.

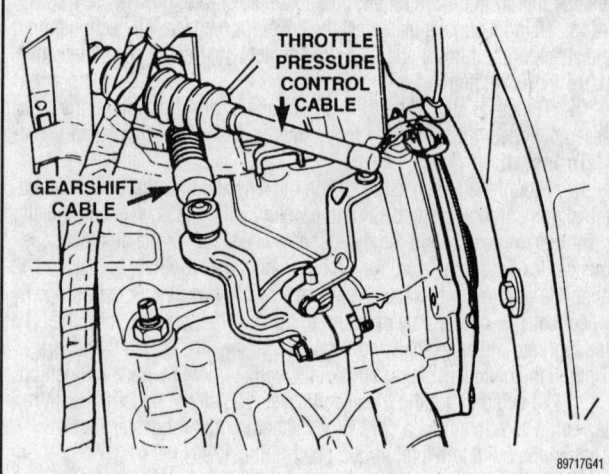

**Fig. 62 Disconnect the gear shift cable end from the transaxle shift lever . . .**

**Fig. 63 . . . then remove the bracket bolt from the transaxle**

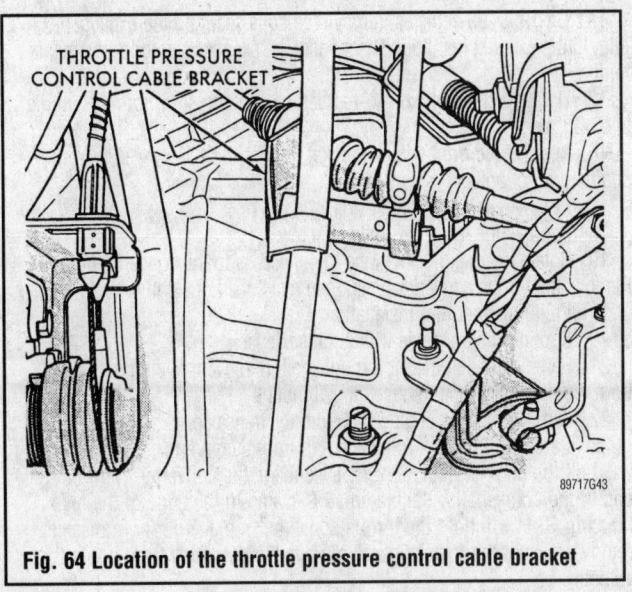

Fig. 64 Location of the throttle pressure control cable bracket

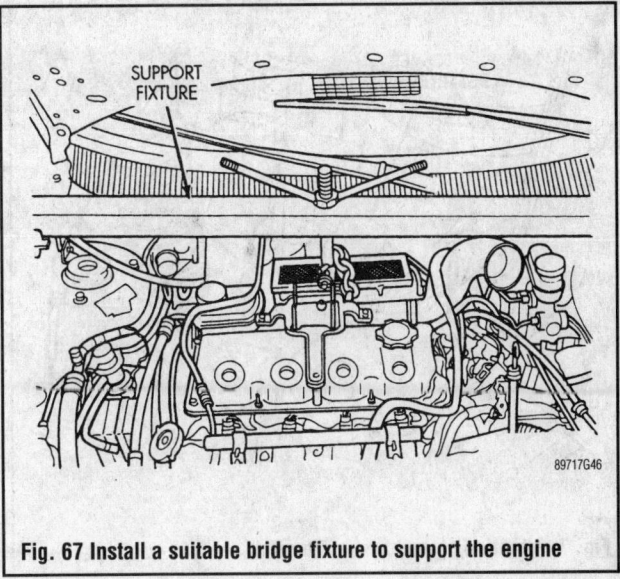

Fig. 67 Install a suitable bridge fixture to support the engine

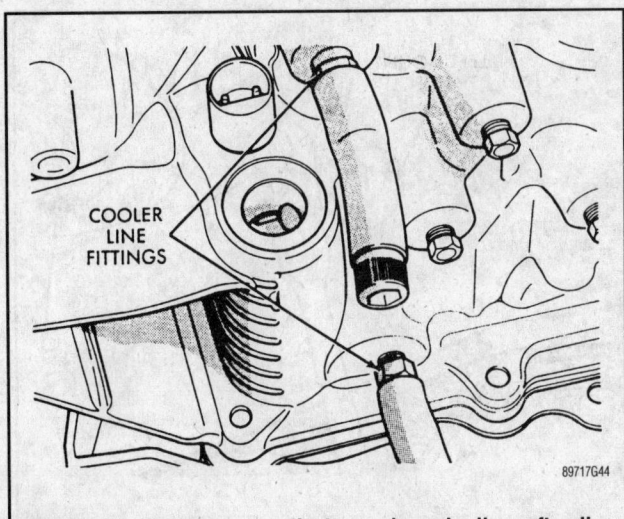
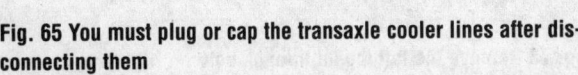

Fig. 65 You must plug or cap the transaxle cooler lines after disconnecting them

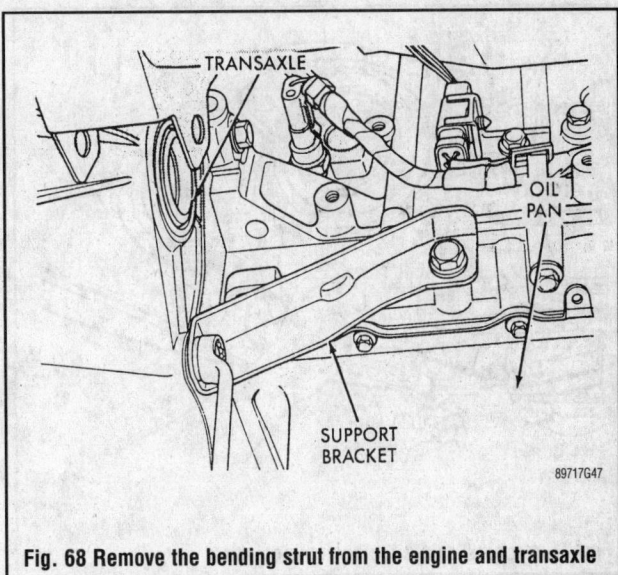

Fig. 68 Remove the bending strut from the engine and transaxle

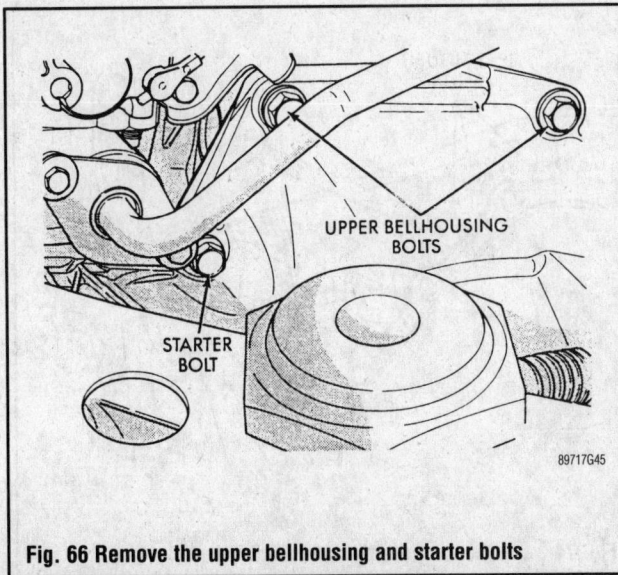

Fig. 66 Remove the upper bellhousing and starter bolts

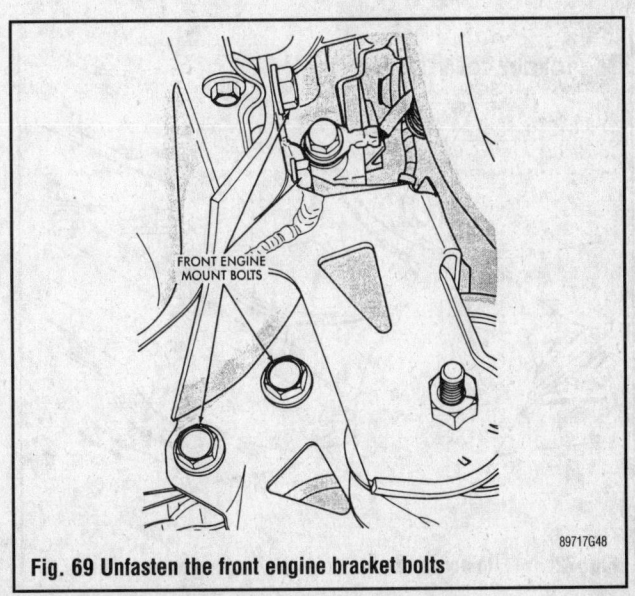

Fig. 69 Unfasten the front engine bracket bolts

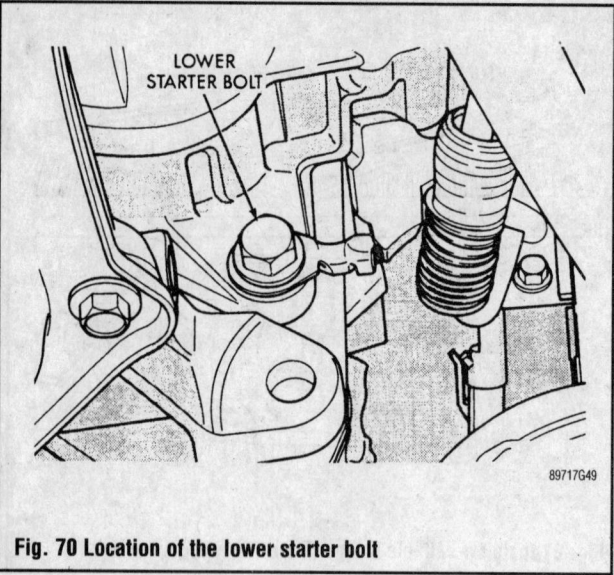

Fig. 70 Location of the lower starter bolt

14. On 1998–99 vehicles, remove the bolts securing the exhaust flex joint to the exhaust manifold. Disconnect the exhaust pipe from the manifold.

15. Unfasten the transaxle-to-rear lateral bending strut from the engine and transaxle.

16. Remove the front engine bracket through-bolt. Remove the front engine bracket bolts.

17. Remove the lower starter bolt.

18. Remove the lower dust shield screw.

19. Rotate the engine clockwise to get access to the converter bolts. Remove the torque converter bolts, then matchmark the converter to the flex plate for alignment during installation.

20. Support the transaxle with a transaxle jack.

21. Remove the left mount through-bolt. Remove the left mount bolts from the transaxle, then remove the left mount.

22. Remove the rear engine bolt from the transaxle.

23. Carefully work the transaxle and torque converter assembly rearward off the engine block dowels. Disengage the converter hub from the end of the crankshaft. Attach a small C-clamp to the edge of the bell housing. This will hold the torque converter in place during transaxle removal. Lower the transaxle and remove the assembly from under the vehicle.

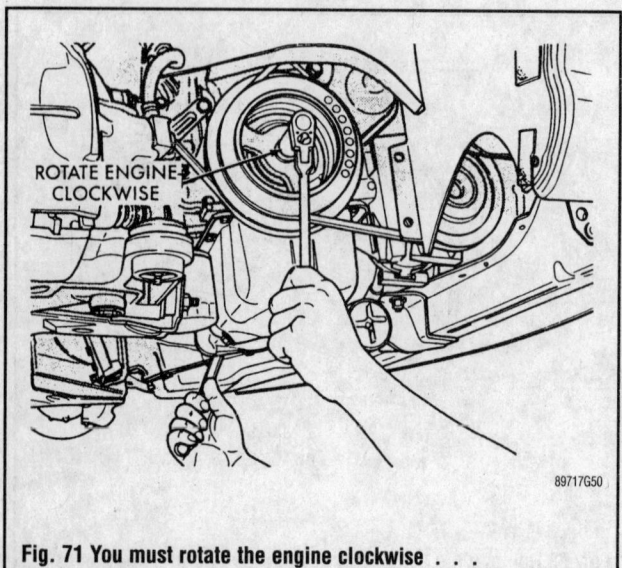

Fig. 71 You must rotate the engine clockwise . . .

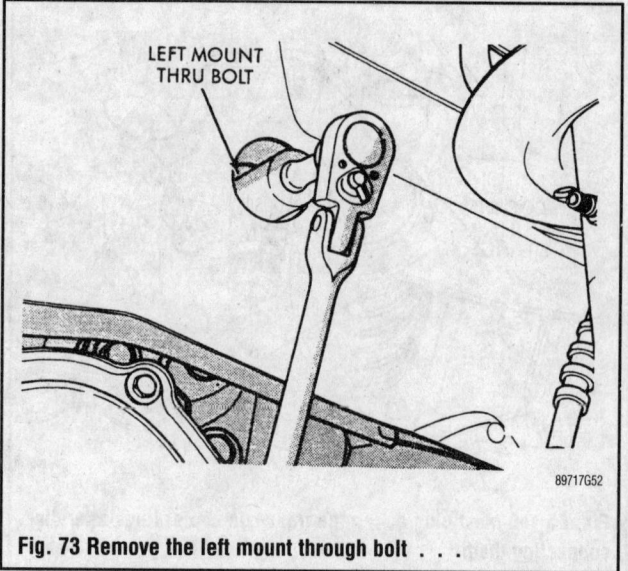

Fig. 73 Remove the left mount through bolt . . .

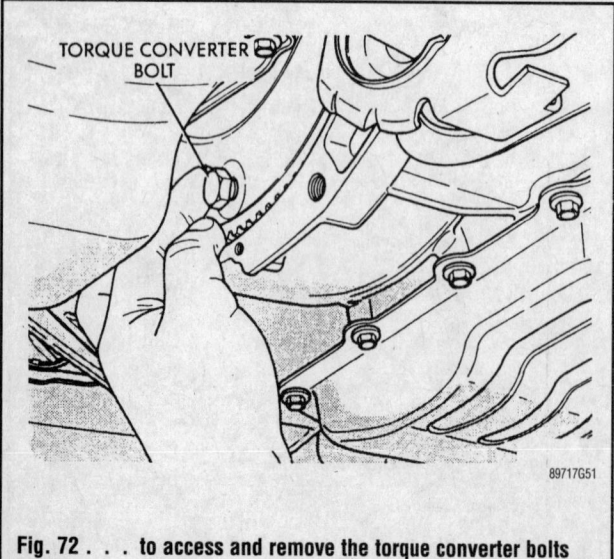

Fig. 72 . . . to access and remove the torque converter bolts

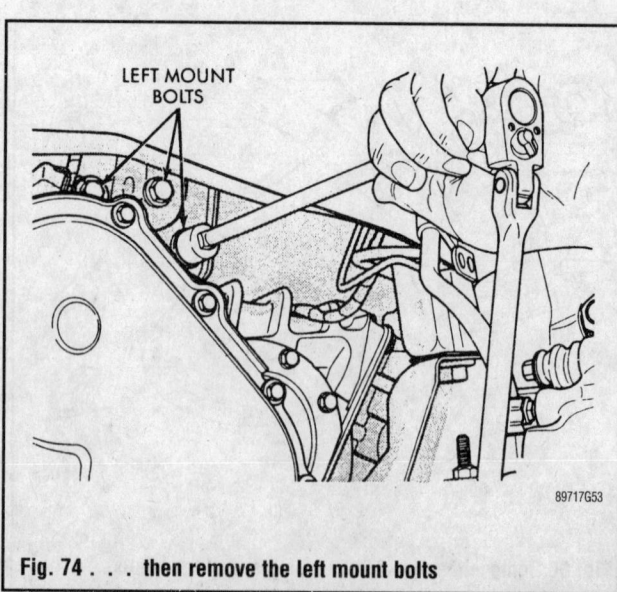

Fig. 74 . . . then remove the left mount bolts

**To install:**

24. Installation is the reverse of the removal procedure. Please note the following important steps.

25. The following items must be tightened to the specifications listed.
- Bell housing cover bolts: 9 ft. lbs. (12 Nm)
- Transaxle oil cooler line-to-radiator connection: 9 ft. lbs. (12 Nm).
- Transaxle oil cooler line connection: 21 ft. lbs. (28 Nm).
- Flex plate-to-crankshaft bolts:70 ft. lbs. (95 Nm).
- Flex plate-to-torque converter bolts: 50 ft. lbs. (68 Nm).
- Left motor mount bolts: 40 ft. lbs. (54 Nm).
- Transaxle-to-cylinder block bolt:70 ft. lbs. (95 Nm).

26. If the torque converter was removed from the transaxle, be sure to align the pump inner gear pilot flats with the torque converter impeller hub flats.

27. Adjust the gearshift and throttle cables.

28. Refill the transaxle with the suitable type and amount of automatic transaxle fluid. For more information, please refer to Section 1 of this manual.

29. Make sure the car's back-up lights and speedometer are working properly.

## ADJUSTMENTS

### Gearshift Cable

▶ See Figure 75

Normal operation of the park/neutral position switch provides a quick check to confirm proper linkage adjustment.

Move the gear selector lever slowly forward until it clicks into the Park position. The starter should operate.

After checking the Park position, move the selector slowly toward the Neutral position, until the lever drops into the N position. If the starter will operate also at this point, the gearshift linkage is properly adjusted. If the starter fails to operated in either position, linkage adjustment is necessary, as follows:

1. Set the parking brake.
2. Remove the floor console, as outlined in Section 10 of this manual.
3. Place the gearshift lever in the Park (P) position.
4. Push down on the tab and unsnap the collar at the shifter cable to allow the cable to be adjusted.
5. Move the gear shift lever on the transaxle to the Park (P) position.
6. Make sure the shift lever and transaxle are in Park. Rotate the collar on the shift cable adjuster end up until it seats against the plastic housing.

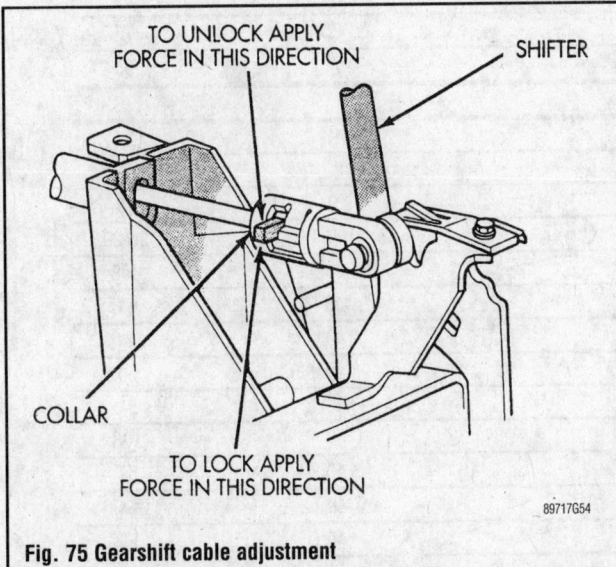

Fig. 75 Gearshift cable adjustment

7. If the collar will not rotate to the fully detented lock position, rotate the collar back to its initial unlocked position. Position the transaxle in the gated Park position. Apply a slight load to the shift lever, fore or aft in the vehicle, while at the same time, rotating the collar up to the LOCK position. The collar must seat against the plastic housing to attain the detented lock position. the gearshift linkage should now be adjusted properly.

8. Check adjustment as follows:
   a. Detent position for Neutral and Drive should be within the limits of the hand lever gate stops.
   b. Key start must occur only when the shift lever is in the Park or Neutral position.

### Throttle Pressure Cable

▶ See Figure 76

The throttle pressure cable adjustment is crucial to the proper operation of the transaxle. This adjustment positions a valve which controls shift speed, shift quality and part throttle downshift sensitivity. If the setting is too long, early shifts and slippage between shifts may occur. If the setting is too short, shifts may be delayed and part throttle downshifts may be sensitive.

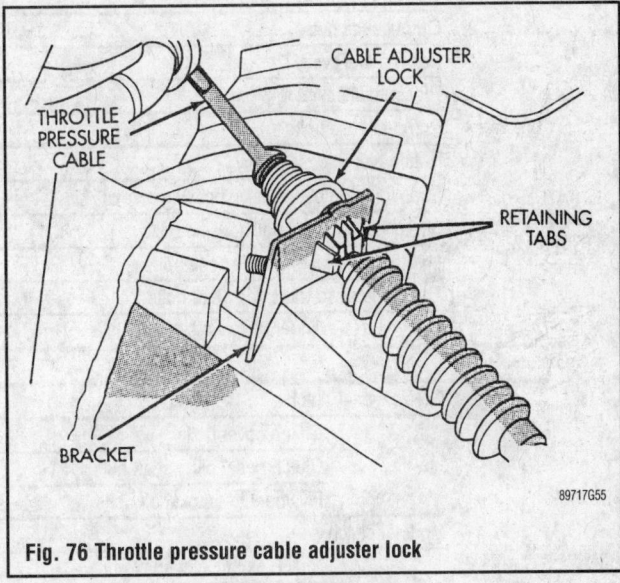

Fig. 76 Throttle pressure cable adjuster lock

1. Perform the transaxle throttle cable pressure adjustment while the engine is at the normal operating temperature.
2. Release the cross-lock on the cable assembly (pull the cross-lock upward).
3. To ensure proper adjustment, the cable must be free to slide all the way toward the engine, against its stop, after the cross-lock is released.
4. Move the transaxle throttle control lever fully clockwise, against its internal stop, and press the crosslock downward into the locked position.

The adjustment is complete and transaxle throttle cable backlash was automatically removed. Test the cable freedom of movement by moving the transaxle throttle lever forward (counterclockwise). Then, slowly release it to confirm the it will return fully rearward (clockwise).

No lubrication is required for any component of the throttle cable system.

## Halfshafts

For halfshaft removal, installation and overhaul, refer to the Halfshaft procedures located under the manual transaxle portion of this section.

## TORQUE SPECIFICATIONS

| Component | ft. lbs. | inch lbs. | Nm |
|---|---|---|---|
| **Automatic Transaxle** | | | |
| Bell housing cover bolts | 9 | | 12 |
| Cooler hose-to-radiator connection | 9 | | 12 |
| Cooler line connection | 21 | | 28 |
| Differential cover-to-case bolt | 14 | | 19 |
| Extension housing-to-case bolt | 21 | | 28 |
| Flex plate-to-crankshaft bolts | 70 | | 95 |
| Flex plate-to-torque converter bolts | 50 | | 68 |
| Fluid filter screw | | 45 | 5 |
| Front motor mount bolt | 40 | | 54 |
| Left motor mount bolts | 40 | | 54 |
| Lower bell housing cover screw | 30 | | 41 |
| Manual cable-to-transaxle case bolt | 21 | | 28 |
| Manual control lever screw | 9 | | 12 |
| Oil pan-to-transaxle case screw | 14 | | 19 |
| Output shaft nuts | 200 | | 271 |
| Park/neutral switch | 25 | | 34 |
| Pressure check plug | | 45 | 5 |
| Pump-to-case bolts | 23 | | 31 |
| Rear cover-to-case screw | 14 | | 19 |
| Speedometer-to-extension housing screw | | 60 | 7 |
| Starter-to-transaxle bell housing bolts | 40 | | 54 |
| Throttle cable-to-transaxle case bolts | 9 | | 12 |
| Throttle lever-to-transaxle shaft bolts | 9 | | 12 |
| Transaxle-to-cylinder block bolt | 70 | | 95 |
| **Clutch** | | | |
| Conventional clutch | | | |
|     Clutch cover bolts | 21 | | 28 |
|     Clutch pedal pivot shaft nut | 30 | | 41 |
|     Flywheel-to-crankshaft bolts | 70 | | 95 |
| Modular clutch | | | |
|     Clutch pedal pivot shaft nut | 30 | | 41 |
|     Drive plate-to-clutch bolts | 55 | | 75 |
|     Drive plate-to-crankshaft bolts | 75 | | 95 |
| **Manual transaxle** | | | |
| Back-up lamp switch | 18 | | 24 |
| Drain plug | 22 | | 30 |
| Dust shield-to-transaxle retainers | 9 | | 12 |
| End plate cover bolts | 19-21 | | 26-29 |
| Front engine mount-to-transaxle retainers | 80 | | 108 |
| Front mount through bolt | 45 | | 61 |
| Front mount-to-engine bolt | 40 | | 54 |
| Lateral bending strut-to-engine bolts | 40 | | 54 |
| Lateral bending strut-to-transaxle retainers | 40 | | 54 |
| Left mount through bolt | 80 | | 108 |
| Left mount-to-transaxle bolts | 40 | | 54 |
| Power hop damper-to-frame bracket | 40 | | 54 |
| Power hop damper-to-transaxle bracket | 40 | | 54 |
| Shift cable bracket-to-transaxle | 21 | | 28 |

89717C01

## TORQUE SPECIFICATIONS

| Component | ft. lbs. | inch lbs. | Nm |
|---|---|---|---|
| Transaxle case bolts | 19-21 | | 26-29 |
| Transaxle-to-engine bolts | | | |
|     1995 vehicles | 23 | | 31 |
|     1996-99 vehicles | 70 | | 95 |
| Transaxle-to-engine intake bracket bolts | | | |
|     1995 vehicles | 23 | | 31 |
|     1996-99 vehicles | 70 | | 95 |
| Vehicle speed sensor bolt | | 60 | 7 |
| Vertical bending strut-to-engine retainers | 80 | | 108 |
| Vertical bending strut-to-transaxle retainers | 80 | | 108 |

89717C02

## Transmission Fluid Indications

The appearance and odor of the transmission fluid can give valuable clues to the overall condition of the transmission. Always note the appearance of the fluid when you check the fluid level or change the fluid. Rub a small amount of fluid between your fingers to feel for grit and smell the fluid on the dipstick.

| If the fluid appears: | It indicates: |
| --- | --- |
| Clear and red colored | • Normal operation |
| Discolored (extremely dark red or brownish) or smells burned | • Band or clutch pack failure, usually caused by an overheated transmission. Hauling very heavy loads with insufficient power or failure to change the fluid, often result in overheating.<br>Do not confuse this appearance with newer fluids that have a darker red color and a strong odor (though not a burned odor). |
| Foamy or aerated (light in color and full of bubbles) | • The level is too high (gear train is churning oil)<br>• An internal air leak (air is mixing with the fluid). Have the transmission checked professionally. |
| Solid residue in the fluid | • Defective bands, clutch pack or bearings. Bits of band material or metal abrasives are clinging to the dipstick. Have the transmission checked professionally. |
| Varnish coating on the dipstick | • The transmission fluid is overheating |

TCCA7C02

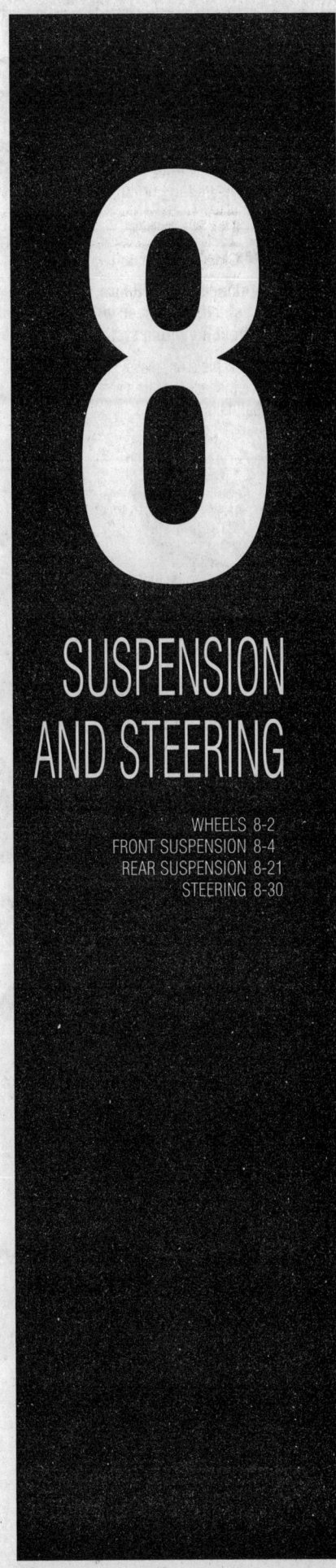

# 8

# SUSPENSION AND STEERING

## WHEELS

### Wheel Assembly

REMOVAL & INSTALLATION

▶ See Figures 1, 2 and 3

➡Vehicles equipped with 13 inch tires have a 4 stud wheel mounting system. Vehicles equipped with 14 inch tires will have either a 4 or 5 stud wheel mounting system.

1. Park the vehicle on a level surface.
2. Remove the jack, tire iron and, if necessary, the spare tire from their storage compartments.

Fig. 1 Pry the center cap off for access to the lug nuts

Fig. 2 You can use the lug wrench supplied with the vehicle to remove the lug nuts

3. Check the owner's manual or refer to Section 1 of this manual for the jacking points on your vehicle. Then, place the jack in the proper position.
4. If equipped with lug nut trim caps, remove them by either unscrewing or pulling them off the lug nuts, as appropriate. Consult the owner's manual, if necessary.
5. If equipped with a wheel cover or hub cap, insert the tapered end of the tire iron in the groove and pry off the cover.
6. Apply the parking brake and block the diagonally opposite wheel with a wheel chock or two.

➡Wheel chocks may be purchased at your local auto parts store, or a block of wood cut into wedges may be used. If possible, keep one or two of the chocks in your tire storage compartment, in case any of the tires has to be removed on the side of the road.

7. If equipped with an automatic transaxle, place the selector lever in **P** or Park; with a manual transaxle, place the shifter in Reverse.
8. With the tires still on the ground, use the tire iron/wrench to break the lug nuts loose.

➡If a nut is stuck, never use heat to loosen it or damage to the wheel and bearings may occur. If the nuts are seized, one or two heavy hammer blows directly on the end of the bolt usually loosens the rust. Be careful, as continued pounding will likely damage the brake drum or rotor.

9. Using the jack, raise the vehicle until the tire is clear of the ground. Support the vehicle safely using jackstands.
10. Remove the lug nuts, then remove the tire and wheel assembly.
**To install:**
11. Make sure the wheel and hub mating surfaces, as well as the wheel lug studs, are clean and free of all foreign material. Always remove rust from the wheel mounting surface and the brake rotor or drum. Failure to do so may cause the lug nuts to loosen in service.
12. Install the tire and wheel assembly and hand-tighten the lug nuts.
13. Using the tire wrench, tighten all the lug nuts, in a crisscross pattern, until they are snug.
14. Raise the vehicle and withdraw the jackstand, then lower the vehicle.

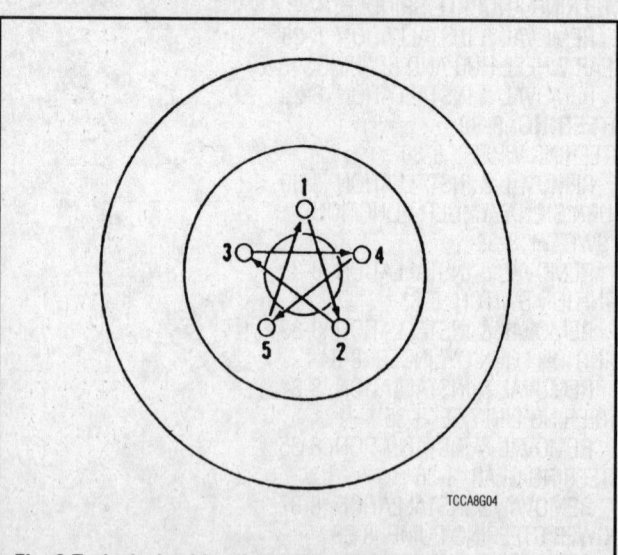

Fig. 3 Typical wheel lug tightening sequence

15. Using a torque wrench, tighten the lug nuts in a crisscross pattern to 100 ft. lbs. ( 135 Nm). Check your owner's manual or refer to Section 1 of this manual for the proper tightening sequence.

### ※※ WARNING

**Do not overtighten the lug nuts, as this may cause the wheel studs to stretch or the brake disc (rotor) to warp.**

16. If so equipped, install the wheel cover or hub cap. Make sure the valve stem protrudes through the proper opening before tapping the wheel cover into position.

17. If equipped, install the lug nut trim caps by pushing them or screwing them on, as applicable.

18. Remove the jack from under the vehicle, and place the jack and tire iron/wrench in their storage compartments. Remove the wheel chock(s).

19. If you have removed a flat or damaged tire, place it in the storage compartment of the vehicle and take it to your local repair station to have it fixed or replaced as soon as possible.

## INSPECTION

Inspect the tires for lacerations, puncture marks, nails and other sharp objects. Repair or replace as necessary. Also check the tires for treadwear and air pressure as outlined in Section 1 of this manual.

Check the wheel assemblies for dents, cracks, rust and metal fatigue. Repair or replace as necessary.

## Wheel Lug Studs

### REMOVAL & INSTALLATION

→Vehicles equipped with 13 inch tires have a 4 stud wheel mounting system. Vehicles equipped with 14 inch tires will have either a 4 or 5 stud wheel mounting system.

**With Disc Brakes**

♦ See Figures 4 and 5

### ※※ WARNING

**If a wheel lug stud needs to be replaced, do NOT try to hammer the stud out of the hub/bearing. If the stud is removed by hammering it out, you can cause damage, leading to bearing failure.**

1. Raise and support the appropriate end of the vehicle safely using jackstands, then remove the wheel.

2. Remove the brake pads and caliper. Support the caliper aside using wire or a coat hanger. For details, please refer to Section 9 of this manual.

3. Lift the rotor off the studs.

4. Install a lug nut on the wheel stud requiring removal, so the threads on the stud are even with the end of the lug nut. Rotate the hub so the stud requiring removal is aligned with the notch cast into the front of the steering knuckle. Install a suitable C-clamp and adapter removal tool, Special tool C-4150 or equivalent, on the hub/bearing flange and wheel stud.

5. Tighten the C-clamp, pushing the wheel stud out of the hub and bearing flange. When the shoulder of the wheel stud is past the flange, remove the tool from the hub and bearing. Then, remove the stud from the flange.

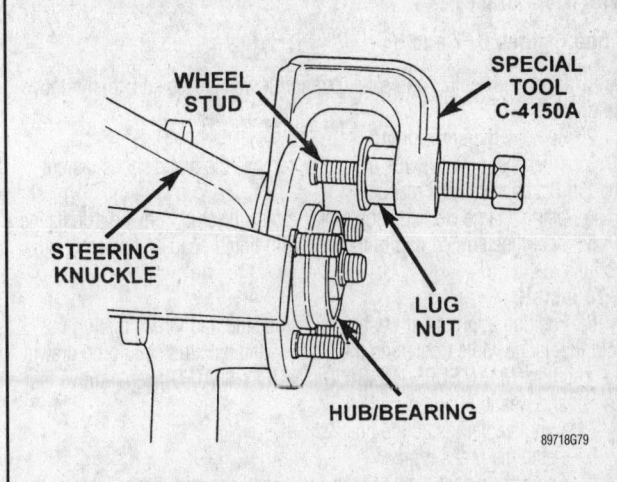

Fig. 4 Removing the wheel stud from the hub and bearing assembly

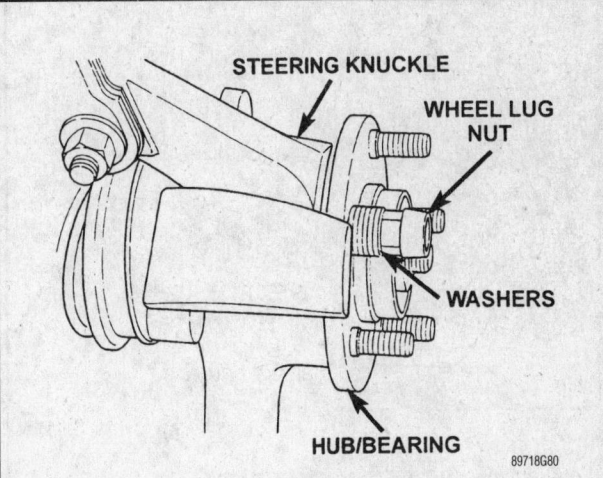

Fig. 5 Place about 5 washers on the stud, then thread on a lug nut with the flat side against the washers

**To install:**

6. Install the replacement stud into the flange of the hub/bearing assembly. Install the about 5 flat washers, and a lug nut on the stud. The lug nut MUST be installed with the flat side of the nut against the washers.

7. Tighten the lug nut. This will pull the stud into the flange of the hub/bearing. When the head of the stud is fully seated against the bearing flange, remove the lug nut and washers from the stud.

8. Place the rotor in position over the wheel lug studs.

9. Install the brake caliper and pads.

10. Install the wheel, then remove the jackstands and carefully lower the vehicle.

11. Tighten the lug nuts to the proper torque.

**With Drum Brakes**

▶ See Figures 6, 7 and 8

1. Raise the vehicle and safely support it with jackstands, then remove the wheel.
2. Remove the brake drum.
3. If necessary to provide clearance, remove the brake shoes, as outlined in Section 9 of this manual.
4. Using a large C-clamp and socket, press the stud from the axle flange.
5. Coat the serrated part of the stud with liquid soap and place it into the hole.

**To install:**

6. Position about 4 flat washers over the stud and thread the lug nut. Hold the flange while tightening the lug nut, and the stud should be drawn into position. MAKE SURE THE STUD IS FULLY SEATED, then remove the lug nut and washers.
7. If applicable, install the brake shoes.
8. Install the brake drum.
9. Install the wheel, then remove the jackstands and carefully lower the vehicle.
10. Tighten the lug nuts to the proper torque.

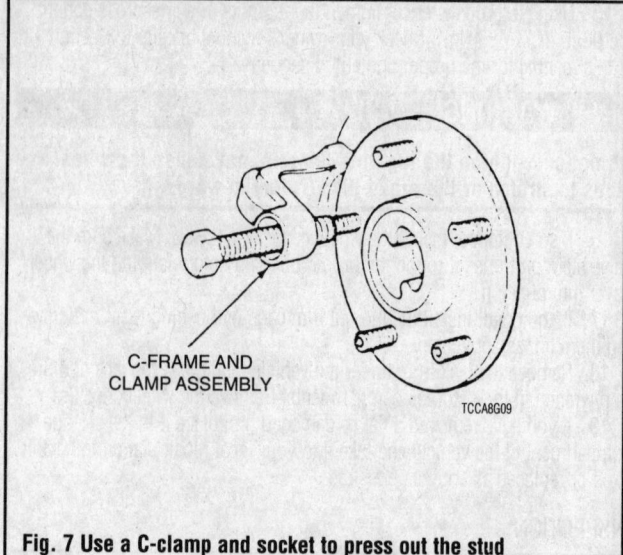

Fig. 7 Use a C-clamp and socket to press out the stud

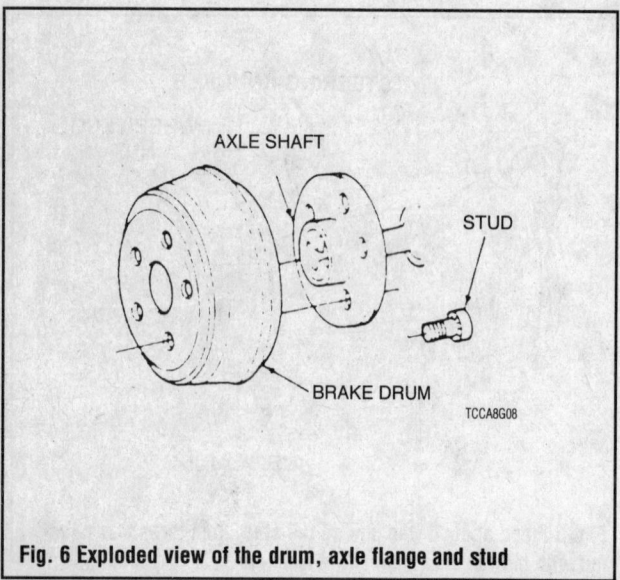

Fig. 6 Exploded view of the drum, axle flange and stud

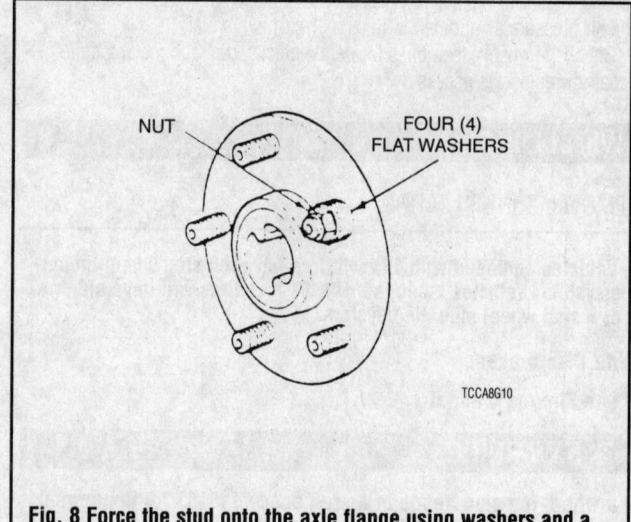

Fig. 8 Force the stud onto the axle flange using washers and a lug nut

## FRONT SUSPENSION

### MacPherson Struts

REMOVAL & INSTALLATION

▶ See Figures 9 thru 17

1. With the vehicle on the ground, loosen the wheel lug nuts.
2. Raise and safely support the vehicle.
3. Remove the wheel and tire assembly.
4. If both strut assemblies are being removed, mark each one right or left, as applicable.
5. Remove the hydraulic brake hose routing bracket and attaching screw from the strut damper bracket. If equipped with ABS, the hydraulic hose routing bracket is combined with the speed sensor cable routing bracket.

➡ The steering knuckle-to-strut assembly attaching bolts are serrated and must not be turned during removal. Remove the nuts while holding the bolts stationary in the steering knuckle.

6. Hold the bolts in place, then remove the 2 nuts securing the strut to the steering knuckle.
7. Remove the 3 nuts attaching the upper mount of the strut to the strut tower of the vehicle. If necessary, partially lower the vehicle for access to the upper mounting nuts.
8. Carefully remove the strut assembly from the vehicle.

**To install:**

9. Install the strut assembly into the strut tower, aligning the 3 studs on the upper strut mount into the holes in the shock tower. Install the 3 upper strut mount retaining nut and washer assemblies. Tighten the 3 nuts to 23 ft. lbs. (31 Nm).

**FRONT SUSPENSION COMPONENT LOCATIONS**

1. Lower control arm
2. Ball joint
3. Tie rod end
4. MacPherson strut
5. Halfshaft
6. Inner CV joint
7. Outer CV joint
8. Stabilizer (sway) bar
9. Power steering gear
10. Crossmember

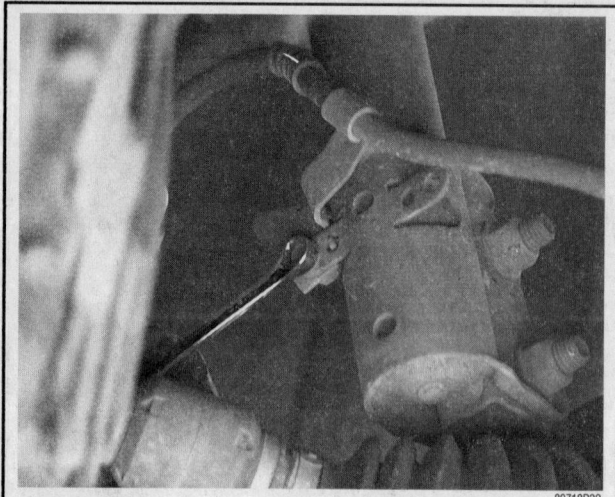

**Fig. 9 Unfasten the bolt securing the brake hose bracket to the strut . . .**

**Fig. 10 . . . then pull the bracket away from the strut**

➡ The steering knuckle-to-strut assembly attaching bolts are serrated and must not be turned during installation. Install the nuts while holding the bolts stationary in the steering knuckle.

10. Align the strut assembly with the steering knuckle. Position the arm of the steering knuckle into the strut assembly, aligning the strut assembly to the steering knuckle mounting holes. Install the 2 strut-to-steering knuckle bolts. The bolts should be installed with the nuts facing the front of the vehicle. Tighten both attaching bolts to 40 ft. lbs. (53 Nm), plus an additional ¼ turn after the specified torque is met.

11. Install the hydraulic brake hose routing bracket and attaching screw onto the strut damper bracket. If the vehicle has ABS, the hydraulic hose routing bracket is combined with the speed sensor cable routing bracket. Tighten the bracket attaching bolts to 10 ft. lbs. (13 Nm).

12. Install the wheel and tire assembly, then tighten the lug nuts in sequence hand-tight.

13. Carefully lower the vehicle then tighten the lug nuts, in sequence, to 100 ft. lbs. (135 Nm).

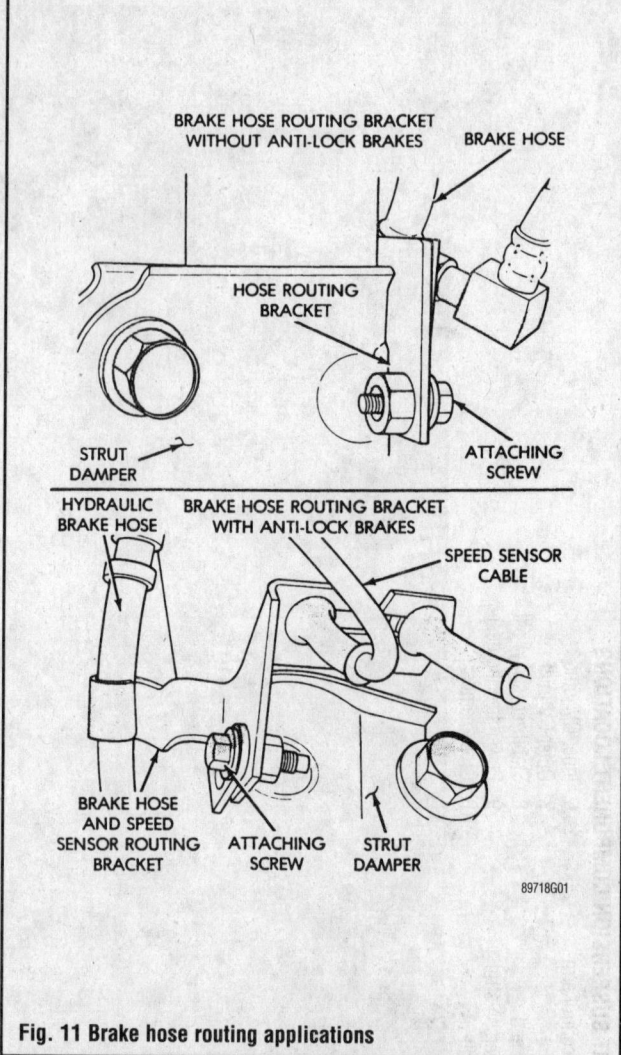

**Fig. 11 Brake hose routing applications**

**Fig. 12 Use a wrench to hold the strut bolt stationary, then loosen the nuts**

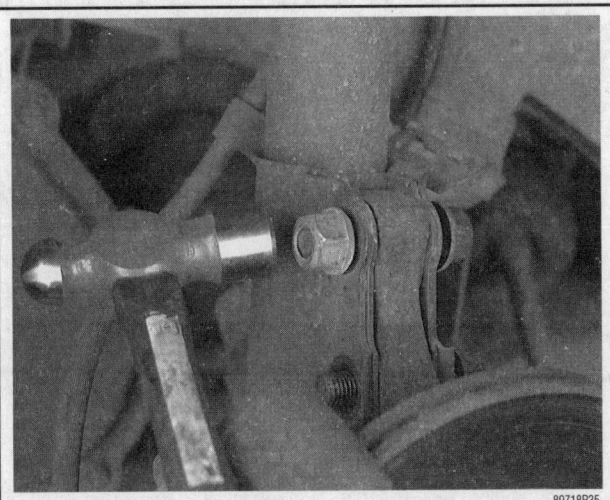

Fig. 13 Sometimes it is necessary to give the nut a sharp rap with a hammer to break it loose

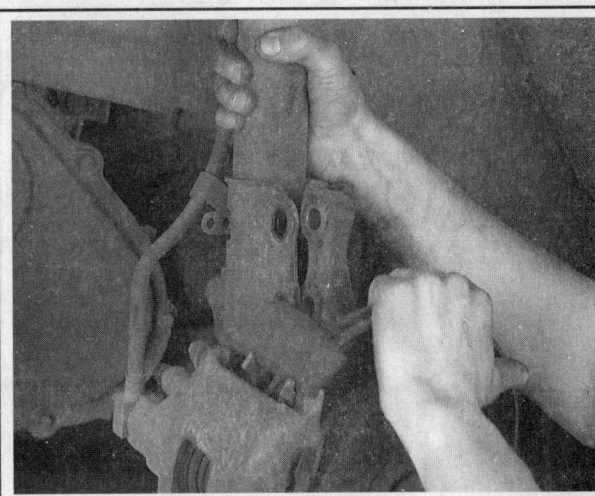

Fig. 16 Pull the steering knuckle away from the strut assembly . . .

Fig. 14 Remove the lower strut mounting bolts. Note the serrations (see arrow)

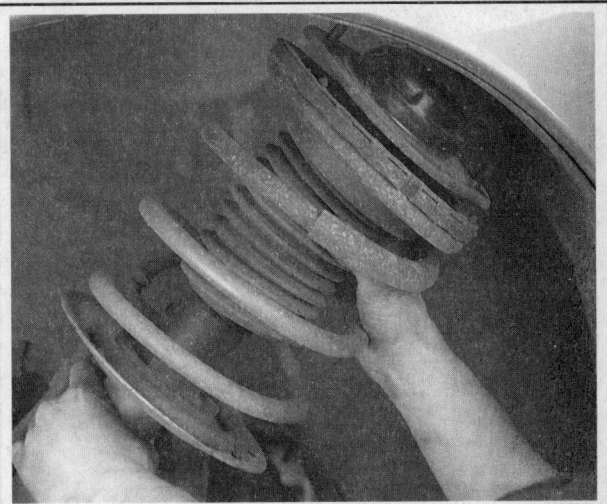

Fig. 17 . . . then carefully remove the strut from the vehicle

Fig. 15 Partially lower the vehicle for access, then remove the 3 upper strut mounting nuts in the engine compartment

## OVERHAUL

▶ See Figures 18, 19, 20 and 21

1. Remove the strut assembly from the vehicle.
2. Clamp the strut in a suitable vise, in a vertical position. When clamping the strut in the vise, do not clamp the strut using the body of the strut, only by the strut clevis bracket, as shown in the accompanying figure.
3. Mark the coil spring and strut assembly right or left, according to which side of the vehicle to strut was removed from, and which strut the coil spring was removed from.

### ❊❊ CAUTION

Do NOT remove the strut rod nut before the strut assembly coil spring is compressed, removing spring tension from the upper spring seat and bearing assembly. When compressing the coil spring for removal from the strut, the first full top and bottom coil of the spring must be held by the jaws of the spring compressor.

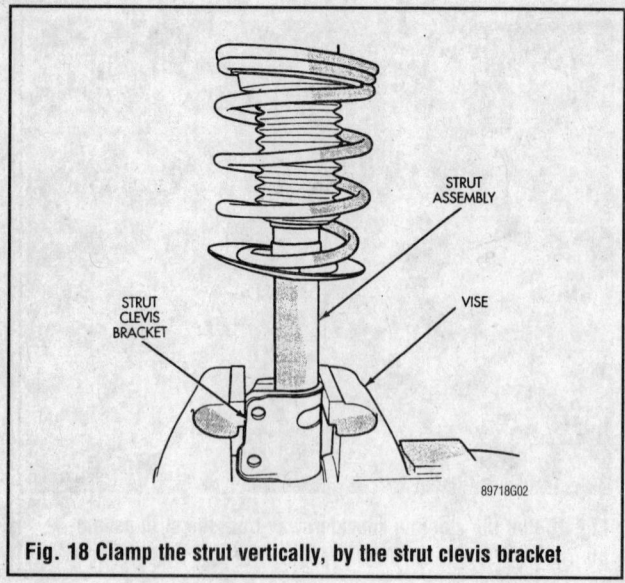

**Fig. 18 Clamp the strut vertically, by the strut clevis bracket**

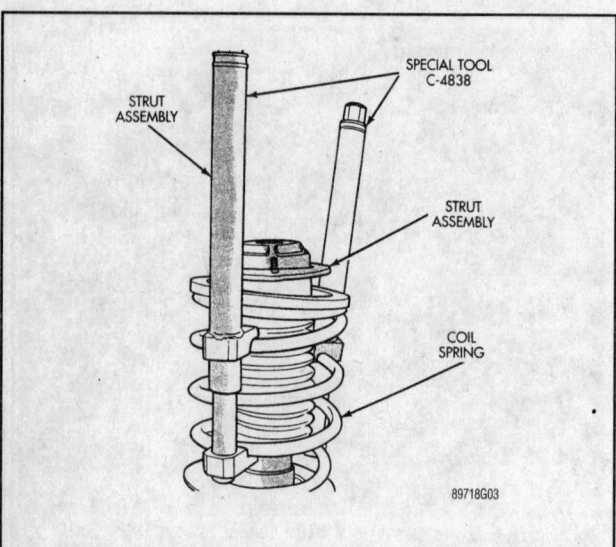

**Fig. 19 Use the proper type of tool to compress the coil spring**

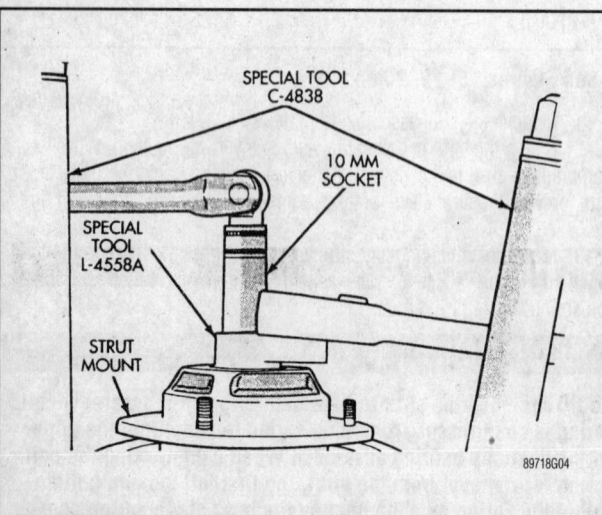

**Fig. 20 Hold the strut shaft in place while removing the shaft retaining nut**

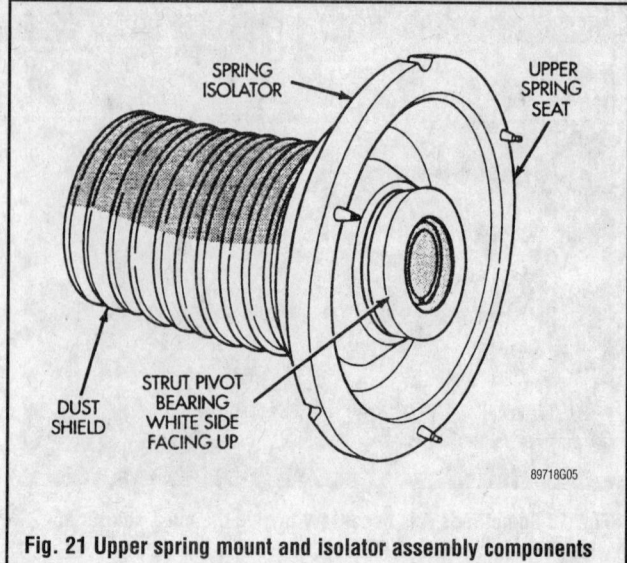

**Fig. 21 Upper spring mount and isolator assembly components**

4. Carefully compress the strut assembly coil spring, using a suitable spring compressor tool.

5. Install a suitable strut nut socket to or an open ended wrench on the strut shaft retaining nut. Then, install a 10mm socket on the hex end of the strut damper shaft. While holding the strut shaft from turning, remove the strut shaft retaining nut.

6. Remove the strut assembly mount/isolator from the strut.

7. Remove the upper spring seat, pivot bearing and dust shield as an assembly from the strut.

8. Remove the jounce bumper from the shaft of the strut assembly.

9. Remove the coil spring from the strut assembly. Mark left and right on the coil springs for their installation back on the correct side of the vehicle.

#### ⁑⁑ WARNING

**If a replacement coil spring is being installed on the strut, then first full top and bottom coil of the spring must be captured by the jaws of the coil spring compressor.**

10. Inspect the strut for any binding of the strut shaft over the full stroke of the shaft.

11. Inspect the strut mount and upper spring seat assembly for any of the following conditions:

• Check the mount for cracks and distortion and the retaining studs for any sign of damage.

• Inspect for severe deterioration of rubber isolator, binding of the strut pivot bearing. If the pivot bearing is replaced, it is to be installed with the while side of the bearing facing up.

• Inspect the dust shield for rips and/or deterioration.

• Check the jounce bumper for cracks and/or signs of deterioration.

12. Replace any components of the strut assembly found to be worn or defective during the inspection, before assembling the strut.

**To install:**

13. Clamp the strut, in a vertical position, in a suitable vise. Only clamp the strut by the clevis bracket, NEVER by the body of the strut.

14. Install the compressed coil spring onto the strut. The spring should be installed with the smaller coil down, so the spring properly seats on the strut.

15. Install the jounce bumper on the strut shaft.

16. Install the dust shield, pivot bearing and upper spring seat as an assembly on the strut.

17. Position the upper spring seat alignment notch with the clevis bracket on the strut assembly.

18. Install the strut mount on the strut assembly and the strut mount retaining nut on the shaft of the strut assembly.

**The following 2 steps must be completely done before the spring compressor tool can be released from the coil spring.**

19. Install strut nut socket or an open end wrench on the strut shaft retaining nut. Then, install a 10mm socket through the center of the socket an on the hex of the strut shaft. While holding the strut shaft from turning, tighten the strut shaft retaining nut to 55 ft. lbs. (75 Nm).

20. Equally loosen both spring compressor tools, until the top coil of the spring is fully seated against the upper spring seat and strut mount. Then, relieve all tensioner from the spring compressors and remove the compressors from the strut spring.

21. Install the strut into the vehicle, as outlined earlier.

## Lower Ball Joint

### INSPECTION

▶ **See Figure 22**

The front suspension ball joints operate with no free-play. The ball joints are replaceable ONLY as an assembly. Do not attempt any type of repair on the ball joint assembly. The ball joint is a press fit into the lower control arm with the joint stud retained in the steering knuckle by the clamp bolt. To check the ball joint, with the weight of the vehicle resting on the road wheels, grasp the grease fitting and without using any tools, attempt to move the grease fitting. If the ball joint is worn the grease fitting will move easily. If movement is noted, replacement of the ball joint is recommended.

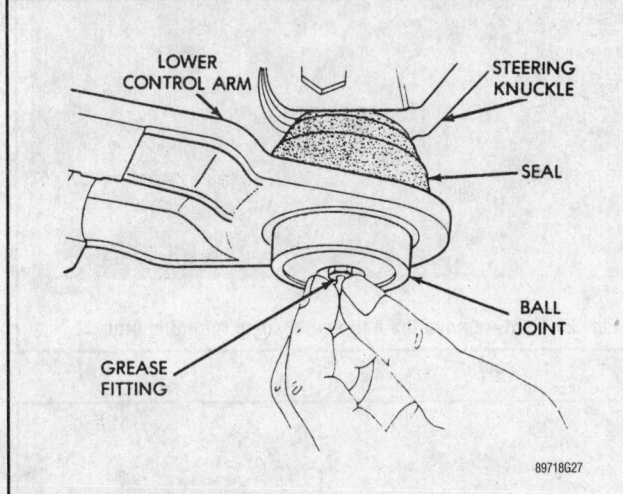

Fig. 22 Wiggle the grease fitting with your fingers. If it moves, the ball joint should be replaced

### REMOVAL & INSTALLATION

▶ **See Figures 23 and 24**

1. Raise and safely support the vehicle. Remove the wheel and tire assembly.
2. Remove the lower control arm from the vehicle, as outlined in this section.
3. Carefully pry the seal boot off the ball joint, using a suitable prytool.
4. Using a suitable press remove the ball joint from the lower control arm.

**To install:**

5. Reinstall the ball joint into the lower control arm with the notch in the ball joint stud facing the front lower control arm bushing.

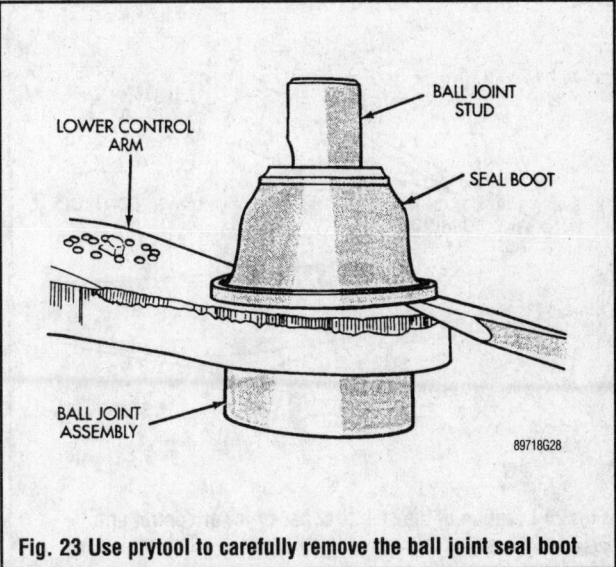

Fig. 23 Use prytool to carefully remove the ball joint seal boot

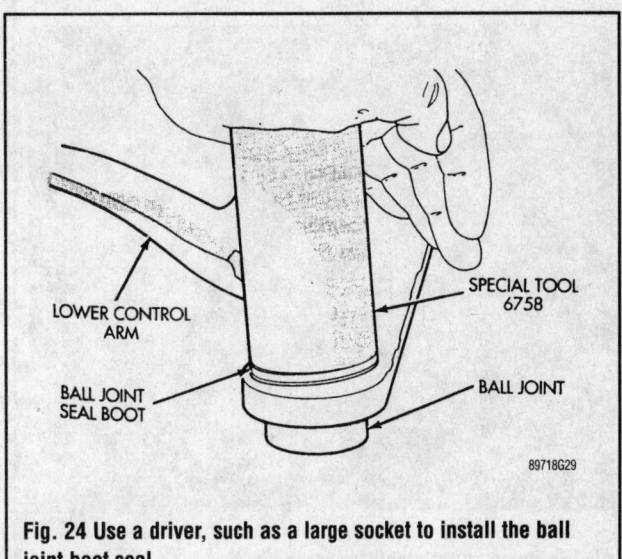

Fig. 24 Use a driver, such as a large socket to install the ball joint boot seal

6. Using a suitable press, press the ball joint into the lower control arm.
7. Reinstall the ball joint boot seal using a suitable driver such as a large socket or suitable sized piece of pipe. Do not use a shop press as was used to install the ball joint as a press exerts too much force.
8. Reinstall the lower control arm, as outlined in this section.
9. Reinstall the wheels and lower the vehicle.
10. The toe should be checked and adjusted as necessary.

## Sway (Stabilizer) Bar

### REMOVAL & INSTALLATION

▶ **See Figures 25 thru 35**

1. Raise and safely support the vehicle.
2. Remove the nuts and stabilizer bar attaching link assemblies from the front lower control arms.
3. Remove the bolts at the front crossmember-to-stabilizer bar bushing retainers. Then, remove the bushing retainers, stabilizer bar and bushings from the front crossmember.

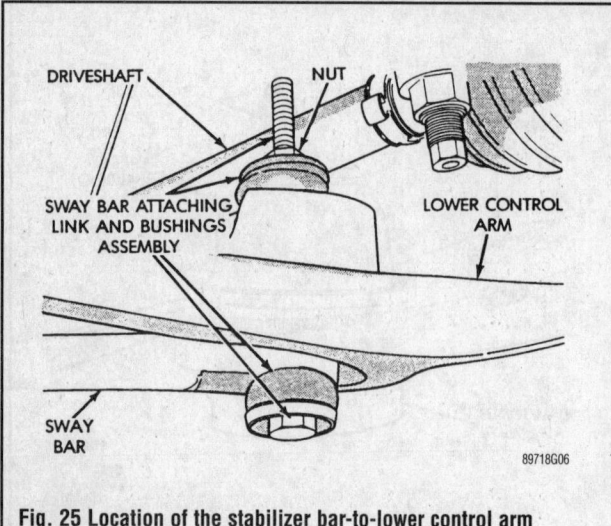

Fig. 25 Location of the stabilizer bar-to-lower control arm attaching links

Fig. 28 Unfasten the bolts from the crossmember-to-sway bar bushing retainers

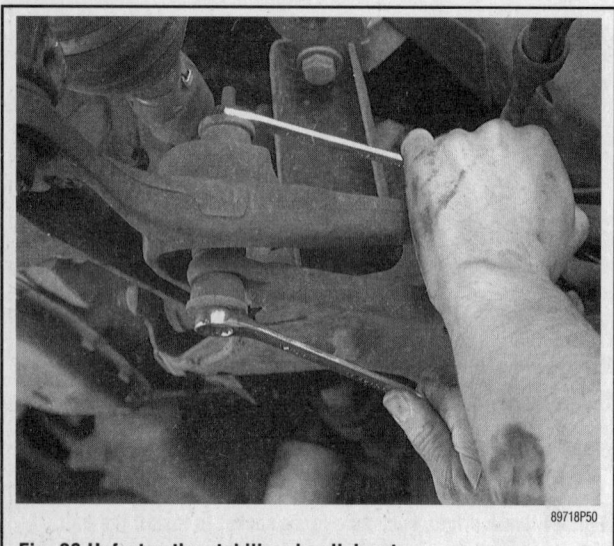
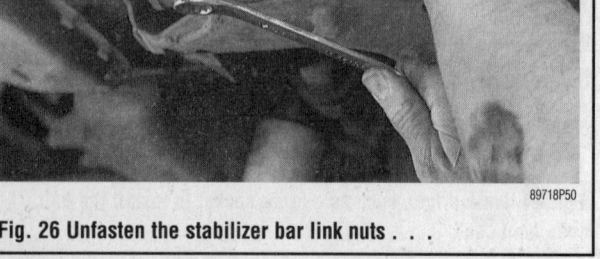

Fig. 26 Unfasten the stabilizer bar link nuts . . .

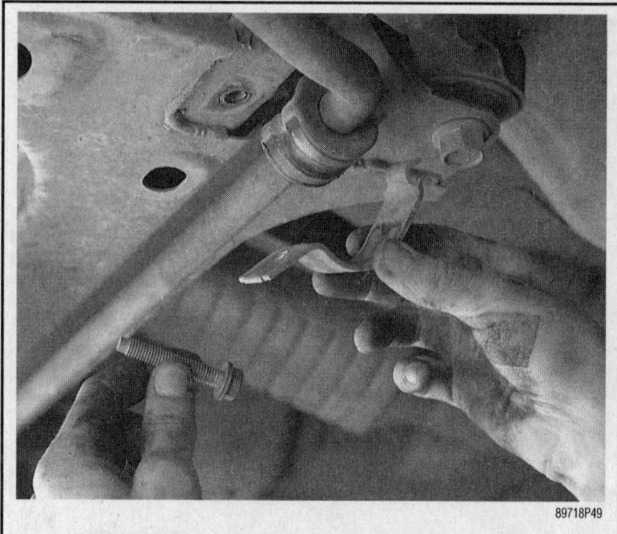

Fig. 29 Then, remove the bolt and bushing retaining bracket

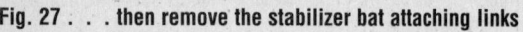

Fig. 27 . . . then remove the stabilizer bat attaching links

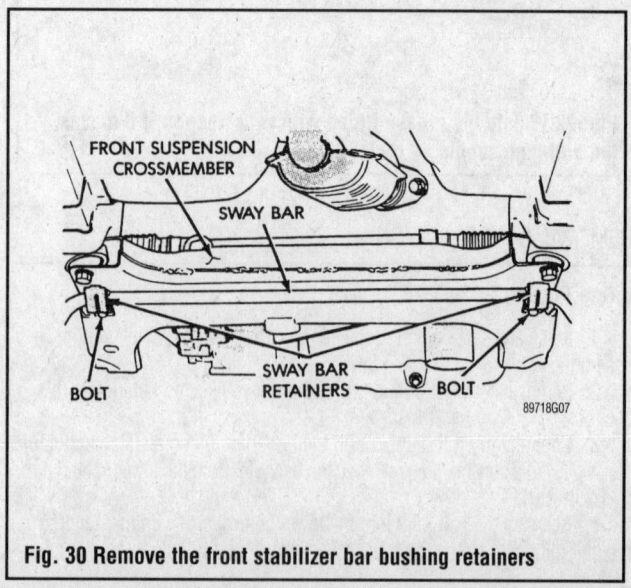

Fig. 30 Remove the front stabilizer bar bushing retainers

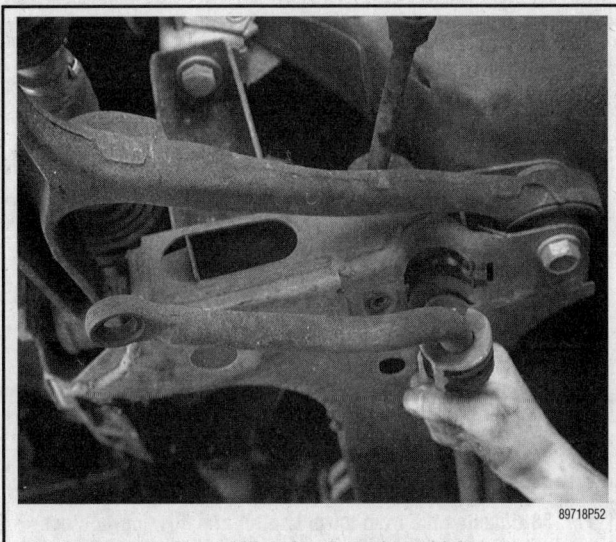

**Fig. 31 Remove the stabilizer bar from the vehicle**

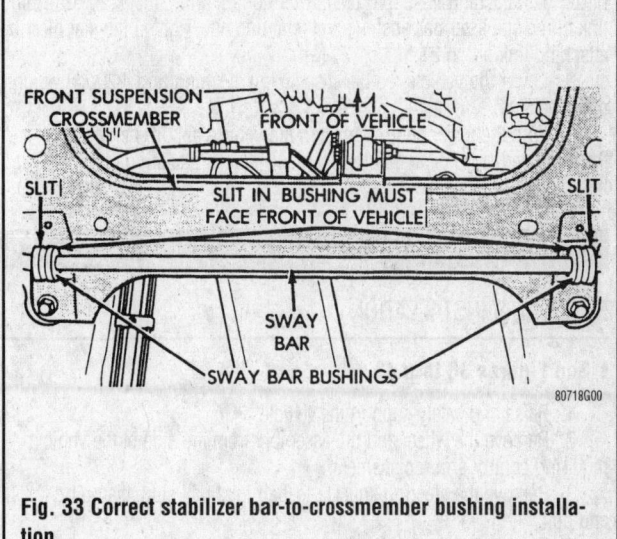

**Fig. 33 Correct stabilizer bar-to-crossmember bushing installation**

4. Inspect for broken or distorted stabilizer bar bushings, bushing retainers and attaching link bolts. If the stabilizer bar-to-front crossmember bushing replacement is necessary, the bushing can be removed from the stabilizer bar by opening the slit and peeling the bushing off the stabilizer bar.

**To install:**

5. If inspection determines replacement of the stabilizer bar-to-lower control arm attachment link bushing is required, replace the bushings before installing the stabilizer bar. Refer to the accompanying figure for the proper orientation of the attaching link bushing components.

6. If the bushings require replacement, install them before installing the stabilizer bar. They are replaced by opening the slit on the bushings and peeling them off the stabilizer bar. Install new bushings on the bar by spreading the bushing at the slit and forcing them on the stabilizer bar. The bushings must be installed on the bar with the slit in the bushing facing the front of the vehicle when the bar is installed.

7. Position the stabilizer bar into the front crossmember, so the cutouts in the bushings are aligned with the raised bead in the crossmember. Install the stabilizer bar bushing retainers onto the crossmember, aligning the raised bead on the retainer with the cutouts in the bushings. Do not tighten the retainers yet.

8. Line the stabilizer bar attaching link and bushing assemblies up with the attaching link mounting holes in the lower control arms. Install the sta-

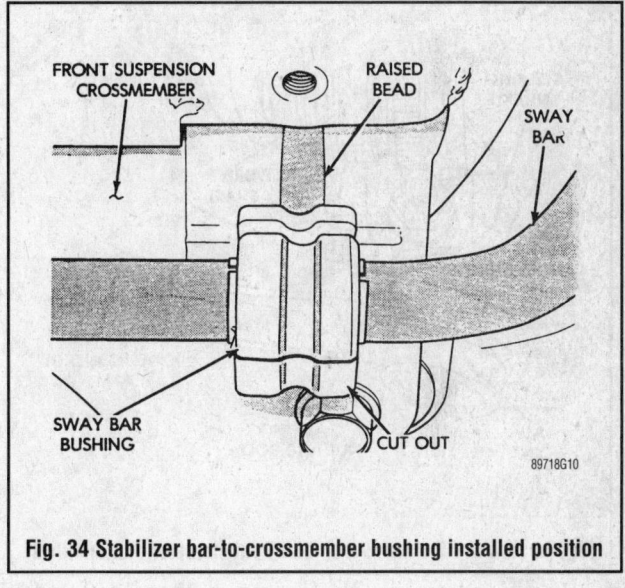

**Fig. 34 Stabilizer bar-to-crossmember bushing installed position**

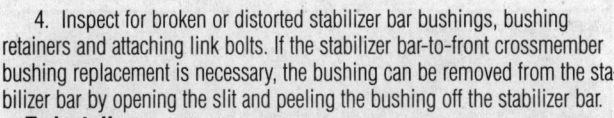
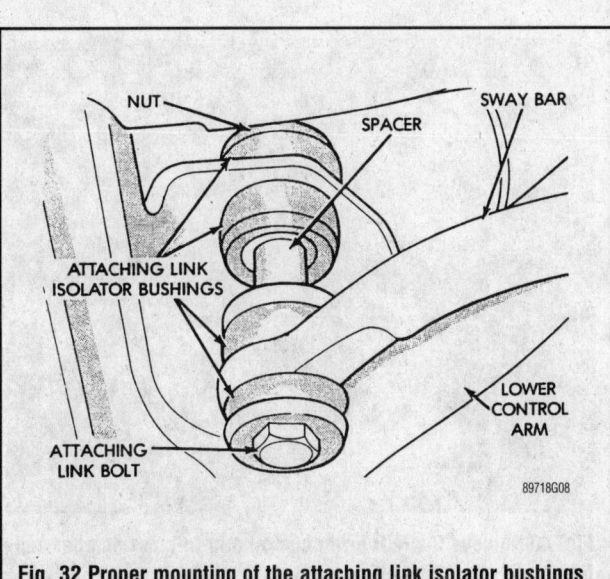

**Fig. 32 Proper mounting of the attaching link isolator bushings**

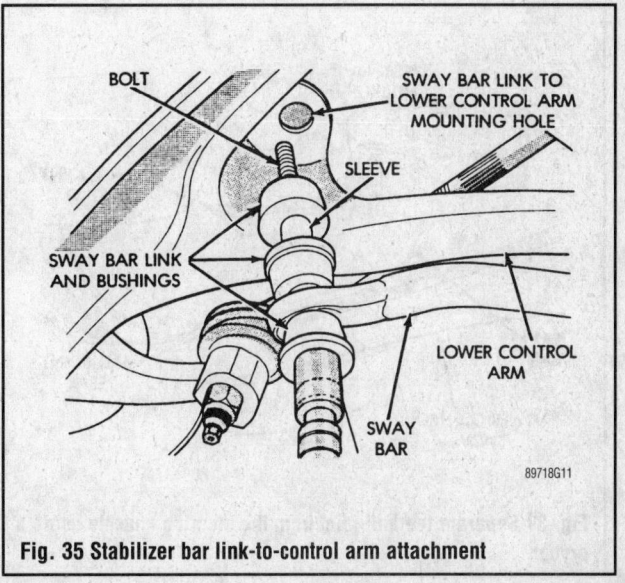

**Fig. 35 Stabilizer bar link-to-control arm attachment**

bilizer bar attaching links into both lower control arms. Install the attaching link to the stabilizer bar bushing and retaining nut. Tighten the stabilizer bar attaching link nut to 21 ft. lbs. (28 Nm).

9. Lower the vehicle, so the suspension is supporting the total weight of the vehicle.

10. With the lower control arms on the vehicle at curb height, tighten the stabilize bar bushing-to-crossmember retainer attaching bolts to 21 ft. lbs. (28 Nm).

## Lower Control Arm

### REMOVAL & INSTALLATION

▶ See Figures 36 thru 43

1. Raise and safely support the vehicle.
2. Remove the wheel and tire assembly from the side of the vehicle requiring control arm replacement.
3. Remove the steering knuckle-to-ball joint ball stud, clamping nut and bolt.
4. Remove the 2 attaching links connecting the stabilizer bar to the lower control arms.

Fig. 38 Unfasten the front lower control arm bushing-to-crossmember attaching nut and bolt . . .

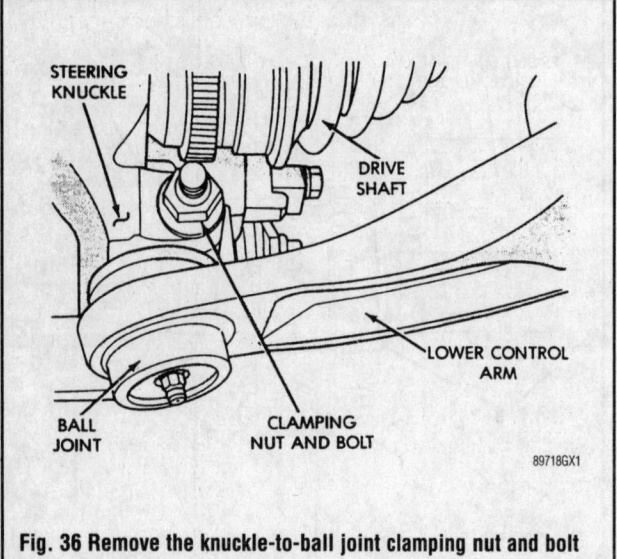

Fig. 36 Remove the knuckle-to-ball joint clamping nut and bolt

Fig. 39 . . . then remove the attaching bolt

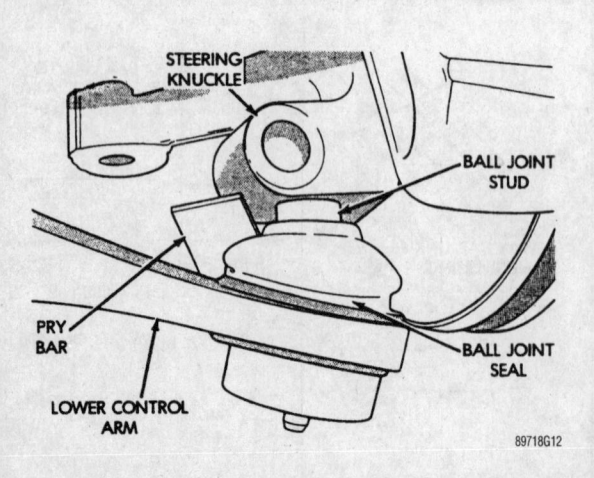

Fig. 37 Separate the ball joint from the steering knuckle using a prybar

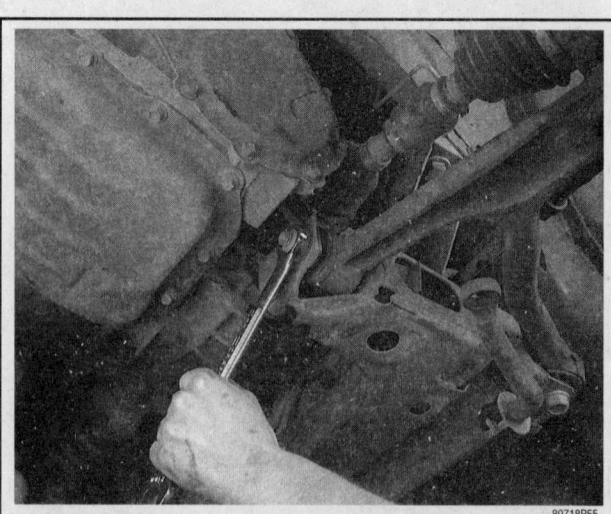

Fig. 40 Remove the rear lower control arm-to-crossmember and frame rail attaching bolt

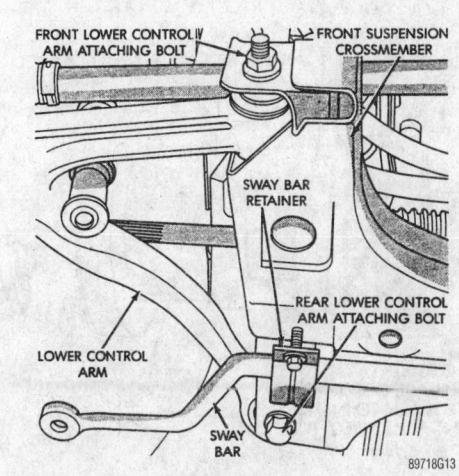

**Fig. 41 Unfasten the lower control arm retainers, then remove the control arm from the vehicle**

**Fig. 43 Installed position of the lower control arm assembly (see arrow)**

5. Loosen, but do not remove the bolts holding the stabilizer bar retainers to the crossmember. Then, rotate the stabilizer bar and attaching links away from the lower control arms.

### ✳✳ WARNING

**Pulling the steering knuckle out from the vehicle after releasing the ball joint can separate the inner CV-joint.**

6. Use a prybar to separate the steering knuckle from the ball joint stud. Be careful when separating the ball joint stud from the knuckle, so the seal does not become damaged.

7. Remove the front lower control arm bushing-to-crossmember attaching nut and bolt. Remove the rear lower control arm-to-crossmember and frame rail attaching bolt. Then, remove the lower control arm from the crossmember.

**To install:**

8. Position the lower control arm into the front crossmember. Install the rear lower control arm-to-crossmember and frame rail attaching bolt. Do NOT tighten the rear bolt at this time. Then, install the front lower control arm-to-crossmember nut and bolt.

9. Tighten the front lower, then the rear control arm nut and bolt to 120 ft. lbs. (163 Nm).

**Fig. 42 Position the lower control arm into the front crossmember**

10. Place the ball joint stud into the steering knuckle. Install the steering knuckle-to-ball joint stud clamping bolt and nut. Tighten the bolt to 70 ft. lbs. (95 Nm).

11. Assemble the stabilizer bar-to-lower control arm link assemblies and bushings.

12. Rotate the stabilizer bar into position, installing the stabilizer bar links into the lower control arms. Install the top stabilizer bar link bushings and nuts. Do NOT tighten the link yet.

13. Install the wheel and tire assembly.

14. Carefully lower the vehicle so the suspension is supporting the total weight of the vehicle.

15. Tighten the stabilizer bar-to-lower control arm links to 21 ft. lbs. (28 Nm).

16. Tighten the stabilizer bar bushing retainer-to-crossmember attaching bolts to 21 ft. lbs. (28 Nm).

### CONTROL ARM BUSHING REPLACEMENT

#### Front Isolator Bushing

▶ **See Figures 44, 45, 46 and 47**

1. Remove the front lower control arm from the vehicle.

2. Mount a suitable C-clamp, C-4212-F in a vise. Install bushing remover tool 6804 and bushing receiver tool 6758 on the C-clamp.

3. Place the lower control arm on the special tools assembled for removal of the front isolator bushing, as shown in the accompanying figure. Be sure the tool are positioned and assembled properly on the C-clamp.

4. Tighten the screw on the C-clamp to press the front bushing out of the lower control arm.

**To install:**

5. Mount installer cup tool C-4214-F on the C-clamp. Then, mount the bushing installer tool 6810 on the screw part of the C-clamp.

6. Start the front bushing into the lower control arm by hand, making sure it is square with its mounting hole in the lower control arm. The bushing is to be installed in the lower control arm from the machined surface side of the lower control arm bushing hole.

7. Install the lower control on the special tools. Make sure the tools are properly installed.

8. Tighten the screw of the C-clamp, pressing the front bushing into the lower control arm until the special tool 6810 is flush on the machined surface of the lower control arm. This will correctly position the front bushing in the lower control arm.

9. Install the lower control arm in the vehicle, as outlined earlier in this section.

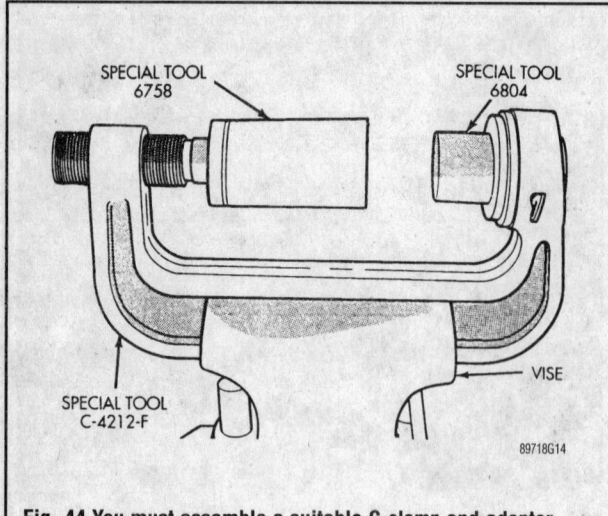

**Fig. 44 You must assemble a suitable C-clamp and adapter tools in a vise**

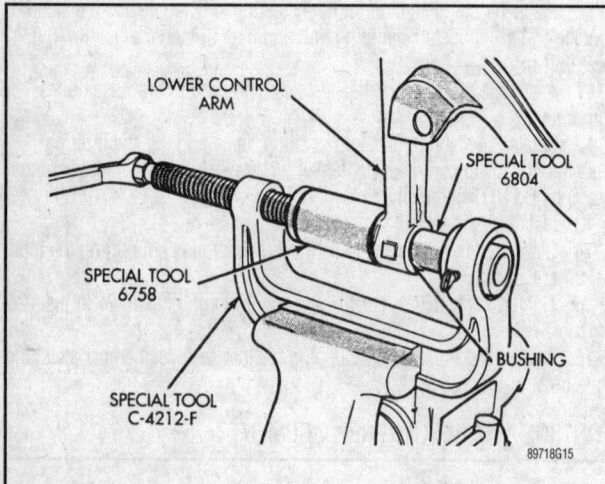

**Fig. 45 Tighten the C-clamp screw to press the front bushing from the lower control arm**

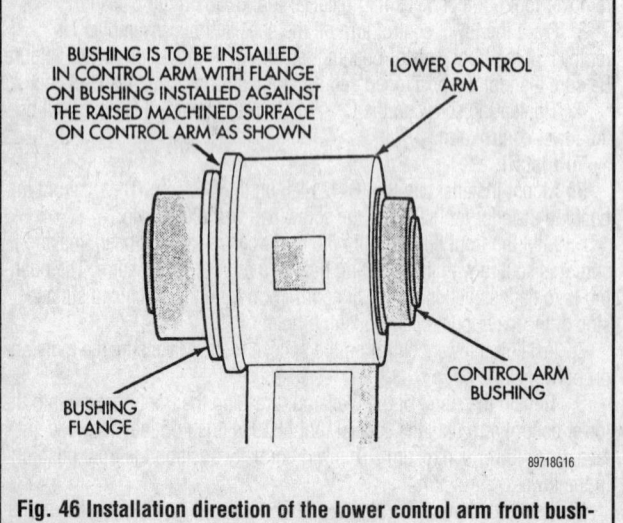

**Fig. 46 Installation direction of the lower control arm front bushing**

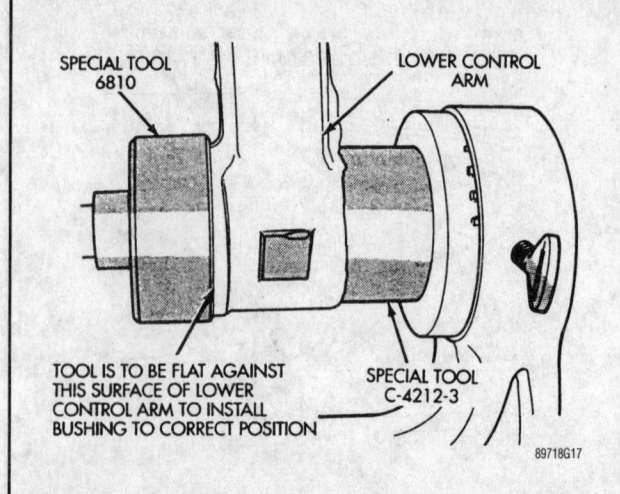

**Fig. 47 Proper installed position of the front lower control arm bushing**

**Rear Isolator Bushing**

▶ See Figures 48, 49, 50 and 51

➡Removal and installation of the rear isolator bushing requires the use of an arbor press and a variety of special tools. Do NOT try to use a different procedure, other than the one given to replace the bushing.

1. Remove the lower control arm from the vehicle.
2. Position the lower control arm in an arbor press supported at the rear bushing using receiver cup tool 6756. Position the remover/installer tool 6758 on top of the rear control arm bushing, as shown in the accompanying illustration.
3. Press the isolator bushing out of the lower control arm.
   **To install:**
4. Install the rear bushing into the lower control arm in the direction indicated in the accompanying figure. The rear bushing must be positioned in the lower control arm with the void in the bushing pointing toward the compression strut of the lower control arm, as shown in the accompanying figure.
5. Place the lower control arm in an arbor press supported at the rear bushing hole using receiver cup 6756. Correctly position the remover/installer tool 6760 on top of the rear control arm bushing.

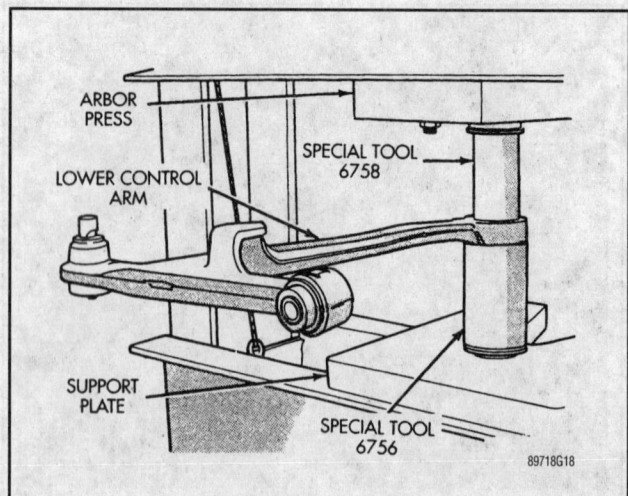

**Fig. 48 Proper assembly of the special tools needed for rear bushing replacement**

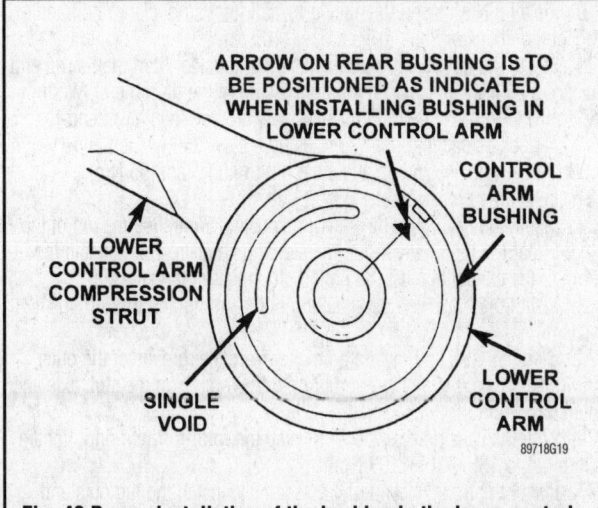

Fig. 49 Proper installation of the bushing in the lower control arm

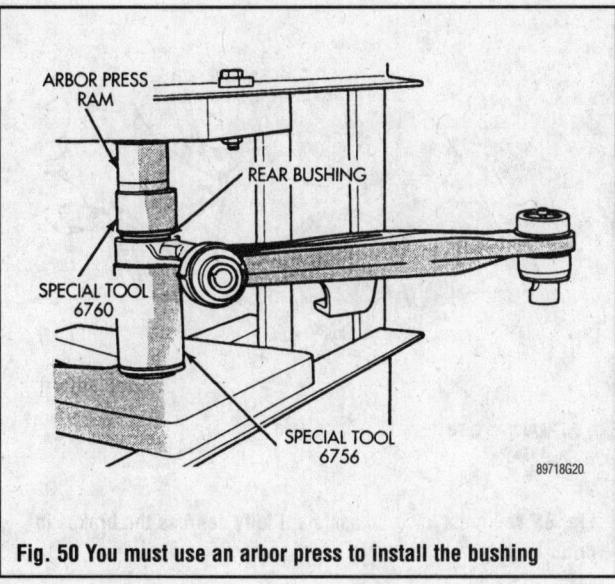

Fig. 50 You must use an arbor press to install the bushing

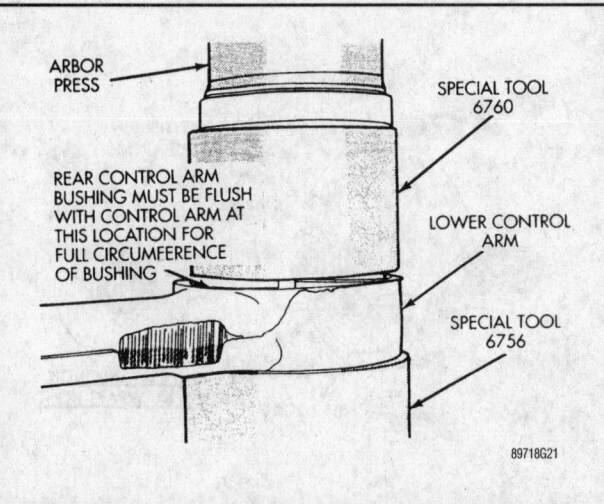

Fig. 51 When the bushing is proper installed, the flange will be flush with the lower control arm machined surface

6. Press the rear bushing into the lower control arm, until the flange on the bushing is flush with the machined surface of the lower control arm.

7. Install the lower control arm into the vehicle.

## Knuckle and Spindle

### REMOVAL & INSTALLATION

▶ See Figures 52, 53, 54, 55 and 56

1. Remove the cotter pin, lock nut and spring washer. Discard the cotter pin.

### ❋❋ WARNING

**The wheel bearing will be damaged If after loosening the hub nut, the vehicle is rolled on the ground or the weight of the vehicle is allowed to be supported by the tires.**

2. With the vehicle still on the ground and the brakes applied, loosen the hub nut. The hub and halfshaft are splined together through the knuckle (bearing) and retained by the hub nut.

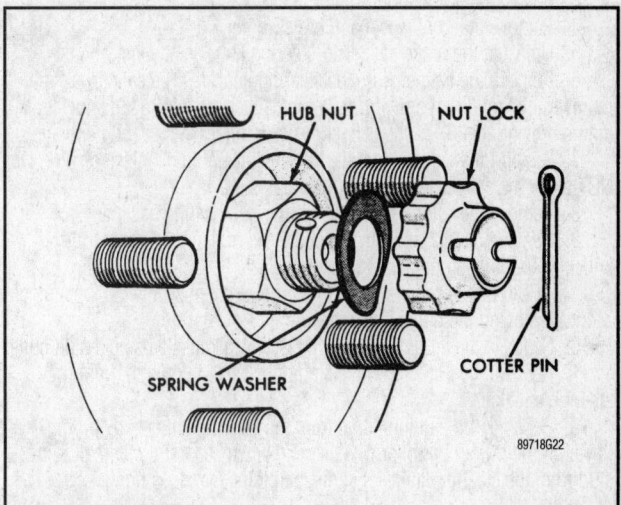

Fig. 52 Remove and discard the cotter pin, then remove the lock nut and washer

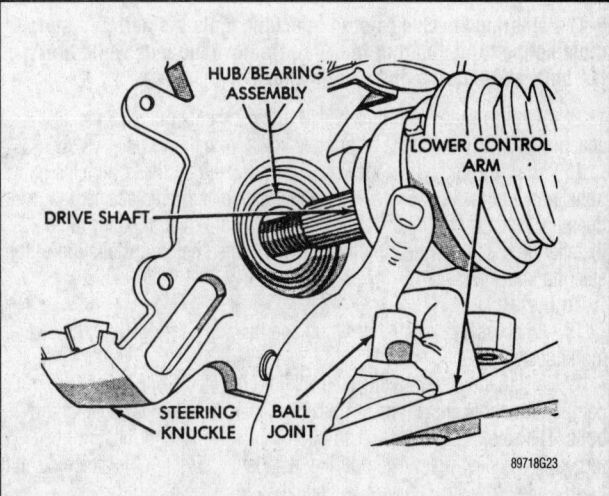

Fig. 53 Pull the steering knuckle out and away from the outer CV-joint

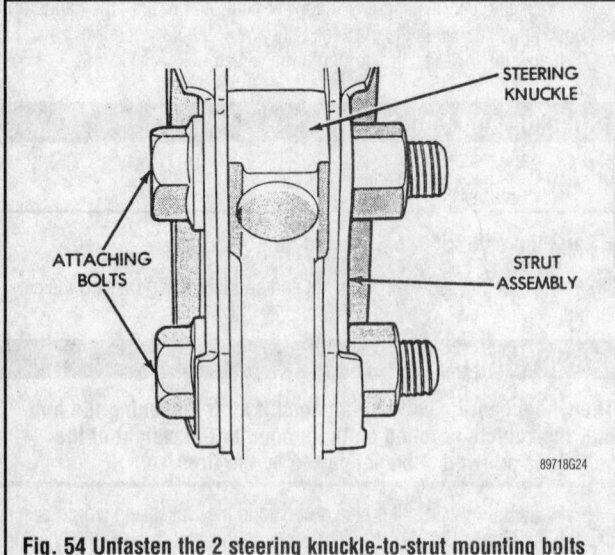

Fig. 54 Unfasten the 2 steering knuckle-to-strut mounting bolts

3. Raise and safely support the vehicle.

4. Remove the front wheel and tire assembly.

5. Unfasten the brake caliper-to-steering knuckle attaching bolts.

6. Remove the caliper from the steering knuckle. The caliper is removed by first lifting the bottom of the caliper away from the knuckle, then removing the top of the caliper out from under the steering knuckle.

7. Support the caliper from the strut using a suitable piece of wire. Do NOT allow the caliper to hang by the brake hose.

8. Remove the rotor from the front hub and bearing assembly.

9. Remove the nut attaching the outer tie rod end to the steering knuckle. The nut can be removed as follows:

 a. Hold the tie rod end stud with an $^{11}/_{32}$ in. socket while loosening and removing the nut with a wrench.

10. Separate the tie rod end from the steering knuckle using a side puller.

11. Remove the nut and bolt, clamping the ball joint stud, from the steering knuckle.

12. Separate the ball joint stud from the steering knuckle by prying down on the lower control arm. Be careful when separating the ball joint stud from the steering knuckle, so the ball joint seal does not get cut.

➡**Be sure not to separate the inner CV-joint during this operation. Do not let the halfshaft hang by the inner CV-joint, the halfshaft MUST be supported.**

13. Pull the steering knuckle out and away from the outer CV-joint.

➡**The steering knuckle-to-strut attaching bolts are serrated and must not be turned during removal. Remove the nuts while holding the bolts stationary in the steering knuckles.**

14. Remove the 2 steering knuckle-to-strut damper clevis bracket attaching bolts. Remove the steering knuckle from the vehicle.

15. The cartridge type front wheel bearing used on these vehicles is not transferable to the replacement steering knuckle. If the replacement knuckle does not come with hub and bearing, a new bearing must be installed. Installation of the new bearing must be performed before installation of the steering knuckle.

**To install:**

16. If necessary, install a new hub and bearing cartridge into the steering knuckle.

17. Install the steering knuckle back into the clevis bracket of the strut damper assembly. Install the strut damper-to-steering knuckle attaching bolts. The steering knuckle-to-strut bolts are serrated and must not be turned in the steering knuckle during installation. Tighten the attaching nuts to 40 ft. lbs. (54 Nm), plus an additional ¼ turn.

18. Slide the halfshaft back into the front hub and bearing. Then, install the steering knuckle onto the ball joint stud.

19. Install a NEW steering knuckle-to-ball joint stud, clamp bolt and nut. Tighten the clamp bolt to 75 ft. lbs. (100 Nm).

20. Install the tie rod end into the steering knuckle. Start the tie rod end-to-steering knuckle attaching nut onto the stud of the tie rod end. While holding the stud of the tie rod end stationary, tighten the tie rod end-to-steering knuckle attaching nut. Then, using a crow foot wrench and $^{11}/_{32}$ in. socket, tighten the tie rod end attaching nut to 40 ft. lbs. (55 Nm).

21. Install the brake rotor.

22. Install the caliper on the steering knuckle. First slide the top of the caliper under the top abutment on the steering knuckle. Then, install the bottom of the caliper against the bottom abutment of the knuckle.

23. Install the brake caliper attaching bolts and tighten to 23 ft. lbs. (31 Nm).

24. Clean all dirt, and/or foreign matter from the threads of the outer CV-joint stub axle. Install the hub nut onto the threads of the stub axle and tighten hand-tight.

25. With the car's brake applied, to keep the rotor from turning, tighten the hub nut to 135 ft. lbs. (183 Nm).

26. Install the front wheel and tire assembly. Install the lug nuts and tighten to 100 ft. lbs. (135 Nm).

27. Carefully lower the vehicle.

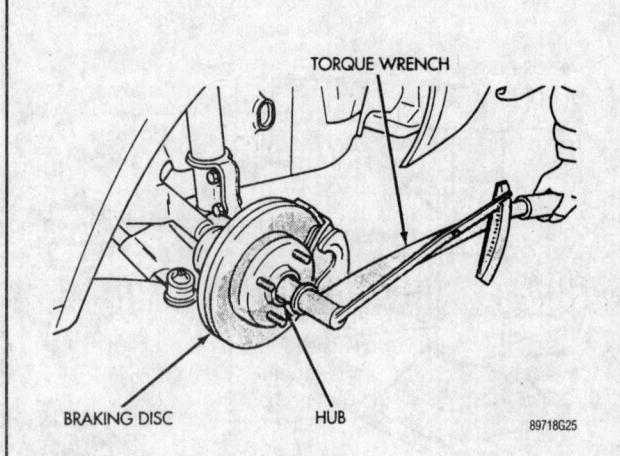

Fig. 55 You must have an assistant fully depress the brakes in order to tighten the hub nut

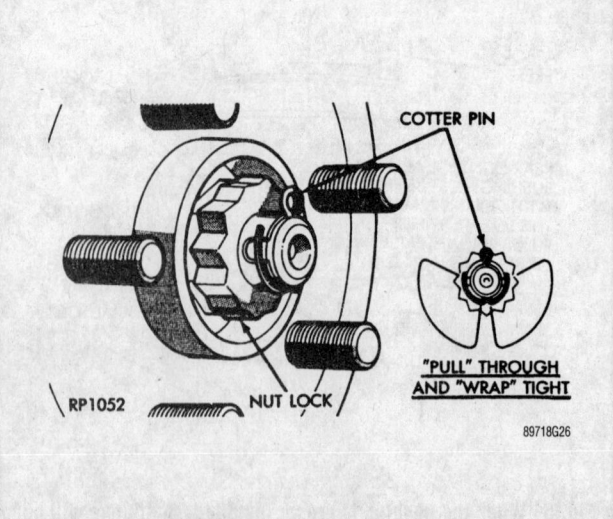

Fig. 56 The new cotter pin must be properly installed

28. Install the spring washer, lock nut and a new cotter pin. Wrap the cotter pin prongs tightly around the lock nut.

29. Take the vehicle to a reputable repair shop to have the toe checked, and adjusted if necessary.

## Front Hub and Bearing

### REMOVAL & INSTALLATION

#### 1995 Vehicles

▶ See Figures 57, 58 and 59

This vehicle uses a sealed for life front hub and bearing assembly attached to the front steering knuckle. The outer CV-joint assembly is splined to the front hub and bearing assembly. The front wheel bearing is called a cartridge bearing. The wheel bearing can be serviced separately from the front steering knuckle and hub assembly. Installation and retention of the front wheel bearing in the steering knuckle is by an interference fit and retained by a snapring. If the front wheel bearing requires replacement, the hub must be removed from the original wheel bearing and transferred to the replacement bearing.

Note that the Neon does not use a rubber lip seal as on past front wheel drive cars to prevent contamination of the front wheel bearing. On this vehicle, the face of the outer CV-joint fits deeply into the steering knuckle using a close fit. This design deters direct water splash on the bearing seal while allowing any water that gets in, to run out the bottom. It is important to thoroughly clean the outer CV-joint and the wheel bearing area in the steering knuckle before it is assembled after servicing.

The steering knuckle MUST be removed to replace both the hub and the front wheel bearing.

1. Remove the front hub cotter pin, nut lock and spring washer. Discard the cotter pin.

#### ✱✱ WARNING

**Wheel bearing damage will result if, after loosening the hub nut, the vehicle is rolled on the ground or the weight of the vehicle is allowed to be supported by the tires.**

2. Loosen the hub nut while the vehicle is on the floor with the brakes applied. The front hub and halfshaft are splined together through the knuckle (bearing) and retained by the hub nut. The front wheel bearing supports the front hub and weight of the vehicle.

3. Raise and safely support the vehicle. Remove the front wheels.

4. Remove the front disc brake caliper from the steering knuckle. The caliper is removed by first lifting the bottom of the caliper away from the steering knuckle and then removing the top of the caliper out from under the steering knuckle. Support the caliper using wire. Do not allow the caliper to hand by the brake hose.

5. Remove the brake rotor from the front hub/bearing assembly.

6. Remove the nut attaching the outer tie rod end to the steering knuckle.

   a. Hold the tie rod end stud with an $^{11}/_{32}$ inch socket while loosening and removing the nut with the wrench.

   b. Remove the tie rod end from the steering knuckle using a puller. Do not hammer wedge-type tools or the steering tie rod end joint will be damaged.

7. Locate and remove the lower control arm ball joint clamping nut and bolt and separate the ball joint stud from the steering knuckle by prying down on the lower control arm. Use care not to damage the steering tie rod end or seal. In addition, use care not to allow the halfshaft to become overextended as the steering knuckle is removed. Do not allow the halfshaft to hang by the inner CV-joint boot. The halfshaft must be supported.

➡The steering knuckle to strut assembly attaching bolts are serrated and must NOT be turned during removal. Remove and reinstall the nuts while holding the bolts stationary in the steering knuckle.

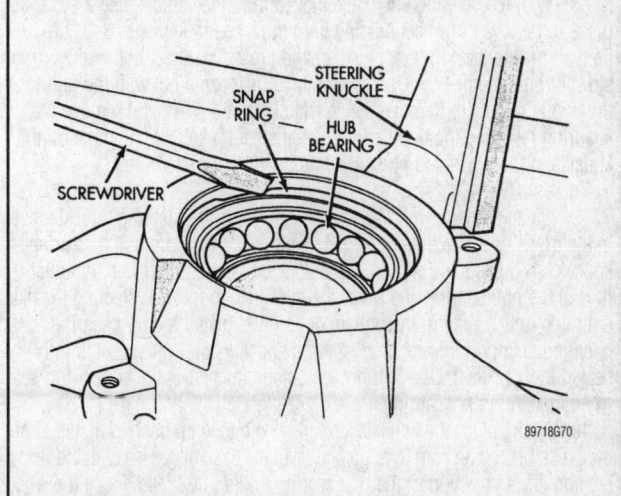

Fig. 57 Use a prytool to carefully remove the snapring from the hub and bearing

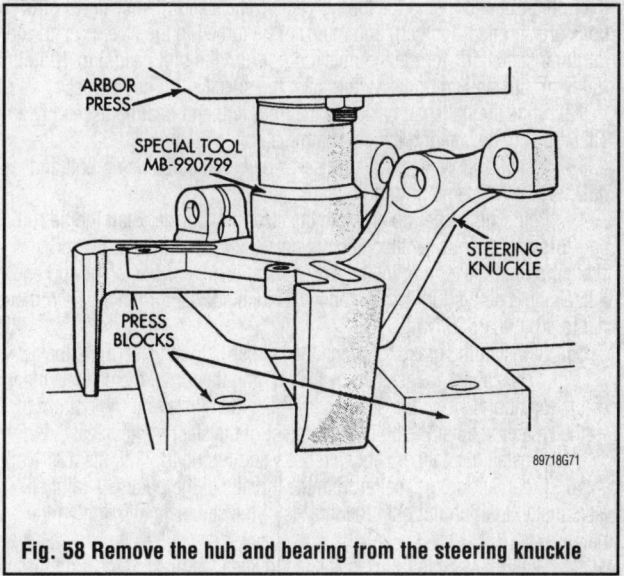

Fig. 58 Remove the hub and bearing from the steering knuckle

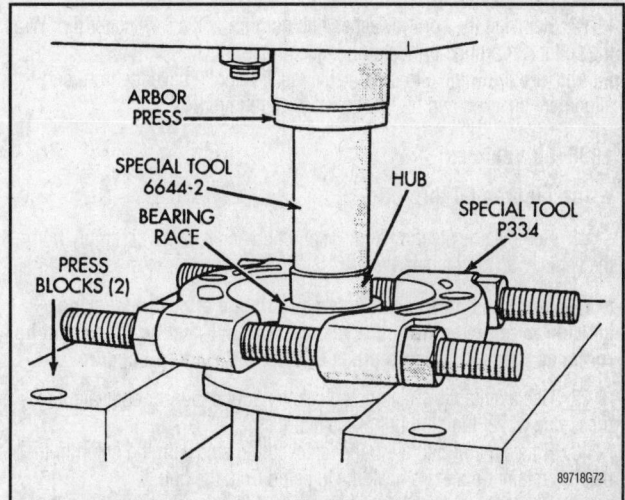

Fig. 59 You must use a suitable press to remove the bearing race from the hub

8. With the steering knuckle removed from the vehicle, use a suitable press to remove the wheel bearing from the steering knuckle. Use care to jig the knuckle level in the press bed and press the wheel hub and bearing slowly from the knuckle. One bearing race may come out with the hub when the hub is removed. Remove the knuckle from the press and remove the snapring retaining the hub bearing in the steering knuckle. Reposition the knuckle in the press and press the hub bearing from its bore.

**To install:**

9. Clean all parts well. Again, use care to jig the steering knuckle level in the press bed. Place the new hub bearing into the bore of the steering knuckle so it is square with the bore. Place a bearing driver on the outer race of the hub bearing and press the hub bearing into the steering knuckle until it is fully seated in the bottom of its bore. Install the hub bearing retaining snapring into its groove in the knuckle bore. Be sure it is fully seated in its groove. Use care not to damage the just-installed bearing seal when installing the snapring.

10. Again, place the knuckle assembly with the hub bearing installed on the press bed using care to align and level the assembly. Use suitable drivers and arbors to support the hub bearing on its inner race. Place the wheel hub in the bearing using care to align it square with the bearing. Using suitable drivers, press the hub into the bearing until it bottoms in the hub bearing.

11. Reinstall the steering knuckle/hub/wheel bearing assembly back into the front strut and install the through bolts. The steering knuckle-to-strut bolts are serrated (toothed) and must not be turned in the steering knuckle during installation. Torque the nuts (do not turn the bolt heads) to 40 ft. lbs. (54 Nm) plus an additional ¼ turn after the specified torque is met.

12. Slide the halfshaft back into the front hub and bearing assembly. Then, install the steering knuckle onto the ball joint stud.

13. Install a NEW steering knuckle-to-ball joint stud, clamp bolt and nut. Torque the clamp bolt to 75 ft. lbs. (100 Nm).

14. Reinstall the tie rod end into the steering knuckle. Start the tie rod end-to-steering knuckle attaching nut onto the stud of the tie rod end. While holding the stud of the tie rod end stationary, torque the tie rod end nut. Using a crow's foot wrench and 11⁄32 inch socket, torque the tie rod end nut to 40 ft. lbs. (55 Nm).

15. Reinstall the brake rotor and the caliper onto the steering knuckle.

a. The caliper is installed by first sliding the top of the caliper under the top abutment on the steering knuckle, then installing the bottom of the caliper against the bottom abutment of the steering knuckle.

b. Install the caliper attaching bolts and torque to 23 ft. lbs. (31 Nm).

16. Clean all foreign matter from the threads of the outer CV-joint stub axle. Install the hub nut onto the threads of the stub axle and tighten the nut.

17. With the vehicle's brakes applied to keep the brake rotor from turning, torque the hub nut to 135 ft. lbs. (183 Nm).

18. Reinstall the wheels and lower the vehicle.

19. Reinstall the spring washer, hub nut lock and a new cotter pin. Wrap the cotter pin prongs tightly around the hub nut lock.

20. Take the vehicle to a reputable repair shop to have the front end alignment checked and the toe adjusted as required.

### 1996–99 Vehicles

▶ **See Figures 60 thru 65**

1. Remove the steering knuckle and hub and bearing assembly from the vehicle, as outlined earlier.

➡ **The hub and bearing can only be replaced after the steering knuckle is removed from the vehicle. The hub and bearing must be removed using a suitable press and the following procedure.**

2. Use a suitable C-clamp and adapter, tool 4150A or equivalent to press one wheel lug stud out of the hub flange.

3. Rotate the hub to align the removed lug stud with the notch in the bearing retainer plate. Remove the lug stud from the hub.

4. Rotate the hub so the hole in the hub that the stud was removed from is facing away from the brake caliper lower rail on the steering knuckle. Install one half of a bearing splitter tool, Special tool 1130 or

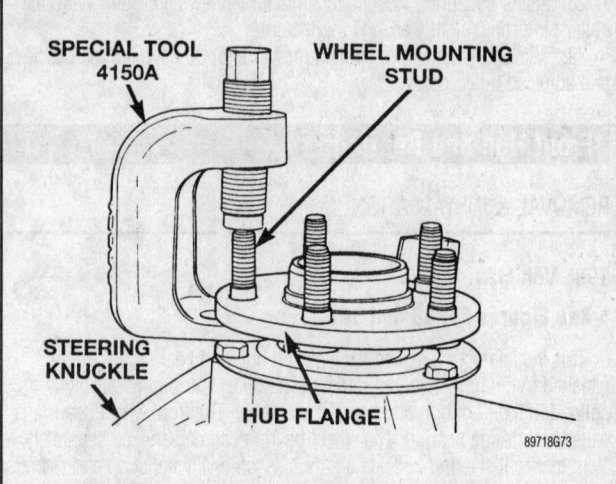

Fig. 60 Use a proper C-clamp and adapter tool to press out one of the lug studs

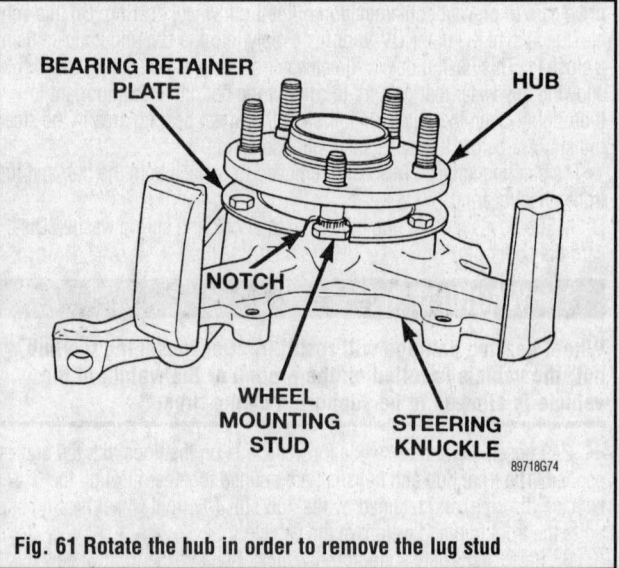

Fig. 61 Rotate the hub in order to remove the lug stud

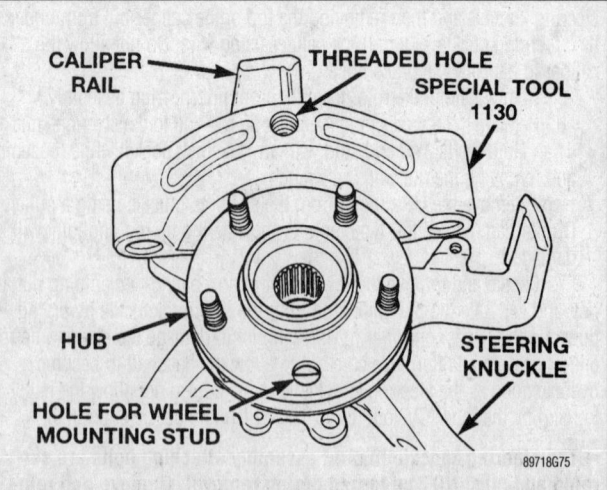

Fig. 62 Install half of a suitable bearing splitter tool on the knuckle

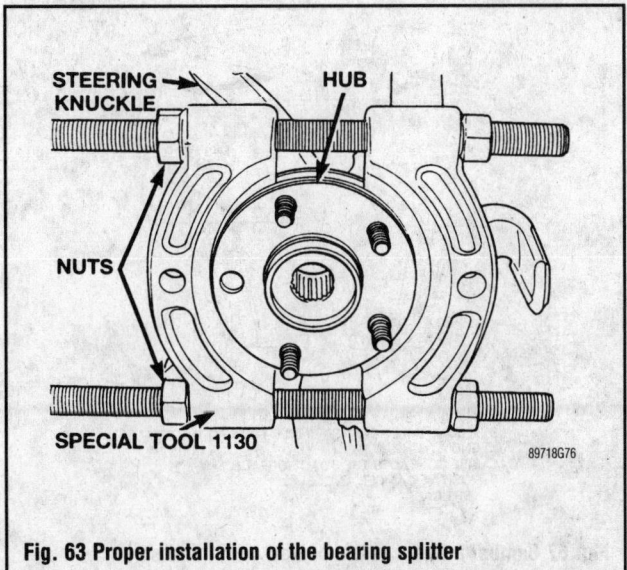

**Fig. 63 Proper installation of the bearing splitter**

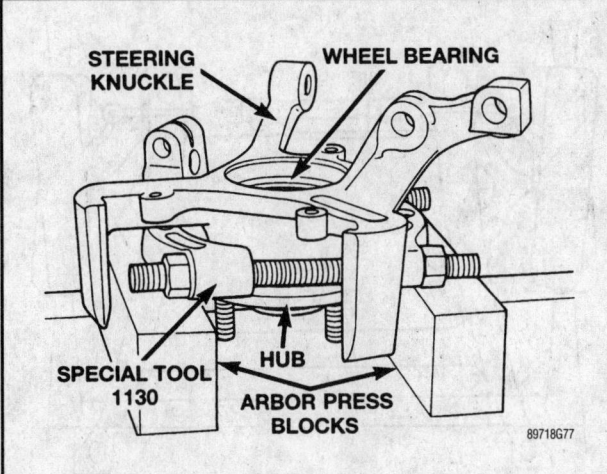

**Fig. 64 The steering knuckle must be properly supported for hub and bearing removal**

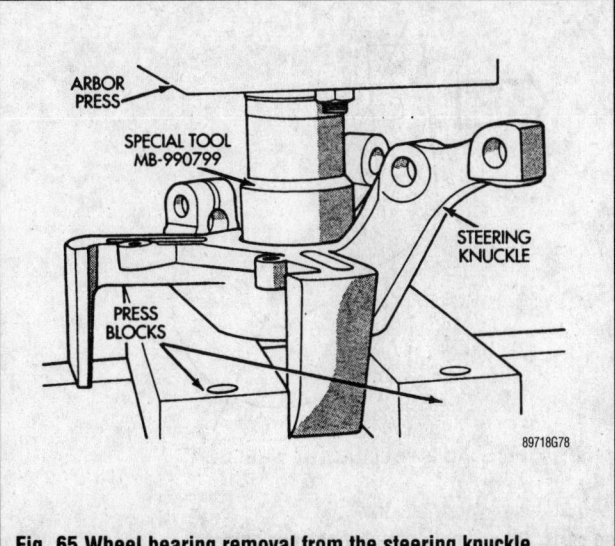

**Fig. 65 Wheel bearing removal from the steering knuckle**

equivalent between the hub and the bearing retainer plate. The threaded hold in this half of the bearing splitter is to be aligned with the caliper rail on the steering knuckle.

5. Install the remaining pieces of the bearing splitter on the steering knuckle. Hand-tighten the nuts to hold the splitter in place on the knuckle.

6. When the bearing splitter is installed, make sure the 3 bolts attaching the bearing retainer plate to the knuckle are contacting the bearing splitter. The bearing retainer plate should not support the knuckle or contact the splitter.

7. Place the steering knuckle in a suitable press, supported by the bearing splitter as shown in the accompanying figure.

8. Position a suitable sized driver on the small end of the hub. Using the press, remove the hub from the wheel bearing. The outer bearing race will come out of the wheel bearing when the hub is pressed out of the bearing.

9. Remove the bearing splitter tool from the knuckle.

10. Place the knuckle in a press supported by the press blocks, as shown in the accompanying figure. The blocks must not obstruct the bore in the steering knuckle so the wheel bearing can be pressed out of the knuckle. Place a suitable driver on the outer race of the wheel bearing, then press the bearing out of the knuckle.

11. Install the bearing splitter on the hub. The splitter is to be installed on the hub so it is between the flange of the hub and the bearing race on the hub. Place the hub, bearing race and splitter in a press. Use a driver to press the hub out of the bearing race.

**To install:**

12. Use clean, dry cloth to wipe and grease or dirt from the bore of the steering knuckle.

13. Clean the rust preventative from the replacement wheel bearing using a clean, dry towel.

14. Place the new wheel bearing into the bore of the steering knuckle. Make sure the bearing is placed squarely into the bore. Place the knuckle in a press with a receiver tool, C-4698-2 supporting the steering knuckle. Place a suitable driver tool on the outer race of the wheel bearing. Press the wheel bearing into the steering knuckle until it is fully bottomed in the bore of the steering knuckle.

➡Only the original or original equipment replacement bolts should be used to mounting the bearing retainer to the knuckle. If a bolt requires replacement when installing the bearing retainer plate, make sure to get the proper type of replacement.

15. Install the bearing retainer plate on the steering knuckle. Install the 3 bearing retainer mounting bolts. Tighten the bolts to 21 ft. lbs. (28 Nm).

16. Install the removed wheel lug stud into the hub flange.

17. Place the hub, with the lug stud installed, in a suitable press supported by adapter tool C-4698-1 or equivalent. Press the wheel lug stud into the hub flange until it is fully seated against the back side on the hub flange.

18. Place the steering knuckle, with the wheel bearing installed, in a press with special receiver tool MB-990799 supporting the inner race of the wheel bearing. Place the hub in the wheel bearing, making sure it is square with the bearing. Press the hub into the wheel bearing until it is fully bottomed in the wheel bearing.

19. Install the steering knuckle in the vehicle, as outlined earlier in this section.

20. Install the wheel and tire assembly, then carefully lower the vehicle.

21. Take the vehicle to a reputable repair shop to have the front end alignment checked and the toe adjusted as required.

## Wheel Alignment

If the tires are worn unevenly, if the vehicle is not stable on the highway or if the handling seems uneven in spirited driving, the wheel alignment should be checked. If an alignment problem is suspected, first check for improper tire inflation and other possible causes. These can be worn suspension or steering components, accident damage or even unmatched tires.

If any worn or damaged components are found, they must be replaced before the wheels can be properly aligned. Wheel alignment requires very expensive equipment and involves minute adjustments which must be accurate; it should only be performed by a trained technician. Take your vehicle to a properly equipped shop.

Following is a description of the alignment angles which are adjustable on most vehicles and how they affect vehicle handling. Although these angles can apply to both the front and rear wheels, usually only the front suspension is adjustable.

## CASTER

### ▶ See Figure 66

Looking at a vehicle from the side, caster angle describes the steering axis rather than a wheel angle. The steering knuckle is attached to a control arm or strut at the top and a control arm at the bottom. The wheel pivots around the line between these points to steer the vehicle. When the upper point is tilted back, this is described as positive caster. Having a positive caster tends to make the wheels self-centering, increasing directional stability. Excessive positive caster makes the wheels hard to steer, while an uneven caster will cause a pull to one side. Overloading the vehicle or sagging rear springs will affect caster, as will raising the rear of the vehicle. If the rear of the vehicle is lower than normal, the caster becomes more positive.

## CAMBER

### ▶ See Figure 67

Looking from the front of the vehicle, camber is the inward or outward tilt of the top of wheels. When the tops of the wheels are tilted in, this is negative camber; if they are tilted out, it is positive. In a turn, a slight amount of negative camber helps maximize contact of the tire with the road. However, too much negative camber compromises straight-line stability, increases bump steer and torque steer.

## TOE

### ▶ See Figure 68

Looking down at the wheels from above the vehicle, toe angle is the distance between the front of the wheels, relative to the distance between the back of the wheels. If the wheels are closer at the front, they are said to be toed-in or to have negative toe. A small amount of negative toe enhances directional stability and provides a smoother ride on the highway.

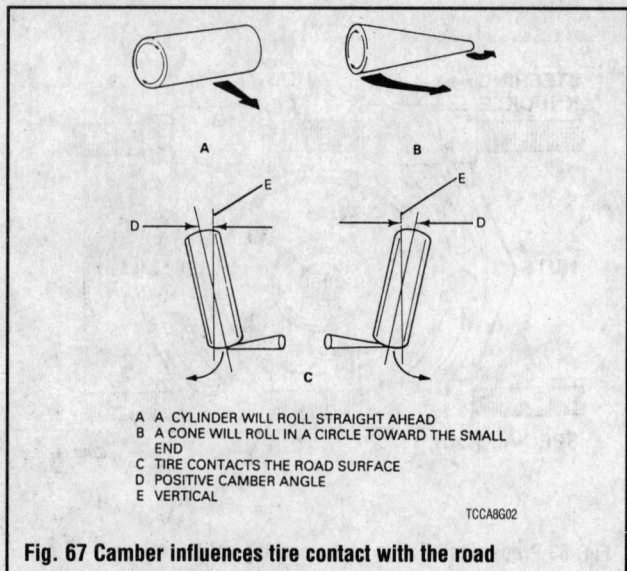

A  A CYLINDER WILL ROLL STRAIGHT AHEAD
B  A CONE WILL ROLL IN A CIRCLE TOWARD THE SMALL END
C  TIRE CONTACTS THE ROAD SURFACE
D  POSITIVE CAMBER ANGLE
E  VERTICAL

TCCA8G02

**Fig. 67 Camber influences tire contact with the road**

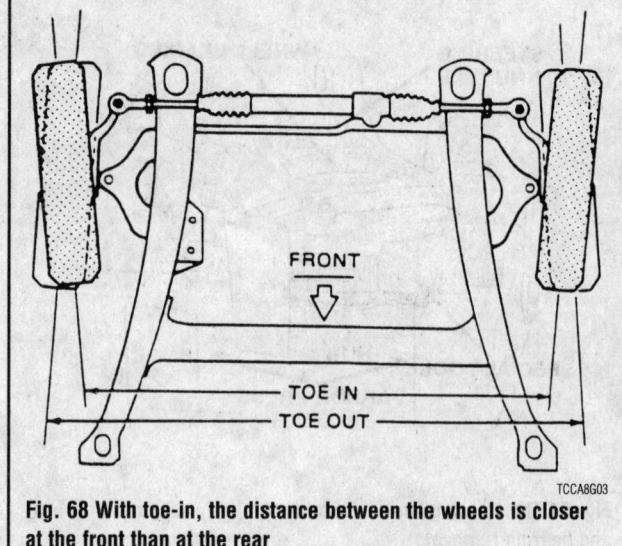

**Fig. 68 With toe-in, the distance between the wheels is closer at the front than at the rear**

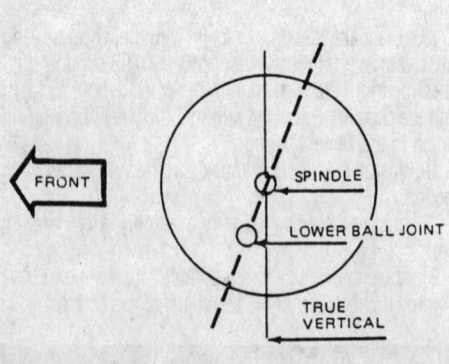

CASTER IS POSITIVE WHEN THE LOAD (LOWER BALL JOINT) IS AHEAD OR PULLING THE SPINDLE.

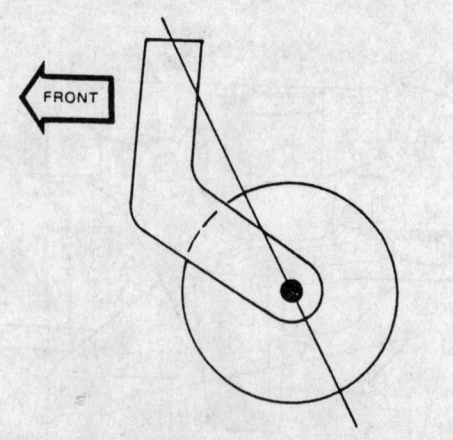

LOAD IS PULLING THE WHEEL

TCCA8G01

**Fig. 66 Caster affects straight-line stability. Caster wheels used on shopping carts, for example, employ positive caster**

**REAR SUSPENSION**

**REAR SUSPENSION COMPONENT LOCATIONS**

1. Strut
2. Rear lateral arm
3. Front lateral arm
4. Rear crossmember
5. Tension strut
6. Tension strut bushing

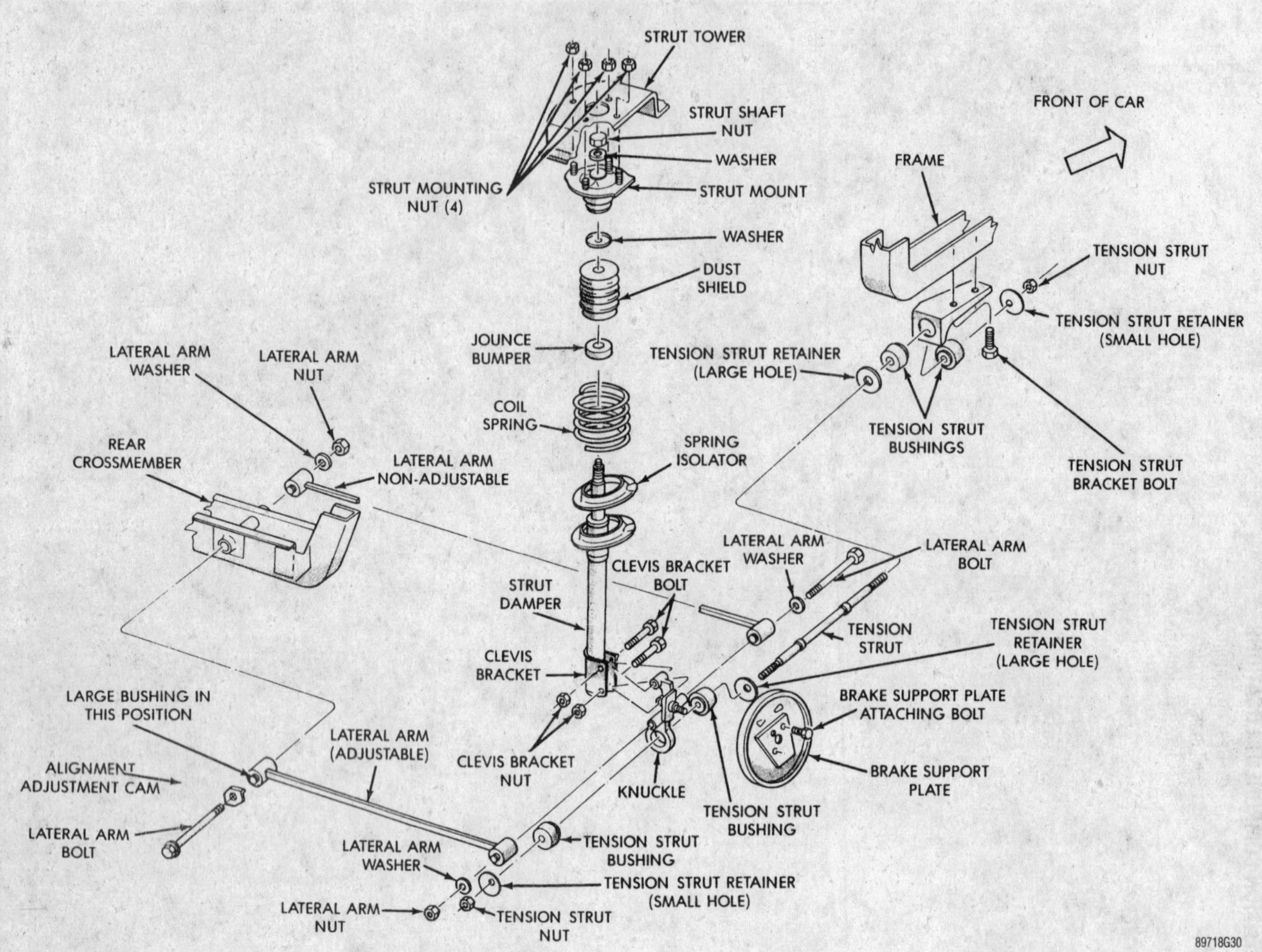

STRUT TOWER

STRUT SHAFT NUT

WASHER

STRUT MOUNT

STRUT MOUNTING NUT (4)

FRONT OF CAR

FRAME

TENSION STRUT NUT

TENSION STRUT RETAINER (SMALL HOLE)

WASHER

DUST SHIELD

LATERAL ARM WASHER

LATERAL ARM NUT

JOUNCE BUMPER

COIL SPRING

TENSION STRUT RETAINER (LARGE HOLE)

TENSION STRUT BUSHINGS

TENSION STRUT BRACKET BOLT

REAR CROSSMEMBER

LATERAL ARM NON-ADJUSTABLE

SPRING ISOLATOR

LATERAL ARM WASHER

LATERAL ARM BOLT

STRUT DAMPER

CLEVIS BRACKET BOLT

TENSION STRUT

TENSION STRUT RETAINER (LARGE HOLE)

CLEVIS BRACKET

BRAKE SUPPORT PLATE ATTACHING BOLT

LARGE BUSHING IN THIS POSITION

ALIGNMENT ADJUSTMENT CAM

LATERAL ARM (ADJUSTABLE)

CLEVIS BRACKET NUT

KNUCKLE

BRAKE SUPPORT PLATE

TENSION STRUT BUSHING

LATERAL ARM BOLT

LATERAL ARM WASHER

TENSION STRUT BUSHING

TENSION STRUT RETAINER (SMALL HOLE)

LATERAL ARM NUT

TENSION STRUT NUT

89718G30

**Fig. 69 Exploded view of the rear suspension components**

## MacPherson Struts

### REMOVAL & INSTALLATION

▶ See Figures 70 thru 75

1. Raise and safely support the vehicle.
2. Remove the wheel and tire assembly.
3. Unfasten the retainer(s), then remove the hydraulic flex hose bracket from the strut bracket. If equipped with ABS, the wheel speed sensor cable routing clip is also attached to the strut assembly bracket.
4. Support the rear knuckle, suspension and brake components before removing the clevis bracket-to-knuckle attaching bolts. Do NOT allow the weight of the knuckle and related components hang without support when the strut is removed.

### ✳✳ WARNING

**The knuckle-to-strut attaching bolts are serrated and must not be turned during removal. Remove the nuts while holding the bolts stationary in the knuckle.**

89718P07

**Fig. 70 Unfasten the brake hose bracket mounting bolt**

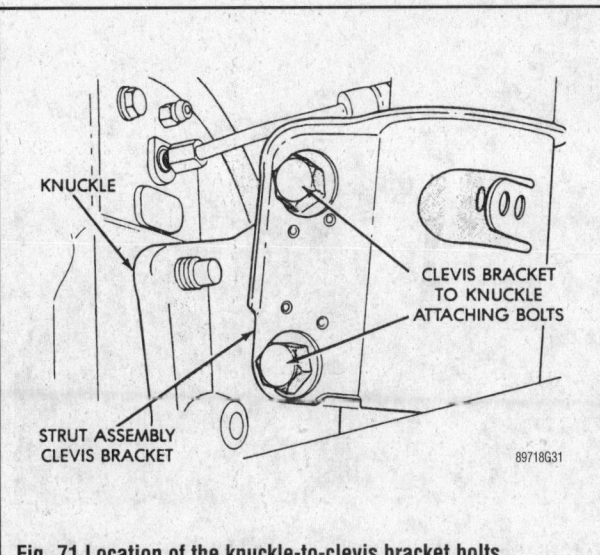

Fig. 71 Location of the knuckle-to-clevis bracket bolts

Fig. 74 Use a ratchet to unfasten the upper strut mounting nuts

Fig. 72 While holding the bolt stationary, loosen the lower strut mounting nuts

Fig. 75 Carefully pull the strut assembly out of the vehicle

Fig. 73 From inside the trunk you can remove the center cap from the strut assembly

5. Hold the bolt with a wrench, then unfasten the 2 clevis bracket nuts attaching the strut to the knuckle.

6. Carefully lower the vehicle, then open the trunk. Access to the rear upper strut mount-to-strut tower attaching bolts is through the trunk of the car.

7. If necessary, remove the carpet from the top of the strut tower. Then, remove the rubber dust shield from the top of the strut tower for easier access to the upper strut nuts.

8. Loosen, but do not remove the 4 upper strut mounting nuts. Then, while supporting the strut assembly, fully remove the 4 strut mount attaching nuts.

9. Remove the strut assembly from the knuckle by sliding the knuckle out of the clevis bracket on the strut, then remove it from the vehicle.

**To install:**

10. Position the strut back into the vehicle with the 4 studs on the strut mount assembly through holes in the strut tower of the vehicle. Install the 4 strut mount-to-body attaching nuts onto the mount studs. Tighten the nuts to 25 ft. lbs. (34 Nm).

11. Install the dust shield into the opening on top of the strut tower. Install the carpeting back on top of the rear strut tower.

12. Raise and safely support the vehicle.

13. Install the knuckle into the clevis bracket on the strut assembly. Install the 2 clevis bracket-to-knuckle attaching bolts and nuts. Hold the bolts with a wrench while tightening the nuts to 70 ft. lbs. (95 Nm).

14. Install the brake hose bracket to the strut bracket and secure with the retaining bolts. If equipped with ABS, the wheel speed sensor cable routing clip is also attached to the strut bracket.

15. Install the wheel and tire assembly on the vehicle. Tighten the lug nuts evenly, in sequence, to 100 ft. lbs. (135 Nm).

16. Carefully lower the vehicle.

17. Have the toe checked and adjusted as necessary.

## OVERHAUL

▶ **See Figures 76 thru 85**

1. Remove the strut requiring overhaul from the vehicle.

2. Position the strut in a vise. Using paint or a marker, matchmark the strut unit, lower spring isolator, spring and upper strut mount for installation purposes.

3. Place suitable spring compressor tools (Special tool C-4838) on the strut spring. Compress the coil spring until all load is removed from the upper strut mount.

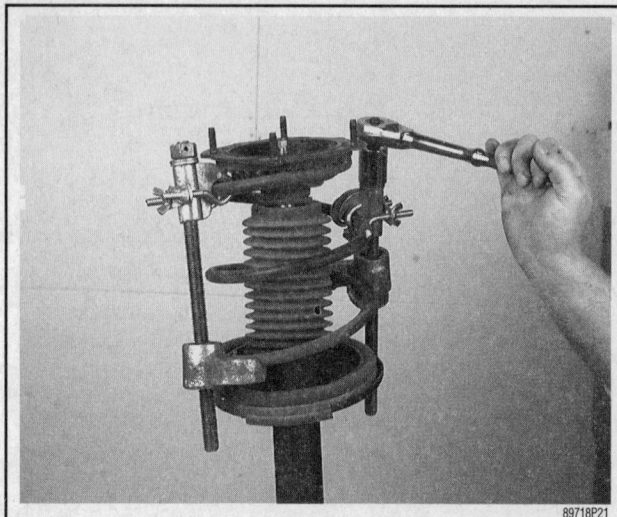
Fig. 78 Use a ratchet to tighten the nut on the spring compressor

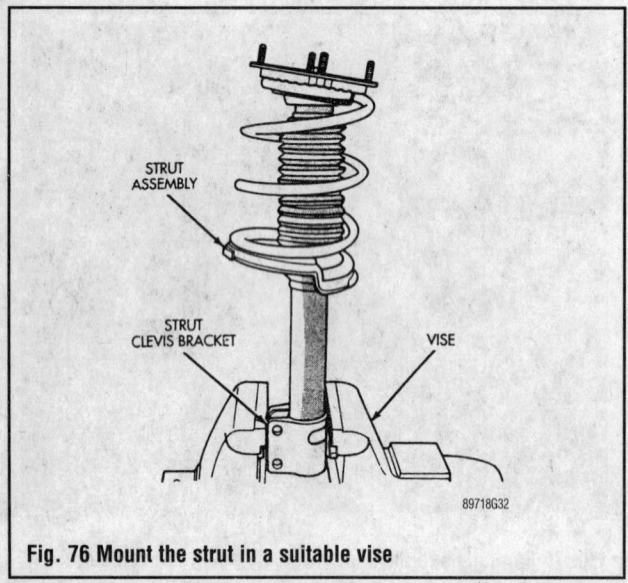
Fig. 76 Mount the strut in a suitable vise

Fig. 79 Use an adjustable wrench to hold the strut shaft in place and loosen the nut

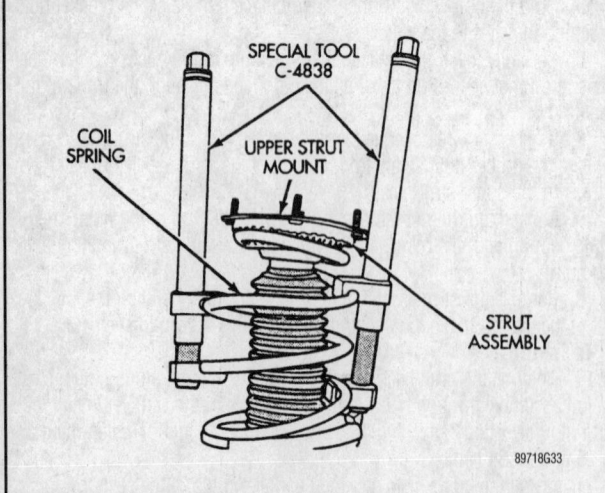
Fig. 77 Carefully compress the coil spring until all tension is relieved from the upper strut mount

Fig. 80 Remove the strut shaft nut and washer

Fig. 81 Remove the upper strut mount and washer

Fig. 84 Remove the dust shield and the jounce bumper from the strut shaft

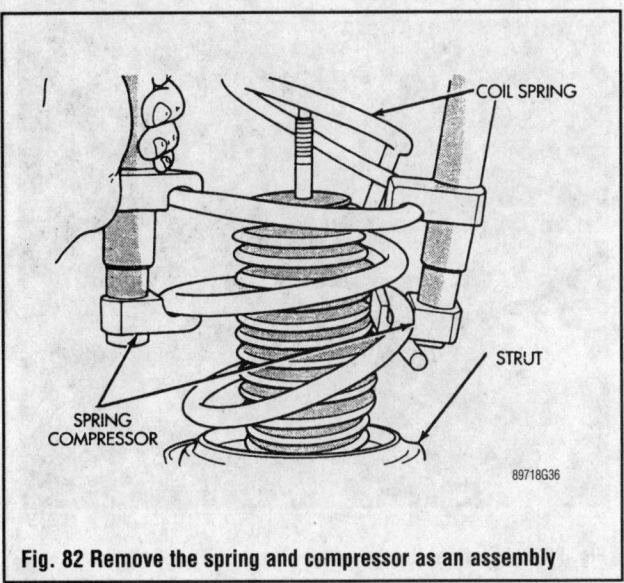

Fig. 82 Remove the spring and compressor as an assembly

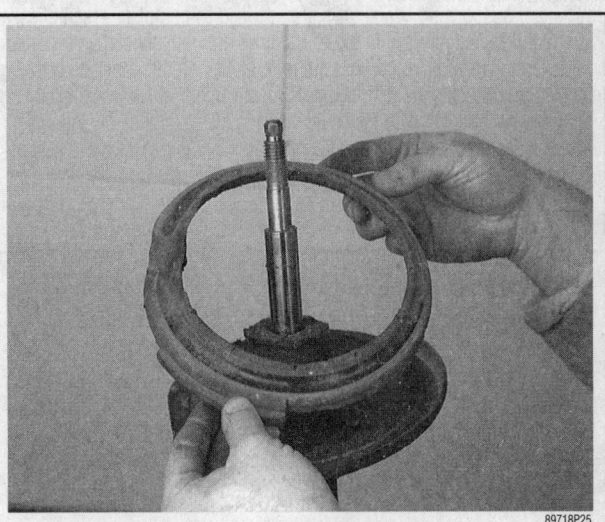

Fig. 85 Remove the coil spring lower isolator

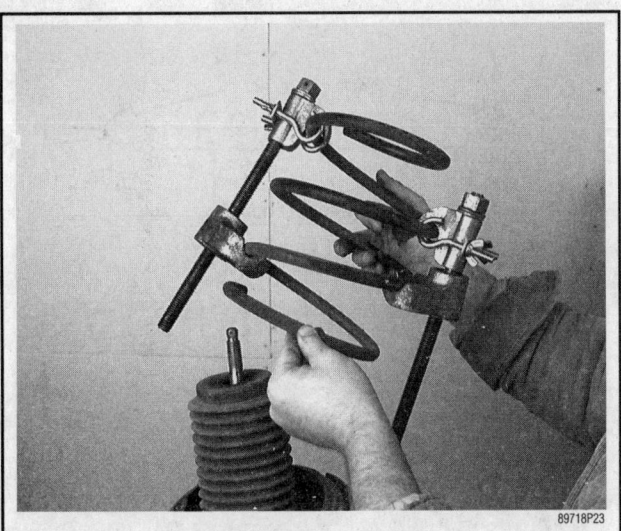

Fig. 83 Carefully lift the spring and compressor from the strut

4. Install a suitable strut nut socket to or an open ended wrench on the strut shaft retaining nut. Then, install a 10mm socket on the hex end of the strut damper shaft. While holding the strut shaft from turning, remove the strut shaft retaining nut.

5. Remove the washer between the strut shaft nut and the upper strut mount and isolator.

6. Remove the upper strut mount assembly from the strut shaft and spring.

7. Remove the washer from the strut shaft that is between the strut upper mount assembly and dust shield.

8. Remove the coil spring and spring compressor as an assembly from the strut.

9. Remove the dust shield from the strut assembly.

10. Remove the jounce bumper from the strut shaft.

11. Remove the coil spring lower isolator from the strut assembly spring seat.

12. Inspect all of the disassembled components for damage, abnormal wear or failure. Check the strut unit for excessive oil leakage and/or loss of oil charge, as follows:

a. Push the strut shaft into the body of the strut and release, the strut shaft should return to its original position.

b. If the shaft does not return to its original position, replace the strut unit.

**To install:**

13. Install the isolator on the lower spring seat of the strut.

14. Install the jounce bumper on the strut shaft.

15. Install the dust shield on the strut assembly.

16. Lower the coil spring onto the strut unit. Position the end of the coil spring against the edge of the spring isolator on the lower spring seat of the strut assembly.

17. Install the washer on the strut shaft with the raised edge of the washer facing upward.

18. Place the strut upper mount onto the strut shaft.

19. Install the washer on the strut upper mount, The washer must be installed with the raised edge of the washer facing down.

20. Install the upper strut mount-to-strut shaft retaining nut.

21. Use a strut rod socket or an open ended wrench and a 10mm socket, to prevent the strut shaft from rotating, tighten the strut shaft nut to 45 ft. lbs. (60 Nm).

22. Equally loosen the spring compressors until the spring is seated on the upper strut mount and all tension is relieved from the spring compressors.

23. Install the strut in the vehicle, as outlined earlier in this section.

24. Have the toe checked and adjusted as necessary.

## Lateral Links

The rear suspension lateral links are serviced as complete assemblies. The isolator bushings used in the lateral links are not serviced as separate components. The rear lateral links are unique, having different size bushings to accommodate the rear toe adjustment cams. The rearward lateral links must be installed with the small bushing sleeve at the knuckle and large bushing sleeve at the rear crossmember. This is necessary to accommodate the rear toe adjustment cam.

### REMOVAL & INSTALLATION

▶ **See Figures 86, 87, 88, 89 and 90**

1. Raise and safely support the vehicle.

2. Remove the wheel and tire assembly.

3. Remove the nut, bolt and washers attaching the lateral links to the knuckle.

4. Unfasten the nut, bolt washer and toe adjustment cam securing the lateral link(s) requiring removal from the rear crossmember. Then, remove the lateral link(s) from the vehicle.

**To install:**

➡ **When installing the rear lateral link(s), they must be positioned and oriented properly on the vehicle.**

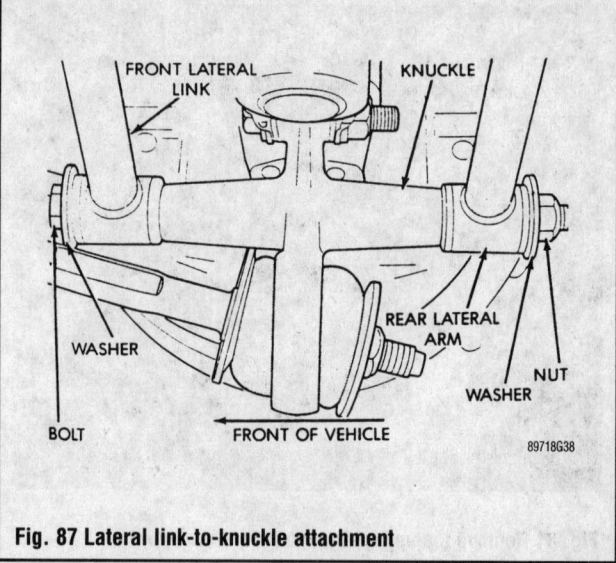

Fig. 87 Lateral link-to-knuckle attachment

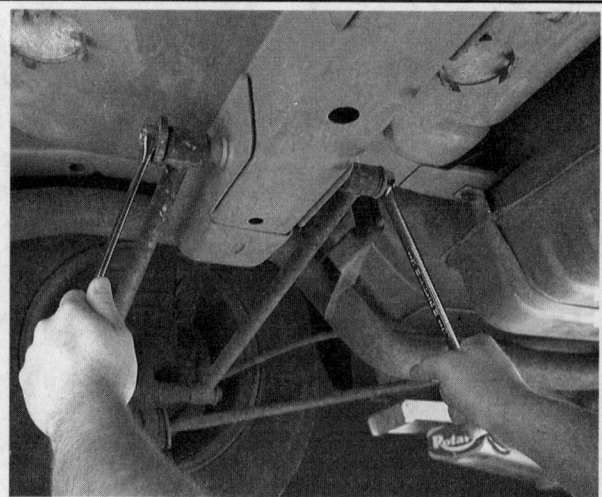

Fig. 88 Rear lateral link removal

Fig. 86 These vehicles are equipped with front (1) and rear (2) lateral links

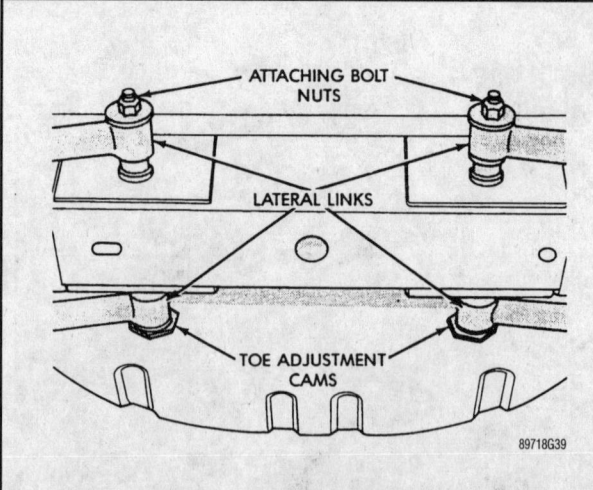

Fig. 89 The lateral link also attaches to the rear crossmember

The lateral link having the same size bushing sleeves, must be mounted to the crossmember and knuckle toward the front of the vehicle. The lateral link with different size bushing sleeves must be mounted to the crossmember and knuckle toward the rear of the vehicle. The lateral link with small and large bushing sleeves must be installed with the small bushing sleeve at the knuckle and the large bushing sleeve at the rear crossmember. This is necessary to accommodate the rear toe adjustment cam at the rear crossmember.

The lateral link mounting bolts are different lengths and need to be installed in specific locations and direction on the vehicle. The lateral link mounting bolt at the knuckle must be installed, with the head of the bolt facing the front of the vehicle. The lateral link mounting bolt at the crossmember must be installed with the head of the bolt facing the rear of the vehicle. The long attaching bolt must be used at the rear crossmember and short bolt used at the knuckle.

5. Install the washer on the short lateral link attaching bolt. Then, install the short lateral link attaching bolt into the lateral link having the same size bushing sleeves. Then install the lateral link, bolt and washer onto the knuckle as an assembly with the head of the bolt facing the front of the vehicle.

6. Install the lateral link with the small and large bushing sleeve on the link attaching bolt in the rear knuckle. Them small bushing sleeve must be installed on the bolt in the rear knuckle with the large bushing sleeve at the crossmember of the vehicle.

7. Install the washer and nut onto the link attaching bolt at the rear knuckle. Do not tighten the lateral link-to-rear knuckle attaching bolt at this time.

8. Install the toe adjustment cam on the long lateral link attaching bolt. Install the long lateral link attaching bolt and adjustment cam into the lateral link toward the rear of the vehicle, having the large bushing sleeve. Then, pass the lateral link attaching bolt into the rear crossmember. The head of the long lateral link-to-crossmember attaching bolt must face to the rear of the vehicle when installed.

9. Position the forward rear lateral link against the rear crossmember. Then pass the lateral link attaching bolt through the front lateral link bushing sleeve.

10. Install the washer and nut onto the lateral link attaching bolt at the rear crossmember. Do NOT tighten the lateral link-to-rear crossmember attaching bolt yet.

11. Install the wheel and tire on the vehicle. Tighten the lug nuts in proper sequence to 100 ft. lbs. (135 Nm).

12. Carefully lower the vehicle.

13. With the weight of the vehicle supported by the suspension, and the lateral links at the proper curb height, tighten both lateral link attaching bolts to 70 ft. lbs. (95 Nm).

14. Have the rear toe checked and adjusted as necessary.

## Stabilizer Bar

### REMOVAL & INSTALLATION

▶ See Figures 91, 92 and 93

1. Raise and safely support the vehicle.
2. Remove both wheel and tire assemblies from the vehicle.
3. Remove the rear stabilizer bar from the 2 stabilizer bar-to-strut attaching links.
4. Rotate the stabilizer bar down slightly to clear the attaching links.
5. Remove the 2 stabilizer bar-to-rear frame rail retainers.
6. Remove the stabilizer bar from the vehicle.
7. Check for broken or distorted retainers and bushings. If bushing replacement Is necessary, perform the following:
   a. Open the slit in the bushing and remove the bushing from around the stabilizer bar.
   b. When the bushings are installed in the bar, the slit must be positioned on the stabilizer bar so it faces the rear of the vehicle when the bar is installed.

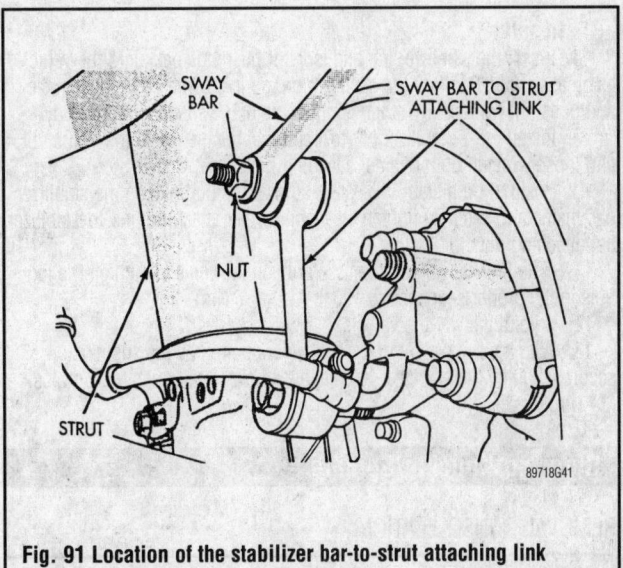

Fig. 91 Location of the stabilizer bar-to-strut attaching link

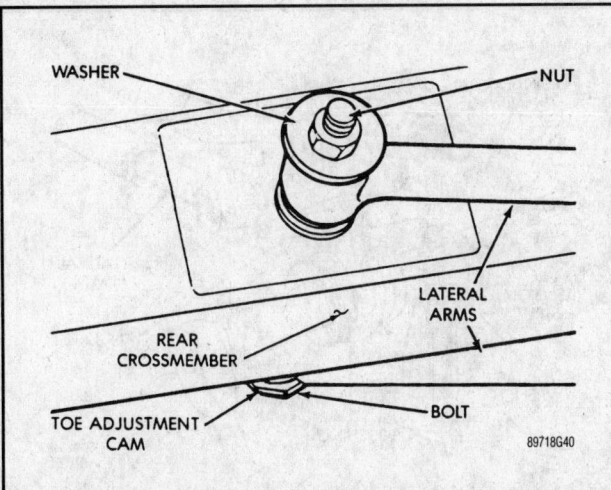

Fig. 90 The lateral links must be oriented and positioned properly for installation

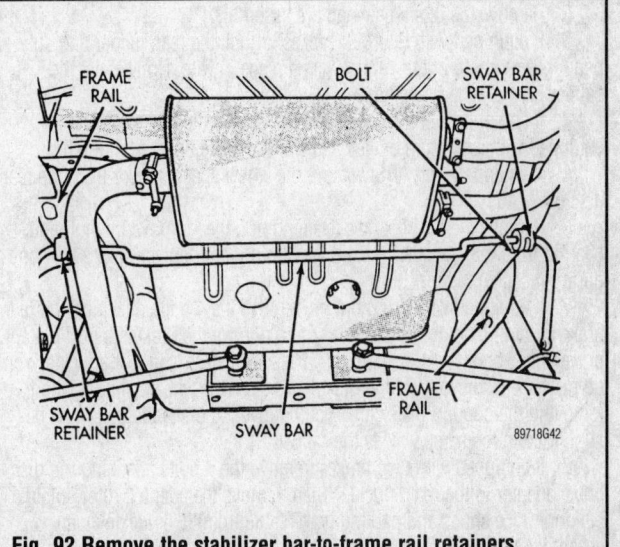

Fig. 92 Remove the stabilizer bar-to-frame rail retainers

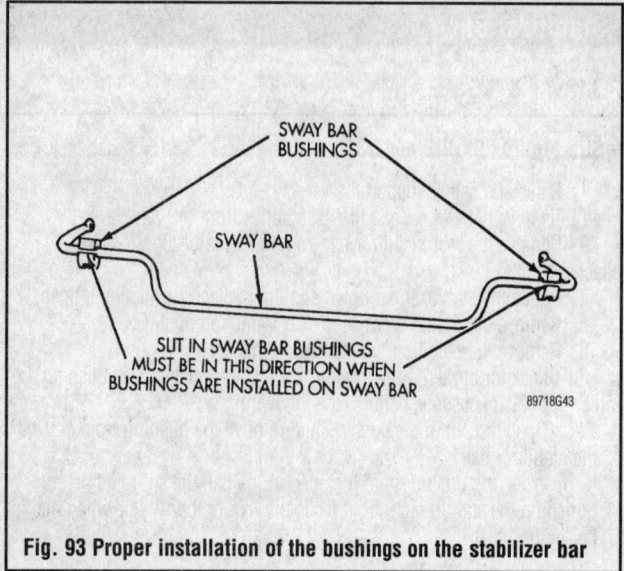

**Fig. 93 Proper installation of the bushings on the stabilizer bar**

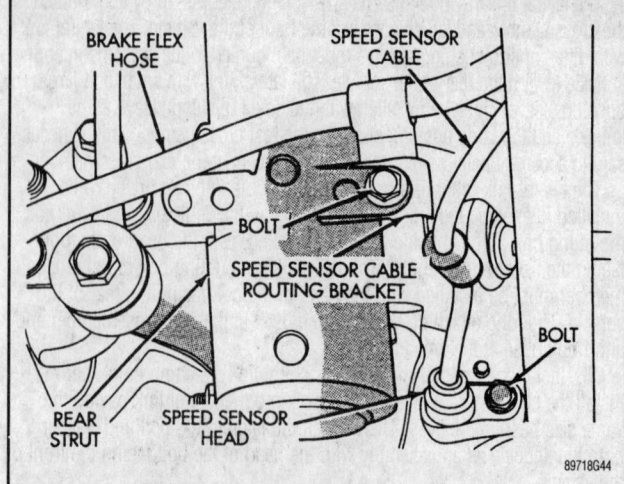

**Fig. 94 Location of the ABS speed sensor-to-disc brake adapter attachment**

**To install:**

8. Install the stabilizer bar and isolator bushings back into the vehicle as an assembly. Position the stabilizer bar so it is centered in the vehicle and does not contact any other components of the suspension or body.

9. Install the 2 stabilizer bar-to-frame rail retainers into the frame rail and loosely install both retainer attaching bolts.

10. Position both stabilizer bar-to-strut attaching links on the stabilizer bar. Install and securely tighten the stabilizer bar attaching link-to-stabilizer bar attaching nuts.

11. Install the wheel and tire assembly on the vehicle. Tighten the lug nuts in the proper sequence to 100 ft. lbs. (135 Nm).

12. Carefully lower the vehicle.

13. With the full weight of the vehicle supported by the suspension, securely tighten the stabilizer bar retainer-to-frame rail bolts to 25 ft. lbs. (34 Nm).

## Steering Knuckle/Spindle

### REMOVAL & INSTALLATION

▶ **See Figures 94, 95, 96 and 97**

1. Raise and safely support the vehicle.
2. Remove the rear wheel and tire assembly.
3. If equipped with rear disc brakes, unbolt the rear caliper and suspend it from frame of the vehicle with a piece of wire. Do NOT let the caliper hang by the brake hose.
4. If equipped with rear disc brakes, remove the brake rotor. If equipped with rear drum brakes, remove the brake drum from the hub.
5. If equipped with ABS, remove the wheel speed sensor from the rear disc brake adapter.
6. Remove the hub/bearing retaining nut, then remove the hub and bearing from the knuckle. Discard the hub nut and replace with a new one during installation.
7. If equipped with drum brakes, remove the 4 bolts attaching the rear brake support plate to the knuckle. Then, remove the brake support plate, brake shoes and wheel cylinder as an assembly from the rear knuckle. You do not have to disconnect the brake hose from the wheel cylinder when removing the support plate. After you remove the brake plate, it must be supported in the same way as the caliper.
8. If equipped with disc brakes, remove the 4 bolts attaching the disc brake adapter to the rear knuckle. Then, remove the adapter, rotor shield, parking brake shoes and parking brake cable from the knuckle as an assembly.

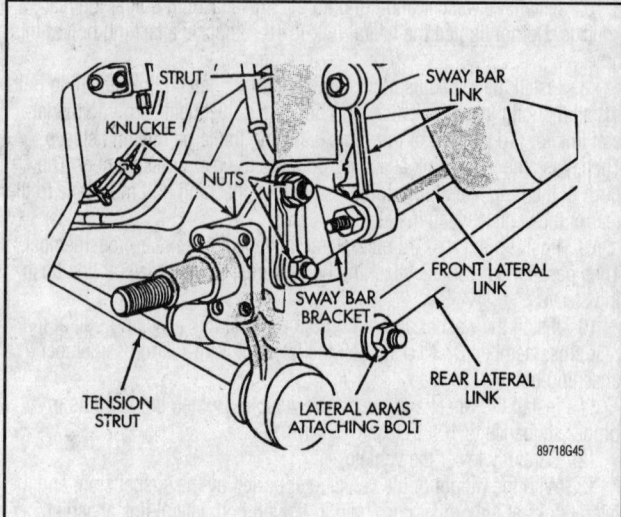

**Fig. 95 Knuckle-to-strut and lateral arm mounting bolts**

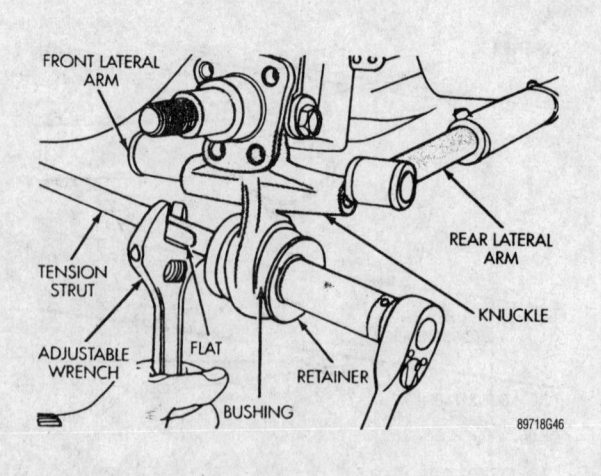

**Fig. 96 Tension strut-to-rear knuckle attachment**

※※ WARNING

**The knuckle-to-strut bolts are serrated and must not be turned during removal. Loosen and remove the nuts while holding the bolts stationary in the knuckle.**

9. Loosen, but do not remove, the 2 strut-to-knuckle bolts. Then, remove the lateral link-to-knuckle attaching bolt.

10. Hold the tension strut from turning using a large adjustable wrench on the flat of the tension strut, then remove the tension strut nut. Then, remove the nut, tension strut retainer and rear tension strut bushing from the tension strut at the rear knuckle.

11. Remove both rear knuckle-to-strut assembly clevis bracket bolts. If the vehicle is equipped with a rear sway bar, also remove the sway bar link-to-strut mounting bracket.

12. Remove the knuckle assembly from the strut by sliding the knuckle straight out of the clevis bracket on the strut. Then, remove the knuckle from the tension strut.

**To install:**

13. Insert the tension strut, tension strut bushing and tensioner strut retainer into the knuckle. Then, install the knuckle into the clevis bracket on the rear strut assembly. Make sure the stepped area of the bushing is squarely seated into the hole in the knuckle.

14. Install the 2 strut clevis bracket-to-knuckle bolts and nuts. Hold the bolts stationary, then tighten the nuts to 70 ft. lbs. (95 Nm).

15. Install the lateral arms-to-knuckle attaching bolt, washers and nut as shown in the accompanying figure. Do NOT tighten the lateral link bolt yet. The vehicle must be at curb height when tightening the link bolts.

16. Install the tension strut bushing, tension strut retainer and nut on the tension strut. When installing the tension strut retainers, the retainers must be installed on the tension strut, with the cupped side of the retainer facing away from the bushing and knuckle.

17. Place a large adjustable wrench on the flat of the tension strut to keep it from turning, then tighten the tension strut nut to 70 ft. lbs. (95 Nm).

18. If equipped with rear drum brakes, install the brake support plate onto the knuckle. Secure with the 4 bolts and tighten to 50 ft. lbs. (68 Nm).

19. If equipped with rear disc brakes, install the adapter on the knuckle. Install the 4 retaining bolts and tighten to 50 ft. lbs. (68 Nm).

20. If equipped with ABS, install the speed sensor head into the brake support plate or disc brake adapter. Tighten the wheel speed sensor mounting bolt to 60 inch lbs. (7 Nm).

※※ WARNING

**The hub/bearing nut must be tightened to, but NOT over, its specified torque value. The proper specification is crucial to the life of the hub bearing.**

21. Install the hub and bearing on the steering knuckle. Install the a new retaining nut and tighten to 160 ft. lbs. (217 Nm).

22. If equipped with rear disc brakes, install the rotor on the hub. Carefully install the caliper over the rotor and on the adapter. Tighten the caliper mounting bolts to 16 ft. lbs. (22 Nm).

23. Install the wheel and tire assembly. Tighten the lug nuts in sequence to 100 ft. lbs. (135 Nm).

24. Carefully lower the vehicle.

25. With the weight of the vehicle supported by the suspension, and the links at the proper height, tighten the lateral link attaching bolts to 70 ft. lbs. (95 Nm).

26. Have the toe checked and adjusted as necessary.

## Rear Wheel Hub and Bearings

REMOVAL & INSTALLATION

▶ **See Figures 98, 99, 100, 101 and 102**

1. Raise and safely support the vehicle.

2. Remove the wheel and tire assembly.

3. If equipped with rear drum brakes, remove the brake drum. If equipped with rear disc brakes, remove the caliper and suspend aside with a piece of wire, then remove the rotor. Do NOT allow the caliper to hang by the brake hose.

4. Remove the dust cap from the rear hub/bearing.

5. Remove the retaining nut securing the hub/bearing assembly to the knuckle/spindle. Discard the hub nut and replace with a new one during installation.

6. Remove the hub/bearing from the spindle buy pulling it off the end of the spindle by hand.

**To install:**

※※ WARNING

**The hub/bearing nut must be tightened to, but NOT over, its specified torque value. The proper specification is crucial to the life of the hub bearing.**

Fig. 97 Installed positions of the tension strut bushings (1), retainer (2) and retainer nut (3)

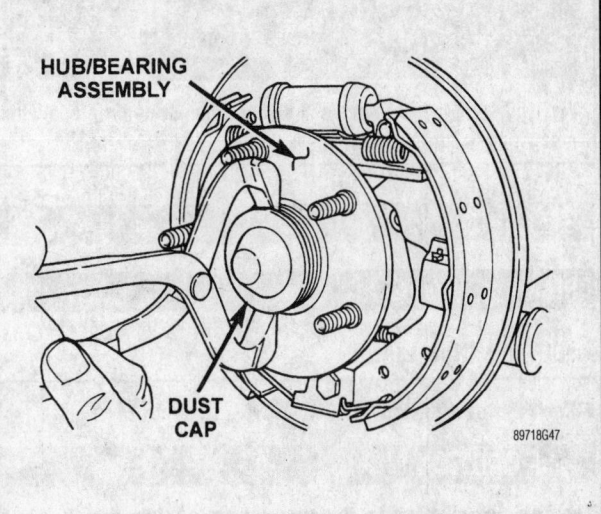

Fig. 98 Use a pair of pincers to remove the dust cap

7. Position the hub/bearing assembly on the rear spindle/knuckle. Install a NEW hub nut and tighten to 160 ft. lbs. (217 Nm).

8. Install the dust cap and seat it using a soft face hammer to carefully tap it into place.

9. If equipped with drum brakes, install the brake drum. If equipped with disc brakes, install the rotor.

10. If equipped with disc brakes, install the caliper and 2 guide pin bolts. Tighten the bolts to 16 ft. lbs. (22 Nm).

11. Install the wheel and tire assembly. Tighten the lug nuts, in a criss-cross pattern, to 100 ft. lbs. (135 Nm).

12. Carefully lower the vehicle.

Fig. 99 Use a ratchet to loosen the hub-to-knuckle retaining nut . . .

Fig. 101 Remove the sealed hub and bearing assembly from the spindle

Fig. 100 . . . then remove and discard the nut and replace with a new one during installation

Fig. 102 Install the dust cap, then seat it properly using a rubber mallet

## STEERING

### Steering Wheel

REMOVAL & INSTALLATION

▶ See Figures 103 thru 112

**✸✸ CAUTION**

The vehicles covered by this manual are equipped with a Supplemental Restraint System (SRS), which uses an air bag. Whenever working near any of the SRS components, such as the impact sensors, the air bag module, steering column and instrument panel, disable the SRS, as described in Section 6.

1. Place steering wheel so the wheels are in the straight ahead position then, rotate the steering wheel ½ turn (180°) to the right (clockwise).

2. Lock the steering column, then remove keys from the ignition.

3. Disconnect and isolate the negative battery cable. Wait at least 2 minutes before continuing the service procedure in order to properly disable the air bag system.

**✹✹ CAUTION**

**Failure to disconnect and isolate the negative battery cable could cause the air bag to deploy and possibly injury.**

4. If equipped, remove the speed control switches and detach the wire connectors or unfasten the screws and remove the covers.

5. Unfasten the driver airbag module screws/bolts from the sides of the steering wheel. Carefully lift the module, then detach the airbag and horn wire connectors. Place the module, inflator side up, on a suitable work bench out of the way.

6. Remove the steering wheel retaining nut. If equipped, remove the steering wheel vibration damper.

7. Attach a suitable puller to the steering wheel, then use it to pull the steering wheel from the shaft. When removing the steering wheel, carefully feed the wires gently through the holes in the clockspring armature.

**To install:**

8. Make sure the following conditions exist:

a. That the steering wheel position is still ½ turn (180°) to the right (clockwise)

b. The steering column is in the **LOCK** position in the ignition cylinder lock.

Fig. 105 Remove the module retaining bolts from the sides of the steering wheel

Fig. 103 Remove the screws from the covers located on the sides of the steering wheel . . .

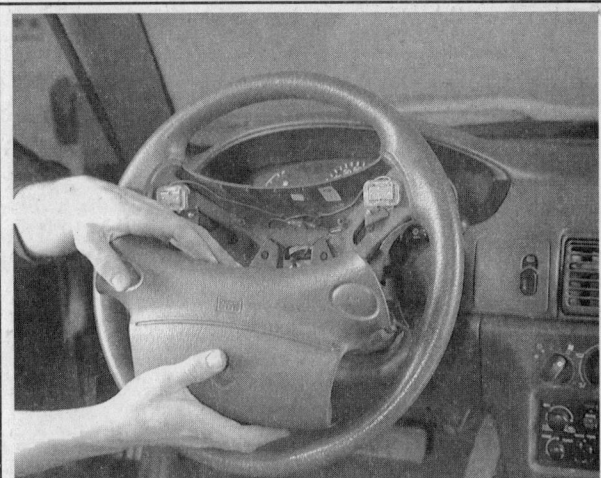
Fig. 106 CAREFULLY lift the airbag module away from the steering wheel

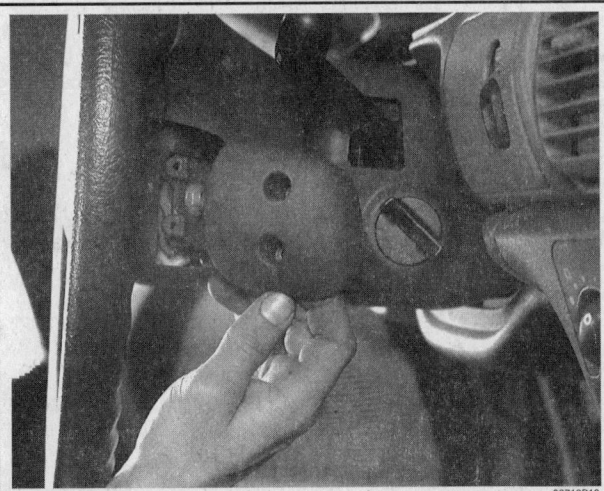
Fig. 104 . . . then remove the covers for access to the airbag module retainers

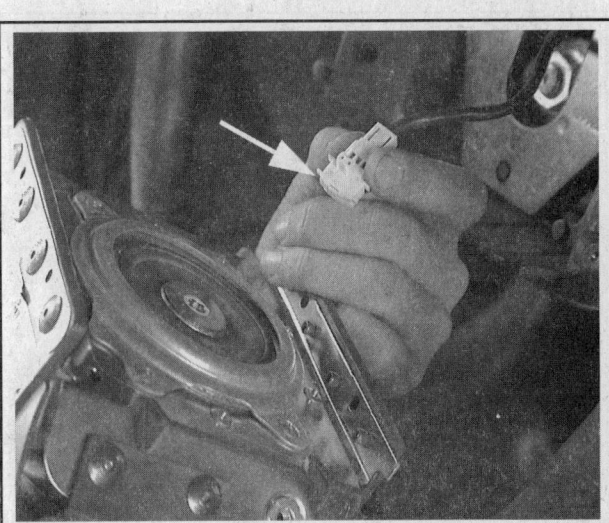
Fig. 107 Unplug the airbag electrical connector (see arrow) . . .

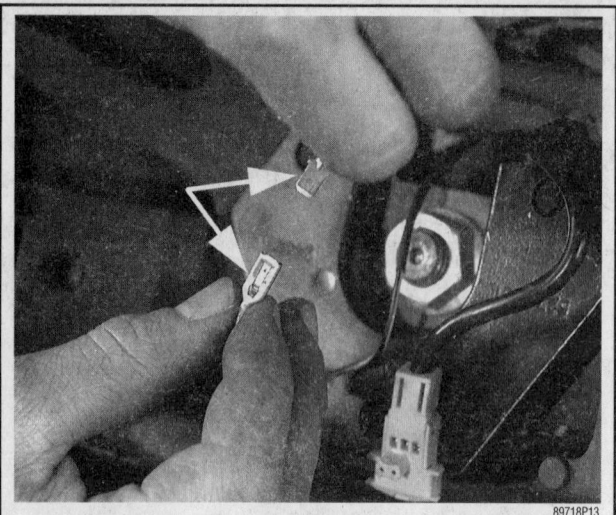

Fig. 108 . . . then detach the horn connector (see arrows)

Fig. 111 Assemble a suitable puller on the steering wheel . . .

Fig. 109 Remove the steering wheel retaining nut

Fig. 112 . . . and use it to pull the steering wheel from the shaft

Fig. 110 Some vehicles are equipped with a vibration damper which must be removed

    c. Turn signal stalk is in the neutral (middle) position.

  9. Installing the steering wheel, making sure the flats on the hub align with the clockspring. Pull the horn lead, airbag and speed control leads through the larger slot. Make sure the leads do NOT get pinched under the steering wheel.

  10. Install the steering wheel retaining nut and tighten to 45 ft. lbs. (61 Nm).

  11. Install the steering wheel air bag module, as follows:

    a. Attach the squib wire to the module. Make sure air bag connection by pressing straight in on the connector. The connector should be fully seated; feel for a snap to indicate proper connection.

    b. Install the retainers and tighten to 7–8 ft. lbs. (10–11 Nm).

  12. Install the non-speed control covers to the steering wheel armature or attach the connectors to the speed control switches and install the switches. Tighten the switch retainers to 20 inch lbs. (2 Nm).

  13. Connect a DRB® or equivalent scan tool to the Data Link Connector (DLC), located at the right side of the steering column and at the lower edge of the lower instrument panel.

  14. Turn the ignition key to the **ON** position. Get out of the vehicle with the scan tool. Make sure you are using the latest version of the proper cartridge.

15. After making sure no one is in the vehicle, remove the tape, then reconnect the negative battery cable.

16. Read and record any stored Diagnostic Trouble Codes (DTCs). If any diagnostic trouble codes are recorded, take your vehicle to a reputable repair shop for diagnosis.

17. If there are no DTCs, and if the airbag warning lamp either fails to light, with the ignition switch **ON**, or the light goes on and stays on, there is a system malfunction. If any of these conditions exist, you should take your vehicle to a reputable repair shop for diagnosis.

## Turn Signal (Multi-function) Switch

### REMOVAL & INSTALLATION

♦ **See Figure 113**

### ✳✳ CAUTION

**Some models covered by this manual may be equipped with a Supplemental Restraint System (SRS), which uses an air bag. Whenever working near any of the SRS components, such as the impact sensors, the air bag module, steering column and instrument panel, disable the SRS, as described in Section 6.**

1. Disconnect and isolate the negative battery cable. Wait at least 2 minutes to allow the air bag system ample time to disarm.

2. Remove both upper and lower steering column covers.

3. Unfasten the multi-function switch mounting screws, then remove the switch from the steering column.

**To install:**

4. Install the multi-function switch and secure with the retaining screws. Tighten the screws to 17 inch lbs. (2 Nm).

5. Install the steering covers and tighten the retainers to 17 inch lbs. (2 Nm).

6. Connect the negative battery cable.

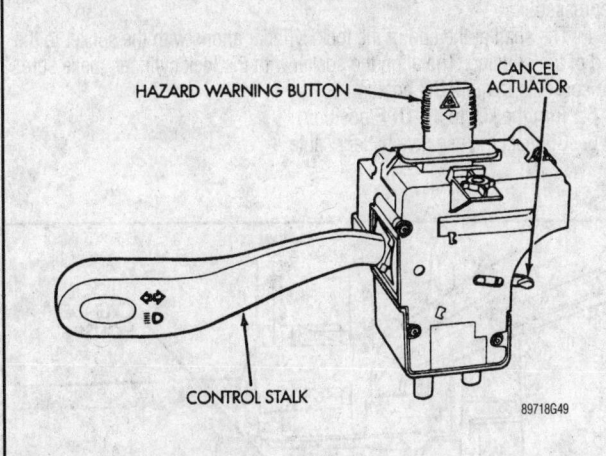

Fig. 113 The multi-function switch is mounted to the steering column

## Ignition Switch

### REMOVAL & INSTALLATION

♦ **See Figures 114, 115, 116, 117 and 118**

The ignition switch is attached to the lock cylinder housing on the end opposite the lock cylinder.

### ✳✳ CAUTION

**Some models covered by this manual may be equipped with a Supplemental Restraint System (SRS), which uses an air bag. Whenever working near any of the SRS components, such as the impact sensors, the air bag module, steering column and instrument panel, disable the SRS, as described in Section 6.**

1. Disconnect and isolate the negative battery cable. Wait at least 2 minutes to allow the air bag system ample time to disarm.

2. Place the ignition key in the **RUN** position. Through the hole in the lower shroud, press the lock cylinder retaining tab, then remove the key cylinder.

3. Unfasten the retainers, then remove the upper and lower steering column shrouds.

4. Detach the ignition switch electrical connectors.

5. Using a #10 Torx® bit, remove the ignition switch mounting screw.

6. Depress the retaining tabs, then pull the ignition switch from the steering column.

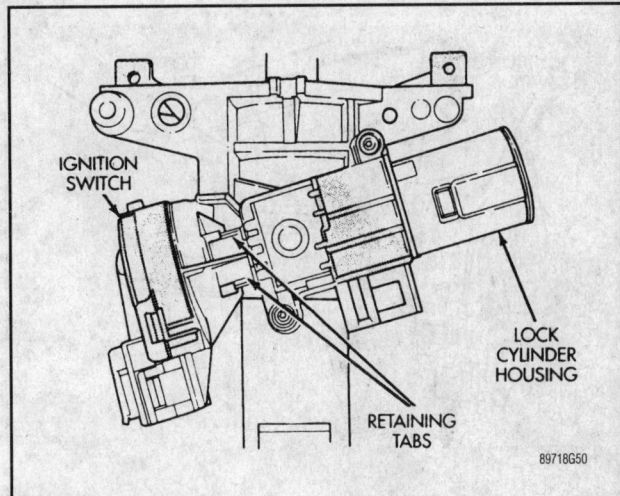

Fig. 114 Location of the ignition switch, as viewed from below the steering column

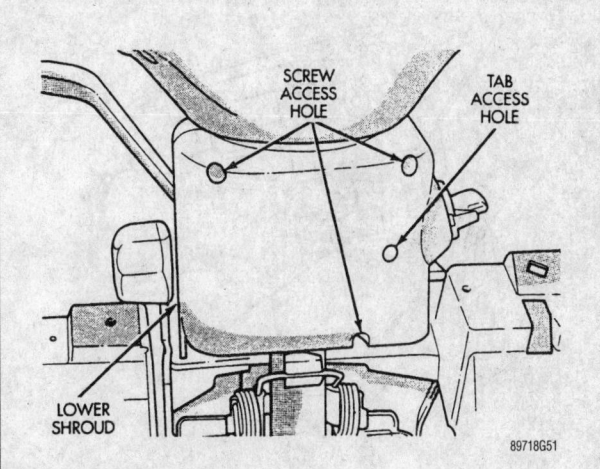

Fig. 115 After removing the retaining screws, you can remove the steering column covers

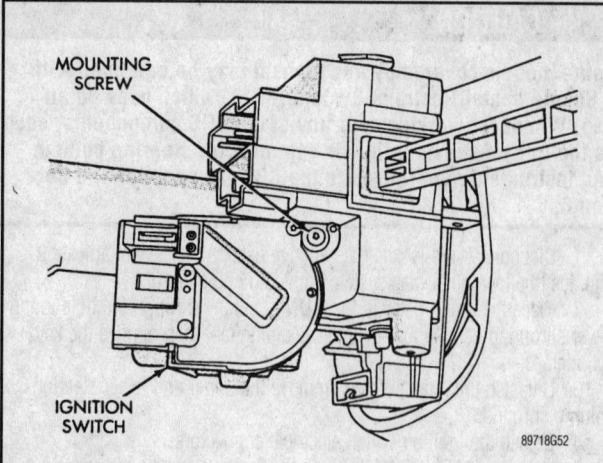

Fig. 116 The ignition switch is secured with a Torx® mounting screw

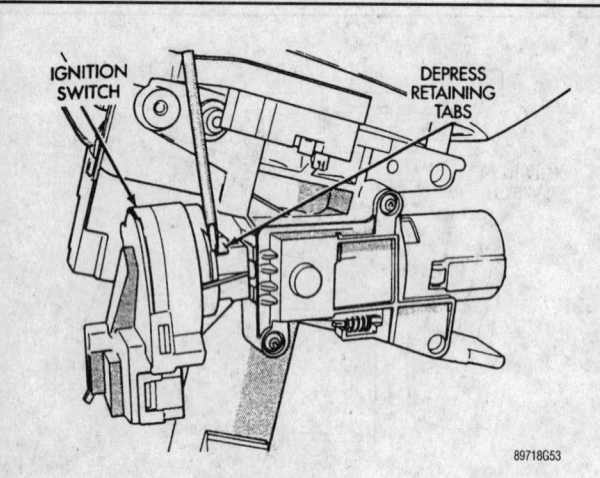

Fig. 117 Use a suitable tool to depress the retaining tabs, then remove the switch from the column

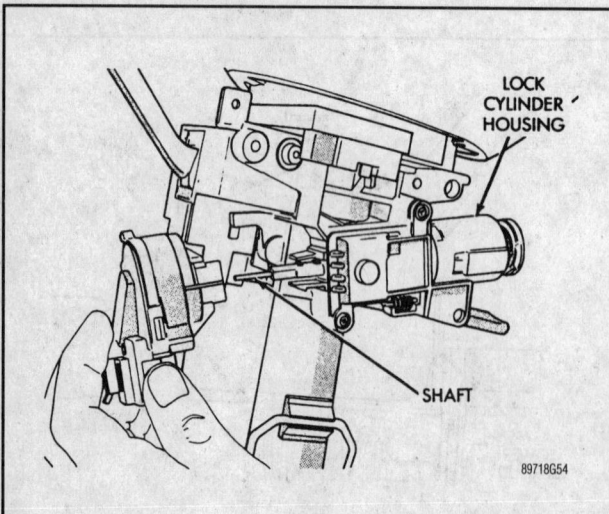

Fig. 118 The ignition switch will snap over the retaining tabs

**To install:**

7. Make sure the ignition switch is in the **RUN** position and the actuator shaft in the lock housing is in the **RUN** position.

8. Carefully install the ignition switch. The switch will snap over the retaining tabs. Install the mounting screw.

9. Attach the ignition switch electrical connectors.

10. Install the upper and lower steering column shrouds.

11. Install the ignition key cylinder (the cylinder retaining tab will depress only in the **RUN** position).

12. Connect the negative battery cable.

13. Check for proper operation of the ignition switch and key-in warning switch.

### Ignition Lock Cylinder

REMOVAL & INSTALLATION

▶ See Figure 119

### ⁛ CAUTION

**Some models covered by this manual may be equipped with a Supplemental Restraint System (SRS), which uses an air bag. Whenever working near any of the SRS components, such as the impact sensors, the air bag module, steering column and instrument panel, disable the SRS, as described in Section 6.**

1. Disconnect and isolate the negative battery cable. Wait at least 2 minutes to allow the air bag system ample time to disarm.

2. Place the ignition key in the **RUN** position. Through the hole in the lower shroud, depress the lock cylinder retaining tab, then remove the key cylinder.

**To install:**

3. Install the key in the lock cylinder. Turn the key to the **RUN** position (position where the retaining tab on the lock cylinder can be depressed).

4. The shaft at the end of the lock cylinder aligns with the socket in the end of the housing. The align the socket with the lock cylinder, make sure the socket is in the **RUN** position.

5. Turn the key to the **OFF** position.

6. Connect the negative battery cable.

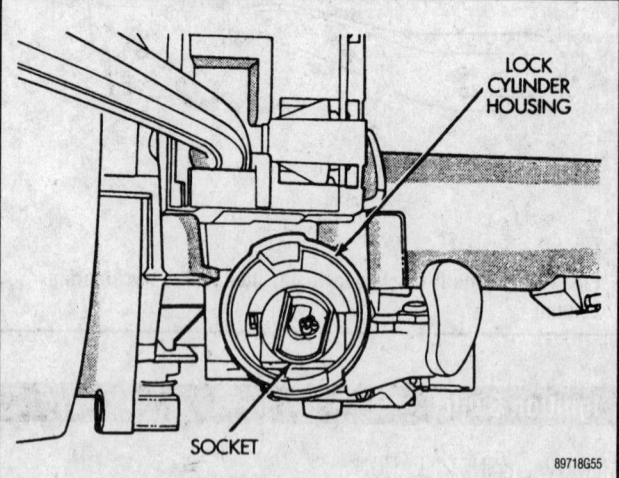

Fig. 119 Align the socket with the cylinder, by making sure it's in the RUN position

## Steering Linkage

### REMOVAL & INSTALLATION

#### Tie Rod Ends

▶ **See Figures 120 thru 128**

1. Raise and safely support the vehicle.
2. Remove the wheel and tire assembly.
3. Remove the nut attaching the outer tie rod end to the steering knuckle. The nut is removed by holding the tie rod end stud with an $^{11}/_{32}$ in. socket while loosening and removing the nut with a wrench.
4. Separate the tie rod end from the steering knuckle using side puller.
5. Loosen the inner tie rod-to-outer tie rod jam nut. Thread the jam nut far enough up the inner tie rod to pull the collar away from the outer tie rod end.
6. For 1998–99 vehicles, pull the collar off the end of the outer tie rod end.
7. Remove the outer tie rod from the inner tie rod by unthreading it, counting the number of turns for proper installation.

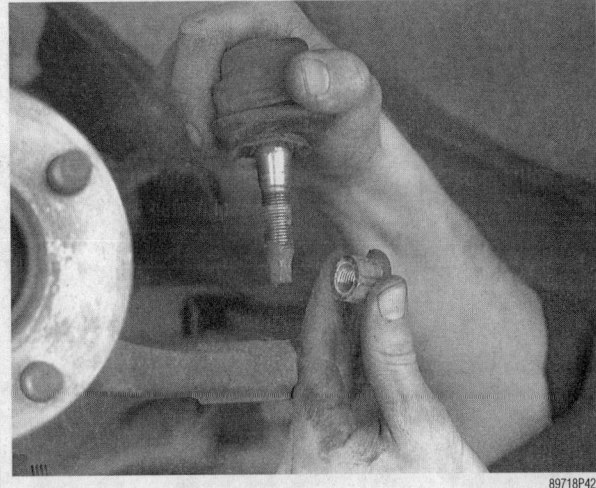

Fig. 122 . . . and separate the tie rod end from the steering knuckle

Fig. 120 Hold the tie rod end stud with a proper socket, then remove the nut with a box end wrench

Fig. 123 Location of the tie rod end jam nut (see arrow)

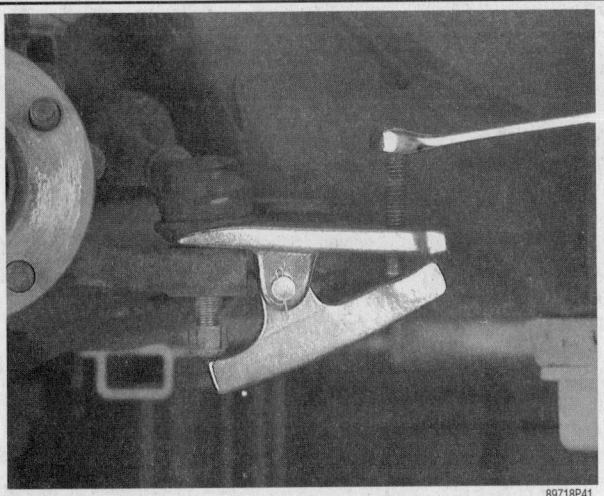

Fig. 121 Install a side puller on the tie rod end-to-steering knuckle connector . . .

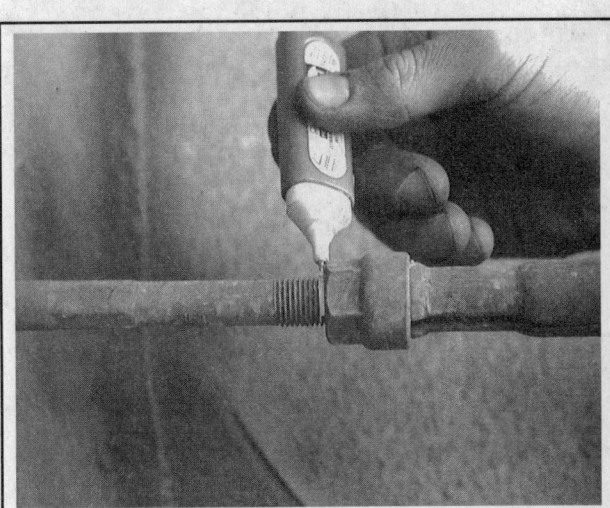

Fig. 124 It's a good idea to matchmark the installed position of the tie rod end before loosening the jam nut

Fig. 125 Loosen the tie rod end jam nut . . .

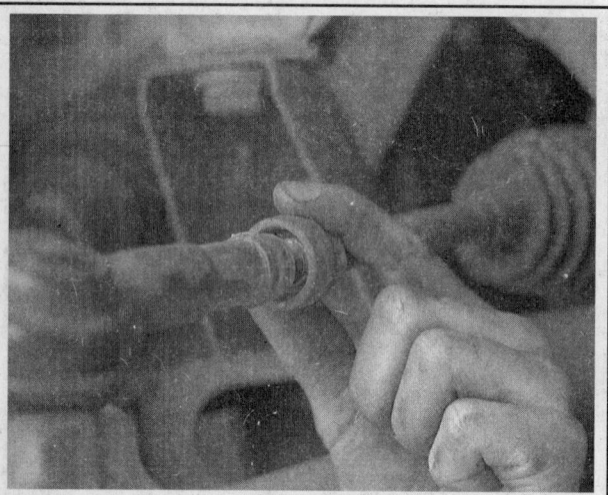

Fig. 126 . . . and pull the collar away from the outer tie rod end

Fig. 127 Count the number of turns you unthread the tie rod end, in order to install it properly

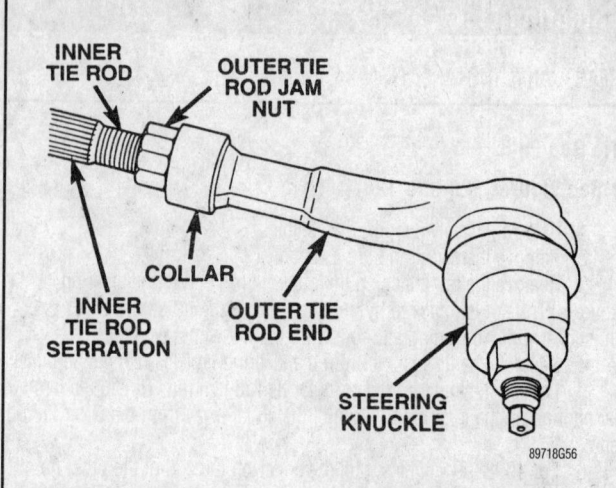

Fig. 128 Outer tie rod end and related components—1998 shown, earlier years similar

**To install:**

8. Install the jam nut on the inner tie rod end.
9. For 1995–97 vehicles, perform the following:
   a. Install the outer tie rod onto the inner tie rod.

➡Make sure the collar is installed on the inner tie rod with the flat end of the collar against the jam nut and the open end of the collar facing the outer tie rod end.

10. On 1998–99 vehicles, perform the following:
    a. Install the collar on the outer tie rod end.
    b. Position the collar around the end of the outer tie rod.
    c. Thread the jam nut down the inner tie rod far enough to hold the collar in place on the outer tie rod. Do NOT tighten the jam nut.
11. Install the tie rod end into the steering knuckle. Start the tie rod end-to-steering knuckle attachment nut onto the stud of the tie rod end. While holding the stud of the tie rod end stationary, tighten the tie rod end-to-knuckle attaching nut. Then, using a crowfoot wrench and an 11/32 in. socket, tighten the tie rod end attaching nut to 45 ft. lbs. (61 Nm).

➡Before tightening the jam nut to the proper specification, check the orientation of the collar, if equipped, to be sure it is in the proper position to fit up against the outer tie rod end.

12. Tighten the tie rod jam nut to 40 ft. lbs. (55 Nm).
13. Take the vehicle to a reputable repair shop to have the toe checked, and adjusted if necessary.

## Steering Gear

The replacement procedure for both the manual and power steering gears is the same. The only additional steps for power steering gear removal and installation is the disconnection and connection of the power steering fluid lines from and to the steering gear

These vehicles are designed and assembled using NET BUILD front suspension alignment settings. This means that the alignment settings are determined as the vehicle is designed by the location of the front suspension components in relation to the body. This is carried out when building the vehicle, by precisely locating the front crossmember, to meter gage holes located in the underbody of the vehicle. With this method of designing and building a vehicle, it is no longer possible to adjust a vehicle's front suspension alignment settings to the required specifications. As a result, whenever the crossmember is removed from a vehicle, it MUST be replaced in the same location on the body of the vehicle it was removed from. The front suspension toe settings can still be adjusted by the outer tie rod ends.

## REMOVAL & INSTALLATION

▶ **See Figures 129 thru 134**

1. From inside the vehicle, disconnect the steering gear coupler, from the steering column shaft coupler.
2. Raise and safely support the vehicle with jackstands.
3. Remove both front wheel and tire assemblies.
4. If equipped, remove the engine/transaxle bobble damper, from the front suspension crossmember. The bobble strut does not have to be removed from the transaxle.
5. Unfasten the nut attaching the outer tie rod end to the steering knuckle. The nut is removed by holding the tie rod end stud with an $^{11}/_{32}$ in. socket while loosening and removing the nut with a wrench.
6. Separate the tie rod ends from the steering knuckles using a side puller, tool MB-991113 or equivalent.
7. If equipped with power steering, perform the following:
   a. Remove the vehicle wiring harness connector from the power steering fluid pressure switch.
   b. Remove the power steering pressure and return hose routing bracket from the front crossmember. The bracket does not have to be removed from the power steering pressure and turn hoses.

c. Remove the power steering fluid, pressure and return hoses from the power steering gear assembly.

### ✴✴ WARNING

**Before removing the crossmember from the vehicle, the location of the crossmember MUST be scribed or marked on the vehicle, as shown in the accompanying figure. This has to be done so the crossmember can be installed in the exact location from which it was removed. If this is not done, the proper NET BUILD alignment specifications will not be obtained and may lead to handling and/or tire wear problems.**

8. Using a paint marker or an awl or equivalent, make a line marking the location where the crossmember is mounted against the body of the vehicle.
9. Place a transmission jack under the center of the crossmember. The jack will be used to lower, support and raise the crossmember when removing the steering gear.
10. Loosen, then remove the front 2 bolts attaching the crossmember to the frame rails of the vehicle. Then, loosen the 2 rear bolts attaching the crossmember and lower control arm to the body of the vehicle. Lower the crossmember while loosening the rear bolts.

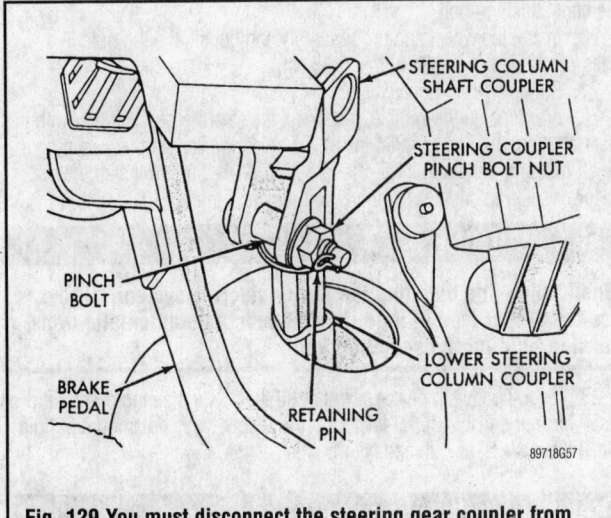

**Fig. 129 You must disconnect the steering gear coupler from inside the vehicle**

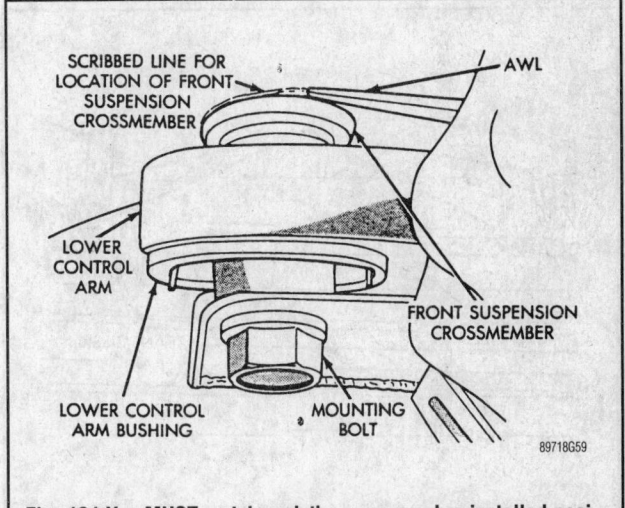

**Fig. 131 You MUST matchmark the crossmember installed position**

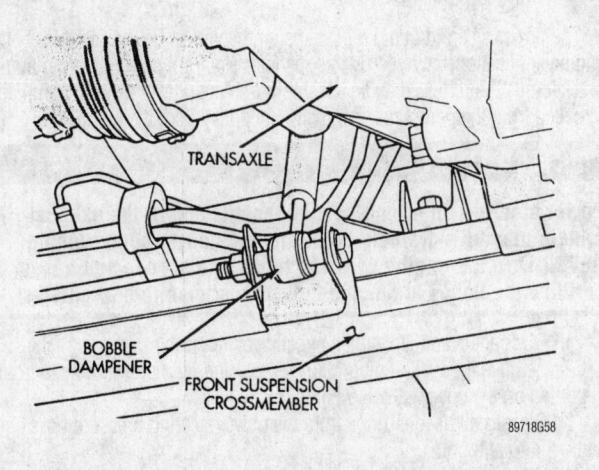

**Fig. 130 Some vehicles are equipped with a bobble damper which must be removed from the crossmember**

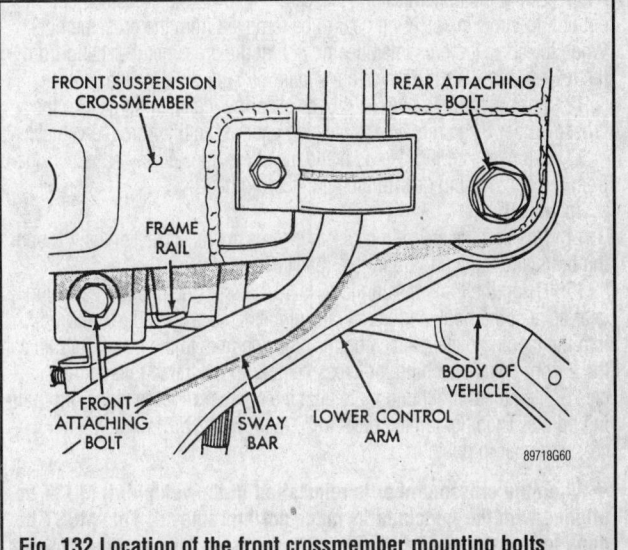

**Fig. 132 Location of the front crossmember mounting bolts**

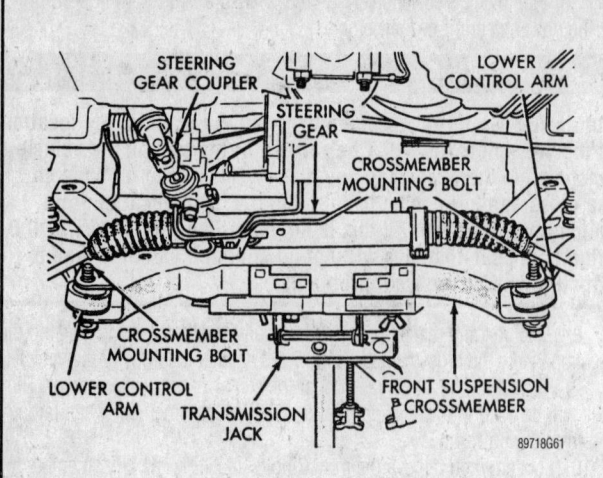

**Fig. 133 You must carefully lower the crossmember for access to the steering gear**

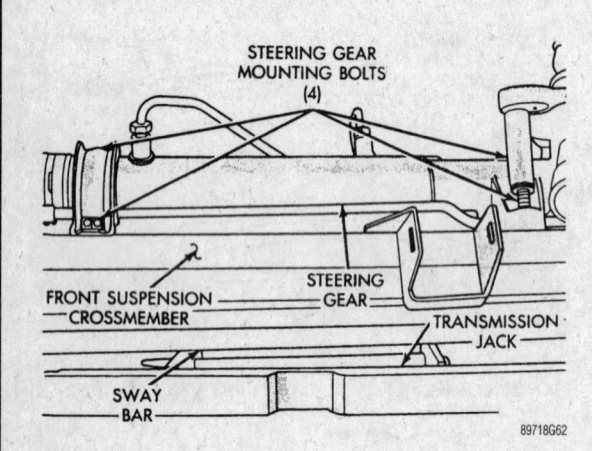

**Fig. 134 Unfasten the mounting bolts, then remove the steering gear from the vehicle**

11. Using the transmission jack, carefully lower the crossmember enough to allow the steering gear to be removed from the crossmember. When lowering the crossmember, do not let the crossmember hang from the lower control arms, the weight should be supported by the jack.

12. Loosen and remove the 4 bolts securing the steering gear to the crossmember. Then remove the steering gear assembly from the vehicle.

13. If a new steering gear is being installed, transfer any necessary parts from the old steering gear to the new steering gear.

**To install:**

14. Position the steering gear on the crossmember. Install the 4 mounting bolts and tighten to 50 ft. lbs. (68 Nm).

15. Using the transmission jack, raise the crossmember and steering gear against the body and frame rails of the vehicle. Start the 2 rear bolts into the tapping plates, attaching the crossmember to the body. Then install the 2 front bolts, attaching the crossmember to the frame rails of the vehicle. Tighten the 4 mounting bolts until the crossmember is at the 4 mounting points. Then tighten the bolts to 20 inch lbs. (2 Nm) to hold the crossmember in position.

➡ **When the crossmember is reinstalled in the vehicle, it MUST be aligned with the matchmarks made during removal. This MUST be done to maintain NET BUILD front suspension alignment settings.**

16. Using a rubber mallet, tap the crossmember into position, until it is aligned with the 2 previously scribed positioning marks on the body. When the crossmember is properly positioned, tighten the 2 rear crossmember/lower control arm bolts to 120 ft. lbs. (163 Nm). Then tighten the 2 front bolts to 120 ft. lbs. (163 Nm).

17. If equipped with power steering, perform the following:

a. Install the power steering fluid pressure and return hoses into the correct fluid ports on the steering gear. Tighten the line-to-steering gear tube nuts to 23 ft. lbs. (31 Nm).

b. Install the power steering pressure and turn hose routing bracket and attaching screw on the crossmember. Tighten the hose routing bracket-to-attaching bolt to 17 ft. lbs. (23 Nm).

c. Install the vehicle wiring harness connector onto the power steering fluid pressure switch on the steering gear assembly. Make sure the locking tab on the wiring harness connector is securely latched to the pressure switch.

18. Install the tie rod end into the steering knuckle. Start the tie rod end-to-steering knuckle attaching nut onto the stud of the tie rod end. While holding the stud of the tie rod still, tighten the tie rod end-to-steering knuckle attaching nut. Then, using a crowfoot wrench and $^{11}/_{32}$ in. socket, tighten the tie rod end attaching nut to 40 ft. lbs. (55 Nm).

19. If equipped, install the engine/transaxle bobble strut back onto the crossmember bracket. Install and securely tighten the dampener-to-crossmember attaching bolt.

20. Install the wheel and tire assembly and tighten the lug nuts in a criss-cross pattern to 100 ft. lbs. (135 Nm).

21. Carefully lower the vehicle.

22. From inside the vehicle, reconnect the steering gear coupler with the steering column shaft coupler. Install the steering gear coupler retaining pinch bolt and tighten to 21 ft. lbs. (28 Nm). Make sure to install the upper-to-lower steering coupler retaining bolt retention pin.

### ✳✳ WARNING

**When filling and bleeding the power steering system, always use the proper type of fluid. NEVER substitute automatic transmission fluid for the specified fluid.**

23. If equipped with power steering, fill the power steering pump fluid reservoir to the FULL-COLD level with the proper type and amount of fluid. Bleed the system, as outlined later in this section.

## Power Steering Pump

### REMOVAL & INSTALLATION

▶ **See Figures 135 thru 141**

The power steering pump replacement procedures are the same for both engine applications covered by this manual. The front power steering pump bracket must be removed as an assembly with the power steering pump and removed from the pump after removing the pulley from the pump.

### ✳✳ CAUTION

**Power steering fluid, engine components and/or the exhaust system may be extremely hot if the engine has been running. NEVER start the engine with any loose or disconnected hoses, or allow the hoses to touch a hot exhaust manifold or catalyst.**

1. Disconnect and isolate the negative battery cable.

2. Remove the banjo bolt and power steering fluid pressure hose from the fitting on the power steering pump.

3. Discard all used O-rings from the power steering pressure hose banjo fitting and bolt.

4. Remove the hose clamp attaching the power steering fluid supply hose to the power steering pump suction fitting. Remove the power steering fluid supply hose from the power steering pump fitting.

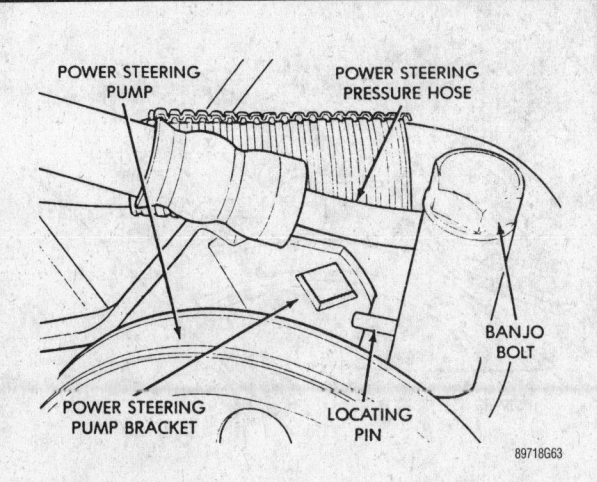

**Fig. 135 Location of the banjo bolt which must be removed from the fitting on the pump**

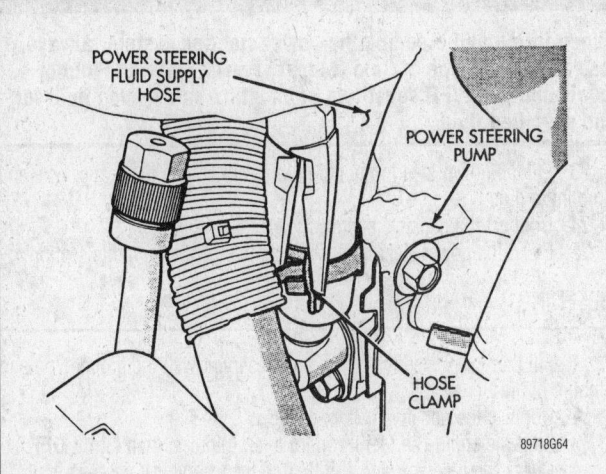

**Fig. 136 Disconnect the fluid supply hose from the power steering pump**

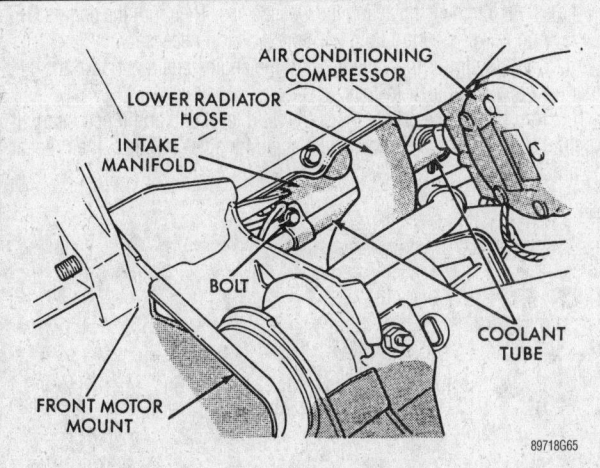

**Fig. 137 On DOHC engines, you must unfasten the coolant tube bolt and position the tube aside**

5. For Dual Overhead Cam (DOHC) engines, perform the following:
   a. Raise and safely support the vehicle.

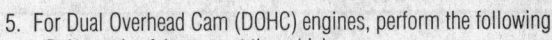

➡**If equipped with a dual overhead cam engine, the bolt attaching the coolant tube to the intake manifold must be removed.**

   b. Remove the bolt attaching the coolant tube to the bottom of the intake manifold. The bolt requires removal in order to allow the coolant tube to be positioned aside for access to the power steering pump mounting bolt. The coolant tube does not need to be removed or the system drained.

6. Remove the 2 power steering pump-to-cast bracket mounting and adjustment bolts.

➡**The power steering pump front mounting bracket is slotted at the bolt securing it to the front engine mount. This bolt only has to be loosened to remove the bracket.**

7. Loosen the bolt attaching the power steering pump front mounting bracket to the front engine mount. Only loosen the bolt enough to slide the bracket out from under the bolt.

8. Remove the power steering pump drive belt from the pump pulley.

9. Remove the power steering pump and front mounting bracket from the engine as an assembly.

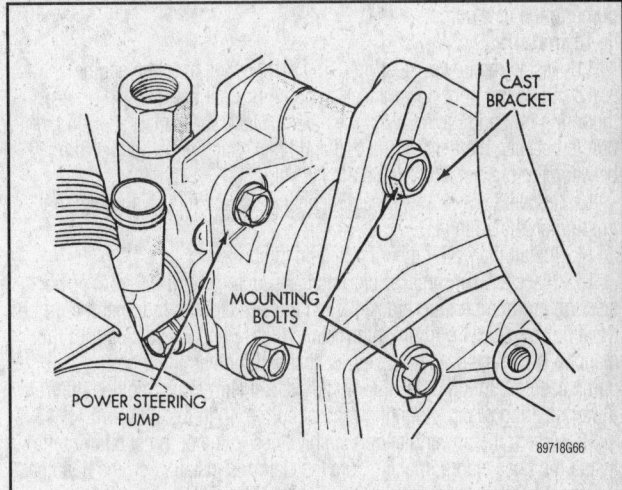

**Fig. 138 Location the of the power steering pump mounting bolts as seen from the rear**

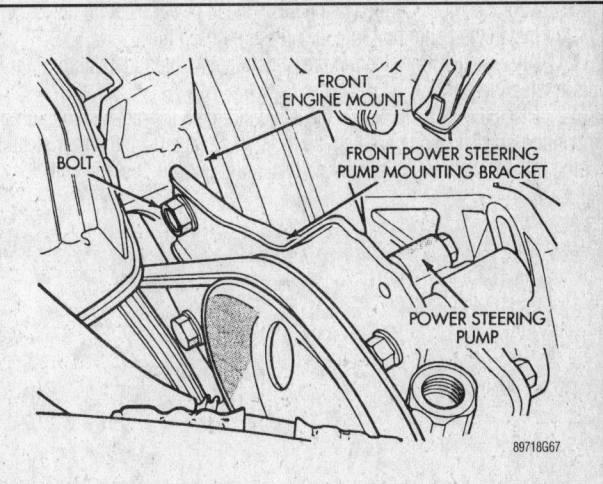

**Fig. 139 Loosen the front mounting bracket bolt enough to remove the bracket**

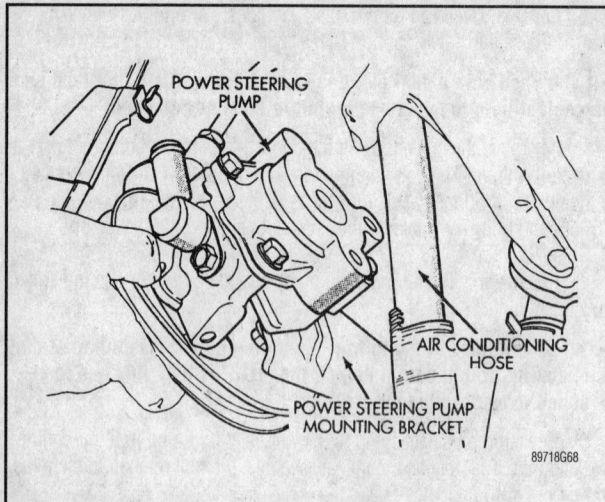

Fig. 140 The power steering pump and bracket are removed as an assembly

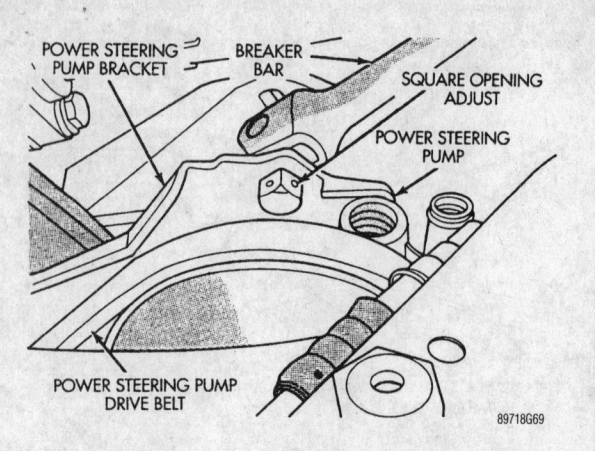

Fig. 141 You must set the power steering belt to the proper tension

10. If installed a new pump, transfer the necessary parts from the old pump to the new pump.

**To install:**

11. Install the power steering pump and bracket onto the engine.

12. Slide the front power steering pump bracket between the bracket mounting bolt and the front engine mount. Make sure the washer on the bolt is between the head of the bolt and bracket and does not get trapped between the bracket and engine mount.

13. Install the 2 pump-to-cast mounting bracket mounting bolts, but do not tighten the bolts yet.

14. Install the power steering belt on the pulley.

15. Place a ½ in. breaker bar into the square hole in the front power steering pump mounting bracket. Then rotate the pump in to get the proper drive belt tension. For more information, please refer to Section 1 of this manual. When the proper tension is obtained, tighten the 2 bolts at the pump case mounting bracket to 40 ft. lbs. (54 Nm). Then, tighten the front power steering pump mounting bracket bolt to 40 ft. lbs. (54 Nm).

16. Attach the power steering supply hose to the pump suction fitting. Install the hose clamp, making sure the clamp is installed on the hose past the upset bead on the power steering pump tube.

17. Using a lint-free towel, wipe all of the open power steering hose ends and pump fittings clean.

18. Install a new O-ring on the end of the power steering pressure hose banjo fitting. Place a new O-ring on the pressure hose banjo fitting bolt.

19. Lubricate both O-rings using fresh, clean power steering fluid.

20. Install the banjo bolt into the pressure hose fitting.

21. Attach the power steering pressure hose on the outlet fitting of the power steering pump.

22. Place the locating pin on the banjo fitting so it is against the pump mounting bracket. While holding the locating pin against the power steering pump bracket, tighten the pump end banjo bolt to 25 ft. lbs. (34 Nm).

**⁂ WARNING**

When filling and bleeding the power steering system, always use the proper type of fluid (Mopar® Power Steering Fluid or equivalent). NEVER substitute automatic transmission fluid for the specified fluid.

23. Fill the power steering pump fluid reservoir with the proper type and amount of fluid.

24. Connect the negative battery cable.

25. Bleed the power steering system, as outlined later in this section.

BLEEDING

1. Fill the power steering pump fluid reservoir with the proper type and amount of fluid.

2. Connect the negative battery cable.

3. Start the engine and let it run for a few minutes, then turn it **OFF**.

4. Check the reservoir and add fluid to the reservoir if necessary.

5. Repeat the preceding 2 steps until the fluid level stays constant after running the engine.

6. Raise the vehicle's front wheels off the ground and support the front of the vehicle securely with jackstands.

7. Start the engine, then slowly turn the steering wheel right and left a few times, until lightly contacting the wheel stops. Then turn the engine **OFF**.

8. Add power steering fluid to the reservoir if necessary.

9. Carefully lower the vehicle. Start the engine again and turn the steering wheel from lock-to-lock.

10. Turn the engine **OFF**. Check the fluid level and add if necessary. If the fluid is very foamy, let the vehicle stand for a few minutes, then repeat the procedure.

### TORQUE SPECIFICATIONS

| Component | ft. lbs. | inch lbs. | Nm |
|---|---|---|---|
| **Front Suspension** | | | |
| McPherson strut | | | |
|   Strut-to-shock tower attaching nuts | 25 | | 34 |
|   Clevis bracket-to-steering knuckle retainers | | | |
|     1995 vehicles | 120 | | 163 |
|     1996-99 vehicles (plus an additional 90° rotation) | 40 | | 54 |
|   Strut shaft nut | 55 | | 74 |
| Steering knuckle | 72-87 | | 98-118 |
|   Ball joint stud-to-steering knuckle nut/bolt | 70 | | 95 |
|   Disc brake caliper bolts | 16 | | 22 |
| Front suspension crossmember | | | |
|   Crossmember-to-body bolts | 120 | | 163 |
|   Lower control arm pivot bolt | 120 | | 163 |
| Stabilizer bar | | | |
|   Bushing retainer-to-crossmember bolts | 21 | | 28 |
|   To control arm attaching link nut | 21 | | 28 |
| Hub and bearing | | | |
|   Front stub axle-to-hub bearing nut | 135 | | 183 |
|   Wheel mounting lug nut | 80-110 | | 109-150 |
| **Rear Suspension** | | | |
| Strut assembly | | | |
|   Strut-to-body attaching nuts | 25 | | 34 |
|   Clevis bracket-to-knuckle nut/bolt | 70 | | 95 |
|   Strut assembly shaft nut | 55 | | 75 |
| Brake support plate | | | |
|   Plate-to-knuckle bolts | 50 | | 68 |
| Stabilizer bar | | | |
|   Bushing retainer-to-frame bolt | 25 | | 34 |
|   Bar-to-strut attaching link nut | 25 | | 34 |
| Tension strut | | | |
|   Shaft nut | 70 | | 95 |
|   Bracket-to-body attaching bolts | 70 | | 95 |
| Lateral link | | | |
|   Attaching nut | 70 | | 95 |
| Disc brake caliper | | | |
|   To adapter mounting bolt | 16 | | 22 |
|   Brake hose-to-caliper mounting bolt | 35 | | 45 |
|   Adapter-to-knuckle mounting bolt | 50 | | 68 |
| Brake hose | | | |
|   Bracket mounting bolt | 17 | | 23 |
| Hub and bearing | | | |
|   Hub and bearing-to-knuckle retaining nut | 160 | | 216 |
|   Wheel stud lug nuts | 80-110 | | 109-150 |
| **Steering** | | | |
| Steering Gear | | | |
|   Steering gear-to-crossmember attaching bolts | 50 | | 68 |
|   Steering gear-to-body attaching bolts | 120 | | 163 |
|   Outer tie rod-to-inner tie rod lock nut | 45 | | 61 |
|   Tie rod end adjusting sleeve nut | 55 | | 75 |

89718C01

## TORQUE SPECIFICATIONS

| Component | | ft. lbs. | inch lbs. | Nm |
|---|---|---|---|---|
| (Steering con't.) | Tie rod end-to-steering knuckle nut | | | |
| | 1995 vehicles | 45 | | 61 |
| | 1996-99 vehicles | 40 | | 54 |
| | Power steering hose tube nuts | 23 | | 31 |
| | Power steering routing bracket at crossmember | 17 | | 23 |
| Steering wheel retaining nut | | 45 | | 61 |
| Steering column upper and lower mounting bracket attaching nuts | | 12.5 | | 17 |
| Power steering pump and lines | | | | |
| | Power steering hose tube nuts | 23 | | 31 |
| | Bracket-to-crossmember attaching bolt | 17 | | 23 |
| Power steering pump | | | | |
| | Pressure hose banjo bolt | 25 | | 34 |
| | Discharge fitting | 55 | | 75 |
| | Pump-to-bracket mounting bolts | 40 | | 54 |
| | Bracket-to-engine mounting bolts | 40 | | 54 |

89718C02

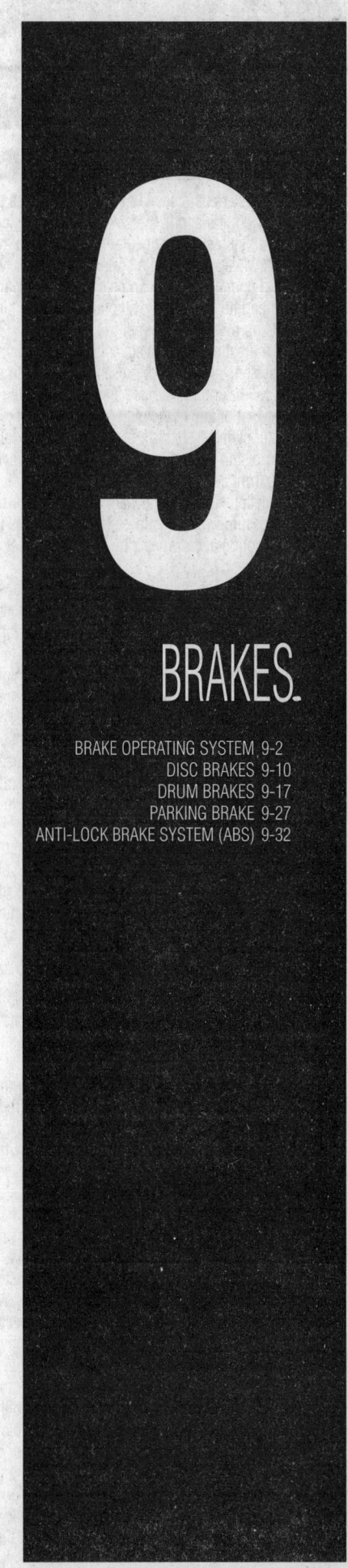

# 9

## BRAKES.

## BRAKE OPERATING SYSTEM

### Basic Operating Principles

Hydraulic systems are used to actuate the brakes of all modern automobiles. The system transports the power required to force the frictional surfaces of the braking system together from the pedal to the individual brake units at each wheel. A hydraulic system is used for two reasons.

First, fluid under pressure can be carried to all parts of an automobile by small pipes and flexible hoses without taking up a significant amount of room or posing routing problems.

Second, a great mechanical advantage can be given to the brake pedal end of the system, and the foot pressure required to actuate the brakes can be reduced by making the surface area of the master cylinder pistons smaller than that of any of the pistons in the wheel cylinders or calipers.

The master cylinder consists of a fluid reservoir along with a double cylinder and piston assembly. Double type master cylinders are designed to separate the front and rear braking systems hydraulically in case of a leak. The master cylinder coverts mechanical motion from the pedal into hydraulic pressure within the lines. This pressure is translated back into mechanical motion at the wheels by either the wheel cylinder (drum brakes) or the caliper (disc brakes).

Steel lines carry the brake fluid to a point on the vehicle's frame near each of the vehicle's wheels. The fluid is then carried to the calipers and wheel cylinders by flexible tubes in order to allow for suspension and steering movements.

In drum brake systems, each wheel cylinder contains two pistons, one at either end, which push outward in opposite directions and force the brake shoe into contact with the drum.

In disc brake systems, the cylinders are part of the calipers. At least one cylinder in each caliper is used to force the brake pads against the disc.

All pistons employ some type of seal, usually made of rubber, to minimize fluid leakage. A rubber dust boot seals the outer end of the cylinder against dust and dirt. The boot fits around the outer end of the piston on disc brake calipers, and around the brake actuating rod on wheel cylinders.

The hydraulic system operates as follows: When at rest, the entire system, from the piston(s) in the master cylinder to those in the wheel cylinders or calipers, is full of brake fluid. Upon application of the brake pedal, fluid trapped in front of the master cylinder piston(s) is forced through the lines to the wheel cylinders. Here, it forces the pistons outward, in the case of drum brakes, and inward toward the disc, in the case of disc brakes. The motion of the pistons is opposed by return springs mounted outside the cylinders in drum brakes, and by spring seals, in disc brakes.

Upon release of the brake pedal, a spring located inside the master cylinder immediately returns the master cylinder pistons to the normal position. The pistons contain check valves and the master cylinder has compensating ports drilled in it. These are uncovered as the pistons reach their normal position. The piston check valves allow fluid to flow toward the wheel cylinders or calipers as the pistons withdraw. Then, as the return springs force the brake pads or shoes into the released position, the excess fluid reservoir through the compensating ports. It is during the time the pedal is in the released position that any fluid that has leaked out of the system will be replaced through the compensating ports.

Dual circuit master cylinders employ two pistons, located one behind the other, in the same cylinder. The primary piston is actuated directly by mechanical linkage from the brake pedal through the power booster. The secondary piston is actuated by fluid trapped between the two pistons. If a leak develops in front of the secondary piston, it moves forward until it bottoms against the front of the master cylinder, and the fluid trapped between the pistons will operate the rear brakes. If the rear brakes develop a leak, the primary piston will move forward until direct contact with the secondary piston takes place, and it will force the secondary piston to actuate the front brakes. In either case, the brake pedal moves farther when the brakes are applied, and less braking power is available.

All dual circuit systems use a switch to warn the driver when only half of the brake system is operational. This switch is usually located in a valve body which is mounted on the firewall or the frame below the master cylinder. A hydraulic piston receives pressure from both circuits, each circuit's pressure being applied to one end of the piston. When the pressures are in balance, the piston remains stationary. When one circuit has a leak, however, the greater pressure in that circuit during application of the brakes will push the piston to one side, closing the switch and activating the brake warning light.

In disc brake systems, this valve body also contains a metering valve and, in some cases, a proportioning valve. The metering valve keeps pressure from traveling to the disc brakes on the front wheels until the brake shoes on the rear wheels have contacted the drums, ensuring that the front brakes will never be used alone. The proportioning valve controls the pressure to the rear brakes to lessen the chance of rear wheel lock-up during very hard braking.

Warning lights may be tested by depressing the brake pedal and holding it while opening one of the wheel cylinder bleeder screws. If this does not cause the light to go on, substitute a new lamp, make continuity checks, and, finally, replace the switch as necessary.

The hydraulic system may be checked for leaks by applying pressure to the pedal gradually and steadily. If the pedal sinks very slowly to the floor, the system has a leak. This is not to be confused with a springy or spongy feel due to the compression of air within the lines. If the system leaks, there will be a gradual change in the position of the pedal with a constant pressure.

Check for leaks along all lines and at wheel cylinders. If no external leaks are apparent, the problem is inside the master cylinder.

### DISC BRAKES

Instead of the traditional expanding brakes that press outward against a circular drum, disc brake systems utilize a disc (rotor) with brake pads positioned on either side of it. An easily-seen analogy is the hand brake arrangement on a bicycle. The pads squeeze onto the rim of the bike wheel, slowing its motion. Automobile disc brakes use the identical principle but apply the braking effort to a separate disc instead of the wheel.

The disc (rotor) is a casting, usually equipped with cooling fins between the two braking surfaces. This enables air to circulate between the braking surfaces making them less sensitive to heat buildup and more resistant to fade. Dirt and water do not drastically affect braking action since contaminants are thrown off by the centrifugal action of the rotor or scraped off the by the pads. Also, the equal clamping action of the two brake pads tends to ensure uniform, straight line stops. Disc brakes are inherently self-adjusting. There are three general types of disc brake:

1. A fixed caliper.
2. A floating caliper.
3. A sliding caliper.

The fixed caliper design uses two pistons mounted on either side of the rotor (in each side of the caliper). The caliper is mounted rigidly and does not move.

The sliding and floating designs are quite similar. In fact, these two types are often lumped together. In both designs, the pad on the inside of the rotor is moved into contact with the rotor by hydraulic force. The caliper, which is not held in a fixed position, moves slightly, bringing the outside pad into contact with the rotor. There are various methods of attaching floating calipers. Some pivot at the bottom or top, and some slide on mounting bolts. In any event, the end result is the same.

### DRUM BRAKES

Drum brakes employ two brake shoes mounted on a stationary backing plate. These shoes are positioned inside a circular drum which rotates with the wheel assembly. The shoes are held in place by springs. This allows them to slide toward the drums (when they are applied) while keeping the linings and drums in alignment. The shoes are actuated by a wheel cylinder which is mounted at the top of the backing plate. When the brakes are applied, hydraulic pressure forces the wheel cylinder's actuating links outward. Since these links bear directly against the top of the brake shoes, the tops of the shoes are then forced against the inner side of the drum. This action forces the bottoms of the two shoes to contact the brake drum by rotating the entire assembly slightly (known as servo action). When pressure within the wheel cylinder is relaxed, return springs pull the shoes back away from the drum.

Most modern drum brakes are designed to self-adjust themselves during application when the vehicle is moving in reverse. This motion causes both shoes to rotate very slightly with the drum, rocking an adjusting lever, thereby causing rotation of the adjusting screw. Some drum brake systems are designed to self-adjust during application whenever the brakes are applied. This on-board adjustment system reduces the need for maintenance adjustments and keeps both the brake function and pedal feel satisfactory.

## Brake Light Switch

### REMOVAL & INSTALLATION

▶ **See Figure 1**

1. Disconnect the negative battery cable.
2. Depress and hold the brake pedal while rotating the brake light switch in a counterclockwise direction, about 30°.
3. Pull the switch rearward, then remove it from its mounting bracket.
4. Detach the electrical connector from the brake light switch, then remove the switch from the vehicle.

**To install:**

➡**Before installing the switch, you must move the plunger into its fully extended position, as described in the following step.**

5. Hold the brake light switch firmly in one hand. Use your other hand to pull outward on the plunger of the switch until it has ratcheted out to its fully extended position.
6. Attach the electrical connector to the brake light switch.
7. Mount the brake light switch into the bracket as follows:
   a. Depress the brake pedal as far down as possible, then install the switch in the bracket by aligning the index key on the switch with the slot at the top of the square hole in the mounting bracket.
   b. When the switch is fully installed in the bracket, rotate the switch clockwise about 30° in order to lock the switch into the bracket.

### ✷✷ WARNING

**Don't use extreme force when you pull on the brake pedal to adjust the switch. If too much force is used, you can damage the brake light switch or striker.**

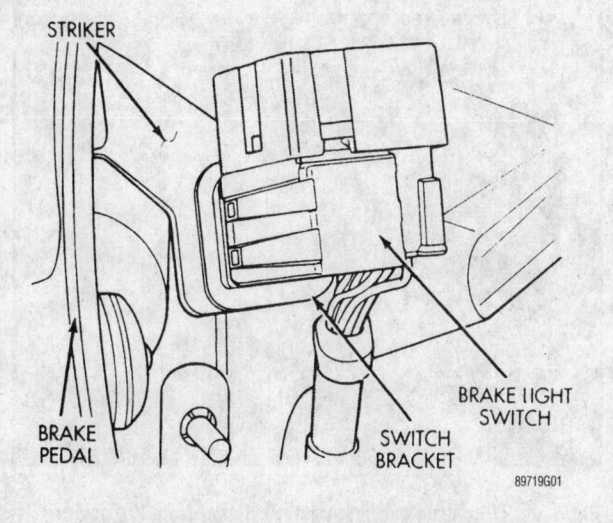

**Fig. 1 The brake light switch is mounted to the brake pedal**

8. Gently pull back on the brake pedal until the pedal stops moving. This causes the switch plunger to ratchet backward to the proper position.
9. Connect the negative battery cable.

## Master Cylinder

### REMOVAL & INSTALLATION

▶ **See Figures 2 thru 12**

### ✷✷ WARNING

**On vehicles equipped with ABS, vacuum in the power booster must be pumped down before removing the master cylinder, in order to prevent thc booster from sucking in any contamination. You can do this by pumping the brake pedal until a firm pedal is attained, with the ignition ON.**

1. Disconnect the negative battery cable.
2. If equipped with ABS, pump the brake pedal about 4–5 times, until a firm pedal is achieved.

**Fig. 2 Using a hand-held vacuum pump siphons the brake fluid out quickly and neatly**

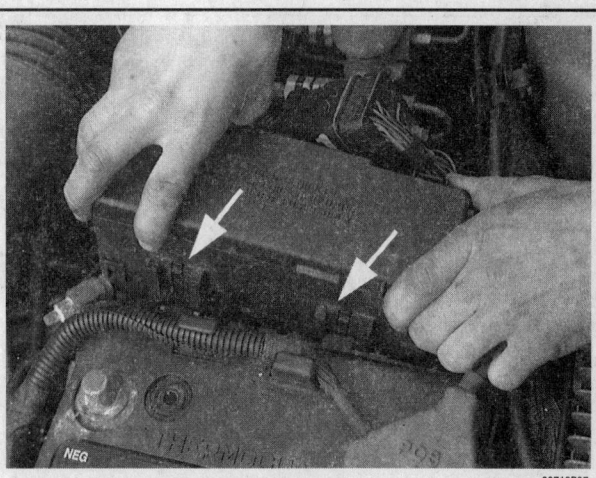

**Fig. 3 On some vehicles you may have to slide the fuse/relay box up and off its retaining clips . . .**

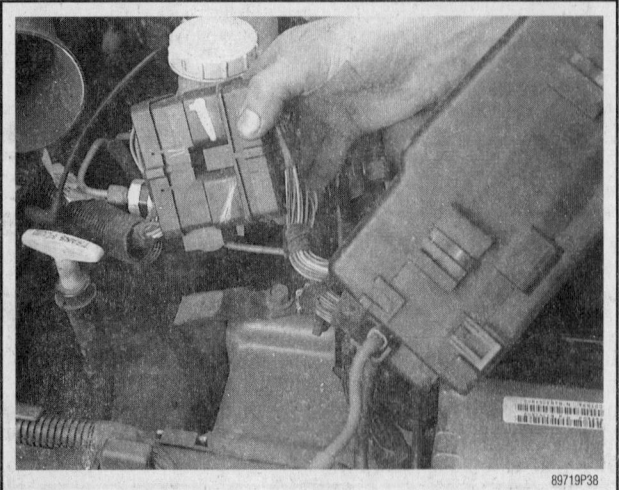

Fig. 4 . . . and reposition the wiring harness and relay box out of the way

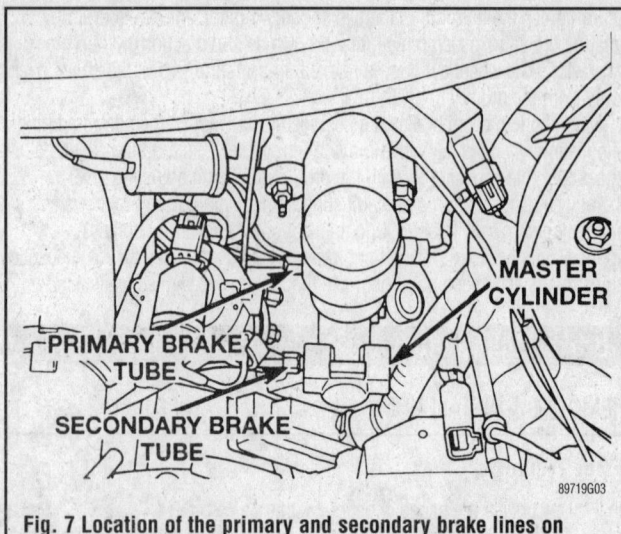

Fig. 7 Location of the primary and secondary brake lines on vehicles equipped with ABS

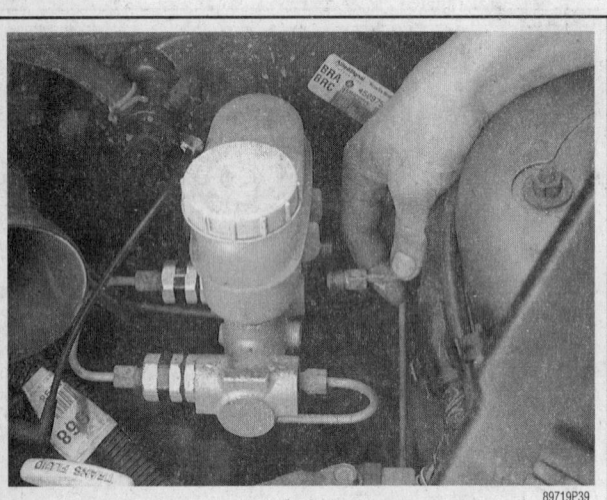

Fig. 5 Disconnect the brake lines from the master cylinder, using back-up wrenches where necessary

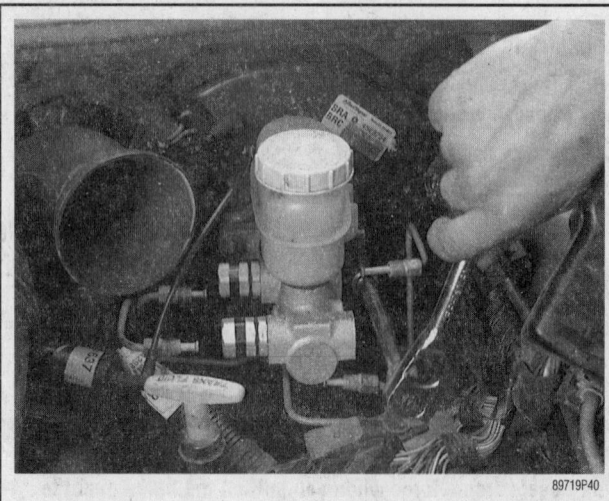

Fig. 8 Unfasten the master cylinder-to-power booster retaining nuts . . .

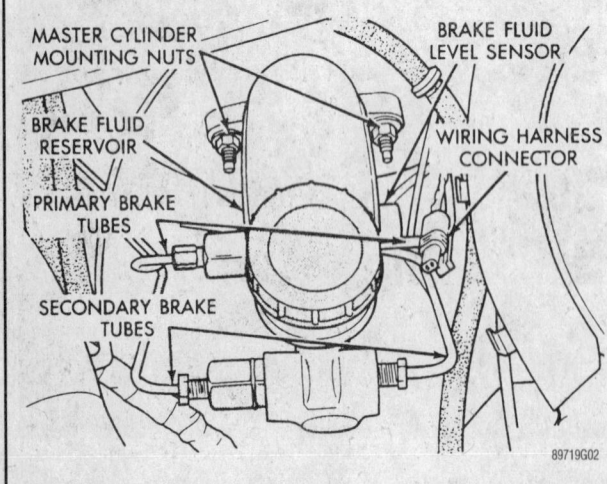

Fig. 6 Primary and secondary brake tube routing—vehicles without ABS

Fig. 9 . . . then remove the master cylinder from the power booster studs

3. Using a vacuum pump or clean turkey baster, remove as much fluid as possible from the master cylinder reservoir.

4. Detach the electrical connector from the brake fluid level sensor in the master cylinder fluid reservoir.

5. Disconnect the primary and secondary brake lines from the master cylinder, then plug all of the brake tube outlets to prevent contamination from entering the brake system.

6. If equipped with ABS, use a suitable cleaner and a rag to clean to area where the master cylinder attaches to the booster.

7. Unfasten the 2 nuts securing the master cylinder housing to the power brake vacuum booster.

### ✳✳ WARNING

**On ABS equipped vehicles, the master cylinder is used to form the seal for holding vacuum in the power brake vacuum booster. The vacuum seal in the front of the booster MUST be replaced whenever the master cylinder is removed from the power brake vacuum booster.**

8. If equipped with ABS, remove the vacuum seal found in the front of the power brake vacuum booster. The vacuum seal is removed by carefully installing a small prytool between the pushrod of the power brake vacuum booster and vacuum seal, then prying the seal from the booster. Do not try the pry the seal from the master cylinder by inserting a tool between the seal and power brake vacuum booster.

**To install:**

### ✳✳ WARNING

**When installing the master cylinder on a vehicle that has ABS, a new vacuum seal must be installed in the power brake vacuum booster. Use only the following procedure to install the seal. Make sure the old seal is removed from the booster before trying to install a new seal.**

9. Lubricate the entire surface of the master cylinder pushrod with Mopar silicone dielectric compound, or equivalent.

10. Install the vacuum seal on the master cylinder pushrod, as shown in the accompanying figure, with the notches on the vacuum seal pointing toward the master cylinder housing. Then slide the seal onto the master pushrod until the seal is seated against the master cylinder housing before installing the master cylinder on the booster.

11. Position the master cylinder on the studs of the power brake unit, aligning the pushrod on the power brake vacuum booster with the master cylinder pushrod.

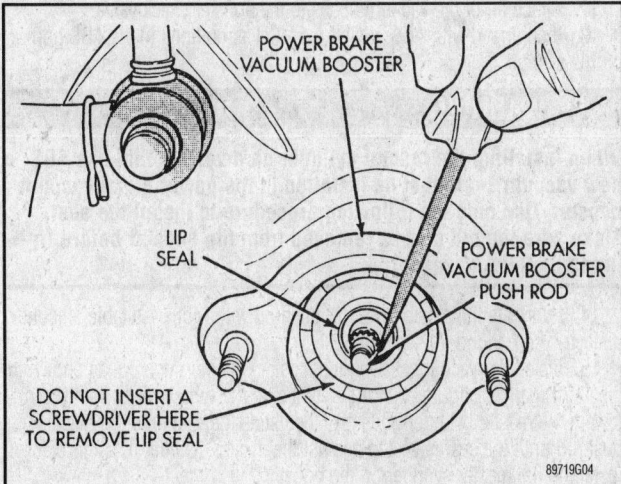

Fig. 10 If equipped with ABS, use a small prytool to carefully remove the seal from the booster

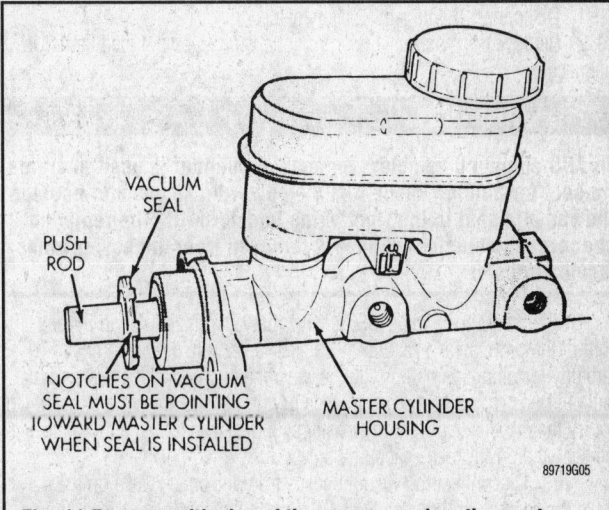

Fig. 11 Proper positioning of the vacuum seal on the master cylinder pushrod

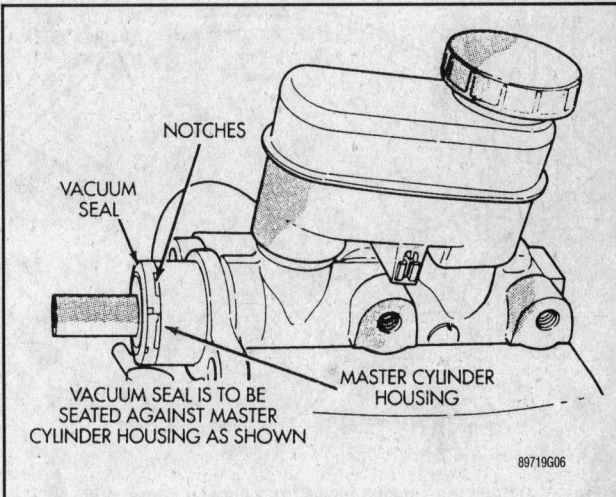

Fig. 12 Correct installed position of the vacuum seal on the master cylinder

12. Install the master cylinder-to-power brake unit mounting nuts and tighten to 21 ft. lbs. (28 Nm).

13. Unplug, then connect the brake lines to the master cylinder primary and secondary ports. Tighten all of the tube nuts to 12 ft. lbs. (17 Nm).

14. Attach the electrical connector to the brake fluid level sensor in the master cylinder fluid reservoir.

15. Connect the negative battery cable.

## Power Brake Booster

### REMOVAL & INSTALLATION

♦ See Figures 13, 14 and 15

### ✳✳ WARNING

**On vehicles equipped with ABS, vacuum in the power booster must be pumped down before removing the master cylinder, in order to prevent the booster from sucking in any contamination. You can do this by pumping the brake pedal until a firm pedal is attained, with the ignition ON.**

1. Disconnect the negative battery cable.
2. Remove the master cylinder from the vehicle, as outlined earlier in this section.

### ✶✶ WARNING

**On ABS equipped vehicles, the master cylinder is used to create the seal for holding vacuum in the power brake vacuum booster. The vacuum seal in the front of the booster MUST be replaced whenever the master cylinder is removed from the power brake vacuum booster.**

3. If equipped with ABS, remove the vacuum seal found in the front of the power brake vacuum booster. The vacuum seal is removed by carefully installing a small prytool between the pushrod of the power brake vacuum booster and vacuum seal, then prying the seal from the booster. Do not try the pry the seal from the master cylinder by inserting a tool between the seal and power brake vacuum booster.
4. Disconnect the vacuum hoses from the check valve on the power brake vacuum booster. Do NOT remove the check valve from the power brake vacuum booster.

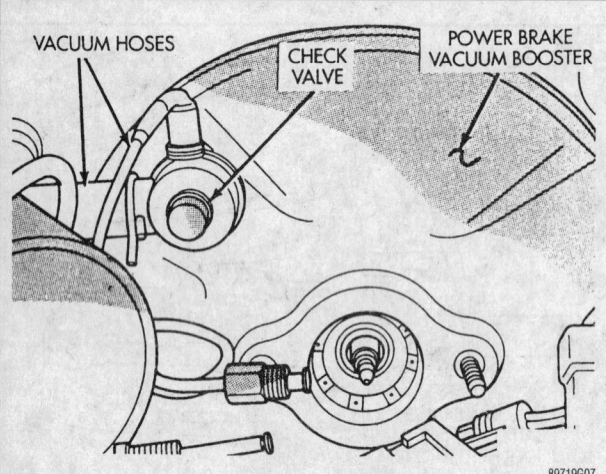

**Fig. 13 Detach the vacuum hoses from booster check valve, but do NOT remove the valve from the booster**

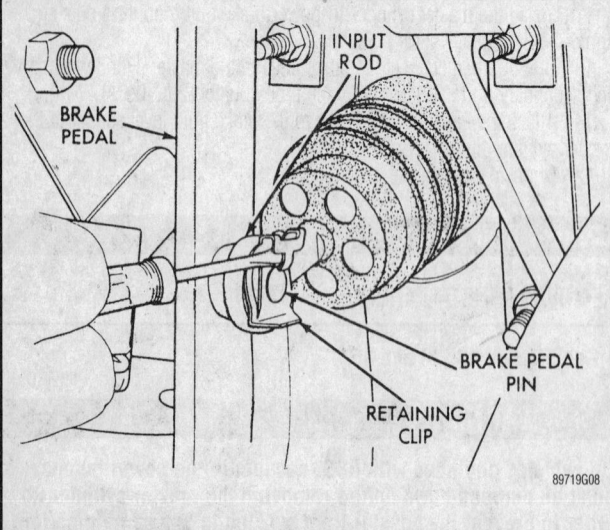

**Fig. 14 Remove the retaining clip with a small prytool**

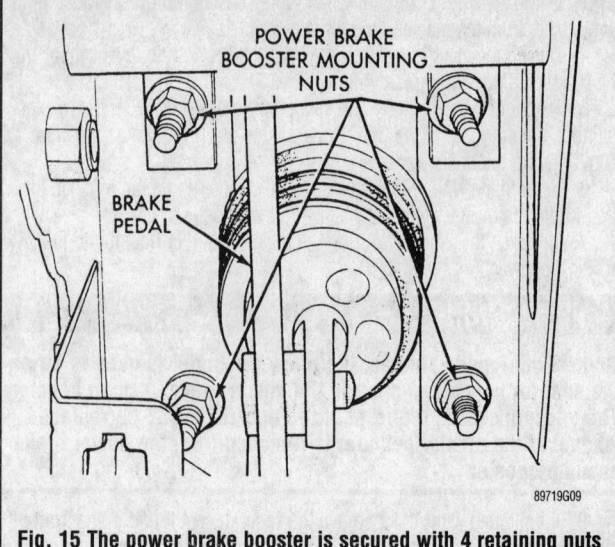

**Fig. 15 The power brake booster is secured with 4 retaining nuts**

5. If the vehicle has ABS, the Hydraulic Control Unit must be removed for access to the power booster. Please refer to the ABS portion of the section for the procedure.
6. Find the power brake vacuum booster input rod-to-brake pedal attachment, located under the instrument panel. Position a small prytool under the center tang of the retaining clip. Rotate the prytool enough to let the retaining clip tank pass over the end of the brake pedal pin. Discard the clip and replace with a new one during installation.
7. Unfasten the 4 nuts securing the power brake vacuum booste r to the dash panel. You can access the nuts from under the instrument panel in the area of the steering column and brake pedal bracket.
8. Slide the power brake vacuum booster forward until the mounting studs clear the dash panel, then tilt the booster up and to the center of the vehicle to remove it from the vehicle.
**To install:**
9. Position the power brake booster onto the dash panel. Install the 2 mounting nuts and tighten to 21 ft. lbs. (29 Nm).
10. Using Lubriplate® or equivalent, coat the surface of the brake pedal pin where it contacts the surface of the vacuum booster input rod.
11. Connect the power brake vacuum booster input rod-to-brake pedal pin, then install a new retaining clip.
12. Attach all of the vacuum hoses to the booster check valve.
13. If equipped with ABS, install the HCU as outlined in the ABS portion of this section.

### ✶✶ WARNING

**When installing the master cylinder on a vehicle that has ABS, a new vacuum seal must be installed in the power brake vacuum booster. Use only the following procedure to install the seal. Make sure the old seal is removed from the booster before trying to install a new seal.**

14. Lubricate the master cylinder pushrod with Mopar suitable silicone dielectric compound, or equivalent.
15. Install the vacuum seal on the master cylinder pushrod, as shown in the accompanying figure, with the notches on the vacuum seal pointing toward the master cylinder housing. Then slide the seal onto the master pushrod until the seal is seated against the master cylinder housing before installing the master cylinder on the booster.
16. Install the master cylinder, as outlined earlier in this section.
17. Connect the negative battery cable.

## Proportioning Valve

REMOVAL & INSTALLATION

### Vehicles Without ABS

▶ See Figures 16, 17, 18 and 19

1. Disconnect the negative battery cable.
2. Using a back-up wrench, unfasten the brake tube from the faulty proportioning valve.
3. Remove the proportioning valve from the master cylinder.

### ✳✳ WARNING

**Never attempt to disassemble a proportioning valve.**

### To install:

4. Lubricate the O-ring seal on the new proportioning valve using clean brake fluid from a fresh, sealed container.
5. Install the proportioning valve in the master cylinder and hand-tighten until the O-ring seal is fully seated in the master cylinder. Tighten the proportioning valve to 30 ft. lbs. (40 Nm).

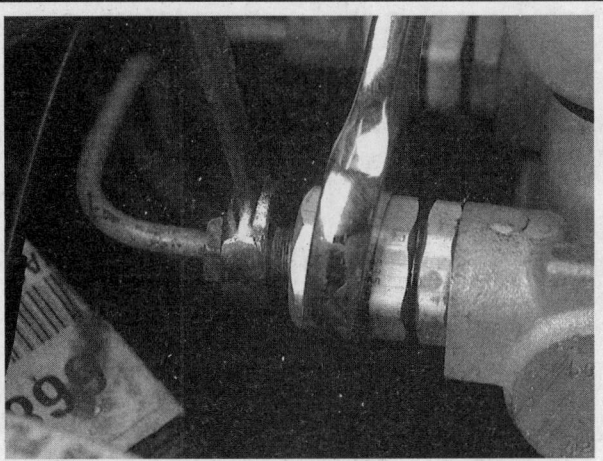

Fig. 16 With a back-up wrench holding the proportioning valve, unfasten the brake line with a flare nut wrench

Fig. 17 Use the proper size wrench to loosen . . .

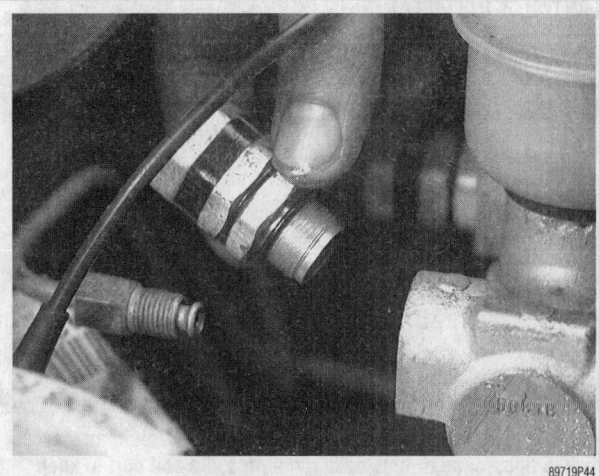

Fig. 18 . . . then remove the proportioning valve from the master cylinder

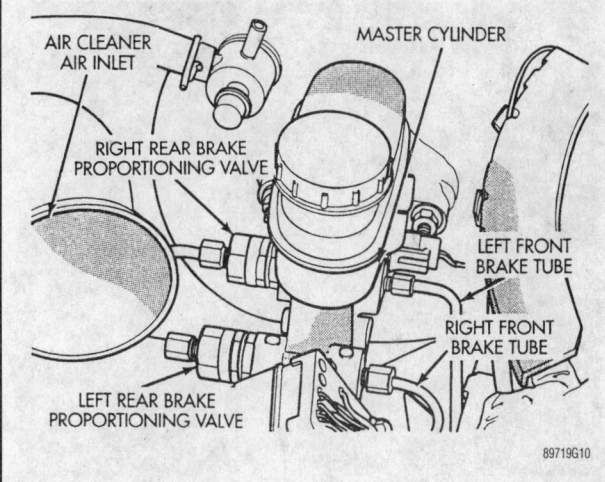

Fig. 19 Location of the 2 proportioning valves on non-ABS vehicles

6. Thread the brake line onto the proportioning valve. Tighten the tube nut to 12.5 ft. lbs. (17 Nm).
7. Connect the negative battery cable.
8. Bleed the brake system, as outlined later in this section.

### Vehicles With ABS

For proportioning valve removal on vehicles with ABS, please refer to the ABS portion of this section.

## Brake Hoses and Pipes

Metal lines and rubber brake hoses should be checked frequently for leaks and external damage. Metal lines are particularly prone to crushing and kinking under the vehicle. Any such deformation can restrict the proper flow of fluid and therefore impair braking at the wheels. Rubber hoses should be checked for cracking or scraping; such damage can create a weak spot in the hose and it could fail under pressure.

Any time the lines are removed or disconnected, extreme cleanliness must be observed. Clean all joints and connections before disassembly (use a stiff bristle brush and clean brake fluid); be sure to plug the lines and ports as soon as they are opened. New lines and hoses should be flushed clean with brake fluid before installation to remove any contamination.

## REMOVAL & INSTALLATION

▶ **See Figures 20 thru 26**

1. Disconnect the negative battery cable.
2. Raise and safely support the vehicle on jackstands.
3. Remove any wheel and tire assemblies necessary for access to the particular line you are removing.
4. Thoroughly clean the surrounding area at the joints to be disconnected.
5. Place a suitable catch pan under the joint to be disconnected.
6. Using two wrenches (one to hold the joint and one to turn the fitting), disconnect the hose or line to be replaced.
7. Disconnect the other end of the line or hose, moving the drain pan if necessary. Always use a back-up wrench to avoid damaging the fitting.
8. Disconnect any retaining clips or brackets holding the line and remove the line from the vehicle.

➡ **If the brake system is to remain open for more time than it takes to swap lines, tape or plug each remaining clip and port to keep contaminants out and fluid in.**

**To install:**

9. Install the new line or hose, starting with the end farthest from the master cylinder. Connect the other end, then confirm that both fittings are

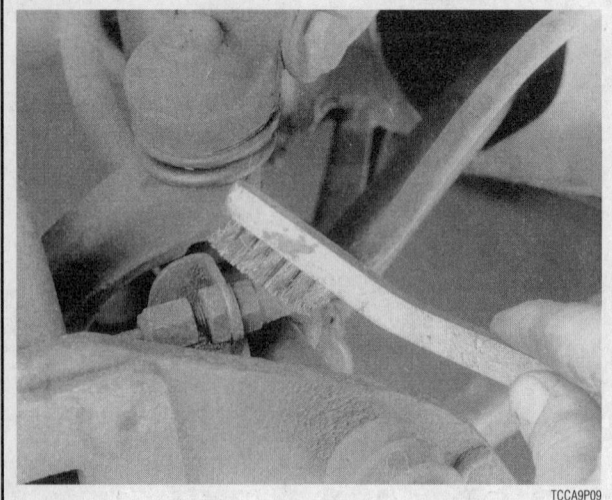

Fig. 20 Use a brush to clean the fittings of any debris

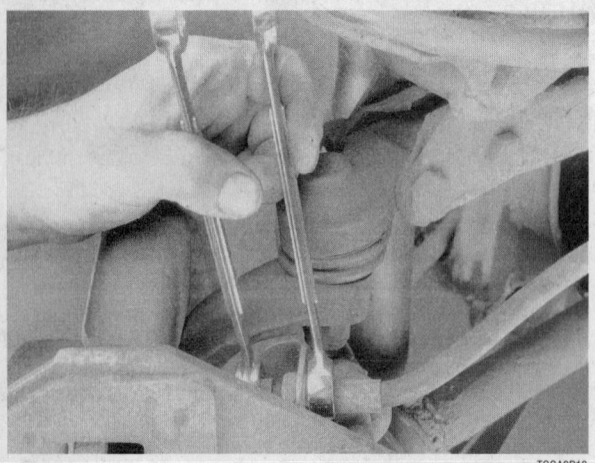

Fig. 21 Use two wrenches to loosen the fitting. If available, use flare nut type wrenches

Fig. 22 Loosen the brake pipe-to-brake hose connection . . .

Fig. 23 . . . then separate the line from the hose

Fig. 24 Disconnect the other end of the brake hose from the caliper

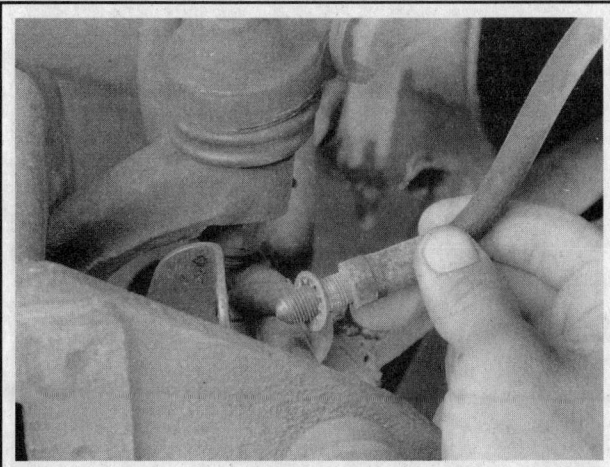

**Fig. 25 Any gaskets/crush washers should be replaced with new ones during installation**

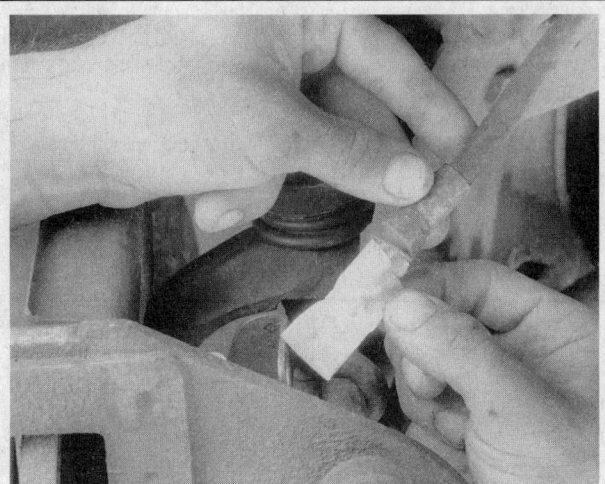

**Fig. 26 Tape or plug the line to prevent contamination**

correctly threaded and turn smoothly using finger pressure. Make sure the new line will not rub against any other part. Brake lines must be at least ½ in. (13mm) from the steering column and other moving parts. Any protective shielding or insulators must be reinstalled in the original location.

## ✳✳ WARNING

**Make sure the hose is NOT kinked or touching any part of the frame or suspension after installation. These conditions may cause the hose to fail prematurely.**

10. Using two wrenches as before, tighten each fitting.
11. Install any retaining clips or brackets on the lines.
12. If removed, install the wheel and tire assemblies, then carefully lower the vehicle to the ground.
13. Refill the brake master cylinder reservoir with clean, fresh brake fluid, meeting DOT 3 specifications. Properly bleed the brake system.
14. Connect the negative battery cable.

## Bleeding the Brake System

➡For vehicles equipped with the Anti-Lock Brake System (ABS), please refer to the bleeding procedure in that section.

The purpose of bleeding the brakes is to expel air trapped in the hydraulic system. The system must be bled whenever the pedal feels spongy, indicating that compressible air has entered the system. It must also be bled whenever the system has been opened or repaired. If you are not using a pressure bleeder, you will need a helper for this job.

## ✳✳ CAUTION

**Never reuse brake fluid which has been bled from the brake system.**

### PRESSURE BLEEDING

When bleeding the brakes, may be trapped in the brake lines or valves far upstream, as much as 10 feet from the bleeder screw. Therefore, it is very important to have a fast flow of a large volume of brake fluid when bleeding the brakes to make sure all of the air is expelled from the system.

The following wheel sequence should be used to be sure all of the air is removed from the system:
- Left rear wheel
- Right front wheel
- Right rear wheel
- Left front wheel

1. You should use bleeder tank tool C-3496-B or equivalent, with the required adapter for the master cylinder reservoir to pressurize the hydraulic system for bleeding. Make sure to follow the manufacturer's directions for using a pressure bleeder.
2. Attach a clear plastic hose to the bleeder screw located at the right rear wheel, then plate the hose into a clean jar that has enough fresh brake fluid to submerge the end of the hose.
3. Open the bleeder screw at least one full turn or more to get a steady stream of fluid.
4. After about 4–8 oz. of fluid has been bled through the brake system and an air-free flow is maintained in the hose and jar, close the bleeder screw.
5. Repeat the procedure at all the other remaining bleeder screws. Then, check the pedal for travel. If pedal travel is excessive or has not improved, enough fluid has not passed through the system to expel all of the trapped air. Be sure to monitor the fluid level in the pressure bleeder. It must stay at the proper level so air will not be allowed to re-enter the brake system through the master cylinder reservoir.
6. Once the bleeding procedure is complete, remove the pressure bleeding equipment from the master cylinder.

### MANUAL BLEEDING

♦ See Figures 27, 28 and 29

➡Proper manual bleeding of the hydraulic brake system will require the air of a helper.

The following wheel sequence should be used to be sure all of the air is removed from the system:
- Left rear wheel
- Right front wheel
- Right rear wheel
- Left front wheel

1. Attach a clear plastic hose to the bleeder screw located at the right rear wheel, then plate the hose into a clean jar that has enough fresh brake fluid to submerge the end of the hose.
2. Have an assistant pump the brake pedal 3–4 times, and hold it down before the bleeder screw is opened.
3. Open the bleeder screw at least one full turn. When the bleeder screw opens, the brake pedal will drop.
4. Close the bleeder screw. Release the brake pedal only AFTER the bleeder screw is closed.
5. Repeat the procedure 4 or 5 times at each bleeder screw. Then check the pedal for travel. If the pedal travel is not excessive, or has not been improved, enough fluid has not passed through the system to expel all of the

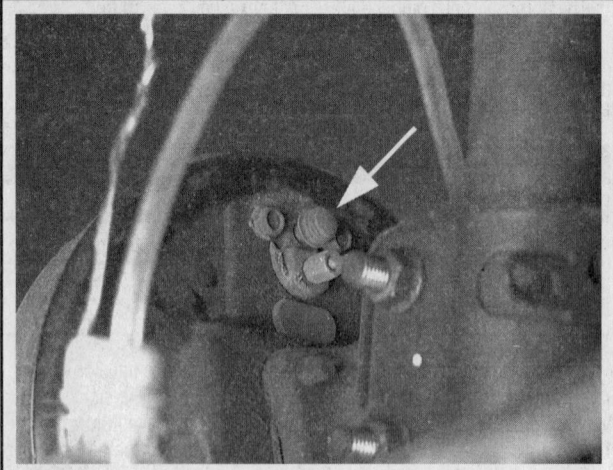

Fig. 27 The bleeder valve has a rubber cap on it that must be removed in order to bleed the brakes

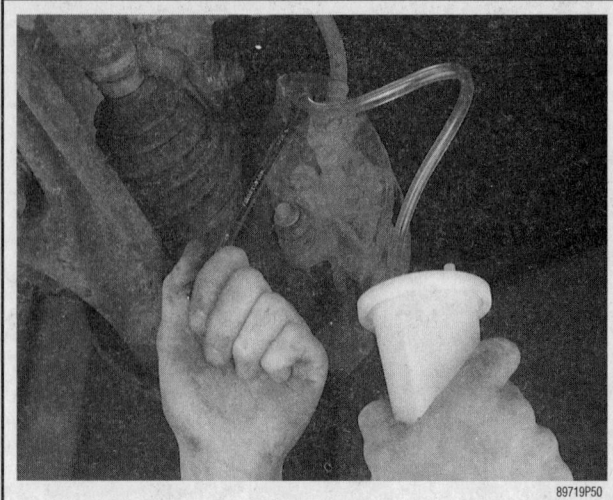

Fig. 29 Bleeding the front disc brake calipers

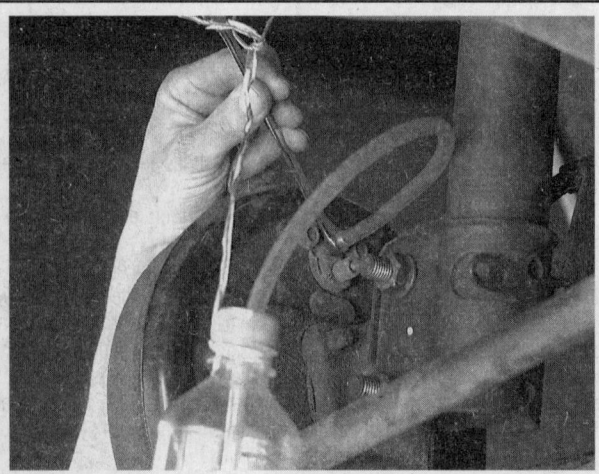

Fig. 28 Attach a hose to the bleeder valve, submerge the other end in clean brake fluid, then open the valve

master cylinder. Position so the outlets of the bleeding tubes will be below the surface of the brake fluid when the reservoir is filled to the proper level.

2. Fill the master cylinder reservoir with DOT 3 brake fluid from a fresh, sealed container.

3. Use a wooden dowel to depress the pushrod slowly, then allow the pistons to return to their released position. You should repeat this several times until all air bubbles are expelled.

4. Remove the bleeding tubes from the master cylinder outlet ports, then plug the ports and install the cap on the master cylinder reservoir.

5. Remove the master cylinder from the vise and install in the vehicle.

trapped air. Make sure to watch the fluid level in the master cylinder reservoir. It must stay at the proper level so air will not reenter the brake system.

6. Test drive the vehicle to be sure the brakes are operating correctly and that the pedal is solid.

## MASTER CYLINDER BLEEDING

▶ See Figure 30

1. Remove the master cylinder from the vehicle and clamp in a soft jawed vise. Attach suitable bleeding tubes (tool 6802 or equivalent) to the

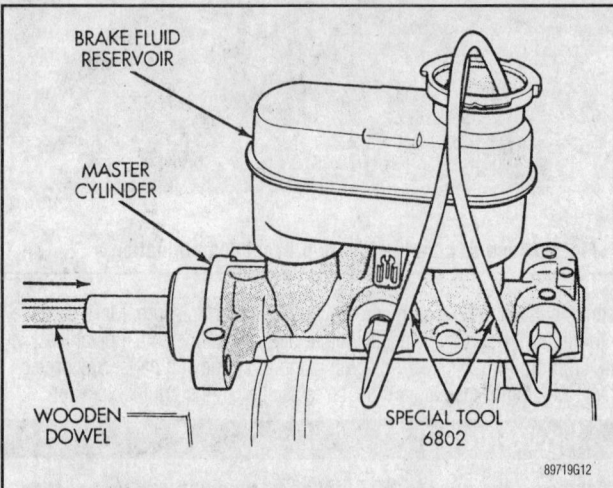

Fig. 30 With the special bleeding tubes attached, depress the pushrod slowly with a wooden dowel

## DISC BRAKES

### ✳✳ CAUTION

Older brake pads or shoes may contain asbestos, which has been determined to be cancer causing agent. Never clean the brake surface with compressed air! Avoid inhaling any dust from any brake surface! When cleaning brake surfaces, use a commercially available brake cleaning fluid.

## Brake Pads

### REMOVAL & INSTALLATION

▶ See Figures 31, 32, 33 and 34

1. Raise and safely support the vehicle.
2. Remove the wheel and tire assembly.

3. Remove the caliper from the vehicle, suspending it from the body with a suitable piece of wire. Do NOT disconnect the brake line, or allow the caliper to hang from the brake hose.

4. Remove the outboard brake shoe by prying the shoe retaining clip over the raised area on the caliper.

5. Pull the inboard brake shoe away from the caliper piston until the retaining clip is out of the cavity in the piston.

**To install:**

6. Apply a suitable multi-purpose lubricant to both steering knuckle abutments.

7. If equipped, remove the protective paper from the noise suppression gasket on the inner and outer brake shoes. Keep in mind that the inner and outer brake shoes are different and are not interchangeable.

8. Install the new inboard brake pad into the caliper piston by firmly pressing it into the piston bore with your thumbs. Make sure the inboard shoe is positioned squarely against the face of the piston.

9. Use the piston compressor tool, a C-clamp or a large pair of pliers to completely retract the caliper piston into the bore.

10. Slide the new outboard brake shoe onto the caliper.

Fig. 31 After unbolting the caliper, use a piece of wire to suspend it from the strut

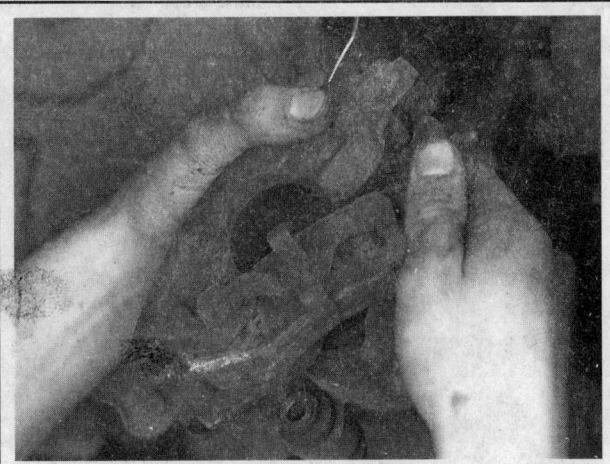

Fig. 32 Pry the outboard shoe retaining clip over the raised area, then remove the shoe from the caliper

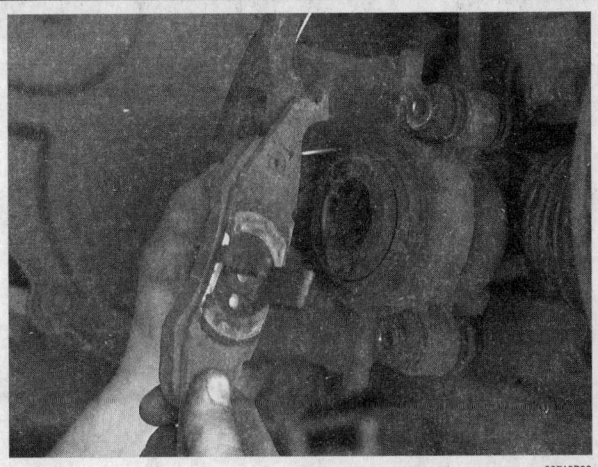

Fig. 33 Pull the inboard pad from the caliper, disengaging the retaining clip from the piston cavity

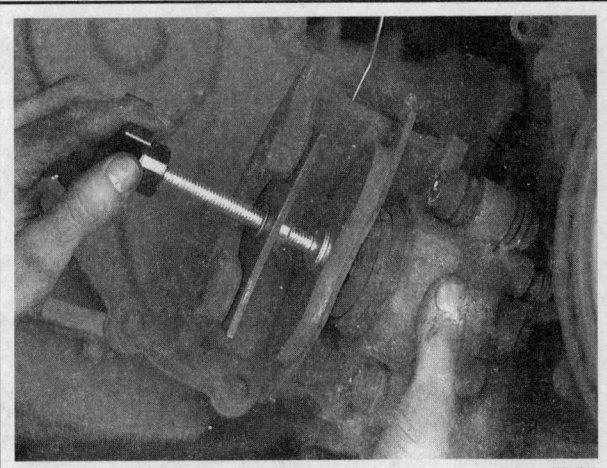

Fig. 34 There are inexpensive tools available to safely and easily retract the caliper piston into the bore

→Be careful when installing the caliper onto the steering knuckle so the seals on the caliper guide pin bushings do not get damaged by the steering knuckle bosses.

11. Install the caliper, then install the wheel and tire assembly.
12. Carefully lower the vehicle.

## INSPECTION

1. If you can't accurately determine the condition of the brake pads by visual inspection, you must remove the caliper, then remove the brake pads.

2. You should measure the combined brake shoe and lining material thickness at the thinnest portion of the assembly.

3. When a set of brake pads are worn to a total thickness of 5/16 in. (7.95mm) for front brakes, or 9/32 in. (7.0mm) for rear brakes, they should be replaced.

4. Replace both brake shoe assemblies (inboard and outboard). It is necessary that both front wheel sets be replaced whenever the brake shoe assemblies on either side are replaced.

5. If the brake shoes do not require replacement, reinstall the assemblies making sure each brake shoe is returned to the original position.

## Brake Caliper

### REMOVAL & INSTALLATION

▸ **See Figures 35 thru 44**

1. Raise and safely support the vehicle.
2. Remove the wheel and tire assembly.
3. If you are removing the caliper for replacement or overhaul, disconnect the fluid line from the back of the caliper.
4. Unfasten the 2 brake caliper-to-steering knuckle guide pin bolts.
5. Remove the caliper from the steering knuckle by firmly rotating the bottom end of the caliper away from the steering knuckle. Then, slide the opposite end of the caliper out from under the machined abutment on the steering knuckle.
6. If you are not removing the caliper for replacement or overhaul, suspend the assembly with a suitable piece of wire from the strut. Do not allow the caliper to hang by the brake line!

**To install:**

7. If you have installed brake pads in the caliper, perform the following:
   a. Use a C-clamp or a pair of large pliers to retract the caliper piston back into the bore of the caliper.
8. Apply a suitable multi-purpose lubricant to both steering knuckle abutments.

### ✳✳ WARNING

**Be careful when installing the caliper onto the steering knuckle so the seals on the caliper guide pin bushings do not get damaged by the steering knuckle bosses.**

9. Carefully position the caliper assembly on the steering knuckle by first hooking the end of the caliper under the edge of the steering knuckle. Then, rotate the caliper into position on the steering knuckle.
10. Install the caliper guide pin bolts. Tighten the bolts to 12–15 ft. lbs.(18–20 Nm) for front calipers or to 16 ft. lbs. (22 Nm). Be very careful not to cross thread the caliper guide pin bolts.
11. If necessary, connect the brake line to the rear of the caliper and tighten the fitting to 35 ft. lbs. (48 Nm).
12. If the brake line was disconnected, bleed the brake system.
13. Install the wheel and tire assembly, then carefully lower the vehicle.

### ✳✳ CAUTION

**Before moving the vehicle, pump the brake pedal a few times to be sure the vehicle has a firm brake pedal.**

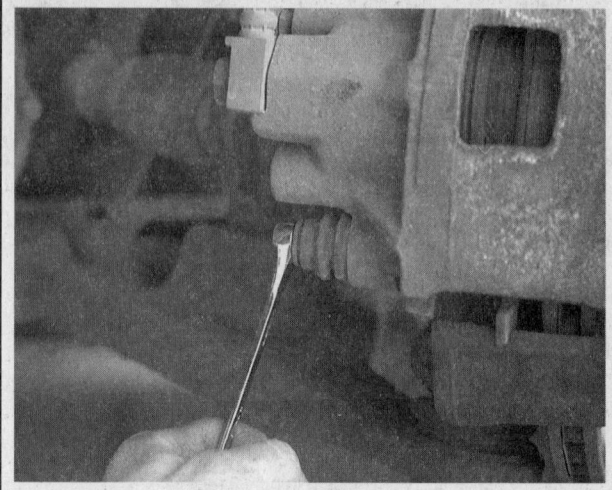

Fig. 36 Loosen the caliper mounting bolts . . .

Fig. 37 . . . then pull the caliper mounting bolt from the bore

Fig. 35 The disc brake caliper is secured to the rotor with two mounting bolts (1) and has a brake fluid line (2) attached to the rear of it

Fig. 38 Rotate the bottom of the caliper away from the knuckle

Fig. 39 . . . then slide the upper end of the caliper out from under the abutment and remove it from the vehicle

Fig. 42 Use a wire brush to clean off the steering knuckle abutments . . .

Fig. 40 If necessary, you can remove the caliper sleeves

Fig. 43 . . . then apply a layer of silicone lubricant to the abutments

Fig. 41 You should lubricate the caliper sleeves before installing them

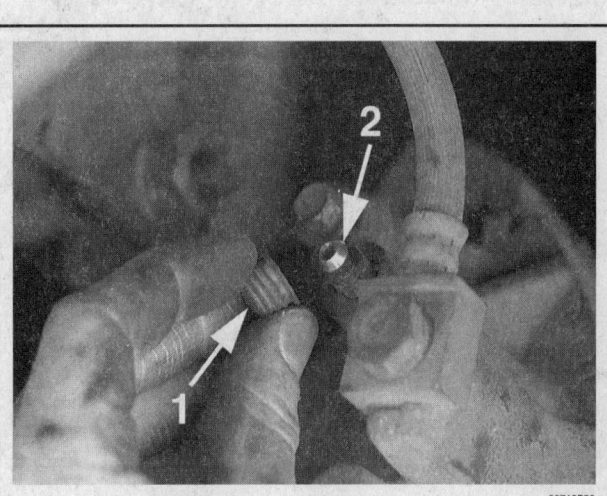

Fig. 44 Remove the rubber cap, (1) exposing the bleeder valve (2)

14. Take the vehicle for a test drive, making several stops to wear off any foreign material on the brakes and also, to properly seat the brake pads.

## OVERHAUL

♦ **See Figures 45 thru 52**

➡ **Some vehicles may be equipped dual piston calipers. The procedure to overhaul the caliper is essentially the same with the exception of multiple pistons, O-rings and dust boots.**

1. Remove the caliper from the vehicle and place on a clean workbench.

### ❈❈ CAUTION

**NEVER place your fingers in front of the pistons in an attempt to catch or protect the pistons when applying compressed air. This could result in personal injury!**

➡ **Depending upon the vehicle, there are two different ways to remove the piston from the caliper. Refer to the brake pad replacement procedure to make sure you have the correct procedure for your vehicle.**

2. The first method is as follows:
   a. Stuff a shop towel or a block of wood into the caliper to catch the piston.
   b. Remove the caliper piston using compressed air applied into the caliper inlet hole. Inspect the piston for scoring, nicks, corrosion and/or worn or damaged chrome plating. The piston must be replaced if any of these conditions are found.
3. For the second method, you must rotate the piston to retract it from the caliper.
4. If equipped, remove the anti-rattle clip.
5. Use a prytool to remove the caliper boot, being careful not to scratch the housing bore.
6. Remove the piston seals from the groove in the caliper bore.
7. Carefully loosen the brake bleeder valve cap and valve from the caliper housing.
8. Inspect the caliper bores, pistons and mounting threads for scoring or excessive wear.
9. Use crocus cloth to polish out light corrosion from the piston and bore.
10. Clean all parts with denatured alcohol and dry with compressed air.
**To assemble:**
11. Lubricate and install the bleeder valve and cap.
12. Install the new seals into the caliper bore grooves, making sure they are not twisted.

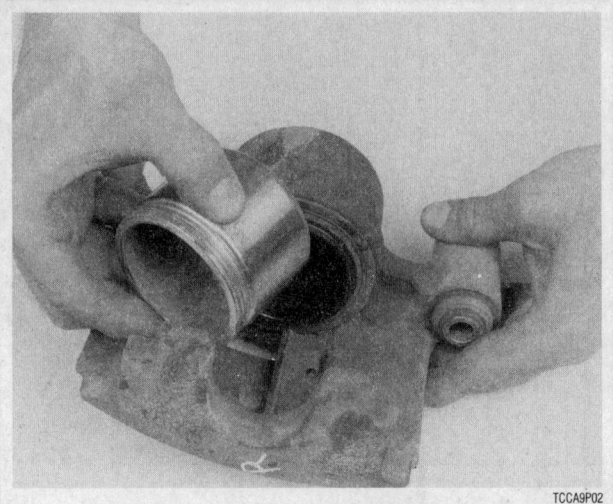

Fig. 46 Withdraw the piston from the caliper bore

Fig. 47 On some vehicles, you must remove the anti-rattle clip

Fig. 45 For some types of calipers, use compressed air to drive the piston out of the caliper, but make sure to keep your fingers clear

Fig. 48 Use a prytool to carefully pry around the edge of the boot . . .

Fig. 49 . . . then remove the boot from the caliper housing, taking care not to score or damage the bore

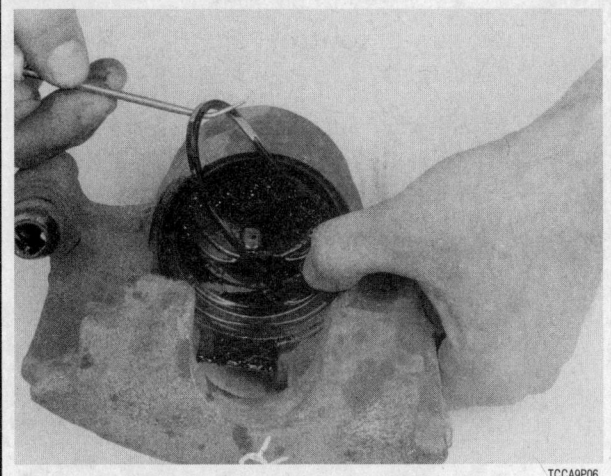

Fig. 50 Use extreme caution when removing the piston seal; DO NOT scratch the caliper bore

Fig. 51 Use the proper size driving tool and a mallet to properly seal the boots in the caliper housing

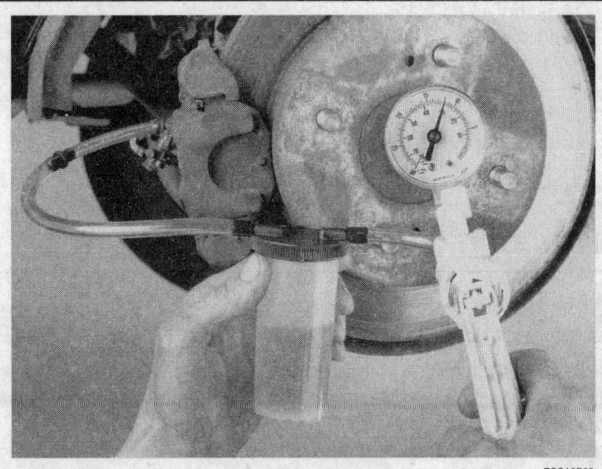

Fig. 52 There are tools, such as this Mighty-Vac, available to assist in proper brake system bleeding

13. Lubricate the piston bore.
14. Install the pistons and boots into the bores of the calipers and push to the bottom of the bores.
15. Use a suitable driving tool to seat the boots in the housing.
16. Install the caliper in the vehicle.
17. Install the wheel and tire assembly, then carefully lower the vehicle.
18. Properly bleed the brake system.

## Brake Disc (Rotor)

REMOVAL & INSTALLATION

▶ **See Figure 53**

1. Raise and safely support the vehicle.
2. Remove the wheel and tire assembly.
3. Remove the caliper from the vehicle, suspending it from the body with a suitable piece of wire. Do NOT disconnect the brake line, or allow the caliper to hang from the brake hose.
4. Remove the brake rotor from the hub by pulling it straight off the wheel lug studs.

Fig. 53 After removing the caliper, pull the rotor straight off the lug studs

**To install:**

5. Install the rotor on the hub, making sure it is squarely seated on the face of the hub.

6. Raise and safely support the vehicle.

7. Remove the wheel and tire assembly.

8. Remove the caliper from the vehicle, suspending it from the body with a suitable piece of wire. Do NOT disconnect the brake line, or allow the caliper to hang from the brake hose.

## INSPECTION

▶ **See Figures 54, 55, 56 and 57**

Whenever the brake calipers are removed, the brake pads are replaced, or any front axle work is performed to the vehicle, inspect the rotors for defects. The brake rotor is an extremely important component of the brake system. Cracks, large scratches or warpage can adversely affect the braking system, and at times, to the point of becoming very dangerous.

Light scoring is acceptable. Heavy scoring or warping will necessitate refinishing or replacement of the disc. The brake disc must be replaced if cracks or burned marks are evident.

Check the thickness of the disc. Measure the thickness at 12 equally spaced points 1 in. (25mm) from the edge of the disc. If thickness varies more than 0.0005 in. (0.013mm) the disc should be refinished, provided equal amounts are out from each side and the thickness does not fall below 0.882 inch (22.4mm) on Chrysler front wheel drive vehicles.

Check the run-out (warpage) of the disc. Total run-out of the disc installed on the car should not exceed 0.005 in. (0.013mm). The disc can be resurfaced to correct minor variations; as long as equal amounts are cut from each side and the thickness is at least 0.882 inch (22.4mm) on Chrysler front wheel drive vehicles after resurfacing.

Check the run-out of the hub (disc removed). It should not be more than 0.002–0.003 inch (0.050–0.076mm) on Chrysler front wheel drive vehicles If so, the hub should be replaced.

All brake discs or rotors have markings for MINIMUM allowable thickness cast on an unmachined surface or an alternate surface. Always use this specification as the minimum allowable thickness or refinishing limit. Refer to a local auto parts store or machine shop, if necessary, shop where brake disc or rotors are resurfaced.

If the brake disc or rotor needs to be replaced with a new part, the protective coating on the braking surface of the rotor must be removed with an appropriate solvent before installing the rotor to the vehicle.

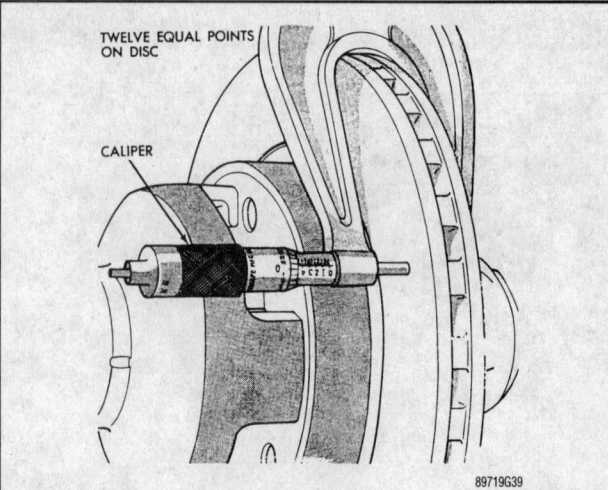

Fig. 55 Use a micrometer to measure the thickness of the rotor at 12 points

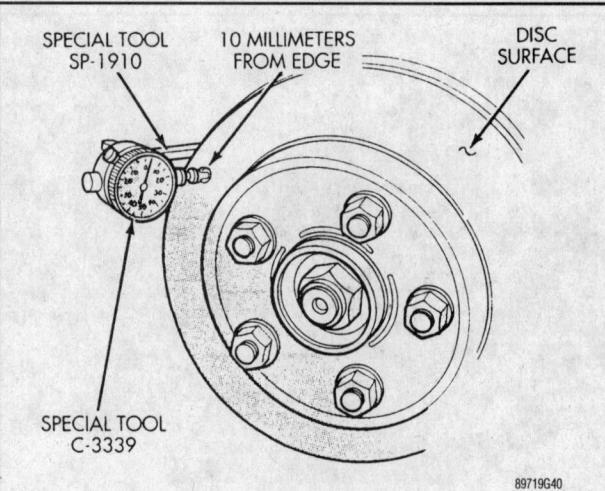

Fig. 56 Use Special Tool C-3339 or its equivalent to measure the run-out (warpage/wobble) of the front disc brake rotors

Fig. 54 Your rotor should have minimum thickness specification stamped on it

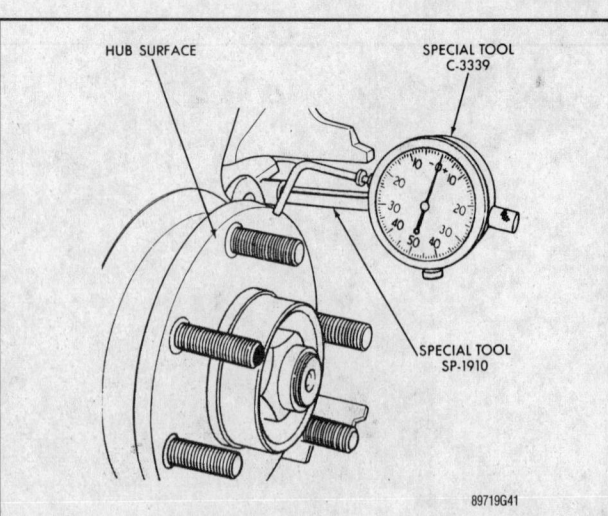

Fig. 57 After checking the rotor for run-out, measure the axle hub in the same manner

**DRUM BRAKES**

REAR DRUM BRAKE COMPONENTS—INSTALLED VIEW

1. Wheel cylinder
2. Return spring
3. Front brake shoe
4. Automatic adjuster lever
5. Hold-down pin
6. Hold-down clip
7. Automatic adjuster screw
8. Automatic adjuster spring
9. Parking brake cable
10. Brake shoe-to-anchor spring
11. Brake anchor plate
12. Rear brake shoe
13. Parking brake lever
14. Parking brake lever pin-to-shoe clip

89719P57

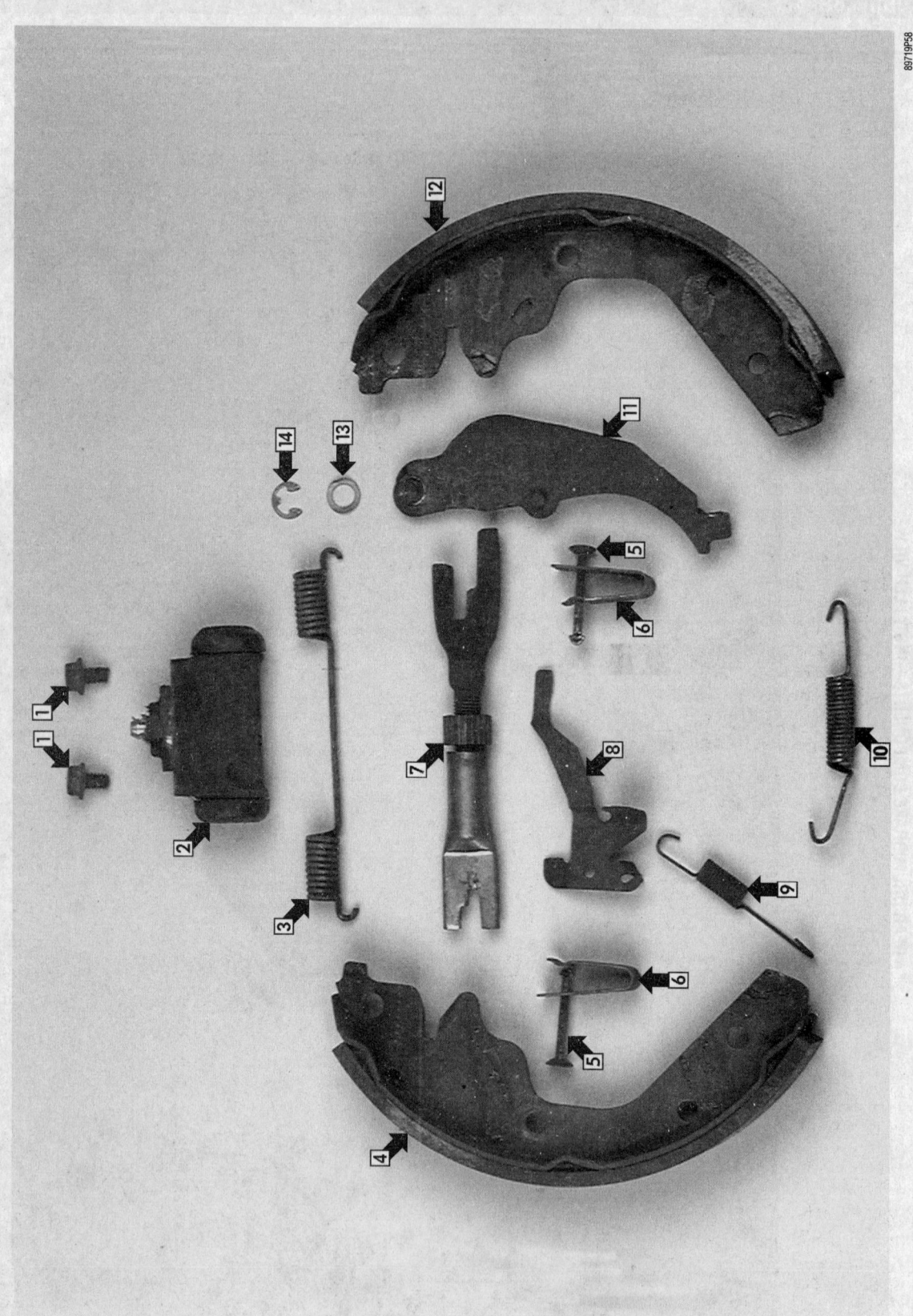

**REAR DRUM BRAKE COMPONENTS—EXPLODED VIEW**

1. Wheel cylinder retaining bolts
2. Wheel cylinder
3. Return spring
4. Front brake shoe
5. Hold-down pin
6. hold-down clip
7. Automatic adjuster screw assembly
8. Automatic adjuster lever
9. Automatic adjuster spring
10. Brake shoe-to-anchor spring
11. Parking brake lever
12. Rear brake shoe
13. Washer
14. Parking brake lever pin-to-shoe clip

89719P58

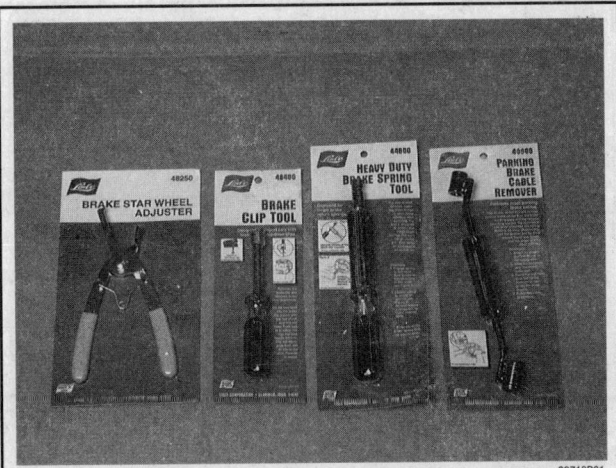

Fig. 58 These are just a few of the special tools that can make servicing your drum brakes a lot easier

### ✳ CAUTION

Older brake pads or shoes may contain asbestos, which has been determined to be cancer causing agent. Never clean the brake surface with compressed air! Avoid inhaling any dust from any brake surface! When cleaning brake surfaces, use a commercially available brake cleaning fluid.

### Brake Drums

#### REMOVAL & INSTALLATION

▶ See Figure 59

1. Raise and safely support the vehicle.
2. Remove the wheel and tire assembly.
3. If equipped, remove the brake drum-to-hub and bearing assembly retaining clips.
4. Remove the brake drum by pulling it straight off the hub and bearing studs.

**To install:**

5. Install the brake drum by positioning it over the hub and bearing assembly studs.
6. If equipped, install the drum retaining clips.
7. Install the wheel and tire assembly, then carefully lower the vehicle.

#### INSPECTION

▶ See Figure 60

Whenever the rear brake drums are removed from the rear hubs, they should be inspected for damage or irregularities. Periodic inspection can help prevent dangerous conditions from developing to the point of personal injury, and can help maintain the quality of the vehicle's driving characteristics.

Measure drum run-out and diameter. If the drum is not to specifications, have the drum resurfaced. Runout should not exceed 0.006 in. (0.1524mm). The diameter variation (oval shape) of the drum braking surface must not exceed either 0.0025 in. (0.0635mm) in 30° or 0.0035 in. (0.0889mm) in 360. All brake drums will show markings of the maximum allowable diameter. All brake drums have markings for MINIMUM allowable thickness. Always use this specification as the minimum allowable thickness or refinishing limit. Refer to a local auto parts store or machine shop if necessary shop where brake drums are resurfaced.

Once the drum is removed from the axle shaft, clean the shoes and springs with a damp rag to remove the accumulated brake dust.

### ✳ CAUTION

Do not use compressed air to blow brake dust off the linings or other brake system parts. Brake dust may contain asbestos, a known cancer causing agent.

Grease on the shoes can be removed with alcohol or fine sandpaper. After cleaning, examine the brake shoes for glazed, oily, loose, cracked or improperly (unevenly) worn linings. Light glazing is common and can be removed with fine sandpaper. Linings that are worn improperly or below specification (refer to the specification chart) should be replaced. A good "eyeball" test is to replace the linings when the thickness is the same as or less than the thickness of the metal backing plate (shoe).

Wheel cylinders are a vital part of the brake system and should be inspected carefully. Gently pull back the rubber boots; if any fluid is visible, it's time to replace the wheel cylinders. Boots that are distorted, cracked or otherwise damaged, also point to the need for service. Check the flexible brake lines for cracks, chafing or wear.

Fig. 59 Pull the brake drum straight off the wheel lug studs

Fig. 60 The brake drum should have a maximum diameter specification stamped into it

Check the brake shoe retracting and hold-down springs; they should not be worn or distorted. Be sure that the adjuster mechanism moves freely. The points on the backing plate where the shoes slide should be shiny and free of rust. Rust in these areas suggests that the brake shoes are not moving properly.

## Brake Shoes

### INSPECTION

The rear brake shoe linings should show contact across the entire width of the lining, and also from the heel to the toe of the lining. It not, the brake shoes should be replaced. You should always replace the brake shoes in axle sets.

Brake shoes that don't contact at the toe or heel might be improperly grounded.

Clean and inspect the brake support plate and adjusting screws. Apply a thin coat of multi-purpose lubricant to the threads of the self adjuster. If it becomes corroded, you should replace the adjusting screw.

### REMOVAL & INSTALLATION

▶ **See Figures 61 thru 79**

1. Raise and safely support the vehicle. Remove the wheel and tire assembly.
2. If equipped, remove the brake drum-to-hub and bearing assembly retaining clips, then remove the brake drum.
3. Remove the adjustment lever-to-leading brake shoe spring.
4. Remove the automatic adjustment lever from the brake shoe.
5. Remove the hold-down clips and pins attaching the leading and trailing brake shoes to the brake support plate.
6. Remove the lower brake shoe-to-anchor plate return spring.
7. Remove the parking brake lever pin-to-rear brake shoe retaining clip.
8. If possible with the hub and bearing in place, remove the leading and trailing brake shoes, upper return spring, and automatic adjuster screw from the brake support (backing) plate as an assembly.
9. If its not possible to remove the brake shoes, spring and adjuster screw as an assembly because the hub is in the way, perform the following:
   a. Pull the leading brake shoe away from the backing plate, unhook the return spring, then remove the shoe from the vehicle.
   b. Unhook the return spring from the trailing shoe, disengage the shoe from the parking brake lever, then remove the shoe from the vehicle.

Fig. 62 Remove the automatic adjustment lever from the brake shoe

Fig. 63 There is a special tool that fits into the grooves of the hold-down clips and pins

Fig. 61 Use a pair of needle-nose pliers to unhook the adjustment lever-to-leading brake shoe spring

Fig. 64 You can use this tool to loosen . . .

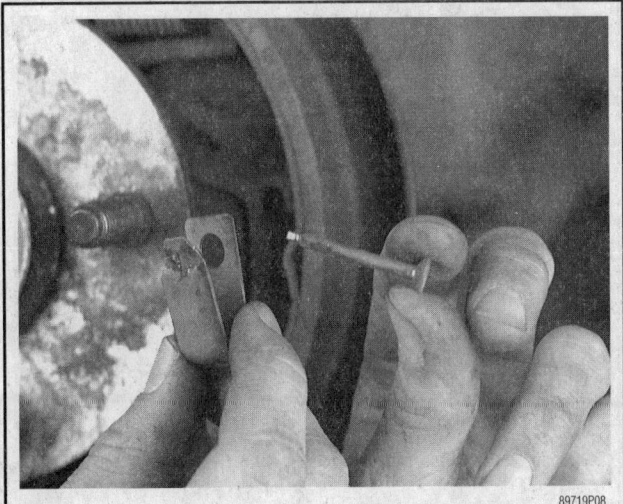

89719P08

Fig. 65 . . . then remove the hold-down clips and pins

89719P14

Fig. 68 Use needle-nose pliers to unhook the lower brake shoe-to-anchor plate return spring . . .

89719P10

Fig. 66 If you don't have the brake tool, a pair of needle nose pliers work just as well to grasp the clip . . .

89719P15

Fig. 69 . . . then remove the spring from the shoes

89719P13

Fig. 67 . . . then turn the clip to free it and pull the pin out of the back of the backing plate

89719P16

Fig. 70 Remove the parking brake lever pin-to-shoe retaining clip

Fig. 71 Pull the leading brake shoe from the backing plate . . .

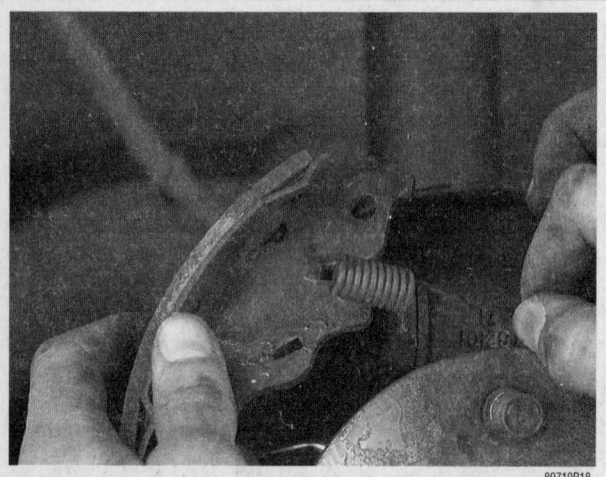

Fig. 72 . . . then unhook the return spring from the shoe and remove the shoe from the vehicle

Fig. 73 Unhook the return spring from the trailing shoe

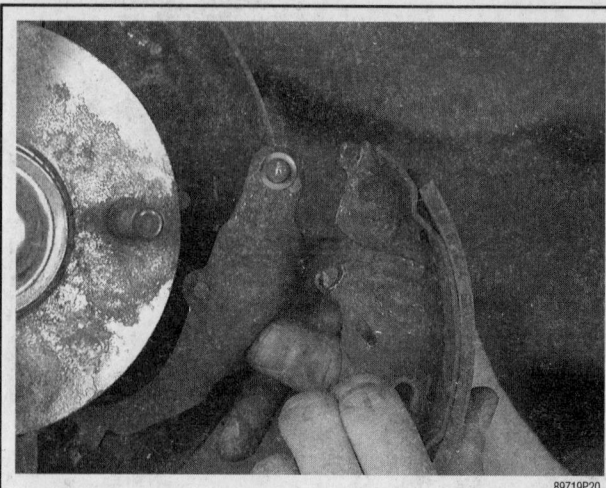

Fig. 74 Disengage the trailing shoe from the parking brake lever and remove the shoe from the vehicle

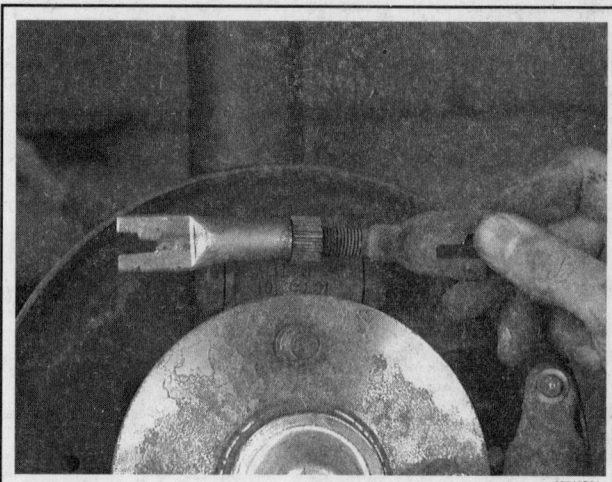

Fig. 75 Now you can remove the automatic adjusting screw from the backing plate

Fig. 76 Hold the parking brake cable with needle-nose pliers, then disengage the parking brake lever from the cable

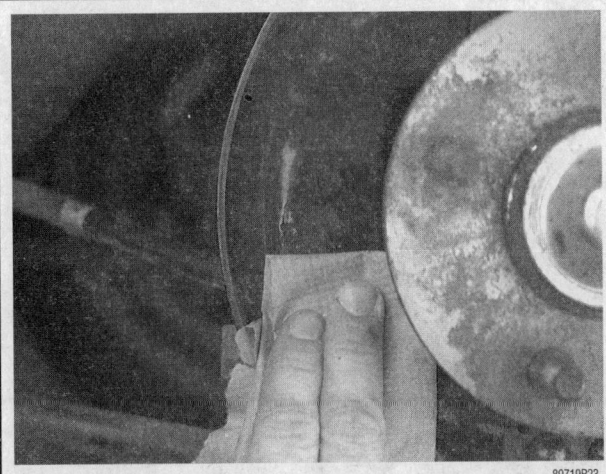

**Fig. 77 Use a rag to clean off the brake support plate contact areas . . .**

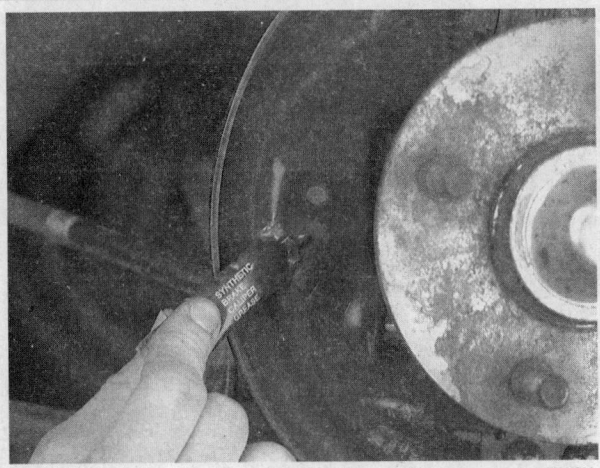

**Fig. 78 . . . then apply a small amount of multi-purpose lubricant to the 8 contact areas**

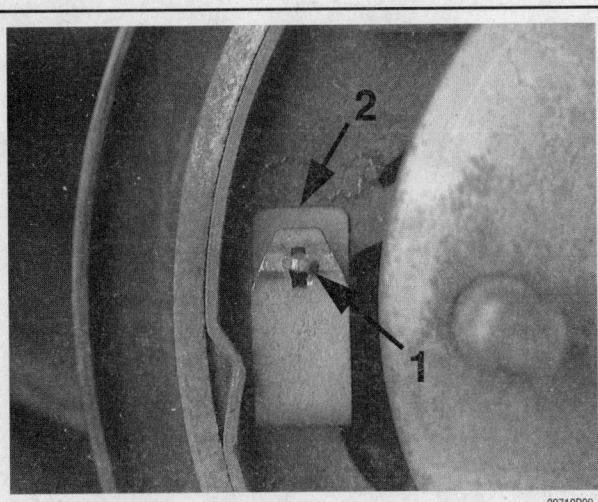

**Fig. 79 Installed view of the hold-down pin (1) and clip (2)**

c. Remove the automatic adjusting screw from the backing plate.

d. If necessary, grasp the sparking brake cable, then detach the parking brake lever from the cable.

**To install:**

10. Lubricate the eight shoe contact areas on the support plate and anchor using a suitable multi-purpose lubricant.

11. Before installation on the brake plate, assemble the front and rear brake shoe assembly, automatic adjuster screw and upper return spring.

12. Install the pre-assembled brake shoe assembly on the brake support plate.

13. Install the wave washer on the pin of the parking brake lever.

14. Install the pin on the parking brake lever into the hole in the rear brake shoe assembly.

15. Install both brake shoes to the brake support plate, then install the hold-down pins and clips.

16. Install the lower brake shoe-to-anchor plate return spring.

17. Install the automatic adjustment lever, on the front brake shoe of the rear brake assembly.

18. Install the automatic adjustment lever to the front brake shoe assembly spring.

19. Adjust the brake shoe assemblies so they don't interfere with the brake drum installation.

20. Install the brake drum on the hub. If equipped, install the retaining clips.

21. Adjust the rear brake shoes, as outlined later in this section.

22. Install the wheel and tire assembly, then carefully lower the vehicle.

## ADJUSTMENTS

▶ See Figures 80 and 81

➡ **Usually, self-adjusting drum brakes do not necessitate manual adjustment. However, in the event of a brake reline, you should make the initial adjustment to speed up the adjustment period.**

1. Make sure the parking brake is fully released.

2. Raise and safely support the vehicle so that all wheels are free to turn.

3. Remove the rear brake adjusting hole rubber plug from the rear of the brake shoe support plate.

4. Insert a suitable brake adjusting tool through the adjusting hole in the support plate and against the star wheel of the adjusting screw. Move the handle of the tool downward until a slight drag is felt when the tire is rotated.

5. Insert a thin screwdriver or equivalent into the adjusting hole. Push the adjusting lever out of engagement with the star wheel. Be very careful

**Fig. 80 Remove the rubber plug (1) from the rear brake adjusting hole (2) in the back of the support plate**

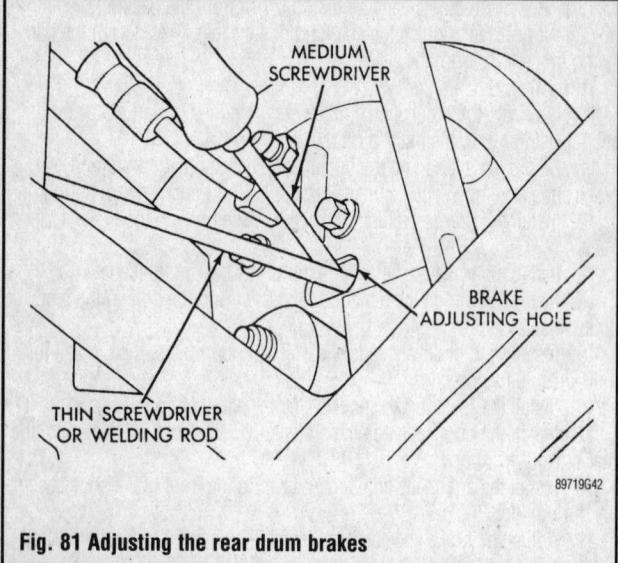

Fig. 81 Adjusting the rear drum brakes

not to bend the adjusting lever or contort the lever spring. While holding the adjusting lever out of engagement with the star wheel, back off the star wheel to guarantee a free wheel with no drag.

6. Repeat the adjustment procedure at the other rear wheel. After the procedure is complete, install the adjusting hole rubber plugs in the rear brake support plates.

7. After adjustment, apply and release the parking brake lever one time.

8. Carefully lower the vehicle.

## Wheel Cylinders

### REMOVAL & INSTALLATION

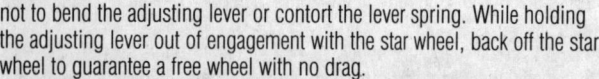

▸ **See Figures 82, 83, 84 and 85**

1. Raise and safely support the vehicle. Remove the wheel and tire assembly.

2. If equipped, remove the brake drum-to-hub and bearing assembly retaining clips, then remove the brake drum.

3. Remove the brake shoes, as outlined earlier in this section. If the brake shoes are wet with grease or brake fluid, due to a leaky wheel cylinder, they must be replaced.

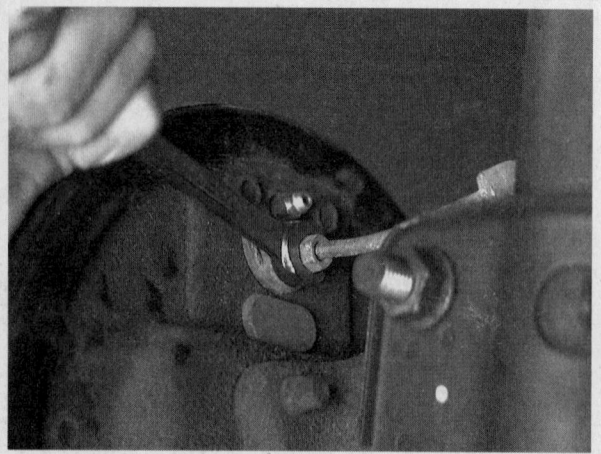

Fig. 82 Disconnect the brake line from the back of the wheel cylinder (bleeder valve cap removed for access)

Fig. 83 Unfasten the 2 wheel cylinder-to-backing plate bolts . . .

Fig. 84 . . . then remove the wheel cylinder from the brake backing plate

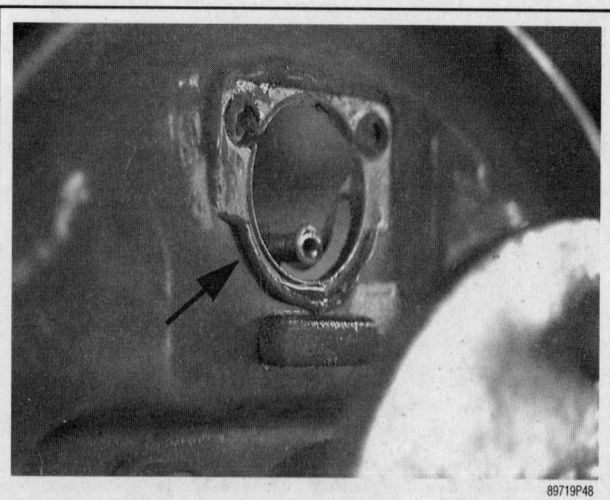

Fig. 85 Apply a thin bead of silicone sealer around the wheel cylinder-to-backing plate mating surface

4. Disconnect the brake hose from the wheel cylinder.

5. Unfasten the wheel cylinder-to-backing plate retaining bolts, then remove the wheel cylinder from the plate.

**To install:**

6. Install a small bead of silicone sealer around the wheel cylinder-to-backing plate mating surfaces.

➡**When installing the wheel cylinder on the backing plate, make sure the it is positioned squarely (horizontal) to the brake shoes.**

7. Position the wheel cylinder on the backing plate and install the attaching bolts. Tighten the bolts to 9.5 ft. lbs. (13 Nm).

8. Attach the brake line to the backing plate, then hand-start the tube nut fitting. Tighten the fitting to 12.5 ft. lbs. (17 Nm).

9. Install the rear brake shoe assemblies, as outlined earlier in this section.

10. Install the rear brake drum and retaining clips (if equipped).

11. Install the wheel and tire assembly. Adjust the brakes.

12. Carefully lower the vehicle, then properly bleed the brake system.

## OVERHAUL

▶ **See Figures 86 thru 95**

Wheel cylinder overhaul kits may be available, but often at little or no savings over a reconditioned wheel cylinder. It often makes sense with these components to substitute a new or reconditioned part instead of attempting an overhaul.

If no replacement is available, or you would prefer to overhaul your wheel cylinders, the following procedure may be used. When rebuilding and installing wheel cylinders, avoid getting any contaminants into the system. Always use clean, new, high quality brake fluid. If dirty or improper fluid has been used, it will be necessary to drain the entire system, flush the system with proper brake fluid, replace all rubber components, then refill and bleed the system.

1. Remove the wheel cylinder from the vehicle and place on a clean workbench.

2. First remove and discard the old rubber boots, then withdraw the pistons. Piston cylinders are equipped with seals and a spring assembly, all located behind the pistons in the cylinder bore.

3. Remove the remaining inner components, seals and spring assembly. Compressed air may be useful in removing these components. If no compressed air is available, be VERY careful not to score the wheel cylinder bore when removing parts from it. Discard all components for which replacements were supplied in the rebuild kit.

4. Wash the cylinder and metal parts in denatured alcohol or clean brake fluid.

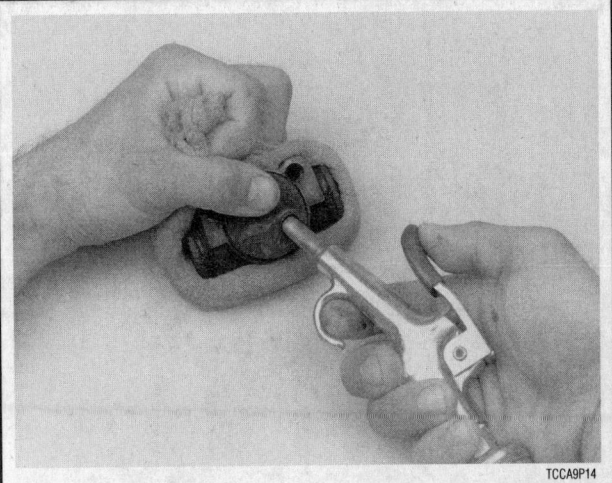

Fig. 87 Compressed air can be used to remove the pistons and seals

Fig. 88 Remove the pistons, cup seals and spring from the cylinder

Fig. 86 Remove the outer boots from the wheel cylinder

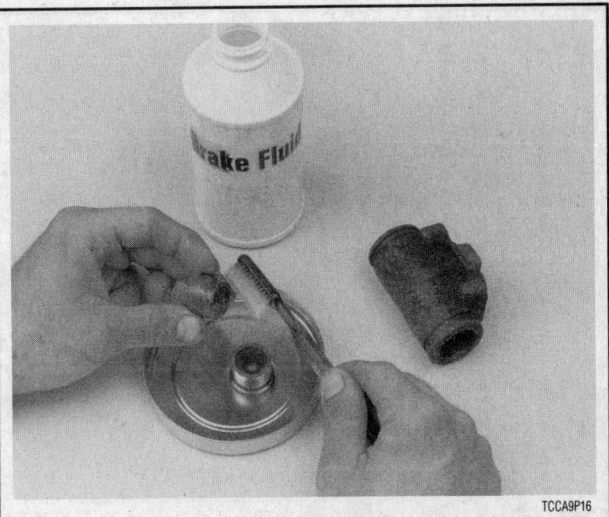

Fig. 89 Use brake fluid and a soft brush to clean the pistons . . .

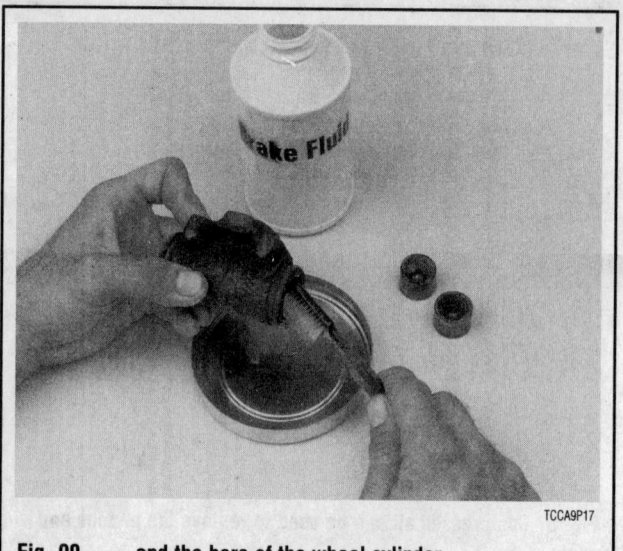

Fig. 90 . . . and the bore of the wheel cylinder

Fig. 91 Once cleaned and inspected, the wheel cylinder is ready for assembly

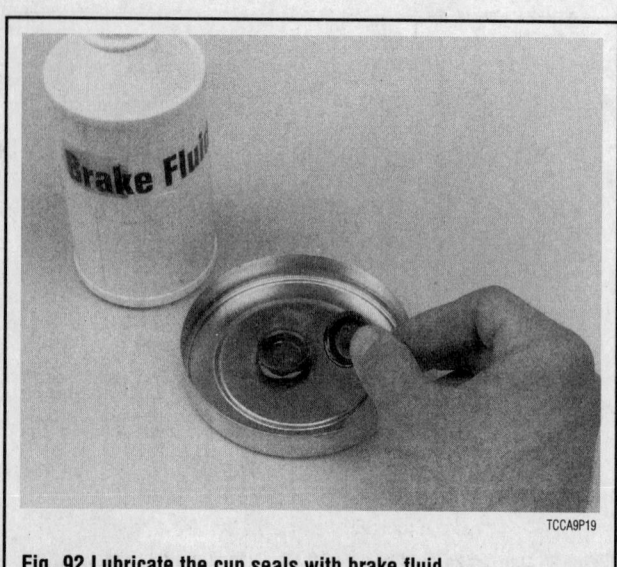

Fig. 92 Lubricate the cup seals with brake fluid

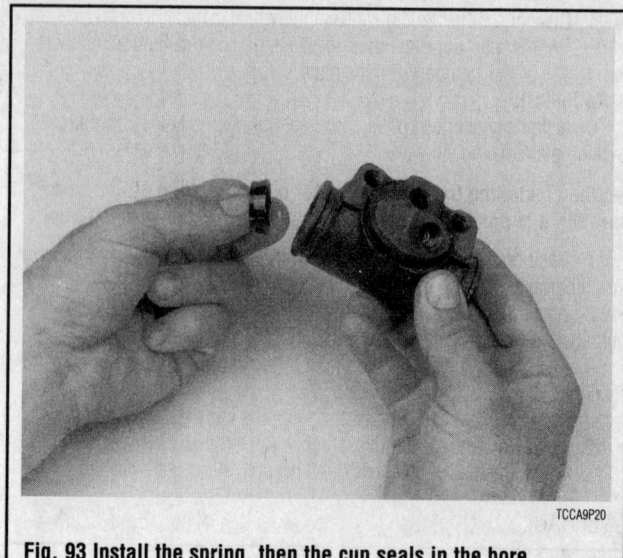

Fig. 93 Install the spring, then the cup seals in the bore

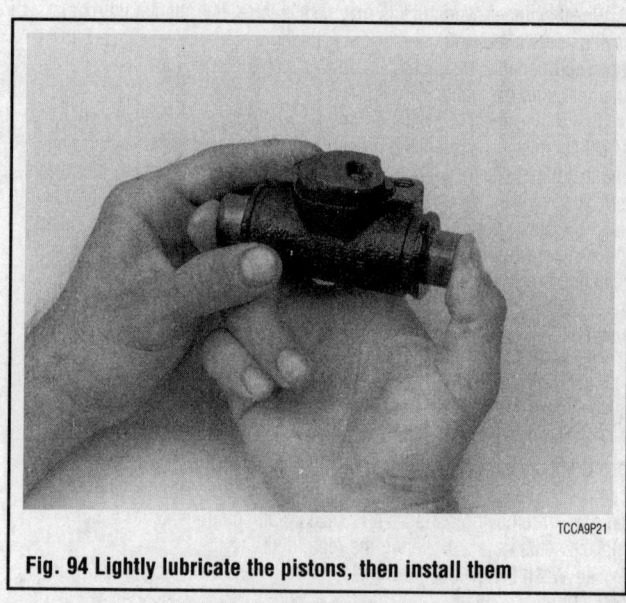

Fig. 94 Lightly lubricate the pistons, then install them

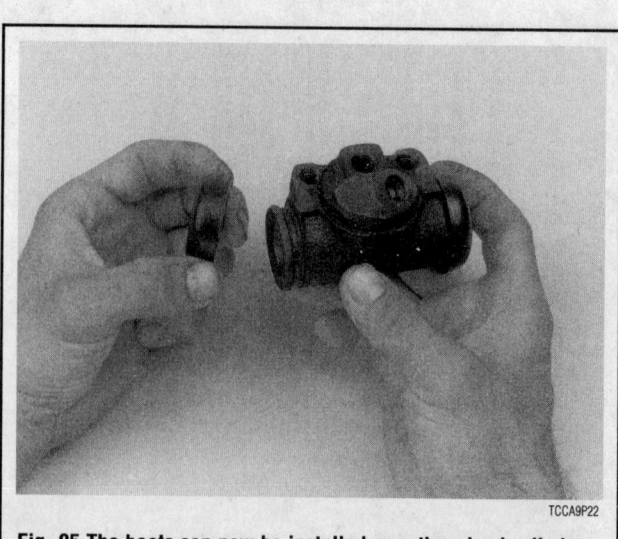

Fig. 95 The boots can now be installed over the wheel cylinder ends

## ✳ WARNING

**Never use a mineral-based solvent such as gasoline, kerosene or paint thinner for cleaning purposes. These solvents will swell rubber components and quickly deteriorate them.**

5. Allow the parts to air dry or use compressed air. Do not use rags for cleaning, since lint will remain in the cylinder bore.

## PARKING BRAKE

### Cables

REMOVAL & INSTALLATION

▶ See Figures 96 thru 109

## ✳ WARNING

**Remove only one rear parking brake cable from the rear brakes at a time. If you attempt to remove both cables at the same time, it will be difficult to connect the cables to the equalizer or parking brake lever at the rear wheel brakes.**

1. From inside the passenger compartment, unfasten the screws securing the rear of the console to the floor pan of the vehicle.
2. Remove the 2 screws found in the cup holders attaching the front of the center console to the console bracket.
3. Raise the parking brake lever as high as it will go for the clearance necessary to remove the console. Remove the center console from the vehicle.

➡ **When repairs to the parking brake hand lever or cables is required, the auto adjuster must be reloaded and locked out.**

4. Lower the parking brake lever handle.
5. Grasp the parking brake lever output cable by hand, then pull it rearward. Keep pulling on the cable until a ³⁄₁₆ in. (5mm) drill bit can be inserted into the handle and sector gear of the parking brake mechanism. This will lock the parking brake mechanism and take tension off the parking brake cables.
6. Remove the rear parking brake cables from the parking brake cable equalizer.
7. Remove the rear seat cushion from the vehicle.

6. Inspect the piston and replace it if it shows scratches.
7. Lubricate the cylinder bore and seals using clean brake fluid.
8. Position the spring assembly.
9. Install the inner seals, then the pistons.
10. Insert the new boots into the counterbores by hand. Do not lubricate the boots.
11. Install the wheel cylinder.

8. Use a prytool to carefully remove the scuff plates from the right and left door sills. The scuff plates are attached to the door sills using clips on the bottom of the scuff plates.
9. Fold the rear carpeting forward to reveal the parking brake cables.
10. Install the box end of a ½ in. wrench over the parking brake cable retainer as shown in the accompanying illustration. Doing this will compress the tabs on the parking brake cable retainers, letting the cable be removed from the console bracket. From under the carpet, grab the parking brake cable housing and pull the cable straight out of the console bracket.

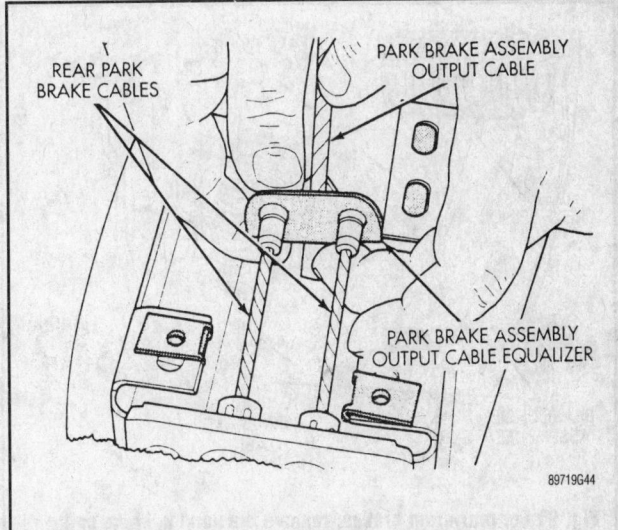

**Fig. 97 Detach the parking brake cables from the equalizer**

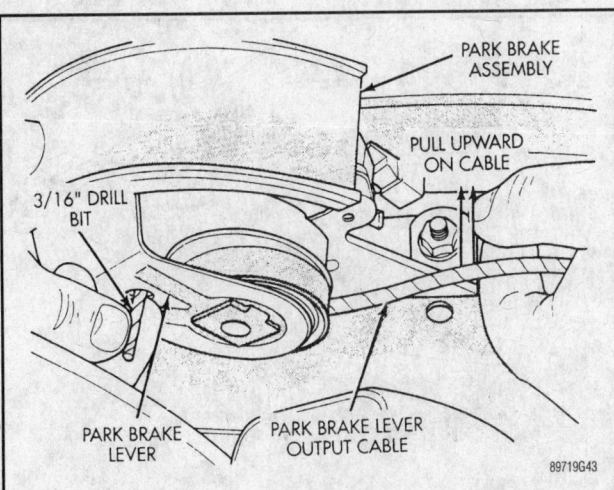

**Fig. 96 Place a drill bit in the handle and sector gear to lock the parking brake mechanism and tension off the cables**

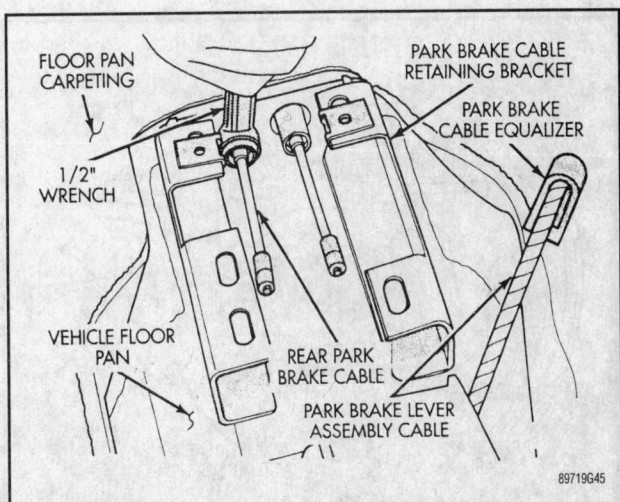

**Fig. 98 You must compress the tabs on the cable retainers in order to remove the cable from the console bracket**

11. Raise and safely support the vehicle, then remove the rear wheel and tire assembly.

12. If equipped with drum brakes, remove the brake drum from the hub and bearing assembly.

13. If equipped with disc brakes, remove caliper and rotor.

14. Remove the dust cap from the rear hub and bearing assembly using a suitable pair of pliers or equivalent as shown in the accompanying illustration.

15. Remove the hub and bearing retaining nut from the spindle, then remove the hub and bearing assembly. Discard the retaining nut and replace with a new one during installation.

16. If equipped with drum brakes, remove the parking brake cable from the parking brake actuating lever. Then, remove the actuating spring from between the brake shoe adjustment lever and the brake shoe assembly.

17. If equipped with rear disc brakes, remove the brake shoe assemblies from the rear disc brake adapter. Then, remove the parking brake actuating lever from the parking brake cable.

18. If equipped with rear drum brakes, remove the parking brake cable from the rear brake support plate. You can remove the cable from the support plate by using a ½ in. wrench to compress the locking tabs on the parking brake cable retainer.

19. If equipped with rear disc brakes, remove the parking brake cable

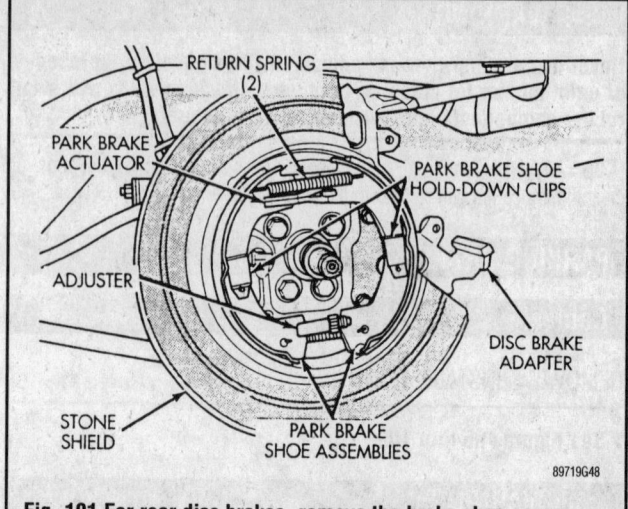

Fig. 101 For rear disc brakes, remove the brake shoe assemblies from the adapter . . .

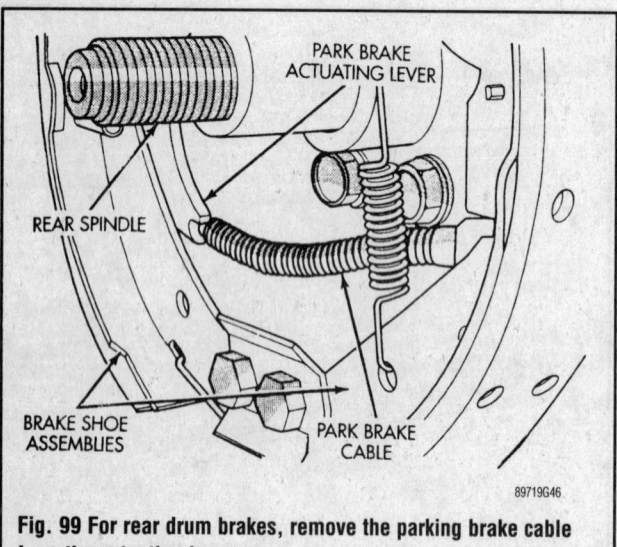

Fig. 99 For rear drum brakes, remove the parking brake cable from the actuating lever . . .

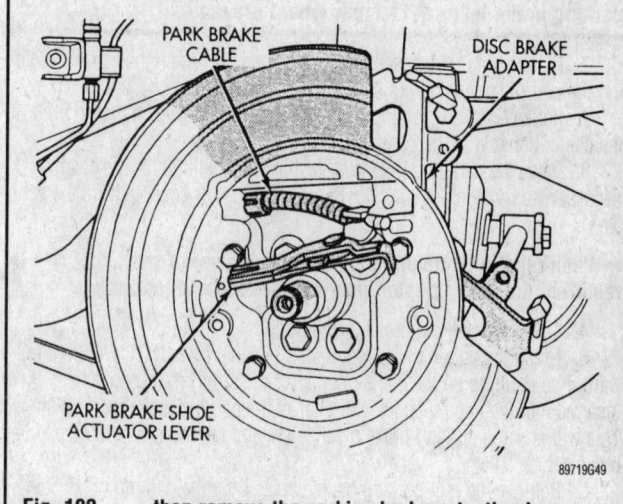

Fig. 102 . . . then remove the parking brake actuating lever from the parking brake cable

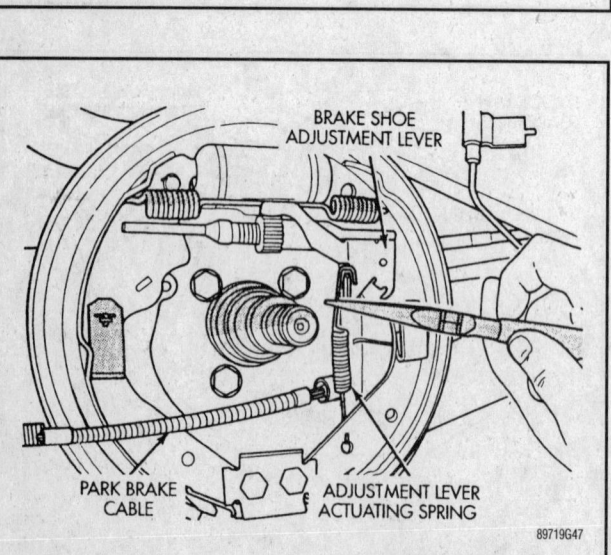

Fig. 100 . . . then remove the actuating spring between the brake shoe adjustment lever and the brake shoe assembly

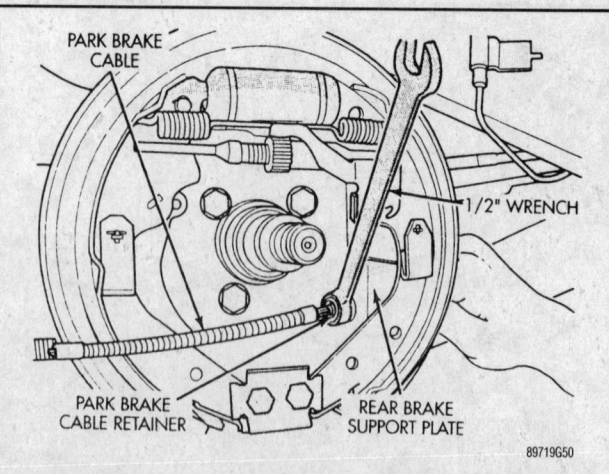

Fig. 103 For rear drum brakes, use a wrench to compress the locking tabs, then remove the parking brake cable from the support plate

from the rear disc brake adapter. Use a small prytool to compress the locking tabs on the parking brake cable retainer.

20. Remove the parking brake cable routing bracket from the vehicle frame rail.

21. Remove the parking brake cable and sealing grommet from the floor pan of the vehicle.

**To install:**

22. Install the parking brake cable into the floor pan of the vehicle, making sure the sealing grommet is installed in the floor pan as far as possible. This will ensure a proper seal.

23. Install the parking brake cable into the brake support plate or rear disc brake adapter. Be sure the locking tabs on the cable retainer are expanded to ensure the cable is securely held in the support plate or adapter.

24. Install the parking brake routing bracket on the frame rail. Install and securely tighten the routing bracket attaching bolt.

25. If equipped with rear drum brakes, install the parking brake cable on the parking brake actuating lever. Then, install the actuating spring between the brake shoe assembly and the brake adjustment lever.

26. If equipped with rear disc brakes, install the parking brake shoe actuator lever on the parking brake cable. Then, install the parking brake shoes on the disc brake adapter.

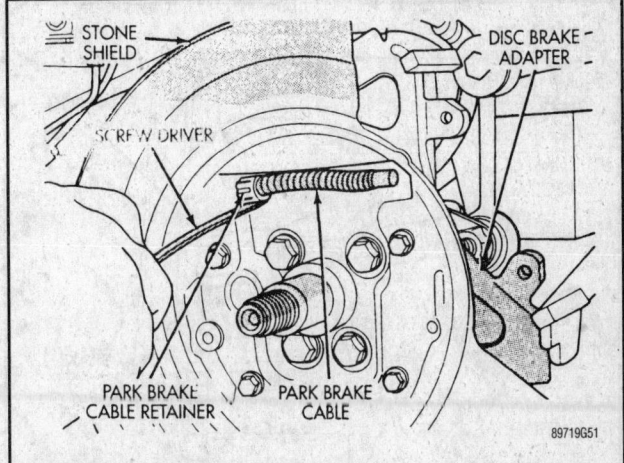

Fig. 106 For rear disc brakes, use a small prytool to compress the locking tabs, then remove the parking brake cable from the brake adapter

Fig. 104 You can also use needle-nose pliers to compress the locking tabs . . .

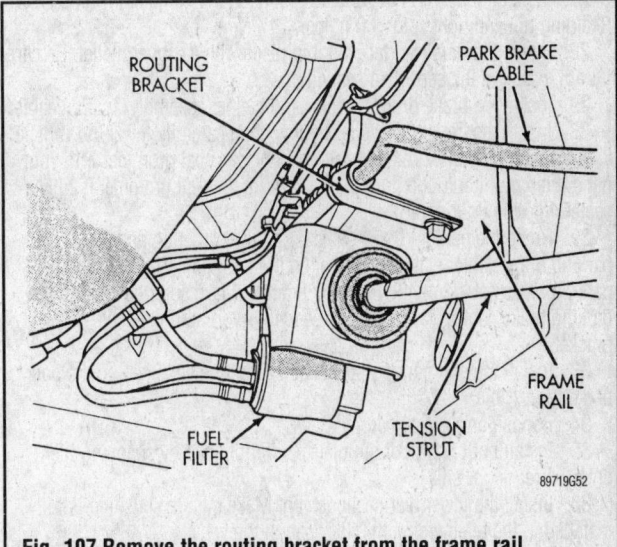

Fig. 107 Remove the routing bracket from the frame rail

Fig. 105 . . . and remove the parking brake cable from the backing plate

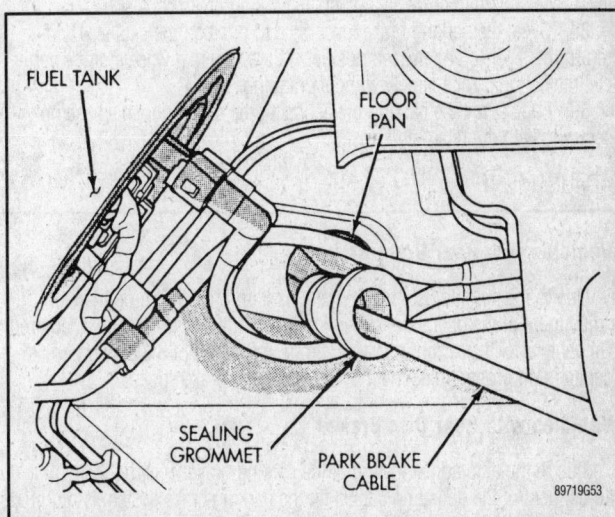

Fig. 108 Disconnect the parking brake cable and sealing grommet from the floor pan

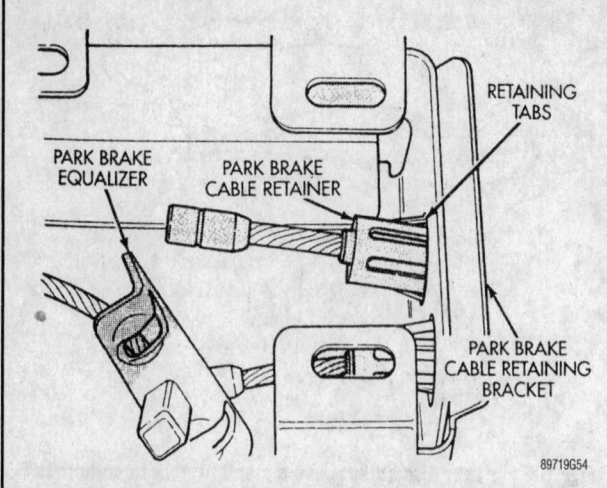

Fig. 109 Make sure the parking brake cable is installed properly in the retaining bracket

27. Install the hub and bearing assembly on the spindle. Install a NEW retaining nut and tighten to 160 ft. lbs. (217 Nm).

28. Install the dust cap, tapping it in place with a rubber mallet. Be careful not to distort the cap when seating it.

29. Install the brake drum, or rotor and caliper assembly, as applicable.

30. Install the tire and wheel assembly, then carefully lower the vehicle.

31. Grab the parking brake cable-to-floor pan seal grommet with your hand, then pull it into the floor pan to be sure the seal grommet is fully seated into the floor pan.

32. Route the parking brake cable under the carpeting and up to the parking brake cable retaining bracket on the floor pan. Then, install the parking brake cable into the retaining bracket. Make sure the tabs on the parking brake cable retainer have expanded out to hold the cable in the bracket.

33. Install the rear parking brake cables into the equalizer on the parking brake lever cable.

34. Reposition the rear carpeting.

35. Install both rear door sill plate scuff moldings by snapping then onto the rear door sills.

36. Install the lower rear seat cushion. Make sure the cushion is fully installed in the retainers on the floor pan of the vehicle.

37. Firmly grab the parking brake lever locking pin and quickly remove it from the parking brake lever mechanism. This will allow the parking brake lever mechanism to correctly adjust the parking brake cables.

38. Cycle the parking brake lever once to position the cables. Then return the lever to its released position. Check the rear wheels of the vehicle, they should rotate freely without dragging.

39. Fully apply the parking brake. Install the center console assembly, securing with the retaining screws.

## ADJUSTMENT

### Vehicles with Rear Drum Brakes

Due to the auto adjust feature of the parking brake lever, no manual adjustment of the operating cables for the parking brake system is required. On vehicles with rear drum brakes, proper operation of the parking brake depends on proper adjustment of the rear drum brake shoes.

### Vehicles with Rear Disc Brakes

Due to the auto adjust feature of the parking brake lever, no manual adjustment of the operating cables for the parking brake system is required. On vehicles that have rear disc brakes, proper adjustment depends on proper adjustment of the drum-in-hat parking brake shoes. Refer to that procedure, located later in this section for details.

## Brake Shoes

### REMOVAL & INSTALLATION

▶ See Figures 110, 111, 112, 113 and 114

➡ This procedure only applies to vehicles with rear disc brakes.

1. Raise and safely support the vehicle. Remove the wheel and tire assembly.

2. Remove the rear disc brake caliper and rotor assembly.

3. Remove the dust cap from the hub and bearing assembly.

4. Remove the hub and bearing assembly retaining nut and washer.

5. Remove the rear brake hose hold-down clip.

6. Turn the brake shoe adjuster wheel until the adjuster is at its shortest length.

7. Remove the adjuster from the parking brake shoe assemblies.

8. Remove the lower shoe-to-shoe spring.

9. Pull the rear brake shoe assembly away from the anchor. Then, remove the rear brake shoe and upper spring.

10. Remove the front brake shoe hold-down clip, then remove the front brake shoe assembly.

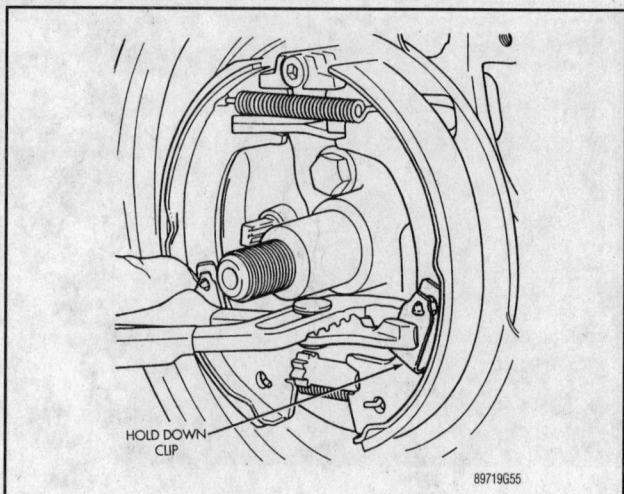

Fig. 110 Use a park of pliers to remove the rear brake shoe hold-down clip

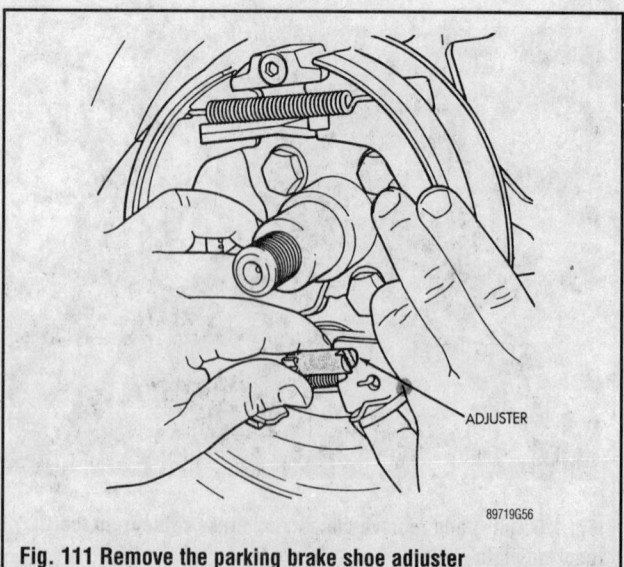

Fig. 111 Remove the parking brake shoe adjuster

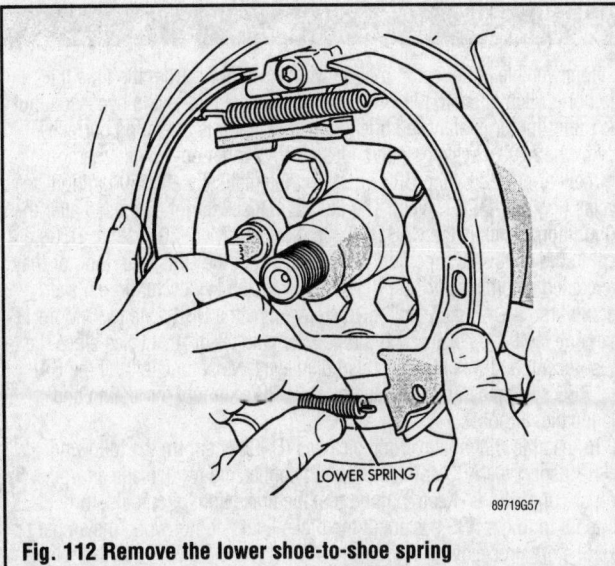

**Fig. 112 Remove the lower shoe-to-shoe spring**

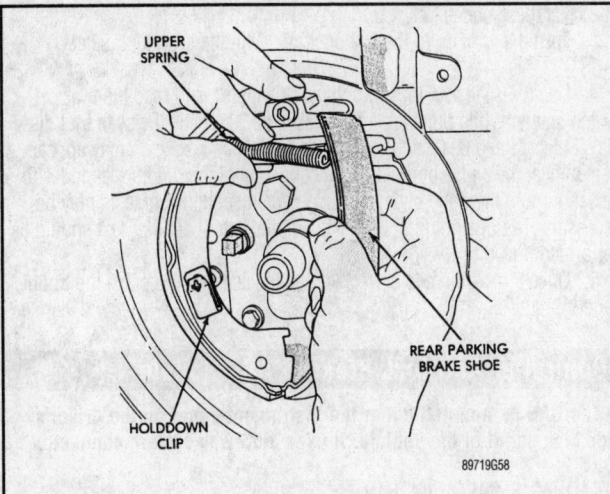

**Fig. 113 Remove the rear shoe and upper spring as an assembly**

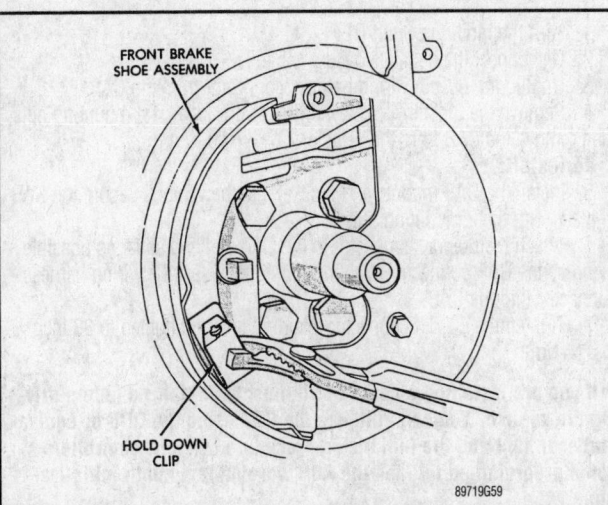

**Fig. 114 Unfasten the front brake shoe hold-down clip, then remove the shoe**

**To install:**

11. Install the front brake shoe and hold-down clip.

12. Install the rear brake shoe and the upper brake shoe-to-shoe return spring.

13. Pull the rear brake hose over the anchor block until it is properly located on the adapter.

14. Install the lower shoe-to-shoe return spring.

15. Install the brake shoe adjuster with the star wheel rearward.

16. Instal the rear brake shoe hold-down clip.

17. Adjust the brake shoes to a diameter of 6.75 in. (171mm).

18. Install the rear hub and bearing on the spindle. Install a NEW hub and bearing retaining nut, and tighten to 160 ft. lbs. (217 Nm). Install the dust cap.

19. Install the rotor and brake caliper assemblies.

20. Install the wheel and tire assembly, then carefully lower the vehicle.

## ADJUSTMENT

➡ The parking brake shoes used in the drum-in-hat parking brake system do not automatically adjust to compensate for brake shoe lining wear. Therefore, it is necessary to manually adjust the parking brake shoes. Manual adjustment is necessary whenever any of the following occurs:

- Excessive travel of the parking brake lever
- Installation of new parking brake shoes
- Performing any service which may effect the location of the parking brake shoes

1. Make sure the parking brake lever is fully released.

2. Raise and safely support the vehicle.

3. Remove the rubber plug from the adjusting hole in the brake shoe backing plate on both sides of the vehicle.

4. For the driver's side (left) adjustment procedure, perform the following:

    a. Insert a medium sized screwdriver through the adjustment hole in the backing plate. Place the screwdriver against the star wheel on the parking brake shoe adjuster mechanism.

    b. Use the screwdriver to rotate the star wheel downward, until a slight drag is felt when turning the rear wheel.

    c. Then, use the screwdriver to rotate the star wheel upward just until the rear wheel can be rotated with no parking brake shoe drag.

    d. From the point where there is no more drag, rotate the star wheel upward a maximum of 2 additional clicks. The parking brake shoe-to-drum clearance is now properly adjusted.

5. For the passenger's side (right) adjustment procedure, perform the following:

    a. Insert a medium sized screwdriver through the adjustment hole in the backing plate. Place the screwdriver against the star wheel on the parking brake shoe adjuster mechanism.

    b. Use the screwdriver to rotate the star wheel upward, until a slight drag is felt when turning the rear wheel.

    c. Then, use the screwdriver to rotate the star wheel downward just until the rear wheel can be rotated with no parking brake shoe drag.

    d. From the point where there is no more drag, rotate the star wheel downward a maximum of 2 additional clicks. The parking brake shoe-to-drum clearance is now properly adjusted.

6. Install the rubber plug into the adjusting hole on the brake shoe backing plate on both sides of the vehicle.

7. Lower the vehicle far enough to get to the parking brake lever, without the rear tires touching the ground.

8. Fully apply and release the parking brakes 2 times after adjusting the parking brake shoes. Then, rotate both rear wheels to be sure the parking brake shoes do not drag on the brake drum following the operation and release of the parking brake.

## ANTI-LOCK BRAKE SYSTEM (ABS)

### General Information

The Bendix ABX-4 type 4 Anti-lock Brake System (ABS) was an option on the 1995–97 Neons. Beginning in 1998, Neons are equipped with the Teves Mark 20 ABS system. Both of these ABS systems operate in basically the same manner, however, they may use some different components.

When conventional brakes are applied in an emergency stop or on ice, one or more wheels may lock. This may result in loss of steering control and vehicle stability. The purpose of the Bendix ABS Anti-lock Brake System (ABS) is to prevent lock up under heavy braking conditions. This system offers the driver increased safety and control during braking. Anti-lock braking operates only at speeds above 3 mph (5 km/h).

Under normal braking conditions, the ABS functions the same as a standard brake system with a diagonally split master cylinder and conventional vacuum assist.

If wheel locking tendency is detected during application, the system will enter anti-lock mode. During anti-lock mode, hydraulic pressure in the four wheel circuits is modulated to prevent any wheel from locking. Each wheel circuit is designed with a set of electrical valves and hydraulic line to provide modulation, although for vehicle stability, both rear wheel valves receive the same electrical signal. The system can build or reduce pressure at each wheel, depending on signals generated by the Wheel Speed Sensors (WSS) at each wheel and received at the Controller Anti-lock Brake (CAB).

### PRECAUTIONS

Failure to observe the following precautions may result in system damage:
• Before performing electric arc welding on the vehicle, disconnect the control module and the hydraulic unit connectors.
• When performing painting work on the vehicle, do not expose the control module to temperatures in excess of 185°F (85°C) for longer than 2 hours. The system may be exposed to temperatures up to 200°F (95°C) for less than 15 minutes.
• Never disconnect or connect the control module or hydraulic modulator connectors with the ignition switch ON.
• Never disassemble any component of the Anti-Lock Brake System (ABS) which is designated unserviceable; the component must be replaced as an assembly.
• When filling the master cylinder, always use brake fluid which meets DOT-3 specifications; petroleum-based fluid will destroy the rubber parts.
• Working on ABS system requires extreme amount of mechanical ability, training and special tools. If you are not familiar have your vehicle repaired by a certified mechanic or refer to a more advanced publication on this subject.

### Diagnosis and Testing

For the proper diagnostic procedure for either the entire ABS system or a single component of the system, a scan tool (DRB or equivalent) is necessary. Because of the complexity of the ABS system and the importance of correct system functioning, it is a good idea to have a qualified automotive mechanic test the system if any problems have been detected.

The self-diagnostic ABS start up cycle begins when the ignition switch is turned to the **ON** position. An electrical check is completed on the ABS components, such as the wheel speed sensor continuity and other relay continuity. During this check the amber anti-lock light is turned on for approximately 1–2 seconds.

Further functional testing is accomplished once the vehicle is set in motion.
• The solenoid valves and the pump/motor are activated briefly to verify function
• The voltage output from the wheel speed sensors is verified to be within the correct operating range

If the vehicle is not set in motion within 3 minutes from the time the ignition switch is set in the **ON** position, the solenoid test is bypassed, but the pump/motor is activated briefly to verify that it is operating correctly.

For the ABX-4 system, fault codes are kept in a non-volatile memory until either erased by the DRB or erased automatically after 50 ignition cycles (key **ON-OFF** cycles). The only fault that will not be erased after the 50 ignition cycles is the CAB fault. On the Teves Mark 20 system, DTCs are kept in the controller's memory until erased with the DRB scan tool, or they are erased automatically after 3,500 miles or 255 key cycles which ever occurs first. A CAB fault can only be erased by the DRB scan tool. More than one fault can be stored at a time. The number of key cycles since the most recent fault was stored is also displayed. Most functions of the CAB and ABS system can be accessed by the DRB scan tool for testing and diagnostic purposes.

To read the Diagnostic Trouble Codes (DTC's) perform the following:
1. Inspect the ABS components and connectors for damage and/or proper connections. Keep in mind that the brake light circuit also provides an input to to the ABS system. If the brake lights do not work, they must be fixed before proceeding.
2. Connect a DRB or equivalent scan tool to the Data Link Connector (located under the drivers side instrument panel). A scan tool must be used to access these codes.
3. Turn the ignition to the **ON** position. Wtih the scan tool, select "ABS".
4. Use the scan tool to select "Inputs/Outputs", and read the brake switch status. While pressing on the brake pedal, check the scan tool display. Select "Read DTC" and record any trouble codes which may appear. Sometimes, the cause of one trouble code may trigger additional codes to be set. If more than one code appear, a certain sequence of tests may be necessary. The beginning of each test will indicate if another test should be performed first.
5. Once the problem is corrected, use the scan tool to erase the trouble code(s).

### Controller Anti-lock Brake (CAB) Module

➡The CAB is mounted under the instrument panel on the driver's side kick panel of the vehicle. It uses a 60-way system connector.

### REMOVAL & INSTALLATION

**Bendix ABX-4 System**

♦ See Figures 115, 116 and 117

1. Turn the ignition switch **OFF**.
2. Disconnect the negative battery cable.
3. Unplug the 60-pin wiring harness connector from the CAB.
4. Remove the 2 controller bracket-to-driver's side cowl mounting nuts, then remove the CAB from the vehicle.

**To install:**
5. Install the CAB module and bracket into the vehicle. Secure the CAB in place with the 2 mounting nuts.
6. Attach the 60-way connector to the CAB by hand as far as possible, then use the CAB connector retaining bolt to fully seat the wiring harness connector into the CAB.
7. Tighten the 60-pin connector retaining bolt and tighten to 38 inch lbs. (4 Nm).

➡If you are installing a new CAB, it must be initialized before driving the vehicle. You can initialize the CAB using the DRB or equivalent scan tool and the initializing procedure. All new controllers come programmed to flash the ABS warning lamp until initialization.

8. Connect the negative battery cable.

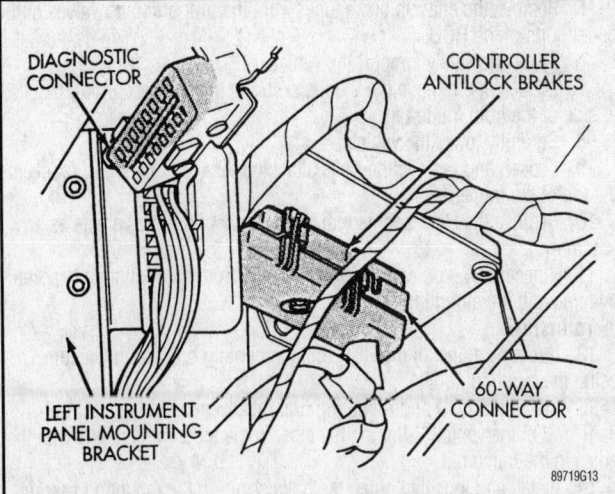

Fig. 115 The CAB is mounted under the instrument panel on the driver's side kick panel

## Teves Mark 20 System

♦ See Figures 118, 119 and 120

➡ To replace the Controller Anti-lock Brakes (CAB) on this vehicles, the Integrated/Hydraulic Control Unit (ICU/HCU) and CAB need to removed from the vehicle as a unit. The CAB can then be separated from the control unit . Do not try to replace the CAB with the control unit in the vehicle.

1. Disconnect the negative battery cable.
2. Remove the ICU/HCU from the vehicle, as outlined in this section.
3. Unplug the pump motor wiring harness from the CAB.
4. Unfasten the 4 bolts attaching the CAB to the HCU, then remove the CAB from the unit.

**To install:**

5. Install the CAB on the HCU. Install the 4 mounting bolts and tighten to 17 inch lbs. (2 Nm).
6. Attach the pump/motor wiring harness to the CAB.
7. Install the ICU/HCU assembly, as outlined in this section.
8. Properly bleed the base brakes and the ABS brakes hydraulic system, as outlined in this section.

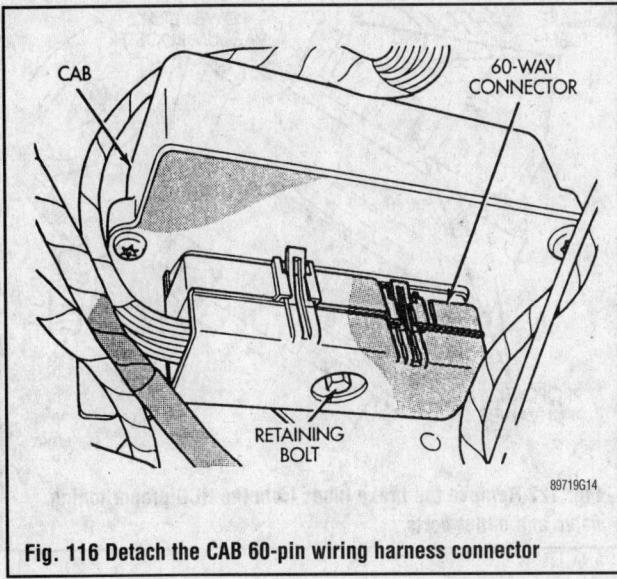

Fig. 116 Detach the CAB 60-pin wiring harness connector

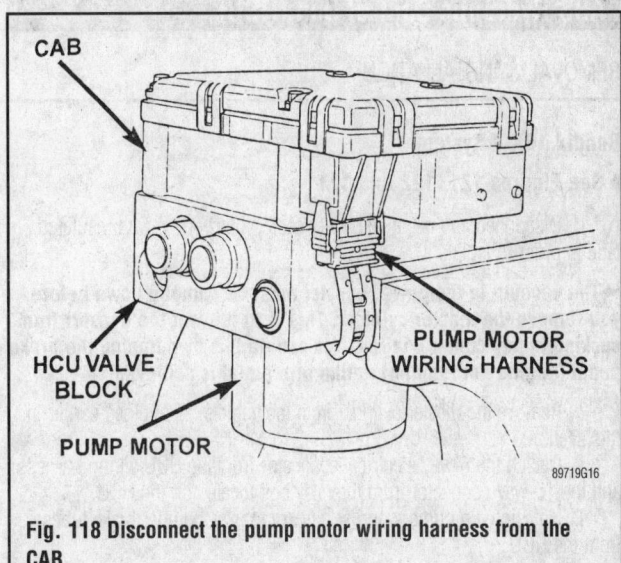

Fig. 118 Disconnect the pump motor wiring harness from the CAB

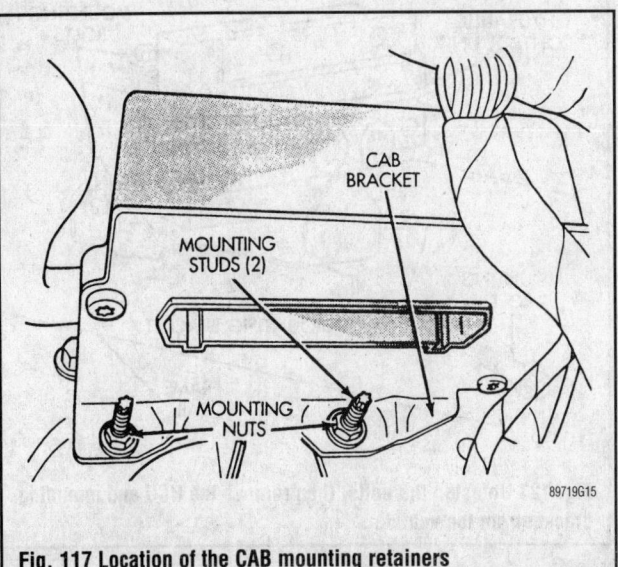

Fig. 117 Location of the CAB mounting retainers

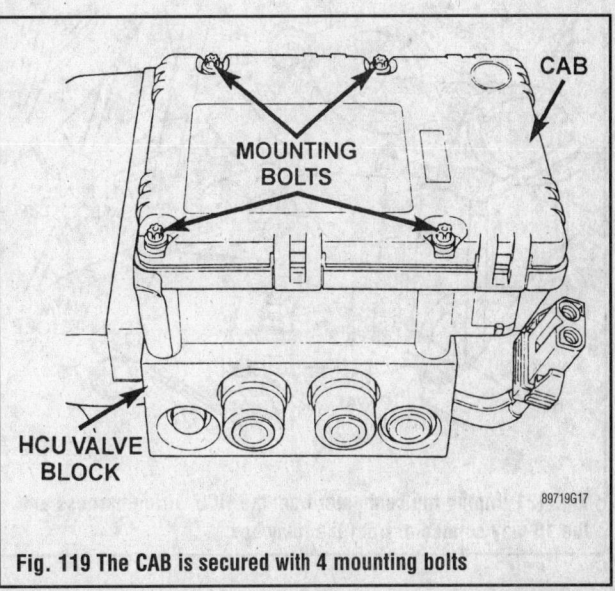

Fig. 119 The CAB is secured with 4 mounting bolts

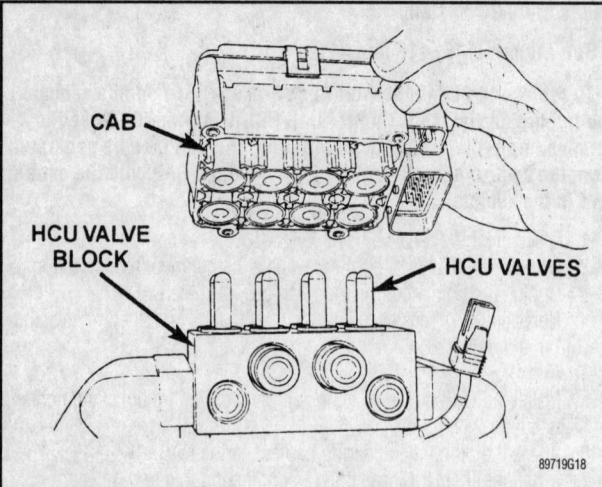

**Fig. 120 After removing the bolts, lift the CAB from the HCU valve block**

## ABS Hydraulic Control Unit (HCU)

### REMOVAL & INSTALLATION

#### Bendix ABX-4 System

♦ See Figures 121, 122 and 123

1. Disconnect the negative battery cable, then wrap it with insulated tape in order to isolate it.

➥The vacuum in the power booster must be pumped down before you remove the master cylinder. This is to prevent the booster from sucking in any contamination. You can do this by pumping the brake pedal (engine not running) until a firm pedal is achieved.

2. Remove the master cylinder from the vehicle, as outlined earlier in this section.

3. Detach the 6-way electrical connector from the HCU wiring harness and the 10-way connector from the relay box located on the HCU.

4. Unfasten the primary and secondary master cylinder brake tubes from the HCU.

5. Remove the chassis brake tubes from the proportioning valves and outlet ports of the HCU.

6. Raise and safely support the vehicle.

7. Loosen and remove the 2 bolts securing the HCU mounting bracket to side of the front frame rail.

8. Carefully lower the vehicle.

9. Loosen and remove the bolts attaching the HCU mounting bracket to the top of the frame rail.

10. Remove the HCU and its mounting bracket from the vehicle as an assembly.

11. If necessary, you can separate the HCU from the mounting bracket by removing the mounting bolts.

**To install:**

12. If removed, install the HCU to the mounting bracket and secure using the mounting bolts.

13. Install the HCU and mounting bracket assembly to the left front frame rail of the vehicle, aligning the tabs on the mounting bracket with the holes in the frame rail.

14. Install and loosely tighten the bolts securing the mounting bracket to the top of the frame rail.

15. Raise and safely support the vehicle.

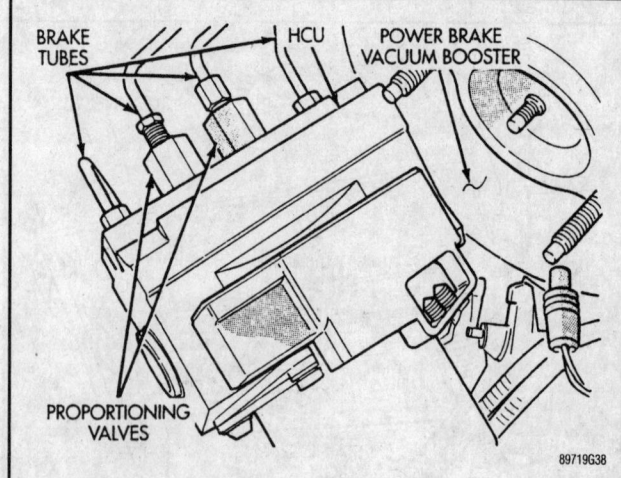

**Fig. 122 Remove the brake tubes from the HCU proportioning valve and outlet ports**

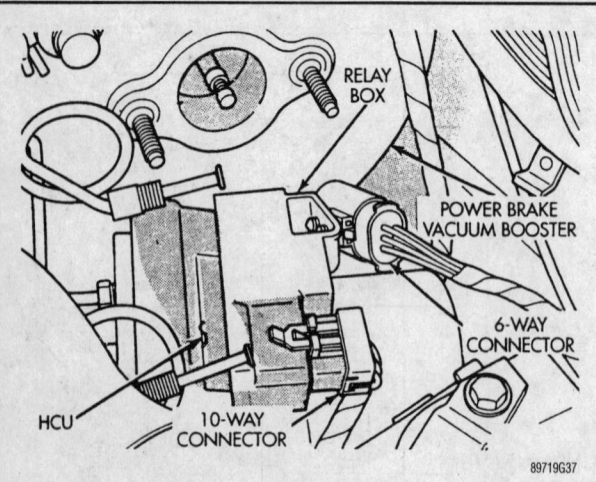

**Fig. 121 Unplug the connector from the HCU wiring harness and the 10-way connector from the relay box**

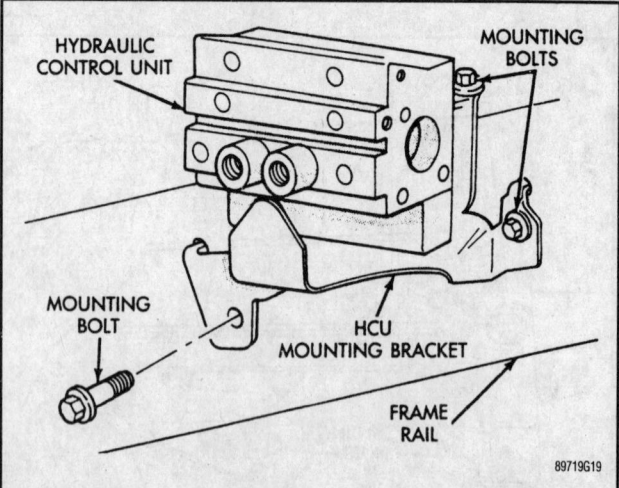

**Fig. 123 Unfasten the bolts, then remove the HCU and mounting bracket from the vehicle**

16. Install the 2 bolts securing the mounting bracket to the side of the front frame rail. Then, tighten both mounting bolts to 21 ft. lbs. (28 Nm).

17. Carefully lower the vehicle.

18. Tighten the bolt securing the mounting bracket to the top of the frame rail to 15 ft. lbs. (20 Nm).

19. Install the 4 chassis brake tubes onto the proportioning valves and outlet ports of the HCU. Tighten the tube nuts to 12.5 ft. lbs. (17 Nm).

20. Attach the master cylinder primary and secondary brake tubes to the HCU and secure the tube nuts hand-tight.

21. Attach the electrical connectors onto the 10-way and 6-way connectors, located on the relay box of the HCU.

22. Install the master cylinder, as outlined earlier in this section. You MUST install a new vacuum seal in the power brake vacuum booster before installing the master cylinder.

23. Remove the tape from the negative battery cable, then connect it to the battery.

24. Bleed the base brake system in the usual fashion.

25. Bleed the modulator assembly following the correct sequences and procedure.

### Teves Mark 20 System

▶ **See Figures 124 thru 130**

1. Disconnect the negative battery cable, then wrap it with insulated tape in order to isolate it.

2. Remove the Power Distribution Center (PDC) from the battery thermoguard, as follows:

    a. Unlatch the 2 retaining clips holding it to the thermoguard.

    b. Pull the PCM straight up off of the thermoguard.

3. Disconnect the vacuum supply hose from the speed control servo.

4. Unfasten the 2 bolts holding the bracket for the speed control servo to the body.

5. Remove the wiring harness connector from the speed control servo. Then, remove the routing clip for the speed control servo wiring harness from the speed control servo mounting bracket.

6. Lay the speed control servo, with the control cable attached, on the top of the engine.

7. Detach the wiring harness connector from the brake fluid level sensor on the master cylinder reservoir.

8. Disconnect the primary and secondary lines from the master cylinder, then plug all of the outlets to avoid contaminating the system.

9. Use a suitable brake cleaner to clean the area where the master cylinder meets the vacuum booster.

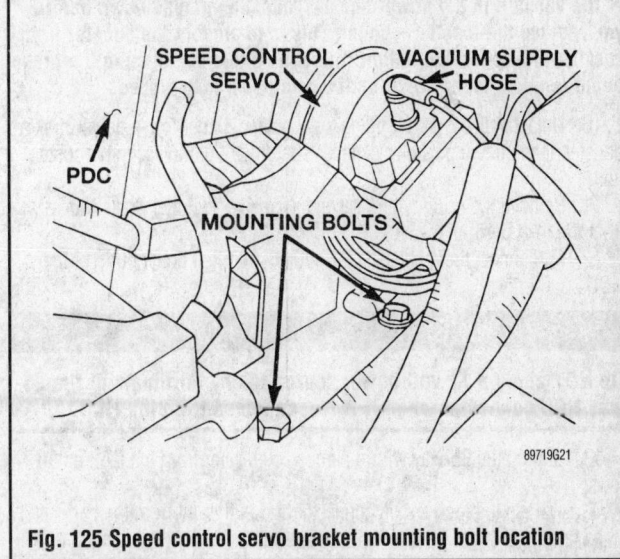

Fig. 125 Speed control servo bracket mounting bolt location

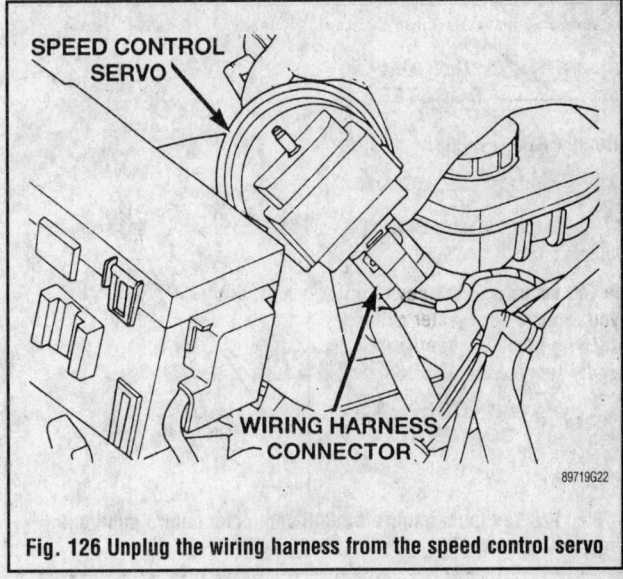

Fig. 126 Unplug the wiring harness from the speed control servo

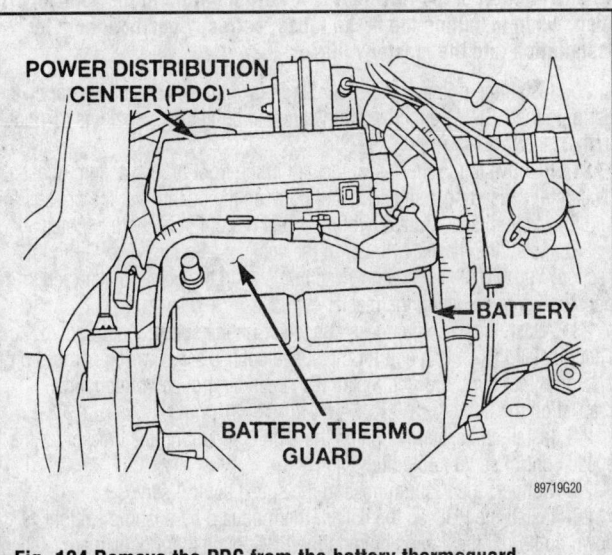

Fig. 124 Remove the PDC from the battery thermoguard

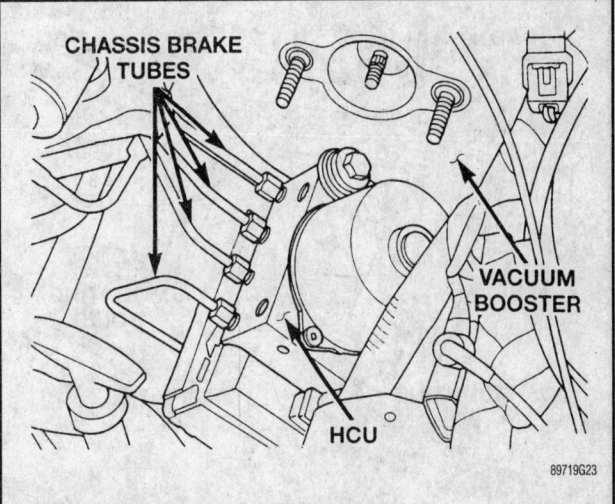

Fig. 127 Disconnect the 4 chassis brake tubes from the outlet ports of the HCU

➡The vacuum in the power booster must be pumped down before you remove the master cylinder. This is to prevent the booster from sucking in any contamination. You can do this by pumping the brake pedal (engine not running) until a firm pedal is achieved.

10. Unfasten the 2 nuts holding the master cylinder to the power brake booster, then slide the master cylinder straight out of the vacuum booster unit.

11. Remove the primary and secondary master cylinder brake tubes from the inlet ports of the HCU.

12. Disconnect the 4 chassis brake tubes from the outlet ports of the HCU.

### ✳✳ WARNING

**Do NOT apply a 12 volt power source to any terminals of the 25-way HCU connector when it is disconnected from the HCU.**

13. Unplug the 25-way wiring harness connector from the CAB as follows:

a. Grasp the lock on the connector and pull it out from the connector as far as it will go. This will unlock and raise the 25-way connector out of the socket on the CAB.

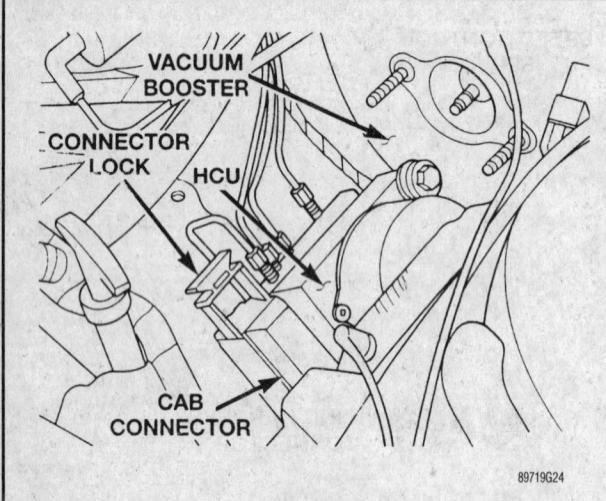

**Fig. 128 You must unlock the CAB connector before unplugging it**

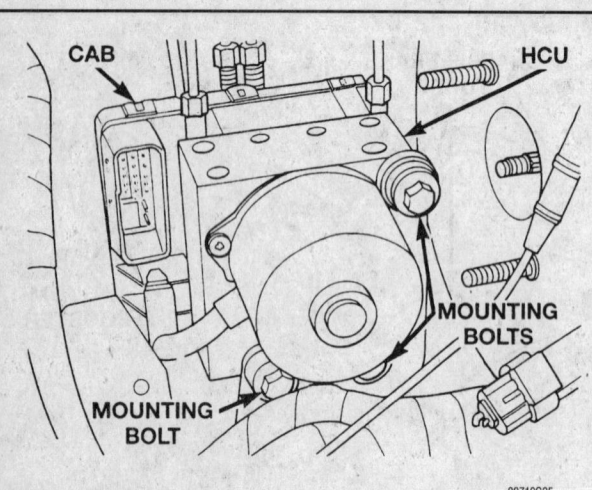

**Fig. 129 Remove the mounting bolts, then you can remove the ICU unit from the vehicle**

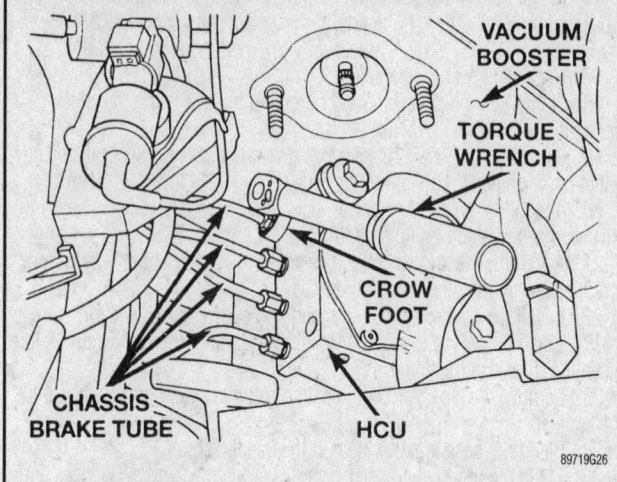

**Fig. 130 Use a crow foot wrench to tighten the chassis tube nuts to the proper specifications**

14. Remove the 3 bolts attaching the CAB and HCU to the mounting bracket.

15. Remove the ICU as a unit from the vehicle.

**To install:**

16. Install the ICU on the mounting bracket.

17. Install the 3 bolts attaching the HCU to the mounting bracket. Tighten the bolts to 97 inch lbs. (11 Nm).

➡Before you install the 25-way connector in the CAB, make sure the seal is properly installed in the connector.

18. Install the 25-way connector into the CAB socket, as follows:

a. Position the connector in the socket on the CAB and carefully push it down as far as it will go.

b. When the connector is fully seated into the CAB socket, push in the connector lock as far as possible.

c. This pulls the connector into the socket and locks it in the installed position.

19. Install the 4 chassis tubes into the outlet ports on the HCU. Use a crow foot wrench to tighten the 4 brake tube nuts to 12.5 ft. lbs. (17 Nm).

➡When installing the master cylinder brake tubes on the HCU, the tube with the small nut is installed in the front inlet port of the HCU. This is the port of the HCU that is toward the front of the vehicle. Also, when installing the brake tubes, correctly position them for installation into the master cylinder.

20. Install the primary and secondary brake tubes from the master cylinder onto the HCU. Use a crow foot wrench to tighten the tube nuts to 12.5 ft. lbs. (17 Nm).

21. Remove the vacuum seal located in the front of the vacuum booster by carefully inserting a small prytool between the pushrod of the booster and the vacuum seal. Carefully pry the seal out of the vacuum booster.

22. Install the master cylinder in the vehicle, as outlined earlier in this section. You MUST install a new vacuum seal in the power brake vacuum booster before installing the master cylinder.

23. Attach the wiring harness connector on the speed control servo. Then, install the routing clip for the speed control servo wiring harness on the servo mounting bracket. Install the speed control servo mounting bracket on the body.

24. Install and securely tighten the 2 bolts mounting the bracket for the speed control servo to the body.

25. Connect the vacuum hose to the speed control servo.

26. Install the PDC on the battery thermoguard by pushing straight down on it until the 2 clips holding the PDC to the thermoguard are latched to the thermoguard.

27. Remove the tape from the negative battery cable, then connect it to the battery.
28. Bleed the base brake system in the usual fashion.
29. Bleed the modulator assembly following the correct sequences and procedure.

## Proportioning Valves

### REMOVAL & INSTALLATION

#### Bendix ABX-4 System

▶ See Figure 131

You do not have to remove the HCU when replacing the proportioning valves.

1. Disconnect the negative battery cable.
2. Disconnect the brake line fitting from the faulty proportioning valve in the HCU.
3. Unscrew and remove the proportioning valve requiring replaced from the HCU.

**To install:**

4. Lubricate the O-ring seal on the new proportioning valve with clean brake fluid, from a fresh sealed container.
5. Install the proportioning valve in the HCU and hand-tighten it until it is fully installed and the O-ring seal is seated in the HCU. Then, tighten the valve to 30 ft. lbs. (40 Nm).
6. Connect the brake line to the proportioning valve and tighten the line nut to 12.5 ft. lbs. (17 Nm).
7. Bleed the base brake system in the usual fashion.

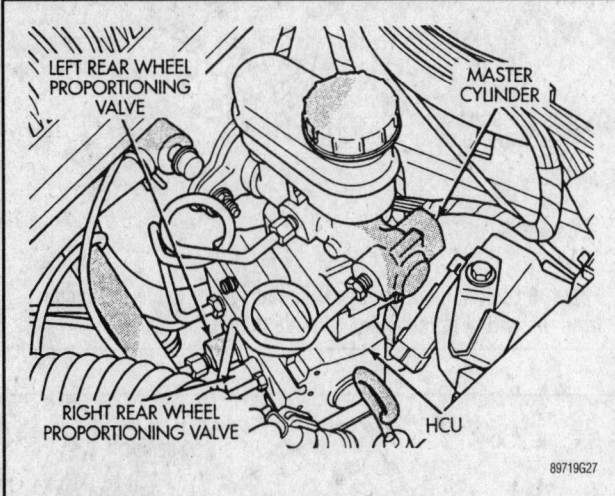

Fig. 131 Location of the rear wheel proportioning valve on the HCU

#### Teves Mark 20 System

▶ See Figure 132

➡ Never attempt to disassemble a proportioning valve.

1. Raise and safely support the vehicle.
2. Remove the chassis brake tube nuts from the proportioning valve controlling the rear wheel of the vehicle which has premature wheel skid.
3. Remove the proportioning valve from the chassis brake tube.

**To install:**

4. Install the proportioning valve in the chassis brake tube.
5. Tighten the 2 chassis brake tube nuts to 12.5 ft. lbs. (17 Nm).
6. Bleed the affected brake line, as outlined in this section.

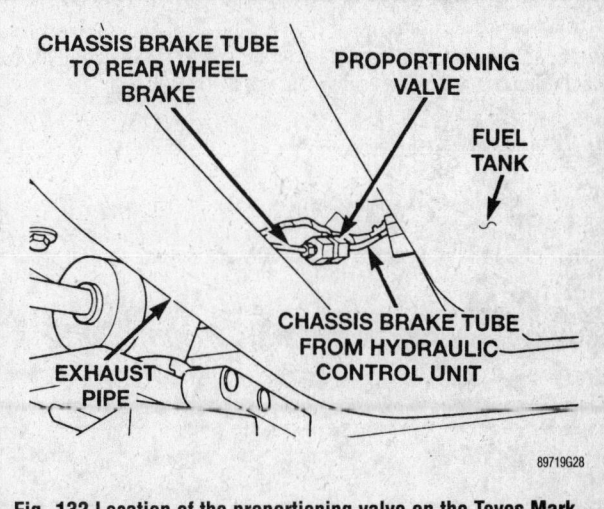

Fig. 132 Location of the proportioning valve on the Teves Mark 20 system

## Relay Box

The ABS relay and pump/motor relay are serviced together as an assembly with the relay box. The relay box mounts directly to the HCU. To remove the relay box from the HCU, you must remove the HCU from the vehicle. This must be done to allow visual access of the relay box-to-HCU electrical connection. Visual access to this connection is necessary to be sure the connection is properly made when installing the relay box on the HCU.

### REMOVAL & INSTALLATION

▶ See Figures 133, 134 and 135

1. Disconnect the negative battery cable, then wrap it with insulated tape in order to isolate it.
2. Remove the Hydraulic Control Unit (HCU) from the vehicle, as outlined in this section.
3. Unclip the 6-way electrical connector from the relay box.
4. Unfasten the 2 screws attaching the relay box to the HCU. Remove ONLY the 2 screws mounting the relay box to the HCU; do NOT remove the pump motor mounting screws.

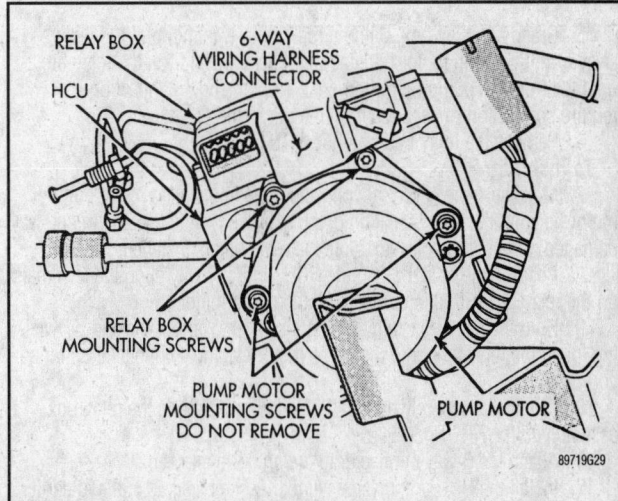

Fig. 133 Make sure to remove the relay box-to-HCU screws, NOT the pump motor mounting screws

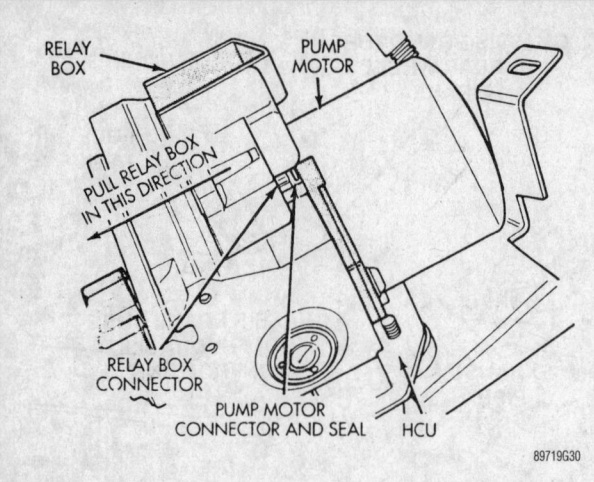

Fig. 134 Firmly pull the relay box away from the pump motor until the connector unplugs

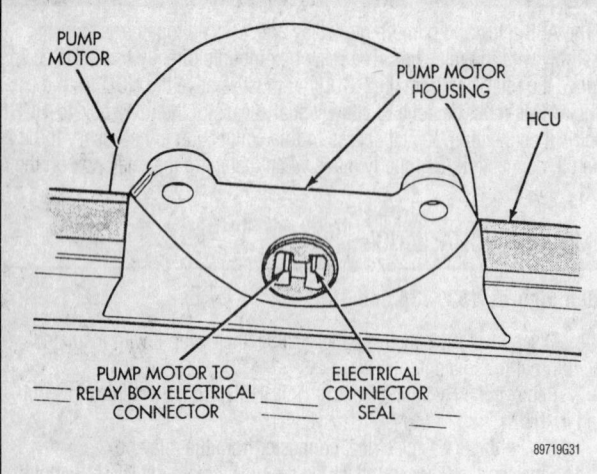

Fig. 135 The pump motor-to-relay box electrical seal must be properly installed

5. Grasp the relay box. Without rocking or twisting, pull the relay box away from the pump motor housing until the connector on the relay box unplugs from the pump motor terminal. This is a tight connection and will require some effort to separate from the pump motor.

6. Remove the relay box from the HCU.

**To install:**

7. Make sure the electrical connector seal in installed in the pump motor housing before installation of the relay body. If the seal is in any way damaged, it must be replaced before the relay box is installed.

8. Position the relay box on the HCU, and carefully align the terminals on the relay box with the terminals on the pump motor.

9. Hold the relay box with both hands. Then, without rocking or twisting, push the relay box onto the pump motor electrical connector as far as you can.

10. Install and securely tighten the 2 screws attaching the relay box assembly to the HCU.

11. Attach the 6-way connector to the onto the relay box.

12. Install the HCU and master cylinder assemblies, as outlined earlier in this section.

13. Connect the negative battery cable.

14. Bleed the base brake system in the usual fashion, then bleed the ABS system following the correct sequences and procedure.

15. Road test the vehicle to be sure the brake system is working properly.

## Wheel Speed Sensors (WSS)

### REMOVAL & INSTALLATION

➡Proper installation of the sensor and its wiring is critical to system function. Make certain that wiring is installed in all retainers and clips. Wiring must be protected from moving parts and not be stretched during suspension movements.

**Front Wheel**

▶ See Figures 136, 137 and 138

1. Disconnect the negative battery cable.

2. Elevate and safely support the vehicle. Remove the wheel and tire assembly.

3. Detach the speed sensor cable connector from the vehicle wiring harness. Remove the clip attaching the speed sensor cable connector to the vehicle body.

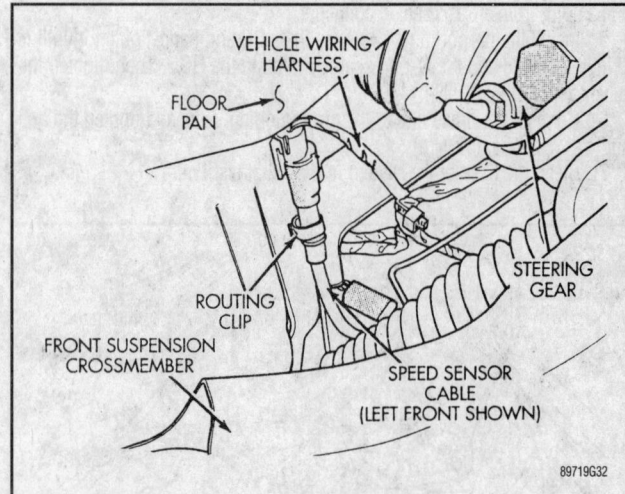

Fig. 136 Unplug the front wheel speed sensor cable connector from the wiring harness and remove the clip

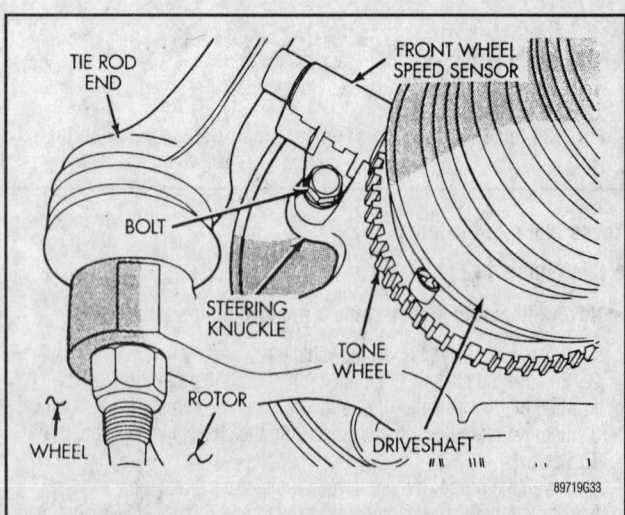

Fig. 137 The front wheel speed sensor is secured with a mounting bolt

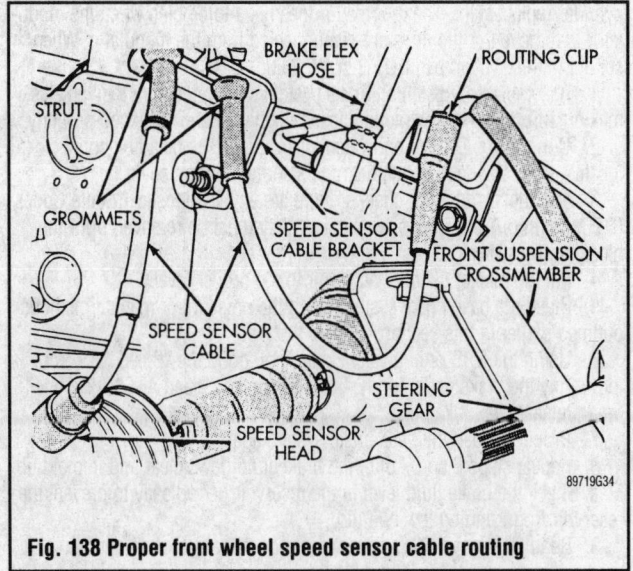

Fig. 138 Proper front wheel speed sensor cable routing

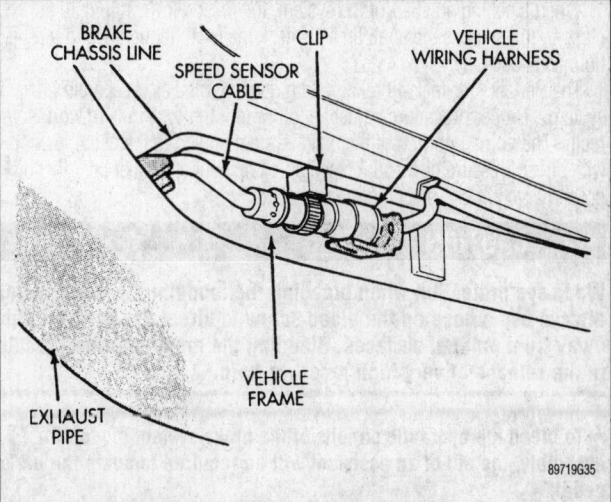

Fig. 139 Location of the rear wheel speed sensor connection to the vehicle wiring harness

4. Unfasten the wheel speed sensor head-to-steering knuckle bolt.
5. Carefully remove the sensor head from the steering knuckle. Do not use pliers on the sensor head; if it is seized in place, use a hammer and small punch to tap the edge of the sensor ear. The tapping and side-to-side motion will free the unit.
6. Remove the speed sensor cable grommets from the retaining bracket. Remove the speed sensor cable routing clip from the frame of the vehicle.

**To install:**
7. Attach the wheel speed sensor cable connector to the vehicle wiring harness.
8. Install the speed sensor cable assembly grommets into the retaining bracket, then fasten the speed sensor cable routing clip onto the frame of the vehicle.
9. Install the wheel speed sensor to the steering knuckle and tighten the retaining screw to 60 inch lbs. (7 Nm).
10. Install the tire and wheel. Lower the vehicle to the ground.
11. Connect the negative battery cable. Road test the vehicle to assure proper brake system operation.

### Rear Wheel

▶ See Figures 139 and 140

1. Disconnect the negative battery cable.
2. Elevate and safely support the vehicle. Remove the wheel and tire.
3. Unplug the speed sensor cable connector from the vehicle wire harness. Remove the clip attaching the speed sensor cable connector to the vehicle body.
4. Remove the speed sensor cable routing bracket from underneath the rear brake hose mounting bracket. Then, remove the speed sensor cable from the routing clips on the rear brake hose and chassis brake tube.
5. Unfasten the bolt securing the rear wheel speed sensor to the disc brake adapter, then remove the cable routing bracket-to-rear strut bolt.
6. Carefully remove the sensor head from the adapter assembly. Do not use pliers on the sensor head; if it is seized in place, use a hammer and small punch to tap the edge of the sensor ear. The tapping and side-to-side motion will free the unit.

**To install:**
7. Before installation, coat the sensor with high temperature multi-purpose grease.
8. Install the sensor head into the brake adapter. Install the wheel speed sensor bolt and tighten the bolt to 5 ft. lbs. (7 Nm).
9. Install the brake hose and wheel speed sensor cable routing bracket on the rear strut bracket.

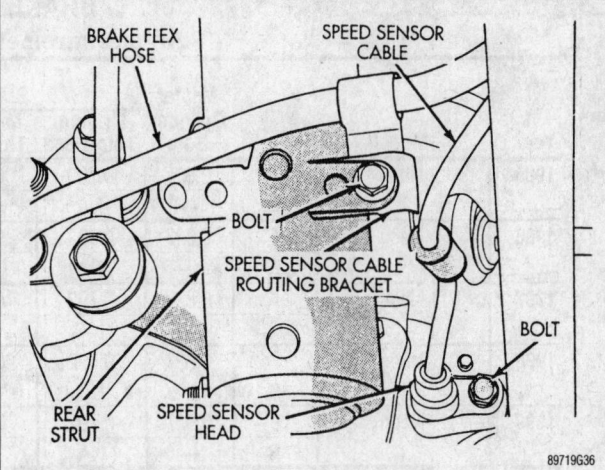

Fig. 140 Rear wheel speed sensor head mounting and cable routing

10. Place the sensor cable into the routing clips on the rear brake flex hose and chassis brake tube.
11. Plug the sensor connector into the vehicle wiring harness, then install the clip attaching the sensor cable connector to the body of the vehicle.
12. Install the tire and wheel, then carefully lower the vehicle to the ground.
13. Connect the negative battery cable. Road test the vehicle to assure proper brake system operation.

### Bleeding The ABS System

➡This bleeding procedure is only applicable for the anti-lock brake modulator unit; bleeding of the master cylinder and wheel cylinders/brake calipers should be performed the same as vehicles without anti-lock systems. A Diagnostic Readout Box (DRB), or the equivalent type of scan tool, is essential to perform the bleeding of the ABS system.

The brake system must be bled any time air is permitted to enter the system through loosened or disconnected lines or hoses, or anytime the modulator is removed. Excessive air within the system will cause a soft or spongy feel in the brake pedal.

When bleeding any part of the system, the reservoir must remain as close to full as possible at all times. Check the level frequently and top off fluid as needed.

The Bendix Anti-lock 4 brake system must be bled as 2 separate brake systems. Proper procedures must be followed if the system is to work correctly. The normal portion of the brake system is bled in the usual fashion with either pressure or manual bleeding equipment and must be fully and properly bled before bleeding the modulator.

### ✳✳ CAUTION

**Wear eye protection when bleeding the modulator assembly and always use a hose on the bleed screw to direct the flow of fluid away from painted surfaces. Bleeding the modulator may result in the release of very high pressure fluid.**

➡ **To bleed the hydraulic circuits of the brake system modulator assembly, the aid of an assistant will be required to pump the brake pedal.**

The Bendix 4 anti-lock brake system modulator does not need to be bled when doing normal servicing procedures such as caliper, hose or wheel cylinder replacement. The modulator does need to be bled when the modulator is removed or the lines are disconnected from the modulator. When servicing this system use DOT 3 brake fluid.

1. Assemble and install all brake system components on the vehicles, making sure all of the hydraulic lines are installed and tightened properly.
2. Connect the DRB or equivalent scan tool to the data link connector, located under the dash panel, near the steering column cover.
3. Use the scan tool to check if there are any Diagnostic Trouble Codes (DTCs) stored. If any codes are present, they must be removed prior to bleeding the system.
4. Fill the master cylinder reservoir to the proper level.
5. Bleed the base brake system using the pressure or manual methods outlined earlier in this section.
6. Using the DRB or equivalent scan tool, go to the "Bleed ABS" routing. Apply the brake pedal firmly, then initiate the "Bleed ABS" cycle one time. Release the brake pedal.
7. Properly bleed the base brake system again.
8. Repeat steps 6 and 7 until the brake fluid flows clear and free of bubbles. Check the brake fluid level in the reservoir periodically to prevent the reservoir from running low on fluid.
9. Road test the vehicle to check for proper brake system operation.

## BRAKE SPECIFICATIONS
All measurements in inches unless noted

| Year | Model | | Master Cylinder Bore | Brake Disc Original Thickness | Brake Disc Minimum Thickness | Brake Disc Maximum Runout | Brake Drum Diameter Original Inside Diameter | Brake Drum Diameter Max. Wear Limit | Brake Drum Diameter Maximum Machine Diameter | Wheel Cylinder or Caliper Bore Front | Wheel Cylinder or Caliper Bore Rear |
|---|---|---|---|---|---|---|---|---|---|---|---|
| 1995 | Neon | F | 0.827 | 0.792 | 0.724 | 0.005 | — | — | — | 0.300 | — |
| | | R | — | NA | NA | NA | 7.88 | NA | NA | — | ① |
| 1996 | Neon | F | 0.827 | 0.792 | 0.724 | 0.005 | — | — | — | 0.300 | — |
| | | R | — | NA | NA | NA | 7.88 | NA | NA | — | ① |
| 1997 | Neon | F | 0.827 | 0.792 | 0.724 | 0.005 | — | — | — | 0.300 | — |
| | | R | — | NA | NA | NA | 7.88 | NA | NA | — | ① |
| 1998 | Neon | F | 0.827 | 0.792 | 0.724 | 0.005 | — | — | — | 0.300 | — |
| | | R | — | NA | NA | NA | 7.88 | NA | NA | — | ① |
| 1999 | Neon | F | 0.827 | 0.792 | 0.724 | 0.005 | — | — | — | 0.300 | — |
| | | R | — | NA | NA | NA | 7.88 | NA | NA | — | ① |

② Rear drum brakes: 0.280

89719C01

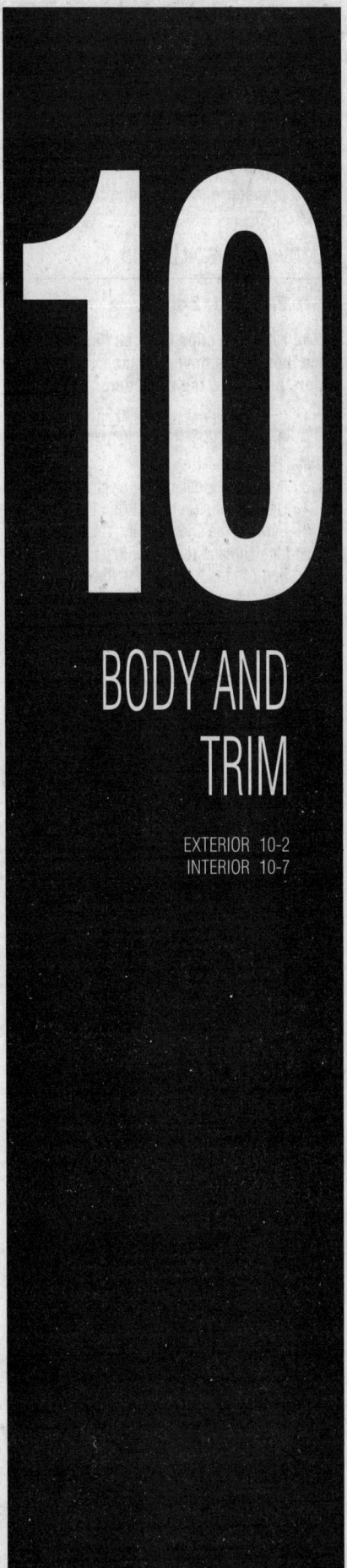

# 10

# BODY AND TRIM

## Doors

➡ **The procedure for removing both the front and rear doors is the same.**

### REMOVAL & INSTALLATION

▶ **See Figures 1, 2 and 6**

➡ **The retaining clips used on the door hinge pins are not reusable once they are removed. Make sure to have new clips on hand before beginning the procedure.**

1. Disconnect the negative battery cable.
2. Open the door, then suitable support it either with the help of an assistant or a padded jack.
3. If equipped, detach the electrical connector at the hinge pillar.
4. Unfasten the bolts securing the door check strap to the hinge pillar.
5. Remove the clip securing the hinge pin in the lower door hinge. Discard the clip and replace with a new one during installation.
6. Remove the pin from the lower hinge.
7. Remove and discard the clip holding the hinge pin in the upper door hinge, then remove the pin from the upper hinge.
8. Carefully remove the door from the vehicle.

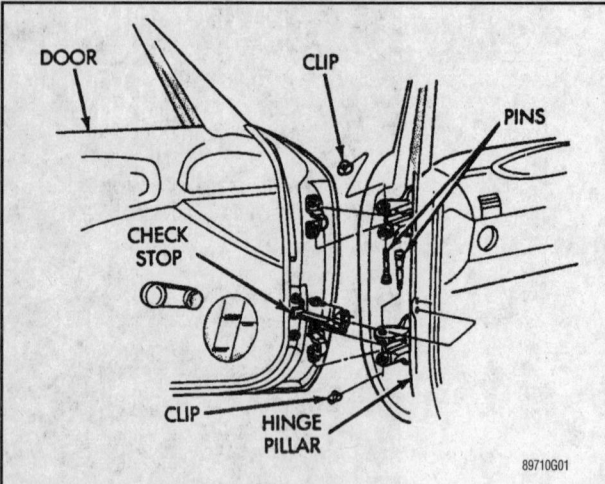

Fig. 1 Exploded view of the door assembly—the procedure is the same for the front and rear doors

**To install:**

9. Apply a suitable multi-purpose grease to the inside of the door hinge bushings.
10. Position the door on the vehicle and install the pin in the upper hinge. Align the knurling on the pin with the grooves in the door hinge before driving the pin in.
11. Install the pin in the lower hinge.

➡ **Make sure the head of each hinge pin is fully seated into the door hinge.**

12. Install a new clip securing the pin in the upper hinge and a new clip to hold the pin in the lower hinge.
13. Install the bolts holding the door check strap to the hinge pillar.

14. If equipped, attach the electrical connector at the hinge pillar.
15. Connect the negative battery cable.

### ADJUSTMENT

▶ **See Figure 2**

➡ **The only adjustment for the doors is a latch adjustment.**

1. Insert a hex wrench through the elongated hole in the door end frame near the latch striker opening.
2. Loosen the socket head screw on the side of the latch linkage.
3. Lift upward on the outside door handle, then release it.
4. Tighten the socket head screw on the latch.
5. Check for proper latch operation.

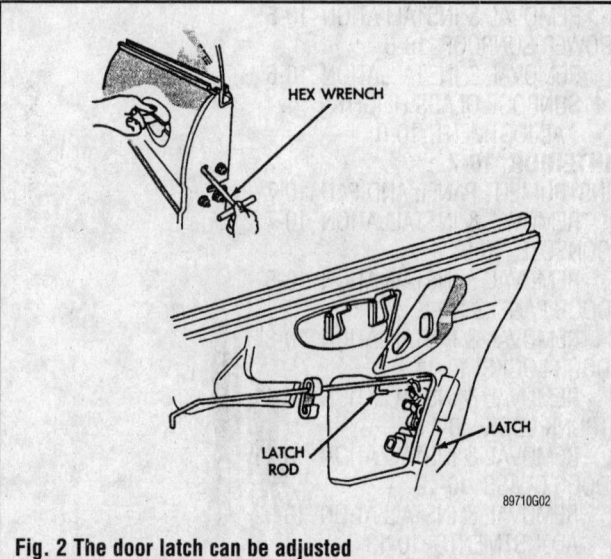

Fig. 2 The door latch can be adjusted

## Hood

### REMOVAL & INSTALLATION

▶ **See Figures 3, 4 and 5**

➡ **You will need an assistant to perform this procedure.**

1. Raise the hood to the full up position.
2. Disconnect the negative battery cable.
3. If equipped, detach the underhood lamp connector from the engine compartment wire harness.
4. Use a grease pencil or paint marker to outline the installed position of all of the bolts and hinges, for alignment during installation. When you are installing the hood, align all of the marks and secure the bolts. The hood should be aligned to a 0.160 in. (4mm) gap to the front fenders and flush across the top surfaces along the fenders.
5. If necessary, disconnect the windshield washer fluid hose from the hood.
6. With an assistant supporting the hood, remove the top bolts holding the hood to the hinge, then loosen the bottom bolts until they can be removed by hand.

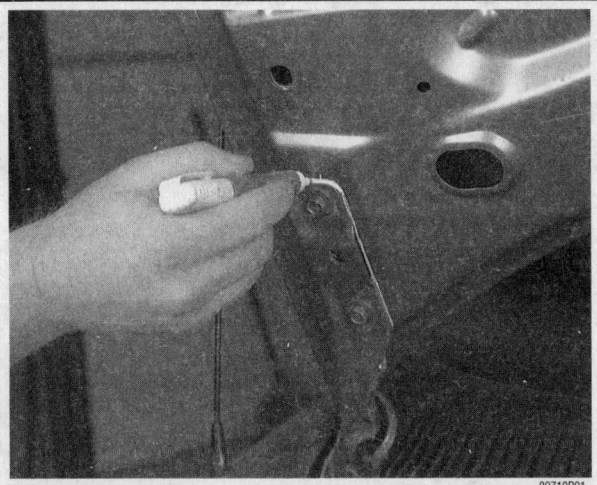

**Fig. 3 Use a suitable pen to matchmark the installed position of the hood hinges**

**Fig. 4 Disconnect the windshield washer fluid hose from the hood**

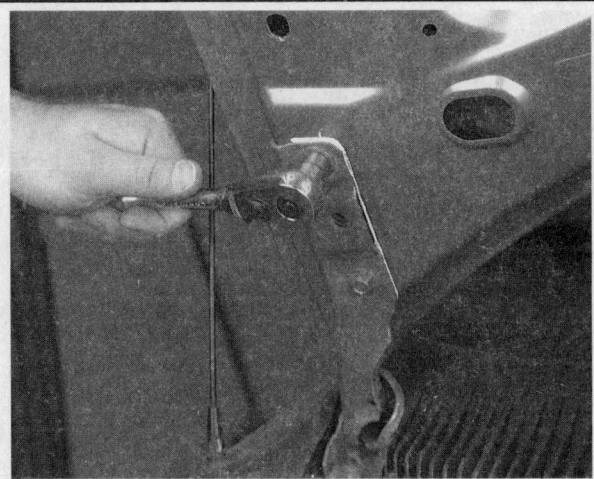

**Fig. 5 With an assistant supporting the hood, unfasten the retaining bolts**

7. With the hood still supported, remove the bottom bolts securing the hood to the hinge.

8. Carefully remove the hood from the vehicle.

**To install:**

9. With the help of an assistant, place the hood in position on the vehicle. Have the assistant hold the hood at the opposite side of the vehicle from which you are working, then install the bottom bolts finger-tight to hold the hood to the hinge.

10. Install the top hood-to-hinge bolts finger-tight.

11. Position the bolts at the marks made during removal, then tighten the bolts securely. The hood should be aligned to a 0.160 in. (4mm) gap to the front fenders and flush across the top surfaces along the fenders.

12. If removed, connect the windshield washer hose to the nipple on the hood.

13. Attach the connector to the underhood lamp, if equipped.

14. Connect the negative battery cable.

15. Check for proper hood operation and alignment.

## Trunk Lid

### REMOVAL & INSTALLATION

▶ **See Figure 6**

1. Disconnect the negative battery cable.

2. Open the trunk lid.

3. Matchmark the bolt locations on the inside of the trunk lid for alignment during installation.

4. Disengage the clips holding the wire harness and trunk lid release cable to the trunk lid.

5. Detach the wire connector and release cable from the trunk latch.

6. Unfasten the bolts holding the top of the hinge to the trunk lid.

7. With an assistant supporting the trunk lid, remove the bolts holding the bottom of the hinge to the trunk lid.

**To install:**

8. Place the trunk lid in position on the vehicle.

9. With an assistant holding the trunk lid in position, install the bolts to hold the bottom of the hinge to the lid.

10. Install the bolts securing the top of the hinge to the trunk lid.

11. Align the trunk lid to obtain equal spacing on all sides and flush across the gaps.

12. Check for proper trunk lid operation and sealing.

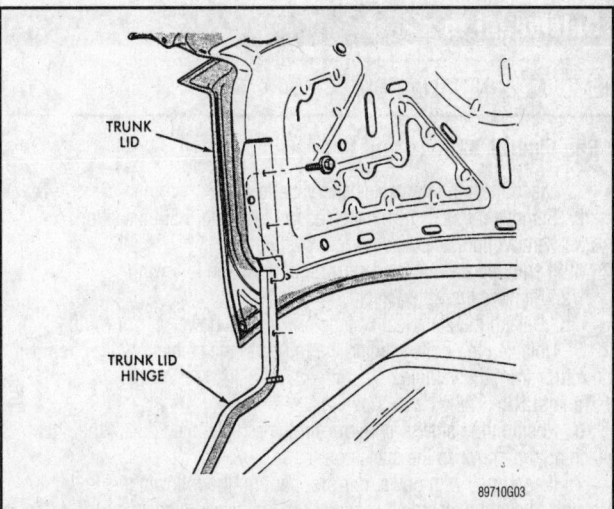

**Fig. 6 Have an assistant support the trunk lid, then remove the mounting bolts**

13. Attach the wire connector and release cable to the latch.
14. Install clips that hold the wire harness and cable to the trunk lid.
15. Connect the negative battery cable.

## Grille

### REMOVAL & INSTALLATION

▶ **See Figure 7**

1. Release the hood latch, then open and support the hood on the pump rod.
2. Remove the screws holding the grille to the parking lamps.
3. Unfasten the screw holding the grille to the radiator closure panel.
4. Remove the grille from the vehicle.

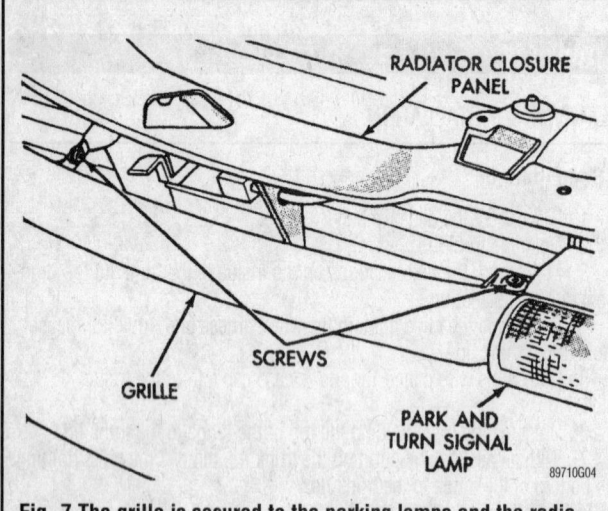

Fig. 7 The grille is secured to the parking lamps and the radiator closure panel

**To install:**
5. Place the grille into position on the vehicle.
6. Install the screw securing the grille to the radiator closure panel.
7. Install the screws holding the grille to the parking lamps.
8. Close the hood.

## Outside Mirrors

### REMOVAL & INSTALLATION

▶ **See Figures 8, 9, 10 and 11**

1. Disconnect the negative battery cable.
2. Remove the door trim panel, as outlined later in this section.
3. Remove the side view mirror cover.
4. If equipped with power mirrors, perform the following:
   a. Remove the water shield.
   b. Detach the electrical connector from the power mirror motor.
5. Unfasten the bolts holding the mirror to the stanchion, then remove the mirror from the vehicle.
**To install:**
6. Position the side view mirror on the vehicle, then install the nuts attaching the mirror to the stanchion.
7. If equipped with power mirrors, perform the following:
   a. Attach the electrical connector to the power window motor.
   b. Install the water shield.
8. Install the door trim panel, as outlined later in this section.

Fig. 8 Remove the side view mirror cover

Fig. 9 Unfasten the nuts securing the mirror to the stanchion . . .

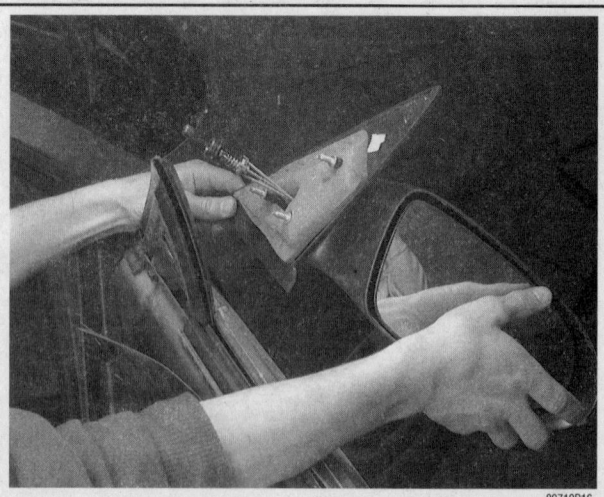

Fig. 10 . . . then carefully remove the side view mirror from the door

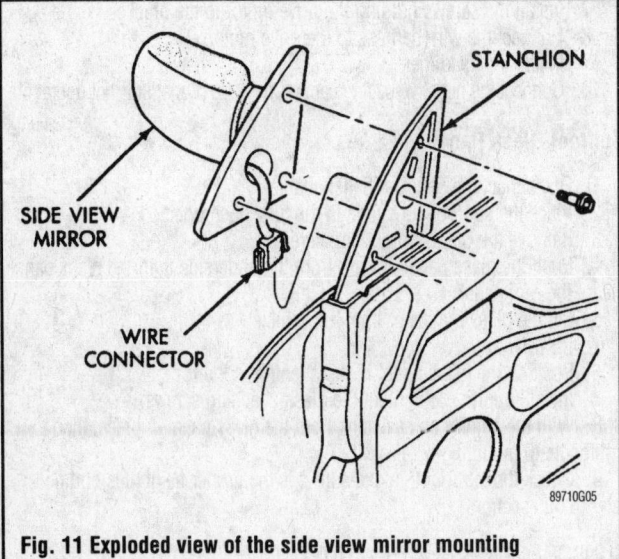

**Fig. 11 Exploded view of the side view mirror mounting**

9. Install the side view mirror cover.
10. Connect the negative battery cable.

## Antenna

### REPLACEMENT

▶ **See Figure 12**

1. Disconnect the negative battery cable.
2. Remove the antenna mast by unscrewing the mast from the antenna body.
3. Locate the antenna lead disconnect in the instrument panel wire harness above the right kick panel. Disconnect the antenna cable from the cable lead.
4. Unfasten the push pins from the rear of the plastic inner fender shield and move the shield to gain access to the mounting screws.
5. Remove the mounting screws, then remove the antenna base and cable assembly from under the fender.
   **To install:**
6. Align the antenna adapter tongue with the groove in the fender hole and push the adapter into the fender.

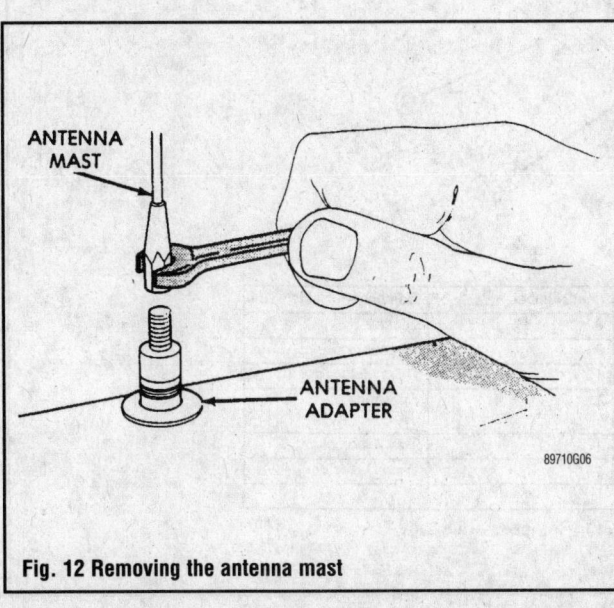

**Fig. 12 Removing the antenna mast**

7. From under the fender, push the antenna base and cable through the adapter in the fender. Tighten the mounting screw to 75 inch lbs. (7 Nm).
8. Seat the grommet in the side panel and attach the cable to the instrument pane harness connector.
9. Install the plastic inner fender shield.
10. Connect the antenna cable to the cable lead.

## Fenders

### REMOVAL & INSTALLATION

1. Disconnect the negative battery cable.
2. Remove all components mounted to the inside of the fender to be removed.
3. Remove the front side marker lamp assembly. For more details, refer to Section 6.
4. Remove the front bumper as necessary to gain clearance to remove the front fender.
5. Remove the front wheel well splash shield.
6. Remove the rocker panel moulding as necessary to clear the front fender.
7. Remove the bolts holding the bottom front fender at the rear of the wheel opening.
8. Remove the bolt holding the front fender at the rear of the wheel well.
9. Remove the bolt holding the front fender at the top of the front door opening.
10. Remove the bolts holding the front fender to the front lower brace and under the radiator closure panel.
11. Remove the bolts holding the front fender to the front of the radiator closure panel.
12. Raise the hood and support the hood with a suitable holding device. Mark the hinge on the fender for installation indexing. Remove the lower hood hinge attaching bolts and separate the hinge from the front fender.
13. Remove the bolts holding the front fender to the inner wheel well along the hood.
14. Separate the front fender from the vehicle.
    **To install:**

➡**When all mounting bolts are installed, adjust the fender to achieve a gap of 0.16 in. (4mm) between the fender and the hood, and a gap of 0.24 in. (6mm) to the front door edge. All surfaces across gaps should be flush.**

15. Position the fender onto the vehicle.
16. Loosely install the bolts to mount the front fender on the inner wheel well along the hood opening.
17. Loosely install the bolts to mount the front fender on the front of the radiator closure panel.
18. Loosely install the bolts to mount the front fender on the lower front brace and under the radiator closure panel.
19. Loosely install the bolts to mount the front fender at the top of the front door opening.
20. Loosely install the bolts to mount the front fender at the rear of the wheel well.
21. Loosely install the bolts to mount the front fender at the rear of the wheel opening.
22. Adjust the front fender to achieve the designated gap between the fender and the front door.
23. Tighten the attaching and mounting bolts.
24. Install the hood hinge-to-fender attaching bolts, the rocker panel moulding and the front wheel well splash shield, then tighten the bolts.
25. Install the front bumper.
26. Install the side marker lamp assembly. Refer to Section 6 for more details.

27. Install any components removed from the inside of the fender. Refer to the necessary procedures depending on the various components.
28. Connect the negative battery cable.

## Power Sunroof

### REMOVAL & INSTALLATION

▶ **See Figure 13**

**Sunroof Drive Motor**

### ✳✳ WARNING

**Do NOT cycle the new motor before installation. The motor is shipped in the closed position. The sunroof vent position is programmed into the motor and is dependent on the closed position of the motor. If the drive motor and sunroof mechanism are not both in the closed position, the sunroof vent height will not be correct.**

1. Remove the headliner until the sunroof drive motor is accessible.
2. If the drive motor is to be reused, cycle the sunroof to the full forward position.
3. Detach the wire harness connector from the motor.
4. Remove the three screws attaching the drive motor-to-sunroof module bracket.
5. Separate the drive motor from the bracket.

**To install:**

6. With the help of an assistant, hold the sunroof glass panel in the closed position and engage the drive motor into the sunroof drive cables.

7. Install the screws holding the drive motor to the bracket.
8. Connect the wire harness to the drive motor.
9. Install the headliner.
10. Connect the negative battery cable. Check for proper sunroof operation.

### Sunroof Glass Panel

1. Disconnect the negative battery cable.
2. Place the sunroof sunshade in the fully open position.
3. Remove the 6 glass mounting screws.
4. Push the glass panel upward from the underside until the glass panel clears the roof panel.
5. Lift the glass the panel from the vehicle.

**To install:**

6. Position the glass panel in the opening in the roof.
7. Install, but do not tighten, the glass attaching screws.
8. With the help of an assistant, hold the glass panel in place, then tighten the 6 mounting screws.
9. Check the sunroof to make sure it is the proper height, as outlined later in this section.

### SUNROOF GLASS HEIGHT ADJUSTMENT

**Flushness Adjustment**

1. Place the sun shade in the fully open position.
2. To adjust the front of the glass, perform the following:
   a. Loosen the front and middle glass attachment screws.
   b. Adjust the front of the sunroof glass panel so that the corners are flush to 1.0mm below the top surface of the roof panel.
   c. Tighten all of the glass attachment screws.
3. To adjust the rear of the glass, perform the following:
   a. Loosen the rear and middle glass attachment screws.

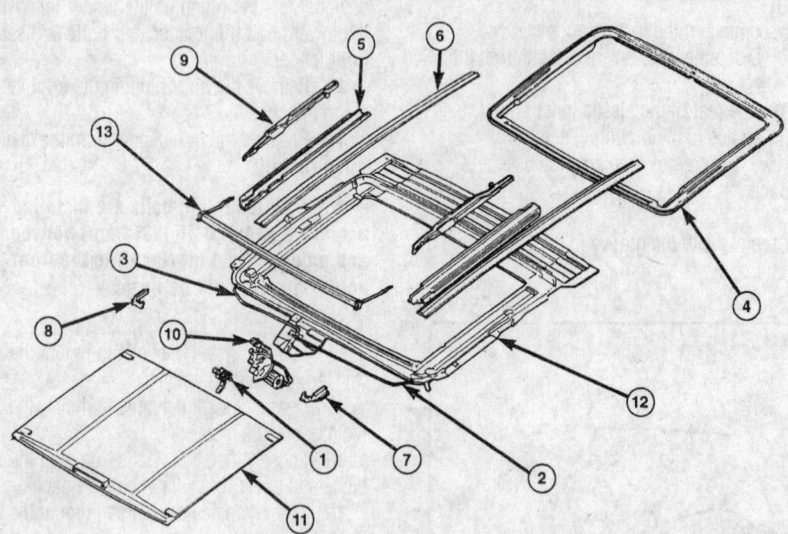

| Item Number | Component Name | Item Number | Component Name |
|---|---|---|---|
| 1 | Drive Tube Locator | 8 | Locator R.H. |
| 2 | Drive Tube L.H. | 9 | Mechanism |
| 3 | Drive Tube R.H. | 10 | Drive Motor |
| 4 | Glass Reinforcment Panel | 11 | Sunshade |
| 5 | Guide | 12 | Tray Assembly |
| 6 | Sunshade Guide | 13 | Wind Deflector |
| 7 | Locator L.H. | | |

89710G07

**Fig. 13 Exploded view of the sunroof glass and related components**

b. Adjust the rear of the sunroof glass panel so that the corners are flush to within 1.0mm of the top surface of the roof panel.

c. Tighten all of the glass attachment screws.

**Vent Height Adjustment**

1. Cycle the sunroof module to the vent position using the drive motor.

2. Check the glass height in tilt using the proper measuring tool.

3. If the vent height is greater than 35mm, use the switch to slowly set to the proper height.

4. After setting the correct height, remove the drive motor.

5. With the motor removed, use the switch to set the tilt by operating the gear to the fully closed position.

6. Using the tilt switch only, operate the motor until it comes to a full stop at the tilt position.

7. Install the drive motor and verify correct operation.

## INTERIOR

### Instrument Panel and Pad

REMOVAL & INSTALLATION

♦ **See Figures 14, 15, 16 and 17**

#### ✳✳ CAUTION

**All models covered by this manual are equipped with a Supplemental Restraint System (SRS), which uses an air bag. Whenever working near any of the SRS components, such as the impact sensors, the air bag module, steering column and instrument panel, disable the SRS, as described in Section 6.**

1. Disconnect and isolate the negative battery cable. Wait at least 2 minutes to begin service to allow the SRS ample time to disarm.

2. Remove the console, as outlined later in this section.

3. Remove the right and left cowl side trim panels.

4. Remove the steering column cover and liner.

5. Remove the top cover and cluster bezel.

6. Remove the right and left trim panels.

7. Remove the defroster upper duct by lifting it up.

8. Remove the center outlet duct by pulling it rearward.

9. Disconnect the heater and A/C control by removing the control cable clips with a small prytool and detaching the wire connector.

#### ✳✳ WARNING

**The steering wheel must be locked in the straight ahead position. This will prevent damaging the clockspring when the steering wheel rotates freely.**

10. Disconnect the steering column at the bottom slap together joint.

11. If equipped with automatic transaxle, disconnect the shifter interlock cable at the shifter.

12. Tag and disconnect any necessary instrument panel wiring.

13. Remove the 4 attaching screws from the center floor pan bracket.

14. Remove the 4 attaching screws from the steering column.

15. Unfasten the 4 cowl top nuts.

16. Remove the attaching screws from the left and right cowl side bracket.

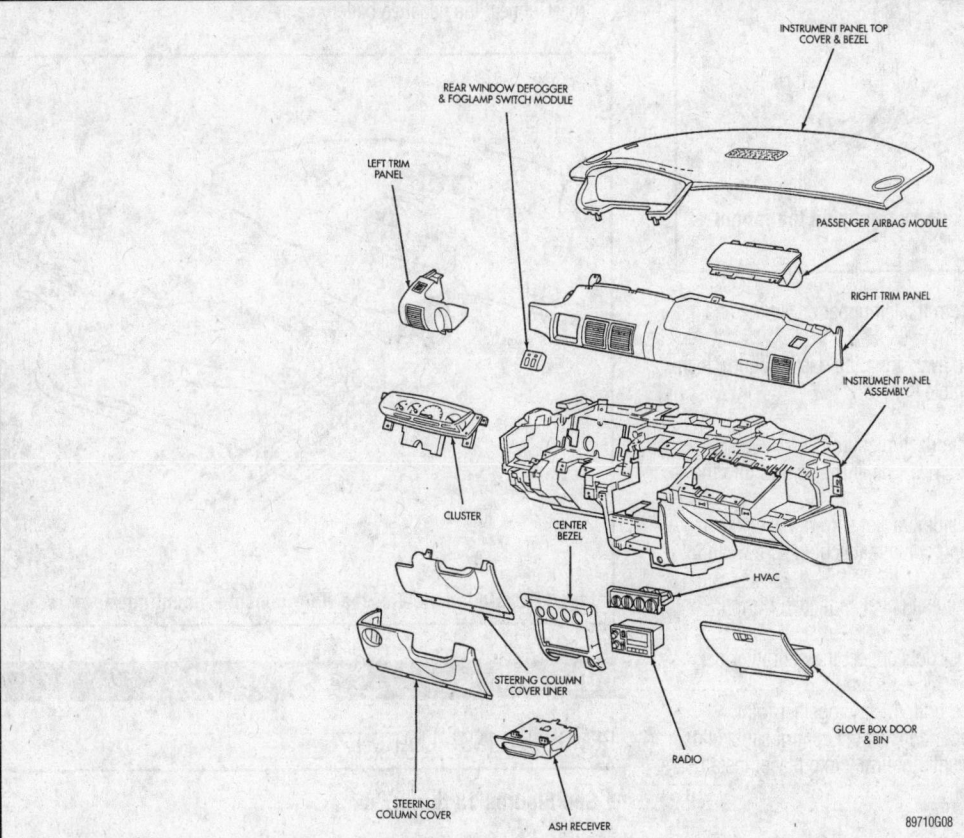

**Fig. 14 Exploded view of the instrument panel, trim panels and related components**

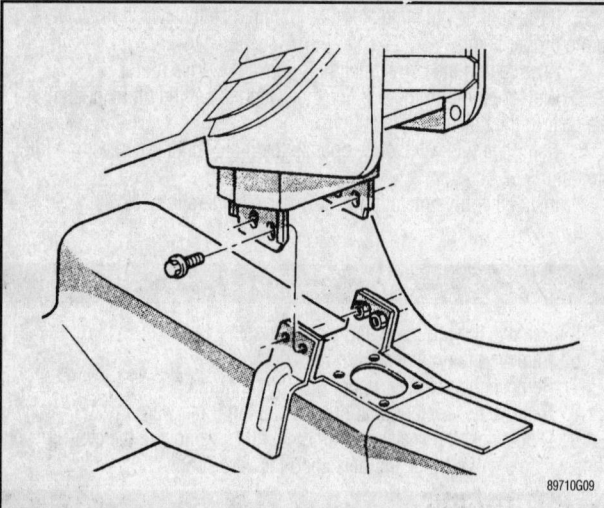

**Fig. 15 Unfasten the screws, then remove the center floor pan bracket**

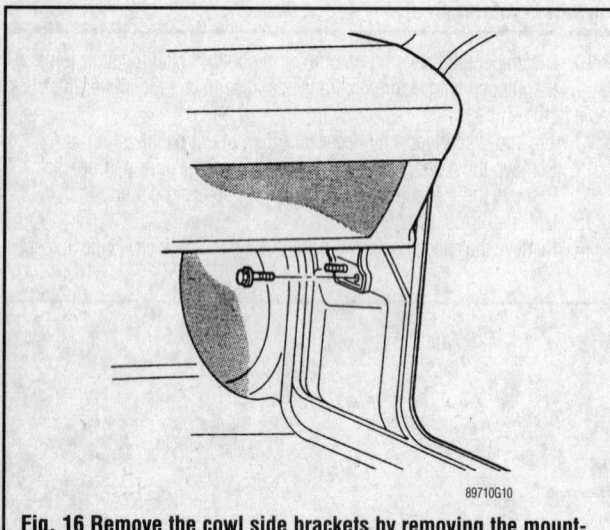

**Fig. 16 Remove the cowl side brackets by removing the mounting screws**

17. Remove the 2 mounting screws from the left upper cowl side and 1 from the right upper cowl side.

18. Pull the instrument panel rearward away from the dash/plenum, then remove the instrument panel from the vehicle.

**To install:**

19. Position the instrument panel to the dash/plenum.

20. Install 1 screw into the right upper cowl side and 2 screws into the left upper cowl side.

21. Install the left and right side cowl side bracket screws.

22. Install the 4 cowl tops nuts, steering column attaching screws and center floor pan bracket screws.

23. Connect all the wiring to the instrument panel as tagged during removal.

24. If equipped with an automatic transaxle, connect the shift interlock cable to the shifter.

25. Connect the steering column at the bottom slap together joint.

26. Attach the heater control connector and install the control cable clips.

27. Install the center outlet duct by pushing it firmly into place. Install the upper defrost duct.

28. Install the right and left trim panels.

29. Install the cluster bezel and top panel.

30. Install the steering column and liner.

31. Install the right and left cowl side trim panel.

32. Install the floor console, as outlined later in this section.

33. Connect the negative battery cable.

## Console

### REMOVAL & INSTALLATION

▶ See Figure 17

### ✳✳ CAUTION

**All models covered by this manual are equipped with a Supplemental Restraint System (SRS), which uses an air bag. Whenever working near any of the SRS components, such as the impact sensors, the air bag module, steering column and instrument panel, disable the SRS, as described in Section 6.**

1. Disconnect and isolate the negative battery cable. Wait at least 2 minutes to begin service to allow the SRS ample time to disarm.

2. If equipped with a manual transaxle, remove the shifter knob.

3. Remove the attaching screws from each side of the cup holder. On vehicles with a non-armrest console, remove the 2 screws from the rear of the console. On vehicles with an armrest console, remove the 4 screws in the console bin.

4. Pull the parking brake lever up all of the way.

5. Lift the console at the rear and guide it out from under the instrument panel.

**To install:**

6. Place the console into proper position in the vehicle.

7. Return the parking brake lever to the fully released.

8. Install the console retaining screws and screws to each side of the cup holder.

9. If equipped with a manual transaxle, install the shifter knob.

10. Connect the negative battery cable.

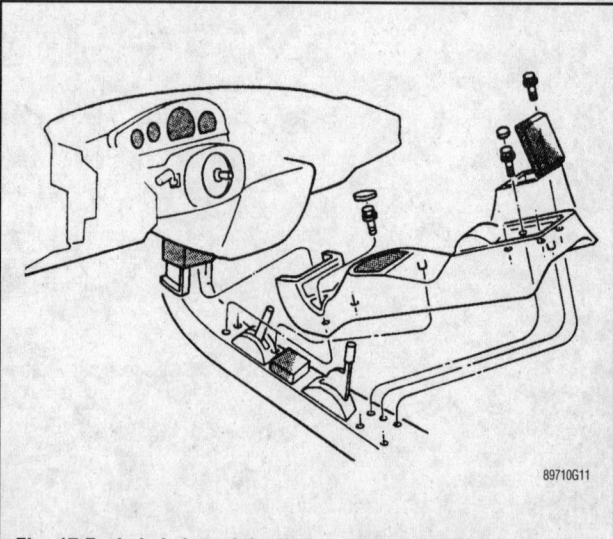

**Fig. 17 Exploded view of the floor console mounting**

## Door Panels

### REMOVAL & INSTALLATION

▶ See Figures 18 thru 27

1. Open the door, then lower the window.

2. Disconnect the negative battery cable.

3. Unfasten the screw attaching the pull cup to the door panel.

Fig. 18 Remove the pull cup-to-door panel retaining screw

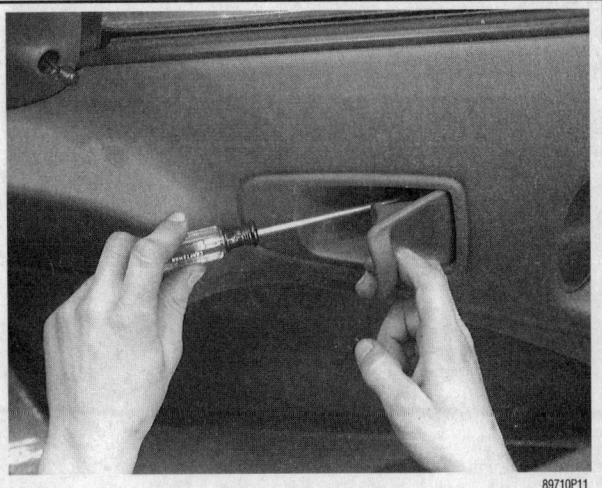

Fig. 19 Pull the door latch handle open, then remove the retaining screw located behind the handle

4. Pull the inside door latch release handle, in order to access the attaching screw, then remove the screw.

5. If equipped with manual windows, slide a window crank removal tool behind the crank to unfasten the retaining clip, then remove the crank.

➡ **Use a fork-type trim panel fastener removal tool to disengage the push-in fasteners. Pulling on the trim panel to disengage the fasteners will damage the panel.**

6. Disengage all hidden push-in fasteners attaching the trim panel to the door. Make sure that all of the fasteners are detached using the removal tool.

7. Tilt the trim panel out to clear the locator pins on the back side of the trim panel.

8. Lift the trim panel to disengage it from the retainer channel on the inner belt weather-strip at the top of the door.

9. Disengage the clip holding the door latch linkage to the back of the inside door handle, then separate the latch rod from the handle.

➡ **Do not let the door trim panel to hang by the wire connector or wiring.**

10. Detach the wire connector(s) from the power door lock switch, mirror switch and/or power window switch, as applicable.

11. Remove the trim panel from the vehicle.

**To install:**

12. Replace any missing or damaged push-in retainers with new ones of the same type and quality.

13. Position the trim panel near the door.

14. Attach the connectors to the power components (window, mirror, locks), as applicable.

15. Insert the latch rod into the inside latch release.

16. Engage the clip holding the door latch linkage to the back of the inside door handle.

17. Place the trim panels into the retainer channel at the top of the door and push it down to seat.

18. Locate the door trim panel to the inner door panel by aligning the locating pins on the backside of the trim panel to the mating holes in the inner door panel. Gently shift the panel forward or rearward, as necessary.

19. Engage the hidden push-in fasteners holding the trim panel to the door from around the perimeter of the trim panel.

20. With the window still all the way down, place the window regulator crank handle approximately. Install the right handle at the 10 o'clock position and the left handle at the 2 o'clock position, if equipped with manual windows.

21. Install the screw securing the trim panel to the door from behind the inside door latch release handle.

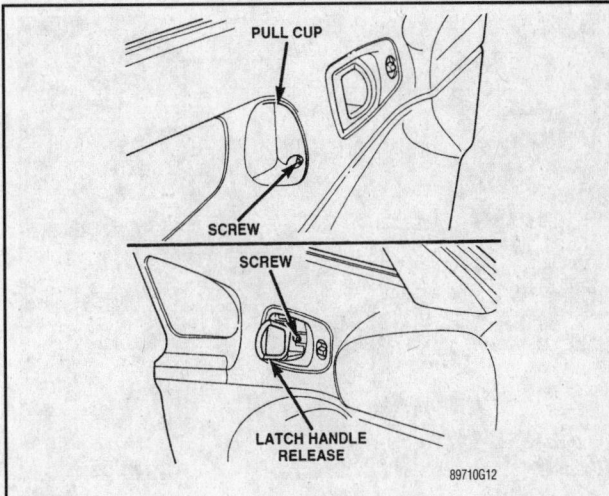

Fig. 20 Location of the pull cup and inside handle screws—rear door panel shown

Fig. 21 If your vehicle has manual windows, insert a suitable removal tool behind the crank . . .

Fig. 22 . . . and remove the window crank (1), washer (2) and retaining clip (3)

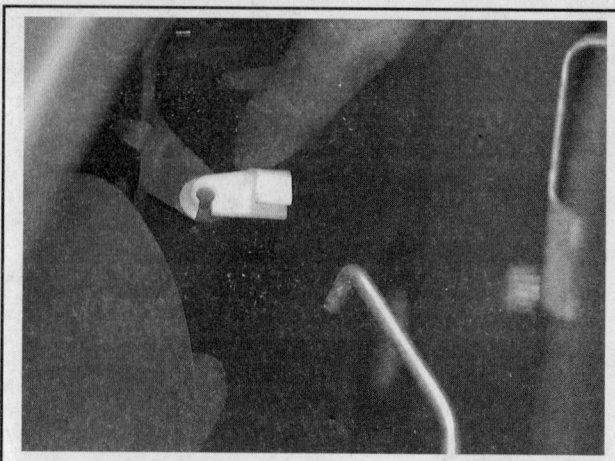

Fig. 25 Disengage the clip securing the door latch linkage to the back of the inside door handle, then remove the trim panel from the door

Fig. 23 After all of the retainers are disengaged, tilt the door panel outward to clear the locator pins

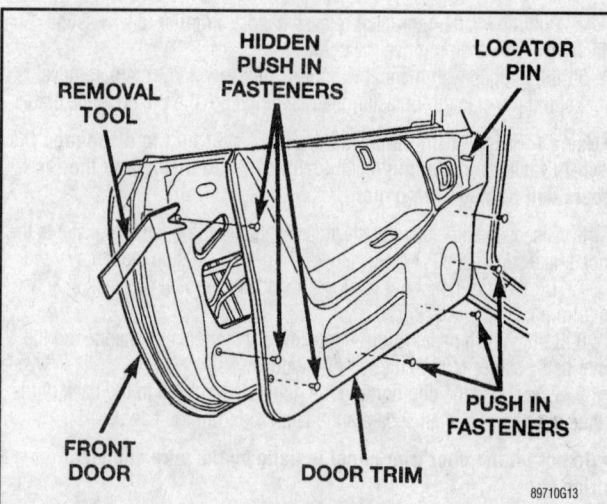

Fig. 26 Exploded view of the door trim panel—front door shown, rear similar

Fig. 24 Lift the door panel to unhook it from the channel on the inner belt weather-stripping at the top of the door

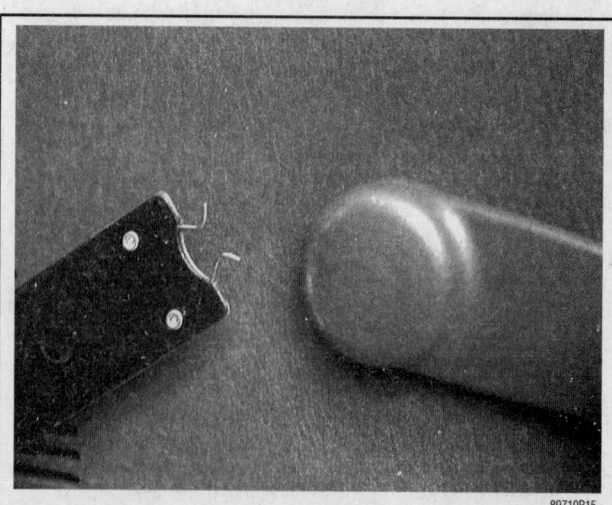

Fig. 27 Use the opposite end of the removal tool to install the window crank handle retaining clip

22. Install the screw inside the pull cup holding door trim panel to the bracket.

23. Connect the negative battery cable.

## Door Locks

### REMOVAL & INSTALLATION

▶ See Figures 28 and 29

1. Remove the door trim panel.
2. Remove the water shield, as follows:
   a. If equipped, remove the door speaker.
   b. Remove the door trim pull cup mount bracket.
   c. Disengage the clip holding the lock linkage to the lock button bell crank.
   d. Carefully peel the water shield away from the adhesive around the edge of the inner door panel.
3. Close the window.
4. Disconnect the door lock rod from the latch.
   a. Remove the clip holding the lock cylinder to the door handle.
   b. Pull the lock cylinder from the door handle.

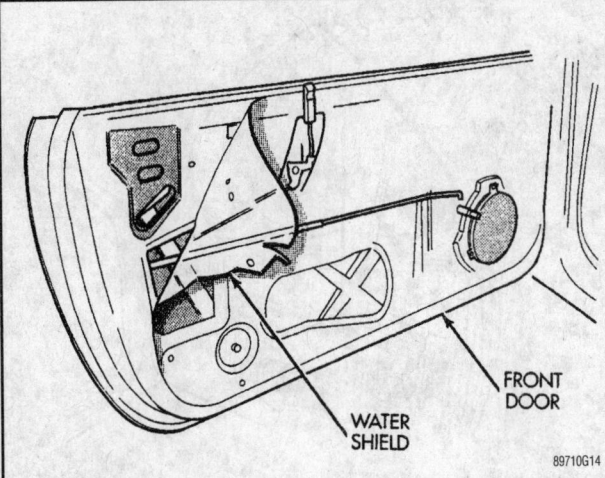

**Fig. 28 Remove the water shield by carefully peeling it away from the inner door panel**

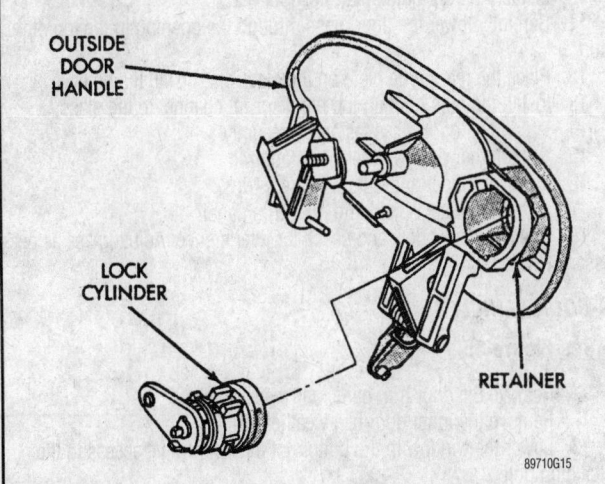

**Fig. 29 The door lock cylinder is mounted in the outside door handle**

**To install:**

5. Push the lock cylinder into the door handle.
6. Install the clip holding the lock cylinder to the door handle.
7. Connect the door lock rod to the latch.
8. Install the water shield, as follows:
   a. Make sure there is enough adhesive to secure the water shield.
   b. Place the water shield in position, then press securely to the adhesive, making sure to properly route the wiring and linkages.
   c. Engage the clip holding the lock linkage to the lock button bell crank.
   d. Install the door trim pull cup mount bracket.
   e. Engage the clip holding the lock linkage to the lock button bell crank.
   f. Install the door trim pull cup mount bracket.
   g. If equipped, install the door speaker.
9. Install the door trim panel, as outlined earlier in this section.
10. Connect the negative battery cable.

## Trunk Lock

### REMOVAL & INSTALLATION

▶ See Figures 30 and 31

1. Remove the trunk latch, as follows:
   a. Open the trunk lid.
   b. Unfasten the bolts securing the trunk latch to the trunk lid.
   c. Disconnect the remote trunk latch release cable from the trunk latch.
   d. Disengage the trunk ajar switch connector from the latch.
   e. Separate the latch from the vehicle.
2. Remove the clip securing the lock cylinder to the trunk lid, then pull the lock cylinder from the trunk lid.

**To install:**

3. Place the lock cylinder in the trunk lid, then install the retaining clip.
4. Install the trunk latch, as follows:
   a. Position the latch in the vehicle and engage the trunk ajar switch connector to the latch.
   b. Connect the remote trunk latch release cable to the trunk latch.
   c. Install the bolts holding the trunk latch to the trunk lid.
   d. Close the trunk lid.

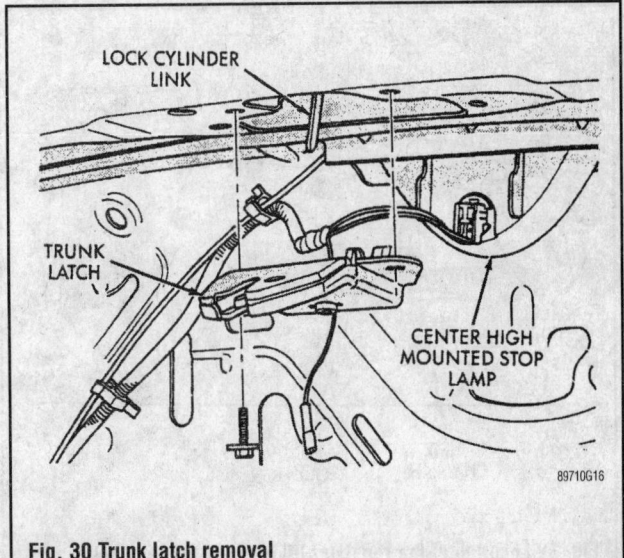

**Fig. 30 Trunk latch removal**

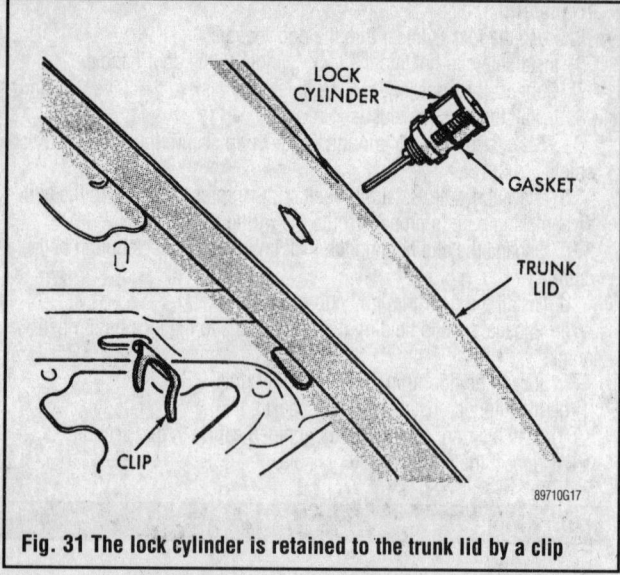

**Fig. 31 The lock cylinder is retained to the trunk lid by a clip**

## Door Glass

### REMOVAL & INSTALLATION

#### Front Door Glass

##### 2-DOOR VEHICLES

▶ See Figures 32, 33 and 34

1. Remove the door trim panel and water shield.
2. Remove the inner and outer door belt weather-strips.
3. Loosen the inner belt stabilizer.
4. Lower the door glass to the bottom of travel to access the glass attachment bolts.
5. Remove the bolts holding the regulator lift channel to the door glass.
6. Remove the bolts holding the rear guide plate from the door glass.
7. Separate the rear guide plate from the door glass.
8. Lift the door glass upward and out of the opening at the top of the door.
9. Remove the front guide plate from the door glass.

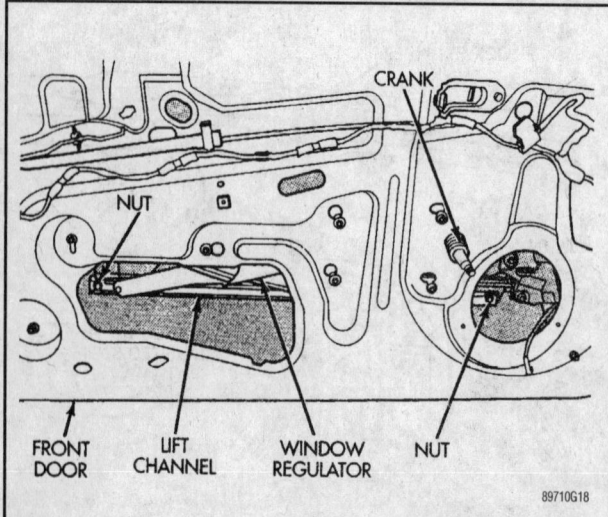

**Fig. 32 Location of the regulator lift channel-to-glass bolts**

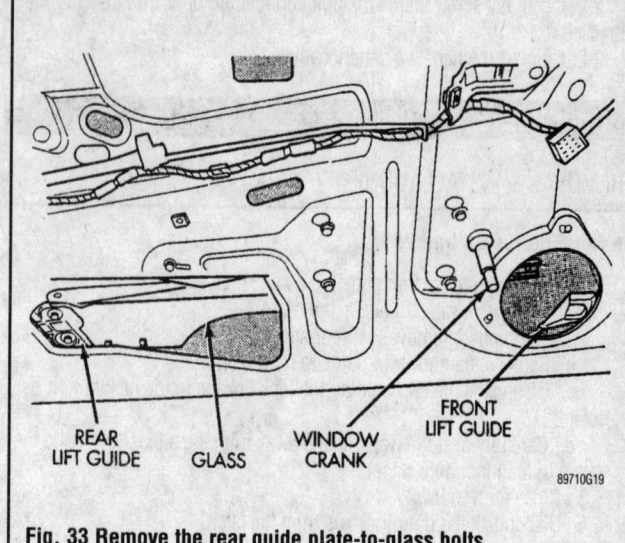

**Fig. 33 Remove the rear guide plate-to-glass bolts**

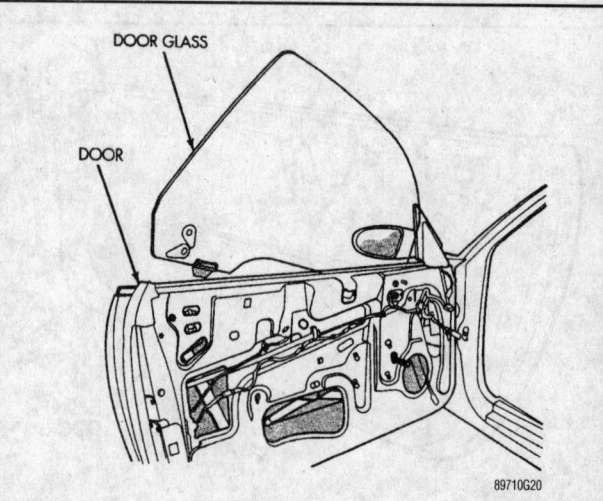

**Fig. 34 Carefully lift the door glass out of the top opening in the door**

**To install:**

10. Install the front guide plate-to-door glass.
11. Carefully lower the door glass through the opening in the top of the door.
12. Place the rear guide plate on the glass and install the bolts.
13. Install the nuts holding the regulator lift channel to the glass.
14. Tighten all door glass fasteners securely.
15. Tighten the window inner belt stabilizer.
16. Install the inner and outer weather-strips.
17. Install the water shield and door trim panel.
18. Operate the window and check for interference. Adjust glass as necessary.

##### 4-DOOR VEHICLES

▶ See Figure 35

1. Remove the door trim panel and water shield.
2. Remove the inner door belt weather-strip.
3. Lower the window to the bottom of the door to get access to the attaching bolts.
4. Remove the bolts holding the door glass to the window regulator lift plates.
5. Disengage the door glass from the regulator.

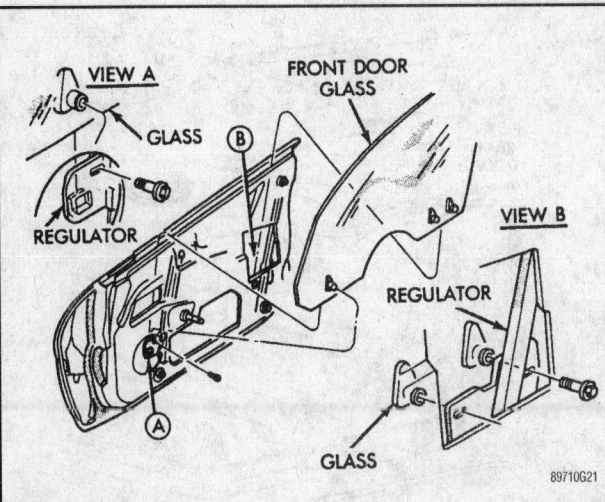

**Fig. 35 Exploded view of the front door glass—4-door vehicle shown**

6. Carefully lift the door glass upward out of the opening at the top of the door.

**To install:**

7. Carefully lower the glass through the opening in the top of the door.
8. Position the door glass into the window regulator lift plates.
9. Install the bolts securing the door glass to the lift plates.
10. Tighten the inner belt stabilizer.
11. Install the weather-strip.
12. Install the water shield and door trim panel.
13. Operate the window and check for interference. Adjust glass as necessary.

### Rear Door Glass

▶ **See Figure 36**

1. Remove the door trim panel and water shield.
2. Remove the inner door belt weather-strip.
3. Loosen the door glass jounce bumper.
4. Lower the glass to the bottom of the door.
5. Remove the nuts holding the door glass to the window regulator lift plate.
6. Disengage the door glass from the regulator.

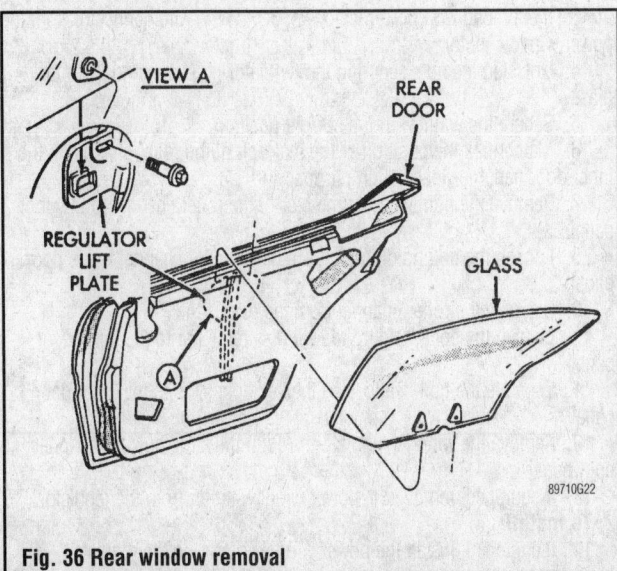

**Fig. 36 Rear window removal**

7. Carefully lift the door glass upward and out of the opening at the top of the door

**To install:**

8. Carefully lower the glass through the opening in the top of the door and into position in the window regulator.
9. Install nuts securing the door glass to the window regulator.
10. Raise the glass and tighten the window inner belt stabilizer.
11. Install the inner door belt weather-strip, water shield and door trim panel.
12. Operate the window and check for interference. Adjust glass as necessary.

## ADJUSTMENTS

### Front Door

▶ **See Figures 37, 38 and 39**

#### *UP-STOP ADJUSTMENTS*

1. Remove the door trim panel.
2. If necessary for access to the adjusters, remove the water shield.
3. Loosen the up-stop nut.
4. Close the door, then raise the door glass.
5. Adjust the up-stop to achieve the proper glass height.
6. Adjust the glass so that a piece of paper can be pulled between the glass and weather-strip with some tension.

➡ **The top edge of the door glass should be beneath the lip of the weather-strip.**

#### *TOP OF GLASS—INBOARD/OUTBOARD ADJUSTMENTS*

1. Remove the door trim panel.
2. If necessary for access to the adjusters, remove the water shield.
3. Using a suitable flare nut socket, loosen the lower jack-screw jam nuts.
4. Close the door, then raise the window.
5. Using a suitable Allen wrench, rotate the jack screws to achieve a proper in/out positioning at the top edge of the glass.
6. Adjust the glass so that a piece of paper can be pulled between the glass and the weather-strip with some tension.
7. Tighten all fasteners.

#### *GLASS—FRONT/REAR ADJUSTMENT*

1. Remove the door trim panel and water shield.
2. Lower the window to the bottom of its travel for access to the glass attachments.
3. Loosen the 3 glass attachment bolts.
4. Raise the glass to the top of its travel and adjust the glass to fit the B-pillar seal. The glass-to-B-pillar appliqué should be about ½ in. (13mm).
5. Tighten the 2 accessible glass fasteners in the full up position.
6. Lower the window to the full down position, then tighten the remaining glass fastener. Raise the glass to the top of its travel, then check positioning.

### Rear Door

▶ **See Figures 39 and 40**

#### *UP-STOP ADJUSTMENTS*

1. Remove the door trim panel.
2. If necessary for access to the adjusters, remove the water shield.
3. Using a suitable flare nut socket, loosen the up-stop eccentric jam-nut.
4. Using a suitable hex wrench to rotate the up-stop eccentric to get the proper glass height.
5. Adjust the glass so that a piece of paper can be pulled between the glass and the weather-strip with some tension.

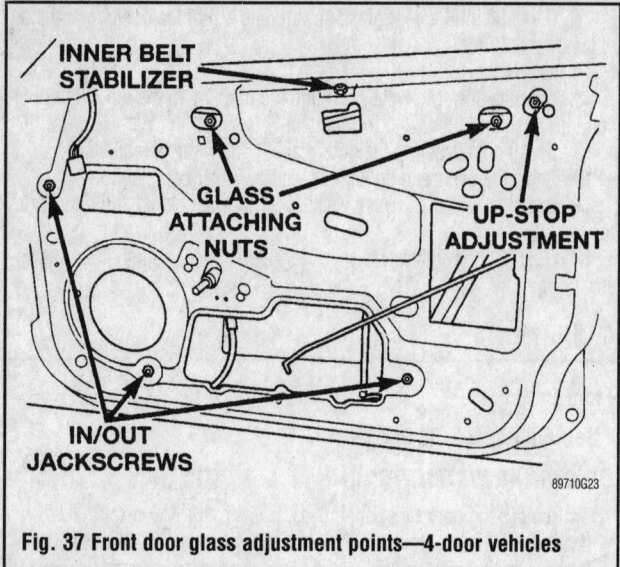

Fig. 37 Front door glass adjustment points—4-door vehicles

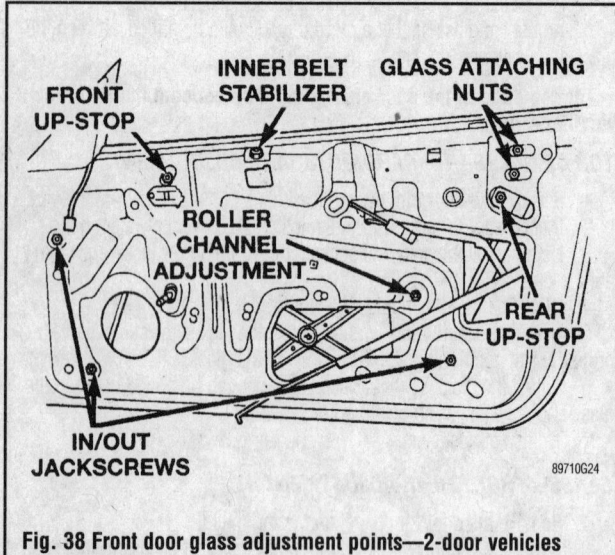

Fig. 38 Front door glass adjustment points—2-door vehicles

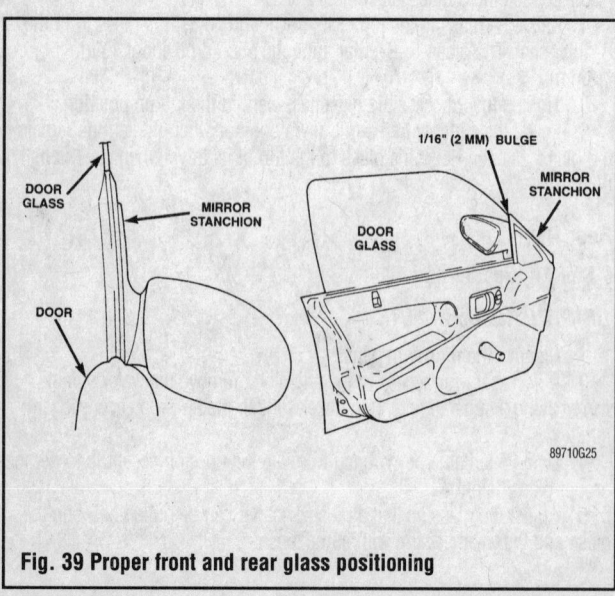

Fig. 39 Proper front and rear glass positioning

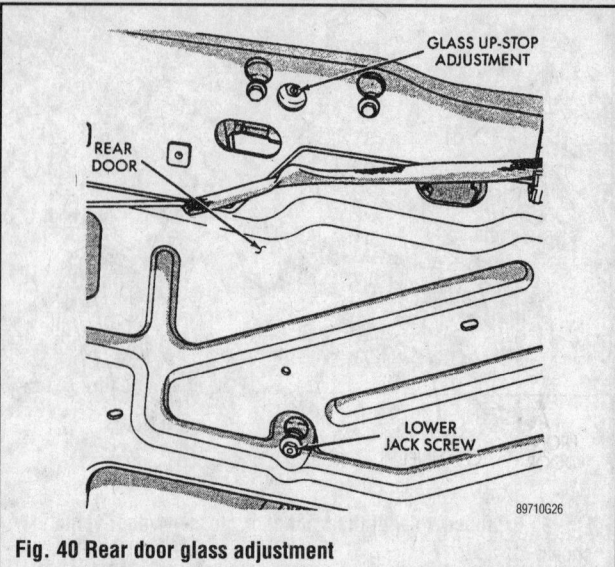

Fig. 40 Rear door glass adjustment

### TOP OF GLASS—INBOARD/OUTBOARD ADJUSTMENTS

1. Remove the door trim panel.
2. If necessary for access to the adjusters, remove the water shield.
3. Using a suitable flare nut socket, loosen the lower jack-screw jam nuts.
4. Using a hex wrench, rotate the jack-screws to achieve proper tensioner at the top of the glass.
5. Adjust the glass so that a piece of paper can be pulled between the glass and the weather-strip with some tension.

## Window Regulator

### REMOVAL & INSTALLATION

➡ Power and manual window regulators are removed and installed using the same procedure.

**2-Door Vehicles**

▶ See Figures 41, 42, 43 and 44

1. Disconnect the negative battery cable.
2. Remove the door trim panel and water shield.
3. If equipped with power windows, detach the wire connector from the power window motor.
4. Unfasten the nuts securing the regulator lift channel to the door glass.
5. Secure the window in the upright position.
6. Matchmark the position of the rear bolt of the roller channel to the inner door panel for installation purposes.
7. Remove the bolt securing the rear of the roller channel to the door panel.
8. Loosen the bolt holding the front of the roller channel to the door panel.
9. Separate the roller channel from the door panel.
10. Loosen the bolts holding the window regulator to the inner door panel.
11. Separate the bolt heads from the key hole slots in the inner door panel.
12. Remove the window regulator through the large hole in the inner door panel.
13. If equipped, remove the power window motor from the regulator.
**To install:**
14. If equipped, install the power window motor on the regulator.

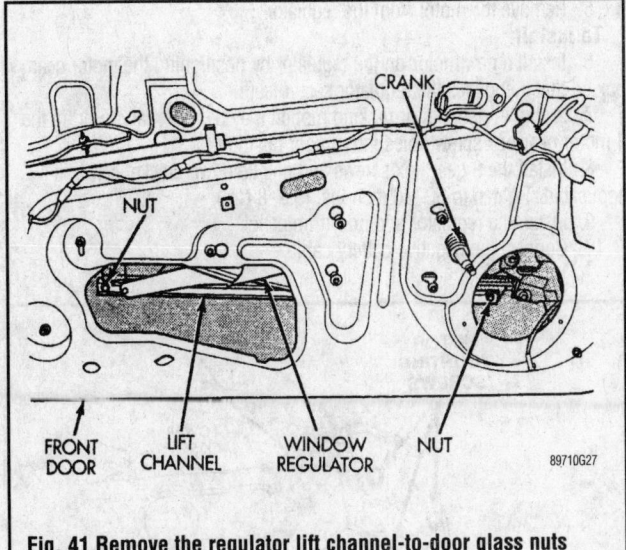

**Fig. 41 Remove the regulator lift channel-to-door glass nuts**

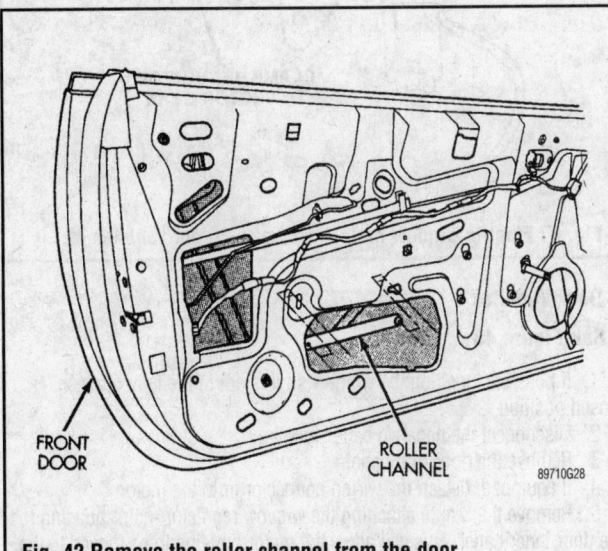

**Fig. 42 Remove the roller channel from the door**

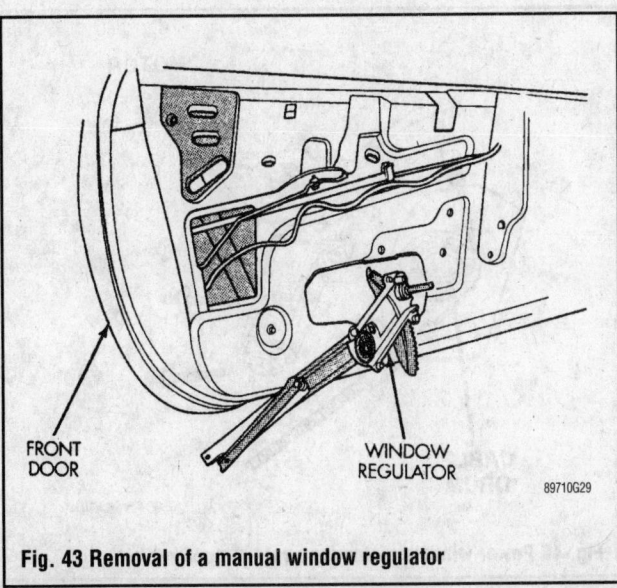

**Fig. 43 Removal of a manual window regulator**

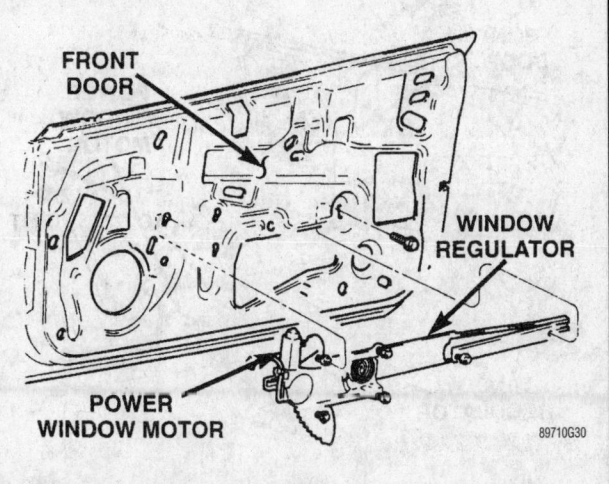

**Fig. 44 After removal, separate the power window motor from the regulator**

15. Move the regulator into position in the door and engage the bolt heads into the key hole slots in the inner door panel and tighten the bolts.
16. Install the roller channel to the door panel.
17. Install the bolt at the rear of the roller channel, making sure to align it to the mark on the inner door panel made during removal.
18. Tighten the front and rear roller channel bolts.
19. Install the nuts holding the regulator lift channel to the door glass.
20. Adjust the window as outlined earlier in this section.
21. If equipped, attach the electrical connector to the power window motor.
22. If equipped, install the door speaker.
23. Install the water shield and door trim panel.
24. Connect the negative battery cable.

### 4-Door Vehicles

▶ See Figures 45 and 46

1. Disconnect the negative battery cable.
2. Remove the door trim panel and water shield.
3. Remove the window glass.
4. If equipped with power windows, detach the wire connector from the power window motor.
5. Remove the nuts securing the top of the regulator to the inner door panel.

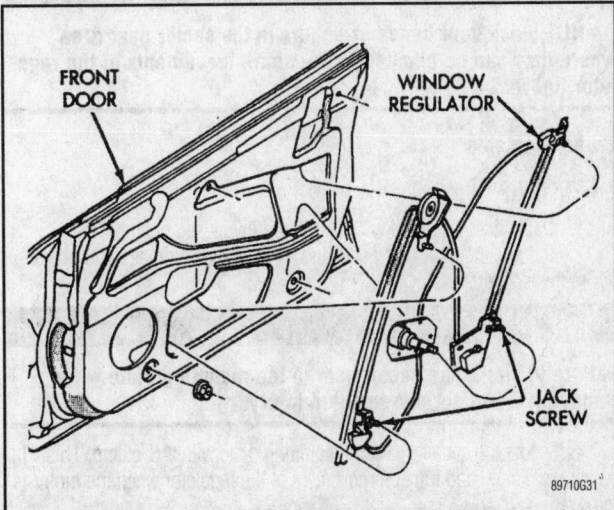

**Fig. 45 Exploded view of the front door manual window regulator**

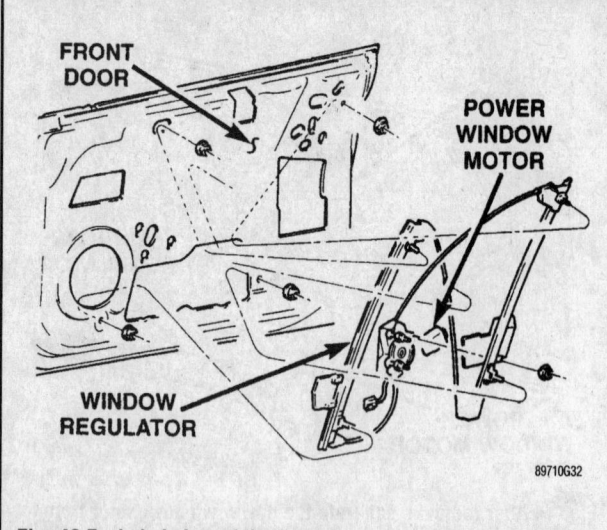

**Fig. 46 Exploded view of the front door power window regulator**

6. Remove the nuts holding the bottom of the regulator to the door panel.

7. Loosen the bolts holding the regulator crank/motor to the door panel.

8. Disengage the bolts from the key hold slots in the door panel.

9. Remove the window regulator from the access hole in the door panel.

10. Remove the power window motor from the regulator, if equipped.

**To install:**

11. If equipped, install the power window motor onto the regulator.

12. Move the window regulator into position in the door and engage the bolt heads in the key slots in the inner door panel.

13. Tighten the bolts attaching the regulator crank/motor to the door panel.

14. Install the nuts holding the top and bottom of the window regulator to the door panel.

15. If equipped, attach the electrical connector to the power window motor.

16. Connect the negative battery cable.

17. Install the door glass. Check and adjust the glass alignment, as necessary.

## Electric Window Motor

REMOVAL & INSTALLATION

### ❊❊ CAUTION

Do NOT place your hands or fingers in the sector gear area where they can be pinched by the small movements of the regulator linkage.

**2-Door Vehicles**

▶ See Figure 47

1. If possible, move the window to the fully closed position.

2. Remove the door trim panel and window regulator, as outlined earlier in this section.

### ❊❊ CAUTION

Failure to clamp the sector gear to the mounting plate when removing the motor can result in injury.

3. Secure the sector gear and mounting plate with a C-clamp. This will prevent a sudden and forceful movement of the regulator when the motor is removed.

4. Remove the 3 mounting screws that secure the motor gear box to the regulator.

5. Remove the motor from the regulator.

**To install:**

6. Install a new motor on the regulator by positioning the motor gear box so that it engages the regulator sector teeth.

7. A slight rotational or rocking motion may be necessary to bring the 3 motor gear box screw holes into proper position.

8. Install the 3 gear box screws and one tie down bracket screw, if applicable. Tighten to 50–70 inch lbs. (5.6–8 Nm).

9. Install the regulator and door trim panel.

10. Connect the negative battery cable.

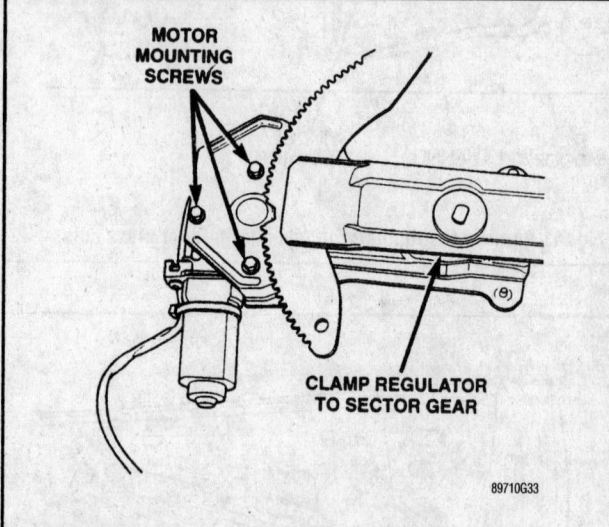

**Fig. 47 Electric window motor removal—2-door vehicles**

**4-Door Vehicles**

▶ See Figure 48

1. If possible, position the window so it is not in the fully open or closed position.

2. Disconnect the negative battery cable.

3. Remove the door trim panel.

4. If equipped, detach the wiring connector from the motor.

5. Remove the 3 nuts attaching the window regulator/motor housing to the door inner panel. This will allow the motor/housing to be moved to the lower door inner panel opening since the cables will flex.

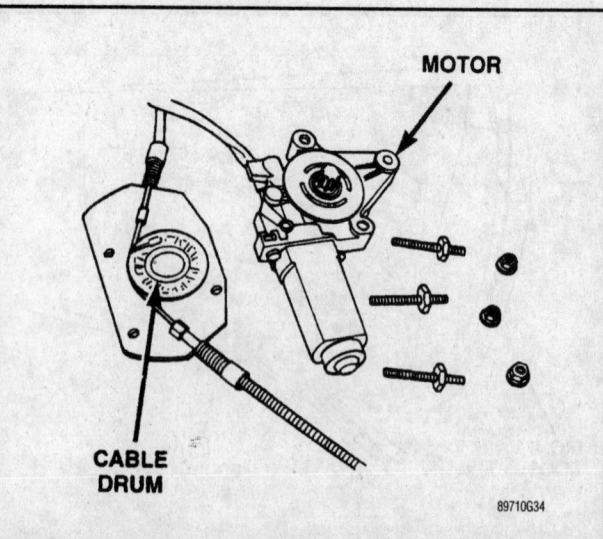

**Fig. 48 Power window motor removal—4-door vehicles**

6. Turn the motor/housing for access to the 3 nuts attaching the motor to the housing.

7. Remove the 3 nuts attaching the motor to the housing.

8. Remove the motor from the housing. Be careful not to pull the cable drum from the housing, as the motor shaft will tend to pull the drum with it.

9. Installation is the reverse of the removal procedure.

## Windshield & Fixed Glass

### REMOVAL & INSTALLATION

If your windshield, or other fixed window, is cracked or chipped, you may decide to replace it with a new one yourself. However, there are two main reasons why replacement windshields and other window glass should be installed only by a professional automotive glass technician: safety and cost.

The most important reason a professional should install automotive glass is for safety. The glass in the vehicle, especially the windshield, is designed with safety in mind in case of a collision. The windshield is specially manufactured from two panes of specially-tempered glass with a thin layer of transparent plastic between them. This construction allows the glass to 'give' in the event that a part of your body hits the windshield during the collision, and prevents the glass from shattering, which could cause lacerations, blinding and other harm to passengers of the vehicle. The other fixed windows are designed to be tempered so that if they break during a collision, they shatter in such a way that there are no large pointed glass pieces. The professional automotive glass technician knows how to install the glass in a vehicle so that it will function optimally during a collision. Without the proper experience, knowledge and tools, installing a piece of automotive glass yourself could lead to additional harm if an accident should ever occur.

Cost is also a factor when deciding to install automotive glass yourself. Performing this could cost you much more than a professional may charge for the same job. Since the windshield is designed to break under stress, an often life saving characteristic, windshields tend to break VERY easily when an inexperienced person attempts to install one. Do-it-yourselfers buying two, three or even four windshields from a salvage yard because they have broken them during installation are common stories. Also, since the automotive glass is designed to prevent the outside elements from entering your vehicle, improper installation can lead to water and air leaks. Annoying whining noises at highway speeds from air leaks or inside body panel rusting from water leaks can add to your stress level and subtract from your wallet. After buying two or three windshields, installing them and ending up with a leak that produces a noise while driving and water damage during rainstorms, the cost of having a professional do it correctly the first time may be much more alluring. We here at Chilton, therefore, advise that you have a professional automotive glass technician service any broken glass on your vehicle.

### WINDSHIELD CHIP REPAIR

▶ **See Figures 49 thru 63**

➡**Check with your state and local authorities on the laws for state safety inspection. Some states or municipalities may not allow chip repair as a viable option for correcting stone damage to your windshield.**

Although severely cracked or damaged windshields must be replaced, there is something that you can do to prolong or even prevent the need for replacement of a chipped windshield. There are many companies which offer windshield chip repair products, such as Loctite's® Bullseye™ windshield repair kit. These kits usually consist of a syringe, pedestal and a sealing adhesive. The syringe is mounted on the pedestal and is used to create a vacuum which pulls the plastic layer against the glass. This helps make the chip transparent. The adhesive is then injected which seals the chip and helps to prevent further stress cracks from developing. Refer to the sequence of photos to get a general idea of what windshield chip repair involves.

➡**Always follow the specific manufacturer's instructions.**

TCCA0P00

**Fig. 49 Small chips on your windshield can be fixed with an aftermarket repair kit, such as the one from Loctite®**

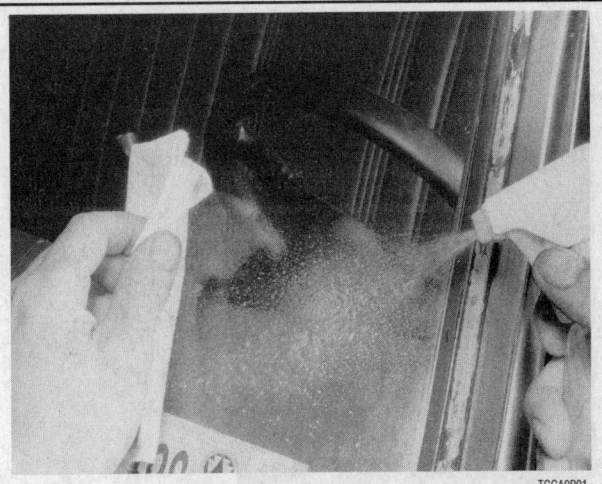
TCCA0P01

**Fig. 50 To repair a chip, clean the windshield with glass cleaner and dry it completely**

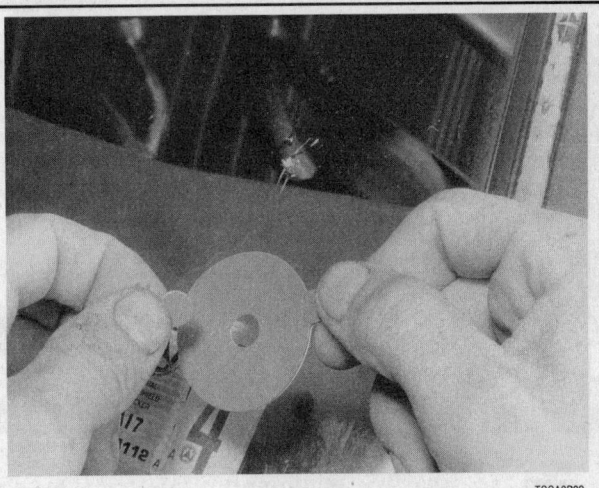
TCCA0P02

**Fig. 51 Remove the center from the adhesive disc and peel off the backing from one side of the disc . . .**

TCCA0P03

**Fig. 52 . . . then press it on the windshield so that the chip is centered in the hole**

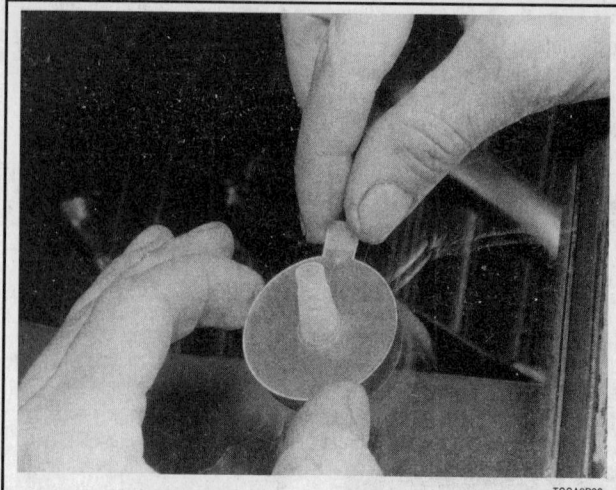

TCCA0P06

**Fig. 55 . . . then position the plastic pedestal on the adhesive disc, ensuring that the tabs are aligned**

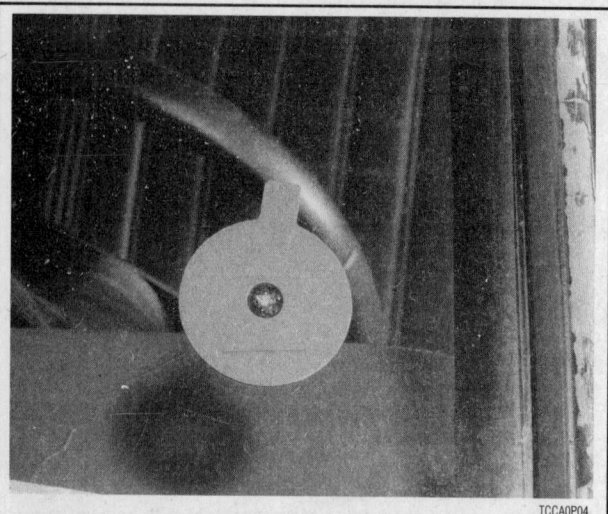

TCCA0P04

**Fig. 53 Be sure that the tab points upward on the windshield**

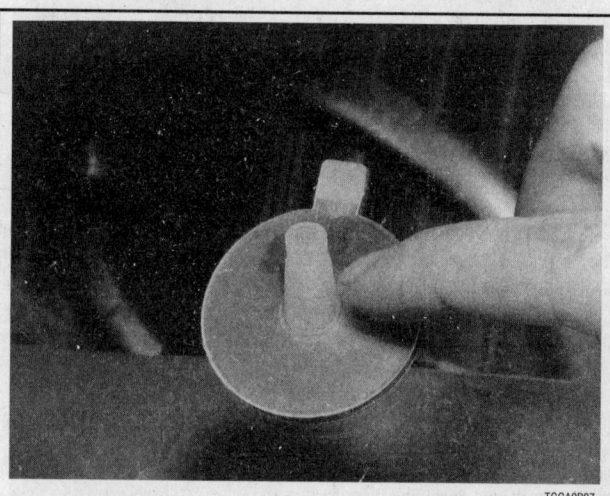

TCCA0P07

**Fig. 56 Press the pedestal firmly on the adhesive disc to create an adequate seal . . .**

TCCA0P05

**Fig. 54 Peel the backing off the exposed side of the adhesive disc . . .**

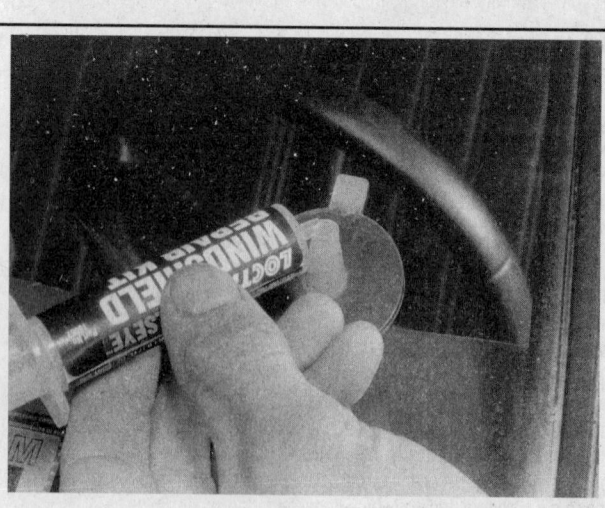

TCCA0P08

**Fig. 57 . . . then install the applicator syringe nipple in the pedestal's hole**

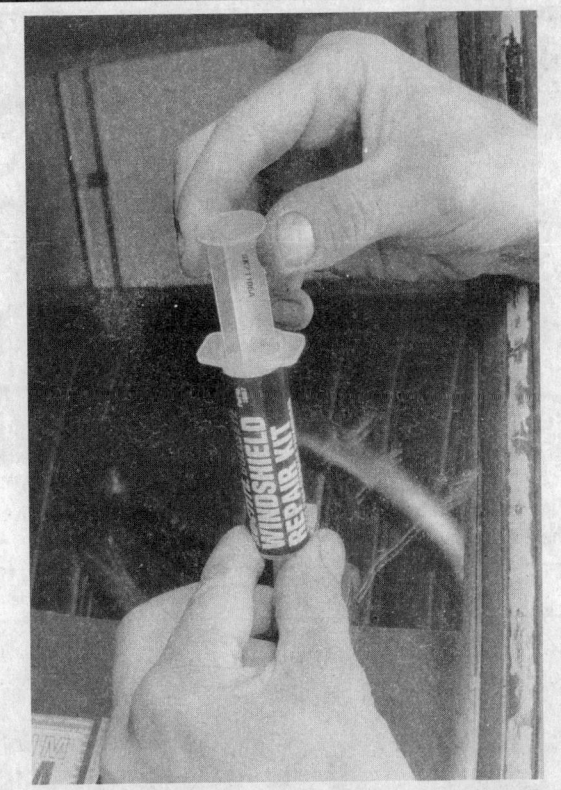

TCCA0P09

**Fig. 58 Hold the syringe with one hand while pulling the plunger back with the other hand**

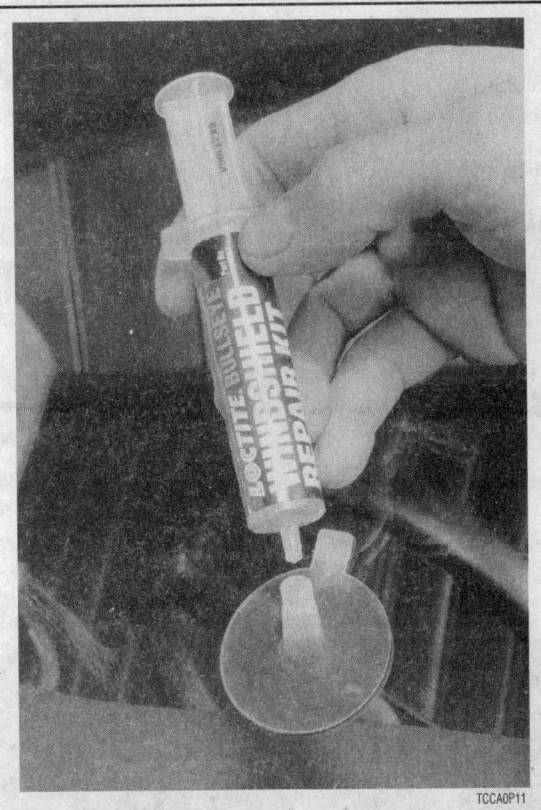

TCCA0P11

**Fig. 60 After the solution has set, remove the syringe from the pedestal . . .**

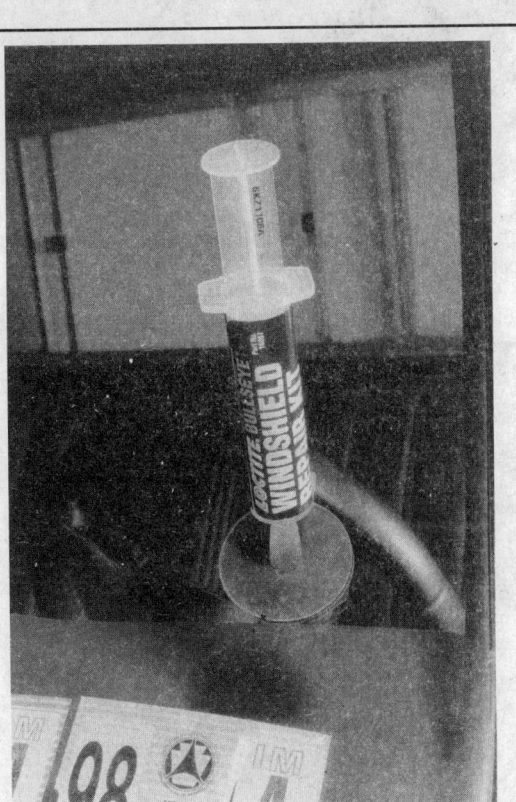

TCCA0P10

**Fig. 59 After applying the solution, allow the entire assembly to sit until it has set completely**

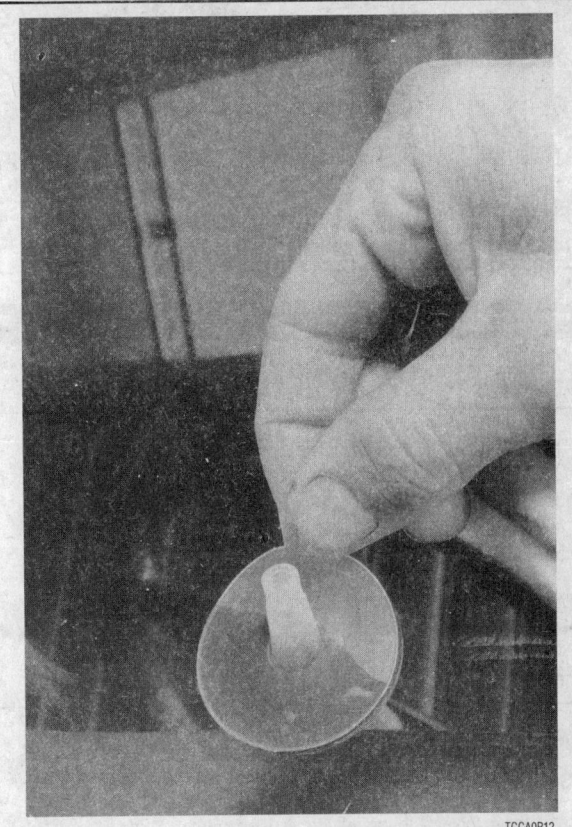

TCCA0P12

**Fig. 61 . . . then peel the pedestal off of the adhesive disc . . .**

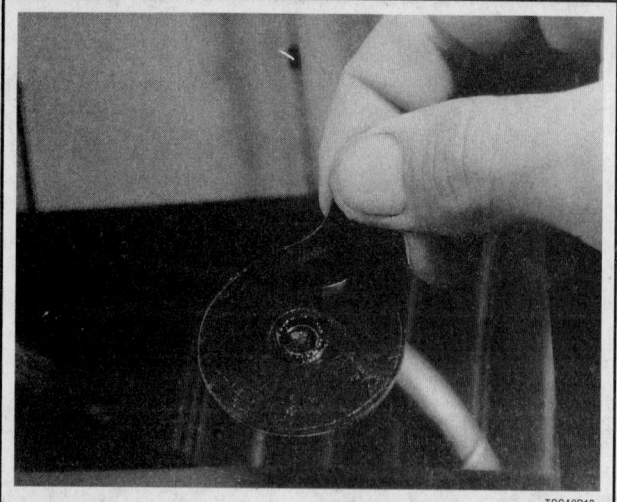

Fig. 62 . . . and peel the adhesive disc off of the windshield

TCCA0P13

89710P19

Fig. 64 Move the seat to the full forward position, then remove the 2 mounting bolts (see arrows)

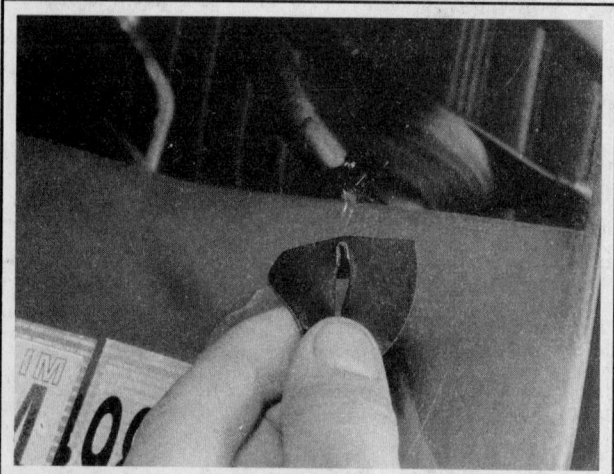

TCCA0P14

Fig. 63 The chip will still be slightly visible, but it should be filled with the hardened solution

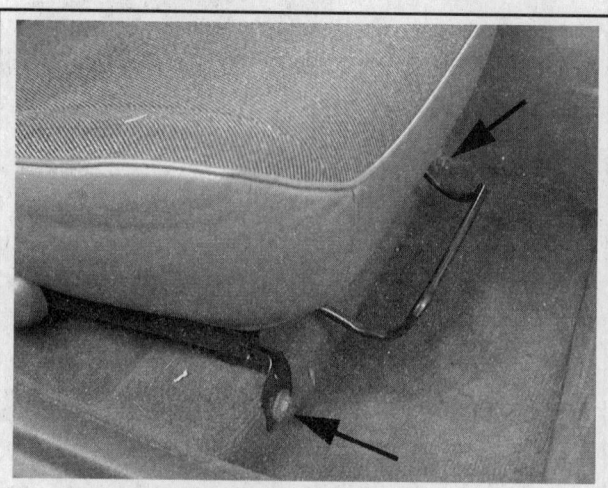

89710P20

Fig. 65 Location of the bolts holding the front of the seat to the floor (see arrows)

## Inside Rear View Mirror

### REPLACEMENT

1. Disconnect the negative battery cable.
2. If equipped, detach the reading lamp wiring connector.
3. Loosen the mirror set screw.
4. Lift the mirror from the mounting bottom.
5. Installation is the reverse of the removal procedure.

## Seats

### REMOVAL & INSTALLATION

**Front Seats**

▶ **See Figures 64, 65 and 66**

1. Move the seat to the fully forward position.
2. Remove the bolts holding the rear of the seat track to the floor.
3. Move the seat to the rearward position.

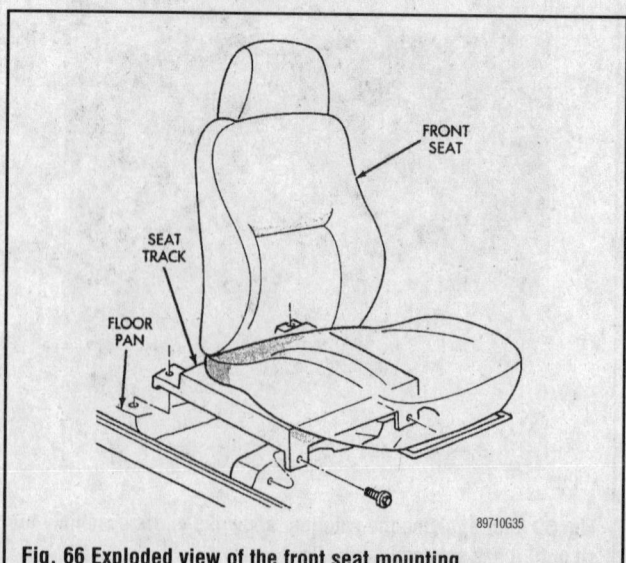

89710G35

Fig. 66 Exploded view of the front seat mounting

4. Remove the bolts securing the front of the seat to the floor.

5. Remove the seat from the vehicle.

**To install:**

6. Move the seat to the fully rearward position and make sure both seat tracks are locked into position.

7. Place the seat in position in the vehicle. Do not use the head restraint, side shield, recliner handle, or the adjuster lift bar to move the seat.

8. Make sure that the locating tabs on the front mounting feet are installed through the slits in the carpet and into the openings in the floor pan crossmember.

9. Install and tighten the front inboard bolt holding the seat track to the floor crossmember. Install and tighten the front outboard bolt holding the seat track to the floor crossmember. Tighten all bolts to 40 ft. lbs. (55 Nm).

10. Move the seat to the forward position. Check to make sure the inboard and outboard tracks are latched in the full forward position.

11. Install the bolts holding the rear of the seat track to the floor, then tighten to 40 ft. lbs. (55 Nm).

## Rear Seats

### REAR SEAT BACK

▶ **See Figures 67, 68, 69, 70 and 71**

1. Remove the rear seat cushion.

2. Unfasten the bolts securing the rear seat back and seat belts to the floor.

3. Push the rear seat back upward to disengage the hooks at the top of the seat back, then remove the seat back from the vehicle.

**To install:**

4. Place the rear seat back into position in the vehicle.

5. Push the seat back downward to engage the hooks at the top of the seat back.

6. Install the bolts holding the rear seat back and seat belts to the floor. Tighten the retainers to 42 ft. lbs. (57 Nm).

7. Install the rear seat cushion.

### REAR SEAT CUSHION

▶ **See Figure 72**

1. Pull upward at each end of the rear seat cushion to disengage the retainer loops from the cups in the floor.

2. Remove the rear seat cushion from the vehicle.

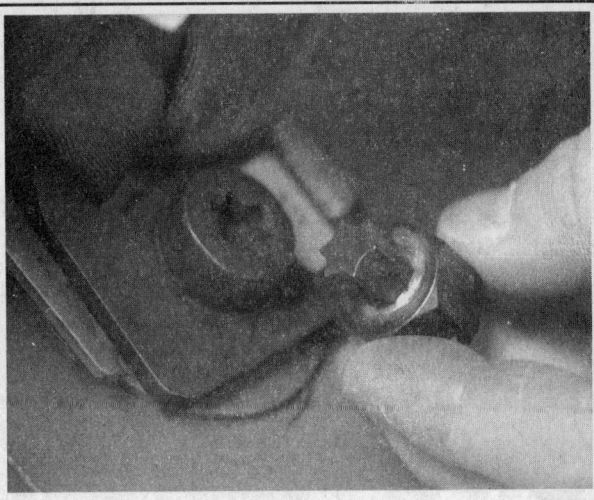

Fig. 68 You must use a special Torx® head driver to loosen . . .

Fig. 69 . . . then remove the bolt to free the seat belt anchor

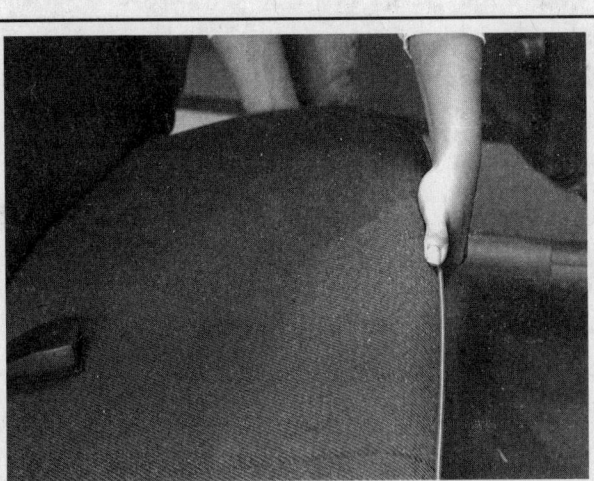

Fig. 67 Remove the rear seat cushion by firmly pulling it up to disengage it from the retaining clips

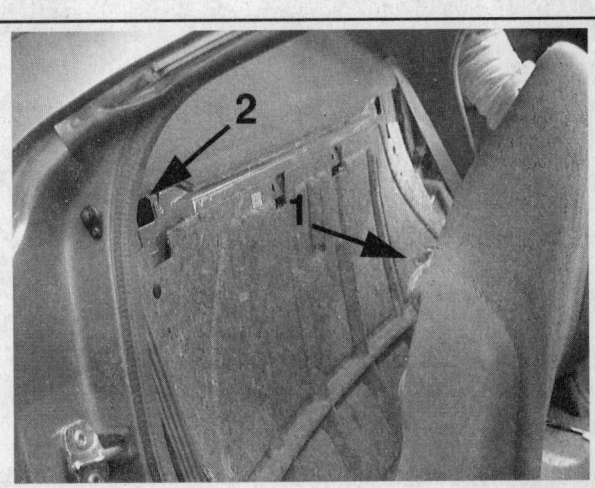

Fig. 70 Pull the rear seat back to unlatch the clips (1) from the mounting holes (2)

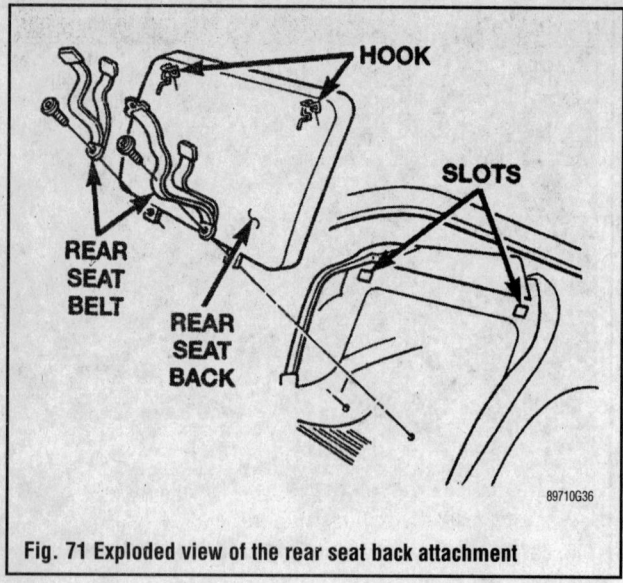

**Fig. 71 Exploded view of the rear seat back attachment**

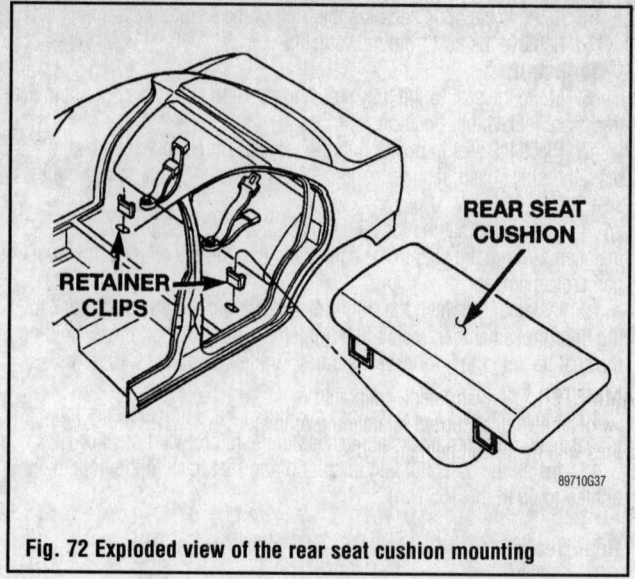

**Fig. 72 Exploded view of the rear seat cushion mounting**

**To install:**
3. Place the rear seat cushion in position under the bottom of the seat back.
4. Position the inboard seat belts on top of the seat cushion.

5. Guide the seat cushion loops into the retainer cups in the floor pan.
6. Push downward on the front corners of the seat cushion to engage the retainers.

## GLOSSARY

**AIR/FUEL RATIO:** The ratio of air-to-gasoline by weight in the fuel mixture drawn into the engine.

**AIR INJECTION:** One method of reducing harmful exhaust emissions by injecting air into each of the exhaust ports of an engine. The fresh air entering the hot exhaust manifold causes any remaining fuel to be burned before it can exit the tailpipe.

**ALTERNATOR:** A device used for converting mechanical energy into electrical energy.

**AMMETER:** An instrument, calibrated in amperes, used to measure the flow of an electrical current in a circuit. Ammeters are always connected in series with the circuit being tested.

**AMPERE:** The rate of flow of electrical current present when one volt of electrical pressure is applied against one ohm of electrical resistance.

**ANALOG COMPUTER:** Any microprocessor that uses similar (analogous) electrical signals to make its calculations.

**ARMATURE:** A laminated, soft iron core wrapped by a wire that converts electrical energy to mechanical energy as in a motor or relay. When rotated in a magnetic field, it changes mechanical energy into electrical energy as in a generator.

**ATMOSPHERIC PRESSURE:** The pressure on the Earth's surface caused by the weight of the air in the atmosphere. At sea level, this pressure is 14.7 psi at 32°F (101 kPa at 0°C).

**ATOMIZATION:** The breaking down of a liquid into a fine mist that can be suspended in air.

**AXIAL PLAY:** Movement parallel to a shaft or bearing bore.

**BACKFIRE:** The sudden combustion of gases in the intake or exhaust system that results in a loud explosion.

**BACKLASH:** The clearance or play between two parts, such as meshed gears.

**BACKPRESSURE:** Restrictions in the exhaust system that slow the exit of exhaust gases from the combustion chamber.

**BAKELITE:** A heat resistant, plastic insulator material commonly used in printed circuit boards and transistorized components.

**BALL BEARING:** A bearing made up of hardened inner and outer races between which hardened steel balls roll.

**BALLAST RESISTOR:** A resistor in the primary ignition circuit that lowers voltage after the engine is started to reduce wear on ignition components.

**BEARING:** A friction reducing, supportive device usually located between a stationary part and a moving part.

**BIMETAL TEMPERATURE SENSOR:** Any sensor or switch made of two dissimilar types of metal that bend when heated or cooled due to the different expansion rates of the alloys. These types of sensors usually function as an on/off switch.

**BLOWBY:** Combustion gases, composed of water vapor and unburned fuel, that leak past the piston rings into the crankcase during normal engine operation. These gases are removed by the PCV system to prevent the buildup of harmful acids in the crankcase.

**BRAKE PAD:** A brake shoe and lining assembly used with disc brakes.

**BRAKE SHOE:** The backing for the brake lining. The term is, however, usually applied to the assembly of the brake backing and lining.

**BUSHING:** A liner, usually removable, for a bearing; an anti-friction liner used in place of a bearing.

**CALIPER:** A hydraulically activated device in a disc brake system, which is mounted straddling the brake rotor (disc). The caliper contains at least one piston and two brake pads. Hydraulic pressure on the piston(s) forces the pads against the rotor.

**CAMSHAFT:** A shaft in the engine on which are the lobes (cams) which operate the valves. The camshaft is driven by the crankshaft, via a belt, chain or gears, at one half the crankshaft speed.

**CAPACITOR:** A device which stores an electrical charge.

**CARBON MONOXIDE (CO):** A colorless, odorless gas given off as a normal byproduct of combustion. It is poisonous and extremely dangerous in confined areas, building up slowly to toxic levels without warning if adequate ventilation is not available.

**CARBURETOR:** A device, usually mounted on the intake manifold of an engine, which mixes the air and fuel in the proper proportion to allow even combustion.

**CATALYTIC CONVERTER:** A device installed in the exhaust system, like a muffler, that converts harmful byproducts of combustion into carbon dioxide and water vapor by means of a heat-producing chemical reaction.

**CENTRIFUGAL ADVANCE:** A mechanical method of advancing the spark timing by using flyweights in the distributor that react to centrifugal force generated by the distributor shaft rotation.

**CHECK VALVE:** Any one-way valve installed to permit the flow of air, fuel or vacuum in one direction only.

**CHOKE:** A device, usually a moveable valve, placed in the intake path of a carburetor to restrict the flow of air.

**CIRCUIT:** Any unbroken path through which an electrical current can flow. Also used to describe fuel flow in some instances.

**CIRCUIT BREAKER:** A switch which protects an electrical circuit from overload by opening the circuit when the current flow exceeds a predetermined level. Some circuit breakers must be reset manually, while most reset automatically.

**COIL (IGNITION):** A transformer in the ignition circuit which steps up the voltage provided to the spark plugs.

**COMBINATION MANIFOLD:** An assembly which includes both the intake and exhaust manifolds in one casting.

**COMBINATION VALVE:** A device used in some fuel systems that routes fuel vapors to a charcoal storage canister instead of venting them into the atmosphere. The valve relieves fuel tank pressure and allows fresh air into the tank as the fuel level drops to prevent a vapor lock situation.

**COMPRESSION RATIO:** The comparison of the total volume of the cylinder and combustion chamber with the piston at BDC and the piston at TDC.

**CONDENSER:** 1. An electrical device which acts to store an electrical charge, preventing voltage surges. 2. A radiator-like device in the air conditioning system in which refrigerant gas condenses into a liquid, giving off heat.

**CONDUCTOR:** Any material through which an electrical current can be transmitted easily.

**CONTINUITY:** Continuous or complete circuit. Can be checked with an ohmmeter.

**COUNTERSHAFT:** An intermediate shaft which is rotated by a mainshaft and transmits, in turn, that rotation to a working part.

**CRANKCASE:** The lower part of an engine in which the crankshaft and related parts operate.

**CRANKSHAFT:** The main driving shaft of an engine which receives reciprocating motion from the pistons and converts it to rotary motion.

**CYLINDER:** In an engine, the round hole in the engine block in which the piston(s) ride.

**CYLINDER BLOCK:** The main structural member of an engine in which is found the cylinders, crankshaft and other principal parts.

**CYLINDER HEAD:** The detachable portion of the engine, usually fastened to the top of the cylinder block and containing all or most of the combustion chambers. On overhead valve engines, it contains the valves and their operating parts. On overhead cam engines, it contains the camshaft as well.

**DEAD CENTER:** The extreme top or bottom of the piston stroke.

**DETONATION:** An unwanted explosion of the air/fuel mixture in the combustion chamber caused by excess heat and compression, advanced timing, or an overly lean mixture. Also referred to as "ping".

**DIAPHRAGM:** A thin, flexible wall separating two cavities, such as in a vacuum advance unit.

**DIESELING:** A condition in which hot spots in the combustion chamber cause the engine to run on after the key is turned off.

**DIFFERENTIAL:** A geared assembly which allows the transmission of motion between drive axles, giving one axle the ability to turn faster than the other.

**DIODE:** An electrical device that will allow current to flow in one direction only.

**DISC BRAKE:** A hydraulic braking assembly consisting of a brake disc, or rotor, mounted on an axle, and a caliper assembly containing, usually two brake pads which are activated by hydraulic pressure. The pads are forced against the sides of the disc, creating friction which slows the vehicle.

**DISTRIBUTOR:** A mechanically driven device on an engine which is responsible for electrically firing the spark plug at a predetermined point of the piston stroke.

**DOWEL PIN:** A pin, inserted in mating holes in two different parts allowing those parts to maintain a fixed relationship.

**DRUM BRAKE:** A braking system which consists of two brake shoes and one or two wheel cylinders, mounted on a fixed backing plate, and a brake drum, mounted on an axle, which revolves around the assembly.

**DWELL:** The rate, measured in degrees of shaft rotation, at which an electrical circuit cycles on and off.

**ELECTRONIC CONTROL UNIT (ECU):** Ignition module, module, amplifier or igniter. See Module for definition.

**ELECTRONIC IGNITION:** A system in which the timing and firing of the spark plugs is controlled by an electronic control unit, usually called a module. These systems have no points or condenser.

**END-PLAY:** The measured amount of axial movement in a shaft.

**ENGINE:** A device that converts heat into mechanical energy.

**EXHAUST MANIFOLD:** A set of cast passages or pipes which conduct exhaust gases from the engine.

**FEELER GAUGE:** A blade, usually metal, or precisely predetermined thickness, used to measure the clearance between two parts.

**FIRING ORDER:** The order in which combustion occurs in the cylinders of an engine. Also the order in which spark is distributed to the plugs by the distributor.

**FLOODING:** The presence of too much fuel in the intake manifold and combustion chamber which prevents the air/fuel mixture from firing, thereby causing a no-start situation.

**FLYWHEEL:** A disc shaped part bolted to the rear end of the crankshaft. Around the outer perimeter is affixed the ring gear. The starter drive engages the ring gear, turning the flywheel, which rotates the crankshaft, imparting the initial starting motion to the engine.

**FOOT POUND (ft. lbs. or sometimes, ft.lb.):** The amount of energy or work needed to raise an item weighing one pound, a distance of one foot.

**FUSE:** A protective device in a circuit which prevents circuit overload by breaking the circuit when a specific amperage is present. The device is constructed around a strip or wire of a lower amperage rating than the circuit it is designed to protect. When an amperage higher than that stamped on the fuse is present in the circuit, the strip or wire melts, opening the circuit.

**GEAR RATIO:** The ratio between the number of teeth on meshing gears.

**GENERATOR:** A device which converts mechanical energy into electrical energy.

**HEAT RANGE:** The measure of a spark plug's ability to dissipate heat from its firing end. The higher the heat range, the hotter the plug fires.

**HUB:** The center part of a wheel or gear.

**HYDROCARBON (HC):** Any chemical compound made up of hydrogen and carbon. A major pollutant formed by the engine as a byproduct of combustion.

**HYDROMETER:** An instrument used to measure the specific gravity of a solution.

**INCH POUND (inch lbs.; sometimes in.lb. or in. lbs.):** One twelfth of a foot pound.

**INDUCTION:** A means of transferring electrical energy in the form of a magnetic field. Principle used in the ignition coil to increase voltage.

**INJECTOR:** A device which receives metered fuel under relatively low pressure and is activated to inject the fuel into the engine under relatively high pressure at a predetermined time.

**INPUT SHAFT:** The shaft to which torque is applied, usually carrying the driving gear or gears.

**INTAKE MANIFOLD:** A casting of passages or pipes used to conduct air or a fuel/air mixture to the cylinders.

**JOURNAL:** The bearing surface within which a shaft operates.

**KEY:** A small block usually fitted in a notch between a shaft and a hub to prevent slippage of the two parts.

**MANIFOLD:** A casting of passages or set of pipes which connect the cylinders to an inlet or outlet source.

**MANIFOLD VACUUM:** Low pressure in an engine intake manifold formed just below the throttle plates. Manifold vacuum is highest at idle and drops under acceleration.

**MASTER CYLINDER:** The primary fluid pressurizing device in a hydraulic system. In automotive use, it is found in brake and hydraulic clutch systems and is pedal activated, either directly or, in a power brake system, through the power booster.

**MODULE:** Electronic control unit, amplifier or igniter of solid state or integrated design which controls the current flow in the ignition primary circuit based on input from the pick-up coil. When the module opens the primary circuit, high secondary voltage is induced in the coil.

**NEEDLE BEARING:** A bearing which consists of a number (usually a large number) of long, thin rollers.

**OHM:** ($\Omega$) The unit used to measure the resistance of conductor-to-electrical flow. One ohm is the amount of resistance that limits current flow to one ampere in a circuit with one volt of pressure.

**OHMMETER:** An instrument used for measuring the resistance, in ohms, in an electrical circuit.

**OUTPUT SHAFT:** The shaft which transmits torque from a device, such as a transmission.

**OVERDRIVE:** A gear assembly which produces more shaft revolutions than that transmitted to it.

**OVERHEAD CAMSHAFT (OHC):** An engine configuration in which the camshaft is mounted on top of the cylinder head and operates the valve either directly or by means of rocker arms.

**OVERHEAD VALVE (OHV):** An engine configuration in which all of the valves are located in the cylinder head and the camshaft is located in the cylinder block. The camshaft operates the valves via lifters and pushrods.

**OXIDES OF NITROGEN (NOx):** Chemical compounds of nitrogen produced as a byproduct of combustion. They combine with hydrocarbons to produce smog.

**OXYGEN SENSOR:** Use with the feedback system to sense the presence of oxygen in the exhaust gas and signal the computer which can reference the voltage signal to an air/fuel ratio.

**PINION:** The smaller of two meshing gears.

**PISTON RING:** An open-ended ring with fits into a groove on the outer diameter of the piston. Its chief function is to form a seal between the piston and cylinder wall. Most automotive pistons have three rings: two for compression sealing; one for oil sealing.

**PRELOAD:** A predetermined load placed on a bearing during assembly or by adjustment.

**PRIMARY CIRCUIT:** the low voltage side of the ignition system which consists of the ignition switch, ballast resistor or resistance wire, bypass, coil, electronic control unit and pick-up coil as well as the connecting wires and harnesses.

**PRESS FIT:** The mating of two parts under pressure, due to the inner diameter of one being smaller than the outer diameter of the other, or vice versa; an interference fit.

**RACE:** The surface on the inner or outer ring of a bearing on which the balls, needles or rollers move.

**REGULATOR:** A device which maintains the amperage and/or voltage levels of a circuit at predetermined values.

**RELAY:** A switch which automatically opens and/or closes a circuit.

**RESISTANCE:** The opposition to the flow of current through a circuit or electrical device, and is measured in ohms. Resistance is equal to the voltage divided by the amperage.

**RESISTOR:** A device, usually made of wire, which offers a preset amount of resistance in an electrical circuit.

**RING GEAR:** The name given to a ring-shaped gear attached to a differential case, or affixed to a flywheel or as part of a planetary gear set.

**ROLLER BEARING:** A bearing made up of hardened inner and outer races between which hardened steel rollers move.

**ROTOR:** 1. The disc-shaped part of a disc brake assembly, upon which the brake pads bear; also called, brake disc. 2. The device mounted atop the distributor shaft, which passes current to the distributor cap tower contacts.

**SECONDARY CIRCUIT:** The high voltage side of the ignition system, usually above 20,000 volts. The secondary includes the ignition coil, coil wire, distributor cap and rotor, spark plug wires and spark plugs.

**SENDING UNIT:** A mechanical, electrical, hydraulic or electro-magnetic device which transmits information to a gauge.

**SENSOR:** Any device designed to measure engine operating conditions or ambient pressures and temperatures. Usually electronic in nature and designed to send a voltage signal to an on-board computer, some sensors may operate as a simple on/off switch or they may provide a variable voltage signal (like a potentiometer) as conditions or measured parameters change.

**SHIM:** Spacers of precise, predetermined thickness used between parts to establish a proper working relationship.

**SLAVE CYLINDER:** In automotive use, a device in the hydraulic clutch system which is activated by hydraulic force, disengaging the clutch.

**SOLENOID:** A coil used to produce a magnetic field, the effect of which is to produce work.

**SPARK PLUG:** A device screwed into the combustion chamber of a spark ignition engine. The basic construction is a conductive core inside of a ceramic insulator, mounted in an outer conductive base. An electrical charge from the spark plug wire travels along the conductive core and jumps a preset air gap to a grounding point or points at the end of the conductive base. The resultant spark ignites the fuel/air mixture in the combustion chamber.

**SPLINES:** Ridges machined or cast onto the outer diameter of a shaft or inner diameter of a bore to enable parts to mate without rotation.

**TACHOMETER:** A device used to measure the rotary speed of an engine, shaft, gear, etc., usually in rotations per minute.

**THERMOSTAT:** A valve, located in the cooling system of an engine, which is closed when cold and opens gradually in response to engine heating, controlling the temperature of the coolant and rate of coolant flow.

**TOP DEAD CENTER (TDC):** The point at which the piston reaches the top of its travel on the compression stroke.

**TORQUE:** The twisting force applied to an object.

**TORQUE CONVERTER:** A turbine used to transmit power from a driving member to a driven member via hydraulic action, providing changes in drive ratio and torque. In automotive use, it links the driveplate at the rear of the engine to the automatic transmission.

**TRANSDUCER:** A device used to change a force into an electrical signal.

**TRANSISTOR:** A semi-conductor component which can be actuated by a small voltage to perform an electrical switching function.

**TUNE-UP:** A regular maintenance function, usually associated with the replacement and adjustment of parts and components in the electrical and fuel systems of a vehicle for the purpose of attaining optimum performance.

**TURBOCHARGER:** An exhaust driven pump which compresses intake air and forces it into the combustion chambers at higher than atmospheric pressures. The increased air pressure allows more fuel to be burned and results in increased horsepower being produced.

**VACUUM ADVANCE:** A device which advances the ignition timing in response to increased engine vacuum.

**VACUUM GAUGE:** An instrument used to measure the presence of vacuum in a chamber.

**VALVE:** A device which control the pressure, direction of flow or rate of flow of a liquid or gas.

**VALVE CLEARANCE:** The measured gap between the end of the valve stem and the rocker arm, cam lobe or follower that activates the valve.

**VISCOSITY:** The rating of a liquid's internal resistance to flow.

**VOLTMETER:** An instrument used for measuring electrical force in units called volts. Voltmeters are always connected parallel with the circuit being tested.

**WHEEL CYLINDER:** Found in the automotive drum brake assembly, it is a device, actuated by hydraulic pressure, which, through internal pistons, pushes the brake shoes outward against the drums.

MASTER
INDEX-